CHARLES DICKENS
A to Z

S0-AAC-910

CHARLES DICKENS
A to Z

The Essential Reference to
His Life and Work

Paul Davis

☑®
Checkmark Books™
An imprint of Facts On File, Inc.

Charles Dickens A to Z

Copyright © 1998 by Paul Davis

First paperback reprint © 1999.

All rights reserved. No part of this book may be reproduced or utilized in any form or by any means, electronic or mechanical, including photocopying, recording, or by any information storage or retrieval systems, without permission in writing from the publisher. For information contact:

Checkmark Books
An imprint of Facts On File, Inc.
11 Penn Plaza
New York NY 10001

Library of Congress Cataloging-in-Publication Data

Davis, Paul B. (Paul Benjamin), 1934–
    Charles Dickens A to Z : the essential reference to the life and work / Paul Davis.
        p. cm.
    Includes bibliographical references and index.
    ISBN 0-8160-29059 (hardcover)
    ISBN 0-8160-4087-7 (pbk.)
    1. Dickens, Charles, 1812–1870—Encyclopedias. 2. Novelists.
English—19th century—Biography—Encyclopedias. I. Title
PR4580.D38 1998   97-26237
823′.8—dc21

Checkmark Books are available at special discounts when purchased in bulk quantities for businesses, associations, institutions, or sales promotions. Please call our Special Sales Department in New York at 212/967-8800 or 800/322-8755.

You can find Facts On File on the World Wide Web at http://www.factsonfile.com

Cover design by Nora Wertz

Printed in the United States of America

VB BVC 10 9 8 7 6 5 4 3 2
   (pbk) 10 9 8 7 6 5 4 3 2 1

This book is printed on acid-free paper.

CONTENTS

For my parents,
George and Mildred Davis

PREFACE

More than any British writer other than Shakespeare, Dickens has engaged the popular imagination with his crowded gallery of memorable characters and his detailed rendering of the life of his times. His stories and people are familiar even to those who have never read the novels: Oliver Twist, Scrooge, and Mr. Pickwick are as well known as Hamlet, Romeo, or Falstaff.

Adapted for the stage almost as soon as they appeared in monthly parts, Dickens's novels have been public property from the beginning. They have been endlessly retold, adapted, imitated, and pirated on both sides of the Atlantic for a century and a half. The cinematic and television adaptations of our time are just the most recent examples of this public appropriation of "Dickens," a process that has sometimes created notions about the novels remarkably different from the original texts.

The most important writer of his time, Dickens is often seen as the quintessential Victorian. "Dickens's England" has almost become synonymous with Victorian England. Since he frequently based his characters on real people and used real places—particularly the streets and neighborhoods of London—as settings for his tales, the connections between his fictional world and the actual world of Victorian England have fascinated his readers. Dickens enthusiasts have often applied themselves—sometimes overzealously—to connecting the people and places in the novels with counterparts in the real world. Understanding the historical context in which Dickens worked is especially important to understanding his life and his novels.

Although his favor with the popular audience has never waned, Dickens was, during the modernist decades of the early twentieth century, largely dismissed by critics who ignored his work as vulgar and simplistic. When Edmund Wilson in his 1941 essay, "Dickens, the Two Scrooges," demonstrated that Dickens was more intellectually challenging than his detractors had allowed, he ushered in an age of serious attention to the novelist. Since that time, Dickens has been explicated and mythologized, analyzed and psychoanalyzed, constructed and deconstructed in a host of critical and academic studies.

Dickens A to Z is a guide to Dickens's works themselves and to the characters he created in them, to the author and the Victorian context in which he worked, and to the critics and scholars who have commented on his novels.

The Works

Each of the fictional works is summarized in a **synopsis.** All of Dickens's novels were originally published in either monthly or weekly serial numbers. The synopses are broken down into these original parts, since they were so important in defining the structure of each work as Dickens imagined it. The **commentary** on each novel discusses Dickens's plans for the work, its composition, and some of the important critical issues it raises. The sections on **criticism** identify and briefly indicate the significance of a few of the more important commentaries on each work. Finally, the section on **adaptations** describes some important theatrical and cinematic versions of the story. Entries for each of Dickens's journalistic essays, occasional sketches, poems, and plays briefly summarize the contents of these works and indicate where they are collected.

The Characters

All of the characters are discussed individually, though members of a single family sometimes appear under the family name or as subsidiary characters under the main character of the entry. Each character is introduced in **boldface** type, either as the subject of the entry or as a character related to the main character in the text of the entry; is characterized, often with a brief description from the novel; and his or her important moments in the story are indicated with parenthetical chapter references. Since all of the characters have their own entries, they are not cross-referenced in the text, except in cases where a character appears under more than one name. Then a capitalized cross-reference in the secondary entries indicates the main entry for the character.

Dickens and His Times

For a general overview of Dickens and his historical context, begin with the entry for Charles Dickens, a chronological biography that cross-references many of his friends and associates, his activities and travels, and his writing career. Individual members of his family, as well as his friends, fellow novelists, publishers, and other business associates, receive separate entries, as do broader social and historical topics, such as the Industrial Revolution, railways, the sensation novel, and the early Victorian period.

Scholarship and Criticism

Many Dickens critics and scholars are mentioned in the commentaries and the summaries of criticism on the individual novels. The most important commentators, especially those who have done a variety of work on Dickens, have separate entries summarizing the nature of their work and indicating their most important books and articles.

I have relied on the work of innumerable scholars and critics in developing the entries for *Dickens A to Z*. Some of my debts are acknowledged in the text, but many more are silent, even unrecognized. I am particularly grateful to generations of Dickensians, writing in journals like *The Dickensian* and *The Dickens Quarterly* whose devotion to Dickens and his works continues to enlarge our understanding of the man, his times, and his novels. I am indebted to Bob Gish, who originally suggested this project, to Michael Fisher, who provided institutional support for it, and to my two graduate assistants, Ann Grigsby and Joyce Flagg, who helped in choosing, chasing down information, and proposing approaches to various entries. I am also grateful to Gary Scharnhorst, Hugh Witemeyer, Gary Harrison, David Johnson, Pat Smith, and Bob Fleming for suggestions on particular entries, and to my wife, Mary, for her patience and for her help in preparing the illustrations. I am especially grateful to Bob Wolf, my editor at Facts On File, whose careful reading and thoughtful criticism did much to improve many of the entries, and to copy editor John Drexel. The inevitable mistakes and omissions in a work of this scope are wholly my own.

Cross-references within the entries are indicated with SMALL CAPITALS. Since all the works and all the characters have individual entries, they are not cross-referenced, except when a secondary entry—e.g., to a character's nickname or alias—indicates a primary entry on the topic. **Boldface** type is used within entries to indicate related subjects, such as family members related to the character who heads the entry. References to scenes or passages from Dickens's works are indicated with parenthetical chapter numbers. The works themselves are identified with short titles and are more fully described in the entry devoted to each work. Works identified by the following short titles appear alphabetically under the longer titles indicated below. Short titles not on the list can be found alphabetically among the entries.

Battle=The Battle of Life

"Bolton"="Mr. Robert Bolton"

Boz=Sketches by Boz

  "Beadle"="The Beadle. The Parish Engine. The Schoolmaster"

  "Broker's"="The Broker's Man"

  "Christening"="The Bloomsbury Christening"

  "Curate"="The Curate. The Old Lady. The Half-pay Captain"

  "Evans"="Miss Evans and the Eagle"

  "Hackney"="Hackney-coach Stands"

  "Last Cab-driver"="The Last Cab-driver, and the First Omnibus Cad"

  "Making a Night"="Making a Night of It"

  "Milliner"="The Mistaken Milliner"

  "Minns"="Mr. Minns and his Cousin"

  "Monmouth Street"="Meditations in Monmouth Street"

  "Neighbour"="Our Next-door Neighbour"

  "Pawnbroker's"="The Pawnbroker's Shop"

  "Porter"="Mrs. Joseph Porter"

  "Sparkins"="Horatio Sparkins"

  Tottle"="A Passage in the Life of Mr. Watkins Tottle"

  "Tuggses"="The Tuggses at Ramsgate"

  "Vauxhall"="Vauxhall Gardens by Day"

  "Winglebury"="The Great Winglebury Duel"

Carol=A Christmas Carol

Chimes=The Chimes

Chuzzlewit=Martin Chuzzlewit

Coquettes=The Village Coquettes

Copperfield=David Copperfield

Cricket=The Cricket on the Hearth

Curiosity Shop=The Old Curiosity Shop

Dombey=Dombey and Son

Dorrit=Little Dorrit

"Doubledick"="The Story of Richard Doubledick"

Drood=The Mystery of Edwin Drood

"English Prisoners"="The Perils of Certain English Prisoners"

Expectations=Great Expectations

"Golden Mary"="The Wreck of the Golden Mary"

"Haunted House"="The Haunted House" (*Christmas Stories*)

Humphrey=Master Humphrey's Clock

Lazy Tour=The Lazy Tour of Two Idle Apprentices

"Marigold"="Doctor Marigold"

Miscellaneous = *Miscellaneous Papers, Plays, and Poems*

    "Bull's Somnambulist" = "Mr. Bull's Somnambulist"

    "Extraordinary Traveller" = "Some Account of an Extraordinary Traveller"

    "Hippopotamus" = "The 'Good' Hippopotamus"

    "Jest-book" = "Proposals for a National Jest-book"

Mudfog = *The Mudfog and Other Sketches*

"Mugby" = "Mugby Junction"

Mutual Friend = *Our Mutual Friend*

Nickleby = *Nicholas Nickleby*

Nightingale = *Mr. Nightingale's Diary*

Notes = *American Notes*

Pickwick = *The Pickwick Papers*

Pictures = *Pictures from Italy*

"Poor Relation" = "The Poor Relation's Story"

Reprinted = *Reprinted Pieces*

    "At Dusk" = "To Be Read at Dusk"

    "Births" = "Births. Mrs. Meek, of a Son"

    "Bore" = "Our Bore"

    "Detective Anecdotes" = "Three 'Detective' Anecdotes"

    "French Folly" = "A Monument of French Folly"

    "French Watering Place" = "Our French Watering-Place"

    "Inspector Field" = "On Duty with Inspector Field"

    "Poor Man's Tale" = "A Poor Man's Tale of a Patent"

    "Workhouse" = "A Walk in a Workhouse"

Rudge = *Barnaby Rudge*

"Silverman" = "George Silverman's Explanation"

Stone = *Charles Dickens' Uncollected Writings from Household Words*, ed. Harry Stone

"Tiddler" = "Tom Tiddler's Ground"

"Tulrumble" = "The Public Life of Mr. Tulrumble"

Twist = *Oliver Twist*

Two Cities = *A Tale of Two Cities*

Uncommercial = *The Uncommercial Traveller*

(1) "His General Line of Business"

(2) "The Shipwreck"

(3) "Wapping Workhouse"

(4) "Two Views of a Cheap Theatre"

(5) "Poor Merchantile Jack"

(6) "Refreshments for Travellers"

(7) "Travelling Abroad"

(8) "The Great Tasmania's Cargo"

(9) "City of London Churches"

(10) "Shy Neighbourhoods"

(11) "Tramps"

(12) "Dullborough Town"

(13) "Night Walks"

(14) "Chambers"

(15) "Nurse's Stories"

(16) "Arcadian London"

(17) "The Italian Prisoner"

(18) "The Calais Night Mail"

(19) "Some Recollections of Mortality"

(20) "Birthday Celebrations"

(21) "The Short-timers"

(22) "Bound for the Great Salt Lake"

(23) "The City of the Absent"

(24) "An Old Stage-coaching House"

(25) "The Boiled Beef of New England"

(26) "Chatham Dockyard"

(27) "In the French-Flemish Country"

(28) "Medicine Men of Civilisation"

(29) "Titbull's Alms-houses"

(30) "The Ruffian"

(31) "Aboard Ship"

(32) "A Small Star in the East"

(33) "A Little Dinner in an Hour"

(34) "Mr. Barlow"

(35) "On an Amateur Beat"

(36) "A Fly-Leaf in a Life"

(37) "A Plea for Total Abstinence"

Young Couples = *Sketches of Young Couples*

Young Gentlemen = *Sketches of Young Gentlemen*

"Aaron" Wrayburn's nickname for RIAH. *Mutual Friend*.

"Aboard Ship" The Traveller's account of sailing on the steamship *Russia* from NEW YORK to LIVERPOOL, of his remembrances of other voyages, his constant awareness of the rolling sea and the ship's engine, and his relief on arriving at Queenstown in Ireland and, finally, at Liverpool. *Uncommercial* (31).

Ackroyd, Peter (1949–) English novelist, poet, critic, and biographer. Dickens has a prominent place in Ackroyd's work. His first novel, *The Great Fire of London* (1982), involves a project for filming *Little Dorrit*, and the novel itself is a continuation of Dickens's story. Ackroyd's controversial biography *Dickens* (1990) presents a compelling portrait of the author as a complex and creative personality. Although it lacks scholarly apparatus, its detailed account of Dickens's life, written with a novelist's intuition, makes it the most readable Dickens biography. Ackroyd has also written introductions to the Heinemann paperback edition of most of Dickens's works and an *Introduction to Dickens* (1991) for the general reader.

Adams (1) Head boy at Dr. Strong's school in Canterbury when David is in attendance there. *Copperfield*.

Adams (2) Clerk to Mr. Sampson, narrator of "Hunted Down."

Adams, Captain Lord Frederick Verisopht's second in the duel with Sir Mulberry Hawk. *Nickleby* (50).

Adams, Jack An acquaintance of Lord Feenix who is the subject of the story he tells at the marriage feast for Dombey and Edith. *Dombey* (31).

Adams, Jane Young housemaid to the Young Couple who reappears as the devoted old servant to the Old Couple in *Sketches of Young Couples*.

Addison, Joseph (1672–1719) One of the 18th-century authors whose works were familiar to Dickens. Although Dickens was not particularly fond of the serious essays of Addison, he found Addison's humorous essays "delightful."

"Address of the English Author to the French Public" Dickens's preface to the French translation of *Nicholas Nickleby* by P. Lorain (1857). Uncollected.

Adelphi A residential complex along the THAMES, between WATERLOO and Hungerford bridges, featuring a terrace of houses raised on arches and facing the river. Dickens had lodgings here as a young man. David Copperfield wanders in the dark arches during breaks from MURDSTONE AND GRINBY's, and later on has rooms there in Mrs. Crupp's house in BUCKINGHAM STREET (*Copperfield* 11, 23). Cornelius Brook Dingwall, M.P., has his residence here (*Boz*, 47). Martin Chuzzlewit takes lodgings in a poor public house (*Chuzzlewit*, 13); Mrs. Edson attempts suicide from Adelphi Terrace ("Lirriper's Lodgings"); Arthur Clennam eavesdrops on the meeting between Miss Wade and Rigaud on the Terrace (*Dorrit*, II:9). OSBORNE'S, the hotel where Wardle and Pickwick stay, is also in this neighborhood (*Pickwick*, 54, 56).

Adelphi Theatre Theater in the STRAND famous for melodrama and comic sketches. The young Dickens saw Charles Mathews perform his comic sketches here. Mentioned in *Pickwick* (31).

Admiral Benbow Inn Hotel at the deserted watering place in "Out of the Season" (*Reprinted*).

Admiralty A guest at Medle's dinner parties. *Dorrit* (I:21).

Adrian, Arthur (1906–) Dickens scholar and critic. In *Georgina Hogarth and the Dickens Circle* (1957), Professor Adrian carefully documents Georgina's life with Dickens, answering those who considered her the scheming cause of Dickens's marital troubles. In *Dickens and the Parent-Child Relationship* (1984), Adrian traces four patterns in the parent-child relationships: orphans, unwanted children, children misguided by their parents, and children forced to assume parental duties.

Affery Longtime maid to Mrs. Clennam and former nurse to Arthur. She is the wife of Jeremiah Flintwinch and lives in constant fear of her husband and her mistress and in bewilderment about their activities. *Dorrit*.

African Knife Swallower   Member of the Vincent Crummles's theater company. He looks and speaks "remarkably like an Irishman." *Nickleby* (48).

Agassiz, Louis (1807–1873)   American scientist, naturalist, and professor. Dickens met Agassiz on his trip to America in 1867. Agassiz attended the farewell party for Dickens when the author left BOSTON for NEW YORK.

"Aged P., The," short for "The Aged Parent"   WEMMICK'S old father; he is well cared for by his son and entertained by the sound of a cannon, which he can hear in spite of his deafness. *Expectations*.

"Aggerawaytor"   Cruncher's epithet for his wife. *Two Cities*.

Agnes   Mrs. Bloss's servant, the object of old Tibb's affections. *Boz*, "Boarding House."

"Agricultural Interest, The"   Uncollected article in the MORNING CHRONICLE (September 17–18, 1834).

Ainsworth, William Harrison (1805–1882)   Editor, publisher; novelist, especially of historical and NEWGATE NOVELS. Ainsworth met Dickens in 1834, the year he published his first novel, *Rookwood*. He introduced Dickens to JOHN FORSTER and to his first publisher, MACRONE. Dickens often attended gatherings of writers at Ainsworth's house and was one of the Trio Club with Ainsworth and Forster. Ainsworth preceded Dickens as editor of BENTLEY'S MISCELLANY. His Newgate novel, *Jack Sheppard* (1839), was often compared to *Twist*.

Akerman   A historical figure, the head jailer at NEWGATE PRISON at the time of the GORDON RIOTS who unsuccessfully tries to defend the prison against the rioters. *Rudge* (64).

Akershem, Sophronia   The "mature young lady," an acquaintance of the Veneerings, who marries Alfred Lammle believing him to be rich (I:10). When the two discover that they have mutually duped each other into marriage, they join forces and agree to prey on others together (I:10). She secretly warns Podsnap, however, of their scheme to entrap his daughter into a marriage with Fledgby (II:16). After going bankrupt, they flee the country (IV:8). *Mutual Friend*.

Albany, The   Chambers for men of fashion, located on the north side of PICCADILLY. Edward Malderton rests his claim as a man of fashion on knowing a former resident of the Albany (*Boz*, "Sparkins"). Fascination Fledgeby has his rooms here, where he is beaten by Lammle and treated to the pepper plaster by Jenny Wren (*Mutual Friend*, III:8).

Albery, James (1838–1889)   Victorian playwright who adapted *Pickwick* for the stage (1871) and whose *Two Roses* (1871) was a popular drama loosely based on *Little Dorrit*.

Albion, The   Public house in LITTLE RUSSELL STREET where Potter and Smithers were regulars. *Boz*, "Making a Night."

Aldersgate Street   The street in London leading north from ST. PAUL'S CATHEDRAL where the warehouse of Chuzzlewit and Son is located. Arthur Clennam comes upon Cavaletto in this street after the foreigner has been run over by a mail coach (*Dorrit*, I:13). Jasper stays in a "hybrid hotel" in a little square behind Aldersgate Street (*Drood*, 23).

Aldgate Pump   A London landmark near the corner of Leadenhall and FENCHURCH STREETs in the CITY. Mr. Blotton, Pickwick's critic in the Pickwick Club, has his residence in **Aldgate High Street** (*Pickwick*, 11), which went east from the pump to Petticoat Lane. Toots, distraught over Walter Gay's attentions to Florence Dombey, walks back and forth from Leadenhall Street to the pump to cool himself (*Dombey*, 56).

Alexander, Francis (1800–1881)   Boston artist who painted Dickens's portrait during his first visit to AMERICA in 1842. The painting was later owned by Dickens's American publisher, James FIELDS.

Alice   Youngest of the FIVE SISTERS OF YORK. With her four sisters she is working on an embroidery which is represented in the Five Sisters window at York Minster. *Nickleby* (6).

Alice, Mistress   Heroine of Magog's tale, the only daughter of the bowyer. *Humphrey* (1).

Alicia, Princess   Eldest daughter of King Watkins the First and heroine of Miss Alice Rainbird's story. "Holiday Romance."

Alick   "A damp, earthy child in red worsted socks" on the GRAVESEND steam packet. *Boz*, "River."

Alicumpaine, Mrs.   A friend of Mrs. Orange. "Holiday Romance."

All the Year Round   Dickens's second general circulation magazine, successor to HOUSEHOLD WORDS. After quarreling with BRADBURY & EVANS over the publication of a notice regarding his separation from his wife, Dickens returned to CHAPMAN & HALL and began this new magazine on April 30, 1859. Like its predecessor, it appeared in a two-column, unillustrated format at twopence for a weekly number, but besides general interest articles and stories, it also ran serialized novels. *A Tale of Two Cities* and *Great Expectations* both first appeared here, as did novels by Wilkie COLLINS, Edward Bulwer LYTTON, Mrs. GASKELL, and others. Dickens also contributed to the special Christmas numbers of the magazine (reprinted in *Christmas Stories*), the essays collected in *The Uncommercial Traveller*, and other miscellaneous papers. Dickens acted as editor and publisher of the magazine, hiring W. H. WILLS as his sub-editor and Chapman & Hall as his agents.

Allegory A narrative that is equated with another story outside of the narrative. Traditionally, allegory was religious, paralleling, for example, the characters and situations in the story to biblical counterparts. Allegorical characters are often personifications of moral traits or abstract ideas. Unlike SYMBOLISM, allegory does not seek to suggest multiple meanings or ambiguities; it establishes a one-to-one relationshp with its referent. The dust heaps in *Mutual Friend*, for example, would be symbolic rather than allegorical, for they suggest several meanings, among them wealth, mortality, pollution, and materialism.

Dickens frequently uses a traditional allegorical motif representing life as a journey. By giving *Twist* the subtitle "the parish boy's progress," Dickens links his story to an allegorical predecessor, John Bunyan's *Pilgrim's Progress* (1672), in which Christian journeys from the City of Destruction to the Celestial City. Master Humphrey says of Little Nell and her journey that she "exist[s] in a kind of allegory," and her story is a kind of progress, ending at the country church where she dies. Dickens's allegorical referent is not so clearly defined as Bunyan's, although *Curiosity Shop* may be the Dickens novel that comes closest to being an allegory.

More often Dickens uses allegorical elements in the novels. Characters with names that suggest their significance—characters like Pip (*seed*), Magwitch (*magic* +

Thomas Worth's illustration of Nell and her grandfather for the American Household Edition (1872–73) depicts the pair as pilgrims in the allegorical tradition of Bunyan's Pilgrim's Progress.

witch?), and Havisham (*have a sham? have is sham? have a shame?*)—have allegorical roots. The strong oppositions in the novels, such as that between Oliver and Fagin, for example, suggest the opposition of innocence and experience, youth and age, good and evil. The parable structure of *Hard Times* with its allusion to the biblical injunction "as ye sow, so shall ye reap," makes the novel, in part, a retelling of the biblical PARABLE.

Many critics have discussed these allegorical aspects of the novels. Janet L. LARSON analyzes the ways in which biblical allusion contributes to allegory, especially in the early novels, and she compares *Twist* with *Pilgrim's Progress*. Jonathan Arac (*Commissioned Spirits*, 1979) provides close allegorical readings of the American episodes in *Chuzzlewit* and the opening chapters of *Dorrit*. Juliet MCMASTER (1987) finds allegorical significance in the opposition of light (Ada) and darkness (Vholes) in *Bleak House*. Sylvere MONOD (1968) and Geoffrey THURLEY (1976) consider the last three novels especially allegorical. Jane Vogel (*Allegory in Dickens*, 1977) offers a reading of all of Dickens's novels as Christian allegories; her interpretations offer some provocative insights into the biblical dimensions of Dickens's vision. Mildred Newcome (*The Imagined World of Charles Dickens*, 1989) sees all of Dickens's novels as developing an extended "allegory of a nineteenth-century Everyman . . . [who] must find the wisdom to permit the natural processes of life, both for himself and for others whom he touches, the freedom to develop, mature, come to fruition, and decay."

Allen, Arabella "A black eyed young lady in a very nice pair of boots with fur round the top" (28), who secretly marries Winkle. Her brother, medical student **Benjamin**, friend and drinking companion of Bob Sawyer, is "a coarse, stout, thick-set young man, with black hair cut rather short, and a white face cut rather long. . . . He presented, altogether, rather a mildewy appearance, and emitted a fragrant odour of full-flavoured Cubas" (30). His plan that Bob marry his sister is foiled when she elopes with Winkle (48). Pickwick reconciles Allen to his sister's marriage. *Pickwick*.

Allonby Seaside town in Cumberland where the two idle apprentices find nothing to keep them occupied. *Lazy Tour* (3).

Alphonse Mrs. Wititterly's little page boy. "If ever an Alphonse carried plain Bill in his face and figure, that page was the boy." *Nickleby* (21).

"Altro" Pancks's nickname for CAVALETTO, based on the foreigner's frequent use of the Italian word meaning "certainly." *Dorrit*.

Amarinta "Bright-eyed" lady "with the obdurate parents" in the narrator's youthful castle in the air. *Miscellaneous*, "Gone to the Dogs." Probably an allusion to Maria BEADNELL.

Amateur Theatricals From early childhood Dickens was entranced by the theater. In his Preface to *The Memoirs of Joseph Grimaldi*, he recalls his excitement at watching the PANTOMIME clowns; before he was nine he wrote a tragedy, *MISNAR, SULTAN OF INDIA;* he spent many hours writing for and performing plays in a toy theater. As a young man, he scheduled an audition at COVENT GARDEN, which illness forced him to cancel. Although he did not follow a theatrical career, his theatrical enthusiasm continued throughout his life, especially in the performances of his amateur theatrical groups in the 1840s and 1850s and in the PUBLIC READINGS of the 1860s.

The Dickens family had produced plays at home, performances in which Charles acted, directed, and stage-managed. His first public performances took place in MONTREAL during his American journey in 1842. There Dickens directed three plays, taking parts in all of them. Between 1845 and 1857, Dickens directed theatrical groups composed of family and friends nearly every year. Regular members of the casts were John FORSTER, Douglas JERROLD, John LEECH, Mark LEMON, Augustus EGG, Frank STONE, Wilkie COLLINS, Mary BOYLE, Catherine DICKENS, Mary DICKENS, and Georgina HOGARTH. Dickens's artist friends designed and constructed sets. Typically the evening included a "serious" play—Ben Jonson's *EVERY MAN IN HIS HUMOUR* and Shakespeare's *Merry Wives of Windsor*, for example—followed by a farce. Dickens directed, managed, and played the leading roles in both plays. Some of the performances were private, for friends and invited guests, like two for Queen VICTORIA and Prince Albert, one in 1851 when the group performed Edward Bulwer LYTTON'S *Not so Bad as We Seem*, and the second in 1857, a performance of Collins's *THE FROZEN DEEP*. Public performances were given for charity; the group raised a good deal of money for indigent writers and the GUILD OF LITERATURE AND ART. In the 1850s the group made several tours of England—especially to MANCHESTER, LIVERPOOL, and BIRMINGHAM—on these charitable enterprises.

During a production of *The Frozen Deep* in 1857, Dickens met Ellen TERNAN, a professional actress hired for the performances in Manchester.

Dickens's favorite roles elicited his histrionic skills. He was said to be "glorious" as the boastful Bobadil in *Every Man in his Humour*; one of the stage carpenters remarked to him, "It was a great loss to the public when you took to writing books!" In a similar vein, Mrs. Frederick YATES exclaimed after one of his performances: "Oh Mr. Dickens what a pity it is you can do anything else!"

Amelia (1) A young girl visiting Ramsgate. *Boz*, "Tuggs."

Amelia (2) The wife of Bill, a criminal defendent being represented by Jaggers. She is so persistent in pleading with Jaggers for his help that the lawyer threatens to drop his client if she does not stop bothering him. *Expectations* (20).

America   Dickens describes his first American tour, in 1842, in *AMERICAN NOTES*. He also used this American experience in *Chuzzlewit*: Young Martin's journey to the New World becomes a Dantesque descent into the heart of darkness where the greed and selfishness that are the themes of the novel emerge in exaggerated form on the American frontier.

His criticisms of the American character in *Notes*—of sharp dealing, suspiciousness, corrupt politics, slavery, and a slanderous press—enraged his American readers in 1842. In an article in *ALL THE YEAR ROUND* in 1862, during the American Civil War, he implies that his assessment has not changed in 20 years (*Miscellaneous*, "Young Man from the Country").

On his second trip to the United States, between November 9, 1867 and April 22, 1868, Dickens gave an exhausting series of PUBLIC READINGS in 16 eastern cities. He repaired the damage of his earlier visit by his kind remarks on the improvements he found after a quarter century. Useful accounts of Dickens's American visits can be found in Michael SLATER's introduction to *Dickens on America and the Americans* (1978) and in Jerome Meckier's *Innocent Abroad* (1990).

"America Junior"   Name used by Putnam SMIF when he writes to Martin Chuzzlewit. *Chuzzlewit* (22).

"American in Europe, An"   Dickens's review of Henry Colman's *European Life and Manners, in Familiar Letters to Friends* for the *EXAMINER* (July 21, 1849). Dickens criticizes Colman's sycophantic fascination with the British aristocracy and his misrepresentations of English life, resulting from his concentration on the luxurious life at country estates. *Miscellaneous*.

American Notes for General Circulation   Dickens's account of his American journey in 1842, largely based on his letters to John FORSTER. The Dickenses sailed from LIVERPOOL on January 3 and visited BOSTON, Springfield, HARTFORD, New Haven, NEW YORK, PHI-

This cartoon from a British magazine on the occasion of Dickens's departure on his American reading tour in 1867 depicts the novelist surrounded by his characters as he bids farewell to John Bull.

Thomas Nast's frontispiece for an American edition of American Notes *(1872–73) depicts the confrontation between Britain and America that angered many American readers of the book.*

LADELPHIA, WASHINGTON, Fredericksburg, RICHMOND, BALTIMORE, HARRISBURG, PITTSBURGH, Cincinnati, LOUISVILLE, CAIRO (Illinois), ST. LOUIS, LEBANON (Illinois; the LOOKING-GLASS PRAIRIE), Columbus, Sandusky, Cleveland, Erie, Buffalo, NIAGARA FALLS, Toronto, KINGSTON, MONTREAL, QUEBEC, Albany, West Point, and a Shaker settlement in LEBANON (New York) before leaving for England from New York City on June 7.

Although Dickens made many friends on the tour, particularly among the literati of Boston, he found the public attentions of the Americans exhausting, and his speeches endorsing international COPYRIGHT alienated some of his American readers. His growing disillusion with America during the journey finds its way into *American Notes* in his critical remarks on the American press, sanitary conditions in the cities, slavery, and American manners, especially the practice of spitting in public. Ironically, *Notes* first appeared in the United States in a pirated version in the periodical *Brother Jonathan*. The book so angered some American readers that it was publicly burned at a theater in New York.

"American Panorama, The"   Article for the EXAMINER (December 16, 1848) recommending "the largest picture in the world," a three-mile-long panorama of the MISSISSIPPI and Missouri rivers from New Orleans to Yellowstone by Mr. Banvard that was currently on display in PICCADILLY. *Miscellaneous.*

Amsterdam, Holland   After the riots, Lord George Gordon flees here, but is refused residence by the "quiet burgomasters" (*Rudge*, 82). After the fall of the House of Clennam, Jeremiah Flintwinch settles in Amsterdam,

where he is known as Mynheer van Flyntevynge (*Dorrit*, II:31).

"Amusements of the People, The"   Two-part article for *HOUSEHOLD WORDS* (March 30, April 13, 1850) describing working-class theaters and arguing for their support and improvement. They should not be closed, Dickens argues much like Sleary in *Hard Times*, because "the people . . . *will be* amused somewhere." Viewing the exhibits at the Polytechnic Institution and reading are not reasonable substitutes for these melodramatic plays in working-class theaters and saloons. *Miscellaneous.*

"Analytical Chemist, The"   The Veneerings's butler who "goes round like a gloomy Analytical Chemist; always seeming to say, after 'Chablis, sir?'—'You wouldn't if you knew what its made of' " (I:2). *Mutual Friend.*

Andersen, Hans Christian (1805–1875)   Danish author and writer of *Fairy Tales*, published from 1835 to 1872. A great admirer of Dickens, he stayed in Dickens's house on his vists to England in 1847 and 1857, but after the second visit, Dickens put a card in the dressing table mirror in the room where Andersen stayed, reading "Hans Christian Andersen slept in this room for five weeks which seemed to the family ages."

Anderson, Mr. and Mrs. John   The neatly dressed and spotless tramps whom the Uncommercial Traveller encounters on the road. John has chalked HUNGRY on the spade that he carries. *Uncommercial*, "Tramps."

Angel (1)   Coaching inn at ISLINGTON on the northern route out of London that Oliver Twist and Noah Claypole pass as they enter the city. *Twist* (8, 42).

Angel (2)   Inn at BURY ST. EDMUNDS, Suffolk, where Sam Weller first meets Job Trotter and where Pickwick receives notice that Mrs. Bardell is suing him for breach of promise. *Pickwick* (15–18). Dickens stayed at the Angel in 1835 while reporting on the parliamentary election.

Angelica   An old girlfriend of the Traveller. *Uncommercial* (9).

Anglers' Inn   The riverside inn where Lizzie Hexam takes Eugene Wrayburn after he is attacked by Bradley Headstone (*Mutual Friend*, IV:10). The original is the Red Lion Hotel in HENLEY-on-Thames.

Anglo-Bengalee Disinterested Loan and Life Assurance Company   The fraudulent investment company promoted by Montague Tigg and David Crimple, with investment capital amounting to "two and as many noughts after it as the printer can get in the line." *Chuzzlewit* (27).

"Animal Magnetism"   Farce by Elizabeth Inchbald (1753–1821) that Dickens read as a child and that he later included in the repertory of his amateur theatrical groups. Dickens, who practiced animal magnetism, or MESMERISM, himself, played a doctor who induced hypnotic spells.

Anne Dombey's housemaid who, when the House of Dombey crashes, marries Towlinson the butler; together they open a grocery store. *Dombey* (59).

Anny An old pauper who summons Mrs. Corney, the matron of the workhouse, to the deathbed of Sally, another pauper who attended Oliver's mother on her deathbed. Sally gives Mrs. Corney a locket and information essential to unravelling Oliver's parentage. *Twist* (24, 51).

"Another Round of Stories by the Christmas Fire" Extra Christmas number of *HOUSEHOLD WORDS*, 1853. Dickens contributed "The Schoolboy's Story" and "Nobody's Story." Among the other contributors were Eliza Lynn LINTON, Adelaide Ann PROCTER, and George SALA.

Antonio A guitar-playing Spanish sailor whom the Traveller meets in Megisson's lodging house. *Uncommercial* (5).

Antwerp, Belgium Rigaud meets Jeremiah Flintwinch's twin brother, Ephraim, here when Ephraim brings the iron box containing the Clennam papers from London. *Dorrit*, (II:30).

Apothecary In the 19th century the apothecary acted as both druggist and general practitioner in treating the poor, especially in rural areas. When old Sally dies in the workhouse, she is attended by an apothecary's apprentice (*Twist* 24). An apothecary attends Nicholas Nickleby's father on his deathbed (*Nickleby*, 1). A "calm Apothecary" attends the ailing Paul Dombey at Blimber's Academy (*Dombey*, 14).

"Appeal to Fallen Women, An" Privately printed leaflet by Dickens (1850) in aid of the URANIA COTTAGE project to rescue prostitutes from the streets.

Arabian Nights, The Dickens read these tales as a child, probably in Jonathan Scott's translation (1811), and they became one of his favorite books. He alludes to the tales frequently in his works, often as representative of the world of FANCY or imagination. Michael SLATER (1983) remarks that such "allusions are a sure sign that his emotions are deeply stirred; they are a guarantee of the genuineness of his romantic feelings."

"Arcadian London" During vacation time when London is deserted, the city becomes an arcadian wilderness in a golden age. The Traveller goes out into the empty streets from his lodging in BOND STREET to be "soothed by the repose" around him and to celebrate the city which has become "the abode of love." *Uncommercial* (16). Originally in *ALL THE YEAR ROUND* (September 29, 1860).

"Archbishop of Greenwich" The fanciful name given to the waiter at the restaurant in GREENWICH where Rokesmith and Bella have their wedding breakfast. *Mutual Friend* (IV:4).

Archetype A term from Jungian psychology for a primordial image or symbol from the "collective unconscious" of the human race that appears repeatedly in MYTHS, dreams, religions, and literature. Such images can awaken the unconscious memories of readers, linking their personal experience to the broader experience of their culture and of humankind. Some of the powerful archetypes that recur in Dickens's works are the city as labyrinth, suggesting that the quest for identity in London is like Theseus's challenge to the Minotaur; the river as both deadly and renewing, producing the drowning/ resurrection motif that appears in several novels, particularly *Expectations, Mutual Friend,* and *Drood;* the lost Eden, in which paradise becomes a deadly garden in *Chuzzlewit* and a "ruined garden" at SATIS HOUSE (*Expectations*); the self as orphan, born to an unknown father like Oliver Twist, a "posthumous" father like Copperfield, or a vindictive father like Harmon (*Mutual Friend*); life as a journey, typified by the ways in which the capsule journeys in *Twist* (8) and *Copperfield* (13) become emblematic of the heroes' lives.

Aristocracy The social range in Dickens's novels is sometimes compared to that in THACKERAY's works. Thackeray's world stretches from servants through the middle class to the mansions of Lord Steyne, and even to the royal receiving rooms. Dickens, by contrast, starts in society's lower depths—in Fagin's den—and moves on to tell of small tradesmen, professionals (especially lawyers), and gentlemen of the upper middle class. Far less frequently than Thackeray does he describes the country estates of the landed aristocracy or the mansions of the silver-fork denizens of London.

If the dimensions of Dickens's world were established by his background and experience, they were also influenced by his Radical political views and his sensitivity to the shifts in power during his lifetime. A strong supporter of parliamentary REFORM in 1832 and an opponent of the CORN LAWS in the mid-1840s, Dickens saw the landed aristocracy as obsolete opponents to progress, and, as a disciple of CARLYLE, as idle parasites who irresponsibly sapped society's wealth without contributing to it. In their occasional appearances in the early novels, in such figures as Sir Mulberry Hawk (*Nickleby*) or Sir John Chester (*Rudge*), they are villains, but in later works they become increasingly absurd, like the Chuzzlewits who trace their lineage back to Adam or the Boodles, Coodles, and Noodles of *Bleak House,* who ritualistically repeat obsolete social rites. More dangerous than old baronets such as Sir Leicester Dedlock, who cannot really grasp the significance of the social changes that have made him obsolete, are the middle-class sycophants who kowtow to aristocratic tradition. Mrs. Nickleby nearly sacrifices Kate to Hawk; Turveydrop's dandiacal imitation of the aristocracy imposes on Prince and Caddy (*Bleak House*).

Dedlock may be an absurd, finally even a pathetic figure, but aristocratic privilege can have destructive implications. The Barnacles who inherit the CIRCUMLOCUTION OFFICE by traditional right prevent social progress and ruin individual lives (*Dorrit*) and self-loathing aristocratic idlers like Harthouse (*Hard Times*) and Gowan (*Dorrit*) bring suffering to those around them.

Insofar as aristocratic power was passed into the hands of the merchants and capitalists, England saved itself from a bloodbath like that of France; but by the end of his life, Dickens clearly wondered whether a powerful bourgeoisie is any better than an oppressive aristocracy. Figures like Bounderby (*Hard Times*), Merdle (*Dorrit*), Veneering and Podsnap (*Mutual Friend*) seem just as destructive in their own ways as the old aristocracy they displaced.

Artful Dodger   The nickname of Jack DAWKINS. *Twist*.

Arundel Street   In the STRAND. The offices of CHAPMAN & HALL, where Dickens bought the issue of the MONTHLY MAGAZINE that contained his first published story, were located here.

Ashford, Nettie   The young lady, "aged half-past six," who is the author of the story of Mrs. Orange in "Holiday Romance," a fantasy about a world where adults and children exchange roles.

"Aspire"   Poem in HOUSEHOLD WORDS (April 25, 1851) urging the reader to affirm the power "in thyself alone . . . / Which strives to reach the light."

"Astley's"   Sketch originally published as "Sketches of London, No. 11" in the EVENING CHRONICLE (May 9, 1835), recalling the narrator's delight as a child at the performances at ASTLEY'S ROYAL EQUESTRIAN AMPHITHEATRE and describing his observations of a family outing to the theater at the present time.

Astley's Royal Equestrian Amphitheatre   An outdoor ampitheater for popular entertainment on WESTMINSTER BRIDGE Road in LAMBETH, South London. Its spectacular productions, mixing theater and circus, always included equestrian performances. Dickens provides a detailed description in "Astley's" (*Boz*). Kit Nubbles takes family outings to Astley's (*Curiosity Shop*, 39, 72). George Rouncewell attends an equestrian show and "is much delighted with the horses and the feats of strength; . . . disapproves of the combats, as giving evidences of unskilful swordsmanship; but is touched home by the sentiments" (*Bleak House*, 21).

Athenaeum   Chief weekly review of books and cultural affairs in England from 1828 to 1921. The *Athenaeum* was somewhat grudging in its reviews of Dickens's early novels, and during the 1840s it often praised the intent of the novels while faulting their liberties in form and style. By the end of Dickens's career, particularly in Henry CHORLEY's reviews of *Expectations* and *Mutual Friend*, the magazine acknowledged Dickens's preeminence among English writers; its obituary notice described the novelist as "one of the greatest and most beneficent men of genius England has produced since the days of Shakespeare."

Athenaeum Club   A club for distinguished and learned men, founded in 1824 and located in London. Dickens was elected to the club in 1838, along with MACREADY, Darwin, and the classical historian George Grote. Among its members during Dickens's time were John FORSTER, THACKERAY, BROWNING, and Anthony TROLLOPE.

Atherfield   **Mrs. Atherfield** and her daughter **Lucy** are passengers on the GOLDEN MARY, the ship that collides with an iceberg in "The Wreck of the Golden Mary," the story by Dickens, Wilkie COLLINS, and others for the Christmas Number of ALL THE YEAR ROUND in 1856. Lucy dies at sea after they abandon ship.

Atlantic Monthly, The   Magazine founded in Boston in 1857 and published by Dickens's American publishers, TICKNOR AND FIELDS. "GEORGE SILVERMAN'S EXPLANATION" appeared here between January and March, 1868. Dickens also contributed an article on his friend Charles FECHTER, "On Mr. Fechter's Acting" (August 1869), when Fechter, an actor and theater manager, was leaving London to resettle in the United States.

Augustus   The dog, "named in affectionate remembrance of a former lover of his mistress to whom he bore a striking personal resemblance," dissected by Professors Muff and Noggs. *Mudfog*.

Aunt, Benjamin Allen's   The aunt with whom Arabella stays in Clifton. *Pickwick* (39).

Aunt, Mr. F's   The crazy old lady who lives with Flora Finching, the aunt of Flora's deceased husband. She is marked by "extreme severity and grim taciturnity; sometimes interrupted by a propensity to offer remarks in a deep warning voice, which, being totally uncalled for by anything said by anybody, and traceable to no association of ideas, confounded and terrified the mind." *Dorrit* (I:13).

Austin Friars   The street in the CITY where Mr. Fips, old Martin Chuzzlewit's solicitor, has his office. *Chuzzlewit* (39).

Austin, Henry (d. 1861)   A lifelong friend of Dickens, he married Dickens's sister Letitia in 1837 and was a frequent visitor at the Dickens home. An architect and artist, Austin supervised the remodeling of TAVISTOCK HOUSE and GAD'S HILL PLACE and painted portraits of Maria BEADNELL when Dickens was courting her.

Australia In the early years of the 19th century, Australia was largely seen as a penal colony to which British convicts had been transported from 1788 onward. Magwitch, after he is recaptured on the marshes, is sentenced to transportation, and he makes his fortune as a sheep farmer in Australia (*Expectations*). "Free settlement" of the continent was encouraged from the 1820s and transportation ceased in 1842. In spite of his dislike of Malthusianism (see MALTHUS), Dickens supported efforts to encourage the poor to immigrate to Australia, and as a director of URANIA COTTAGE, he encouraged some of the women to begin a new life there. This policy also informs the resettlement of Martha Endell and Little Em'ly in *Copperfield*, who go off to the colony with Daniel Peggotty and the Micawbers (57), where they successfully establish a new life. Dickens encouraged two of his sons, Alfred and Edward, to immigrate and take up sheep farming in the outback. (See DICKENS, ALFRED and DICKENS, EDWARD.) In 1862, Dickens himself seriously considered making a reading tour of Australia.

Autobiography Dickens was reserved, even secretive, about some parts of his life and never wrote an autobiography. He destroyed some letters from friends and members of his family—especially those from his father—and instructed his heirs to destroy others. He did write a brief account of his childhood experience in the BLACKING FACTORY, which he shared only with John FORSTER. This fragment, reprinted in Forster's biography, is sometimes referred to as Dickens's Autobiography.

Modern commentators have assumed that Dickens's failure to write an autobiography resulted from the fact that many of his memories were too painful to commit to paper, but Dickens may not have considered himself a fit subject for such a work. Many Victorian autobiographies—those of J. S. MILL and Newman, for example—were accounts of intellectual development; others, like TROLLOPE's, were records of achievements. The romantic, confessional mode, which Dickens's autobiographical fragment represents, was out of fashion.

The novels provided an outlet for Dickens's autobiographical impulses and also enabled Dickens to mask direct personal revelation behind such characters as Pip or David Copperfield, the most directly autobiographical of Dickens's heroes. In their first-person accounts, Dickens could write his life and mask it at the same time, much as BROWNING was able to disguise self-revelation behind the characters in his dramatic monologues.

Although *Copperfield* and *Expectations* have often been treated as autobiographical fictions by Dickens critics, nearly all of Dickens's writings are, in a broad sense,

Fred Barnard's vignette of Dickens as a despondent child, sitting in the window of Warren's Blacking, where he pastes labels on the blacking bottles.

autobiographical. They provide a record of the inner life of their author, of the traumas remembered from his childhood, of his repeated attempts to accept his father's irresponsibility and his mother's hard-heartedness, and of his own domestic failures and public successes. Many of Dickens's journalistic writings provide an account of more mundane events in his life: travels; visits to schools, hospitals, and prisons; evenings in the theater and at public entertainments; observations of people at work or at leisure.

Avenger The nickname for Pip's servant boy, PEPPER. *Expectations* (27).

Avignon, France City northwest of MARSEILLES that is the home of Hortense, Lady Dedlock's French maid (*Bleak House*, 12). Cavaletto does odd jobs here (*Dorrit*, I:11). Captain Richard Doubledick recovers from his wounds nearby ("Seven Poor Travellers"). Dickens's visit here is described in *Pictures from Italy*.

Axton, William (1926–) Professor at the University of Louisville and an editor of *Dickens Studies News-*

letter and *Dickens Annual*. In *Circle of Fire* (1967), Axton discusses Dickens's debt to the popular Victorian theater. A classic article, "Keystone Structure in Dickens' Serial Novels" (*University of Toronto Quarterly*, 1967), explores the larger structural patterns in the monthly serials, noting the special importance of parts 5, 10, and 15 in the overall pattern. Axton has also published articles on *Pickwick*, *Dombey*, and other Dickensian topics. *Convivial Dickens* (1983), written with Edward Hewett, describes and supplies recipes for the drinks in Dickens's novels.

Aylmer, Felix (1889–1979)   Penname of Felix Edward Aylmer Jones, English actor and writer. For *Dickens Incognito* (1959) he combed Dickens's diaries to uncover coded references to the author's relationship with Ellen TERNAN, including his controversial and later discredited discovery of a child born to the couple. In *The Drood Case* (1965) Aylmer argued that Drood was not murdered and that Jasper, though arrested for the crime, was to be exonerated in the conclusion of the novel. His theatrical adaptation of the novel in collaboration with Jane Bacon in 1951 developed dramatically this solution to the Drood mystery.

Ayresleigh, Mr.   A "pale and haggard" debtor whom Pickwick meets at Namby's sponging house. *Pickwick* (40).

B., Master Ghost in Dickens's Christmas story, "The HAUNTED HOUSE," a projection of the lost youth of John the narrator.

Baber Junior clerk in Tapenham's department who "represented the turf," "made a book, and wore a speckled blue cravat and top-boots." *Miscellaneous*, "Cheap Patriotism."

Babley, Richard The given name of Mr. DICK. *Copperfield*.

Bachelor, The Kindly old gentleman who lives with the clergyman in the rural village where Nell and her grandfather end their wanderings. In the village he is known only as the Bachelor, "the active spirit of the place, . . . the universal mediator, comforter, and friend" (52). He turns out to be Mr. Garland's brother, and one of his letters reveals the location of Nell and her Grandfather to those who are searching for them (68). *Curiosity Shop*.

Badger, Bayham Doctor with whom Richard Carstone studies medicine. A cousin of Kenge, John Jarndyce's solicitor, Dr. Badger, "a pink, fresh-faced, crisp-looking gentleman, with a weak voice, light hair, and surprised eyes" (13), is perhaps most notable as Mrs. Bayham Badger's third husband. His wife, **Laura**, is the widow of Captain Swosser, R. N., and of Professor Dingo. *Bleak House*.

Bagman, The One-Eyed The traveling salesman who tells two of the INTERPOLATED TALES in *Pickwick*, "The BAGMAN'S STORY" (14) and "The Story of the BAGMAN'S UNCLE" (49). The Pickwickians meet him at the PEACOCK in EATANSWILL (14) and again at the BUSH INN at BRISTOL (48).

"Bagman's Story, The" In this INTERPOLATED TALE in *Pickwick*, Tom Smart, a traveling salesman, stops at a country inn where a "grim-looking high-backed chair" in his room turns into an old man during the night and advises him to expose Jinkins, the adulterous suitor of the widow who owns the inn, and to marry the widow himself. *Pickwick* (14).

Bagman's Uncle See MARTIN, JACK.

"Bagman's Uncle, Story of the" One of two INTERPOLATED TALES told by the Bagman in *Pickwick*. After drinking too much one evening in Edinburgh, Jack Martin, the Bagman's uncle, falls asleep in a derelict coach and imagines himself back in the 18th century, a passenger in the mail coach from Edinburgh to London. With him in the coach is a beautiful young woman, the son of the Marquess of Filletoville who has abducted her, and the Marquess's henchman. Jack rescues the girl and races off with her in the coach, pursued by the villains. Before they can catch him, he wakes up to find himself sitting in a derelict coach on a cold and rainy morning in Edinburgh. *Pickwick* (49).

Bagnet, Matthew ("Lignum Vitae") Ex-artilleryman, bassoon player, and proprietor of a small musical instrument shop. An army friend of George Rouncewell, he acts as guarantor of George's loan from Grandfather Smallweed. "An ex-artilleryman, tall and upright, with shaggy eyebrows, and whiskers like the fibres of a cocoanut, not a hair upon his head, and a torrid complexion. His voice, short, deep, and resonant, is not at all unlike the tones of the instrument to which he is devoted. Indeed, there may be generally observed in him an unbending, unyielding, brass-bound air, as if he were himself the bassoon of the human orchestra" (27). When George is unable to repay the loan, Smallweed threatens the meager finances of the Bagnet family. **Mrs. Bagnet ("the Old Girl")** manages his household and advises him on all the important decisions in his life. When George Rouncewell is arrested for the murder of Mr. Tulkinghorn, she goes off to Lincolnshire to find Mrs. Rouncewell and reunites George with his mother from whom he has long been separated (52). "A strong, busy, active, honest-faced woman, . . . so economically dressed (though substantially), that the only article of ornament of which she stands possessed appears to be her wedding-ring; around which her finger has grown to be so large since it was put on, that it will never come off again until it shall mingle with Mrs. Bagnet's dust" (27). Their three children, **Quebec**, **Malta**, and **Woolwich**, are named for military bases where the family has been stationed. *Bleak House*.

Bagstock, Major Joseph Retired army officer who lives across the way from Miss Tox; "a wooden-featured, blue-faced major, with eyes starting out of his head, . . . [who] tickled his vanity with the fiction that [Miss Tox] was a splendid woman, who had her eye on him. This he had several times hinted at the club: in connexion with little jocularities, of which old Joe Bagstock, old Joey Bagstock, old J. Bagstock, old Josh Bagstock, or so forth, was the perpetual theme. . . . 'Joey B., Sir,' the Major would say, . . . '[is] tough, Sir, tough and de-vilish sly!' " (7) He keeps an Indian servant whom he abuses and calls "the Native." Reactionary and self-absorbed, Bagstock worms his way into Dombey's confidence, accompanies him to LEAMINGTON, where he promotes his marriage to Edith Granger (26), acompanies him to DIJON, but then abandons him after the bankruptcy (58). *Dombey.*

Bailey, Benjamin ("Bailey Junior") Houseboy at Todgers, "a small boy with a large red head and no nose to speak of" (8). A streetwise and resiliant Cockney, he leaves Todgers to become a groom for Tigg Montague (27), is nearly killed in a coach accident (42), and eventually becomes a partner in Poll Sweedlepipe's bird business (52). *Chuzzlewit.*

Bailey, Captain David's presumed rival for the attentions of the eldest Miss Larkins. *Copperfield* (18).

Baillie "Baillie Mac something and four syllables after it," a friend of the Bagman's Uncle. *Pickwick* (49).

Bald-Faced Stag, The A coaching inn where Tom Pinch stops on the road to London from SALISBURY. *Chuzzlewit* (36).

Balderstone, Thomas ("Uncle Tom") Mrs. Gatterton's rich brother who remembers all of Shakespeare's plays word for word and disrupts the performance of *Othello* with his unnecessary promptings. *Boz*, "Porter."

Balim A young ladies' young gentleman, "so profusely decked with scarfs, ribands, flowers, and other pretty spoils, that he looked like a lamb . . . adorned for the sacrifice." *Young Gentlemen.*

Ball's Pond A district on the undeveloped north edge of London in Dickens's time. Mr. and Mrs. Theodosious Butler have a house near a brickfield here (*Boz*, "Sentiment"); Mr. Perch, Dombey's messenger, also lives here (*Dombey*, 18).

Baltimore, Maryland Being served by slaves on his first visit to Baltimore in 1842 left Dickens "with a sense of shame and self-reproach," though he appreciated Barnum's Hotel, the only one in America "where the English traveller will find curtains to his bed." He also spent a memorable evening here with Washington IRVING, sharing an enormous mint julep. On his second visit in 1868, Dickens found the city still haunted by "the ghost of slavery." Dickens describes his 1842 visit in *Notes*, 8–9.

Bamber, Jack One of the law clerks Pickwick meets at the MAGPIE AND STUMP (20), "a little, yellow high-shouldered man [with a] . . . shrivelled face, . . . remarkable features, . . . [and] a fixed grim smile." He tells the "Tale of the QUEER CLIENT" (*Pickwick*, 21). Pickwick proposes him for membership in Master Humphrey's circle (*Humphrey*, 4).

Banger, Captain Vestryman of Wilderness Walk. *Reprinted*, "Vestry."

Bangham, Mrs. The charwoman and messenger in the MARSHALSEA PRISON who attends Mrs. Dorrit at the birth of her daughter Amy. *Dorrit* (I:6).

Bank of England Dickens mentions this CITY landmark in several of his novels. Boz describes an omnibus ride that ends at the Bank (*Boz*, "Omnibuses"); the Gordon rioters vainly attack the bank (*Rudge*, 67); and the Traveller meditates on the bank and its treasures during his night walks (*Uncommercial*, 13). The bank is also mentioned in *Nickleby* (35), *Dombey* (13), and *Dorrit* (I:26).

Banks, Major Meltham assumes the disguise of this retired East India Company director to trick Julius Slinkton. "Hunted Down."

Bantam, Angelo Cyrus The Master of Ceremonies in the Pump Room at BATH, a dandy, "a charming young man of not much more than fifty," who introduces Pickwick to the society at Bath. *Pickwick* (35).

Baps The dancing master at Dr. Blimber's academy, "a grave gentleman, with a slow and measured manner of speaking" (14). He and his **wife** attend the going-away party at the beginning of the school holiday. *Dombey.*

Baptista, Giovanni Genoese narrator of the story of Clara and Signor Dellombra. *Reprinted*, "At Dusk."

Baptiste Soldier billeted on the poor water-carrier in the French town where Langley, the misanthropic Englishman, stays. "Somebody's Luggage."

Bar The barrister with "his insinuating Jury droop and . . . persuasive double eyeglass," who represents the Law and is one of Merdle's guests. *Dorrit* (I:21).

Barbara The Garland's servant girl, "tidy, modest and demure" (22). She is jealous of Kit Nubbles's devotion to Little Nell, but later marries him. Her **mother** becomes friendly with Mrs. Nubbles on the excursion to ASTLEY'S (39), and later goes with her daughter to visit Kit in prison (63). *Curiosity Shop.*

Barbary, Miss Lady Dedlock's stern sister who lives at WINDSOR; the "godmother" who raises Esther Summerson. "She was a good, good woman! She went to church three times every Sunday, and to morning prayers on Wednesdays and Fridays, and to lectures whenever there were lectures; and never missed. She was handsome; and if she had ever smiled, would have been . . . like an angel—but she never smiled." *Bleak House* (3).

Barbary, Mrs. Captain, of Cheltenham   Owner of a horse that Captain Maroon attempts to sell. *Dorrit* (I:12).

Barbican   District in the CITY of London where Simon Tappertit and the 'PRENTICE KNIGHTS hold their meetings at an inn (*Rudge*, 8). It is also mentioned in *Twist* (21), *Chuzzlewit* (37), and *Dorrit* (I:13).

Barbox Brothers   A bill-brokering house off LOMBARD STREET with a reputation for hard dealing. When Young Jackson, the last remaining member of the firm, retires, the firm is closed down. He is known by the nickname "Barbox Brothers." "Mugby."

Bardell, Mrs. Martha   Pickwick's landlady in GOSWELL STREET. "A comely woman, of bustling manners, and agreeable appearance; with a natural genius for cooking" (12), she is the widow of a government clerk who had been "knocked on the head with a quart pot in a public house cellar" (34). After she misconstrues Pickwick's questions about keeping a servant as a proposal of marriage (18), she files a breach-of-promise suit against him and is represented in the action by the unscrupulous lawyers Dodson and Fogg. When Pickwick refuses to pay the costs of the trial, the lawyers turn on her and she too is imprisoned in FLEET PRISON (47). She is released when Pickwick agrees to pay the costs. **Tommy**, Mrs. Bardell's spoiled son, is used by the lawyers to elicit sympathy for his mother at the Bardell versus Pickwick trial (34). *Pickwick*.

"Bardell and Pickwick"   Along with *A Christmas Carol*, this reading from *Pickwick* was the most popular of Dickens's PUBLIC READINGS. Dickens first performed this reading, also titled "The Trial from Pickwick," in 1858.

Barham, Richard Harris (1788–1845)   Clergyman and author of *The Ingoldsby Legends*, which were originally published in *BENTLEY'S MISCELLANY* when Dickens was its editor.

Bark   Lodging-house keeper and receiver of stolen goods visited by Inspector Field: "a red villain and a wrathful, with a sanguine throat that looks very much as if it were expressly made for hanging." *Reprinted*, "Inspector Field."

Barker, Fanny   The name given to Fanny BROWN in "The Lamplighter's Story," the prose adaptation of Dickens's play *The Lamplighter*.

Barker, Phil   One of Fagin's cohorts, drunk at the THREE CRIPPLES. *Twist* (26).

Barker, William (Bill Boorker, "Aggerwatin' Bill")   The first London Omnibus conductor or cad. *Boz*, "Last Cab-Driver."

Barkis   The carrier between BLUNDERSTONE and Yarmouth who drives David Copperfield. After eating a piece of Peggotty's cake, he entrusts David with the message "Barkis is willin' " to deliver to Clara PEGGOTTY (5), whom he marries (10). Although he is tight with his money, he is a loving husband and he leaves Peggotty comfortably well-off after he goes "out with the tide" (30). *Copperfield*. Barkis was based on a carrier named Barker who lived at Blundestone, a town near Yarmouth.

Barley, Clara   Herbert Pocket's fiancée, a "pretty, slight, dark-haired girl of twenty or so," who arranges to hide Magwitch, under the name of Campbell, in her father's house until he can be smuggled abroad. She cares for her invalid father, **Old Bill Barley**, a retired ship's purser who is "totally unequal to the consideration of any subject more psychological than Gout, Rum and Purser's Stores" (46). "A captive fairy whom that truculent Ogre, Old Barley, had pressed into his service" (46), Clara does not marry Herbert until after her father has died. *Expectations*.

Barlow   Pedantic tutor in the popular didactic story for children, *Sanford and Merton*. He reminds the Traveller of his own tutor. Every boring lecture, condescending remark, or didactic moment recalls Mr. Barlow. *Uncommercial* (34).

Barnaby Rudge: A Tale of the Riots of Eighty   Dickens's fifth novel, published as a weekly serial in *Mas-*

Browne's (Phiz's) depiction of Barnaby with his pet raven, Grip.

ter *Humphrey's Clock*, 1841, illustrated by BROWNE and CATTERMOLE; issued in a single volume, 1841. A historical story based on the GORDON RIOTS of 1780, *Rudge* was the first novel Dickens planned to write. He contracted for the story, to be published in three volumes in 1836, then put it aside as *Pickwick* became a popular best-seller; returned to it in 1839 and wrote the first three chapters; put it down again until 1841 when he completed the novel as a weekly serial. Commentators have considered *Rudge* to be two novels awkwardly put together: a gothic melodrama about the murder of Reuben Haredale and a historical tale about the No Popery riots of 1780. Although the connections between the two are sometimes strained, Dickens develops similar themes in the two stories, suggesting that the social order reflects the domestic world where the troubled relationships between fathers and sons produce violence and rebellion.

SYNOPSIS

Part 1 (February 13, 1841)
(1) On the stormy evening of March 19, 1775, a stranger stops at the MAYPOLE INN near CHIGWELL north of London and asks about the Haredale family, owners of the WARREN, a country estate nearby. He learns that the current residents are Sir Geoffrey Haredale, a Catholic landowner, and his niece Emma, the daughter of Reuben Haredale, who was murdered exactly 22 years before, on March 19, 1753. Both the gardener at the Warren and the steward, Barnaby Rudge, disappeared after the crime. They were the primary suspects in the crime, but when a body thought to be that of Rudge was found at the bottom of a well, the gardener was assumed to be the murderer.

Part 2 (February 20, 1841)
(2) On the road to London, Gabriel Varden, a gentle locksmith, is accosted by the stranger from the Maypole, who collides with Varden's carriage and threatens him. (3) When Varden gets to London, he meets the son of Rudge, young Barnaby, a mentally-defective young man, born on the day after the murder. Barnaby is standing over the body of a man who has been robbed, wounded, and left by the road.

Part 3 (February 27, 1841)
(4) Varden takes the wounded man, Edward Chester, to the house of Barnaby's mother, the widow Rudge. (5) The next evening, while Varden is checking on the patient, Mrs. Rudge is called away and frightened by the stranger who had threatened the locksmith on the road, but she prevents Gabriel from detaining the man.

Part 4 (March 6, 1841)
(6) Edward Chester tells Varden that his attacker was the stranger from the Maypole.
(7) When Varden returns to his home, the Golden Key, he finds his household in as much disarray as the life in the streets. His temperamental wife, Martha, accuses him of neglecting her.

Part 5 (March 13, 1841)
(8) Varden's apprentice, Simon Tappertit, sneaks out of the house at night to attend a secret meeting of the 'Prentice Knights, a society of disgruntled apprentices who plan to overthrow their masters. (9) When he returns from the meeting, Sim finds that Miggs, Mrs. Varden's maid, has blocked the keyhole so that he cannot get back into the house without her help.

Part 6 (March 12, 1841)
(10) Edward Chester's father, Sir John Chester, engages young Barnaby to carry a message to Geoffrey Haredale asking for a meeting. (11) The regulars at the Maypole speculate that when the two old rivals meet, there will be a fight.

Part 7 (March 27, 1841)
(12) At the meeting, Haredale is irascible and short-tempered, Chester distant and cool, refusing to be ruffled by Haredale's rudeness. Although they dislike each other, they agree that they have a common interest to prevent a match between Edward and Emma. Chester wants his son to marry a wealthy heiress; Haredale wants Emma to marry a Catholic.

Part 8 (April 3, 1841)
(13) On March 25, Joe Willet, son of the Maypole's innkeeper, goes to London to pay the Maypole's annual vintner's bill. He stops at the Vardens's house, hoping to see Dolly, Gabriel's pretty daughter, but Dolly only speaks to him in passing, and Mrs. Varden appropriates the bouquet he brought for her daughter. (14) On his way home, Joe meets Edward Chester on the road. They stop by the Warren, but Edward's assignation with Emma there is interrupted by Haredale, who forbids him to see the girl again. When Edward learns that his father has been conferring with Haredale, he returns to the city.

Part 9 (April 10, 1841)
(15) The next day, Edward goes to his father's rooms in the TEMPLE. His father wants him to marry a rich woman in order to replenish the family fortune so that Mr. Chester can live in the luxurious style to which he is accustomed. Chester objects to Emma, because she is poor, a Catholic, and the daughter of a murdered man.

(16) That evening the widow Rudge is again shadowed by the mysterious and secretive stranger.

Part 10 (April 17, 1841)
(17) He follows her home. She recognizes him as her husband, the elder Barnaby Rudge, and shrinks from him, but he warns her against turning him in, and, describing himself as "a spirit, a ghost upon the earth, a thing from which all creatures shrink," he tells her that he will not be taken alive. He hides in a closet when his son returns home and secretly watches the boy with his mother. (18) After young Barnaby falls asleep, his father leaves and wanders in the streets until dawn.

Part 11 (April 24, 1841)
(19) Edward asks Dolly Varden to take a letter to Emma at the Warren. (20) Dolly delivers the letter; as she is

leaving with Emma's reply, Haredale stops her and offers her a position as Emma's companion.

Part 12 (May 1, 1841)
(21) On her way back to the Maypole, Dolly is assaulted by Hugh, the Maypole's ostler, who comes out of the woods, holds her in his arms, and threatens her. Joe Willet finds her there, upset and crying; she realizes that she doesn't have the letter or the bracelet that Emma entrusted to her. (22) Joe accompanies her part of the way back to London.

Part 13 (May 8, 1841)
(23) Hugh takes Emma's letter to Mr. Chester, who chastises him for also stealing the bracelet. (24) Then Simon Tappertit, who is secretly in love with Dolly and jealous of Joe Willet's attentions to her, calls on Chester and urges him to stop Dolly from acting as a messenger between Edward and Emma, and to "put Joseph Willet down, sir. Destroy him. Crush him."

Part 14 (May 15, 1841)
(25) Fearful of her husband and his power over her, Mrs. Rudge returns to the Warren for the first time in 22 years. She tells Haredale that she can no longer accept an annuity from him, because she can no longer control where the money goes. She says that she plans to leave the house in London that he provides for her to resettle in a secret location. (26) When Haredale asks Gabriel what Mrs. Rudge's motives might be, Varden tells of meeting the stranger at her house. The two men go to the house, but she has left it and Sir John Chester is there instead.

Part 15 (May 22, 1841)
(27) Chester flatters Mrs. Varden and enlists her help in breaking the engagement between his son and Emma. (28) When Hugh brings him another letter that he has taken from Dolly, Chester warns him to give no public indications of their connection.

Part 16 (May 29, 1841)
(29) At the Warren, Chester accosts Emma as she walks in the garden. He lies to her, telling her that his son plans to plead poverty and break off their relationship, and that he opposes his son's scheme and has tried to dissuade him. Haredale interrupts this conversation and is outraged by Chester's hypocrisy.

(30) When Joe Willet is "put on parole" by his father and not allowed to leave the Maypole, Joe decides that he must leave home.

Part 17 (June 5, 1841)
(31) He visits Dolly, but she treats him coquettishly and does not admit her love for him, so he joins the army. (32) The same day, Edward defies his father and is disowned.

Part 18 (June 12, 1841)
(33) Five years later, on the stormy night of March 19, 1780, a frightened Solomon Daisy, one of the regulars at the Maypole, tells his drinking companions of hearing a voice in the church and seeing a ghost in the churchyard. (34) Taking Hugh as his guide, John Willet goes to the Warren to tell Haredale what Daisy has seen. Haredale thanks him but seems distracted and distraught.

Part 19 (June 19, 1841)
(35) On their way back to the Maypole, Willet and Hugh meet Lord George Gordon, leader of the No Popery movement. He is on his way to London with Gashford, his opportunistic secretary, and John Grueby, one of his aides. They stop for the night at the Maypole. (36) Before going to bed, Gordon and Gashford discuss their anti-Catholic movement, now 40,000 strong, and mention Sim Tappertit, Mrs. Varden, and Miggs among their London followers.

Part 20 (June 26, 1841)
(37) Gordon and his party are welcomed in London by their supporters. Gashford swears Dennis the hangman into the cause as a future leader. (38) Hugh also joins the movement and becomes a member of Dennis's brigade.

Part 21 (July 3, 1841)
(39) At the Boot Tavern, London headquarters for the No Popery movement, Hugh meets Simon Tappertit, who makes him a member of the United Bulldogs, the latest incarnation of the 'Prentice Knights, one of the groups that has sworn allegiance to the Protestant cause. (40) Leaving the Boot in the middle of the night, Hugh reports back to Chester, telling him that he has joined the movement and met Dennis. After Hugh leaves, Chester ruminates on how Hugh will serve his ends and bring retribution on Haredale.

Part 22 (July 10, 1841)
(41) Gabriel Varden prepares to take part in the parade of the Royal East London Volunteers. His wife wishes that he would support the No Popery cause, but she is impressed by his uniform nonetheless. (42) When Gabriel returns from the parade, Haredale is waiting for him. He tells Varden of his fruitless search for Mrs. Rudge and Barnaby, now missing for five years. Haredale is staying secretly at their former house in London.

Part 23 (July 17, 1841)
(43) A pistol beside him, Haredale keeps a nightly vigil in Mrs. Rudge's house. One day on his way there from Vauxhall, he meets Gashford, Lord George Gordon, and Chester in a crowd of Protestants at Westminster Hall. Chester provokes Haredale into expressing his support for the Catholic position and his detestation of Gashford as a snivelling, unscrupulous toady. (44) Gashford tells Hugh and Dennis that any destruction they bring on Haredale's house will be approved.

Part 24 (July 24, 1841)
(45) Stagg, the blind associate of the elder Barnaby Rudge, comes to the village of straw workers, where Mrs. Rudge and Barnaby have lived in secret poverty for five years. He tells the widow that he is allied with the man from whom she fled and he demands £20. (46) She offers

all her savings, but he says that £7 is insufficient. She promises more money in a week. That evening she tells Barnaby that they must disappear into the crowds in London.

Part 25 (July 31, 1841)

(47) Mrs. Rudge and Barnaby make their way to London, getting occasional bits of change by having Grip, Barnaby's pet raven, perform along the way. On June 2, 1780, they arrive in the city. (48) It is the day when Lord George Gordon and his followers have gathered to present their petition to Parliament. As they sit by WEST-MINSTER BRIDGE, Barnaby is given the blue cockade of the protestors and is recruited into the movement by Gordon himself. At ST. GEORGE'S FIELDS Barnaby meets Hugh and joins his regiment. Banned from the field, Mrs. Rudge loses sight of her son.

Part 26 (August 7, 1841)

(49) The contingents of protestors make their way in four divisions to the House of Commons. Barnaby, bearing the flag of the movement, goes with Hugh and Dennis at the head of one of the divisions. As they are about to storm their way into the chamber, word comes that soldiers are gathering outside. Barnaby and Hugh confront the Horse Guards. With his flagstaff Barnaby knocks one of the guards from his horse. (50) Later that evening, Gashford tells them that the cause has failed in Parliament by a vote of 192 to 6, and that Barnaby and Hugh are being sought for their attack on the guards. Hugh leads Barnaby and Dennis into the streets, where they join in looting Catholic churches.

Part 27 (August 14, 1841)

(51) Drunk and exhilarated, Sim returns from the riots and gives up his position as Varden's apprentice. Gabriel tries unsuccessfully to detain him. (52) The next morning, Hugh, Dennis, and Sim plan the attack on the Warren. They do not include Barnaby, for fear that he will protect the Haredales. When they go out that evening to raid Catholic churches and homes for relics, altar furnishings, and household items to burn in their bonfires, Gashford asks them with annoyance, "Can you burn nothing whole?"

Part 28 (August 21, 1841)

(53) The next day Gashford urges the attack on Haredale's house, and counsels "no mercy, no quarter, no two beams of the house, to be left standing." Leaving Barnaby on watch at the Boot, Hugh, Dennis, and Sim lead a band of rioters off to Chigwell. Gashford sits on the roof of his house, watching for a fiery glow in the night sky to the north. (54) The rioters arrive at the Maypole. They take food and drink, then ransack and vandalize the building. Dennis wants to hang John Willet, but Hugh prevents him. They bind the innkeeper to a chair before setting off for the Warren.

Part 29 (August 28, 1841)

(55) As John Willet sits tied in the chair, the stranger, not recognized as the elder Rudge, enters the inn, takes some food, and inquires about the rioters. He and Willet see a glow in the sky and hear the sounds of the rioting as the mob breaks into the Warren, loots it, and burns it to the ground.

(56) Meanwhile, Solomon Daisy and two companions are on their way into London when they meet Mr. Haredale on horseback headed toward his home. Taking Solomon with him, he stops at the Maypole and finds Willet dazed and incoherent, claiming he has seen a ghost. When they get to the Warren, the house is an empty ruin. Everyone seems to be gone, but Haredale discovers the stranger hiding in the tower. Haredale attacks him, names him Barnaby Rudge, accuses him of Reuben Haredale's murder, and takes him captive.

Part 30 (September 4, 1841)

(57) Meanwhile, Barnaby stands watch at the Boot as Lord Gordon and his aide, John Grueby, pass by. Gordon praises him as a hero, but Grueby advises him to hide and warns him that he will be hanged. Barnaby stays at his post until the soldiers arrest him. (58) In spite of his pleas, the soldiers—among them a one-armed man—refuse to give him Grip, his pet raven. But when he is taken in irons to a cell in NEWGATE PRISON, Grip is there.

Part 31 (September 11, 1841)

(59) During the burning of the Warren, Hugh and Dennis have captured Emma and Dolly, taking them to a hideout on the outskirts of London. Sim Tappertit reveals his amorous designs on Dolly, and there is talk of Gashford's similar interest in Emma. (60) When Hugh and Dennis return to the Boot, they are warned that soldiers have occupied it, so instead they go to FLEET MARKET. There a one-armed man, injured and bandaged around his head, tells them that Barnaby has been arrested and taken to Newgate. The rioters plan to attack the prisons and release the prisoners.

Part 32 (September 18, 1841)

(61) Mr. Haredale takes the murderer Rudge into London. He goes to the MANSION HOUSE, but the LORD MAYOR, fearful of the rioters, refuses to hear Haredale's case for having Rudge imprisoned. Magistrate Sir John FIELDING does listen and commits the captive to Newgate. (62) There, in the prison yard, the elder Barnaby meets his son and reveals his identity to him.

Part 33 (September 25, 1841)

(63) The weak Lord Mayor declines to take decisive action against the rioters, and the mob controls the city. That evening the rioters gather to storm Newgate. On the way, they stop to enlist Gabriel Varden to force the locks on the prison gates, but Gabriel valiantly refuses to go with the rioters. Miggs, however, helps them gain entry to the house. They capture Varden and his tools and head for the prison. (64) When Gabriel refuses to force the lock, the mob threatens to kill him, but the one-armed man and his accomplice break through the crowd and spirit Gabriel away. Then the rioters set fire

to the prison door; slowly it burns away and they gain entry to the prison.

Part 34 (October 2, 1841)
(65) Rudge cowers in a corner of his cell, fearing that the mob will wreak vengeance on him. But they free him along with his son and the other prisoners. Dennis, looking forward to future hangings, tries to prevent the release of four prisoners on death row, but Hugh insists and they too are freed.

(66) Haredale has been searching unsuccessfully for his niece. Tired and dazed from exertion and lack of sleep, he goes to Newgate when he hears of the attack on the prison, but he is too exhausted to prevent Rudge's release. Langdale, a compassionate distiller, takes him to his house and cares for him. Grueby, who has left Gordon and become a servant to Langdale, brings back news of the rioters as they sack and burn the houses of Lord Mansfield and the city magistrates.

Part 35 (October 9, 1841)
(67) The next day there are soldiers in the streets, but the rioters are undeterred. During the day they issue threats; at night they set fires. They attack Langdale's house. Disguised as rioters, Edward Chester and a one-armed Joe Willet rescue Haredale and Langdale as the rioters break into the house.

(68) Meanwhile, freed from Newgate, Barnaby and his father hide in an empty shed in Finchley. Rudge sends his son in search of Stagg, but Barnaby is unable to find the blind man. Drawn by the crowd to the riot at Langdale's house, Barnaby sees Hugh knocked from his horse and wounded, and he takes him back to Finchley.

Part 36 (October 16, 1841)
(69) Before they can escape to the country, however, Dennis, who has turned traitor, turns them over to the soldiers who arrest Rudge, Barnaby, and Hugh, and shoot Stagg as he tries to run away. (70) Then Dennis gets Miggs to aid in Gashford's plan to kidnap Emma and Dolly to the continent.

Part 37 (October 23, 1841)
(71) This scheme is thwarted by Haredale, the Vardens, Joe Willet, and Edward Chester, who rescue Emma and Dolly and arrest the miscreants. (72) Joe is reunited with his father, who has difficulty believing his son has lost an arm. Dolly, changed by her experience, realizes how coquettish she has been. Joe tells her of his idle dream of returning rich to marry her.

Part 38 (October 30, 1841)
(73) By Friday of the week of riots, order has been restored. Recovered from her illness, Mrs. Rudge visits Barnaby in prison and urges him to say nothing about his relationship to his father. She urges the elder Rudge to confess his crime, but he refuses, cursing her and their son. Lord George Gordon is imprisoned in the Tower for high treason.

(74) Dennis, taken prisoner on the testimony of Gabriel Varden, is locked up in the same cell with Hugh.

He fears Hugh's retribution, but Hugh simply wants to live as comfortably as he can until he and Dennis are hanged.

Part 39 (November 6, 1841)
(75) A month later, Gabriel Varden has learned that Hugh, who is to hang the next day, is the illegitimate son of Sir John Chester by a gypsy woman who was hanged at TYBURN. He pleads unsuccessfully with Chester to acknowledge his son. (76) At Newgate the prisoners await their execution: Barnaby waits with his mother; Dennis cowers desperately hoping for a last-minute reprieve; Hugh remains exultantly defiant.

Part 40 (November 13, 1841)
(77) On the day of execution, Hugh remains defiant and takes the blame for luring Barnaby into the riots. Barnaby faces death bravely. Dennis remains fearful and cowardly.

(78) Joe tells his father that he plans to go to the West Indies to work there with Edward Chester, but Dolly interrupts the conversation, admits that she loves Joe, and the two are reunited.

Part 41 (November 20, 1841)
(79) At the time of the executions, Gabriel Varden's friends gather at the Golden Key, Gabriel's restored house and shop. The distraught Mrs. Rudge is also there. Mr. Haredale asks his niece's forgiveness and blesses her union with Edward Chester. He plans to enter a monastery on the Continent. Then Gabriel returns home, bringing Barnaby with him. He and Haredale have secured a last-minute pardon for the boy. Barnaby is restored to his mother. (80) Later, while the Vardens celebrate the reunion of Joe and Dolly, Miggs returns to claim her old place as Mrs. Varden's maid, but they send her away again.

Part 42 (November 27, 1841)
(81) At the end of August, Haredale makes a final visit to the ruins of the Warren. There he meets Sir John Chester and accuses him of engineering the destruction of his house and family. The two duel, and Chester is killed. (82) Haredale escapes to the Continent. Sir George Gordon is found not guilty of high treason, but he continues in his fanaticism, finally converting to Judaism. Convicted of libel, he dies in prison. Gashford becomes a government informer; Tappertit, a shoeblack; Miggs, a prison turnkey. Joe and Dolly Willet restore the Maypole. Barnaby and his mother reside happily on the Maypole farm.

COMMENTARY

It was probably inevitable that Dickens, when planning a subject for his first novel in 1836, would choose a historical subject. Sir Walter SCOTT, who had died only four years earlier, was still the defining novelist in Britain; his influence dominated the 1830s, leading such popular novelists of the period as Edward Bulwer LYTTON and

William Harrison AINSWORTH to specialize in historical romances.

Dickens's choice of the Gordon Riots for his subject may acknowledge a particular indebtedness to Scott. The year 1836 was only 56 years after the events the novel proposed to relate; there were people still alive who could remember the happenings and give personal accounts of them. In his Scottish history novels, Scott chose events that were close enough in time to possess this personal connection. By doing so he was better able to make history relevant to the present of his readers.

Contemporary relevance was particularly important to Dickens, for, as John BUTT and Kathleen TILLOTSON (1957) point out, he wanted to link the Gordon Riots with the Chartist agitations and the religious intolerance of his own time. Reactions to the NEW POOR LAW in the late 1830s had prompted petitions to Parliament and mass demonstrations, particularly in the north of England. By 1838 this anti-Poor Law movement had coalesced into CHARTISM, a working-class movement determined by mass action to force such democratic reforms as universal manhood suffrage and the secret ballot. One wing of the movement, the "physical force Chartists" led by Fergus O'Connor, advocated violent rebellion as the only means to achieve their ends, and several mass meetings in 1838 and 1839 erupted into violent confrontations between demonstrators and civil authorities.

Religious differences were also becoming more heated in 1839 when the newly founded Protestant Association used mass meetings and petitions to Parliament to oppose legislation that would liberalize restrictions on Catholics. Their organizational tactics and violent rhetoric recalled Gordon's Association of 1779–80. *Barnaby Rudge*, or, as it was originally titled, *Gabriel Varden, the Locksmith of London*, would be a warning of the dangers of religious intolerance and of mob action emerging from mass political movements. Dickens wanted his novel to address the current condition of England by showing its analogue in the past.

Dickens apparently thought of the Gordon Riots in his novel as similar to the Porteous Riots in Scott's *Heart of Mid-Lothian* (1819), because they brought together historical forces larger than the individual participants. The central figure in the novel, a fool like Scott's Madge Wildfire, could symbolize the inability of the individual to control or even to understand the significance of the historical situation in which he was embroiled.

Much of Barnaby's story is clichéd gothic melodrama: He is shadowed by a mysterious stranger who will turn out to be his father and whose crime, committed on the day his son was born, has left the boy a symbolically wounded mental defective. Young Barnaby is one of several sons in the novel whose father bears responsibility for his role in the riots. Maimed by his father's crime and abandonment and forced into secretive isolation with his mother, Barnaby acts from instinct rather than reason. He makes Hugh his hero and gets caught up in the public frenzy.

Maypole Hugh, another son abandoned and denied by his father, leads one of the rebellious batallions. The natural (i.e., illegitimate) son of Sir John Chester by a gypsy woman, Hugh has never known his father and has been abandoned to wildness. An ostler, he lives with animals in the stable and is himself illiterate, savage, and sexually aggressive. Ironically, the father who denies him is as highly civilized as Hugh is wild. Effete, unnaturally restrained and controlled, Chester cooly manipulates others for his own selfish ends.

Chester's other son, Edward, suffers not from neglect but from restraint. His father refuses to sanction his marriage to Emma Haredale, demanding instead that he "must marry well and make the most of [him]self" (15) so that he can enable his father, who has squandered his own inheritance, to live luxuriously. "Every man has a right to live in the best way he can, or he is an unnatural scoundrel" (15), the parasitic father tells his son. So Edward, if he is to recoup the extravagance of his father's past, must marry against his desire. He escapes this excessive and cynical restraint by running off to the West Indies.

Similarly Joe Willet's father denies his son the chance to choose his own life by treating him as a boy who will never grow up. Old John refuses to give Joe a responsible role at the Maypole, and he does not take Joe's interest in Dolly Varden seriously. As Chester imposes on Edward to maintain the comforts of his past, so John Willet refuses to allow Joe to grow up in order to maintain the Maypole as an unchanging representative of an idyllic past. The nostalgic picture of the inn that opens the novel suggests the fantasy of "old England" that governs Willet's consciousness. The old house, with "its floors sunken and uneven, its ceilings blackened by the hand of time," and its regular customers who retell its legends, is a reminder of the past, "hale and hearty though, still" (1). Still, but not unchanging, for the storm that opens the novel presages the storms to come and the stranger in the Maypole represents the murder of Reuben Haredale, one of several unresolved issues from the past that will lead to the riots and the destruction of the Maypole and the Warren. Like Edward, unnaturally restrained by his father and the past, Joe runs off to the army.

The last of the father-son relationships in the novel leads more directly to the riots. Although Gabriel Varden and Sim Tappertit are not biologically related, their relationship as master and apprentice repeats the issues of freedom and restraint in the other father-son pairs. When we first see Varden in the novel, he is counseling John Willet to treat his son as an adult and not encourage an "ill-timed rebellion" (3). Although Varden treats his apprentice with understanding and forebearance, Tappertit is nonetheless rebellious and unreasonably characterizes Gabriel as one of the "Tyrant Masters (of whose grievous and insupportable oppression, no 'prentice could entertain a moment's doubt)" (8).

Tappertit's disaffection stems from political and personal causes. The secret society of 'Prentice Knights, who have organized to restore "their ancient rights and holidays" (8), encourages him to entertain an idyllic fantasy of the past, similar to the Maypole fantasy, when apprentices were free from restraining masters. But Sim, "little more than five feet high, and thoroughly convinced in his own mind that he was above the middle size" (4), also has a Napoleon complex. He thinks that Varden does not recognize his talents, that Dolly does not acknowledge his physical attractiveness, and the 'Prentice Knights convince him that in the past things would have been different. Sim differs from Edward and Joe in that he, not Gabriel, harbors the fantasy of the past and of himself as victim of arbitrary oppression.

Gabriel is, in fact, the representative of reason and moderation in the novel. While he frequently joins the Maypole community, he does not live in the past. His house is in the center of London and is central to the issues raised by the novel, for as a locksmith, Varden is a technician of restraint. Appropriately he is a member of the citizen's militia that keeps order in the city and, at the climax of the novel, he refuses to unlock the gates of Newgate Prison, even under the threat of losing his life. He remains true to his commitment to social order. Thus Varden becomes the primary link between the father-son motif in the first half of the novel and the story of the riots in the second half. His household is a microcosm of the larger social issues: Mrs. Varden and Miggs are fanatical Protestants who sympathize with Gordon and the rioters; Tappertit, a disgruntled "son," is "oppressed" and denied sexual fulfillment by his constraining father/master; Dolly, Varden's "madcap" daughter, softens the harshness of his wife, but disturbs the order in the household by attracting Sim's adoration and raising Miggs's jealousy.

Dolly is a key figure in the sexual drama. The object of both Joe Willet's and Sim Tappertit's attentions, her coquetry increases Joe's frustrations and prompts him to join the army while her rejection of Sim reinforces his resentment against Gabriel. Dolly also acts as a go-between for Edward and Emma and is sexually attacked and later kidnapped by Hugh. Her presence reveals the sexual energies of the sons that would break the restraints of the fathers and challenge the hegemony of the old order.

These family and sexual issues have seemed to some readers far removed from the political and religious forces that culminate in the riots. *Rudge* has often appeared to be two novels, the first a gothic, domestic romance and the second a historical novel about the riots. If the devices that Dickens uses to connect the two stories are sometimes mechanical or clumsy, they are nonetheless thought out. Dickens believed that the public life is grounded in the private life, the family a microcosm of the larger society. By grounding the riots in the private lives of the participants, he reveals the mixed motives and personal issues that complicate issues of state. At the same time, he knew that history was not always a rational process of competing interests struggling for control. By making the central figures in the riots either fools, or madmen, or self-serving manipulators, he shows the destruction that emerges when the irrational mob mirrors its leaders.

The second half of the novel pairs Lord George Gordon with Barnaby Rudge. A historical figure, Gordon was viewed in his own time as mad, a fanatical Puritan, restless, "wild and ungovernable" (35). Goaded on by Gashford, his cynical, self-serving secretary, and by the adulation of his followers, Gordon does not control the demonstrations and he loses sight of the issues that brought him to London. His leaders in the field—Hugh, Barnaby, Simon, and Dennis—exemplify the ungovernable forces he unleashed. They have no ideological commitment to the Protestant cause. When Gordon leads the mob shouting, "No Popery," Hugh shouts, "No Property!" and Dennis, the renegade hangman, concludes with "Down with everybody, down with everything!" (38) The fury of the mob has no political end. It is simply nihilistic, primitive energy.

Dickens originally planned to make three escapees from Bedlam the leaders of the riot, a way of indicating the insanity of the mob. His friend John FORSTER discouraged that tack, so instead Dickens made the same point with Barnaby and Hugh, mad sons abandoned by their fathers, mentally defective and illiterate. Neither understands nor controls the mob he leads. Dennis the hangman is a somewhat different case, for, as a corrupt and renegade government functionary, he represents the power of the state run amok.

While the mob is a mad monster, the established authority is little better. The Lord Mayor, too frightened to take action to control the mob, in effect encourages the riots. The country magistrate who tries to buy Grip and threatens Barnaby and his mother is an unthinking oppressor (47). Only Varden represents a restrained middle course; he is neither weak nor an oppressor. The Golden Key and its owner are the true representatives of traditional England, but Varden's virtues are insufficient to save the Golden Key from attack during the riots, and his firm heroism cannot prevent the gates of the prison from being breached.

The destruction wrought by the riots purges some stains from the past. Old Rudge the murderer and Sir John Chester the parasitic aristocrat are both killed. But Geoffrey Haredale, who brings them both to justice, is vindicated only to retreat to a monastery on the Continent where he will soon die. Barnaby is rescued from the gallows, but he still hears the sounds of the past and remains a fool; Joe Willet, who has lost an arm freeing himself from his father's oppression, restores the Maypole. The toll may be best represented in the destruction of Lord Mansfield's house, especially his extensive law library: for when violence resolves the issues, the rule of law is itself one of the casualties.

CRITICISM

Rudge has not engaged the attention of many critics. Those who have written about the novel usually consider it less than successful, finding its melodrama clichéd and its two halves unconnected. It is often viewed as a precoursor to Dickens's later historical novel, *A Tale of Two Cities*, especially in its depiction of the mob and the riots, generally thought to be the best section of the novel. Steven MARCUS (1965) challenges some of these judgments and finds the novel unified around the theme of fathers and sons. In the most extensive essay on the novel, Myron Magnet (*Dickens and the Social Order*, 1985) makes a convincing case that Dickens's political analysis, grounded in the rationalism of the Enlightenment, is thoughtfully considered and carefully articulated in the novel. Ian Duncan places *Rudge* into the tradition of Scott in *Modern Romance and Transformations of the Novel* (1992) and Butt and Tillotson (1957) describe the composition of the novel and its contemporary relevance.

ADAPTATIONS

Several stage adaptations were on the boards in London before the novel completed its serial run. Some of these early dramas concentrated on the melodrama of the murder of Reuben Haredale and did not include the riots at all; Edward STIRLING's *Barnaby Rudge: or The Riots of London in 1780* (1841) did include the riots, but did not attract an audience. In most of the early productions, women played the role of Barnaby.

Later in the century stage adaptations focused on Dolly Varden and many of them, like G. Murray Wood's 1873 adaptation, were titled *Dolly Varden*.

Thomas BENTLEY made a silent film (1914), notable for its recreation of the riots, using a cast of extras numbering more than a thousand. The BBC produced a 13-part television serial of the novel in 1960.

Barnacle   The important and extensive family that controls the CIRCUMLOCUTION OFFICE, Dickens's satiric representation of aristocratic priviledge in the higher levels of the government bureaucracy. "The Barnacles were a very high family, and a very large family. They were dispensed all over the Public Offices, and held all sorts of public places. . . . Wherever there was a square yard of ground in British occupation under the sun or moon, with a public post upon it, sticking to that post was a Barnacle" (I:10,34). **Lord Decimus Tite Barnacle**, cabinet Minister of Circumlocution, considers his duties "to set bounds to the philanthropy, to cramp the charity, to fetter the public spirit, to contract the enterprise, to damp the independent self-reliance" of the people (I:34). His wife, **Lady Jemina Bilberry**, is the daughter of the 15th Earl of Stiltstocking and the Honorable Clementina Toozellem (I:17). His nephew **Tite Barnacle** is a senior official in the Circumlocution Office, an "altogether splendid, massive, overpowering, and inpracticable" man who "wound and wound folds of tape and paper round the neck of the country"(I:10). His son **Clarence Barnacle (Barnacle Junior)** is also an official in the Office, an empty-headed and callow young man, "the born idiot of the family" (I:26). Other family members catalogued in *Little Dorrit* include **Ferdinand**, private secretary to

Lord Decimus, **William**, a Member of Parliament "who had made the ever-famous coalition with Tudor Stiltstocking" (I:34), and others who attend the wedding of Henry Gowan and Minnie Meagles (I: 34). *Dorrit*.

Barnard Castle   Nicholas Nickleby stops at the King's Head Inn in this market town in Durham on the recommendation of Newman Noggs (*Nickleby*, 7). Dickens and Hablot BROWNE stayed at the inn in 1838 when they were investigating the Yorkshire Schools.

Barnard, Frederick (1846–1896)   Illustrator best known for his illustrations to the English HOUSEHOLD EDITION of Dickens's works (1871–79). He also produced a series of "Character Sketches from Dickens" in the 1880s. Examples of Barnard's work appear in the following illustrations in this volume: figure 4 (AUTOBIOGRAPHY); 48 (HEEP); 69 (PECKSNIFF); 70 (PHILANTHROPY); 73 (PROSTITUTION); 79 (RAILWAYS); 89 (*A TALE OF TWO CITIES*).

Barnard's Inn   One of the INNS OF COURT, now defunct. Located in HOLBORN, it is "the dingiest collection of buildings ever squeezed together in a rank corner as a club for Tom Cats"; where Herbert Pocket and Pip share rooms when Pip first arrives in London. *Expectations* (21).

Barnet, Hertfordshire   In Dickens's time, this town, 11 miles or so north of the CITY, was an important staging point on the route out of London. Oliver Twist meets the Artful Dodger here when he arrives in London (*Twist*, 8). Esther Summerson stops here on her way to Bleak House and during her pursuit of Lady Dedlock with Mr. Bucket (*Bleak House*, 6, 57).

Barnett, Charles Zackery   Victorian playwright, a contemporary of Dickens, who produced melodramatic adaptions of *Twist*, *Rudge*, *A Christmas Carol*, and *Cricket* for the stage.

Barney   Jewish waiter at the THREE CRIPPLES who helps Fagin plan the Chertsey robbery. *Twist*.

Barnstaple, Devon   Coastal town at the mouth of the Taw Estuary in north Devon; setting of "A Message from the Sea."

Barnwell, George   Hero of *The London Merchant, or the History of George Barnwell* (1731), a domestic tragedy by George Lillo. The work tells the story of a London apprentice who steals from his master and murders his uncle to satisfy the demands of his seductress, Sarah Millwood. When the stolen money gives out, the two give evidence against each other and both are hanged. Dickens alludes to the play in several works, most notably in *Great Expectations* where Pip attends Wopsle's reading of the play during the time of his apprenticeship to Joe Gargery (15).

"Baron of Grogswig, The" INTERPOLATED TALE about a German baron and his scolding wife, told by a merry-faced gentleman to his fellow travelers on the London-to-Yorkshire coach. Burdened with financial troubles and thirteen children, the baron is about to commit suicide when the Spirit of Suicide and Despair convinces him that his life can be happy if he takes up hunting and controls his wife. He does so and lives a long and satisfying life. *Nickleby* (6).

Barroneau After the death of Marseilles innkeeper **Henri Barroneau**, his young widow, **Madame Barroneau**, marries Rigaud, who murders her for her money. (*Dorrit*, I:1).

Barrow Dickens's mother's family. **Charles** (1759–1826), Dickens's maternal grandfather, was "Chief Conductor of Monies in Town" at the Navy Pay Office, responsible for transfering money to the ports of Plymouth, PORTSMOUTH, Sheerness, and CHATHAM. In 1810 he admitted embezzling money from the office and escaped to the Isle of Man without repaying what he had taken. His daughter Elizabeth (1789–1863) married John DICKENS in 1809 (see Elizabeth Barrow DICKENS). His son **John Henry** (1796–1869) was a Barrister in GRAY'S INN and the founder and editor of the *MIRROR OF* PARLIAMENT. His younger son **Edward** (1798–1869) was, like Dickens and his father, a shorthand reporter for the paper which printed verbatim accounts of Parliamentary proceedings. John Henry taught Dickens the Gurney system of shorthand. He was Dickens's sub-editor on the *DAILY NEWS.* Edward's wife, Janet Ross, a painter of miniatures, may have been the original for Miss LaCreevy in *Nickleby.* She painted the earliest authenticated portrait of Dickens.

Barrymore, Lionel (1878–1954) American stage and screen actor whose annual portrayal of Scrooge on the radio between 1934 and 1953 made him the American Scrooge of the period and informed his role as Potter, the Scroogelike banker in Frank Capra's 1946 film *It's a Wonderful Life.* Barrymore also portrayed Daniel Peggotty in George Cukor's 1935 film version of *Copperfield.*

Bart, Lionel (1930–) British playwright and composer of stage musicals; author of the most popular modern adaptation of *Twist*—the musical *Oliver!*, first produced in 1960 and later made into a film (1968).

Barsad, John Alias of Solomon PROSS. *Two Cities.*

Bartholomew's Close A back street near Jaggers's office in LITTLE BRITAIN where Pip observes Jaggers's clients waiting to see the lawyer. *Expectations* (20).

Barton, Jacob Mrs. Malderton's brother, a grocer who embarrasses his nouveaux riches relatives by frequently speaking of his business. *Boz*, "Sparkins."

Bastille, The Notorious Parisian prison that became a symbol for the tyranny of the ancien régime in France because of the many prisoners, like Doctor Manette in *A Tale of in Two Cities*, who were held there without trial, simply on the order of a powerful aristocrat. The storming of the Bastille on July 14, 1789, the initial event in the FRENCH REVOLUTION, is described in *Two Cities*, II:21. Dickens's description closely follows that of CARLYLE in *The French Revolution*.

"Bastille Prisoner, The" A public reading from *A Tale of Two Cities* that Dickens prepared in 1861 but never performed.

Bates, Belinda One of the guests in the haunted house, "a most intellectual, amiable and delightful girl, . . . [who] 'goes in' . . . for Women's mission, Women's rights, Woman's wrongs, and everything that is woman's with a capital W." "Haunted House."

Bates, Charley Member of Fagin's kennel of pickpockets; he exhibits "some very loose notions concerning the rights of property" (10). After the murder of Nancy and the death of Sikes, Master Bates reforms and becomes "the merriest young grazier in all Northamptonshire" (53). *Twist.*

Bath, Somerset Dickens took the name Pickwick from Moses PICKWICK, a coach operator and hotel keeper in this spa town. The Pickwickians spend some time here: Pickwick meets Angelo Cyrus Bantam, the master of ceremonies in the Assembly Rooms; he discovers the manuscript of Prince Bladud, legendary founder of the city, in his rooms on the Royal Crescent; Winkle gets entangled with the Dowlers; Sam attends the footmen's "swarry" (*Pickwick*, 35–37). Bath is also mentioned as the residence of Volumnia Dedlock (*Bleak House*, 28).

Battens Oldest male resident of Titbull's AlmsHouses; he complains of neglect by the trustees. *Uncommercial* (29).

Battle Bridge Old name for King's Cross in London, site of a bridge over the River Fleet where a battle between the Romans and Britons took place. In *Sketches by Boz*, Dickens describes it as a place inhabited by "proprietors of donkey-carts, boilers of horseflesh, makers of tiles, and sifters of cinders" ("First of May"). BOFFIN'S BOWER and its dust mounds is nearby (*Mutual Friend*). Also mentioned in *Twist* (31) and *Dombey* (31).

Battle of Life, The. A Love Story Fourth of Dickens's CHRISTMAS BOOKS, published in December 1846, with illustrations by DOYLE, LEECH, MACLISE, and STANFIELD. Like the other Christmas Books, *Battle* tells of a change of heart, but one that is not brought about by a supernatural agency.

SYNOPSIS

(1) On a battlefield that once ran with blood many generations ago, a calm domestic life has now settled in. The memory of the battle and why it was fought is all but forgotten. On the morning of the anniversary of the battle, Doctor Jeddler's two daughters, Grace and Marion, dance in the orchard as pickers take fruit from the trees. When they are done, they join a ceremonial breakfast for Alfred Heathfield, Doctor Jeddler's ward, who is about to set out on a foreign tour. It is both Alfred's and Marion's birthday, and he has just come of age. The lawyers Snitchey and Craggs have come to draw up the legal documents officially ending Jeddler's guardianship. At breakfast they discuss the doctor's philosophy that the world is "a gigantic practical joke: . . . something too absurd to be considered seriously, by any rational man." The lawyers suggest that the law is serious, but the doctor, using the battle fought on the site as his illustration, insists on the futility of human aspirations and argues that "the same contradictions prevail in everything. One must either laugh or cry at such stupendous inconsistencies; and I prefer to laugh." His servant, Benjamin Britain, echoes his master: "Humanity," he says, "that's the joke."

After breakfast Alfred bids farewell to his love, the younger Jeddler daughter Marion, and asks her calm and serene sister to watch over her for him. As his coach goes off into the distance, Marion falls sobbing on Grace's neck.

(2) Three years later, Snitchey and Craggs are advising one of their clients, Michael Warden, a spendthrift who has burdened his estate in debt with expensive living and now "means to repent and be wise." They counsel him to flee to Europe and live frugally for some time in order to nurse his estate back to financial health. He tells them that he is in love with Marion Jeddler and will agree to follow their advice only after a month has passed, so that he has time to save Marion from Alfred's return, which "she dreads, and contemplates with misery."

A month later, during the Christmas season, Warden's departure is set for the same day as Alfred's scheduled return. The Doctor plans a grand party to celebrate Alfred's homecoming; but Clemency Newcome, the Jeddlers' maid, has forebodings of disaster when she observes, in the "dark and doubtful night that lay beyond the threshold," a secret assignation between Marion and Warden. Alfred plans to surprise the family by arriving on foot at a side door. There he finds a distressed Clemency Newcome with Grace; they announce that Marion is gone.

(3) Six years later, Michael Warden appears at The Nutmeg-Grater, an inn run by Benjamin Britain and his wife, the former Clemency Newcome, who enriches her husband's life with her "plain, straight-forward thrift, good-humour, honesty, and industry." Clemency concludes from Warden's black dress and manner that Marion has died and that Grace is to be told of her

sister's fate next day on the anniversary of the battle, which is also Marion's birthday and the anniversary of Grace and Alfred's wedding. Their marriage is a happy one, blessed by Alfred's rewarding medical practice among the poor, and by their two children, Marion and Clem. Only the loss of Marion casts a dark shadow on their lives.

At sunset on the anniversary day, Marion returns. She tells them that she left home to enable Grace to marry Alfred, for she knew how much her sister loved him and had sacrificed for her. Warden's flight to the Continent had given her a cover for her disappearance; she had actually gone to stay with her Aunt Martha, Doctor Jeddler's sister. Now that her sacrifice has enabled Grace and Alfred to marry, she can return.

Marion's sacrifice changes the doctor. He no longer believes the world a joke. "It's a world full of hearts," he says, "and a serious world, with all its folly, . . . a world on which the sun never rises, but it looks upon a thousand bloodless battles that are set-off against the miseries and wickedness of Battle-Fields, . . . a world of sacred mysteries."

Michael Warden makes Ben Britain the owner of the Nutmeg Grater, and Britain changes the name to "The Nutmeg-Grater and Thimble" and posts Clemency's inscriptions in the parlor, "Do as you would be done by!" and "Forget and Forgive!" Michael Warden and Marion marry and, by the time the story is told, they have honored the countryside with their presence for 35 years.

COMMENTARY

Battle is the least successful of the five Christmas books. THACKERAY called it "a wretched affair" and the reviews were generally not laudatory. Even Lord JEFFREY admitted to Dickens, "The general voice, I fancy, persists in refusing it a place among your best pieces."

Though excited by the initial idea for the book, Dickens had difficulty writing it. Away from London and living in Switzerland and also attempting to get *Dombey* under way, he struggled with *Battle*, dreaming for a whole week that the story "was a series of chambers impossible to be got to rights or got out of, through which I wandered drearily all night."

Like the other Christmas books, *Battle* treats a change of heart, but one that involves no supernatural agency. Doctor Jeddler is won to the belief that the world is "serious" and not a joke by the self-sacrificing behavior of his two daughters. First Grace suppresses her love for Alfred Heathfield because she believes her sister loves him. Then Marion, in an even greater sacrifice, disappears for six years to give Grace time to marry Alfred. The melodrama of Marion's disappearance and return is clumsily linked to the story of Michael Warden, but otherwise unconnected to the plot. The central characters, especially Alfred and Marion, are notable for their absence. Doctor Jeddler's misguided philosophy lacks the negative energy of Scrooge's miserliness or Redlaw's painful memories.

Battle is also a period piece. Set in the late 18th century, the story was frequently compared to GOLDSMITH's *Vicar of Wakefield* by early reviewers. But there is no compelling reason for this historical distance, which also distanced the story from contemporary relevance.

Dickens was right to be excited by his initial conception for the story—linking the historical battlefield with the domestic battlefield of everyday struggles—and the opening scene describing Grace and Marion dancing in a fruitful orchard that centuries before was a bloody field is probably the best thing in the story. But it was, as Dickens later recognized, the germ of a much bigger book. In fact, Thackeray's *Vanity Fair*, a very big novel that would begin its run in monthly parts in January 1847, made a similar linkage, connecting the Napoleonic wars and the Battle of Waterloo with the battle of the sexes in the drawing rooms of London and Paris. Dickens just did not have room in a short Christmas book to give his idea adequate development.

The principle that underlay Dickens's idea for the book—that the larger public life is implicit in the domestic life—was one that would inform many of Dickens's longer novels, especially such late works as *Bleak House* and *Our Mutual Friend*. *Battle* is also interesting for its foreshadowing of characters in the later novels. Marion and Grace prefigure Dora and Agnes in *Copperfield*, though Dora will die to give David the deserving Agnes. Marion's sacrifice also prefigures Sydney Carton's in *Two Cities*. Clemency Newcome, the down-to-earth servant, has long been recognized as an early version of Peggotty in *Copperfield*, less developed and more didactic than her loving successor.

CRITICISM

Battle has received little critical discussion. Michael SLATER (1971) provides a useful introduction to it in his Penguin edition of the Christmas books. Steven MARCUS (1965) suggests an interesting biographical reading of the story.

ADAPTATIONS

To upstage the pirates, Dickens sold the proof-sheets of *Battle* to the KEELEYS, actor-managers at the Lyceum Theatre. They secured Albert SMITH to write a script and they opened on December 21, 1846. Six other productions, largely based on Smith's version, appeared in the first few months. George Dibden Pitt's melodramatic adaptation for the Brittania, Hoxton, added a duel between Heathfield and Warden and a suicide attempt by Grace when she learns that Marion is missing. Charles DICKENS, JR., son of the novelist, adapted the story for the theater in 1873, and Walter Ellis's *Marion* was a popular stage adaptation in the 1890s. No films of *Battle* have been made.

Bayham Street, Camden Town   The Dickens family lived at No. 16 in 1823, the house that is probably the original of Bob Cratchit's (*Carol*) and of the one occcupied by the Micawbers and Traddles (*Copperfield*, 27).

Bayton   When **Mrs. Bayton** dies of starvation, her poor husband, **Mr. Bayton**, can only afford the "porochial" funeral which Oliver Twist attends as an apprentice to undertaker Sowerberry. *Twist* (5).

Bazzard   Grewgious's gloomy clerk and author of the unproduced tragedy, *The Thorn of Anxiety*. "Possessed of some strange power over Mr. Grewgious," he intimidates his employer. *Drood* (20).

"Beadle, The. The Parish Engine. The Schoolmaster"   Opening sketch in *Our Parish*, the first section of *Boz*. Originally published in the EVENING CHRONICLE (February 28, 1835) as "Sketches of London No. 4, The Parish," it mixes satire and humor in its descriptions of the institutions of local government—the beadle, the fire brigade, and the poor schoolmaster. *Boz*.

Beadle, Harriet ("Tattycoram")   Orphan companion and maid to Pet Meagles, whose nickname combines the diminutive of Harriet with an allusion to Coram's Hospital, the orphanage from which she comes. "A sullen, passionate girl," she is subject to fits of rage and is instructed by Mr. Meagles to count to 10 before speaking. In one of these fits, she runs from the Meagles and joins Miss Wade as her companion (I:27), but the relationship sours and Tattycoram returns penitently to the Meagles, bringing with her the papers concerning Little Dorrit and Mrs. Clennam that had been in Miss Wade's possession (II:33). *Dorrit*.

Beadnell, Maria (1810–1886)   Youngest daughter of London banker George Beadnell. Dickens fell in love with her in 1830, but her parents objected to the relationship, forbade the courtship, and sent their daughter off to school in Paris. The difficult courtship ended in 1833 and Maria subsequently married Henry Winter, a merchant. Dickens portrays the youthful Maria in Dora Spenlow in *Copperfield*; the matronly Mrs. Winter, the woman she became, whom he met again in 1855, is depicted in the garrulous Flora Finching in *Little Dorrit*. Maria's older sister **Anne** married Dickens's friend Henry KOLLE in 1833.

Bear, Prince   Prince Bull's adversary, representative of Russia in Dickens's ALLEGORY of the Crimean War. *Reprinted*, "Prince Bull."

Beard, Thomas (1807–1891)   Journalist and Dickens's lifelong friend. The two worked together as shorthand reporters and Beard helped Dickens obtain a position on the *Morning Chronicle* in 1834. Beard was the best man at Dickens's wedding and godfather to Charley, Dickens's eldest son. His younger brother, **Dr. Francis Carr Beard** (1814–93), Dickens's regular physician after 1859, attended the author on his deathbed.

David Copperfield is introduced to the captivating Dora Spenlow, a character based on Maria Beadnell.

Beauvais, France Birthplace of Dr. Manette and a stopping point on Charles Darnay's return journey to France. *Two Cities* (III:1,10).

Beaver, Nat A sea captain with "a world of watery experiences in him," and a guest in the haunted house. "Haunted House."

Bebelle Pet name of Gabrielle, the orphan girl loved and cared for by Corporal Théophile and later adopted by Langley. "Somebody's Luggage."

Beckwith, Alfred Alias adopted by MELTHAM in his scheme to trick Julius Slinkton. "Hunted Down."

Becky Barmaid at the RED LION INN, where Bill Sikes and Oliver Twist stop on their way to the CHERTSEY robbery. *Twist* (21).

Bedford Hotel, Brighton One of the best hotels in BRIGHTON, where Mr. Dombey stays when he visits his son Paul (*Dombey*, 10). Dickens stayed here in 1848, 1849, and 1861.

Bedford Street, Strand When WARREN'S BLACKING WAREHOUSE was moved from HUNGERFORD STAIRS to this street in the STRAND, Dickens was humiliated by having to work in a window in view of those passing by as he pasted labels on the blacking bottles.

Bedlam Contracted form of Bethlehem Hospital, the lunatic asylum in London whose name is synonymous with madhouse. The Traveller speculates on madness outside the walls of the Hospital in *Uncommercial* (13).

Bedwin Mr. Brownlow's housekeeper, "a motherly old lady," and a staunch believer in Oliver's innocence. *Twist*.

"Begging-Letter Writer, The" In this article for *HOUSEHOLD WORDS* (May 18, 1850), Dickens catalogs the frauds perpetrated by these "public robbers" who write letters asking for aid. Dickens distinguishes between the poor, who do not write such letters, and those engaged in "one of the most shameless frauds and impositions of this time." *Reprinted*. At the end of *Chuzzlewit*, Pecksniff becomes a begging-letter writer.

Begs, Mrs Ridger Married name of Emma MICAWBER. *Copperfield* (63).

Belinda A lovelorn young woman from Bath who writes to Master Humphrey seeking help in finding her lover. *Humphrey* (2).

Bell Alley, Coleman Street A "narrow and dark street" in the CITY, location of Namby's sponging house. *Pickwick* (40).

Bell Yard A narrow lane off FLEET STREET where Mrs. Blinder cares for the Neckett children. *Bleak House* (15).

Bell, Knight, M.R.C.S. A speaker at the medical section of the Mudfog Association. *Mudfog*.

Bella (1) Younger of two sisters detained for prostitution. She hides her face in shame as she climbs into the police van. *Boz*, "Prisoner's Van."

Bella (2) Miss Pupford's housemaid, who leaves Miss Kimmeens by herself. "Tiddler."

Belle Scrooge's fiancée. She rejects him because of his love of money. *Carol* (2).

Belle Sauvage Inn Coaching inn on LUDGATE HILL, west of ST. PAUL'S CATHEDRAL, that is the headquarters of Tony Weller, who calls it "my nat'ral-born element." *Pickwick*.

Beller, Henry Former toastmaster who drank a great deal of foreign wine and is reported to be a convert to the Brick Lane Branch of the United Grand Junction Ebenezer Temperance Association. *Pickwick* (33).

Belling, Master One of Squeers's pupils, "a diminutive boy, with his shoulders drawn up to his ears," who travels up to YORKSHIRE with Nicholas. *Nickleby* (4, 5).

Bellows, Brother   A barrister who is a guest at one of Merdle's dinner parties. *Dorrit* (I:21).

Bell's Life in London and Sporting Chronicle
A weekly journal to which Dickens contributed 12 "Scenes and Characters" sketches in 1835–36. The sketches were later collected in *Boz*.

Bell's Weekly Magazine   Dickens's sketch "Sentiment" (*Boz*) originally appeared in this magazine for June 7, 1834.

Bells, Goblins of the   The goblins seen by Trotty Veck as he climbs the belfrey on New Year's Eve. *Chimes.*

"Belltott"   Nickname of Mrs. Isabella TOTT.

Belmore, George (1829–1876)   Late Victorian comic actor who played several Dickensian roles in the 1860s and 70s, including Sam Weller in *Pickwick*, Noggs in *Nickleby*, Grandfather in *Curiosity Shop*, Daniel Peggotty in *Copperfield*, and Wegg in *Mutual Friend*.

Belmore, Lionel (1867–1953)   A member of a multi-generational theatrical family, this British character actor played Brownlow (1921) and Bumble (1933) in film versions of *Twist*.

Belvawney, Miss   Member of Crummles's theatrical company, "who seldom aspired to speaking parts, and usually went on as a page in white silk hose, to stand with one leg bent and contemplate the audience." *Nickleby* (23).

Ben (1)   Mail-coach guard whom Sikes overhears telling of Nancy's murder. *Twist* (48).

Ben (2)   Waiter at the ROCHESTER inn, where the meal is prepared for the "Seven Poor Travellers."

Ben (3)   Servant at the Two Robins Inn. *Lazy Tour.*

Bench   One of Merdle's important dinner guests. *Dorrit* (I:21).

Benjamin   Member of the 'Prentice Knights. *Rudge* (8).

Benjamin, Thomas   Plaintiff in a divorce suit conducted by Mr. Spenlow and David Copperfield. *Copperfield* (33).

Bennett, Arnold (1867–1931)   English novelist, one of the realists whose extreme dislike of Dickens characterizes and exaggerates the modernist rejection of the Victorians. In a letter, Bennett wrote: "Of Dickens, dear friend, I know nothing. About a year ago, from idle curiosity, I picked up *The Old Curiosity Shop*, & of all the rotten vulgar un-literary writing . . . ! Worse than George Eliot's."

Benson, Lucy   A village coquette, daughter of **Old Benson**, a small farmer, and brother to **Young Benson**. She flirts for a while with Squire Norton, but she comes to her senses in time and returns to her humble lover, George Edmunds. *Village Coquettes.*

Bentley, Richard (1794–1871)   Publisher and founder of the firm of Richard Bentley & Son. In August, 1836, when Dickens was just establishing himself with *Pickwick*, Bentley contracted with him to provide two three-volume novels at £500 each and to edit a new magazine, BENTLEY'S MISCELLANY. The subsequent success of *Pickwick* and disagreements with Bentley led Dickens to break off his agreements with the publisher in 1839 after only one of the two novels, *Oliver Twist*, had been published.

Bentley, Thomas (c. 1880–1950)   British actor and film director. After portraying Dickens characters on the stage, Bentley went on to produce and direct many film versions of the novels, among them *Pickwick* (1921), *Twist* (1912), *Chimes* (1914), *Curiosity Shop* (1914), *Rudge* (1915, 1921), and *Hard Times* (1915). His *David Copperfield* (1913) was the first eight-reel British feature film, and his adaptation of *Curiosity Shop* (1935) was the first feature-length sound film based on Dickens.

Bentley's Miscellany   An illustrated monthly magazine started by publisher Richard BENTLEY in January 1837. Dickens was its initial editor and continued with the magazine until February 1839, in spite of disagreements with the publisher. *Oliver Twist* first appeared in 24 serial installments in the magazine. Dickens also contributed "The Mudfog Papers," "The Pantomime of Life," "Some Particulars Concerning a Lion," and "Familiar Epistle from a Parent to a Child aged Two Years and Two Months" to the *Miscellany*.

Benton, Miss   Master Humphrey's housekeeper. Briefly the object of Tony Weller's affections, she later marries Slithers. *Humphrey.*

Berenthia (Berry)   Mrs. Pipchin's middle-aged niece "and devoted slave, . . . possessing a gaunt and iron-bound aspect, and much afflicted with boils on her nose." *Dombey* (8).

Berg Collection   Substantial collection in the New York Public Library, containing many Dickens materials, including Dickens's diary for 1867, a memoranda book for 1855–70, as well as manuscripts of several minor works, proof sheets for *Mutual Friend*, and several publishers' agreements. An anthology of Dickens materials in the Berg Collection was edited by Lola L. Szladits in commemoration of the centennial of Dickens's death in 1970.

Berkeley Heath, Glostershire   Pickwick's coach changed horses at the Bell Inn here on his journey from Bristol to Birmingham. *Pickwick*, 50.

Berners Street, Oxford Street   A street running north out of Oxford Street, where Dickens as a child saw the "White Woman," possibly an original for Miss Havisham. *Miscellaneous*, "Where We Stopped Growing."

Berry, Miss   Nickname for BERENTHIA. Dombey.

"Best Authority, The"   In this article for HOUSEHOLD WORDS (June 20, 1857) Dickens describes his search for the Best Authority, a personification of the source for much of the gossip that is purveyed in London society. When he finally captures the person purported to be Best Authority, he turns out to be the narrator's cousin Cackles, "the most amiable ass alive." *Miscellaneous*.

Bet (Betsy)   Prostitute and companion to Nancy, on rather friendly terms with Tom Chitling. After identifying Nancy's body, she goes mad. *Twist*.

Bethnal Green   A squalid area in the East End of London where Sikes and Nancy live (*Twist*) and where Eugene Wrayburn leads Bradley Headstone in an aimless pursuit (*Mutual Friend*, III:10).

Betley   One of Mrs. Lirriper's first lodgers. "Lirriper's Lodgings."

Betsey   Nurse to the Britain children. *Battle of Life*.

Betsey Jane   Mrs. Wickam's cousin, who "took fancies to people [and] . . . they all died" (8). Wickam warns Miss Berry not to get too close to young Paul, who might have a similar effect. *Dombey*.

Betsy   Mrs. Raddle's "dirty, slipshod" servant girl who waits on Bob Sawyer's dinner party. *Pickwick* (36).

"Betting-Shops"   An article for HOUSEHOLD WORDS (June 26, 1852) describing the betting shops in London and some of their questionable practices. *Miscellaneous*.

Beulah Spa, Norwood   A fashionable health spa in southeast London in the 1830s. *Boz*, "Tottle."

Bevan   Kindly American whom Martin Chuzzlewit meets at PAWKINS's boarding house in New York. Bevan is far less chauvinistic than his fellow countrymen. He sends Martin money to enable him to leave EDEN and return to England. *Chuzzlewit*.

Bevan, Mrs.   A former neighbor of Mrs. Nickleby. *Nickleby* (41).

Bevis Marks   A street off WHITECHAPEL in East London where Sampson Brass has his house and office. *Curiosity Shop* (33).

Bib, Mr. Julius Washington Merryweather   Boarder at the National Hotel, "a gentleman in the lumber line," who is present at the levee for Elijah Pogram that Martin Chuzzlewit attends in America. *Chuzzlewit* (34).

Bible   In his novels, Dickens alludes more to the Bible than to any other text. Bentley, Micheal SLATER and Burgis (1988) provide a list of the main biblical allusions in the novels. The most frequent references are to Genesis and to the Gospels, especially the parables.

Dickens's retelling of the New Testament for his children, THE LIFE OF OUR LORD, presents a simplified version of Jesus' life, emphasizing the parables and moral teachings, for Dickens regarded the New Testament, as he wrote to his son Edward (see DICKENS, EDWARD), as "the best book that ever was or will be known in the world, . . . because it teaches you the best lessons by which any human creature who tries to be truthful and faithful to duty can possibly be guided." He was more dubious about the Old Testament, which he suggested might be "thrown overboard . . . 'to lighten the sinking ship of Christianity.' " Some of his most vindictive characters—Mrs. Clennam, for example—base their heartless faith on the Old Testament.

Several recent critics have written on Dickens's use of the Bible. Alexander WELSH (1971) discusses its role in Dickens's treatment of death and his celebration of the feminine; Dennis WALDER discusses his use of the Bible in the broader context of his religion; Bert G. HORNBACK (1972) traces some of the images and symbols from Genesis; Jane Vogel (*Allegory in Dickens*, 1977) finds biblical allegory in all of Dickens's works, centering on the power of a New Testament vision to redeem a world corrupted by Old Testament sins; Janet L. LARSON, in the most sustained discussion of Dickens's use of the Bible, argues that Dickens, like his fellow Victorians, inherited a "broken scripture," so that he often uses the Bible not as a coherent or simple story, but rather as "a paradoxical code that provides him with contradictory interpretations of experience."

Bibliography   The most important bibliographical resources on Dickens are listed below. Two general bibliographies provide categorized lists of available materials by and about Dickens: The British Museum, *Dickens: An Excerpt from the General Catalogue* (1960), and Philip COLLINS the Dickens section from *The New Cambridge Bibliography of English Literature* (1970).

The most important bibliographies of Dickens's works are J. C. Eckel, *The First Editions of the Writings of Charles Dickens* (1932); Walter E. Smith, *Charles Dickens in the Original Cloth*, 2. vols. (1981; 1983). Two older bibliographies remain the primary resource on Dickens's minor writings: F. G. KITTON, *The Minor Writings of*

Dickens (1900), and T. Hatton and A. H. Cleaver, *A Bibliography of the Periodical Works of Dickens* (1933). William Miller's *The Dickens Student and Collector* (1946), remains useful, especially for its coverage of dramatic adaptations, plagiarisms, and other Dickensiana.

Dickens criticism up to 1970 is listed in *Charles Dickens, A Centenary Bibliography* (1971), edited by Joseph GOLD. R. C. CHURCHILL's *A Bibliography of Dickensian Criticism, 1836–1975* (1975) annotates its entries and prints excerpts from the critics; John J. Fenstermaker, in *Charles Dickens, 1940–1975* (1979), provides an index of critical materials indicating which critics discuss various themes and features in each of the novels. Garland Press, beginning in 1981, has been publishing comprehensive annotated bibliographies of Dickens criticism for each of the novels.

Biddy Wopsle's great aunt's granddaughter. An orphan like Pip, she assists in the dame school where Pip receives his earliest education: "her hair always wanted brushing, her hands always wanted washing, and her shoes always wanted mending and pulling up at heel" (7). After Pip's sister is injured, Biddy comes to look after the Gargery house and becomes Pip's close friend, but Pip does not recognize her love for him and treats her with snobbish condescension (17–19). After losing his fortune, Pip plans to propose to her, but he arrives home to discover that she has just married Joe Gargery (57–58). *Expectations.*

Bigby, Mrs. Mrs. Meeks's mother, "never known . . . to yield any point whatever, to mortal man." *Reprinted,* "Births."

Bigwig Family The "stateliest" family, devoted to ruling those beneath them. "Nobody's Story."

Bilberry, Lady Jemima Wife of Lord Decimus Tite Barnacle and daughter of the 15th earl of Stiltstocking. *Dorrit* (I:17).

Bildungsroman Novel describing the maturation of a young man or woman, also known as the Apprenticeship Novel or the Novel of Initiation. Derived from such European models as Goethe's *Wilhelm Meister's Apprenticeship* (1796), these novels typically concern a young person from the provinces who, dissatisfied with the social and intellectual restrictions of provincial life, leaves home to make his way in the city. There he is initiated into the truth about the world, often through painful love affairs, and he loses his illusions and accommodates himself to the newly discovered reality. Two of Dickens's novels, *David Copperfield* and *Great Expectations*, are among the English classics of the genre. Jerome H. BUCKLEY discusses these two works as examples of the Bildungsroman in *Season of Youth.* In "Young Man from the Country," Dickens characterizes himself as the typical bildungsroman hero, a young man from the country who went to America and had his idealism dashed by

his experiences there. Although the bildungsroman usually has a young man as its protagonist, Dickens's Esther Summerson (*Bleak House*) can be included among the minority of young women in such works.

"Biler" Nickname of Robin TOOTLE. *Dombey.*

Bilkins "The only authority on taste." *Reprinted,* "French Watering Place."

Bill (1) Coachman who drives Mr. Minns to Stamford Hill. *Boz,* "Minns."

Bill (2) Gravedigger who buries Mrs. Bayton. *Twist* (5).

Bill (3) Criminal defended by Jaggers, husband of Amelia. *Expectations* (20).

"Bill, Aggerawatin' " Nickname of William BARKER. *Boz,* "Omnibus Cad."

Bill, Black NEWGATE prisoner visited by Pip and Wemmick. *Expectations* (32).

"Bill, Uncle" "The wit of the party" among a group taking tea in a public tea garden. *Boz,* "London Recreations."

Billickin, Mrs. ("The Billikin") Landlady of the London lodging house where Rosa Bud is placed by Mr. Grewgious. She takes Miss Twinkleton to be her enemy and maintains an ongoing feud with her. "Personal faintness and overpowering personal candor" were her distinguishing characteristics. *Drood* (22).

Billingsgate The fish market in the CITY of London. Mentioned in *Dorrit, Expectations,* and *Uncommercial Traveller.* Slang for foul and vituperative language—such as that heard in a fish market.

Billsmethi, Signor (i.e., Bill Smith) The proprietor of a dancing academy in GRAY'S INN LANE, who, aided by his son and daughter, **Master** and **Miss Billsmethi**, extorts £20 from Augustus Cooper by threatening a breach of promise suit. *Boz,* "Dancing Academy."

"Bill-sticking" In an interview with the King of the Bill-Stickers, the narrator learns about the history and procedures of the business of poster advertising. Article for HOUSEHOLD WORDS (March 22, 1851). *Reprinted.*

Bilson and Slum Business for whom Tom Smart is a traveling salesman. *Pickwick* (14).

Bintrey Walter Wilding's solicitor, who helps to track down and expose Obenreizer. "No Thoroughfare."

Birmingham   Dickens visited this city in the industrial MIDLANDS of England many times and gave the first of his PUBLIC READINGS, a performance of *A Christmas Carol*, here in 1853.

Pickwick travels to Birmingham to inform Mr. Winkle of his son's marriage (50). Birmingham is also the original of the factory town that Nell and her Grandfather pass through (*Curiosity Shop*, 43–44). It is the home of John, the poor inventor (*Reprinted*, "Poor Man's Patent"). Birmingham is also mentioned in *Twist* (48), *Nickleby* (27), *Dombey* (20), and *Uncommercial* (25).

"Birthday Celebrations"   The Traveller remembers many birthday celebrations he has attended: a childhood party; a tedious visit to an Orrery (a precursor to a planetarium) with Olympia Squires; a schooltime celebration with a hamper of food; his 21st birthday; later celebrations of Flipfield's and Mayday's birthdays; the DULLBOROUGH festivity for Shakespeare's birthday. *Uncommercial* (20). Originally in ALL THE YEAR ROUND (June 6, 1863).

" 'Births. Mrs. Meek, of a Son' "   George Meek's account of the disruptions in his household brought about by the birth of his son, Augustus George, and the presence of his mother-in-law, Mrs. Bigby, and the maternity nurse, Mrs. Prodgit. The sketch originally appeared in HOUSEHOLD WORDS, February 22, 1851. *Reprinted*.

Bishop   Guest at Merdle's party, the representative of the church hierarchy. *Dorrit*.

Bishops   Older waiter who acts as a mentor to Christopher as he learns the trade. "Somebody's Luggage."

Bishopsgate   The street in the CITY of London where Brogley, the broker who takes possession of the WOODEN MIDSHIPMAN, has his shop. *Dombey* (9).

Bit, Charley   Under this name (short for Blitheringtonfordbury), Gabblewig disguises himself as an actor who once played in the same company with Slap. *Nightingale*.

Bitherstone, Bill   One of Paul Dombey's fellow boarders with Mrs. Pipchin, "whose relatives were all in India" (*Dombey*, 8). Major Bagstock knew his father, **Bill**, in the Army.

Bitzer   Star pupil at Mr. Gradgrind's school, he goes to work for Bounderby's bank. There he spies on Tom Gradgrind and reports his illegal activities. "His skin was so unwholesomely deficient in the natural tinge, that he looked as though, if he were cut, he would bleed white" (I:2). *Hard Times*.

Black, Mrs.   One of Mrs. Lemon's pupils. "Holiday Romance."

Black and **Green**   Policemen who accompany Inspector Field. *Reprinted*, "Inspector Field."

Black Badger, The   The pub frequented by the Game Chicken. *Dombey* (22).

Black Boy Inn, The   The inn at Chelmsford where Tony Weller picks up Jingle and Trotter. *Pickwick* (20).

Black Boy and Stomach-ache   Oldcastle inn where the second meeting of the Mudfog Association is held. *Mudfog*.

Black Bull Inn   The inn in HOLBORN where Sarah Gamp and Betsey Prig nurse Lewsome. *Chuzzlewit* (25).

Black Country, The   Dickens's most surreal account of the industrial MIDLANDS of England appears in his description of Little Nell's journey through the Black Country, based on his own impressions of the area while traveling on the road from BIRMINGHAM to WOLVERHAMPTON. *Curiosity Shop* (43–45). He describes a rail journey between the two towns in a winter snowstorm in "Fire and Snow." *Miscellaneous*.

"Black Eagle in a Bad Way, A"   Description of the state of Vienna in 1851, divided by class differences, dominated by the presence of the military, and characterized as "the most inhospitable capitol in Europe." An article for HOUSEHOLD WORDS (November 22, 1851) written with E. C. Grenville Murray and Henry Morley. *Stone*.

Black Lion Inn   The inn in WHITECHAPEL freqented by John and Joe Willet. *Rudge* (13, 71, 72.)

"Black Veil, The"   Story of a young surgeon whose first patient is a mysterious woman in a black veil. She engages him to come to her house in a remote section of WALWORTH at nine in the morning. There the surgeon is asked to revive the body of her son, a criminal who has just been hanged. Afterward the surgeon becomes a daily visitor to the mother, who has been driven mad by the event. *Boz*.

Blackboy, Mr.   The name Barkis has painted on his money box. *Copperfield* (31).

Blackey   A beggar who "stood near London Bridge these five-and-twenty years, with a painted skin to represent disease." *Reprinted*, "Inspector Field."

Blackfriars Bridge   One of the principal bridges across the THAMES in the CITY of London. Built in 1760, its toll houses were burned and robbed by the Gordon rioters in 1780 (*Rudge*, 67). David Copperfield is robbed of his box of belongings and his money in **Blackfriars Road**, the street leading to the bridge, as he makes his way out of London (*Copperfield*, 12). Mr. George crosses the bridge on his way to visit the Bagnets (*Bleak House*, 27). Clennam and Plornish cross the bridge on their way to visit MARSHALSEA PRISON (*Dorrit*, I:12), just as Dickens had done as a boy when he went from WARREN'S BLACKING warehouse (See also BLACKING WAREHOUSE) to visit his family in the debtor's prison. The bridge is also mentioned in *Expectations* (46), and *Reprinted*, "Down with the Tide."

Blackheath A village on the outskirts of London, southeast of the city along the DOVER road. David Copperfield's SALEM HOUSE SCHOOL is nearby, and he passes through Blackheath on his way to Dover (13). John and Bella Rokesmith settle here after their marriage (*Mutual Friend*, IV:4). The Traveller passes through on his way to the Continent (*Uncommercial*, 7).

Blacking Warehouse Factory for the manufacture of shoe polish. Dickens was sent to work at WARREN'S BLACKING as a boy of 12 while his father was imprisoned for debt in MARSHALSEA PRISON. In the fragmentary AUTOBIOGRAPHY that he gave to John FORSTER, Dickens described this period in his life as one of "humiliation and neglect." Placed in a window where he could be observed from the street, Dickens was assigned the task of pasting labels on the blacking bottles. His fellow workers were two working-class boys, Bob FAGIN and Poll GREEN, who referred to him as "the young gentleman."

Dickens "suffered in secret," humiliated by "this companionship" and in despair that his hopes of a better life had been dashed forever.

This experience in his childhood was so traumatic for Dickens that even as an adult he could not talk about it and he could not go back to HUNGERFORD STAIRS, the site of Warren's factory, until after they were torn down. He confided to Forster that "even now, famous and caressed and happy, I often forget in my dreams that I have a dear wife and children; even that I am a man; and wander desolately back to that time of my life."

Most contemporary commentators, following the lead of Edmund WILSON (1941), consider the blacking warehouse episode the psychic wound that prompted Dickens's creative impulse. It appears only thinly disguised as MURDSTONE AND GRINBY'S wine-bottling warehouse in *Copperfield*. It has also been considered the source of Pip's apprenticeship in Joe Gargery's forge (*Expectations*) and Oliver's "imprisonment" in Fagin's den (*Twist*).

Blackmore, Edward Junior partner in the law firm of ELLIS AND BLACKMORE, for whom Dickens worked as an office boy after leaving school at age 15. A friend

View of Hungerford Stairs by the Thames, where Warren's Blacking Warehouse was located.

of the boy's parents, Blackmore hired Dickens for 13s. 6d. (13 shillings and sixpence) a week and considered him "a bright, clever-looking youth."

Blackpool, Stephen   A power-loom weaver in Bounderby's mill; he is "a rather stooping man with a knitted brow, a pondering expression on his face, and a hard-looking head sufficiently capacious, on which his iron grey hair lay long and thin" who finds life "a muddle" (I:10). He loves Rachael, another Coketown factory hand, but he is unable to marry her because he is already married. His **wife** is a drunken woman who appears, disappears, and reappears. When he seeks advice from Bounderby about how to obtain a divorce, he is rebuffed by his employer as a troublemaker (I:11), and when he refuses to join the union he is ostracized by his fellow workers (II:4). When Blackpool leaves Coketown to look for work, Tom Gradgrind manages to throw suspicion onto Blackpool in the bank robbery (III:4). As he returns to clear his name, Blackpool falls into an empty mineshaft and dies shortly after he is rescued (III:6). *Hard Times.*

"Blacksmith, The"   Poem celebrating "the iron Blacksmith," whose work shows "what A MAN can do." Published in ALL THE YEAR ROUND (April 20, 1859).

Blackwood's Magazine   Magazine founded in 1817 in Edinburgh as a Tory rival to the Whig *Edinburgh Review.* During the Victorian period it became one of the primary venues for serial fiction. Novels by John Galt, Samuel Warren, Edward Bulwer LYTTON, Anthony TROLLOPE, and George ELIOT appeared in its pages, but in the 1840s it inveighed against "low" novelists like Dickens.

"Bladud, True Legend of Prince"   One of the INTERPOLATED TALES in *Pickwick*, this story is in a manuscript Pickwick finds in his rooms at BATH. Dickens's variant on the usual legend of the founding of the city tells how Prince Bladud, broken-hearted because his love has married another, wandered tearfully to the site of Bath, where he wished that his tears "might flow forever." When "his hot tears welled up through the earth," his wish was granted and the springs at Bath have been warm ever since. *Pickwick* (36).

Bladud, Prince   The mythical founder of the public baths at Bath, whose story appears in *Pickwick* (36).

Blake, "Warmint"   An "out-and-out young gentleman." *Young Gentlemen.*

Blandois, Monsieur   The alias adopted by RIGAUD in England. *Dorrit.*

Blank   An exhibitor at the Mechanical Science Section of the Mudfog Association. *Mudfog.*

Blanquo, Pierre   Our Bore's Swiss mountain guide. *Reprinted,* "Bore."

Blathers   BOW STREET runner summoned with Duff to investigate the robbery at Mrs. Maylie's house: "a stout personage, of middle height, aged about fifty, with shiny black hair cropped pretty close, half whiskers, a round face, and sharp eyes" (31). *Twist.*

Blaze and Sparkle   London jewelers who cater to the "fashionable people" and not to the "general public." *Bleak House* (2).

Blazes   Sam Weller's name for TUCKLE, a footman dressed in a crimson livery. *Pickwick* (32).

Blazo, Sir Thomas   A fellow cricket player with Jingle in the West Indies: "Played a match once—single wicket—friend the Colonel—Sir Thomas Blazo—who should get the greatest number of runs." *Pickwick* (7).

Bleak House   Two houses in ST. ALBANS have been suggested as the likely originals of Dickens's Bleak House. Fort House in BROADSTAIRS, the building where Dickens spent many holidays, has been renamed Bleak House, but it has no connection with the house in the novel.

Bleak House   Dickens's ninth novel, published in monthly parts in 1852–53, with illustrations by Hablot Knight BROWNE ("Phiz"), issued in one volume in 1853. Often characterized as the first of the late novels, *Bleak*

Browne's (Phiz's) illustration for the controversial scene in Bleak House *in which Guppy and Jobling discover that Krook has disappeared by spontaneous combustion.*

House describes England as a bleak house, devastated by an irresponsible and self-serving legal system, symbolically represented by the Lord Chancellor ensconced in foggy glory in the CHANCERY. Dickens uses two narrators: a third-person narrator who reports on the public life in the worlds of law and fashion, and a first-person narrator, Esther Summerson, a young woman who tells her personal history. By this double narration, he is able to connect and contrast Esther's domestic story with broad public concerns. Esther's narrative traces her discovery of her identity as the illegitimate child of Lady Dedlock. Abandoned in infancy and raised by an abusive aunt, Esther is a self-denying, unassertive young woman, grateful for any recognition she receives from the patriarchal society around her. Her situation encapsulates that of the larger society, in which traditions of aristocratic privilege deny human needs and desires and patriarchal institutions such as the courts make orphans of society's children, enable slums and disease to flourish, and suppress individual autonomy by a "philanthropy" that makes dependents of its recipients.

SYNOPSIS

Part 1 (March 1851)

(1) A foggy November afternoon. At the heart of the fog, the Court of Chancery is entangled in the Jarndyce and Jarndyce case, a dispute over a will that has dragged on for several generations. The Lord Chancellor considers the disposition of two young people in the suit.

(2) My lady Dedlock is bored to death during the rainy season at Chesney Wold, her place in Lincolnshire. So she and her husband, Sir Leicester Dedlock, a baronet 20 years her senior, come up to London. There they consult with Mr. Tulkinghorn, the family lawyer. When he shows them some inconsequential documents pertaining to the Jarndyce case, she asks who copied them, faints, and is taken to her room.

(3) Esther Summerson begins the story of her life by telling of her lonely and oppressed childhood. She was raised by Miss Barbary, a "godmother" who tells her that she is her mother's "disgrace" and that it would have been far better had she never been born. After her godmother's death, she is sent off to Greenleaf School for six years before being summoned to London by John Jarndyce, the primary living representative of the Jarndyce family, to become a companion to Ada Clare. Ada is one of two wards in the Jarndyce case, assigned to the care of Jarndyce by the Court of Chancery. As Esther leaves the court with Ada and the other ward, Richard Carstone, the three young people meet a little mad woman, obsessed with the judgments of the Court, who greets them as representatives of "youth, hope, and beauty." (4) Then, Mr. Guppy, a law clerk, conducts them to the house of Mrs. Jellyby, a friend of Jarndyce, where they are to spend the night. The house is in complete disorder: The children are neglected, there is no hot water, stair carpets are loose, dinner is served almost raw. Mrs. Jellyby devotes all of her time and attention to an African mission in Borrioboola Gha. Her daughter Caddy, who acts as her secretary, complains of the "disgraceful house" and falls asleep with her head in Esther's lap.

Part 2 (April 1852)

(5) The next morning they again meet the little mad woman, Miss Flite. She takes them to her room on the top floor of Krook's Rag and Bottle Warehouse, where she shows them the caged birds, with names like Youth, Hope, and Beauty, that she plans to set free when the court decides her case. She leads them past the dark door of the another lodger, a law writer called Nemo, and introduces them to her landlord, the junk dealer Krook, who has earned the nickname "Lord Chancellor" because he collects legal documents and papers among the items in his shop. Although he cannot read, he spells out letter by letter *J-a-r-n-d-y-c-e* and *B-l-e-a-k h-o-u-s-e*, words he has learned from his documents. (6) Then the three young people set out for Bleak House, the home of their guardian in ST. ALBANS. When they arrive, Jarndyce suggests that they meet as old friends even though they have not met before. He shows them their rooms in the irregular house and surprises Esther by giving her the household keys. They also meet a guest in the house, Harold Skimpole, an artist, composer, and doctor who does not work and claims to have no understanding of money. He sponges from Jarndyce and persuades Esther and Richard to pay a debt to keep him from being arrested. When Jarndyce finds out that they have given him money, he gets them to promise never to do so again.

(7) Mrs. Rouncewell, the housekeeper at Chesney Wold, presides while the Dedlocks are away. The weather remains wet in Lincolnshire. When Guppy tours the house, he is struck by a portrait of the current Lady Dedlock, who seems strangely familiar to him. He also wants to hear the story of the Ghost's Walk, but Mrs. Rouncewell waits until he leaves before she tells the story to her grandson Watt and Rosa, a pretty young servant. The story explains the sound of footsteps on the terrace, the footsteps of a Lady Dedlock of the 17th century who was crippled by her Cavalier husband when she opposed him and aided the Roundheads. She vowed to walk the terrace until the pride of the house was humbled (7).

Part 3 (May 1852)

(8) At breakfast Skimpole delightfully develops his "philosophy" that drones should be honored over those who are as busy as bees. Jarndyce shows them the Growlery, a room where he retreats when he is out of humor. He talks of the blight of Chancery and urges Richard to choose a profession. One of Jarndyce's acquaintances, Mrs. Pardiggle, a local "philanthropist," recruits Esther and Ada to accompany her to a nearby brickmaker's house. On the way the Pardiggle children complain to Esther that their allowances are taken by their mother for charity. They intrude into the brickmaker's house and discover that an infant child has died. Esther covers the little corpse with her handkerchief. (9) Lawrence Boythorn, an old schoolfellow, visits Jarndyce, filling Bleak

House with boisterous superlatives and irrepressible hyperbole. Mr. Guppy also comes to Bleak House. He proposes to Esther, suggesting that he can act on her behalf. She rejects him, but she both laughs and cries over the proposal.

(10) Tulkinghorn inquires of Snagsby, the stationer who provides copying services for the legal community, who copied the affidavit that Lady Dedlock saw. Together they go to Krook's, and he leads them up to Nemo's room. There is a smell of opium in the darkness and Nemo does not respond to Krook's "Hallo."

Part 4 (June 1852)
(11) They find Nemo dead. While Krook is out of the room, Tulkinghorn removes some papers from Nemo's portmanteau. At the inquest the next day at Sol's Arms, no significant additions are made to the story; the one witness who knew Nemo, Jo, a poor crossing sweeper, is not allowed to testify. Nemo is buried in a pauper's cemetery. Jo sweeps the step into the burial ground. (12) In January Sir Leicester and Lady Dedlock return to Chesney Wold. The weather has cleared. Lady Dedlock annoys Hortense, her French maid, by complimenting the beauty of a local servant girl, Rosa. Tulkinghorn tells Lady Dedlock of Nemo's death. Assuming her characteristic manner, she apparently listens to the story only to divert herself from the tedium of Chesney Wold.

(13) After vaguely considering the navy, the army, and the law, Richard chooses medicine and goes to study with Mr. Bayham Badger. Ada confesses to Esther that she and Richard love one another.

Part 5 (July 1852)
(14) Caddy tells Esther that she is secretly engaged to a dancing master, and Esther goes with her to the Academy, where they meet the hard-working Prince Turveydrop and his idle and parasitic father, a latter-day dandy who considers himself the model of deportment. At Miss Flite's, where Caddy has been learning household skills, they meet Jarndyce, Krook, and Allan Woodcourt, the young physician in attendance at Nemo's death. Esther is chilled when she passes the dark room where Nemo died. (15) Skimpole tells Esther and Jarndyce of the death of Neckett, the bill collector, who "has been arrested by the great Bailiff," and they seek out Neckett's orphaned children. They find the two younger ones, Tom and Emma, locked in a tenement room in BELL YARD while Charley, the oldest, is out doing laundry. The neighbors, Mrs. Blinder and Mr. Gridley, keep an eye on the children and tell of their admiration for Charley.

(16) Sir Leicester remains alone in Lincolnshire. In London, Jo, the illiterate crossing sweeper, who was a friend of the dead copywriter, wonders at his darkened world. He lives in TOM-ALL-ALONE'S, a slum blighted because it is caught up in a Chancery suit, and he is surprised when a woman, dressed as a servant, seeks him out and has him guide her to Snagsby's, Krook's, and the cemetery where Nemo is buried. She gives the boy a golden sovereign before she disappears.

Part 6 (August 1852)
(17) Richard is not committed to medicine. He proposes that the law would be a more engaging pursuit, and Jarndyce agrees to the change, but that evening Esther finds her guardian in the Growlery. There he tells her the little he knows of her personal history. Meanwhile, Allan Woodcourt, a physician devoted to his profession, announces that he is going to the East as a medical man. Caddy brings Esther some flowers that Woodcourt left at Miss Flite's. (18) In midsummer, while visiting Boythorn in Lincolnshire, Esther is disturbed by seeing Lady Dedlock's face, which calls up memories of childhood and a haunting sense that she has seen her before. When they meet in a garden house at Chesney Wold, Lady Dedlock's voice also unsettles Esther.

(19) Taking tea at Snagsby's, Guppy learns that the Reverend Chadband's wife was formerly Miss Rachel, servant to Esther's godmother. When Jo is brought to Snagsby by a constable who has arrested him for not "moving on," Jo tells them of the lady who gave him a sovereign.

Part 7 (September 1852)
(20) Guppy continues to pursue the mysteries surrounding Nemo's death. He convinces his friend Tony Jobling to take Nemo's room at Krook's, so that he can spy on Krook and gather information about Nemo. (21) Nearby, Trooper George, an ex-soldier, runs a shooting gallery. He has borrowed the money for the business from Grandfather Smallweed, a small-time moneylender, and each month George manages to pay enough interest to renew the loan for the principal amount. (22) Tulkinghorn is also pursuing the Nemo mystery. When Snagsby tells him Jo's story of the lady who gave him a sovereign, the lawyer sends Snagsby and Detective Bucket to Tom-All-Alone's to find the boy. When they bring Jo back, there is a veiled lady in Tulkinghorn's rooms. At first Jo thinks it is the woman he guided through the streets, but when she removes her gloves he sees that her hands are not so delicate nor her rings so precious as those on the woman who gave him the sovereign. This woman is Hortense, Lady Dedlock's former maid. Tulkinghorn and Bucket are pleased to have established that Jo's woman was a lady disguised as Hortense.

Part 8 (October 1852)
(23) Hortense offers herself to Esther as a maid, but Esther turns her down. Richard reveals that he is bored with the law and in debt. Caddy asks Esther to go with her when she announces her engagement to their parents. Mr. Turveydrop agrees to the marriage when Caddy and Prince promise to take care of him. Mrs. Jellyby, continuing her mission work in spite of her husband's bankruptcy, refuses to take Caddy seriously. Esther is surprised to learn that Mr. Jarndyce has hired Charley as her maid.

(24) Richard moves from the law to the army. Jarndyce asks Ada and Richard to break their engagement because they are too young and unsettled. Richard com-

plies resentfully. To prepare for his new profession, Richard takes fencing and shooting lessons from Trooper George at the shooting gallery where Gridley, the man from Shropshire, now ill and a fugitive from the law, is hiding. Just as Bucket comes to arrest him, Gridley dies.

(25) Mrs. Snagsby has convinced herself that Jo is her husband's son. At an oration by Chadband hinting at this connection, Jo falls asleep. Snagsby quietly gives the boy a half crown and commends him for saying nothing about the the lady with a sovereign.

Part 9 (November 1852)
(26) Grandfather Smallweed asks George for a sample of the handwriting of Captain Hawdon, George's former officer in the army. Smallweed is acting on behalf of Tulkinghorn, and George, reluctant to give it to him until he knows why it is wanted, agrees to go with Smallweed to see Tulkinghorn. (27) The lawyer will not reveal why he wants the writing. George feels vaguely threatened, so he consults with his old Army comrade, Mat Bagnet, whose wife advises him to stay out of things he doesn't understand. George refuses to turn over the writing.

(28) Meanwhile, Rouncewell the Ironmaster, the elder son of Mrs. Rouncewell, proposes to remove Rosa from Chesney Wold and educate her to be a fit wife for his son Watt. Sir Leicester is scandalized to learn that Rouncewell does not value Rosa's training as a servant at Chesney Wold; he knows that "the whole framework of society" has cracked. (29) Guppy tells Lady Dedlock that he has linked her portrait with Esther's face, her story with those of Miss Barbary and Captain Hawdon, that Hawdon was the real name of Nemo the dead law writer, that Esther is his daughter, and that Lady Dedlock herself was the lady who gave Jo the sovereign. He offers to obtain a sheaf of Hawdon's letters for her. After he leaves, she falls on her knees, crying "O my child!"

Part 10 (December 1852)
(30) Esther serves as Caddy's bridesmaid. On the wedding day, Jarndyce's good spirits overcome differences between Mrs. Jellyby's preoccupied philanthropic friends and Turveydrop, who thinks the Jellybys lack deportment. (31) Over Skimpole's objection, Esther and Charley take in Jo, who is sick with fever, but by the next morning Jo has mysteriously disappeared. Charley comes down with the fever and Esther cares for her, but when Charley recovers, Esther contracts the disease. The fever is so bad that Esther goes blind.

(32) Guppy and Jobling wait in Nemo's old rooms to meet an appointment with Krook at midnight, when he will turn over Nemo's letters to them. They are bothered by an oppressiveness in the air and by oily soot on the windowsills and walls. When the clock strikes 12, they go downstairs and find the cat snarling at a spot on the floor. That is all that remains of Krook, who has died from spontaneous combustion.

Part 11 (January 1853)
(33) COOK'S COURT can talk of nothing else but the strange events at Krook's. The Smallweeds claim the

building as the property of Mrs. Smallweed, Krook's sister. Guppy tells Lady Dedlock that he does not have the letters, and that they were probably destroyed. (34) Smallweed demands that George pay the principal of his loan, but George does not have the money and Mat Bagnet, his cosigner, is threatened. Tulkinghorn agrees to restore matters to their old footing for a sample of Hawdon's writing. George gives in.

(35) After several weeks, Esther awakens from her illness and gradually recovers her sight. She notices that the mirrors in her rooms are gone and realizes that this means that she is scarred by the disease and has lost her "old face." Miss Flite visits and tells of Woodcourt's heroism in saving the survivors of a shipwreck. Esther admits that she used to think Woodcourt loved her, but now she is grateful that she is disfigured and won't have that to worry about anymore.

Part 12 (February 1853)
(36) At Boythorn's house, where she goes to recuperate, Esther finds a mirror in her room with a curtain pulled across it. After Charley has gone to bed, Esther pulls back the curtain, looks in the mirror, and tearfully accepts her changed face. On one of her daily walks in the park at Chesney Wold, Esther is confronted by Lady Dedlock, who reveals that she is Esther's mother and, kneeling before her, asks her forgiveness. Esther is unsettled; walking on the Ghost's Walk and hearing her hollow footsteps, she thinks she is the calamity in the Chesney Wold legend. Gradually she comes to accept her birth and to believe that she was intended to live. (37) Esther asks Skimpole to discourage Richard's obsession with the Jarndyce case, his distrust of Mr. Jarndyce, and his reliance on his new attorney, Vholes. Skimpole says he is incapable of such "responsibility." (38) Esther asks Guppy to abandon his pursuit of her personal history. Guppy, disconcerted by her changed appearance, agrees to do so, and makes her swear that she turned down his original proposal and that she understands that it cannot be renewed.

Part 13 (March 1853)
(39) Tulkinghorn inquires about Guppy's business with Lady Dedlock, but Guppy tells him nothing. (40) At Chesney Wold, where the Dedlocks have gathered, Tulkinghorn tells the story of an ironmaster who forbade his daughter to associate with a great lady when he learned that the great lady had suppressed a secret affair and a child she had borne out of wedlock many years before. Lady Dedlock leaves the room, (41) but later she confirms Tulkinghorn's story and tells him of her plan to flee. He threatens her with immediate exposure. That night Tulkinghorn sleeps unaware of the distaught figure pacing on the Ghost's Walk. (42) When Tulkinghorn returns to the city, Snagsby complains that Mademoiselle Hortense has been lingering near his house and raising Mrs. Snagsby's suspicions. Tulkinghorn threatens to have her thrown in prison if she persists. She demands his aid in securing a new position and leaves threatening revenge.

Part 14 (April 1853)

(43) Esther worries that she will reveal her mother's secret. When Sir Leicester Dedlock calls and invites her to visit Chesney Wold, she is disconcerted. She seeks advice from Mr. Jarndyce, telling him that Lady Dedlock is her mother (43). Jarndyce agrees that she must avoid further meetings with Sir Leicester. Then he asks her to send Charley "this night a week" for a letter from him. The letter turns out to be a proposal asking her to be "mistress of Bleak House." He assures her that nothing will change in his feelings for her, whatever she decides. Esther thinks that devoting her life to Jarndyce's happiness "was to thank him poorly," yet she cries over her good fortune. Then she burns Woodcourt's dried roses. After several days she agrees to be mistress of Bleak House. (45) Esther goes down to the town of Deal, in Kent, where Richard has sold his commission and is preparing to leave the army. While she is there, Allan Woodcourt returns from India. Esther asks him to be a friend and advisor to Richard.

(46) Back in London, in Tom-All-Alone's, Woodcourt comes upon the sickly Jo. The boy tells him that he was taken from Bleak House by Bucket, who put him in a hospital and then gave him some money and told him to "move on" and stay away from London. He has returned to Tom-All-Alone's to die.

Part 15 (May 1853)

(47) Woodcourt takes the sick boy to George's shooting gallery. There the boy dies as he repeats the Lord's Prayer after Woodcourt. (48) Lady Dedlock turns Rosa over to Rouncewell. Tulkinghorn takes this act as a breach of their agreement, but he will not tell her when he plans to inform Sir Leicester of her secret. That night a shot rings out, and the next morning the people who come to clean Tulkinghorn's house discover his body. (49) The next day Bucket appears at Mrs. Bagnet's birthday dinner. He charms the family with his stories and songs and leaves with George, who is white and drawn. On their way home, Bucket arrests George for Tulkinghorn's murder.

Part 16 (June 1853)

(50) After the birth of Caddy's sickly baby, Esther nurses Caddy through an illness. Prince, Mr. Turveydrop, and Woodcourt are frequent visitors to the sickroom. Esther tells Caddy and Ada of her agreement to marry Jarndyce. After Caddy's recovery, Esther returns home and feels a "shade" between herself and Ada. (51) Ada confesses to Esther that she and Richard have married. (52) Esther is now alone in Jarndyce's house. Woodcourt, who serves as both Caddy's and Richard's doctor, tells her of their conditions. When he tells her of George's arrest, they visit the trooper in prison and offer to help him, but he so distrusts lawyers that he refuses any legal aid. Mrs. Bagnet decides to seek out George's mother, whom she believes is still alive and living in Lincolnshire.

(53) Bucket investigates the murder. He observes those attending Tulkinghorn's funeral, studies anonymous letters implicating Lady Dedlock, and he learns from Sir

Leicester's footman that Lady Dedlock went out walking on the night of the murder.

Part 17 (July 1853)

(54) Bucket reveals the true story of Lady Dedlock to Sir Leicester, advising him to buy Captain Hawdon's letters now in Grandfather Smallweed's possession. Then he apprehends Hortense and charges her with Tulkinghorn's murder. (55) When Mrs. Bagnet finds George's mother, she turns out to be Mrs. Rouncewell. George has been estranged from his family ever since he ran away from home as a young man. When Mrs. Rouncewell reveals herself to her son, George falls on his knees, asks her forgiveness, and says he is innocent. She asks Lady Dedlock to do anything she can for her son. Guppy tells Lady Dedlock that Hawdon's letters have been found and that Sir Leicester has been told her story. Lady Dedlock writes to Sir Leicester, telling him that she followed Tulkinghorn on the evening of the murder, but that she is innocent of the crime. (56) Sir Leicester collapses on the floor of the library, suffering from a stroke. When he learns of Lady Dedlock's disappearance, he summons Bucket and, by writing on a slate, asks the detective to find his wife and forgive her. Bucket hires horses and a carriage, and, at one in the morning, comes to Esther's house to secure her aid in the search.

Part 18 (August 1853)

(57) Bucket and Esther go to a police station where the detective files a description of Lady Dedlock, then to a place by the river where suicides are recovered; they then head north, picking up a trail that leads to the brickmaker's houses outside St. Albans. There Bucket learns that Jenny, the brickmaker's wife, and Lady Dedlock have gone off in opposite directions. They follow Lady Dedlock's trail to the north, but they lose it about evening. Then Bucket heads back toward London, to follow Jenny's trail.

(58) Meanwhile, Sir Leicester, attended by George, awaits his wife's return.

(59) At three in the morning Esther and Bucket reach the outskirts of London. They go on to Chancery Lane, where they learn from Snagsby's servant that she has directed a ragged woman to the graveyard where Nemo is buried. There they find Lady Dedlock, dressed in Jenny's clothes, dead on the pavement before the cemetery gate.

Parts 19–20 (September 1853)

(60) After Lady Dedlock's death, Esther settles in London to be near Ada and Richard. They worry about Richard's declining health. Ada tells Esther that she is pregnant and that she hopes Richard's child will draw him away from his destructive obsession with the Jarndyce case. (61) Esther asks Skimpole to stop seeing Richard. He agrees, seeing no point in making himself part of Richard's unhappy poverty. One evening, as he accompanies Esther home from Richard's, Woodcourt reveals his love and admiration for her, but Esther turns down his proposal because she is not free to love him. With

tears in her eyes, she watches him leave. (62) Esther tells Jarndyce to set the time when she will become mistress of Bleak House. Meanwhile, Grandfather Smallweed has found a Jarndyce will, more recent than any other, that reduces John Jarndyce's interest in favor of Richard's and Ada's.

(63) Visiting his brother the ironmaster in the iron district, George is welcomed as an honored guest and invited to stay there. But George returns to settle at Chesney Wold.

(64) Jarndyce plans to go to Yorkshire to see about Woodcourt's new position there as a physician to the poor. He asks Esther to accompany him. There he shows her a house for Woodcourt furnished like Bleak House and he tells her that his proposal was a mistake. Both he and Woodcourt encourage her to marry Allan and to live in the new Bleak House. She is very happy. Back in London Guppy renews his proposal and is again refused. (65) Allan and Esther set out for Chancery on the day the Jarndyce will is to be decided. They are late for the session and when they arrive, the proceedings are already over. Jarndyce and Jarndyce is decided. The new will is valid, but all the money has been absorbed in legal costs. Richard, weak and with his mouth full of blood, talks of the dream being over, of beginning in the world. He reconciles with Jarndyce. But he will begin in the next world. As he dies, Miss Flite releases her birds.

(66) Chesney Wold is quiet. Sir Leicester, accompanied by George, can be seen riding by Lady Dedlock's grave and stopping in quiet respect. The house is dark and vacant.

(67) Seven years later, Esther lives a settled life with Allan and their two daughters in Yorkshire, where they are visited by Caddy, by Ada and her son Richard, and by Jarndyce, for whom they have added a growlery to their house (67).

COMMENTARY

Bleak House, along with *Copperfield* and *Expectations*, is one of the books most often described as Dickens's best novel. A voluminous body of criticism attests to its academic popularity. Published in 1852–53, *Bleak House* is often considered the first of the late novels, coming just after the autobiographical *Copperfield*, which divides Dickens's career. Though there are some comic characters and humorous scenes, it is a dark novel that presents England as diseased, and apocalyptically warns of a coming day of judgment. Like the other late novels, it is focused around a central theme and dominant symbol, the fog which represents the pervasive influence of the COURT OF CHANCERY in all areas of British life. Dickens began this social critique with a contemporary scandal: In 1850, the *Times* began publishing articles exposing the Court, its endless delays, repetitive proceedings, and interminable cases. They cited several cases that had gone on for years and, like Jarndyce, ended by exhausting all the resources in court costs. Dickens began with

this scandal and turned it into a story symbolically anatomizing the condition of England in 1852.

The most notable technical feature in Dickens's conception is the use of two contrasting narrations—a third-person narration marked by the usual Dickensian hyperbole and rhetorical effects and a first-person narration by Esther Summerson. Critics have debated endlessly about why Dickens used this narrative strategy and just how successful it was, particularly in telling Esther's story.

The third-person narration that opens the novel is a generalizing, highly rhetorical voice with a panoramic view of the world. In the famous description of the fog that begins the first chapter, he links London's present fogginess to Noah's flood, suggesting that it is far more than a weather condition, and then to the Court of Chancery, where the foggy wigs of the judges and lawyers symbolize the pervasive confusion that they bring to the condition of England. Then, in the second chapter, the narrative focus moves to Lincolnshire and finds that the "waters are out" there as well. Satirical, symbolic, authoritative, these opening chapters present a public view; they are highly stylized reportage of the worlds of Chancery and Fashion by a very capable reporter, sure of his effects. The voice is clearly male.

Esther Summerson is just as clearly female. Her narration, which begins in chapter 3, is hesitant, self-deprecating, personal, an account of the narrow world she inhabits. From her opening sentence—"I have a great deal of difficulty in beginning to write my portion of these pages, for I know I am not clever" (3)—she counters the assurance and objectivity of the male narrator. Philip COLLINS (1990) has pointed out that Esther's style and language still have many characteristic Dickensian traits, but many readers have nonetheless found her narrative tedious. Esther is too passive, too deferential to others, too repressed, too coy; she conceals or withholds her feelings about her mother and about Allan Woodcourt, and she dutifully accepts the role of "little woman." Among those who find Esther a tiresome bore, there is disagreement about whether Dickens was celebrating her as an ideal woman or using her to show the oppressiveness of patriarchal institutions.

Esther has much in common with Dickens's other "orphan" heroes. Like Oliver Twist, she bears a name that does not indicate her parentage, and her godmother oppresses her psychologically much as Oliver is oppressed by parish authorities. Like David Copperfield, Esther has a host of nicknames, indicative of her uncertainty about her identity and her willingness to accept the identities others give her. Her situation as a woman exaggerates the identity crisis faced by these Dickensian orphans, for the opportunities available to her are fewer than those available to David or Pip. Yet for all her reticence, Esther is not totally passive. She does, for example, resist Mr. Guppy's attempts to claim her and her story.

Esther's "progress" is like that of the heroine of Charlotte Bronte's *Jane Eyre* (1847), a popular novel published just a few years before *Bleak House*, passing through a series of symbolic bleak houses. She begins in the house of a cruel aunt who tells her, "It would have been far better . . . that you had never been born" (3), and teaches her to use "submission, self-denial, [and] diligent work" as ways to compensate for her guilty presence. After a respite at Greenleaf—a marked contrast to Jane's unhappy Lowood School—Esther is called to be the housekeeper at Bleak House, where, like Jane, she will also be tempted to marry the master of the house. On the way there, she stays at the house of Mrs. Jellyby, whose "telescopic philanthropy" leads to her preoccupation with Africa and to her neglect of her own children. Mrs. Jellyby represents the bleak house of imperial England, engaged around the world but out of touch with the problems at home. Krook's rooming house is another emblem of such waste and neglect. In his rag-and-bottle shop, he hoards the detritus of legal London that surrounds him, and his apartments house the victims of Chancery, little Miss Flite and the dying law-writer Nemo.

In sharp contrast to the poverty and decay in the urban slums stands Chesney Wold, the opulent country estate of Sir Leicester Dedlock, but it too has been wasted by the flood that has fogged in London. The floodgates have been opened, Sir Leicester repeatedly complains, and the waters are out in Lincolnshire. Lady Dedlock, "bored to death," acts out the devastation that has been wrought on the landed aristocracy and the legend of the Ghost's Walk foretells the judgment that will fall upon the house.

Removed from the neglect and decay in London, the actual Bleak House seems far from bleak. Located in St. Albans, an old settlement well away from the city, it provides a refuge in its irregular rooms and gardens where its owner, John Jarndyce, has withdrawn to this rural retreat to escape the city and the Jarndyce case. But the devastation of Chancery reaches St. Albans; Jarndyce's attempt to escape to the country proves as illusory as Skimpole's charade as an irresponsible child. Jarndyce must have the Growlery to retreat to when the east wind blows, for the ills of London appear at Bleak House as Skimpole's parasitism, Mrs. Pardiggle's oppressive philanthropy, the sufferings of the brickmakers, and the smallpox that Jo, the diseased child of urban neglect, brings from Tom-All-Alone's to St. Albans.

The bleakness that afflicts all of these houses is in various ways connected to the law and the system of injustice that serves itself but ignores the human effects of its operations. The law is represented by the Lord Chancellor, the interminable Jarndyce suit, and the many lawyers in the novel, especially Tulkinghorn, whose house in Lincoln's Inn is the bleak house of the law: "Formerly a house of state . . . it is let off in sets of chambers now; and in those shrunken fragments of its greatness, lawyers lie like maggots in nuts. . . . Here, among his many boxes labelled with transcendent names, lives Mr. Tulkinghorn. . . . Everything that can have a lock has got one; no key is visible" (10). The allegorical significance of Tulking-

horn is indicated by the Allegory painted on the ceiling of his rooms. Locked up and secretive as an oyster, dressed in rusty black like an agent of fate, his motives for acting are never clear. He does not seem to serve the best interests of his clients, but rather to seek power for its own sake. His machinations are part of a legal system that simply serves itself, and which in doing so, wreaks havoc on society. Allegorically, all of England is a bleak house devastated by the law.

The other metaphor that underlies the novel is disease. Dickens is here following the lead of Thomas CARLYLE, who coined the phrase "Condition of England" in his essay on *Chartism* (1839), to describe the social turmoil of the times as a form of disease. In *Bleak House*, the infection of Chancery is seen in the Jarndyce case—its name suggestively close to jaundice—in Tom Jarndyce who has blown his brains out before the beginning of the story, and in Richard Carstone, who catches the disease and slowly wastes away and dies. These cases are echoed in the stories of other Chancery suitors: Gridley, "The Man from Shropshire," and Miss Flite, for example.

The disease metaphor has its most bizarre expression in the figure of Krook, the illiterate rag-and-bottle merchant, who acts an underworld parody of the Lord Chancellor. He compulsively collects legal documents and papers, but, unable to understand their contents, he can make no use of them. His papers cannot aid the cause of justice; they are simply instruments of the law. Like the gin that courses through Krook's veins and arteries, this narcissistic, self-gratifying use of law is ultimately self destructive. In Krook's improbable death by spontaneous combustion, an episode that drew much adverse criticism, there is a warning for the established legal system: When the law becomes totally absorbed with itself and its own procedures, it will destroy itself. Dickens defended his use of spontaneous combustion on scientific grounds, citing cases and scientific studies that confirmed the possibilty, but his real defense would argue on symbolic grounds. Krook's explosion is a small version of Legal England ending in fire.

The disease metaphor is most fully developed in Jo, the illiterate crossing-sweeper. He is the product of Tom-All-Alone's, the slum in the heart of London created by Chancery, for the money that would repair and maintain the houses there is tied up in the Jarndyce case. The child is as neglected as the buildings. In a society with no public education, Jo is allowed "to know nothink," to be less educated than a dog who has at least been trained to herd sheep. This neglected child, forced by the law to "move on," carries the fever from the festering slum to St. Albans. There Esther is exposed and her illness brings her identity story to its crisis, precipitating the action that leads to Lady Dedlock's death.

A constitutional society grounded in the law that neglects its citizens is like an irresponsible parent who neglects or abuses his children. Jo and Esther—and numerous other children in the novel—represent these victims of neglect. The law is not the only bad parent.

Dickens also blames religion: the cruel Calvinism that engenders the psychological abuse inflicted by Esther's aunt; the hypocritical Evangelicism of the Chadbands that concentrates on converting street children like Jo rather than feeding their hunger; the "telescopic philanthropy" of those like Mrs. Jellyby who are so obsessed with missionary work in Africa that they neglect the children of England. Dickens also blames "Fashion": the class system that leads Lady Dedlock to suppress her past relationship with Captain Hawdon and "abandon" her child; the dandyism that turns Turveydrop into an imitator of the idle aristocracy and into a parasite who exploits his son. Finally, Dickens blames the artists who, like Skimpole, celebrate beauty and pretend to be children in order to avoid taking responsibility for the ugliness around them.

Faced with such systemic ills—with a national bleak house—Jarndyce's philanthropy seems trivial and ineffective. Indeed, Jarndyce cannot save Richard from Chancery nor Jo from smallpox. His kindness to Skimpole may, in fact, hasten Jo's illness and death. Although he is more enlightened and less self-interested than Mrs. Jellyby and Mrs. Pardiggle, Jarndyce's philanthropy does not represent the solution to bleakness. His strategy is one of retreat and withdrawal; he is basically passive. In spite of his kindness, he is allied with the old order. He can preserve Bleak House, even build a replica of it, but he cannot create a new order.

Jarndyce's inability to change things may account for the unfinished ending of the novel. It breaks off, midsentence, in Esther's narrative. She is again revealing her sense of inferiority—or her coyness—and seems not to have been changed at all psychologically by the events of the novel. The scars of parental abandonment are so lasting and the wounds of her childhood so deep, that she will carry them forever, in spite of a happy marriage and loving family. There is ample textual support for this despairing conclusion.

Yet there are also some reasons for hope in the final chapters of the novel. If a self-serving legal system, an obsolete aristocracy, and a narrow and repressive religion collude to deny possibilities for change and growth, there are a few characters in *Bleak House* who are not blinded by self-interest or enfeebled by the past. One such character is Rouncewell the Ironmaster, one of the new captains of industry. He is not intimidated by Sir Leicester's title and position: he challenges the Dedlock candidate in the election and wins, and he removes Rosa from Chesney Wold to better educate her for a useful place in society. Inspector Bucket is also one of the new class, a professional who takes pride in his work and who carries out his duties for his client; he is one of the new metropolitan police who represent a new way of administering the law. Finally, Allan Woodcourt, much more than the romantic hero of the novel, is the doctor who serves his patients and ministers to the poor. If anyone can heal the diseased condition of England, it will be such a man.

CRITICISM

Bleak House has probably generated more criticism than any other Dickens novel, an indication of its importance on academic reading lists. Two collections of criticism bring together some of the better articles: one edited by Jacob Korg (1968), the other by A. E. DYSON (1969). The Norton Critical Edition of the novel, edited by George H. FORD AND SYLVÈRE MONOD (1977), includes some critical articles as well as useful background materials. Robert Newsom's *Dickens on the Romantic Side of Familiar Things: Bleak House and the Novel Tradition* (1977) analyzes the mixture of romantic and realistic elements in the novel as a way of describing Dickens's work more broadly and his relation to the central tradition of the novel. Volume 19 of *DICKENS STUDIES ANNUAL* (1990) contains five articles on *Bleak House*, including one by Philip COLLINS, "Some Narrative Devices in *Bleak House*," which addresses key critical issues in the novel. Audrey JAFFE (1991) offers an interesting recent analysis of the double narrative and point of view in the novel.

ADAPTATIONS

Nearly all of the early stage adaptations of *Bleak House* concentrated on Jo and were given such titles as *The Adventures of Joe the Crossing-Sweeper, Joe the Orphan*, or *Outcast Joe; or, The London Arab*. The most famous portrayer of the child was Jennie LEE, who first played the role in San Francisco in 1875. She continued playing in *Jo; or Bleak House*, a version of the novel done by her husband, J. P. Burnett, until 1921. The other frequently dramatized story from the novel was that of Lady Dedlock. Several actresses, the most famous being Fanny Janauschek, played both Lady Dedlock and Hortense in these adaptations.

Four silent films were made from the novel, in 1910, 1918, 1920, and 1922. The last of these films starred Sybil Thorndike as Lady Dedlock. Bransby WILLIAMS made a short sound film in 1933 of his characterization of Grandfather Smallweed. The BBC has done two television adaptations of the novel, an 11-part serial by Constance COX in 1959, and an eight-part serial by Arthur Hopcraft, directed by Jonathan Powell (1985).

Bleeding Heart Yard An urban tenement in HOLBORN, situated in "a maze of shabby streets," that takes its name from the Bleeding Heart Pub. The property is owned by Casby, and the rents are collected by Pancks. Plornish lives here and his wife has her small shop here; Doyce and Clennam's factory is also located in the Yard. *Dorrit*.

Blessington, Marguerite, Countess of (1789–1849) Widowed in her second marriage to Charles John Gardiner, first Earl of Blessington, the countess, a friend of Byron who had lived many years in France, returned to England in 1831 and established one of the most notable salons in Regency London. The scandal surrounding her relationship with Alfred, Count D'ORSAY, both her stepson and lover, made her house off-limits to many in London society, but artists, writers, dandies, and politicians attended her gatherings at Gore House. In 1836 Dickens was introduced to her salon, where he met Walter Savage LANDOR, Benjamin DISRAELI, Edward Bulwer LYTTON, William MACREADY, and William Harrison AINSWORTH. She wrote novels and memoirs, edited the *Book of Beauty* and *The Keepsake*, and contributed to the *Daily News* when it was under Dickens's editorship. Bankrupted in 1849, she fled to Paris with D'Orsay and died there.

Blight, Young Mortimer Lightwood's office boy. *Mutual Friend*.

Blimber, Doctor Headmaster of the school that Paul Dombey attends in BRIGHTON, "a great hothouse in which all the boys blew before their time. . . . Every description of Greek and Latin vegetable was got off the driest twigs of boys under the frostiest circumstances"(11). Blimber's forcing system speaks to Mr. Dombey's desire to rush his son into adulthood, but it does not work in Paul's case. The boy gradually declines during his time at Blimber's and when he leaves at the end of the autumn term, he is too ill to dance at the Christmas party (14). Blimber is assisted by his **wife**, who runs the household and his daughter, **Cornelia**, "working in the graves of deceased languages," who is Paul's particular tutor. *Dombey*.

Blinder, Bill The hostler who dies and leaves his lantern to Tony Weller. *Humphrey*.

Blinder, Mrs. The kindly woman in BELL YARD who cares for the Neckett children after their father's death. *Bleak House* (15).

Blinkins The Latin master at Our School, "a colorless, doubled-up, near-sighted man, with a crutch; who was always cold." *Reprinted*, "Our School."

Blockitt, Mrs. The nurse who attends Mrs. Dombey at the birth of Paul, "a simpering piece of faded gentility." *Dombey* (1).

Blockson, Mrs. Miss Knag's charwoman. *Nickleby* (18).

Blogg The parish beadle who enables Betty Higden to adopt Sloppy. *Mutual Friend* (I:16).

Bloomsbury Square The site of Lord Chief Justice Mansfield's house, which is attacked and sacked by the Gordon rioters (*Rudge*, 66). Two of the rioters are later hanged here (77).

"Bloomsbury Christening, The" Story of the christening of Frederick Charles William Kitterbell, whose godfather, Nicodemus Dumps, "the most miserable man in the world," disrupts the christening party by losing the silver mug he bought for the child and by giving a speech listing the hazards that might afflict the child, thus driving the infant's mother into hysterics. Originally published in the MONTHLY MAGAZINE (April 1834). *Boz*.

Blose, Dr. Laon Headmaster of Queen Elizabeth's Royal Free Grammar-School at Thistledown; "he is stout, but every limb betrays his laxity of fibre; his coat is fluffy; his hands are unclean. He evidently lives in an unwholesome atmosphere." *Stone*, "Free (and Easy) School."

Bloss, Mrs. The wealthy and vulgar widow who boards at Mrs. Tibbs's. "Having nothing to do, and nothing to wish for," she becomes a hypochrondriac, eventually marrying another hypochrondriac, Mr. Gobler. *Boz*, "Boarding House."

Blotton, Mr. The member of the Pickwick Club who calls Mr. Pickwick "a humbug." The controversy is resolved when Blotton agrees that he meant the term only "in its Pickwickian sense." *Pickwick* (1).

Blower, Captain, R. N. One of Gabblewig's disguises; he has presumably been made ill by taking Slap's mustard and milk cure. *Nightingale*.

Blowers, Mr. An eminent attorney involved in the case of JARNDYCE AND JARNDYCE. *Bleak House* (1).

Blubb Member of the Mudfog Association. *Mudfog*.

Blue Boar (1) The coaching inn at Aldgate in WHITECHAPEL where David first arrives in London and is met by Mr. Mell. *Copperfield* (5).

Blue Boar (2) One of Tony Weller's hangouts, in Leadenhall Market. While waiting for his father here, Sam writes his valentine to Mary. *Pickwick* (33).

Blue Boar (3) Inn near the forge, where Pip and Joe sign Pip's apprenticeship papers and where Pip stays when he returns from London to his home town. *Expectations* (13, 28, 30, 43).

Blue Dragon, The The inn near SALISBURY, owned by Mrs. Lupin, where old Martin Chuzzlewit stays when he is hounded by relatives. Mark Tapley plans to change the name to "The Jolly Tapley" after he marries Mrs. Lupin. *Chuzzlewit* (3, 53).

Blue Lion Inn, Muggleton The dinner that follows the great Muggleton versus Dingley Dell cricket match is held here. *Pickwick* (7, 9).

Blue Lion and Stomach Warmer Inn   Headquarters of the Gentlemen's Whist Club of Winglebury Buffs, where Horace Hunter stays. *Boz,* "Winglebury."

Blues and Buffs   The colors of the Tory and Whig parties, respectively, in the EATANSWILL election (*Pickwick,* 13). The two inns at Great Winglebury are also Blue and Buff institutions, respectively. *Boz,* "Winglebury."

"Bluffy"   The name given to Trooper George ROUNCEWELL by the Bagnet children. *Bleak House.*

Blumb, R. A.   Artist that Our Bore takes to see "the finest picture in Italy." *Reprinted,* "Bore."

Blunderbore, Captain   Officer in the Horse Marines and an authority on horses. *Mudfog.*

Blunderstone   The village in Suffolk where David spends his earliest years, based on the village of Blundestone, which Dickens visited in 1848. *Copperfield.*

Blunderum   Member of the Mudfog Association who contributes a paper on the last moments of the learned pig. *Mudfog.*

"Boarding-house, The"   Two sketches, originally published in the MONTHLY MAGAZINE (May, August 1834), describing romantic intrigues in Mrs. Tibbs's boarding house in GREAT CORAM STREET. In the first, the three male boarders (Mr. Simpson, Mr. Septimus Hicks, and Mr. Calton) each arrange secret marriages to Mrs. Maplestone and her two daughters. In the second, the presence of Mrs. Bloss, a hypochrondriac widow, prompts romantic intrigues among the male boarders. *Boz.*

Bob   Turnkey at the Marshalsea (see MARSHALSEA PRISON and godfather to Amy. *Dorrit.*

"Bob Sawyer's Party"   One of the most popular of Dickens's PUBLIC READINGS, based on chapter 32 of *Pickwick.*

Bobbo   The best friend of the hero of Jemmy's story, "the cleverest and bravest and best-looking and most generous of all the friends that ever were." "Lirriper's Lodgings."

Bobster, Cecilia   The girl that Newman Noggs confuses with Madeline Bray. He arranges a secret meeting between Nicholas and the girl, and the mistake is discovered just in time for Nicholas to avoid her tyrannical **father**. *Nickleby* (40, 51).

Bocker, Tom   A 19-year-old orphan suggested by Milvey for adoption by the Boffins. *Mutual Friend* (I:9).

Bodgers   Name on a burial tablet in the Blunderstone Church. *Copperfield* (2).

Boffer   A stockbroker expelled from the Exchange whose ruin prompts Wilkins Flasher and Frank Slimmery to bet on the chances of his suicide. *Pickwick* (55).

Boffin, Henrietta ("Henrietty")   The kind and simple wife of Nicodemus, who befriends Bella Wilfer and discovers in Rokesmith the John Harmon she had loved as a child. "A stout lady of rubicund and cheerful aspect, she pretends to be a "highflyer at Fashion" (I:5), but she is a down-to-earth, commonsensical woman. *Mutual Friend.*

Boffin, Nicodemus (Nick or Noddy Boffin; "The Golden Dustman")   Unlettered former servant of old John Harmon, the dust contractor, who inherits his master's wealth when Harmon's son, the primary heir, is presumed drowned in the THAMES. "A broad, round-shouldered, one-sided old fellow. . . . Both as to his dress and to himself he was of an overlapping, rhinoceros build, with folds in his cheeks, and his forehead, and his eyelids, and his lips, and his ears; but with bright, eager, childishly-inquiring grey eyes, under his ragged eyebrows and broad-brimmed hat" (I:5). He hires Silas Wegg to read to him (I:5) and Rokesmith as his secretary (I:8). To make up for Bella's loss of a chance at fortune, he invites her to live with them (I:9) and he and his wife adopt a child to replace the John Harmon who was lost. But his kindness appears to be undermined when he develops an interest in misers (III:4–5), dismisses Rokesmith for his mercenary intentions in proposing to Bella (III:15), and causes Bella to leave his house. His change in character, however, proves to be a pious fraud, a pretense to bring Bella to her senses (IV:13). *Mutual Friend.* Boffin is probably based on Henry Dodd, a dust contractor in ISLINGTON who was said to have given his daughter a dust heap as a wedding present.

Boffin's Bower   The house among the dust heaps where the Boffins lived before moving to their fashionable house on CAVENDISH SQUARE. Boffin hires Wegg to live at the Bower and be its caretaker. *Mutual Friend.*

Bogles, Mrs.   The landlady at the Traveller's London boardinghouse who is arrested for debt. *Uncommercial* (6).

Bogsby, James George   Landlord of SOL'S ARMS. *Bleak House* (33).

"Boguey"   Weevle's nickname for KROOK. *Bleak House* (32).

"Boiled Beef of New England, The"   Article for ALL THE YEAR ROUND (August 15, 1863), describing a visit to a cooperative eating establishment for working people. England is shabbier than almost any other country, Dickens asserts, and the shabby fashion of the poor usually simply imitates that of the rich. One of the qualities of the English working man, however, is his independence; that quality is apparent in the new "self-supporting Cooking Depot for the Working Classes" in WHITECHAPEL, a gathering place for the creators of a new England. *Uncommercial* (25).

Boiler, The Rev. Boanerges   The tedious preacher from the Traveller's childhood whose "lumbering jocularity" was never amusing to the child. *Uncommercial* (9).

Bokum, Mrs.   "The dearest friend of Mrs. MacStinger, whom she considered a pattern for her sex." She acts as Mrs. MacStinger's bridesmaid. *Dombey* (60).

Bolder   One of Squeers's pupils at DOTHEBOYS HALL, "an unhealthy-looking boy, with warts all over his hands." *Nickleby* (8).

Boldheart, Captain   Pirate and captain of the schooner *Beauty* and the nine-year-old hero of the story told by nine-year-old Robin Redforth. He enters a life of piratical adventure after being "spited by a Latin-grammar master." "Holiday Romance."

Boldwig, Captain   An imperious and self-important neighbor of Sir Geoffrey Manning, who has Pickwick taken to the village pound when he finds him on his property in a wheelbarrow, sleeping off the effects of cold punch. "A little fierce man in a stiff black neckerchief and blue surtout." *Pickwick* (19).

Boles   Inhabitant of a "high, bleak" house "in the Down-country" and father of **Miss Boles**, "a blessed creature, a Divinity," whom the narrator visits on several New Year's Days. *Miscellaneous*, "New Year's Day."

Bolo, Miss   An ancient spinster lady who was Pickwick's card partner at BATH. She became so distressed by his play that she "rose from the table considerably agitated and went straight home, in a flood of tears and a sedan chair." *Pickwick* (35).

Bolter, Morris   Noah CLAYPOLE'S alias as a member of Fagin's gang. *Twist*.

Bolton, Robert   Shorthand writer for the press who engrosses his audience at the Green Dragon pub with his account of a baker who murdered his son. *Mudfog*, "Bolton."

Bonchurch   Town on the Isle of Wight where Dickens spent his summer holiday in 1849.

Bond Street   Fashionable shopping street in the West End of London. The Maldertons shop here (*Boz*, "Sparkins"); Cousin Feenix stays at Long's Hotel when he comes to England for Edith Grainger's wedding (*Dombey*, 31). Bond Street is also mentioned in *Nickleby* (32), *Mutual Friend* (III: 8), and *Uncommercial* (16).

Bones, Banjo and Mrs. Banjo   Comic entertainers at a pub for sailors. *Uncommercial* (5).

Bonney   Promoter of the United Metropolitan Improved Hot Muffin and Crumpet Baking and Punctual Delivery Company. *Nickleby* (2).

Boodle, Lord   One of Sir Leicester Dedlock's friends who tells him that the choices for a new government "would lie between **Lord Coodle** and **Sir Thomas Doodle**—supposing it to be impossible for the **Duke of Foodle** to act with **Goodle**, which may be assumed to be the case in consequence of the breach arising out of that affair with **Hoodle**. Then, giving the Home Department and the Leadership of the House of Commons to **Joodle**, the Foreign Office to **Moodle**, what are you to do with **Noodle**? You can't offer him the Presidency of the Council; that is reserved for **Poodle**. You can't put him in the Woods and Forests; that is hardly good enough for **Quoodle**. What follows? That the country is shipwrecked, lost, and gone to pieces" (12). *Bleak House*.

"Boofer Lady"   Little Johnny's name for Bella WILFER. *Mutual Friend* (II:9).

Booley   Retired gentleman from ISLINGTON who has taken an extraordinary series of travels—up the Mississippi, Missouri, Ohio, and Nile rivers; to Australia, New Zealand, India, Egypt; and, most recently, to the Arctic—all by means of the panoramas on display in London. He describes his travels in lectures to the Social Oysters. *Miscellaneous*, "Extraordinary Traveller," "A Card." Booley also provides an allegorical interpretation of the LORD MAYOR's Parade in "Mr. Booley's View of the Last Lord Mayor's Show." *Miscellaneous*.

Boot Inn   The disreputable alehouse that is the headquarters for the Gordon rioters. *Rudge* (38).

Boot-jack and Countenance   Oldcastle inn where the second meeting of the Mudfog Association is held. *Mudfog*.

Boots and Brewer   Two guests at the Veneerings's dinner parties who reiterate the banalities of "the social chorus." *Mutual Friend*.

"Boots at the Holly Tree Inn"   One of Dickens's PUBLIC READINGS, derived from the Christmas story for 1855, "The Holly-Tree Inn."

Boozey, William   Captain of the foretop on the schooner *Beauty* in the tale of Captain Boldheart. "Holiday Romance."

Boozle The temperamental actor who refuses to take over Flimkins's part. *Young Gentlemen.*

Borough, The Area of London south of LONDON BRIDGE including SOUTHWARK and parts of Bermondsey, LAMBETH and Rotherhithe. The MARSHALSEA PRISON was situated on the **Borough High Street**, connecting the area with the traumatic period in Dickens's childhood when his father was in the prison. The WHITE HART INN, where Pickwick first meets Sam Weller, is located here and was similar to the George Inn in the Borough High Street, the only remaining galleried inn in London. Bob Sawyer's lodgings are in LANT STREET (*Pickwick*, 10, 32), a street where David Copperfield, like Dickens himself, also had rooms. Much of the first half of *Little Dorrit*, centered around the Marshalsea, takes place in the Borough.

Boroughbridge, Yorkshire A town that Nicholas passes through on his return to London after beating Squeers. Smike joins him here. *Nickleby* (13).

Borrioboola-Gha African village that is the focus of Mrs. Jellyby's missionary activities. *Bleak House* (4).

Borum, Mrs. A patron of Crummles's Theater Company, who takes a box and brings her **husband** and six children, among them **Augustus**, **Charlotte**, and **Emily**, to see the Crummles's productions. *Nickleby* (24).

Boston, Massachusetts Dickens landed in Boston on his first visit to America in 1842. Many of his American friends were members of the Boston intelligentsia that he met at this time—Henry Wadsworth LONGFELLOW, Cornelius FELTON, Richard Henry DANA, Charles SUMNER, and William PRESCOTT. He describes his impressions of the city in *Notes* (3). On his reading tour in 1867–68, Dickens gave several readings in Boston and renewed many of his old friendships.

"Bottle-nosed Ned" Nickname of Edward TWIGGER. *Mudfog.*

Bottles John's stableman, "a phenemenon of moroseness not to be matched in England," whose deafness makes him untouched by the ghosts in the house. "Haunted House."

Boucicault, Dion (1820–1890) This Irish-born Victorian playwright, with almost 200 plays to his credit, wrote two popular stage adaptations of Dickens: *Smike: or Nicholas Nickleby* (1859) and *Dot: A Fairy Tale of Home* (1859), an adaptation of *Cricket*. He also played Lord Frederick Verisopft in an 1839 production of *Nickleby.*

Bouclet, Madame Langley's French landlady, "a compact little woman of thirty-five or so." **Monsieur Bouclet** is "great at billiards." "Somebody's Luggage."

Boulogne, France A seaport town on the English Channel, near CALAIS, where Dickens frequently went on holiday, described in "Our French Watering Place" (*Reprinted*). It is also mentioned in *Boz* ("Boarding House"); in *A Tale of Two Cities* (II:3); and in *Reprinted* ("A Flight").

"Bound for the Great Salt Lake" The Traveller visits an emigrant ship carrying 800 Mormons who are beginning their journey to Utah. He expects "to bear testimony against them," but he is astonished to find their demeanor exemplary and their social arrangements in perfect order. *Uncommercial* (22).

Bounderby, Josiah Coketown banker and mill owner and friend of Mr. Gradgrind: "A big, loud man, with a stare, and a metallic laugh. A man made out of coarse material, which seemed to have been stretched to make him. . . . A man who could never sufficiently vaunt himself a self-made man. . . . A man who was the Bully of humility" (I:4). To maintain the myth that he is self made, Bounderby hides away his mother, **Mrs. Pegler**, who has sacrificed to give him an education and a place in the world. He bullies his employees, convinced that they are a rebellious lot who want to "be set up in a coach and six, and . . . fed on turtle soup and venison, with a gold spoon"(I:11). He at first pursues Stephen Blackpool, one of his mill hands accused of robbing his bank, and later the actual robber, Tom Gradgrind, who works in the bank. His marriage to Louisa GRADGRIND is a loveless union that ends when she leaves him and returns home (II:12). The truth about his origins is revealed at the close of the novel (III:5). *Hard Times.*

Bow The rural district in East London where the Nicklebys live in the cottage rented to them by the Cheeryble brothers. The mad Gentleman in Small Clothes lives next door. *Nickleby* (35).

Bow Street Police Court The main Metropolitan court in London, established in 1749. Here Barnaby Rudge is questioned and one of the rioters hanged (*Rudge*, 58, 77). The trial of the Artful Dodger takes place at Bow Street (*Twist*, 43), as does that of the two girl prostitutes (*Boz*, "Prisoners' Van"). The **Bow Street Runners**, the only detective force until the establishment of the Metropolitan Police in 1829, worked out of the Bow Street Court. Blathers and Duff, the runners who investigate the robbery at Mrs. Maylie's house (*Twist*, 31), are Dickens's fullest description of these officers.

Bowes, Yorkshire Site of William Shaw's School, the original for DOTHEBOYS HALL, which Dickens visited in 1838. *Nickleby.*

Bowley, Sir Joseph An elderly Member of Parliament. Although he poses as "The Poor Man's Friend and Father," the "one great moral lesson" which he would teach the poor is their "entire Dependence on myself." His son, **Master Bowley**, is being groomed to continue his father's paternalism. **Lady Bowley**, his equally condescending wife, has introduced eyelet-hole making as an occupation for the men of the village. *Chimes*.

Bowyer, The The rich man who is Mistress Alice's father and Hugh Graham's master in Magog's story. *Humphrey* (1).

Boxer John Peerybingle's dog. *Cricket*.

"Boy at Mugby, The" The epithet by which Ezekiel, the narrator of chapter three of "Mugby Junction," who describes the operations of the refreshment room at the station, is known.

Boyle, Hon. Mary (1810–1890) Niece of Mrs. Richard WATSON, whom Dickens met at ROCKINGHAM CASTLE in 1849. They were close friends for the rest of his life. She often performed in Dickens's theatricals, usually playing opposite him; he described her as "the very best actress I ever saw off the stage, and immeasurably better than a great many I have seen on it." She was at Gad's Hill when he died.

"Boys to Mend" Article by Henry MORLEY and Dickens for *HOUSEHOLD WORDS* (September 11, 1852) on juvenile offenders, with an extensive description of the system of reformation employed at the Farm School at Red Hill in East Surrey. *Stone*.

Boythorn, Lawrence The impetuous and boisterous friend of John Jarndyce, who speaks with a "vigorous healthy voice," spilling out a "very fury of . . . superlatives, which seem . . . to go off like blank cannons and hurt nothing" (9). His boisterousness is belied by the pet canary he often carries upon his shoulder. He maintains an ongoing litigation over property lines with his neighbor, Sir Leicester Dedlock. He offers his house to Esther Summerson for her recuperation from smallpox. *Bleak House*. Boythorn was, according to Dickens, "a most exact portrait" of the poet Walter Savage LANDOR.

"Boz" The pen name Dickens used at the beginning of his career. Most of the magazine sketches that would be collected as *Sketches by Boz* were originally published under this pseudonym, as were *The Pickwick Papers* and the early numbers of *Oliver Twist*. The name derived from Dickens's nickname for his younger brother, Augustus, whom he had dubbed "Moses" in honor of *The Vicar of Wakefield*. The child nasally mispronounced the name as "Boses" and it then was shortened to "Bose" and finally "Boz." When Dickens reappropriated the name for his own pseudonym, he commented, "Boz was a very familiar household word to me, long before I was an author." He was fond of characterizing his works as the spectacular performances of a magician or a theatrical performer, characterizing himself as "The Inimitable Boz."

"Boz's Annual Register and Obituary of Blue Devils" A CHRISTMAS BOOK that Dickens agreed to write for CHAPMAN & HALL in 1837; however, he did not complete the project.

Bradbury, William (1800–1869) Partner in the publishing firm that replaced CHAPMAN & HALL as Dickens's publisher in 1844. There was occasional friction between Dickens and Bradbury, especially when Dickens thought that Bradbury was unnecessarily interfering with his editing of the *DAILY NEWS* and when Bradbury refused to print in *PUNCH* Dickens's explanation of his separation in 1858, but the two remained good personal friends in spite of these differences.

Bradbury & Evans Dickens's publishers from 1844 to 1858. With them Dickens published all his major novels from *Dombey* through *Little Dorrit*, the CHRISTMAS BOOKS from *The Chimes* on, and the weekly magazine *HOUSEHOLD WORDS*. They were also the publishers of the *DAILY NEWS*, the paper which Dickens edited briefly in 1846. When they refused to publish his explanation of his separation in *PUNCH*, Dickens left them and returned to CHAPMAN & HALL.

Braham, John (1774?–1856) Tenor and theater manager who sang in Dickens's opera *The Village Coquettes* and acted in his two farces, *The Strange Gentleman* and *Is She His Wife?*, which he produced at the ST. JAMES'S THEATRE in 1836–37.

Brandley, Mrs. The society woman with whom Estella stays in RICHMOND and who sponsors her coming out in London. She has a daughter, **Miss Brandley**, who is considerably older than Estella. "The mother looked young, and the daughter looked old; the mother's complexion was pink, and the daughter's was yellow; the mother set up for frivolity, and the daughter for theology" (38). *Expectations*.

Brass, Sally Sampson's sister, an "amazon at common law," who acts as his partner, clerk, co-conspirator, and housekeeper (33). Masculine in appearance and manner, she looks enough like her brother to be mistaken for him. But she is tougher than he, refusing to give in when their schemes are discovered (66). The MARCHIONESS is probably her child by Quilp. In the end she escapes the clutches of the law and becomes a vagrant (73). The Brasses are the children of **Old Foxey**, a lawyer as unscrupulous as they are (36). *Curiosity Shop*.

Brass, Sampson Quilp's legal advisor, "an attorney of no very good repute from Bevis MARKS, . . . a tall, meagre man, with a nose like a wen, a protruding forehead, retreating eyes, and hair of a deep red. . . . He had a cringing manner but a very harsh voice, and his blandest smiles were so extremely forbidding, that . . . one would have wished him out of temper that he might only scowl" (11). He serves Quilp in his possession of the old Curiosity Shop (11), by hiring Swiveller as his clerk (33), and by framing Kit Nubbles for robbery (59). But he testifies against Quilp after the scheme is discovered (66). *Curiosity Shop.*

Bravassa, Miss   Member of the Crummles theatrical company. *Nickleby.*

Bray, Madeline   The girl with whom Nicholas falls in love when he first sees her outside the employment office; she has "a countenance of most uncommon beauty, though shaded by a cloud of sadness" (16). Later, when she seeks help from the Cheerybles, they employ Nicholas to act as their agent in aiding the girl and her father (46). Nicholas discovers that Bray has agreed to marry his daughter to the old miser, Arthur Gride, in exchange for having his debts forgiven (47). On the wedding day, Nicholas rescues Madeline and takes her away to his mother's home (54). He eventually marries her (65). *Nickleby.*

Bray, Walter   The embittered and tyrannical father of Madeline Bray. A debtor living within the rules of the KING'S BENCH PRISON, Bray agrees to marry his daughter to the old miser, Arthur Gride, who has learned that Madeline is heiress to a considerable fortune. In exchange for his daughter, Bray's debts to Ralph Nickleby will be forgiven, but he falls dead on the day of the wedding and saves his daughter from the unwanted marriage (54). *Nickleby.*

Break-Neck Stairs   Stairs leading to the THAMES at the foot of the street where Wilding and Co. is located. "No Thoroughfare."

Break of Day Inn, The   The inn at Chalons-sur-Saone where Rigaud and Cavaletto are briefly reunited as they are traveling northward. *Dorrit* (I:11).

Brentford, Middlesex   A town along the THAMES, six miles west of London. Oliver and Sikes pass through on their way to the Maylie robbery (*Twist*, 21). Betty Higden lived in one of "the complicated back settlements of muddy Brentford" (*Mutual Friend*, I: 16). Compeyson had a house nearby (*Expectations*, 42).

Brewer   One of the pair of Veneering sycophants, Boots and Brewer. *Mutual Friend.*

Brick, Jefferson   War correspondent of the *New York Rowdy Journal*—"a small young gentleman of very juvenile appearance, and unwholesomely pale in the face; partly, perhaps, from intense thought, but partly, there is no doubt, from the excessive use of tobacco"—who is convinced that "the aristocratic circles of England quailed before the name of Jefferson Brick" (16). His

wife, "a sickly little girl . . . with tight round eyes" (16), cares for two young children and attends lectures on the Philosophy of the Soul and the Philosophy of Vegetables. *Chuzzlewit.*

Brick Lane   Street in WHITECHAPEL, site of the meeting hall of the United Grand Junction Temperance Association. *Pickwick* (33).

Brickmaker, The   Abusive husband of Jenny. *Bleak House.*

Bricusse, Leslie (1931–)   British screenwriter and lyricist; he wrote the lyrics for Wolf Mankowitz's musical adaptation of *Pickwick* (1963) and the screenplay and lyrics for the musical film *Scrooge* (1970).

Bridewell   Workhouse and prison near Blackfriars where Miss Miggs becomes the turnkey. *Rudge.*

Brieg, Switzerland   Town at the foot of the Simplon Pass, the starting point for Vendale's and Obenreizer's journey over the mountains and site of Vendale's marriage to Marguerite. "No Thoroughfare."

Brig Place, India Docks   "On the brink of a little canal near the India Docks" (9), this street is the site of Mrs. MacStinger's house, where Captain Cuttle lodges. *Dombey.*

Briggs   Student at Blimber's Academy with whom Paul shares a room. *Dombey* (12).

Briggs, Mr. and Mrs.   Friends of the egotistical young couple. *Young Couples.*

Briggs, Mrs.   A widow with three daughters, including **Julia** and **Kate**, and two sons, **Samuel**, an attorney, and **Alexander**, his apprentice. They all go on the steam excursion and seek to outshine their rivals, the Tauntons. *Boz,* "Excursion."

Brighton   Fashionable seaside resort on the Sussex coast where Dickens was a frequent visitor, usually staying at the **Bedford Hotel**, where Mr. Dombey stays when visiting his son there. Brighton figures most significantly in *Dombey;* young Paul stays at Mrs. Pipchin's establishment here (8) and attends Dr. Blimber's Academy (11). Mr. Turveydrop deports himself near the Pavilion built by his hero and mentor, the Prince Regent (*Bleak House,* 14). Brighton is also mentioned in *Boz* ("Tuggses") and in *Nickleby* (50).

Bristol   As a young reporter, Dickens was sent to the port city of Bristol in 1835 to report on Lord John Russell's election campaign. He stayed at the BUSH INN, where Pickwick and Mr. Winkle stay (*Pickwick,* 38, 48). There the Pickwickians also reconnect with Bob Sawyer, who has set up his medical practice in Bristol; Ben Allen is in the town and his sister is living outside of Bristol with an aunt when Winkle finds her and proposes.

Britain, Benjamin ("Little Britain")   Doctor Jeddler's manservant, "a small man with an uncommonly sour and discontented face." He matches his master's belief that everything is a joke, with the nihilistic philosophy: "I don't know anything; I don't care for anything; I don't make out anything; I don't believe anything; and I don't want anything." After he marries **Clemency Newcome** and becomes manager of The Nutmeg Grater Inn, he learns the value of love. The couple have **two sons** and a daughter **Clem**. *Battle.*

"Britannia, The"   The steamship on which Dickens crossed the Atlantic on his way to America in 1842. After a sometimes rough and stormy crossing, the other passengers selected Dickens to present Captain Hewitt with an engraved plate commending his courage and competence during a hazadarous journey. *Notes* (1).

Britannia Theatre, Hoxton   A popular theater uniting "vastness with compactness" visited by the Uncommercial Traveller. *Uncommercial* (4).

"British Lion, The"   Satirical verses Dickens wrote for the *DAILY NEWS* in 1846, characterizing the old aristocratic order as a lion by repute that turns out to be a boar.

British Museum   As soon as he was 18, Dickens secured a ticket to the old British Museum Reading Room, and he spent many hours as a young man reading there. He describes the place and some of the readers in *Boz*, "Shabby-genteel People."

Brittles   Mrs. Maylie's man-of-all-work, "who entered her service a mere child and was treated as a promising boy, though he was something past thirty" (28). He is the younger of the two servants who surprise Oliver when Sikes lowers the boy into the house in CHERTSEY. *Twist.*

Brixton   In Dickens's time, a comfortable, middle-class suburb in South London. Wilkins Flasher, the stockbroker, lives here (*Pickwick*, 55), and the Misses Malderton hope to find husbands among the eligible bachelors of Brixton. *Boz*, "Sparkins."

Broad Court   Off BOW STREET, COVENT GARDEN, the home of Mr. Snevellicci. *Nickleby* (30).

Broadstairs, Kent   The coastal resort where Dickens spent many holidays between 1837 and 1851. Dickens describes it in "Our English Watering Place" (*Reprinted*). FORT HOUSE, one of the places where Dickens stayed, has been renamed Bleak House and contains a Dickens museum. An annual Dickens festival is held in Broadstairs.

Brobity, Ethelinda   Mrs. Sapsea's maiden name. *Drood.*

Brock, Charles E. (1870–1938)   Book illustrator and portrait painter, contributor to *PUNCH* and the *Graphic*, who illustrated several of Dickens's novels, including *Pickwick, Nickleby*, and *The Christmas Books*. The *DICKENSIAN* described his work as true to the spirit of Phiz, but characterized by humor rather than caricature.

Brogley, Mr.   Second-hand furniture dealer and broker who takes possession of the WOODEN MIDSHIPMAN when Sol Gills cannot pay his debts (9). Walter Gay stays with Brogley after he returns from overseas (48–49). *Dombey.*

Brogson   An elderly guest at the Budden's dinner party. *Boz*, "Minns."

"Brokers' and Marine-store Shops"   Survey of the stores dealing in second-hand furniture, clothing, and personal items in various areas of London. Originally in the *MORNING CHRONICLE* (October 10, 1834) as "Street Sketches No. 5." *Boz.*

"Broker's Man, The"   Three anecdotes in which Mr. Bung describes his work as an agent for broker Fixem. Originally published as "Sketches of London No. 18, Our Parish" in the *EVENING CHRONICLE* (July 28, 1835). *Boz.*

Brook Street   A fashionable street in London's West End, running from BOND STREET to GROSVENOR SQUARE. Feenix's London house, where Mrs. Skewton stays and where Florence last sees Edith, is here (*Dombey*, 61). Mr. Dorrit stays in a hotel on Brook Street when he returns to London from Italy (*Dorrit*, II:16).

Brooker, Mr.   Ralph Nickleby's former clerk and a returned convict who tries to blackmail his former employer with his knowledge that Smike is Ralph's son; "a spare, dark, withered man . . . with a stooping body and a very sinister face" (44). *Nickleby.*

Brooks (1)   A pieman, Sam Weller's landlord, who makes pies from cats. "I seasons 'em for beefsteak, weal, or kidney 'cordin' to the demand" (*Pickwick*, 19).

Brooks (2)   One of five boys occupying the same bed at DOTHEBOYS HALL. *Nickleby* (7).

"Brooks of Sheffield"   The name Murdstone uses for David when he tells Quinion and Passidge about Mrs. Copperfield in young David's presence. *Copperfield* (2).

Brougham, Henry Peter, Lord (1778–1868)   Whig politician, Lord Chancellor 1830–34; prolific writer and social commentator; head of the Society for the Diffusion of Useful Knowledge. His assertion that factory women could hire wet nurses for their infant children and thus had no need for a 10-hours bill limiting their hours of employment made him the butt of PUNCH satire and, perhaps, one of the models for Sir Joseph Bowley in *Chimes*.

Brougham, John (1810–1880) Irish-American actor-manager who played many Dickens roles, among them Crummles, Cratchit, Bagstock, Captain Bunsby, Micawber, and Turveydrop. He adapted many of the novels for the New York stage, including *Dombey* (1848), *Haunted Man* (1849), *Copperfield* (1851), *Bleak House* (1853), *Dorrit* (1873), *Message from the Sea* (1860), and *Gold Dust* (1871, from *Mutual Friend*). His most famous adaptation was *Little Nell and the Marchioness* (1867), in which Lotte Crabtree played both of the lead female roles, performing a banjo solo as the Marchioness.

Browdie, John The hearty Yorkshireman who meets Nicholas at Fanny Squeers's tea party (9). He helps Nicholas to escape from DOTHEBOYS HALL after he thrashes Squeers (13). On his wedding trip to London with his bride, Matilda Price, he arranges Smike's escape from Squeers (39). *Nickleby*.

Brown (1) The violincelloist in the amateur orchestra for the Gattletons's theatricals. *Boz*, "Porter."

Brown (2) Member of the Mudfog Association. *Mudfog*.

Brown (3) One of Mrs. Lemon's pupils. "Holiday Romance."

Brown (4) Friend of Mrs. Nubbles, "supposed to be then a Corporal in the East Indies." *Curiosity Shop* (21).

Brown and O'Brien Eligible young men who are passengers on the THAMES excursion. *Boz*, "River."

Brown, Alice Daughter of Good Mrs. Brown, the child of her seduction by Edith Granger's uncle. Alice bears a striking physical resemblance to Edith; "a solitary woman of some thirty years of age; tall; well-formed; handsome; miserably dressed; the soil of many country roads in varied weather—dust, chalk, clay, gravel—clotted on her grey cloak" (33). Ruined and abandoned by James Carker, Alice was transported for theft. She returns bent on revenge (34), and she aids her mother in discovering Carker's whereabouts to Dombey (52), but she regrets doing so (53). She is befriended by Harriet Carker, to whom she tells her story before she dies (58). *Dombey*.

Brown, Captain John Captain of the ship *Polyphemus* in one of Sol Gill's seafaring tales. *Dombey* (4).

Brown, Conversation Feenix's friend, a "four-bottle man at the Treasury Board." *Dombey* (61).

Brown, Emily Cause of the Great Winglebury duel. *Boz*, "Winglebury."

Brown, Fanny Stargazer's niece; he thinks she is destined to marry Tom Grig. *Lamplighter*.

Brown, "Good Mrs." The ironic name of the thief and receiver of stolen goods who kidnaps Florence Dombey in the street; "a very ugly old woman, with red rims around her eyes, and a mouth that mumbled and chattered of itself when she was not speaking" (6). She is the mother of Alice BROWN (alias **Alice Marwood**), the child of her seduction by Edith Granger's uncle, and Alice bears a striking physical resemblance to Edith. Mrs. Brown hates James Carker, who has ruined Alice, and she aids Dombey's discovery of Carker to avenge this wrong (52). *Dombey*.

Brown, The Misses Three spinsters who are "enthusiastic admirers of the curate" in "our parish." *Boz*, "Ladies' Societies."

Brown, Mrs. Landlady of one of the parish paupers. *Boz*, "Beadle."

Brown of Muggleton The maker of Rachel Wardle's shoes—shoes that enable Wardle and Pickwick to track her down in London. *Pickwick* (10).

Browndock, Miss Nicholas Nickleby's father's cousin, who, according to Mrs. Nickleby, "made her fortune in no time at all" by winning ten thousand pounds in the lottery. *Nickleby* (17).

Browne, Hablot Knight ("Phiz") (1815–1882) Dickens's chief illustrator, Browne, who took the pseudonym "Phiz" to complement Dickens's "Boz," worked with Dickens on nearly all his major works from *Pickwick* through *A Tale of Two Cities*. He learned his craft as an apprentice at Finden's, prominent steel engravers of the period, and his selection as the illustrator to replace Seymour and Buss on *Pickwick*—over Thackeray, who also applied for the position—established his career when he was only 20. The collaboration was successful from the beginning, one of Phiz's first pictures being the memorable "First appearance of Mr. Samuel Weller." The high points in their collaboration came with the great middle novels, *Dombey, Copperfield,* and *Bleak House,* in which Browne's evocative pictures extend the texts. His "dark plates" for *Bleak House,* employing a new technique developed for the novel, are particularly apt in rendering the mood of the work. Dickens dropped Browne after his disappointing illustrations for *Two Cities* and the two parted with some bitterness, but by 1860 Browne's style, grounded in the graphic-satiric tradition of Hogarth, was no longer appropriate for the more realistic novels of the period. Browne also worked as an illustrator for many other novelists, including William Harrison AINSWORTH, Edward Bulwer LYTTON, Anthony TROLLOPE, and Charles LEVER, and for the major illustrated periodicals of the period. Notable discussions of the collaboration between Browne and Dickens appear in HARVEY (1970), STEIG (1978); Jane R. Cohen, *Charles Dickens and his Original Illustrators* (1980). Examples of his work appear in the following illustrations in this volume: 5 (*BARNABY RUDGE*); 6 (Maria BEADNELL); 8 (*BLEAK HOUSE*); 22 (*DAVID COPPERFIELD*); 29 (Dombey); 30 (*DOMBEY AND SON*); 45 (Gamp); 52 (*LITTLE DORRIT*); 57 (*MARTIN CHUZZLEWIT*); 63 (*NICHOLAS NICKLEBY*); 94 (TOM-ALL-ALONE'S); 96 (WELLER).

Browning, Robert (1812–1889)   English poet and dramatist, best known for his dramatic monologues and *The Ring and the Book* (1868–69); one of John FORSTER's circle of friends, along with Dickens. Forster also advised Browning on literary matters. Few records of Dickens's friendship with Browning remain. The two met, through Forster and William Henry AINSWORTH, in the 1830s and occasionally dined or went to the theater together. Dickens admired Browning's plays, and was especially moved by the story of Mildred's love and death in *A Blot in the 'Scutcheon* (1843). Although Browning considered vulgar Dickens's penchant for naming his children after famous people and thought him theologically inconsistent, he admired and praised his work in a tribute presented to Dickens before the latter left on his American reading tour in 1867.

Brownlow   The kindly old man who befriends Oliver Twist, "a very respectable-looking personage, with a powdered head and gold spectacles" (10). He is as idealistic and trusting as his friend Grimwig is cynical. After Oliver is arrested for picking his pocket, he believes in the boy's innocence, refuses to testify against him, and takes him to his home (10–12). When Oliver is retaken by Sikes and Nancy and seems to have run away, Brownlow maintains his belief in him (14). Later he adopts Oliver and aids him in establishing his identity as Edward Leeford's child. *Twist.*

Bucket   Police detective employed by Tulkinghorn to inquire into Lady Dedlock's interest in Hawdon's grave. "With his attentive face, and his hat and stick in his hands, and his hands behind him, [he is] a composed and quiet listener" (22). After Tulkinghorn's murder, he and **Mrs. Bucket**, "a lady of a natural detective genius" (53), work together to solve the crime. He is also employed by Sir Leicester Dedlock to follow Lady Dedlock when she runs from CHESNEY WOLD (57). *Bleak House.* Although Dickens denied it, Bucket was probably based on INSPECTOR FIELD of the Metropolitan Police.

Buckingham Street, Strand   A street in the ADELPHI where David Copperfield takes rooms in Mrs.

Crupp's house at No. 15 (*Copperfield*, 23), the rooms Dickens himself occupied in 1834.

Buckley, Jerome H. (1917–)   Professor, Harvard; prolific writer on Victorian literature. In *Season of Youth* (1974), Buckley discusses *Copperfield* and *Expectations* as examples of the English BILDUNGSROMAN. *Expectations* is the greater of the two, he suggests, for it offers a much fuller characterization of the narrator, making him a more profound portrait of the author.

Bud, Rosa (Rosebud, Pussy)   "Pet pupil" at Miss Twinkleton's school, "wonderfully pretty, wonderfully childish, wonderfully whimsical" (3). An orphan, she has been "willed" to Edwin Drood by her father who was a friend to Edwin's father. Because their fate is decided for them, she acts with pettish childishness toward Edwin, and he condescendingly takes her for granted. Before it is too late, both of them reevaluate their relationship and in an earnest consultation agree to be brother and sister to each other rather than husband and wife (13). After Edwin's disappearance and presumed death, Rosa flees from Jasper, who frightens her with his vehement protestations of love for her (19). As the novel breaks off, she seems to be attracted to Tartar (20). *Drood.*

Budden, Octavius   A prosperous corn chandler who retires to a cottage in the country with his wife, **Amelia**, and his precocious only son, **Alexander Augustus Budden**. Budden unsuccessfully tries to secure the interest of his cousin Minns for his son. *Boz*, "Minns."

Budger, Mrs.   ROCHESTER widow, "whose rich dress and profusion of ornament bespoke her a most desirable addition to a limited income," whom Dr. Slammer is courting when Jingle cuts in on him. *Pickwick* (2).

Buffer, Dr.   Member of the Mudfog Association. *Mudfog.*

Buffers, Two Other Stuffed   Guests of the Veneerings. *Mutual Friend* (2).

Buffle, Mr.   A disagreeable tax-collector who is taken in, with his **wife** and daughter **Robina**, by Mrs. Lirriper and Major Jackman after his house burns down. "Lirriper's Legacy."

Buffum, Oscar   Leader of the group at the National Hotel in America that holds the levee for Elijah Pogrom. *Chuzzlewit* (34).

Buffy, The Rt. Hon. William, M.P.   Political friend of Sir Leicester Dedlock; he contends that "the shipwreck of the country—about which there is no doubt— . . . is attributable to Cuffy. If you had done with Cuffy what you ought to have done, when he first came into Parliament, and had prevented him going over to Duffy, you would have got him into alliance with Fuffy." *Bleak House* (12).

Bulder, Colonel Commander of the ROCHESTER garrison, he attends the ball at the BULL (3) with his **wife** and **daughter**. *Pickwick* (2).

Bule, Miss The girl of eight or nine, the leading lady in John's "seraglio" at Miss Griffin's School. "Haunted House."

Bull The "Tom Brown" of the National Jest-Book, the mediator of the jests. *Miscellaneous*, "Jest-Book."

Bull, Prince The representative of England and the antagonist to Prince Bear, representing Russia, in Dickens's ALLEGORY of the Crimean War. *Reprinted*, "Prince Bull."

Bull (1), The This coaching inn in Aldgate, WHITE-CHAPEL, in London's East End is the starting point for Tony Weller's coach going to Ipswich. *Pickwick* (20).

Bull (2), The Also known as the Bull and Gate and the Black Bull, this is the coaching inn at 121 HOLBORN, where Mrs. Gamp tends Lewsome. *Chuzzlewit* (25).

Bull (3), The Located in ROCHESTER, KENT, the Bull and Victoria Inn, more commonly known just as the Bull, figures in several of the novels. It is the site of the Winkle's confrontation with Dr. Slammer (*Pickwick*, 2). It is also the original of the BLUE BOAR, the inn where Pip stays when he returns home (*Expectations*), and of the Winglebury Arms (*Boz*, "Winglebury").

Bullamy Porter in the offices of the Anglo-Bengalee Assurance Company, "a wonderful creature in a vast red waistcoat and a short-tailed pepper-and-salt coat" (27). After the collapse of the company, he and Crimple abscond with the remaining assets. *Chuzzlewit*.

Bullfinch Business advisor to the Traveller who shares a "nasty little dinner" in Namelesston with him. *Uncommercial* (33).

Bullman Plaintiff represented by Dodson and Fogg in the case of Bullman and Ramsey. *Pickwick* (20).

Bullock Defendant in an excommunication case in DOCTORS' COMMONS handled by David Copperfield. *Copperfield* (29).

Bull's Eye Bill Sikes's white shaggy dog. After Nancy's murder, Sikes, fleeing from the law, attempts to drown the dog (48), but Bull's Eye escapes and shows up at JACOB'S ISLAND just before his owner arrives (50). When Sikes falls from the roof of the hideout and hangs himself, the dog leaps for his body, misses, and dashes his brains out on a stone (50). *Twist*.

Bulph The pilot at whose house the Crummles stay in PORTSMOUTH. *Nickleby* (23, 30).

Bulwer Edward Bulwer, who added his mother's surname to his own in 1843, is usually known as LYTTON, even though he should be properly identified as Bulwer or Bulwer-Lytton.

Bumble Self-important parochial beadle of the workhouse where Oliver Twist is born. "A fat man and a choleric" (2), Bumble oversees Oliver's childhood and apprenticeship. He marries **Mrs. Corney**, matron of the workhouse, with an eye to "a joining of hearts and housekeepings" (27), but she rules him in an unequal marriage. When the two are being questioned about their involvement in suppressing Oliver's identity, Brownlow prompts Bumble's most famous speech by stating that the law supposes that Mrs. Bumble acts under the direction of her husband. "If the law supposes that," Bumble responds, "the law is a ass, a idiot. If that's the eye of the law, the law is a bachelor; and the worst I wish the law is, that his eye may be opened by experience" (51). The Bumbles lose their positions as a result of their actions in Oliver's case and end their lives as inmates in the workhouse they once administered. *Twist*.

Bumple Plaintiff in a brawling case being heard in DOCTORS' COMMONS. The defendant, Sludberry, is accused of using the expression, "You be blowed." *Boz*, "Doctors' Commons."

"Bundle of Emigrant's Letters, A" Article for *HOUSEHOLD WORDS* (March 30, 1850) describing the efforts of Mrs. Caroline CHISHOLM—who became the model for Mrs. Jellyby in *Bleak House*—and the Family Colonisation Loan Society, which enabled English working class families to immigrate to the colonies. The article reprints the letters from Australia of several English emigrants supplied by Mrs. Chisholm. *Stone*.

Bung Former broker's man who is the successful candidate for beadle in "Our Parish." *Boz*.

Bunkin, Mrs. Mrs. Bardell's neighbor, mentioned by Mrs. Sanders in her testimony at the trial. *Pickwick* (34).

Bunsby, Captain Jack Friend of Captain Cuttle and skipper of the *Cautious Clara*, "a bulk head—human and very large—with one stationary eye in the mahogany face, and one revolving one, on the principle of some lighthouses" (23). Cuttle seeks out his advice, which is inscrutable and laced with nautical terminology. Bunsby does enable Cuttle to escape Mrs. MacStinger, only to be caught himself by the widow, whom he marries in the end. *Dombey*.

Burdett-Coutts, Angela Georgina (1814–1906)
Daughter of the radical politician and reformer Francis Burdett, she hyphenated her surname and devoted her life to philanthropy after inheriting the fortune of her maternal grandfather, banker Thomas Coutts, in 1837. Dickens, a member of her father's social circle that also included Wordsworth and Byron, met her in 1838 or 1839 and the two became lifelong friends. Dickens investigated, recommended, and administered many of her philanthropic projects, including aid to RAGGED SCHOOLS; URANIA COTTAGE, a project to rehabilitate prostitutes; and a slum-clearance, low-cost housing project in BETHNAL GREEN. Baroness Coutts was privy to Dickens's marital troubles and attempted unsuccessfully to reconcile the author and his wife. Edgar JOHNSON collected many of Dickens's letters to Miss Coutts in *The Heart of Charles Dickens* (1952).

Burgess and Co.   Mr. Toots's tailors. *Dombey* (12).

Burlington Arcade   A fashionable shopping arcade off PICCADILLY. *Uncommercial,* "Arcadian London."

Burnett, Henry (1811–1893)   Singer, music teacher, and husband of Dickens's sister **Frances Elizabeth** (see DICKENS, FRANCES ELIZABETH). He spent some of his childhood in BRIGHTON, where he sang before George IV at the Pavilion. He met his wife while they were both students at the Royal Academy of Music. They sang several concerts together in 1835–36 and married in 1837. Their sickly, deformed child, **Henry Jr.** (d. 1849), was the inspiration for Tiny Tim and young Paul Dombey. Burnett played Squire Norton in *The Village Coquettes* and for a few years was a member of MACREADY's theatrical company at COVENT GARDEN, before he and Fanny moved to MANCHESTER, where he worked as a music teacher.

Burton, Thomas   One of the converts to teetotalism mentioned at the Brick Lane Temperance meeting, "a purveyor of cat's meat to the Lord Mayor and sheriffs." *Pickwick* (33).

Bury, George   Old John's wife's father who left her a legacy of £128 10s. *Reprinted,* "Poor Man's Tale."

Bury St. Edmunds   The "handsome little town" in Suffolk where Jingle tricks Pickwick into hiding in the courtyard of the girls' school (*Pickwick,* 15, 16). Dr. Chillip, the doctor who delivers David Copperfield, settles down here (*Copperfield,* 60). The Pickwickians stay at the ANGEL INN (*Pickwick,* 16).

Bush Inn, Bristol   This inn, owned by Moses PICKWICK, operator of the London-to-Bath coach, is where both Winkle and Pickwick stay when they are in Bristol. *Pickwick* (38, 39, 48, 50).

Buss, Robert William (1804–1875)   Graphic artist hired by CHAPMAN & HALL to provide two illustrations for the third number of *Pickwick* after the suicide of Robert SEYMOUR. Buss, who had not done any steel engraving prior to his work for the novel, submitted pictures of the Fat Boy in the arbor and the Muggleton cricket match that disappointed the publishers. Although they were included in the monthly numbers, the illustrations were later replaced with work by BROWNE. Though Buss was upset by the way Chapman & Hall treated him and by his abrupt dismissal from the project, he remained a lifelong admirer of Dickens. He produced several paintings on Dickensian subjects for Royal Academy exhibitions. His watercolor, "Dickens' Dream," done after the author's death and at the end of Buss's own life, has become a Dickensian icon. It shows the author surrounded by the figures of his imagination, several of them unfinished.

Butcher, The Young   The bully, "the terror of the youth of Canterbury," who fights with David Copperfield and other boys at Dr. Strong's school. *Copperfield* (18).

Butcher, William   Chartist who explains society's laws regarding the poor to old John the inventor. *Reprinted,* "Poor Man's Tale."

Butler (1)   Dr. Blimber's butler "in a blue coat and bright buttons, who gave quite a winey flavor to the table beer; he poured it out so superbly." *Dombey* (12).

Butler (2)   Mrs. Skewton's "silver-headed retainer." *Dombey* (30).

Butler (3)   The Chief Butler in Merdle's establishment, who comments on the suicide of his employer: "Mr. Merdle never was the gentleman, and no ungentlemanly act on Mr. Merdle's part would surprise me." *Dorrit* (II:25).

Butler (4)   The Veneerings's "ANALYTICAL CHEMIST." *Mutual Friend.*

Butler, Theodosius   The conceited young man, author of "Considerations on the Policy of Removing the Duty on Bees'-Wax," who elopes with Lavinia Brook Dingwall. He adopts the alias of Edward M'Neville Walter. *Boz,* "Sentiment."

Butt, John (1906–1965)   Professor, University of Edinburgh, scholar of 18th-and 19th-century literature. His pioneering study of Dickens's methods of composition, *Dickens at Work* (1957), done with Kathleen TILLOTSON, stessed the importance of the serial form of Dickens's novels and made use of Dickens's notes, diaries, and number plans to establish his conscious artistic designs.

Button, William   "The tailor of Tooley Street," a role acted by Signor Jupe as the clown in Sleary's Circus. *Hard Times* (I:3).

Buxom Widow, The   Proprietor of the inn on MARBOROUGH DOWNS in "The BAGMAN'S STORY." Tom Smart informs her of Jinkins's bigamous scheme to marry her, and then marries her himself. *Pickwick* (14).

Buzfuz, Serjeant   The barrister "with a fat body and a red face" who represents Mrs. Bardell in court. He bullies the witnesses at the trial, especially confusing Winkle into giving incriminating testimony. *Pickwick* (34). He is thought to be based on Serjeant Bompas, a prominent lawyer of the period.

"By Rail to Parnassus"   Article for *HOUSEHOLD WORDS* (June 16, 1855) by Henry Morley and, perhaps, Dickens. It describes the imaginings of the narrator that are prompted by reading Leigh HUNT's *Stories in Verse* as he rides on the train to Southampton on a dismal day for a job interview. The implicit praise it gives to Hunt may have been Dickens's way of making up for his portrayal of Hunt as Skimpole in *Bleak House*. *Stone*.

C

Cackles Cousin of the narrator of "The Best Authority," the "most amiable ass alive." *Miscellaneous*.

Cadogan Place Fashionable street in west London where the Wititterleys live, "the connecting link between the aristocratic pavements of BELGRAVE SQUARE, and the barbarism of CHELSEA." *Nickleby* (41).

"Cain in the Fields" Article by R. H. Horne for *HOUSEHOLD WORDS* (May 10, 1851) with some significant additions and revisions by Dickens. It describes several recent murders in the countryside, suggests the social conditions—ignorance, poor education, poverty—that prompt these murders, and attacks the barbarism of the public executions held in the countryside. *Stone*.

Cairo, Illinois Illinois town at the junction of the Ohio and MISSISSIPPI rivers that Dickens used as the model for EDEN in *Chuzzlewit*. He described the settlement as "a breeding-place of fever, ague, and death. . . . A dismal swamp, on which the half-built houses rot away: . . . teeming, then, with rank unwholesome vegetation, in whose baleful shade the wretched wanderers who are tempted hither, droop, die, and lay their bones." *Notes* (12).

Calais, France This seaport town across the English Channel from DOVER was a place of refuge for those escaping English justice. Mr. Sparsit retreats to Calais to escape bankruptcy (*Hard Times*, I:7) as do the Veneerings (*Mutual Friend*, IV:17). Clennam and Meagles seek out Miss Wade who has gone into hiding here "in a dead sort of house" (*Dorrit*, II:20). Roger Cly spies on Charles Darnay as he boards the channel boat in Calais (*Two Cities*, II:3). The Traveller gives his impressions of the port and the town (*Uncommercial*, 18).

"Calais Night Mail, The" The Traveller's account of crossing the Channel from DOVER to CALAIS and boarding the night train to PARIS. *Uncommercial* (18).

Calcroft Executioner for the county of Suffolk who was unavailable to carry out the execution of Maria Clarke. *Miscellaneous*, "Finishing Schoolmaster."

Callow Doctor who prescribes "rhubarb and calomel, low diet, and moderate exercise" for Our Bore. *Reprinted*, "Bore."

Calton Superannuated beau, a boarder at Mrs. Tibbs's who "had never been married, but was still on the look-out for a wife with money." He leaves Mrs. Matilda Maplestone at the altar and is sued for breach of promise. *Boz*, "Boarding House."

Camberwell Well-to-do rural suburb southeast of London. Home of the Maldertons (*Boz*, "Sparkins") and of the brass and copper founder who hires Ruth Pinch as a governess (*Chuzzlewit*, 9). Pickwick has carried out some of his investigations here (*Pickwick*, 1), and Wemmick's marriage to Miss Skiffins takes place in a church near Camberwell Green (*Expectations*, 55).

Camden Town Poor suburb on the northern edge of London where the Dickens family lived at 141 BAYHAM STREET in 1822–23. When John Dickens was imprisoned for debt, Charles Dickens went to live with Mrs. ROYLANCE in LITTLE COLLEGE STREET. In *Boz*, Camden Town is the home of city clerks ("Streets—Morning"), of Miss Evans, and of the shabby-genteel engraver ("Shabby-Genteel People"). Heyling's despised father-in-law retreats to a run-down lodging in Camden Town (*Pickwick*, 21); Stagg's Gardens, home of the Toodles, is surrounded by railway construction in "Camberling Town" (*Dombey*, 6); and the Micawbers rent a house here where Traddles subleases a room (*Copperfield*, 27–28).

Camilla, Mrs. Matthew Pocket's sister who, with her husband, **Raymond**, is one of the parasitic Pocket relatives who gather at Miss Havisham's hoping for inclusion in her will (11). She claims her concern for Miss Havisham keeps her awake at night, so she receives £5 in the will "to buy rushlights to put her in spirits when she wake[s] in the night" (56). *Expectations*.

Campbell Alias assumed by MAGWITCH when he is in hiding at Mrs. Whimple's house. *Expectations* (46).

Canada Dickens visited Canada at the end of his American tour in 1842, going from NIAGARA FALLS to Toronto, KINGSTON, and MONTREAL before returning to New York (*Notes*, 14–15). Though he found Canadian hotels vile—Rasco's Hotel in Montreal he described as "the worst in the whole wide world"—he found Canadians' manners more English than those of their southern

Dickens and his parents lived in this house on Bayham Street in Camden Town after moving to London from Chatham in 1822.

neighbors. Describing Canada as "full of hope and promise," he praised qualities he found lacking in the United States: "the commerce, roads, and public works, all made *to last*; the respectability and character of the public journals" (*Notes*, 15). The climax of his visit to Canada came in two evenings of theatrical performances at Montreal starring and directed by himself. He also visited HALIFAX, Nova Scotia, when his steamship stopped there on its way to BOSTON (*Notes*, 2).

Cannana, Hamet Safi Arabian gentleman organizing the subscription campaign to erect a monument to the Good Hippopotamus. *Miscellaneous*, "Hippopotamus."

Canterbury, Kent This cathedral town near GAD'S HILL was one of Dickens's favorite places to take visitors. It has a major role in *Copperfield* as the site of Dr. Strong's school and the home of the Wickfields and Heeps (15–19). Passing through on his way to DOVER, David describes "[t]he sunny streets of Canterbury, dozing as it were in the hot light; and with the sight of its old houses and gateways, and the stately gray Cathedral, with the rooks sailing round the towers" (13).

Cape Violonist in the amateur orchestra for the Gattleton's theatricals. *Boz*, "Porter."

Capper, Mr. and Mrs. Hosts to Mincin, the Very Friendly Young Gentleman. *Young Gentlemen.*

Captain Member of Parliament and "a very old frequenter of Bellamy's." *Boz*, "Parliamentary Sketch."

"Card from Mr. Booley, A" Note in HOUSEHOLD WORDS (May 18, 1850) from Booley recognizing the contributions of several artists to the panoramas described in his earlier article "Some Account of an Extraordinary Traveller." *Miscellaneous.*

Carey, Lea, and Blanchard Philadelphia publishing firm that pirated several of Dickens's early works and then made an agreement with the author to buy advance copies of the proofs of his novels from his English publishers.

Carey, John (1934–) In *The Violent Effigy: A Study of Dickens' Imagination* (1973; published in the U.S. as *Here Comes Dickens: The Imagination of a Novelist*, 1974), Carey, Professor at Merton College, Oxford, considers Dickens as a comic writer who turns the animate inanimate and the inanimate animate, embodying an essentially dualistic vision of life.

Caricature A concept from the visual arts in which characteristic features are exaggerated for satiric or comic effect. Dickens was familiar with the work of the English graphic satirists William HOGARTH (1697–1764), James Gillray (1757–1815), and Thomas Rowlandson (1756–1827), who use caricature to good effect in their work. The characterization in *Boz* and the physical comedy in the early works owes a good deal to these visual satirists.

Dickens adapts caricature techniques in several ways in his novels. He frequently uses descriptions like the one of the French and English monarchs in the opening chapter of *Two Cities*, which reduces each of the rulers to a single physical marker: "There were a king with a large jaw and a queen with a plain face, on the throne of England; there were a king with a large jaw and a queen with a fair face, on the throne of France." Dickens's characters are often constructed around a few significant visual markers; James Carker's (*Dombey*) feline characteristics place him in the caricature tradition that reduces humans to animals. Working in a verbal medium, Dickens is able to use more than just visual tags; Jingle (*Pickwick*), for example, is characterized by his telegraphic manner of speaking.

Though caricature is traditionally satiric, exaggerating grotesque or ugly features, Dickens does not always employ such exaggeration for ridicule. Mr. Chillip, the doctor who delivers David Copperfield, is made sympathetic by likening him to a bird who cocks his head to one side, and Peggotty's popping buttons (*Copperfield*) are emblematic of her embracing love for young David. In reviewing the work of John LEECH, an inheritor of the tradition of Hogarth, Dickens praised the artist as "the very first English caricaturist . . . who has considered beauty as being perfectly compatible with his art. He almost always introduces into his graphic sketches some beautiful faces or agreeable forms." Similarly, Dickens used exaggeration for sympathetic and humorous effect as well as for ridicule.

Although Dickens was profoundly influenced early in his career by the graphic satirists and their use of caricature, he moved away from these models later on. Michael STEIG (1978) has traced this movement toward greater realism in Dickens's work. Dickens's use of caricature and his indebtedness to the graphic satire tradition has also been discussed by John HARVEY, Nancy Hill (*A Reformer's Art*, 1981), and Michael Hollington (*Dickens and the Grotesque*, 1984).

Carker, James　Manager at Dombey and Son, "thirty-eight or forty years old, of a florid complexion, and with two unbroken rows of glistening teeth, . . . [he] bore so wide a smile upon his countenance . . . that there was something in it like the snarl of a cat" (13). Sybaritic and self-serving, Carker is obsequious to Dombey but secretly resents his authority. When Dombey employs him as a go-between to negotiate the terms of his relationship with Edith (42), Carker insinuates himself into a position of power over her and elopes with her to Dijon (47). Then she rejects him, revealing that she loathes him and simply used him to humiliate her husband (54). Fleeing from Dombey, who has discovered his whereabouts from Alice Marwood, his former mistress, Carker falls in front of a passing train and is torn limb from limb (55). *Dombey.*

Carker Family　Family of white-collar workers associated with the firm of Dombey and Son. The younger brother, **James Carker**, has risen to become manager, second in command in the firm. His elder brother **John**, called **Carker the Junior** because of his low position in the firm, is held down as a punishment for embezzling from the firm as a young man. He befriends Walter Gay and lives penitently in a simple cottage with his sister **Harriet**—a "slight, small, patient figure, . . . who . . . went over to him in his shame and put her hand in his, and with a sweet composure and determination, led him hopefully upon his barren way" (33). Harriet also befriends Alice Marwood, but she is rebuffed when Alice learns that she is James Carker's sister (33, 34). During their years of humiliation, John and Harriet are befriended by Mr. Morfin, who ultimately marries Harriet (62). When they inherit James's fortune, they use the money to provide an income for the bankrupt Dombey (58). *Dombey.*

Carlavero, Giovanni　Italian wine maker who was once a political prisoner and was released through the efforts of an English visitor. *Uncommercial* (17).

Carlo　One of Jerry's performing dogs. *Curiosity Shop* (18).

Carlton Chronicle, The　Weekly newspaper in which Dickens first published "The Hospital Patient" (August 6, 1836). *Boz.*

Carlton, William J. (1886–1973)　Dickens scholar and avid Dickensian whose many articles in the DICKENSIAN most often concern aspects of Dickens's early life. He was also the author of *Dickens and Shorthand* (1926).

Carlyle, Thomas (1801–1866)　Scottish essayist, historian, novelist, and philosopher. He met Dickens in 1840, and the two became lifelong friends. Dickens dedicated *Hard Times* to him. Carlyle's influence is pervasive in Dickens's works. The idealism of *Sartor Resartus* (1833–34), Carlyle's philosophical BILDUNGSROMAN, shaped Dickens's autobiographical novels, *Copperfield* and *Expectations*. The novel's critique of DANDYISM influenced *Bleak House*, and its spiritual and psychological themes helped to define Arthur Clennam's personal crisis in *Dorrit*. Carlyle's social philosophy, developed in works like *Chartism* (1839) and *Past and Present* (1843), shaped the critique of Mammonism in *Chuzzlewit* and *Dorrit*, and the attacks on UTILITARIANISM in *Hard Times* and

Maclise's portrait of a youthful Carlyle.

on aristocratic privilege in *Bleak House* and *Dorrit*. Dickens relied on Carlyle's history of *The French Revolution* (1837) for much of the background in *Two Cities*. Dickens valued Carlyle's reactions to his work as well as those of Carlyle's wife, **Jane Welsh**. Although Carlyle criticized Dickens as a mere entertainer, saying on one occasion, for example, that "Dickens had not written anything which would be found of much use in solving the problems of life," he was more generous on other occasions, describing him after his death as "the good, the gentle, ever friendly noble Dickens,—every inch of him an Honest Man!" Dickens's relationship with Carlyle is treated by Michael GOLDBERG (1972) and by William Oddie (*Dickens and Carlyle: The Question of Influence*, 1972).

Carnaby Street   Near Oxford Circus in London, the street where the Kenwigs live. *Nickleby*.

Carolina   Beautiful maid to the English bride haunted by the face in her dreams. *Reprinted*, "At Dusk."

Caroline   Wife of one of Scrooge's debtors. She and her husband are moved by Scrooge's death because it temporarily relieves them of the nececessity of paying what they owe him. *Carol* (4).

Carstone, Richard   Ward of Chancery, committed by the court to the guardianship of John Jarndyce (3). He falls in love with his cousin and fellow ward, Ada Clare. Jarndyce tries to give direction for his life by encouraging him to enter a profession. Richard tries medicine (13), the law (17), and the Army (24), but he is unable to settle on anything because of his unhealthy preoccupation with the Jarndyce case. Finally he falls into the clutches of the lawyer Vholes, who feeds his obsession with the suit (37). Estranged from Jarndyce and wasting away, Richard secretly marries Ada (51), but she cannot restore him to health. When the Jarndyce suit ends with all proceeds absorbed in court costs, Richard dies, leaving Ada and his unborn child to the care of Jarndyce (65). *Bleak House*.

Carter   Head of the Mechanical Section of the Mudfog Association. *Mudfog*.

Carton, Captain George   Commanding officer of the expedition to Silver-Store Island. He leads the expedition against the pirates and shoots Christian George King. He marries Marion Maryon and later becomes Admiral Sir George Carton, Bart. "English Prisoners."

Carton, Sydney   The dissipated barrister who works as a researcher for Mr. Stryver. The "idlest and most unpromising of men," he lounges about the court "with his hands in his pockets, staring at the ceiling" (II:5). His physical resemblance to Charles Darnay enables Stryver to confuse the witnesses at Darnay's trial and secure his acquittal. Carton falls hopelessly in love with Lucie Ma-

nette and promises to offer any sacrifice for her. His opportunity comes when Darnay, now her husband, is sentenced to execution. He uses his likeness to Darnay to change places with him in prison and to take his place at the guillotine. As he goes to his death, Carton states the famous closing lines of the novel, "It is a far, far better thing that I do, than I have ever done; it is a far, far better rest that I go to than I have ever known" (III: 15). *Two Cities*.

Casby, Christopher ("Patriarch")   Father of Flora Finching and slumlord of BLEEDING HEART YARD and other properties, his "shining bald head, . . . the long grey hair at its side and back, like floss silk or spun glass . . . looked so benevolent . . . that various old ladies spoke of him as The Last of the Patriarchs" (I:13). He employs Pancks as his rent collector, enabling the odium that properly should fall on him, to be directed instead at his agent. In the end Pancks exposes his employer by cutting his locks and leaving him shorn in the middle of Bleeding Heart Yard (II:34). *Dorrit*.

Castle Street   Street in HOLBORN where Traddles has lodgings. *Copperfield* (36).

Cateaton Street   Street in the CITY—now Gresham Street—where the warehouses of Tom Smart's employers, Bilson and Slum, were located. *Pickwick* (49).

Catholic Church   As a liberal Protestant, Dickens had mixed feelings about Roman Catholicism. On the one hand, he attacked religious intolerance; *Rudge* is a testament to his belief that British Catholics had a right to practice their religion without constraint. The Catholic *Dublin Review* noted that the novel opposes "a sturdy, highminded Catholic gentleman, and . . . a mean, vindictive Protestant villain." But Dickens was not so kindly disposed toward Catholicism when it was the dominant religion. In *Child's History* he characterizes Catholic England as benighted, and in *Pictures from Italy* he blames the poverty, oppression, and suffering of the Italian people on corrupt rulers and a reactionary Catholic Church. He sympathized with the Italian revolutionaries and, in Geneva during the 1846 revolution, he supported the overthrow of the Jesuits, commenting in a letter that "I have a sad misgiving that the religion of Ireland lies as deep at the root of all its sorrows, even as English misgovernment and Tory villainy." In an article for HOUSEHOLD WORDS in 1850, after the Pope proposed to elevate Dr. Wiseman to cardinal, Dickens has Mrs. John Bull warn her children against the Bulls of Rome, describing them as "an insolent, audacious, oppressive, intolerable race" that perpetuates "misery, oppression, darkness, and ignorance" ("A Crisis in the Affairs of Mr. John Bull").

Catlin, George (1796–1872)   Ethnographer and artist who lived with various Indian tribes, producing the classic *Illustrations of the Manners, etc. of the North*

Catlin's portrait of Pitchlynn, an Indian chief whom Dickens met on his American journey in 1842.

American Indians (1857). Dickens criticizes him as one of the purveyors of the superstitious idea of the Noble Savage. *Reprinted*, "Noble Savage."

Cattermole, George (1800–1868) Watercolorist and illustrator who was Dickens's personal friend and the husband of Dickens's cousin. Cattermole contributed about 40 illustrations for *Master Humphrey's Clock, Curiosity Shop*, and *Rudge*. His work, which concentrated on architectural subjects, especially on romantically-depicted old buildings, was particularly apt for the old churches in *Curiosity Shop* and the historical buildings in *Rudge*. Another example of his work appears in illustration 65 (*OLD CURIOSITY SHOP*).

Cautious Clara Captain Jack Bunsby's ship. *Dombey* (23).

Cavaletto, Signor John Baptist ("Altro") Petty Italian smuggler imprisoned with Rigaud in MARSEILLES (1). He makes his way to London, where he is employed by Arthur Clennam, who calls him "Altro," an Italian word meaning "certainly," which Cavaletto uses as "a confirmation, an assertion, a denial, a taunt, a compliment, a joke, and fifty other things" (I:1). Cavaletto aids in the search for Rigaud in London and nurses Clennam in MARSHALSEA PRISON. *Dorrit*.

Cavendish Square Madame Mantalini has her millinery business near this fashionable neighborhood in

MARYLEBONE (*Nickleby*). Silas Wegg's post outside the corner house that the Boffins later occupy is near the Square (*Mutual Friend*).

Caveton The Throwing-off Young Gentleman. *Young Gentlemen*.

Cecil Street Street off the STRAND where Watkins Tottle lives during his married days. *Boz*, "Tottle."

Celia Charity girl who meets her charity-boy lover in a deserted CITY churchyard. *Uncommercial* (23).

Certainpersonio, Prince Alicia's bridegroom in Alice Rainbird's tale. "Holiday Romance."

Cervantes Saavedra, Miguel de (1547–1616) Spanish novelist and dramatist; his *Don Quixote* (1605, 1615) has often been considered the first novel in Western literature. Among the treasured books of his childhood, *Quixote* provided Dickens with a model for his own work. Its loosely connected series of adventures that take place on a journey, its use of interpolated tales, and its fundamental opposition of illusion and reality, were important features in many of the English novels of the 18th and early 19th centuries. Dickens's early works, especially *Pickwick*, whose hero was described by an early reviewer as "the Cockney Quixote of the nineteenth century," use these Cervantean features. Pickwick's steadfast commitment to principle is similar to Quixote's belief in his chivalric mission and his relationship with Sam Weller echoes that of Quixote and Sancho Panza. In "Dingley Dell and the Fleet," W. H. Auden compares and contrasts *Quixote* and *Pickwick* (*The Dyer's Hand*, 1962). Alexander WELSH (1981) discusses *Pickwick* as a primary example and redefinition of the Quixotic tradition.

Chadband, The Reverend Mr. Unctuous dissenting clergyman admired by Mrs. Snagsby, he is the model of cant and hypocrisy: "a large yellow man, with a fat smile, and a general appearance of having a good deal of train oil in his system" (19). He speaks in a homiletic style, asking empty rhetorical questions, and he "never speaks without first putting up his great hand, as delivering a token to his hearers that he is going to edify them" (19). His **wife**, "a stern, severe-looking, silent woman" (19), turns out to be Mrs. Rachel, Esther Summerson's childhood nurse. Chadband sermonizes Jo on "Terewth" (25). He joins with the Smallweeds in an attempt to blackmail Sir Leicester Dedlock and is thwarted by Bucket (54). *Bleak House.*

Chalk, Kent Dickens spent his honeymoon at this town in KENT, and it was a regular stop on his walks from GAD'S HILL. With HIGHAM, it served as the model for Pip's village in *Expectations*.

Chalons, France Rigaud and Cavaletto meet briefly at the Break of Day Inn near this town on the Marne, east of Paris. *Dorrit* (I:11).

"Chambers" The Traveller describes the loneliness of chambers in the various INNS OF COURT, where single men live in dusty rooms that have never known the liveliness of marriages, children, and family festivals. *Uncommercial* (14).

Chancellor, The Lord High Presiding judge over the Court of CHANCERY who, at the beginning of *Bleak House*, sits in the center of the fog in LINCOLN'S INN HALL with "a foggy glory round his head" (1).

Chancery, Court of Supreme court in England for the resolution of Equity cases, such as those involving contested trusts and legacies; presided over by the LORD CHANCELLOR. Dickens suffered the ineffectiveness of the court when he unsuccessfully attempted to recover damages from a magazine that had pirated *A Christmas Carol*. In *Pickwick* he describes some long-term prisoners languishing in jail as a result of disputed wills (41, 43). Dickens also attacked court abuses in articles for *HOUSEHOLD WORDS*. His most extended criticism appears in *Bleak House*, in which the court's delays, obfuscation of issues, and self-serving procedures lead to indolence, despair, and suicide and produce such social ills as festering slums. Dickens's treatment of the court in the novel echoed widespread criticisms in the press in the early 1850s. The court was abolished in 1873 and its functions taken over by the newly established Supreme Court of Justice for England and Wales.

Chancery Lane This street in the legal area of London where the Court of CHANCERY is situated is a major setting in *Bleak House*; Krook's rag and bottle shop, Snagsby's stationer's business, and SOL'S ARMS are located here. Watkins Tottle is imprisoned for debt in nearby CURSITOR STREET (*Boz*, "Tottle"); Pickwick is confronted by a bail tout here (*Pickwick*, 40); Rokesmith stops Boffin in Chancery Lane to offer his services as secretary (*Mutual Friend*, I:8).

Chancery Prisoner, The "A tall, gaunt, cadaverous man . . . with sunken cheeks, and a restless, eager eye" who sublets his room in the FLEET PRISON to Pickwick. *Pickwick* (42).

Cattermole's predilection for architectural subjects is illustrated in his rendering of the Maypole Inn for Barnaby Rudge *(1841).*

Chaplain, Drunken One of Pickwick's fellow prisoners in FLEET PRISON. *Pickwick* (42).

Chapman, Edward (1804–1880) Partner in the publishing firm CHAPMAN & HALL. The more literary of the two partners, Chapman conceived the idea for *Pickwick*. In a letter to him in 1839, Dickens described the firm as "the best of booksellers past, present, or to come."

Chapman, Frederic (1823–1895) Cousin of Edward CHAPMAN. He became a partner in CHAPMAN & HALL in 1847, and its head in 1864.

Chapman & Hall Publishing firm founded by Edward CHAPMAN and William HALL, which, with BRADBURY & EVANS, was one of the two firms that published most of Dickens's works. In 1836, when they contracted with Dickens for *Pickwick*, the two partners gambled their fledgling firm on the innovative idea of serial publication. When the novel became a runaway best-seller, they had established the firm and introduced a mode of publication that would be widely adopted by other novelists. They went on to publish *Nickleby*, and, in 1840, became Dickens's regular publishers, buying up the rights to *Boz*, *Twist*, and other early works from MACRONE and BENTLEY. Their relationship with Dickens soured, however, when *Chuzzlewit* and *A Christmas Carol* did not produce the financial returns that Dickens expected, so he moved to Bradbury & Evans in 1844, staying with them until 1859. After quarreling with Bradbury & Evans over the publication of his explanation of the separation from his wife, Dickens returned to Chapman & Hall. He published *ALL THE YEAR ROUND* and the novels of the 1860s with them. Chapman & Hall collaborated with Bradbury & Evans on the CHEAP EDITION and LIBRARY EDITION of Dickens's works. In 1861 they bought the rights to the novels owned by Bradbury & Evans. Among other Victorian writers published by the firm were Thomas CARLYLE, Edward Bulwer LYTTON, Robert BROWNING and Elizabeth Barrett Browning, Elizabeth GASKELL, Anthony TROLLOPE, and George Meredith. Dickens's relationship with the firm is discussed at length in PATTEN (1978).

Characterization All Dickens criticism is in some way about characterization, for Dickens is known for his characters, many of whom, like Scrooge, Oliver Twist, or Mr. Micawber, are familiar figures in the popular culture. Dickens's gallery of characters is crowded with a wider range of diverse and memorable people than that of any other writer in English since Shakespeare.

Most of Dickens's people are what E. M. FORSTER in 1927 described as "flat characters," figures defined by one or two exaggerated traits who "can be expressed in one sentence such as 'I never will desert Mr. Micawber.'" George ELIOT observed that these defining characteristics were "external traits" and that Dickens "scarcely ever passes from the humorous and external to the emotional and tragic." This method of characterization, John Ruskin and other critics have asserted, is that of an entertainer, not that of a serious writer who observes and describes the ways in which experience changes people and enables them to grow. Except for David Copperfield and Pip, these flat characters are said to lack an internal life and remain unchanged by their experiences. "Those who dislike Dickens have an excellent case," Forster admits. "He ought to be bad. He is actually one of our big writers."

The problem for critics, then, has been to explain how Dickens, working primarily with simple, flat characters, was able to create a complex and serious vision of the world. V. S. Pritchett (*The Living Novel*, 1947), suggested an approach that many later critics have followed. For all their eccentricities, Dickens's characters have certain things in common. "The distinguishing quality of Dickens's people," Pritchett argues, "is that they are solitaries. They are people caught living in a world of their own. They soliloquize in it. They do not talk to one another; they talk to themselves. . . . The solitariness of people is paralleled by the solitariness of things. Fog operates as a separate presence, houses quietly rot or boisterously prosper on their own. . . . The people and things of Dickens are all out of touch and out of hearing of each other, each conducting its own inner monologue, grandiloquent or dismaying." Solitary, eccentric, individualized, the world that Dickens's characters inhabit is defined by separation and isolation.

Raymond WILLIAMS (*English Novel*, 1974) argues that this dramatic and emphatic use of flat characters was a "method . . . uniquely capable of expressing the experience of living in cities, . . . a way of seeing men and women that belongs to the street. There is at first an absence of ordinary connection and development. These men and women do not so much relate as pass each other and then sometimes collide. Nor often in the ordinary way do they speak to each other. They speak past each other, each intent above all on defining through his words his own identity and reality." In these collisions, Williams goes on to say, relationships and connections emerge, as if forced to consciousness.

Many critics have explored the ways in which these unfamiliar urban relationships reveal themselves: how characters double, mirror, and repeat each other; how the characters articulate multiple parts of the self that have been separated from one another; how the characters act as projections of each other. Dickens's characters often relate to others in unusual or grotesque ways, like the figures in a dream rather than realistically. Taylor STOEHR (1965) and Mark SPILKA (1963) analyze the ways in which they act as parts of a dream or fantasy; Williams suggests that they express a fragmented urban consciousness. Although many of the characters are self-created and self-defined, they are still part of a larger vision, pieces in an imagined world. They have, as James Davies describes it, "a textual life" (*The Textual Life of Dickens's Characters*, 1990). They cannot be removed from their novels without simplification or misrepresentation.

Many Dickensians, especially in the early decades of this century, were engrossed in discovering the ORIGINALS of Dickens's characters, the figures in real life on whom they were based. Although Dickens admittedly drew on real people for many of his characters, he usually transformed them into a different order of being in the novels. Doris Alexander (*Creating Characters with Charles Dickens*, 1991) reverses the process to study the ways in which the originals are transformed by Dickens's artistic imagination as he gives his characters textual life.

Charing Cross   This crossroads in central London adjoining Trafalgar Square is notable in several of the novels. The Pickwickians begin their journeys from the GOLDEN CROSS HOTEL (2) where David Copperfield stays (*Copperfield*, 19); Eugene Wrayburn meets Mr. Dolls in the street near Charing Cross (*Mutual Friend*, III:10).

Charitable Grinders   Charity school to which Mr. Dombey sends Polly Toodles's eldest son, earning the boy the nickname Rob the Grinder. The uniform that Rob wears, "a nice, warm, blue baize tailed coat and cap, turned up with orange-coloured binding; red worsted stockings; and very strong leather small-clothes" (5), was characteristic of charity school uniforms of the day. *Dombey.*

Charker, Corporal Harry   Gill Davis's comrade-in-arms who is killed in the battle to protect the colony of Silver-Store Island from pirates. "He had always one most excellent idea in his mind. That was, Duty." "English Prisoners."

Charles and Louisa   Cool Couple who suffer "apathy and dulness" on the rare occasions when they are alone together. *Young Couples.*

Charles Dickens Edition   Last collected edition of Dickens's works published during his lifetime. Issued by CHAPMAN & HALL in monthly volumes beginning in June 1867, each volume contained eight illustrations. Dickens supplied new prefaces and descriptive headlines for the pages.

Charles, Old   Waiter in a West Country Hotel, "by some considered the "Father of Waitering." "Somebody's Luggage."

Charley (1)   "Shambling pot-boy, with a red head" at the MAGPIE AND STUMP. *Pickwick* (20).

Charley (2)   Second-hand clothing dealer to whom David sells some clothes on his way to DOVER. *Copperfield* (13).

Charley (3)   Nickname of Charlotte NECKETT. *Bleak House.*

Charley (4)   Bashful narrator of "The Holly Tree" who, thinking himself jilted by Angela Leath, sets off for AMERICA but gets snowed in at the Holly Tree Inn on the way and there learns that Angela really loves him.

Charlotte (1)   Edward's exasperating wife in the Contradictory Couple. *Young Couples.*

Charlotte (2)   Sowerberry's slatternly maid who embezzles from her employers and runs off to London with Noah Claypole. *Twist.*

Charlotte (3)   Cruel schoolmate who encouraged Miss Wade's infatuation for her. *Dorrit* (II:21).

Charlotte (4)   Old John's daughter, whose husband has left her and thus forced her and her three children to live with her parents. *Reprinted*, "Poor Man's Tale."

Chartism   Working-class movement that emerged in 1838 out of the Anti–Poor Law agitation, bringing together several working class groups. Its name derived from the People's Charter, a document based on six points: universal manhood suffrage, equal electoral districts, payment for members of Parliament, elimination of the property qualification for Parliament, vote by ballot, and annual Parliaments. The Chartists circulated petitions calling for these reforms and, in 1839, 1842, and 1848, they massed in London to present their demands to Parliament, each time without success. The mass meetings and several violent confrontations with authorities led many to fear a violent revolution led by the Chartists. A split in the movement between the "physical force" and the "moral force" factions contributed to the popular perception that many Chartists were dangerous and violent agents of French radicalism. Although the movement died after 1848, it was an important precursor to the socialist movement later on. All of the Chartist reforms, except annual parliaments, were adopted by the end of the 19th century.

Dickens supported the radical goals of the Chartists and agreed with Thomas CARLYLE, who blamed an idle aristocracy and an unresponsive Parliament for the rise of the movement. Dickens sympathy is probably most directly expressed in *Chimes* in his treatment of Will Fern, a victim of agricultural distress who is radicalized into an incendiary terrorist by the mistreatment he receives from the rich. *Rudge*, also a response to Chartism, parallels the GORDON RIOTS to the Chartist agitations; its condemnation of mob action can be taken as a warning against physical force Chartism. In "The Poor Man's Tale of a Patent," an inventor, similar to Daniel Doyce in *Dorrit*, develops sympathy for the Chartists after his frustrating experiences in dealing with the government bureaucracy.

Château des Moulineaux, Boulogne   Castle in BOULOGNE that Dickens leased for his summer holidays in 1853 and 1856.

Chatham   Seaport town in KENT, located at the estuary of the Medway where it meets the THAMES; twin city with ROCHESTER. Pickwick describes the lively seaport town in the following terms: "The principal production . . . appears to be soldiers, sailors, Jews, chalk, shrimps, officers and dockyard men. The commmodities chiefly exposed for sale in the public streets are marine stores, hardbake, apples, flat fish and oysters. The streets present a lively and animated appearance, occasioned chiefly by the conviviality of the military" (2). Dickens spent his happiest childhood years here between 1817 and 1823 while his father served as a pay clerk at the naval station. The family lived at 2 Ordinance Terrace, the house where Dickens found his father's library of novels and avidly read the works of FIELDING, SMOLLETT, CERVANTES and others. His father often walked with his son in the countryside surrounding the town; on one of these walks he advised the boy that if he worked hard he could one day own a house like GAD'S HILL PLACE. Chatham appears as MUDFOG and DULLBOROUGH (*Uncommercial*, 12, 26); Pickwick's first journey takes him to neighboring Rochester, where he meets Wardle and where Winkle nearly duels with Dr. Slammer (2, 4); David sells some clothes here on his way to DOVER (*Copperfield*, 13). Chatham also appears in "Seven Poor Travellers" and *Reprinted*, "Detective Police."

"Chatham Dockyard"   The Traveller's account of day-dreaming by the river in CHATHAM and then visiting the dockyard where the warship *Achilles* is under construction. As he meditates on ropemaking, the Traveller is "spun into a state of blissful indolence, wherein my rope of life seems to be so untwisted by the process as that I can see back to very early days indeed." *Uncommercial* (26).

Cheap Edition   First collected edition of Dickens's works, issued by BRADBURY & EVANS and CHAPMAN & HALL in both monthly parts and separate volumes, beginning in 1847. Dickens wrote new prefaces for the novels; each volume included a frontispiece by a well-known artist, but was otherwise unillustrated. These cheap editions were designed to appeal to a new audience rather than to compete with more expensive editions of the novels that were also available at the time.

"Cheap Patriotism"   A retired civil servant, Mr. Tapenham, tells of his experiences in the government bureaucracy and of the reforms that came with each new government. These reforms were, however, "cheap patriotism," for they always went after junior bureaucrats and never changed anything at the top of the department. *Miscellaneous*.

Cheapside   Street near ST. PAUL'S CATHEDRAL in the CITY. Here Pickwick meets Tony Weller for the first time at an inn (20); Mr. Mould lives nearby and listens to the traffic in Cheapside (*Chuzzlewit*, 25). Also mentioned in *Boz*, "Minns," "Christening"; *Dombey* (13); *Expectations* (48).

Cheerful   Proprietor of a betting shop in the vicinity of the offices of HOUSEHOLD WORDS. *Miscellaneous*, "Betting-shops."

Cheeryble, Charles and Edwin (Ned)   Twin brothers, wealthy merchants who hire Nicholas Nickleby and become his benefactor. Charles, "a sturdy old fellow in a broad-skirted coat, . . . with . . . a pleasant smile playing about his mouth, and . . . a comical expression of mingled slyness, simplicity, kind-heartedness, and good-humour, lighting up his jolly old face" is matched by his brother, whose "slight additional shade of clumsiness in his gait and stature formed the only perceptible difference between them" (35). They are benefactors to Madeline Bray and it is through working for them that Nicholas meets her (46). When they retire, they leave the business to Nicholas and their nephew **Frank**, a "sprightly, good-humoured, pleasant fellow" who reminds Nicholas of the brothers (43). Frank marries Kate Nickleby (63). *Nickleby*. The Cheeryble brothers were based on William and Daniel Grant, MANCHESTER calico merchants whom Dickens met in 1838.

Cheeseman, Old   Subject of "The Schoolboy's Story." He had been a student at the school who was left there, like Scrooge, to spend the holidays alone. Then he had been hired as second Latin master and was considered a traitor by the other boys, who organized a society to torment him. However, when he inherits a fortune and is kind to the boys, they change their mind about him.

Cheggs, Alick   Market-gardener and brother to **Miss Cheggs**, Sophy Wackles's close friend. He is Dick Swiveller's rival for Sophy. She tries to heighten Swiveller's interest by her attentions to Cheggs just as Dick is scheming to marry Nell (8). Cheggs wins the contest and marries Sophy. *Curiosity Shop*.

Chelsea   District in London along the THAMES south of KENSINGTON. In Dickens's time a village, it is where Dickens was married at ST. LUKE'S Church and where he often visited Thomas CARLYLE, the sage of Chelsea. The tearful Job Trotter is compared to the Chelsea Waterworks (*Pickwick*, 28); Swiveller visits Sophy Wackles at her house in Chelsea (*Curiosity Shop*, 8); Gabriel Varden and his regiment march to the Chelsea Bun House (*Rudge*, 42); Mr. Bayham Badger practices medicine here (*Bleak House*, 13); John stays with Thomas Joy in Chelsea when he comes to London to secure a patent (*Reprinted*, "Poor Man's Tale").

Chertsey   Village along the THAMES in Surrey where Bill Sikes takes Oliver to rob Mrs. Maylie's house (*Twist*, 22). Betty Higden passes through on her way up the Thames (*Mutual Friend*, III:8).

"Cherub, The" Bella's pet name for her father, Reginald WILFER. *Mutual Friend*.

Chesney Wold The Dedlocks' house in Lincolnshire (2), where Lady Dedlock's portrait attracts Guppy's attention (7), and where the legend of the Ghost's Walk haunts Lady Dedlock. *Bleak House*. Dickens based Chesney Wold on ROCKINGHAM CASTLE in Northamptonshire.

Chester, Edward Son of **Sir John Chester**, "a young man of about eight-and-twenty, . . . of a somewhat slight figure, gracefully and strongly made" (1). Disowned by his father for his relationship with Emma Haredale, he goes off to the West Indies (32), returning at the time of the riots when he and Joe Willet save Geoffrey Haredale, Emma, and Dolly Varden from the vengeance of the mob (67, 71). He marries Emma and returns to the West Indies (79). *Rudge*.

Chester, Sir John A "smooth man of the world," who hides a ruthless cynicism, selfishness, and hypocrisy behind a mask of affability. The enemy of Geoffrey Haredale from their schooldays together, Chester seeks to prevent the marriage of his son **Edward** (see CHESTER, Edward) to Haredale's niece Emma and force the boy to marry a rich heiress so as to restore the family fortunes (12, 15). Using Hugh as his agent, he is also behind the destruction of the Warren (40, 56), though he later refuses to acknowledge Hugh as his illegitimate son by a gypsy woman and perhaps save him from hanging (75). After the GORDON RIOTS he goes to the ruined house where he meets Haredale and is killed in a duel (81). *Rudge*. Dickens based Sir John Chester on Lord Chesterfield (1694–1773) who, in Dickens's view, cynically advised his son to cultivate a smooth manner while exploiting the weaknesses of others.

Chesterton, G. K. (1874–1936) English novelist; social, political, religious, and literary critic; poet; and journalist. Chesterton, a Londoner like Dickens, challenged the modernist criticisms of Dickens and became the novelist's primary apologist at the beginning of the 20th century. In *Charles Dickens* (1903), *Charles Dickens: A Critical Study* (1906), *The Victorian Age in Literature* (1913), and in numerous introductions to the novels and journalistic essays, Chesterton wrote about the life-affirming, magical world of Dickens. He considered all of Dickens's works part of a single vision revealing an archetypal realm, filled with magic, fantasy, and mystery. Dickens, he claimed, was "the last of the great mythologists."

Chestle Hop-grower from KENT who marries the eldest Miss Larkins. *Copperfield* (18).

Chib Head vestryman, "a remarkably hale old gentleman of eighty-two." *Reprinted*, "Our Vestry."

Chick, Mrs. Louisa Sister of Mr. Dombey who claims that Mrs. Dombey died in childbirth because she was not a true Dombey and did not "make an effort" (3). She invites her friend, Miss Tox, to aid in finding a nurse for young Paul and encourages her to entertain hopes of Dombey's matrimonial interest, but when Dombey selects Edith, she ends her friendship with Miss Tox (29). She explains Dombey's ruin as the result of his not making an effort. Her husband, **John**, "a stout bald gentleman, with a very large face, and his hands continually in his pockets," has a habit of whistling at inopportune moments (2). *Dombey*.

Chickenstalker, Mrs. Anne Owner of a general store to whom Trotty Veck owes some small debts, "a good-humoured comely woman of some fifty years of age." In Trotty's dream she has married Tugby, Sir Joseph Bowry's former porter, and he forces Meg to give up the rooms she rents from them when she is unable to pay the rent. *Chimes*.

Chicksey, Veneering and Stobbles Drug firm near Mincing Lane in the CITY for whom Reginald Wilfer is a clerk. Veneering is the sole surviving partner "who had signalised his accession to supreme power by bringing into the business a quantity of plate-glass window and French-polished mahogany partition, and a gleaming and enormous door-plate" (I:4). *Mutual Friend*.

Chickweed, Conkey Subject of an anecdote told by Blathers, he was the keeper of a tavern near BATTLE BRIDGE who faked a burglary in order to solicit public sympathy and donations. *Twist* (31).

Chiggle "Immortal" American sculptor who, Martin is told, "made the celebrated Pogram statter in marble, which wrose so much con-test and preju-dice in Europe." *Chuzzlewit* (34).

Chigwell Town in Essex that was a favorite resort of Dickens. The King's Head Inn here, "a delicious old inn" Dickens told John FORSTER, is the original of the MAYPOLE in *Rudge*.

Childers, E. W. B. Equestrian performer with Sleary's Circus, "a remarkable sort of Centaur . . . celebrated for his daring vaulting act as the Wild Huntsman of the North American Praries" (I:6). He stands up to Gradgrind and Bounderby when they disparage Sissy's father (I:6) and he later helps Tom to escape to LIVERPOOL (III:7,8). He is married to Sleary's daughter **Josephine**, and their three-year-old **son** is billed as "The Little Wonder of Scholastic Equitation" (III:7). *Hard Times*.

Childhood Dickens has a surprising number of child characters, many of them like Oliver Twist, Tiny Tim, and David Copperfield among the most memorable figures in his works. This was something new in the novel, as Kathleen TILLOTSON (1956) notes: "To put a child at the centre of a novel for adults was virtually unknown when Dickens wrote *Oliver Twist* and *The Old Curiosity Shop*."

Dickens had an essentially romantic view of the child. Like Wordsworth's "best Philosopher," the Dickens child is often more in touch with his immortal origins than are the adults around him. Louisa Gradgrind (*Hard Times*) still sees visions in the fire, in spite of her Utilitarian education (see UTILITARIANISM), as does Lizzie Hexam (*Mutual Friend*), even in the depths of LIMEHOUSE HOLE. These "philosophical" children have a sensitivity and prescience described in Paul Dombey's case as being "old fashioned." Even in the most oppressive circumstances they maintain their innocence, as Oliver does in Fagin's den.

Many of Dickens's children are victims of the Victorian world around them. Although Dickens did not write directly about the children laboring in the cotton factories or the mines, he was aware of these exploited children and wrote the *Carol* partly as a response to a Parliamentary report describing the cruel abuse of children working in the mines. Tiny Tim is not a factory child, but his maimed legs are caged in iron, symbolic of the oppression brought about by the INDUSTRIAL REVOLUTION. Dickens also writes frequently about the effects of urbanization on the children of his day, children like Jo the crossing sweeper and Charley Neckett (*Bleak House*) who are orphans of the city streets, abandoned to Ignorance and Want—the two spectres of childhood revealed to Scrooge by the Spirit of Christmas Present (*Carol*).

Besides these physical and material ills, Dickens's children are often oppressed by hard-hearted, narrow-minded religion, like the Calvinism of the Murdstones (*Copperfield*) or Mrs. Clennam (*Dorrit*) that views children as naturally sinful and in need of harsh treatment to correct their corrupt condition. Such children as Pip (*Expectations*), who is told that all children are "naterally wicious," and Esther Summerson (*Bleak House*), whose birthday is remembered only as a day of shame, are denied their childhoods by this dark and cruel world view.

Dickens symbolized the situation of the Victorian child in his depiction of the family. The lost childhood is frequently represented as a condition of orphanhood where the child must fend for himself and find his own way in the world. In doing so he must give up his childhood and go to work at MURDSTONE AND GRINBY like David Copperfield or prepare for a place in the firm of Dombey and Son like young Paul. Even children whose parents are living may be abandoned, as are Jenny Wren (*Mutual Friend*) and Little Nell (*Curiosity Shop*), who must take parental roles with their irresponsible parents. Dickens frequently inverts the child and adult roles as a way of showing the lost childhood in Victorian England.

Frank Donovan (*Dickens and Youth*, 1968) surveys the children in Dickens's novels. Arthur ADRIAN (1984)

writes specifically about the relations between parents and children.

Children's Hospital, Great Ormond Street, Bloomsbury   Dickens served as Chairman at a fundraising dinner for this hospital in 1858 and gave a moving speech on its mission. Betty Higden's great-grandson Johnny dies in the hospital before the Boffins can complete their plan to adopt him. *Mutual Friend*, (II: 9).

"Child's Dream of a Star, A"   Sentimental story of a boy who dreams after his sister dies that she has become an angel. Although he wishes to join her when his younger brother, mother, and his own daughter die, his wish is only granted when he becomes an old man. *Reprinted*. This story originally appeared in the second issue of *HOUSEHOLD WORDS* (April 6, 1850). The sister is often taken to refer to Dickens's sister Frances (see Frances Elizabeth DICKENS).

Child's History of England, A   Dickens's narrative history of England from its beginnings in 55 B.C. up to the Glorious Revolution of 1688, written for children and published serially in *HOUSEHOLD WORDS* from January 25, 1851 to December 10, 1853 and issued in three volumes with frontispieces by F. W. TOPHAM in 1854. Based on Thomas Knightley's *History of England* (1839), Dickens's work is particularly Protestant—sympathetic to Cromwell while attacking Popish plots and Catholic kings like James I, who is called "his sowship." Dickens characterizes the rule of William and Mary when the Protestant religion was established in England as the time when "England's great and Glorious Revolution was complete."

"Child's Story, The"   Allegorical story describing the journey of life from childhood to old age. One of Dickens's two contributions to *A Round of Stories by the Christmas Fire*, the Christmas number of *HOUSEHOLD WORDS*, 1852.

Chill, Uncle   Miserly uncle of Michael, the poor relation, who disinherits his nephew when he wants to marry a poor woman. "Poor Relation."

Chillip   BLUNDERSTONE doctor who attends David's birth, "the mildest of little men" who carries "his head on one side, partly in modest deprecation of himself, partly in modest propiation of everybody else" (1). After his second marriage, Chillip moves his practice to BURY ST. EDMUNDS, where his **wife** has some property (59). *Copperfield*.

Chimes, The. A Goblin Story of Some Bells that Rang an Old Year Out and a New Year in   Second of the five CHRISTMAS BOOKS, published in December 1844 by CHAPMAN & HALL, with illustrations by Daniel MACLISE, John LEECH, Richard DOYLE, and Clarkson

STANFIELD. More topical than the *Carol*, *The Chimes* addressed controversial and social issues of the day.

SYNOPSIS

(1) At his post on a doorstep, Toby ("Trotty") Veck, a poor ticket porter, keeps watch on a windy winter day, the last day in the old year. He is heartened by the sound of the chimes in the church tower, which seem to tell him "Toby Veck, Toby Veck, keep a good heart, Toby!," but he also wonders whether the poor "have any business on the face of the earth," and whether they are intruders who are born bad and "have no right to a New Year." His daughter Meg brings him a dinner of hot tripe, Trotty's favorite dish, and tells him that she and her beau, Richard, plan to marry the next morning on New Year's Day. They realize that things will not change for the poor so there is no reason to put off marriage until their lot improves.

As Trotty enjoys his dinner, the door in which he is standing opens and a footman and three gentlemen emerge. Mr. Filer lectures Trotty about political economy, pointing out to him that tripe is an extravagant dish and that by eating it he is depriving widows and orphans of food. He also condemns Meg and Richard for their imprudent and "wicked" plan to marry. Alderman Cute puts down Trotty's belief that people are starving, telling him that "there's a great deal of nonsense talked about Want." The third gentleman extols "the good old times" and asserts that "it's of no use talking about any other times, or discussing what people are in *these* times." By the end of their harangue, Meg is in tears, Richard is downcast, and Trotty is convinced that he is an intruder who does not belong on earth. The bells now seem to be saying, "Put 'em down! Put 'em down!" Convinced that he has no business with the New Year, Trotty wishes to die.

(2) Trotty takes a letter from Alderman Cute to Sir Joseph Bowley, M. P., who is in London for a few hours to clear up his accounts so he can begin the new year owing nothing to anyone. He calls himself the "Poor Man's Father and Friend" and asserts that the great lesson the poor man must learn is his "entire dependence on myself." He advises Trotty to clear up all his obligations for the new year, but Trotty has some debts that he cannot afford to pay. Cute's letter seeks Sir Joseph's permission to arrest for vagrancy Will Fern, a rural laborer who has come to London seeking work. Sir Joseph

In November 1844 Dickens returned to England from Italy to read The Chimes *to a group of his friends. Maclise's sketch of the occasion identifies those who attended.*

knows Fern in the country as someone who refuses to be dependent, an ungrateful and rebellious troublemaker. He grants Cute's request. Toby trots back to Cute with Sir Joseph's answer and then, as he hurries home hoping to avoid hearing the unhappy message of the bells, he meets Fern, who is seeking Alderman Cute so he can clear up his case before the new year. Trotty warns him that he will be arrested and invites him to his house. With his last sixpence Trotty purchases some tea and a rasher of bacon for Will and his nine-year-old niece Lilian, and then provides places for them to spend the night. Helping Will and his niece makes Trotty happy and hopeful, but when he reads his newspaper before the fire, he is again brought to despair by accounts of crime and violence. As the chimes ring they seem to be calling to him and saying, "Haunt and hunt him, break his slumbers." Trotty goes out to the bell-tower and finding the door open, he climbs up to the top of the belfrey, feeling his way in the darkness. There he falls into a swoon.

(3) When Trotty regains consciousness, he sees the many goblin spirits of the bells. The Goblin of the Great Bell accuses him of doubting the message of advancement and improvement and of hearing in the bells only a cry of despair. By doing so, the Spirit of the Great Bell claims, Trotty has wronged the bells. The Goblin sends him off with the Spirit of the Chimes, a child who shows Trotty his own corpse lying at the foot of the tower. Then Trotty sees a series of visions of a time nine years after his death: Meg works late into the night to earn enough just barely to survive; Sir Joseph Bowley and his associates are shocked by the suicide of Deedles the banker; Will Fern, a vagabond in and out of prison, gives a revolutionary speech calling for better conditions for the poor; Lilian, now a young woman, has escaped grinding poverty by going on to the streets.

(4) In a vision of a later time Trotty sees Meg and her drunken husband Richard living in squalor in a room in Mrs. Chickenstalker's house. When Richard dies, Meg, unable to pay the rent, is evicted by Tugby, Mrs. Chickenstalker's husband, formerly Sir Joseph's footman. Meg goes to the river with her infant daughter and is about to plunge in when Trotty pleads with the Spirit to save her, protesting that he has learned the message of the bells. "I know that we must trust and hope," he tells the Spirit, "and neither doubt ourselves, nor doubt the Good in one another."

Trotty awakens by his hearth as the bells chime in the New Year and Mrs. Chickenstalker brings some celebratory punch. She turns out to be the friend that Will Fern was seeking in the city. They all prepare for the wedding of Meg and Richard.

COMMENTARY

If Dickens set out to make a "sledge-hammer blow" on behalf of the Poor Man's Child in the *Carol*, that political message was largely ignored by his readers, so a year later he made his social message more explicit in *The Chimes*. The second Christmas Book concentrated on so-cial and political issues. Agricultural distress, Chartist agitation (See CHARTISM), and intense debate over the CORN LAWS made these issues especially urgent in the mid-1840s. Sympathetic with the Chartist demands, incensed by the insensitivity of the ARISTOCRACY, and outraged by the Parliamentary reports on the exploitation of children, Dickens became increasingly radical during these years. In *The Chimes* he took up the issue of who was to blame for the distress of the poor.

Trotty Veck, the poor ticket-porter at the center of the tale, is a traditional member of the lower orders. Deferential, an errand boy for his superiors, he knows his place; he can always be found at his station on the street corner when he is not off on an errand. So deferential is he, in fact, that he takes to heart the cant that the poor are responsible for their lot, that they have "no business on the face of the earth" and "no right to a New Year." He is a victim in a society that blames the victims for their situation.

The gentlemen from the upper classes that Trotty has to deal with represent a cluster of attitudes that combine to "put down" the poor. Filer is the "philosopher," one of the political economists from the school of hard facts that Dickens also attacks in *Twist* and *Hard Times* (see POLITICAL ECONOMY). Filer has taken MALTHUS to

Leech's sketch of Toby Veck for The Chimes *(1844).*

heart. His specious argument that Trotty has stolen his tripe from the mouths of widows and orphans is humbug—or tripe. It echoes a criticism of the *Carol* leveled by the economist Nassau SENIOR who asked how many people went without food so that Scrooge could give Bob Cratchit the prize turkey. Filer also echoes Malthus in counseling Meg and Richard not to marry. The gentleman in the red waistcoat who celebrates the past and takes no interest in the present satirizes reactionary Toryism, like that of the Young England Movement which idealized medieval peasants and ignored the Victorian poor. Alderman Cute, sharp-tongued and sharp-witted, was based on Sir Peter Laurie, a Middlesex magistrate who vowed to stop the poor from committing suicide by punishing those who tried. Finally, Sir Joseph Bowley, "The Poor Man's Friend and Father," represents a paternalism that demanded dependency as the price the poor had to pay for his support and help. Although Bowley seems to be a Tory landholder, his oppressive paternalism was an attitude found among both Whigs and Tories. Together these men represent the privileged class that takes no responsibility for the poverty around them. They treat the poor as counters or ciphers without individual identity. By blaming them for being poor, they deny their right to a decent life.

The factors that bring about Trotty's conversion from despair to hope are not so clear as those that transform Scrooge. The visions of the bells would seem more calculated to increase his despair, for they show him Meg in an unhappy marriage and then attempting suicide, Lilian surviving by prostitution, and Will Fern radicalized into an incendiary terrorist by the unfair treatment he has received. Nor is Trotty's change brought about by any change in the attitudes of the rich. The separation between rich and poor is not bridged as it was at the end of the *Carol*. Trotty chooses hope because he cannot live in despair. His belief that there are things worth living for is supported in the end by the community of the poor who gather round him—Will and Lilian, Mrs. Chickenstalker, Meg and Richard. The vision of *The Chimes* is of England as two nations that have no connection with each other, the separate nations of rich and poor. Trotty hopes that the community among the poor is enough to enable them to survive, in spite of the neglect and irresponsibility of the rich.

CRITICISM

The most useful work on *The Chimes* is by Michael SLATER in his introduction to the Penguin edition of the Christmas books and in his articles on the topicality of the story (1970) and its composition (1966). Michael GOLDBERG (1972) discusses the social themes in the story and its indebtedness to Thomas CARLYLE.

ADAPTATIONS

Compared to the *Carol*, *The Chimes* has prompted few adaptations. Its initial production, *The Chimes; a Goblin Story of some Bells that rang the Old Year out and the New Year in*, was staged at the ADELPHI THEATRE. The adaptation was done by Gilbert Abbott à Beckett and Mark LEMON from proof sheets supplied by Dickens. Edward STIRLING did a version for the KEELEYs at the Lyceum, but there were only a few other scattered productions in the 1840s. Another significant production did not appear until 1872, when John TOOLE played the lead in *Trotty Veck*, a new version at the Gaiety Theatre in London.

Two silent films of *The Chimes* were produced in 1914 and 1920, but no later film versions have appeared.

Chinaman, Jack   Opium den operator across the court from Princess Puffer. *Drood* (1).

"Chinese Junk, The"   Article describing the junk anchored in the THAMES that offers Londoners an instant visit to China. From the *EXAMINER* (June 24, 1848). *Miscellaneous*.

Chips   Shipwright who makes a deal with the devil in one of the ghost stories told to the Traveller by his childhood nurse. *Uncommercial* (15).

"Chips"   Corrections, additions, or clarifications to articles in *HOUSEHOLD WORDS* appeared under the rubric "Chips." Dickens was responsible for several such pieces in relation to "A Free (and Easy) School" (December 6, 1851); " 'Household Words' and English Wills" (November 16, 1850); "The Samaritan Institution" (May 16, 1857); "Small Beginnings (April 5, 1851). *Stone*.

Chirrup, Mr. and Mrs.   The Nice Little Couple. "Mr. Chirrup has the smartness, and something of the brisk, quick manner of a small bird. Mrs. Chirrup is the prettiest of all little women." The Chirrups are thought to have been based on Dickens's publisher William HALL and his wife. *Young Couples*.

Chisholm, Caroline (1808–1877)   Wife of a captain in the service of the East India Company, Mrs. Chisholm spent time in India and AUSTRALIA before returning in 1848 to England, where she continued and extended her efforts to aid immigrants to the colonies, especially to Australia. Dickens aided her work with the Family Colonisation Loan Society and she provided the letters which he reprinted in "A Bundle of Emigrants' Letters." After visiting her home to collect the letters, Dickens wrote to Angela COUTTS: "I dream of Mrs. Chisholm, and her housekeeping. The dirty faces of her children are my continual companions." She served as the model for Mrs. Jellyby in *Bleak House*.

Chitling, Tom   Member of Fagin's gang who has recently returned from prison and taken up with Betsy. He is at Jacob's Island when Sikes is killed. *Twist*.

Chivery Family   **John** is the turnkey at the MARSHALSEA PRISON during William Dorrit's time there and father to **Young John**, his "sentimental son," who is hopelessly in love with Amy Dorrit. Young John is "small of stature, with rather weak legs, and very weak light hair. . . . But he was great of soul. Poetical, expansive, faithful" (I:18). He pines for Amy by sitting alone amid the laundry (I:22) but is faithful to her to the end, aiding Pancks in uncovering her history (I:35) and forcing Arthur to see how much Amy loves him (II:27). His mother, **Mrs. Chivery**, a "comfortable-looking woman, much respected about HORSEMONGER LANE for her feelings and her conversation" (I:22), has a small tobacconist's shop. *Dorrit.*

Choke, General Cyrus   General in an American militia, member of the WATERTOAST ASSOCIATION OF UNITED SYMPATHIZERS, and "one of the most remarkable men in the country." He introduces Martin to Scadder, agent for the Eden Land Corporation. *Chuzzlewit* (21).

Chollop, Major Hannibal   American frontiersman in EDEN, "esteemed for his devotion to rational liberty; for the better propagation whereof he usually carried a brace of revolving pistols in his coat pocket. . . . He always introduced himself to strangers as a worshipper of Freedom; was the consistent advocate of Lynch law, and slavery" (33). *Chuzzlewit.*

Chopper   William Tinkling's great-uncle, who brings a "shabby" gift to the christening of William's baby brother. "Holiday Romance."

Chopper, Mrs.   Mother of Mrs. Merrywinkle of the Couple who Coddle Themselves. *Young Couples.*

Chops   Dwarf in a sideshow whose real name was Stakes and who performed as Major Tpchoffki of the Imperial Bulgraderian Brigade. After he wins £12,500 in a lottery, he goes into society, fulfilling a lifelong ambition. However, he learns that performing in society is no different from performing in a sideshow, so he returns to the show, where he dies. "Going into Society."

Chorley, Henry (1808–1872)   Reviewer for the ATHENAEUM who reviewed many of Dickens's later novels and wrote the magazine's obituary on Dickens. He was a close friend of the novelist during the last two decades of his life, taking part in some of Dickens's theatricals.

"Chowley"   Nickname of Charles MACSTINGER. *Dombey.*

Chowser, Colonel   One of Ralph Nickleby's questionable dinner guests. *Nickleby* (19).

Christiana   Sweetheart of Michael, the poor relation, she gives him up when his Uncle Chill disinherits him. "Poor Relation."

Christina, Donna   Jingle's Spanish conquest: "splendid creature—loved me to distraction—jealous father—high-souled daughter—handsome Englishman—Donna Christina in despair—prussic acid—stomach pump in my portmanteau—operation performed—old Bolaro in ecstasies—consent to our union—join hands and floods of tears—romantic story—very." *Pickwick* (2).

Christmas   No writer has been more identified with Christmas than Dickens. Largely on the basis of the *Carol* and the other CHRISTMAS BOOKS, Dickens has been variously described as "Father Christmas" and the "inventor" of Christmas; he deserves some credit for helping to rescue the holiday from dour Calvinists, many of whom condemned the traditional Christmas celebrations as pagan rites.

The Dickens Christmas, described in the Pickwickians' celebration at Dingley Dell and in in the festivities in the *Carol*, is one of feasting, storytelling, and merrymaking; present-giving has a very secondary role. It is also a time for reflection—especially on the losses of the past year—and for expressing one's common humanity in charity. Scrooge's nephew Fred characterizes Dickens's view of the holiday as "the only time I know of, in the long calendar of the year, when men and women seem by one consent to open their shut-up hearts freely, and to think of people below them as if they really were fellow-passengers to the grave, and not another race of creatures bound on other journeys" (*Carol*, 1).

Storytelling—especially the telling of ghost stories—is one of the traditions celebrated in *Pickwick* and the Christmas books. It was also the basis for the special Christmas numbers of HOUSEHOLD WORDS and ALL THE YEAR ROUND. For these issues Dickens typically wrote a frame narrative and then collected stories by several other writers to fit the frame. Dickens's contributions to these group efforts are collected as the CHRISTMAS STORIES, even though many of the stories are not about Christmas.

If celebration and feasting predominates in *Pickwick* and the *Carol*, the darker, more reflective side of Christmas is central to some of the other works, particularly the later novels. Redlaw's dark and brooding Christmas (*Haunted Man*) is a prelude to the Christmas season in the later novels: in *Two Cities* Dr. Manette is kidnapped and forced to tend the victims of the St. Evrémondes's oppression during the Christmas season, an episode that leads to his imprisonment and to Madame Defarge's revolutionary anger; Pip's meeting with the convict on the marshes that shadows his later life is the dark Christmas story that begins *Expectations*; the mysterious disappearance of Edwin Drood takes place on an apparently murderous Christmas Eve.

Dickens's ideas about Christmas, especially in the early works, are discussed by Paul Davis (*The Lives and Times of Ebenezer Scrooge*, 1990). Katherine Carolan considers the dark Christmases of the later novels ("Dickens' Last Christmases," *Dalhousie Review*, 1972).

Christmas Books   Dickens gave this title to the volume in the CHEAP EDITION collecting the five stories he had written for Christmas between 1843 and 1848: *A Christmas Carol* (1843); *The Chimes* (1844); *The Cricket on the Hearth* (1845); *The Battle of Life* (1846); and *The Haunted Man* (1848). Although later editions sometimes call them CHRISTMAS STORIES, Dickens used that title for the stories collected from Christmas numbers of *HOUSEHOLD WORDS* and *ALL THE YEAR ROUND*.

Christmas Carol in Prose, A. A Ghost Story of Christmas   First of the five CHRISTMAS BOOKS, published in December 1843 by CHAPMAN & HALL, with illustrations by John LEECH. Although Dickens was motivated by the economic controversies of the time to write the *Carol*, the book was taken as an affirmation of Christmas rather than as a controversial tract. The best known of all Dickens's works, it has become the modern classic of Christmas literature.

SYNOPSIS

(1) Seven years to the day after the death of his partner Jacob Marley, the miser Ebenezer Scrooge works in his

Leech's well-known picture of Scrooge confronting the Spirit of Christmas Present.

counting house on Christmas Eve. The fire is so low and the room so cold that his clerk, Bob Cratchit, attempts to warm his fingers by a candle flame. Scrooge's icy manner chills the office even more than the weather, and his "Bah! Humbug!" dampens the season. He turns down his nephew's invitation to Christmas dinner, drives a caroling boy from his door, and refuses to give anything to charity, suggesting that the poor would be better off dead and thus decreasing "the surplus population." He grudgingly grants Bob a holiday on Christmas, and the clerk plans a grand family celebration on his meager weekly salary of 15 shillings.

Scrooge takes his dinner alone at a "melancholy tavern," then returns home. As he opens his door, he is surprised by the face of his late partner, Jacob Marley, in the door knocker. But he checks the house and finds nothing unusual. Then, as he sits by the fire before retiring, he hears the sound of chains rattling and bells ringing, and the Ghost of Marley enters the room. Scrooge tries to dismiss it as a humbug induced by indigestion, but the ghost convinces him of his reality. He says that he has come to warn Scrooge of his fate, of the chains that his hard-heartedness is forging, and to tell him of his opportunity to change. Marley tells Scrooge that he will be haunted by three spirits, who will show him how to "shun the path I tread." After delivering this message, Marley goes out through the window and joins a crowd of phantoms in the air outside. Scrooge attempts to say "Humbug," but manages only the first syllable. Then he goes to bed.

(2) When the clock strikes one, Scrooge notices a light in his room and sees "a strange figure—like a child: yet not so like a child as like an old man," standing by his bed. This Ghost of Christmas Past takes Scrooge on a journey to view past Christmases in Scrooge's life: a Christmas when Scrooge as a child was left at school alone for the holidays, taking consolation for his loneliness by reading the *Arabian Nights* and *Robinson Crusoe*; a later Christmas when his sister Fan came to the school and took him home for a family celebration; the Christmas in London when Scrooge was apprenticed to old Fezziwig and he and Dick Wilkins helped to turn the warehouse into a festive hall for a Christmas dance and party; the Christmas when Belle, Scrooge's fiancée, returned his ring, telling him that he was more interested in money than in her; finally, a later Christmas when Belle joyfully celebrates the holiday with her husband and children. Shaken by these visions of the past and by what he has lost, Scrooge asks the Spirit to haunt him no longer. Then, taking the Spirit's extinguisher cap, he snuffs out the light of the Spirit as if it were a candle flame, and sinks into a heavy sleep.

(3) The clock again strikes one, but Scrooge sees no sign of another spirit. Then, noticing a light coming from the next room, he opens the door and is presented with a blazing fire and a gigantic spirit enthroned atop a cornucopia of Christmas treats. This Ghost of Christmas Present takes Scrooge into the streets and markets filled with the good will and abundance of the season. Then

he takes him to Bob Cratchit's house, where Mrs. Cratchit and the children are preparing Christmas dinner. After Bob returns from church with Tiny Tim, his crippled son, the family make a feast of their modest board, eating every scrap of goose, mashed potatoes and gravy, applesauce, and Christmas pudding. Then they gather at the hearth and Bob salutes the season, "A Merry Christmas to us all, my dears. God bless us!" and his toast is echoed by Tiny Tim's "God bless us every one!" Moved by the scene, Scrooge asks the Spirit "if Tiny Tim will live," and is told, "If these shadows remain unaltered by the Future, the child will die." Then the Cratchits share family stories and songs, and, with some reluctance on Mrs. Cratchit's part, toast Scrooge as the "founder of the feast." The Spirit then takes Scrooge on a quick tour of the city streets, a poor miner's cabin, a solitary lighthouse, and a ship at sea where simple celebrations are in progress. Finally, they observe the Christmas party at the house of Scrooge's nephew Fred, where Scrooge wishes he could join in the singing and games, even the game of Yes and No where "Uncle Scrooge" becomes the subject of some good-natured mockery as the bear who denies the holiday. As the Spirit ages and prepares to end his "life upon this globe," Scrooges notices two urchins under the Spirit's robe. They are Ignorance and Want, clinging to the Spirit because they have been rejected by mankind. As he disappears, the Spirit warns Scrooge that these children spell Doom.

(4) In the mist and darkness in which the Spirit has vanished, Scrooge sees a phantom "shrouded in a deep black garment, which concealed its head, its face, its form, and left nothing of it visible save one outstretched hand." This Ghost of Christmas Yet to Come shows Scrooge some city businessmen talking unfeelingly about the death of one of their colleagues; a pawnbroker's den where the belongings of the dead man are being sold by his servants; and a darkened room with a corpse laid out on a bed. Scrooge is unwilling to uncover the face and identify the dead man. When Scrooge asks if there is anyone moved by this man's death, the Spirit shows him a couple rejoicing that it has relieved them of their debts, at least for a time. The Spirit then takes Scrooge to the Cratchit house, where the family mourns Tiny Tim. When Scrooge is ready to learn the identity of the dead man, the Spirit takes him to a churchyard and shows him his own tombstone. Shaken, Scrooge insists, "I am not the man I was. . . . Why show me this, if I am past all hope?" He promises to honor Christmas in his heart, to "live in the Past, Present, and Future," and, as he kneels before the Specter and prays to have his fate reversed, the Phantom dwindles into the bedpost on his bed.

(5) Scrooge repeats his prayers and his promises and exclaims that "the shadows of the things that would have been, may be dispelled. They will be. I know they will!" He runs to the window, throws open the shutter, and it is morning. He learns from a boy in the street below that it is Christmas Day. Scrooge is exultant, for he hasn't missed the holiday. He sends the boy to the poulterer's to buy the prize Christmas turkey for the Cratchits. Going out into the streets, he wishes everyone he sees a merry Christmas, gives a large donation to help the poor, attends a Christmas service at church, and goes to his nephew's house for a "wonderful party, wonderful games, wonderful unanimity, won-der-ful happiness!"

The next morning Scrooge waits in the office for Bob Cratchit, who arrives 18 minutes late, apologizing for his tardiness and promising that it will not happen again. Putting on his stern voice, Scrooge asserts, "I am not going to stand this sort of thing any longer, . . . and therefore I am about to raise your salary!" That afternoon, master and clerk share a bowl of Christmas punch. Scrooge "became as good a friend, as good a master, and as good a man, as the old city knew, . . . [and] he knew how to keep Christmas well, if any man alive possessed the knowledge. May that truly be said of us, and all of us! And so, as Tiny Tim observed, God bless Us, Every One!"

COMMENTARY

Early in 1843, in response to a parliamentary report on the exploitation of child laborers in the mines and factories, Dickens promised to strike a "sledge-hammer blow . . . on behalf of the Poor Man's Child." That blow turned out to be *A Christmas Carol*. In September, while visiting MANCHESTER, Dickens conceived the specific idea for the story, and by the middle of December it was on the booksellers' shelves, even though he was also writing the monthly numbers of *Chuzzlewit* at the same time.

Many of *Chuzzlewit*'s themes are also found in the *Carol*. Both stories are about selfishness. Scrooge, like the Chuzzlewits, particularly Jonas and his father, is obsessed with money. Charity, the virtue preached by the Christmas story, is satirically represented in the novel by Pecksniff's shrewish daughter. Bob Cratchit's mild and deferential manner is exaggerated in Tom Pinch's blind admiration for his hypocritical master. Both stories are about a change of heart, Scrooge's overnight transformation and young Martin's painful recognition of his obsession with himself. However, whereas Scrooge's conversion enables him to join the rest of humanity, giving the *Carol* an exultantly positive ending, *Chuzzlewit* remains a much darker story. At the end Martin may enter a caring community with Mary Graham, Tom and Ruth Pinch, and John Westlock, but the unconverted Chuzzlewits remain as selfish as ever. Dickens's intense engagement with the writing of the *Carol* may have been due in part to the relief it offered from the dark world of the novel.

At the heart of the *Carol* Dickens had an economic message: a society in which the masters are only concerned with the bottom line and take no responsibility for the general welfare is a death-dealing society. Scrooge knows nothing about Bob Cratchit and his family; he only knows that Bob makes 15 shillings a week and would cheat his employer by demanding a paid holiday on Christmas day. By taking no interest or responsibility for his clerk's situation, Scrooge becomes morally responsible for Bob's inability to afford medical treatment for Tiny Tim; Scrooge's obsession with money has chained him to cash boxes and caged Tim's legs in steel. All this hardware objectifies Scrooge's (screw, gouge) hard heart. Unless he changes, Scrooge and Tiny Tim will both die; their fates are linked. The condition of the poor is the responsibility of the rich.

Although Dickens's message arose as a response to the exploitation of children in factories and mines, he does not direct his PARABLE specifically at the abuse of working children. Tim's crippled condition is similar to the injuries sustained by factory children, but Dickens blames those who allow ignorance and want to persist for the maimed children, not the spinning and weaving machines. Charity was needed by the society as a whole.

The celebratory impact of the story was more important to its original readers than was its economic message. The wonderful catalogs of the fruits and delicacies in the markets, the descriptions of Fred's Christmas party and the Cratchits' Christmas dinner: these were the striking passages in the story for the Victorian audience. For the *Carol* proved that one didn't need a baronial country house, a burning Yule log, and a sumptuous feast to have Christmas. The holiday could be just as festive in Fezziwig's city warehouse, and the modest meal shared by the urban Cratchit family could have its moments of celebration—as when Mrs. Cratchit delivers the Christmas pudding or Tim blesses "every one."

The simplicity of the story, its neat three-part structure, and Scrooge's overnight conversion, have bothered some critics who want a more realistic tale. In the real world, they suggest, Tiny Tim would die. But Dickens's purpose was to take an old nursery tale and give it "a higher form." He uses fantasy in the manner of the FAIRY TALE, giving the story a timelessness that makes it like Cinderella or Little Red Riding Hood, a folk story that seems to have been in the culture forever. The avuncular narrator increases this effect, telling the story as if it is an oral tale passed down from a time before the invention of writing.

Yet for all its simplicity, the *Carol* has complexity and ambiguity as well. Even before his conversion, Scrooge is more than the stereotypical miser. He enjoys taking on the believers in Christmas and revels in his wit, asserting, for example, that "every idiot who goes about with 'Merry Christmas,' on his lips, should be boiled with his own pudding, and buried with a stake of holly through his heart" (1). His zest for the confrontations with Fred and the charity solicitors is not that of a man who only prefers to be "solitary as an oyster" (1). As we learn something of his life, there are suggestions of painful episodes in the past, like the death of his sister, that may have contributed to his negativism, but Dickens leaves much of this sympathy for Scrooge to the imagination of the reader. Even as he weeps for Tiny Tim, Scrooge is reluctant to reveal the change that is occurring within him. So when the change occurs in Stave 5, the climax is evocative. We share Scrooge's joy as he learns from the boy in the street, a boy he characterizes as "a most intelligent boy," that he has not missed Christmas day.

Dickens imagined his story in musical terms, a carol to be sung or heard, each of its chapters one of five "staves." His timing in this basically oral tale is impeccable, expecially the brevity with which he tells the final stave. When he turned it into the first, and the most popular, of his PUBLIC READINGS, the story took to the platform as if it had been written to be performed aloud.

CRITICISM

Michael SLATER's edition of the Christmas books includes a good introduction to the *Carol*. Paul Davis, in *The Lives and Times of Ebenezer Scrooge* (1990), discusses the many adaptations of the story and the ways in which they articulate different readings of it.

ADAPTATIONS

The *Carol* has been adapted for stage, screen, and other media more than any other of Dickens's works. Eight stage adaptations were in production within two months of its first publication, and new adaptations continue to appear on an almost annual basis. Edward STIRLING (1843), C. Z. BARNETT (1843), J. C. Buckstone (1901), Bransby WILLIAMS (1928), Maxwell Anderson (1954), Barbara FIELD (1977), and Israel Horowitz (1978) are among the playwrights who have adapted the story. Notable film versions include Sir Seymour HICKS's 1935 cinematic version of a role he had played for years on the stage; Alastair SIM's masterful portrayal of a tormented Scrooge (1951); Albert Finney's "counterculture" Scrooge in the 1970 musical; and George C. Scott's 1984 performance in a film for television. Other famous Scrooges include Bransby Williams, Lionel BARRYMORE, Alec GUINNESS (also remembered for his portrayal of Marley in the 1970 musical *Scrooge*), Sir Ralph Richardson, and Patrick Stewart.

The *Carol* has also been a perennial favorite for illustrators. Leech's original pictures have been complemented by the later work of EYTINGE, BARNARD, RACKHAM, C. E. BROCK and innumerable others. Noteworthy contemporary illustrators who have pictured the story include Ronald Searle (1960), Michael Foreman (1983), Michael Cole (1985), Lisbeth Zwerger (1988), Roberto Innocenti (1990), and Ida Applebroog (1993).

The story is so embedded in the popular culture that it is annually translated, parodied, and adapted in various ways to speak to changing times. Recent translations into "Muppet" (1982) and "Disney" (1983), and Bill Murray's modernization in *Scrooged* (1988) are among the most recent in the ongoing folk process of adapting the story.

"Christmas Carol, A" Song celebrating the Christmas season sung by Wardle in *Pickwick* (28). It was set to music when the novel first appeared and was later included in *The Book of British Song*.

"Christmas Dinner, A" Sketch describing a family Christmas at the home of Uncle and Aunt George. Originally published as "Scenes and Characters No. 10. Christmas Festivities" in BELL'S LIFE IN LONDON (December 27, 1835). *Boz*.

"Christmas in the Frozen Regions" Article by Dickens and Robert McCormick, surgeon aboard the Antarctic expedition in 1834–43, describing Christmas on the expedition, for the Christmas number of HOUSEHOLD WORDS (December 21, 1850). *Stone*.

Christmas Stories Title given to collections of Dickens's stories for the Christmas numbers of HOUSEHOLD WORDS and ALL THE YEAR ROUND. Typically Dickens wrote a frame narrative and then invited other writers to submit stories fitting the frame. The collections include only the frame narratives and the stories that Dickens wrote, except for "No Thoroughfare," which he wrote with Wilkie COLLINS. The following stories were included in the CHARLES DICKENS EDITION and the LIBRARY EDITION: "The Seven Poor Travellers," "The Holly Tree," "The Wreck of the Golden Mary," "The Perils of Certain English Prisoners," "Going into Society," "The Haunted House," "A Message from the Sea," "Tom Tiddler's Ground," "Somebody's Luggage," "Mrs. Lirriper's Lodgings," "Mrs. Lirriper's Legacy," "Doctor Marigold," "Two Ghost Stories" ("To Be Taken with a Grain of Salt" and "No. 1 Branch Line: The Signalman"), "The Boy at Mugby," and "No Thoroughfare." Later editions added the rest of "Mugby Junction," "What Christmas Is as We Grow Older," "A Christmas Tree," "The Poor Relation's Story," "The Child's Story," "The Schoolboy's Story," "Nobody's Story," and "The Lazy Tour of Two Idle Apprentices." Stories indicated as *Christmas Stories* in this volume follow the contents for the OXFORD ILLUSTRATED EDITION.

"Christmas Tree, A" Dickens's essay for the Christmas number of HOUSEHOLD WORDS, 1850. As he looks at a Christmas tree, he remembers the Christmases of his childhood: the toys he played with; the toy theaters and the pantomime; fairy tales and Arabian Nights stories; ghost stories told around the Christmas fire. *Christmas Stories*.

Christopher Sixty-one-year-old waiter who "comes from a family of Waiters"; he narrates "Somebody's Luggage." He acquires some luggage left by a hotel guest, discovers some manuscripts in the bags, and gets them published.

Chuckster Witherden's clerk and a member of the GLORIOUS APOLLOS with his friend Dick Swiveller (14). He is jealous of Kit Nubbles's favor in the eyes of the Garlands and distrusts the boy, condemning him as a snob. *Curiosity Shop*.

Chuffey Anthony Chuzzlewit's devoted clerk, "a little blear-eyed, weazen-faced, ancient man. . . . He looked as if . . . somebody had just found him in a lumber-closet" (11). After Anthony's death, he lives with Jonas and Mercy and transfers his loyalty to Mercy. To silence him, Jonas places him in the care of Mrs. Gamp (46), but after Jonas is exposed, Chuffey tells of the young man's abortive attempts to poison his father (51). *Chuzzlewit*.

Church Street Jenny Wren and Lizzie Hexam share lodgings in this street off SMITH SQUARE in Westminster. *Mutual Friend*.

Churchill, R. C. (1916–) Journalist, literary historian and critic. *A Bibliography of Dickensian Criticism, 1836–1975* (1975) provides an annotated bibliography of criticism on each of the novels and on a range of Dickensian topics and includes many apt quotations from the works cited. Churchill's essay on "The Genius of Charles Dickens" in *From Dickens to Hardy*, ed. B. Ford (1958; 1982) discusses Dickens as the Shakespeare of the Victorian age, assesses the reasons for his popularity, especially as a comic writer; and summarizes his career from an unusual perspective which judges *Chuzzlewit*, *Bleak House*, and *Dorrit* his "major achievements."

Chuzzlewit, Martin The name of two central figures in *Chuzzlewit*. **Old Martin** is "a strong and vigorous old man with a will of iron" who obstinately believes that everyone is out to secure his money. He trusts no one. Even the grandson that he has groomed to become his heir, **Young Martin**, earns his distrust when he disobeys his grandfather and falls in love with Mary Graham. He too bears the family traits of stubbornness and preoccupation with self. After he is turned out, young Martin goes to study architecture with Pecksniff, a relative who his grandfather detests (5). When he is dismissed by Pecksniff at old Martin's prompting (12), Martin goes off to America to seek his fortune (15). There he falls ill and nearly dies (33). His experiences in America make him more aware of the needs of others and of his own selfishness. His grandfather also seems to be changed at the same time, to realize how his suspicions and his need for control soured his relations with others, but his earlier paranoia can also be interpreted as a pious fraud adopted to force the growth of his grandson. In the end the two Martins are reunited and the old man blesses his grandson's marriage to Mary Graham (52). *Chuzzlewit*.

Chuzzlewit Family Old family at the center of *Martin Chuzzlewit* that is "descended in a direct line from

Adam and Eve" (1). Dickens satirically traces their lineage through British history, including the Chuzzlewit who arrived with William the Conqueror and Chuzzlewit Fawkes of the Gunpowder Plot. Their claim to aristocratic connections derives from **Diggory**, who "was in the habit of perpetually dining with Duke Humphrey" (i.e. going without food), and **Toby**, whose dying words identified his grandfather as "Lord No Zoo" (1). The family patriarchs at the time of the novel are **Old Martin**, the rich family head who is so beseiged by fawning relatives hoping to inherit his wealth that he trusts no one, and his brother **Anthony**, a businessman "sharpened by the wariness and cunning of his life" (4). Tightfisted, greedy, and close, Anthony raised his son **Jonas** to similar virtues. Both of them measure value solely in monetary terms; both seek to control others. After Anthony becomes aware that Jonas is trying to poison him for his inheritance, he dies a broken man, realizing that his teaching and example have been too effective (18). Jonas, "conducted from his cradle on the strictest principles of the main chance" and taught "to overreach everybody," has no sympathy for anyone else (8). His marriage to Mercy Pecksniff (26) is a commercial transaction, and he abuses and demeans her. After Montague plays on his greed and threatens him with knowledge of his plot to poison Anthony, the cornered Jonas turns murderous. He clubs Montague to death (47) and after he is captured he poisons himself (51). Among the other Chuzzlewit relatives who seek old Anthony's wealth are **George**, "a gay bachelor cousin . . . inclined to corpulency" (4), **Mrs. Ned**, widow of old Martin's brother, and her three daughters; **Mrs. SPOTTLETOE**, a niece; and **Chevy SLYME**, a nephew. *Chuzzlewit.*

Cicero Ex-slave whom Mark Tapley meets in New York; he bears the physical scars from his mistreatment as a slave. When he got too old to work, his master allowed him to buy his freedom. *Chuzzlewit* (17).

Circumlocution Office, The Dickens's satiric representation of the Civil Service in *Dorrit*, written in the wake of the bureaucratic bumbling during the Crimean War. Staffed on the principles of nepotism and aristocratic privilege and entangled in red tape, the Circumlocution Office is the special preserve of the Barnacle family: "No public business of any kind could possibly be done at any time, without the acquiescense of the Circumlocution Office. . . . Whatever was required to be done, the Circumlocution Office was beforehand with all the public departments in the art of perceiving—HOW NOT TO DO IT" (I:10). The Office makes it impossible for Daniel Doyce to secure a patent for his invention, a theme Dickens also develops in "A Poor Man's Tale of a Patent."

Circus From childhood on Dickens was fascinated by the circus, a form of popular entertainment that appeared in England in the mid-18th century when Philip

Astley opened his circus near WESTMINSTER BRIDGE in 1769. Dickens describes the elaborate equestrian performances at ASTLEY'S in *Boz*. As the young Dickens might have done, Kit Nubbles takes his mother there when he receives his first quarter's pay from the Garlands (*Curiosity Shop*, 39). Dickens reports his delight in clowns in the preface to Joseph GRIMALDI's memoirs. The traveling showmen in *Curiosity Shop* and Mr. Chops's career as a performer in *Going into Society* involve entertainments related to the circus, but Dickens's most extensive use of the circus is in *Hard Times* where it functions as the symbolic counter to Coketown and the school of hard facts. Sleary and company represent the realm of imagination and they make up a community where the cynicism, opportunism, and exploitation of Coketown is absent. In Coketown, where imagination is suppressed, the serpents and elephants of the circus have been perverted: "It was a town of machinery and tall chimneys, out of which interminable serpents of smoke trailed themselves forever and ever, and never got uncoiled, . . . and where the piston of the steam-engines worked up and down, like the head of an elephant in a state of melancholy madness" (I:5).

Articulating Sleary's—and Dickens's—principle that "people must be amused," the circus also challenges those who wanted to suppress such popular entertainments, particularly on Sundays. Dickens frequently attacked such killjoys.

Paul SCHLICKE (1985) describes the Victorian circuses that Dickens knew and makes a detailed analysis of the circus in *Hard Times*.

City, The The old City of London as defined by its original boundaries. In the nineteenth century—and now—the City is largely the financial district, around the area of ST. PAUL'S CATHEDERAL, in the center of London. It does not include the West End and such famous landmarks as Buckingham Palace or the Houses of Parliament.

"City of London Churches" The Traveller tells of a year of making Sunday visits to the dusty old churches in the CITY which "remain the tombs of the old citizens who lie beneath them and around them, Monuments of another age." *Uncommercial* (9).

City of London Theatre Theater in Norton Folgate, Spitalfields, where Potter and Smithers drunkenly disturb the performance and are ejected. *Boz*, "Making a Night."

"City of the Absent, The" The Traveller's account of his visits to obscure CITY churchyards. *Uncommercial* (23).

City Road, North London The Micawbers live in WINDSOR TERRACE off this thoroughfare when David boards with them (*Copperfield*, 11). Florence Dombey is kidnapped by old Mrs. Brown in the City Road as Polly is watching for her son returning from school (*Dombey*, 6).

Clapham Residential area in south London where the stockbroker Mr. Gattleton lives at Rose Villa, Clapham Rise (*Boz*, "Porter"). The Poor Relation has lodgings in Clapham Road ("Poor Relation").

Clara English bride haunted by Signor Dellombra. *Reprinted*, "At Dusk."

Clare, Miss Ada Ward in CHANCERY who is committed by the court to the guardianship of John Jarndyce (3). Esther Summerson, who refers to Ada as "my beauty," is chosen to be her companion. Although she is in love with her fellow ward, Richard Carstone, she is also worried about his restless and suspicious behavior. She secretly marries him shortly before his death (51) and is left with an infant son to be cared for by Jarndyce (67). *Bleak House*.

Clare Market Slum quarter of London's HOLBORN district, noteworthy for its ostentatious gin-shops (*Boz*, "Gin Shops"). The MAGPIE AND STUMP was located nearby (*Pickwick*, 20).

Clarendon Edition Definitive scholarly edition of Dickens's works inaugurated in 1966 with Kathleen TILLOTSON's edition of *Oliver Twist* and published by Oxford University Press. Under the general editorship of John BUTT and Kathleen TILLOTSON, the Clarendon edition provides critical texts of the novels, indicating variations in the manuscript and the editions published during Dickens's lifetime. By 1995 about half of the novels had been issued in this edition.

Clark Wharf manager who turns over Florence Dombey to Walter Gay after she has been kidnapped. *Dombey* (6).

Clark, Betsy Flirtatious maid who shows an interest in Mr. Todd's young man. *Boz*, "Streets—Morning."

Clark, Mrs. Potential employer to whom the agency sends Madeline Bray. *Nickleby* (16).

Clarke, Joseph Clayton ("Kyd") Late Victorian illustrator whose watercolor *Characters from Charles Dickens* (1889) are among the best known renderings of Dickens in the late 19th century. Kyd also illustrated editions of *Copperfield* and *Expectations* in the 1880s. Another example of his work appears in illustration 60 (MICAWBER).

Clarke, Maria Woman scheduled for hanging on Easter Tuesday, 1851, a "decent compliment to the fes-

Kyd's (Joseph Clayton Clarke's) rendering of Mr. Jingle.

tival of Easter," Dickens satirically remarks. *Miscellaneous*, "Finishing Schoolmaster."

Clarke, Mary Cowden (1809–1898) Author of the *Complete Concordance to Shakespeare* (1844–45), she met Dickens in 1848 and joined his theatrical group, playing Dame Quickly in *Merry Wives of Windsor*, Tib in *Every Man in His Humour*, and Mrs. Hilary in *Love, Law, and Physic*. A lifelong friend, she wrote of Dickens and his "indefatigable vivacity, cheeriness, and good humour" in *Recollections of Writers* (1878).

Clarke, Susan Maiden name of Tony Weller's second wife. *Pickwick*.

Clarkson Lawyer who defends Shepherdson and his confederates in "The Butcher's Story" narrated by Sergeant Mith. *Reprinted*, "Detective Police."

Clarriker Young shipping broker who is looking for a partner and from whom Pip buys the place for Herbert Pocket (52). After his own loss of expectations, Pip himself joins the firm (58). *Expectations*.

Clatter   Physician who diagnoses Our Bore's complaint as "Accumulation of fat about the heart." *Reprinted*, "Bore."

"Clause for the New Reform Bill, A"   Article by Dickens and Wilkie COLLINS for *HOUSEHOLD WORDS* (October 9, 1858), proposing a new reform bill that would instruct mayors not to decorate their cities for a visit from the Queen, thus allowing the Queen to see her people "in *their* natural characters." *Stone*.

Claypole, Noah   Charity boy who is Sowerberry's assistant, "a large-headed, small-eyed youth, of lumbering make and heavy countenance" (5). Noah bullies and taunts Oliver and when he insults Oliver's mother, Oliver strikes back (6). Noah runs off to London with Charlotte (42), joins Fagin's gang (43), and, using the alias Morris Bolter, spies on Nancy for Fagin (46). He testifies against Fagin and takes up a profession as a police informer (52). *Twist*.

Cleaver, Fanny ("Jenny Wren")   The crippled doll's dressmaker with whom Lizzie Hexam takes lodgings after her father's death. Although she is only an adolescent, she is "sharp" beyond her years and sharp-tongued; she has the manner and responsibilities of an adult, earning a living by her craft and caring for her alcoholic father, **Mr. Cleaver ("Mr. Dolls")**, as if he were her child. She is also a visionary, aware of a spiritual world unsullied by materialistic reality. With Riah she aids Lizzie's escape from London and keeps the secret of her whereabouts. But her father reveals the secret for some gin money from Wrayburn (III: 16). She is called to Eugene's bedside after his beating and attends his recuperation (IV: 9). The final chapters suggest that a marriage to Sloppy may be in her future. *Mutual Friend*.

Clennam, Arthur   "The son . . . of a hard father and mother. . . . The only child of parents who weighed, measured, and priced everything; for whom what could not be weighed, measured, and priced, had no existence. Strict people as the phrase is, professors of a stern religion, their very religion was a gloomy sacrifice of tastes and sympathies that were never their own, offered up as part of a bargain for the security of their posessions"

Arthur Clennam's imprisonment in the Marshalsea externalizes the imprisoning inner guilt that defines his character. An illustration for the Household Edition by James Mahoney.

(I:2). Arthur is the love child of **Mr. Clennam** and a dancer and the adopted son of his "mother," **Mrs. Clennam**. She controls the family business from her invalid chair in a crumbling house in London, and adopts the boy to raise him in righteousness and retribution. The Clennams' loveless marriage, arranged for financial reasons by Mr. Clennam's uncle, the miserly **Gilbert**, leads to guilt and regret. Knowing that Arthur's natural mother has gone mad and died, the guilty Gilbert adds a codicil to his will, leaving £1,000 to the youngest daughter or cousin of her benefactor, Frederick Dorrit, a provision that makes Little Dorrit the beneficiary of the will. But along with supressing the story of her husband's prior liason, Mrs. Clennam suppresses this codicil. At the beginning of the novel, Arthur returns from 20 years in China, where he has been working unhappily in the family business until the death of his father. His harsh upbringing has left him without will and purpose in his life. He suspects that his parents have a guilty secret, and when he sees Little Dorrit working as his mother's servant, he intuitively links her with the suppressed secret and undertakes to learn her story, which will ultimately reveal his own. Arthur leaves the family business (I:5), becomes a partner to Daniel Doyce (I:23), and encourages the investigation by Pancks that uncovers Mr. Dorrit's inheritance (I:35). He has a disillusioning reunion with his garrulous childhood sweetheart, Flora Finching (I:13), half-heartedly considers courting Pet Meagles but withdraws in the face of Henry Gowan's interest in her (I:28), and only after convincing himself that he is too old for romantic impulses realizes that he loves Little Dorrit (II:29) and marries her (II:34). The Calvinist Mrs. Clennam attempts to keep the stories of the past suppressed, but Arthur's suspicions, the investigation that he promotes, and the machinations of Rigaud (Blandois), who has obtained the codicil and other Clennam papers, finally reveal the truth. Mrs. Clennam rises from her paralysis, secures the forgiveness of Little Dorrit, and escapes the collapse of her house—which kills Blandois—only to live on speechless and paralyzed for three more years. *Dorrit*.

"Cleopatra" Name by which Mrs. SKEWTON is known, based on a sketch of her entitled "Cleopatra," published when she was a young woman. *Dombey* (21).

Clergyman (1) Wardle's guest at DINGLEY DELL who recites "The Ivy Green" and tells the story of "The CONVICT'S RETURN." *Pickwick* (6).

Clergyman (2) The kindly old pastor of the village church where Little Nell is keeper of the keys and is finally buried, "a simple-hearted old gentleman . . . very little acquainted with the world." *Curiosity Shop* (52).

Clerkenwell Area of London north of HOLBORN. The Artful Dodger and Charley Bates pick Mr. Brown-low's pocket at a bookstore near Clerkenwell Green (*Twist*, 10); Gabriel Varden's house and locksmithing business is located here (*Rudge*, 4); Phil Squod worked as a tinker in Clerkenwell (*Bleak House*, 26); Jarvis Lorry lives in Clerkenwell when it is still something of a suburb (*Two Cities*, II:6); Mr. Venus has his taxidermy business in Clerkenwell (*Mutual Friend*, I:7).

Cleverly, William and Susannah Mormon brother and sister on their way to Salt Lake. *Uncommercial* (22).

Click (1) Gas-fitter and fellow lodger of the sidewalk artist who narrates "His Brown-Paper Parcel." "Somebody's Luggage."

Click (2) Inhabitant of Rats' Castle, a thieves' den in ST. GILES. *Reprinted*, "Inspector Field."

Clickett ("The Orfling") "A dark-complexioned young woman, with a habit of snorting" who serves as the Micawber's maid. She is an orphan from ST. LUKE'S WORKHOUSE. *Copperfield* (11).

Clickett, Miss "The youngest Miss Clickett but one" is the object of the boyish affections of the narrator and his rival, "the Fiend Paynter." *Miscellaneous*, "New Year's Day."

Clickit, Mr. and Mrs. Plausible Couple praised by Bobtail Widgers. *Young Couples*.

Clifford's Inn Oldest of The Inns of CHANCERY, among the the INNS OF COURT established in 1345 on the north side of FLEET STREET opposite the TEMPLE. Jack Bamber tells Pickwick the tale of a suicide that occurred here (*Pickwick*, 21); Melchisedech's offices are located here (*Bleak House*, 34); Tip Dorrit languishes here as a clerk (*Dorrit*, I:7); Boffin discusses employing Rokesmith as a secretary in the courtyard of the Inn (*Mutual Friend*, I:8).

Clifton, Gloucestershire Suburb of BRISTOL where Arabella Allen is sequestered with her aunt. *Pickwick* (38).

Clip Hairdresser who is among the group listening to Robert Bolton's tale. *Mudfog*, "Bolton."

Clissold, Lawrence Clerk who embezzles £500 from his employer and lays the blame on Tregarthen. "The Message from the Sea" clears up the crime.

Clive Clerk at the CIRCUMLOCUTION OFFICE. *Dorrit* (I:10).

Clocker　Grocer in a seaside village who has heard the cry of distress from an emigrant ship. *Reprinted*, "Out of Season."

Cloisterham　Cathedral town that is the setting for *Drood*—a thinly disguised version of ROCHESTER.

Clubber, Sir Thomas　Commissioner of the Chatham Dockyard who creates "a great sensation" when he enters the charity ball at the BULL INN, ROCHESTER with **Lady Clubber** and his **two daughters**. *Pickwick* (2).

Cluppins, Mrs. Elizabeth　A friend of Mrs. Bardell and sister of Mrs. Raddle. "A little, brisk, busy-looking woman, she gives evidence at the Bardell versus Pickwick trial. *Pickwick* (34).

Cly, Roger　The former servant of Charles Darnay who gives evidence against him at the trial (II:3). Later he is buried in a sham funeral (II:14). Eventually he finds his way to France as a spy and ends up on the guillotine (III:15). *Two Cities*.

"Co."　After Martin Chuzzlewit makes him an equal partner in his American architectural firm, Chuzzlewit and Co., Mark TAPLEY refers to himself as "Co." and is known by that appellation in EDEN. *Chuzzlewit* (21).

Coaches　In the popular imagination, Dickens is often associated with the stagecoach and the inns where the coaches stopped to change horses. This image may be largely derived from *Pickwick*, in which the Pickwickians travel about England by coach, but coach journeys are important in many of the novels, especially those prior to *Dombey*. In retrospective works like *Copperfield* and *Expectations*, coach journeys also play an important role, and the latter novel is structured in "stages" that turn Pip's life into a coach journey. Humphry HOUSE points out that the age of the coach was largely past by the time Dickens began writing; indeed, the transition from the coach to the RAILWAY symbolized for most Victorians the tumultuous changes wrought by the INDUSTRIAL REVOLUTION. So the coach, even for the Victorians, was a nostalgic reminder of another time. House sums up the special significance of the coach to Dickens and other writers of his generation: " 'Coaching' has thus become idealized in the popular memory not merely as a striking and picturesque feature of a vanished world, but because a whole generation, in which there were many writers, caught by admiration of the coaches in their short-lived pride [during their boyhood years], was unable to work off in the boredom of adult experience the glamorous ambitions of boyhood."

"Coavinses"　Skimpole's name for NECKETT, derived from Neckett's employment as an agent for Coavinses' Sponging House. *Bleak House* (6).

Cobb, Tom　General chandler and post office keeper at CHIGWELL and a regular at the MAYPOLE. *Rudge*.

Cobbey　Pupil at DOTHEBOYS HALL who receives 18d. in pocket money from his sister that is appropriated by Mrs. Squeers. *Nickleby* (8).

Cobbler, The　Prisoner with whom Sam Weller shares a room in FLEET PRISON. *Pickwick* (44).

Cobbs　Boots at the HOLLY TREE who tells Charley, the narrator, the story of Master Harry Walmers and Norah. "Holly Tree."

Cobham　Village in KENT near GAD'S HILL to which Mr. Tupman retreats after Rachel Wardle runs off with Jingle (*Pickwick*, 11). The LEATHER BOTTLE, the inn where Tupman stays, and the town itself were favorite destinations for Dickens and remain sites of Dickensian pilgrimage.

Cochrane and M'Crone　Publishers of the MONTHLY MAGAZINE, in which Dickens published several early sketches.

Cocker, Indignation　Patron of the Temeraire who objects to the arithmetic on his restaurant bill, interrupting the waiter who is serving the Traveller. *Uncommercial* (33).

Cockney School, The　Genre of popular fiction at the end of the 19th century, represented by such works as Arthur Morrison's *Tales of Mean Streets* (1894), Arthur St. John Adcock's *East End Idylls* (1897), Somerset Maugham's *Liza of Lambeth* (1897), and the works of Edwin PUGH and William Pett Ridge. Dickens was an important influence on these writers, both for his depiction of life in London's inner city as, for example, in TOM-ALL-ALONE's in *Bleak House* and the LIMEHOUSE of *Mutual Friend*, and for such great Cockney characters as Sam Weller and Sairey Gamp.

Codger, Miss　Literary lady at the levee for Elijah Pogram. *Chuzzlewit* (34).

Codlin, Thomas　Proprietor of a PUNCH AND JUDY show and partner of Harris, or Short, with whom Nell and her Grandfather travel in their wanderings. Devious and suspicious, he plans to sell Nell's secret to anyone who will pay for it, but Nell slips away from him at the races before he is able to do so (19). Later he tells the single gentleman of his association with her (37). *Curiosity Shop*.

Coiler, Mrs.　Neighbor to Matthew and Belinda Pocket, "a widow lady of that highly sympathetic nature that she agreed with everybody, blessed everybody, and shed smiles and tears on everybody, according to circumstances." *Expectations* (23).

Coketown   Industrial town that serves as the setting for *Hard Times*; "a town of machinery and tall chimneys, out of which interminable serpents of smoke trailed themselves forever and ever, and never got uncoiled. It had a black canal in it, and a river that ran purple with ill-smelling dye, and vast piles of building full of windows where there was a rattling and trembling all day long, and where the piston of the steam-engine worked monotonously up and down like the head of an elephant in a state of melancholy madness" (I: 5). Commentators have disagreed over whether the original of Coketown was MANCHESTER or PRESTON; it is safe to say that it is neither, but rather a town based on Dickens's impressions of both places and of other industrial towns in the north of England.

Charles Collins's cover for the serial parts of Edwin Drood, *completed before illness forced him to abandon the project, has fed speculation about Dickens's intentions for the unfinished portions of the story.*

Colburn, Henry (d. 1855)   Publisher and magazine proprietor; partner of Richard BENTLEY from 1829 to 1832. He published the *PIC-NIC PAPERS* (1841).

Coldbath Fields   Site of The Middlesex House of Correction in CLERKENWELL, noted for its introduction of the Silent System in 1834, under which prisoners were required to remain absolutely silent. *Boz*, "Last Cab-Driver."

Colden, David C. (1797–1850)   American lawyer and public servant, son of the Mayor of New York City, who acted as Dickens's host in NEW YORK on the author's first visit to AMERICA in 1842. He first met Dickens in England in 1840.

Coleshaw, Miss   Passenger on the *Golden Mary* who is on her way to California to join her brother. "Golden Mary."

Collins   Policeman keeping order in the House of Commons. *Boz*, "Parliamentary Sketch."

Collins, Charles Allston (1828–1873)   PRE-RAPHAELITE painter, essayist, and novelist (*Bar Sinister*, 1864); younger brother of Wilkie COLLINS. He was a contributor to *HOUSEHOLD WORDS* and *ALL THE YEAR ROUND*; he also designed the cover for *Drood*, but ill health prevented him from illustrating the novel. He married Dickens's daughter Kate (see Kate Macready DICKENS) in 1860.

Collins, Philip (1923–   )   Professor at the University of Leicester, author of numerous books and articles on Dickens and Victorian literature; perhaps the most important contemporary Dickens scholar. His *Dickens and Crime* (1962) and *Dickens and Education* (1963) were pioneering studies of two areas of Victorian culture that are central in Dickens's novels. In numerous articles, critical essays, and reviews he has discussed and contributed to nearly every aspect of Dickens studies. As editor of the *Letters* (1960–63), *Dickens: The Critical Heritage* (1971), *The Public Readings of Charles Dickens* (1975), and *Dickens: Interviews and Recollections* (1981), Collins has greatly enlarged our understanding of the cultural and literary context in which Dickens worked. He has also provided important bibliographical studies of Dickens's works and of Dickens scholarship and criticism in *The Cambridge Bibliography* (1970) and in George H. FORD's *Victorian Fiction* (1978).

Collins, (William) Wilkie (1824–1889)   English novelist, playwright, and journalist who collaborated with Dickens on several projects and who was among Dickens's closest companions during the last two decades of Dickens's life. Dickens met Collins in 1851 when Collins was in the company performing Edward Bulwer LYTTON's *Not so Bad as We Seem*. Collins joined the staff

Wilkie Collins.

of HOUSEHOLD WORDS in 1856 and serialized his two best-known novels, *The Woman in White* (1860) and *The Moonstone* (1868), in ALL THE YEAR ROUND. The two novelists collaborated on *The Lazy Tour of Two Idle Apprentices* (1857), on several Christmas numbers of *Household Words* and *All The Year Round*, and on essays for the same periodicals. Dickens produced Collins's plays *The Lighthouse* (1855) and *The Frozen Deep* (1857). Collins's unconventional and bohemian way of life made him a congenial, accepting colleague, friend, and traveling companion. For a discussion of Collins's possible influence on Dickens as a writer of DETECTIVE STORIES, see T. S. ELIOT's essay "Wilkie Collins and Dickens" (1932).

Colonel Forger awaiting execution in NEWGATE PRISON who offers Wemmick some portable property. *Expectations* (32).

Colosseum Building in Regent's Park in which a panoramic view of London from the top of ST. PAUL'S CATHEDRAL, 64 feet high and covering the circumference of the building, was on display. *Boz*, "Greenwich Fair."

Commercial Road Street in WHITECHAPEL where Captain Cuttle buys the ballad of "Lovely Peg" (*Dombey*, 9); also mentioned in *Uncommercial* (3).

"Common Sense on Wheels" Article for HOUSEHOLD WORDS (April 12, 1851) by Dickens, William Henry WILLS, and E. C. Grenville MURRAY, discussing the need for reforms of the hackney coach trade and describing the regulations in several European cities. *Stone*.

Compact Enchantress, The French actress who shares the train compartment with the narrator on a journey from London to Paris. *Reprinted*, "Flight."

Compeyson Fast-talking forger, swindler, and conman who deceives Miss Havisham in order to secure her money and then jilts her on the day of the wedding. He is Magwitch's accomplice, who uses his boarding-school polish and good looks—in spite of the scar on his face—to cast blame on Magwitch and get himself a lighter sentence, thus prompting Magwitch's vengeance and desire to create a gentleman. Compeyson is captured on the marshes as he fights with Magwitch, whose desire for vengeance overcomes his will to escape (5). Compeyson learns of Magwitch's return to England and aids the police in capturing him, though Compeyson drowns in the struggle (53–55). He is married to **Sally**, whom he physically abuses. *Expectations*.

Conciergerie Ancient French prison in which Charles Darnay is held when Sydney Carton changes places with him. *Two Cities* (III:13).

"Confession Found in a Prison in the Time of Charles the Second, A" Story included in *Master Humphrey's Clock*, narrated by an officer in the army of King Charles II as he awaits execution for murdering his nephew. The officer tells how the murder came about, of his guilt after committing it, and how he was caught by two bloodhounds who entered his garden and exposed the grave where he had buried the boy. *Humphrey* (2).

"Convict's Return, The" INTERPOLATED TALE in *Pickwick*, told by the parish clergyman at DINGLEY DELL about one of his parishiners, John Edmunds. Raised by a drunken father and a mother who spoiled him, Edmunds is transported for robbery. When he returns anonymously to the village many years later, he meets his father; the stressful reunion causes the father's death from a ruptured blood vessel and prompts the reformation of the son, who then enters the service of the clergyman. He dies three years later. *Pickwick* (6).

Conway, General Historical figure, soldier and politician Henry Seymour Conway (1721–95). He stands up to the Gordon rioters and prevents their incursion into the House of Commons. *Rudge* (49).

Cook, Captain   Commander of the Cunard steamship *Russia* on which the Traveller sails from NEW YORK to LIVERPOOL. *Uncommercial* (21).

Cook's Court   Street off CHANCERY LANE where Snagsby has his stationary shop. Based on Took's Court. *Bleak House* (10).

Coolidge, Archibald C. (1928–   )   Professor, University of Iowa, whose work on *Dickens as a Serial Novelist* (1967) was among the early studies of the ways in which serial publication affected the literary qualities of Dickens's novels.

Cooling, Kent   Village at the edge of the marshes northeast of ROCHESTER that served as one of the models for Pip's village in *Expectations*. Dickens was fond of walking here on his rambles from GAD'S HILL, though he reduced the number of "little stone lozenges" that marked the graves of Pip's five brothers from the 13 such gravestones in Cooling churchyard. *Expectations* (1).

Cooper, Augustus   Young man "in the oil and colour line" whose mother, "having managed her husband and *his* business in his lifetime, took to managing her son and *his* business after his decease." Augustus, to escape his mother's control, takes dancing lessons at Signor Billsmethi's Academy, is sued for breach of promise by Miss Billsmethi, and is rescued by his mother. *Boz*, "Dancing Academy."

Cooper, Frederick Fox   Victorian adaptor of Dickens's works for the theater, Cooper turned at least seven of Dickens's novels into plays, most notably *Master Humphrey's Clock* (1840), and *Hard Times* (1854). He was not scrupulous in maintaining fidelity to the original text; his adaptation of *Two Cities, The Incarcerated Victim of the Bastille* (1860), for example, managed to save Carton's life.

Copperfield, Clara   David Copperfield's mother, a "childish widow" (1) before the birth of David, her first child. Youthful, weak, vain, and sickly, she is described by Aunt Betsey as "a very Baby" (1). She marries a second husband, Mr. Murdstone (3), but she fades under his regime of "firmness" and, with her infant **son** from the second marriage, dies while David is still a boy (9). *Copperfield*.

Copperfield, David   Author who narrates his personal history in the eponymous novel to let his readers decide "whether [he] shall turn out to be the hero of [his] own life" (1). Posthumous son of **David Copperfield** of Blunderstone, who died before he was born, and **Clara Copperfield**, a young, pretty, and weak widow, David dislikes her second husband, Murdstone, challenges his authority and bites his thumb (4). He is sent away to SALEM HOUSE School, where he is mistreated and forms a close friendship with James Steerforth

(5–9). After his mother's death, he is sent to London to work in MURDSTONE AND GRINBY's wine-bottling warehouse (10), flees from there to Dover to his Aunt Betsey Trotwood (12), who sends him to school in CANTERBURY (15). After school he is apprenticed to the law (23); unwisely marries **Dora Spenlow**, his boss's daughter (42); and gradually becomes a well-known author. After the deaths of his wife (53) and Steerforth (55), and after learning the pain of "an undisciplined heart," he eventually settles his life and marries the steady **Agnes Wickfield** (62). David is the most autobiographical of Dickens's characters; his initials reverse those of the author, and many of the episodes in Copperfield's history are based on Dickens's own experiences. *Copperfield*.

Coppernose   Member of the Mudfog Association. *Mudfog*.

Copyright   As a professional writer who had to support a large family with his pen alone, Dickens was interested in the business of writing and the protection of the writer's intellectual property rights. The English Copyright Act (1709)—the first such law in the world—was only a little more than a century old when Dickens began writing. He supported the extension of the Act, sponsored by his friend Sir Thomas Noon TALFOURD, which passed in 1842. His most intense involvement with the issue of copyright, however, came on his American tour in 1842 when he spoke out for an INTERNATIONAL COPYRIGHT agreement between Britain and the United States. American publishers had been pirating the works of Dickens and other English writers. In speeches at BOSTON and Hartford, Dickens appealed to the self-interest of his American audience, arguing that an American literature would not develop as long as it was cheaper for American publishers to steal the works of foreigners than to pay for the works of Americans. His statements enraged the American newspaper editors—many of them among the pirates—and Dickens was vilified in the press as a money-grubbing, ungrateful guest. Dickens responded with letters on the issue to British journals and with his satire of the American press in *Notes* and *Chuzzlewit*.

Corn Laws   These tariffs on grain imported into England were supposed to protect British agriculture and stabilize the price of grain, but the Whigs who took power after the 1832 REFORM BILL saw the Corn Laws as remnants of privilege for the landed agricultural aristocracy and the most glaring violation of the principle of free trade. The Anti-Corn Law League, formed in 1838 to seek repeal of the tariffs and led by Radicals John Bright and Richard Cobden, was most active during the tumultuous early years of CHARTISM. The anti-Corn Law activists and the Chartists agreed that the Corn Laws raised the price of grain, making food unnecessarily expensive for the poor. A bad grain harvest and the Irish potato famine forced the issue to a crisis in 1845–46, just as Dickens was beginning his brief tenure as editor of the *DAILY NEWS.* He considered repeal one of the central missions of his paper.

Cornberry   Rich old man who died leaving his fiancée, Miss Julia Manners, all his money. *Boz,* "Winglebury."

Corney, Mrs.   Matron of the workhouse where Oliver Twist is born; she later marries Bumble (27) and makes his life miserable. *Twist.*

Cornhill   This thoroughfare in the CITY, running from LEADENHALL STREET to the BANK OF ENGLAND, is the site of Dodson and Fogg's offices (*Pickwick,* 20) and the GEORGE AND VULTURE (*Pickwick,* 26). Bob Cratchit slides on the ice on Cornhill on his way home from the office (*Carol,* 1). Bradley Headstone's grudging proposal to Lizzie is delivered in ST. PETER'S churchyard here (*Mutual Friend,* II:15).

Cornhill, The   Monthly periodical established in 1860 and edited by THACKERAY. Dickens contributed a memorial to Thackeray in the February 1864 issue.

"Countess, The"   Nickname of Liza GRIMWOOD. *Reprinted,* "Detective Anecdotes."

County Inn   Inn where Mr. Dick stays on his visits to David in CANTERBURY. Based on the Royal Fountain Hotel.

Cour, Capitaine de la   Commander of the soldiers stationed in VAUBAN, the French village where Langley goes. "Somebody's Luggage."

"Court Ceremonies"   Article for The *EXAMINER* (December 15, 1849) commenting on the death of Adelaide, the Queen Dowager, and her request for a simple funeral. Her request makes this an appropriate occasion on which to note how outdated and preposterous most ceremonies of the English court are and how much they are in need of being updated. *Miscellaneous.*

Courts   As a clerk in a law office, a shorthand reporter in Doctors' Commons, and a litigant in CHANCERY, Dickens had numerous opportunities to observe the legal system in action. He describes a number of different courts in his writings. He mentions two debtors' courts: the **Insolvent Debtor's Court**, described by Boz as one of the haunts of shabby-genteel people (*Boz,* "Shabby-genteel"; *Pickwick,* 43; *Dorrit,* I:7), and the **Palace Court** or **Marshalsea Court**, where Tip Dorrit briefly finds work in an attorney's office (*Dorrit,* I:7). The Insolvent Debtor's Court was abolished in 1861 when personal indebtedness was no longer cause for imprisonment. Tigg compares the **Court of Requests**, a court where the poor could sue for recovery of debts, to the Blue Dragon dunning Chevy Slyme to pay his bill (*Chuzzlewit,* 7). Pickwick is tried for breach of promise

in the **Common Pleas Court** (*Pickwick,* 34), the main court for civil actions which, in 1881, would be absorbed into the Queen's Bench Court. David Copperfield trains to become a proctor (*Copperfield,* 23, 33, 39), one of the attorneys practicing in **Doctors' Commons**, a civil court that handled marriage licenses and divorces, as well as ecclesiastical and naval matters. Here Jingle gets a license to marry Rachael Wardle (*Pickwick,* 10) and Tony Weller seeks advice on a will (*Pickwick,* 54). Dickens satirized the court in *Boz* ("Doctor's Commons") and clearly regarded it as an institution that had outlived its usefulness. It was abolished in 1857. The **Court of Chancery**, supreme court for issues involving legacies, wills, and trusts, is attacked in *Bleak House* as an obsolete, self-serving, and dilatory institution. It was absorbed into the Supreme Court in 1873. Dickens describes the OLD BAILEY, the main criminal court for London, in *Boz* ("Criminal Courts"), as a place where "every trial seems a mere matter of business. There is a great deal of form, but no compassion." Mentioned frequently in the novels, this court is the one in which Charles Darnay is tried for spying (*Two Cities,* II:2).

Coutts, Angela   Angela BURDETT-COUTTS, philanthropist and friend of Dickens, is sometimes identified simply as Miss Coutts. Born Angela Burdett, she added her maternal grandfather's surname, Coutts, to her own name after inheriting his forune.

Covent Garden   This area of London—west of the CITY and north of the STRAND where the central fruit and vegetable market was located—was a familiar wandering place for the young Dickens as it was for David Copperfield (12). Several characters have lodgings here, among them Augustus Minns (*Boz,* "Minns"); Arthur Clennam (*Dorrit,* I:13); and the Uncommercial Traveller (1). Copperfield goes to Covent Garden Theatre (19) and Pip takes rooms in Hummums Hotel when Wemmick warns him not to go home (*Expectations,* 45). Job Trotter spends the night in a vegetable basket (*Pickwick,* 47) and Mr. Dolls is tormented by street urchins in Covent Garden (*Mutual Friend,* IV:9).

Coventry   Pickwick and his friends change horses here on their way from BIRMINGHAM to London (*Pickwick,* 51). The city where Nell learns to be a guide for Mrs. Jarley's Waxworks may be based on Coventry (*Curiosity Shop,* 27).

Cox, Constance (1915–)   English playwright, actress, and adaptor of many 19th-century novels for the stage. She did the scripts for many of the BBC television serial adaptations of Dickens's novels, among them, *Bleak House* (1959), *Twist* (1962), *Curiosity Shop* (1963), *Chuzzlewit* (1964), and *Two Cities* (1965).

Crabtree, Carlotta   An American actress of the later 19th century, known as "Lotta," famous for her dual portrayal of the Marchioness and Little Nell in stage productions of *Curiosity Shop*. She enhanced her performance as the Marchioness with a banjo solo.

Crackit, Toby   Member of Fagin's gang, "Flash Toby" is Sikes's accomplice in the attempted break-in at Mrs. Maylie's house (22). His hideout on JACOB'S ISLAND is where Sikes seeks refuge in the end (50). *Twist.*

Craddock, Mrs.   Landlady of the house in the Royal Crescent in BATH where Pickwick and the Dowlers take lodgings. *Pickwick* 36.

Craggs, Thomas   Law partner of Jonathan Snitchey, "a cold, hard, dry man, dressed in grey and white, like a flint; with small twinkles in his eyes, as if something struck sparks out of them." His **wife**, Mrs. Snitchey's closest friend, is "on principle suspicious of Mr. Snitchey." *Battle.*

Cratchit, Bob   Scrooge's poor clerk, who struggles to support his family on 15 shillings a week. He lives with

Sol Eytinge's picture of Bob Cratchit and Tiny Tim for an 1867 American edition of the Carol *was the first rendering of this iconographic subject.*

his **wife** and six children in a four-room house in CAMDEN TOWN. There, Scrooge observes their Christmas dinner in his vision of Christmas Present, seeing Mrs. Cratchit assisted by **Belinda**, her second daughter, and the other children, preparing the feast; **Martha**, the eldest daughter who works as a milliner, surprising her father when he returns from church; **Peter**, the eldest son, preparing to go out to work; and the whole family making their Christmas toasts, climaxing with the prayer of the crippled **Tiny Tim**, "God bless us every one!" (3). In Christmas Yet to Come, Scrooge observes the family mourning the death of Tiny Tim (4). A changed Scrooge raises Bob's salary and provides care for his crippled son (5). *Carol.*

Craven Street   Street near CHARING CROSS where Mr. Brownlow takes up residence after returning from the West Indies. *Twist* (41).

Crawley   Young man at BATH whose father has "eight hundred a-year, which dies with him." *Pickwick* (35).

Creakle   Headmaster of SALEM HOUSE School, a brutal man who delights "in cutting at the boys, which was like the satisfaction of a craving appetite" (5). He has almost no voice and speaks in a whisper, confiding to David that he is "a Tartar." His **daughter**, whom young David considers "of extraordinary attractions," is thought by the boys to be in love with Steerforth. "Thin and quiet" **Mrs. Creakle** informs David of his mother's death (9). Later, Creakle becomes a Middlesex magistrate and warden of the prison where the hypocritical Heep and Littimer are his model prisoners (61). *Copperfield.* Creakle was based on William JONES, headmaster of WELLINGTON HOUSE ACADEMY.

Creeble, Miss   Schoolmistress whom Mr. Booley encounters on some of his travels. *Miscellaneous*, "Extraordinary Traveller."

Crewler, Sophy   Tommy Traddles's fiancée, "the dearest girl" and one of ten daughters of the **Reverend Horace Crewler**, a poor curate in Devonshire. Traddles has difficulty securing his consent to the marriage because Sophy helps to care for **Mrs. Crewler**, an invalid, and her many sisters, among them **Caroline**, **Sarah**, **Louisa**, **Margaret**, and **Lucy**. Traddles and Sophy finally marry after a long engagement (59). *Copperfield.*

Cricket on the Hearth, The. A Fairy Tale of Home
The third of Dickens's CHRISTMAS BOOKS, published by BRADBURY & EVANS in December 1845, with illustrations by MACLISE, DOYLE, LEECH, LANDSEER, and STANFIELD. Returning to a domestic story after the politics of *The Chimes*, Dickens puts the conversion of the hardhearted man in the background and focuses this Christ-

mas story on a humble couple and the threat to their marriage.

SYNOPSIS

(1) Dot Peerybingle puts the kettle on as she waits for her husband, John, a carrier and delivery man, to return from work. The kettle hums and a cricket chirps. Dot believes that the cricket brings them luck. "To have a Cricket on the Hearth," she says, "is the luckiest thing in all the world!" When John arrives, he surprises his wife by bringing with him a stranger, a deaf old white-haired man he has found sitting by the roadside. The stranger thinks Dot is John's daughter, she seems so much younger than her husband. Dot is also surprised by one of the packages John is delivering, a wedding cake for the gruff and selfish old toymaker, Tackleton, who plans to marry in three days, on the first anniversary of John and Dot's wedding. When Tackleton comes to collect the cake, he compares his impending marriage to theirs, for he, like John, is marrying a much younger woman. He also urges them to get rid of the annoying cricket. Dot is briefly overcome by some unexplained terror, but she returns to herself and goes about her household tasks as John smokes his pipe and meditates on the Cricket's visions of his happy hearth and home.

(2) Caleb Plummer, Tackleton's assistant, and his blind daughter Bertha work together in their toymaking workshop. He makes Noah's arks and rocking horses; she is a doll's dressmaker. Caleb acts as her eyes, making their lot seem far happier than it really is. He describes their shabby rooms as colorful and happy, his own ragged clothes as new and stylish, and their hard-hearted employer as benevolent and good-natured. He assures Bertha that all of Tackleton's cynicisms are merely jokes, and Bertha believes Tackleton to be a noble and kind man. She is pleased that he is to marry her friend, May Fielding, but she admits that she envies May, for she too loves Tackleton. Caleb regrets that he has deceived his daughter about the harsh old man.

The stranger, who has taken lodgings with the Peerybingles, accompanies them on their weekly picnic with Caleb and his daughter. Bertha senses something familiar in his step, and Dot is distracted and agitated in his presence. During the gathering, Tackleton takes John Peerybingle to the toy warehouse and shows him Dot in an assignation with the stranger, who has removed his white-haired wig and is now a handsome young man. On their way home, John cannot ride in the cart with Dot. He walks beside his horse, brooding on what he has seen.

(3) John spends the night before the fire, thinking about Dot, about the difference in age between them, about the "shadow of the stranger" in their home. He seeks guidance from the Spirit of the Cricket on the Hearth, and he concludes that he was not understanding enough of Dot's situation. He decides to release her from the marriage to return to her parents' home if she should choose to do so. John surprises Tackleton in the morning when he tells him of this decision. He is in turn surprised to discover that the stranger is missing from his room.

Caleb admits to his daughter that he has deceived her, and he enlightens her about their situation, and their employer. When the stranger returns, he is revealed to be Edward Plummer, the son whom Caleb thought had died in South America. He has claimed May as his bride and they have just been married. Dot and John also renew their vows on this anniversary of their wedding day. When Tackleton learns what has happened, he sends them the wedding cake, for he has been changed by observing the generosity of John Peerybingle during his trial. Everyone joins to celebrate Edward and May's marriage and John and Dot's anniversary as the cricket chirps on the hearth.

COMMENTARY

In its review of *Cricket*, *Chambers's Edinburgh Journal* remarked: "We are happy to find that Mr. Dickens . . . has left the question of social wrongs and rights to the discussion of those who can consider them in a calmer and less partial spirit and turned his attention to a subject of purely moral interest." Many Victorian readers shared this view. The politics of *The Chimes* had seemed contentious and inappropriate for a Christmas book. Like the reviewer, they preferred *Cricket*'s "picture of humble life, contemplated in its poetic aspects, and at its more romantic crises"; they bought, according to John FORSTER's somewhat exaggerated figures, more than twice as many copies of *Cricket* than of the earlier Christmas books. Seventeen dramatic productions of the story were staged within a month of its publication. It was a runaway best-seller.

Modern readers, however, have agreed with Lenin, who, according to ORWELL, walked out of a dramatic production of *Cricket* because he "found Dickens's 'middle-class sentimentality' so intolerable." The idealization of home and hearth which led Dickens's Victorian readers to canonize him as, in Margaret Lane's words, "a humorous but Puritan god of the domestic hearth," make modern readers remark on his hypocrisy and turn to those of his other works that treat marriage more realistically.

Dickens's idea for *Cricket* began as the name for a magazine that would promote the "*Carol* philosophy, cheerful views, sharp anatomization of humbug, jolly good temper, . . . a vein of glowing, hearty, generous, mirthful, beaming reference in everything to Home and Fireside." When he abandoned the magazine project, he used the idea for his Christmas book, making "the Cricket a little household god—silent in the wrong and sorrow of the tale, and loud again when all went well and happy."

The central action of the story occurs at the Peerybingles' hearth, the residence of the cricket. There the stranger is introduced who will disrupt Tackleton's marriage plans and threaten the Peerybingles' happiness. There John broods through the night as he considers

Dot's supposed infidelity. There Tackleton learns of John's heroic decision and himself abandons his claim to May Fielding. The cricket is a chirping or silent presence as these crises are faced and overcome. It is the supernatural agency in this fairy tale, comparable to the spirits in the *Carol*.

The dramatic plot on which the story turns, set off by the arrival of the white-haired stranger, is clichéd and predictable, as is the story of blind Bertha Plummer, who is predictably enlightened by the events of the tale. The more interesting story involves the threat to Dot and John's marriage, an action doubled in the marriage of Tackleton and May Fielding scheduled to take place on the first anniversary of the Peerybingle's wedding. Both are January-and-May unions, bringing together a young woman and an older man. But Tackleton irritates Dot when he presumes to call attention to their similarity, for she had not thought of her own marriage as unequal or unfulfilling, and she—and everyone else except blind Bertha Plummer—knows that Tackleton is not an appropriate husband for young May, Dot's former schoolmate.

Tackleton is a relative of Scrooge. A man who should have been a moneylender or a sharp attorney, he became instead a toy maker and "a domestic Ogre, who had been living on children all his life, and was their implacable enemy" (1). Like Scrooge, he also exploits his worker, Caleb Plummer, yet he expects gratitude and obedience from him. Tackleton's interest in May is not explained, but there are suggestions that he is indulging an unhealthy desire to control the young woman. We do not know enough of Tackleton to understand his character; he is presented in terms of his external contradictions rather than his interior desires. His change of heart at the end of the story mirrors John Peerybingle's coming to terms with the inequality in his own marriage; it does not seem to arise from anything within Tackleton.

Potentially, John Peerybingle is the most interesting character in the story; his decision to free Dot from the demands of the marriage suggests a depth of uncertainty and sensitivity not apparent in any other character. But Dickens does not let the reader know enough about John and about his meditations during the decisive night by the hearth to enable an understanding of his character. In a story where the central action is internal, Dickens's dramatic method of mirroring Tackleton and Peerybingle is insufficient to present and develop the plot.

CRITICISM

Little has been written about *Cricket*. Michael SLATER (1971) has a useful introduction to the story in his edition of the CHRISTMAS BOOKS.

ADAPTATIONS

Dickens released the proof sheets for *Cricket* to the KEELEYS, who engaged Albert SMITH to adapt the story for the Lyceum Theatre. That production opened on December 20, 1845, the same day that the book appeared.

Within a month, 16 more productions of *Cricket* appeared on the London stage. Of the two dozen theaters in London, only six did not stage a version of the story. The roles created by the leading actors were those of Dot and Caleb Plummer; in two productions, male actors took the part of Tillie Slowboy.

The most important 19th-century adaptation of the story was Dion BOUCICAULT's *Dot*, which opened in New York in 1859 and, occasionally retitled as *Caleb Plummer* or *A Christmas Story*, was produced regularly on both sides of the Atlantic during the rest of the century. Boucicault added a Shakespearean frame with Titania and Oberon in an enchanted wood. The story was also adapted for the French theater; the production that Lenin walked out of was that of the Moscow Art Theater early in the 20th century.

Four silent films, including one by D. W. GRIFFITH (1909), have been made from the story. Karl Goldmark's opera *Das Heimchen am Herd* (1896), originally staged at the State Opera House in Vienna, has been performed in both England and the United States.

Crime Crime fascinated Dickens. From the brutal murders committed by Bill Sikes and Jonas Chuzzlewit to the confidence games of Jingle and Tigg and the white-collar crimes of Uriah Heep and Merdle, there is crime in nearly every novel. Beginning with the FLEET PRISON in *Pickwick*, prisons are omnipresent. NEWGATE PRISON shadows Pip with "the taint of prison and crime" (*Expectations*, 32), and the MARSHALSEA PRISON becomes symbolic of the human condition in *Dorrit*. *Bleak House*, in which Inspector Bucket pursues Lady Dedlock and Tulkinghorn's murderer, is among the first DETECTIVE NOVELS.

Dickens accompanied the police on their rounds and reported on these excursions in articles for his magazines, in "On Duty with Inspector Field" and "Down with the Tide," for example. He visited prisons, witnessed public executions, and walked at night through the crime-ridden areas of London. In observing and writing about crime, Dickens may have been trying to exorcise the taint in his own past, for he seemed to associate his father's imprisonment for debt with criminality. Crime was also a way to represent dramatically the dark side of human nature.

Many critics have written on the thematic significance of the crimes in the various novels. Philip COLLINS's *Dickens and Crime* (1962) is a classic on this topic, placing the crimes in the novels into the context of the growing awareness of crime in Victorian England. In *The Novel and the Police* (1983), D. A. Miller makes a deconstructive analysis of crime and public order in several Victorian novels, among them *Bleak House*.

"Criminal Courts" Originally published as "Street Sketches No. 3. The Old Bailey" in the MORNING CHRONICLE (October 23, 1834), this sketch describes a boy leaving NEWGATE PRISON in the company of his mother, a trial at the OLD BAILEY in which the accused is found guilty, and the trial of a 13-year-old for picking pockets. *Boz.*

Crimple, David A pawnbroker (then known as Crimp, 13) who becomes Tigg Montague's cohort in the ANGLO-BENGALEE insurance scam (27). After Montague's murder, he and Bullamy leave the country with the remaining funds (51). *Chuzzlewit.*

Crinkles Exhibitor at the meeting of the Mudfog Association who has invented a machine to pick pockets. *Mudfog.*

Cripple Corner Courtyard where Wilding and Co. is located. "No Thoroughfare."

"Crippler, The" Vessel of Captain Swosser on which he fell in love with the future Mrs. Bayham Badger. *Bleak House* (13).

Cripples, Mister He lives with his son, **Master Cripples**, and operates a nightschool in the building where Frederick Dorrit lives. *Dorrit*, (I:9).

Cripps, Tom Bob Sawyer's shop boy who advertises Sawyer's apothecary business by leaving bottles of pills at the wrong addresses. *Pickwick* (38).

"Crisis in the Affairs of Mr. John Bull, A" In this essay from *HOUSEHOLD WORDS* (November 23, 1850), Dickens writes an allegorical fable in which Mrs. John Bull instructs her children on the dangers of associating with Master Wiseman, Young England, and the Bulls of Rome who "perpetuate misery, oppression, darkness, and ignorance." The article was written in response to the restoration of the Catholic hierarchy in England on September 29, 1850. When the pope returned the English divisions of the Catholic Church to the status of regular dioceses and named Bishop Wiseman as a cardinal and Bishop of Westminster, his action, which seemed to ignore the authority of the Anglican hierarchy, aroused English Protestants and prompted a bill in Parliament, which prohibited the assumption of ecclesiastical titles already held by the clergy in the Church of England. In a letter to Miss COUTTS, Dickens condemned the restoration of Catholic titles in even stronger terms: "*Now*, a war between the Roman Catholic Religion—that curse upon the world—and Freedom, is inevitable." *Miscellaneous.*

Crisparkle, The Reverend Septimus Minor canon of the Cloisterham Cathedral, a muscular Christian who is "fair and rosy, and perpetually pitching himself head-foremost into all the deep running water in the surrounding county, . . . early riser, musical, classical, cheerful, kind, good-natured, contented, and boy-like" (2). He lives with his mother, **Mrs. Crisparkle**, a "cheerful and calm" old lady whose "dress is as the dress of a china shepherdess" (6). He agrees to tutor Neville

Landless and seeks to curb the wildness in the boy's character, remaining convinced of Neville's innocence when the boy is suspected of murdering Drood. *Drood.*

Crofts Barber who shaves Mr. Harvey of the Old Couple. *Young Couples.*

Crocus, Doctor Scotch phrenologist on a lecture tour of America whom Dickens met in Belleville, Illinois. *Notes* (13).

Crookey Attendant at Namby's lock-up who "looked something between a bankrupt grazier, and a drover in a state of insolvency." *Pickwick* (40)

Cropley, Miss Friend of Mrs. Nickleby at Exeter. *Nickleby* (33).

Cross Keys Inn Inn on WOOD STREET, CHEAPSIDE, from where coaches left for ROCHESTER. Pip, like Dickens, first arrived in London here (*Expectations*, 20). Cavalletto is run over in a nearby street (*Dorrit*, I:13). Also mentioned in *Boz*, "Omnibuses"; *Nickleby* (33); *Uncommercial* (12).

Crotch, W. Walter (1874–1947) Editor in chief of the International Press Bureau in Paris; editor of the revived *Household Words*; one of the founding members of the DICKENS FELLOWSHIP in 1902; president of the Fellowship from 1915 to 1920. Author of several books on Dickens, including *Charles Dickens as Social Reformer* (1913).

Crowl Newman Noggs's neighboring garret-dweller, "a hard-featured square-faced man, elderly and shabby." *Nickleby* (14).

Crown Inn, Golden Square Newman Noggs's favorite inn. *Nickleby* (7).

Crowquill, Alfred (1804–1872) Penname of writer and illustrator Alfred Henry Forrestier. An associate of George CRUIKSHANK, Crowquill drew for *PUNCH* in its early years and wrote for *BENTLEY'S MISCELLANY* and the *NEW MONTHLY MAGAZINE*. He illustrated *Pickwick* (1841) and other novels before concentrating in his later work on illustrations for children's books. An example of Crowquill's work appears in illustration 71 (*Pickwick Papers*).

Crozier Inn Cloisterham inn where Datchery stays when he first comes to town. Based on the Crown Inn, ROCHESTER. *Drood* (18).

Cruikshank, George (1792–1878) Artist, caricaturist, and illustrator, Cruikshank was the preeminent exponent in early Victorian England of the tradition of graphic satire stemming from HOGARTH. Among the nearly 900 works that he illustrated in a long career were

Cruikshank's illustration for the "Public Dinners" sketch in Boz *includes Dickens as the second adult from the left in the procession and Cruikshank himself as the second from the right. Some commentators identify the two stewards leading the procession as Chapman and Hall.*

several by Dickens. He was Dickens's first illustrator, commissioned by John MACRONE to illustrate *Sketches by Boz.* He also did illustrations for *Mudfog, Grimaldi,* and BENTLEY'S MISCELLANY when Dickens was its editor, and, most important, for *Oliver Twist.* His illustrations for *Twist* have sometimes been regarded as the finest original illustrations for any of the novels. Although there were occasional professional disagreements during these projects, the two were close friends socially in the 1840s. Their relationship cooled in the late '40s when Dickens criticized, in "Frauds on the Fairies," Cruikshank's teetotalism and his retellings of classic fairy tales. By the end of his life, Cruikshank became embittered and implausibly claimed that he originated much of the story and many of the characters in *Oliver Twist.* Other examples of Cruikshank's work appear in illustrations 36 (FAGIN); 66 (OLIVER TWIST); and 83 (SKETCHES BY BOZ).

"Cruikshank's 'The Drunkard's Children' " Dickens's "gentle protest" at Cruikshank's pictorial analysis of the effects of gin chides the artist for ignoring the social misery that produces drunkenness while blaming the gin. Although Dickens praised the art and the ob-

servation of social reality in the pictures, his criticism strained his relationship with the artist. The article first appeared in the EXAMINER, July 8, 1848. *Miscellaneous.*

Crummles Family   Theatrical family who lead the repertory company that Nicholas Nickleby joins during their run in PORTSMOUTH. **Vincent**, manager of the company, a large man with "a very full underlip, a hoarse voice, as though he were in the habit of shouting very much, and very short black hair, shaved off nearly to the crown of his head—to admit . . . of his more easily wearing character wigs of any shape or pattern" (22), acts leading roles in many of their productions. His **wife**, "a short, portly female, apparently between forty and fifty, in a tarnished silk cloak" (23), is a versatile actress, as are his children, **Charles**, **Percy**, and **Ninetta** (**"the Infant Phenemenon"**), "a little girl in a dirty white frock" who has been 10 for the last five years (23). Nicholas reconnects with the family later on as they are about to depart for America (48). *Nickleby.*

Crumpton, Misses Amelia and Maria   Spinster sisters who operate Minerva House, a finishing school in HAMMERSMITH, where young women acquire "a smattering of everything, and a knowledge of nothing." *Boz,* "Sentiment."

Cruncher, Jeremiah (Jerry)   Messenger for TELLSON'S BANK and a "RESURRECTION MAN," who takes bodies from graves and sells them as anatomical specimens. He has "stiff black hair, standing jaggedly all over" his head, "more like the top of a strongly spiked wall than a head of hair" (I:3). His avocation as a grave robber enables him to know that Roger Cly is not really dead (II:14). **Mrs. Cruncher's** Evangelical fervor is an aggravation to her husband, who objects to her "flopping herself down and praying agin me" (II:1). **Young Jerry**, his look-alike son, spies on his father's grave-robbing and wants to take up the same profession. When the elder Jerry accompanies Mr. Lorry to Paris, the Reign of Terror so frightens him that he vows to give up his resurrection business and to be more kindly to his wife (III: 14). *Two Cities.*

Crupp, Mrs.   David Copperfield's landlady in the ADELPHI. She suffers from "the spazzums," a complaint relieved by David's brandy (26). When David falls in love with Dora, she is aware that there is "a lady in the case" (26). *Copperfield.*

Crushton, the Honorable Mr.   Lord Mutanhed's obsequious friend. *Pickwick* (35–36).

Cummins, Tom   The man "in the chair" during an adventurous evening described by one of Dodson and Fogg's clerks. *Pickwick* (20).

"Curate, The. The Old Lady. The Half-pay Captain"   Second of the sketches comprising "Our Parish" in *Boz*, it describes a handsome young curate whose popularity is effaced by a new clergyman at the chapel-of-ease; a benevolent old lady; and a retired naval officer on half pay. The sketch originally appeared as "Sketches of London No. 12. Our Parish" in the *EVENING CHRONICLE* (May 19, 1835).

Curdle, Mr. and Mrs.   Patrons of the drama in PORTSMOUTH who subscribe to Miss Snevellicci's benefit. Mr. Curdle has written a pamphlet on the character of the nurse's deceased husband in *Romeo and Juliet*. *Nickleby* (24).

"Curious Dance Round a Curious Tree, A"   Article for *HOUSEHOLD WORDS* (January 17, 1852), written with William Henry WILLS, describing a visit to a holiday party for the inmates of St. Luke's Hospital for the insane, showing the positive effects of humane and loving treatment of the patients. *Stone.*

"Curious Misprint in the 'Edinburgh Review' "   Article for *HOUSEHOLD WORDS* (August 1, 1857) in which Dickens challenges the *Edinburgh*'s reviewer for suggesting that novelists were not qualified to discuss social issues, and, in particular, his claim that the Post Office and Rowland Hill's career there show that the CIRCUMLOCUTION OFFICE does not exist. Dickens describes the obstacles to reform that Hill faced for many years from the government establishment. *Miscellaneous.*

Cursitor Street   Street running east from CHANCERY LANE where John Dounce (*Boz*, "Dounce") and Snagsby (*Bleak House*, 10) live. Solomon Jacobs' sponging house where Watkins Tottle is held (*Boz*, "Tottle") and Coavinses (*Bleak House*, 15), the sponging house where Neckett works, are both located here.

Curzon, Thomas   Hosier to whom Mark Gilbert, one of the 'PRENTICE KNIGHTS, is apprenticed. Curzon's **daughter** spurns the young man. *Rudge* (8, 39).

Cute, Alderman   Malthusian city magistrate claiming to be a plain and practical man who has made his mission in life putting down the poor. He views as cant all talk of poverty, distress, and starvation, and he is particularly intent on putting down suicide. He warns Trotty against claiming deprivation, and he lectures Meg and Richard on the imprudence of their marriage plans (1). *Chimes.* Dickens based Cute on Sir Peter LAURIE, a garrulous and officious magistrate and LORD MAYOR of London. See also Thomas Robert MALTHUS.

Cutler, Mr. and Mrs.   Friends of the Kenwigs. *Nickleby* (14).

Cuttle, Captain Edward (Ned)   Retired sea captain, friend to Sol Gills, whose shop he watches when Sol goes off in search of Walter Gay, "a gentleman in a wide suit of blue, with a hook instead of a hand. . . . He wore a loose black silk handkerchief round his neck, and such a very large coarse shirt collar, that it looked like a small sail" (4). He is intimidated by his landlady, the widow McStinger, but escapes her clutches to care for the Wooden Midshipman and Florence (25). After Sol's return he becomes a partner in the business (66). He is fond of remarking, "When found, make a note of." *Dombey.*

Cuttris's Hotel, James Street, Covent Garden   Hotel where Dickens stayed when he returned to London from Italy in 1844 to give a reading of *The Chimes.*

D

Dabber, Sir Dingleby Fashionable artist imagined by Mrs. Nickleby as the painter of Kate's portrait after she marries Sir Mulberry Hawk. *Nickleby*, (27).

Dadson Writing master at MINERVA HOUSE who attends the half-yearly ball in "a white waistcoat, black knee-shorts, and ditto silk stockings, displaying a leg large enough for two writing masters." His **wife** is "in green silk, with shoes and cap-trimmings to correspond." *Boz*, "Sentiment."

Daily News Liberal daily newspaper which began publication on January 21, 1846, with Dickens as editor. The main investors—Joseph PAXTON, William BRADBURY, and Frederick EVANS, capitalized the project with money from railway speculation. Dickens was excited by the opportunities to promote liberal causes like the repeal of the CORN LAWS and, by paying top salaries, to assemble a staff of such first-rate journalists as W. H. WILLS, John FORSTER, W. J. FOX, and Douglas JERROLD. John DICKENS was put in charge of the reporters, a position he held until his death. Dickens found the demands of a daily paper too taxing and objected to Bradbury's interference with his direction, so he resigned the editorship on February 9, 1846. He did continue to write occasional pieces for the paper.

Daisy Steerforth's pet name for DAVID COPPERFIELD.

Daisy, Solomon Parish clerk and bell-ringer at CHIGWELL, and a regular at the MAYPOLE INN, who "had little round black shiny eyes like beads; moreover this little man wore at the knees of his rusty black breeches, and on his rusty black coat, and all down his long flapped waistcoat, little queer buttons like nothing except his eyes; . . . he seemed all eyes from head to foot" (1). Daisy tells the story of Reuben Haredale's murder (1), is startled by the ghost of Rudge in the church many years later (33), and accompanies Haredale when he returns to the Warren after its destruction (56). *Rudge*.

Daleski, H. M. (1926–) Professor at Hebrew University in Jerusalem who has written on Joseph Conrad, D. H. Lawrence, and other 19th-and 20th-century writers. In *Dickens and the Art of Analogy* (1970), Daleski discusses repeated patterns (analogies) that act as thematic focal points in the novels. In the analysis of *Great Expectations*, for example, he treats expectation and hidden relationships as the central analogies in the novel.

Damiens Prisoner who was tortured, executed, and mutilated for making an attempt on the life of Louis XV. *Two Cities*, (II:15).

Dana, Richard Henry Jr. (1815–82) American author of *Two Years before the Mast* (1840) and other works whom Dickens met on his tours to America. Dickens considered Dana "a very nice fellow"; Dana described Dickens as "far from well bred" but "full of life."

"Dancing Academy, The" Originally published as "Scenes and Characters. No. 3" in BELL'S LIFE IN LONDON (October 11, 1835), this sketch describes the attempt of naive Augustus Cooper to escape the control of his mother by taking dancing lessons at Signor Billsmethi's Academy. He is set up and sued for breach of contract by Miss Billsmethi and must be rescued by his mother, who supplies a cash settlement of £20 and regains control of her son. *Boz*.

Dando Head boatman at Searles Yard on the THAMES. *Boz*, "River."

Dandyism A movement of the Regency period in the 1810s that promoted a male ideal in dress and behavior. Beau Brummel (1778–1840) and the Prince Regent, George IV, were its most notable exemplars; preoccupied with clothes and with their public appearance, they represented the narcissism and dedication to genteel idleness that characterized the dandy. An extravagant and flashy dresser, Dickens—particularly as a young man—was often described as a dandy, but he never affected a posture of idleness.

In *Sartor Resartus* (1833–34), Thomas CARLYLE defined the dandy as "a Clothes-wearing Man, a man whose trade, office, and existence consists in the wearing of Clothes." He satirically analyzed dandyism as a religion devoted to the worship of self. The dandies in Dickens's novels fit this Carlylean pattern. Steerforth (*Copperfield*), Harthouse (*Hard Times*), and Gowan (*Dorrit*), all cultivate an aristocratic insouciance and boredom and seek only self-gratification. Sydney Carton (*Two Cities*), and Eugene Wrayburn (*Mutual Friend*) are more positive versions of the dandy figure; both transcend their dandiacal tendencies in a concern for others.

Dickens most fully explores dandyism in *Bleak House.* Old Mr. Turveydrop with his padded clothes and his ideal of "Deportment" is the Regency dandy surviving into what he calls "degenerate times." His idleness and parasitism, however, are representative of a new "Dandyism of a more mischievous sort, that has got below the surface and is doing less harmless things" (12). The Dedlocks and their aristocratic company represent this new Dandyism as they idly perpetuate their own interests and justify their unconcern for anyone else as a rejection of "the Vulgar." Harold Skimpole imitates this mode of being in his irresponsible dilettantism. In its various manifestations, this subsurface dandyism characterizes the self-serving society of *Bleak House.*

Ellen Moers discusses dandyism, Dickens as dandy, and the dandies, in his novels in *The Dandy* (1960).

Danton "Young man of about five-and-twenty, with a considerable stock of impudence, and a very small share of ideas" who attempts to be the life of the Kitterbells' christening party. *Boz,* "Christening."

Darby Police Constable who accompanies Bucket and Snagsby to TOM-ALL-ALONE'S. *Bleak House,* (22).

Darby, Mr. and Mrs. Keepers of a disreputable lodging house near the LIVERPOOL docks. *Uncommercial* (5).

Darnay, Charles The English name taken by **Charles D'Aulnais,** "a young man of about five-and-twenty, well-grown and well-looking, with a sunburnt cheek and a dark eye. His condition was that of a young gentleman" (II:2). Although he is heir to the title Marquis ST. EVRÉMONDE after the death of his father and the assassination of his uncle, Charles has renounced his title and chosen to live in England and earn his living there. Through the machinations of his servant Roger Cly and the influence of his uncle, Charles is tried for treason in London and acquitted due to his physical resemblance to Sydney Carton (II:3). He marries **Lucie** Manette. During the Revolution he returns to France to testify for a family servant, Gabelle, and is himself arrested as an emigré. Through the efforts of Doctor Manette, he is released (III:6), only to be rearrested and convicted, largely on the basis of a manuscript condemning the St. Evrémonde family written by the doctor while he was in prison (III:10). Sydney Carton substitutes himself for Darnay in the condemned cell, and Darnay returns with his wife and daughter to England. *Two Cities.*

Dartle, Rosa Mrs. Steerforth's tormented and vindictive companion and distant relative; "she had black hair, and eager black eyes, and was thin, and had a scar upon her lip" (20). The scar, inflicted by Steerforth with a hammer when they were children, is a visible manifestation of the wounds she bears from his denial of affection. When Steerforth elopes with Emily, Rosa vows revenge upon the girl and when Emily returns to Lon-don, Rosa pursues her and heaps contempt upon her (50). After Steerforth's death, she remains as Mrs. Steerforth's companion. *Copperfield.*

Datchery, Dick Mysterious stranger, "a white-haired personage with black eyebrows" (18), who appears in CLOISTERHAM and takes lodgings with the Topes, apparently to keep an eye on Jasper, who lives in the Gatehouse next door. *Drood* (18, 23). Commentators have speculated that he is one of the other characters—Drood, Bazzard, Helena Landless, or Tartar—in disguise. *Drood.*

Davenport, Jean (1829–1903) Actress who has been identified as the original of Ninetta CRUMMLES, though this identification has been contested. She went with her parents to America in 1838 and was presented as a child prodigy for several years. She played Dot in several productions of *Cricket.*

David Cheeryble's butler, "of apoplectic appearance, and with very short legs" (37). *Nickleby.*

David, Old Sexton's assistant in the village where Little Nell dies. *Curiosity Shop,* (54).

David Copperfield, The Personal History of (Serial Title: *The Personal History, Adventures, Experience & Observation of David Copperfield the Younger, of Blunderstone Rookery. [Which He never meant to be Published on any Account.]*) Dickens's eighth novel, published in monthly parts by BRADBURY & EVANS, May 1849–November 1850, with illustrations by BROWNE. Published in one volume, 1850. Written at the midpoint in Dickens's career, *Copperfield* uses materials from the author's own life in David's fictional autobiography. The novel is usually considered the dividing point in Dickens's career between the early and late novels. Although it appears to have the formlessness of the 18-century "personal histories" on which it is modeled, *Copperfield* is a carefully crafted and unified novel, presenting its hero as a Victorian everyman seeking self-understanding.

SYNOPSIS

Part 1 (May 1849)

(1) "Whether I shall turn out to be the hero of my own life, or whether that station will be held by anybody else, these pages must show." With these words David Copperfield begins the story of his life. He tells of his birth six months after his father's death, a "posthumous child," born into a loving household composed of his sweet and doting mother, Clara Copperfield, and her housekeeper, Clara Peggotty. His father's sister, his aunt Betsey Trotwood, came for the occasion, but when she learned that the child was a boy and not the girl she expected, "she vanished like a discontented fairy . . . and never came back any more." (2) David remembers his early child-

hood, his house, his visits to church, and Mr. Murdstone, who accompanies his mother home from church. (3) When his mother has Peggotty take David on a holiday to YARMOUTH, they visit her brother, Daniel Peggotty, and stay in his house, a boat turned upside-down on the beach. There David meets Ham and Mrs. Gummidge and spends long hours playing by the sea with Little Em'ly, Daniel's orphaned niece. When he returns to BLUNDERSTONE, he discovers that Mr. Murdstone has married his mother.

Part 2 (June 1849)
(4) Murdstone suppresses his wife's sympathy for her son and introduces a regime of "firmness," bringing in his steely sister, Miss Jane Murdstone, to oversee the household. David finds secret solace reading the books his father left in a little room upstairs. When Murdstone beats him for confusing his lessons, David bites him on the thumb and is locked in his room for five days. Through the keyhole Peggotty tells him that he will be sent away to school. (5) On the way to school, the carrier, Mr. Barkis, asks him to tell Peggotty that "Barkis is willin'." In London David is met by Mr. Mell, a master at SALEM HOUSE. On the way to the school they stop at an alms-house where Mell visits his mother and plays the flute

Browne's (Phiz's) illustration of the boy David ordering his lunch at a London pub exaggerates David's youth in contrast to the towering adult world of the city.

for her. When they arrive at Salem House, deserted for the school holiday, David is directed to wear a placard stating "Take care of him. He bites." (6) Mr. Creakle, the headmaster, warns David that he is "a Tartar," but the boys are more friendly. The head boy, James Steerforth, takes charge of David's seven shillings, spending the money for a late-night supper at which he promises to be young David's protector (6).

Part 3 (July 1849)
(7) David idolizes Steerforth, who encourages David to tell nightly stories to the other boys, repeating the stories he had read in his father's library. One day Steerforth challenges Mr. Mell as an "impudent beggar." When Steerforth reveals that Mell's mother is in an almshouse, something he has learned from David, Creakle fires the schoolmaster. David feels implicated in Steerforth's mean action, but he keeps silent, and when Mr. Peggotty and Ham visit the school, he introduces them to Steerforth.

(8) On his way home for the holiday, David promises Barkis that he will tell Peggotty that "Barkis is waitin' for an answer." When he arrives, the Murdstones are out and David spends an idyllic afternoon with his mother, Peggotty, and his new baby brother. But after the Murdstones return, the regime of firmness is reinstated and David is miserable until it is time to go back to Salem House. (9) In March, on his birthday, David is called to Creakle's office and told that his mother has died. On his way home he stops at the shop of Mr. Omer, the undertaker, where he is fitted for funeral clothes and listens to the hammer as his mother's coffin is being constructed. Peggotty describes his mother's death, her gradual decline under the rule of firmness, her concern for her "fatherless boy," and her desire to have her baby buried with her should he die at the same time. After the funeral, David ruminates: "The mother who lay in the grave, was the mother of my infancy; the little creature in her arms, was myself, as I had once been, hushed for ever on her bosom."

Part 4 (August 1849)
(10) Murdstone dismisses Peggotty, but she arranges to take David to Yarmouth for a holiday. There David renews his ties with Little Em'ly and the others and, on a "wonderful day," David and Em'ly accompany Peggotty and Barkis to their wedding and David dreams of marrying Em'ly. Back at Blunderstone, David is idle and neglected until Murdstone announces that he is not returning to school but rather is to be sent to London to work at MURDSTONE AND GRINBY's, a wine business.

(11) In London David begins life on his own account, washing and pasting labels on wine bottles. He contrasts his fellow workers, Mick Walker and Mealy Potatoes, to his former companions at Salem House and describes the "secret agony," "misery," and "shame" that he feels in his new situation. He is introduced to Mr. Micawber, with whom he has lodgings. He soon learns of Micawber's financial difficulties, offers to lend the family money from his meager wages, and helps them by taking items to the pawnbroker's. When Micawber is imprisoned for debt, David takes lodgings near the prison. (12) After he

is released from prison, Micawber decides to go to Plymouth where he hopes something will "turn up." David also decides to leave London and to seek out his Aunt Betsey in DOVER. After work on a Saturday evening, David puts his plan into effect, but the young man he hires to carry his box to the coach steals the box and the half guinea David has borrowed from Peggotty for travel expenses. So David begins his journey on foot, "taking very little more out of the world, towards the retreat of my aunt, Miss Betsey, than I had brought into it, on the night when my arrival gave her so much umbrage."

Part 5 (September 1849)
(13) On his six-day journey, David sustains himself by selling his vest and coat. He sleeps outside—one night in a field near Salem House—and arrives in Dover ragged and tired. His aunt, acting on the advice of her weak-minded lodger, Mr. Dick, bathes and feeds the boy. (14) The Murdstones come to Dover and make it quite clear that they will have nothing more to do with David if he does not return to Blunderstone. Aunt Betsey castigates them and sends them away. She becomes David's guardian and decides to call him Trotwood Copperfield. (15) David soon becomes best friends with Mr. Dick. They fly kites made from pages of Mr. Dick's Memorial, an autobiographical memoir he writes to seek redress from the LORD CHANCELLOR, but he inevitably gets entangled in discussing his obsession with King Charles's head and must discard each successive draft. When Aunt Betsey decides that David should go to school in CANTERBURY, he stays at the home of Mr. Wickfield, her solicitor, and meets Wickfield's daughter, Agnes, and his clerk, Uriah Heep. As she leaves to return to Dover, Aunt Betsey counsels David: "Never . . . be mean in anything; never be false; never be cruel. Avoid these three vices, Trot, and I can always be hopeful of you."

Part 6 (October 1849)
(16) David begins at Doctor Strong's school, where he meets the old scholar and his young wife, Annie. David senses some uneasiness between Mr. Wickfield and Doctor Strong when they talk of Jack Maldon, Annie's cousin, and he observes Annie's distress when Maldon goes off to India. (17) Mr. Dick visits David regularly and becomes a good friend of the doctor. He tells David of a strange man who loiters outside Betsey Trotwood's house and gets money from her. David also gets to know the fawning Uriah Heep. When he goes to tea at Uriah's house, David is "pumped" by the clerk and his mother about his former life. While he is there, Mr. Micawber passes the open door, sees David, and introduces himself to Heep. The Micawbers are in Canterbury seeking employment. David is uneasy when he sees Heep with Micawber the next day. He enjoys a lavish dinner with the Micawbers before they return to London, but Micawber leaves David a letter detailing his desperate financial situation.
(18) In a retrospective chapter, the first of several such chapters (see also 43, 53, and 64), in which David sums up a stage in his life and prepares for an important change, David remembers the infatuations of his school-

days—his love for Miss Shepherd, his fight with a young butcher over her, and, later on when he has become head boy at Doctor Strong's, his infatuation for the eldest Miss Larkins. These retrospective chapters stress the importance of memory in the novel.

Part 7 (November 1849)
(19) David finishes school and plans a vacation at Yarmouth before settling into a profession. Before he leaves, Agnes reveals her worry about her father's alcoholism and Uriah Heep's role in encouraging it. David also learns that Maldon wants to return from India, and he observes Mr. Wickfield's distrust of Annie Strong. On his way to Yarmouth, David unexpectedly meets Steerforth in London. (20) He spends a few days at Steerforth's home in HIGHGATE, where he meets Steerforth's mother, who dotes upon her son, and Rosa Dartle, her contradictory companion who bears a scar across her lip. She got the scar as a child when Steerforth threw a hammer at her. (21) David also meets Littimer, Steerforth's respectable servant, whose condescending manner makes David feel young. David takes Steerforth to Yarmouth, where they celebrate Ham's engagement to Em'ly. Steerforth charms the company with his stories and affability.

Part 8 (December 1849)
(22) When Steerforth falls into a spell of dejection, he confesses to David that he lacks purpose in his life and wishes he could "guide [himself] better." He tells David that he has bought a boat that he plans to call "The Little Em'ly." Miss Mowcher, a dwarf hairdresser, gossips with Steerforth as she fixes his hair.

Em'ly befriends Martha Endell, one of her coworkers who has been ruined. Afterward, Em'ly tearfully tells Ham that she is unworthy of him.

(23) David follows Aunt Betsey's suggestion that he become a proctor at Doctors' Commons. As they go together to Mr. Spenlow's office to arrange his articles, Aunt Betsey is accosted by a strange man who gets money from her. She arranges rooms for David at Mrs. Crupp's. (24) David invites Steerforth and two of Steerforth's college friends to a housewarming. After drinking too much wine at dinner, they go to the theater where the drunken David sees Agnes. He awakens the next morning bitterly remorseful.

Part 9 (January 1850)
(25) Agnes warns David of Steerforth's influence. She also tells him that her father is about to make Uriah Heep his partner. Uriah boasts of his changed relationship with Wickfield and outrages David when he reveals his aspiration to marry Agnes.

(26) When David spends a weekend at Mr. Spenlow's, he falls hopelessly in love with Spenlow's daughter Dora. He is disconcerted to find Miss Murdstone acting as Dora's companion, but they agree to keep confidential their past relationship.

(27) David meets Traddles, a former schoolmate at Salem House, who tells David of his struggle to establish himself as a lawyer and of his engagement to a curate's daughter. David is surprised to discover that Traddles lodges with Micawber.

Part 10 (February 1850)
(28) At a dinner in David's lodgings, Mrs. Micawber urges her husband to advertise for work and David learns that Micawber's financial difficulties have entangled Traddles. Afterward, Steerforth brings a letter from Peggotty informing David that Barkis is dying. David plans to go to Yarmouth after spending a day at Steerforth's home, (29) where Rosa Dartle questions him to learn what she can of Steerforth's movements. (30) In Yarmouth, David sees Barkis as he "goes out with the tide" and notices that Em'ly seems restless. (31) After the funeral, Ham receives a letter from Em'ly saying that she is running off with Steerforth. Dan'l Peggotty resolves "to seek [his] niece through the wureld . . . and bring her back."

Part 11 (March 1850)
(32) Miss Mowcher tells David of Steerforth's treachery. When David and Dan'l Peggotty call on Mrs. Steerforth, she is haughty and unsympathetic. Rosa Dartle too scorns Em'ly. Dan'l Peggotty sets out on his journey.

(33) David spends an ecstatic day at Dora's birthday picnic. Afterward, with the help of Miss Mills, Dora's friend, he arranges a tryst with Dora. They are engaged, but decide to keep it secret from Mr. Spenlow. (34) David discovers Betsey Trotwood with Mr. Dick, two birds, a cat, and all her worldly belongings "like a female Robinson Crusoe," sitting in the middle of his apartment. She tells David that she is ruined.

Part 12 (April 1850)
(35) David is determined to help his aunt out of her difficulties, and he tries unsuccessfully to resign his articles and recover some of the premium. Agnes suggests that he apply to work as a secretary for Doctor Strong, who has retired to London. (36) Doctor Strong hires David for £70 a year. David also decides to learn shorthand with an eye to becoming a parliamentary reporter. Mr. Dick takes up legal copying and proudly contributes his earnings to Betsey Trotwood. Heep, now the dominant partner in Wickfield and Heep, hires Micawber as a clerk. Before he leaves for Canterbury, Micawber "repays" Traddles with an IOU. (37) David tries to tell Dora of his changed circumstances, but she refuses to listen.

Part 13 (May 1850)
(38) Traddles helps David learn shorthand by reading parliamentary speeches for him to copy.

When Mr. Spenlow learns of David's relationship with Dora from Miss Murdstone, who has discovered one of David's letters, he demands that the affair be broken off. The same evening Spenlow dies suddenly, without a will, his affairs in disarray. Dora goes to live with her two maiden aunts in Putney.

(39) At Canterbury David finds Micawber unwilling to speak about Heep, Wickfield lamenting his partner's interest in his daughter, and Heep suspicious of David, whom he considers a rival for Agnes's affections.

(40) One snowy night David meets Daniel Peggotty, who tells of his unsuccessful search for Em'ly in France,
Italy, and Switzerland. David notices that Mr. Peggotty is being followed by Martha Endell.

Part 14 (June 1850)
(41) Dora's aunts, Miss Clarissa and Miss Lavinia Spenlow, agree to allow David to visit Dora on certain stated conditions. Aunt Betsey becomes a regular caller at their house. David worries that all, including his aunt and himself, treat Dora "like a plaything." (42) When Agnes and her father come to London to visit the Strongs, David introduces Agnes to Dora.

Heep tells Doctor Strong that he suspects Annie of infidelity with Maldon and indicates that David and Wickfield share his suspicions. The Doctor refuses to believe Annie unfaithful and blames himself for any unhappiness she feels. Afterward, David angrily strikes Heep for involving him.

(43) In a retrospective chapter, David remembers his 21st birthday and how his career changes from successful shorthand reporter to successful author. He remembers his wedding to Dora.

Part 15 (July 1850)
(44) David and Dora begin housekeeping and Dora proves utterly incapable of managing a home. David asks his aunt to counsel her, but she refuses to interfere in their lives. Dora asks David to think of her as his "child-wife."

(45) Mr. Dick notices the "cloud" between Doctor Strong and his wife and tells David that he will set things right. A few weeks later, Dick escorts Annie into the presence of her husband. She kneels before the Doctor, reiterates her love and respect for him, and tells of the awkward position she has been in because of the dishonorable behavior of Jack Maldon. David ruminates on two things she says: "There can be no disparity in marriage like unsuitability of mind and purpose," and "I should be thankful to him for having saved me from the first mistaken impulse of my undisciplined heart."

(46) About a year after his wedding, David is summoned to Steerforth's house. There Littimer tells him that Steerforth has left Em'ly and that she has disappeared. Rosa Dartle exults over Em'ly's suffering.

Part 16 (August 1850)
(47) David goes with Daniel Peggotty to seek out Martha Endell and enlist her aid in locating Emily should she come to London. They trace Martha to the edge of the THAMES and prevent her from drowning herself.

When David returns home he sees Aunt Betsey give some money to a man in her garden. She tells David that the man is her husband.

(48) David gives up parliamentary reporting and takes up writing full-time. Dora sits by his side as he works, but they quarrel about domestic issues. David attempts to "form Dora's mind," but the effort is unsuccessful, so he accepts her limitations and loves her as his "child-wife." During the second year of their marriage, Dora's health begins to fail so that David must carry her up and down stairs.

(49) Mr. Micawber has become secretive, irritable, and depressed. When David and Traddles meet him in London, he is so troubled that he is unable even to make punch. Suddenly he explodes with a denunciation of his employer, "HEEP," and then, just as abruptly, he leaves. He makes an appointment to meet them in Canterbury in a week, when he will expose the villain.

(50) Martha conducts David to her rooms, where they find Rosa Dartle berating Emily. Knowing that Daniel Peggoty has been told of Emily's whereabouts, David does not interfere. Just as Rosa leaves, Daniel arrives and Emily faints into his arms.

Part 17 (September 1850)
(51) Mr. Peggotty recounts the story of Emily's escape from Steerforth, her illness and recuperation in Italy, and her return to England. He plans to immigrate to Australia with her and "begin a new life over theer." Ham confesses that he feels partly responsible for Emily's ruin because she was trying to avoid marrying him. He asks David to tell Emily of his feelings.

(52) On the appointed day David, Aunt Betsey, and Traddles meet Micawber in Canterbury. At the office of Wickfield and Heep, Micawber reads off his accusations against the "HEEP of Infamy," charging him with forgery, misrepresentation, and embezzlement. Aunt Betsey learns that Heep, not Wickfield, was responsible for her losses. Traddles takes over the legal prosecution and assembles the evidence that Micawber has gathered. Although his mother urges him to "be 'umble and make terms," Uriah is defiant. He attacks David as the one responsible for his comeuppance: "I have always hated you. You've always been an upstart, and you've always been against me."

(53) In a retrospective chapter, David recalls Dora's decline and how, in her final hours, she regretted their childish marriage and asked to speak with Agnes. As Dora lingered, David meditated on his "undisciplined heart." As her dog Jip expired in his Chinese house, Dora passed away upstairs.

Part 18 (October 1850)
(54) Traddles and Micawber sort out Wickfield's business and Heep's schemes. They recover Aunt Betsey's money and liquidate Wickfield's firm without bankruptcy. Betsey praises David for meeting the test of financial hardship "nobly—persevering, self-reliant, self-denying." She arranges to pay off Micawber's debts and enables him to settle in Australia. Back in London, she reveals that her husband has died.

(55) David decides to deliver Emily's reply to Ham in person. At Yarmouth he finds himself in a tumultuous storm, "the greatest ever known to blow upon that coast," and it jumbles his thoughts and recollections. Drawn to the beach by news that a schooner is breaking up just offshore, David finds Ham preparing to attempt to rescue the lone sailor who clings to the mast of the sinking ship. But the attempt fails and, "beaten to death by a great wave," Ham's generous heart is stilled forever. The body of the lone sailor also washes up on the

shore. It is Steerforth. (56) David returns to London with Steerforth's body. Mrs. Steerforth's spirit is broken, but Rosa Dartle's pride and anger rise to a fever pitch and she curses David and the "evil hour that you ever came here."

(57) David bids farewell to the Micawbers and Mr. Peggotty as they leave for Australia. Daniel is taking Martha, as well as Emily and Mrs. Gummidge, with him.

Parts 19–20 (November 1850)
(58) While David spends three years in a Swiss village where he overcomes the "brooding sorrow . . . that fell on my undisciplined heart," he realizes that he loves Agnes and he thinks he has "thrown away the treasure of her love."

(59) Back in England, David learns that Traddles has married and that Murdstone has driven his new wife mad. He is reunited with Betsey, Dick, and Peggotty, who is now Miss Trotwood's housekeeper. (60) At Canterbury, David finds Agnes running a school for girls, but he is troubled by the thought that she is not happy.

(61) When David accepts an invitation to visit a model prison from Mr. Creakle, now a Middlesex magistrate, he is surprised to find Littimer and Uriah Heep among the model prisoners. Littimer forgives Emily "her bad conduct toward myself," and Heep hopes that "Mr. W. will repent, and Miss W., and all of that sinful lot." David leaves the prison convinced that the system merely encourages hypocrisy and false humility.

(62) David seeks to learn the secret of Agnes's unhappiness. He confesses to her his hope that she might be "something more than a sister" to him. She breaks into tears of joy and reveals that she has loved him all her life. Two weeks later, on their wedding day, Agnes tells David that Dora on her deathbed had given her "this vacant place."

(63) Ten years later, Mr. Peggotty surprises the Copperfields with a visit. He reports his success as a farmer, Emily's goodness and kindness to others, Martha's marriage, and Micawber's rise to become Port Middlebay District Magistrate. David also reads in an Australian paper of Doctor Mell of Colonial Salem House Grammar School.

(64) David closes with a final retrospect. He describes Aunt Betsey, a firm and upright woman of 80; Peggotty teaching his youngest son to walk as she taught him; and Mr. Dick continuing work on his memorial. He also remembers Mrs. Steerforth, whose life stopped on the day of her son's death; Julia Mills and Jack Maldon, who are "in society"; Doctor Strong, who still works on his dictionary; and Traddles, successful in the law, now a judge, and happy in his marriage to Sophy. Most of all, David tells of Agnes, "one face shining on me like a heavenly light by which I see all other objects."

COMMENTARY

In his 1867 Preface to *Copperfield*, Dickens described the novel as his "favourite child" and spoke of the difficulty of "dismissing some portion of himself into the shadowy world." The book may have had such personal importance to him because it was the most autobiographical of all his novels. Some of the most painful episodes of his life were only thinly disguised in the novel. These oblique revelations contained in *Copperfield* gave it a special place for him and contribute to its truthfulness and power as a novel.

The most important autobiographical materials involve the months he spent at WARREN'S BLACKING, his courtship of Maria BEADNELL, and his journalistic and writing career. As John FORSTER and others have pointed out, these episodes are essentially factual. The descriptions of David's labor at Murdstone and Grinby's repeat verbatim much of Dickens's description of his experiences at the BLACKING WAREHOUSE in the fragmentary *AUTOBIOGRAPHY* that he gave to Forster. David's fascination with Dora Spenlow draws on Dickens's own attraction to the flirtatious Maria Beadnell, and the outlines of David's career—from Doctors' Commons, to shorthand reporter, to novelist—follow those of his creator.

Yet all these episodes—as well as the other autobiographical materials in the novel—are also transformed by art. The villainous Murdstone is very different from the well-intentioned James LAMERT, Dickens's cousin who was responsible for placing him at Warren's Blacking. David's resolution to run away from the wine bottling warehouse ends his time there on a courageous note; Dickens, embittered by his mother's desire that he continue working, was saved by his father, who removed him from the factory to attend school. In the story of Maria Beadnell, recreated as Dora Spenlow in the novel, David marries the girl who spurned Dickens, and, perhaps indulging in some ex post facto wish-fulfilment, Dickens "kills" the father who has frustrated the courtship. David's literary career seems far less hectic and demanding than that of Dickens and his achievement far less spectacular. David's modesty about such matters would not alone account for these differences in temperament and achievement. Some of these transformations may be explained as the result of Dickens telling his life as he wished it might have been, but they must also be seen as indications of Dickens's conscious artistry, taking the materials of autobiography and giving them thematic relevance and coherence. In the end, Copperfield is David's autobiography, not Dickens's.

David begins his account by stating: "Whether I shall turn out to be the hero of my own life, or whether that station will be held by anybody else, these pages must show" (1), suggesting that even he is unsure of the resolution of this issue and that the test of his heroism will come in the writing of his story. In this Victorian quest narrative, the pen will be mightier than the sword, and the reader will be left to judge those qualities of the man and the writer that constitute heroism.

David's opening statement implies one of the standards by which to judge his heroism: that he, rather than someone else, will determine his life. The form of David's narrative exaggerates this test. Even though he narrates the story, David often seems to disappear. Other characters have a physical presence that he lacks. By contrast to Micawber, Heep, or Steerforth, he often appears colorless and passive. Several commentators have noted that we have no clear physical impression of David; in the illustrations he tends to be out of the center of the picture, often facing away from the viewer. To judge whether he becomes the hero of his life, then, we need to read his story in a different way from the way we would read a hero's saga. Instead of measuring David's great deeds, we need to study his refractions in other characters. What does Steerforth, or Micawber, or Heep, or Dora, tell us about David? And we must look at the narration itself for signs of the writer's heroism.

David's difference from two other writers in the story may suggest some of the tests for heroic narrative. Doctor Strong and Mr. Dick are both engaged in writing projects. Strong's dictionary will never be completed; by the end of the novel he is laboring "somewhere about the letter D" (64). Like the project of writing one's life, the dictionary will be "finished" only with the death of the author. Mr. Dick—whose name and connection with King Charles I links him to Charles Dickens—is engaged on an explicitly autobiographical project. His memorial gives surreal exaggeration to the test David faces as a writer. Can he overcome incoherence and inconclusiveness as he attempts to tell his life? Can he take control of his story? Can he unify it, give it a beginning, middle, and end? Can he transcend the traumas of the past—the severing of King Charles's head—to make sense of the present and give direction to the future? David's ability as a storyteller to pull together an account of his whole life, including the painful and traumatic episodes as well as his successes, is one measure of his heroism as a writer.

The pull of the past is especially strong on David. Born "a child of close observation" (2), he is an adult of extraordinary memory. His account of his childhood is so concretely realized that we forget, as he sometimes seems to, that he is remembering the past rather than describing events as they happen. He remarks on the powers of memory and marks the passages in his life with "retrospective" chapters. In many ways, *Copperfield* is a novel about memory and the ways in which it provides the imagination with the materials to make experience whole.

George ORWELL remarked on Dickens's ability to enter into the child's point of view, "to stand both inside and outside the child's mind." The opening chapters of *Copperfield* are a beautiful example of this double vision, combining the child's perspective with that of the narrator who knows that David's innocence and security will pass. Even before Murdstone intrudes as his stepfather or his mother dies, young David has intimations of his mortality in such scenes as the "Brooks of Sheffield" episode (2), and he knows that childhood has ended when he sees his infant brother, the image of himself, dead on his mother's breast (9).

David's life is in a way a series of lives, each one of them ending in a radical disjunction from what follows. The boy who goes to work at Murdstone and Grinby's is a different person from the child of Blunderstone Rookery or the boy at Salem House, and David seems to think that his survival depends on keeping these parts of himself disconnected from one another. When, as a schoolboy in Canterbury, for example, he meets Micawber again while he is having tea at Uriah Heep's house (17), he is terrified that Heep might connect him with the waif the Micawbers knew in London. These radical breaks in David's life are often marked by his changing name. When he runs away to Dover and begins a new life as Trotwood Copperfield under his aunt's protection, he remarks, "Thus I began my new life, in a new name, and with everything new about me. Now that the state of doubt was over, I felt, for many days, like one in a dream. . . . The two clearest things in my mind were, that a remoteness had come upon the old Blunderstone life—which seemed to lie in a haze of an immeasurable distance; and that a curtain had for ever fallen on my life at Murdstone and Grinby's" (14). In remembering and telling his story, David attempts to connect these separate lives into one.

"A posthumous child" (1), David is born after his father's death. His aunt acts out his identity problem, his "orphanhood," on the day of his birth when she abandons him because he was supposed to be a girl. His early years, spent in a community of women centering on his mother, Clara Copperfield, and his nurse, Clara Peggotty, further undermine his sense of masculine identity. He develops a feminine sensibility—trusting, unworldly, innocent, and insecure like his orphan mother. Young David is characterized as Daisy, Steerforth's feminine nickname for him. If he is to avoid his mother's fate and survive in the world with a masculine identity, he must find a father figure to replace the father he never knew.

Murdstone is the first of his male role models. He darkens David's childhood with "firmness," a principle missing in David's parents and in his life up until the time Murdstone appears. Murdstone and his metallic spinster sister bring order to the household, but they stifle and eventually kill its love and care. David's resistance to Murdstone is both a challenge to the usurper who has stolen his mother's love and an act of rebellion that liberates him from their regime of firmness. In Micawber, David finds another ineffectual father, one very different from Murdstone. Micawber lacks firmness and responsibility; he does not lack imagination and love. His marriage is grounded in fidelity and devotion, and, in spite of the recurrent setbacks in his life, his outlook is one of eternal optimism, always believing that something will "turn up." As a member of the Micawber household, David must adopt a semi-parental role and help the Micawbers with their financial difficulties.

Among David's other male role models are Heep, Traddles, and, especially, Steerforth. Heep acts as a kind of negative mirror to David, magnifying qualities that David represses or denies. Heep exploits his humble origins with a false humility as a way of evoking sympathy and disguising his ruthless ambition. Although David suppresses his humble past and hides his ambition under a veneer of genteel diffidence, he is also a self-seeking social climber. Heep's ambition, like Murdstone's firmness, is unbalanced by any tempering feminine qualities.

Steerforth appears to David to be everything that Heep is not. He has been born to his place as a gentleman, and even though he has no visible ambition, no apparent purpose in life, he is a commanding person; but his unacceptability as a male ideal is suggested long before he steals Emily from Yarmouth to ruin her in Italy. It appears in his brutality to Rosa Dartle, which has scarred her for life, and in his cruelty to Mr. Mell. His condescending attitude and selfish exploitation of others are contrasted to Daniel Peggotty's selflessness and love. Although David comes to realize Steerforth's villainy, he is still drawn to Steerforth's charismatic gentility, even as he sees him dead on the sands at Yarmouth, "lying with his head upon his arm, as I had often seen him at school" (55).

Though lacking Steerforth's charisma, Traddles is, in the long run, a far better model for David. In many ways, Traddles and David are alike, but Traddles is less easily manipulated by others. He possesses a moderation and restraint that David sometimes lacks. Born neither to humbleness nor wealth, he too must find his own place in the world. Love tempers Traddles's ambition, patience restrains his passion, and justice is more important to him than social position.

David's personal history makes it harder for him to achieve such balance in his life, for he seems fated to reenact the mistakes of his parents. He is inevitably attracted to Dora, for she possesses the same delicate and captivating femininity as his mother, and she is just as frivolous. The chapters describing their courtship and marriage are among the most successful in the novel, for they capture David's painful ambivalence. He is both infatuated with Dora and frustrated by her helplessness, incompetence, and lack of discipline. While he loves her, he attempts to change her and "form her mind." In doing so, he is forced to recognize his own need for "firmness" and his discomfiting kinship with Murdstone.

David's Aunt Betsey dramatizes the struggle to achieve a balance between firmness and softness, rationality and sympathy. Aunt Betsey, whose repressed personal history has forced her into a masculine role, is a proponent of firmness and discipline. Her tough-mindedness prompts her to abandon the infant David and to decry the weakness of his parents, but it is tempered by her own experience of suffering and by her sympathy for Mr. Dick, who modifies her rationality with his irrational foolishness and down-to-earth advice. In spite of her rationality, Aunt Betsey cannot control her world: She cannot make the infant David a girl, save herself from Heep's machinations, or resist her husband's entreaties for money. She can see David's "blindness," but she cannot prevent his marriage to Dora. Ironically, it is Mr. Dick, prompted by intuition and feeling, who can act to aid Micawber in exposing Heep and to heal the misunderstandings between the Strongs.

The story of Doctor Strong's marriage to his young wife, Annie, which counterpoints David's marriage to Dora, illustrates the mixture of firmness and feeling necessary to take control of one's life. While Dora is dying and David attempts to understand his role in his marriage, he watches the Strongs sort out their relationship. Two statements by Annie Strong lodge in his memory. When she tells why she rejected Jack Maldon, she thanks her husband for saving her "from the first mistaken impulse of my undisciplined heart" and asserts that "there can be no disparity in marriage like unsuitability of mind and purpose"(45). David repeats these words to himself, acknowledging their relevance to his marriage to Dora and underscoring their thematic importance in the novel. Discipline must be tempered with love, firmness balanced with feeling.

This recognition and the painful memories that he suffers following Dora's death enable David to overcome his blindness and acknowledge his love for Agnes, the woman Dickens identified in his notes for her first appearance in the story as the "true heroine" of the novel. With the saintly aura of the stained-glass window surrounding her, Agnes has disappointed many readers. She is more of a conscience or ideal than a real person; she brings discipline and responsibility into David's life, but she seems to lack the human qualities that make Dora so attractive.

The ending has also annoyed some readers, who find the Micawbers' exile to Australia a convenient but unconvincing way to "clean up" David's identity, allowing him to achieve respectable maturity by removing them from his presence. If David has achieved a "disciplined heart" by the end of his autobiography, he has done so, these critics suggest, by diminishing the richness and complexity of his life, for he sacrifices Dora to death and the Micawbers to emigration. It is not the story itself but the tone of its telling that lingers. In the narration, David's success as a novelist and his happy marriage to Agnes are mixed with memories of his losses. Whatever heroism there is for him by the end of his story, he has not been left unscathed in achieving it.

Some critics find David unconvincing as a portrait of the artist. David tells us little about the books that he writes, and he is not self-dramatizing in the manner of the Inimitable Boz. In spite of the novel's autobiographical passages, Dickens does not seem to be presenting David as his own self-portrait in the novel. In some ways, Micawber comes closer to filling that role. The most triumphant creation in *Copperfield*, he is the character who possesses the power of self creation. He does so through language, and we remember him not for his story but for his words. His story is inconsistent: Who can believe that Heep would hire him, that this perenially unsuccessful man could pull together the case against Heep, or that he could achieve such success in Australia? It is Micawber's grandiloquent and inflated rhetoric that

transforms the world, even if it inevitably ends, like Micawber, unable to sustain itself and, in short, deflated. His most famous speech exemplifies this self-creating, self-affirming, and deflating rhetorical pattern:

> "My other piece of advice, Copperfield," said Mr. Micawber, "you know. Annual income twenty pounds, annual expenditure nineteen nineteen six, result happiness. Annual income twenty pounds, annual expenditure twenty pounds ought and six, result misery. The blossom is blighted, the leaf is withered, the God of day goes down upon the dreary scene, and—and in short you are for ever floored. As I am" (12).

If Dickens was "floored" in ending this novel, unable to sustain the richness of the story he had spun, nevertheless we remember the wonderful invention in the telling and accept the inevitability in the end.

CRITICISM

Overall *Copperfield*, Dickens's favorite of all his novels, has been his readers' favorite as well. Its unity of style and tone, its serious theme leavened by the wonderful comic scenes with the Micawbers, and its fundamentally optimistic view of life have made it a perennial favorite. The vivid account of David's childhood has also given it recognition as a story for children, though its popularity as a school text is probably due at least as much to its moral earnestness.

Two good general introductions to *Copperfield* are those by Sylvère MONOD (1967), whose chapters on the novel are particularly good on the part structure and the style, and by Philip COLLINS (*Charles Dickens: David Copperfield*, 1977), who discusses David's life in relation to Dickens's life, and David as child, adult, and narrator of the novel. Q. D. LEAVIS (1970) compares *Copperfield* with *War and Peace*, making a case for Dickens's novel as an important influence on Tolstoy and analyzing the serious and adult insights in both novels. She is especially good on David's relationship with Dora. Gwendolyn Needham's classic essay "The Undisciplined Heart of David Copperfield" (*Nineteenth Century Fiction*, 1954) analyzes a central theme in the novel. Jerome H. BUCKLEY (1974) discusses *Copperfield* along with *Expectations* as examples of the BILDUNGSROMAN. Alexander WELSH (1987) spends several chapters exploring the novel as the culmination of Dickens's autobiographical attempt in the middle works to come to terms with his role as a novelist. Finally, J. B. Priestley's discussion of Micawber (*English Comic Characters*, 1966) explains his conclusion that "with the one exception of Falstaff, [Micawber] is the greatest comic figure in the whole range of English literature."

ADAPTATIONS

Malcolm MORLEY claims that after *Twist* and *Cricket*, *Copperfield* has inspired more dramatic adaptations than any other work by Dickens. During the 1850s alone there were at least 25 productions. The first stage adaptation, *Born with a Caul* by George Almar, produced before the serial had completed its run, took great liberties with the story; he saved Steerforth from drowning to marry Little Em'ly and added a character named Hurricane Flash whose role was to kill Murdstone. Most other early adaptations were more faithful to the text.

Later in the Victorian period, Andrew HALLIDAY's *Little Em'ly* (1869) provided a model for many other adaptations. Telling only the story of Em'ly, Halliday's play and its imitations replaced nearly all other adaptations in the last three decades of the 19th century.

In the 20th century, Mr. Micawber has proved a more engaging focus. He was central in Louis Napoleon Parker's 1914 stage adaptation in which Sir Herbert Beerbohm Tree played both Micawber and Daniel Peggotty. Bransby WILLIAMS doubled in the same two roles (1923). Williams, famous for his one-man shows of characters from Dickens, also included Uriah Heep in his repertory.

The popularity of the story is attested to by the seven silent film adaptations of the novel that appeared early in the century, but the two great cinematic versions were sound films made in 1934 and 1970. In the first, produced for MGM by David O. Selznick and George Cukor, Edna May Oliver played Aunt Betsey; Lionel BARRYMORE, Daniel Peggotty; Maureen O'Sullivan, Dora; W. C. FIELDS, Micawber; and Freddie Bartholomew, the child David. The 1970 film had an equally distinguished cast. Directed by Delbert Mann for Twentieth Century Fox, it included Edith Evans (Aunt Betsey), Susan Hampshire (Agnes), Laurence Olivier (Mr. Creakle), Michael Redgrave (Daniel Peggotty), Emlyn WILLIAMS (Mr. Dick), and Ralph Richardson (Micawber).

The BBC has produced several television adaptations of the novel, most notably a 13-part adaptation by Vincent Tilsley, produced twice (1956; 1966); Hugh Whitemore's six-part adaptation (1974); and James Andrew Hall's 10-part version (1986). Adaptations have also been produced for American (1954), French (1967), and Australian (1985) television.

Davis, Earle R. (1905–   )   Professor, Kansas State University, whose *The Flint and the Flame: The Artistry of Charles Dickens* (1963) provides useful discussions of the influence of Victorian theater on Dickens's novels and of Wilkie COLLINS's influence on Dickens.

Davis, Eliza   Wife of **J. P. Davis**, the British Jewish banker who bought TAVISTOCK HOUSE in 1860. She wrote to Dickens in 1863 stating that his portrayal of Fagin in *Twist* had done "a great wrong" to her people. Dickens wrote back defending his portrayal of Fagin, but he was clearly troubled by the suggestion that the novel was anti–Semitic. In *Our Mutual Friend* he included Riah and the circle of Jews who take in Lizzie Hexam partly to redress the balance in his treatment of the Jews. After the later novel appeared, Mrs. Davis sent him a copy of Benisch's Hebrew and English Bible, inscribed: "Presented to Charles Dickens, in grateful and admiring recognition of his having exercised the noblest quality men can possess—that of atoning for an injury as soon as conscious of having inflicted it."

Davis, Gill   Illiterate retired private in the Royal Marines who narrates "The Perils of Certain English Prisoners" to Lady Carton, one of the former colonists whom he has been instrumental in rescuing from the pirates on Silver-Store Island. A poor and ignorant man, he envies the comfortable life of the colonists, but his admiration and love for Marion Maryon prompts his heroic efforts on their behalf. He tells the story late in his life when he has become a "poor, old, faithful, humble" retainer of Lord and Lady Carton. "English Prisoners."

Dawes, Mary   Nurse in the nobleman's family where Miss Wade works as a governess. Miss Wade is convinced that she will turn the children against her. *Dorrit* (II:21).

Dawkins, John (The Artful Dodger)   Youthful pickpocket who is a member of Fagin's gang and recruits Oliver Twist: "one of the queerest looking boys that Ol-

The Artful Dodger greets Oliver Twist as he arrives in London. Illustration by Harry Furniss (1910).

iver had ever seen. He was a snub-nosed, flat-browed, common-faced boy, . . . but he had about him all the airs and manners of a man" (8). He robs Brownlow at the bookstore, a crime for which Oliver is arrested (10). When he appears in court, he gamely tries to put the judge and the court itself on trial, but his strategy fails and he is sentenced to transportation for life (43). *Twist.*

Daws, Mary   Dombey's kitchen maid who worries that her wages won't be paid after the bankruptcy. *Dombey* (59).

Dawson, Doctor   Physician in Our Parish who delivers Mrs. Robinson's daughter. *Boz,* "Four Sisters."

Deaf Gentleman   Companion to Master Humphrey, who is like a brother to him even though he has never told him his name. *Humphrey* (1).

Deal   Seacoast town in KENT where Esther visits Richard Carstone as he is leaving the Navy. While there she also meets Allan Woodcourt, who has just returned from the East. *Bleak House* (45).

Dean, Abigail   Mr. Bull's sleepwalking housekeeper, a satiric representation of the Earl of Aberdeen, prime minister from 1852 to 1855: "Abby Dean. Phlegmatic temperament. Bilious habit. Circulation, very sluggish. Speech, drowsy, indistinct, and confused. Senses, feeble. Memory, short. Pulse, very languid. A remarkably slow goer. At all times a heavy sleeper, and difficult to awaken." *Miscellaneous,* "Bull's Sonambulist."

Dean of Cloisterham   Dignitary of the Cathedral in Cloisterham on whom Mr. Sapsea models himself (4). *Drood.*

Death   At the beginning of *Charles Dickens Resurrectionist,* Andrew SANDERS takes two pages just to list the more important deaths that occur in Dickens's works, giving substance to the common impression that deaths and deathbed scenes occur frequently in the novels. Dickens was not simply exploiting the sentimental possibilities of such scenes; he was describing a reality of his times. Death was much more frequent in Victorian times than in modern England, especially in the cities, and the dying more present, for they were more likely to die at home than in hospital. Dickens was probably not guilty of exaggerating the facts about death in Victorian England. The five little stone lozenges on the graves of Pip's five siblings who died in infancy in the opening chapter of *Expectations* were based on an actual grave in a country churchyard at CHALK near GAD'S HILL, where there were 13 such markers on one family's plot.

Oscar Wilde's remark that one would need a heart of stone not to laugh at Little Nell's death marks a major change in sensibility between the 19th and 20th centu-

ries. Like Wilde, most modern readers find Dickens's deathbed scenes, particularly those describing the deaths of children, oppressively sentimental and overdone. Yet these were often the scenes most prized by Victorian readers, both in the novels and in the stage adaptations. The deaths of Nell, Paul Dombey, and Jo the crossing sweeper (*Bleak House*) moved them to tears and were climactic moments on the stage. The Victorians were much more willing to cry, women and men alike, than are modern readers.

Dickens's SENTIMENTALITY in handling such scenes, particularly the deaths of young women like Little Nell, is often linked to the death of Mary HOGARTH, his sister-in-law, who died at 17. Dickens, who was holding her in his arms at the moment of her death, removed a ring from her finger and wore it for the rest of his life. She became the model for Nell, Florence Dombey, Little Dorrit, and Dickens's other saintly young women. They are, as Alexander WELSH (1971) suggests, angels who act as intermediaries between this world and the next, agents both of death and immortality.

Death also has a didactic role in the novels, for by showing us how to die it teaches us how to live. In an increasingly secular world, death is a reminder of the spiritual dimension in this life and the promise of an afterlife—at least an afterlife in the memories of those who remember the good deeds of the dead. The narrator of the *Carol* expresses this didactic function of the death scenes as Scrooge contemplates his body on its bier:

> Oh cold, cold, rigid, dreadful Death, set up thine altar here, and dress it with such terrors as thou hast at thy command, for this is thy dominion! But of the loved, revered, and honored head, thou canst not turn one hair to thy dread purposes, or make one feature odious. It is not that the hand is heavy, and will fall down when released; it is not that the heart and pulse are still: but that the hand was open, generous, and true, the heart brave, warm, and tender, and the pulse a man's. Strike, Shadow, strike! And see his good deeds springing from the wound, to sow the world with life immortal! (4)

Dickens's theology in this passage seems to suggest that in the death of the good man there is immortality, for his good deeds will be remembered by the living.

The most thorough discussion of Dickens's treatment of death is Sanders (1982). Welsh (1971) offers several provocative chapters on the idealized young woman as an angel of death and immortality.

Debtors Prisons   When Dickens was a boy of twelve, his father was imprisoned in the MARSHALSEA PRISON for debt, an event at the center of the most traumatic episode in Dickens's youth. Although John DICKENS was only held from February 20 to May 28, 1824, Charles was humiliated by the dishonor to the family and by the degrading work he was sent to do at WARREN'S BLACKING warehouse. Dickens used this period in his life as the basis for the episodes in *Copperfield* dealing with Mr.

Micawber's imprisonment and David's employment at MURDSTONE AND GRINBY's; he wrote about it directly in the fragment of AUTOBIOGRAPHY that he gave to John FORSTER at about the same time.

Personal insolvency was subject to imprisonment during most of Dickens's lifetime, although the penalty was not often exacted in the two decades before it was finally abolished in 1869. During Dickens's youth, however, imprisonment for debt was common. Typically the debtor was arrested and detained for a few days in a sponging house or halfway house—such as that with which Neckett is connected (*Bleak House*, 6)—in order to allow time to raise the money to pay the debt. If he was unable (or unwilling, as in *Pickwick*'s case) to pay, the debtor was sent to prison. Dickens writes about each of the three main debtors' prisons in London: Pickwick is imprisoned in the FLEET (*Pickwick*, 41–47), a debtors' prison dating back to the 13th century, which was demolished in 1846. Micawber is held in the KING'S BENCH in SOUTHWARK (*Copperfield*, 11), a prison destroyed during the GORDON RIOTS, rebuilt afterward, and finally demolished in 1880. Mr. Dorrit, like Dickens's father, was imprisoned in the Marshalsea, also in Southwark, which was closed in 1842.

"December Vision, A" Article for *HOUSEHOLD WORDS* (December 14, 1850) describing the Spirit of Death coming over the world through Ignorance, Disease, and Injustice. Those who recognize that these social ills need to be overcome, nonetheless acquiesce to despair, remarking that "it will last my time." The Spirit points out that their time is in Eternity and that they will be forever condemned for doing nothing to change things. *Miscellaneous*. The essay allegorizes the criticism of CHANCERY that Dickens develops in *Bleak House*.

Dedlock Family Landed family with an estate in Lincolnshire, CHESNEY WOLD; they represent the ARISTOCRACY in *Bleak House*. **Sir Leicester**, baronet and patriarch of the Lincolnshire Dedlocks, laments the passing of the old order. "He has a general opinion that the world might get on without hills, but would be done up without Dedlocks. . . . He is an honourable, obstinate, truthful, high-spirited, intensely prejudiced, perfectly unreasonable man" (2). He married beneath him, a woman 20 years his junior. **Lady Honoria**—beautiful, cold, repressed—hides her guilt about her past beneath a facade of being "bored to death," but she cannot conceal from Tulkinghorn, the family lawyer, her interest in a particular law writer. Tulkinghorn pursues her story and learns of her relationship with Captain Hawdon and of their illegitimate daughter, Esther SUMMERSON. Lady Dedlock reveals herself to Esther (36), but she runs from Chesney Wold when Sir Leicester learns of her past (56). Disguised as a poor brickmaker's wife, she makes her way to London where she dies by the graveyard where Hawdon is buried (59). When Sir Leicester learns her story, he forgives her, and, even though weakened by a stroke, he sends Bucket to find her and bring her back (56). After Lady Dedlock's death, **Volumnia**, a proud and poor spinster related to Sir Leicester, becomes mistress of Chesney Wold. *Bleak House*.

Deedles Banker who surprises Alderman Cute by committing suicide. *Chimes*.

Defarge Family Husband and wife representing the revolutionary Jacquerie in *Two Cities*. **Ernest**, keeper of a wineshop in the ST. ANTOINE section of Paris that is a center for revolutionary activity, was formerly a servant of Dr. Manette. He takes in the old man when he is released from prison. During the storming of the Bastille, he goes to the cell formerly occupied by Manette and finds the manuscript left there by the doctor (II:21) that will later be used to convict Charles Darnay (III:10). "A bull-necked, martial-looking man of thirty," he is a ringleader in the Revolution; "he was a dark man altogether, . . . good-humoured looking on the whole, but implacable-looking, too" (I:5). He and his wife, **Madame Thérèse**, are ringleaders of the Revolution. She is "a stout woman, . . . with a watchful eye that seldom seemed to look at anything," and she records the atrocities of the aristocracy by knitting them into a list that will condemn them to the guillotine. Her special thirst for vengeance against the Evrémonde family is a result of the fact that her sister and brother were raped and killed by the Evrémondes. Determined that none of the St. Evrémonde family shall live, she attempts to detain Lucie before she flees from Paris, but she arrives at the Darnay apartment after all but Miss Pross have fled. In a struggle with Pross, Madame Defarge is killed by her own gun (III:14). *Two Cities*.

Defoe, Daniel (1660–1731) One of the 18th-century writers whom Dickens, like David Copperfield, read as a child. *Robinson Crusoe* is frequently mentioned in Dickens's works, most notably in *Pickwick* (7, 30, 44); *Carol* (2); *Chuzzlewit* (5, 21); *Dombey* (4, 39); *Copperfield* (4, 5, 24, 26, 34); *Bleak House* (8); *Dorrit* (I:13, 25); *Mutual Friend* (IV:17).

Defresnier et Cie Swiss wine merchants, represented in England by Jules Obenreizer. "No Thoroughfare."

De la Rue, Emile and Augusta Swiss banker and his wife who were neighbors of the Dickenses in GENOA in 1844–45. Dickens attempted through MESMERISM to treat Mrs. De la Rue's psychosomatic maladies that induced sleeplessness and hallucinations. His late-night treatments aroused Catherine's jealousy and engaged Dickens's attentions as "doctor" almost obsessively.

Dellombra, Signor Gentleman who possesses the evil face that haunts the dreams of the English bride. He kidnaps her and they disappear. *Reprinted*, "At Dusk."

Delmonico's The NEW YORK restaurant at which a grand press banquet was held for Dickens during his reading tour in the United States in 1867. In his speech here Dickens spoke positively about AMERICA and the American press, hoping to heal the wounds caused by his criticisms after his 1842 visit.

"Demeanour of Murderers, The" Article for *HOUSEHOLD WORDS* (June 14, 1856), in which Dickens comments on the trial of murderer William Palmer (1824–56), a case that aroused intense public interest. Known as the Rudgeley Poisoner, Palmer was convicted in 1856 of poisoning his friend John Parsons, as well as his wife and brother. Dickens notes that many people have been suprised by the "complete self-possession" and "profound composure" of Palmer during his recent trial, but, comparing Palmer to other famous murderers, he suggests that such equanimity is characteristic of ruthless killers who have lost all natural human feeling and are confident of acquittal. *Miscellaneous.*

Demented Traveller Englishman whose faculties are "entirely absorbed in hurry." He is in the narrator's compartment on the train to Paris. *Reprinted*, "Flight."

Demerara Colony in British Guiana. Jingle and Job Trotter immigrate there (*Pickwick*, 53); Fred Trent is sent there by his Grandfather (*Curiosity Shop*, 23); Sol Gills stops there on his journey in search of Walter Gay (*Dombey*, 56).

Demple, George Pupil at SALEM HOUSE, a doctor's son. *Copperfield* (5).

Denham, Edmund Name taken by Edmund LONGFORD to maintain his anonymity as Redlaw's student. *Haunted Man* (2).

Dennis, Edward Public hangman who becomes one of the leaders of the GORDON RIOTS, "a squat, thickset personage, with a low, retreating forehead. . . . A dingy handkerchief twisted like a cord about his neck, left its great veins exposed to view, and they were swoln and starting, as though with gulping down strong passions, malice, and ill-will" (37). Dennis takes an unwholesome pride in his work and relishes the commissions that will be produced by the riots. Although he becomes an informer for the authorities (69), he is arrested and condemned (74), reduced to grovelling cowardice by the sentence (77), and eventually hanged (79). *Rudge.*

Deptford Dock area along the south side of the THAMES, east of London. Tony Jobling retreats here to recover financially (*Bleak House*, 20); Toby Magsman tells the story of Chops the dwarf here, "Going into Society."

Deputy ("Winks") Boy hired by Durdles to pelt him with stones and drive him home when he is wandering aimlessly under the influence of drink. Deputy is a servant at the Travellers' Twopenny, a cheap lodging house for transients. *Drood.*

Derrick, John Valet to the narrator of the ghost story "To Be Taken with a Grain of Salt." "Marigold."

"Dectective Police, The" A group of Scotland Yard detectives tell anecdotes of their exploits at a gathering in the offices of *HOUSEHOLD WORDS*. The names of the policemen thinly conceal actual policemen of the time: Witchem (Whicker) tells of capturing Tally-ho Thompson, a horse thief; Wield (FIELD) tells of taking Fikey, a forger; Mith (Smith) tells of capturing Shepherdson by disguising himself as a butcher; Dornton (Thornton) tells of tracing Aaron Mesheck, a con man, to New York. Originally in *Household Words* (July 27 and August 10, 1850). *Reprinted.*

Detective Story Edgar Allan POE is usually described as the originator of the detective story: a novel or story in which a crime—usually a murder—is solved by a detective who logically follows a series of clues to discover the identity of the perpetrator. Dickens's *Bleak House* is often listed along with Poe's stories as one of the earliest such novels, but *Bleak House* does not allow the reader to follow along with Inspector Bucket's processes of deduction and hence it lacks some of the intellectual appeal usually found in such stories. However, as Karen Chase (*Eros and Psyche*, 1984) points out, its plot, does use the techniques of the detective story to unravel the hidden and suppressed identities in the novel.

Some detective figures appear prior to *Bleak House*. The runners from the BOW STREET POLICE COURT are called in to help solve the robbery at Mrs. Maylie's house in CHERTSEY (*Twist*, 31); Nadgett, a private investigator working for Tigg, uncovers Jonas Chuzzlewit's guilt (51). The most significant detective in the later novels is the Inspector in *Mutual Friend* who solves the Harmon murder.

By including detectives in his novels, Dickens was reflecting the major changes in policing during his lifetime. Peel's Metropolitan Police Force was established in 1829, replacing the army and such semiprivate operations as the Bow Street Runners as keepers of public order. The Detective Department came into being in 1842, so the evolution of the detective in Dickens's novels from Bow Street Runner to private investigator to Department inspector reflects this historical transition. Several of Dickens's magazine articles describe the work of these new policemen and detectives, most notably, "The Detective Police," "Three 'Detective' Anecdotes," "On Duty with Inspector Field," and "Down with the Tide" (*Reprinted*).

Had Dickens finished *Drood*, that novel might have most completely fulfilled the definition of the detective story. Written under the influence of Wilkie COLLINS, it seems to have a crime in the murder or disappearance of Drood, and Datchery may be a detective in disguise.

Ian Ousby (*Bloodhounds of Heaven: The Detective in English Fiction from Godwin to Doyle*, 1976) includes Dickens's detectives among those he discusses.

Devasseur, Loyal   Landlord who rents two country houses to visitors at the French Watering Place; "a portly, upright, broad-shouldered, brown faced man" and a great admirer of Napoleon. *Reprinted*, "French Watering Place."

Devonshire House   Duke of Devonshire's house in PICCADILLY where Dickens and his troupe of actors presented Edward Bulwer-LYTTON's *Not so Bad as We Seem* at a benefit for the GUILD OF LITERATURE AND ART, a performance attended by the queen and prince consort on May 16, 1851. After a second performance on May 27, the duke gave a ball and supper for the actors.

Devonshire Terrace   Dickens lived at number 1 in this street off Marylebone Road, Regent's Park, London, from 1839 to 1851.

Dexter Collection, J. F.   Dickens materials acquired by the British Library in 1969, catalogued in *Charles Dickens: The J. F. Dexter Collection* (1974). The collection includes the manuscripts of two essays, many letters, the Preface to *Twist*, proof copies of illustrations by BROWNE and CRUIKSHANK, and some sets of the novels in parts.

Dexter, Walter (1877–1944)   Author and editor of numerous books relating to Dickens; editor of The DICKENSIAN, 1925–44; leader in the effort to secure DICKENS HOUSE for a library and museum. Dexter wrote a brief biography of Dickens (1927) and several volumes on Dickensian TOPOGRAPHY; he also made several collections of Dickens's letters, culminating in the collection for the NONESUCH EDITION, still the scholarly edition of the LETTERS for the years not yet covered by the Pilgrim Edition.

Dialect   Dickens uses a wide range of regional and class dialects in the novels, usually marking such speech with a few recognizable characteristics, rather than attempting to represent a totally accurate transcription. Compare, for example, John Browdie's Yorkshire speech in *Nickleby* with the much fuller rendering of a Yorkshire dialect in Emily Brontë's sometimes unintelligible Joseph in *Wuthering Heights*. Dickens represents class dialects more fully, especially the languages used by various London subcultures, from the thieves' slang in *Twist* to the upper-class dialect spoken at the Veneering's supper ta-

The house in Devonshire Terrace occupied by Dickens and his family from December 1839 until November 1851.

ble in *Mutual Friend*. G. L. Brook (*The Language of Dickens*, 1970) and Robert Golding (*Idiolects in Dickens*, 1985) undertake linguistic analyses of the various dialects that appear in the novels.

Diamond Edition American edition of Dickens's works with illustrations by Sol EYTINGE, published by TICKNOR AND FIELDS in 1867.

Dibabs, Jane Acquaintance of Mrs. Nickleby who married a man much older than herself. Mrs. Nickleby uses her example to justify the appropriateness of Madeline Bray marrying Gride. *Nickleby* (55).

Dibble, Sampson A blind old man and his wife, **Dorothy**, who are among the Mormon emigrants. *Uncommercial* (22).

Dibdin, The Late Mr. Poet whose song "The Jolly Young Waterman" is explicated as a celebration of abstinence by Anthony Humm at a meeting of the Brick Lane Temperance Association. *Pickwick* (33).

Dick (1) Pauper orphan friend of Oliver Twist at Mrs. Mann's baby farm. *Twist* (7, 17).

Dick (2) Guard on the coach that takes Nicholas to YORKSHIRE. *Nickleby* (5).

Dick (3) Tim Linkinwater's blind blackbird: "there was not a bird of such methodical and business-like habits in all the world, as the blind blackbird, who dreamed and dozed away his days in a large snug cage, and had lost his voice, from old age, years before Tim first bought him" (37). *Nickleby*.

Dick (4) Ostler at the SALISBURY inn where Tom Pinch meets Martin. *Chuzzlewit* (5).

Dick (5) The name by which Christopher's father is known. "Somebody's Luggage."

Dick (6) Fiancé of Sally, nurse at the FOUNDLING HOSPITAL. "No Thoroughfare."

Dick, Mr. Name by which Richard BABLEY is known, but which he cannot bear to hear spoken. A harmless lunatic and distant connection of Betsey Trotwood, whom she has rescued from the asylum where he was placed by his brother. She describes him as "the most friendly and amenable creature in existence" (14), and relies on his good advice. He keeps busy writing a memorial of his life for the LORD CHANCELLOR, always trying to avoid mention of King Charles's head, which inevitably finds its way into his account. Then he makes kites of the manuscripts spoiled by his obsession. Though mad, he advises Betsey to keep and care for David and to educate him at CANTERBURY. He also sorts out the misunderstandings between Doctor Strong and his wife, Annie (45). *Copperfield*.

Dickens, Alfred Allen (1813–1814) Dickens's younger brother, who died in infancy.

Dickens, Alfred D'Orsay Tennyson (1845–1912) Dickens's fourth son, named for his two godfathers, and nicknamed "Skittles" by his father. He was not suited for the military career which Dickens encouraged and, at age 20, he immigrated to Australia, where he married Jessie Devlin, "the Belle of Melbourne," and had a successful career with the London and Australia Agency Company Ltd. After his father's death, he lectured on Dickens's life and works in England and America. He died in NEW YORK on one of his lecture tours. He wrote "My Father and His Friends" (*Nash's Magazine*, 1911).

Dickens, Alfred Lamert (1822–1860) Dickens's younger brother; a civil engineer and sanitary inspector who left a widow and five children when he died. Dickens aided the family but found his sister-in-law **Helen** irritating.

Dickens, Augustus (1827–1866) Dickens's youngest brother. It was his infant pronunciation of his nickname "Moses" that produced "Boses" and, eventually, "Boz." Although Dickens helped to find him a job in London, Augustus deserted his wife and eloped to America with another woman. He died penniless in Chicago. Dickens contributed to the support of his American family and the deserted wife in England.

Dickens, Catherine Hogarth ("Kate") (1815–1879) Dickens's wife, and mother to his 10 children. The eldest daughter of George HOGARTH, music critic on the *MORNING CHRONICLE* and editor of the *EVENING CHRONICLE* when Dickens as a young man was working as a journalist, she married Dickens on April 2, 1836. An amiable, conventional, and domestic woman, she deferred to her husband who increasingly found her unresponsive, clumsy, indolent, and an incompetent mother and housekeeper. Some of her duties as housekeeper and hostess were assumed by her younger sister Georgina HOGARTH, who moved into the household after the trip to America in 1842. During the 1850s the marriage gradually deteriorated until, in 1857, Charles and Catherine took separate bedrooms, and in 1858 legally separated. Catherine moved into London with Charley, her oldest child; the other children and Georgina remained at GAD'S HILL with Dickens. Bitter and self-pitying, Catherine nonetheless remained loyal to her husband. Hebe Elsna (*Unwanted Wife: A Defence of Mrs. Charles Dickens*, 1963) describes Catherine's relationship with her husband from her point of view.

Dickens, Charles Culliford ("Charley") (1837–1896) Dickens's oldest child. Educated at Eton, he entered a business career, working for Baring's Bank and then going into trade with China. After he went bankrupt in 1868, Dickens made him a subeditor on *ALL THE YEAR ROUND*. He accompanied his father on the final reading tour and owned GAD'S HILL for a time after Dickens's death. In 1862, he married **Elizabeth ("Bessie") Evans**, daughter of Dickens's former publisher. Dickens, who had quarreled with BRADBURY & EVANS, disapproved of the marriage and did not attend the wedding, but he was reconciled with them and his first grandchild, Mary Angela DICKENS, at Christmas 1862. Charley and Bessie had eight children. Charley, who gave public readings of his father's work and lectures about him, published "Dickens as an Editor" (*English Illustrated Magazine*, 1889) and "Glimpses of Charles Dickens" (*North American Review*, 1895). His "Reminiscences of my Father" appeared in *Windsor Magazine* in 1934.

Dickens, Charles John Huffam ("Boz") (1812–1870)   Charles Dickens was born on February 7, 1812 in PORTSMOUTH the second child of John DICKENS a clerk in the Navy Pay Office there, and Elizabeth Barrow DICKENS. The family moved a good deal during Dickens's childhood, as his father was transferred from one station to another: in 1815 to London while John worked at SOMERSET HOUSE, and in 1817 to CHATHAM in KENT, where the boy spent the happiest years of his childhood. Here he roamed in the countryside, watched the activities in the bustling seaport town, and began his education with William GILES, the son of the local Baptist minister, who thought him an exceptional student. In 1822, John Dickens was transferred to London, where the family took up residence at 16 BAYHAM STREET, CAMDEN TOWN, but their straitened finances meant that Charles was not able to attend school. When his mother undertook to increase the family income by operating a school, the family moved, in 1823, to a house suitable for the project at 4 GOWER STREET, but the school failed to attract any pupils. Meanwhile, Charles's older sister Fanny DICKENS began as a student at the Royal Academy of Music, where she would study until 1827.

Early in February 1824, with the family nearing financial ruin, Charles was sent to work at WARREN'S BLACKING warehouse, HUNGERFORD STAIRS, the STRAND, a job obtained for him by his cousin James LAMERT. On February 20 John Dickens was arrested for debt and imprisoned in the MARSHALSEA PRISON. His wife and three of the younger children joined him in the prison; Charles took lodgings with Mrs. ROYLANCE, a friend of the family, at her house in Camden Town. In late April, John's mother, Elizabeth DICKENS, died, leaving him £450 which paid some of his creditors, and on May 28, after successfully negotiating a settlement, John was released from prison. Later that summer, over his mother's objections, Dickens was removed from Warren's Blacking to start school at WELLINGTON HOUSE ACADEMY, where he would be a student for the next three years. There he won a Latin prize and with his schoolmates wrote and produced plays for a toy theater. The family lived at 29 JOHNSON STREET, SOMERS TOWN during this time and, in 1825, John Dickens retired from the Navy Pay Office with a small pension and went to work as a reporter.

When the family again fell into financial difficulties in 1827, they were evicted from their house for nonpayment of rent. Fanny withdrew from the Royal Academy of Music and Charles left Wellington House to go to work as a solicitor's clerk in the offices of ELLIS AND BLACKMORE, GRAY'S INN. There he learned shorthand and in 1828 became a shorthand reporter in Doctors' Commons. As he developed his skill over the next few years, he moved on in 1831 to record verbatim the proceedings in Parliament for the *mirror of parliament,* a paper managed by his uncle, John Henry BARROW, and in 1832 to become a regular reporter for the *TRUE SUN*. During this period, he met John FORSTER, drama critic and journalist, who would become his closest friend. He also entertained ideas of becoming an actor, but illness forced him to cancel an audition at COVENT GARDEN Theatre in 1832.

Meanwhile, in May 1830, he met Maria BEADNELL, the flirtatious daughter of a banker, whose family looked with disdain at young Charles. They sent their daughter off to the Continent to cool the romance, which waxed and waned over the next three years and was finally broken off in May 1833. This was an eventful year for the young reporter, for his first story, "A Dinner at Poplar Walk," appeared in the December issue of the *MONTHLY MAGAZINE.*

In 1834, Dickens published six more sketches in the magazine and five in the *MORNING CHRONICLE,* a daily newspaper for which he had become a reporter. He also met Catherine HOGARTH, the daughter of the music critic on the paper, and began courting her. When his father was again arrested for debt in November and held in a sponging house, Dickens moved out of the family house and into rooms at FURNIVAL'S INN. He continued to publish his sketches; 20 "Sketches of London" appeared in the *EVENING CHRONICLE* in 1835; 12 in *BELL'S LIFE IN LONDON*. In February 1836 the sketches were collected into the first series of *Sketches by Boz* and their popularity earned him notice as a writer and a contract for a monthly serial, *The Pickwick Papers*, which began its run at the end of March, 1836. On the strength of these literary successes, Dickens married Catherine on April 2 and the couple went to CHALK for a brief honeymoon. When Robert SEYMOUR, illustrator for *Pickwick*, committed suicide on April 20, Dickens took over the dominant role in the project and, after interviewing several candidates to replace Seymour, he selected Hablot K. BROWNE, the illustrator who would work with him through most of his career. After some of his dramatic farces were produced and *Pickwick* became increasingly successful, Dickens left the *Morning Chronicle* in November to devote himself full time to his literary work.

In January 1837, the month in which his first child, Charles Culliford Boz ("Charley") DICKENS was born, Dickens issued the first number of *BENTLEY'S MISCELLANY,* the magazine in which *Oliver Twist* began appearing at the end of the month. For much of the year, both *Pickwick* and *Twist* were appearing monthly. The publication of both novels was suspended for a month in May, however, after the sudden death of Mary HOGARTH, Catherine's younger sister, who was living with the Dickenses. Dickens was holding her in his arms at the moment of her death and was deeply grieved; he took a ring from her finger which he wore to the end of his life. Charles and Catherine left their newly acquired house at 48 DOUGHTY STREET and retired to a farm in HAMPSTEAD to recover. Later in the summer they went to BROADSTAIRS for the first of many holidays they would spend at that seaside town in KENT. At the end of the year the completed *Pickwick* was published in book form.

With a new project in mind, Dickens went to YORKSHIRE with Browne in January 1838 to observe the infamous YORKSHIRE SCHOOLS and in March he began *Nickleby*, the novel in which his exposé of such schools would appear. His literary fame had brought him nominations to the GARRICK CLUB and the ATHENAEUM CLUB and his circle of friends included many writers and artists, among them AINSWORTH, CRUIKSHANK, MACREADY, MACLISE, and Forster. His second child, Mary DICKENS, was also born in March. By the end of the year *Twist* was completed. *Nickleby* continued its serial run until October 1839, the same month in which his second daughter, Kate Macready DICKENS, was born. To house this growing family, Dickens moved from

Doughty Street to 1 DEVONSHIRE TERRACE at the end of 1839.

The new project was *Master Humphrey's Clock*, a weekly periodical begun in April, 1840, in which Dickens serialized his next two novels, *The Old Curiosity Shop* (1841) and *Barnaby Rudge* (1841). By the end of 1841, Dickens was exhausted. The two novels, a fourth child, Walter Landor DICKENS, born in February, an active public life that earned him an invitation to stand as the Liberal candidate for Parliament from Reading which he refused, and an operation for a fistula in October, left him tired and weak. He decided to take a trip to the United States to recuperate.

Charles and Catherine sailed from Liverpool on January 4, 1842. Their American journey took them to BOSTON, Worcester, Springfield, HARTFORD, New Haven, NEW YORK, PHILADELPHIA, WASHINGTON, RICHMOND, BALTIMORE, HARRISBURG, PITTSBURGH, Cincinnati, LOUISVILLE, ST. LOUIS, Buffalo, NIAGARA FALLS, Toronto, MONTREAL, and many stops in between. They made many American friends, especially with such writers as Washington IRVING, Richard Henry DANA, and Henry Wadsworth LONGFELLOW. Dickens was traveling as a private citizen, but he was feted nearly everywhere he went and was expected to address the local population. Although he began with high expectations, the draining public schedule and the crititicism in the American newspapers, prompted in part by his advocacy for an INTERNATIONAL COPYRIGHT agreement, changed his perspective and he wrote back to Macready that America was "not the republic of my imagination." After they returned to England in July, Georgina HOGARTH, Catherine's younger sister, joined the household to help with the housekeeping and the care of the children. Dickens's book describing his travels, *American Notes* (1842), infuriated many Yankees, especially for its criticisms of the press, and their reaction prompted Dickens to plan a satirical account of AMERICA for his next novel, *Martin Chuzzlewit* (1844).

A dark story of money and murder, *Chuzzlewit* did not attract as large an audience as some of the earlier novels and his publishers, CHAPMAN & HALL, talked of having to reduce Dickens's monthly payment. To fend off financial troubles, Dickens conceived the idea of publishing a story directed to the Christmas market. The first of the CHRISTMAS BOOKS, *A Christmas Carol*, was published for Christmas 1843. Although it was a critical and popular success, it did not bring the hoped for financial rewards. A fifth child, Francis Jeffrey DICKENS, born in January 1844, and the continued disappointing sales of the novel led Dickens to change publishers to BRADBURY & EVANS and to pack up his family to live more cheaply in Italy. After *Chuzzlewit* was completed in July, they left for GENOA, where they would stay for nearly a year. There Dickens wrote the next Christmas book, *The Chimes* (1844), and notes for the travel articles that would become *Pictures from Italy* (1846). He also became deeply involved in using MESMERISM to treat the hysteria of Mrs. DE LA RUE, a neighbor in Genoa. After returning

Dickens in 1839, based on the portrait by Maclise.

to England in the summer of 1845, Dickens organized the first of his AMATEUR THEATRICALS, playing Bobadil in Jonson's *Every Man in his Humour*; a sixth child, Alfred D'Orsay Tennyson DICKENS, was born; and the third Christmas book, *The Cricket on the Hearth*, appeared.

The year 1846 began with Dickens's short-lived attempt to edit a daily newspaper. The liberal *DAILY NEWS* commenced publication on January 21; on February 9, burdened by the demands of a daily paper and at odds with some of its sponsors, Dickens gave up the editorship. In May he took his family off to Switzerland, where he wrote *The Battle of Life*, the Christmas book for 1846, and began *Dombey and Son* (1848). After three months in PARIS, the family returned to London in February 1847. In April another child, Sydney Smith Haldimand DICKENS, was born, and during the summer, Dickens organized another series of amateur theatrical performances. URANIA COTTAGE, a philanthropic project to redeem fallen women from the streets, which he organized with Angela BURDETT-COUTTS, opened in November. He planned another Christmas book, but after beginning *The Haunted Man* (1848), he put it off until the next Christmas. By the time that year had passed, *Dombey* was complete and Dickens's sister Fanny had died of consumption.

Fanny's crippled son, nine-year-old Henry BURNETT, the original of Tiny Tim and Paul Dombey, died a few months later in January 1849, the same month in which Dickens's seventh child, Henry Fielding DICKENS, was born. In February Dickens began work on his "favorite child," *David Copperfield* (1850), and later in the year he conceived the idea for *HOUSEHOLD WORDS,* a weekly magazine that began publication in March 1850. His work with Urania Cottage and the amateur theatricals continued. After *Copperfield* was completed in October 1850, while preparing a theatrical performance at KNEBWORTH, Edward Bulwer LYTTON's country house, Dickens and Lytton came up with the idea for the GUILD OF LITERATURE AND ART. Meanwhile, *A Child's History of England* (1852–53) was appearing in weekly installments in *Household Words*.

Dickens began work on *Bleak House* (1853) at the end of 1851, a very trying year. In early March Catherine had suffered a nervous breakdown and at the end of that month Dickens's father died. His infant daughter, Dora Annie DICKENS, born August 16, 1850, died eight months later in April 1851. While attending to these family matters, Dickens was also preparing a theatrical performance to be attended by Queen VICTORIA on May 16. Life improved after a family holiday at Broadstairs. Catherine recovered her spirits and, under the pseudonym Lady Maria Clutterbuck, wrote a cookbook, *What Shall We Have for Dinner?* Dickens moved the family from Devonshire Terrace to the larger TAVISTOCK HOUSE in BLOOMSBURY.

Dickens's 10th and last child, Edward Bulwer Lytton DICKENS, was born on March 13, 1852. In the same year his theatrical troupe made an extensive tour of sev-

Dickens in 1852.

eral towns in the north of England, performing Lytton's *Not so Bad as We Seem* for the benefit of the Guild of Literature and Art. After the tour was completed, the Dickenses took their first holiday in BOULOGNE, a French seaside town on the English Channel. Dickens returned there the next summer to recover from exhaustion after finishing *Bleak House*. After a trip to ITALY with Wilkie COLLINS and Augustus EGG in the autumn of 1853, he returned to England in time to give the first PUBLIC READING of the *Carol* at the BIRMINGHAM Town Hall on December 27.

Early in 1854, Dickens traveled up to PRESTON in Lancashire to observe the manufacturing town during a strike in preparation for *Hard Times* (1854), the novel he planned to serialize in *Household Words*. He completed the novel in July while again spending the summer in Boulogne.

When he received a letter from Maria Beadnell, now Mrs. Maria WINTER, in February, 1855, Dickens had fantasies of reviving their romance after a quarter century; but instead of the flirtatious girl he imagined, Mrs. Winter turned out to be a garrulous and silly middle-aged woman who would provide the model for Flora Finching in *Dorrit* (1857), the new novel he began in the Spring of 1855. He continued to work on the novel during a summer holiday at FOLKSTONE and an extended stay in Paris over the next winter; the first number, which appeared in December, sold nearly 40,000 copies by the end of the year.

After another summer in Boulogne, the Dickens family returned to London in September 1856, and Dickens began preparations to perform Collins's THE FROZEN DEEP. He also took possession of GAD'S HILL PLACE, the mansion outside ROCHESTER that he had dreamed of owning as a boy. The first performances of *The Frozen Deep* in January were held at Tavistock House. In July the troupe held a benefit performance for Douglas JERROLD's widow; for the final performances at MANCHESTER in August, Dickens employed some professional actresses, one of whom was Ellen TERNAN. Restless, painfully aware of his premature aging, and unhappy in his marriage, Dickens was attracted to the young actress. In September he and Wilkie Collins took a tour through the north of England, described in *The Lazy Tour of Two Idle Apprentices* (1857), which ended at DONCASTER, where Ellen was performing.

In the spring of 1858, Dickens's marital unhappiness reached a crisis. In March, he wrote that "the domestic unhappiness remains so strong upon me that I can't write, and (waking) can't rest, one minute. I have never known a moment's peace or content, since the last night of The Frozen Deep"; in May he and Catherine agreed to separate. After financial and legal arrangements were worked out by Forster and Mark LEMON, Catherine agreed to move to a separate residence with her son Charley. In June, upset by rumors circulating about his relations with Georgina and Ellen Ternan, Dickens published a defense of his conduct in *Household Words* against the advice of his friends and publishers. Angered by what he perceived as their lack of support, Dickens turned away from some of his old friends, and, over the next few years, surrounded himself with a circle of admiring young men, among them Collins, Edmund YATES, Percy FITZGERALD, Marcus STONE, and Charles FECHTER. Because his publishers, Bradbury & Evans, refused to publish his statement in *PUNCH,* he resigned the editorship of *Household Words* and planned a new magazine with Chapman & Hall. His resentment continued; three years later he refused to attend the wedding of his son Charley to Evans's daughter Bessie. The controversy also led to differences with William Makepeace THACKERAY, which erupted in a bitter quarrel between the two novelists over the membership of Edmund Yates in the Garrick Club. Dickens and Thackeray were not reconciled until 1863, shortly before Thackeray's death.

In the midst of all this turmoil, Dickens began giving public readings from his works for his own benefit. After some readings in London in April and May 1858, he undertook an extensive provinicial reading tour of 87 performances in the summer and fall. The new magazine, named ALL THE YEAR ROUND, began publication in April 1859, running weekly installments of *A Tale of Two Cities* (1859). When that novel ended late in the year, he began publishing *The Uncommercial Traveller* (1860), a series of essays that would be collected into a volume for the first time later in the year. He asked other novelists to contribute serial fiction to the new magazine, among them Wilkie Collins, Elizabeth GASKELL, Charles READE, and George ELIOT, and in the summer of 1860 he moved his household from Tavistock House in London to take up permanent residence at Gad's Hill.

Dickens concentrated on the new magazine and the pubic readings. When the magazine's circulation declined during the publication of Charles LEVER's *A Day's Ride,* he undertook to restore its audience by replacing Lever's novel with *Great Expectations* (1861). He did a second series of readings in London during the spring of 1861, a second provincial tour later in the year, and another series in London the next spring. Meanwhile his old friends and associates were dying. Arthur SMITH died in 1861 a few days before Henry AUSTIN, and in 1863–64 Augustus Egg, Thackeray, John LEECH, both his and Catherine's mothers, and his son Walter died within a few months of each other. Georgina suffered a severe illness in 1862, and Dickens himself had pain and lameness in his left foot. His relationship with Ellen Ternan was in the background throughout this period, hinted at occasionally in letters, in unexplained absences from London, and in visits to France. Returning from one of these journeys in June 1865, he and Ellen were involved in the STAPLEHURST RAILWAY ACCIDENT. Although they were not injured in the incident which killed 10 and injured 50, Dickens was emotionally shaken by it and by his experience of caring for those who were hurt.

In mid-1864 Dickens began his last long 20-part novel, *Our Mutual Friend* (1865). After completing it

Dickens in 1861.

Dickens in 1868.

and another volume of *Uncommercial Traveller* essays late in 1865, he planned another tour of 50 readings for the spring of 1866 and toyed with the possibility of giving readings abroad, in Australia and the United States. Even though a lingering cold, exhaustion, and sleeplessness plagued him during the tour, he counted the readings a success and undertook another series the next spring. Afterward he was so drained that he was unable to walk, but the promises of huge profits induced him to set out on an American tour. He arrived in Boston in mid-November, 1867, and for the next five months, during a severe winter while harboring a persistent cold, he gave readings up and down the east coast. Although he made a net profit on the American tour of about £19,000, it left him homesick and exhausted. After six months back in England, however, he undertook another series of English readings. Early in 1869, he introduced into his repertory a new reading, "Sikes and Nancy." A rendering of Nancy's murder and the pursuit of Sikes from *Oliver Twist*, it excited and taxed both the audience and Dickens and he insisted on performing it in spite of his physician's advice to the contrary. In April, tired and suffering paralysis on the left side, he was forced to cancel his remaining engagments and return to London.

In spite of failing health, Dickens planned a new series of readings for 1870 and began work on a new novel,

The Mystery of Edwin Drood (1870). He began his final series of readings in mid-January and gave his final performance, a reading of the *Carol* and the trial from *Pickwick*, on March 15. The first installment of the new novel appeared at the beginning of April, and on June 9, 1870, after spending the afternoon at work on the novel, he suffered a stroke and died that evening. He was buried in WESTMINSTER ABBEY on June 14.

Forster was Dickens's first biographer. His *Life of Charles Dickens* (1872–74), based on his intimate relationship with Dickens and on the novelist's many letters to him and others, is by far the best account from those who knew Dickens. Forster suppressed what he knew of Dickens's relationship with Ellen Ternan, and his dislike of some of the young men who surrounded Dickens in the 1860s colors his biography, but overall it is a remarkably objective and comprehensive account. The most useful edition of Forster's book is that edited and annotated by J. W. T. LEY (1928). The standard scholarly biography is still Edgar JOHNSON's *Charles Dickens: His Tragedy and Triumph* (1952), a detailed and thoroughly annotated version of Dickens's life. The revisions in Johnson's account necessitated by more recent scholarship are made in Fred KAPLAN's *Dickens, A Biography* (1988), a more contemporary and psychological portrait. Peter ACKROYD's imaginative and readable *Dickens* (1990) provides another contemporary version of the novelist's life.

Dickens, Dora Annie (1850–1851)   Dickens's ninth child, born while *Copperfield* was appearing and named for David's wife. A frail infant, she died at the age of eight months on April 14, 1851.

Dickens, Edward Bulwer Lytton ("Plorn") (1852–1902)   Dickens's 10th and youngest child, a favorite of his father. Sensitive and shy, he did not do well in school and in 1868, at age 17, he was sent by his grieving father to join his brother Alfred DICKENS in AUSTRALIA, where he never prospered. He died there in 1902.

Dickens, Elizabeth Ball (1745?–1814)   Dickens's paternal grandmother, a servant in the household of John Crewe, a Member of Parliament.

Dickens, Elizabeth Barrow (1789–1863)   Dickens's mother. She married John DICKENS in 1809. Charles was the second of eight children. Although she taught him as a child, he never forgave her for suggesting that he continue to work at WARREN'S BLACKING after her husband was released from prison. He caricatured her as the garrulous Mrs. Nickleby and used her more sympathetically as the original of Mrs. Micawber (*Copperfield*).

Dickens, Frances Elizabeth ("Fanny") (1810–1848)   Dickens's older sister and his fast friend in childhood. Dickens envied her opportunity to study at the

Royal Academy of Music while he was working in the BLACKING WAREHOUSE. She received a scholarship and was awarded a silver medal in 1824. She continued at the Academy, on and off, until 1834. In 1837 she married **Henry Burnett**, a fellow student at the Academy, and they settled in MANCHESTER. Their crippled son, **Henry, Jr.**, who died in 1848, was the model for Paul Dombey and Tiny Tim. Fanny appears in the *Carol* as sister Fan who rescues Scrooge from school, and in "A Child's Dream of a Star." She died of consumption at age 38.

Dickens, Francis Jeffrey ("Frank") (1844–1886) Dickens's fifth child, named after his godfather, Francis JEFFREY. He went to India in 1863 and served in the Bengal Mounted Police, returning to England in 1871. Eventually he joined the Canadian Northwest Mounted Police. He died in America.

Dickens, Frederick (1820–1868) Dickens's younger brother. He lived with Dickens and traveled to ITALY with him, but he offended his brother by using Dickens's name to obtain credit and by sponging from him. Dickens may have had him in mind when creating Fred Trent in *Curiosity Shop*. On his death, Dickens remarked, "It was a wasted life, but God forbid that one should be hard upon it, or upon anything in this world that is not deliberately and coldly wrong."

Dickens, Harriet (1819–?) Dickens's sister, fifth child in the family, who died in childhood.

Dickens, Sir Henry Fielding ("Harry") (1849–1933) Dickens's eighth child, the most successful of his children. Educated at BOULOGNE and ROCHESTER, Harry started the *GAD'S HILL GAZETTE* with his brother Edward DICKENS. Harry went on to Cambridge, won a scholarship and an essay prize, and afterward pursued a distinguished career in the law, becoming a Queen's Counsel. He was knighted in 1922. In 1876, he married **Marie Thérèse Louise Roche**; they had seven children. In 1904 he gave public readings of his father's work. He published *Memories of My Father* (1928), "A Chat about my Father" (*Harper's Magazine*, 1914), and *Recollections* (1934).

Dickens, John (1785–1851) Dickens's father. A clerk in the Navy Pay Office, he married **Elizabeth Barrow** in 1809. They had eight children. John's work took him from London to PORTSMOUTH, where Charles was born in 1812; back to London in 1815; to CHATHAM in 1817; and finally back to London in 1822. A convivial man but a poor money manager, he was always in debt; in 1824, he was imprisoned in the MARSHALSEA for three months for a debt of £40. His conviviality led to his being chosen the chairman of the prisoners committee in the short time he was there. After his release, he became a reporter, but he was again arrested for debt in 1834 and rescued by his son. In later years, he traded

on Charles's fame to obtain credit and he became a financial and emotional burden on his son, who deplored his financial irresponsibility. He served as a model, at least in part, for Micawber in *Copperfield* and for William Dorrit.

Dickens, Kate Macready ("Katey") (1839–1929) Dickens's third child, goddaughter of the actor William MACREADY. Temperamental and high-spirited, she had a talent for art and studied at Bedford College. She took her mother's side in the separation. In 1858 she married the painter Charles Allston COLLINS, prompting her father to conclude that she did so to get away from home. After Collins's death, she married Carlo Perugini, also a painter. Her interviews with Gladys STOREY many years later gave her version of her father's relationship with Ellen TERNAN and were the basis of Storey's revelatory book *Dickens and Daughter* (1939).

Dickens, Laetitia Mary (1816–1893) Dickens's younger sister. She married architect and artist **Henry Austin** in 1837 and was widowed in 1862. Acting as her advocate, Dickens secured a government pension for her.

Dickens, Mary ("Mamie") (1838–1896) Dickens's second child and eldest daughter. Gentle and mild-tempered, she was nicknamed "Mild Glos'ter" by her father, who had named her for Mary HOGARTH, who died a year before her birth. She remained with Dickens after the separation, serving with Georgina HOGARTH as his housekeeper and companion, and she did not visit her mother until after her father's death. She continued to live with Georgina, editing her father's LETTERS with her. She published her reminiscences in *My Father as I Recall Him* (1897).

Dickens, Mary Angela ("Mekitty") (1862–1948) Dickens's first grandchild, eldest child of Charley DICKENS. She and the other grandchildren called Dickens "Venerables" because he disliked the title Grandfather. In "My Grandfather as I Knew Him" (*Nash's Magazine*, 1911), she recounts the mixture of awe and fear that she felt in Dickens's presence and the "dreadful moment" of seeing him cry at the final reading of the *Carol*.

Dickens, Monica (1915–1992) Dickens's great granddaughter, grandchild of Henry. Author of numerous works of fiction and nonfiction, she remembers her grandfather's performances of his father's works and discusses her literary inheritance from Dickens in *An Open Book* (1978).

Dickens, Sydney Smith Haldimand (1847–1872) Dickens's seventh child, nicknamed "Ocean Spectre" for the faraway look in his eyes, as if he were gazing out to sea. Although Dickens was pleased by the boy's choice of a naval career, he was irritated by his extravagance and refused him financial help. Sydney died at sea at age 25 on his way back to England for sick leave.

Dickens, Walter Savage Landor (1841–1863)
Dickens's fourth child, named for his godfather, the poet
LANDOR. With the help of Miss Burdett COUTTS, he was
nominated to a cadetship in the East India Company
and sailed to India in 1857. He rose to the rank of lieutenant in the 42nd Highlanders and distinguished himself
during the Indian Mutiny. Although he was granted sick
leave, he died in Calcutta before returning to England,
leaving many unpaid debts for his father to settle.

Dickens, William Jr. (1719–1785) Dickens's paternal grandfather, a butler at Crewe Hall.

Dickens Fellowship Organization that works to
promote Dickens's works and to preserve his memory.
Founded in 1902 and headquartered in London, the Fellowship has local branches throughout the English-
speaking world. It administers the DICKENS HOUSE at 48
DOUGHTY STREET as a museum and library and publishes the *DICKENSIAN* a quarterly devoted to Dickens
and his work.

Dickens House The house at 48 DOUGHTY STREET,
London, where Dickens lived from 1837 to 1839, and
where he wrote some of *Pickwick* and *Twist*, all of *Nickleby*, and the beginnings of *Rudge*. It is now the headquarters of the DICKENS FELLOWSHIP and houses a
Dickens museum and library.

Dickens Project An organization of American teachers, scholars, and other Dickensians, founded by Murray
Baumgarten and headquartered at the University of California, Santa Cruz. It sponsors the Dickens Universe, an
annual seminar for teachers and others on one of Dickens's novels; an annual scholarly conference on topics
relating to Dickens; and various other activities to promote interest in Dickens and his works. It publishes an
occasional newsletter, the *Dickens Round.*

Dickens Quarterly Initiated in 1984 as the successor
to *DICKENS STUDIES NEWSLETTER,* this scholarly journal
published by the DICKENS SOCIETY contains articles on
Dickens, reviews of recent books, a checklist of recent
publications, and announcements of Dickensian activities
in America and elsewhere.

Dickens Society Founded in 1970 by Robert B.
Partlow, Jr., the society is dedicated "to conduct, encourage, foster, further, and support research, publication, instruction and general interest in the life, times,
and literature of Charles Dickens." It holds an annual
meeting and dinner during the convention of the Modern Language Association, publishes the DICKENS QUAR-
TERLY, and sponsors the Robert B. Partlow prize for the
best first article-length publication during the preceding
year.

Dickens Studies American academic journal devoted
to Dickens, founded and edited by Noel PEYROUTON
and published quarterly from 1965 to 1969.

Dickens Studies Annual Successor to *DICKENS STUD-
IES,* this annual collection of articles on Dickens and,
recently, on Victorian literature generally, often includes
several articles on a particular novel or topic and has, in
recent years, published several papers from the annual
conference of the DICKENS PROJECT.

Dickens Studies Newsletter Begun in 1970 as the
publication of the American DICKENS SOCIETY, this publication gradually evolved into more of a scholarly journal than a newsletter, becoming the DICKENS
QUARTERLY in 1984.

Dickensian, The Journal of the DICKENS FELLOW-
SHIP, which began publication as a monthly magazine in
January 1905 under the editorship of B. W. MATZ. Frederic KITTON was originally supposed to edit the journal,
but he died before its inception. Matz remained editor
until his death in 1925. The journal was published
monthly until 1919, when a rise in the cost of paper
increased production costs and the journal became a
quarterly. CHAPMAN & HALL was its publisher until
1921. Later editors include Walter DEXTER (1925–44),
Leslie STAPLES (1944–68), Michael SLATER (1968–77),
Andrew SANDERS (1978–86), Margaret Reynolds (1986–
91), and Malcolm ANDREWS (1991–   ). The character
of the journal has changed over the years following
trends in Dickens studies. In the early years many articles
on biographical, topographic, and historical points appeared, as well as numerous appreciations of Dickens
and his works. As Dickens criticism became more professional in the 1940s and '50s and Dickens of greater
academic interest, the journal devoted more space to academic criticism. In recent years the journal has become
so academic that it has seemed, to some of its readers,
too serious, though it remains the best source for information on Dickensiana, biography, and illustrations. Articles by most important Dickens scholars and critics
appear in the journal. Among the significant contributors
to the journal in its early years—sometimes referred to
as the great "amateur scholars" of the early 20th century—were Matz, J. W. T LEY, J. Cuming Walters, Arthur WAUGH, Dexter, Willoughby MATCHETT, J. H.
MCNULTY, T. W. HILL, Malcolm MORLEY, and W. J.
CARLTON.

Diego, Don Inventor of a flying machine. *Reprinted,*
"Flight."

Digby SMIKE's stage name with the Crummles Company. *Nickleby* (30).

Dijon The city in France to which Carker and Edith
Dombey elope. *Dombey* (52).

Dilber, Mrs. Scrooge's charwoman, who sells some
of his belongings to Old Joe in Scrooge's vision of Christmas Yet to Come. *Carol.*

Dilke, Charles Wentworth (1789–1864) Journalist and editor of the *ATHENAEUM,* Dilke was a fellow clerk with John DICKENS at SOMERSET HOUSE when Charles was working at WARREN'S BLACKING. When John introduced the boy to his friend, Dilke gave him a half-crown and received a very low bow in return. Many years later, when John FORSTER told Dickens of Dilke's memory of this episode, Dickens was deeply disturbed, and Forster felt he "had unintentionally touched a painful place in his memory."

Dingley Dell Village in KENT where Wardle's MANOR FARM is located. The Pickwickians first visit the farm on their initial journey (4–9) and later celebrate CHRISTMAS there (28–30). The original is thought to be the village of SANDLING near MAIDSTONE. *Pickwick.*

Dingo, Professor Famous botanist who was the second husband of Mrs. Bayham Badger. *Bleak House* (13).

Dingwall, Cornelius Brook, M. P. The "haughty, solemn, and portentous" member of Parliament who had "a very great idea of his own abilities, which must have been a great comfort to him, as no one else had." He and his **wife** place their daughter **Lavinia** in the Misses Crumptons' school in HAMMERSMITH and she runs off with Theodosius Butler. Their spoiled infant son **Frederick** wears "a blue tunic with a black belt a quarter of a yard wide, fastened with an immense buckle—looking like a robber in a melodrama, seen through a diminishing glass." *Boz,* "Sentiment."

"Dinner at Poplar Walk, A" Dickens's first published story appeared in the *MONTHLY MAGAZINE* (December 1833). In *Boz* it was retitled "MR. MINNS AND HIS COUSIN."

Diogenes Florence Dombey's "blundering, ill-favoured, clumsy, bullet-headed dog" (18). A gift from Toots, the dog was formerly a resident of Blimber's Academy and was especially friendly with young Paul. *Dombey.*

"Discovery of a Treasure near Cheapside" Article written with Henry MORLEY for *HOUSEHOLD WORDS* (November 13, 1852), describing the smelting of gold and other precious metals at Wingrove's Wood Street Smelting Works. *Stone.*

"Dismal Jemmy" Nickname of Jemmy HUTLEY. *Pickwick.*

Disraeli, Benjamin (1804–1881) Politician and novelist, first Earl of Beaconsfield. Although Dickens had known Disraeli in the 1830s as one of the other authors who regularly attended Lady BLESSINGTON's salon, he had never liked him. In the heat of the battle for repeal of the CORN LAWS, Dickens, an advocate of repeal, described Disraeli, leader of the conservative Young England movement and an opponent of repeal, as an

"impostor and Humbug." Disraeli is probably the politician satirized as "the honourable member for Verbosity" in Dickens's essay "Our Honourable Friend." As a novelist, Disraeli is best known for his trilogy of political novels: *Coningsby* (1844), *Sybil* (1845), and *Tancred* (1847). A leader of the Conservative right, he served as prime minister in 1868 and again from 1874 to 1880.

Diver, Colonel Editor of the New York *Rowdy Journal* whose expression combines "vulgar cunning and deceit." He meets the *Screw* at the dock and introduces Martin to the Pawkins's boarding house. *Chuzzlewit* (16).

Divinities of Albion, or Galaxy Gallery of British Beauty Tony Jobling's prize possession, a collection of copper-plate pictures "representing ladies of title and fashion in every variety of smirk that art, combined with capital, is capable of producing." It includes a picture of Lady Dedlock. *Bleak House* (20).

Divorce Divorces were difficult to obtain and very expensive in Victorian England. They required a decree from the ecclesiastical court in Doctors' Commons, followed by a private act of Parliament. The only acceptable grounds were a wife's adultery or a husband's adultery if accompanied by cruelty, incest, bigamy, or bestiality. When Stephen Blackpool asks how much a divorce would cost, Bounderby summarizes the procedure and costs for him: "Why, you'd have to go to Doctors' Commons with a suit, and you'd have to go to a court of Common Law with a suit, and you'd have to go to the House of Lords with a suit, and you'd have to get an Act of Parliament to enable you to marry again, and it would cost you (if it was very plain sailing), I suppose from a thousand to fifteen hundred pound" (*Hard Times,* I:11). Blackpool's frustration at being trapped by the marriage laws has sometimes been seen as representing Dickens's growing unhappiness in his own marriage at the time. In 1850, in "The Murdered Person," he criticized those who supported strict divorce laws for not taking into account those who suffered under such laws.

When Dickens's marriage disintegrated in 1857, he ruled out a divorce as too expensive. He was thinking both of the money an action would cost and of the damage to his reputation and career. Instead of a divorce, Dickens and his wife worked out a separation, with the details negotiated by John FORSTER and Mark LEMON.

In 1857 Parliament passed the Divorce and Matrimonial Causes Act, which slightly liberalized the grounds for divorce and moved the action from the ecclesiastical to a civil court. However, the act did not equalize the grounds for men and women, nor did it significantly broaden the grounds for divorce. It did not sanction divorce on grounds of incompatability, the reason Dickens gave for his own domestic unhappiness.

Dobble Host of the New Year's Eve party who is saluted along with his **wife,** **son,** and **daughters** (including **Julia**), by Tupple, one of his junior clerks. *Boz*, "New Year."

Dobbs, Julia   Young woman on her way to GRETNA GREEN to marry a young lord. She gets caught in the mistaken identities of *The Strange Gentleman* and ends up eloping with Walter Trott.

Doche, Madame   Woman selling animals at the Calf Market in Poissy. *Reprinted*, "French Folly."

"Doctor Dulcamara, M. P."   Article for HOUSE-HOLD WORDS by Dickens and Wilkie COLLINS (December 18, 1858) expressing their dislike of the formalism and dogmatism of the Oxford Movement, which sought to reform the Church of England by returning to the rituals of the CATHOLIC CHURCH and by reconciling Anglican and Catholic doctrines. The article challenges the quackery of Mr. Sidney Herbert, who promulgates the outlandish idea that Charlotte Yonge's Puseyite (after Edward Pusey, one of the leaders of the Oxford Movement) novel, *The Heir of Redclyffe* (1853), is a work second only to the Bible. *Stone.*

"Doctor Marigold"   Title given to the two framing chapters Dickens wrote for "Doctor Marigold's Prescriptions" when collected in *Christmas Stories.*

"Doctor Marigold's Prescriptions"   Christmas number of ALL THE YEAR ROUND, 1865. The narrator of the frame narrative, Doctor Marigold is a cheap jack, a traveling peddler and auctioneer, who adopts a deaf-and-dumb girl after his own daughter dies. He teaches her to read and write and then places her with a tutor for two years. While she is away, he makes a special "library cart" for her. But she falls in love with a deaf-and-dumb young man at the school, and, even though she chooses to return to Marigold, she is clearly denying her love. Marigold unites the two young lovers. They go off to China, returning with their daughter on Christmas Eve, 1864, to be reunited with Marigold. Dickens also wrote one of the stories, "TO BE TAKEN WITH A GRAIN OF SALT," for the book of stories, *Doctor Marigold's Prescriptions*, that Marigold prepared for his adopted daughter. *Christmas Stories.*

"Doctors' Commons"   Originally published in the *MORNING CHRONICLE* (October 11, 1836) as "Sketches by Boz. New Series. No. 2," this sketch describes a visit to the Arches Court and the Perogative Office where wills are recorded. *Boz.*

Dodger, The Hon. Ananias   Subject of a story about "one of the largest acquisitions of dollars ever made in this country" told by an American traveler to the narrator of "At Dusk." *Reprinted.*

Dodson and Fogg   The firm of unscrupulous attorneys, "mean, rascally, petifogging robbers"(53), who take on speculation Mrs. Bardell's breach of promise suit against Pickwick. When Pickwick refuses to pay the costs of the trial because of his outrage at these lawyers, they imprison Mrs. Bardell in debtor's prison, where Sam Weller discovers her and his kindhearted master pays the fine so that she can be released from the FLEET PRISON (53). *Pickwick.*

Dodson, Mr.   Partner in the law firm of DODSON AND FOGG; "a plump, portly, stern-looking man, with a loud voice"(20), he always acts as the spokesman for the firm. *Pickwick.*

Do'em   Captain Fitz-Whisker Fiercy's servant, a pantaloon in *The Pantomime of Life.*

Dogginson   Vestryman who thinks that vestrymen Banger and Tiddypot should settle their differences with their fists. *Reprinted*, "Our Vestry."

Dolby, George (d. 1900)   Manager of Dickens's reading tours from 1866 until Dickens's death. Though he began as a servant to the "Chief," he became a trusted friend and companion, "as tender as a woman and as watchful as a doctor." He described his days with Dickens in *Charles Dickens as I Knew Him: The Story of the Reading Tours, 1866–1870* (1885).

Dolloby   Dealer in used clothing to whom David sells his waistcoat for ninepence while on the road to DOVER. *Copperfield* (13).

"Dolls, Mr."   Nickname of Jenny Wren's father. See CLEAVER.

Dolphin's Head   Old coaching inn failing as a result of the coming of the railway. *Uncommercial* (24).

Dombey Family   Family of rich CITY merchants who pass their wealth and power from one male generation to the next in the firm of Dombey and Son. **Paul**, current head of the firm, is reserved, distant, and controlling, his wealth a sign that he possesses the Dombey trait, characterized by his sister **Mrs. Chick**, as "making an effort" (1). He is a model of patriarchy: "rather bald, rather red, and though a handsome, well-made man, too stern and pompous in appearance, to be prepossessing" (1). He grooms his infant son, **young Paul**, to carry on the firm, but the sensitive and sickly boy, who has "a strange, old-fashioned, thoughtful way . . . of sitting brooding in his miniature arm-chair, when he looked (and talked) like one of those terrible beings in fairy tales, who, at a hundred and fifty or two hundred years of age, fantastically represent the children for whom they have been substituted" (8), cannot adapt to the monetary mundanity of the Dombey world. A loving and otherworldly child, he dies at age six (16). His older sister **Florence (Floy)**, is neglected and abused by her father, who thinks of her as "merely a piece of base coin that couldn't be invested—a bad Boy—nothing more" (1). She blames herself for his neglect and desperately seeks

Browne's (Phiz's) suggestions to Dickens for the visual image of Mr. Dombey.

his love and approval, but he resents her and wishes she had died rather than his son. Dombey's first wife, **Fanny**, dies giving birth to Paul (1). After his son's death, Dombey marries **Edith Granger**, a beautiful young widow with aristocratic connections who is as cold and arrogant as her husband, expecting that she will bear him another son. Resentful that she has become a property in the marriage market (27), Edith challenges Dombey's dominance, and their marriage becomes a protracted struggle for control. Dombey humiliates Edith by employing Carker, his business manager, to negotiate the terms of their relationship. Edith in turn humiliates Dombey by running away to France with Carker (54). After his marriage breaks up and his business fails, Dombey, depressed and suicidally deranged, finally recognizes the value of Florence and accepts the love she offers him. In the closing days of his life he lavishes the love he denied his own children on Florence's two children, Paul and Florence (62). *Dombey.*

Dombey and Son (Full Title: *Dealings with the Firm of Dombey and Son, Wholesale, Retail, and for Exportation*) Dickens's seventh novel, published in monthly parts by BRADBURY & EVANS, October 1846 to April 1848, with illustrations by BROWNE; published in one volume, 1848. Conceived by Dickens as a novel about pride, *Dombey* exhibits more careful planning and execution than the novels that precede it. Its characters and situations all contribute to the development of the main theme, which the novel expresses in the symbolic opposition of the railway and the sea. This overall organization and symbolic centering have led some critics to consider it the first of the later novels.

SYNOPSIS

Part 1 (October 1846)
(1) Dombey, 48 years old, sits in front of the fire with Son, 48 minutes old. He exults that the House will once again be Dombey and Son, for his cosmos is predicated on the perpetuation of the male line and his marriage has produced no other issue, except a daughter, Florence, "a piece of base coin that couldn't be invested—a bad Boy—nothing more." Meanwhile, Mrs. Dombey's life ebbs away and she drifts out upon the "dark and unknown sea that rolls round all the world." (2) A nurse

must be found for the new baby. Polly Toodle, mother of a large family, is hired with the stipulations that she take the name Richards and that after her job is done she will sever all ties with the Dombeys. (3) Polly feels imprisoned in Dombey's house, a blank tomb of a building where the furniture is shrouded in dust covers. When Polly encourages Florence to play with young Paul, Susan Nipper, Florence's nurse, objects because she has been instructed to keep Florence out of sight of her father. But Polly convinces Dombey to allow the two children to play together by suggesting that young Paul will benefit from the interaction.

(4) At the Wooden Midshipman, an old-fashioned marine instruments shop that does little business, Sol Gills celebrates the first day of his nephew, Walter Gay, with Dombey and Son. They share the next-to-last bottle of some special Madeira with Captain Cuttle, tell sea stories, and imagine Walter's progress to the top of the firm. They even imagine Walter marrying Dombey's daughter as they toast the future of "Dombey—and Son—and Daughter."

Part 2 (November 1846)
(5) To thank Miss Tox, a spinster friend of the family, for her help in securing a nurse, Dombey considers making her young Paul's godmother, but he doesn't want his gesture misunderstood. He has no intention of marrying again, for with a son his life is complete. On the cold day of the christening, the house is icy and the church cold and funereal. Dombey bestows chilly compliments and calculated gifts—a bracelet to Miss Tox, and a place in the Charitable Grinder's School for Polly's oldest son. (6) The next day, Polly and Susan take Florence and Paul to STAGG'S GARDENS, where the Toodle family live in a jerry-built row of houses in the midst of railway construction. Polly visits her younger children, and then, hoping to see Rob, her oldest son, on his way home from school, she takes a roundabout route home. As they are rescuing Rob from some bullies and evading a runaway coach, they lose Florence, who is "found" by an old crone, Good Mrs. Brown. She leads the child back to her hovel, and there takes her clothes, and considers cutting off her hair. Afterward she abandons Florence in the streets of the City, where, two hours later, Walter Gay discovers her. When Dombey learns of the episode, he dismisses Polly for endangering his son.

(7) Miss Tox inhabits a dark little house in a dead-end street in a neighborhood of illustrious people. The situation is especially important to Miss Tox's neighbor,

Browne's (Phiz's) illustration of the Dombey wedding party for the tenth number of the novel recalls Hogarth's crowd scenes, such as the execution of Tom Idle from Industry and Idleness.

Major Joey Bagstock, who boasts of his neighbors at his club, carries on a vague flirtation with Miss Tox, and is annoyed that young Paul has diverted her attention from him. Meanwhile Miss Tox studies Dombey's bracelet, apparently entertaining romantic notions about the giver.

Part 3 (December 1846)
(8) As Paul grows up, he becomes a curious mixture of youth and age. Sitting in his small armchair, he often seems more an old philosopher than a child. One day he asks his father, "What is money?" When Dombey replies, "Money, Paul, can do anything," the boy wishes to know why it didn't save his mother and cannot make him as strong as Florence. The doctor recommends sea air for the boy's frail health, so Paul is sent to stay with Mrs. Pipchin, who keeps a juvenile boarding house in BRIGHTON. Paul strikes up a curiously frank relationship with the old woman, and he enjoys being pushed in his wheelchair out by the ocean to listen to the waves.

(9) When a broker takes possession of the Wooden Midshipman for a debt of £370 that Sol is unable to pay, Captain Cuttle advises Walter to ask Mr. Dombey for help.

(10) Seeing Walter's request as a chance to show Paul "how powerful money is," Dombey asks the boy to decide. Paul watches Florence's tears turn to joy as he grants the loan.

Part 4 (January 1847)
(11) When Paul is six, Dombey places him in Dr. Blimber's Academy in Brighton to get the boy past his "childish life." Florence is to remain in Brighton for a term so that Paul can be gradually "weaned" from her. Paul enters Blimber's educational hothouse an uncultivated plant ready for forcing, but when his father and Florence leave him there, he feels very old, "weary, weary! very lonely, very sad." (12) Dr. Blimber lectures the boys on Roman history as they eat; after dinner they loiter outside for half an hour, but do nothing "so vulgar as play." Paul's tutor, Cornelia Blimber, confuses the boy with lengthy assignments, but with the help of Florence, who buys copies of his books and studies the assignments ahead of him, he begins to learn. Paul watches at the window for Florence, who passes the school each evening. Occasionally Dombey himself does the same.

(13) When Dombey needs to fill a junior position in Barbados, he sees it as an opportunity to get rid of Walter Gay, who reminds him of his daughter. Walter has also annoyed James Carker, Dombey's second-in-command, by unwittingly mentioning his brother, Mr. Carker the Junior, a clerk kept in a lowly position as a punishment and reminder of his youthful mistake of stealing from the firm. Both Dombey and Carker thus have reasons to want Walter out of the way.

Part 5 (February 1847)
(14) As the boys at Blimber's Academy prepare for their summer holiday. Cornelia gives Paul his "analysis," not-

ing that he has a tendency to be singular or "old-fashioned" in his character and conduct. By the end-of-term dance, Paul is so ill that he just sits and watches the party. Afterward he must stay at Mrs. Pipchin's for several days to regain strength before returning to London.

(15) Unable to tell his uncle that he is to go to Barbados, Walter asks Cuttle to break the news, but the Captain delays until he can first urge Mr. Dombey to change his mind. (16) Meanwhile Paul is fading. He watches the sunlight, the "golden water" as it ripples on the walls of his room. He asks Floy, "Are we all dead, except you?" and urges his father to "remember Walter. I was fond of Walter." Then he goes out to that "old, old fashion—Death."

Part 6 (March 1847)
(17) Paul's illness has prevented Cuttle's proposed interview with Dombey, and when Walter returns to the Wooden Midshipman, Cuttle has not managed to break the news to Sol. When he finally does tell Sol, describing it as a grand chance for Walter, Sol is dispirited. As the time for Walter's departure nears, Cuttle seeks to confirm his sense of Walter's future with Carker. Flattered by the urbane manager, Cuttle thinks that he gains Carker's agreement about Walter's prospects, even his prospect of winning Florence.

(18) Dombey orders a tombstone describing Paul as his "only child" and withdraws into his darkened rooms. Upstairs alone, Florence watches a family across the street. A motherless family of daughters, the eldest replacing the mother in her attentions to her loving father, they become a wish of what Florence would have her life be. Although she goes down in the darkness to her father's rooms, his door is always shut. One evening Florence finds his door open. She goes in to him, but he retreats from her, and sends her back upstairs. Then he locks the door and cries for his lost boy.

(19) Before Walter leaves for Barbados, Florence asks him to be her "brother" and presents him with a purse she had made for Paul. Sol and Cuttle take Walter to his ship, the *Son and Heir*.

Part 7 (April 1847)
(20) To recuperate from his son's death, Dombey goes to LEAMINGTON Spa with Joey Bagstock. On the train, Dombey feels blighted and, haunted by the memory of Florence's face the night before, he wishes that she, rather than Paul, had died. (21) At Leamington they meet Mrs. Skewton and her beautiful widowed daughter, Edith Granger. Dombey admires Edith's accomplishments as artist, harpist, and pianist, but he does not recognize the song Florence used to sing to Paul when Edith performs it.

(22) Back in London, James Carker takes charge of Dombey and Son. He goes through the mail, reading a letter from Mr. Dombey very carefully, noting the impossibility of carrying out Dombey's request to prevent Walter from sailing. He secures a place for Rob Toodle with Sol Gills and tells the boy that he wants to know

the details of Sol's life and his connections with Florence. As Carker passes Dombey's house, Florence's dog barks and growls at the catlike manager.

Part 8 (May 1847)
(23) Alone in the dark and empty house, Florence meditates on loving her father and winning his heart. When no news of Walter comes, she seeks out Sol Gills and finds him restless and distracted. (24) Florence spends her time observing other children to see if she can learn the secret of their loving relationships with their parents. She longs for such parental love and blames herself for its denial. Her life is a greater trial than an orphan's, for "not an orphan in the wide world can be so deserted as the child who is an outcast from a living parent's love." When Carker offers to take a message to her father, she sends only her love. She reads in Carker's manner or smile that nothing is yet known of Walter's ship, and when Carker leaves, she shudders.

(25) Cuttle learns that Sol has disappeared, so he takes charge of the Midshipman, keeping it against Walter's and Sol's return.

Part 9 (June 1847)
(26) At Leamington, while Carker reports to Dombey, Bagstock and Mrs. Skewton arrange the marriage of Edith and Dombey. (27) On a walk in the countryside early the next morning, Carker sees a woman whose face suggests intense internal struggle. Later he recognizes Edith as the troubled woman he had seen on his walk.

After touring Warwick Castle with Carker as their guide, Edith sketches for Dombey, plays the piano, and sings to his command. Later she tells her mother that "he has bought me," comparing herself to a slave and racehorse, an object traded in the market.

(28) When Dombey introduces Edith to his daughter, Florence thinks that perhaps she can learn from "her new and beautiful Mama, how to gain her father's love."

Part 10 (July 1847)
(29) Mrs. Chick, Dombey's sister who had sponsored Miss Tox in Dombey's home, so surprises Miss Tox when she tells her about Dombey's impending marriage that Miss Tox faints. Mrs. Chick acts shocked and surprised to "learn" that Miss Tox had entertained hopes of an alliance with her brother and she snobbishly breaks off any connection with her.

(30) During the week before the wedding, Florence stays with Edith and her mother, but when Mrs. Skewton surprises Dombey by suddenly revealing Florence hidden under her shawl, Dombey is speechless and Florence distressed by his discomfort. Edith's insistence that Florence go home after the ceremony and not stay to be corrupted by Mrs. Skewton causes a rift between Edith and her mother. (31) After the ceremony Dombey and Edith depart for Paris. Florence returns to the newly refurbished room where Paul once slept.

Part 11 (August 1847)
(32) Cuttle goes to Dombey and Son to verify a newspaper report of the sinking of the *Son and Heir*. Carker

confirms the news, refuses to say a good word for Walter's prospects, and, after accusing Cuttle and Sol of dark schemes, ejects him from the office. Shaken, Cuttle goes back to the Midshipman and commits Walter's body to the deep.

(33) James Carker's house is luxuriously furnished with books, paintings, and games, a parrot who sits in a hoop that looks like a great wedding ring, and especially with a portrait of a woman resembling Edith Dombey. On the other side of London, John Carker and his sister Harriet occupy a modest cottage surrounded by vines and flowers. When a stranger who knows John's story comes to the door and offers to help them, Harriet refuses his aid, saying that John's reward is the self-respect he has achieved by his repentence. That afternoon Harriet comforts a weary traveler who also resembles Edith Dombey. She takes her in out of the rain, washes her bleeding feet, and gives her some money.

(34) As Good Mrs. Brown huddles before the fire in her hovel in the heart of London, the traveler enters and identifies herself as her daughter Alice, returned from a sentence of transportation, resentful of her mother's neglect and bitter about her betrayal by James Carker. When she realizes that the woman who gave her the money was Harriet Carker, she returns to the cottage and throws the money on the ground in front of the startled sister and brother.

Part 12 (September 1847)
(35) Florence asks Edith to instruct her to become the loving child of her father, but Edith tells her that she is not a good teacher of love. That night Florence dreams of trying to help her father, but of not being able to set him free. Then she dreams that she sees Paul, the river, and a grave with the body of Edith in the bottom. (36) At their housewarming, Dombey's guests do not mix with Edith's guests. Afterward, in Carker's presence, Dombey criticizes Edith for not being a better hostess. (37) The next day, Carker apologizes to Edith for his helplessness the night before, professing that as Dombey's "mere dependent," he was powerless to leave. Then, insinuating his influence over Dombey, he warns her that Florence's continued association with Cuttle and the group at the Midshipman will bring her husband's displeasure. After he leaves, Edith learns that her mother has had a paralytic stroke.

(38) Miss Tox, abandoned by Mrs. Chick, seeks out Polly Toodle, hoping to learn about the Dombeys from her.

Part 13 (October 1847)
(39) A year after Sol's disappearance, Cuttle, living alone in the Midshipman like Crusoe on his island, opens the letter that Sol left. It is Sol's will, leaving everything to Walter—or to Cuttle in lieu of Walter. Cuttle notes that the letter was opened and then puts it away again.

(40) Proud Dombey hates Florence in his heart because she has stolen his bride as she stole his son. Resolved to show his wife that he is supreme, he tells her she displeases him by her treatment of his guests, by her

extravagance, and by the company she keeps. He requires that she defer to him and threatens to use Carker as an emissary to see that his demands are met. Edith, thinking of Florence, suppresses her anger, but she tells him that he will never get homage from her. She reminds him that their lives are bound up with others. Dombey repeats his ultimatum.

Attended by Edith and Florence, Mrs. Skewton is sent to Brighton for her health. On the Downs outside Brighton, Edith and her mother meet another mother and daughter—Mrs. Brown and Alice—who appear as DOUBLES to them. Mrs. Skewton gives some money to Mrs. Brown, telling her that she is an "excellent woman, and a good mother." Alice tells Edith that good looks and pride will not save them. (41) Florence tearfully visits Paul's old school. Mrs. Skewton dies. Dombey goes to Brighton for the funeral.

Part 14 (November 1847)
(42) Back in London, Dombey asks Carker to tell Edith that any show of devotion to his daughter displeases him. As he rides back to the City, Dombey is thrown from his horse and injured. Florence is shaken by the news, but Edith accepts it calmly. (43) When her father is brought home, he is guarded by Mrs. Pipchin and Florence is unable to see him. One night she slips downstairs, finds him alone, and stares at his sleeping face, unclouded by any consciousness of her. When she returns upstairs, she finds Edith still awake, bearing a self-inflicted wound on her hand, and wondering what her life might have been had she not been tormented by pride and self-rejection. As dawn breaks, Edith seeks comfort in the company of Florence, watching over her as she sleeps. (44) The next morning, Susan Nipper tells Dombey of Florence's kindness, gentleness, and love for him and is dismissed from Dombey's service. (45) Meanwhile, Carker informs Edith that she has displeased Dombey by being unsubmissive, and that Florence will suffer if Edith remains partial to her. Insinuating his control over her, Carker kisses her gloved and wounded hand as he leaves.

Part 15 (December 1847)
(46) Carker rides through the street, attended by Rob Toodle and observed by Alice and Mrs. Brown, who question Rob about his master. At the office Carker tells his brother that everyone there secretly wishes to see Dombey humbled; then he returns to Dombey's house, thinking of his growing power over Edith.

(47) Florence worries that she has caused Edith to be more distant and cold to her, but Edith tells her the change is on the surface only. Florence is alone again, living with the images of the people she loves rather than the people themselves. When Dombey humiliates Edith because she refuses to attend his dinner for their second wedding anniversary, Edith asks to be released from the marriage. Carker supports her request for a separation. Later that evening, Florence sees Carker slip out of Edith's rooms and then she meets Edith on the staircase,

as Edith cringes against the wall and descends past Florence without touching her. The next morning Dombey finds Edith gone and all the clothes and ornaments from her marriage scattered about on the floor of her room. He feels utterly dishonored. Florence goes to him with outstretched arms, but he strikes her across the heart, knocking her to the floor. She runs out of the house with "no father upon earth." (48) Sobbing and confused, Florence goes into the streets at dawn, wanders to the Wooden Midshipman, and there faints into the arms of Captain Cuttle. He prepares a room at the top of the house for her.

Part 16 (January 1848)
(49) The Captain cares for Florence, but she is troubled by the "darkening mark of an angry hand" on her breast. On her second evening, Cuttle tells the story of a shipwreck, and of the survival of three members of the crew, one of them a boy beloved of all his shipmates. As Florence realizes that it is Walter's story, he appears and "brother and sister" are restored to each other. (50) Learning from Florence the reasons for her "exile," Walter realizes that he cannot urge her to return home. He confesses that he loves her. She returns his love.

(51) Dombey retreats from the world, refusing help from Mrs. Chick, Feenix, and Bagstock. He is unaware of Miss Tox's interest in his condition, of the gossip in the servant's quarters, or the speculation at the office about who will fill Carker's position.

Part 17 (February 1848)
(52) From Mrs. Brown and Alice, who worm the information out of Rob Toodle, Dombey learns of Carker's whereabouts—that Carker and Edith have gone abroad separately and plan to meet in DIJON.

(53) When Dombey dismisses John Carker the Junior from the firm because his presence reminds him of the unfaithful manager, Harriet tells her brother of a stranger who has promised to help them. The stranger turns out to be Mr. Morfin, one of Dombey's assistants. He offers to help John find another position and tells him of James's reckless and self-serving investments in the name of the firm. Regretting that she helped Dombey to learn Carker's whereabouts, Alice asks Harriet to warn her brother that he is in danger.

(54) When Carker and Edith meet at midnight in a luxurious apartment in Dijon, she resists his advances, telling him that she only used him to humiliate her husband. She wished Dombey to think her unfaithful so that she could humble him. She also wanted to compromise Carker so that he could not reveal the truth without humiliating himself. When Dombey knocks on the door, Edith disappears into another room and slips out a secret passage. Carker, discovering her gone, escapes by the same route.

Part 18 (March 1848)
(55) Pursued by Dombey, Carker flees back to England. He stops at a country inn beside the railway, but he is

tormented by visions and by the noise of passing trains and cannot sleep. Arising at dawn to continue his journey, he sees Dombey, steps back onto the tracks into the path of a passing train, and is torn limb from limb.

(56) Walter and Florence plan their wedding. On the day before the wedding, Sol Gills returns and joins the celebration. (57) Florence and Walter visit Paul's grave on their way to the church in the CITY where they are to be married. After the ceremony they set out on a year-long journey to China.

Parts 19–20 (April 1848)

(58) A year later, the world buzzes with talk of the failure of Dombey and Son. Meanwhile, Harriet asks Mr. Morfin to arrange for James Carker's money—which she and John have inherited because James died without a will—to be secretly used to give a life income to Mr. Dombey. Then she calls on Alice, who is gravely ill, and learns that Alice is the child of Edith's father's brother. Harriet reads to her of Christ's compassion for the woman taken in adultery. After she leaves, Alice dies. (59) The fall of Dombey causes the breakup of the household. The servants leave and the furnishings are sold at auction. Polly Toodle is employed to occupy the house and watch over Dombey, who has retreated into the darkness of his rooms. Dombey broods on his life and on what he has given up. In particular he is aware that he has lost Florence. In the dead of the night, he climbs the stairs to the children's room and lies on the bare floorboards weeping. At daybreak he goes downstairs again, returning again the next night. Seeing his wasted image in a mirror, he wonders how long it would take for a trickle of blood from a dying man to be discovered in the empty house. Suddenly his daughter returns, asks forgiveness, and tells him of her own child. She leads him out of the house. Polly closes up the mansion and goes home.

(60) A series of marriages takes place: Cornelia Blimber marries Mr. Feeder, schoolmaster at the Academy; Susan Nipper marries Toots; Cuttle's friend, Captain Jack Bunsby, marries Mrs. MacStinger.

(61) Weak, incoherent, and distracted, Dombey gradually regains his senses under Florence's care, but he has very little strength. One evening, Feenix takes Florence to meet Edith. Edith rejects Florence's offer to secure Dombey's forgiveness for her. She tells Florence she is innocent and intends to resettle in the south of Italy. (62) The group at the Wooden Midshipman, including Mr. Dombey, drink the last bottle of Madeira to celebrate Walter and his wife. Mr. Dombey lives on a sum that arrives each year anonymously. Mr. Morfin has married Harriet and John Carker lives with them. The Wooden Midshipman—now Gills and Cuttle—prospers. Walter has an important position with the shipping firm that sent him to China and is helping to build a new "edifice," a new "Dombey and Son." An old man, Dombey walks on the beach with his grandchildren—his grandson, who is a strong version of young Paul, and his grand-

daughter for whom he has profound and unspoken affection.

COMMENTARY

While he was at work on *Dombey*, Dickens told John FORSTER that the novel "was to do with Pride what [*Chuzzlewit*] had done with Selfishness." *Dombey* is, however, a considerable advance over its predecessor in terms of structure and control. Kathleen TILLOTSON (1956) has shown how carefully Dickens planned and worked out the novel. The extravagant comic invention of a Mrs. Gamp may be missing in *Dombey*, but each of the characters and episodes in the novel is made relevant to its developing theme. *Dombey* is the first novel for which Dickens wrote out detailed plans. It is clear from these notes—and from Dickens's letters to Forster—that he had the story well in mind from the beginning, especially the central action involving Mr. Dombey, young Paul, and Florence. At the same time, Dickens's notes also indicate that he could change his mind about things as the story developed. He altered his plans for both Edith and Walter Gay as he worked on the story and saved both of them from the deaths he had planned. He also prevented Walter from falling into idleness and ruin, a story he saved for Richard Carstone in *Bleak House*.

Dickens's careful planning for the novel, his subordination of character and incident to the development of theme, and his use of the contrasting symbols of the railway and the sea to center the novel, make *Dombey* more akin to the later novels—those following *Copperfield*—than to the novels that preceded it. Even though Dickens's career has traditionally been divided at *Copperfield* into early and late periods, there are strong reasons, as several critics have argued, for making *Dombey* the turning point.

The novel's title, as the brilliant opening chapter makes clear, perfectly links the domestic and the public spheres, for Dombey and Son refers both to the 48-year-old father with his infant son and to the family business. As a business magnate, Dombey thinks of his new son not as a human child but as the continuation of the firm. On the one hand, he reduces everything to its commercial value: Young Paul counts only as the "and Son" and his sister doesn't count at all, for she is "merely a piece of base coin that couldn't be invested—a bad Boy—nothing more" (1). On the other hand, Dombey grandiosely inflates his own importance to a blasphemous extreme: Dombey and Son, "those three words conveyed the one idea of Mr. Dombey's life. The earth was made for Dombey and Son to trade in, and the sun and moon were made to give them light. Rivers and seas were formed to float their ships; . . . stars and planets circled in their orbits, to preserve inviolate a system of which they were the centre. Common abbreviations took new meanings in his eyes, and had sole reference to them: A.D. had no concern with anno Domini, but stood for anno Dombei—and Son" (1). Dombey's pride, based in wealth and social position, raises him above the rest of mankind to live in a delusion of divine power beyond the reach of mortal limitation. He is the controlling figure in his House—the firm of Dombey and Son—and in his household—both a merchant prince whose underlings feed his pride and a patriarch who rules his family. At the end of chapter one, mortality appears to upset his rule when his wife dies, but Dombey is untouched. She has served her purpose in bearing his son and has no further usefulness. She leaves his temporal and mechanical world—symbolized by the watches in the opening chapter—and drifts "out upon the dark and unknown sea that rolls round all the world" (1).

By the end of the opening chapter, Dickens has established several of the crucial oppositions on which the novel turns. The spheres of business and family, public and private, and male and female, are established and contrasted. The public sphere of business recognizes external achievement and denies or represses the private world of internal feeling. Material, mechanical, and male, it opposes the immaterial, natural, and female. After Fanny's death, the Toodle family enter as representatives of the "other" side. Humble people who are as low in the social scale as Dombey is high, the Toodles are devoted to their children—both male and female— and their love and concern for each other is apparent in the interview with Dombey and in their natural "apple" faces. Even though Dombey tries to control Polly's relationship with his son by restraining her in the terms of their contract and by giving her a male name, Richards, Polly's natural feelings come out.

Dickens ends the first monthly number with a chapter introducing the Wooden Midshipman, the household of sea people which symbolically counters Dombey's destructive commercial empire. There Sol Gills and Captain Cuttle nurture Walter Gay on stories about the sea, stories which Walter will reenact as he rescues Florence from the kidnapping or later as he returns from the sea to rescue and marry her. Walter is a creature of legend, particularly the legend of Dick WHITTINGTON, the story of a poor boy who, through trading ventures, rose to become the LORD MAYOR of London. His miraculous return and fairy-tale romance are, as Harry STONE (1979) has shown, part of the fairy tale method of the CHRISTMAS BOOKS that Dickens adapts to a longer novel in *Dombey*.

But the sea people and Walter are elaborations on the central story of Mr. Dombey and Florence. As he began the novel, Dickens described his plan to Forster in the following terms:

> I design to show Mr. D. with that one idea of the Son taking firmer and firmer possession of him, and swelling and bloating his pride to a prodigious extent. As the boy begins to grow up, I shall show him quite impatient for his getting on, and urging his masters to set him great tasks, and the like. But the natural affection of the boy will turn towards the despised sister . . . When the boy is about ten (in the fourth number), he will be taken ill, and will die; and when he is ill, and when he is dying,

> I mean to make him turn always to the sister still, and keep the stern affection of the father at a distance. So Mr. Dombey—for all his greatness, and for all his devotion to the child—will find himself at arm's length from him even then, and will see that his love and confidence are all bestowed upon his sister. . . . The death of the boy is a death-blow, of course, to all the father's schemes and cherished hopes; and "Dombey and Son," as Miss Tox will say at the end of the number, "is a Daughter after all."

Dickens moved Paul's death to the fifth number and Miss Tox's observation comes much later, in chapter 59, but the central focus of the story on Mr. Dombey is clear in Dickens's summary and in the novel itself.

Dombey is a difficult hero. Icy, remote, reserved, and unfeeling, he presents only surfaces and hides whatever depths are within him. We get only brief and infrequent glimpses of the man beneath the surface in such scenes as the one where he secretly watches Florence as he sits in the drawing room with a handkerchief over his head (35). Withdrawn from the world, he acts through intermediaries: Bagstock arranges his wedding; Carker manages his business and negotiates the terms of his marriage. His decline and fall elicits little sympathy from the reader, who may agree with Hippolyte Taine, a French critic of the Victorian period, who noted that when Dombey is transformed at the end "he becomes the best of fathers, and spoils a fine novel" (Philip COLLINS, *Heritage*, 1971).

Florence, on the other hand, is a sympathetic figure, but the SENTIMENTALITY in her presentation has put off many modern readers. Like David Copperfield and Little Nell, Florence seems small for her age; even when she is in her late teens and runs from home, she is described as if she were a much younger child. This appearance of childlike innocence, though it may increase the pathos in her presentation, does not endear her to her father. For him she is, as Alexander WELSH (1989) points out, an angel of death. She is at her mother's side and at Paul's side when they die. Her name and its contraction, Floy, suggest her connection with the waters of death and immortality, but Dombey, who denies death and whose only notion of immortality involves the longevity of the firm, blames her for his son's death. The more she seeks his love, the more he resents and hates her. A passive victim of her father's neglect, she never abandons her hopeless love for him, even after he strikes her and drives her out of the house. Her devotion strains credulity, even though we may recognize in her the prototype of the abused child who blames herself for the treatment she receives. The episodes in which Florence studies other children in order to learn how to gain her father's love and asks Edith to teach her how to love him embody painful psychological truth.

The story of Dombey and daughter seems headed toward the tragic conclusion that Taine expected and preferred, a 19-century version of *King Lear* in which Dombey would recognize too late that the child he treasured was "a daughter after all." But Dombey is saved from Lear's fate at the last minute. After financial ruin, madness, and an attempt at suicide, he is rescued by Florence, removed from his funereal house, and granted a chance to walk by the sea with his grandchildren. This final moment in the novel, narrated as if it is dream or vision rather than reality, suggests how close Dombey came to completing the tragedy his life appeared to be reenacting.

Dombey's mythic story of father and daughter and its parable of pride is embedded in the 1840s, a period of rapid social and material change. The Whigs who assumed power after the passing of Parliamentary REFORM BILL OF 1832 introduced a long agenda of legislation designed to reform governmental and social institutions and to respond to industrialization and urbanization. The railway boom during the period made the INDUSTRIAL REVOLUTION visible and turned England from a coaching nation to one run on "steam." Beneath the story of Dombey's progress and redemption is an embedded historical fable on the theme of social change. A merchant prince who has inherited the family trading business from his father and grandfather, Dombey represents the mercantile era of the 17th and 18th centuries. He is not one of the new captains of industry, not a member of Marx's bourgeoisie controlling the means of production. He comes from a pre-industrial society where merchants may have had money, but where power reposed in the hands of landed aristocrats who looked down on those like Dombey who acquired their riches in trade. Indeed, Dombey's rigid pride may derive in part from his sense of inferiority in a society based on aristocratic rules, an inferiority that makes him easily manipulated by Bagstock and attracted to Edith, both of whom have a tincture of the nobility he lacks. It also makes him incapable of seeing Mrs. Skewton for what she is, an embodiment of the artificial, false, and outdated aristocracy.

Trapped in outmoded habits of mind, Dombey not only overvalues the past, he is incapable of understanding and dealing in the present. He employs intermediaries like Bagstock to manage his life and his business, and they in turn manage him. James Carker represents a new class of professional managers, replacing the former owner-operators of the CITY. Ambitious, manipulative, class-conscious, and resentful, Carker asserts that there is no one of Dombey's employees "who wouldn't be glad at heart to see his master humbled: who does not hate him, secretly: who does not wish him evil rather than good: and who would not turn upon him, if he had the power and boldness" (46). Expressed at the same time that Marx and Engels were composing *The Communist Manifesto* (1848), Carker's worldview also envisions society as class war. Carker may manage and manipulate, but he does not own the means of production and he does not control the course of history—or his own destiny. Appropriately, he is killed by a train, symbol of the new industrialism that was radically changing Victorian England.

The famous description of the railway construction at Staggs's Gardens in chapter six compares the turmoil to "a great earthquake" in its destruction and to the Tower of Babel in its confusion. It is both a source of "dire disorder" and of "civilization and improvement." For Dombey and for Carker, the railway will become "the remorseless monster, Death" (20), but for Toodles, it offers opportunity. He rises to become an engineer and even though his old neighborhood is "cut up root and branch" (15), a new neighborhood emerges from the destruction and confusion:

> There were railway patterns in its drapers' shops, and railway journals in the windows of its newsmen. There were railway hotels, office-houses, lodging-houses, boarding-houses; railway plans, maps, views, wrappers, bottles, sandwich-boxes, and time-tables; railway hackney-coach and cabstands; railway omnibuses, railway streets and buildings, railway hangers-on and parasites, . . . There was even railway time observed in clocks, as if the sun had given in. . . . To and from the heart of this great change, all day and night, throbbing currents rushed and returned incessantly like its life's blood (15).

The Toodle family thrives by adapting their natural energy to this new life force. Dombey cuts himself off; his class pride even causes him to reject Mr. Toodle's sympathetic condolences after Paul's death (20).

If Dombey's pride is in part a product of a consciousness that fails to adapt to changes in his society and its class system, it is also an expression of patriarchal power in a radically gendered society. In a world based on what Thomas CARLYLE called "the cash nexus," where all relationships were defined by contract in monetary terms, Dombey values his son as "capital" for what he represents to the business, and he devalues his daughter as a "base coin" (1). His marriages are contracts and when he hires a wet nurse to nurture his son, the terms of the relationship are strictly contractual. Most of the women in the novel collude with this system of male power which turns them into commodities on the market. Many become sycophantic hangers-on, like Miss Tox or Mrs. Chick. A few, like Alice Marwood and Edith, resent their degraded position. Edith defines the limits of her contract when she tells her mother: "There is no slave in a market; there is no horse in a fair: so shown and offered and examined and paraded, mother, as I have been, for ten shameful years. . . . He sees me at the auction, and he thinks it well to buy me. Let him! . . . When he would have me show one of [my accomplishments], to justify his purchase to his men, I require of him to say which he demands, and I exhibit it. I will do no more" (27). She resentfully acquiesces to the system and accepts the marriage contract contractually.

To acquiesce to patriarchy and reduce all relationships to money is to choose death over life. The precocious young Paul uncovers this truth when he asks his father, "What is money?" and elicits the answer, "Money, Paul, can do anything." The boy's response, "If it's a good thing, and can do anything . . . I wonder why it didn't save me my Mama" (8), underscores the impotence of a culture that divides the world; placing thought, action, material control on one side and feeling, acceptance, and spiritual understanding on the other; elevating the former and devaluing the latter. Dombey's systematic decline, Carker's destruction, Edith's self-destructive resentment, Mrs. Skewton's sycophantic emptiness, and Alice Marwood's obsessive bitterness are among the discontents of this divided civilization. The power to heal the division and restore some balance flows from the waters of immortality, is heard in the voice of the waves, and returns from a honeymoon at sea to unite a broken old man with his grandchildren. The tenuous account and the sentimental distance in the final pages make the novel seem much more assured in its analysis of the disease than in its expectations for a cure.

CRITICISM

Tillotson (1954 and 1957) describes Dickens's careful planning and composition of the novel and the resulting unity in theme, character, and incident. Steven MARCUS (1965) treats the novel as "a comprehensive, unified presentation of social life by depicting how an abstract principle conditions all experience. That principle is change, and the novel's key words, so to speak, are change, alteration and time." Raymond WILLIAMS (Introduction to the Penguin edition, 1970) discusses the historical context of these changes as expressed in the novel, seeing Dickens's characters and incidents as expressions of a popular urban culture. Stone (1979) analyzes the images and motifs from fairy tale that run through the novel as part of a much fuller and more integrated use of such materials than in the earlier novels. Susan HORTON (1979) employs *Dombey* as a case study in which she explores the role of the reader in the process of interpretation. Denis Donoghue ("The English Dickens and *Dombey and Son*," *Nineteenth Century Fiction*, 1970) considers the novel in Wordsworthian terms as a celebration of the primacy of feeling. Nina Auerbach's feminist analysis ("Dickens and Dombey, a Daughter after All," *Dickens Studies Annual*, 1976) discusses the novel as an exploration of the separation between male and female spheres and suggests that Dickens failed to connect the two, arriving in the end only at a "troubled, tragic awareness of the gulf between the sexes."

ADAPTATIONS

The first play from the novel, T. P. Taylor's "Dombey and Son, or Good Mrs. Brown the Child Stealer" (1847), appeared in London when the novel had completed only half of its serial run; a male actor played Mrs. Brown. W. Sydney's "Dombey and Son" (1849), produced after the completion of the novel, nonetheless amplified the story by adding three visions of Christmas to it. Early American adaptations usually featured Captain Cuttle. W. E. Burton's performance of the part in John BROUGHAM's adaptation (1848) was popular for more

than two decades; other adaptations, including Andrew HALLIDAY's popular "Heart's Delight" (1873), gave similar prominence to the Captain.

Two silent films were based on the novel: the very early "What Are the Wild Waves Saying Sister?" (1903) and "Dombey and Son" (1917), adapted by Eliot Stannard. A sound film, "Rich Man's Folly" (1931), directed by John Cromwell and adapted by Grover Jones and Edward Paramore, Jr., modernized the story, making Dombey into a rich shipbuilder.

The BBC produced a 13-episode television version written by Hugh Leonard in 1969, and a 10-part serial adapted by James Andrew Hall in 1983.

Sir Harry Johnston's novel *The Gay-Dombeys* (1919), in which the title figures are descendants of Dickens's characters, derives many of its characters from *Dombey* and other Dickens novels.

Donny, Misses Twin sisters who operate Greenleaf School, near READING, where Esther Summerson is a pupil. *Bleak House* (3).

"Doom of English Wills, The" Article by Dickens and William Henry WILLS for *HOUSEHOLD WORDS* (September 28, 1850), calling attention to the deplorable state of public records in England. Antiquarian William Wallace, a fictional character based on William Downing Bruce, searches for documents in the registry at an unnamed cathedral based on Lincoln and Litchfield. There he confronts officious and uncooperative clerks, uncovers neglected and rotting documents, and discovers some unrecognized treasures. *Stone*.

"Doom of English Wills: Cathedral Number Two, The" A second article by Dickens and William Henry WILLS for *HOUSEHOLD WORDS* (October 5, 1850) on the deplorable state of public records in England. William Wallace goes to the Registry of Public Documents at York, where he finds the papers stored in a totally inadequate building, ill-catalogued and unprotected. Some documents have even been sold to private parties. *Stone*.

Doppelgänger German term for the DOUBLE, especially in romantic literature, in which a ghost, apparition, or dream figure replicates a living person.

Dor, Madame Obenreizer's Swiss housekeeper; Marguerite's friend and protector. "No Thoroughfare."

Dorker Pupil at DOTHEBOYS HALL who dies in spite of Squeers's last minute attempts to save him. *Nickleby* (4).

Dorking Town in Surrey where Mrs. Weller maintains the inn, the MARQUIS OF GRANBY. *Pickwick* (27, 33, 52).

Dornton, Sergeant   Detective policeman from Scotland Yard, "about fifty years of age, with a ruddy face and a high sunburnt forehead," who tells the Adventures of a Carpet Bag. *Reprinted*, "Detective Police."

Dorrit Family   Family whose transformation from poverty to riches defines the action of *Little Dorrit*. The family is led by **William**, who has been in the MARSHALSEA debtor's prison so long that he is known as the "Father of the Marshalsea." His brother **Frederick**, who subsists outside of prison as a struggling theater musician, "a retired and simple man [who] had shown no particular sense of being ruined, at the time when that calamity fell upon him, further than that he left off washing himself when the shock was announced, and never took to that luxury any more" (I:7). The family's fortunes change when Arthur Clennam takes an interest in **Amy**, William's youngest child, uncovering an inheritance that secures William's release from prison. The family travels to Italy, where William attempts to impose on the family the pretentious and ostentatious life style of the newly rich. His two elder children are spoiled by the inheritance and their father's dishonesty. **Edward** ("Tip"), a restless ne'er-do-well, ruins himself with drink. His sister **Fanny**, a gold digger who works as a dancer during the prison years, marries Edmund Sparkler for his social position and leaves to Amy the care of her neglected children. Frederick does not adapt to the manner of the newly rich and defends Amy's similar refusal to do so. Even William is unable to sustain the pretense. He falls ill at Mrs. Merdle's dinner party in Rome, and, believing himself back in prison, dies (II:19). Frederick dies kneeling beside his brother's deathbed (II:19). *Dorrit*.

Dorrit, Amy ("Little Dorrit," "Child of the Marshalsea")   Youngest child of **William Dorrit**, she was born in the prison and with self-denying industry worked to provide for her father and the rest of the family. "Her diminutive figure, small features, and slight spare dress gave her the appearance of being much younger than she was. A woman, probably of not less than two-and-twenty, she might have been passed in the street for little more than half that age" (I:5). Amy works in the Clennam household, where she draws Arthur's interest; he believes that his family is responsible for her situation and he seeks to have the Dorrits released from prison. When the family is released from prison, Amy is reluctant to leave (I:36), and she is unhappy living in luxury in Italy (II:4). After her father's death and the financial collapse of the family, Amy returns to England, where she cares for Arthur Clennam in prison, eventually marrying him. *Dorrit*.

Dorrit, William ("Father of the Marshalsea")   Little Dorrit's father, "a very amiable and very helpless middle-aged gentleman" (I:6), has been in the MARSHALSEA PRISON for 25 years, longer than any other prisoner. He patronizes the other inmates as his inferiors, accepting monetary "testimonials" from them and from

visitors to the prison. Brought up a gentleman, he is incapable of providing for himself and he refuses to acknowledge that he survives by depending on others, particularly his daughter **Amy**, who works as a servant for Mrs. Clennam to support him. He accuses her of ingratitude when she refuses John Chivery's proposal (I:19), and after Clennam and Pancks discover that he is heir to a large fortune, he criticizes her unwillingness to adopt a lavish way of life. But he dies suddenly in Rome, imagining that he is back in the prison (II:19), and the family then learns that he has lost his fortune by investing in Merdle's financial schemes. *Dorrit*.

D'Orsay, Alfred Count (1801–1852)   French aristocrat and artist who moved to London in the 1820s and became a leader in fashion, the "Prince of Dandies." His scandalous relationship with Lady BLESSINGTON and her husband made him the talk of London. He presided over her fashionable salon at Gore House, where Dickens probably met him in 1840. D'Orsay was godfather to Dickens's sixth child, Alfred.

Dostoyevsky, Feodor Mikhailovich (1821–1881)   Russian novelist, author of *Crime and Punishment* (1866), *The Idiot* (1868), *The Brothers Karamazov* (1880) and other works; a great admirer of Dickens. He knew Dickens's novels well and drew on them for inspiration and as models for his own fiction, most notably in his protrayal of Prince Myshkin in *The Idiot*, based, in part, on Pickwick. Like Dickens, Dostoyevsky frequently made use of the DOUBLE and explored the role of irrationality and crime in his novels. Although Dickens's darker novels, such as *Bleak House* and *Little Dorrit*, are often considered "Dostoyevskian," the Russian found Dickens's works "idealistic" and "calming" and was more drawn to the earlier works. Extended studies of the relationship between the two authors include: Donald FANGER (1965); N. M. Lary, *Dostoyevsky and Dickens* (1973); Loralee MacPike, *Dostoyevsky's Dickens* (1981).

Dotheboys Hall   School run by Squeers in the YORKSHIRE village of Dotheboys in "a long cold-looking house, one story high, with a few straggling outbuildings behind, and a barn and stable adjoining" (7). Like the notorious "Yorkshire Schools" that Dickens was attacking, Dotheboys takes unwanted and illegitimate children, keeping them far away from their families in the south of England. Dotheboys was based on William SHAW's Bowes Academy at GRETA BRIDGE, which Dickens visited in 1838. *Nickleby*.

Double   A character who replicates, diametrically contrasts, or represents part of another character. Dickens bases his character thematics on this technique from romantic literature. He sometimes uses doubling as a form of incremental REPETITION, as, for example, with the Cheeryble Brothers (*Nickleby*), the Flintwinch brothers (*Dorrit*), or Charity and Mercy Pecksniff (*Chuzzlewit*). Such characters underscore each other through repetition. Doubles are also often contrasting figures. Their relationship as doubles may be indicated in their physical appearance, their names, or family connections, but in other respects they are opposites to each other, as, for example, are John and James Carker (*Dombey*), Oliver Twist and Monks (*Twist*), or Samuel Pickwick and Sam Weller (*Pickwick*). By combining and mixing repetition and contrast, Dickens can suggest complexity in his characters and ambiguity in theme. Edith Dombey and Alice Marwood, cousins who physically resemble each other and who both have manipulative mothers, appear to be social opposites, one living at the top of society and the other at the bottom, but both are "sold" in the sexual marketplace and both become entangled with James Carker (*Dombey*). Their stories both contrast and repeat each other.

In psychological terms the double represents an alter ego, a part of the self split off from conscious recognition

Furniss's illustration (1910) of Sydney Carton and Charles Darnay for A Tale of Two Cities *emphasizes their roles as doubles.*

and experienced as other. Dickens's identity plots are often based on this psychological assumption. When David Copperfield asks whether he "shall turn out to be the hero of [his] own life, or whether that station will be held by anybody else" (1), his story frames that question in terms of a series of doubles that he must recognize and deal with to achieve an integrated sense of himself. Nearly every character in David's account of his life is a partial double to him: Micawber, for example, represents the incompetence David inherits from his father; Murdstone his desire for firmness and order; Heep his ambition and "humbleness"; Steerforth his snobbery. David must connect these parts of himself to overcome the psychological decomposition of his character and to "turn out to be the hero" of his own life. Dickens repeats this mode of characterization and psychological analysis in novel after novel, achieving a greater degree of integration or composition in the later novels.

The doubles in the later novels also articulate the MYTH of the double as described in Freudian terms by Otto Rank (*The Double*, 1971). The stories of Charles Darnay and Sydney Carton, or Eugene Wrayburn and Bradley Headstone, for example, depend on a dynamic where the survival of one of the doubled characters depends on the sacrifice of the other.

Lawrence FRANK (1984) discusses Dickens's use of the double in several novels; his analysis of *Copperfield*, while based on similar premises, is markedly different from that offered by Loralee MacPike (*Dostoyevsky's Dickens*, 1981). Julian Moynahan's "The Hero's Guilt: The Case of *Great Expectations*" (*Essays in Criticism*, 1960) is the classic analysis of the use of doubling in *Expectations*.

Doubledick, Richard   Young man who joins the army after being jilted, who is saved from a life of dissipation by his commanding officer. After the death of his officer, he is restored to the woman he loved by the mother of his officer friend. "Doubledick."

Doughty Street   Dickens lived at No. 48 on this street in BLOOMSBURY from 1837 to 1839, and he finished *Pickwick* and *Twist*, wrote all of *Nickleby*, and began *Rudge* here. Since 1921 the house has served as the headquarters of the DICKENS FELLOWSHIP and as a Dickens library and museum.

Dounce, John   A steady old boy, this widower and retired glovemaker makes himself ridiculous by courting a young lady in blue who sells oysters. After she rejects his proposal, he eventually marries his cook. *Boz*, "Dounce."

Dover   Channel port in KENT mentioned frequently in Dickens's novels, most importantly as Betsey Trotwood's home (*Copperfield*, 13). Arthur Clennam returns from China via Dover (*Dorrit*, I:3). Lorry meets Lucie Manette at the Royal George Hotel here (*Two Cities*, I:3). The Traveller passes through Dover on journeys to the continent (*Uncommercial*, 7, 18).

Dickens lived in this house on Doughty Street, now a Dickens museum, from April 1837 to December 1839.

Dover Road   David's trek to DOVER in search of his Aunt Betsey (*Copperfield*, 13) and Lorry's coach journey on his way to Paris (*Two Cities*, I:2) describe the route between London and Dover.

Dowdles, Misses   Kate Nickleby's school mistresses in Devon, described by Mrs. Nickleby as "the most accomplished, elegant, fascinating creatures." *Nickleby* (26).

Dowler   A retired army officer and his **wife** who travel to BATH on the coach with Pickwick; they share lodgings in the Royal Crescent with the Pickwickians. "A

stern-eyed man of about five-and-forty, who had a bald and glossy forehead, . . . and large black whiskers," Dowler is fierce in the middle of the night, threatening to cut Winkle's throat when he thinks the young man has pursued his pretty wife. But the next morning he is cowardly and timorous. *Pickwick* (35–38).

"Down with the Tide"   An account of a night spent with "Pea," a supervisor of the THAMES Police, on his regular patrol of the river. Pea shows the narrator the haunts of various criminals. They also visit "Waterloo," the toll-taker on WATERLOO BRIDGE, who tells them about suicides from the bridge and about the strange people he has seen there. *Reprinted.*

Doyce, Daniel   Engineer and inventor, friend of Meagles; he takes Arthur Clennam as a partner in his business: "a short, square, practical looking man, whose hair had turned grey, and in whose face and forehead there were deep lines of cogitation" (I:10). Clennam unsuccessfully undertakes to secure support from the CIRCUMLOCUTION OFFICE for Doyce's invention (II:8). While Doyce is abroad where his work is more appreciated, Clennam invests the firm's assets in Merdle's ruinous ventures (II:26). When Doyce returns to England, he forgives his partner and helps to secure his release from prison. *Dorrit.*

Doylance, Old   John's former schoolmaster. "Haunted House."

Doyle, Richard (1824–1883)   Illustrator for *PUNCH.* He contributed illustrations—usually those on the initial page of the separate chapters—for *Chimes, Cricket,* and *Battle.* Dickens did not know Doyle well and there was little or no consultation between them about the illustrations.

Doze, Professor   Member of the Mudfog Association. *Mudfog.*

Drama   Dickens's fascination with the theater was evident from childhood on. His earliest known work, written when he was just a child, was the tragedy *Misnar, the Sultan of India.* He also wrote several farces that were produced in London during the early years of his writing career: *The Strange Gentleman* (1836), *The Village Coquettes* (1836), *Is She His Wife?* (1837), *The Lamplighter* (1838). Later he collaborated with Mark LEMON on *Mr. Nightingale's Diary* (1851) and with Wilkie COLLINS on *The Lighthouse* (1856), *The Frozen Deep* (1857), and *No Thoroughfare* (1867).

Although Dickens was a mediocre dramatist, his novels adopt many conventions of the theater and the drama to prose narrative. William AXTON (1966) discusses the ways in which the Victorian theater influenced his vision and style. Robert E. GARIS (1965) describes Dickens's novels themselves as theatrical performances.

After illness forced him to cancel an audition at COVENT GARDEN Theatre in 1831, Dickens's ambitions as an actor were satisfied in his AMATEUR THEATRICALS and PUBLIC READINGS. He counted theater people, especially William MACREADY and Charles FECHTER, among his close friends.

His novels contain many scenes in the theater, from his sketches in *Boz* of private theaters to his hilarious account of Wopsle's *Hamlet* in such a theater (*Expectations*, 31). The episodes describing the Crummles Theatrical Company are pivotal, both structurally and theatrically, in *Nickleby*. Edgar and Eleanor JOHNSON's anthology (*The Dickens Theatrical Reader*, 1964) collects many of these passages. In *Dramatic Dickens* (1989), Carol MacKay has collected a series of papers on various aspects of Dickens's work in relation to the drama. All of Dickens's novels were adapted for the stage, even before they had completed their serial run. These adaptations are described by Malcolm MORLEY in a series of articles for the *DICKENSIAN* (1946–56), by F. Dubrez Fawcett (*Dickens the Dramatist*, 1952), and by Robert BOLTON (1987).

Drawley, Mr.   Member of the Mudfog Association. *Mudfog.*

Dream Allegory   A common form in medieval literature in which the narrator falls asleep and dreams the allegorical story that the work has to tell. Bunyan used the form in *The Pilgrim's Progress*, a work that Dickens alludes to frequently. Dickens employs a version of dream allegory, in which a transforming vision or dream prompts a change of heart, in some of the CHRISTMAS BOOKS. Dickens's dream allegories differ from their medieval predecessors in that the dreams are not those of his narrators.

Dreary   Narrator of "The Poor Man and his Beer." *Miscellaneous.*

Dringworth Bros.   Firm in America Square, London, that employs Tregarthen and Clissold. "Message from the Sea."

Drooce, Sergeant   Royal Marine Sergeant on the expedition to Silver-Store Island, "the most tyrannical noncommissioned officer in His Majesty's service." "English Prisoners."

Drood, Edwin   John Jasper's nephew, a young engineer who plans to go to Egypt and help to develop an undeveloped country. He has accepted the destiny decreed by his father's will, that he should marry Rosa Bud, but his condescension toward her and his taking her for granted bother both John Jasper and Neville Landless, who are each infatuated with the girl. After earnestly discussing their relationship, Edwin and Rosa decide to be brother and sister rather than husband and wife (13), but they do not tell either Jasper or Landless of their decision. Jasper jealously provokes a quarrel between Landless and Drood (8) that makes Neville a prime suspect in Drood's disappearance (14). *Drood.* Although Edwin's disappearance has generally been thought to be the result of his murder, some completions of the unfinished novel have Drood reappearing in the denouement of the story.

"Drooping Buds"   Essay by Dickens and Henry MORLEY for *HOUSEHOLD WORDS* (April 3, 1852), occasioned by the opening of the Hospital for Sick Children in Great Ormond Street. It describes the problem of infant mortality at the time and a visit to the new hospital. In the middle of the essay Dickens reflects on the deaths of some children—and some adults he had known as children—who had been close to him: his infant daughter Dora; his sister Fanny (see Frances Elizabeth DICKENS) and her son, Henry BURNETT; and Mary HOGARTH. *Stone.*

Drowvey, Miss   Co-proprietor with Miss Grimmer of the school that Alice Rainbird and Nettie Ashford attend. "Holiday Romance."

Drum, The   Trotty Veck's "private friend" who salutes Margaret's marriage. *Chimes* (4).

Drummle, Bentley ("The Spider")   Pip's fellow student at Matthew Pocket's; from a rich family in Somersetshire, he is "heavy in figure, movement, and comprehension . . . idle, proud, niggardly, reserved, and suspicious" (25). Jaggers names him "the Spider." Estella marries him for his money, but he beats and abuses her. He is, in turn, kicked and killed by a horse that he has ill-treated (58). *Expectations.*

Drummond Street   In this street off EUSTON SQUARE in northwest London, Dickens and his schoolmates from WELLINGTON HOUSE pretended to be beggars. Miss Amelia Martin maintains her millinery and dressmaking establishment at No. 7. *Boz*, "Mistaken Milliner."

"Drunkard's Death, The"   Life story of a drunkard: his wife dies in wretched poverty; his sons are transported or killed; his daughter leaves him; and, finally, he drowns himself in the THAMES. This story was written for the Second Series of *Boz.*

Drury Lane   Street in central London famous for the **Drury Lane Theatre**, where Miss Petowker of the Crummles Company performed (*Nickleby*, 14); Dick Swiveller's lodgings are located over a tobacconist's shop here (*Curiosity Shop*, 7); David Copperfield orders beef at an à la mode restaurant here (11), as Dickens himself had done as a boy. The graveyard where Captain Hawdon is buried is nearby (*Bleak House*). Also mentioned in *Boz*, "Astley's," "Broker's,'," "Gin-shops," "Pawnbroker's," "Shabby-genteel People"; *Uncommercial* (4, 25, 35).

Dubbley   A constable at IPSWICH, "a dirty-faced man, something over six feet high, and stout in proportion," who helps in the arrest of Mr. Pickwick during the confrontation with Peter Magnus. *Pickwick*, 24–25.

Ducrow, Andrew (1793–1842) Famous equestrian performer who became manager of ASTLEY'S ROYAL EQUESTRIAN AMPITHEATRE. *Boz*, "Astley's."

"Duelling in France" Article for *HOUSEHOLD WORDS* (June 27, 1857), by Eliza Lynn LINTON and Dickens, though Dickens's contribution was small. The article gives a historical account of duelling in France by telling the stories of a number of duels. *Stone*.

Duff Bow Street runner and colleague of Blathers: "a red-headed, bony man, in top-boots; with a rather ill-favoured countenance, and a turned-up sinister-looking nose" (31). He investigates the CHERTSEY robbery. *Twist*.

Duke's Place Street of second-hand clothing shops near Sampson Brass's office in BEVIS MARKS, Aldgate. *Curiosity Shop* (33).

Duke Street (1) Off LINCOLN'S INN Fields. Location of the Sardinian Chapel destroyed by the Gordon rioters. *Rudge* (50).

Duke Street (2) A quiet street off PICCADILLY where Mr. Twemlow has his lodgings over a livery stable. *Mutual Friend*, (I:2).

Dull Vice-president of the Umbugology and Ditch-wateristics Section of the Mudfog Association. *Mudfog*.

Dullborough The Traveller's version of CHATHAM, his boyhood home. "Most of us come from Dullborough who come from a country town." *Uncommercial* (12).

"Dullborough Town" The Traveller visits the town where he was a boy and finds it much changed, "mysteriously gone, like my own youth." Then he meets Joe Specks, a boyhood friend, and their shared memories make the visit a rewarding one. *Uncommerical* (12).

Dulwich Village south of London where Pickwick settles in retirement. *Pickwick* (57).

Dumas, Alexandre (1802–1870) French novelist and dramatist, author of *The Count of Monte Cristo* (1844) and other works. Dickens visited Dumas in Paris in 1844 with William MACREADY and attended a performance of his play *Christine*.

Dumbledon Parlor-boarder at "Our School," an "idiotic goggle-eyed boy" whose favored treatment leads his fellow students to believe he is wealthy. *Reprinted*.

Dumkins, Mr. Star batsman for the All-Muggleton Cricket Club. *Pickwick* (7).

Dummins "Eccentric" and "rather wild" Out-and-out Young Gentleman. *Young Gentlemen*.

The dustheaps in Victorian London provided subsistence for scavengers and made some of their owners rich men, like the elder John Harmon in Our Mutual Friend.

Dummy Member of the Mudfog Association. *Mudfog.*

Dumps, Nicodemus Misanthropic bachelor uncle of Charles Kitterbell, who disrupts the christening party for Kitterbell's son by toasting the infant with a list of the dangers he faces in the world. As a result, Dumps is not asked again to sponsor one of his nephew's children. *Boz,* "Christening."

Dunchurch The Warwickshire village where Pickwick stops on his way to London from BIRMINGHAM. *Pickwick* (51).

Dundey, Dr. Irish bank robber whom Sergeant Dornton follows to America. *Reprinted,* "Detective Police."

Dunkle, Dr. Ginery Spokesman for the deputation at the National Hotel that waits on Elijah Pogram, "a shrill boy . . . of great poetical elements." *Chuzzlewit* (34).

Dunstable During Christmas dinner, Pumblechook describes this village butcher's especially adept method of killing a pig as a good reason for Pip to be glad that he was not born a pig (4). *Expectations.*

"Durden, Dame" One of Esther SUMMERSON's nicknames, from a song celebrating the Dame's excellence as a housewife. *Bleak House.*

Durdles Drunken stonemason who carves the tombstones for Cloisterham Cathedral; "in a suit of coarse flannel with horn buttons, a yellow neckerchief with draggled ends, an old hat more russet-colored than black, and laced boots of the hue of his stony calling, Durdles leads a hazy gipsy sort of life, carrying his dinner about with him in a small bundle" (4). Sapsea employs him to carve his wife's epitaph (4), and Jasper gets him to lead him on a guided tour of the catacombs beneath the cathedral and to demonstrate how he identifies old tombs (12). *Drood.*

Dustheaps Central symbol in *Mutual Friend,* these heaps of rubbish are the source of John Harmon's wealth and comprise the inheritance he passes on to his son and the Boffins.

"Dying Clown, The" Alternate title for "The STROLLER'S TALE" in *Pickwick.* Robert SEYMOUR was working to meet Dickens's objections to his illustration for this tale just before he committed suicide.

Dyson, A. E. (1928–) Scholar and literary critic, especially interested in the Christian dimensions of literary works: editor of Dickens's criticism (*Modern Judgments on Dickens,* 1968; *Casebook on "Bleak House",* 1969) and author of *The Inimitable Dickens* (1970), a celebration of Dickens works with critical essays on 12 of the novels, especially on Christian thematic elements in them.

Eagle Inn Famous pleasure garden and tavern in the CITY ROAD in northeast London where musical entertainments were held. Dickens describes it in "Miss Evans and the Eagle" (*Boz*) and in "Amusements of the People" (*Miscellaneous*).

"Early Coaches" Humorous sketch describing the difficulties in taking an early-morning coach. Originally published as "Sketches of London No. 3" in the *EVENING CHRONICLE* (February 19, 1835). *Boz*.

Early Victorian Age Although VICTORIA did not take the throne until 1837, the Victorian period is usually dated from 1832, the year of the First REFORM BILL and the death of Sir Walter SCOTT, and extends to the turn of the century with Victoria's death in 1901. The Early Victorian Period, from 1832 to 1851, the year of the Crystal Palace Exhibition, was characterized by rapid social and political change, vigorous public controversy, and near revolution in the Chartist Movement of the 1840s (See CHARTISM). In literature the period is marked by the emergence of the novel as the dominant literary form. Dickens produced half of his major works during this period; his prolific output, comic exuberance, and social concerns were typical of the novels of the time. G. K. Young's *Early Victorian England* is a standard history of the period; Kathleen TILLOTSON's *Novels of the Eighteen Forties* (1956) is the classic study of the early Victorian novel.

East India House Headquarters of the East India Company in LEADENHALL STREET in the CITY of London, just around the corner from Dombey and Son. It is a "magnificent" building, "teeming with suggestions of precious stuffs and stones, tigers, elephants, howdahs, hookahs, umbrellas, palm trees, palanquins, and gorgeous princes of a brown complexion sitting on carpets" (*Dombey*, 4). Bob Sawyer and Ben Allen both go abroad on surgical appointments with the East India Company (*Pickwick*, 57).

Easthope, John (1784–1865) Stockbroker, liberal politician, and publisher of the *MORNING CHRONICLE*. He took over the paper in 1833 and hired Dickens in 1834. An irascible and premptory man, he was known as "Blasthope" to his employees. Dickens, during his years working as a reporter on the paper from 1834 to 1836, represented the reporters in a successful negotiation with him.

Eatanswill Fictitious town in East Anglia where the Pickwickians observe the election between the Blues and Buffs, respectively Tories and Whigs (13). Although it is generally thought to be based on SUDBURY, where Dickens covered an election as a reporter in 1834, IPSWICH, BURY ST. EDMUNDS, and NORWICH have also been suggested as models. The contentiousness of the election is apparent in the town's two rival newspapers, the *Eatanswill Gazette*, edited by Pott, and the *Eatanswill Independent*, edited by Slurk, a rivalry that comes to blows between the two editors (51). *Pickwick*.

Eaton Square A developing area in Belgravia, in west London, where Boz notices that door knockers are being replaced by bells. *Boz*, "Next-Door Neighbor."

Eddard The intelligent donkey who pulls the cart that takes Wegg to Boffin's Bower. *Mutual Friend* (I:5).

Eden The town on the MISSISSIPPI where the Eden Land Corporation is selling lots. Martin Chuzzlewit buys land here sight unseen from General Choke and Mr. Kettle, only to discover that the place is a swamp "choked with slime and matted growth" (23). Martin's dream of setting up an architectural firm in Eden ends when he contracts fever and nearly dies (33). *Chuzzlewit*. Dickens based Eden on a settlement in CAIRO, ILLINOIS, that he saw on his American trip in 1842.

Edinburgh, Scotland Dickens went to Edinburgh as a reporter for the *MORNING CHRONICLE* in 1834 and subsequently set "The Story of the BAGMAN'S UNCLE" in Canongate. He gave readings here in 1858, 1861, and 1869.

"Edinburgh Apprentice School Association" Article from the *EXAMINER* (December 30, 1848), reporting on the success of the Edinburgh night school for apprentices and working men. *Miscellaneous*.

Editor, Dickens as Throughout most of his writing career, Dickens was also engaged as the editor of various periodicals for which he both himself wrote and for which he also solicited and edited the work of other writers. These editorial enterprises included *BENTLEY'S MIS-CELLANY* (February 1837–April 1839), *MASTER HUMPHREY'S CLOCK* (April 4, 1840–December 4, 1841), *DAILY NEWS* (January 21, 1846–February 9, 1846), *HOUSEHOLD WORDS* (March 27, 1850–May 28, 1859), and *ALL THE YEAR ROUND* (April 30, 1859–his death). Although W. H. WILLS served as Dickens's sub-editor on the most important of these projects, Dickens was an active copyeditor, reworking and even co-writing many of the articles. He was also an active editor-in-chief, particularly in soliciting materials from other writers and guiding the content of the magazines.

Detailed discussions of Dickens's practices as an editor, particularly of *HOUSEHOLD WORDS,* can be found in the introductions to Harry STONE (1968) and Anne Lohrli's index and reference book on *Household Words* (1973). R. C. Lehman's collection of Dickens's letters to WILLS, *Charles Dickens as Editor* (1912), gives some insight into Dickens's role as editor.

Edkins "A pale young gentleman in a green stock, and spectacles of the same, a member of the honourable Society of the Inner Temple," who goes on the steam excursion. *Boz,* "Steam Excursion."

Edmunds, John The subject of "The Convict's Return," the tale told by the Clergyman at DINGLEY DELL. *Pickwick* (6). Abused by his father, Edmunds is transported for robbery. When he returns and confronts his father, the old man dies.

Edson One of Mrs. Lirriper's lodgers who deserts his pregnant wife, **Peggy**. She dies shortly after, and Mrs. Lirriper adopts their infant son, **Jemmy**. Years later Mrs. Lirriper takes the boy to France where he meets his father on his deathbed. "Lirriper's Lodgings," "Lirriper's Legacy."

Education Dickens's own formal education was limited to a year or so with William GILES in CHATHAM and almost three years at WELLINGTON HOUSE ACADEMY after his father was released from the DEBTORS PRISON. Beyond this he was largely self-educated, teaching himself shorthand to become a parliamentary reporter and reading at the BRITISH MUSEUM, for which he obtained a reader's ticket as soon as he was eligible at age 18. Perhaps because his own education had been so restricted or because he wrote so often about the lives of children, Dickens had a great deal to say about education in his articles and novels, and he depicted schools and teachers in many of his books. Philip COLLINS's *Dickens and Education* (1963), the standard work on this topic, takes four pages to list the articles and novels that include schools or remarks on education.

Dickens was a lifelong advocate of national schools, which were not approved by Parliament until 1870, the year of his death. At the same time, he opposed condescending education for the poor, designed to teach them to know their place. He satirized such efforts in the Charitable Grinders School in *Dombey* and in the school where Uriah Heep learned false humility in *Copperfield.*

Many of the schools in the novels exemplify other kinds of educational abuse. DOTHEBOYS HALL (*Nickleby*) illustrated the neglect and brutality of the Yorkshire schools, where unwanted children were relegated to oblivion. SALEM HOUSE, Creakle's school in *Copperfield,* based on Dickens's experience at Wellington House, also makes liberal use of corporal punishment and judges its students by their family's social standing. Dr. Blimber's Academy (*Dombey*) is an educational hothouse that forces its students to premature growth—and death—with its heady regimen of classical languages and history. M'Choakumchild's classroom of hard fact in *Hard Times* may be Dickens's most famous school; it offers a satiric version of a utilitarian education, wholly devoted to fact and absolutely opposed to fancy (See UTILITARIANISM). It has the predictable effect of leaving its graduates incapable of acting on feeling or of making ethical choices. Bradley Headstone's (*Mutual Friend*) preparation as a schoolmaster is similar to that of M'Choakumchild. Both are products of the new teachers training institutes. Bradley's learning and teaching is "mechanical" and does not enable him to govern his passions.

The most positively presented school in the novels is Doctor Strong's Academy (*Copperfield*). Although Dickens does not give details of the school's curriculum, he does show how David learns from the Doctor and his young wife the most important lesson for his own life—the need for "a disciplined heart."

Edward With his wife, Charlotte, half of the contradictory couple. *Young Couples.*

Edwards, Miss Young lady, "motherless and poor," a teaching apprentice at Miss Monflathers's school, who befriends Little Nell. She is secretly reunited with her younger **sister**. *Curiosity Shop* (31, 32).

Edwin Charley's schoolmate and his supposed rival for the affections of Angela Leath. They meet at the HOLLY TREE INN when Edwin is on his way to GRETNA GREEN to marry Angela's cousin Emmeline. "Holly Tree."

Edwin Drood See *MYSTERY OF EDWIN DROOD.*

Eel-Pie Island An island in the THAMES that Morleena Kenwigs proposes to visit. *Nickleby* (52).

Egg, Augustus (1816–1863) Artist and friend of Dickens who participated in many of Dickens's AMATEUR THEATRICALS, acting and designing costumes. He went to Italy with Dickens and Wilkie COLLINS in 1853. In the mid-1850s, he proposed to Dickens's sister-in-law, Georgina HOGARTH, but she refused to marry him.

Eigner, Edwin (1931–) Professor, University of California, Riverside; founding member of the DICKENS PROJECT; scholar and writer on Dickens, Stevenson, and other Victorian writers. *The Metaphysical Novel in England and America: Dickens, Bulwer, Hawthorne, Melville*, (1978) discusses a sub-genre in which Dickens and other writers were working. These novels mixed romance and realism and were based in an idealistic aesthetic derived from Kant and Hegel rather than in the realistic tradition coming from Locke and Aristotle. In *The Dickens Pantomime* (1989), Eigner explores elements of traditional PANTOMIME in Dickens's novels, especially in *David Copperfield*, where Micawber is a triumphant version of the pantomime clown.

Eisenstein, Sergei (1898–1948) Russian film director and pioneer in cinematography; his films include *Potemkin* (1915), *Ten Days that Shook the World* (1927–28). *Alexander Nevsky* (1938), and *Ivan the Terrible* (1943–46). He developed the use of MONTAGE as the basic technique of cinematic storytelling. In "Dickens, Griffith, and the Film Today" (in *Film Form*), Eisenstein described Dickens's "head-spinning tempo of changing impressions" as part of the "urbanism" of his work, and he analyzed some scenes from *Twist* for their cinematic qualities, especially for their use of montage. A. L. Zambrano (*Dickens and Film*, 1977) shows how the rhythm in Eisenstein's films, his use of parallel montage, and his associating of characters with objects derives from Dickens.

Elections Dickens is not particularly kind to members of Parliament in the novels. Venal, egotistical, and devoted to humbug, they usually represent established power rather than act as agents of reform. He may have developed this image of politicians as a young man while recording parliamentary proceedings from the press gallery. His famous description of the EATANSWILL election in *Pickwick* (13) was based on his experience covering the election in SUDBURY in 1835 for the *MORNING CHRONICLE*. His account of the contest between the Dedlock forces and Rouncewell the Ironmaster in *Bleak House* (40) dramatizes the shift from landed to industrial power in the years following the REFORM BILL OF 1832. Veneering's "election" (*Mutual Friend*, II:3) is simply a matter of buying the right to represent the borough of Pocket-Breeches, apparently unchanged by reforms in the electoral process. Humphry HOUSE (1941) summed up Dickens's attitude toward the electoral process:

> He saw almost from his boyhood that the imperfections of Parliament were largely caused by the initial corruption of its members through the very process of election. Influence, whether financial or social, counted for more than merit; the influence was more often than not corruptly exercised; and even when technical corruption did not enter in, the far more subtle corruption of electioneering promises and party propaganda undermined the morale of an M.P. from the start. Nearly all his attacks on Parliament can be reduced to this suspicion of the personal sincerity and independence of its members.

So when a group of liberal electors from READING invited Dickens to run for Parliament, he declined to do so on the grounds that he was unwilling to give up his independence.

"Election for Beadle, The" Originally appeared as "Sketches of London No. 16. Our Parish" in the *EVENING CHRONICLE* (July 14, 1835). An account of the contest between Bung and Spruggins for Parish Beadle in which the main issue is the number of children each man has. *Boz.*

Elephant and Castle The district in south London where the Bagnets live (*Bleak House*, 27). Its name comes from the famous public house at its center where the roads to KENT and Surrey come together.

Eliot, George (pseud. of Mary Ann Evans) (1819–1880) Though he once described Eliot and George LEWES as "the ugliest couple in London," Dickens was a great admirer of Eliot's work, especially *Adam Bede*, and he hoped to get her to write for *ALL THE YEAR ROUND.* Long before she revealed her identity, Dickens, when reading *Scenes of Clerical Life*, identified the author as a woman. On first meeting Dickens, Eliot found his appearance "disappointing—no benevolence in the face and I think little in the head." After dining with him some years later, she discovered "a strain of real seriousness along with his keenness and humour."

Eliot, Thomas Stearns (1888–1965) Anglo-American poet, playwright, and critic; spokesman for and exemplar of literary modernism; best known for *The Waste Land* (1922). In "Wilkie Collins and Dickens" (*Times Literary Supplement*, 1927), Eliot compared Dickens, preeminently a creator of character, with Collins, a master of plot. He suggested that much could be learned about both writers by studying their collaboration.

While he was working on *The Waste Land*, Eliot was reading *Our Mutual Friend*, and he took the poem's original title from Betty Higden's remark that "Sloppy is a beautiful reader of the newspaper. He do the Police in different voices" (I:16). Although Eliot later changed the title, his initial choice suggests the novel's influence on the method of the poem, which presents a series of vignettes in different voices.

Calling *Mutual Friend* "Dickens' Waste Land," Edgar JOHNSON (1952) compares the poem with the novel, noting the use of dust heaps, the polluted THAMES, and the MYTH of resurrection in both works.

Eliot, William Greenleaf (1811–1887) Founder of Washington University in St. Louis, grandfather of the poet, T. S. ELIOT, he was Dickens's host in ST. LOUIS on his 1842 tour of AMERICA.

Elizabeth, Miss   One of the inhabitants of the corner house whom Silas Wegg imagines he serves and to whom he gives fictitious names. *Mutual Friend*, I:5.

Elliotson, John (1791–1868)   Professor of Medicine at the University of London and the leading English theorist of MESMERISM. He was the author of *Human Physiology* (1840) and *On Numerous Cases of Surgical Operations Without Pain in the Mesmeric State* (1843) and the founder and editor of *The Zooist*, a journal of mesmerism and phrenology. He was a good friend of Dickens, influencing the novelist's interest and participation in mesmerism.

Ellis   An admirer of the parlour orator, "a sharp-nosed, light-haired man in a brown surtout reaching nearly to his heels." *Boz*, "Parlour Orator."

Ellis and Blackmore   The law firm located in GRAY'S INN to which Dickens was apprenticed in 1827. Dickens found the routine legal work on this job tedious.

Elm Cottage, Petersham   Dickens's summer house in 1839 while he was working on *Nickleby*.

Elwes, John (1714–1789)   A historical figure, one of the misers upon whom Boffin supposedly models his change to miserliness. Through scrimping and saving, Elwes cleared an encumbered estate from debt and left a fortune worth £500,000. *Mutual Friend* (III:5).

Ely Place   Street in the CITY off HOLBORN Hill. Agnes stays here with the Waterbrooks when she visits London. *Copperfield* (25).

Emanuel Chapel   The church in DORKING where Stiggins is an official. *Pickwick* (52).

Emerson, Ralph Waldo (1803–1882)   American essayist, poet, transcendentalist. Dickens dined with him, Thomas CARLYLE, and John FORSTER in London in 1848. Carlyle, fulminating during the meal on the moral decline of England, shocked Emerson by proclaiming that male chastity was a thing of the past. Dickens continued the joke by assuring Emerson that if his son were "particularly chaste," he would be concerned about his health. After attending one of Dickens's readings in Boston in 1867, Emerson told Annie FIELDS: "I am afraid he has too much talent for his genius; it is a fearful locomotive to which he is bound and can never be free from it nor set it at rest. . . . He is too consummate an artist to have a thread of nature left. He daunts me! I have not the key!"

Emigration   Dickens's frequent attacks on Thomas MALTHUS's doctrine of surplus population would lead one to expect him to reject emigration, one of Malthus's cures for the problem. However, in the novels, in his work with URANIA COTTAGE, and in his journalism, Dickens promoted emigration as a solution to poverty. In "A Bundle of Emigrants' Letters," for example, he wrote: "It is unquestionably melancholy that thousands upon thousands of people, ready and willing to labour, should be wearing away life hopelessly in this island, while within a few months' sail—within a few weeks' when steam communication with Australia shall be established—there are vast tracts of country where no man who is willing to work hard . . . can ever know want." The women at Urania Cottage were encouraged to emigrate and start a new life there, as Em'ly and Martha Endell do in *Copperfield*. Dickens also encouraged his own sons Frederick and Edward to settle in AUSTRALIA.

In the novels, emigration is often a convenient way to dispose of such criminal figures as Monks (*Twist*), Fred Trent (*Curiosity Shop*), or Tom Gradgrind (*Hard Times*). It can also be a test and a way to temper the arrogance of a character like young Martin Chuzzlewit, who is transformed by his time in AMERICA, or Pip, who learns to provide for himself in Egypt (*Expectations*). The novel that most fully exploits emigration as a way to resolve its themes is *Copperfield*, written at the height of Dickens's involvement with Urania Cottage. The Micawbers, Dan'l Peggotty, Mrs. Gummidge, Em'ly, Martha Endell, and Mr. Mell all end up successful in Australia, and their absence from England conveniently simplifies David's life.

Norris Pope (*Dickens and Charity*, 1978) discusses the controversy about emigration and Dickens's place in it.

Emile   The soldier billeted at the clockmaker's in the French town where Langley goes. "Somebody's Luggage."

Emilia   Mrs. Orange's baby. "Holiday Romance."

Emily   A brazen young prostitute taken off in the prisoner's van with her sister Bella. *Boz*, "Prisoner's Van."

Em'ly, Little   Daniel Peggotty's orphan niece who is raised in his boat-house on the YARMOUTH sands and is David's infant sweetheart (3). She goes to work as a seamstress in Omer's shop and is about to marry her cousin Ham when David introduces Steerforth into the Yarmouth circle (21). Steerforth seduces Em'ly, running off to ITALY with her on the eve of her marriage (31). Daniel spends years seaching for the girl, and the two are reunited when Em'ly returns to London after Steerforth tires of her (50). She immigrates to AUSTRALIA with Daniel, Mrs. Gummidge, and Martha Endell (57). *Copperfield*.

Emma (1)   One of the servant girls at DINGLEY DELL whom Pickwick kisses under the mistletoe. *Pickwick* (28).

Emma (2)   The waitress "with the bright eyes and the pretty smile" at an English angler's inn. "Holly Tree."

Emmeline Angela Leath's cousin, a young woman of property who elopes with Edwin. They marry and have seven children. "Holly Tree."

"Empty Chair, The" Famous watercolor painting by Luke FILDES, painted on the day of Dickens's death, showing the novelist's study with an empty chair by the writing desk.

Endell, Martha A schoolmate of Little Em'ly who also works as an apprentice at Omer's. After she is seduced and disgraced, Em'ly gives her money to go to London (22). There she becomes a prostitute (46, 47), but she redeems herself by helping Daniel Peggotty in his search for Em'ly and eventually immigrates to AUSTRALIA with the Peggottys (57). *Copperfield.*

Engel, Monroe (1921–) American novelist, critic, Harvard professor, Engel has written on Dickens's social, political, and aesthetic ideas; in *The Maturity of Dickens* (1959), he made extensive use of Dickens's journalism to explore these aspects of the novels.

"Enlightened Clergyman, An" Note from *ALL THE YEAR ROUND* (March 8, 1862), reporting on the objections raised by two clergymen to public readings of Wilkie COLLINS's story "Picking up Waifs at Sea" and Dickens's "The Bloomsbury Christening," which, according to the clergyman, "trifles with a sacred ordinance." *Miscellaneous.*

Epping Forest An old growth forest northeast of London, a destination for holiday excursions like those of the Young Ladies' Young Gentleman (*Young Gentlemen*) and the inmates of Titbull's Almshouses (*Uncommercial*, 29). CHIGWELL, site of the MAYPOLE INN, is on the south edge of the forest. *Rudge.*

"Epsom" Article by William Henry WILLS and Dickens for *HOUSEHOLD WORDS* (June 7, 1851), describing a tour of Epsom Downs, its stables and track, before race day and concluding with Dickens's masterful set piece on race day at Epsom. *Stone.*

Epsom Races Horse races held on the downs near Epsom, Surrey; the most famous race, the annual Derby, first run in 1780, is described in "Epsom," an article for *HOUSEHOLD WORDS.* Compeyson met Abel Magwitch at the races (*Expectations*, 42). The races are also mentioned in *Reprinted*, "Three Detective Stories."

An engraving based on Fildes's painting of "The Empty Chair."

Esau Slodge   The river boat that takes Martin Chuzzlewit's appeal for help from EDEN to Mr. Bevan in NEW YORK. *Chuzzlewit* (33).

Essex Street   The street between the STRAND and the river where Pip finds lodgings for Magwitch. *Expectations* (40).

Estella   Daughter of Magwitch and Molly, who is adopted by Miss Havisham to be the agent of her vengeance against men. When Pip is recruited as a child to play with her (8), Estella taunts and humiliates him. But when Pip receives his expectations (18), he believes that Miss Havisham is his benefactor and that she also plans to marry him to Estella. While Pip lives as a gentleman in London, Estella continues to tantalize and torment him (32, 33, 38), though at the same time warning him that she has "no heart, . . . no softness there, no—sympathy—sentiment—nonsense" (29). Even after he learns that she is not his intended, Pip is distressed when she plans to marry Bentley Drummle (44), who abuses her so that she separates from him. In the final ending that Dickens wrote for the novel (59), Estella meets Pip at the ruins of SATIS HOUSE, and as they leave "the ruined place," Pip says that he sees "no shadow of another parting from her." But in the suppressed original ending, Pip and Estella meet and part on a London street with no suggestion that they will meet again. *Expectations*.

Etc. Etc.   "Devilish gentlemanly fellow" who requests admission for himself and a friend to Master Humphrey's circle. His application is refused. *Humphrey* (1).

Eugène   Soldier billeted at the tinman's in the French town where Langley goes. "Somebody's Luggage."

Euston Square   Site of the first London railway terminus, built in 1838. Miss Martin's house in Drummond Street next to the Square preceded the railway there. *Boz*, "Mistaken Milliner."

Evangelicalism   Revival movement in the Church of England, stemming from 17th-century Puritanism and reaching fulfillment in the career of John Wesley (1703–91), whose conversion in 1738 is usually considered the beginning of the Evangelical movement. Evangelicals stressed the consciousness of sin; the experience of conversion; rigorous rules of personal conduct; the evangelical mission of the church, both at home and abroad, to convert others to Christ; and the responsibility of Christians for social reform. While some Evangelicals left the Church of England to form splinter sects, most notably the Methodists or Wesleyans, others remained within the Anglican Church. Evangelicalism was influential well into the 19th century in giving impetus to movements for prison reform and the abolition of slavery; in promoting temperance, Sunday closing, and strict standards of behavior; and in promoting enthusiastic and participatory forms of worship.

Dickens often allied himself with Evangelicals on issues of social reform, as with Lord SHAFTESBURY on factory reform and the bill to limit the working day to 10 hours. He was strenuously opposed, however, to their sabbatarianism; in *Sunday under Three Heads* (1836), in other essays, and in the novels, he frequently attacked those who wanted to deny necessary amusement to working people.

Nearly all of his portraits of Evangelicals are satiric. Stiggins' Emmanuel Chapel (*Pickwick*), Little Bethel (*Curiosity Shop*), Melchisedech Howler's chapel of the "ranting persuasion" (*Dombey*) and Chadband's congregation (*Bleak House*) are all versions of the enthusiastic meeting house that duped susceptible women like Mrs. Weller, Mrs. Nubbles, Mrs. McStinger, and Mrs. Snagsby into becoming true believers. The enthusiastic preachers are nearly always hypocrites like Stiggins, who professes teetotalism but bears the red nose of drink, or like Chadband, who stuffs himself with muffins as he feeds the starving Jo only with words. Although he is not a clergyman, Pecksniff (*Chuzzlewit*) is the triumphant rendering of this Tartuffian strain in Evangelicalism.

Dickens was harsher in his treatment of the repressive and earnest negativism of the Evangelicals. There is nothing comic in his presentation of Mrs. Clennam (*Dorrit*), whose consciousness of sin and hypocrisy blight Arthur's childhood, produce her paralysis, and lead to her destruction. Even though they are not presented as figures defined by their religion, the Murdstones (*Copperfield*) and the unconverted Scrooge (*Carol*) possess similar repressive Evangelical earnestness.

The best discussion of Dickens and Evangelicalism appears in Norris Pope (*Dickens and Charity*, 1978).

Evans   "A tall, thin, pale young gentleman with extensive whiskers" who plays Roderigo in the Gattleton's production of *Othello*. *Boz*, "Porter."

Evans, Frederick Mullet   Senior partner in the publishing firm BRADBURY & EVANS, a rotund, good-humored man, known as "Pater" to the staff of *PUNCH*. When Evans refused in 1858 to publish in *Punch* Dickens's statement about his marital troubles, Dickens broke with him and two years later refused to attend the wedding of his son Charles to Evans's daughter Bessie (see Charles Culliford DICKENS). Their friendship was never renewed.

Evans, Jemima ("Jemima Ivins")   The young lady of CAMDEN TOWN whose **maternal parent**, sister **Tilly**, and **youngest sister** take considerable interest in her courtship by Samuel Wilkins. The couple's excursion to the EAGLE TAVERN, however, ends in a brawl. *Boz*, "Miss Evans."

Evans, Richard   One of Marton's pupils, "an amazing boy to learn; blessed with a good memory; with a good voice and ear for psalm-singing." *Curiosity Shop* (52).

Evans, Superintendent   Officer of the Thames Police who takes the narrator on an inspection tour of his "beat." *Reprinted*, "Down with the Tide."

Evening Chronicle   The newspaper edited by Dickens's father-in-law, George HOGARTH, to which in 1835 Dickens contributed a number of sketches which were later collected in *Boz*.

Evenson, John   One of Mrs. Tibbs's boarders, "a thorough radical" who has a running feud with Mr. Wisbottle. He arouses Mrs. Tibbs's suspicions about secret assignations in the maid's storeroom. *Boz*, "Boarding-House."

Every Man in His Humour   The play (1598) by Ben JONSON that Dickens's amateur players performed on numerous occasions, beginning in 1845. Dickens directed and played the role of Bobadil.

Examiner, The   Liberal weekly journal of politics and literature founded by John and Leigh HUNT in 1808. John FORSTER served as its literary editor from 1835 and as managing editor from 1847 to 1855. Dickens contributed a number of reviews and articles to the paper, most of which are included in *Miscellaneous Papers*.

"Exchange or Barter"   Nickname of a pupil at SALEM HOUSE, son of a coal merchant who secures his tuition in exchange for coal. *Copperfield* (6).

Exchequer Coffee-house   The address that John Harmon gives when posing as Julius Handford (*Mutual Friend*, I:3). Supposed to be in PALACE YARD, Westminster, but probably fictitious.

Exeter   The town in Devon where Mrs Wittitterley danced at the election ball with the baronet's nephew. *Nickleby* (21).

Exeter Change   A building on the north side of the STRAND in London that housed a wild animal menagerie until 1828. *Boz*, "Thoughts about People."

Exeter Hall, Strand   A meeting hall built in 1830–31, used for conventions and for religious meetings, especially the annual meeting of Evangelicals in May (see EVANGELICISM). Dickens satirizes it as the HAVEN OF PHILANTHROPY (*Drood*, 17). It is also briefly mentioned in *Nickleby* (5) and in *Boz*, "Ladies' Societies."

Exmouth   Town in Devon where Richard Doubledick was born. "Seven Poor Travellers."

Eyre, Edward John (1815–1901)   Colonial governor in Jamaica whose harsh imposition of martial law to

Eytinge's frontispiece to an 1869 American edition of A Christmas Carol *shows Scrooge confronting the three spirits.*

suppress a native rebellion in 1865 provoked intense controversy in Britain. John Stuart Mill's Jamaica Committee attempted unsuccessfully to prosecute Eyre for murder. Dickens, along with CARLYLE, RUSKIN, TENNYSON, and others, joined in the defense of Eyre, arguing that stern measures were called for to prevent further violence.

Eytinge, Solomon (1833–1905)   American genre painter and book illustrator who illustrated a number of early American editions of Dickens's works, most notably the DIAMOND EDITION of Dickens's works (1867) and an edition of *A Christmas Carol* (1869). Dickens said of Eytinge's illustrations: "They are remarkable alike for a delicate perception of beauty, a lively eye for character, a most agreeable absence of exaggeration, and a general modesty and propriety which I greatly like." Another example of his work appears in illustration 20 (CRATCHIT).

Ezekiel   The name of the serving boy at Mugby Junction. *Mugby*.

F

F., Mr. The abbreviation Flora FINCHING uses when referring to her late husband. *Dorrit.*

Face-Maker, The "A corpulent little man in a large white waistcoat" who performs at a Flemish country fair, changing his face into "a thousand characters." *Uncommercial* (27).

Fagin Receiver of stolen goods and leader of a gang of young thieves and pickpockets, "a very old shrivelled Jew, whose villainous-looking and repulsive face was obscured by a quantity of matted red hair" (8). The Artful Dodger introduces Oliver Twist into Fagin's gang (8) and Oliver's half-brother, Monks, employs Fagin to corrupt his innocent sibling. To this end, Fagin teaches Oliver to pick pockets and involves him in Sikes's robbery of Mrs. Maylie's house (22). Fagin attempts but fails to recapture Oliver after the Maylies take him in, and as his own capture approaches, he desperately urges Sikes to murder Nancy (47). After his capture, as he awaits hanging, Fagin is visited in prison by Oliver and Mr. Brownlow. Mad with fear, he attempts to leave his cell with the boy (52). *Twist.* Dickens took Fagin's name from **Bob Fagin**, a boy who worked with him at the WARREN'S BLACKING in 1824. Fagin has often been considered an anti-Semitic caricature, based on a stereotype. Alec GUINNESS's portrayal of the Jew in David LEAN's 1948 film was censored before it could be shown in the United States. Eliza DAVIS, a Jewish acquaintance of Dickens, communicated her objections to him and he included Riah in *Mutual Friend* as a way of achieving a balance in his depictions of JEWS.

Fair Freedom The "lovely princess" who is Prince Bull's wife. *Reprinted,* "Prince Bull."

Fairfax, Mr. The censorious young gentleman, "a remarkably clever person." *Young Gentlemen.*

Fairy Tales Dickens frequently alludes to fairy tales, traditional folk stories for children in which spirits from an invisible world intervene in the lives of the characters. Dickens treasured such stories from his own childhood; indeed, he credited them with saving him from despair during his dark days in the BLACKING WAREHOUSE.

Cruikshank's famous rendering of Fagin awaiting execution for the original edition of Oliver Twist *(1839).*

They "kept alive my fancy," he wrote, "and my hope of something beyond that place and time."

Dickens knew well the "Mother Goose" tales retold by PERRAULT in France, the folk stories collected by the brothers Grimm in Germany, and similar collections of British tales, many of which first appeared during Dickens's childhood. He was particularly fond of the oriental fairy tales in THE ARABIAN NIGHTS, translated into English in the 18th century, and of James Ridley's mutations of such stories in the *Tales of the Genii* (1764). Allusions to all of these traditional stories appear frequently in nearly all of the novels. Although Dickens also knew the work of such 19th-century fabulists as E. T. A. Hoffmann and Hans Christian ANDERSEN, who wrote original fairy tales, he does not draw on their stories as he does on the traditional ones.

So central are these traditional stories to Dickens's work that he developed what Harry STONE (1979) calls a "fairy tale method," in which particular stories or motifs from fairy tales provide a basis for the SYMBOLISM of the novel. Dickens thought these stories nurtured fancy or imagination in the child and reminded the adult of an inner life unconstrained by mundane concerns and expectations. That is why he strenuously objected, in "Frauds on the Fairies," to CRUIKSHANK's retelling of traditional tales to promote teetotalism and other versions of such children's stories to teach a moral or serve didactic purposes.

Stone (1979) describes the evolution of Dickens's fairy tale method from scattered references in the early novels, to his conscious intent to give a "higher form" to old nursery stories in the CHRISTMAS BOOKS, to his integrated and systematic use of such materials in the novels from *Dombey* on.

"Familiar Epistle from a Parent to a Child"
Dickens's letter to the readers of *BENTLEY'S MISCELLANY* (February 1839) as he turned over to William AINSWORTH the editorship of the magazine, his child. *Mudfog.*

Family Pet Nickname of the thief that Duff blames for a robbery in Edmonton. *Twist* (31).

Fan Scrooge's younger sister, who comes to take him home from school for Christmas. She is also the mother of Scrooge's nephew Fred. *Carol* (2). She is based on Dickens's sister Fanny.

Fanchette Daughter of a Swiss innkeeper who nurses "Our Bore." *Reprinted,* "Bore."

Fancy Although Coleridge distinguished the powers of imagination and fancy, Dickens uses the terms interchangeably. His project, as he described it in the "Preliminary Word" to *HOUSEHOLD WORDS,* was to bring fancy to bear on the grim realities of life:

> In the bosoms of the young and old, of the well-to-do and of the poor, we would tenderly cherish that light of Fancy which is inherent in the human breast. . . . to show to all, that in all familiar things, even in those which are repellent on the surface, there is Romance enough, if we will find it out:—to teach the hardest workers at this whirling wheel of toil, that their lot is not necessarily a moody, brutal fact, excluded from the sympathies and graces of imagination.

The transforming powers of Fancy could create a better world in the imagination and provide an ideal for which to strive. Dickens repeated this idea in the preface to *Bleak House,* in which he said that in the novel he had "purposely dwelt upon the romantic side of familiar things." The function of fancy—or imagination—then, was to transform the real world.

Dickens takes up the opposition of Fact and Fancy most directly in *Hard Times,* in which COKETOWN's utilitarian commitment to fact suppresses "the robber Fancy." The lives of both Louisa and Tom Gradgrind are blighted by their inability to imagine the world as different from what it is, to see the romantic possibilities in things.

Garrett STEWART (1974) traces the effects of imagination on the style of Dickens's novels; Robert NEWSOM (1977) discusses dwelling on the "romantic side of familiar things" as a fundamental principle in Dickens's work.

Fang Magistrate who hears the case against Oliver Twist for picking Mr. Brownlow's pocket. "His face was stern, and much flushed. If he were really not in the habit of drinking rather more than was exactly good for him, he might have brought an action against his countenance for libel, and have recovered heavy damages" (11). He bullies Oliver, browbeats Mr. Brownlow, and sentences the boy to three months in prison without any evidence. When the bookseller exonerates Oliver, Fang threatens to bring charges against Brownlow. *Twist.* Fang was modeled on the notorious magistrate Allan Stewart LAING of HATTON GARDEN Police Court.

Fanger, Donald (1929–) Professor of Slavic and comparative literature at Harvard. In *Dostoyevsky and Romantic Realism* (1965), Fanger considers Balzac, Dickens, and Gogol as precursors to Dostoyevsky and all of them as "romantic realists" who used the novel form to explore and mythologize the transformation to modernity in the 19th-century cities they all wrote about.

Fanny "One of the prettiest girls that ever was seen," sweetheart of the narrator as a young man. "Child's Story."

Faraday, Michael (1791–1867) Leading chemist and physicist of his time; Faraday's most significant achievement was the discovery of electromagnetic induction. Dickens requested Faraday's lecture notes as a source for several scientific articles that appeared in *HOUSEHOLD WORDS* in 1850. Faraday's remarks on SPONTANEOUS COMBUSTION there may have bolstered Dickens's position in the debate over Krook's death in *Bleak House*: "It is said that spontaneous combustion does happen sometimes; particularly in great spirit drinkers. I don't see why it should not, if the system were to become too inflammable."

Fareway Aristocratic family that determines the course of George Silverman's life. After he tutors the second **son** of the family, a young man whose "abilities were much above the average; but he came of a rich family, and was idle and luxurious," **Lady Fareway**, "a handsome well-preserved," and manipulative woman offers Silverman a small living in north Devon on the condition that he will also serve as her secretary and tutor her daughter. In Devon he secretly falls in love with the daughter, **Adelina**, but, considering himself unworthy, he marries her to Granville Wharton instead of claiming her for himself. "Silverman."

"Fast and Loose" Allegorical essay for *HOUSEHOLD WORDS* (March 24, 1855), describing the lies by which the rich and powerful control those beneath them, telling them that their situation is the result of "Providence" and that it would be "unparliamentary" to attempt to change it. *Miscellaneous.*

Fat Boy, The The epithet by which Wardle's servant JOE is known. *Pickwick.*

The chalet on the grounds of Gad's Hill that Dickens used as a study. The building was given to the novelist by Charles Fechter and is now housed at the Dickens Museum in Rochester.

"Father of the Marshalsea" The title given William DORRIT in the MARSHALSEA PRISON.

Fechter, Charles (1822–1879) Swiss actor and theater manager, one of Dickens's close friends in the 1860s. He made his name in Paris; when Dickens saw him in *La Dame aux Camélias*, he exclaimed that "a man who can do this can do anything." Fechter moved to London in 1860 and in 1863, with Dickens as his financial backer, became the lessee of the Lyceum Theatre. Dickens especially praised his performances in *Hamlet* and *Othello* and in 1868, when Fechter moved on to America, contributed an essay to the *Atlantic Monthly* "On Mr. Fechter's Acting." Fechter played Jules Obenreizer, the leading role in *No Thoroughfare*, the play by Wilkie COLLINS and Dickens that was produced in 1868. Fechter gave Dickens the little Swiss chalet that he used as his writing place at GAD'S HILL.

Fee, Dr. W. R. A medical member of the Mudfog Association. *Mudfog.*

Feeder, Mr., B. A. Assistant master to Dr. Blimber, "he was a kind of human barrel-organ, with a little list of tunes, at which he was continually working over and over again, without any variation" (11). He drills the boys in Greek and Latin grammar. After Blimber retires, Feeder is married by his brother, the **Reverend Alfred**, to Cornelia BLIMBER and takes over the management of the school. *Dombey.*

Feenix, Lord (Cousin Feenix) Edith Dombey's cousin, "a man about town forty years ago" (31), he now makes his home in Baden-Baden. He is fond of referring to such friends as Conversation Brown, Billy Jopler, Tommy Screwzer, and others in his conversation, assuming that his listeners will know those he talks about. He represents Edith's family at her wedding and he takes her in after she leaves her husband (61). *Dombey.*

Felton, Cornelius (1807–1862) Professor of Greek at Harvard whom Dickens met on his American tour in 1842. They became good friends and regular correspondents. Dickens described Felton as "one of the jolliest and simplest of men, and not at all starry, or stripey." Felton reviewed *American Notes* enthusiastically, even though most of his countrymen were disturbed by the book and by Dickens's "ingratitude." Felton called Dickens "the most original and inventive genius since Shakespeare!" He visited Dickens in England in 1853.

Fenchurch Street The street in the CITY where, at the corner of MINCING LANE, Bella Wilfer waits for her father to come from his office. *Mutual Friend* (II:8).

Fendall, Sergeant   A London police inspector, "a prodigious hand at pursuing private inquiries of a delicate nature." *Reprinted*, "Detective Police."

Ferdinand, Miss   A lively girl at Miss Twinkleton's school who "surprised the company with a sprightly solo on the comb-and-curlpaper." *Drood* (13).

Fern, Will   A country laborer who comes to London with his orphan niece **Lillian** in search of work. He is found sleeping in a shed, arrested for vagrancy, and taken before Alderman Cute, who is "determined to put this sort of thing down." Trotty Veck takes the couple in and they become part of his New Year vision, Will as a rick-burning Chartist (see CHARTISM) and Lillian as a prostitute. *Chimes*.

Féroce   The "gentle and polite" owner of a bathing machine at the French Watering Place. *Reprinted*, "French Watering Place."

Fetter Lane   A street running between HOLBORN and FLEET STREET, in the CITY, where the residence of Mr. Augustus Cooper is located. *Boz*, "Dancing Academy."

"Few Conventionalities, A"   Humorous article for *HOUSEHOLD WORDS* (July 12, 1851), in which Dickens lists conventional phrases and actions used in government, in the theater, at public dinners and meetings, and in social discourse. Such phrases, he suggests, disguise and soften the truth. *Miscellaneous*.

Fezziwig   Scrooge's employer when he is a young man, a jovial "old gentleman in a Welsh wig" who turns his warehouse into a Christmas dancehall. His **wife** is "one vast substantial smile" and the **three Miss Fezziwigs** are "beaming and lovable." *Carol* (2).

Fibbitson, Mrs.   The old woman who sits by the fire like "a bundle of old clothes" during Mr. Mell's visit to his mother at the BLACKHEATH almshouse. *Copperfield* (5).

Field, Barbara (1935–)   Contemporary American playwright who adapted the *Carol* for the Gutherie Theater in Minneapolis (1975) and *Great Expectations* for the Seattle Children's Theater (1983).

Field, Inspector   A real person, Charles F. Field, a well-known member of the detective police force. Dickens describes going on rounds with the policeman in "On Duty with Inspector Field" (*Reprinted*). He also writes about him as Charley Wield in "Detective Police" and "Three Detective Anectotes" (*Reprinted*). Field was also the model for Inspector Bucket in *Bleak House*.

Gustave Doré's picture of a police constable shining his bull's-eye lantern on a group of homeless people in the streets of London recalls Dickens's visits to the London slums with Inspector Field.

Field, Kate (1838–1896)   American journalist, playwright, and lecturer; friend of Walter Savage LANDOR, the BROWNINGs, and Anthony TROLLOPE. Her *Pen Photographs of Dickens's Readings* (1871) gives a firsthand account of Dickens's public readings in America in 1867–68, "twenty-five of the most delightful and most instructive evenings of my life."

Field Lane   One of London's most disreputable slums during Dickens's time, the part of SAFFRON HILL between Charles Street and HOLBORN. Described in *Twist* (26).

Fielding, Emma   Described as both a bride and an old woman in *Sketches of Young Gentlemen* and *Sketches of Young Couples*.

Fielding, Henry (1707–1754)   English novelist and playwright, justice of the peace for Middlesex, who, with his half brother John FIELDING, reorganized the police force and established the Bow Street Runners (see BOW

This engraving of the notorious slum of Field Lane alludes to Dickens with the names "Scrooge" and "Fagan" [sic] on the shop signs.

STREET POLICE FORCE). Dickens, like David Copperfield (4), read his *Tom Jones* (1749) as a boy. Although Dickens is said to have preferred Tobias SMOLLETT to Fielding, he acknowledged his debt to the latter by naming his sixth son for him.

Fielding, Sir John (1721–1780) Blind half brother of novelist Henry FIELDING, who succeeded his brother as chief magistrate at Bow Street (see BOW STREET POLICE FORCE). He presides over the committal of the elder Barnaby Rudge to NEWGATE PRISON (*Rudge*, 58). Dickens stretches historical truth with this incident; Fielding was on his deathbed by the time of the GORDON RIOTS.

Fielding, Kenneth J. (1924–) Prolific scholar, critic, and editor of Dickens. His numerous articles cover biographical, editorial, critical, and historical topics. His *Charles Dickens: A Critical Introduction* (1958; revised 1965) remains one of the best introductions to Dickens's life and works; his edition of *The Speeches of Charles Dickens* (1960) is a model of scholarly editing.

Fielding, May Dot Peerybingle's pretty schoolmate and Edward Plummer's intended who agrees to marry the sour curmudgeon Tackleton when she thinks that Edward has died in South America. She is saved when Plummer returns in disguise and marries her on the day she was to become Tackleton's wife. Her mother, **Mrs. Fielding**, is a "genteel and patronising" old woman. *Cricket.*

Fields, James Thomas (1817–1881) Dickens's American publisher, senior partner in TICKNOR & FIELDS. As a young man, he saw Dickens on his first American tour; he and his wife, **Annie** (1834–1915), became close friends with the author in 1859 when they visited him at GAD'S HILL. He urged and organized Dickens's reading tour in AMERICA in 1867 and hosted him in BOSTON. The Fields again visited Dickens in England in 1869. On that trip Dickens took them on several excursions, including one to the opium den in London's East End described in *Drood*. Fields's memories of Dickens are recorded in *Yesterdays with Authors* (1872). Annie's journals, which describe her impressions of Dickens, were published as *Memories of a Hostess*, ed. M. A. De Wolfe Howe (1923).

Fields, W. C. (1880–1946) American film actor and comedian, most famous perhaps for his unforgettable portrayal of Mr. Micawber in the 1935 film of *David Copperfield.*

Fiercy, Captain the Hon. Fitz-Whisker A swaggering officer who, with his servant Do'em, operates a con game in which they take goods on credit and sell them for cash. "Pantomime of Life."

Fikey A forger arrested by Inspector Wield. *Reprinted,* "Detective Police."

Fildes, Luke (1843–1927) Painter and illustrator. As a young artist he was recruited by Dickens to do the illustrations for *Drood*, displacing the ailing Charles COLLINS, who had done some preliminary sketches. Fildes redesigned the cover that Collins had done and produced 12 pictures for the unfinished novel. After Dickens's death, Fildes painted a watercolor, "The Empty Chair," depicting Dickens's study and writing desk with an empty chair (see illustration 34, "The Empty Chair"). The picture was engraved for the 1870 Christmas number of *The Graphic* and has become one of the most memorable images associated with the author. Another example of Fildes's work appears in illustration 64 ("The Nightly Scene in London").

Filer Friend of Alderman Cute, "a low-spirited gentleman of middle age, of a meagre habit, and a disconsolate face" who has a political economist's faith in statistics.

He "proves" by numbers that Trotty, by eating tripe, has deprived widows and orphans of sustenance. *Chimes*.

Filletoville, Son of the Marquis of   The young man in "The BAGMAN'S STORY" who abducts the lady rescued by the Bagman's uncle. *Pickwick* (49).

Films   From the beginning of motion pictures, Dickens's stories have provided material for filmmakers. One of D. W. GRIFFITHS's favorite authors, Dickens suggested techniques of visual storytelling easily translated from novel to film. Sergei EISENSTEIN found in Dickens's extensive use of MONTAGE the fundamental technique of the cinema.

A. L. Zambrano (1977) discusses Dickens's influence on the cinema and many of the film adaptations of his novels. She also provides a checklist of film adaptations. Robert BOLTON (1987) also catalogs film adaptations. Michael Pointer (*Charles Dickens on the Screen*, 1996),

provides a complete filmography for all of the silent and sound film adaptations as well as for all television versions of Dickens's novels, and discusses and evaluates the most important works of each type.

Finchbury, Lady Jane   Amateur painter mentioned by cousin Feenix, a "woman with tight stays" who has sketched the village church. *Dombey* (41).

Finches of the Grove   Dining club that Pip, Herbert Pocket, Drummle, and Startop belong to. "The object of which institution I have never divined, if it were not that the members should dine expensively once a fortnight, to quarrel among themselves as much as possible after dinner, and to cause six waiters to get drunk on the stairs." *Expectations* (34).

Finching, Flora   Widowed daughter of Casby and childhood sweetheart of Arthur Clennam. In middle age,

Fildes's picture of Edwin and Rosa for the first number of Edwin Drood *is characteristic of the realistic illustrations of the 1860s.*

she has become garrulous and silly: "Flora, always tall, had grown to be very broad too, and short of breath; but that was not much. Flora, whom he had left a lily, had become a peony; but that was not much. Flora, who had seemed enchanting in all she said and thought, was diffuse and silly. That was much. Flora, who had been spoiled and artless long ago, was determined to be spoiled and artless now. That was a fatal blow" (I:13). She refers frequently to her late husband, whom she calls Mr. F., and she is constantly attended by Mr. F's aunt, a woman given to remarks of total irrelevancy. In spite of her garrulousness and sentimental illusions, Flora is kindhearted, and she befriends Little Dorrit. *Dorrit*. Flora was modeled on Maria BEADNELL.

Finching, Mrs.   Friend of the Plausible Couple, the Widgers. *Young Couples*.

Finchley   In Dickens's time, a village on the northern outskirts of London. The Garland's Abel Cottage, with its "thatched roof and little spires at the gable ends and pieces of stained glass in some of the windows," is in Finchley (*Curiosity Shop*, 22). Barnaby Rudge escapes to a shed in Finchley (*Rudge*, 68). Also mentioned in *Dombey* (32). Dickens had lodgings in Finchley while he was writing *Chuzzlewit*.

"Finishing Schoolmaster, The"   Article from *HOUSEHOLD WORDS* (May 17, 1851), commenting on the applicants who volunteered to stand in for the regular hangman who was unavailable for the execution of Maria Clarke. Their letters of application, which Dickens reprints, are testimony to their illiteracy and to the education offered by a society that cannot agree to teach the Lord's Prayer but can agree on the educational efficacy of public hanging. *Miscellaneous*.

Fips, Mr.   Solicitor of Austin Friars retained by old Martin Chuzzlewit to employ Tom Pinch as a librarian. *Chuzzlewit* (39).

"Fire and Snow"   Essay for *HOUSEHOLD WORDS* (January 21, 1854) describing a Christmastime visit to WOLVERHAMPTON when the factories are shut down for the holiday and the BLACK COUNTRY is covered with snow. *Miscellaneous*.

"First Fruits"   Article by Dickens and George Augustus SALA for *HOUSEHOLD WORDS* (May 15, 1852) describing "primaries," first experiences in life. Dickens records his first picture book, first oyster, first visit to the theater, and the first time he was taken for a man. *Stone*.

"First of May, The"   This sketch from the second series of *Boz* first appeared in the *LIBRARY OF FICTION*, no. 3 (1836), as "A Little Talk about Spring and the Sweeps." It laments the changes in the celebrations on the first of May, which have declined from a general celebration of the coming of spring, to the parades and dancing of the chimney sweeps, until, today, even the sweeps' festivities have largely disappeared.

First-Person Narrative   Mode of narration in which one of the characters tells the story in the first person. Such narration is often contrasted to omniscient narration, in which an unidentified narrator outside the story—often said to be the author or a traditional storyteller—narrates the story from a position of complete knowledge of its events and characters. By contrast, the first-person narrator is limited to his own knowledge and understanding of the events in the story.

Dickens frequently wrote his short fiction and journalistic essays using a first-person point of view, as, for example, in the Mrs. Lirriper stories, "The Signal Man's Story," or "George Silverman's Explanation." However, he used first-person narration in only three of the novels. In *Copperfield* and *Expectations*, the narration is appropriate to the autobiographical subject matter. There are moments in *Copperfield* when the demands of first-person narration strain the reader's credulity, as, for example, when David watches Rosa Dartle torment Em'ly without intervening (50). The confessional mode in *Expectations* makes such scenes less likely. In *Bleak House*, the limitations of the first-person narration are used to contrast with the expansiveness in the third-person narration, making evident by contrast the constrictions in Esther's situation and psyche.

Fish   Sir Joseph Bowley's secretary, "a not very stately gentleman in black." *Chimes*.

Fisher, Mr. and Mrs. Fanny   Members of the English colony on Silver-Store Island who are attacked and taken captive by pirates. At the end of the story they are reunited with their child who they thought had been killed in the raid. "English Prisoners."

Fithers   Artist friend of Bobtail Widgers. *Young Couples*.

Fitz Binkle, Lord and Lady   Philanthropic couple who chair the dinner of the Indigent Orphans' Friends' Benevolent Institution. *Boz*, "Public Dinners."

Fitzgerald, Percy (1834–1925)   Irish author and journalist; frequent contributor to *HOUSEHOLD WORDS* and *ALL THE YEAR ROUND*; one of the group of "Mr. Dickens's young men" along with YATES, SALA, AND PAYN. He was a frequent visitor to GAD'S HILL in the 1860s and Dickens hoped his daughter Mamie might marry him (see Mary DICKENS). Founder of the Boz Club to celebrate Dickens's memory, he wrote several adulatory books and articles about Dickens, among them *History of Pickwick* (1891), *Memoirs of an Author* (1895), *Life of Charles Dickens* (1905), and *Memories of Charles Dickens* (1913).

Fitz-Legionite, Percival   One of the aristocratic junior members of Tapenham's government department. *Miscellaneous*, "Cheap Patriotism."

Fitz-Marshall, Captain Charles   Alias that Alfred JINGLE adopts in IPSWICH. *Pickwick.*

Fitz-Osborne, The Hon. Augustus Fitz-Edward Fitz-John   Flamwell suggests this to be Sparkins's real identity. *Boz*, "Sparkins."

Fitzroy Street   Dickens lived with his parents on this street in MARYLEBONE in 1832–33.

Fitz-Sordust, Colonel   The commander of the military young gentlemen. *Young Gentlemen.*

"Five New Points of Criminal Law"   Satirical article for ALL THE YEAR ROUND (September 24, 1859), describing five ways in which the proposed revisions in the criminal law embody the underlying assumption "that the real offender is the Murdered Person." *Miscellaneous.*

"Five Sisters of York, The"   INTERPOLATED TALE told by a gray-haired passenger on the London-to-York coach which explains the origins of the famous stained-glass windows in YORK Minster. During the reign of Henry IV, the five sisters are reprimanded by a monk for spending their time frivolously embroidering. He urges them to enter a convent, but they refuse. Gradually they leave the garden of their youthful happiness to marry. Their husbands—knights and courtiers—die; then their youngest sister, Alice, the most beautiful and innocent of them all, also dies. The monk repeats his advice, but they again refuse. As they die, their embroideries are made into stained glass that becomes the window in the Cathedral known as the Five Sisters. *Nickleby* (6).

Fixem   Broker who employed Bung before Bung became parish beadle. *Boz*, "Broker's Man."

Fizkin, Horatio   The Buff candidate for Parliament in EATANSWILL who is defeated by the Hon. Samuel Slumkey. *Pickwick* (13, 18).

Fizzgig, Donna Christina   In Jingle's account, this daughter of the Spanish Grandee **Don Bolaro Fizzgig** commits suicide when her father refuses to consent to her marriage to Jingle. *Pickwick* (2).

Flabella, Lady   Heroine of a romantic novel that Kate Nickleby reads to Mrs. Wititterly. *Nickleby* (28).

Fladdock, General   American militia officer introduced to Martin Chuzzlewit by the Norrises. After he condemns the pride and "the artificial barriers set up between man and man" in Europe, he is outraged to be considered a "fellow" passenger with Martin, who was traveling in steerage on the *Screw*. *Chuzzlewit* (17).

Flair, The Hon. Augustus   Friend of Lord Peter. *Boz*, "Winglebury."

Flam, The Hon. Sparkins   Squire Norton's friend, whose plan to abduct Rose is thwarted by the Squire's change of heart. *Village Coquettes.*

Flamwell   Name-dropping friend of the Maldertons, "one of those gentlemen of remarkably extensive information whom one occasionally meets in society, who pretend to know everybody, but in reality know nobody." *Boz*, "Sparkins."

Flanders, Sally   Childhood nurse of the Traveller, who took him as a child to her husband's funeral. *Uncommercial* (26).

"Flash Toby"   Nickname of Toby CRACKIT. *Twist.*

Flasher, Wilkins   The stockbroker who transfers the securities left to Tony Weller by his wife. *Pickwick* (55).

Flay, George   John Lost's manservant. *Miscellaneous*, "Narrative of Extraordinary Suffering."

Fledgeby, "Fascination"   "An awkward sandy-haired, small-eyed youth" who is self-conscious about his youthful looks and his lack of whiskers. He is a moneylender who operates as PUBSY & CO. and employs Mr. Riah as his front man. His father, **Mr. Fledgeby, Senior**, had also been a moneylender and his mother, **Mrs. Fledgeby**, one of the Snigsworth family, had married her husband when she was unable to repay a loan. When the Lammles fail in their attempt to marry Georgina Podsnap to Fledgeby, he calls in their loans. He is beaten in turn by Lammle, and afterward Jenny Wren puts pepper into the wounds (IV:9). *Mutual Friend.*

Fleet Market   On the present site of Farringdon Street, this meat, fish, and vegetable market "was a long irregular row of wooden sheds and pent-houses" that the Gordon rioters use as a stronghold (*Rudge*, 60). Sam Weller tells Pickwick the story of Prisoner "number twenty" who longs to go out of the gates of the FLEET PRISON and see the market (*Pickwick*, 41).

Fleet Prison   Debtors prison in Farringdon Street, east London. The original structure, dating from the thirteenth century, was burnt down during the GORDON RIOTS in 1780 (*Rudge*, 67). Pickwick is imprisoned in the rebuilt structure that remained in use until 1842 (*Pickwick*, 41–47, 51).

Fleet Street   A street that Dickens knew well; there are numerous references to it in the novels. He wandered the street as a child, like David Copperfield who looks

The racket-ground in the yard of Fleet Prison. The groups of prisoners who congregate here are described in Pickwick *as "worth looking at, if it were only in idle curiosity" (45).*

into the windows of food shops on Fleet Street during his lunch hour at MURDSTONE AND GRINBY (*Copperfield*, 11). Tellson's Bank is here (*Two Cities*). The street is also mentioned in *Boz, Pickwick, Chuzzlewit, Bleak House, Expectations*, and "Holly Tree."

Fleetwood This family, **Mr. and Mrs. Fleetwood** and their **son**, are guests at the steam excursion. *Boz*, "Steam Excursion."

Fleming, Agnes Oliver Twist's mother and sister of **Rose Maylie**. Seduced by Edwin Leeford, "she was weak and erring" (53), but her gravestone is a shrine for the son who never knew her. *Twist.*

Fletcher, Angus (d. 1862) Scottish sculptor whom Dickens met in London in the 1830s. He produced busts of the famous writers and artists of the time, including one of Dickens in 1841. He acted as the Dickenses' guide on their tour of Scotland in 1841, stayed with them at BROADSTAIRS and ALBARO, and amused them with his eccentricities. Dickens nicknamed him "Kindheart." On his death, Dickens remarked: "Poor Kindheart! I think

of all that made him so pleasant to us, and am full of grief."

"Flight, A" Article from *HOUSEHOLD WORDS* (August 30, 1851), describing a "magic carpet" trip to Paris in a compartment on the South-Eastern Railway, in the company of both French and English travelers. *Reprinted.*

Flimkins, Mr. and Mrs. An acting couple at the Surrey Theatre. *Young Gentlemen.*

Flintwinch, Jeremiah Confidential clerk and business partner of Mrs. Clennam. "A short, bald old man, in a high-shouldered black coat and waistcoat, drab breeches, and long drab gaiters. . . . There was nothing about him in the way of decoration but a watch. . . . His head was awry, and he had a one-sided, crab-like way with him, as if his foundations had yielded at about the same time as those of the house, and he ought to have been propped up in a similar manner" (I:3). He has an intimate knowledge of Mrs. Clennam's affairs. When Arthur returns from China, he gives documents concerning

Arthur and Little Dorrit to his twin brother **Ephraim** to take abroad for safekeeping (I:3), but Rigaud gets possession of the papers and blackmails Mrs. Clennam (I:30). When Rigaud's scheme is foiled by the collapse of the house, Flintwinch escapes to Holland. Jeremiah's wife, **Affery**, is bewildered by his activities. *Dorrit*.

Flipfield Friend of the Uncommercial Traveller who describes Flipfield's birthday celebration, a party attended by his mother, **Mrs. Flipfield**, his sister, **Miss Flipfield**, and his long-lost brother **Tom**, who "came to light in foreign parts." *Uncommercial* (20).

Flite, Miss "A little mad old woman in a squeezed bonnet" (3) who haunts the Court of CHANCERY, for she believes that a judgment in her case is immanent. She befriends Esther (whom she calls Fitz-Jarndyce) and invites her to her lodgings at the top of Krook's house (5). There she keeps a cage of birds named Hope, Joy, Youth, Peace, Rest, Life, Dust, Ashes, Waste, Want, Ruin, Despair, Madness, Death, Cunning, Folly, Words, Wigs, Rags, Sheepskin, Plunder, Precedent, Jargon, Gammon, and Spinach. When the Jarndyce case is settled, she sets the birds free (65). *Bleak House*.

Flopson One of Mrs. Pocket's maids who cares for the distracted mother's children. *Expectations* (22, 23).

Florence Dickens describes this "magnificently stern and sombre" city, one of the last places he visits on his tour of ITALY, in *Pictures*.

Florence, William. J. (1831–1891) American comic actor famous for his portrayals of Captain Cuttle and Jules Obenreizer in the 1860s.

Flounceby An especially obstinate purveyor of gossip on "The Best Authority." *Miscellaneous*.

Flower Pot Inn in BISHOPSGATE Street where Minns catches the coach to STAMFORD HILL. *Boz*, "Minns."

Flowers Mrs. Skewton's maid, who presides over the mysteries of Cleopatra's cosmetics and dress. *Dombey*.

Fluggers Member of Crummles's theatrical company who does the "heavy business." *Nickleby* (30).

Flummery Member of the Mudfog Association. *Mudfog*.

"Fly-leaf in a Life, A" The Traveller describes his experiences during a period of withdrawal and rest brought on by exhaustion. He realized the similarities in his "case" and that of Mr. Merdle in *Dorrit*, both victims of "pressure." He also was advised on his spiritual condition by intrusive clergymen and badgered by begging letter writers. *Uncommercial* (36). This article, first published in ALL THE YEAR ROUND (May 22, 1869), de-

scribes Dickens's respite from PUBLIC READINGS in the final months of his life.

Fogg Silent partner in the firm of DODSON AND FOGG, the lawyers who represent Mrs. Bardell. "An elderly, pimply-faced, vegetable-diet sort of man, . . . who seemed to be an essential part of the desk at which he was writing, and to have as much thought or sentiment" (20). *Pickwick*.

Folair, Augustus (Tommy) Pantomimist with the Crummles theatrical company who tries to instigate a feud between Lenville and Nicholas. *Nickleby* (23–25, 29, 30).

Foley One of Cousin Feenix's acquaintances. *Dombey* (41).

Folkestone Dickens had a summer home at this seaside town in KENT in 1855 while he was working on *Dorrit*. Described as PAVILIONSTONE in *Reprinted*, "Out of Town."

Folly Ditch The ditch separating JACOB'S ISLAND from the south bank of the THAMES at Bermondsey. The ditch could be filled at high tide by opening sluice gates. Toby Crackit's house from which Sikes tries to escape at the end of *Twist* is situated along the ditch.

Fonblanque, Albany (1793–1872) Journalist and friend of Dickens. While editor of the EXAMINER, he introduced John FORSTER to *Sketches by Boz* and assigned him to review a performance of *The Village Coquettes*. He was a leader (i.e., editorial) writer on the DAILY NEWS when Dickens was editor.

Ford, George H. (1914–1995) Most important contemporary scholar writing on Dickens's reputation. In numerous articles and in his classic study *Dickens and His Readers: Aspects of Novel Criticism since 1836* (1955), he charts reactions to Dickens's works from his own day to the present. In *The Dickens Critics* (1961), Ford and Lauriat Lane, Jr., collect critical articles representing this changing critical response to Dickens. Ford's edition of *Hard Times*, done with Sylvère MONOD in 1966, is the best available edition of that novel.

Foreign Gentleman A guest at Georgiana Podsnap's birthday party. Podsnap condescendingly dismisses him as "not English" (I:11). *Mutual Friend*.

"Foreigners' Portraits of Englishmen" To this article for HOUSEHOLD WORDS (September 21, 1850), written with William Henry WILLS and E. C. MURRAY, Dickens contributed descriptions of some absurd depictions of Englishmen in continental theaters. *Stone*.

Formiville SLAP's stage name. *Miscellaneous*, "Nightingale."

Forster, E. M. (1879–1970)   British novelist and critic, best known for *A Passage to India* (1924). As a critic, Forster represents a modernist point of view, largely unsympathetic to Dickens. His well-known distinction between "flat" and "round" characters in *Aspects of the Novel* (1927) assesses Dickens as one-sided:

> Dickens' people are nearly all flat (Pip and David Copperfield attempt roundness, but so diffidently that they seem more like bubbles than solids). Nearly every one can be summed up in a sentence, and yet there is this wonderful feeling of human depth. Probably the immense vitality of Dickens causes his characters to vibrate a little, so that they borrow his life and appear to lead one of their own. It is a conjuring trick; at any moment we may look at Mr. Pickwick edgeways and find him no thicker than a gramophone record.

Forster, John (1812–1876)   Journalist, biographer, historian; Dickens's closest friend, advisor, literary executor, and first biographer. The son of a Newcastle butcher, Forster came to London, took a degree at University College, and proceeded to make himself a man of letters. When Dickens met him in 1836, Forster was drama critic for the EXAMINER, a magazine he would edit from 1847 to 1855. There he reviewed Dickens's early plays negatively and Boz enthusiastically. Nicknamed "Fuz" by CARLYLE and "Beadle of the Universe" by Thornton Hunt, Forster was a heavy, portentous, and dictatorial man, but he was also a man of great common sense and a true friend to many fellow writers of the time, especially Carlyle, Leigh HUNT, Charles Lamb, Edward Bulwer LYTTON, and Dickens. Dickens shared his works in progress with him and Forster read proof on nearly all the novels. He advised Dickens on financial, literary, and personal matters. Dickens corresponded regularly with him and told him, while he was working on *Copperfield*, the secret of his childhood employment in the BLACKING WAREHOUSE. In the last decade of Dickens's life, when the novelist struck up a close friendship with Wilkie COLLINS, Forster was jealous of Dickens's young friends and his relationship with the novelist was not as close as it had formerly been. But Forster remained Dickens's Boswell, producing his *Life of Charles Dickens* two years after the author's death. Although he suppressed some facts about Dickens's life, notably about the novelist's relationship with Ellen TERNAN, this remains one of the great biographies of the period. Besides numerous journalistic essays, Forster also wrote historical works about the 17th century; among his many biographies, those on Goldsmith, Defoe, Swift, and LANDOR are noteworthy. Dickens caricatured his friend in *Dorrit*'s Podsnap. A useful recent book on Forster is James A. Davies, *John Forster* (1983).

Forster Collection (Victoria and Albert Museum)   The most extensive collection of manuscripts and proof-sheets of Dickens's works is that donated by

John Forster.

John FORSTER to the Victoria and Albert Museum in London. It includes complete manuscripts for 11 of the novels and for several minor works, as well as proof sheets for many works. The Forster Collection also includes many letters, printed documents, pamphlets, and pictures. A catalog of some of the materials was prepared by the museum for a centenary exhibition in 1970.

Fort House   One of the houses where Dickens stayed on holidays in BROADSTAIRS, KENT. It is now a Dickens museum.

Fort Pitt   A deserted fortification near CHATHAM where Dickens played as a child. The abortive duel between Winkle and Dr. Slammer takes place here. *Pickwick* (2).

Foulon   A historical figure, Joseph-François Foulon (1715–1789), a financier who was hated by the Jacquerie for asserting "The people may eat grass." His massacre is described in *Two Cities* (II:22). Dickens bases his description of Foulon's death on Thomas CARLYLE's account in *The French Revolution*.

Foundling Hospital   Established in 1739 by Captain Thomas Coram, a retired merchant seaman, this orphanage took in illegitimate and abandoned children. The building, sometimes called Coram's Hospital, was in Guildford Street, BLOOMSBURY, in what are now called Coram's Fields. The Meagles adopt Tattycoram from this institution, giving her an allusive name (*Dorrit*, I:2). "No Thoroughfare" involves a similar adoption.

Fountain Court   One of the courtyards in The TEMPLE where Ruth Pinch and John Westlock rendezvous. *Chuzzlewit* (45, 53).

"Four Sisters, The"   First published as "Sketches of London No. 14. Our Parish" in the *EVENING CHRONICLE* (June 18, 1835), this sketch tells of the four Willis sisters who are so inseparable that when one of them marries, no one in the parish can ascertain which of the four sisters is the bride. The arrival of a child settles the issue. *Boz*.

Fox-under-the-Hill, The   A pub along the THAMES that Dickens and David Copperfield visited in their youth.

Fox, W. J. (1786–1864)   Journalist, Unitarian clergyman, Radical utilitarian (see UTILITARIANISM). He was present in the circle of friends who gathered in 1844 to hear Dickens's prepublication reading of *The Chimes*. He was also a leader (i.e., editorial) writer on the *DAILY NEWS* under Dickens. His commitments to repeal of the CORN LAWS and educational reform made him an ally of Dickens politically.

Foxey   Member of the Mudfog Association. *Mudfog*.

Foxey, Old   Father of Sampson and Sally Brass, whose maxim was "always suspect everybody." *Curiosity Shop* (66).

Frame Story   A story framing another story or group of stories, as the story of the Canterbury pilgrimage frames the tales in Chaucer's *Canterbury Tales*. Dickens used this convention for many of the CHRISTMAS STORIES in *HOUSEHOLD WORDS* and *ALL THE YEAR ROUND*. Usually he would write the frame narrative and then recruit other writers to contribute stories to the project.

France   From the time of his first visit to France in 1844, Dickens frequently crossed the English Channel to visit or spend extended periods of time there. After an extended stay in Paris in 1846–47, he claimed to be "an accomplished Frenchman," speaking the language like a native. In PARIS he visited several French writers, among them HUGO, Sue, DUMAS, Gautier, Lamartine, Chateaubriand, and Scribe. In 1853, 1854, and 1856, Dickens

spent the summers with his family at BOULOGNE, a seaside resort on the Channel southwest of CALAIS which he describes in "Our French Watering Place." In the 1850s and 1860s, he lived in Paris for several extended visits. He describes the journey from London to Paris in "A Flight." In the mid-1860s he kept a house at Condette, a village south of Boulogne, where he frequently stayed, often with Ellen TERNAN.

Dickens describes some of his visits to France in *Pictures from Italy* and in *The Uncommercial Traveller* (7, 18, 27). In the novels, France is most prominent in *Two Cities*. Carker meets Edith in DIJON (*Dombey* 54); *Dorrit* begins in MARSEILLES where Clennam is in quarantine on his return from China; Mrs. Lirriper goes to SENS to meet Jemmy's dying father "Lirriper's Legacy").

Francis, Father   Name given to Maître VOIGT in the dramatized version of "No Thoroughfare."

François (1)   Waiter who serves Carker and Edith in DIJON. *Dombey* (54).

François (2)   Butcher who is buying calves at the Calf Market in Poissy. *Reprinted*, "French Folly."

Frank, Lawrence (1933–)   Professor, University of Oklahoma, whose *Charles Dickens and the Romantic Self* (1984) discusses the self in Dickens's novels as a construct created by the individual and provides psychoanalytic readings of several of the novels.

Frank, Little   "A diffident boy," the young cousin who Michael, the poor relation, imagines as his loving companion. "Poor Relation."

"Frauds on the Fairies"   Dickens's critical review in *HOUSEHOLD WORDS* (October 1, 1853) of CRUIKSHANK's retellings of classic FAIRY TALES to promote teetotalism. Dickens argues that we nurture our imagination on such stories and to make them serve such political causes removes the FANCY from them; "a nation without fancy, without some romance, never did, never can, and never will, hold a great place under the sun." Then he presents a retelling of "Cinderella" according the politically correct principles of the day in support of his final admonition: "The world is too much with us, early and late. Leave this precious escape from it, alone." *Miscellaneous*.

Fred   Scrooge's nephew and son of Fan, who thinks of Christmas "as a good time: a kind, forgiving, charitable, pleasant time: the only time I know of, in the long calendar of the year, when men and women seem by one consent to open their shut-up hearts freely" (1). He invites his uncle to Christmas dinner and is refused. The spirits show Scrooge Fred's party and his **wife**, "exceedingly pretty. With a dimpled, surprised-looking, capital face; a ripe little mouth, that seemed made to be kissed; . . . and the sunniest pair of eyes you ever saw" (3). After his conversion, Scrooge goes to Christmas dinner at Fred's house (5). *Carol.*

"Free (and Easy) School, A"   Article for *HOUSE-HOLD WORDS* by Dickens and Henry MORLEY (November 15, 1851), investigating the operation of free grammar schools by visiting Queen Elizabeth's Royal Grammar-school at Thistledown. There the narrator finds the master of the school, Dr. Laon Blose, separating the free pupils from his private pupils, a common violation of the intent of such schools brought about by allowing the masters to supplement their inadequate salaries by taking private students. *Stone.*

Freeman's Court   On the north side of CORNHILL in the CITY of London, site of DODSON AND FOGG's offices. *Pickwick.*

Freemason's Hall   In Queen Street, HOLBORN. A banquet honoring Dickens was held here on the eve of his departure for AMERICA in 1867.

French Revolution   Dickens's second historical novel, *A Tale of Two Cities* (1859), is set during the French Revolution of 1789. Dickens indicates in his preface to the novel his indebtedness to CARLYLE's history of *The French Revolution*, from which he derived many of the incidents for the novel as well as its "philosophy," which found the cause of the conflict in the excesses of the French aristocracy in their treatment of the peasants. Dickens also develops this theme in "Judicial Special Pleading," in which he challenges the notion that the French peasants revolted to secure political rights. "It was," he submits, "a struggle on the part of the people for social recognition and existence. It was a struggle for vengeance against intolerable oppressors. It was a struggle for the overthrow of a system of oppression, which in its contempt of all humanity, decency, and natural rights, and in its systematic degradation of the people, had trained them to be the demons that they showed themselves, when they rose up and cast it down for ever."

"Friend of the Lions, The"   While painting Dickens as a rat-catcher in one of his paintings, LANDSEER complains about how the lions at the London Zoo are housed and fed. An article for *HOUSEHOLD WORDS* (February 2, 1856). *Miscellaneous.*

Frith, William P. (1819–1909)   Painter often compared to Dickens for his realistic depiction of Victorian life. Several of his works have been used as cover illustrations for recent editions of Dickens. A great admirer of Dickens's work, Frith painted several pictures of Dolly VARDEN, prompting Dickens to ask him to paint miniatures of Dolly and Kate Nickleby for him. Afterward, the two became friends. Frith asked to be one of the illustrators for the LIBRARY EDITION, for which he provided two illustrations for *Dorrit*. John FORSTER commissioned Frith's famous portrait of Dickens in 1859.

"From the Raven in the Happy Family"   Three articles for the first volume of *HOUSEHOLD WORDS* (May 11, June 8, August 24, 1850) in the voice of a raven who complains of Buffon's characterization of ravens as gluttons and thieves and gets back by describing human beings from a raven's point of view (1). Then he satirizes ostentatious funerals and identifies undertakers as the ravens among humankind (2). He completes his natural history of human beings with a horse's view of man's stupidity, irrationality, and conceit (3). *Miscellaneous.*

Frome   The quiet town in Somerset where Dick Doubledick goes to tell Mrs. Taunton that her son has died at Badajoz. "Seven Poor Travellers."

Frost, Miss   Mistress at our school. *Reprinted*, "Our School."

Frozen Deep, The   Play by Wilkie COLLINS from an idea of Dickens. On a polar expedition, Richard Wardour discovers that the man he has vowed to kill for stealing his love is also a member of the expedition. He contrives to go off into the arctic wastes with his rival, intending to carry out his revenge, but instead he saves his life and, in the end, dies in the grateful arms of the woman he loves. Dickens's amateur company performed the play with great success at TAVISTOCK HOUSE in January 1857 and in July for the Queen and Prince Albert. Dickens's performance as Wardour was generally acclaimed. In August he took the play to MANCHESTER with three professional actresses, Mrs. TERNAN and her daughters Ellen and Maria, in the main female roles.

Frye, Northrop (1912–1991)   Canadian literary theorist and critic, especially of English romanticism, whose comprehensive scheme for classifying literary works along archetypal lines has greatly influenced American literary criticism. His most sustained discussion of Dickens appears in "Dickens and the Comedy of Humours" (in *The Stubborn Structure*, 1970), which characterizes the typical Dickens novel in terms of the traditions of classical New Comedy.

Fulham   Riverside village west of London where Florence visits Sir Barnet and Lady Skettles (*Dombey*, 24). Arthur Clennam passes through on his way to TWICKENHAM (*Dorrit*, I:16).

"Full Report of the First Meeting of the Mudfog Association"   Second of three *Mudfog Papers* published in *BENTLEY'S MISCELLANY* (October 1837). Boz's report of the proceedings in the Zoology and Botany, Anatomy and Medicine, Statistics, and Mechanical Science sections of the conference at Mudfog satirizes the proceedings of the British Association for the Advancement of Science. *Mudfog*.

"Full Report of the Second Meeting of the Mudfog Association"   This second satirical report of the proceedings of the Mudfog Association appeared in *BENTLEY'S MISCELLANY* (September 1838) and added a section on Umbugology and Ditchwateristics. *Mudfog*.

Furniss, Harry (1854–1925)   Caricaturist, author, lecturer, illustrator for many London magazines, notably *PUNCH*. Among his many projects were illustrated complete editions of the works of Dickens and THACKERAY. His edition of Dickens (*The Charles Dickens Library*, 1910) contains over 500 of his illustrations and includes a volume on the original illustrations to Dickens's works. Other examples of his work appear in illustrations 23 (DAWKINS), 31 (DOUBLE), and 47 (*HARD TIMES*).

Furnival's Inn   One of the INNS OF COURT located in HOLBORN. Its use as a legal community was discontinued in 1818 and the buildings were rented out as chambers. Dickens lived here from 1834 to 1837, writing most of *Pickwick* during his time here. John Westlock has rooms in the Inn (*Chuzzlewit*, 36); Rosa Bud stays in the hotel in the Inn (*Drood*, 11, 20). It is also mentioned in *Boz* ("Steam Excursion," "Christening").

Harry Furniss, a self-portrait.

G

Gabblewig Lawyer who, by a series of impersonations, promotes his claim to Rosina Nightingale's affections and saves her uncle from Slap's extortion schemes. *Nightingale*.

Gabelle, Théophile Postmaster in the village near the St. Evrémonde chateau. After the murder of the Marquis, Charles Darnay puts Gabelle in charge of some of the business affairs of the estate. When Gabelle is arrested by the revolutionary court, Darnay returns to France to testify for him and is arrested himself. *Two Cities*.

Gabriel Vardon, the Locksmith of London The first novel that Dickens contracted to write in an agreement with publisher John MACRONE in 1836. He did not fulfill that contract, but the novel he had in mind was eventually published as *Barnaby Rudge* in 1841.

Gad's Hill Place Dickens's home for the last decade of his life. Located on a hilltop on the road between GRAVESEND and ROCHESTER, the house was one that Dickens had admired as a boy, his father telling him that if he worked very hard he might live there one day. Dickens purchased the house in 1856 for £1,790, moved there in 1860, and died there in 1870. The house is now a girls schoool.

Gad's Hill Gazette The family newspaper produced by Dickens's two sons, Henry and Edward, started in 1863 and published irregularly over the next few years. It included family news of visitors, excursions, and diversions. Dickens made some joking contributions to it. (See also Henry DICKENS and Edward DICKENS.)

Gallanbile Sabbatarian member of Parliament who advertises for a cook: "Fifteen guineas, tea and sugar, and servants allowed to see male cousins, if godly. . . . No vituals whatever, cooked on the Lord's Day, with the exception of Dinner for Mr. and Mrs. Gallanbile, which, being a work of piety and necessity, is exempted." *Nickleby* (16).

"Game Chicken, The" Boxer employed by Mr. Toots to teach him to fight by "knocking him about the head three times a week for the small consideration of ten and six a visit." *Dombey* (22).

Gamfield Chimney sweep "whose dark and villainous face was a regular stamped receipt for cruelty" (3). The magistrate, noting Oliver's fear of the man, refuses to approve the apprenticeship papers drawn up by the workhouse guardians. *Twist*.

Gamp, Mrs. Sarah (Sairey) Professional nurse who attends Anthony Chuzzlewit, Lewsome, and old Chuffey, "a fat old woman. . . . with a husky voice and a moist eye, which she had a remarkable power of turning up, and only showing the white of it. . . . She wore a very rusty black gown, rather the worse for snuff, and a shawl and bonnet to correspond. . . . The face of Mrs. Gamp— the nose in particular—was somewhat red and swollen; and it was difficult to enjoy her society without becoming conscious of a smell of spirits" (19). She has a habit of appealing to the authority of an imaginary friend, Mrs. Harris, and her cockney speech is larded with mispronounciations and malapropisms. She prepares the body of Anthony Chuzzlewit for burial (19), tends Chuffey while Jonas is in the country (25, 26), and, splitting her duties with Betsy Prig, she cares for Lewsome at the Bull Inn

Gad's Hill Place.

Mrs. Gamp shares a toast with Betsey Prig.

(29). She aids Westlock in securing Chuffey's testimony at the final exposure of Jonas (51). *Chuzzlewit*.

Gander, Mr. Gentleman "of a witty turn" who boards at Todgers. *Chuzzlewit* (9).

Ganz, Dr. Physician at Neuchâtel who helps to prove George Vendale's identity. "No Thoroughfare."

Garden Court The court in the TEMPLE where Pip and Herbert Pocket have rooms (*Expectations*, 39). Ruth Pinch also waits here to meet Tom and John Westlock (*Chuzzlewit*, 45).

Gargery, Joe Blacksmith and husband of Pip's older sister, **Georgiana Maria (Mrs. Joe)**, "this gentle Christian man" (57) is as "mild, good-natured, sweet-tempered, [and] easy-going" (2) as his wife is shrewish. He befriends Pip as a boy and speaks of the "larks" they will share together. Pip confesses to Joe his lies about Miss Havisham (9) and as Joe's apprentice he regretfully learns the trade of blacksmith (13). Although Pip is snobbish and condescending to him, Joe remains loyal to Pip (27) and nurses him when he falls ill after Magwitch's death (57). Mrs. Joe, "tall and bony" with "such a prevailing redness of skin, that I sometimes used to wonder whether it was possible she washed herself with a nutmeg-grater instead of soap" (2), resentfully brings up Pip "by hand" and indulges in "Ram-pages" at the boy and her husband. Her mean temper is stilled after she is struck over the head by an unknown assailant (16), a wound which partly paralyzes her, leaves her speechless, and leads to her early death (34). Biddy takes over Mrs.

Joe's duties as housekeeper and eventually marries Joe (58). They have one son, **Pip**. *Expectations*.

Garis, Robert E. (1925–) Professor at Wellesley whose controversial book *The Dickens Theatre* (1965) describes Dickens in his novels as a performer, a master of ceremonies who presents externally described characters who are also performers. Garis suggests that this popular mode separates Dickens from such novelists as Jane Austen and George ELIOT who develop more interior worlds in their novels.

Garland, Mr. and Mrs. A kindly old couple who befriend Kit Nubbles and hire him as their groom. With the help of attorney Witherden they defend Kit from the false charges made by Quilp and Sampson Brass. Their son **Abel**, who resembles his father "in face and figure, though wanting something of his full round cheerfulness, and substituting in its place a timid reserve" (14), works with Witherden and eventually becomes his partner. Mr. Garland's brother, **The Bachelor**, resides in the country village where Nell and her grandfather end their journey. He befriends them and informs Mr. Garland of their whereabouts, but Nell dies before Garland and the Single Gentleman get there (71). *Curiosity Shop*.

Garraway's Coffee house on Change Alley in the CITY, a gathering place for businessmen, where Pickwick writes his "chops and tomata sauce" note to Mrs. Bardell (34), Nadgett keeps watch on Jonas Chuzzlewit (27), and Jeremiah Flintwinch conducts business (*Dorrit*, I:29). The Traveller finds it closed on Sunday (*Uncommercial*, 21).

Garrick Club A London men's club founded in 1831 and including many theatrical people among its members. The Theatrical Young Gentleman thinks that being a member of the club would be "one of the highest gratifications the world can bestow" (Young Gentlemen). Dickens was elected to membership in 1837, but his involvement with the club over the years was sometimes a stormy one. He resigned the first time in 1838 when William MACREADY left the club over a personal slight. In 1858, when his friend Edmund YATES was expelled from the Club for not apologizing to THACKERAY after publishing an offensive article about him, Dickens defended Yates and enraged Thackeray. The two novelists were not reconciled until shortly before Thackeray's death. Dickens again resigned from the club in 1865 after William Henry WILLS was turned down for membership.

Gashford Lord George Gordon's ruthless and hypocritical secretary, "angularly made, high-shouldered, bony, and ungraceful. . . . His manner was smooth and humble, but very sly and slinking. He wore the aspect of a man who was always lying in wait for something" (35). A former Catholic, Gashford urges the rioters to extreme acts, such as the burning of the Warren (44). He tries to use the riots as a means of seducing Emma Haredale, but his scheme is foiled by Edward Chester and Joe Willet (71). He abandons Gordon, becomes a government spy, and eventually poisons himself (82). *Rudge*. Gashford's suicide seems to be based on that of Robert Watson, who claimed to have been Gordon's secretary shortly before he hanged himself in 1838.

Gaskell, Elizabeth (1810–1865) MANCHESTER novelist whose first novel, *Mary Barton* (1848), prompted Dickens to place her among the first writers he solicited to contribute to HOUSEHOLD WORDS; "I do honestly know," he wrote, "that there is no living English writer whose aid I would desire to enlist in preference to the authoress of *Mary Barton* (a book that most profoundly affected and impressed me)." She became a regular contributor to the magazine. "Lizzie Leigh" began in the first issue; *Cranford* appeared in eight installments between 1851 and 1853; she allowed *North and South* to be serialized in the magazine (1854–55), but objected to the ways in which it was compressed, cut, and adapted for serial publication, and requested that the "novel not be revised, even by Mr. Dickens." She also wrote numerous other stories and articles for *Household Words*, and, even though she disapproved of Dickens's public airing of his marital difficulties, she also contributed some articles to ALL THE YEAR ROUND, but not the novel that Dickens requested. She attended the dinner to launch *Copperfield*. Dickens visited her and her husband, a Unitarian minister, when he was in Manchester.

"Gaslight Fairies" Article for HOUSEHOLD WORDS (February 10, 1855) on the actors who play the walk-on roles in the theaters, like the fairies in the pantomime. Dickens wonders about their lives between pantomime seasons and, by imagining the Fairy family, supported by the meager earnings of the 23-year-old daughter who plays one of the fairies, he urges his readers not to condemn the shabby people who take these parts. *Miscellaneous*.

Gaspard After his child is killed by the Marquis St. Evrémonde's coach, Gaspard pursues the Marquis and assassinates him (II:9). He is hanged for the crime (II:15). *Two Cities*.

Gattleton, Mr. A stockbroker living comfortably at Rose Villa, CLAPHAM Rise, whose family is "infected with the mania for private theatricals." His "good-tempered, vulgar" **wife** and his four children, including **Caroline**, **Lucina**, and **Sempronius**, put on *Othello* in their dining room, a production spoiled by their neighbor, Mrs. Joseph Porter. *Boz*, "Porter."

Gay, Walter Sol Gills's nephew, "a cheerful looking, merry boy, . . . fair-faced, bright-eyed, and curly-haired" (4). He is employed by the House of Dombey as a junior clerk and is instrumental in returning Florence to her home after she is abducted by Mrs. Brown (6), an act which earns the friendship of young Paul and the displeasure of his father. At the instigation of James Carker, who fears Walter as a rival for Florence's affections, Dombey sends Walter to Barbados (13), but his ship, the *Son and Heir*, is lost at sea. Unwilling to give up hope, Sol Gills goes off in search of Walter. The boy has survived the wreck. He returns to London (49), marries Florence (57), and goes to sea again with his bride. When they return, the ruined Dombey lives with them and loves their children. *Dombey*.

Gazingi, Miss Member of the Crummles theatrical company. *Nickleby* (23).

General, Mrs. The "dignified and imposing" widow of a commissariat officer, employed as a chaperone and "polisher" of Amy and Fanny Dorrit. "If her eyes had no expression it was probably because they had nothing to express" (II:2). She counsels her charges to practice their elocution by repeating "Papa, potatoes, poultry, prunes and prism" (II:15). Mr. Dorrit's death thwarts her design to secure him as her second husband. *Dorrit*.

Geneva During the month or so that Dickens spent in this Swiss city in 1846, he completed *The Battle of Life* and admired the Swiss revolutionaries who overthrew Catholic rule: "They are a genuine people, these Swiss. . . . They are a thorn in the sides of European despots, and a good wholesome people to live near Jesuit-ridden Kings on the brighter side of the mountains."

Genoa Between July 1844 and June 1845, Dickens and his family spent nearly a year, off and on, in Genoa, a seaport town on the northwest coast of ITALY. He wrote *The Chimes* here, returning to England in December to read the finished story to his friends. He describes the city, its environs and attractions in "Genoa and its Neighbourhood" (*Pictures*). He visited Genoa again in 1853 with Wilkie COLLINS and Augustus EGG.

Genre Painting Popular school of painting during the Victorian period. Genre painters rendered realistic scenes of everyday life in pictures that often implied a story and a moral message. Genre painting had its roots in Dutch domestic realism of the 17th century and was an important influence on such realistic novelists as George ELIOT, who frequently compared her work to Dutch realistic painting.

Dickens was an admirer of the work of Sir David WILKIE, the Scottish artist whose scenes of the life of the poor influenced such later Victorian artists as FRITH and FILDES. In a tribute to Wilkie after the artist's death in 1841, Dickens described him as "devoted to all that was true and beautiful, and elevating, in art and nature, . . . who made the cottage hearth his grave theme, and who surrounded the lives, and cares, and daily toils, and occupations of the poor, with dignity and beauty." Dickens's scenes in Dan'l Peggotty's boat-house (*Copperfield*) and in Joe Gargery's forge (*Expectations*) are very much in the same tradition that he praised in Wilkie's work.

Gentleman in Small-clothes, The   The madman who lives with his keeper next door to Mrs. Nickleby at BOW. He courts her by throwing vegetables over the garden wall (37), and makes a dramatic entrance into her cottage by coming down the chimney. But when he sees Miss La Creevy, he deserts Mrs. Nickleby for the artist (49). *Nickleby.*

Gentleman in the White Waistcoat, The   Member of the workhouse board who is convinced that Oliver, "that audacious young savage," will "come to be hung." *Twist* (7).

George (1)   Eldest son in the family party at ASTLEY'S, a boy of 14 "who was evidently trying to look as if he did not belong to the family." *Boz,* "Astley's."

George (2)   "A young man . . . bearing the reputation of a rake" present at the Kenwigs' dinner party. *Nickleby* (14).

George (3)   Guard on the coach that takes David to SALEM HOUSE. *Copperfield* (5).

George (4)   Guard on the coach that Charley takes to the Holly Tree Inn. "Holly Tree."

George (5)   An insolvent coachman and friend of Tony Weller. *Pickwick* (43).

George (6)   Driver of Mrs. Jarley's touring van who eventually marries her. *Curiosity Shop* (26, 28, 47).

George (7)   Assistant to Christopher the head waiter. "Somebody's Luggage."

George (8)   Clerk to Buffles, the tax collector. "Lirriper's Legacy."

George, Master   Wegg's name for one of the residents of the house near CAVENDISH SQUARE where he sets up his stall. *Mutual Friend* (I:5).

George, Mrs.   Guest at Mrs. Quilp's tea party who says that she would kill herself before standing in awe of a man. *Curiosity Shop* (4).

George, Trooper   Nickname of George ROUNCEWELL. *Bleak House.*

George, Uncle and Aunt   Hosts of the family Christmas party. *Boz,* "Christmas Dinner."

George III (1738–1820)   The "King with a large jaw" described in the opening paragraphs of *Two Cities* who is on the English throne at the time of the French Revolution.

George IV (1762–1830)   Prince regent from 1811 to 1820 and King of England from 1820 to 1830. The first of the dandies, he is worshipped by Mr. Turveydrop as the model of Deportment (*Bleak House,* 14).

George and New Inn   The inn at GRETNA BRIDGE, Yorkshire, where the coach leaves Squeers and his party when they arrive from London. *Nickleby* (6).

George and Vulture Inn   Inn on LOMBARD STREET in the CITY where Pickwick takes rooms when he comes up to London to deal with Mrs. Bardell's suit (26). He is also arrested and taken to the FLEET PRISON from here (40) and returns here when he is released from prison (50). The Winkles also stay here after their marriage (54). *Pickwick.*

"George Silverman's Explanation"   Short story written for the *ATLANTIC MONTHLY* (January–March 1868; also in *ALL THE YEAR ROUND,* February 1, 15, 29, 1868). George Silverman, an elderly clergyman, tells the story of his life, from his harsh childhood in a PRESTON cellar; to his early orphanhood and youth under the guardianship of Brother Hawkyard, an enthusiastic and hypocritical chapel preacher; to his sucess at Cambridge as a scholarship student and tutor; to his modest living in a parish in Devon controlled by Lady Fareway. There he fell in love with Adelina Fareway, but he eschewed so unequal a marriage and encouraged her relationship with Granville Wharton. When he married them secretly, Lady Fareway accused him of profiting from the union and he resigned the living. Throughout his life Silverman has been accused of worldliness and self-seeking, but his "explanation," told when he is 60, reveals that the judgments of others fail to understand a diffident, self-denying, and unworldly man. *Reprinted.*

Georgiana   One of Miss Havisham's relatives "who called her rigidity religion, and her liver love" (25), who hopes to inherit her aunt's fortune. She receives £20 in the will. *Expectations.*

Gerrard Street   The street in SOHO where Jaggers lives. *Expectations* (26).

"Ghost of Art, The"   The narrator, a bachelor lawyer and art connoisseur, meets a man on a steamship during a thunderstorm whom he is sure he has met before. The man turns out to be an artist's model whom the narrator has seen in many different roles in many different paintings. Two years later the model reappears on another stormy night at the narrator's rooms. He announces himself as "The Ghost of Art" and has resurrected his career by growing a beard which expresses the characters he now represents in various paintings. Article from *HOUSEHOLD WORDS* (July 20, 1850). *Reprinted.*

Ghosts of Christmas The three spirits of Christmas who bring about Scrooge's conversion. The **Ghost of Christmas Past**, "a strange figure—like a child: yet not so like a child as like an old man," dressed in a white tunic and emitting a beam of light from its head, shows Scrooge scenes of his childhood and his early working years (2). The **Ghost of Christmas Present**, a jolly giant surrounded by a cornucopia of abundance and spreading Christmas cheer, takes Scrooge to the Cratchit's Christmas dinner and his nephew's party (3). The **Ghost of Christmas Yet-to-Come**, a hooded specter, shows Scrooge his own and Tiny Tim's deaths (4). *Carol.*

Ghost Story Dickens was introduced to this traditional form of storytelling by his childhood nurse, Mary WELLER, whose tales of the macabre and GROTESQUE fascinated and horrified the boy. He describes these "Nurse's Stories" in *Uncommercial* (15). Although he was skeptical of the "truth" of such tales, Dickens knew their appeal. He includes ghost stories among the INTERPOLATED TALES in the early novels. Particularly noteworthy is "The Story of the Goblins who Stole a Sexton" (*Pickwick*, 29), the first version of his most famous ghost story, *A Christmas Carol* (1843), subtitled "A Ghost Story of Christmas." The CHRISTMAS BOOKS, which blended fantasy and realism to give a "higher form" to old nursery tales, are partly conceived in the tradition of the oral stories—often ghost stories—told to those gathered at the Christmas hearth. *The Haunted Man*, the other ghost story in the series, is based on Dickens's belief that Christmas was an especially appropriate time for the living to remember the dead. Among the ghost stories in the Christmas numbers of Dickens's magazines, "The Signal-Man" (1866) is the most memorable.

Dickens occasionally uses motifs from the ghost story in the longer novels, as in the shadowy presence of Barnaby Rudge's father (*Rudge*), the apparitions that haunt the guilty Lewsome (*Chuzzlewit*, 48), or the vision of the hanging woman that Pip sees on two occasions at SATIS HOUSE (*Expectations*, 8, 48).

Peter Haining's introduction to *The Complete Ghost Stories of Charles Dickens* (1982) summarizes Dickens's involvement with the genre. Harry STONE (1979) discusses ghost stories as one of the types of children's literature important in Dickens's work.

Ghost's Walk, The The terrace at CHESNEY WOLD where ghostly footsteps are sometimes heard. Legend has it that they are those of the Lady Dedlock from the 17th century whose sympathy for the Puritan cause made her a traitor to King Charles and to the Dedlocks. *Bleak House* (7).

Gibbs, William Hairdresser who is the subject of Sam Weller's story. *Humphrey* (5).

Giggles, Miss A pupil, "deficient of sentiment," at Miss Twinkleton's. *Drood* (9, 13).

Gilbert, Mark Hosier's apprentice and member of the 'PRENTICE KNIGHTS. He later becomes Tappertit's lieutenant. *Rudge* (8, 39).

Giles Mrs. Maylie's butler who fires the shot at Oliver and raises the alarm about the robbery (22). *Twist.*

Giles, William (1798–1856) Son of a Baptist clergyman in CHATHAM; Dickens's first schoolmaster. He recognized the boy's unusual abilities and gave him individual instruction. When Dickens moved to London at age 11, Giles gave him a copy of Goldsmith's *Bee*, a volume of essays which Dickens treasured. Although his father was a formidable preacher and may have been the model for some of Dickens's unsympathetic portraits of dissenting ministers, young Giles was remembered with great affection by his former pupil.

Gill, Mr. and Mrs. Clients of Sarah Gamp. Mrs. Gill is noteworthy for her ability to "name the very day and hour" when she would give birth. *Chuzzlewit* (29).

Gills, Solomon (Old Sol) Walter Gay's uncle and the proprietor of the WOODEN MIDSHIPMAN, a nautical instrument shop, "a slow, quiet spoken, thoughtful old fellow, with eyes as red as if they had been small suns looking at you through the fog" (4). When Walter is lost at sea, Sol goes off in search of him, leaving Captain Cuttle in charge of the shop (25). He comes back after a long absence to find that Walter has returned and is about to marry Florence (56). In the end, Sol makes Cuttle his partner. *Dombey.*

Gimbel, Colonel Richard (1898–1970) American merchant, bibliophile, collector of Dickens materials, including the manuscripts of several minor works. He donated much of his collection to Yale University.

Gimblet, Brother An "expounder" in the dissenting congregation to which he and Brother Hawkyard, his rival expounder, belong. "Silverman."

"Gin-shops" Sketch describing "a great vice in England," the gin shops in the slums where the poor seek "temporary oblivion," particularly one such establishment in the ROOKERY OF ST. GILES at the bottom of Tottenham Court Road. Originally published as "Sketches of London No. 2" in the *EVENING CHRONICLE* (February 19, 1835). *Boz.*

Gissing, George (1857–1903) Late-Victorian novelist and critic, best known for *New Grub Street* (1901). His *Charles Dickens, A Critical Study* (1898) and *Critical Studies of the Works of Charles Dickens* (1924) defend Dickens as a realist against the criticisms of such contemporaries as George Henry LEWES and Henry JAMES. Although Gissing did not celebrate the romantic side of Dickens and his more fanciful inventions, he was profoundly influenced by Dickens's social vision, and he reminds us that much that may seem fantastic in Dickens's work is grounded in careful observation of the social conditions at the time.

Glamour, Bob Regular at the SIX JOLLY FELLOWSHIP PORTERS. *Mutual Friend.*

Glasgow Dickens opened the Athenaeum at this Scottish city on December 28, 1847. He also gave several successful PUBLIC READINGS of his works in the city, the first in 1858.

Glavormelly, Mr. A deceased actor and friend of Mr. Snevellicci. *Nickleby* (30).

Glibbery The name used for Bob GLIDDERY when he is first introduced (I:6). *Mutual Friend.*

Gliddery, Bob The pot-boy at the SIX JOLLY FELLOWSHIP PORTERS. *Mutual Friend.*

Globson, Bully "A big fat boy, with a big fat head, and a big fat fist," who bullies the Traveller at school. *Uncommercial* (20).

Glogwog, Sir Chipkins An aristocratic friend of the Egotistical Couple. *Young Couples.*

Glorious Appollers "A select convivial circle" devoted to drinking and glee-singing. Dick Swiveller is Perpetual Grand Master and Chuckster a member. *Curiosity Shop* (13).

Gloucester Place Dickens lived at no. 57 on this street near HYDE PARK in 1864 when he was beginning work on *Mutual Friend.*

Glubb, Old The old sailor who pushes Paul's invalid chair and tells him stories of the deep. *Dombey* (8, 12).

Glumper, Sir Thomas One of the guests at the Gattleton's private theatricals. *Boz,* "Porter."

Goat and Boots, The The inn where Our Curate addresses an antislavery meeting. *Boz,* "Curate."

Gobler Hypochrondriac who boards at Mrs. Tibbs's and marries Mrs. Bloss, also a hypochrondriac. *Boz,* "Boarding-house."

Goblins, King of the The leader of the pack of goblins who capture and torment Gabriel Grub in Wardle's Christmas story, "The Goblins who Stole a Sexton." *Pickwick* (29).

"Goblins Who Stole a Sexton, The Story of the" INTERPOLATED TALE told by Wardle on Christmas Eve about Gabriel Grub, a morose sexton. When Grub digs a grave on Christmas Eve and drinks himself into a stupor, he has a dream in which he is tormented by goblins. The dream changes his life: Ashamed of his

misanthropy, he leaves his village and wanders for 10 years before returning as a ragged and repentant man. *Pickwick* (29). The story is often considered the precursor to *A Christmas Carol.*

Gog and Magog Two giant figures in the GUILDHALL—guardian spirits of the CITY of London—who come to life and tell stories and legends of the city's past; Joe Toddyhigh overhears "MAGOG'S TALE" of Hugh Graham. *Humphrey* (1). In "Gone Astray" the boy lost in the city seeks out the giants during his wanderings.

Goggle-eyed Gentleman Madman on the train that John the narrator takes to the north. "Haunted House."

"Going into Society" Dickens's story for *House to Let,* the Christmas number of HOUSEHOLD WORDS, 1858. Toby Magsman, former tenant of the house to let and proprietor of Magsman's Amusements, tells of Mr. Chops, a performing dwarf who won the lottery and left the show to go into society. After spending all his money he learned that society is itself a kind of sideshow, and he returned to the show and died soon after. *Christmas Stories.*

Gold, Joseph (1933–) Professor, University of Waterloo (Ontario); compiler of *The Stature of Dickens: A Centenary Bibliography* (1971), a list of materials on Dickens and his works from the Victorian period to 1970; author of *Charles Dickens: Radical Moralist* (1972), a provocative introduction to Dickens, with essays on all the novels, emphasizing their moral and, especially, their religious themes.

Goldberg, Michael (1930–) Professor, University of British Columbia; editor and critic of the works of CARLYLE, Dickens, and other Victorian and modern writers. He has written on Dickens in relation to D. H. Lawrence, George Bernard SHAW, and, especially, Carlyle. In *Carlyle and Dickens* (1972), Goldberg discusses the relationship between the two men and the influence of Carlyle, venerated by Dickens as a literary mentor and hero, on the novelist's work.

Golden Cross Hotel, The Coaching inn on the present site of Trafalgar Square from which Pickwick begins his travels on May 13, 1827 (*Pickwick,* 2). David Copperfield stays here, "a mouldy sort of establishment in a close neighborhood," when he comes up to London from DOVER (19). Dickens describes the inn on a winter morning in *Boz,* "Early Coaches."

"Golden Dustman, The" Nickname of NICODEMUS BOFFIN. *Mutual Friend.*

Golden Mary Cargo ship carrying emigrants bound for California, it collides with an iceberg and sinks off Cape Horn. "Golden Mary."

Golden Square   The once-fashionable square in SOHO where many of the old mansions have been turned into lodgings by the time Ralph Nickleby has his office there (*Nickleby*, 2, 4). The home of the Kenwigs is nearby (*Nickleby*, 14). Mr. Peggotty recovers Little Em'ly in the vicinity of the square (*Copperfield*, 50).

Golding, Mary   One of the bathers recognized by Captain Waters at RAMSGATE, who "in her bathing costume, looked as if she were enveloped in a patent mackintosh of scanty dimensions." *Boz*, "Tuggses."

Goldsmith, Oliver (1728–1774)   Dramatist, novelist, and essayist; one of the 18th-century authors whom Dickens read as a child. Dickens received a collection of Goldsmith's essays from William GILES when he left CHATHAM; his nickname BOZ ultimately derived from *The Vicar of Wakefield*; Goldsmith was among the writers he read in his course of self-study at the BRITISH MUSEUM. Goldsmith's sentimentality and his benevolent characters such as the Reverend Primrose exerted the greatest influence on Dickens.

Goldstraw, Mrs. Sarah (Sally)   Nurse at the FOUNDLING HOSPITAL who later becomes Wilding's housekeeper and tells him of the mistake made in his identity. "No Thoroughfare."

"Gone Astray"   In this article from *HOUSEHOLD WORDS* (August 13, 1853), Dickens describes an experience when he was eight or so of being separated from the person he was with and finding himself lost in the CITY. He spent the day visiting London's landmarks, imagining himself as Dick WHITTINGTON, and going to a play. In the evening he went to a police station and his father was called to retrieve him. *Miscellaneous*. The essay is echoed in Florence Dombey's "kidnapping" and in David Copperfield's wanderings in the streets of London.

"Gone to the Dogs"   Article for *HOUSEHOLD WORDS* (March 10, 1855), in which Dickens describes the ways in which his own life and that of the nation has gone to the dogs. The only competitor Posterity has for the treasures that may be handed down to them, he asserts, are the Dogs. The romantic castles he once built in the air have gone to the dogs; Bob Temple, friend of his youth, has succumbed to gambling; whole streets of buildings have fallen into ruin; the nation is sending its soldiers to vanish in Balaklava. *Miscellaneous*. The "romantic castles" obliquely allude to Dickens's infatuation with Maria BEADNELL.

" 'Good' Hippopotamus, The"   Article for *HOUSEHOLD WORDS* (October 12, 1850), satirizing the use of public funds to provide for idle aristocrats in its description of the proposed subscription to erect a monument to H. R. H. (His Rolling Hulk) the Hippotamus. *Miscellaneous*.

Goodchild, Francis   One of two idle apprentices who "would take upon himself any amount of pains and labour to assure himself that he was idle." *Lazy Tour*.

Goodwin   Mrs. Pott's maid who "rendered herself useful in a variety of ways, but in none more so than in the particular department of constantly aiding and abetting her mistress in every wish and inclination opposed to the desires of the unhappy Pott" (18). *Pickwick*.

Goody, Mrs.   "An inconvenient woman," the grandmother of a child whom Reverend Milvey suggests the Boffins might adopt. *Mutual Friend* (I:9).

Gooseberry, Old   One of the pseudonyms by which those paying testimonials refer to William DORRIT. *Dorrit*.

Gordon, Colonel   Member of Parliament who opposes his kinsman Lord George GORDON and who, with General Conway, prevents the rioters from entering the Houses of Parliament. *Rudge* (49).

Gordon, Emma   Tightrope walker in Sleary's Circus who comforts Sissy after her father abandons her (I:6). She marries an admiring cheesemonger (III:7). *Hard Times*.

Gordon, Lord George (1751–1793)   Youngest son of the duke of Gordon, he was the fanatical leader of the Protestant Association during the No Popery riots protesting the Catholic Relief Act in July 1780. After he gathered 60,000 supporters in a massive but unsuccessful petition of Parliament for repeal of the bill, mob violence broke out and in several days of rioting 450 people were killed or wounded. After the riots Gordon was arrested for high treason and acquitted. He converted to Judaism and eventually died in NEWGATE PRISON, where he was imprisoned for libel. Dickens holds to the facts of Gordon's life in *Rudge*, in which he presents Gordon as misguided and muddled rather than malevolent, a man "of a slender make, and sallow complexion, with an aquiline nose, and long hair of a reddish brown, . . . in a full suit of black, quite free of any ornament, and of the most precise and sober cut. The gravity of his dress, together with a certain lankness of cheek and stiffness of deportment, added nearly ten years to his age, but his figure was that of one not yet past thirty" (35). *Rudge*.

Gordon Riots   Disturbances in London in June 1780 stemming from demonstrations to secure the repeal of the Catholic Relief Act of 1778, which had removed some of the civil disabilities against Catholics. Led by Lord George GORDON, who formed the Protestant Association in 1779 to protest the act and deliver a petition to Parliament, the demonstrations assembled a mob of thousands who virtually held London in thrall for a week while Catholic chapels, the homes of Roman Catholics, and several public buildings were pillaged and burned.

Gordon was arrested, tried for treason, and acquitted on the grounds that he had no treasonous intent. The Catholic Relief Act was not repealed. In *Rudge*, Dickens writes as if the rioters are trying to prevent passage of the bill. For his readers in 1841, the Gordon Riots had remarkable similarities to the Chartist demonstrations going on in London and other English cities at the time (see CHARTISM).

Goswell Street   Now known as Goswell Road, this street in the CITY is the site of Mrs. Bardell's house, where Pickwick has his lodgings. As Pickwick surveys his neighborhood, "Goswell Street was at his feet, Goswell Street was on his right hand—as far as the eye could see Goswell Street extended on his left; and the opposite side of Goswell Street was over the way" (2). *Pickwick.*

Gothic Novel   A type of novel popular in the late 18th and early 19th centuries that featured supernatural occurrences, mysterious events and characters, and medieval castles with trapdoors, mysterious passageways, and chambers of horrors. Horace Walpole's *Castle of Otranto* (1764) is usually considered the originator of the form; among its prominent English practitioners were Matthew ("Monk") Lewis, Mary Shelley, and Anne Radcliffe.

Although none of Dickens's novels can be considered a gothic novel, Dickens did use devices and motifs from the gothic in his fiction, such as surrealistic elements of dream, sharp contrasts between light and dark worlds and between country and city, themes of imprisonment and death, and ruined and horrifying houses, such as SATIS HOUSE (*Expectations*), CHESNEY WOLD with its Ghost's Walk (*Bleak House*), or Mrs. Clennam's crumbling house (*Dorrit*). Larry Kirkpatrick ("The Gothic Flame of Charles Dickens," *Victorian Newsletter*, 1967), includes these features as part of what he describes as a "gothic substructure" in the novels. Archibald C. COOLIDGE (1967) discusses Dickens's use of techniques derived from the gothic novels of Ann Radcliffe. Thomas Loe ("Gothic Plot in *Great Expectations*," *Dickens Quarterly*, 1989) dicusses the gothic plot as one of three plot lines in the novel.

Governor, Jack   One of the visitors to the haunted house and an old friend of the narrator, "a portly, cheery, well-built figure of a broad-shouldered man, with a frank smile, a brilliant dark eye, and a rich dark eyebrow." "Haunted House."

Gowan, Henry   An indolent and snobbish young gentleman who takes up a career as an artist for lack of something better to do. He falls in love with Pet Meagles and marries her, much to the distress of her parents. After a continental honeymoon, the couple return to England where Gowan snubs his wife's parents while condescending to accept an annual allowance from them. His mother, **Mrs. Gowan**, widow of "a commissioner

of nothing in particular," is as snobbish and condescending as her son. She lives in HAMPTON COURT PALACE. *Dorrit.*

Gradgrind Family   Lancashire family representing the new ruling class in the north of England brought to wealth by the INDUSTRIAL REVOLUTION and to power by the REFORM BILL OF 1832. **Thomas**, a retired merchant and member of Parliament for Coketown, is a spokesman for POLITICAL ECONOMY and UTILITARIANISM. He sponsors a school devoted to teaching his philosophy of hard facts and suppressing imagination. "A man of realities—a man of facts and calculations—a man who proceeds upon the principle that two and two are four, and nothing over, and who is not to be talked into allowing for anything over" (I:2). His **wife**, "stunned by some weighty piece of fact," is a woman "of surpassing feebleness mentally and bodily" (I:4). Gradgrind's heartless philosophy has its harshest effects on his children, **Louisa**, who marries Bounderby in a loveless union because she can come up with no convincing reason not to, and **Tom ("The Whelp")**, whose utitlitarian education makes him consummately selfish. Louisa is unprepared for Harthouse's seductions, which enable her to see the emptiness of her marriage and prompt her to leave her husband. Tom exploits his sister's devotion to him and ends up robbing Bounderby's bank. Gradgrind has another daughter, **Jane**, and two more sons, **Adam Smith** and **Malthus**, whose names bespeak their father's philosophical commitments. *Hard Times.*

Graham, Hugh   The hero of Magog's tale, a 16th-century apprentice who is in love with his master's daughter, Mistress Alice. After she is seduced and ruined by a nobleman, Hugh protects her, kills the offending nobleman, and is himself killed in the ensuing riot. *Humphrey.*

Graham, Mary   The young, beautiful, and selfless companion of old Martin Chuzzlewit, suspected by his relatives of having designs on the old man's money. She has agreed to be his companion on the understanding that she will inherit nothing. She loves young Martin, and remains loyal to him during his absence in America, while Pecksniff presses his opportunistic attentions on her and Tom Pinch adores her from afar. When Martin returns, Pecksniff is exposed and Mary and Martin marry. *Chuzzlewit.*

Grainger   One of Steerforth's friends who attends David's bachelor dinner party at his rooms in Mrs. Crupp's house. *Copperfield* (24).

Gran, Mrs.   Jemmy Lirriper's name for Mrs. LIRRIPER in the story he tells. "Lirriper's Legacy."

Granby, Marchioness of   Tony Weller's nickname for Mrs. WELLER, proprietor of the MARQUIS OF GRANBY. *Pickwick.*

Grandfather, Little Nell's The "name" by which Mr. TRENT is most often identified. *Curiosity Shop.*

Grandmarina, Fairy Godmother of Princess Alicia, to whom she gives the magic fishbone. "Holiday Romance."

Grandpapa and Grandmamma Guests at the Christmas dinner party. *Boz,* "Christmas Dinner."

Granger, Edith Edith DOMBEY's name from her first marriage, before she marries Dombey. *Dombey.*

Grannett Overseer in the workhouse where Oliver Twist is born, admired by Bumble and Mrs. Corney for his harsh treatment of the paupers. *Twist* (23).

Grant, William and Daniel Merchants and manufacturers in MANCHESTER, so famous for their philanthropy that John DICKENS held them up as models to his son. Charles Dickens met them in 1839 and used them as models for the Cheeryble Brothers in *Nickleby.* Although he assured his readers "that the Brothers Cheeryble live; that their liberal charity, their singleness of heart, their noble nature, and their unbounded benevolence, are no creations of the Author's brain," many readers have found them impossible and tiresome, and, as Aldous Huxley described them, "gruesome old Peter Pans."

Grapes Inn Tavern in Narrow Street, LIMEHOUSE, original of the SIX JOLLY FELLOWSHIP PORTERS. *Mutual Friend.*

Graves, Robert (1895–1985) English poet and novelist whose *The Real David Copperfield* (1933) is a modernist "rewriting for the ordinary reader." It eliminates repetitions and prolixity of style necessitated by the original serial form, reducing the novel to what Graves calls "its natural length and plot." In doing so, he removes much about David and Agnes and makes the sexual content in David's relationships with Emily and Dora more explicit. Although Graves claimed that he undertook the project because of his admiration for Dickens, most Dickensians have considered his efforts as expressing contempt for the original. George H. FORD's (1955) reaction is representative: Graves' "*jeu d'esprit* is about as effective as Pope's attempts to translate Donne's satires into elegant neo-classical verses and will remain an equally amusing specimen for future literary historians."

Gravesend Port on the THAMES estuary in KENT about halfway between London and CHATHAM. The steam excursion boat from London to Gravesend is described in *Boz,* "River." David Copperfield bids farewell to the Australian emigrants at Gravesend (57). Caddy Jellyby spends her honeymoon with Prince here (*Bleak House,* 30). Pip and Herbert row beyond Gravesend a

they attempt to smuggle Magwitch out of England (*Expectations,* 54).

Graymarsh Pupil at DOTHEBOYS HALL whose aunt thinks Squeers "too good for this world." *Nickleby* (8).

Grayper, Mr. and Mrs. Neighbors of Mrs. Copperfield at BLUNDERSTONE at whose house she meets Murdstone. *Copperfield* (2).

Gray's Inn One of the INNS OF COURT, located in HOLBORN west of Gray's Inn Road. Dickens worked here in 1827 as a clerk for ELLIS AND BLACKMORE. The Traveller describes the inn as "one of the most depressing institutions in brick and mortar" (*Uncommercial,* 14). Lawyers Perker and Phunkey (*Pickwick*) have their legal offices at the inn; Percy Noakes (*Boz,* "Excursion") and Tommy Traddles (*Copperfield*) have lodgings here. Flora Finching proposes to meet Arthur Clennam in Gray's Inn Gardens (*Dorrit,* I:13).

Gray's Inn Lane Now called Gray's Inn Road, this street running north from HOLBORN is the site of Signor Billsmethi's dancing academy (*Boz,* "Dancing Academy") and of Micawber's lodgings when he is going under the alias Mortimer (*Copperfield,* 36). Casby lives in a side street off the Lane (*Dorrit,* I:13).

Grazinglands, Alexander Gentleman of property from the MIDLANDS who comes to London with his wife **Arabella** to transact some business at the BANK OF ENGLAND. They receive poor service at JAIRING'S HOTEL and when they complain the waiter tells them that "when indiwiduals is not staying in the 'Ouse, their favours is not as a rule looked upon as making it worth Mr. Jairing's while." *Uncommercial* (6).

"Great Baby, The" Article from HOUSEHOLD WORDS (August 4, 1855) opposing proposals to close taverns on Sunday. The members of Parliament who intend to do so are under the influence of Monomaniacs who view the People as a Great Baby, influenced by strong drink and bad company in taverns, and thus incapable of acting responsibly. *Miscellaneous.*

Great Coram Street Now known as Coram Street, this is the site in Bloomsbury of Mrs. Tibbs's boarding house. *Boz,* "Boarding House."

"Great Exhibition and the Little One, The" Essay by Dickens and R. H. HORNE for HOUSEHOLD WORDS (July 5, 1851) contrasting the Great Exhibition at the Crystal Palace with a little exhibition of Chinese articles at the Chinese Gallery in HYDE PARK. It is a "comparison between Stoppage and Progress," between a Chinese culture "crippled by conceited absolutism and distrust" and the Western industrial culture which is "moving in a right direction towards some superior condition of society—politically, morally, intellectually, and religiously." *Stone*.

Great Expectations Dickens's 13th novel, published in 36 weekly parts in *ALL THE YEAR ROUND* (December 1, 1860–August 3, 1861), unillustrated. Published in three volumes by CHAPMAN & HALL, 1861. A BILDUNGSRO-MAN narrated in the first person by its hero, *Great Expectations* recalls *David Copperfield*, but Pip's story is more tightly organized than David's and Pip is more aware of his shortcomings. Pip tells his story in three equal parts, casting his life as a journey in three stages: his childhood and youth in KENT, when he wishes he could overcome his humble origins and rise in the world; his young manhood in London after he receives his great expectations; and his disillusionment when he learns the source of his good fortune and realizes the emptiness of his worldly values. The novel's concise narration, balanced structure, and rich SYMBOLISM have made it the most admired and most discussed of Dickens's works.

SYNOPSIS

Stage I:

Part 1 (December 1, 1860)
(1) Philip Pirrip, known as "Pip," remembers the day when he was seven and gained his "first most vivid and broad impression of the identity of things." Then, while visiting the graves of his parents in the churchyard on a

Pip and Joe by the hearth at the forge in John McLenan's illustration for the original American serial of Great Expectations *in* Harper's Weekly. *The simultaneous British serial in* All the Year Round *was unillustrated.*

dreary Christmas Eve, the child Pip is surprised by an escaped convict who threatens to kill him if he does not bring him food and a file. (2) Back at the house of his sister, who has brought him up "by hand," Pip is punished for getting home late, but he has the sympathic companionship of his sister's husband, Joe Gargery the blacksmith. At supper Pip secretly saves his bread, and early on Christmas morning, after taking a pork pie and some brandy from the larder and a file from the forge, he slips out of the house and on to the marshes.

Part 2 (December 8, 1860)
(3) There he is surprised by another escaped convict, a young man with a scar on his face. When he finds the ragged man who scared him the day before, Pip watches compassionately as the man devours the food and files the manacle from his leg, but he arouses the convict's anger when he tells him of the other escapee on the marshes. (4) At Christmas dinner, while he guiltily awaits the discovery of the theft from the larder, Pip is admonished by his Uncle Pumblechook and the other guests to "be grateful" and to overcome the tendency of boys to be "naterally wicious." As his sister goes to the larder to fetch the pork pie that he stole for the convict, a troop of soldiers appears at the door.

Part 3 (December 15, 1860)
(5) The soldiers ask Joe to repair some handcuffs. Then Joe and Pip follow them as they pursue the convicts. The two escapees are captured as they fight with each other on the marshes. Before he is returned to the prison ship anchored in the THAMES, Pip's convict confesses to stealing some food from Mrs. Joe's larder. Joe forgives him, saying, "We don't know what you have done, but we wouldn't have you starved to death for it, poor miserable fellow-creatur.—Would us, Pip?"

Part 4 (December 22, 1860)
(6) Pip is unable to tell Joe the truth about the theft from the larder. (7) As he awaits the time when he will be apprenticed to Joe, Pip gets some rudimentary education from Mr. Wopsle's great aunt and her granddaughter Biddy, enough to realize that Joe cannot read. About a year after the convict episode, Mrs. Joe announces that her Uncle Pumblechook has arranged for Pip to play at the house of Miss Havisham, a rich recluse in the nearby market town.

Part 5 (December 29, 1860)
(8) Pumblechook delivers the boy to SATIS HOUSE the next morning. There Pip meets Estella, a supercilious young woman not much older than he, and Miss Havisham, an old woman in a tattered bridal dress, inhabiting rooms in the ruined house where everything is yellowed with age and all the clocks have stopped at 20 minutes to nine. She orders Pip and Estella to play cards and urges Estella to break Pip's heart. Pip fights back tears when Estella ridicules him as coarse and common,

and he escapes into the garden to cry. There he has a sudden vision of Miss Havisham in the abandoned brewery, hanging from a beam and calling to him.

Part 6 (January 5, 1861)
(9) When Pumblechook and Mrs. Joe ask about Miss Havisham, Pip caters to their imaginings by telling them a fantastic tale about a black velvet coach, four dogs, and a silver basket of veal cutlets. Later he confesses to Joe that he made up the story because he felt "common," but Joe assures him that he is "oncommon small" and an "oncommon scholar." (10) Pip enlists Biddy's help in teaching him to be "uncommon." One Saturday evening, Pip finds Joe at the Jolly Bargeman with a "secret-looking" stranger who stirs his drink with a file and gives Pip a shilling wrapped up in two one-pound notes. Pip fears that his connection with the convict will come to light.

Part 7 (January 12, 1861)
(11) When Pip returns to Miss Havisham's, her relatives have gathered at Satis House for her birthday. Estella insults him, slaps him, and dares him to tell on her. Miss Havisham shows him a table spread with a decaying feast, including the remains of a wedding cake, where she will be laid out when she dies. She points out the places her relatives will occupy at this table when she is dead. She again orders Pip to play cards with Estella and to admire her beauty. When he goes out into the garden, Pip meets a pale young gentleman there who challenges him to fight. Pip reluctantly enters the match, but he knocks the young man to the ground and gives him a black eye. After the fight, Estella invites him to kiss her.

Part 8 (January 19, 1861)
(12) Pip's visits to Satis House become more frequent. He pushes Miss Havisham around her rooms in a wheelchair and plays cards with Estella as the old lady murmurs, "Break their hearts, my pride and hope!" One day, Miss Havisham, noting that Pip is growing tall, asks him to bring Joe Gargery to Satis House. (13) Two days later, in his Sunday clothes, Joe accompanies Pip to Miss Havisham's. She asks Joe whether Pip has ever objected to becoming a blacksmith and if Joe expects a premium for taking Pip on as an apprentice. Joe, speaking through Pip, replies no to both questions, but she gives him 25 guineas anyway to pay for Pip's apprenticeship. The Gargerys celebrate the occasion with a dinner at the Blue Boar, but Pip is wretched, convinced he will never like Joe's trade.

Part 9 (January 26, 1861)
(14) Pip does not tell Joe of his unhappiness, but as he works at the forge he remembers his former visits to Satis House and sees visions of Estella's face in the fire. (15) Although Joe advises against it, Pip takes a half-holiday to visit Miss Havisham. His fellow worker, Dolge Orlick, a surly and contrary man, envies Pip and demands equal time off, but when he offends Joe with some derogatory remarks about Mrs. Joe, the blacksmith knocks him to the ground. At Satis House, Pip learns that Estella has gone abroad to be educated. Miss Havisham tells him that he can visit her each year on his birthday, but he is to expect nothing from her. Back at the forge, he discovers that someone has broken into the house and that Mrs. Joe has been knocked senseless by an unknown assailant.

Part 10 (February 2, 1861)
(16) The weapon was an old convict's leg iron. Convinced that it is the manacle from his convict's leg, Pip feels guilty, as if he struck the blow himself. Mrs. Joe is left unable to speak and partly paralyzed, but she changes character and becomes good-tempered. Although Orlick is suspected of the crime, Mrs. Joe is conciliatory to him. Biddy, Pip's schoolmate and teacher, comes to the forge to take over housekeeping duties. (17) On his birthday Pip visits Miss Havisham, receives a guinea, and is told to come again next year. It becomes his regular custom. Meanwhile, Pip and Biddy develop a close friendship and he confesses to her his desire to become a gentleman "on Estella's account." She wisely asks him whether he wants "to be a gentleman, to spite her or to gain her over?" As Pip and Biddy walk through the countryside, Orlick follows them.

Part 11 (February 9, 1861)
(18) In the fourth year of his apprenticeship, Pip is surprised by Mr. Jaggers, Miss Havisham's lawyer from London, who announces that Pip has "great expectations." If Joe will release him from his apprenticeship, Pip is to move to London and become a gentleman. He is to be known as Pip and not to ask the identity of his benefactor. Joe refuses any compensation for Pip's release, but there is a touch of sadness in his celebration of Pip's good fortune. (19) After they burn the apprenticeship papers, Pip talks of what he will do to raise Joe up. He bids farewell to Pumblechook, who takes credit for Pip's good fortune, and to Miss Havisham. After an awkward parting from Joe, Pip sets out for London.

Stage II:

Part 12 (February 23, 1861)
(20) In London, Jaggers, a criminal lawyer, is to act as the representaive of Pip's unnamed benefactor. At Jaggers's office near SMITHFIELD MARKET, Pip finds a host of shady characters clamoring for the lawyer's attention. While he waits, Pip visits NEWGATE PRISON nearby. (21) Jaggers has his clerk, John Wemmick, take Pip to BARNARD'S INN, where he is to stay with Herbert Pocket, the son of his tutor. When he meets Herbert, Pip recognizes him as the pale young gentleman he fought in Miss Havisham's garden.

Part 13 (March 2, 1861)
(22) Herbert teaches Pip the manners of a gentleman and nicknames him "Handel" (in honor of that composer's

"Harmonious Blacksmith"). He tells him of Estella, adopted by Miss Havisham to wreak vengeance on men, and of Miss Havisham's own past: Daughter of a wealthy brewer, she and her half brother inherited their father's business. She fell in love with a fast-talking con man who proposed to marry her and convinced her to buy her brother's share in the brewery at a high price. Then he split the proceeds with her brother and jilted her on her wedding day, the day when she stopped the clocks at 20 minutes to nine and withdrew into Satis House.

Part 14 (March 9, 1861)

(23) At the home of Matthew Pocket, Herbert's father who is to act as Pip's tutor, Pip meets his fellow pupils: Drummle, a disagreeable young man from a wealthy family, and Startop, a delicate and friendly fellow. The Pocket household is in disarray. Matthew, educated at Harrow and Cambridge, is impractical and a poor manager; his wife, Belinda, daughter of a knight, is obsessed with social position and pays no attention to housekeeping. (24) When Pip goes to secure Jaggers's approval for his plan to live at Barnard's Inn with Herbert, he has an opportunity to watch the lawyer's intimidating courtroom manner, and to become further acquainted with Wemmick, Jaggers's clerk. Wemmick shows Pip the death masks of some of their former clients; advises him to "get hold of portable property"; and tells him, when he goes to Jaggers's house for dinner, to observe the housekeeper, whom he describes as "a wild beast tamed." He also invites Pip to visit at his home in the suburbs.

Part 15 (March 16, 1861)

(25) Although some of the Pockets resent Pip, thinking that he has intruded on their rightful portion of Miss Havisham's fortune, Matthew, who has refused to curry favor with Miss Havisham, bears him no ill will. Pip's studies progress nicely. When he visits Wemmick at his home in WALWORTH, he finds him very different from the hard and materialistic clerk he met in the City. Wemmick lives in a bucolic little castle, surrounded by a moat, gardens, and animal pens, and he maintains a domestic establishment with his Aged Parent. Jaggers knows nothing of Wemmick's private life, for Wemmick's policy is to keep office and home totally separate. (26) When Pip goes to Jaggers's house for dinner with Startop and Drummle, the lawyer makes his housekeeper, Molly, display her strong and scarred wrists. Fascinated with Drummle, Jaggers calls him "the Spider," and provokes him to boast of his strength and to reveal his dislike for Pip. As they leave, Jaggers advises Pip to keep clear of Drummle.

Part 16 (March 23, 1861)

(27) Joe visits Pip in London. Dressed uncomfortably in his best clothes and intimidated by Pip's formality and servant boy, he addresses his old companion as "sir." He tells Pip that Wopsle has come to London to be an actor, that Estella has returned and would be glad to see him,

and that Pip is always welcome at the forge. Then he leaves. (28) Pip immediately sets out to see Estella. On the coach he rides with two convicts, one of whom talks of once delivering two one-pound notes to a boy in the town. Pip is shaken by this coincidence. Once he is home, Pip decides to stay at the Blue Boar Inn rather than at the forge.

Part 17 (March 30, 1861)

(29) Pip is disturbed to find Orlick working as the porter at Satis House, but Estella is more beautiful than ever. She warns him that she has "no heart," but Miss Havisham urges him to "Love her, love her, love her!" Pip is convinced that Miss Havisham has chosen him for Estella. He is uneasy that he has not gone to visit Joe.

Part 18 (April 6, 1861)

(30) As Pip walks through town, the tailor's boy mocks his snobbery and elegance in the street by pretending not to know him. Pip warns Jaggers about Orlick and the lawyer promises to dismiss him from Miss Havisham's service. Back in London, Pip confesses to a dubious Herbert that he loves Estella. Herbert reveals that he is secretly engaged to Clara Barley, daughter of a ship's purser. (31) Pip and Herbert see Mr. Wopsle, the parish clerk from Pip's village with ambitions for the stage, perform *Hamlet*. After the wretched but hilarious production, they invite the actor, whose stage name is Waldengarver, to dinner.

Part 19 (April 13, 1861)

(32) When Estella asks Pip to meet her coach in London, he arrives hours early. While he is waiting, Wemmick takes him through Newgate Prison. He returns just in time to see Estella's hand waving to him in the coach window. (33) She tells him that she is going to be introduced into society and that he may visit her in Richmond. Pip takes this as part of Miss Havisham's plan for them (33).

Part 20 (April 20, 1861)

(34) Pip falls into lavish spending habits. He and Herbert list their debts, but then, with the other members of their club, the Finches of the Grove, they get even further into debt. When Pip learns that his sister has died, (35), he returns home for the funeral. There Biddy tells him that his sister's last words were "Joe," "Pardon," and "Pip." Pip is annoyed when Biddy doubts his promise to come often to see Joe.

Part 21 (April 27, 1861)

(36) On his 21st birthday, Pip receives £500 from Jaggers to pay his debts. Jaggers says that he will receive the same sum each year until his benefactor reveals himself. Pip asks Wemmick to help him use some of the money to advance Herbert's prospects. When Wemmick gives his "deliberate opinion in this office" against doing so, Pip asks to solicit his opinion at Wemmick's home. (37) There Wemmick suggests that Pip buy Herbert a position with Clarriker, an up-and-coming shipping bro-

ker. Wemmick has Skiffins, his fiancée's brother, arrange it so that Herbert will not know the source of his good fortune.

Part 22 (May 4, 1861)

(38) Pip visits Estella frequently. Although she warns him to beware of her, she also drives him to jealous distraction. When the two of them visit Satis House, Miss Havisham delights to hear of Estella's conquests, but she accuses her of being cold and indifferent to her. "I am what you have made me," Estella replies, proud and hard. Unable to sleep that night, Pip observes Miss Havisham walking the halls of Satis House moaning. Back in London, he is outraged when Drummle toasts Estella at a meeting of the Finches. Pip warns her against him; she says that she is simply out to "deceive and entrap" him.

Part 23 (May 11, 1861)

(39) A week after his 23rd birthday, late on a stormy night, Pip is suprised by someone calling his name on the stairs outside his door. It is a man of about 60 with iron-gray hair, dressed like a sea voyager. When the man holds out his hands, as if to embrace him, Pip recognizes the convict from the marshes. He has been a sheep farmer in New South Wales and reveals that he is the source of Pip's expectations. The convict looks around Pip's rooms with the pride of ownership, especially at this gentleman. "I'm your second father," he tells Pip, but Pip is horrified and speechless, and troubled by knowing that the convict will be hanged if he is discovered in England. Gradually he realizes that all his ideas about Miss Havisham and Estella were a dream and that he deserted Joe and Biddy to be linked with a criminal.

Stage III:

Part 24 (May 18, 1861)

(40) The next morning Pip learns that his benefactor is Abel Magwitch, going by the name Provis, and that he has returned to England for good, even though he will be sentenced to death should he be caught. Pip dresses him like a prosperous farmer and secures rooms for him in a nearby lodging house. Jaggers confirms Magwitch's identity as Pip's benefactor by not denying it; the lawyer says that he warned Magwitch not to return to England. When Herbert returns to London, Magwitch swears him to silence.

Part 25 (May 25, 1861)

(41) Pip and Herbert agree that Pip should take no more of Magwitch's money and that Magwitch must be gotten out of England. (42) Magwitch tells them the story of his life: About 20 years earlier he became an accomplice of a gentleman named Compeyson, a forger and swindler who with a Mr. Arthur had just bilked a rich lady of her fortune. Arthur, near death at the time, had nightmares about a woman in white who tried to cover him with a shroud. When Magwitch and Compeyson were arrested

and tried for their crimes, Magwitch was sentenced to 14 years. Compeyson, presenting himself as a gentleman, received a light sentence and Magwitch vowed revenge. Finding himself on the same prison ship with Compeyson, he struck him, scarring his face, and then escaped from the ship, only to learn that Compeyson had also escaped. In assuring Compeyson's recapture, Magwitch was also taken and sentenced to transportation for life. He doesn't know what happened to Compeyson. After hearing the story, Herbert tells Pip that Arthur was Miss Havisham's brother and Compeyson her lover.

Part 26 (June 1, 1861)

(43) Pip returns home to see Estella. At the Blue Boar, he finds Drummle attended by Orlick. Drummle is also there to see Estella. (44) Pip accusingly tells Miss Havisham and Estella of his benefactor. Miss Havisham admits to leading him on, but tells him he made his own snares. She justifies her actions as a way of tormenting her avaricious relatives. Pip pours out his love for Estella, but she says he touches nothing in her breast and that she plans to marry Drummle. Distraught, Pip walks back to London, arriving late at night. The watchman on the gate to his rooms has a note for him from Wemmick. It reads, "Don't go home."

Part 27 (June 8, 1861)

(45) After a restless night in a hotel, Pip learns from Wemmick that his rooms are being watched by Compeyson and that he must get Provis out of the country. (46) Pip arranges with Provis, now known as Mr. Campbell, to watch for him as he rows on the river. He and Herbert plan to keep a boat at the TEMPLE stairs and to make a regular practice of rowing up the Thames. When the time is right, they will get the convict from his hiding place and take him to the Continent.

Part 28 (June 15, 1861)

(47) As Pip waits for the signal from Wemmick that the time has come to take Magwitch out of the country, he and Herbert regularly row down the river. One evening after attending one of Wopsle's dramatic performances, Pip learns from the actor that the second convict taken on the marshes was sitting behind him in the theater. Pip knows that Compeyson is watching him and he writes to Wemmick of the growing danger. (48) During dinner at Jaggers's house, Pip notices Molly's hands. They remind him of Estella's hand as she waved from the coach window. Wemmick tells him what he knows of Molly's story: that she was tried for the strangulation murder of a woman much larger than herself; that Jaggers's concealed the strength of her hands during the trial and argued that she was physically incapable of the crime; that she was suspected of destroying her three-year-old daughter at the time of the trial to avenge herself on the father; and that, after being acquitted, she went to work for Jaggers.

Part 29 (June 22, 1861)
(49) Pip goes to Satis House to learn more of Estella's story. A remorseful Miss Havisham tells Pip how she took the child supplied by Jaggers and turned the girl's heart to ice, that she knows nothing of Estella's parentage, and that Estella is now married and in Paris. She supplies Pip with money to pay for Herbert's position with Clarriker's and asks him to forgive her. As he walks in the ruined garden outside the house, Pip again sees the vision of Miss Havisham hanging from a beam. When he returns to bid her farewell, her dress is suddenly set afire by the flames in her grate. Pip extinguishes the flames, burning his hands in the process. That evening, as he leaves for London, the seriously injured old woman mutters distractedly, "What have I done?" (50) Herbert cares for Pip's burns and tells him what he has learned of Magwitch's story: Magwitch had a daughter of whom he was fond, but he lost touch with her when he went into hiding during the trial of the child's mother. Compeyson controlled him by threatening to reveal his whereabouts to the authorities. The child, had she lived, would be about Pip's age. Pip is sure that Magwitch is Estella's father.

Part 30 (June 29, 1861)
(51) Pip challenges Jaggers to confirm his conclusion about Estella's parentage. Jaggers obliquely does so, telling Pip that he hoped to save one of the many lost children by giving Estella to Miss Havisham. Jaggers asserts that it will do no one any good—not Molly, nor Magwitch, nor Estella—to reveal the truth now, and he advises Pip to keep his "poor dreams" to himself. (52) When Wemmick signals that the time has come to smuggle Magwitch to the Continent, Pip's hands are still too badly burned to row the boat. He enlists the aid of Startop. Before they can set out, however, Pip receives a mysterious letter telling him to come that evening to the limekiln on the marshes near his home if he wants "information regarding *your uncle Provis.*"

Part 31 (July 6, 1861)
(53) In the dark sluice house, Pip is suddenly attacked and bound by a noose. The attacker is Orlick, who plans to kill him. Orlick accuses Pip of causing him to lose his job with Miss Havisham and of coming between him and Biddy. He admits that he struck Mrs. Joe with the manacle, but claims "it warn't Old Orlick as did it; it was you." He knows about Magwitch. As he is about to strike Pip with a hammer, Startop, Herbert, and Trabb's Boy come to the rescue. Exhausted and ill from the ordeal, Pip is now very concerned about Magwitch's safety.

Part 32 (July 13, 1861)
(54) The next morning, Pip, Startop, and Herbert set out on the river. After picking up Magwitch, they row out to an isolated inn to spend the night before rowing out to meet the Hamburg packet steamer the next morning. Pip is uneasy when he sees two men examining their boat. The next morning, they are followed by a four-oared boat and ordered to turn over Abel Magwitch. Compeyson is in the other boat. In the confusion that follows, Compeyson and Magwitch both go overboard, locked in struggle. Only Magwitch surfaces. Afterward Pip accompanies Magwitch, injured and having difficulty breathing, back to London. He no longer feels any aversion to the wretched man who holds his hand in his. Pip knows that all Magwitch's property will be forfeited to the Crown.

Part 33 (July 20, 1861)
(55) Magwitch's trial is set for a month from the time of his arrest. Meanwhile Herbert, now a shipping broker, prepares to go to Egypt, where he will be in charge of Clarriker's Cairo office. He offers Pip a clerk's position there. Jaggers and Wemmick both deplore the fact that Pip did not act to secure Magwitch's property. Wemmick invites Pip to breakfast at Walworth. Afterward Pip accompanies Wemmick when he and Miss Skiffins are married in an impromptu ceremony. (56) Pip visits Magwitch daily in the prison hospital and holds his hand at the trial when he is condemned to hang. But Magwitch is gravely ill, and he dies with Pip at his side before the sentence is carried out. On his deathbed he thanks Pip for not deserting him. Pip tells him that his daughter lives and that he loves her.

Part 34 (July 27, 1861)
(57) Pip, deeply in debt, is very ill. When the arresting officers come, he is delirious and loses consciousness. He awakens from the fever to discover Joe, gentle as an angel, caring for him. As he slowly recuperates he learns from Joe that Miss Havisham has died, leaving all of her property to Estella except for £4,000 left to Matthew Pocket. He also learns that Orlick is in jail for assaulting Pumblechook. As Pip recovers, Joe becomes more distant. After Joe returns home, Pip learns that he has paid his debts. Pip considers his options: to return to the forge and ask Biddy to take him back or to go to Cairo to work with Herbert.

Part 35 (August 3, 1861)
(58) No longer a man of property, Pip gets a cool reception at the Blue Boar and from Pumblechook. When he returns to the forge, he discovers that it is Joe and Biddy's wedding day. He asks their forgiveness, promises to repay the money that Joe gave to pay his debts, and goes off to Egypt. There he lives with Herbert and Clara, repays his debts, and rises to become third in the firm. Only then does Clarriker tell Herbert that Pip had originally paid for his position. (59) After 11 years in Egypt, Pip returns home to visit Joe, Biddy, and their son, Pip. At the ruins of Satis House, he finds Estella, a widow who suffered at the hands of an abusive husband. She asks Pip's forgiveness "now, when suffering has been stronger than all other teaching, and has taught me to understand what your heart used to be." They vow

friendship and as they leave the ruined garden, Pip takes her hand and sees "no shadow of another parting from her."

COMMENTARY

Although Dickens's original plan seems to have been to publish *Great Expectations* in monthly numbers, he opted to write it as a weekly serial for *All the Year Round* when the magazine's sales slipped during the tedious run of Charles LEVER's *A Long Day's Ride*. *Expectations* restored the audience for the magazine, but it changed Dickens's novel from what it would have been in monthly parts. Each weekly number comprised only one or two short chapters, and, like the other novels in the magazine, it was unillustrated. This format forced Dickens to adopt concise and focused chapters, to concentrate on a single story line, and to work out, almost mathematically, the overall structure of the novel. He divided the story into three equal "stages," with 12 of the 36 weekly parts devoted to each. The three-stage structure reinforces the underlying metaphor of the novel which casts life as a journey.

As he began work on the novel, Dickens wrote to John FORSTER that "the book will be written in the first person throughout, and during these first three weekly numbers, you will find the hero to be a boy-child, like David." Dickens reread *Copperfield* just to make sure that there were "no unconscious repetitions" of the earlier novel. There are many similarities. Both boys are essentially orphans and both suffer from a feeling of hopelessness as they labor at pasting labels on bottles or working at a forge. Blacksmithing is the later novel's version of the BLACKING WAREHOUSE, for both novels are essentially autobiographical.

Expectations is more realistic than its autobiographical predecessor. Written at a time when novels like George ELIOT's *Adam Bede* (1859) were in vogue, *Expectations* is more restrained stylistically and more consistent in tone than many of the earlier novels. George GISSING (1898) defines its difference from earlier works by comparing Joe Gargery and Dan'l Peggotty: "If we compare the two figures as to their 'reality,' we must decide in favor of Gargery. I think him a better piece of workmanship all round; the prime reason, however, for his standing out so much more solidly in one's mind than Little Emily's uncle, is that he lives in a world, not of melodrama, but of everyday cause and effect."

Although *Expectations* has no Dan'l Peggotty and no Mr. Micawber, it is not lacking humorous scenes or memorable characters. The descriptions of Pip's Christmas dinner (4), Wopsle's Hamlet (31), or Wemmick's wedding (55) are among the great comic scenes in the novels. Its unforgettable characters include the lawyer Jaggers, with his intimidating forefinger, his habit of washing his hands, and his conversation by cross-examination; the divided Wemmick, at the office smiling mechanically with his "post-office" mouth as he advises Pip to secure "portable property," and at home in his castle, a loving son who refuses to talk business; and Miss Havisham, the bizarre recluse who lives in a ruined mansion, dressed in the tattered bridal gown that she has worn since she was left standing at the altar many years before. Neither the comic scenes nor the eccentric characters are independent of the story. They are absolutely organic to the plot and theme of the novel.

In *Copperfield*, David defines himself by establishing his difference from the other characters in his life. Although he sees himself as a victim of others' cruelty—of Murdstone's tyranny and neglect, for example—he is more industrious than Pip in pursuing a career and establishing a place for himself in society. David admires Steerforth's genteel indolence, but he does not adopt it as a way of life. When the tempest comes, he is able to view Steerforth's body on the beach with only a twinge of regret. He does not consciously connect his own undisciplined heart with Steerforth or link Steerforth's death to Dora's. Implicitly, the novel suggests that David survives and is successful because he is not Steerforth.

Pip's is a more interior story. His expectations make him passive, waiting to discover what others have in store for him. He adopts a life of idleness and is frequently made aware of his connections with Drummle, Orlick, and the convict. He is also more present in the narrative as an older and wiser man judging the mistakes of his past. The stormy night that brings Magwitch to Pip's door in the Temple forces him to acknowledge his connection with the convict, to abandon his illusions, and to reconstruct his life on totally different assumptions. David seems unconscious of the losses and rejections that have been necessary to secure his respectable position as a successful novelist; Pip is painfully aware of what he has left behind or lost, and *Great Expectations* has a pervasive mood of disillusionment. Joe articulates one of the central themes of the novel when he tells Pip that "life is made of ever so many partings welded together" (27). If David's story is truer to the outward facts of Dickens's life, Pip's may be more revealing of Dickens's inner autobiography.

The difference is apparent in the opening chapters of the two novels. *Copperfield* begins with an account of David's birth; *Expectations* opens with Pip's psychological "birth," when, at age seven or so, he comes to his "first most vivid and broad impression of the identity of things." The setting is bleak: an empty churchyard at dusk on a cold and gray winter day, a "wilderness," "overgrown with nettles," where the only distinguishing features are a gibbet and a beacon. A "small bundle of shivers," Pip is delivered into consciousness by an escaped convict who picks him up, turns him upside down, places him on a tombstone, fills him with fear and terror, and makes him promise to bring food and a file. Every detail in this short chapter simultaneously contributes to the realistic picture of the marsh country on a bleak December evening and to the primal story of Pip's psychological birth.

Appropriately this encounter takes place on Christmas Eve and together the first five chapters of the novel—the first three numbers published in the first three weeks of December 1860—form a kind of Christmas story, similar to the CHRISTMAS BOOKS that Dickens published in the mid 1840s. It includes Pip stealing the Christmas pie from the larder and delivering it to the convict, and a wonderfully humorous Christmas dinner at which the guilty child awaits exposure while the adults at the table lecture him about the ingratitude and natural viciousness of boys. This Christmas story culminates with the pursuit on the marshes, which ends with Pip exonerated by the captured convict, who confesses to stealing the pie himself. Joe states the Christmas theme of the story when he assures the convict "we don't know what you have done, but we wouldn't have you starved to death for it, poor miserable fellow-creature.—Would us, Pip?" (5)

This Christmas story and its message of empathy and compassion is pushed into the background as Pip goes on to tell the main story of his life, which begins with his introduction to Satis House (8). Although he is occasionally reminded of the odd and terrifying incident in his childhood—by the man who stirs his drink with a file (10), for example—Pip treats the Christmas story as if it were an unusual and bizarre event, part of the story of his life but unconnected with its plot.

Pip divides his life between external reality and interior wishes. The realities include his abuse by Mrs. Joe, who brings him up "by hand"; his apprenticeship to Gargery the blacksmith, and the likelihood of his becoming Joe's partner and successor; and his humiliating visits to the decaying Satis House, where he is taunted and abused. His wish is to be a gentleman and his unspoken scenario makes him Miss Havisham's heir, chosen to inherit her money and to marry Estella, her adopted daughter. By the time Jaggers announces Pip's "great expectations" (18), Pip has so internalized these wishes and elaborated their implications in his mind, that he is not surprised. He accepts his elevation to gentility as inevitable and deserved, and he rejects his humble beginnings, the forge, and Joe, and represses his memory of the traumatic Christmas on the marshes.

Pip's wishes so control his consciousness that he is unable to see the truth. Joe appears to him an illiterate country bumpkin and Pip condescendingly tells Biddy how he will educate Joe and "remove [him] into a higher sphere" (19). Only much later does Pip recognize Joe for the "gentle Christian man" (57) he is. While Pip is unable to see the depths in Joe's character, he cannot see the surfaces in Miss Havisham's either. In spite of the decay, ruin, and madness at Satis House, and the harsh teaching that makes Estella his tormentor, Pip wishes for the old woman's riches and to be selected, like Estella,

as her protégé. By rejecting Joe's true gentility and idealizing Miss Havisham's sham, Pip abandons himself to illusions.

This division indicates Pip's fractured sense of self. In Wemmick, Pip can observe someone who divides his life into public and private parts, surviving in both worlds by keeping them separate. Pip is unable to do so. He attempts to repress the dark and humble sides of his life, but Orlick and Drummle shadow him and criminals remind him of the "taint of prison and crime" (32) that seems to cling to him. When he rejects Joe and avoids the forge on his visits to his home town, Trabb's boy follows him in the streets and taunts him as a snob with the refrain, "Don't know yah" (30). In the novel's psychological parable, many of the characters in the story can be seen as fragments of Pip's self that he has failed to integrate into a full understanding of who he is.

Herbert Pocket acts as Pip's foil during his years in London. Although he is not Pip's equal in strength or expectations, he has a more realistic view of the world. He recognizes Miss Havisham's madness and Estella's cruelty, and he has no unwarranted hopes of inheriting Miss Havisham's money, even though he is related to her. His modest ambition is based on a realistic view of his situation and expectations.

The story reaches its crisis in chapter 39 when Pip, alone in his apartment on a stormy winter evening, is forced in a way to reenact the traumatic Christmas Eve on the marshes. Suddenly the story that seemed merely a curious and disconnected episode in his childhood becomes the defining text for his life. Pip's surprise mirrors that of the reader, who has also constructed Pip's rags-to-riches tale as a fairy-tale romance. The convict's revelation redirects the reader's expectations in this sensational turn of events in this SENSATION NOVEL. By making our reading of the story mirror Pip's self-understanding, Dickens engages our wishes and expectations. The romance that Pip has imagined his life to be is the romance that we wish for him—and for ourselves. But Magwitch's revelation strips Pip of his wishes and of the fairy-tale scenario he has constructed for himself. In the final stage of his life, Pip must redefine the relationships that he has taken for granted, such as his friendship with Herbert, his business relationship with Jaggers, and, especially, his relationships with Miss Havisham and Estella; he must also come to terms with those parts of himself that he has repressed and rejected—with Drummle, Orlick, Magwitch, and Joe.

In the novel's psychological theme, Pip's reconciliation with Joe is linked with his acceptance of Magwitch. They represent two related aspects of the father that have both contributed to Pip's identity. When he denied the criminal father, he also rejected Joe, the companion with whom he could share "larks." Pip's acceptance of Magwitch has several stages: At first, Pip hopes to get him out of the country; then he plans to go with him to the Continent; after the failed escape attempt, Pip accompanies him back to London, appears beside him in court, and attends him as he dies. Critics debate just how complete Pip's final acceptance of Magwitch is; his refusal to secure Magwitch's money seems to indicate that he still believes that he can be free of the taint of Newgate, and his final prayer at Magwitch's bedside, "O Lord, be merciful to him a sinner!" (56), can be read as the condescending words of a Pharisee. But Pip also publicly acknowledges his connection with Magwitch by holding the convict's hand as he is sentenced to hang (56). By such acts, Pip gives up his great expectations and can be reconciled with Joe. Though he is no longer young enough or innocent enough to share larks with the blacksmith, he can recognize Joe's true gentility and prepare to start life on his own in Egypt.

Jaggers, the novel's third father figure, embodies aspects of both Joe and Magwitch and represents a darkly realistic assessment of the human condition. As a criminal lawyer, he knows that the taint of Newgate is pervasive and that darkness and violence define the human psyche. Cynical, secretive, and pessimistic, he has abandoned whatever illusions, or, as he calls them, "poor dreams," that he may once have had. Nevertheless, he acts in ways to redress injustice and impose order. He "saves" Magwitch's daughter from abandonment, for example, and controls Molly's violent strength. Yet his cynical realism, his lack of expectations, makes him a discomfiting and morally ambiguous figure.

Pip's relationships with the women in his life are, if anything, even more complicated than those with the men. Just as Joe and Magwitch and Jaggers represent for Pip various aspects of the father, Mrs. Joe, Miss Havisham, Estella, and Biddy represent various aspects of the feminine. Mrs. Joe's harsh abuse may teach him resentment and cause him subconsciously to wish for the blow that Orlick inflicts on her, as Orlick suggests when he is taunting Pip in the sluice house (53). She also has a share in introducing Pip to Miss Havisham and encouraging him to think of the madwoman in white as a potential benefactress, thus prompting both his illusions and his masochism as Pip seeks the pain of his visits to Satis House as exquisite testimony to his desires. Pip may wish that Mrs. Joe and Miss Havisham suffer for the pain they cause him. He is indirectly implicated in both of their deaths and painfully burned while attempting to extinguish the fire that mortally injures Miss Havisham (49). Only Estella survives the suffering that Pip may subconsciously wish for her. At their final meeting, she acknowledges a changed understanding of him; "suffering has been stronger than all other teaching," she tells him, "and has taught me to understand what your heart used to be" (59).

Estella's statement appears in both versions of the final chapter that Dickens wrote for the novel and would seem to be central to his final thematic point. Dickens changed the original ending after Edward Bulwer LYTTON read the proofs and urged him to do so. In the original ending, which is included as an appendix in many editions of the novel, Pip returns to England after eight years in Egypt and while he is walking with little Pip, Joe and Biddy's child, on a street in London, he meets Estella, who has married a Shropshire doctor after her unhappy marriage to Drummle. She assumes that the child is Pip's and he does not tell her otherwise; then she confides that suffering has changed her. Pip concludes the original ending by remarking: "I was very glad afterwards to have had the interview; for, in her face and in her voice, and in her touch, she gave me the assurance, that suffering had been stronger than Miss Havisham's teaching, and had given her a heart to understand what my heart used to be." This tough ending has seemed to many readers more consistent with the tone of the novel than the revised ending. John Forster described it as "more consistent with the drift, as well as natural working out, of the tale."

Forster does not take note of the imagery in the second ending, however, that makes it, as George Bernard SHAW put it, "artistically much more congruous than the original." In many ways *Great Expectations* is a poetic novel, constructed around recurring images: the desolate landscape of the marshes; twilight; chains binding us to home, the past, and painful memories; fire; hands that manipulate and control; wishes as remote and distant as stars; the river linking past, present, and future. In the second ending, Dickens changed the meeting place from London to Satis House at twilight as evening mists are rising, mists that recall the mists as Pip left for London at the end of stage one, an allusion to the rising mists in Milton's *Paradise Lost* as Adam and Eve leave Eden. The imagery in the altered ending, then, seems to suggest a new beginning for Pip and Estella, and many readers consider it a "happy" ending, promising the union of the two lovers. But Dickens's words are more ambiguous than that. The imagery of rising mists and the broad expanse of light may suggest a new beginning, but Pip only concludes that at that moment "I saw no shadow of another parting from her." Even if Pip and Estella remain together, the ending would seem to suggest that the human condition, so aptly symbolized in the bleak graveyard of the opening chapter, will remain bleak in the ruined garden that was once Satis House. Shaw, who recognized that the atmosphere that Dickens added to the second ending improved it, nevertheless objected to the happy, marital implication. The perfect ending, he suggested, would consist of a sentence added to the revised ending: "Since that parting I have been able to think of her without the old unhappiness; but I have never tried to see her again, and I know I never shall." If, as the ambiguity in the final sentence allows, Pip and

Estella make a final parting as they leave Satis House, never again to see each other—or part from each other—then the second ending confirms the disillusioning note with which the novel began and is the novel's final statement of Joe's theme, that "life is made of ever so many partings welded together." In either case, the final sentence does not describe a historical fact but rather an expectation: "As the morning mists had risen long ago when I first left the forge, so, the evening mists were rising now, and in all the broad expanse of tranquil light they showed to me, I saw no shadow of another parting from her" (59). This concluding sentence confirms a central truth in the novel, that humans, in spite of all suffering, survive by expectation.

CRITICISM

The criticism of *Great Expectations* is voluminous. Richard Lettis and W. E. Morris have collected several standard essays on the novel in *Assessing Great Expectations* (1960), including Dorothy VAN GHENT's (1953) classic discussion of its modes of characterization and Julian Moynahan's "The Hero's Guilt: the Case of *Great Expectations*" (*Essays in Criticism*, 1960), a psychological analysis of Pip and his doubles. Janice Carlisle's recent edition of the novel (1995) includes essays by several prominent critics, among them Peter Brooks and Edward Said, representing psychoanalytic, deconstructive, feminist, and cultural criticism as ways to approach the novel. The autobiographical roots of the story are discussed by Ada NISBET in "The Autobiographical Matrix of *Great Expectations*" (*Victorian Newsletter*, 1959). Q. D. LEAVIS (1970) provides a close reading of the novel as an example of psychological realism. Many commentators write on Pip as narrator, including Robert B. Partlow, "The Moving I: A Study of Point of View in *Great Expectations*" (*College English*, 1961) and Robert E. GARIS (1965). Beth Herst (*The Dickens Hero: Selfhood and Alienation in the Dickens World*, 1990) discusses Pip as an example of the alienated hero in Dickens's later novels. Bert G. HORNBACK (1987) offers a useful introduction to the novel and the various critical issues it raises.

Great Expectations was first published as a serial in *All the Year Round*, and, consistent with the format of that magazine, was unillustrated. Some critics, most notably Q. D. Leavis (1970), have suggested that the realism of the novel made illustrations—especially caricatures in the manner of BROWNE—inappropriate. However, there have been many successfully illustrated later editions of the novel. The first American edition—the serial published in *Harper's Weekly*—was illustrated by John McLenan. Since it was printed from advance proofs sent from England and appeared a week before the English serial, this edition could be said to be the first edition of the novel. Dickens had Marcus STONE illustrate the LIBRARY EDITION of the novel in 1862. Es-

pecially noteworthy among later illustrators of the novel are F. W. Pailthorpe (1885), Harry FURNISS (1910), and Gordon Ross (1937).

ADAPTATIONS

Although several theatrical adaptations of *Great Expectations* appeared in the United States during the 1860s, the first British adaptation was W. S. Gilbert's *Great Expectations*, produced at the Court Theater in London in 1871. In this production and in some of the American versions, the role of Pip was played by an actress; Adah Isaacs Menken became famous touring the United States as Pip in her adaptation of the story. Noteworthy among later stage versions are those by Alec GUINNESS (1939), in which Guinness played Herbert Pocket, and Barbara FIELD (1983). An opera by Dominick Argento and John Olon-Scrymgeour, *Miss Havisham's Fire*, appeared in 1979.

Paramount produced a silent film based on the novel in 1917, and in 1921 a Danish company filmed an adaptation by Laurids Skands. Universal made a talking picture in 1934, an adaptation by Gladys Unger directed by Stuart Walker, in which the grotesque elements in the novel are given realistic treatment; Miss Havisham wears her wedding dress, for example, only on the annual anniversary of the day on which she was jilted. David LEAN's 1946 film for Cineguild, one of the great cinematic adaptations of Dickens, stars John MILLS (Pip), Bernard Miles (Joe Gargery), Martita Hunt (Miss Havisham), Jean Simmons (Estella), Francis L. SULLIVAN (Jaggers), Alec Guinness (Herbert Pocket), and Finlay Currie (Magwitch).

The BBC produced a 13-part serial in 1959, a 10-part serial written by Hugh Leonard in 1967, and a 12-part version by James Andrew Hall in 1981. NBC has produced two American television adaptations: a 1954 production with Roddy McDowall as Pip, and Sherman Yellen's 1974 adaptation, starring James Mason as Magwitch. A six-hour serial produced in Britain in 1989 featured Anthony Hopkins as Magwitch and Jean Simmons, who played the young Estella in Lean's 1947 film, as Miss Havisham.

Great International Walking Match   A 13-mile walking race in BOSTON refereed by Dickens during his reading tour in the United States in February 1868. The two contestants—Dickens's manager, George DOLBY, representing Great Britain, and the junior partner of his American publishing firm, James OSGOOD—traveled with Dickens on the tour and engaged in various frivolous competitions. A passionate walker himself, Dickens, who was suffering from a persistent cold, did not participate, but he laid out the course, nicknamed the contestants ("Man of Ross" and "The Boston Bantam"), gave a celebratory dinner for the participants and friends afterward, and wrote up the whole affair in his letters and journals.

Great Marlborough Street   The street in central London running from REGENT STREET to SOHO where the Taunton family live. *Boz*, "Excursion."

Great Queen Street   The street in HOLBORN where Dick Swiveller has bought a pair of shoes on credit, so he can take it only after the shops have closed. *Curiosity Shop* (8).

Great Russell Street   In BLOOMSBURY, site of Charles Kitterbell's house. *Boz*, "Christening."

Great St. Bernard Pass   The pass over the Alps between SWITZERLAND and ITALY where the hospice of St. Bernard is located. The Dorrits traveling from England meet the Gowans and Rigaud at the hospice when their journeys cross there. *Dorrit* (II:1).

Great White Horse, The   The "overgrown tavern" in IPSWICH where Pickwick and Peter Magnus stay when Pickwick surprises Miss Witherfield by by mistaking her room for his own. *Pickwick* (22). Dickens stayed at the inn when reporting on the election of 1835.

"Great Tasmania's Cargo, The"   The Traveller's indignant report of a visit to the LIVERPOOL Workhouse where the discharged soldiers from the *Great Tasmania* were recuperating from a voyage from India on which they had been starved and subjected to disease. Although Pangloss, the government official who accompanies him, takes no responsibility for the diseased and dying men, it is evident to the Traveller that the government has neglected its duty. *Uncommercial*, (8). Originally in ALL THE YEAR ROUND (April 21, 1860).

Great Winglebury   The fictitious town "exactly forty-two miles from Hyde Park Corner" where the great Winglebury duel takes place. *Boz*, "Winglebury." It was based on ROCHESTER.

"Great Winglebury Duel, The"   When Alexander Trott tries to avoid fighting a duel with Horace Hunter over the hand of Emily Brown by soliciting the influence of the mayor of Winglebury, he inadvertently becomes entangled with Lady Julia Manners and Lord Peter. The duel is averted, but Trott is taken for Lord Peter. When he is bundled off in a carriage with Lady Julia, the two decide to marry, thus allowing Emily Brown to marry Horace Hunter. *Boz*. Dickens dramatized the story as *The Strange Gentleman*.

Greaves, John (1899–1976)   Ardent Dickensian; Secretary of the Dickens Fellowship from 1948 to 1976;

performer of scenes and characters from Dickens's works. He was the author of numerous articles and books on various points of Dickensian lore, including *Dickens at Doughty Street* (1975), an account of Dickens's early years at the house that is now DICKENS HOUSE; *Who's Who in Dickens* (1972); and *The London of Charles Dickens* (1970, with Gwen Major), a centenary guide to Dickens sites in contemporary London.

Greedy   One of Mrs. Lemon's pupils. "Holiday Romance."

Greeley, Horace (1811–1872)   American journalist, Whig political leader, editor of the New York *Tribune*. He was one of the few American journalists who supported Dickens's views on COPYRIGHT during Dickens's first visit to AMERICA. He introduced Dickens at the press banquet at Delmonico's in New York during the reading tour in 1868.

Green (1)   Law writer and acquaintance of Nemo. *Bleak House* (11).

Green (2)   Police constable in WHITECHAPEL. *Reprinted*, "On Duty."

Green (1), Charles (1840–1898)   Artist and illustrator, particularly noted for his pen drawings. He provided the illustrations for *Curiosity Shop* in the English HOUSEHOLD EDITION (1876). He also did several watercolor paintings of subjects from Dickens and an oil painting of Pickwick addressing the Pickwick Club that is now in the SUZANNET COLLECTION at the DICKENS HOUSE. An example of his work appares in illustration 77 (*Old Curiosity Shop*).

Green (2), Charles (1785–1870)   Balloonist who made the first ascent in a gas balloon. Of his more than 500 ascents, many were made from VAUXHALL, including one in 1836 that covered 480 miles, ending in Nassau, Germany. *Boz*, "Vauxhall."

Green, Lucy   Childhood sweetheart of the Traveller whom he meets as Dr. Specks's wife when he returns to DULLBOROUGH. *Uncommercial* (12).

Green, Miss   Friend of the Kenwigs. *Nickleby* (14).

Green, Mrs.   Neighbor of Mrs. Nubbles who lodges at the cheesemonger's around the corner. *Curiosity Shop* (21).

Green, Paul (Poll)   One of the boys who worked with Dickens in the BLACKING WAREHOUSE, the son of a fireman who worked at the DRURY LANE Theater.

Green, Tom Alias taken by Joe WILLET in the army. *Rudge* (58).

Green Dragon Public house in Westminster where Robert Bolton holds forth. *Mudfog*, "Bolton."

Green Lanes The area in MARYLEBONE that is the meeting place of the Gordon rioters. *Rudge* (44).

Greene, Graham (1904–1991) British novelist and essayist. His classic essay "The Young Dickens" (1950; reprinted in *The Lost Childhood*, 1951) describes Dickens as a writer of "secret prose" that presents "a mind speaking to itself with no one there to listen" and characterizes the world of *Oliver Twist* as Manichaean, a world without God in which "we can believe in evil-doing, but goodness wilts into philanthropy."

Greenleaf The school near READING where Esther Summerson is educated under the tuteledge of the Misses Donny. *Bleak House* (3).

Greenwich The riverside town east of London where Bella Wilfer and her father run off for a private dinner at the SHIP INN (II:8), and where later Bella and John are married (IV:4). *Mutual Friend*. Dickens describes the annual fair held here on Easter Monday in *Boz*, "Greenwich Fair."

"Greenwich, Archbishop of" Head waiter at the restaurant in GREENWICH where Bella Wilfer and John Rokesmith have their wedding dinner. *Mutual Friend* (IV:4).

"Greenwich Fair" Account of the annual fair at GREENWICH held on Easter Monday, particularly of the itinerant theatrical performance and the temporary ballroom. Originally published in the *EVENING CHRONICLE* (April 16, 1835) as "Sketches of London No. 9." *Boz*.

Greenwood One-eyed tramp who has seen the ghost in the haunted house. His name is JOBY, but he answers to Greenwood. "Haunted House."

Greenwood, Miss Young woman who speculates on the marital prospects of the Censorious Young Gentleman. *Young Gentlemen*.

Gregory Foreman at MURDSTONE AND GRINBY's warehouse. *Copperfield* (11).

Gregsbury A member of Parliament, "a tough, burly, thick-headed gentleman, with a loud voice [and] a pompous manner," who offers Nicholas a position as his secretary, which Nicholas turns down. *Nickleby* (16).

Greta Bridge The town in YORKSHIRE near DOTHEBOYS HALL where Squeers and his party leave the coach from London. *Nickleby* (6, 7). Dickens visited the town with H. K. BROWNE in 1838 when collecting material for the novel.

Gretna Green This town in Scotland, just over the border north of Carlisle, has traditionally been the destination of runaway lovers, because Scottish law allowed an immediate marriage to be performed by an innkeeper or a blacksmith. The two couples in "The Great Winglebury Duel" both are married by the blacksmith in Gretna Green (*Boz*, "Winglebury"). Harry and Norah are on their way to Gretna Green when they stop at the Holly Tree Inn and meet Edwin and Emmeline, who are on a similar journey ("Holly Tree").

Grewgious, Hiram Lawyer of STAPLE INN and Rosa Bud's guardian. An "angular" man whom Nature seems to have left unfinished, Grewgious "still had some strange capacity in him of making on the whole an agreeable impression" (9). His gentle questioning leads Edwin to consider seriously whether he wants to marry Rosa (11). He cares for Rosa when she flees to London and finds a place for her to stay (21). With Crisparkle and Tartar, he is committed to clearing Neville Landless of suspicion (20). He also seems to suspect Jasper of the presumed murder. *Drood*.

Grey, The Misses Amelia and her **sister** are friends of Felix Nixon, the Domestic Young Gentleman. *Young Gentlemen*.

Gride, Arthur An old miser and moneylender who is involved with Ralph Nickleby in underhanded schemes, "a little old man of about seventy or seventy-five years of age, of a very lean figure, much bent and slightly twisted. . . . The whole expression of the face was concentrated in a wrinkled leer, compounded of cunning, lecherousness, slyness and avarice" (47). He has illegally obtained a document indicating that Madeline Bray will inherit £12,000 when she marries and, with Ralph's help, he gets Bray's consent to marry his daughter in return for paying off her father's debts (47). But Mr. Bray dies on the wedding day and Nicholas carries off the bride (54). Gride's housekeeper, Peg Sliderskew, steals the documents that will reveal his duplicity, but Gride is murdered by burglars before he can be called to account (65). *Nickleby*.

Gridley ("The Man from Shropshire") A frustrated victim of the Court of CHANCERY whose continuing and violent efforts to gain a hearing of his grievances lead to his repeated imprisonment for contempt of court. "A tall sallow man with a careworn head, . . . a combative look; and a chafing, irritable manner"

(15), he dies in George's Shooting Gallery while trying to escape arrest (27). *Bleak House.*

Griffin, Miss   Principal of the school where John the narrator had secretly played Haroun Alraschid as a child: "We knew Miss Griffin to be bereft of human sympathies." "Haunted House."

Griffith, D. W. (1875–1948)   American film director—best known for *The Birth of a Nation*—often considered the father of film. From Dickens, Griffith's favorite author and the source for many of his cinematic ideas, the filmmaker learned how to place romantic melodrama in a romantic setting, how to use detail to build narrative rhythm and tension, and, especially, how to use the cutback, or parallel cutting, to switch between narrative lines and thereby give rhythm and dynamism to the story.

Grig, Tom   Poor lamplighter whom Stargazer thinks is the person predicted by the stars to marry his niece. *Lamplighter.*

Griggins   He justifies his characterization as "the funny young gentleman" by his clowning at Mrs. Brown's party. *Young Gentlemen.*

Griggs   A family among the Nupkins's social circle in IPSWICH. *Pickwick* (25).

Grimaldi, Joseph (1778–1837)   Famous clown and star of PANTOMIME during Dickens's childhood years. Dickens edited his MEMOIRS (1838) for BENTLEY in 1838. Dickens was eight when he first saw a performance by Grimaldi, "in whose honor I am informed I clapped my hands with great precosity." Throughout his life Dickens was fond of imitating Grimaldi's clowning.

Grimble, Sir Thomas   Mrs. Nickleby unrealistically speculates that Smike may have dined with this wealthy YORKSHIRE landowner while he was a pupil at DOTHEBOYS HALL. *Nickleby* (35).

Grime, Professor   A member of the mechanical section of the Mudfog Association. *Mudfog.*

Grimmer, Miss   Miss Drowvey's partner in managing the school where Nettie Ashford is a pupil. "Holiday Romance."

Grimwig   Mr. Brownlow's cynical lawyer friend who is as suspicious of Oliver as Brownlow is trusting, "a stout old gentleman, rather lame in one leg, who was dressed in a blue coat, striped waistcoat, nankeen breeches and gaiters, and a broad-brimmed white hat" (14). He underscores his cynical predictions with the hyperbolic

promise to "eat my head," should they not come true. He appears to be delighted when his suspicions are confirmed by Oliver's disappearance with Brownlow's books and money (16), but underneath he is good-hearted and wishes the best for the boy. By the end of the story, he and Dr. Losberne have become close friends (53). *Twist.*

Grimwood, Eliza ("The Countess")   Murder victim whose case is investigated by Inspector Field. *Reprinted,* "Detective Anecdotes."

Grinder   A traveling showman with a small company consisting of himself, and a young gentleman and young lady on stilts. Little Nell and her grandfather meet them on the road. *Curiosity Shop* (17).

Grinders, The Charitable   The sponsors of the Cschool to which Mr. Dombey nominates Robin Toodle. *Dombey* (5).

Grip   Barnaby Rudge's pet raven: "He fluttered to the floor and went to Barnaby—not in a hop, or walk, or run, but in a pace like that of a very particular gentleman with exceedingly tight boots on, trying to walk over loose pebbles" (*Rudge*, 6). Dickens had two ravens as pets in the 1840s.

Gritts, Right Honorable Mr.   Member for Sordust whose administration of Tapenham's department is noteworthy for corrupt appointments. *Miscellaneous,* "Cheap Patriotism."

Groffin, Thomas   A druggist who is called for jury duty in the Pickwick and Bardell trial and who asks to be relieved for fear his errand boy may poison one of his customers while he is gone. *Pickwick* (34).

Groggles   Member of the Common Council who recommends a restaurant where Snoady can get turtle soup. There Snoady sees the resemblance between the turtle and his friend. *Miscellaneous,* "Lively Turtle."

Grogzwig, Baron of   The title of the Baron von KOËLDWETHOUT in the INTERPOLATED TALE told by the "merry-faced gentleman" on the London to YORK coach. *Nickleby* (6).

Grompus   The "ogre" who Mrs. Podsnap presents as a dancing partner to her daughter at her birthday party. *Mutual Friend* (I:11).

Groper, Colonel   A member of the group that welcomes Mr. Elijah Pogram. *Chuzzlewit* (34).

Grosvenor Square   A fashionable square in the West End of London where Mr. Tite Barnacle has his residence at 24 Mews Street, just off the square, where the houses are "abject hangers-on to a fashionable situation" (*Dorrit*, I:10). During the GORDON RIOTS Lord Rockingham's house on the square was barricaded against the rioters (*Rudge*, 67).

Grotesque, The   The use of exaggeration and fantasy in art and literature to make unfamiliar the familiar and to reveal the tensions and contradictions beneath the surface of things. It emerges in the obsessions of the comedy of humours, in the traditional figures of PANTOMIME on stage, in the exaggerations of visual CARICATURE that reduce humans to animals, or in romantic irony that makes the monstrous simultaneously repellent and attractive. Dickens's use of the grotesque is most apparent in his animation of the material world and his reification of the human. Dorothy VAN GHENT (1950) developed the classic description of this aspect of Dickens's work, in which "the course of things demonically possessed is to imitate the human, while the course of human possession is to imitate the inhuman." Michael Hollington (*Dickens and the Grotesque*, 1984) explores the subject in detail.

Groves, James (Jem)   Landlord of the VALIANT SOLDIER, where Nell's grandfather meets the gamblers who win his money and persuade him to rob Mrs. Jarley. *Curiosity Shop* (29, 30, 73).

Growlery, The   John Jarndyce's den at Bleak House to which he escapes when the "east wind" has blown him out of humor. *Bleak House*.

Grub, Gabriel   The "ill-conditioned cross-grained surly" sexton who is the subject of Wardle's Christmas story in *Pickwick* (29).

Grubble, W.   Landlord of the Dedlock Arms. *Bleak House* (37).

Grudden, Mrs.   Member of the Crummles theatrical company who handles many of the backstage chores and occasional bit parts. *Nickleby* (23–5, 30, 35, 48).

Grueby, John   Lord George Gordon's loyal servant, "self-possessed, hard-headed, imperturbable" (35), who tries to save Gordon from his followers and his fanaticism. He helps Haredale escape the wrath of the mob (43). *Rudge*.

"Gruff and Glum"   An old pensioner with wooden legs who is present at the marriage of Bella Wilfer and John Rokesmith (IV:4). *Mutual Friend*.

"GruffandGrim"   Herbert Pocket's nickname for Old Bill Barley. (See Clara BARLEY). *Expectations*.

Gruff and Tackleton   The firm of toymakers that employs Caleb Plummer. *Cricket*.

Grummer, Daniel   Constable at IPSWICH, "an elderly gentleman in top boots, who had been a peace officer, man and boy, for half a century at least," who arrests Pickwick for Magistrate Nupkins. *Pickwick* (24–25).

Grummidge, Dr.   Member of the medical section of the Mudfog Association. *Mudfog*.

Grundy   One of the law clerks who Pickwick meets at the MAGPIE AND STUMP. *Pickwick* (20).

Guard, The   Attendant on the train that leaves Young Jackson at Mugby Junction. *Mugby* (1).

Gubbins   Ex-churchwarden who presents Our Curate with an inkstand as a token of the parish's esteem. *Boz*, "Our Parish."

Guild of Literature and Art, The   Scheme developed in 1850–51 by Dickens and Edward Bulwer LYTTON to create an endowment for the support of indigent and deserving artists and writers. Performances by Dickens's theatrical company of a play by Lytton were to provide initial funding for the project. Lytton also donated some land on his estate for a small artists colony to be established. Dickens served as chairman of the endowment for several years and gave considerable time to the project, but it failed to generate widespread and substantial support.

Guildford   Near this town in Surrey is the site of Dora's birthday picnic (*Copperfield*, 33). Nicholas first meets Crummles as he is traveling from Guildford back to London (*Nickleby*, 22).

Guildhall   Seat of civic government on Gresham Street in the CITY of London where the statues of GOG AND MAGOG are housed in the great hall. The Court of Common Pleas was held here until 1873. The trial of Bardell vs. Pickwick takes place here. *Pickwick* (34).

Guinness, Sir Alec (1914–)   British actor and playwright. His adaptation of *Great Expectations* (1939) for the stage was widely performed in the 1940s. Guinness played Herbert Pocket in the initial production, a role he also performed in David LEAN's masterful film adaptation of the novel (1946). His controversial performance as Fagin in Lean's *Oliver Twist* (1948), which exaggerated stereotypical Jewish traits in the character, was significantly edited in early American prints of the film. Guinness has also played Marley in the musical film

Scrooge (1970) and William Dorrit in the film of *Little Dorrit* (1988).

Gulpidge, Mr. and Mrs.   Dinner guests of the Waterbrooks. Mr. Gulpidge has something to do with the law business of the Bank. *Copperfield* (25).

Gummidge, Mrs.   Widow of Daniel Peggotty's fishing partner, who serves as his housekeeper. She suffers from fits of depression and describes herself as "a lone lorn creetur" (3). She remains at Daniel's house when he goes off in search of Em'ly (32); in the end, her spirits lifted, she immigrates with the Peggottys to AUSTRALIA (57). *Copperfield*.

Gunter   One of the guests at Bob Sawyer's bachelor party, "a gentleman in a shirt emblazoned with pink anchors." *Pickwick* (32).

Guppy, William   Clerk for Kenge and Carboy, a brash and vulgar young man who proposes to Esther Summerson and is refused (9). He investigates Esther's identity and learns Lady Dedlock's secret (29), but Krook's surprising death destroys the corroborating documents that he has arranged to buy (32). After Esther's illness, he formally withdraws his proposal (38), only to renew it once again (64). When he is again refused, Guppy's protective and doting mother, **Mrs. Guppy**, indignantly rises to her son's defense (64). *Bleak House*.

Gurney, Jeremiah (1812–1886)   American portrait photographer for the New York firm of J. Gurney and Son, which secured exclusive rights to photograph Dickens on his American reading tour in 1868. Dickens was ill at the time the pictures were taken, and the photographs reveal his age and exhaustion.

Gusher   One of Mrs. Pardiggle's missionary friends, "a flabby gentleman, with a moist surface, and eyes so much too small for his moon of a face, that they seemed to have been originally made for somebody else." *Bleak House* (15).

Guster   Mrs. Snagsby's maid, a young woman from the workhouse who is subject to fits. *Bleak House*.

Guy's Hospital   A teaching hospital in SOUTHWARK where Bob Sawyer is a medical student (*Pickwick*, 30) and where Mrs. Gamp's husband dies (*Chuzzlewit*, 19).

Gwynn, Miss   The writing and ciphering teacher at Westgate House, the school in BURY ST. EDMUNDS where Pickwick is caught after hours hiding in the courtyard. *Pickwick* (16).

H

"H. W." Article by Dickens and Henry MORLEY for *HOUSEHOLD WORDS* (April 16, 1853) describing the process by which the magazine is produced, from choosing the contents, to preparing the plates and running the steam presses, to distributing it to news dealers. *Stone.*

"Hackney-coach Stands" Originally published as "Sketches of London No. 1" in the *EVENING CHRONICLE* (January 31, 1835). This sketch describes the hackney coach, "a remnant of past gentility . . . progressing lower and lower in the scale of four-wheeled degradation, until at last it comes to—a *stand!" Boz.*

Haggage Drunken doctor in the MARSHALSEA PRISON who delivers Amy Dorrit. *Dorrit* (I:6, 7).

Half Moon and Seven Stars, The An obscure alehouse in Pecksniff's village where Anthony, Jonas, Tigg, and Slyme stay. *Chuzzlewit* (4).

Halifax Dickens visited this capitol city of Nova Scotia on his American tour in 1841. He describes his "most pleasant impression" of the town and its legislative assembly in *American Notes* (2).

Hall, William (1801–1847) Partner in the publishing firm of CHAPMAN & HALL. The business half of the firm with a head for numbers, Hall sold Dickens the copy of the *MONTHLY MAGAZINE* that contained his first published work. Dickens remembered him and the excitement of that moment when he negotiated the terms for *Pickwick.* In 1843 Hall annoyed Dickens by tactlessly suggesting that the poor sales of *Chuzzlewit* might force the firm to reduce the author's payments, prompting Dickens to change publishers to BRADBURY & EVANS.

Halliday, Andrew (1830–1877) Scottish playwright who adapted several of Dickens's novels for the stage, including *Nicholas Nickleby* (1875); *Nell, or; The Old Curiosity Shop* (1871); *Heart's Delight* (*Dombey*, 1873); and *Little Em'ly* (*Copperfield*, 1869), an adaptation praised by Dickens.

Ham House This baroque mansion in Surrey across the Thames from TWICKENHAM is the site of the duel between Sir Mulberry Hawk and Lord Frederick Verisopht that leaves the latter dead. *Nickleby* (50).

"Hamlet's Aunt" The name given by Copperfield to Mrs. Henry SPIKER. *Copperfield* (25).

Hammersmith The Thames-side town southwest of London where the Misses Crumpton operate Minerva House, a "finishing establishment for young ladies" (*Boz,* "Sentiment"), and where the Matthew Pocket family resides (*Expectations,* 21). Oliver passes through Hammersmith on his way to the CHERTSEY robbery (*Twist,* 21).

Hammond, W. J. (1799–1848) Manager and chief comedian at the Strand Theatre in London, famous for his portrayal of Sam Weller in MONCRIEFF's adaptation of *Pickwick.* He toured England in the late 1830s playing his famous Weller character in productions that were only very loosely derived from Dickens.

Hampstead Village north of London. Dickens had lodgings here in 1832. After Mary HOGARTH's death, Dickens and his wife rented a cottage at Collins's Farm (now Wylde's Farm) on Hampstead Heath. He and John FORSTER often walked from DOUGHTY STREET to Jack Straw's Castle, an inn near the Heath.

Hampstead is mentioned frequently in the novels. Pickwick's fame derived in part from his paper on "The Source of the Hampstead Ponds" (*Pickwick,* 1). Mrs. Bardell is arrested at the SPANIARDS Inn by the Heath as she has tea with some friends (*Pickwick,* 46). Bill Sikes crosses the Heath on his way out of London after killing Nancy (*Twist,* 48). Dick Swiveller settles in Hampstead with the Marchioness (*Curiosity Shop,* 73). The Gordon rioters make an abortive expedition to destroy Caen Wood (now Kenwood) House (*Rudge,* 66). David Copperfield walks out to Hampstead for breakfast (*Copperfield,* 35). Miss Griffin's school is located near the Hampstead Ponds (*Haunted House*).

Hampton Mortimer Lightwood and Eugene Wrayburn have a cottage by the THAMES RIVER in this village (*Mutual Friend,* I:12). Twist passes through (21); Hawk and Verisopht attend the Hampton races (*Nickleby,* 50).

Hampton Court Palace This royal palace, presented to Henry VIII by Cardinal Wolsey in 1526, was, in the 19th century, a residence for royal pensioners. Mrs. Gowan has apartments here on the strength of her husband's diplomatic post. *Dorrit* (I:17, 26).

Hancock and Floby, Messrs.   Owners of the dry-goods store where Putnam Smif was a clerk. *Chuzzlewit* (22).

"Handel"   Herbert Pocket's nickname for PIP, an allusion to George Frideric Handel's "Harmonious Blacksmith" (1718); "We are so Harmonious, and you have been a Blacksmith, would you mind Handel for a familiar name?" *Expectations* (22).

Handford, Julius   The pseudonym used by John Harmon when he goes to view the body believed to be his own own (I:3). *Mutual Friend*.

Hanging-Sword Alley   This narrow alley off WHITEFRIARS Street in east London is the unsavory neighborhood where Jerry Cruncher lives (*Two Cities*, II:1). George Rouncewell notes its military significance as he passes by (*Bleak House*, 27).

Hannah   Miss La Creevy's servant girl "with an uncommonly dirty face." *Nickleby* (3).

Hanover Square   Off REGENT STREET in Mayfair, the site of the Hanover Square Rooms where Dickens's AMATEUR THEATRICAL company gave several performances of LYTTON's *Not so Bad as We Seem* in 1851 and where he later gave PUBLIC READINGS.

Hard Times, for these times   Dickens's 10th novel, serialized in *HOUSEHOLD WORDS* (April 1–August 12, 1854), unillustrated. Published in one volume by BRADBURY & EVANS, 1854. This controversial book, the shortest of Dickens's novels, takes up the issues of industrialism and education and offers a moral fable challenging some of the dominant ideologies of the Victorian era.

SYNOPSIS

I. Book the First. Sowing.

Part 1 (April 1, 1854)
(I:1) Mr. Gradgrind instructs schoolmaster M'Choakumchild that the one thing needful in life is Facts. (I:2) Sissy Jupe is the only "little vessel" in Gradgrind's school that is not filled with facts. Bitzer, the star pupil, shows off his ability to recite all the physical characteristics of a horse. These children are "regulated and governed" by fact; they are never to imagine. M'Choakumchild, a factory-produced teacher, will fill them with facts and kill the robber fancy lurking within. (I:3) On his way home to Stone Lodge, Thomas Gradgrind passes the circus and discovers his children Tom and Louisa peeping into the tent. He reprimands them by repeating, "What would Mr. Bounderby say?"

Part 2 (April 8, 1854)
(I:4) Banker and manufacturer, Mr. Bounderby, the "Bully of Humility," is bullying Mrs. Gradgrind, a

Portrait of Gradgrind by Harry Furniss (1910).

woman of surpassing feebleness, with the story of his neglected and abused childhood. Bounderby ascribes Louisa and Tom's deliquency to the influence of Sissy Jupe, a circus performer's daughter. He and Gradgrind decide to ask Signor Jupe to persuade his daughter to refrain from encouraging the idle curiosity of the Gradgrind children. As they leave to find Jupe, Bounderby kisses Lousia good-bye and she tries to rub off the mark of the kiss. (I:5) Coketown, a red-brick town founded upon fact, is totally utilitarian and functional—blackened by the "serpent-like" smoke from factory chimneys. On the way to Pod's End, Gradgrind and Bounderby meet Sissy, who is being chased through the streets by Bitzer. They halt the pursuit and go on with the girl.

Part 3 (April 15, 1854)
(I:6) But when they get to the Pegasus's Arms, Jupe is not there. The circus people tell them that Jupe has

probably "cut," run off because his talents were slipping, and deserted both the circus and his daughter. Bounderby berates Jupe's irresponsibility. Gradgrind offers to take Sissy into his home if she will promise to cut herself off from the circus. Sissy tearfully agrees. As they leave, Sleary, the circus manager, counters Gradgrind's harsh judgment of the circus by reminding him that "People must be amuthed," and asking him to "make the betht of uth, not the wurtht."

Part 4 (April 22, 1854)
(I:7) Mrs. Sparsit, grandniece to Lady Scadgers, acts as Bounderby's housekeeper. He exploits her privileged background as a contrast to his story of deprivation. She tolerates, but inwardly resents, this vulgar exploitation. Sissy is told to pay proper deference to Mrs. Sparsit, to forget her own past and the circus, and to begin her life anew as a servant to Mrs. Gradgrind. (I:8) The keynote of Gradgrind's system is "never wonder." But Tom and Louisa sit before the fire and wonder about the "something missing" in their lives and about the future. Tom wants to leave home, to join Bounderby's bank, where he plans to manage Bounderby by playing on the banker's affection for his sister. When Mrs. Gradgrind discovers the two children "wondering," she reprimands them for disobeying their father.

Part 5 (April 29, 1854)
(I:9) Sissy does not do well in school. She cannot take facts seriously and cannot remember them. Given statistical problems, she ignores the percentages and attends only to individuals who are suffering, no matter how small their numbers. She tells Louisa of her father, a clown, and of the stories she read to him from the *Arabian Nights*. She continues to hope for his return.

(I:10) After work, Stephen Blackpool, a weaver in Bounderby's mill, walks home with Rachael, the woman he loves, telling her of his unhappiness and of his belief that life is a muddle. When he gets to his own apartment, he discovers that his wife of many years has returned and is lying drunk on his doorstep.

Part 6 (May 6, 1854)
(I:11) Stephen seeks Bounderby's advice about getting a divorce. Bounderby warns him not to be a malcontent and tells him that he married for better or worse and that there is no way that he, a poor man, can dissolve the bond. Stephen's response, "Tis a muddle," shocks Mrs. Sparsit and prompts Bounderby to assert, "I see traces of turtle soup, and venison, and gold spoon in this." (I:12) Outside Bounderby's house, Stephen meets an old woman who tells him that she comes to town once a year to look at Bounderby. Later, as he works at his loom, Stephen sees the old woman in the street, looking at the factory building with admiration.

Part 7 (May 13, 1854)
(I:13) At home, Stephen finds Rachael attending his ailing wife. He sleeps fitfully in a chair, dreaming that he is on stage and that everyone in the world shuns him. Then, half awake, he sees his wife get up from the bed

and take a bottle of poison from the table. He is powerless to stop her, inwardly wishing to be free of her. Just as she is about to drink it, Rachael awakens and takes the bottle away from her. As Rachael leaves, Stephen blesses her as "an angel" who "changest me from bad to good."

(I:14) Some years later, Mr. Gradgrind has become a member of Parliament, while Sissy has been dismissed from school, liked by Gradgrind in spite of her academic failings. Tom works in Bounderby's bank. When her father makes an appointment to talk with Louisa about marriage, Tom urges her to remember him. Louisa looks into the "factory" of her self and finds it mute, noiseless, and secret.

Part 8 (May 20, 1854)
(I:15) Gradgrind tells Louisa that Bounderby has proposed to marry her. When she asks if she is expected to love Bounderby, Gradgrind advises her just to look at the facts: she is 20, Bounderby is 50. There is a disparity in their ages, but not in their means or positions. In sum, he says, Bounderby has asked her to marry him. The question now is whether she will. Louisa observes the smoke pouring from the Coketown chimneys, wonders about the shortness of her life, and then accepts the proposal. "Let it be so," she says, "what does it matter?" Sissy looks at Louisa in wonder, in pity, in sorrow. Mrs. Gradgrind worries about what she will call her son-in-law. (I:16) When Bounderby announces his intentions to Mrs. Sparsit, she responds with compassion, simultaneously wishing him happiness and treating him as "a Victim." She accepts his offer of a position at the bank. At the wedding Bounderby speaks of Louisa as deserving of him and Tom bids her good-bye as "a game girl" and a "first-rate sister."

Book the Second. Reaping.

Part 9 (May 27, 1854)
(II:1) On a hot summer day, Mrs. Sparsit and Bitzer, now the bank's light porter, look out of her window above the bank and see a stranger with an "air of exhaustion." He brings an introduction to the Bounderbys from Mr. Gradgrind and inquires if Mrs. Bounderby is quite the formidable philosopher her father makes her out to be.

Part 10 (June 3, 1854)
(II:2) Bored with serving in the Dragoons and the foreign service, traveling to Jerusalem, and yachting about the world, the stranger, James Harthouse, has decided to go in for hard fact. He flatters Bounderby by agreeing with him on the necessity of smoke, the pleasantness of the work in the mills, and the unreasonable demands of the Hands. But he is puzzled and challenged by the cold, unrevealing face of Louisa. He believes any set of ideas as good as any other; she seems to believe in nothing. Only when Tom arrives does Harthouse discover something that will "move that face." So he cultivates "the whelp" and secures him as a guide back to his hotel. (II:3)

Harthouse plies Tom with cigars and liquor and pumps him for the truth about his sister, who married Bounderby for Tom's sake. He also asks about Mrs Sparsit, who had her cap set for Bounderby herself, and, inadvertently, about Tom himself. The whelp leaves in a fog, not remembering what he has revealed.

Part 11 (June 10, 1854)
(II:4) Slackbridge, the union organizer, urges the working men of Coketown to shun Blackpool as a traitor for refusing to join them. Stephen defends himself before the men, saying that he remains their friend and will work by himself among them, but the loneliness of being shunned is difficult, for Stephen is afraid even to contact Rachael. After four lonely days, Bitzer informs Stephen that Bounderby wishes to see him. (II:5) Bounderby asks him why he refuses to join the union, but Stephen declines to reveal his reason. He defends the men against Bounderby's charges that they are rebellious, and, taking courage from looking at Louisa's face, he describes "the muddle" and condemns the rich who blame everything on the workingmen. By the end of the interview, Bounderby is so angry that he fires Stephen.

Part 12 (June 17, 1854)
(II:6) In the street, Stephen meets Rachael and the old lady whom he had met once before outside Bounderby's house. Stephen tells Rachael that he has been fired and that he plans to leave Coketown to search for work. She knows it was because of his promise to her not to join the union. They go to Stephen's home, where Mrs. Pegler, the old woman, questions Stephen about Bounderby's wife. Their tea is interrupted by Louisa and Tom. Louisa offers Stephen help for his journey. Tom engages him to wait outside the bank on the evenings before he sets out, telling him that he hopes he can do something for him and that Bitzer will bring a message. But no message comes. After the third night, Stephen sets out on his journey.

Part 13 (June 24, 1854)
(II:7) Harthouse gains the trust of Gradgrind and Bounderby and takes an increasing interest in Mrs. Bounderby. He visits her at the country house that Bounderby has acquired by repossession. There he learns that she has given Tom a good deal of money to cover his gambling debts, but Tom is short with her because she has refused him more money. In a private interview with Tom, Harthouse offers to help him with his debts and urges him to be nicer to his sister. That evening, Tom is indeed much nicer to her. Harthouse observes the gratitude in her face.

Part 14 (July 1, 1854)
(II:8) During the night the bank is robbed by someone using a forged key. Bitzer and Mrs. Sparsit had seen Blackpool loitering outside the bank, and the disgruntled hand is suspected. After this "explosion," Mrs. Sparsit comes to stay at the Bounderby country house; she pays particular attention to Bounderby, playing cards with him and fixing his favorite drinks. Louisa is shocked

by the news of the robbery. When she asks Tom if he has anything to tell her, she gets only a sullen and resentful reply.

Part 15 (July 8, 1854)
(II:9) Mrs. Sparsit takes over her old role as Bounderby's housekeeper. Louisa is indifferent, but Mrs. Sparsit's involvement with Bounderby frees Louisa to spend more time with Harthouse. When Louisa is called back from the country to the bedside of her gravely ill mother, Mrs. Gradgrind tries to tell her daughter of something that has been missing from her life, but she dies without communicating her message. (II:10) Mrs. Sparsit imagines a staircase and, as she contemplates this mental image, she watches Louisa descending. Bounderby informs them that Blackpool and an old woman are the prime suspects in the robbery. That evening Mrs Sparsit watches Harthouse and Louisa talking in the garden. They are talking about Blackpool: Harthouse found him "dreary," but Louisa believed in him.

Part 16 (July 15, 1854)
(II:11) Mrs. Sparsit continues to watch Louisa's descent. When she learns that Harthouse, who is away hunting in Yorkshire, will return while Bounderby is away on business, she hastens to the country house, and, hiding in the heavy shubbery, she spies on the couple as Harthouse presses his suit. Louisa resists, but appears finally to give in. Mrs. Sparsit cannot overhear the arrangements, however, for a thunderstorm drowns out their words. In the rain, she follows Louisa to the train, but she loses track of her when they arrive in Coketown. (II:12) Louisa goes to her father, tells him that his training has made her empty and confused, that she has left a husband she despises, that Harthouse has proposed to elope with her, and that she has not disgraced her father. She tells him that his philosophy has brought her to this pass and asks him to save her. Then she collapses at his feet.

Book the Third. Garnering.

Part 17 (July 22, 1854)
(III:1) Shaken by his daughter's revelations, Gradgrind tells Louisa the next morning that he has neglected the wisdom of the heart for the wisdom of the head. Sissy, who has brought such understanding into the Gradgrind household, offers to help Louisa. (III:2) That evening, Sissy goes to Harthouse and tells him that he should forget Louisa and leave Coketown. Harthouse is struck by how "absurd" and "ridiculous" he will appear to be just walking away from Coketown, but he is "vanquished" by Sissy and decamps for Egypt and the pyramids.

Part 18 (July 29, 1854)
(III:3) When Bounderby appears at Stone Lodge with Mrs. Sparsit to inform Gradgrind that Louisa has run off, he learns that she is in her father's house. Although Gradgrind tells Bounderby that Louisa is suffering from

the education he gave her and needs time with Sissy to recuperate, Bounderby demands that she return to his house by noon the next day. When she doesn't appear, he gets rid of her things and resumes his bachelor life. (III:4) Bounderby pursues his investigation into the bank robbery. Rachael assures him that Stephen will return to clear his name; she sends a letter to Stephen telling of the accusations against him, but he does not return.

Part 19 (August 5, 1854)
(III:5) Sissy assures Rachael that the people of Stone Lodge still believe in Stephen. The two women plan to walk out in the countryside to search for him on the route he would take back to Coketown. Meanwhile, Mrs. Sparsit has apprehended the old lady, who is suspected along with Stephen. The woman turns out to be Bounderby's mother, Mrs. Pegler. She humiliates her son by giving a very different account of his childhood than the story he tells.

(III:6) In the country, Sissy and Rachael find Stephen's hat lying on the ground near the entrance to an abandoned mine—the Old Hell Shaft. With help, they find Stephen at the bottom, injured but still alive. Stephen tells of hurrying to return to Coketown, cutting across open country at night, and falling into the pit. He also tells of a star he has watched from the bottom of the pit and of his wish that all men might live together peacefully. He tells Gradgrind of Tom's request that he wait outside the bank. Then he dies.

Part 20 (August 12, 1854)
(III:7) Tom disappears from the group gathered around the Old Hell Shaft. Gradgrind realizes his son's guilt and Sissy tells him that she directed Tom to go to Sleary's circus. There they find Tom dressed as a clown taking part in the show. He blames Louisa for his crime, for she did not give him the money he needed, and he excuses himself by citing figures to prove his dishonesty was predictable. They prepare to send him abroad, but just as he is about to leave, Bitzer arrives to arrest him. (III:8) Gradgrind tries to appeal to Bitzer's good nature, which is lacking, and to his self-interest, but Bitzer thinks he can take over Tom's position at the bank only if he apprehends him. Finally Sleary distracts Bitzer and Tom is spirited away. Sleary explains the circus philosophy to Gradgrind: Sissy's faith that her father will return is a sign, he says, that there is love in the world and "not all [is] self interest after all." His other message to Gradgrind is that "People mutht be amuthed. They can't be alwayth a-learning, nor yet they can't be alwayth a-working." Thus Sleary challenges the two central propositions of Gradgrind's shattered worldview.

(III:9) Bounderby, outraged by the Mrs. Pegler episode, dismisses Mrs. Sparsit and sends her off to live with her relation, Lady Scadgers. The future shows Bitzer rising in business; Bounderby dying of a fit in the street; Gradgrind adopting the philosophy of Faith, Hope, and Charity and exonerating Blackpool; Tom dying penitent abroad; Sissy marrying and raising a loving family; and Louisa, remaining unmarried, loving Sissy and her children (III:9).

COMMENTARY

Dickens wrote *Hard Times* for *Household Words*, and the novel seems almost tailored to articulate the aims of the magazine, stated in its first issue: "No realities, will give a harsh tone to our *Household Words*. . . . We would tenderly cherish that light of Fancy which is inherent in the human breast; which, according to its nurture, burns with an inspiring flame, or sinks into a sullen glare, but which (or woe betide that day!) can never be extinguished."

Yet Dickens had difficulty with the short installments called for in the weekly magazine serial, and as he worked on the novel, he thought of it in terms of monthly parts. Compared to the other monthly serials, however, *Hard Times* is a very short novel. Its five monthly numbers (two for "Sowing", two for "Reaping", and one for "Garnering") make it only a quarter of the standard length. Even when compared with the other weekly serials, such as *A Tale of Two Cities* or *Great Expectations*, *Hard Times* is a short novel. Its spare and unembellished prose, its simple fable, and its overt didacticism reinforce the impression that the shortest of Dickens' novels is also the simplest. So uncharacteristic is it that many Dickensians have considered it insignificant; F. G. KITTON (1900), for example, placed it along with the magazine articles, travel books, and CHRISTMAS BOOKS among Dickens's "minor writings."

The novel's controversial subject matter has put off many readers like Macaulay, who dismissed it as "sullen socialism," but *Hard Times* has also had defenders; RUSKIN considered it the most important of Dickens's novels and its view of industrialism "the right one, grossly and sharply told." This Victorian controversy, which pitted the novel's detractors, who decried its lack of Dickensian humor, against those who praised its social insights, has continued to the present, supercharged in 1948 by what may be the single most controversial essay on Dickens written in the 20th century, F. R. LEAVIS's "Note" on *Hard Times* in *The Great Tradition*. After excluding Dickens from the great tradition of the English novel as an "entertainer" in whose works "the adult mind doesn't as a rule find . . . a challenge to an unusual and sustained seriousness," Leavis added an appendix describing *Hard Times* as a "masterpiece" and an exception to this rule. He praised the tight construction of the novel as a "moral fable," its systematic critique of UTILITARIANISM, and its poetic expression. His eccentric evaluation—reprinted in slightly revised form in 1970 in *Dickens the Novelist*—aroused many Dickensians to respond. Many made the case for the greatness of the other novels, often at the expense of *Hard Times*, which was frequently described as misinformed on the issues, humorless, and lacking convincing and engaging characters.

Certainly Dickens's intent in the novel was serious. When he dedicated it to CARLYLE, he told him "I know it contains nothing in which you do not think with me." The critique of industrialism and utilitarianism in the novel is as Carlylean as the history of the French Revolution in *Two Cities*. Carlyle described Victorian times as diseased, hardened by a belief in "mechanism" and "machinery," and he attacked the economic philosophers of the day for using an analytic method that reduced everything to numbers and statistics. The utilitarians, he asserted, did not consider individuals and they denied the truths of intuition and spirit.

Gradgrind represents the utilitarians in the novel. Appropriately he schools his own children to become creatures of fact like himself. He does not see these children as living creatures filled with wonder, but rather as empty vessels to be stuffed with facts. The contrast between the living, organic world that he stifles and the deadly realm of fact that drains life from the children is presented in the contrast between Sissy Jupe and Bitzer as they are caught in a shaft of sunlight entering the schoolroom. Sissy "was so dark-eyed and dark-haired, that she seemed to receive a deeper and more lustrous colour from the sun, when it shone upon her, the boy was so light-eyed and light-haired that the self-same rays appeared to draw out of him what little colour he possessed. . . . His skin was so unwholesomely deficient in the natural tinge, that he looked as though, if he were cut, he would bleed white" (I:2). This contrast between the natural and unnatural is fundamental to Dickens's analysis in the novel. By reducing everything to material fact, Utilitarianism was unnatural and destructive. It fragmented the world into unnatural pieces—like the "facts" in Bitzer's definition of a horse—and failed to see anything whole as it naturally appeared in the world.

Dickens is sometimes criticized for creating an unrecognizable caricature of Utilitarianism, the rational-empiricist philosophy of Jeremy Bentham (1748–1832), James Mill (1773–1836), and Mill's son, the great political philosopher John Stuart Mill (1806–73). Bentham based his philosophy on a binary opposition between sensations of pleasure and pain, and on the principle of maximizing pleasure and minimizing pain. The philosophy's quantifiable social goal was to achieve the greatest happiness of the greatest number of people. Bentham and his followers were particularly interested in principles of social organization that facilitated progress toward this goal. While Gradgrind's philosophy may not be intellectually rigorous, it is grounded in a binary opposition between fact and fancy, and it constructs "reality" from analytically dervied pieces.

Gradgrind's educational program has often been compared to the one James Mill developed for his son, a rigorous discipline in mathematics, logic, and language, instilled from early childhood, but Gradgrind's system with its commitment to the "—ologies" may be more scientific than the one Mill devised. Both schemes, however, were unsuccessful. In his *Autobiography* John Stuart Mill described a nervous breakdown he suffered in his 20s when he realized that he really did not care about the social and rational principles he had been taught; he

overcame the depression only when he allowed the truths of feeling, especially as expressed in Wordsworth's poetry, to counter the absolute rationalism of his upbringing. In the novel, Louisa, Tom, and Bitzer also discover that their EDUCATION in Gradgrind's school, by denying feeling and imagination, has not prepared them to live fulfilling lives.

Louisa has no resources to enable her to respond to Bounderby's proposal of marriage. When she asks her father's advice, he can only suggest that she treat the issue "simply as one of Tangible Fact," and then he reduces the fact to numbers, to the 20-year difference in their ages, which he then evaluates statistically. Although Louisa has a vague sense that something more should be at issue, she does not know what it might be and she acquiesces to the marriage, saying, "What does it matter?" (II:15) Tom, who has learned the principle of self-interest, but who has no empathy for anyone but himself, robs Bounderby's bank and frames Blackpool. Bitzer, the model analyst who reduces the world to bits, also evaluates everything in terms of self-interest. When Gradgrind tries to bribe him to allow Tom to escape arrest, the calculating Bitzer responds from pure self-interest: "Knowing that your clear head would propose that alternative," he tells Gradgrind, "I have gone over the calculations in my mind; and I find that to compound the felony, even on very high terms indeed, would not be as safe and good for me as my improved prospects in the Bank" (III:8).

The reductionism inherent in Utilitarianism was exaggerated in the principles of POLITICAL ECONOMY, the popular economic philosophy of the time which reduced all human relationships to economic self-interest. The names of Gradgrind's younger children—Adam Smith and MALTHUS—suggest the alliance between the Utilitarians and political economists that Dickens was attacking. Coketown and Mr. Bounderby are the most blatant expressions of the new economics in the novel. A town of red brick, smoke and ashes, machinery and tall chimneys, Coketown articulates the philosophy that created it: "Fact, fact, fact, everywhere in the material aspect of the town; fact, fact, fact, everywhere in the immaterial" (I:5). Like the schoolchildren who are reduced to "vessels," Coketown's inhabitants are reduced to "hands," "people equally like one another, who went in and out at the same hours, with the same sound upon the same pavements, to do the same work, and to whom every day was the counterpart of the last and the next" (I:5). What signs there are of imagination have been perverted into repetitive madness by the iron laws of economics that define the town's existence: from the chimneys "interminable serpents of smoke trailed themselves for ever and ever, and never got uncoiled. . . . [and] the piston of the steam engine worked monotonously up and down like the head of an elephant in a state of melancholy madness" (I:5).

Bounderby, the Captain of Industry who represents the triumph of economics, also perverts imagination. Like Dickens's great comic figures—Micawber, Tony

Weller, or Sarah Gamp, for example—Bounderby claims to be self-created, but his story of rising from abandonment to become Josiah Bounderby of Coketown is a lie. Unlike Gradgrind, who is humbled and changed by Louisa's fall, Bounderby is simply reinforced in his fatuous dishonesty. He bullies Gradgrind's humility and rejects Louisa.

Stephen Blackpool's double bind shows how the "laws" of Coketown constrain and oppress the worker. When he seeks to escape "the muddle," Bounderby accuses him of rebelliousness and of being a dupe of some "mischievous stranger" (I:11), but when Stephen refuses to go along with Slackbridge and join the UNION, he is shunned by his fellow workmen. The marriage laws and the laws of political economy conspire to deny Stephen love, community, and identity. Although Stephen can imagine a better life for himself, he dies as an industrial martyr, killed by falling into the hell-shaft of industrial England. He cannot escape the muddle.

Harthouse's cynical fatalism—"What will be will be" (II:8)—is an apt expression of the fundamental truth of a world without imagination, and it echoes Louisa's "What does it matter?" If fact rules everything, then human choice and action can have no effect. Harthouse is ironically named, for he is as empty inside as Bounderby, but he does act as a catalyst to make Louisa aware of her own heart, her own inner needs. Their climactic rendezvous takes place outside Coketown in a natural setting during a cleansing rainstorm (II:11), and it releases Louisa's natural impulses that have been so long repressed.

Sissy Jupe is the real representative of heart. She acts from a higher law than the law of fact, and she alone can reduce Harthouse to absurdity and convince him to leave Coketown. She affirms the centrality of love. Her loyalty to her father, even after he abandons her, is in marked contrast to Bounderby's immediate rejection of Louisa after she returns to her father. Sissy's connections with the circus also enable Tom to escape the inevitability of "the law."

The CIRCUS embodies the alternative to Coketown's philosophy of fact. Its world of illusion expresses its commitment to FANCY, to imagination. Its horses are not fettered to mechanical routines like the melancholy elephants in Coketown, and the circus people know and understand them from experience, not from textbook definitions of them. So a real horse can dance rings around Bitzer and foil his attempt to arrest Tom (III:8). There is a community among the circus people, derived from another power of the imagination, the power to empathize with others, to imagine oneself in another's place. Sleary sums up the philosophy of Fancy when he tells Gradgrind "that there ith a love in the world, not all Thelf-interetht after all," and that Fancy "hath a way of ith own of calculating or not calculating, whith Thomehow or another ith at leath ath hard to give a name to" (III:8). These mysterious powers of love, empathy, and imagination offer hope, comfort and amusement.

The circus has sometimes been criticized as an inadequate symbol to represent the alternative to Fact. Certainly the amusing circus vagabonds were a less established social institution than the factories and schools of fact in Victorian England. Its power to counteract the destructive effects of industrialism is very limited. It saves Tom from arrest, but he will soon die far from home. It may be the basis of Sissy's ability to achieve happiness, but it cannot remove the blight of Coketown from Louisa, who will never know the happiness of her own family. Coketown has blighted their lives and the lives of every other inhabitant. The circus changes Gradgrind, but he is scorned by his former associates and Coketown goes on as before. The marginality of the circus may suggest just how important its presence was in Victorian England, even if its unspoken philosophy of Fancy was accessible only to those who could translate the truths in Sleary's boozy prose.

CRITICISM

Leavis's essay, first included in *The Great Tradition* (1948) and later in slightly revised form in *Dickens the Novelist* (1970), defined many of the critical issues in *Hard Times* and threw down a gauntlet to other critics by describing the novel as a "masterpiece." John Holloway ("*Hard Times*: A History and a Criticism," *Dickens and the Twentieth Century*, ed. Gross and Pearson, 1962) responded to Leavis by arguing that the novel was a shallow and simplistic rendering of Utilitarianism. Robin Gilmour ("The Gradgrind School: Political Economy in the Classroom," *Victorian Studies*, 1967), on the other hand, showed that Dickens understood in some depth the educational philosophy and schools that he was attacking. Michael GOLDBERG (1972) discusses Dickens's debt to Carlyle in the novel. Paul SCHLICKE (1985) describes Victorian circuses and analyzes the symbolism of the circus in the novel. Kate Flint (*Dickens*, 1986) suggests that Dickens failed to confront the structural and social issues in his critique of industrial capitalism and chose instead to offer a sentimental vision of Sleary's Circus as an anarchic alternative to Coketown. George H. FORD and Sylvère MONOD, in their edition of the novel, include a selection of contemporary background pieces and responses to the novel as well as Leavis's essay and some responses to it.

ADAPTATIONS

Very few dramatic versions of *Hard Times* have been produced. The first, a melodramatic adaptation by Frederick Fox COOPER, appeared at the close of the novel's serial run, but it radically changed the story by rehabilitating nearly every character. Tom returned the stolen money to the bank, Blackpool lived through his accident to marry Rachael, and Louisa was reunited with Bounderby, who ended the play bestowing gifts on everyone.

Thomas BENTLEY made a silent film version (1915) with Bransby WILLIAMS as Gradgrind. Arthur Hopcraft's four-part television adaptation appeared on Granada TV in 1977; a four-part serial for the BBC (1994), directed and written by Peter Barnes, presented Bob Peck as Gradgrind and Alan Bates as Bounderby.

Hardwick, Michael (1924–1991) and Mollie Writers, dramatists, novelists, compilers, and editors, this industrious couple has written radio and TV plays, produced records, and compiled, edited, and written numerous books—many on Victorian topics, several on Dickens. Their *Charles Dickens Encyclopedia* (1973) lists the works, characters, places, and people of Dickens and provides a large and well-chosen selection of the most memorable passages in Dickens's works. Also on Dickens: *The Charles Dickens Companion* (1965); *Dickens's England* (1970); *As They Saw Him: Charles Dickens* (1970).

Hardy, Barbara Contemporary Victorian scholar; Professor at Birkbeck College, University of London, who has written on Austen, THACKERAY, ELIOT, and Hardy as well as on Dickens. In *The Moral Art of Dickens* (1970), Hardy provides a probing analysis of the moral dimensions of Dickens's characters and the pattern of conversion that underlies most of the novels.

Hardy, Mr. "Practical joker, immensely popular with married ladies," who plans the steam excursion with Percy Noakes. *Boz*, "Steam Excursion."

Haredale Family Landed CATHOLIC family whose country seat, The WARREN near the MAYPOLE INN, is sacked during the No Popery riots. Dickens's sympathetic treatment of the Catholic squire has sometimes been taken as an indication of his tolerance for religious views differing from his own. **Geoffrey**, generally believed responsible for the death of his brother **Reuben**, devotes his life to proving his innocence and to caring for Reuben's daughter **Emma**. When his old enemy Sir John Chester enlists his aid to prevent the marriage of Emma to Chester's son Edward, he reluctantly agrees (12), but Chester's excesses make him regret his decision. During the riots Geoffrey proves his innocence and apprehends the elder Barnaby Rudge for Reuben's murder (56). In spite of her uncle's opposition, Emma keeps in contact with Edward through Dolly Varden, her companion and friend. The two girls are captured during the riots (59), and Gashford and Sim Tappertit plot their seduction (59), but the girls are rescued by Edward Chester and Joe Willet (71). Then Geoffrey blesses his niece's marriage to Edward (79) and duels with Sir John Chester, killing him (81). *Rudge*.

Harker Officer in charge of the jury for the murder trial. "Marigold."

Harker, The Reverend John Vicar of Groombridge Wells who acts as a reference for Mrs. Miller when she adopts Walter Wilding. "No Thoroughfare."

Harleigh Musical friend of the Gattletons who is the principal singer in their amateur production of *Masaniello*. *Boz*, "Porter."

Harley Street The Merdles live in "the handsomest house" on this fashionable street north of CAVENDISH SQUARE. *Dorrit* (I:20).

Harmon, John The "mutual friend" of the title whose several identities indicate his alienation from his father and his uncertainty about his own place in the world. His father, **Old John Harmon**, "a tremendous old rascal who made his money by Dust," leaves his estate to his son on the condition that he marry Bella Wilfer, chosen because of her petulence. The dustman's son, **John** (a.k.a. **Julius Handford, John Rokesmith, "the Man from Somewhere"**), decides to return to England in disguise in order to size up his potential bride, but his scheme to switch identities with another man is foiled when the other man is drowned and his body is taken for Harmon's (I:2). Taking the alias Rokesmith, Harmon becomes secretary to Boffin (I:15), who has inherited the estate in his place, and he courts Bella, but is refused (II:13). Only after his proposal is finally accepted and he is married (IV:4), after he is cleared of the suspicion of murdering Harmon, and after he is recognized by the Boffins, does he finally reveal his identity and accept his fortune (IV:12). *Mutual Friend*.

Harmonic Meeting These entertainments, held in public houses, combined refreshment with group singing led by professional singers and were the precursors to the later music hall. A typical harmonic meeting is described in *Boz*, "Streets—Night." Harmonic meetings are held regularly at SOL'S ARMS. *Bleak House* (33).

Harmony Jail The name by which BOFFIN'S BOWER was known in the days of Old John Harmon. *Mutual Friend*.

Harper and Brothers New York publishing firm with whom Dickens negotiated agreements for the publication of several of his works, in some cases sending them the proof sheets prior to English publication so that they could beat the pirates into print. *Great Expectations* and *Edwin Drood* were both published in **Harper's Weekly** from the proof sheets. *Expectations* appeared a week in advance of its appearance in ALL THE YEAR ROUND, making the *Harper's Weekly* serial literally the first published edition of the novel.

Harris (1) Law stationer and friend of John Dounce. *Boz*, "Dounce."

Harris (2) Greengrocer in BATH whose shop is the site of the footmen's "swarry" attended by Sam Weller. *Pickwick* (37).

Harris, Mr. (a.k.a. "Short Trotters," "Short," "Trotters") Codlin's partner in the Punch-and-Judy show with whom Nell and her grandfather travel to the race meeting. "A little merry-faced man with a twinkling eye and a red nose, who seemed to have unconsciously imbibed something of his hero's character" (16). *Curiosity Shop.*

Harris, Mrs. Mrs. Gamp's imaginary friend, used to supply Mrs. Gamp with topics of conversation and authoritative support for her opinions: "There were conflicting rumours on the subject; but the prevalent opinion was that she was a phantom of Mrs. Gamp's brain . . . created for the express purpose of holding visionary dialogues with her on all manner of subjects, and invariably winding up with a compliment to the excellence of her nature" (25). Mrs. Gamp also imagines Mrs. Harris's little **Tommy** "as calls me his own Gammy" (49). *Chuzzlewit.*

Harrisburg, Pennsylvania A "very cheerful city" where Dickens put up at a "snug hotel" and visited a model prison on his 1842 journey to AMERICA. *Notes* (9).

Harrison Orphan suggested by Reverend Milvey as suitable for the Boffins to adopt. *Mutual Friend* (I:9).

Harrow Famous public school in Middlesex, just west of London. Matthew Pocket was an old Harrovian. *Expectations* (23).

Harry (1) Stableman at the GOLDEN CROSS. *Boz,* "Early Coaches."

Harry (2) "A genteel-looking young man" locked up for debt in Solomon Jacobs's sponging house. *Boz,* "Tottle."

Harry (3) Peddler selling stain remover who meets Bill Sikes in a pub and offers to remove the bloodstain from his hat. *Twist* (48).

Harry (4) Marton's favorite pupil, a young boy who falls ill and dies: "His hair still hung in curls about his face, and his eyes were very bright; but their light was of Heaven, not earth" (25). *Curiosity Shop.*

Harte, (Francis) Bret (1836–1902) California novelist, humorist, and journalist, often compared to Dickens. According to Mark Twain, Harte described himself as "the best imitator of Dickens in America." Harte's sentimentality, his use of child characters and angelic women, and his method of characterization through peculiarities were aspects of his work most often described as Dickensian.

Dickens read "The Luck of the Roaring Camp" (1868) and "Outcasts of Poker Flat" (1869) shortly before his death and wrote to Harte to tell him how the stories impressed and moved him, and he invited Harte to contribute to ALL THE YEAR ROUND. Dickens was dead and Harte had written his memorable tribute to his literary mentor, "Dickens in Camp" (July 1870), before Harte received Dickens's letter. The memorial poem described a group of California miners sitting around an open campfire and reading aloud *The Old Curiosity Shop.*

Hartford, Connecticut During his 1842 visit to AMERICA, Dickens spent four days in this town, "beautifully situated in a basin of green hills," visiting the lunatic asylum and the prison. *Notes* (5).

Harthouse, James A good-looking gentleman of 35, who comes to look over Coketown as a potential parliamentary candidate. "Had tried life as a Cornet of Dragoons, and found it a bore; and had afterwards tried it in the train of an English minister abroad, and found it a bore; and had then strolled to Jerusalem, and got bored there; and had then gone yachting about the world, and got bored everywhere" (II:2). He insinuates his way into Louisa Bounderby's affections by his apparent interest in her brother Tom (II:7). When Bounderby is away, he meets her in the garden of her country house and urges her to run off with him, but she returns to her father's home (II:11–12). Sissy Jupe confronts him and persuades him to leave Coketown (III:2). *Hard Times.*

Harvey Young man to be married to Miss Emma Fielding. *Young Couples.*

Harvey, John (1942–) British novelist, artist and printmaker on the faculty of Emmanuel College, Cambridge. In *Victorian Novelists and Their Illustrators* (1970), Harvey analyzes the effect of the graphic satire tradition on Dickens and his illustrators.

Hatfield Town in Hertfordshire to which Sikes escapes after Nancy's murder; however he is driven away from the pub here by a peddler who insists on removing the bloodstain from Sikes's hat (*Twist*, 48). The Lirripers spend their honeymoon here at the Salisbury Arms, where Dickens himself had stayed in 1838 ("Lirriper's Lodgings"). Mrs. Lirriper is buried in the Hatfield churchyard ("Lirriper's Legacy").

Hatton Garden Street in HOLBORN where the police court presided over by Magistrate Fang is located (*Twist,* 11). It is on Phil Squod's beat as a tinker (*Bleak House,* 26). The Jellybys take lodgings here after Mr. Jellyby's bankruptcy (*Bleak House,* 30).

"Haunted House, A" Satiric article for HOUSEHOLD WORDS (July 23, 1853), describing Mr. Bull's haunted house in Westminster, a scene of confused babbling made worse by members of Bull's family who go into the countryside, into towns like Burningshame, bringing ill will, depravity, and corruption. *Miscellaneous.*

"Haunted House, The" Christmas number of ALL THE YEAR ROUND, 1859. Dickens wrote two of the eight chapters, "The Mortals in the House" and "The Ghost in Master B.'s Room." John, the narrator of the story, rents a house in the north of England, even though he is told that it is haunted. After all of his servants are frightened away by various supernatural happenings and their own imaginings, he invites a group of his friends to spend the Christmas season in the house with him. They plan to share their supernatural experiences at the close of their stay. John takes Master B.'s room and there encounters the ghost of "my own childhood, the ghost of my own innocence, the ghost of my own airy belief," as he remembers the innocent recreation of Haroun Alraschid's seraglio that he enacted with his schoolmates, as well as the traumatic death of his father. *Christmas Stories.*

Haunted Man and The Ghost's Bargain, The: A Fancy for Christmas-Time Fifth and last of the CHRISTMAS BOOKS, published for Christmas 1848 by BRADBURY & EVANS, with illustrations by TENNIEL, STANFIELD, and LEECH. Returning to a story of a Christmas conversion, Dickens tells how Redlaw, a chemist who is given a gift that enables him to eradicate painful memories, learns how important such memories are in enabling love and understanding between people.

SYNOPSIS

(1) Redlaw, a professor of chemistry, sits before his fire on Christmas Eve, brooding on the past and looking like a haunted man. It is a cold and windy night and even in his vaultlike dwelling, part library and part laboratory, he is chilled and depressed in the gathering darkness. The keeper of the college, William Swidger, comes to stir the fire and lay the table for dinner. As he does so, he talks of his wife, Milly, and of her concern for a sick student and for a street urchin whom she has taken in. When she arrives with the dinner, her father-in-law, 87-year-old Philip Swidger, comes with her, bringing bunches of holly to decorate the college rooms for Christmas. He remembers past Christmases, even the painful ones, and the memories make him "merry and happy."

After they leave, Redlaw is troubled by painful memories of his own—of a friend who betrayed him by stealing his fiancée, and of his sister's death. He finds that each Christmas only adds "more figures in the lengthening sum of recollection that we work and work at to our torment." As he ruminates, his DOUBLE appears out of the gloom and stands behind his chair. This phantom rehearses the wounds of Redlaw's past, and when the chemist wishes to "forget my sorrow and my wrong," the specter offers him the opportunity to do so. He even goes a step further: Because the chemist has recognized that "the memory of sorrow, wrong, and trouble is the lot of all mankind," he will also be granted the power to erase the memories of those he meets. After the specter melts away, the chemist hears a cry in the lecture hall adjoining his rooms. He finds there the ragged waif that Milly has taken in; the child is looking for her.

(2) At the Tetterby house in Jerusalem Buildings, Mr. Tetterby lovingly tends his rambunctious children. When Mrs. Tetterby comes home with supper, she is upset and tells her husband that she envies those in the market with more money and resents being poor. But after she is at home for a while, she remembers their trials together as a family and her heart is softened. The Tetterbys are surprised by Redlaw, who comes to their flat, seeking the sick student. As he leaves, the once happy family, influenced by his power, begins fighting.

The student turns out to be Edmund Denham, the quietest and most retiring of all Redlaw's students. He explains that his real name is Edmund Longford and that he is the son of the woman that Redlaw once loved. He chose another name in order to be judged only on his own merits. After telling Redlaw of his admiration for him, Denham steps forward to touch the chemist, but Redlaw, to avoid physical contact with the boy, backs away, throwing a purse to him as he does so. Hurt and insulted, Denham returns the purse, but Redlaw grasps him by the arm and the student forgets his past, his obligations, and his resentments.

When Milly comes to visit him, Denham is curt with her, suggesting that she makes more of his illness than it deserves and asking what payment she expects for her attentions. Hurt and rejected, Milly leaves.

Redlaw is distressed by his influence on others. "I am infected," he cries, "I am infectuous! I am charged with poison for my own mind, and the minds of all mankind. Where I felt interest, compassion, sympathy, I am turning into stone." Hating his new power, Redlaw seeks solitude. Then he remembers the urchin, the one person who would seem able only to benefit from his powers. He finds the boy and asks that he take him to the slum where he comes from. As they go along, Redlaw realizes that "the expression on the boy's face was the expression on his own," that they are doubles. Redlaw believes that taking away the memories of sorrow, wrong, and trouble that torment those in the slum can do no harm. But his power affects an abused woman so that she is not softened by memories of her family, and it hardens a repentant George Swidger against reconciliation with his father and brother. Old Philip, denied his softening memories, becomes instantly senile, aware only that he is 87. Alarmed by the destructiveness of his power, Redlaw rushes back to his flat with the boy and locks himself in. Milly comes to the door, begging him to help her deal with the sorrowful changes that have occurred, but he refuses. He prays for the phantom to return and take back the gift.

(3) Back in his rooms with the boy, Redlaw again confronts the phantom. When he asks that the curse he has laid on others be withdrawn, the phantom tells him to seek out Milly. Then the phantom explains that the boy is the one creature who is not changed by Redlaw, because he has no softening memories to lose.

The next morning the Tetterbys are still fighting, regretting that they ever married and ever had children. But when Milly comes to their house, they are reconciled and restored to a loving family. Milly tells them that Redlaw came to her very early on Christmas morning, and together they went to the slum, where the abused woman regained soothing memories of her family and George Swidger again became penitent. Now at the Jerusalem Buildings the Tetterbys are reconciled and Edmund Longford asks forgiveness for his cruel treatment of Milly. Redlaw can see in those around him how much he has lost.

Back at the Swidger's rooms, Milly restores the good feeling in her family and reunites Redlaw with Mr. Longford, who many years before had wronged Redlaw by jilting his sister and stealing his fiancée. Now a penitent, Longford has returned to seek Redlaw's forgiveness and that of Edmund, the son that he abandoned. Edmund is also reunited with his fiancée, reminding Redlaw of his own love many years before. In the end all are brought together in the old College hall, where they celebrate Christmas dinner beneath the portrait of the college founder. After the events of Christmas Eve, the prayer of the founder has taken on new meaning for Redlaw: "Lord, keep my memory green."

COMMENTARY

Dickens began *Haunted Man* in the fall of 1847, but he found that it diverted his attention from *Dombey and Son* and quickly abandoned his original intention of releasing the book for Christmas. As a result, 1847 was the first year in five in which Dickens did not write a Christmas Book. When he resumed work on the story in the autumn of 1848, he found the writing difficult, and the manuscript, now in the collection of the Pforzheimer Foundation in New York, shows considerably more revision than usual. One of the original reviewers, writing in *Macphail's Edinburgh Ecclesiastical Journal* (January 1849), was so displeased with the tale that he advised the author to "quit the *twenty-fifth of December*, and take to the *first of April*." Many modern readers have have also been unmoved by the story, described by Edgar JOHNSON (1952) as "feeble," "slapdash," "sentimental," and "overmoralistic."

Haunted Man follows Dickens's plan for all of the Christmas books of giving a "higher form" to an "old nursery tale." The presence of ghosts and phantoms that turn Redlaw's wishes into magical and destructive powers; the countering effect of the "fairy godmother," Milly Swidger; and the sudden transformations of the chemist and of several other characters are all elements that Dickens took from FAIRY TALES, especially from the stories of E. T. A. Hoffmann. In this use of fairy tale conventions and motifs, *Haunted Man* is, of all the Christmas Books, most like *A Christmas Carol*.

Dickens shapes his fairy tale to a higher form by injecting into the story realistic commentary on the social conditions of his time, especially through the figure of the orphan waif. This neglected slum child has never experienced love or caring from others and thus has no humanizing memories to counter his brutish ignorance. He is a warning to Victorian England of the results of social neglect. He is also a double to Redlaw, a perverse projection of the scientist's wish to alleviate human suffering by suppressing painful memories of the past.

Haunted Man also achieves its higher form by using the fairy story to explore the psychology of the chemist and his wish to free himself and humanity from painful memories. That wish—one of the central desires of scientific rationalism—is shown to lack psychological and spiritual understanding of the human condition. For, deprived of such memories, mankind loses community; relationships formerly based on shared suffering are reduced to cash transactions.

The opening chapter, "The Gift Bestowed," presents the haunted man, the chemist Redlaw, inhabiting his college fortress like an ogre in his castle. His apartment and his laboratory are separated only by a curtain. His rooms suggest that his inner life is all mind, "part library and part laboratory." Nevertheless, Redlaw is not an enlightened man; instead he is surrounded by darkness and gloom, engulfed in a paralytic cloud of despair and self-pity. As the darkness of Christmas Eve descends, his depression deepens. The good nature of the Swidgers and their preparations for Christmas cannot penetrate his gloom. Unlike old Philip Swidger, who hangs Christmas greens while keeping green the memories of his long life, Redlaw is tormented by his painful memories.

As he dwells on these memories, Redlaw's gloom deepens until it calls up a phantom, the chemist's double who grants the Redlaw's wish to cast out the poisonous memories in his mind just as a chemist might counter poisons in the body with a chemical antidote. But the phantom's gift will not be limited to Redlaw alone. Articulating the benevolent scientist's desire to aid mankind with his knowledge, the phantom also gives Redlaw the power to be mankind's benefactor: "Your wisdom has discovered that the memory of sorrow, wrong, and trouble is the lot of all mankind, and that mankind would be happier, in its other memories, without it. Go! Be its benefactor! Freed from such remembrance, from this hour, carry involuntarily the blessing of such freedom with you."

This gift turns out to be a Faustian bargain rather than a blessing. The second chapter, "The Gift Diffused," shows its effects on Redlaw and others. He blights the loving Tetterby family, the CRATCHITs of this story, who, lacking the memories of shared suffering symbolized by the remnants of their past occupations in their shop window, focus on present distress and blame each other for their difficulties. Redlaw's presence also prevents George Swidger's reconciliation with his family, for without memory, George lacks reasons for penitence and the family lacks sources for forgiveness. And with his own memories gone, Redlaw loses his former benevolence; when he unfeelingly offers money to minister to the sick student's illness, mechanical charity has replaced fellow feeling.

Only two characters remain untouched by Redlaw's power. The urchin child has no healing memories to counter the unrelenting pain of his life. He has no ties to others. By the end of the second chapter, Redlaw, locked in his rooms with the urchin, realizes that he is like the child: Stripped of his memories, he has lost his ties to others. His gift, in its effects on himself and on those he touches, is revealed to be a curse. Milly Swidger is the other person untouched by Redlaw's power. Her love for those around her, from her family to the students who affectionately call her "Swidge," derives from her memories, especially from the painful memory of a lost child. In the final chapter, "The Gift Reversed," her counterinfluence restores the Tetterbys to a loving family, reconciles George Swidger and his family, restores Longford to health and reconciles him with Redlaw. In the process, she restores Redlaw's repressed memories and, by bringing them to light, she frees him from the neurotic denial that has paralyzed him and darkened his life. By the end, he has discovered the truth of the founder's prayer for his own life, "Lord, keep my memory green."

The higher form that Dickens's tale takes, then, is one which challenges Redlaw's enlightenment rationalism, showing its one-sidedness in its stress on intellect and its denial of emotion. Redlaw is not just wrong in his rationalism; he is also emotionally paralyzed, unable to act positively or lovingly. In the fable of freeing the chemist from these psychological neuroses, Dickens foreshadows the Freudian analysis of Redlaw's condition. For Dickens, however, the final form that the fable takes is spiritual. Milly represents more than psychological liberation, more than an embodiment of Redlaw's emotional "better wisdom." When Redlaw thanks Milly, "who through the teaching of pure love, has graciously restored me to the memory which was the memory of Christ upon the cross, and of all the good who perished in His cause," he is reminded of the Christian doctrine of suffering and the story becomes a Christmas Christian ALLEGORY.

CRITICISM

Harry STONE analyzes the style and structure of the story in "Dickens's Artistry and *The Haunted Man*" (*South Atlantic Quarterly*, 1962) and its fairy-tale techniques in *Dickens and the Invisible World* (1979). Deborah Thomas (*Dickens and the Short Story*, 1982) discusses the ways in which reading contributes to humanizing memory.

ADAPTATIONS

Haunted Man has not been as popular with theatrical and film adaptors as most of Dickens's other works. Although about 14 different stage versions appeared between 1848 and 1850, there have been few later adaptations. The first adaptation, by Mark LEMON, "by express permission of the author," was staged for 42 performances at the ADELPHI THEATER, London, between December 20, 1848 and February 7, 1849. Among other early stage adaptations was one by Edward STIRLING, the last of Dickens's works that he adapted. Stirling's version does not seem to have been performed. No film or television adaptations of the story have been made.

Brett HARTE's parody of Dickens's Christmas books, "The Haunted Man. A Christmas Story. By CH__R__S D__CK__N__S," in his *Condensed Novels* (1867), is partly based on *Haunted Man*.

Havisham, Miss Eccentric old woman who lives in SATIS HOUSE and who hires Pip to play with her adopted protégée, Estella. "She was dressed in rich materials—satins, and lace, and silks—all of white. Her shoes were white. And she had a long white veil dependent from her hair, but her hair was white. . . . I saw that everything within my view which ought to be white, had been white long ago, and had lost its lustre, and was faded and yellow" (8). She retreated into seclusion after being jilted by Compeyson and she is training Estella to carry out her revenge by despising men. She brings Pip to Satis House as a victim for Estella to practice on (8) and she uses him to taunt her relatives into thinking him a rival for her money (11). She pays for his apprenticeship (13), leading Pip to believe that she is the source of his great expectations. After he learns otherwise, he rescues her from burning (49), but her injuries prove fatal. She leaves most of her money to Estella (57). Her brother, **Arthur**, a drunken ne'er-do-well, plotted with Compeyson to defraud her. *Expectations*.

Hawdon, Captain ("Nemo") Retired military officer and law writer who, using the alias Nemo (Latin for *nobody*), lives in abject poverty on the middle floor of Krook's house and is found dead there, probably from an opium overdose (10). He is mourned only by Woodcourt, the doctor who attended him, and Jo, a crossing sweeper. Tulkinghorn and Guppy, suspicious of his identity, discover his secret, that he was Lady Dedlock's lover before her marriage and the father of Esther Summerson. Their pursuit of this secret leads to Lady Dedlock's flight, which ends with her death by the gate of the cemetery in the heart of TOM-ALL-ALONE's, where he is buried. *Bleak House*.

Hawk, Sir Mulberry A dissolute aristocrat and gambler who lives by fleecing rich young men. While he and Ralph Nickleby are engaged in taking Lord Frederick Verisopht's money, he meets Kate Nickleby and determines to seduce her (19). Nicholas thwarts this scheme by beating Hawk and marking his face for life (32). Hawk kills Verisopht in a duel, then flees to France (50). *Nickleby*.

Hawkins (1) New member of Parliament whom the Political Young Gentleman thinks it may be necessary "to bring . . . down on his knees for that vote on the miscellaneous estimates." *Young Gentlemen.*

Hawkins (2) Middle-aged baker of PENTONVILLE whom Miss Rugg successfully sues for breach of promise. *Dorrit* (I:25).

Hawkinson, Aunt Georgiana Podsnap's aunt, who left her the necklace that she offers to the Lammles to help them out of their financial difficulties. *Mutual Friend* (IV:2).

Hawkyard, Brother Verity Dissenting preacher and dry-salter who acts as George Silverman's guardian. The story implies that he has appropriated properties that rightfully belong to Silverman, but the self-denying Silverman writes a letter exonerating Hawkyard from any guilt. "Silverman."

Haymarket Turveydrop likes to dine at a restaurant in this street off PALL MALL in London's West End. George's shooting gallery is nearby. *Bleak House.*

Haynes, Inspector A police officer in the BOROUGH. *Reprinted*, "Inspector Field."

Headstone, Bradley Schoolmaster who trains Charley Hexam and then falls in love with Lizzie, Charley's sister. "In his decent black coat and waistcoat, and decent white shirt, and decent formal black tie, and decent pantaloons of pepper and salt, with his decent silver watch in his pocket, and his decent hair guard round his neck, [he] looked a thoroughly decent young man of six-and-twenty. There was a kind of settled trouble in the face" (II:1). By mechanical work and mechanical study, Bradley has risen from low origins to his position as schoolmaster, but his learning is insufficient to enable him to control his passion and jealousy. When he meets Eugene Wrayburn, he is intensely aware of his social inferiority (III:6). The two become rivals for Lizzie's affections, shadow each other in the streets of London, and feverishly compete with each other to discover Lizzie's whereabouts. Bradley pursues Eugene up the THAMES (IV:1), spies on his assignation with Lizzie, and murderously attacks and nearly kills him (IV:6). Rogue Riderhood uncovers Headstone's guilty secret, attempts blackmail, and the two of them drown together as they struggle in each other's arms (IV:15). *Mutual Friend.*

"Heart of Mid-London, The" Article for *HOUSEHOLD WORDS* (May 4, 1850) by William Henry WILLS and Dickens, describing the overcrowding and brutality at the SMITHFIELD livestock market and recommending that a suburban market replace it. *Stone.* A description of a mad bull rampaging through the streets is reminiscent of the scene of Florence's kidnapping. *Dombey* (6).

"Heart's Delight" Captain Cuttle's pet name for Florence DOMBEY. *Dombey.*

Heathfield, Alfred Doctor Jeddler's ward, who is in love with Marion Jeddler. When she discovers that her sister Grace also loves him, she disappears; in time, Alfred falls in love with **Grace** and marries her. They have a daughter, **Marion**. Heathfield becomes a village doctor, ministering to the poor. *Battle.*

Heep, Uriah Wickfield's clerk and eventual partner, "a red-haired person . . . whose hair was cropped as close as the closest stubble; who had hardly any eyebrows, and no eyelashes, and eyes of a red-brown, so unsheltered and unshaded, that I remember wondering how he went to sleep" (15). He is a writhing, hypocritical opportunist who pretends to humility while he contrives to take over Wickfield's business, marry his daughter, and defraud the firm's clients. His schemes ruin Betsey Trotwood (34), but Micawber eventually exposes his villainy (52). Imprisoned for fraud, he becomes a model prisoner (61). His widowed mother, **Mrs. Heep**, "the dead image of Uriah, only short" (17), is as "'umble" as her son and is devoted to him. *Copperfield.*

Fred Barnard's portrait of Uriah Heep.

Helps, Sir Arthur (1813–1875) Clerk to the Privy Council; author; friend of Dickens, especially during the 1860s. He arranged Dickens's audience with Queen VICTORIA on March 9, 1870. His obituary tribute to Dickens (*Macmillan's Magazine*, 1870) describes the author as unusually observant, humorous, orderly, disciplined, and attentive.

Helves, Captain An uninvited guest brought on the steam excursion by the Tauntons. A braggart and swindler, he entertains the party with exaggerated tales of his military exploits. *Boz*, "Steam Excursion."

Hendon A village on the outskirts of London to which Sikes escapes after murdering Nancy, but "all the people he met—the very children at the doors—seemed to view him with suspicion." *Twist* (48).

Henley This village along the THAMES in Oxfordshire is the original of the town where Eugene Wrayburn is attacked by Bradley Headstone. The ANGLER'S INN, where he recuperates, is based on the RED LION INN. Hurley Lock, about six miles down river from Henley, became Plashwater Weir Mill Lock. *Mutual Friend*.

Henri Employee of a Swiss inn who disappears during the night and turns out to have been murdered. "Holly Tree."

Henrietta Sweetheart of Tom, the pavement artist, who agrees to "walk" with him "on the understanding that softer sentiments may flow." She does not know that Tom is the artist who created the pictures on the pavement in PICCADILLY that she admires. When Tom criticizes the impostor who claims the pictures as his own, Henrietta rejects him. She later marries the impostor. "Somebody's Luggage."

Henry Cousin of Maria Lobbs in "The Parish Clerk," a tale told by Sam Weller to Mr. Pickwick. He is Nathaniel Pipkin's rival for Maria's affections and he eventually marries her. *Pickwick* (17).

Henry, Mr. Pawnbroker's assistant, "the gentleman behind the counter, with the curly black hair, diamond ring, and double silver watch guard." *Boz*, "Pawnbroker's."

Henry VIII (1491–1547) King of England, 1509–47, described by Dickens as "a most intolerable ruffian, a disgrace to human nature, and a blot of blood and grease upon the History of England." *Child's History*.

Herbert, Henry (1734–1794) Tenth earl of Pembroke, member of Parliament, a historical figure who, in *Rudge* during the debate on Catholic Emancipation,

points out Lord Gordon's presence in the chamber, wearing the blue cockade of the rioters. *Rudge* (73).

Herschel, John Cousin of the narrator of "The Haunted House." He and his **wife** are part of the group assembled to investigate the hauntings.

Hexam Family Family from the lower depths of society in LIMEHOUSE; they play a contrasting role to surface people like the Veneerings in *Mutual Friend*. **Jessee (Gaffer)**, "the nightbird of the Thames," is a waterman who patrols the river, looking for corpses. He finds the body that is taken to be John Harmon's (I:1). Later Gaffer is himself found drowned in the THAMES (I:14). His daughter, **Lizzie**, "a dark girl of nineteen or twenty" (I:1), rows the boat as he observes the water and she refuses to leave this unsavory occupation even though she is discomfited by the work and offered chances to do so. She does enable her brother **Charley** to leave home and go off to school (I:6). He is ambitious and selfish and desires respectability above all else. When she refuses to marry Headstone (II:15), Charley rejects her, just as he later turns on Headstone when he learns of his complicity in the maiming of Wrayburn. After her father's death, Lizzie moves in with Jenny Wren (II:1), but the unwonted attentions of both Headstone and Wrayburn drive her into seclusion and, aided by Riah, she finds refuge in a mill town up the Thames. When Wrayburn discovers her there (IV:1), he is attacked by Headstone and saved from death by Lizzie (IV:6), who nurses him back to consciousness and finally marries him (IV:11). *Mutual Friend*.

Heyling, George Subject of Jack Bamber's "Tale about the Queer Client." After his wife, **Mary**, and their **infant son** die while he is in debtor's prison, he devotes his life to wreaking revenge on his wife's father, whom he blames for the tragedy. *Pickwick* (21).

Hicks, Septimus "A tallish, white-faced young man, with spectacles, and a black ribbon round his neck," with a passion for Byron, who marries Matilda Maplesone and then deserts her. *Boz*, "Boarding House."

Hicks, Seymour (1871–1941) British actor, theater manager, and dramatist. He played in everything from music hall to serious drama. He was famous for his portrayal of Scrooge, both in Buckstone's adaptation of the story and in music hall sketches. He played Scrooge in the 1935 film version of the *Carol*.

Hickson Subscriber who gives one guinea to the Indigent Orphans' Friends' Benevolent Institution. *Boz*, "Public Dinners."

Hickson, Mr. and Mrs. Couple attending the Gattleton's private theatricals. *Boz*, "Porter."

"Hidden Light" Poem in *HOUSEHOLD WORDS* (August 26, 1854) by Adelaide Anne PROCTER and Dickens proclaiming the goodness inherent in "the soul of all mankind." *Stone*.

Higden, Mrs. Betty An old woman, nearly 80, who keeps a "minding school" and does ironing on a mangle operated by Sloppy, one of the boys she has taken in. Mrs. Boffin wants to adopt her great-grandson Johnny (I:16), but the child dies before the adoption can be arranged (II:9). His death breaks Betty's heart; she takes to the road as a peddler of needlework (II:14). Terrified of the workhouse, she dies by the side of the road in the arms of Lizzie Hexam (III:8). *Mutual Friend*.

Highgate Village north of London where Dickens and his parents lived in 1832. His parents and his infant daughter, Dora Annie, are buried in Highgate Cemetery. The village is significant in *Copperfield*, the novel he was writing when his daughter died. Mrs. Steerforth's house, the retirement cottage of Dr. Strong, and the cottages of Betsey Trotwood and David himself, are in Highgate. The village is also mentioned in *Twist* and *Bleak House*.

Higham The village in KENT which, along with CHALK, was the original for the village of Joe Gargery and his forge in *Great Expectations*.

Hill, Mrs. Jane Seymour Dickens's contemporary, a dwarf chiropodist who recognized herself as the original for Miss Mowcher, the dwarf hairdresser in *Copperfield* (22). She wrote to Dickens objecting to the portrait, and in response, Dickens radically changed Miss Mowcher's character on her next appearance in the novel (32).

Hill, T. W. (1866–1953) Active Dickensian; secretary of the DICKENS FELLOWSHIP, 1914–19; frequent contributor to the *DICKENSIAN*, most remembered for his explanatory notes to the novels published in that journal.

Hilton Master of ceremonies at the annual dance of Minerva House School. *Boz*, "Sentiment."

"Hiram Powers' Greek Slave" Poem from *HOUSEHOLD WORDS* (October 26, 1850), saluting Powers's statue of a shackled Greek slave as a work of art that can "shame the strong" and overthrow serfdom.

Historical Novel A form of the novel, developed by Sir Walter SCOTT, in which historical persons and a historical situation are combined with fictional characters and a fictional story. For Scott, the historical situation usually involved two cultures in conflict, one dying and the other being born, and a period close enough to be within memory of some living persons. In Scott's novels, the fictional characters participate in historical events along with the historic figures. His heroes usually have divided loyalties between the conflicting historical forces.

Influenced by Scott, nearly every major Victorian novelist attempted at least one historical novel; some, like William Harrison AINSWORTH and G. P. R. James, made historical fiction their vocation. The first novel that Dickens planned, *Gabriel Vardon, the Locksmith of London*, was to be a historical novel in the manner of Scott. Although he set aside the project when *Pickwick* became popular, he eventually completed the novel as *Barnaby Rudge* (1841), a story of the GORDON RIOTS in the 1780s. Although Dickens did not employ the elaborate editorial devices that Scott often used to establish the link between his historical subject and the present, *Rudge* had contemporary relevance in 1841, for the Gordon Riots provided an easily recognized parallel to CHARTISM.

Although some of Dickens's shorter stories are set in the past—*The Battle of Life*, for example, takes place in the late 18th century—the only other novel that qualifies as historical is *A Tale of Two Cities* (1859), a novel about the FRENCH REVOLUTION in which Dickens inserted the tale of Charles Darnay, an expatriate French aristocrat, into the Revolution, the depiction of which he based mainly on CARLYLE's history. Andrew Sanders discusses Dickens as a historical novelist in *The Victorian Historical Novel, 1840–1880* (1979).

Hobler, Francis LORD MAYOR's clerk at the MANSION HOUSE Police Court, famous for his jokes at court proceedings. *Boz*, "Last Cab-driver."

Hockley-in-the-Hole A slum area in CLERKENWELL through which the Artful Dodger leads Oliver on his way into London. *Twist* (8).

Hogarth, George (1783–1870) Dickens's father-in-law. A Scot, educated for the law at Edinburgh, he practiced law for many years in Scotland, acting as Sir Walter SCOTT's attorney. He was also a violoncellist and composer and the music critic for the *Edinburgh Courant*. In 1830 he left the law for journalism and established the *Halifax Guardian*. In 1834 he became music critic for the *MORNING CHRONICLE* in London. It was there that he met Dickens, who was writing "Street Sketches" for the paper. When he became editor of the newly established *EVENING CHRONICLE* in 1835, he asked Dickens to contribute sketches to that paper as well. He was hired as music critic for the *DAILY NEWS* under Dickens's editorship, continuing in that position for 20 years. In 1814 he married Georgina Thomson, daughter of a fellow musician. Three of their daughters had important roles in Dickens's life: **Catherine** (1815–79), the eldest, who became his wife (See Catherine DICKENS); **Mary**, whose early death deeply affected Dickens; and **Georgina**, Dickens's companion and housekeeper.

Hogarth, Georgina (1827–1917) Georgina joined the Dickens household after the Dickenses returned from AMERICA in 1842. Gradually she took more and more responsibility for managing the household and, after siding with Dickens during the separation, she remained with him until the end of his life, prompting scandalous and unfounded rumors about Dickens's relationship with her. After his death, she and Mamie DICKENS edited the first collection of Dickens's LETTERS (1880–82).

Hogarth, Mary Scott (1819–1837) Dickens's sister-in-law. Mary, a pretty and lively girl, four years younger than Catherine (see Catherine DICKENS), moved into the Dickens's household in 1836, shortly after the marriage. A year later, on May 6, 1837, she was suddenly taken ill, dying the next day in Dickens's arms. Dickens missed a month of *Twist*, ascribing the interruption to "the sudden death of a very dear young relative to whom he was most affectionately attached and whose society had been for a long time the chief solace of his labours." For her tombstone he wrote: "Young, beautiful, and good, God in his mercy numbered her with His angels at the early age of seventeen." He took a ring from her finger and wore it until his own death. Biographers have suggested that Mary was the model for many of Dickens's sweet and innocent young women, particularly Little Nell in *Curiosity Shop*, whose death reminded Dickens of Mary's.

Hogarth, William (1697–1764) Painter and engraver; graphic satirist and moralist whose works profoundly influenced Dickens; especially important were the progresses, series of narrative pictures telling exemplary stories. Dickens had 48 prints by Hogarth hanging at GAD'S HILL, and he subtitled *Oliver Twist* "The Parish Boy's Progress," indicating his debt to such Hogarth works as "The Harlot's Progress" (1731), "The Rake's Progress" (1735), and "Industry and Idleness" (1747), as well as to John Bunyan's *Pilgrim's Progress* (1678). John HARVEY (1971) discusses Dickens's debt to Hogarth.

Hoghton Towers A deserted mansion on the road between PRESTON and Blackburn which Dickens visited in 1867. George Silverman is sent to the farmhouse to recover his health. "Silverman" (5).

Holborn This section of London and its main thoroughfare, running westward from the CITY to TOTTENHAM COURT ROAD, is frequently mentioned in Dickens's works. Job Trotter runs up Holborn Hill to fetch Perker when Pickwick decides to leave the FLEET (*Pickwick*, 47); Oliver Twist and Sikes take this route on their way to

CHERTSEY (*Twist*, 21). During the GORDON RIOTS, Langdale's distillery on Holborn Hill is burned down (*Rudge*, 68). Mrs. Gamp has rooms in KINGSGATE STREET off High Holborn, and she and Betsey Prig nurse Lewsome at the BLACK BULL in Holborn (*Chuzzlewit*, 25). On her arrival in London, Esther Summerson goes to THAVIES INN via Holborn through a thick fog (*Bleak House*, 4).

"Holiday Romance" A collection of four short stories, supposedly written by four children, which Dickens wrote for the American magazine *Our Young Folks*, appearing there between January and May, 1868, and simultaneously in ALL THE YEAR ROUND. The two boys tell the stories of William TINKLING and Captain BOLDHEART, the girls the fairy tale of Princess ALICIA and a romance about a country where the adults obey the children.

Holland, Captain J. B. Proprietor of the MONTHLY MAGAZINE, he was Dickens's first publisher, accepting "A Dinner at Poplar Walk" for the December 1833 issue. Altogether he published nine of Dickens's early sketches in his magazine.

Holland, Lady Augusta-Mary (1770–1845) Autocratic hostess of a famous literary and Whig political salon at Holland House. Dickens was introduced there in 1838.

Holliday, Arthur The "reckless, rattle-pated, open-hearted, and open-mouthed" son of a rich manufacturer who is the protagonist of Doctor Speddie's story of the dead medical student who comes back to life. *Lazy Tour*.

Hollingshead, John (1827–1904) Journalist and, later, theater manager; a frequent contributor to HOUSEHOLD WORDS and ALL THE YEAR ROUND. He described Dickens as "an inspired Cockney" and himself as "a Dickens young man." Dickens is said to have characterized him as "the most ignorant man on the staff [of *Household Words*], but he'll cram up the facts, and won't give us an encyclopaedical article."

Holloway Rural suburb north of London where the Wilfer family live. *Mutual Friend* (I:4).

"Holly-Tree, The" The Christmas number of HOUSEHOLD WORDS for 1855. Dickens wrote three parts of this five-part story, retitling them "The Holly Tree: Three Branches" when he reprinted them in CHRISTMAS STORIES. "The Guest" tells of Charley, a jilted lover, who gets snowed in at the Holly Tree Inn on his way to LIVERPOOL to sail for AMERICA, spending his time remembering stories about the many inns where he has stayed. In the second section, Cobbs, the boots of the inn, tells Charley "The Boots," a story of two children who try to elope to GRETNA GREEN. In "The Bill," Charley learns that he has not been jilted and is reunited with his sweetheart.

Holly Tree Inn, The Inn on the YORKSHIRE moor that is the setting for "The Holly Tree." It is thought to be based on the GEORGE AND NEW INN in GRETA BRIDGE, where Dickens had stayed in 1838.

Holywell Street Street running parallel to the STRAND on the north, "despised" for its unsavory collection of old clothes dealers. *Boz,* "Monmouth Street."

"Home for Homeless Women" Article for *HOUSEHOLD WORDS* (April 23, 1853) describing the operation and philosophy of a successful home for women from the streets. Although it is not named in the article, the institution was URANIA COTTAGE, a charitable enterprise in which Dickens had a guiding hand. *Miscellaneous.*

Hominy, Mrs. Major Pretentious and conceited American "philosopher and authoress" to whom Martin Chuzzlewit is introduced at the National Hotel; she signs her letters from abroad "The Mother of the Modern Gracchi" (22). "She was very straight, very tall, and not at all flexible in face or figure. On her head she wore a great straw-bonnet, with trimmings of the same, in which she looked as if she had been thatched by an unskilful labourer" (22). *Chuzzlewit.*

Honeythunder, The Reverend Luke Professional philanthropist, director of the Haven of Philanthropy, brother-in-law of Mrs. Crisparkle, and guardian of Neville and Helena Landless; a bullying, overbearing man whose "philanthropy was of that gunpowderous sort [so] that the difference between it and animosity was hard to determine" (6). He is quick to assume Neville's guilt and give up his guardianship of the Landless twins (17). *Drood.*

Honner, Robert (1809–52) and Maria (1812–1870) Actor and theater manager; as manager of Sadler's Wells in the 1840s, he produced and took leading roles in several Dickens adaptations. Among Honner's roles were Fagin, Quilp, Scrooge, the Mysterious Stranger in *Rudge,* and Mrs. Brown in *Dombey.* His wife, Maria, played Oliver, Little Nell, Dot Peerybingle, Clemency Newcome, and Edith Granger.

Hood, Thomas (1799–1845) Poet and wit and a friend of Dickens during first half of the 1840s. His appreciative review of *Curiosity Shop* in the ATHENAEUM brought Dickens an "unusual glow of pleasure and encouragement." In his 1848 preface to the novel, Dickens goes on to remark: "Long afterwards, and when I had come to know him well, and to see him, stout of heart, going slowly down into his grave, I knew the writer of that essay to be Thomas Hood."

Hood's Magazine and Comic Miscellany One of several literary magazines edited by Thomas HOOD in the course of his career. He began this journal in 1844 and it continued for three years after his death. Dickens's essay "A Threatening Letter to Thomas Hood, from an Ancient Gentleman" appeared in the May 1844 issue. *Miscellaneous.*

Hook, Theodore (1788–1841) Tory wit, dramatist, comic writer, and silver-fork novelist, Hook was appointed editor of the *New Monthly Magazine* in 1837, charged to challenge the success of BENTLEY'S MISCELLANY under the editorship of Dickens. Although Hook serialized novels by himself, Mrs. Trollope, and MARRYAT in the magazine, it did not seriously challenge Bentley's magazine.

Hop Pole Inn, Tewkesbury Inn in Gloucestershire where Pickwick, Bob Sawyer, and Ben Allen stop on their way to BIRMINGHAM. *Pickwick* (50).

Hopkins (1) Candidate for beadle. *Boz,* "Election for Beadle."

Hopkins (2) The Bashful Young Gentleman. *Young Gentlemen.*

Hopkins, Captain Fellow inmate with Micawber in KING'S BENCH, a prisoner "in the last extremity of shabbiness." *Copperfield* (11).

Hopkins, Jack Fellow medical student with Bob Sawyer who, at the bachelor party, tells the story of the child who swallowed a necklace. *Pickwick* (32).

"Horatio Sparkins" One of five "Tales" in *Boz,* it tells of a draper's assistant who poses as a gentleman, fooling the snobbish Maldertons. Originally published in the MONTHLY MAGAZINE (February 1834).

Horn Coffee House The establishment near the FLEET PRISON to which Pickwick sends for wine to celebrate Winkle's marriage. *Pickwick* (44).

Hornback, Bert G. (1935–) Professor, University of Michigan; performer of dramatic readings from Dickens; scholar and critic of Victorian literature, especially Dickens. In *Noah's Arkitecture; A Study of Dickens' Mythology* (1972), Hornback suggests a mythopoeic reading of the novels based largely on the Eden and Noah stories from Genesis. Concentrating on *Copperfield* in *"The*

Hero of My Life" (1981), Hornback explores Dickens's central theme, the function of imagination in creating human wisdom. *Great Expectations: A Novel of Friendship* (1987) offers an introduction to the novel, directed to undergraduates.

Horne, Richard Hengist (1803–1884)   Poet, journalist, and friend of Dickens, he was on the staff of the DAILY NEWS and HOUSEHOLD WORDS, even though WILLS was not always satisfied with his work. He performed minor roles in some of Dickens's theatricals, even though Dickens thought him "the very worst actor that the world ever saw." He included a chapter on Dickens in *A New Spirit of the Age* (1844). He immigrated to Australia as a Commissioner of Public Lands in 1852, but continued to submit occasional essays to Dickens's periodicals.

Hornsey   An area of north London where Pickwick has carried out "unwearied researches" (*Pickwick*, 1). Betsey Trotwood's husband is buried in the Hornsey churchyard (*Copperfield*, 54).

Horse Guards   The building in WHITEHALL that houses the War Department. Gabriel Varden sets up Sim Tappertit as a shoeblack under an archway near the Horse Guards (*Rudge*, 82). Peggotty takes Mr. Dick to see the guards at the entrance (*Copperfield*, 35). Also mentioned in *Nickleby* (41).

Horsemonger Lane   On this street in the BOROUGH stood the Horsemonger Lane Gaol where Dickens in 1849 saw the execution of the notorious MANNINGS, which prompted him to write a letter to the *Times* calling for the abolition of public executions. He later based the character of Hortense in *Bleak House* on Mrs. Manning. Mrs. Chivery's tobacco shop is located at 5 Horsemonger Lane (*Dorrit*, I:18).

Hortense   Lady Dedlock's passionate French maid, who becomes insanely jealous when she is supplanted by Rosa: "a large-eyed brown woman with black hair: who would be handsome, but for a certain feline mouth, and general uncomfortable tightness of face, rendering the jaws too eager, and the skull too prominent. There is something indefinably keen and wan about her anatomy; and she has a watchful way of looking out of the corners of her eyes without turning her head, which could be pleasantly dispensed with—especially when she is in an ill-humour and near knives" (12). She aids Tulkinghorn's investigation, but when he does not reward her appropriately, she murders him (48). Bucket and his wife pursue and arrest her (54). *Bleak House.* She is loosely based on Mrs. MANNING, the notorious murderess whose execution Dickens witnessed in 1849.

Horton, Susan (1941–)   Professor, University of Massachusetts, Boston; interested in the ways in which Dickens creates his audience and the ways in which his

readers create the novels. Horton explores in *Interpreting Interpreting: Interpreting Dickens's "Dombey"* (1979) the various ways of reading and interpreting *Dombey and Son,* showing how different interpretive contexts shape the reader's understanding of the novel. *The Reader in the Dickens World* (1981) explores the contradictions in Dickens's rhetorical voice that produce conflicting expectations in the reader.

Hosier Lane   A street beside SMITHFIELD MARKET along which Oliver goes with Bill Sikes. *Twist* (21).

"Hospital Patient, The"   Originally published in *The Carlton Chronicle* (August 6, 1836), this sketch describes a young woman in hospital from a brutal beating who, just before dying, refuses to identify her lover as the man who beat her. *Boz.*

Houghton, Arthur Boyd (1836–1875)   Painter and illustrator, he provided frontispieces for *Hard Times* and *Mutual Friend* in the CHEAP EDITION.

House, Humphry (1909–1955)   Oxford don and, with Edmund WILSON, one of the pioneers of contemporary Dickens studies. His classic work, *The Dickens World* (1941), places Dickens in his social and historical contexts and traces his growing awareness of the systematic social problems of Victorian England. The original editor of the Pilgrim Edition of Dickens's LETTERS, his role was assumed by **Madeline House** and **Graham Storey** after his early death.

Household Edition   Popular edition of Dickens's works issued in monthly parts by CHAPMAN & HALL between 1871 and 1879. This edition included John FORSTER's *Life of Dickens,* as well as the novels; it was generously illustrated by several new illustrators, notably James Mahoney, Charles GREEN, H. French, F. A. Fraser, A. B. Frost, Gordon Thomson, E. G. Dalziel, and, most significantly, Frederick BARNARD, who depicted nine of the novels. The **American Household Edition**, issued simultaneously by Harper & Brothers, replaced several of the British illustrators with American artists C. S. Reinhart, Thomas Worth, W. L. Shepperd, E. A. Abbey, and Thomas Nast.

"Household Narrative of Current Events, The"   Monthly supplement to HOUSEHOLD WORDS, begun in April 1850 and discontinued in December 1855, providing a chronicle of the important events during the preceding month. Dickens wrote the announcement describing the "Narrative" for the April 13, 1850 issue. *Stone.*

Household Words   Weekly magazine "conducted" and edited by Dickens from March 30, 1850 to May 28, 1859. It took its title from Shakespeare, "Familiar in their mouths as Household Words" (Henry V, Act IV, sc.3), and among its stated purposes was "to show to all, that in all familiar things, even in those which are repellant on the surface, there is Romance enough, if we will find it out." The magazine, sold at 2d. for a weekly issue, was also issued in monthly form and in bound annual volumes. Articles were unsigned and many were edited or coauthored by Dickens or his subeditor, W. H. WILLS. Although serialized novels were not part of the original plan, Dickens ran *Hard Times* in the magazine after the circulation dropped in 1853. Besides the many articles he wrote or collaborated on for the magazine, Dickens wrote the frame narratives and occasional stories for the annual Christmas numbers. After quarreling with BRADBURY & EVANS over the publication of a statement about his separation, Dickens discontinued *Household Words* and incorporated it into ALL THE YEAR ROUND.

Ann Lohrli compiled the contents of the magazine, identified its contributors, and developed summaries of their work for the magazine (*Household Words*, 1973).

"House to Let, A"   Christmas number of HOUSEHOLD WORDS for 1858. Dickens contributed the third chapter, "Going into Society"; he collaborated with Wilkie COLLINS on another, "Let at Last."

Howler, The Reverend Melchisedech   Evangelical preacher who acts as Mrs. MacStinger's spiritual guide and performs the wedding ceremony when she marries Bunsby (60): He "announced the destruction of the world for that day two years, at ten in the morning, and opened a front-parlour for the reception of ladies and gentlemen of the Ranting persuasion" (15). *Dombey*.

Hubble Mr. and Mrs.   Friends of the Gargerys who attend Christmas dinner at the blacksmith's house. Mr. Hubble is the village wheelwright "with his legs extraordinarily wide apart: so that in my short days I always saw some miles of open country between them when I met him coming up the lane" (4). *Expectations*.

Huffam, Christopher   Dickens's godfather, a prosperous naval rigger who lived in LIMEHOUSE. Dickens made several memorable visits to him when his family lived in BAYHAM STREET in 1822–23.

Hugh   Wild young ostler at the MAYPOLE INN who becomes a leader of the Gordon rioters, "a young man, of a hale athletic figure, and a giant's strength, whose sunburnt face and swarthy throat, overgrown with jet black hair, might have served a painter for a model. . . . The negligence and disorder of the whole man, with something fierce and sullen in his features, gave him a picturesque appearance" (11). Hugh acts as an agent for Sir John Chester, stealing Emma Haredale's letters to Edward Chester for him (21, 28). Recruited to the No Popery cause by Gashford (38), Hugh leads the rioters in several actions, but he protects Barnaby and takes the blame for leading him into the riots (77). Although Varden discovers that Hugh is the illegitimate son of Sir John Chester and a gypsy woman, his father refuses to do

anything to acknowledge his son or save him from execution (75). *Rudge*.

Hughes, Rev. Stephen and Rev. Hugh   Historical figures, two brothers who were clergymen in the neighboring parishes of Llanallgo and Penrhos in Wales. In an essay for ALL THE YEAR ROUND, "The Shipwreck," Dickens praised their ministry to the survivors and the dead from the shipwreck of the *Royal Charter* on its way from Melbourne to LIVERPOOL on October 26, 1859. *Uncommercial* (2).

Hugo, Victor (1802–1885)   French novelist, poet, and dramatist; best known for *The Hunchback of Notre Dame* (1831) and *Les Misérables* (1862); one of the French authors Dickens met on his visit to Paris in 1844. Dickens was sometimes compared to Hugo; both novelists used horror and eccentric characters, both utilized the serial format.

Hullah, John (1812–1884)   Composer who wrote the music for Dickens's comic operetta *The Village Coquettes*.

Humm, Anthony   "A converted fireman, now a schoolmaster, and occasionally an itinerant preacher," who is the president of the Brick Lane Branch of the United Grand Junction Ebenezer Temperance Association. *Pickwick* (33).

Hummums Hotel   The inn in COVENT GARDEN where the FINCHES OF THE GROVE hold their meetings and where Pip spends the night after being warned by Wemmick not to go home. *Expectations* (33, 45).

Humphrey, Master   Narrator of MASTER HUMPHREY'S CLOCK, "a misshapen, deformed old man" who gathers a group of friends around him who contribute manuscripts that they read to each other and store in his clock case. He extends his role, in what must be an authorial afterthought, when he identifies himself as the "Single Gentleman," the brother of Nell's grandfather, in *Curiosity Shop*. After the completion of *Barnaby Rudge*, the Deaf Gentleman, one of the circle of friends, tells of Master Humphrey's peaceful death. *Humphrey*.

Hungerford Market   A long-established market that had fallen into decay in the early years of the 19th century when Dickens spent odd hours there while working in the BLACKING WAREHOUSE. A new market replaced the old buildings in 1833 and CHARING CROSS Station was built on the site in 1862. Mr. Dick has rooms in the vicinity of the market (35), and the Micawbers leave for AUSTRALIA from the nearby **Hungerford Stairs** (57). *Copperfield*.

Hunt   Captain Boldwig's gardener. *Pickwick* (19).

Hunt, Leigh (1784–1859)   Poet, essayist, and editor of literary journals, Hunt was a friend of Keats, Byron,

Shelley, Moore, and Lamb. John FORSTER introduced him to Dickens in 1838 and the two became friends. When Dickens based Harold Skimpole on Hunt, however, the friendship was strained. Dickens claimed that only some of Hunt's more delightful characteristics informed the character, but he later admitted that "I suppose that he is the most exact portrait that was ever painted in words! . . . It is an absolute reproduction of a real man."

Hunt, William Holman (1827–1910)   Artist and member of the PRE-RAPHAELITE Brotherhood who was the best man at the wedding of Charles COLLINS to Dickens's daughter Kate in 1860 (see Kate Macready DICKENS).

"Hunted Down"   Short story published in the *New York Ledger* (August 20 and 27 and September 3, 1859) and in *ALL THE YEAR ROUND* (April 4, 11, 1860). Based on the case of the notorious poisoner Thomas Wainewright, the story is narrated by Mr. Sampson, an insurance man who holds a policy on the life of Alfred Beckwith, an intended victim of Julius Slinkton, the beneficiary. Beckwith is, in fact, Meltham, an insurance actuary in disguise, determined to trap Slinkton for the earlier murder of his niece, the girl Meltham loved. After the crimes are brought to light, Slinkton commits suicide and Meltham fades and dies of a broken heart. *Reprinted*.

Hunter, Horace   Emily Brown's lover, who challenges his rival, Alexander Trott, to a duel. He eventually marries Emily. *Boz*, "Winglebury."

Hunter, Mrs. Leo   Poetess and literary hostess of "The Den" in EATANSWILL. **Mr. Leo Hunter**, her "grave" husband, delivers to Pickwick and his followers the invitation to attend her fancy dress "*fête champêtre*," where they will meet other literary lions and hear his wife recite her "Ode to an Expiring Frog." *Pickwick* (15).

Hutley, Jemmy ("Dismal Jemmy")   A strolling actor and brother to Job Trotter who tells "The Stroller's Tale" to the Pickwickians in ROCHESTER. *Pickwick* (3).

Hutter, Albert D. (1941–)   Professor, UCLA; mystery writer; psychoanalyst. Hutter has written several articles on psychological issues in the novels and their roots in Victorian culture, among them "The High Tower of His Mind: Psychoanalysis and the Reader of *Bleak House*" (*Criticism*, 1977) and "Nation and Generation in *A Tale of Two Cities*" (*PMLA*, 1978). "Dismemberment and Articulation in *Our Mutual Friend*" (*Dickens Studies Annual*, 1983), analyzes the role of Mr. Venus, the taxidermist and articulator of bones, connecting it with the death and resurrection story at the center of the novel, especially in the Harmon murder plot, and with the fragmentation and dismemberment of Victorian society.

Hyde Park   Dickens had lodgings at several addresses in the neighborhood of the park during the 1860s. Oliver and Bill Sikes pass Hyde Park Corner on their way to CHERTSEY. *Twist* (21).

Hyppolite, Private   Soldier billeted at the perfumers's in VAUBAN. "Somebody's Luggage."

"Hymn of the Wiltshire Labourers, The"   Verses by Dickens, published in the *DAILY NEWS* in 1846, expressing sympathy for the agricultural workers in Wiltshire, who were suffering from hunger and oppression.

"Idea of Mine, An" Article for *HOUSEHOLD WORDS* (March 13, 1858), proposing to reconnect the fine arts with reality by withdrawing all artists' models from service, an action which might force the artists to concentrate on the "telling of stories and conveying of ideas." *Miscellaneous*.

Idle, Thomas One of the two lazy apprentices, based on William HOGARTH's apprentices from *Industry and Idleness*. Idle is a thinly disguised version of Wilkie COLLINS. *Lazy Tour*.

"Idiots" Article for *HOUSEHOLD WORDS* (June 4, 1853) by W. H. WILLS and Dickens, describing current knowledge about idiocy and advocating humane institutions for the care and instruction of idiots. A visit to the Asylum for Idiots in HIGHGATE shows the effectiveness of such institutions. *Stone*.

"Ignorance and Crime" Article for the *EXAMINER* (April 22, 1848), reporting on the figures released by the goverment indicating how many of those convicted of various crimes in 1847 had no occupational skills and were illiterate. Ignorance, Dickens suggests, is almost always allied with crime, disease, and misery. *Miscellaneous*.

Ikey (1) Assistant to Solomon Jacobs, the bailiff who imprisons Watkins Tottle. *Boz*, "Tottle."

Ikey (2) Stableboy at the inn near the Haunted House. "Haunted House."

Illustrations Nearly all of Dickens's novels were illustrated in their serial and first editions. Only *Hard Times* and *Great Expectations*, which first appeared in Dickens's unillustrated magazines, made their first appearance without pictures.

Pickwick, Dickens's first novel, was originally conceived as a series of sporting prints by Robert SEYMOUR for which Dickens was to provide editorial copy. Dickens took the opportunity provided by Seymour's suicide to reorient the project and to give more prominence to the verbal narrative. Dickens seems to have thought of *Twist*, which he subtitled "The Parish Boy's Progress," as a narrative in the manner of William HOGARTH, whose progresses told stories in series of pictures. Visual narrative, then, had an important place in Dickens's developing idea of the novel. The illustrators with whom Dickens worked on these early novels, BROWNE and CRUIKSHANK, were both practitioners in the graphic satire tradition descended from Hogarth.

In his standard serial format, each monthly number included two illustrations, so a 20-part novel contained 40 illustrations by the time it was completed. During his career, Dickens worked with 18 different illustrators, among them some of the foremost artists of his day, including Cruikshank, LEECH, MACLISE, LANDSEER and FILDES. His principal collaborator was Hablot Browne ("PHIZ"), who illustrated most of the novels from *Pickwick* through *Two Cities*.

The illustrations for the later novels are generally considered to be less successful than those for the earlier books. This decline has been variously attributed to the displacement of visual caricature by more realistic illustration, the increased literacy of Dickens's readers, and Dickens's own diminished interest in the illustrations.

J. R. HARVEY (1971) discusses the Dickens illustrations in relation to the tradition of graphic satire. Jane R. Cohen (*Charles Dickens and his Original Illustrators*, 1980) describes the contributions of each of the 18 original illustrators and the nature of their relationship with Dickens. Michael STEIG (1978) discusses the collaboration between Dickens and Browne and how the illustrations affect the reader's understanding of the novels.

Many later artists have also undertaken to illustrate the novels or to represent the characters. Among the more noteworthy are EYTINGE, BARNARD, "Kyd" (J. C. CLARKE), Charles GREEN, FURNISS, C. E. BROCK, Gordon Ross.

Impressionism A technique in writing in which events or scenes are described in terms of how they appear at a precise moment from an individual's point of view. Derived from impressionistic painting, literary impressionism's most notable practitioners were such turn-of-the-century novelists as Stephen Crane and Joseph Conrad. Although he was writing without the example of Monet, Manet, and their fellow painters to draw on, Dickens made occasional use of impressionistic technique, as in the opening chapter of *Expectations*. There Pip describes the convict picking him up and turning him upside down in the following terms: "The man, after looking at me for a moment, turned me upside down, and emptied my pockets. There was nothing in them but a piece of bread. When the church came to itself—for he was so sudden and strong that he made it go head over heels before me, and I saw the steeple under my feet—when the church came to itself, I say, I was seated on a high tombstone, trembling, while he ate the bread ravenously."

"In and Out of Jail"   Review of Frederic Hill's *Crime: Its Amount, Causes, and Remedies* (1853) for *HOUSEHOLD WORDS* (May 14, 1853) by Henry MORLEY, with considerable revisions and additions by Dickens. The essay concludes with a strong statement of Dickens's views that prisons should punish and that the lives of prisoners should not be more comfortable than those of the poor. *Stone*.

"In the French-Flemish Country"   On a journey to the Flemish area of France, the Traveller goes to a performance of a provincial theater company and to a fair where he sees the ventriloquist and the Face-maker, a mime who makes a thousand faces. *Uncommercial* (27).

Industrial Revolution   Historians usually date the Industrial Revolution from about 1760, when a series of inventions began to transform the manufacture of textiles. The impact of these inventions was not generally recognized, however, until the early 19th century, when the application of steam to power the new machines created a number of new industrial cities in the north of England and railways made them easily accessible from the south. Dickens and other Victorian novelists born during the second decade of the century were the first generation of writers to acknowledge the emergence of industrial England.

The first description of industry in Dickens's works appears in Little Nell's journey through the BLACK COUNTRY in *Curiosity Shop* (43–45), but Dickens's most sustained depiction of industrial England is in *Hard Times*, in which Coketown is based on his observations of life in MANCHESTER and PRESTON. Dickens wrote about these industrial towns as an outsider, a southerner with little day-to-day experience of life there, and he has been criticized for simplifying and misunderstanding the industrial north, especially the trade UNIONS. However, he does not attempt in *Hard Times* to provide a realistic description of the factories or of life in the new industrial cities as Mrs. GASKELL, a resident of Manchester, had done in *Mary Barton* (1848). Nor does he take on such issues as child labor or industrial safety. He directs his attention instead to the hard-fact empiricism that produced industrialization and its effects on education and domestic life.

As a novelist of urban life, of the anomie and isolation in the cities and the reification of the human that turned men into machines, Dickens, more than any other early Victorian novelist, responded to the changes brought about by industrialization. His use of the RAILWAY in *Dombey* and other novels symbolizes the changes brought about by "steam." Raymond WILLIAMS, in his various writings on Dickens, discusses the ways in which Dickens's works responded to industrialization and urbanization.

"Inexhaustible, The"   Nickname of John and Bella Harmon's baby. *Mutual Friend* (IV:12).

Infant Mortality   Although the infant mortality rate in Victorian England was the lowest among all but the Scandinavian countries in Europe, it was nevertheless approximately 10 times the current rate. In 1840, the reported rate was 143 out of 1,000 live births, and this figure is probably low, since many physicians did not report stillbirths.

The death of a newborn or of the mother was not uncommon. Dickens's daughter Dora died in her first year, not long after the deaths in his novels of Fanny Dombey after the birth of young Paul and of David Copperfield's infant brother. Even though the five little stone lozenges marking the graves of Pip's siblings (*Expectations*, 1) may exaggerate the average figures, they reduced the 13 graves in the churchyard at COOLING that Dickens had in mind to a more believable number.

Victorians often blamed the high infant mortality rate on the practice of baby farming, putting infants into foster facilities like that of Mrs. Mann in *Twist* (2), where Oliver's friend, young Dick, becomes a statistic. Dickens attacked the practice of baby farming in his articles on one such institution in "Paradise at Tooting."

"Infant Phenomenon, The"   Stage name of Ninetta CRUMMLES. *Nickleby*.

"Inimitable Boz, The"   The name Dickens sometimes gave himself, turning his nom de plume into the appellation of a theatrical or circus performer. (See also BOZ.)

Inns of Court   Located near the law courts in HOLBORN, these institutions were originally the premises of four societies empowered to admit persons to the Bar: GRAY'S INN, LINCOLN'S INN, the Inner TEMPLE and Middle TEMPLE. By the middle of the 19th century, chambers in the inns could be rented by people other than barristers and law students. Pip and Herbert Pocket, for example, have rooms in the Temple. There were also several lesser inns, known as the Inns of CHANCERY, that offered such lodgings: BARNARD'S INN, CLIFFORD'S INN, FURNIVAL'S INN, SERGEANT'S INN, STAPLE INN, and SYMOND'S INN.

Insolvent Debtors' Court   Court in Portugal Street, west London, where Solomon Pell practiced (*Pickwick*, 43). Here insolvent debtors who could prove that their personal belongings were worth less than £20 could appeal for relief from imprisonment. The court was abolished in 1861.

Inspector, The Policeman in charge of the Thames station who investigates the deaths of John Harmon and, later, of Gaffer Hexam. *Mutual Friend*.

"Insularities" Article for HOUSEHOLD WORDS (January 19, 1856), describing patterns of unreasonable or ridiculous behavior that the English fail to question: resistance to innovative dress and beards, denigration of "theatrical" paintings, contempt for the innocent recreations of the poor, and servile adulation of aristocracy and royalty. *Miscellaneous*.

International Copyright On his first trip to AMERICA in 1842, Dickens raised a considerable controversy when he delivered three speeches—in BOSTON, HARTFORD, and NEW YORK—calling for a system of international copyright. Although copyright laws had been adopted in the 18th century protecting the works of American authors, such protection did not extend to works by foreigners. The novels of Dickens and works by other English authors were commonly reprinted in American papers that specialized in pirating the works of foreigners. Dickens argued that this practice not only denied the authors their rightful reward, but it also created unfair competition for native writers and discouraged the development of a national literature. His remarks prompted American writers to circulate a petition to Congress urging an international copyright agreement, but his speeches were also attacked as greedy and self-serving in several American newspapers—many of them profiting by piracy. In response, Dickens attacked the American press in *Notes*, satirized it in *Chuzzlewit*, and urged his fellow English writers to deal only with reputable American publishers. An international copyright agreement was not passed until 1891. See also COPYRIGHT.

"International Copyright" Letter that appeared in the *EXAMINER* (July 16, 1842) and in other English papers, discussing the issue of INTERNATIONAL COPYRIGHT and urging Dickens's fellow English writers not to deal with American publishers who opposed an agreement. *Miscellaneous*.

Interpolated Tales Stories inserted or added to a narrative that are not integral to the main plot or story. Dickens modeled his use of interpolated tales on the work of Henry FIELDING and Tobias SMOLLETT, two of his favorite authors as a child. The several interpolated tales in *Pickwick* were long viewed as extraneous to the story, but recent critics have argued that they are necessary to present the dark side of life that the innocent Pickwick otherwise fails to notice. Interpolated tales appear in several of the early novels—*Pickwick, Nickleby*, and *Master Humphrey's Clock*—but Dickens abandoned the practice in his later, more carefully structured works. Miss Wade's "History of a Self-Tormentor" (*Dorrit*, II:21)

has the appearance of an interpolated tale but is organic to the thematic development of the novel.

Ipswich The town in Suffolk where Pickwick, in pursuit of Jingle, is brought before magistrate Nupkins after his misunderstanding with Miss Witherfield and Peter Magnus at the WHITE HART INN. *Pickwick* (22–25).

Iron Bridge Southwark Bridge over the THAMES, built in 1818, a favorite walking place of Little Dorrit (*Dorrit*, I:9, 18).

Irving, Sir Henry (1838–1905) Victorian actor, known for his ability to play many kinds of roles. Among the Dickens characters that he portrayed were Jingle, Bill Sikes, Nicholas Nickleby, Mr. Domby, John Peerybingle, and Digby Grant, a character based on Mr. Dorrit. He gave performances of Dickens characters for charity. In recognition of his success in these performances, the Dickens family gave him the desk and gas lighting system that Dickens used in his PUBLIC READINGS.

Irving, Washington (1783–1859) American author whose *Sketch-Book* provided an important model for Dickens's *Sketches by Boz*. After corresponding with him, Dickens met Irving on his American tour in 1842. At the Dickens Dinner in NEW YORK, Irving supported Dickens's controversial call for an INTERNATIONAL COPYRIGHT agreement when he noted in his toast to the visitor, "It is but fair that those who have laurels for their brows should be permitted to browse on their laurels." Dickens described Irving as "a *great* fellow. We have laughed most heartily together. He is just the man he ought to be."

Is She His Wife? or Something Singular A one-act farce performed at the St. James's Theatre, March 6, 1837. It deals with the misunderstandings that arise when two married couples, the Lovetowns and the Limburys, and a neighboring squire, Felix Tapkins, misrepresent their marital status and flirt with each other.

Isaac Sheriff's officer who takes Mrs. Bardell to the FLEET PRISON. *Pickwick* (46).

Islington In the 19th century, this village on the north edge of London was an important way station on the great north road out of London. Either the ANGEL or the PEACOCK INN is mentioned as a landmark or stopping place in *Boz* ("Prisoners' Van"), *Rudge* (31, 68), *Nickleby* (39), *Twist* (8, 12), *Bleak House* (59). Potter and Smithers (*Boz*, "Making a Night"), Tom and Ruth Pinch (*Chuzzlewit*, 36, 37), and Mr. Morfin (*Dombey*, 13) live in Islington.

"It Is Not Generally Known" Article for HOUSEHOLD WORDS (September 2, 1854), arguing against Sunday closing laws. Such laws are promoted, Dickens suggests, by those who base legislation on the worst members of society and justify closing public amusements on Sunday because the notorious criminal Sloggins declares that "Amusements done it." *Miscellaneous*.

"Italian Prisoner, The" The Traveller recounts a commission given to him by an English friend to deliver a letter to Giovanni Carlavero while on a tour of ITALY. Calavero, a wine maker, was once a political prisoner who was released through the efforts of the English letter-writer. His gratitude is unbounded and he gives the Traveller a huge bottle of wine to take back to England—a commission that leads to countless difficulties on the return journey. *Uncommercial* (17).

Italy Dickens made two trips to Italy. He spent a year there with his family in 1844–45, first staying at GENOA for several months and later touring the north of Italy, ROME, and NAPLES. The letters he wrote to John FORSTER during this trip provided the basis for *Pictures from Italy* (1846). He went to Italy a second time in 1853 with Augustus EGG and Wilkie COLLINS, visiting Genoa, Naples—where they climbed Vesuvius—Rome, FLORENCE, VENICE, and Turin. Dickens was able to appreciate Italy as a tourist because he was not generally recognized as a famous author there and he did not expect it to exemplify his political ideals, as he had AMERICA. He was unsympathetic to the CATHOLIC CHURCH, however, which he saw as allied with tyranny and oppression, and he described church ceremonies as fraudulent "mummery."

Dickens drew on his Italian experiences for his descriptions of the Dorrit family in Venice and Rome (II:3–7, 11, 14–15, 19). Em'ly flees from Steerforth and hides in a fishing village near Naples (*Copperfield*, 46, 50).

"Ivins, J'mima" The common pronunciation of the name of Jemima EVANS. *Boz*, "Miss Evans."

"Ivy Green, The" A poem written by the clergyman at DINGLEY DELL. *Pickwick* (6).

Izzard One of the welcoming committee for Elijah Pogram. *Chuzzlewit* (34).

J

Jack (1) Prisoner charged with beating to death the woman he lived with. *Boz,* "Hospital Patient."

Jack (2) Mrs. Lupin's manservant. *Chuzzlewit* (36).

Jack (3) One of the policemen who arrest Jonas Chuzzlewit. *Chuzzlewit* (51).

Jack (4) The man of all work at the riverside inn where Pip and Magwich stay as Pip attempts to spirit Magwich out of England. *Expectations* (54).

Jack (5) A common sailor as a type described in "Poor Merchantile Jack." *Uncommercial* (5).

Jackman, Major Jemmy Mrs. Lirriper's lodger, a good-hearted but irregular man who becomes joint guardian to Jemmy Lirriper. "Lirriper's Lodgings" and "Legacy."

Jackson (1) DODSON AND FOGG's clerk. He delivers the writs to the Pickwickians (31) and later arrests Mrs. Bardell (46). *Pickwick.*

Jackson (2) Acquaintance of Cousin Feenix who runs a boxing establishment in BOND STREET. *Dombey* (61).

Jackson (3) A former turnkey of the MARSHALSEA PRISON. *Dorrit* (I:19).

Jackson, Michael Bucket's fictional informant about Lady Dedlock's visit to the brickmaker's. *Bleak House* (57).

Jackson, Mr. and Mrs. Friends of the Plausible Couple. *Young Couples.*

Jackson, Thomas A. (1879–1955) In *Charles Dickens: The Progress of a Radical* (1938), a Marxist reading of the novels, Jackson finds many points of agreement between Marx and Engels and Dickens. He describes the late novels from *Bleak House* on as the culmination of Dickens's developing class analysis of his society.

Jackson, Young He works his way up in the firm of BARBOX BROTHERS until he is the only member. Then he dissolves the firm. *Mugby.*

Jacksonini, Signor Clown at the Cloisterham Theatre, "quite as large as life and almost as miserable." *Drood* (14).

Jacobs, Solomon Bailiff who arrests Watkins Tottle for debt. *Boz,* "Tottle."

Jacob's Island Island in the THAMES RIVER off Bermondsey where Toby Crackit's house is located in a festering slum. Sikes ends his life here. *Twist* (50).

Jacques The name taken by the revolutionaries, the "Jacquerie," connected with Monsieur Defarge. **Jacques Four** is the epithet assumed by Defarge himself. **Jacques Five** is the road mender who watches the Marquis St. Evrémonde and later becomes a woodsawyer in Paris. *Two Cities.*

Jaffe, Audrey Contemporary scholar and critic, professor, Ohio State University. In *Vanishing Points: Dickens, Narrative, and the Subject of Omniscience* (1991), Jaffee discusses the NARRATOR and POINT OF VIEW in Dickens's novels, describing his omniscient narrator as occupying a position between a disembodied voice outside the novel and a presence within it, a tension produced by the problematical status of omniscience itself in Victorian England. She also discusses several "semi-omniscient" characters, figures like Florence Dombey, Esther Summerson, David Copperfield, and John Harmon, who mediate between the action in the novel and our consciousness of it, becoming in the process "vanishing points" in the narration.

Jaggers Lawyer with offices in LITTLE BRITAIN who serves both Miss Havisham and Magwich. "He was a burly man of an exceedingly dark complexion, with an exceedingly large head and a corresponding large hand. . . . His eyes were set very deep in his head, and were disagreeably sharp and suspicious" (11). Pip first meets him at Miss Havisham's house (11). Later, he announces to Pip his great expectations (18), and he represents Pip's benefactor, whose identity is withheld from Pip. He practices criminal law, employing some questionable strategies to defend his clients, but he is also a compassionate man who attempts in small ways to mitigate the evil in the world. He arranges, for example, for Miss Havisham to adopt Estella, saving the child from the criminal underworld into which she was born. *Expectations.*

Jairing's Hotel   The London hotel where reputable "families and gentlemen" from the MIDLANDS stay; the Grazinglands eat a desultory meal here served by a waiter who would rather they dine somewhere else. *Uncommercial* (6).

James (1)   Bayham Badger's butler. *Bleak House* (13).

James (2)   Brook Dingwall's servant. *Boz*, "Sentiment."

James (3)   Servant in Mrs. Tibbs's boarding house. *Boz*, "Boarding-house."

James (4)   Son of Old John who is shot in India as a soldier. *Reprinted*, "Poor Man's Tale."

James (5)   Twin brother to John, in business together at Goodman's Fields. He has a premonition of his brother's death. *Reprinted*, "Dusk."

James (1), Henry (1843–1916)   American born novelist and critic. As a realist and modernist, James is often remembered as antagonistic to Dickens. He expressed his reservations about Dickens's superficiality and philosophical incoherence, and the lack of universal humanity in his eccentric characters, in his review of *Our Mutual Friend*, written for *The Nation* when James was only 22. Nevertheless, in later autobiographical writings, James recalled the powerful hold Dickens had on his childhood imagination and in his *Notebooks* he describes meeting "the master" during the older novelist's 1867 reading tour in AMERICA. George H. FORD (1955) discusses James's mixed feelings about his predecessor and speculates about Dickens's influence on James's work, especially *The Princess Casamassima* (1886).

James (2), Henry   Captain of the *Defiance*, the ship that reported the wreck of the *Son and Heir*, the ship on which Walter Gay was sailing. *Dombey* (32).

James, Sir Jasper   "Remarkable man of business" who is twice appointed with changes in governments to reform Tapenham's department. *Miscellaneous*, "Cheap Patriotism."

Jane (1)   Waitress, "the Hebe of Bellamy's." *Boz*, "Parliamentary Sketch."

Jane (2)   A young visitor at Ramsgate. *Boz*, "Tuggses."

Jane (3)   Maidservant to the Kitterbells. *Boz*, "Bloomsbury Christening."

Jane (4)   Mrs. Potts's maidservant. *Pickwick* (13).

Jane (5)   Wardle's maidservant. *Pickwick* (5).

Jane (6)   Sister of the old lord's fiancée, who offends Miss Knag by insisting that she be waited on by Kate Nickleby. *Nickleby* (18).

Jane (7)   Pecksniff's maidservant. *Chuzzlewit* (31).

Jane (8)   Miss Wozenham's maidservant. "Lirriper's Lodgings."

Jane (9)   Mrs. Orange's maidservant. "Holiday Romance."

Jane (10)   One of the suicides at "Mr. Baker's trap." *Uncommercial* (3).

Jane Aunt (1),   Wife of Uncle Robert, a guest at the Christmas dinner. *Boz*, "Christmas Dinner."

Jane Aunt (2),   One of Wegg's imagined inhabitants of the corner house. *Mutual Friend* (I:5).

Janet   Betsey Trotwood's maidservant, "a pretty blooming girl, of about nineteen or twenty, . . . one of a series of protégées whom my aunt had taken into her service expressly to educate in the renouncement of mankind, and who had generally completed their abjuration by marrying the baker" (13). She marries a tavern keeper (60). *Copperfield*.

Jarber   The man who reads aloud the story of the "House to Let." "Going into Society."

Jarley, Mrs.   Proprietor of a traveling waxworks, "a Christian lady, stout and comfortable to look upon" (26), who befriends Little Nell and her grandfather and hires Nell as a show woman for her "calm and classical" exhibit. She marries her driver George (47). *Curiosity Shop*.

Jarndyce, John   Present owner of Bleak House and court-appointed guardian to Richard Carstone and Ada Clare, an "upright, hearty and robust" man, "nearer sixty than fifty," who has "a handsome, lively, quick face" (6). He devotes his life to the practice of private philanthropy. He avoids any involvement with the case of Jarndyce and Jarndyce and advises others to do so, advice that would have been useful to his great uncle, **Tom Jarndyce**, who "in despair blew his brains out at a Coffee House in Chancery Lane" (1). He is unsuccessful in preventing Richard's entanglement in the case. When such things put him out of humor, he says "the wind's in the east" and retreats to his Growlery. He adopts Esther Summerson, sending her to school and then engaging her as a companion to Ada (3). He later proposes marriage to her (44); she accepts out of gratitude and obligation, but when he realizes that she really loves Woodcourt, he arranges their marriage, providing a new Bleak House for them in the north (64). *Bleak House*.

Jarndyce and Jarndyce   The lawsuit at the center of *Bleak House* that has been winding on interminably in CHANCERY for several generations. John Jarndyce avoids a destructive obsession with the case, but his great-uncle Tom, Richard Carstone, and others are ruined by it. When it is finally settled at the end of the novel, all proceeds from the will have been used up in legal costs. Dickens based the case on actual cases in Chancery that prompted a movement for court reform at the time the novel was being written.

Jarvis   Clerk to the wine merchants, Wilding and Co. "No Thoroughfare."

Jasper, John (Jack)   Edwin Drood's uncle, "a dark man, of some six-and-twenty, with thick lustrous, well-arranged black hair and whiskers. . . . His voice is deep and good, his face and figure are good, his manner is a little sombre" (2). Although he is choir director at Cloisterham Cathedral, he is also an opium addict and a frequenter of Princess Puffer's den in London's East End. He is devoted to his nephew Edwin, but he is also secretly in love with Edwin's fiancée, Rosa Bud. Although he tries to implicate Neville Landless in the disappearance of Drood, Jasper himself is the most likely suspect at the close of the unfinished novel. *Drood*.

Jean Marie   An Alpine guide in the drama, but not the story, of *No Thoroughfare*.

Jean Paul   An Alpine guide in the drama, but not the story, of *No Thoroughfare*.

Jeddler Family   Family whose house on an ancient battlefield provides the metaphor for their latter-day domestic struggles. For **Doctor Anthony**, a philosophical widower, "the heart and mystery of his philosophy was, to look upon the world as a gigantic practical joke; as something too absurd to be considered seriously, by any rational man." His daughters, **Grace** and **Marion**, however, take life more seriously. Grace, the elder daughter, is earnest and self-denying and performs the mother's role in the household. When Marion, the more frivolous younger daughter, realizes that Grace loves her fiancé, Alfred Heathfield, she disappears, and by doing so, enables Grace and Alfred to marry. She stays secretly with the Doctor's maiden sister **Martha** and returns home after six years to clear her name and eventually to marry Michael Warden. Marion's sacrifice causes the doctor to give up his belief that the world is a joke and to take life seriously. *Battle*.

Jeffrey, Francis (Lord Jeffrey) (1773–1850)   Scottish judge, member of Parliament, literary critic and the editor and founder of the *Edinburgh Review*. An early admirer of Dickens's work, especially *Twist, Curiosity Shop, Carol*, and *Dombey*, Jeffrey became one of Dickens's close friends and a frequent correspondent. Dickens

visited him in Scotland in 1841, dedicated *Cricket* to him, and named his fifth child Francis Jeffrey DICKENS.

Jellyby Family   London family thrown into chaos and confusion by the "mission" of **Mrs. Jellyby** that causes her to neglect her domestic responsibilities. Drawn from Mrs. Caroline CHISHOLM, Mrs. Jellyby is a "pretty, very diminuitive, plump woman of from forty to fifty, with handsome eyes, though they had a curious habit of seeming to look a long way off, as if . . . she could see nothing nearer than Africa" (4). Her "telescopic philanthropy" causes her neglect of her family, evident when her young son **Peepy** gets his head caught in the area railing (4) and when **Mr. Jellyby**, her mild-mannered husband, goes bankrupt (23). She employs her daughter **Caroline (Caddy)** as her amanuensis but neglects instructing her in domestic skills or personal grooming. Caddy, "a jaded and unhealthy-looking, though by no means plain girl" (4), resents this exploitation and confesses her resentment to Esther. Caddy escapes her chaotic home by marrying Prince Turveydrop (30). When Mrs. Jellyby's mission in Africa fails, she takes up the cause of women's rights (67). *Bleak House*.

Jem (1)   The "sallow-faced red-haired sulky boy" who is the doorkeeper at Solomon Jacobs's sponging-house. *Boz*, "Tottle."

Jem (2)   One of Wardle's farm hands. *Pickwick* (28).

Jemima   Polly Toodle's sister who took over the care of Polly's children when she went to work for the Dombeys. *Dombey* (2,6).

Jenkins (1)   Friend of the Contradictory Couple. *Young Couples*.

Jenkins (2)   Sir Mulberry Hawk's manservant. *Nickleby* (50).

Jenkins, Miss   Pianist at the Gattleton's theatricals. *Boz*, "Porter."

Jenkinson   Messenger at the CIRCUMLOCUTION OFFICE. *Dorrit* (I:10).

Jennings (1)   Robe maker, friend of John Dounce. *Boz*, "Dounce."

Jennings (2)   Secretary to Nicholas Tulrumble, mayor of Mudfog. *Mudfog*.

Jennings (3)   Pupil at DOTHEBOY'S HALL. *Nickleby* (7).

Jennings, Miss   Pupil at Nun's House, Miss Twinkleton's school. *Drood* (9).

Jenny   Brickmaker's wife visited by Mrs. Pardiggle accompanied by Esther (8). When her infant dies, Esther covers the child with her handkerchief (8). She trades coats with Lady Dedlock, thus misleading Bucket's pursuit (57). *Bleak House*.

Jerdan, William (1782–1869) Editor of the *Literary Gazette* from 1817 to 1850 who urged Dickens, after he introduced Sam Weller into *Pickwick*, to develop his character "to the utmost." Dickens invited him to the dinner celebrating the completion of the novel. Jerdan also contributed to BENTLEY'S MISCELLANY when it was under Dickens's editorship.

Jerrold, Douglas William (1803–1857) Dramatist, radical satirical journalist and wit, best known for his play *Black-eyed Susan* (1829). Jerrold was one of Dickens's close friends, a man Dickens described as "the gentlest and most affectionate of men." He edited *Douglas Jerrold's Shilling Magazine* and *Douglas Jerrold's Weekly Newspaper*. He worked with Dickens on the DAILY NEWS and on several of the AMATEUR THEATRICALS. After his death Dickens organized several performances of *The Frozen Deep* for the benefit of Jerrold's widow and family. Jerrold's son, **William Blanchard** (1826–84), was a frequent contributor to HOUSEHOLD WORDS.

Jerry "A tall, black-whiskered man, in a velveteen coat" who manages a troupe of performing dogs. *Curiosity Shop* (18, 19, 37).

Jerusalem Buildings The row of shops that houses the Tetterby's shop and lodgings and the rooms of the poor student, Edmund Longford. *Haunted Man*.

Jerusalem Coffee House One of the oldest such establishments in the CITY of London, this coffee house was frequented by merchants, like Jeremiah Flintwinch, who were engaged in trade with China, India, and Australia. *Dorrit* (I:29).

Jewby One of Snagsby's clients. *Bleak House* (10).

Jews The two important Jews in Dickens's novels are Fagin in *Twist* and Riah in *Mutual Friend*. Fagin has often been viewed as an anti-Semitic stereotype and Riah as Dickens's attempt to atone for Fagin. There is a good deal of truth to this characterization, for Dickens was prompted to include Riah in the later novel by Mrs. Eliza DAVIS, who complained of his anti-Semitism in *Twist* and urged him to make amends. Attitudes toward Jews were changing during Dickens's lifetime, and, as Harry STONE (1959) points out, the treatment of Fagin was representative of the anti-Semitism of its time. By 1865, many of the earlier attitudes toward Jews and the social restrictions placed on them had changed. Riah, then, represents both a change in societal attitudes during the period and Dickens's conscious attempt to right an injustice, however unconscious his earlier anti-Semitism had been.

Jilkins Physician who treats Our Bore with sherry and mutton chops. *Reprinted*, "Bore."

Jingle, Alfred A strolling actor and adventurer "of No Hall, Nowhere." "The thinness of his body and the length of his legs gave him the appearance of being much taller. The green coat had been a smart dress garment in the days of swallow-tails, but had evidently in those times adorned a much shorter man, for the soiled and faded sleeves scarcely reached to his wrists. . . . His face was thin and haggard, but an indescribable air of jaunty impudence and perfect self-possession pervaded the whole man"(2). He enters the novel when he rescues Pickwick from an altercation with a cab driver (2), and entertains the Pickwickians with his telegraphic speech on the journey to ROCHESTER:

> Ah! you should keep dogs—fine animals—sagacious creatures—dog of my own once—Pointer—surprising instinct—out shooting one day—entering enclosure—whistled—dog stopped—whistled again—Ponto—no go; stock still—called him—Ponto, Ponto—wouldn't move—dog transfixed—staring at a board—looked up, saw an inscription—'Gamekeeper has orders to shoot all dogs found in this enclosure'—wouldn't pass it—wonderful dog—vaulable dog that—very (2).

In Rochester, his outrageous behavior prompts the challenge from Dr. Slammer (2). Introduced to Wardle by Pickwick, he elopes with Rachael (9) and is bought off by Wardle (10). In EATANSWILL, he appears at Mrs. Leo Hunter's party as Captain Fitz Marshall (15) and is pursued by Pickwick to BURY ST. EDMUNDS, where his scheme to seduce Nupkin's daughter is exposed (25). Jingle and his servant, Job Trotter, eventually turn up in the FLEET, imprisoned for debt (42). The two are given a chance to begin life anew in the West Indies when Pickwick pays their debts and releases them from prison (53). *Pickwick*.

Jiniwin, Mrs. Mrs. Quilp's mother, "laudably shrewish in her disposition and inclined to resist male authority" (4). She encourages her daughter to rebellion, even though she is terrified of Quilp. A condition of her daughter's second marriage is that Mrs. Jiniwin will not be part of the household (73). *Curiosity Shop*.

Jinkins (1) "An unshaven, dirty, sottish-looking" customer in the pawnbroker's shop. *Boz*, "Pawnbroker's."

Jinkins (2) The suitor of the widow innkeeper who is bested by Tom Smart in the BAGMAN'S STORY. *Pickwick* (14).

Jinkins (3) The oldest boarder at Todgers's, "a fish-salesman's book-keeper aged forty" (9). *Chuzzlewit*.

Jinkinson Barber in Sam Weller's tale—"easy shavin' was his natur', and cuttin'and curlin' was his pride and glory"—who spent all his money on bears. *Humphrey* (5).

Jinks   Clerk to Magistrate Nupkins, mayor of IPSWICH. *Pickwick* (24).

Jip (short for **Gypsy**)   Dora Spenlow's spoiled little dog, who has a little pagoda for a doghouse and who dies at the same moment as his mistress (53). *Copperfield*.

Jo ("Toughy")   Illiterate crossing-sweeper and street urchin, "he sums up his mental condition, when asked a question, by replying that he 'don't know nothink' " (16). Befriended by Nemo, he testifies at the inquest into his death (11), is employed by a veiled lady to show her Nemo's grave (16), and is hounded out of London by the police who force him to "move on." He carries smallpox to Bleak House, infecting Charley and Esther (31). He dies at George's shooting gallery, attended by Woodcourt (47). *Bleak House.* Jo is based, in part, on an interview with George Ruby, an illiterate 14-year-old crossing sweeper, published in the *EXAMINER* (January 12, 1850) and later reprinted in *HOUSEHOLD WORDS* (HOUSEHOLD NARRATIVE, January 1850).

Jobba   Member of the Mudfog Association who invents a machine for bringing "railway shares prematurely to a premium." *Mudfog*.

Jobling, Dr. John   Unscrupulous physician who acts as the medical officer for the ANGLO-BENGALEE DISINTERESTED LOAN AND LIFE ASSURANCE COMPANY. He attends the dying Anthony Chuzzlewit and Lewsome, Mrs. Gamp's patient at The BULL inn. *Chuzzlewit*.

Two crossing-sweepers at work, from Henry Mayhew's London Labour and the London Poor *(1851).*

Jobling, Tony ("Weevle")   Guppy's friend who takes Nemo's rooms after the law writer's death in order to keep an eye on Krook for Guppy (20). He waits with Guppy for the appointed hour when Guppy is supposed to get Hawdon's papers from Krook, and the two of them discover the old man's extraordinary disappearance (32). Tony also goes with Guppy when he renews his proposal to Esther (64). *Bleak House.*

Jobson   An extensive family of Mormon emigrants beginning their journey from London to Utah. *Uncommercial* (22).

Joby   One-eyed tramp also known as GREENWOOD. "Haunted House."

Jock   Serving boy at the Cumberland inn where Idle's sprained ankle is treated. *Lazy Tour*.

Jodd   Member of the welcoming committee for Elijah Pogram. *Chuzzlewit* (34).

Joe (1)   Waiter at the HYDE PARK hotel where Rose Maylie is staying. *Twist* (39).

Joe (2)   Receiver of stolen goods who bargains for Scrooge's belongings after his death in the vision of Christmas Yet to Come. *Carol* (4).

Joe (3)   Laborer who fetches Walter Gay to take charge of Florence when she is lost on the docks after her kidnapping by Good Mrs. Brown. *Dombey* (6).

Joe (4)   Coachman on the coach taking Mr. Lorry from London to Dover. *Two Cities* (I:2).

Joe (5)   Driver of the Cloisterham bus. *Drood*.

Joe, ("The Fat Boy")   Wardle's page, a "red-faced boy in a state of somnolency," who is always either eating or sleeping. He is awake, though, when he spies on Tupman courting Rachael Wardle in the garden at DINGLEY DELL and reports what he sees to Mrs. Wardle (8). *Pickwick*.

Joey, Captain   A bottle-nosed regular at the SIX JOLLY FELLOWSHIP PORTERS. *Mutual Friend*.

Jogg, Miss   An artist's model. *Bleak House* (29).

John (1)   The Poetical Young Gentleman. *Young Gentlemen*.

John (2)   The dying pantomime clown who is the subject of "The Stroller's Tale." *Pickwick* (3).

John (3)   An unemployed laborer, pitied by Florence during her visit to the Skettles. *Dombey* (24).

John (4) Narrator and lessee of the POPLARS, the haunted house where he gathers his friends together. "Haunted House."

John (5) Unemployed boilermaker visited by the Traveller. *Uncommercial* (32).

John (6) Servants and waiters in *Boz* ("Sparkins," "Tottle"); *Young Gentlemen; Is She His Wife?; Pickwick* (51); *Strange Gentleman*.

John, Old Narrator and an inventor who spends all his money on bureaucratic fees as he tries to secure a patent. *Reprinted*, "Poor Man's Tale."

Johnny Betty Higden's great-grandson whom the Boffins wish to adopt and name John Harmon. He dies at the CHILDREN'S HOSPITAL watched over by Bella Wilfer, "the boofer lady" (II:9). *Mutual Friend*.

Johnson (1) Nicholas NICKLEBY's stage name. *Nickleby* (16).

Johnson (2) One of Dr. Blimber's pupils, who cannot suppress his convulsions at the doctor's dinner table. *Dombey* (12).

Johnson, Andrew (1808–1875) President of the United States from 1865 to 1868. Dickens met with him in WASHINGTON on February 5, 1868, just a few weeks before Johnson's impeachment trial. Dickens found him "a man not to be turned or trifled with. . . . who must be killed to be got out of the way."

Johnson, Edgar (1912–1995) Biographer and critic; professor, New York University; Dickens's foremost modern biographer. His *Charles Dickens: His Tragedy and Triumph* (1952) remains the standard scholarly biography. Thoroughly researched and copiously documented, it was reissued in revised and abridged form in 1977. He was the author of numerous articles on Dickens, and editor of Dickens's letters to Angela BURDETT-COUTTS, *The Heart of Charles Dickens* (1952). With Eleanor Johnson, he also collected a volume of Dickens's writings about the theater, *The Dickens Theatrical Reader* (1964).

Johnson, John Young man who elopes to GRETNA GREEN with Mary Wilson. *Strange Gentleman*.

Johnson, Tom Acquaintance of Cousin Feenix, the "man with cork leg from White's." *Dombey* (41).

Johnson Street Street in SOMERS TOWN, north London, where the Dickens family lived in 1825 while Charles attended WELLINGTON HOUSE ACADEMY.

Jollson, Mrs. Woman who lived at number 9 Brig Place before Mrs. MacStinger. *Dombey* (39).

Jolly Boatman Public house in Mudfog that is denied a license by Mayor Tulrumble, who has statistically figured out that the number of beer patrons served by the pub contributes to the increasing depravity of the town. *Mudfog*.

Jolly Sandboys, The "A small road-side inn of pretty ancient date" where Nell and her grandfather stay on the recommendation of Codlin and Short. *Curiosity Shop* (18).

Joltered, Sir William President of the zoology section of the Mudfog Association. *Mudfog*.

Jonathan A regular at the SIX JOLLY FELLOWSHIP PORTERS. *Mutual Friend*.

Jones (1) Witty barrister's clerk and friend of John Dounce. *Boz*, "Dounce."

Jones (2) Dinner guest of the Buddens, "a little smirking man with red whiskers." *Boz*, "Minns."

Jones (3) Shop clerk for Blaze and Sparkle, fashionable jewelers. *Bleak House* (58).

Jones, George A regular at the SIX JOLLY FELLOWSHIP PORTERS. *Mutual Friend* (6).

Jones, Mary A 19-year-old woman executed for shoplifting in 1771, leaving behind a **husband** and **two children**. *Rudge* (37).

Jones, Master CANTERBURY schoolboy, "a boy of no merit whatever," who is David Copperfield's rival for the attentions of Miss Shepherd. *Copperfield* (18).

Jones, William (1786–1836) Welsh headmaster of WELLINGTON HOUSE ACADEMY, which Dickens attended between 1824 and 1827. His sadistic treatment of the students, caning them or striking them across the palms with "a bloated mahogany ruler," made him the probable model for Mr. Creakle in *Copperfield*.

Jonson, Ben (1572–1637) Renaissance playwright, best known for *Volpone* (1606) and *The Alchemist* (1610). A practitioner of the comedy of humors, in which, as Jonson himself described it in *Every Man out of His Humour* (1599), "some one peculiar quality/ Doth so possess a man, that it doth draw/ All of his affects, his spirits, and his powers,/ In their confluctions, all to run one way." Jonson's characters are driven by a single obsession, such as greed, jealousy, or suspiciousness, and, at the end of the play, they are called to account for their vices. *Every Man in His Humour* (1598) was a fixture in the repertory of plays performed by Dickens's AMATEUR THEATRICAL groups. Dickens took the role of the boastful coward Bobadil.

The conventions of humors comedy influenced Dickens's flat characters, who are defined by a single central trait; his names, which often suggest the moral character of the figures who bear them; and his comic plots, which expose the failings of such characters as the hypocritical Pecksniff or the ambitious Uriah Heep. The novel in which the influence of the humors tradition is most apparent is *Chuzzlewit* (See MARTIN CHUZZLEWIT: Commentary).

Joper, Billy   Acquaintance of Cousin Feenix, "man with a glass in his eye." *Dombey* (41).

Joram   Assistant to Omer the undertaker who marries Minnie, Omer's daughter, and becomes a partner in the business. *Copperfield* (9).

Jorgan, Captain Silas Jonas   Native of Salem, Massachusetts, "American born. . . . but he was a citizen of the world," who found Hugh Raybrock's message. "Message from the Sea."

Jorkins   Spenlow's junior partner, "a mild man of a heavy temperament, whose place in the business was to keep himself in the background, and be constantly exhibited by name as the most obdurate and ruthless of men" (23). *Copperfield*.

Joseph (1)   Head waiter at the Slamjam Coffee-house. "Somebody's Luggage."

Joseph (2)   Charity boy whose tryst with **Celia** in a CITY churchyard is observed by the Traveller. *Uncommercial* (23).

Jowl, Joe   A gambler, "a burly fellow, of middle age; with black whiskers, broad cheeks, a coarse wide mouth, and bull neck," who, with others at the VALIANT SOLDIER pub, fleeces Nell's grandfather and tries to persuade him to rob Mrs. Jarley. *Curiosity Shop* (29, 42).

Joy, Thomas   A London carpenter who puts John up when he comes to London to seek a patent. *Reprinted*, "Poor Man's Tale."

"Judicial Special Pleading"   Article for the EXAMINER (December 30, 1848), chiding Mr. Baron Ald-

erson, judge in the trial of the physical force Chartists, for his gross oversimplification of the situation that brought on the FRENCH REVOLUTION. Such special pleading, Dickens argues, can easily be challenged by the Chartists. *Miscellaneous*. See also CHARTISM.

Julia   Sweetheart of the narrator of "The Ghost of Art." *Reprinted*.

Jupe, Cecelia (Sissy)   Daughter of the circus clown and dog trainer, **Signor Jupe**; when her father thinks himself too old to perform anymore, he disappears, leaving behind his daughter and his dog, Merrylegs. Sissy is taken into the Gradgrind household and unsuccessfully educated, as "Girl number twenty," at Gradgrind's school. She becomes a loving influence among the Gradgrinds. She convinces Harthouse to leave COKETOWN after his fateful meeting with Louisa at the country house (III:2); she discovers the dying Stephen Blackpool in the Old Hell Shaft (III:6); and she accompanies Gradgrind and Louisa when they go to Sleary's circus in search of Tom (III:7). *Hard Times*.

Juvenile Crime   There was growing concern in the 1820s and '30s at the increase in juvenile crime, now generally attributed to the dislocations resulting from industrialization. At the time, no distinction was made between juvenile and adult offenders, and children as young as eight could be imprisoned or transported as adults. The jails, like the criminal rookeries in the slums of the major cities, became schools in criminality where children like Oliver Twist were trained for a life of crime. Dickens was an active supporter of the reform movement, led by Mary Carpenter and Lord SHAFTESBURY, that sought to distinguish juvenile from adult offenders and to provide education for children in hopes of preventing criminal activity. Their efforts led to the Juvenile Offenders Act (1847), which distinguished adult offenders from children under 14 and gave judges the discretionary power to dismiss charges against youthful offenders. In the 1840s and '50s the reformers also established RAGGED SCHOOLS, reformatory schools, and industrial schools designed to educate children away from a life of crime. These institutions are generally credited with lowering the juvenile crime rate after 1860.

Kags Convict who has returned illegally from transportation and is hiding in Toby Crackit's house on JACOB'S ISLAND when Sikes comes to hide out there: "a robber of fifty years, whose nose had been almost beaten in in some old scuffle, and whose face bore a frightful scar" (50). *Twist.*

Kaplan, Fred (1937–) Professor, City University of New York; scholar of Victorian literature and culture; biographer. Besides his definitive modern biography of CARLYLE (1983), Kaplan has written a scholarly biography of *Dickens* (1988), particularly revealing in its account of Dickens's personal and family life; *Dickens and Mesmerism* (1975), an account of Dickens's involvement with hypnotism and its effect on his novels; and *Sacred Tears: Sentimentality in Dickens, Thackeray and Carlyle* (1985). Kaplan has also edited Dickens's memorandum book in the collection of the New York Public Library (1981).

Kate (1) Wife of Harry, a debtor in Solomon Jacobs's sponging house. *Boz,* "Tottle."

Kate (2) Maria Lobbs's "arch, impudent, bewitching little" cousin. *Pickwick* (17).

Kate (3) An orphan girl who visits the Skettles's house in FULHAM when Florence is staying there. *Dombey* (24).

Kedgick, Captain Proprietor of the National Hotel, where Martin Chuzzlewit stays on his way going to and coming from EDEN. *Chuzzlewit* (22, 34).

Keeley, Robert (1793–1869) He and his wife, **Mary Goward** (1806–99), were actors and theater managers who, in the 1840s, produced many dramas based on Dickens's works. Mrs. Keeley established her reputation as a portrayer of Dickens's children: Oliver, Smike, Nell, and Young Bailey. She also played Meg Veck, Dot Peerybingle, and Clemency Newcome before she gave up Dickensian roles. Her husband was best known for his portrayal of Sairey Gamp. Their daughter **Louise** played Dot in Dion BOUCICAULT's version of *Cricket* (1862). Dickens first met the Keeleys when they were performing in Edward STIRLING's adaptation of *Nickleby* in 1839. They remained friends throughout his life. After Robert Keeley's death, Dickens described him

on stage as "a master of pathos" and remarked that "in private, he had the heart of a child, and the integrity of the noblest man."

Keepsake, The An illustrated annual edited by the Countess of BLESSINGTON. Dickens published a verse satire, "A Word in Season" (1843) and a story, "To be read at Dusk" (1852), in this annual.

Kenge ("Conversation Kenge") Mr. Jarndyce's solicitor with the firm of Kenge and Carboy: "a portly, important-looking gentleman, dressed all in black, with a white cravat, large gold watch seals, a pair of gold eyeglasses, and a large seal ring upon his little finger.... He appeared to enjoy beyond everything the sound of his own voice" (3). *Bleak House.*

Kenilworth Medieval castle in Warwickshire, an important setting in Sir Walter SCOTT's *Kenilworth* (1821), to which Dombey takes Edith Granger during their courtship (*Dombey*, 27). Dickens stayed at the castle with H. K. BROWNE in 1838.

Kennington The south London district where Mr. Vholes lives in a country cottage with his three daughters (*Bleak House,* 39). When Jemmy Lirriper gets lost he is found by the Kennington police. "Lirriper's Lodgings."

Kensington Fashionable suburb of London, south of HYDE PARK, where Gabriel Parsons meets Fanny secretly (*Boz,* "Tottle"); it is the home of Sam Weller's man of principle who dies from eating crumpets (*Pickwick,* 44). Prince Turveydrop teaches in a Kensington dancing academy (*Bleak House,* 4).

Kent County southeast of London and to the south of the THAMES, where Dickens spent some of the happiest years of his childhood in CHATHAM and the last decade of his life at GAD'S HILL PLACE. Kentish locations—especially Chatham, ROCHESTER, and CANTERBURY—provide many settings for the novels. David Copperfield's journey to DOVER in search of Betsey Trotwood follows the **Kent Road** out of London (*Copperfield,* 13).

Kent, William Charles (1823–1902) Journalist and editor; contributor to *HOUSEHOLD WORDS* and *ALL THE YEAR ROUND.* His enthusiastic review of *Dombey* in the

Sun led to his friendship with Dickens. He organized the reading tour in 1867 and compiled a record of Dickens's readings from papers supplied by the author, published as *Charles Dickens as a Reader* (1872).

Kentish Town   An area in north London, home of Mrs. Kidgerbury, the Copperfield's charwoman. *Copperfield* (44).

Kenwigs Family   Family that lives in the house on GOLDEN SQUARE where Newman Noggs lodges. **Mr. Kenwigs** is an ivory turner; his wife, **Susan**, from a "very genteel family" (14), is the niece of Mr. Lillyvick, a collector of water-rates. The Kenwigs hope that Lillyvick will provide for their three daughters, but their expectations are dashed when he marries Miss Petowker, only to be revived again when she leaves him. Nicholas is hired to teach French to the three Kenwigs girls, **Morleena** and two others. The Kenwigs also have an infant son, **Lillyvick**. *Nickleby*.

Ketch, Professor John   Member of the Mudfog Association who exhibited the skull of a notorious murderer, James Greenacre. *Mudfog*.

Kettle, La Fayette   Secretary of the Watertoast Association of United Sympathisers whom Martin meets on the train on his way to EDEN. He is languid, listless, and suspicious. "He had bright dark eyes, which he kept half closed; only peeping out of the corners, and even then with a glance that seemed to say, 'Now you won't overreach me: you want to, but you won't.' " *Chuzzlewit* (21, 22).

Kibble, Jacob   A passenger with John Harmon back from the Cape Colony in southern Africa who gives testimony at the inquest into the murder (IV:12). *Mutual Friend*.

Kidderminster   "A diminutive boy with an old face" who assists E. W. B. Childers in his equestrian act in Sleary's Circus. "Made up with curls, wreaths, wings, white bismuth, and carmine, this hopeful young person soared into so pleasing a Cupid as to constitute the chief delight of the maternal part of the spectators; but in private, where his characteristics were a precocious cutaway coat and an extremely gruff voice, he became of the Turf, turfy" (I:6). *Hard Times*.

Kidgerbury, Mrs.   "The oldest resident of KENTISH TOWN," hired by David and Dora Copperfield as a charlady, even though she is "too feeble to execute her conceptions of that art." *Copperfield* (44).

Kimmeens, Kitty   Pupil of Miss Pupford who, left alone at Miss Pupford's school, seeks out human contact and comes upon the Traveller who takes her to Tom Tiddler's Ground. "Tiddler."

Kincaid, James R. (1937–   )   Professor, University of Southern California; scholar of Victorian literature who has written on TENNYSON, TROLLOPE, Carroll, and, especially, Dickens. *Dickens and the Rhetoric of Laughter* (1972) studied the ways in which Dickens used laughter to castigate his characters' weaknesses and correct them to produce a world of "freedom, justice, rebirth, flexibility." In *Child Loving: The Erotic Child and Victorian Culture* (1992), which considers the Victorian child figure and its relevance to current concerns about pedophilia and the eroticized child in contempory culture, Kincaid briefly discusses Paul Dombey, Little Nell, David Copperfield, and Oliver Twist. *Annoying the Victorians* (1995) devotes much of its attention to Dickens as it mocks and parodies the obsessions of contemporary literary criticism.

Kinch, Horace   Prisoner in the KING'S BENCH PRISON who has succumbed to the "Dry Rot" and who dies in confinement. *Uncommercial* (13).

Kindheart   The Traveller's friend (see Angus FLETCHER) in ITALY, "an Englishman of an amiable nature, great enthusiasm, and no discretion." *Uncommercial* (26).

"King of the Bill-Stickers"   Purveyor of advertising posters who is interviewed in his van as it circulates, covered with advertisments, in the streets of London. *Reprinted*, "Bill-sticking."

King, Christian George   Native pilot of the sloop *Christopher Columbus* who betrays the colonists to the pirates. He is shot by Captain Carton. "English Prisoners."

King's Bench Prison   Last of London's debtors prisons, this prison in SOUTHWARK on the BOROUGH ROAD became exclusively a debtors prison in the late 18th century. In 1780 it was burnt down by the Gordon rioters (*Rudge*, 67) but was later rebuilt. It was demolished in 1869. The Traveller describes the prison in *Uncommercial* (13). Mr. Micawber is imprisoned here while David is staying with the Micawber family (*Copperfield*, 11). Mr. Bray has permission to live in the rules of the prison—that is, to live in an area surrounding the prison, for which he paid a fee (*Nickleby*, 46, 47, 51).

King's Bench Walk   An area in the TEMPLE where Sydney Carton walks before going to his job at Stryver's office. *Two Cities* (II:5).

Kingsgate Street   Street in HOLBORN where Mrs. Gamp lives "at a bird-fancier's next door but one to the celebrated mutton-pie shop, and directly opposite to the original cat's-meat warehouse." *Chuzzlewit* (19).

Kingston, Ontario   Town in Ontario, CANADA, visited by Dickens on his 1842 tour of AMERICA; he described it as "a very poor town, rendered still poorer in the appearance of its market-place by the ravages of a recent fire." *Notes* (15).

Kingston, Surrey   Betty Higden goes through this town along the THAMES on her final journey (*Mutual Friend*, III:8). Magwich tells of being in jail here (*Expectations*, 42). Gowan sketches here (*Dorrit*, I:17).

Kitt   The "young creature in pink" at Dora's birthday picnic with whom David flirts when Dora's attentions are monopolized by "Red Whisker." Her "**mother** in green" also attends the picnic. *Copperfield* (33).

Kitten   Vice-commissioner at Silver-Store Island, "a small, youngish, bald, botanical and mineralological gentleman." "English Prisoners."

Kitterbell, Charles   He invites his uncle, Nicodemus Dumps, to the christening of his son **Frederick Charles William**. But Dumps loses the christening cup and casts a pall over the celebration with a misanthropic speech. **Jemima**, Charles's wife, is "one of those young women who almost invariably . . . recall to one's mind the idea of a cold fillet of veal." *Boz*, "Christening."

Kitton, Frederic G. (1856–1904)   Dickens bibliographer, compiler, and scholar who did pioneering work on Dickens's writings and illustrations. He was one of the founders of the *DICKENSIAN* and was slated to be its first editor, but he died before the magazine made its debut. Among his works on Dickens, *Dickensiana* (1886), *The Minor Writings of Charles Dickens* (1900), *Charles Dickens by Pen and Pencil* (1890), and *Dickens and His Illustrators* (1899) contain some still useful material.

Klem Family   The summer caretakers of the Traveller's London lodgings. **Mrs. Klem** is "an elderly woman, laboring under a chronic sniff" and her **husband** "a meagre and mouldy old man, whom I have never yet seen detached from a flat pint of beer in a pewter pot." Their daughter, **Miss Klem**, is "apparently ten years older than either of them." *Uncommercial* (16).

Knag, Miss   Madame Mantalini's forewoman, "a short, bustling, over-dressed female" (17). At first she is friendly with Kate Nickleby, but then she becomes jealous and opposes Kate's role in the firm (20, 21). She eventually takes over the business (44). Her brother **Mortimer** is the melancholy proprietor of a small circulating library near TOTTENHAM COURT ROAD (18). *Nickleby*.

Knebworth   Stately home of Sir Edward Bulwer LYTTON in Hertfordshire. Lytton invited Dickens's amateur theatrical company to perform *Every Man in His Hu-* *mour* there in the fall of 1850, and at that time he and Dickens conceived the plan for the GUILD OF LITERATURE AND ART. As part of this scheme, three gothic houses for writers and artists were built on the estate and were dedicated in 1865.

Knight, Charles (1791–1873)   Publisher, journalist, regular contributor to *HOUSEHOLD WORDS*; member, with Dickens, of the Shakespeare Society, one of the organizers of Dickens's AMATEUR THEATRICALS. Dickens shared Knight's passion for educating the common man and the two celebrated their friendship by dining together each year on Knight's birthday. Knight described his relationship with Dickens in *Passages of a Working Life* (1864).

Knowles, James Sheridan (1784–1862)   Dramatist. In 1832 Dickens had an audition for a part in Knowles's play, *The Hunchback*, but a cold and a sore throat prevented his keeping the engagement. Dickens was active in charitable efforts to provide Knowles with financial aid during his old age.

Koëldwethout, Baron von, of Grogzwig   Subject of the tale told by the merry-faced gentleman to his fellow passengers when the Yorkshire coach breaks down. *Nickleby* (6).

Kolle, Henry (1808?–1881)   A friend of Dickens's youth, he exchanged letters with the author. He married Maria BEADNELL's sister Anne.

Krook ("Lord Chancellor")   A drunken and illiterate rag-and-bone dealer, who amasses miscellaneous artifacts and papers in much the same way as the Court of CHANCERY collects documents, earning him the nickname "Lord Chancellor." "An old man in spectacles and a hairy cap. He was short, cadaverous, and withered; with his head sunk edgeways between his shoulders, and the breath issuing in visible smoke from his mouth, as if he were on fire within" (5). Nemo occupies rooms on the middle floor of his house and Miss Flite the top floor. After Nemo's death, Jobling takes his rooms (20). On the night Krook is to give some of Nemo's papers to Guppy, the old man spontaneously combusts, taking the documents with him (32). When Krook is discovered to have been Mrs. Smallweed's brother, the Smallweeds take over his effects and discover the missing Jarndyce will among his papers (33). *Bleak House*.

Kucich, John (1952–)   Professor, University of Michigan; psychological critic of Victorian fiction. In a postmodern analysis, *Excess and Restraint in the Novels of Charles Dickens* (1981), Kucich concentrates on the tension between the desire to transcend boundaries and the constraints imposed by society and the human condition. Using this dichotomy, he analyzes the patterns of melodrama in the novels, the nature of villainy, and the ways the endings reconcile this tension. In *Repression in Victorian Fiction: Charlotte Brontë, George Eliot, and Charles Dickens* (1987), Kucich studies the ways in which three Victorian novelists use psychological repression to express the interiority of their characters.

Künstlerroman   A subgenre of the BILDUNGSROMAN that describes the maturation of an artist. The most notable example in English is James Joyce's *Portrait of the Artist as a Young Man* (1916). Technically, *David Copperfield* fits this form, but the novel makes little attempt to describe the artist as different from any other successful young man. Indeed, David's success as a novelist would seem to be the same as that open to a diligent and disciplined person in any field of endeavor.

Kutankumagen, Dr.   Member of the medical section of the Mudfog Association. *Mudfog*.

Kwakley   Member of the statistical section of the Mudfog Association. *Mudfog*.

"Kyd"   Penname of illustrator Joseph Clayton CLARKE.

L

La Cour, Capitaine de   French officer billeted at Madame Bouclet's. "Somebody's Luggage."

La Creevy, Miss   Miniature painter, "a mincing young lady of fifty" (3), with whom the Nicklebys take lodgings when they first come to London. A bright and cheerful optimist, she stands by Kate in her troubles and eventually marries Tim Linkinwater (63). She has a brother **John** in the country (31). *Nickleby.*

La Force   Parisian prison in which Charles Darnay is incarcerated before he is taken to La CONCIERGIE. *Two Cities.*

"Ladies' Societies, The"   Originally published as "Sketches of London No. 20. Our Parish" in the EVENING CHRONICLE (July 28, 1835), this sketch describes the competition between the Child Examination Society and the Bible Distribution Society for dominance in Our Parish. *Boz.*

Ladle, Joey   Superstitious cellarman for Wilding and Co. who accompanies Marguerite Obenreizer on her journey to SWITZERLAND to rescue Vendale. "No Thoroughfare."

Lady Jane   Krook's tigerish cat. *Bleak House* (5).

Lagnier   Alias used by RIGAUD. *Dorrit.*

Laing, Allan Stewart   The magistrate from HATTON GARDEN whose "harshness and insolence" made him the model for Magistrate Fang in *Oliver Twist.*

Lambert, Miss   Partner of Hopkins, the Bashful Young Gentleman, in the quadrille. *Young Gentlemen.*

Lambeth   Slum area south of the THAMES across from Westminster where Peg Sliderskew hides after stealing the papers from Arthur Gride (*Nickleby*, 57). In nearby WALCOT SQUARE is the house that Mr. Guppy has taken with the prospect of marrying Esther Summerson (*Bleak House*, 64). The Gordon rioters attack **Lambeth Palace**, residence of the Archbishop of Canterbury (*Rudge*, 67).

Lamert, James   Stepson of Dickens's mother's sister, he lived with the Dickens family in CHATHAM and in CAMDEN TOWN after they moved to London. He built a toy theater for young Charles and introduced him to the theater in Chatham. He also arranged for the boy to work in the BLACKING WAREHOUSE that he managed for his brother-in-law George Lamert. James's father, **Dr. Matthew Lamert**, an army surgeon in Chatham, was probably the model for Dr. Slammer in *Pickwick.*

Lammle, Alfred   "A mature young gentleman with too much nose on his face, too much ginger in his whiskers, too much torso in his waistcoat, too much sparkle in his studs, his eyes, his buttons, his talk, his teeth" (I:2). An opportunistic friend of Veneering and an unscrupulous adventurer, he marries **Sophronia Akershem**, a "mature young lady," for her money. Equally opportunistic, she has married him for his money and on the honeymoon they discover that each has been deceived about the financial situation of the other. So they join forces to dupe others as they have been duped (I:10). Sophronia, however, has misgivings about their scheme to marry Georgiana Podsnap to Fascination Fledgeby, and she secretly warns the Podsnaps (II:16). Later the Lammles try to replace Rokesmith and Bella Wilfer in the Boffin household (IV:2), but they fail to fool Boffin, who pays them £100 to escape overseas from their debts. *Mutual Friend.*

Lamplighter, The   Farce written by Dickens for MACREADY in 1838. The astrologer Stargazer, convinced that the stars have predicted the marriage of his niece to Tom Grig, a cockney lamplighter, has his scheme thwarted by Betsy Martin, his maid, who convinces him that he has misread the omens and that his son, Galileo Isaac Newton Flamstead, is the predicted suitor. Macready, unconvinced of the play's commercial potential, did not produce it. Dickens turned it into a short story—"The Lamplighter's Story" (1841)—for the PIC-NIC PAPERS.

"Lamps"   Porter at Mugby Junction who is devoted to his crippled daughter Phoebe and composes comic songs to sing to her. *Mugby.*

Lancaster   Dickens stayed at the King's Arms Inn in this Lancashire town with Wilkie COLLINS in September

1857 and made it the setting for the ghost story of The Bride's Chamber in *Lazy Tour*.

Landless, Neville and Helena Orphaned twins, born in Ceylon, now under the guardianship of the Reverend Honeythunder; "an unusually handsome lithe young fellow, and an unusually handsome little girl; much alike; both very dark, and very rich in color; she of almost the gipsy type; something untamed about them both" (6). Honeythunder places them in Cloisterham to be educated and "civilized." Helena is enrolled at Miss Twinkleton's school where she becomes Rosa Bud's roommate and close friend; Neville is placed under the tutelage of the Reverend Crisparkle. When Drood's patronizing way with Rosa annoys Neville, the two men quarrel (8), and when Drood disappears, Neville becomes the prime suspect in his presumed murder (15–16). Supported by Crisparkle and Grewgious, he leaves Cloisterham and takes lodgings in London. There he is visited by Helena as well as by Crisparkle, who seems to be interested in her (21). *Drood*.

Landon, Letitia Elizabeth ("L. E. L") (1802–1838) Poet and historical novelist who used the initials L. E. L. as her nom de plume and who, like Byron, had a reputation for scandal. Dickens knew her as a member of Lady BLESSINGTON's circle at Gore House. She was engaged briefly to John FORSTER and later married George Maclean, Governor of the Gold Coast. Three months after her marriage, she was found dead of poison under suspicious circumstances.

Landor, Walter Savage (1775–1864) Poet and essayist, friend of Dickens. John FORSTER introduced the young novelist to the old poet in 1836. The two admired each other's work and quickly became friends. On one of his annual birthday visits to Landor at BATH in 1840, Dickens came up with the idea of Little Nell, the character most loved by Landor of all of Dickens's creations. Landor was godfather to Dickens's second son and the model for Boythorn in *Bleak House*, whose hot temper, warm heart, and addiction to superlatives were all characteristic of the poet.

"Landor's Life" Review of John FORSTER's biography of W. S. LANDOR for *ALL THE YEAR ROUND* (July 24, 1869). Dickens writes of his associations with the poet, giving a portrait that shows how fully Boythorn embodies the qualities Dickens saw in his friend. *Miscellaneous*.

Landseer, Sir Edwin Henry (1802–1873) Painter and sculptor, best known for his paintings of animals and for the lions on Nelson's Monument in Trafalgar Square. He was one of Dickens's many artist friends and a member of "the Portwiners" club along with FORSTER, THACKERAY, LYTTON, MACREADY, LEMON, and MA-

Landseer's only illustration for Dickens was this picture of John Peerybingle's dog Boxer for The Cricket on the Hearth.

CLISE. He looked after Grip, Dickens's pet raven, while the novelist was in ITALY and was deeply moved by Dickens's death. He is the artist in "Friend of the Lions."

Lane, Miss Distracted governess tending the unruly Borum children. *Nickleby* (24).

Langdale A historical figure, this kindly vintner and distiller gives the exhausted Haredale a place to sleep and shelters him from the mob. His house is attacked and burned by the rioters. *Rudge* (61, 66–68).

Langley (M. L'Anglais or "Mr. The Englishman") English visitor who has come to the French town of Vauban to forget the daughter he has rejected. While he is there he watches Corporal Théophile, a soldier stationed in the town, as he loves and cares for a small orphan girl, Bebelle. When the corporal is killed in a fire, Langley adopts the child and forgives his daughter. "Somebody's Luggage."

Langley, Noel (1911–1980) British novelist, dramatist, screenwriter, and filmmaker who adapted *A Christmas Carol* (1951) and adapted and directed *Pickwick Papers* (1952) for the screen.

Lant Street On this street in SOUTHWARK Dickens had lodgings while he worked at the BLACKING WAREHOUSE in 1822–23. Bob Sawyer lodges here in Mrs. Raddle's house, where "the majority of the inhabitants either direct their energies to the letting of furnished apartments, or devote themselves to the healthful and invigorating pursuit of mangling." *Pickwick* (32).

"Larkey Boy, The" Prizefighter who demolishes "The Game Chicken." *Dombey* (44).

Larkins, The Eldest Miss Object of the youthful David Copperfield's romantic fantasies, "a tall, dark, black-eyed, fine figure of a woman" (18). Her **father** is "a gruff old gentleman with a double chin, and one of his eyes immovable in his head" (18). *Copperfield*.

Larkins, Jem Amateur actor, performing under the name Horatio St. Julien, whose speciality is "genteel comedy." *Boz*, "Private Theatres."

Larson, Janet L. (1945–   ) Professor, Rutgers University; editor-at-large for the *Christian Century* who writes on the relationship between religion and literature. In *Dickens and the Broken Scripture* (1985), she studies the increasingly problematic role of biblical allusion in Dickens's novels as his assurance in biblical texts eroded along with that of his contemporaries.

"Last Cab-driver, and the First Omnibus Cad, The" Sketch first published in *BELL'S LIFE IN LONDON* as "Scenes and Characters No. 6. Some Account of an Omnibus Cad" (November 29, 1835). It describes in particular the "red cab-driver," whose defiance of his fares lands him in COLDBATH FIELDS prison, and William Barker, the first omnibus cad. *Boz*.

"Last Words of the Old Year, The" Article for *HOUSEHOLD WORDS* (January 4, 1851) written in the vein of Carlylean prophecy. On his deathbed, the year 1850, a venerable old man, catalogs his accomplishments and failures, particularly noting the failure to do anything to educate the 45% of English children who are illiterate, and he bequeaths to the new year "a vast inheritance of degradation and neglect in England." *Miscellaneous*.

Latin-Grammar Master, The Antagonist to Captain Boldheart in Robin Redforth's tale of piratical adventure. "Holiday Romance."

Laughton, Charles (1899–1962) British actor who played Pickwick on the London stage (1928), produced a version of *Bleak House* in New York (1953), and originally was intended for the role of Micawber in the 1935 MGM film of *Copperfield*—a role that instead established W. C. FIELDS's Dickensian reputation.

Laurence, Samuel (1811–1884) Artist who did portraits of many literary figures, including CARLYLE, THACKERAY, and BROWNING. He painted portraits of Dickens and his wife in 1837 while Dickens was at work on *Pickwick*.

Laurie, Sir Peter (1808–1877) London magistrate who mounted a campaign to prevent suicide by sentencing those who tried and failed to the treadmill. Dickens satirized him as Alderman Cute in *The Chimes*. Laurie, who knew Dickens and had taken Catherine DICKENS to a LORD MAYOR's dinner, described the Christmas book as "most disgraceful" and said Dickens was "a dangerous man to meet."

Lausanne Swiss town on Lake Geneva where Dickens stayed with his family for several months in 1846. He began *Dombey* here and wrote *Battle of Life*. He later drew on his Swiss experiences in describing the Dorrits' journey to Italy.

Law Terms The traditional schedule for the law courts in Westminster set four terms in which the courts were open: Hilary, January 11–31; Easter, April 15–May 8; Trinity, May 22–June 12; and Michaelmas, November 2–25. The Long Vacation described the period between Trinity and Michaelmas terms. Although the Judicature Act of 1873 abolished the terms for the courts, they are still informally recognized in various other functions.

Layard, Austen Henry (1817–1894) British archeologist who excavated Ninevah and other Middle Eastern sites; writer on art and other subjects; member of Parliament, 1852–57; friend of Dickens. The novelist met Layard on an ascent of Vesuvius in 1853. After visiting the Crimea during the Crimean War, Layard formed the Administrative Reform Association to press for changes in the bungling government bureaucracy. Dickens supported his ultimately unsuccessful efforts with several articles in *HOUSEHOLD WORDS* in 1855. He addressed the Association on June 27, 1855.

Lazarus, Abraham Thief whom Jaggers is engaged to prosecute for stealing a plate. His **brother** pleads with Jaggers to represent him, but is refused. *Expectations* (20).

Lazy Tour of Two Idle Apprentices, The Semi-fictional account by Wilkie COLLINS and Dickens of their tour of the north of England in August 1857. The story appeared in five parts in *HOUSEHOLD WORDS* (October 1857).

(1) Two apprentices to the trade of writing set out on an idle walking tour. Taking their names, Francis Goodchild (Dickens) and Thomas Idle (Collins), from HOGARTH's *Industry and Idleness*, they walk five miles out of London before turning around and taking the train to Carlisle. They go into the Cumberland highlands and climb Carrock Mountain on a misty day. There Idle sprains his ankle on the way down. (2) The travelers go on, stopping first at Wigton and then at an unnamed town where a doctor is called to examine Tom's injury. Goodchild returns to Doctor Speddie's surgery with him and hears the story of Arthur Halliday, the son of a manufacturer, who stopped one night in DONCASTER, where the only room he could find turned out to have a dead man in the second bed. As Arthur, unable to sleep, watched the body, he saw signs of life and called in Speddie, then a doctor in Doncaster, who revived the man. Now, many years later, Speddie thinks that his strange assistant, Lorn, resembles the young man whom he revived in Doncaster. (3) The apprentices go on to Allonby on the Cumberland coast to give Tom a healing rest, but the town is so boring that they leave and spend time

at a railway station instead. (4) Going on to LANCASTER, they take a room at an inn where Goodchild hears the story of The Bride's Chamber from the ghost of the man who murdered both the bride and the young man who tried to save her. (5) Then the two go on to Doncaster for race week, where Goodchild gets caught up in the crowds and activity while Idle nurses his foot at the hotel, the one idler in Doncaster not involved with the races.

Leacock, Stephen (1869–1944)   Canadian humorist, essayist, biographer; political scientist and economist at McGill University. His *Fiction and Reality: A Study of the Art of Charles Dickens* (1916) and *Charles Dickens: His Life and Work* (1933) are the work of a critic who wrote against the modernist denigration of Dickens at the time; they are particularly interesting for their treatment of Dickens as a humorist and caricaturist and for Leacock's comparisons of Dickens with Mark Twain.

Leadenhall Market   In the CITY on **Leadenhall Street**. Sam Weller writes his valentine to Mary at the BLUE BOAR (*Pickwick*, 33). The fictional WOODEN MIDSHIPMAN is located here, based on the actual marine instrument shop of Norie and Wilson at No. 157 Leadenhall Street. (*Dombey*).

Leamington   Dickens and H. K. BROWNE stayed at Copps's Royal Hotel at this spa town in Warwickshire in 1838. Dombey and Major Bagstock have the same accommodations when Dombey meets Edith Granger. *Dombey* (20).

Lean, David (1908–1991)   British film director (*Doctor Zhivago, A Passage to India*) whose two adaptations from Dickens, *Great Expectations* (1946) and *Oliver Twist* (1948) are among the most successful film versions of Dickens's novels. Their masterful use of black-and-white photography, montage, and period settings mix realism with fantasy in particularly Dickensian ways.

Leath, Angela   Fiancée of Charley, the bashful narrator of "Holly-Tree." When he thinks she has left him for his friend Edwin, Charley plans to run off to America, but he learns that she has not jilted him and they are reunited and married, becoming the parents of eight children.

Leather Bottle Inn, The   Inn at COBHAM, KENT where Tupman retreats after he is deserted by Rachel Wardle (*Pickwick*, 11). The inn has become a site of Dickensian pilgrimage.

Leaver   Member of the Mudfog Association. *Mudfog*.

Leaver, Augustus and Augusta   The Loving Couple, who are totally dependent on each other's attentions. *Young Couples*.

Leavis, F(rank) R(aymond) (1905–1978)   Professor, Cambridge University; founder and editor of *Scrutiny*; literary critic who wrote widely on literary issues, particularly of the 19th and 20th centuries, and established a standard of moral seriousness by which he judged literary works. His controversial discussion of the 19th- and 20th-century novel, *The Great Tradition* (1948), discovered sufficient seriousness in only five major novelists: Austen, George ELIOT, Henry JAMES, Conrad, and Lawrence. Dickens, described as an "entertainer," achieved such seriousness, Leavis argued, only in *Hard Times*, which Leavis discussed in a note appended to the main text of his work. In 1970 he revised his views and with his wife, **Q(ueenie) D(orothy)** (1900–82), he published *Dickens the Novelist*. Chapters on *Dombey, Copperfield, Bleak House, Hard Times, Dorrit,* and *Expectations* compared Dickens with Tolstoy and Blake and considerably expanded the Leavises' view of the serious Dickens canon. Their critical work is characterized by close reading of the text and careful analysis of the psychological and moral situations in the novels. Even when they are wrong, their views are provocative and thoroughly grounded in the text.

Lebanon, Illinois   Town where Dickens stayed when he went out from St. Louis to see the Looking Glass Prairie, "lonely and wild, but oppressive in its barren monotony." *Notes* (13).

Lebanon, New York   Site of the "grim" Shaker village that the Dickenses visited in 1842. Afterward Dickens commented: "I so abhor, and from my soul detest that bad spirit, no matter by what class or sect it may be entertained, which would strip life of its healthful graces, rob youth of its innocent pleasures, pluck from maturity and age their pleasant ornaments, and make existence but a narrow path towards the grave." *Notes* (15).

Le Cat, Claude Nicolas (1700–1768)   Renowned French surgeon cited by Dickens in the Preface to *Bleak House* as the source for a report of a recent case of SPONTANEOUS COMBUSTION.

Ledbrain, X.   Member of the Statistics Section of the Mudfog Association. *Mudfog*.

Ledrook, Miss   Member of the Crummles Theatrical Company, a special friend of Miss Snevellicci. *Nickleby* (23).

Lee, Jennie (1850–1925)   Stage actress whose fame was largely based on her performance as Jo in *Bleak House*, a role she first performed in the 1870s, giving her last performance in 1921 when she was in her 70s. She was said by the ATHENAEUM, to play the part "with a realism and a pathos difficult to surpass . . . the slouching, dejected gait, and the movement of some hunted animal, were admirably exhibited." She was particularly affecting as she recited the Lord's Prayer.

Leech, John (1817–1864) Illustrator and caricaturist, especially for *PUNCH*; friend who often dined and occasionally took holidays with Dickens; a participant in the Dickens theatricals. A friend of THACKERAY from Charterhouse School and his associate on *Punch*, Leech also applied unsuccessfully to replace SEYMOUR as the illustrator for *Pickwick*. He illustrated *A Christmas Carol* and provided some illustrations for all of the other CHRISTMAS BOOKS. Dickens praised the beauty and idealism in his CARICATURES and considered his work "truer to life than even HOGARTH." Other examples of his work appear in illustrations 14 (*The CHIMES*) and 15 (*A CHRISTMAS CAROL*).

"Leech's 'The Rising Generation'" Review of LEECH's collection of 12 drawings from *Punch* for the *EXAMINER* (December 30, 1848). Describing Leech as "the very first English caricaturist . . . who has considered beauty as being perfectly compatible with his art," Dickens concentrates on the humor, rather than the satire, in Leech's pictures. *Miscellaneous*.

Leeford, Edward ("Monks") Villainous half-brother of Oliver Twist, "a tall man wrapped in a cloak" (33), who plots with Fagin to corrupt Oliver into a life of criminality (26). If he succeeds, Monks will inherit the estate of their father **Edwin**, whose will otherwise left most of his property to Oliver on the condition that he remain uncorrupted. Monks plotted with his mother to suppress the will, but after he robbed and deserted her, she revealed the truth before dying. Nancy reveals his dealings with Fagin to Brownlow (40) and Monks is forced to leave the country. He dies in prison in America (52). *Twist*.

"Legal and Equitable Jokes" Satiric article for *HOUSEHOLD WORDS* (September 23, 1854). The narrator, a barrister, rejects Graham Willmore's proposed legal reforms on the grounds that what they address are just practical jokes played by the legal system about which Willmore has no sense of humor. *Miscellaneous*.

Leicester Square Area in west London, "a centre of attraction to indifferent foreign hotels and indifferent foreigners, racket courts, fighting men, swordsmen, old china, gaming houses, exhibitions, and a large medley of shabbiness and shrinking out of sight" (*Bleak House*, 21), where Trooper George has his shooting gallery. Known as **Leicester Fields** at the time of the GORDON RIOTS, it was the site of the mansion of Sir George Saville, sponsor of the Catholic Relief Bill in Parliament, which was burned by the demonstrators (*Rudge*, 56).

"Leigh Hunt. A Remonstrance" Article reviewing the biography of HUNT by his son for *ALL THE YEAR ROUND* (December 24, 1859) in which Dickens admits that he based the delightful side of Skimpole on Hunt, but claims that Skimpole's vices were not drawn from the poet. *Miscellaneous*.

Leigh, Mary Ann Maria BEADNELL's closest friend and confidante, the original for Julia Mills, Dora Spenlow's friend in *Copperfield*. She flirted with Dickens, gossiped about his relationship with Maria, and earned his displeasure when some of the gossip got back to him.

Lemon, Mark (1809–1870) Playwright, novelist, and founding editor of *PUNCH* from 1841 to 1870. Dickens met Lemon in 1843 and their mutual love of the theater, good company, and conviviality made them close friends. Dickens soon recruited Lemon for his AMATEUR THEATRICAL enterprises and Lemon acted in most of Dickens's productions, performing especially well as Sir John Falstaff in *The Merry Wives of Windsor* in 1848. Dickens collaborated with Lemon on a farce, *Mr. Nightingale's Diary* (1851), and Lemon adapted for the stage two of Dickens's CHRISTMAS BOOKS, *The Chimes* and *The Haunted Man*. Although he was a regular visitor in Dickens's household and was "Uncle Mark" to Dickens's children, Lemon was rejected by Dickens after he represented Catherine DICKENS in the negotiations for the separation in 1858. The two were reconciled at THACKERAY's funeral in 1863, but their close friendship was never resumed.

Leech's familiar rendering of Fezziwig's Ball for A Christmas Carol *(1843).*

Lemon, Mrs. Friend of Mrs. Orange who takes in all of Mrs. Orange's "children" in Nettie Ashford's tale. She is the mother of **Tootleumboots**. "Holiday Romance."

Lenville, Thomas Member of the Crummles Theatrical Company; "his age did not appear to exceed thirty, although many at first sight would have considered him much older, as his face was long and very pale, from the constant application of stage paints" (33). When his professional jealousy is aroused by Nicholas, he challenges him and threatens to "pull his nose" in retaliation (29). His **wife**, "in a very limp bonnet and veil" (23), is also a member of the company. *Nickleby*.

Le Sage, Alain René (1668–1747) French novelist and dramatist, one of the early practitioners of the PICARESQUE. *Gil Blas* (1715–35; translated by SMOLLETT, 1749) was one of the cherished books of both Copperfield and Dickens. Dickens also refers to Le Sage's satirical novel *Le Diable boiteux* (*The Devil upon Two Sticks*, 1707), in which a student releases from captivity Asmodeus, a small, lame demon, and is rewarded by seeing Madrid with all the rooftops pulled away so that he can know the guilty secrets of those living beneath. Dickens alludes to this invention significantly in *Curiosity Shop* (33) and *Dombey* (47).

Leslie, Charles Robert (1794–1859) Artist, illustrator, friend of Dickens. Introduced to Dickens by Washington IRVING, whose books he had illustrated, Leslie was a frequent visitor in Dickens's house. He painted a portrait of Dickens in the role of Bobadil (1846) and did the frontispiece for the CHEAP EDITION of *Pickwick*.

Letters Before he died, Dickens burned many of the letters he had received and requested his correspondents to do likewise, so many of his letters are forever lost. The first collection of his remaining letters, selected and sometimes severely edited by his daughter Mamie DICKENS and Georgina HOGARTH appeared in three volumes in 1880–82. The next general selection was done in 1938 by Walter DEXTER for the NONESUCH EDITION; this collection is the one that has been used until recently by scholars. It is now gradually being replaced by the Pilgrim Edition of *The Letters of Charles Dickens*, which includes all the letters and is throughly edited and annotated by Madeline HOUSE, Graham STOREY, Kathleen TILLOTSON, and others. The first volume was issued in 1965; the most recent, volume 7, brings the collection up to the year 1855. Several volumes of letters to particular correspondents—among them BEARD, Miss COUTTS, Maria BEADNELL, KOLLE, WILLS, and LEMON—have also appeared over the years.

Lettis, Richard (1928–) Professor, C. W. Post University; critic of Victorian fiction. Lettis's two volumes, *The Dickens Aesthetic* (1989) and *Dickens on Literature* (1990), describe the novelist's writings on literature and aesthetics and are especially useful for their use of Dickens's journalism and editorial advice. Lettis has also made a useful collection of critical materials in *Assessing Great Expectations* (1965; with R. Morris).

Lever, Charles (1806–1872) Irish physician, novelist, and humorist; contributor to HOUSEHOLD WORDS and ALL THE YEAR ROUND; best known for *The Confessions of Harry Lorrequer* (1839) and *Charles O'Malley* (1841). Although Lever's work was often compared to that of Dickens, the two were not close friends, perhaps because the advertisements for *Lorrequer* suggested that it was superior to *Pickwick*. Nevertheless, Dickens, who admired Lever's work, commissioned a serial from him in 1860 for *All the Year Round*. Unfortunately, the novel, *A Day's Ride*, did not interest readers, and Dickens was forced to serialize *Great Expectations* simultaneously to restore the magazine's circulation. Dickens assuaged Lever's hurt feelings over the episode by helping him to negotiate a contract for the novel with CHAPMAN & HALL and by encouraging him to submit more stories and articles to the magazine.

Lewes, George Henry (1817–1878) Author, reviewer, and scientist; he lived with Mary Ann Evans (George ELIOT) as her husband from 1854 until his death; friend of Dickens. Lewes performed in Dickens's production of *Every Man in His Humour* in 1847; carried on a public controversy with Dickens over the SPONTANEOUS COMBUSTION in *Bleak House*, which he considered unscientific; and, after Dickens's death, he enraged John FORSTER with some remarks about Dickens suggesting that the novelist had an "animal intelligence" rather than one that transformed sensations into ideas.

Lewsome Mrs. Gamp is hired by John Westlock, his old schoolmate, to attend this physician's assistant during a serious illness. In exchange for forgiving a gambling debt, Lewsome had supplied Jonas Chuzzlewit with poison and he believes that Jonas used it to murder his father (48). After he confesses this guilty secret to Westlock, John and others confront Jonas (51). *Chuzzlewit*.

Ley, J. W. T. (1879–1943) Journalist; president of the National Union of Journalists, 1939–40; Dickensian; Honorable Secretary of the DICKENS FELLOWSHIP from 1904 to 1909. He contributed innumerable articles to the *DICKENSIAN* and stated in 1926 that only six issues of the magazine had appeared that didn't include something by him. He edited a still useful annotated edition of John FORSTER's *Life of Dickens* and authored many books on Dickens, including a volume on Dickens's friendships, *The Dickens Circle* (1918), though much in the latter work has since been outdated.

Library Edition Edition of Dickens's works issued in monthly volumes jointly by BRADBURY & EVANS and CHAPMAN & HALL, beginning in January 1858. Initially unillustrated, it was reissued by Chapman & Hall alone in 1861–62 with the original illustrations.

Library of Fiction, The   Monthly periodical published by CHAPMAN & HALL from April 1836 to July 1837. Dickens published two sketches in it which were later included in *Boz*—"Tuggses" and "First of May."

Licensed Victualler, Mr.   Host of a LIVERPOOL pub for merchant seamen. *Uncommercial* (5).

Life of Our Lord, The   Narrative life of Jesus that Dickens wrote for his own children in 1846 under the title *The Children's New Testament*. When it was first published in 1934—after the death of his last surviving child, Henry—it was given the title by which it is now known. The narrative is cast in simple language and emphasizes the parables and the moral teachings in the gospels.

Lighthouse, The   Melodrama by Wilkie COLLINS that Dickens produced with his group of amateur players in 1855. Dickens played with great success the role of the lighthouse keeper, Aaron Gurnock, and composed a poetic prologue and "The SONG OF THE WRECK" for the play.

Lighterman Arms   Public house in Mudfog where Nicholas Tulrumble spends the evenings with his friends before he becomes mayor. *Mudfog.*

Lightwood, Mortimer   A solicitor and intimate friend of Eugene Wrayburn. He is one of the Veneerings' "oldest friends," a frequent member of their dinner parties where he tells the dinner guests the unfolding saga of "the man from somewhere," the story of John Harmon. *Mutual Friend.*

"Lignum Vitae"   Nickname of Matthew BAGNET, meaning "tree of life." The narrator says that the name, given to him by his regiment, acknowledged his honesty and his "stolid face" (27). *Bleak House.*

Lillerton, Miss   The fastidious woman who is the object of the matrimonial intentions of both Watkins Tottle and the Reverend Timson. She engages the unwitting Tottle to carry a note to Timson setting the date for her wedding to the clergyman. *Boz*, "Tottle."

Lillo, George (1693–1739)   Dramatist; author of the domestic tragedy *The London Merchant, or The History of George Barnwell* (1731), in which an apprentice is seduced into robbing his employer and murdering his uncle. Dickens frequently alludes to the play, most notably in *Rudge*, where Sim Tappertit compares himself to Barnwell (4), and in *Expectations*, where Wopsle reads the play to the apprentice Pip (15).

Lillyvick   Mrs. Kenwig's uncle, a collector of water rates; "a short old gentleman, in drabs and gaiters, with a face that might have been carved out of *lignum vitae*" (15). Smitten by Miss PETOWKER, the actress, he follows her to PORTSMOUTH, where she is playing with the Crummles Company and marries her (25). After she abandons him for a half-pay captain, he returns to London, restoring the hopes of the Kenwigs that their children will inherit his money (52). *Nickleby.*

Limbkins   Chairman of the Board of Guardians at the workhouse where Oliver is born, "a red-faced gentleman in the high chair." *Twist* (2).

Limbury, Mr. and Mrs. Peter   Friends of the Lovetowns who are caught up in their attempt to make each other jealous. *Is She His Wife?*

Limehouse   Dockside area in east London, site of the GRAPES Inn, original of the SIX JOLLY FELLOWSHIP PORTERS. Rogue Riderhood and the Hexams live nearby in **Limehouse Hole**. Pleasant Riderhood's leaving shop is also located here. *Mutual Friend.*

Lincoln's Inn   One of the INNS OF COURT. In 1827 Dickens worked as a clerk in the offices of Molloy, a solicitor here in New Square. Serjeant Snubbin has his chambers in Old Square (*Pickwick*, 31) as do Kenge and Carboy (*Bleak House*, 20). Much of the action of *Bleak House* takes place in the Inn and its neighborhood: The Court of CHANCERY is held here in **Lincoln's Inn Hall** (1); Tulkinghorn's house, modeled on the house of John FORSTER, is at no. 58, **Lincoln's Inn Fields** (10), a residential square next to the Inn. The Gordon rioters gather in the Fields before going on to NEWGATE PRISON (*Rudge*, 63); Betsey Trotwood stays in a hotel here (*Copperfield*, 23).

Lincolnshire   County about 125 miles north of London where CHESNEY WOLD, country seat of the Dedlocks, is located. *Bleak House.*

Linda   Dickens's pet St. Bernard who, Dickens wrote to Annie FIELDS, on his return to GAD'S HILL after the reading tour in AMERICA, "was greatly excited, weeping profusely, and throwing herself on her back that she might caress [his] foot with her great forepaws."

Linderwood, Lieutenant   Officer in command of the 24 Royal Marines dispatched to Silver-Store Island. He is ill when they arrive at the colony. "English Prisoners."

Lindsay, Jack (1900–)   Prolific Australian-born poet, novelist, social critic, editor, and translator. His critical biography *Charles Dickens* (1950) approaches its subject from a Marxist and Freudian point of view and offers many original and provocative insights.

Linkinwater, Tim   "Fat, elderly, large-faced clerk, with silver spectacles and a powdered head" (35), who has loyally served the Cheeryble Brothers for 44 years. Nicholas is hired to relieve him of some of his duties (35).

He has a pet blackbird, Dick, and his **sister**, his female counterpart, attends the Cheerybles' festivities (37). He befriends the Nicklebys and eventually marries Miss LA CREEVY (65). *Nickleby*.

Linseed, Duke of   A begging letter-writer who asks Boffin to subscribe to the Family Party Fund. *Mutual Friend* (I:17).

Linton, Mrs. Eliza Lynn (1822–1898)   Novelist and journalist; regular contributor to HOUSEHOLD WORDS and ALL THE YEAR ROUND. A friend of Walter Savage LANDOR, who introduced her to Dickens, she earned Dickens's respect for her journal articles: "Good for anything, and thoroughly reliable." In *My Literary Life* (1899), she describes Dickens as "one, who wrote so tenderly, so sentimentally, so gushingly, [yet] had a strain of hardness in his nature which was like a rod of iron in his soul." She sold GAD'S HILL PLACE, which she inherited from her father, to Dickens.

Linx, Miss   "Sharply observant" pupil in Miss Pupford's Lilliputian College. "Tiddler."

Lion   Henry Gowan's dog, who attacks Rigaud and is later found poisoned. *Dorrit* (I:17, II:6).

Lion, The   "Miserable old public house" where David sometimes gets a plate of bread and cheese and a glass of beer for dinner when he is working at MURDSTONE AND GRINBY's. *Copperfield* (11).

Lirriper, Mrs. Emma ("Gran")   Narrator of "Mrs. Lirriper's Lodgings" and "Mrs. Lirriper's Legacy." Widowed in the second year of her marriage and left with her husband's debts, she opened the lodging house at 81, NORFOLK STREET, STRAND, that she has managed for 38 years. Kind and good-natured, she is only irritated by her rival lodging-house keeper, Miss Wozenham, but after she saves her rival from bankruptcy the two become friends. She tells of the servants that have worked for her and of her lodgers, especially Major Jackman, her parlor boarder, and the Edsons, a young married couple whose child she adopts and names **Jemmy Jackman Lirriper** after Mrs. Edson is abandoned and dies giving birth to the boy. She and the Major dote upon Jemmy, who loves them in return, telling them a fictionalized version of his life in "Lodgings" (2). In "Legacy," Mrs. Lirriper and the Major take the boy to SENS, FRANCE, where he meets his dying father.

List, Isaac   One of the group of gamblers at the VALIANT SOLDIER who fleece Nell's grandfather and persuade him to rob Mrs. Jarley. *Curiosity Shop* (29, 30, 42).

Lithers, Thomas   Landlord of the Water-Lily Hotel at Malvern, where Nightingale comes to take the water cure. *Nightingale*.

Littimer   Steerforth's smug, deferential, and respectable manservant; "he surrounded himself with an atmosphere of respectability, and walked secure in it. It would have been next to impossible to suspect him of anything wrong, he was so thoroughly respectable" (21). His demeanor intimidates David and provides cover for his machinations to arrange Steerforth's affair with Em'ly. He reports Steerforth's wanderings on the Continent (46) and is offered Em'ly when Steerforth tires of her. After he embezzles from his master and his villainy is discovered by Miss Mowcher, he ends up as a "model" prisoner (61). *Copperfield*.

"Little Blossom"   Betsey Trotwood's nickname for David's wife, DORA. *Copperfield*.

Little Britain   Street in the CITY where Jaggers's office is located. *Expectations* (20).

Little College Street   Street in CAMDEN TOWN where Dickens boarded with Mrs. ROYLANCE in 1824 while his father was in the MARSHALSEA PRISON.

"Little Dinner in an Hour, A"   The Traveller and his friend Bullfinch endure a dreadful dinner at the Temeraire in Namelesston. *Uncommercial* (33).

"Little Dombey, The Story of"   Dickens's public reading from *Dombey and Son*. Developed in 1858, the first of the PUBLIC READINGS from one of the longer novels, it presented the life and death of Paul Dombey. A sad reading, it was not performed as often as many of the others.

Little Dorrit   Dickens's 11th novel, published in monthly numbers (December 1855–June 1857) by BRADBURY & EVANS, illustrated by BROWNE. Published in one volume, 1857. *Little Dorrit* may be the most difficult of Dickens's novels. Its passive hero and heroine, obscure and complex inheritance plot, and unremittingly bleak picture of society make it a dark and ambiguous story. It anatomizes Victorian Britain as a nation obsessed with wealth and power, imprisoned by traditions of class privilege, and diminished by oppressive and negative religion. Arthur Clennam and Amy Dorrit struggle to overcome these imprisoning forces and the novel ends on a redemptive and hopeful note as they seem to begin a more authentic and fulfilling way of life.

SYNOPSIS

Book I: Poverty

Part 1 (December, 1855)
(I:1) On a bright August day in MARSEILLES 30 years ago, two prisoners linger in a dark cell, Monsieur Rigaud, charged with murdering his wife, and John Baptist Cavalletto, a small-time Italian smuggler. (I:2) At the same time, several English travelers returning from the East are in quarantine in Marseilles: the Meagles, a re-

In "The Marshalsea becomes an Orphan," Browne (Phiz) depicts the Dorrits leaving the prison after Mr. Dorrit comes into his fortune.

tired banker and his wife, their pampered daughter Pet and her servant Tattycoram; Miss Wade, a bitter and unforgiving spinster; and Arthur Clennam, returning to London after many years working in the family business in China. Clennam speaks of his lack of purpose and will. (I:3) Arthur arrives in London on Sunday and remembers the oppressive Sundays of his childhood. He finds his mother's house unchanged: decaying and rusting, blackened by the smoke of the city, and propped up by huge timbers. His invalid mother, confined to a chair in an upper room, is also unchanged. She greets him coldly. (I:4) Meanwhile, Affery Flintwinch, Mrs. Clennam's maid, sees her husband with his DOUBLE in the middle of the night. After sending the double away, Flintwinch tells her she has been dreaming.

Part 2 (January, 1856)
(I:5) The next day Arthur offends his mother by withdrawing from the family business and by asking if his late father had any guilty secret that he might have wanted to set right. Mrs. Clennam takes Flintwinch into the business in Arthur's place. Arthur wonders if his family's guilty secret has to do with his mother's servant, Amy Dorrit.

(I:6) Amy, also known as Little Dorrit, was born in the MARSHALSEA, a debtors prison where her father, William Dorrit, has been a prisoner longer than any other inmate and is known as "the Father of the Mar-

shalsea." Other inmates and visitors acknowledge his importance by giving him small monetary tributes. (I:7) Amy grew up as "the Child of the Marshalsea." After her mother died when she was eight, she became the "mother" of the family, keeping the accounts and providing for her ungrateful older sister Fanny and her ne'er-do-well brother Tip. Amy goes out to work each day for Mrs. Clennam. (I:8) Curious about Amy, Arthur follows her to the Marshalsea. There he meets her father, William Dorrit, pays his respects, and leaves a tribute. He asks Little Dorrit's forgiveness for intruding in her life. When he attempts to leave the prison, he discovers that the gates have been closed and he must spend the night.

Part 3 (February 1856)
(I:9) Arthur's interest in Amy and her family continues. Amy tells him that getting her father out of prison is hopeless and she worries that he could not survive outside the Marshalsea. Arthur learns that Dorrit's primary creditor is Tite Barnacle of the CIRCUMLOCUTION OFFICE (I:10). Devoted to the process of How Not To Do It, the Circumlocution Office has long been the preserve of the Barnacle family. After inquiring for Tite Barnacle several times and never getting to see him, Arthur is finally introduced to Barnacle Junior who, after aimless conversation, sends him to Tite Barnacle's home in Mews Street behind GROSVENOR SQUARE. There Ar-

thur finds Tite Barnacle posing for a portrait; after more fruitless questioning he is sent back to the Circumlocution Office, where he is given a lot of forms. As he leaves, Arthur meets Meagles with Daniel Doyce, an inventor who has unsuccessfully attempted to secure support at the Circumlocution Office for his invention. Instead of helping Doyce, the bureaucrats treat him as a public offender.

(I:11) The scene shifts to the Break of Day, a small inn in Chalons, France, where Rigaud and Cavaletto, the two prisoners from Marseilles, meet again. Since they are both on their way north, Rigaud suggests that they travel together, but at dawn Cavaletto slips out of the inn and goes off on his own.

Part 4 (March, 1856)
(I:12) Seeking information about the Dorrits, Clennam goes to BLEEDING HEART YARD, a slum tenement, and there engages Plornish, an unemployed plasterer, to act as his agent in securing the release of Tip, Amy's brother, from the Marshalsea. (I:13) Arthur finds Mr. Casby, landlord of the tenement and father of his childhood sweetheart, unchanged after 20 years. His daughter Flora, now the widow of Mr. Finching, has gained weight, but she is still silly, garrulous, and flirtatious. After an uncomfortable dinner with them, Arthur leaves with Pancks, Casby's rent collector. They aid a foreigner—Cavaletto—who has been run over by a mail van. After this eventful day, Arthur ruminates on his life: "From the unhappy suppression of my youngest days, through the rigid and unloving home that followed them, through my departure, my long exile, my return . . . down to . . . this day with poor Flora, . . . What have I found!" As he asks this question, Little Dorrit appears at his door. (I:14) She tells him that Tip has been released from prison by the good agency of an unknown benefactor whom she is not allowed to thank. She asks Arthur to give no more money to her father. Then she spends the cold night in the streets, the first night she has ever spent outside the Marshalsea.

Part 5 (April 1856)
(I:15) Affery overhears her husband and Mrs. Clennam quarreling. Flintwinch accuses Mrs. Clennam of not putting Arthur's doubts about his father to rest. He warns her that he will not submit to being ruled by her. He also tries to discredit Little Dorrit, but Mrs. Clennam refuses to hear him out.. Affery is convinced that something is wrong in the house.

(I:16) Arthur and Daniel Doyce go to the Meagles's country place for a weekend. Arthur thinks about courting Pet and offering to become Doyce's business partner. (I:17) Arthur takes an immediate dislike to Henry Gowan, an arrogant and unsuccessful painter who comes to visit Pet. Doyce tells Arthur that Meagles dislikes Gowan so much that he took Pet away to Europe.

(I:18) Meanwhile, young John Chivery, son of the Marshalsea turnkey who looks to the Dorrits as the aristocracy of the prison, is infatuated with Amy. One Sunday, after bringing his tribute of cigars to Mr Dorrit, he

seeks out Amy on the IRON BRIDGE, a place where she goes seeking solitude, and asks her if he "may say it." She tells him that he should never say it and never again seek her out on the bridge. She wishes him happiness and a good wife. He goes home imagining the epitaph on his tombstone.

Part 6 (May, 1856)
(I:19) The Dorrit brothers are a study in contrasts. William, the prisoner, is strong and healthy; Frederick, who lives outside the prison and works as a musician, is weak and depressed. William wonders whether his brother would have been better off in prison, but he decides that he would not have had the strength of character for it.

When Chivery, the turnkey, is short with him, William blames Amy for rejecting Chivery's son. As he eats the meal she has prepared for him, he pities himself and asks, "What am I worth to anyone?" She is so upset that she sits up the whole night, watching over him as he sleeps. (I:20) When Amy asks her sister about a bracelet she is wearing, Fanny takes her to Mrs. Merdle's house in HARLEY STREET, CAVENDISH SQUARE. There Amy learns that Mrs. Merdle has offered Fanny presents—the bracelet, dresses, money—to prevent a romance between Fanny and her son, Edmund Sparkler. Fanny justifies making Mrs. Merdle pay for her class snobbery and she accuses Amy of acting in ways that encourage such people to despise them as paupers. (I:21) Later, at a dinner party at the Merdles' home, Bar and Bishop, Treasury and Admiralty, flatter their host, Mr. Merdle the financier, and speculate about his wealth. Mrs. Merdle displays her husband's jewels on her bosom. But there is a shadow over the party: Merdle has a physical complaint, even though his doctor can find nothing wrong with him.

(I:22) Once he stops paying tribute to Mr. Dorrit, as Amy has requested, Clennam does not rise in the estimation of the Father of the Marshalsea. Nevertheless he continues to visit. One Sunday Clennam sees young John Chivery, disconsolate and melancholy, pining for Little Dorrit. Clennam is surprised, for he has not thought of Little Dorrit in romantic terms. When he breaks his promise and sends some money to her father, Clennam is puzzled by the intensity of Amy's distress.

Part 7 (June, 1856)
(I:23) Arthur buys a partnership in Doyce's factory in Bleeding Heart Yard, and he recruits Pancks to secure information about the Dorrits. (I:24) Flora wants to employ Little Dorrit, but she makes Amy uncomfortable by spilling out the story of her life and relationship to Arthur. Amy is also intimidated by Pancks, who observes her closely and tells her fortune. After he describes her family with uncanny accuracy and tells her that she "shall live to see," she retreats to her room. There she tells Maggy, a retarded woman who regards Amy as her "Little Mother," the story of the Princess and the little woman who works at her wheel and has a secret shadow hidden in her closet. When the little woman dies, the Princess cannot find the shadow and believes that it has gone, as the little woman said it would, into her grave

with her. (I:25) Cavalletto moves into Bleeding Heart Yard, where the residents teach him English and notice that he peers out into the streets as if he is fearful of someone.

Part 8 (July 1856)
(I:26) Had Arthur decided to court Pet, he would have intensely disliked Henry Gowan. Gowan does bother Mr. Meagles. When Clennam goes with Gowan to visit his mother at HAMPTON COURT, Arthur meets a group of condescending aristocratic parasites. Mrs. Gowan asserts that Pet is just a social climber trying to "catch" her son, but Arthur, angered by her snobbery and condescension, assures her that Mr. Meagles is not pleased by the courtship. (I:27) When Meagles asks Clennam to help him search for Tattycoram, who has run away, they find the girl living with Miss Wade. She tells Tattycoram that Meagles wants to take her back to be "a foil to his pretty daughter, a slave to her pleasant wilfulness, and a toy in the house showing the goodness of the family," and the girl refuses to go. (I:28) After several attempts to change her mind, Meagles decides she is irrecoverable. Meanwhile Gowan continues to pursue Pet. When Pet confides to Arthur that she is going to marry Gowan, he goes to the edge of the river at night and scatters some roses on the flowing water.

(I:29) Back in the city, Mrs. Clennam wonders why Pancks is inquiring into Little Dorrit's life, and she questions the girl about her situation and seems to be consoled by Amy's uncomplaining answers.

Part 9 (August 1856)
(I:30) Rigaud, the Marseilles prisoner, who now calls himself Blandois and describes himself as a man of no country, arrives at Mrs. Clennam's door with a letter of credit to Clennam and Co. He flatters Mrs. Clennam, admires her husband's portrait and watch, and learns that the initials on the watch—"DRF"—stand for "do not forget." She tells him that her monotonous existence does not allow her to forget "to be sensible of having (as we all have every one of us, all the children of Adam!) offences to expiate and peace to make."

(I:31) Little Dorrit walks from Bleeding Heart Yard to the Marshalsea with Old Nandy, a workhouse resident. Fanny is scandalized that her sister would be seen in the streets with a pauper. Her father is also distressed and tells her that he has been humiliated and that she lacks "Spirit," but a letter from Clennam containing a banknote puts him in a better frame of mind. At tea, he is obsequious with Clennam, patronizing with Nandy, who sits on a window ledge like a serf in a baronial hall, and angered by Tip, who shows his "proper spirit" by insulting Clennam. (I:32) Arthur tells Amy not to be concerned over the "insults" he has suffered; he would gladly suffer them to see her. When he asks her to rely on him, she weeps uncontrollably. He confides to her his realization, prompted by his loss of Pet, that he is too old for love and romance; he asks her to confide similarly in him. Maggy suggests that she tell the story of the prin-

cess, but she tells Arthur it is merely a fairy story. Pancks informs Arthur that he is on the verge of a breakthrough in the search for Little Dorrit's story.

Part 10 (September 1856)
(I:33) Although Meagles will pay Gowan's debts, Mrs. Gowan still considers her son's marriage a demeaning alliance in Society's eyes. Mrs. Merdle complains that her husband does not accommodate himself to Society, that he is preoccupied with business. She wants him to "seem to care about nothing." Merdle wanders through his house as if he doesn't belong there. (I:34) Gowan complains that he is a disappointed man. But then, he philosophizes, we are all disappointed. Even his impending marriage does not diminish his disappointment. At the wedding, the differences between the Society Barnacles and the business Meagles cause uneasiness.

(I:35) Pancks discovers that Mr. Dorrit is heir to a landed fortune. When Arthur breaks the news to Little Dorrit, she faints. When they tell Mr. Dorrit, he is so upset that he just shakes. Little Dorrit wonders that her father "should have lost so many years and suffered so much, and at last pay all the debts as well. It seems to me," she remarks, "hard that he should pay in life and money both." (I:36) On his last day in prison, Mr. Dorrit gives a baronial dinner for the inmates and then, at noon, leads his family out to a waiting coach. Little Dorrit is not with them. She has fainted in her room. Clennam finds her and carries her to the carriage, where Fanny is scandalized because Amy is wearing her old dress. The carriage drives off, leaving Clennam behind in the street.

Book II: Riches

Part 11 (October 1856)
(II:1) The Dorrits—William, Frederick, Fanny, Tip, and Amy—who are traveling from SWITZERLAND to ITALY stop for the night at the monastery at the Pass of the GREAT SAINT BERNARD. There they meet the Gowans and Blandois, who are on their way to Rome. Amy comforts Pet after the young bride faints during dinner. Blandois watches Amy, making her uncomfortable. (II:2) Traveling with the Dorrits is Mrs. General, daughter of a clerical dignitary and widow of a commissariat officer, who has been engaged to "form the minds" of Fanny and Amy. (II:3) As the Dorrits make their descent into Italy, Little Dorrit is haunted by the image of Blandois watching their carriage. At Martigny, Mr. Dorrit is offended because the hotel room he has reserved has been taken by Mrs. Merdle and her son Edmund Sparkler. Mrs. Merdle does not acknowledge either Fanny or Amy, but as her coach pulls away Sparkler peers at them through the back window.

In Italy, cut off from familiar people and places, Amy lives in her memories. At VENICE she becomes known as the little English girl who sits alone on her balcony looking out on the canal. (I:4) Amy writes to Arthur from Venice to tell him that she has met Pet, and that she senses something is not right in the marriage, something that even Pet may not be aware of. She thinks Pet needs a husband more "steadfast and firm." She tells him of the "unreality" of her trip and how she thinks about the people in England. She asks him not to think of her in any way different from the poor girl he knew from the prison.

Part 12 (November 1856)
(II:5) Mrs. General reports to Mr. Dorrit that Amy has no force of character and no self-reliance. He directs Amy to submit to Mrs. General's instruction, and says that she alone of the family reveals the taint of the prison. Frederick defends Amy and confronts the family: "I protest against pride. I protest against ingratitude. I protest against any one of us here who have known what we have known, and have seen what we have seen, setting up any pretension that puts Amy at a moment's disadvantage, or to the cost of a moment's pain." The other Dorrits are outraged and agree that he is crazy. (II:6) When Little Dorrit visits the Gowans, she finds Henry painting in his studio with Blandois as his model. After his dog growls at Blandois, Gowan knocks the animal to the floor and kicks it. On the way home, Little Dorrit observes that Gowan treats his wife like a child. Fanny notices Sparkler following their gondola and says that she will make a slave of him. (II:7) When Little Dorrit sees Pet again, they are shadowed by Blandois and Pet tells her that Blandois has poisoned Gowan's dog. Fanny astounds Amy with the news that Mrs. General has designs on their father. Little Dorrit realizes that Society in Italy is a "superior sort of Marshalsea." From Venice they go on to ROME, where they meet the Merdles once again.

Part 13 (December 1856)
(II:8) Back in London, Arthur seeks support for Doyce's invention and sorely misses Little Dorrit. (II:9) One day he sees Tattycoram in a London street with a foreigner; he secretly follows them and observes their clandestine meeting with Miss Wade. (II:10) A few days later Arthur is disturbed to meet the insolent foreigner, now identified as Blandois, at his mother's house.

(II:11) Little Dorrit writes to Arthur of Pet's devotion to her husband, of their new son, and of the Meagles's discomfort with Gowan. She also tells of Fanny's suitor and of her own homesickness.

Part 14 (January 1857)
(II:12) Merdle's wealth gives him power. He uses his influence with Sir Decimus Barnacle to secure a position in the Circumlocution Office for Edmund Sparkler. (II:13) His influence spreads throughout England and there is a boom in Merdle's enterprises and an epidemic of speculation in Merdle's shares. Even Pancks has invested £100. Arthur is cautious, but he considers placing the Doyce and Clennam money in Merdle's stock. (II:14) In Rome, Sparkler's new position is the talk of the English community. Fanny must make up her mind about mar-

rying him and returning to England with him. She recognizes that she is a willful person who would not submit to a clever husband; Sparkler's dull-wittedness suits her desire to rule her husband. Marriage to Sparkler also offers her a chance to get back at Mrs. Merdle.

Part 15 (February 1856)
(II:15) Fanny asks Amy whether she should rush her marriage or delay it. Amy counsels delay, but Fanny sees a quick marriage as a way to get one up in her struggle with Mrs. Merdle. So she marries quickly and returns to London with her husband, accompanied by Mr. Dorrit. Amy is left behind with Mrs. General. (II:16) In London the Sparklers take over Mrs. Merdle's rooms in the Merdle's house. Mr. Dorrit buys into Merdle's securities and becomes increasingly aware that Fanny's marriage has moved him ahead in the world. (II:17) Before he leaves London, Mr. Dorrit goes to Mrs. Clennam to learn what he can about the disappearance of Blandois, but she tells him very little. Dorrit is unsettled by her secrecy, by Affery's fear of noises in the house, by Flintwinch's dispatch, and by the realization that the house is being watched. (II:18) He is also upset by a visit from young John Chivery, who reminds him of his prison days. On the way back to Rome, Dorrit builds castles in his mind, contemplating marriage to Mrs. General.

Part 16 (March 1856)
(II:19) Back in Rome, Mr. Dorrit is unwell. He is prepared to propose to Mrs. General, but he does not find an opportune moment. At Mrs. Merdle's going-away party, crowded with all the important English people in Rome, he seems confused. When he rises to deliver a speech, he reverts to his old manner as Father of the Marshalsea. He thinks he is back in the prison. Amy manages to get him home. She cares for him, but he continues in his old identity and dies 10 days later attended by Frederick, who also dies, kneeling at his brother's bedside.

(II:20) Hoping to learn something about Blandois, Arthur Clennam seeks out Miss Wade, who is sequestered in CALAIS with the unhappy Tattycoram. She suggests that Arthur ask Gowan about Blandois, her sarcasm revealing her hatred for the artist and his wife, and she gives Arthur a document. (II:21) The document is Miss Wade's life story, "The History of a Self-Tormentor." An orphan who became a governess, Miss Wade learned in childhood to distrust others who patronized and condescended to her. She is insanely jealous and distrustful of friends and lovers, and hateful toward those who abandoned her or interfered in her life. She especially detests Gowan, a former lover, and Pet, who stole him from her. She sees in Tattycoram an orphan patronized and mistrusted as she was.

(II:22) Unsuccessful in securing support for his work in England, Doyce goes abroad to work for a "barbaric" power that believes in getting things done. He leaves the financial affairs of Doyce and Clennam in Arthur's hands, advising him only to avoid speculation. Clennam learns that his worker, Cavaletto, knows Blandois as Rigaud, an accused murderer.

Part 17 (April 1856)
(II:23) Arthur tells his mother that Blandois is an accused murderer, and even though she is taken aback, she will reveal nothing about her dealings with the foreigner. Affery tells him of noises, rustlings, and tremblings in the house, but is afraid to tell him its "secrets."

(II:24) Three months after the deaths of the Dorrit brothers, the Sparklers spend a hot summer evening alone in London. They were calculated to "shine in society," Fanny asserts, but now that she is pregnant, she is incapable of shining. She vows that she will guard against their being alone anymore. Mr. Merdle appears at their door. He is distracted, speaks of having much to do, borrows a penknife, and sets out for home. (II:25) A little while later, Merdle's physician is called away from a dinner party, where the guests are speculating on rumors circulating about Merdle's finances, to the baths down the street. There he finds Merdle, a suicide, lying in a pool of blood. A note to the physician indicates that Merdle's complaint was simple forgery and robbery. (II:26) Arthur had invested all of his company funds in Merdle's enterprises. He sends a letter to their creditors, telling them that payment will be stopped and exonerating Doyce from any blame. He is arrested for debt, taken to the Marshalsea, and placed in the Dorrits' former rooms.

Part 18 (May 1857)
(II:27) In the Marshalsea, John Chivery attends Arthur, but Arthur senses an undercurrent of anger in Chivery's manner. Finally John accuses Arthur of not being honest and insists that he admit that he loves Little Dorrit. He tells Arthur that Little Dorrit loves him. Arthur is stunned. He broods on Little Dorrit's importance in his life. (II:28) Ten or 12 weeks later, Cavalletto and Pancks bring Blandois to the prison. Blandois admits that he sells anything that commands a price—that he sold information about the Gowans to Miss Wade, that he has something to sell to Mrs. Clennam and that she has a week to respond to his offer. (II:29) Arthur, stifled and despondent, is unable to sleep for the next week. On the sixth day he finds a bouquet of flowers beside his bed. He is vaguely aware of a quiet figure in the room. It is Little Dorrit. He weeps and embraces her. She offers him all of her money, but he cannot accept that sacrifice. John Chivery escorts her home and returns with the message that she sends Arthur her undying love.

Parts 19–20 (June 1857)
(II:30) On the seventh day, Pancks and Callavetto bring Blandois to Mrs. Clennam's house. Blandois reveals that he knows Mrs. Clennam's secret: Arthur is not her child, but rather is her husband's child by another woman. She has suppressed the truth and brought up Arthur in a spirit of revenge, "that the child might work out his release in bondage and hardship." She has also suppressed a codicil to Arthur's uncle's will that made Little Dorrit an heiress. Blandois has given copies of the papers he

has to Little Dorrit, instructing her to open them if no one claims them before the gates of the Marshalsea close. In shock, Mrs. Clennam rises out of her chair for the first time in 15 years and runs out of the house. (II:31) She runs through the unfamiliar streets, crosses LONDON BRIDGE, and goes to the Marshalsea. There she asks Little Dorrit to read the papers and learn how she has been wronged. But Amy forgives Mrs. Clennam and promises not to tell Arthur until after Mrs. Clennam is dead. As they return to the house, it crumbles into a ruin, killing Blandois, who is sitting inside. Mrs. Clennam falls paralyzed to the street. She lives on for three more years but is unable to speak or move.

(II:32) Pancks blames himself for recommending Merdle's shares to Clennam and, the more unhappy he is with himself, the more unhappy he becomes with Casby. When Casby tells him that he is not squeezing enough from the tenants, Pancks knocks off Casby's hat, cuts off his long flowing locks, and resigns his position, leaving the patriarch standing in the middle of Bleeding Heart Yard, looking foolish and not in the least venerable.

(II:33) Amy worries that the originals of Blandois's documents will come to light, so she asks Meagles to retrieve them. The search ends at Miss Wade's in Calais, but she denies having any documents. Afterward Tattycoram appears in London with the papers. She asks to become one of Meagles's family once again.

(II:34) On an autumn day after Arthur has recovered, Little Dorrit tells him he must leave the prison. When he learns that they have both been ruined in Merdle's collapse and are poor, he embraces her. The next morning they are married in the church next to the prison. Then they go down together into the roaring streets.

COMMENTARY

Little Dorrit is a complex novel, the epitome of the later Dickens works that Lionel Stevenson characterized as the "dark novels." Its inheritance plot is so intricate that John Wain has described the novel as "plotless" and "a labyrinth," and the editor of the Penguin edition provides an unravelling summary of its intricacies in an appendix. Yet even when these plot complications are clarified, the novel remains a puzzling and disturbing book.

The devices from gothic melodrama used to resolve the plot—the fall of Mrs. Clennam's house, for example, and the machinations of Blandois—seem to break with the realistic temper of much of the rest of the novel and do not really resolve the story. The reader, with a little help, learns the details of Arthur's parentage and Little Dorrit's inheritance, but Arthur is never fully informed about the facts and the lack of knowledge that contributed to his sense of guilt at the beginning of the novel continues even after its apparently "happy" conclusion. The human situation, the novel seems to suggest, is an imprisoning muddle.

Many of Dickens's initial readers found these frustrations in the story daunting. *Frazer's Magazine* declared it "decidedly the worst" of Dickens's novels and E. B. Hanley characterized the novel as a "wilderness." These early reviewers usually attributed their disappointment to the lack of comedy in the novel and called for Dickens to return to such figures as Pickwick and Mrs. Gamp.

Modern critics, however, have been as positive as the original reviewers were negative. Lionel Trilling's classic introduction (1953), declared *Little Dorrit* "one of the three great novels of Dickens' great last period," along with *Bleak House* and *Our Mutual Friend*. Many others have followed to suggest that the ambiguities in the plot and irresolution at the end are part of Dickens's Dostoyevskian strategy to respond to the condition of England in the wake of the Crimean War.

Although the novel is set in the mid-1820s, it directly addresses several topical issues of the 1850s. The Circumlocution Office, for example, is an attack on the abuses brought to light by a Parliamentary inquiry of 1853 which criticized the incompetence of the civil service during the Crimean War and the methods for recruiting civil servants. Merdle's story drew on the case of Michael Sadleir, a bank director and member of Parliament, who committed suicide in 1856 after falling heavily into debt. The Marshalsea Prison, the main symbol in the novel, however, comes from an earlier period. Imprisonment for debt had been declining since the mid-1840s, and the prison itself had been closed in 1849.

Trilling describes the novel as "about society in its very essence." The social range of the novel is very broad, reaching from the aristocratic Barnacles and Gowans at the top, down to Nandy's workhouse and the proletarian housing complex at Bleeding Heart Yard at the bottom. The figure most representative of English society in the 1850s is Merdle, the speculator and securities dealer who attracts attention and money from all quarters. His wife is the epitome of a society matron, a statuesque bust where Merdle displays his wealth in jewels, and his dinners are attended by representatives of all the dominant institutions. These dinner guests are not individualized but are identified only by their roles in society: Bar, Treasury, Bishop, and so forth. Yet Merdle, in spite of financial power and adulation from all sectors of established society, suffers from "some deep-seated recondite complaint" (I:21), a feeling of unease that his doctor cannot diagnose.

Merdle's complaint and his power to infect so many others have prompted Edwin B. Barnet ("*Little Dorrit* and the Disease of Modern Life," *Nineteenth Century Fiction*, 1970) to suggest that the controlling metaphor in the novel is disease. Disease links the speculators with the paralyzed, like the guilty Mrs. Clennam, and the neurotic, like the self-tormenting Miss Wade. The novel's diagnosis of the condition of England finds the whole society infected with Merdle's complaint. The more accepted analysis, however, identifies the prison as the novel's dominant symbol.

The Marshalsea, the debtors prison where Dickens's father was imprisoned in 1824, crystallizes the prison imagery in the novel. William Dorrit has been held there

so long that his youngest child, who is 17 at the start of the novel, was born there. She is the Child of the Marshalsea and he, its longest inmate, its Father. He sees his position as one of honor, a belief reinforced by the deference and monetary tributes he receives from other inmates and visitors. He thinks of himself as the patriarch of the prison and as a father who provides for his family; he cannot acknowledge that his children work outside the prison to provide for him. These patriarchal delusions echo those of the society outside the prison that admires the idle gentleman as a social ideal and establishes a class hierarchy with idle aristocratic parasites like the Barnacles or wealthy swindlers like Merdle at the top.

Dickens is mocking the absurdity of the bureaucracy in the Circumlocution Office and attacking the pretensions of the Barnacles. There was a sharp and bitter edge to his satire in 1856, for the inefficiency, incompetence, and infighting between various departments of the civil service had produced a series of fatal disasters during the Crimean War. The army was inadequately fed and clothed, supplies did not reach the troops, and the medical care for the wounded was insufficient and unsanitary. The unnecessary suffering and deaths caused by administrative mismanagement were tallied daily in the British press from reports telegraphed from the front. Dickens was in the vanguard of those calling for reform of the civil service, for purging unnecessary departments, paper work and red tape, and for choosing bureaucrats on the basis of their competence rather than their family connections. Edmund Sparkler's appointment to a government job and the incompetent Barnacle dynasty at the Circumlocution Office represent the abuses that Dickens thought needed correction. His critique goes well beyond the shortcomings of aristocratic privilege. When even such good people as the Meagles collude to keep such incompetents as the Barnacles in positions of power, more than the civil service needs to change. The class system itself imprisons people, blinding them to the truth and leading to delusion, loneliness, and despair.

Nearly all of the settings in the novel elaborate the theme of imprisonment: the quarantine station in Marseilles where the novel opens, the prison where Rigaud and Cavaletto share a cell, the crumbling house in which Mrs. Clennam is confined to her wheelchair, the slum tenement in Bleeding Heart Yard, the convent at the top of the Simplon Pass, the palaces in Venice. Each in its own way articulates an imprisoning mode of consciousness. Dark, haunted by unnerving sounds and secretive strangers, Mrs. Clennam's house, for example, contains the repressed secrets of the Clennam family, secrets that threaten to undermine the building; and the house, like its occupant, must rely on crutches to avoid collapse. The house is more than simply a projection of Mrs. Clennam's paralyzing and debilitating psychology. It also represents the oppressive Calvinism that afflicts her to the point of paralysis, blights the lives of all around her, and makes Sunday in England a day of oppressive monotony, where "melancholy streets in a penitential garb of soot, steeped the souls of the people who were condemned to look at them out of windows, in dire despondency" (I:3).

Arthur is one of the victims of this imprisoning Calvinism, which has left him with a large measure of guilt and little sense of self-worth. His lack of will is rooted in this cultural ideology that causes Mrs. Clennam's paralysis, but Arthur, unlike his mother, refuses to live in bad faith. He gives up his place in the family business, and, convinced that he and his family have some responsibility for William Dorrit's situation, he sets out to release Dorrit from prison. With Pancks's help, he does liberate the Dorrits, but that does not free him from the debilitating sense of guilt that eventually leads him to acquiesce to his own imprisonment as a just punishment for his mishandling of the funds of Doyce and Clennam.

For many readers, Arthur is not an engaging hero. A middle-aged failure, burdened by a sense of guilt into depression and passivity, he withdraws from life, giving up his place in the family business, his courtship of Pet, his hopes for Doyce and Clennam. His diffidence and self-punishment are not extraordinary. He is, rather, a Victorian everyman at mid-life, uncertain of his origins, wounded and guilt-ridden as a result of his harsh Calvinistic upbringing, alienated from the dishonesty and hypocrisy in his materialistic society, and incapable of acknowledging and acting from spontaneous feeling. He is, as several chapter titles suggest, "a Nobody" (I:16, 17, 26, 28). Dickens's original title for the novel, *Nobody's Fault*, suggested, along with its sarcasm about the buck-passing in the Circumlocution Office, Clennam's debilitating sense of guilt as the central theme of the novel. By changing the title to *Little Dorrit*, Dickens stressed some more positive aspects of his theme.

Amy Dorrit may be, as Trilling describes her, "the Beatrice of the *Comedy*, the Paraclete in female form," but her redemptive role in the story does not make her without conflict or flaws, an innocent untouched by the imprisoning society in which she lives. She is the "Child of the Marshalsea" and a product of the prison that nurtured her. She rejects the pretenses adopted by her father, Tip, and Fanny and accepts the need to work for a living, but Amy also supports her father's delusions and pretensions and worries that he could not survive outside the prison, a concern that his death in Rome proves to be justified. Little Dorrit's concern for her father is also a concern for herself, for she is, to use a contemporary term, codependent with him. She justifies her life by caring for him and by maintaining the lies that feed his delusions. Clennam's project to free Mr. Dorrit threatens Amy as well as her father. Her inability to adapt to a life of idle gentility in Italy mirrors her father's inability to suppress his memories of the prison and Arthur's inability to overcome his guilt. Amy and Arthur are both prisoners of their parentage and their pasts. If Arthur suffers from mid-life crisis, Amy reveals arrested development, her child-like "littleness" at odds with the adult responsibilities she assumes and the complex mixture of truth and complicity that forms her character. She may be

unbelievable, but she is not simplistically boring as some commentators have suggested.

Paradoxically it is the acceptance of imprisonment that finally liberates Amy and Arthur. She does not respond to the teaching of Mrs. General and embarrasses her family by failing to develop "a truly refined mind [which] will seem to be ignorant of anything that is not perfectly proper, placid, and pleasant" (II:5). She remains true to an inner sense of self and to the truth of her situation: She is a child of the Marshalsea. Similarly, Arthur's guilt causes him to seek imprisonment, even though Daniel Doyce does not blame him for losing the firm's money by speculating in Merdle's enterprises. By acknowledging his responsibility and refusing to deny or repress his guilt, Arthur acknowledges that he too is a child of the Marshalsea. Once he is there he can recognize and accept his love for Little Dorrit. Both Amy and Arthur go through imprisonment in order to transcend it.

Most of the other characters in the novel lack the inner resources to enable them to admit and go beyond their imprisonment. Fanny resists Mrs. General but gives herself to a loveless marriage with Sparkler in order to establish her power over Mrs. Merdle. Though good-hearted, Mr. and Mrs. Meagles alienate Tattycoram by their condescending treatment of her, and their toadying to the Barnacles may enable Pet's disastrous marriage to Gowan. Although Frederick Dorrit has managed to eke out a living outside the prison and is more clear-sighted than William about the family's position, he cannot survive the death of his defining brother-double. William Dorrit and Arthur's father represent the dishonesty and delusions of patriarchy; Casby dramatizes it as a patriarchal impostor who grinds the faces of the poor in Bleeding Heart Yard. Pancks, his agent, has been turned into a machine, a "laboring steam-engine" to carry out Casby's oppression; and even though he helps to free the Dorrits from prison and publicly humiliates Casby in the end, Panks is not saved from ruin when Merdle's financial bubble bursts. Merdle, the avatar of this diseased society, fradulent and vacuous, destroys himself, a victim of his lies and delusions, the most extreme of the many characters in the novel who are, in Miss Wade's term, "self tormentors."

Two characters stand out as free spirits. The inventor Daniel Doyce receives no support from English institutions and he clearly has little head for business, but he continues his creative work in spite of frustrations with the Circumlocution Office. When he is discouraged from working in England, he finds opportunities abroad. He does not succumb to despair and paralysis. When Arthur, against Doyce's instructions, speculates with the firm's money, Doyce nonetheless forgives him and maintains their partnership. His energy, creativity, and independence help to sustain Arthur and bring him out of the prison of despair.

Flora Finching is the other notable exception to the rule of passivity and vacuousness in the novel. She too is inventive and in her profusions of language she connects in a random and associative way the disparate pieces of her life. She blends absurdity with benevolence, shrewdness with excess; she is one of Dickens's great comic figures, in a novel notably short on comedy. Like Doyce, she is a figure of energy, overwhelming the passive and reserved Clennam with her physical and vocal presence. She also intimidates Little Dorrit by ignoring the social distance between them and spilling out the details of her life to her. In garrulous middle age, Flora may be a peony rather than a lily, but she brings a natural energy to a novel where many of the characters have been reduced to objects or machines; her organic presence—indicated by her botanic and ornithological name—blesses the wedding of Arthur and Amy (II:34). Unlike the roses that Arthur has tossed on the river when he gave up any notion of courting Pet (I:28), Flora is a flower that he retains, one of the autumn blooms flourishing when Arthur is restored to health (II:34).

Neither Arthur nor Amy have the extraordinary creative powers of Doyce and Flora. They are survivors rather than victors. Both are products of their time and place, children of the Marshalsea who have been wounded in childhood and have struggled to free themselves. It may be their very imperfections that make the justly famous final paragraphs of the novel so moving. These paragraphs sum up their imperfections, their honesty, and their choice to transcend the past, leave the prison, go into the streets, and live as fully as they can in the here and now:

> They paused for a moment on the steps of the portico, looking at the fresh perspective of the street in the autumn morning sun's bright rays, and then went down.
>
> Went down into a modest life of usefulness and happiness. . . . They went quietly down into the roaring streets, inseparable and blessed; and as they passed along in sunshine and shade, the noisy and the eager, and the arrogant and the froward and the vain, fretted, and chafed, and made their usual uproar (II:34).

CRITICISM

Lionel Trilling's introduction (reprinted in *The Opposing Self*, 1955) is the classic essay on the *Little Dorrit*. He describes society's effect on the individual will as the central concern of the novel, an analysis he compares to Freud's theory of neurosis. J. C. Reid's *Charles Dickens: Little Dorrit* (1967) is a useful general introduction to the novel; George Holoch analyzes the interlocking mystifications that constitute the novel's social order in "Consciousness and Society in Little Dorrit" (*Victorian Studies*, 1978). F. R. LEAVIS (1970) offers a controversial analysis of the novel that compares Dickens to Blake and describes Little Dorrit as an agent of the real. P. J. M. Scott (*Reality and Comic Confidence in Charles Dickens*, 1979), extends and modifies Leavis's view in an essay that characterizes the novel as Dickens's "triumph of reality." David Holbrook (*Charles Dickens and the Image of Woman*, 1993), also takes issue with Leavis's praise of Amy Dorrit and Arthur Clennam; he finds them repre-

sentatives of "duty" rather than spokespersons for the reality principle. Kathleen Woodward ("Passivity and Passion in Little Dorrit," *Dickensian*, 1975) discusses the women characters in the novel; she finds Amy "unconvincing and boring" as a portrait of a mature woman and Miss Wade "the only woman in the book who possesses sexuality and mystery."

ADAPTATIONS

The least dramatized of all Dickens's novels, *Little Dorrit* prompted only one unsuccessful adaptation, by F. Fox COOPER, during its initial appearance. James Albery's *The Two Roses* (1870) starred Henry Irving as Digby Grant, a character modeled on William Dorrit. Albery's play was a popular production during the rest of the 19th century and was probably the basis for a silent film (1910). Four more silent films—one American (1913), one German (1917), one British (1920), and one Danish (1924)—were produced. A German adaptation, *Klein Dorrit*, appeared as a sound film in 1934 and the Stanislavsky Theater in Moscow produced a Russian adaptation in 1953. The most successful dramatization of the novel is the film adaptation written and directed by Christine Edzard (1987). The most ambitious cinematic adaptation of any Dickens novel, and one of the most successful, Edzard's film echoes the structure of the novel in its two three-hour sections. The first part, "Nobody's Fault," tells Arthur's version of the story; the second half is "Little Dorrit's Story." Major roles are played by Sarah Pickering (Amy), Derek Jacobi (Arthur), Joan Greenwood (Mrs. Clennam), and Alec GUINNESS (William Dorrit).

"Little Dorrit" Appellation by which Amy DORRIT is usually known. *Dorrit*.

Little Em'ly Daniel Peggotty's niece. See EM'LY, LITTLE. *Copperfield*.

Little Gosling Street Street near the London docks where Flora and Mr. Finching "settled down" at no. 30 after their honeymoon on the continent. *Dorrit* (I:24).

Little Nell Epithet given to Nell TRENT. *Curiosity Shop*.

Little Russell Street At the ALBION Hotel on this street in BLOOMSBURY, Potter and Smithers "Make a Night of It." *Boz*.

Lively Receiver of stolen goods on SAFFRON HILL, "a salesman of small stature, who had squeezed as much of his person into a child's chair as the chair would hold" *Twist* (26).

"Lively Turtle" Satiric article for *HOUSEHOLD WORDS* (October 26, 1850) celebrating the virtues of the turtle—who enjoys comfort and desires to be left alone—

as the virtues of England. Snoady, the narrator, sees a similarity between his friend Groggles, a member of the London city council, and the turtles kept by a restaurant for soup, and he deduces the political significance of the turtles. *Miscellaneous*.

Liverpool Dickens sailed from this port in northwest England when going to AMERICA in 1841 and 1867. Several of his characters also embark for foreign destinations from Liverpool: Lummy Ned (*Chuzzlewit*, 13), Richard Carstone (*Bleak House*, 24), Tom Gradgrind (*Hard Times*, III:7), Tip Dorrit (*Dorrit*, I:7), Captain Jorgan ("Message from the Sea"), Charley ("Holly Tree"), Captain Ravender ("Golden Mary"). The Traveller describes a visit to the slums near the Liverpool docks where sailors gather (*Uncommercial*, 5). Dickens's theatrical troupe performed in Liverpool in 1847 and Dickens gave several public readings in the city.

Liz Brickmaker's wife and friend of Jenny. "An ugly woman . . . [who] had no kind of grace about her, but the grace of sympathy; but when she condoled with the woman, and her own tears fell, she wanted no beauty" (8). *Bleak House*.

Lobbs Family **Maria Lobbs** is the daughter of a rich saddler, **Old Lobbs**, and the object of the secret affections of Nathaniel Pipkin, a parish clerk, in the tale of "The Parish Clerk." *Pickwick* (17).

Lobley Tartar's servant and boatman, "the dead image of the sun in old woodcuts, his hair and whiskers answering for rays all round him" (21). *Drood*.

Lobskini, Signor Singing master at Minerva House. *Boz*, "Sentiment."

Loggins Actor who plays Macbeth under the stage name **Beverly** in one of London's private theaters (*Boz*, "Private Theatres"), similar to the theater where Wopsle plays Hamlet in *Expectations* (31).

Lombard Street Street in east London connecting the BANK OF ENGLAND with FENCHURCH STREET. Maria BEADNELL's house was located here, next to the bank of Smith, Payne and Smith, where her father worked. Access to the GEORGE AND VULTURE through George Yard leads from this street (*Pickwick*, 26); Mr. Merdle's bank (*Dorrit*, II:16) and the offices of Barbox Brothers ("Mugby") are located here. The Traveller speculates about all the money in the banks on the street (*Uncommercial*, 23).

London Donald FANGER notes that "the romantic realists—notably Balzac, Dickens and Gogol—were the first fully to realize the potentialities of the metropolis as a subject of fiction." What Paris was to Balzac and Petersburg to Gogol, London was to Dickens. There is now a London, based on the real city of his time, that we

think of as "Dickens' London." Maps of this city are available at the DICKENS HOUSE and numerous guide books direct visitors to Dickensian sites.

Much of the work in Dickens TOPOGRAPHY was done around the turn of the century by such Dickensians as KITTON, MATZ, and DEXTER, though many of the sites they identified no longer exist. *A Dickens Atlas* (1923) by A. A. Hopkins and N. F. Read provides maps of Dickensian sites identified by the topographers and suggests appropriate walking tours. Two recent volumes provide more up-to-date information on Dickens's London: London Transport's centenary guide, *The London of Charles Dickens* (1970), offers an alphabetical listing of Dickensian sites in and around the city; Tony Lynch's *Dickens's England: A Travellers' Companion* (1986) lists sites throughout England that can still be visited.

Jacob Korg's *London in Dickens' Day* (1960) collects writings by Dickens and his contemporaries about Victorian London.

London Bridge Two London Bridges appear in Dickens's novels. The old bridge is the one referred to in *Rudge* (5, 8, 16, 43, 49); *Pickwick* (32), and the one where David goes during his intervals away from work in the wine-bottling factory (*Copperfield*, 11). The new bridge, opened in 1831 (now in Lake Havasu, Arizona), is the one with the stairs going down to the river where Claypole spies on Nancy as she talks with Brownlow and Rose Maylie (*Twist*, 46) and where Jonas tosses his bundle of bloody clothes into the river (*Chuzzlewit*, 51).

London Coffee House Tavern in LUDGATE STREET where Arthur Clennam stays when he first returns to England from China. *Dorrit* (I:3).

"London Recreations" Originally appeared in the *EVENING CHRONICLE* (March 17, 1835) as "Sketches of London No. 6." It describes the rich man who takes pride in possessing a garden and directing his gardeners, the retired middle-class couple who spend many hours happily working in their garden, and the working-class family that gather on a summer afternoon at a suburban public tea garden. *Boz*.

London Tavern Public meetings were often held at this institution in BISHOPSGATE STREET. The United Metropolitan Improved Hot Muffin and Crumpet Baking and Punctual Delivery Company organizes here (*Nickleby*, 2). Dickens chaired a meeting of the General Theatrical Fund here in 1836.

London *Times* Founded in 1785, the *Times* (London) was, by the mid-19th century, the organ of the upper middle class, the class brought into power by the first REFORM BILL OF 1832, which the paper supported. Though it was mildly reformist in the 1820s and '30s, it was not nearly as liberal as the *MORNING CHRONICLE* and the *DAILY NEWS*, two papers with which Dickens was associated. Dickens may have written some penny-a-line pieces for the paper as a boy, but he was unsuccessful in gaining employment with the *Times* as a young man; he worked for the rival *Morning Chronicle* instead, taking great delight in the competition to scoop the rival paper in covering the news. When he started the *Daily News*, the *Times* refused to advertise the new paper and was uneasy with its new radical competitor. Representing its class bias, the *Times* criticized Dickens's vulgarity—both in his writing and his behavior—but it also praised some of his works, especially his early writings. After his death, it called for Dickens to be buried in WESTMINSTER ABBEY.

Dickens wrote letters to the *Times* on January 12, 1861 (asserting the rights of authors to prevent theatrical adaptation of their works), October 8, 1863 (giving his impressions of a recent earthquake), and September 4, 1867 (denying rumors that he is ill).

Long Acre   East-west street running just north of COVENT GARDEN, one of the haunts of young men who idle about the theaters and taverns (*Boz*, "Shabby-genteel"). Dick Swiveller, who has ordered a meal from an establishment in Long Acre and not paid for it, is obliged to put the street on his list of those he cannot enter (*Curiosity Shop*, 8).

Long Ears, The Hon. and Revd.   Member of the Mudfog Association. *Mudfog*.

Longfellow, Henry Wadsworth (1807–1882) American poet, professor of modern languages at Harvard. Dickens met him on his first American tour in 1842. Longfellow then described Dickens as "a glorious fellow . . . a gay free-and-easy character, with a bright face . . . and withal a slight dash of the Dick Swiveller about him." Dickens thought the poet "a frank accomplished man as well as a fine writer" and invited him to stay with him in London. Longfellow visited Dickens in England in 1842 and his host gave him a night tour of the London slums. He visited again in 1856 and 1868.

Long's Hotel   Fashionable hotel in BOND STREET where Cousin Feenix stays. *Dombey* (31).

"Long Voyage, The"   The narrator remembers the many stories of sea travel and shipwrecks that have fascinated him from childhood on. He particularly remembers the story of the *Halsewell*, which broke up on the rocks, and the story of a ship's steward who cared for a small boy after their ship was wrecked off the coast of Africa. *Reprinted*. Originally in *HOUSEHOLD WORDS* (December 31, 1853).

Longford, Edmund   Redlaw's student, he takes the name **Edmund Denham** to conceal his identity as the son of Redlaw's one-time fiancée. Poor and ailing, he is cared for by Molly Swidger. When Redlaw's gift releases him from his memories, he turns against Milly, but her loving influence restores him to his better self. *Haunted Man*.

Looking-Glass Prairie   Dickens describes his somewhat disappointing visit to this prairie near LEBANON, ILLINOIS, in *Notes* (13).

Lord Chancellor   Head of the British judicial system, appointed by the prime minister, a member of the cabinet, he is the presiding judge in the Court of CHANCERY. He is "at the very heart of the fog" in the opening chapter of *Bleak House* and is the judge who appoints Jarndyce as guardian over Richard Carstone and Ada Clare. *Bleak House* (3).

"Lord Chancellor"   KROOK's nickname. His rag and bottle establishment parodies the court with its mountains of papers. *Bleak House* (5).

Lord Mayor   Title granted to chief officer of a city or borough, especially the head of the Corporation of London, the group that administers the CITY of London from the GUILDHALL. In London this largely ceremonial position, usually held by an important businessman, dates back to 1192. Among the lord mayors of London was Dick WHITTINGTON, who held the position three times, in 1397, 1406, and 1419. His story of a poor boy who makes good in business and rises to become lord mayor is the ARCHETYPAL version of the rags to riches tale. Dickens alludes frequently to the Whittington legend, especially in *Dombey*, in which Walter Gay is being groomed for a Whittington-like career.

Lorn   Dr. Speddie's pale assistant; he is probably the medical student whom Speddie revived many years before. *Lazy Tour* (2).

Lorry, Jarvis   A confidential clerk in TELLSON'S BANK, he served as Dr. Manette's financial advisor before his imprisonment. After Mrs. Manette died, he brought their two-year-old daughter to England and he undertakes the mission to reunite the daughter with her father when Dr. Manette is "recalled to life" (I:2). He remains a close friend and advisor to the doctor. In PARIS on bank business during the FRENCH REVOLUTION, he assists the Manettes and brings Lucie and Charles back to England after Sydney Carton takes Darnay's place on the guillotine (III:13). *Two Cities*.

Losberne   Surgeon and friend of the Maylies; he believes Oliver innocent and protects him from the inquiries of the Bow Street Runners; "known . . . as 'the doctor,' [he] had grown fat, more from good humour than from good living: and was as kind and hearty, and withal as eccentric an old bachelor, as will be found" (29). When he retires from his practice, he settles near Rose and Harry (53). *Twist*.

Lost, John   Retired businessman of the Maze, Ware, who becomes lost in Bradshaw's railway schedule and goes mad trying to find his way home. *Miscellaneous*, "Narrative of Extraordinary Suffering."

"Lost Arctic Voyagers, The"   Two-part article for *HOUSEHOLD WORDS* (December 2 and 9, 1854) in which Dickens responds to Dr. John Roe's conclusion that the members of the Franklin expedition to the Arctic resorted to cannibalism in their attempts to survive. Dickens points out that Franklin was prepared to die on an earlier expedition and did not consider cannibalism then. He also questions the veracity of the Eskimo stories on which Roe based his conclusions. In the second article, Dickens reviews many cases of alleged cannibalism to show how uncommon and unnatural the practice is, particularly for civilized Europeans. *Miscellaneous*. Roe answered Dickens's objections in a letter printed in *Household Words* on December 23, 1854 (*Stone*). Wilkie COLLINS's play, *THE FROZEN DEEP* (1856), prompted by an idea from Dickens and written in collaboration with him, was based on the Franklin expedition.

Louis (1)   Employee of a Swiss inn who murders Henri, a fellow employee who has discovered him stealing from their employer. "Holly-tree" (1).

Louis (2)   The Traveller's servant on his journey to France. *Uncommercial* (7).

Louisa   Wife of Charles of the Cool Couple who have very little to do with each other. *Young Couples*.

Louisville, Kentucky   Dickens stopped overnight at this "regular and cheerful" town on his way from Cincinnati to ST. LOUIS. *Notes* (12).

"Loving Ballad of Lord Bateman, The"   Cockney version of a traditional ballad, illustrated by CRUIKSHANK and published by Charles Tilt in 1849. Dickens wrote a preface and some notes for the volume.

Lovetown, Mr. and Mrs. Alfred   Recently married couple who are bored with each other. They reawaken each other's romantic interest by flirting with others—Alfred with Mrs. Limbury and Mrs. Lovetown with Felix Tapkins. *Is She His Wife?*

Lowell, Massachusetts   Dickens gives an idealized description of this New England factory town, remarking on the orderly and well-appointed factories, the well-dressed young women who worked in them, and the regimen which allowed them time for education and for writing for the *Lowell Offering*, their literary magazine. Although he explicitly refrains from comparing these American mills to their European counterparts, he notes that if he did so "it would be between the Good and Evil." *Notes* (4).

Lowestoft   Coastal town in Suffolk where Murdstone takes young David. *Copperfield* (2).

Lowfield, Miss   Young woman smitten with Caveton, the Throwing-off Young Gentleman. *Young Gentlemen*.

Lowten   Perker's "puffy-faced young" clerk who introduces Pickwick to the society of law clerks at the MAGPIE AND STUMP (20). *Pickwick*.

Lucas, John (1937–)   Professor, Loughborough University; writer on many Victorian novelists, especially Dickens, "the greatest novelist in the language." His Marxist reading of the novels in *The Melancholy Man: A Study of Dickens's Novels* (1970) presents Dickens as a truth-teller, the conscience of his age, who was at the same time its greatest entertainer. Lucas's Dickens, "far and away the most intelligent of all English novelists," seeks to reconcile these sometimes competing impulses in his art. In *Charles Dickens: the Major Novels* (1992), an introduction to six of Dickens's major works, Lucas again seeks to place the novelist into the context of his time as "the great informant of and for his age, as well as its great conscience."

Lucas, Solomon   EATANSWILL costume dealer from whom the Pickwickians rent costumes for Mrs. Leo Hunter's fancy-dress breakfast. "His wardrobe was extensive—very extensive—not strictly classical perhaps, nor quite new, nor did it contain any one garment made precisely after the fashion of any age or time, but everything was more or less spangled; and what *can* be prettier than spangles!" *Pickwick* (16).

Ludgate Hill   Street running from ST. PAUL'S CATHEDRAL to FLEET STREET. Smike lingers here just before he is captured by Squeers (*Nickleby*, 38); Betsey Trotwood and David are confronted by her husband here (*Copperfield*, 23); the LONDON COFFEE HOUSE where Arthur Clennam stays on returning to England is located here (*Dorrit*, I:3).

Luffey   Star player on the Dingley Dell Cricket Club. *Pickwick* (7).

Lumbey, Dr.   Doctor who delivers Mrs. Kenwig's baby; "a stout bluff-looking gentleman, with no shirt-collar, to speak of, and a beard that had been growing since yesterday morning; for Doctor Lumbey was popular, and the neighbourhood was prolific; and there had been no less than three other knockers muffled, one after the other, within the last forty-eight hours" (36). *Nickleby*.

Lummy Ned   Guard on the SALISBURY coach whose immigration to the United States prompts Martin to follow suit. *Chuzzlewit* (13).

Edward Bulwer Lytton in an engraving by Daniel Maclise.

Lupin, Mrs.   Landlady of the BLUE DRAGON INN, "a widow, but years ago had passed through her state of weeds, and burst into flower again" (3). Her admiration for Pecksniff is destroyed when he dismisses Tom Pinch (31). She welcomes Martin and Mark back from AMERICA (43) and eventually marries Mark (53). *Chuzzlewit.*

"Lying Awake"   Article from *HOUSEHOLD WORDS* (October 30, 1852) describing the author's abortive attempts to go to sleep. Meanwhile, his mind wanders from George III to NIAGARA FALLS, to the MANNINGS' execution, to balloon ascents, to the PARIS morgue. Finally he gives up trying to sleep and goes for a night walk. *Reprinted.*

Lytton, Edward Bulwer, First Baron Lytton (1803–1873)   Popular novelist, playwright, journalist, politician. A colleague and friend, Dickens named his youngest child for him. Dickens shared his views on political reform and occasionally followed his lead as a novelist. *Oliver Twist* was often linked with Lytton's earlier NEWGATE NOVELS, and Dickens changed the ending of *Expectations* after Lytton objected to the original ending. In 1850, Dickens's theatrical group gave three performances at KNEBWORTH PARK, the Lytton estate in Hertfordshire. At that time the two men conceived the scheme for the GUILD OF LITERATURE AND ART; although some cottages for writers and artists were constructed at Knebworth, the scheme never gained widespread support. Dickens dedicated *Bleak House*, "as a remembrance of our friendly union, to my companions in the Guild of Literature and Art." Lytton's *A Strange Story* was serialized in *ALL THE YEAR ROUND* in 1861. Though he thought Dickens incapable of presenting "characters of intellectual depth or refinement," he nonetheless considered him "one of the greatest geniuses in fiction the world has produced."

Mac Coorts of Mac Coort   The "great Highland family" from whom Mrs. Woodcourt's late husband was descended. *Bleak House* (30).

M'Choakumchild   Schoolmaster in Gradgrind's school of hard facts. "He and some one hundred and forty other schoolmasters, had been lately turned out at the same time, in the same factory, on the same principles, like so many pianoforte legs. He had been put through an immense variety of paces, and had answered volumes of head-breaking questions. Orthography, etymology, syntax, and prosody, biography, astronomy, geography, and general cosmography, the sciences of compound proportion, algebra, land-surveying and levelling, vocal music, and drawing from models, were all at the ends of his ten chilled fingers. . . . If he had only learnt a little less, how infinitely better he might have taught much more!" (I:2). *Hard Times.*

McCormick, Dr. Robert (1800–1890)   Surgeon on the *Erebus* during Sir James Clark Ross's *Voyages of Discovery in the Arctic and Antarctic Seas, and Round the World* (1884). He described "Christmas in the Frozen Regions" aboard the *Erebus* for the Christmas number of HOUSEHOLD WORDS (1850), an article which Dickens edited and expanded. *Stone.*

Macey, Mr. and Mrs.   Colonists on Silver-Store Island. She is the sister of Marion Maryon. "English Prisoners."

Mackenzie, Norman (1921–   )   Novelist, biographer, professor, University of Sussex, who collaborated with his wife, **Jeanne** (1922–86), on several biographical and historical studies of Victorian writers and social thinkers, especially members of the Fabian Society. Their biography, *Dickens: A Life* (1979), is a readable account of the author's life that ascribes his energy and artistic productivity to his abandonment by his parents as a young child.

Mackin, Mrs.   Client in a DRURY LANE pawn shop; "a slipshod woman, with two flat irons in a little basket." *Boz*, "Pawnbroker's."

Macklin, Mrs.   Woman at No. 4 on a street in the suburbs who buys muffins from a street-seller on a cold winter evening. *Boz*, "Streets-Night."

Maclise, Daniel (1806–1870)   Irish-born painter of historical and literary subjects; member of the Royal Academy from 1835; a close friend and companion of Dickens, especially during the 1840s. Introduced to Dickens by W. H. AINSWORTH, the artist quickly became one of a nearly inseparable triumvirate with John FORSTER and Dickens. He made several portraits and sketches of Dickens and other members of his family, including the famous frontispiece for *Nicholas Nickleby*, commissioned

Maclise's frontispiece for The Battle of Life *(1846).*

222

by CHAPMAN & HALL in 1839. He provided one illustration for *Curiosity Shop* and several for *Chimes, Cricket*, and *Battle*, but the strain of the collaboration also strained the relationship between the two men. In the 1860s, while he was working on his frescoes for the House of Lords, Maclise became remote and reclusive. He died shortly before Dickens, whose last public speech was a tribute to his friend, "the gentlest and most modest of men, . . . incapable of a sordid or ignoble thought, gallantly sustaining the true dignity of his vocation, without one grain of self-ambition, wholesomely natural at the last as at the first, 'in wit a man, simplicity a child.' " Other examples of his work appear in illustrations 10 (CARLYLE); 13 (*The CHIMES*); 25 (Charles DICKENS); 53 (LYTTON); 58 (MARTINEAU); 90 (TALFOURD); 93 (THACKERAY).

Macmanus   Midshipman on the *Halsewell*. Reprinted, "Long Voyage."

McMaster, Juliet (1937–   )   Professor, University of Alberta, who has written on Austen, TROLLOPE, and THACKERAY as well as Dickens. In *Dickens the Designer* (1987), she considers the visual dimensions of seven of Dickens's novels and focuses on the ways in which the physical appearance of the characters articulates their personalities and roles within the novels.

McNulty, J. H. (d. 1954)   Early 20th-century journalist, editor of *The Old Lady of Threadneedle Street*, journal of the Bank of England; frequent contributor to the *DICKENSIAN* from 1916 to 1950. Many of his articles are fantasies taking off from Dickens's novels or characters. Some of his writings on Dickens are collected in *The Dethronement of Shakespeare* (1926), *Concerning Dickens and other Literary Characters* (1933), and *The Return of Mr. Pickwick* (1936).

Macready, William (1793–1873)   Distinguished actor and theater manager; one of Dickens's closest friends from 1837, when John FORSTER introduced them, until the end of his life. They dined together frequently, traveled together, and were regular correspondents. Macready was a great admirer of Dickens's work: He was deeply grieved at the death of Little Nell, cried at Dickens's reading of *The Chimes*, and described Dickens's reading of "Sikes and Nancy" as "two Macbeths." He was godfather to Dickens's daughter Kate. Dickens gave the celebratory speech at Macready's retirement from the stage in 1851 and was a constant friend to the actor and his family until the end of his life. His review of Macready's production of *Lear*, "The Restoration of Shakespeare's 'Lear' to the Stage," (*EXAMINER*, February 4, 1838), commended Macready for abandoning Nahum Tate's revision of the play and restoring Shakespeare's original text, expecially the character of the fool. Dickens also praised "Macready as 'Benedict' " in a review of *Much Ado about Nothing* for the *Examiner* (March 4,

W. C. Macready.

1843), challenging those who expected Macready to perform only the great tragic roles. *Miscellaneous*.

Macrone, John (1809–1837)   Dickens's first publisher. He paid Dickens £100 for the rights to the first series of *Boz*, collected from the various magazines and newspapers in which they had already been published. The success of this production, which he had illustrated by CRUIKSHANK, prompted Macrone to pay £150 for a second series of sketches and to contract for a three-volume novel, *GABRIEL VARDEN, THE LOCKSMITH OF LONDON* for £200. These agreements led to some difficult negotiations when Dickens moved to CHAPMAN & HALL, to whom Macrone sold the copyright for *Boz*. After Macrone's untimely death in 1837, Dickens and AINSWORTH planned a collection of writings and illustrations to benefit his widow that eventually appeared as *THE PIC-NIC PAPERS* (1841), edited by Dickens.

MacStinger, Mrs.   Captain Cuttle's landlady, "a widow lady, with her sleeves rolled up to her shoulders, and her arms frothy with soap-suds and smoking with hot water" (9), who holds him captive at no. 9 BRIG PLACE, near the India Docks, terrifying him with her matrimonial intentions. After he escapes to the WOODEN MIDSHIPMAN (25), she traces him down, but he is saved by Captain Bunsby, who eventually marries her (60). Her three children are **Charles** ("Chowley"), **Juliana**, "the image of her parent" (60), and **Alexander**. *Dombey*.

Maddox, John Farm boy in love with Rose. She briefly deserts him to flirt with Sparkins Flam, a fop from London. *Coquettes*.

Madgers, Winifred One of Mrs. Lirriper's serving maids, a Plymouth Sister who goes off with a Plymouth Brother. "Lirriper's Legacy."

Madman, The Author and narrator of "A MADMAN'S MANUSCRIPT." Writing from his lunatic's cell, he describes the progress of his disease, which he claims is hereditary, culminating in his plot to murder his wife and her family, and hence to his incarceration. *Pickwick* (11).

"Madman's Manuscript, A" One of the INTERPOLATED TALES in *Pickwick*, this document, given to Pickwick by the clergyman at DINGLEY DELL, purports to be a madman's account of his disease and his plot to murder his wife and her family. Before it can be fully executed, his scheme is thwarted by his capture. *Pickwick* (11).

Mag, Mary Anne John Lost's confidential domestic who purchases the Railway Guide that drives her employer mad. *Miscellaneous*, "Narrative of Extraordinary Suffering."

Magg Vestryman who insists that there should be no interference with local self-government. *Reprinted*, "Our Vestry."

Maggy Mentally retarded granddaughter of Mrs. Bangham, a fellow inmate in the MARSHALSEA PRISON with Amy Dorrit, to whom she is devoted. She calls Amy, who cares for her, "Little Mother." "She was about eight-and-twenty, with large bones, large features, large feet and hands, large eyes and no hair. . . . There was also that attentive listening expression in her face, which is seen in the faces of the blind; but she was not blind, having one tolerable serviceable eye. Her face was not exceedingly ugly, though it was only redeemed from being so by a smile" (I:9). After the Dorrits go off to Italy, Maggy is cared for by the Plornishes (II:4). *Dorrit*.

"Magic Fishbone, The" Children's story told by Alice Rainbird. Given a magic fishbone by Fairy Grandmarina, Princess Alicia knows when to use the charm to save her father, King Watkins the First, from financial ruin. She is rewarded with the hand of Prince Certainpersonio. "Holiday Romance."

Magnus, Peter The "red-haired man, with an inquisitive nose and blue spectacles" who travels with Pickwick to IPSWICH, where he plans to propose to a Miss Witherspoon (22). After Pickwick inadvertently stumbles into Miss Witherspoon's room in the middle of the night, the jealous Magnus is so enraged that she fears a duel between Magnus and Pickwick and so she has Pickwick arrested by the magistrate (24). *Pickwick*.

Magog See GOG AND MAGOG.

"Magog's Tale" Story of Hugh Graham, apprentice to a wealthy Bowyer at the time of Elizabeth. He falls in love with Mistress Alice, his employer's daughter, but she runs off with a gentleman and is ruined. When she returns Hugh protects her, kills her seducer, and is killed himself in the ensuing riot. *Humphrey* (1).

Magpie and Stump Gathering place for Lowten and his fellow law clerks, this tavern could have been based on either the George IV or the Old Black Jack, which were both located in Portsmouth Street, LINCOLN'S INN Fields. *Pickwick* (20, 21).

Magsman, Robert (Toby) Proprietor of the sideshow where Mr. Chops the Dwarf performs, "a grizzled personage in velveteen, with a face so cut up by varieties of weather, that he looked as if he had been tattooed"; the narrator of "Going into Society."

Magwitch, Abel Unnamed escaped convict for whom Pip steals the Christmas pie from his sister's larder (2): "a fearful man, all in coarse grey, with a great iron on his leg. A man with no hat, and with broken shoes, and with an old rag tied round his head. A man who had been soaked in water, and smothered in mud, and lamed by stones, and cut by flints, and stung by nettles, and torn by briars; who limped and shivered" (1). Out of gratitude to the boy and a desire to get even with the gentlemen who imprisoned him, Magwitch secretly uses his earnings as an Australian sheep farmer to provide Pip's great expectations. When he returns to England to see his gentleman, he surprises Pip and repels him with his commonness and his claim to be Pip's "second father" (39). While Pip makes plans to smuggle him out of England, he takes the aliases **Provis** and **Campbell** and tells Pip the story of his life (42), of his entanglement with Compeyson, of his relationship with MOLLY, and of their daughter, who turns out to be ESTELLA. He is arrested during Pip's abortive attempt to escape with him to the Continent (54). Sentenced to hang, he dies in the prison hospital before the sentence can be carried out (56). *Expectations*.

Maiden Lane This street in HOLLOWAY, described in *Boz* as "inhabited by proprietors of donkey-carts, boilers of horse-flesh, makers of files, and sifters of cinders" ("First of May"), is where BOFFIN'S BOWER and its dust heaps are located. *Mutual Friend* (I:5).

Maidstone Village in KENT, generally believed to be the original of MUGGLETON. *Pickwick* (7).

"Making a Night of It"   Sketch describing two young CITY clerks who celebrate their quarterly payday by getting drunk, going to the theater, being ejected for disrupting the performance, and finally getting arrested for disorderly conduct. It first appeared in *BELL'S LIFE IN LONDON*, October 18, 1835. *Boz.*

Malderton Family   Snobbish CAMBERWELL family. **Mr. Malderton**, who had made his money in a few successful speculations, is "hospitable from ostentation, illiberal from ignorance, and prejudiced from conceit." His **wife** hopes to marry her two daughters—**Teresa**, "a very little girl, rather fat," age 28, and **Marianne**—to high-class suitors. The two sons, **Frederick** and **Thomas**, threaten to undermine Theresa's marital prospects with their "low" conversation. *Boz*, "Sparkins."

Maldon, Jack   Annie Strong's cousin, "rather a shallow sort of young gentleman . . . with a handsome face, a rapid utterance, and a confident bold air" (16). He sponges off Doctor Strong, who sponsors Maldon's trip to India (16). Maldon returns without having established himself in a profession and pursues a flirtation with Annie which leads to malicious gossip about the doctor's young wife. *Copperfield.*

Mallard   Serjeant Snubbin's elderly law clerk. *Pickwick.*

Mallet   Member of the Mudfog Association. *Mudfog.*

Mallowford, Lord   Arthur Gride's former client who burnt to death in his bed. *Nickleby* (51).

Malthus, Thomas Robert (1766–1834)   English clergyman and economist who argued in *An Essay on the Principle of Population* (1798) that as the population grew geometrically, the food supply would increase only arithmetically. His solutions to this problem of "surplus population" were harsh: He advocated sexual abstinence for the poor, emigration, and the denial of charity to the poor, thus forcing them to adopt more prudent ways of life. Although Dickens shared Malthus's belief in emigration as a remedy for poverty, he was outraged by the economist's harsh views on charity. He frequently attacked "philosophers" like Malthus in his broad condemnation of the Utilitarians and the school of "hard facts" (See UTILITARIANISM). His most direct attacks on Malthus appear in the *Carol* and *Chimes*, and in *Hard Times*, in which Gradgrind names one of his children for the economist.

Malvern Wells   Spa in Worcestershire where the hypochondriacal Mr. Nightingale comes to take the water cure. *Nightingale.*

"Man from Shropshire, The"   Epithet by which GRIDLEY is generally known. *Bleak House.*

Manchester   This Lancashire center of cotton manufacture in the 19th century was often used symbolically to represent industrial England. COKETOWN is sometimes said to be based on Manchester, but Dickens also connected the town with nearby PRESTON, which he visited during a bitter strike while he was writing *Hard Times*. Dickens's sister Fanny lived in Manchester after her marriage and Dickens visited her there several times. During one such visit in 1843, he came up with the idea for *A Christmas Carol*, in which Tiny Tim—like the later Paul Dombey—was based on Fanny's sickly son, Henry BURNETT. Dickens and his troupe performed their AMATEUR THEATRICALS in Manchester and Dickens gave several PUBLIC READINGS in the city on his English tours.

Manchester Buildings   A group of houses near WESTMINSTER BRIDGE in London, "a narrow and dirty region, the sanctuary of the smaller members of Parliament" (*Nickleby*, 16), where Nicholas interviews for a position as secretary to Mr. Gregsbury, M.P. Also mentioned in *Boz*, "Parliamentary."

Manette Family   French doctor's family who become entangled in the FRENCH REVOLUTION through their connections with the aristocratic St. Evrémondes and the revolutionary Defarges. **Doctor Alexandre** was, in 1757, a physician in Beauvais who was taken by the Marquis St. Evrémonde and his twin brother and forced to attend a peasant girl who had been raped by the younger brother; he also cared for the girl's brother, wounded while defending her honor. After the patients died, the St. Evrémondes had the doctor, who knew too much, thrown into the BASTILLE to keep him quiet. There he remained for 18 years. Two years after his imprisonment began, his English wife, **Madame Manette**, died and their "orphaned" infant daughter, **Lucie**, was taken to England by Jarvis Lorry, the family's financial advisor. *Two Cities* begins when Manette is released from prison and "recalled to life." Lorry escorts the 17-year-old Lucie, who has never seen her father, to Paris to bring the doctor back to England (I:2–6). At first the doctor, who has worked as a shoemaker in prison, fails to recognize Lorry or his daughter, but her loving care and her physical resemblance to his wife, especially her golden hair, gradually restore him. When Lucie marries Charles Darnay, a French emigré in England, however, the doctor temporarily reverts to his prison occupation as a shoemaker on learning that Darnay is really the Marquis St. Evrémonde, nephew of the Marquis who had him imprisoned (II:18). When Charles is arrested in Paris, Manette works to save him, but a manuscript he wrote in prison describing the crimes of the St. Evrémondes is revealed by Defarge and Darnay is condemned to death (III:10). *Two Cities.*

Manheim, Leonard (1902–1983)   Professor, University of Hartford; psychoanalytic critic and literary theorist; founder and editor of *Literature and Psychology*;

one of the important psychoanalytic critics of Dickens's novels. His work appears in articles in *American Imago* ("The Personal History of *David Copperfield*," 1953; "The Law as Father," 1955); *Texas Studies in Language and Literature* ("Floras and Doras: The Women in Dickens' Novels," 1965); and other journals.

Mann, Mrs. Operator of the baby farm, "a branch workhouse . . . where twenty or thirty other juvenile offenders against the poor laws, rolled about the floor all day, without the inconvenience of too much food or too much clothing" (2), where Oliver lives until he is nine. "A woman of wisdom and experience; she knew what was good for the children; and she had a very accurate perception of what was good for herself. So, she appropriated the greater part of the weekly stipend to her own use, and consigned the rising parochial generation to an even shorter allowance than was originally provided for them" (2). *Twist*.

Manners, Julia "Buxom, richly-dressed female of about forty" whose planned rendezvous with Lord Peter gets entangled with the elopement schemes of Alexander Trott. She ends up eloping with Trott. *Boz*, "Winglebury."

Manning, Frederick George and Maria Notorious murderers who conspired to kill Mrs. Manning's young lover. Dickens attended their public execution in 1849 and wrote two letters to the TIMES (London) describing the "brutal mirth or callousness" of the crowd there. He proposed that future executions be held secretly within prison walls. He describes being haunted by their execution in "Lying Awake" (*Reprinted*). Mrs. Manning has sometimes been considered the original of Hortense, Lady Dedlock's French maid in *Bleak House*.

Manning, Sir Geoffrey Wardle's neighbor on whose lands the Pickwickian hunting party takes place. *Pickwick* (18).

Manning, Sylvia (1943–) Professor, University of Southern California. In *Dickens as Satirist* (1971), Manning does not survey the satiric passages in the novels, but rather discusses the profoundly ironic view of life that Dickens reaches in the later novels in which the characters attempt to survive and grow in "a world somehow dying, with life and vitality yielding to torpor, rigidity, or death."

Manor Farm Wardle's home at DINGLEY DELL where the Pickwickians visit (2–4) and later spend Christmas (29–30). *Pickwick*.

Mansel, Miss Passenger on the *Halsewell*. *Reprinted*, "Long Voyage."

Mansfield, Lord Historical figure, Lord Chief Justice at the time of the GORDON RIOTS. Angered by his support for the Catholic Relief Bill, the rioters burned his house in BLOOMSBURY and planned to burn his country estate at Kenwood near HAMPSTEAD. *Rudge* (66–67).

Mansion House Official residence of the LORD MAYOR in the CITY of London, it is also the name given to its immediate neighborhood. Nicodemus Dumps sets out from Mansion House for the Kitterbell's Christening (*Boz*, "Christening"); preparations for the lord mayor's Christmas celebration are described in *Carol* (1). With the lord mayor as chief magistrate, Mansion House was also the site of the London Police Court where the red cab driver delights the court with his wit (*Boz*, "Last Cab-driver"); Kit Nubbles is taken to this court (*Curiosity Shop*, 60); Haredale petitions the Lord Mayor to have Mr. Rudge imprisoned during the GORDON RIOTS (*Rudge*, 61).

Mantalini, Madame Fashionable dressmaker whose indulgence of her ne'er-do-well younger husband, **Alfred**, gets her financially entangled with Ralph Nickleby, who induces her to hire Kate (10). Her husband's extravagance bankrupts the business (21), so Madame Mantalini, "a buxom person, handsomely dressed and rather good-looking, but much older than the gentleman in the Turkish trousers, whom she had wedded some six months before" (10), finally immune to Alfred's blandishments, turns the business over to her assistant, Miss Knag (44). Alfred, whose "name was originally Muntle . . . had married on his whiskers; upon which property he had previously subsisted, in a genteel manner, for some years" (10). He supports himself by flattering his vain wife and comparing her to the countess he gave up to marry her. But after he embezzles money from her (34), he is imprisoned and is last seen mangling for the laundress who pays to release him from DEBTORS PRISON (64). *Nickleby*.

Maplesone, Mrs. Matilda Widow who has unsuccessfully made the rounds of the spas for four seasons with her two eligible daughters, **Matilda** and **Julia**. Their luck with the gentlemen at Mrs. Tibbs's boarding house is better: Julia marries Mr. Simpson, but then elopes six weeks later with a half-pay officer; Matilda marries Septimus Hicks, who then abandons her; and Mrs. Maplesone, jilted by Mr. Calton, sues him for breach of promise and wins £1,000. *Boz*, "Boarding House."

Marlborough Downs Old inn on the downs in Wiltshire. Tom Smart, in "The BAGMAN'S STORY," meets the mysterious chair which turns into an old man at his room in the inn. *Pickwick* (14).

"Marchioness, The" Dick Swiveller's nickname for the little servant kept locked in the cellar at BEVIS MARKS by the Brasses: "a small slipshod girl in a dirty coarse apron and bib, which left nothing visible but her face and feet. She might as well have been dressed in a violincase" (34). Dick gives her food and beer to make up for the short rations which Sally Brass allows her, and teaches her to play cribbage (57). When Dick is dismissed by Sampson and falls ill, she runs away from Bevis Marks and cares for him (64). Her testimony about the Brasses' and Quilp's scheme to frame Kit Nubbles leads to Sampson's imprisonment and Kit's pardon (66). After coming into his inheritance, Dick names her **Sophronia Sphinx**, pays for her education, and marries her (73). *Curiosity Shop*. Dickens's manuscript indicates that the Marchioness was the child of Sally Brass by Quilp, but he removed the relevant passage before publication.

Marcus, Steven (1928–) Professor, Columbia University; writer on Victorian cultural and literary history, on Freud, Engels, and other Victorians, and on the psychological and social dimensions of literature. *Dickens: from Pickwick to Dombey* (1965) is one of the most important books on the early novels; although its Freudian approach has been controversial, its thorough grounding in Victorian social history yields insightful and provocative readings of the novels.

Margaret The senior Mr. Winkle's housemaid. *Pickwick* (50).

Margaret, Aunt She married a poor man without her mother's consent, but at the family Christmas celebration, her husband turns out to be a "nice man." *Boz*, "Christmas Dinner."

Margate The snobbish Tuggses choose RAMSGATE over this competing seaside resort in KENT because they thought only tradespeople went to Margate (*Boz*, "Tuggses"). Abel Garland visited Margate as a boy with his schoolmaster (*Curiosity Shop*, 14); during the long vacation, Margate is a destination for "young clerks . . . madly in love" (*Bleak House*, 19); Captain Boldheart seeks out his bride while she is bathing at Margate ("Holiday Romance").

Marigold, Doctor Cheap jack—a traveling peddler and auctioneer—who follows the profession of his father, **Willum**, and narrates an account of his life. "I was born on the Queen's highway, but it was the King's at that time. A doctor was fetched to my own mother by my own father, when it took place on a common; and in consequence of his being a very kind gentleman, and accepting no fee but a tea-tray, I was named Doctor, out of gratitude and compliment to him. There you have me. Doctor Marigold." His temperamental **wife** abuses their daughter, **Sophy**. After his wife, daughter, and dog die, Marigold adopts a deaf-and-dumb girl, names her **Sophy** after his daughter, educates her, and blesses her marriage to a deaf-and-dumb young man. "Marigold."

Marker, Mrs. Client of the employment office who is seeking a cook: "Two in family, and see very little

company. Five servants kept. No man. No followers." *Nickleby* (16).

Markham One of Steerforth's Oxford friends who is invited to David's housewarming dinner. He speaks of himself in the third person as "a man." *Copperfield* (24–25).

Markleham, Mrs. ("The Old Soldier") Annie Strong's mother, called "the Old Soldier" by the boys in the school "on account of her generalship, and the skill with which she marshalled great forces of relations against the Doctor" (16). Her machinations increase the suspicions about her daughter's relations with Jack Maldon, and her selfish indulgence in her own pleasures makes her insensitive to Annie's suffering (45). *Copperfield*.

Marks, Will John Podgers's nephew, "a wild, roving young fellow of twenty" who accepts the commission to watch for witches and becomes involved in a Cavalier conspiracy to bury one of their hanged comrades. *Humphrey*.

Marley, Jacob Scrooge's deceased partner who died on Christmas Eve seven years before the time of the story. He appears to Scrooge as a ghost, first in the knocker on Scrooge's door, and then as an apparition "in his pigtail, usual waistcoat, tights and boots. . . . The chain he drew was clasped about his middle. It was long, and wound about him like a tail; and it was made . . . of cash boxes, keys, padlocks, ledgers, deeds, and heavy purses wrought in steel" (1). He has come with a warning: Scrooge also bears a chain and will suffer a fate similar to his own unless he heeds the visions of the three spirits and changes his life. *Carol*.

Maroon, Captain Horse trader to whom Tip Dorrit owes money: "gentleman with tight drab legs, a rather old hat, a little hooked stick, and a blue neckerchief" (I: 12). *Dorrit*.

Marquis of Granby Tavern in DORKING kept by Tony Weller's second wife; "a model of a road-side public-house of the better class—just large enough to be convenient, and small enough to be snug" (27). *Pickwick*.

Marryat, Captain Frederick (1792–1848) Prolific popular novelist, particularly of novels about the sea; friend of Dickens during the 1840s, who, John FORSTER notes, was "one of the first of Dickens' liking." Both were regulars at Lady BLESSINGTON's salon at Gore House. Marryat's critical *Diary in America* (1839) is often compared with *Notes*. He chaired the dinner to welcome Dickens home from America in 1842. Like Dickens he was profoundly influenced by such picaresque novelists as LE SAGE and SMOLLETT, and his novels often had orphan-waif heroes who may have influenced such Dickens's heroes as Oliver Twist.

The Marshalsea.

Marseilles   Seaport in southern FRANCE where Arthur Clennam is held in quarantine on his way back to England from China (*Dorrit*, I:1). Dickens passed through Marseilles several times during his year in ITALY; he considered the city "a dirty and disagreeable place" with "dust, dust, dust, everywhere" (*Pictures*). Herbert Pocket is in Marseilles on business when Magwitch appears at Pip's door in London (*Expectations*, 39).

Marshall, Mary   Richard Doubledick's sweetheart, who jilts him and then marries him many years later after he has been wounded in battle and is near death in Brussels. "Doubledick."

Marshall, Miss   One of the young ladies who wonders about the mysterious Mr. Fairfax, the Censorious Young Gentleman. *Young Gentlemen*.

Marshalsea Prison   DEBTORS PRISON often referred to simply as The Marshalsea, located in the BOROUGH HIGH STREET, SOUTHWARK, where Dickens's father was imprisoned in 1824. Much of the first half of *Dorrit* takes place in the prison, "an oblong pile of barrack buildings, partitioned off into squalid houses, standing back to back, so that there were no back rooms; environed by a narrow paved yard, hemmed in by high walls duly spiked at the top" (*Dorrit*, I:6). It is also the setting for the Old Man's Tale About the Queer Client, where "want and misfortune are pent up in the narrow prison; an air of gloom and dreariness seems . . . to hang about the scene, and to impart to it a squalid and sickly hue" (*Pickwick*, 21).

Martha (1)   Gabriel Parsons's serving maid. *Boz*, "Tottle."

Martha (2)   Palsied old workhouse inmate who sees Mrs. Corney get from Old Sally the pawn ticket that leads to the locket proving Oliver's identity. *Twist* (23–24).

Martha (3)   "Ugly, misshapen, peevish, ill-conditioned" but "best-beloved" daughter of John, the laborer that Florence meets at the Skettles's. *Dombey* (24).

Martin (1)   Arabella Allen's surly groom. *Pickwick* (39).

Martin (2)   Gamekeeper at DINGLEY DELL. *Pickwick* (19).

Martin, Amelia The mistaken milliner—"pale, tallish, thin, and two-and-thirty"—who attempts to become a singer. *Boz*, "Milliner."

Martin (1), Betsy One-eyed charwoman converted by the Brick Lane Branch of the United Grand Junction Ebenezer Temperance Association, who "thinks it not impossible that if she had always abstained from spirits, she might have had two eyes by this time." *Pickwick* (33).

Martin (2), Betsy Stargazer's servant who foils the astronomer's misguided scheme to marry his niece to Tom Grig. *Lamplighter*.

Martin, Captain MARSHALSEA prisoner whom Mr. Dorrit uses as an example to Amy, urging her to respond favorably to John Chivery's proposal; Martin encouraged his daughter to entertain the attentions of the turnkey's son. *Dorrit* (I:19).

Martin, Jack The Bagman's uncle, "one of the merriest, pleasantest, cleverest fellows that ever lived." *Pickwick* (49).

Martin, Miss Bartender and bookkeeper at the hotel where Christopher works. "Somebody's Luggage."

Martin, Tom A butcher imprisoned in the Fleet. *Pickwick* (42).

Martin Chuzzlewit, The Life and Adventures of (Serial Title: *The Life and Adventures of Martin Chuzzlewit, his Relatives, Friends and Enemies: Comprising all his Wills and his Ways, with an Historical Record of What he did, and What he didn't; showing, moreover, who inherited the Family Plate, who came in for the Silver Spoons, and who for the Wooden Ladles: the Whole forming a Complete Key to the House of Chuzzlewit, edited by "Boz"*) Dickens's sixth novel, published in monthly parts (January 1843 to July 1844), with illustrations by BROWNE. Published in one volume by CHAPMAN & HALL, 1844. A transitional novel between the loosely structured early works and the more carefully planned later ones, *Chuzzlewit* combines improvisation and indulgent characterization with the more consciously developed central theme of selfishness. To expose the materialism of the Chuzzlewits and, by extension, of Victorian society, Dickens mixed satire, sentimental comedy, humours comedy, and the comedy of the absurd, and he created two of his most memorable characters, Seth Pecksniff and Sairey Gamp.

SYNOPSIS

Part 1 (January 1843)
(1) The Chuzzlewit family is one of extreme antiquity, "descended in a direct line from Adam and Eve." Their importance renders them "highly improving and acceptable acquaintance to all right-minded individuals."

Browne's (Phiz's) illustration of Pecksniff discharging Tom Pinch depicts the central theme of Martin Chuzzlewit—*the struggle between selfishness and altruism.*

(2) On a windy afternoon in late autumn, Seth Pecksniff, an architect, arrives home, only to have the wind blow shut his front door and knock him to the ground where he is rescued by his younger daughter, Mercy. At tea, Pecksniff's assistant, Tom Pinch, tries unsuccessfully to reconcile architect Pecksniff with his student, John Westlock, but as he leaves for London Westlock tells Pinch, who defends his employer, that Pecksniff is a self-serving hypocrite.

(3) At the Blue Dragon, the local inn, a sick old man and a young woman have taken refuge. Since the apothecary is unavailable, Mrs. Lupin, the innkeeper, asks Pecksniff as a prominent member of the community to visit the sick man. She tells Pecksniff that she thinks the old man's illness stems from guilt over his association with an unmarried young woman. Pecksniff discovers the invalid to be his relative, old Martin Chuzzlewit. When the old man awakens, he tells Pecksniff that he is pursued by greedy relatives and has no friends because his wealth dooms him "to try the metal of all other men and find it false and hollow." He says that he trusts only Mary Graham, the young orphan who travels with him. He has told her that she will inherit nothing from him, so she has nothing to gain by his death. Pecksniff advises

old Martin to provide for his grandson, young Martin. The old man assumes Pecksniff's pleading is "a new plot" and as the architect leaves, old Martin mutters, "Oh self, self, self! at every turn nothing but self!"

Part 2 (February 1843)
(4) Rejected by old Martin, Pecksniff nonetheless is determined "to return good for evil," so he keeps watch over the old man, peering in on him though the keyhole of his room. One day he finds a vagabond dressed in grandiloquent and tattered clothes at the keyhole before him. It is Montague Tigg, friend of Chuzzlewit's nephew Chevy Slyme. Tigg asserts Slyme's claim upon old Martin and tells Pecksniff that other relatives have discovered the old man's whereabouts and are gathering in the town. Soon all available accommodations are taken by Chuzzlewits, each suspicious of the others, all suspicious of Tigg and Mary Graham, who are not members of the family. Pecksniff calls them all together at his house, where they agree that Mary Graham "casts a shadow of disgrace and shame upon this family." But they fight about everything else. Meanwhile old Martin secretly slips away.

(5) Tom Pinch goes to SALISBURY to meet Pecksniff's new architectural pupil, young Martin Chuzzlewit. In pleading the young Chuzzlewit's case to old Martin, Pecksniff had been indirectly pleading his own. On the way Tom gives a ride to Mark Tapley, the man-of-all-work at the Blue Dragon who is going off to seek work elsewhere that will present more of a challenge to his good humor. Tom and young Martin quickly become friends. Tom even confides to Martin his joy in playing the organ at the parish church and reveals how smitten he is by a beautiful young woman who listens to him play, and, with tears in his eyes, he tells Martin of Pecksniff's goodness. When they arrive at Pecksniff's house, the architect and his two daughters, Charity and Mercy, appear to be unprepared for their arrival, but Tom notes that the supper is unusually lavish. The girls pay particular attention to the new student.

Part 3 (March 1843)
(6) The next morning, Pecksniff announces that he and his daughters are going to London for a week; he leaves young Martin in charge of the household, instructing him to design a grammar school for an architectural competition while he is gone. Martin is disconcerted to have his education interrupted so soon. That evening Martin tells Tom of his expectations from his grandfather and of the old man's obstinacy and selfishness in opposing his love for Mary Graham. Obstinacy and selfishness, Martin asserts, are Chuzzlewit traits, and he promises to respond to his grandfather's obstinacy with "firmness." He has come to study with Pecksniff because of his grandfather's "inveterate dislike" for the architect.

(7) While Martin works on the grammar school and Tom goes over Pecksniff's accounts, Montague Tigg comes to Pecksniff's house as an ambassador from Chevy Slyme. They are being detained at the Dragon because they cannot pay their bill, so Martin pays Mrs. Lupin just to get the two out of town. Tigg coaxes an extra 10 shillings out of Pinch.

(8) Meanwhile, on the London coach, Pecksniff and his daughters are joined by Anthony Chuzzlewit, old Martin's brother, and his son Jonas, who are returning home to London.

Part 4 (April 1843)
(9) At the heart of the labyrinth of London streets, not far from the MONUMENT, is the boardinghouse for gentlemen presided over by Mrs. Todgers. The men of the house, led by Jinkins the senior resident, plan a festive dinner to honor the visiting Pecksniffs. Meanwhile, Pecksniff, his daughters, and Mrs. Todgers deliver a letter from Tom Pinch to his sister, who is working as a governess in CAMBERWELL. Pecksniff condescends to Ruth, hoping for an introduction to the snobbish copper founder for whom she works, but he is only asked to stay off the grass and leave the premises. At the dinner party, Charity and Mercy are honored by the gentlemen of Todgers's; Pecksniff drinks too much, makes up to Mrs. Todgers, falls into the fireplace, and is carried upstairs. There he is subdued and locked in his room. Young Bailey, the energetic house boy of the establishment, keeps watch at his door. (10) Pecksniff's business in London is to meet with old Martin Chuzzlewit, who urges the obsequious architect to dismiss the ungrateful young Martin as his student.

Part 5 (May 1843)
(11) At the end of the week, Jonas calls for Charity, arousing the jealous envy of Mercy. He takes the two girls sightseeing to the free attractions in London. Although he is ostensibly interested in Charity, he keeps inquiring about "the other one." Jonas's interest in his cousins throws the gentlemen of Todgers into despair. They serenade the girls on their last night in town and then bid their coach farewell the next morning. Jonas and his father also come to see the Pecksniffs off.

(12) While Pecksniff is in London, Martin works on the design for the grammar school and treats Pinch with condescension. John Westlock, to celebrate coming into an inheritance, invites Pinch and Martin to dine with him at the best hotel in Salisbury. There Martin learns that John, much to the consternation of the naive Tom Pinch, thinks Pecksniff "the most consummate scoundrel on the face of the earth." After Martin tells John how Tigg imposed on Pinch, John returns the loan and advises Tom to lend no more money to Tigg.

On his return from London, Pecksniff snubs Martin and refuses to speak to him. When Martin demands an explanation, Pecksniff renounces him and charges him with deception and depravity. Martin leaves abruptly, telling Tom that he will go to America.

Part 6 (June 1843)
(13) Out in the rain, Martin looks into the book that Tom has given him as a parting gift and finds the half sovereign that Tom had once lent Tigg. He makes his way to London, pawning his belongings to get by. Five

weeks after arriving in the city, penniless and despairing of ever reaching America, Martin receives a letter with £20 in it and, at the same time, Mark Tapley appears at his door and offers to go to AMERICA with him as his servant. Mark tells Martin that Mary Graham is in London. (14) When they meet in ST. JAMES'S PARK, Martin tells Mary that he has asked Tom Pinch to protect her. She gives him a diamond ring as a parting gift and he smugly asserts that "she is worthy of the sacrifices I have made." (15) During the crossing to America, Mark cares for other passengers in the steerage of the *Screw*, especially helping a mother with three small children who is on her way to join her immigrant husband. Martin reprimands Mark for not paying more attention to him and he spends the whole voyage inside the cabin because he does not want to be seen on deck as someone who could only afford to travel in steerage.

Part 7 (July 1843)
(16) When the *Screw* arrives in NEW YORK, newsboys and newspaper editors meet the ship and Martin goes off with Colonel Diver, editor of the New York *Rowdy Journal*. At the newspaper offices Martin meets Jefferson Brick, the paper's youthful war correspondent, who is presented to him, like every other American, as "one of the most remarkable men" in the country. (17) At Major Pawkins's Boarding House Martin meets an exception to this rule, Mr. Bevan, who is simply a kind physician from BOSTON. When Mark hires an ex-slave to help him with their luggage and is outspoken about the contradiction in a country that is devoted to liberty and yet harbors slavery, Bevan warns them that Mark's frankness may get him into trouble. They visit the Norrises, a family of abolitionists who nevertheless believe in the necessity of separating the races. They also preach the superiority of American liberty but are obsessed with the British aristocracy. When they learn that Martin crossed in steerage, they snub him. After less than a day in America, Martin begins to despair about his plan to establish himself as an architect.

Part 8 (August 1843)
(18) Back in London, Jonas Chuzzlewit taunts his father for not dying and leaving his money to his son. The old man delights in his son's tight-fisted ways. While Pecksniff negotiates with Anthony a possible marriage between Jonas and his daughter, the old man falls ill. Jonas tells Pecksniff that the architect's fortunate presence in the house means that people won't be able to accuse Jonas of causing his father's illness. But neither Pecksniff nor Jonas, nor Chuffey, Anthony's old clerk who genuinely cares for his master, can prevent Anthony from dying.

(19) Pecksniff seeks out Mrs. Gamp, the nurse and midwife recommended by the undertaker, to prepare the body for burial. Jonas orders an expensive and elaborate funeral and appears to the undertaker to be the very model of a bereaved son. Only old Chuffey's sobbing mars the ceremony and unsettles Jonas. (20) After the funeral Jonas plans to spend some time at Pecksniff's

house in the country. On the way there he elicits a promise that Pecksniff will provide a dowry of £4,000 should either of his daughters marry. But when Jonas proposes to Mercy, Pecksniff is surprised and Charity is beside herself. Jonas asks Pecksniff for an extra £1,000 for choosing the more difficult daughter, but their negotiations are interrupted when Pinch announces that old Martin and Mary Graham are approaching the house.

Part 9 (September 1843)
(21) Back in the United States, on a train going west, Martin and Mark meet General Choke, who introduces them to Mr. Scadder, agent for the Valley of Eden Land Corporation, who operates out of a small shed containing a grand map of the settlement. Assured that there is work for an architect in the developing town of Eden, Martin buys into the scheme, in spite of Mark's skepticism. Using Mark's money for the purchase, Martin makes him an equal partner in the firm of Chuzzlewit and Co. Then they go to a meeting of the Watertoast Sympathisers, a group devoted to putting down the British lion and celebrating liberty. When the group learns that an Irish politician they have supported because of his anti-British position also opposes slavery, they renounce him and disband the organization. (22) Captain Kedgick, proprietor of the National Hotel, where they are staying, requires Martin to hold a levee, a reception for nearly everybody in town, including Mrs. Hominy, an authoress of moral sentiments who attaches herself to Martin for the next two days. Meanwhile, Mark gathers supplies for their new life in Eden. As they are about to set off on the steamboat for the settlement, Mark asks Kedgick why they hold the levees. "Our people like excitement," Kedgick tells him, and "nobody as goes to Eden ever comes back a-live." (23) As the steamboat goes farther and farther on its journey, the settlements become increasingly rude and primitive. Eden is simply a few rotting cabins set in a fetid swamp. Most of the settlers have left or died and the few who remain are weak and sickly. Martin cries, expecting to die there; Mark tries to set things in order and raise Martin's spirits.

Part 10 (October 1843)
(24) Back in England, old Martin and Mary Graham are again staying at the Blue Boar and visiting Pecksniff. The architect has difficulty presenting a harmonious household to old Martin. Charity, jealous and resentful that Jonas has chosen her sister, is at odds with Mercy. Jonas, described by Pecksniff as a model son, nonetheless is suspicious and hostile to everyone around him. When Tom escorts Mary and the old man back to their inn, his praise of Pecksniff convinces Martin that Tom is just another of Pecksniff's toadies, and when Tom confronts the surly Jonas and knocks him to the ground, he earns Charity's grateful approval.

Old Martin asks Mercy whether she loves Jonas. She says she hates him and will marry to tease him and get the better of him. After she toys with Jonas about a date for the wedding, he vows to punish her once they are married.

(25) Mrs. Gamp has been hired to care for Chuffey while Jonas is in Wiltshire. She also holds a second position as a night nurse for a young man at the BULL INN. On her first night there, the patient surprises her by feverishly exclaiming in the middle of the night, "Chuzzlewit! Jonas! No!" (26) Later, when the newly married Jonas and Mercy return to the city, Mrs. Gamp does not think that the bride looks very merry. Old Chuffey raises his trembling hands above his head saying, "Oh! woe, woe, woe, upon this wicked house!"

Part 11 (November 1843)
(27) Jonas meets with Tigg Montague (formerly Montague Tigg) who has established the Anglo-Bengalee Disinterested Loan and Life Assurance Company, a lavish-appearing operation which conceals several confidence schemes. He impresses Jonas with his head for business and invites him to buy into the company. After Jonas leaves, Tigg employs Nadgett, his private investigator, to find out as much about Jonas as he can. (28) Later, at an opulent dinner at Montague's house, Jonas is plied with liquor until he agrees to join the firm. Young Bailey, formerly Mrs. Todgers's houseboy and now Montague's liveried footman, takes the drunken Jonas home at three in the morning. There the boy finds Mercy looking broken and dispirited and he hears Jonas threaten her.

(20) As Mrs. Gamp prepares Lewsome, her patient from the Bull, for a journey to the country to recuperate from his illness, the sick man asks his friend John Westlock if he can confide a terrible secret to him. Westlock invites him to do so, but Lewsome is not yet ready to reveal his secret.

Part 12 (December 1843)
(30) Charity leaves home for London, so Pecksniff invites old Martin to move into his house with him. To improve his chances for the old man's money, Pecksniff decides he must marry Mary. When he meets her alone in the woods, however, she rejects him and threatens to tell old Martin of his unwanted advances. Pecksniff promises to injure young Martin should she do so. (31) After this confrontation, Pecksniff goes into the church to rest and, while he hides in one of the pews and listens to Tom Pinch playing the organ, he also overhears a conversation between Tom and Mary. She tells him of Pecksniff's treachery and Tom is finally convinced that Pecksniff is not the man he thought him. That evening, in the presence of old Martin, Pecksniff dismisses Tom, accusing him of making overtures to Mary Graham. Tom leaves for London, adjusting to a world in which "there was no Pecksniff; there never had been a Pecksniff."

(32) Ensconced at Todgers, Charity works on the affections of Augustus Moddle, the youngest of the gentleman boarders, who was driven to thoughts of suicide by Mercy's marriage. Although he is interested in Charity only because she reminds him of "Another," he finally offers her "a blighted heart," which she accepts.

Part 13 (January 1844)
(33) Back in America, on the day after his arrival in Eden, Martin falls ill of fever. When Mark goes to the neighbors for help, they turn out to be the family he cared for on the ship. They help him tend Martin, who is so ill he nearly dies. When Martin finally begins to recover, Mark falls ill. Martin and the neighbors care for him. Mark has at last found a situation that challenges his ability to maintain his good spirits, and Martin, during his illness, realizes how selfish he has been. Desperate to leave Eden, he writes to Mr. Bevan asking for help. Several weeks later a letter arrives with money in it and Martin and Mark begin their journey home. (34) On the steamboat back to New York, they meet Elijah Pogram, a member of Congress and another remarkable man. Mr. Bevan offers them money for their passage back to England, but Mark arranges to pay for it by signing on as a cook on the ship. As they leave, Mark speculates on how he would represent the American eagle: "like a Bat, for its shortsightedness; like a Bantam, for its bragging; like a Magpie, for its honesty; like a Peacock, for its vanity; like an Ostrich, for putting its head in the mud." Martin adds, "and like a Phoenix, for its power of springing from the ashes of its faults and vices, and soaring up anew into the sky." (35) A year after they left, Martin and Mark arrive back in England. Surprised to see Pecksniff in the port town, they learn that he is there to lay the cornerstone for his new building. Martin is outraged to discover that the building is the grammar school he designed.

Part 14 (February 1844)
(36) In London, Tom finds his unhappy sister patronized and put down by the copper founder she works for, so he gives the man a piece of his mind and takes Ruth away from her demeaning job. They find a flat in ISLINGTON. (37) Tom meets Charity Pecksniff and Augustus Moddle and goes with them to Todgers's. There he finds Mercy looking much altered. Tom is grateful for Mrs. Todgers's concern for the girl.

(38) After shadowing Jonas for some time, Nadgett reports to Montague. When Montague whispers something to Jonas after this interview, Jonas looks disturbed and agrees to put more money into the enterprise.

Part 15 (March 1844)
(39) John Westlock comes to Tom's Islington flat with news that Tom has been offered a position at £100 per annum. At the dark and dusty offices of Mr. Fips, an attorney in AUSTIN FRIARS, Tom learns that he is to catalogue a room full of books for an unnamed employer. (40) Tom regularly collects his wages from Fips, but he learns nothing more about his employer.

On one of his regular morning walks to the steamboat piers, Tom is asked to deliver a letter to a person boarding the steam packet for Antwerp. The passenger turns out to be Jonas and the letter shocks him, calling him off the boat to meet Montague, who is waiting to take him to the CITY. (41) Jonas admits that he was trying to escape. Threatening to disclose Jonas's secret that Nadgett has uncovered, Montague demands that he put more money into the firm and help in a scheme to fleece Pecksniff.

Part 16 (April 1844)
(42) Reluctantly Montague undertakes a journey to the country with Jonas. It is a stormy night and Montague imagines that Jonas is about to attack him with a bottle. Then the coach overturns and Montague is just barely saved from having his head crushed by the horses that Jonas is manuevering. Young Bailey, who has accompanied them on the coach, is badly injured in the accident and is left in the road for dead.
(43) Meanwhile, Mark and Martin arrive at the Dragon to a joyful reunion with Mrs. Lupin, who tells them all that has transpired in their absence. The next morning they go to Pecksniff's, where Martin unsuccessfully seeks reconciliation with his grandfather, who seems to be under Pecksniff's influence. After a brief reunion with Mary, Martin leaves Pecksniff's house just as Jonas is arriving. (44) Jonas arouses Pecksniff's greed with his surly talk of Montague's scheme, and by evening Pecksniff has agreed to commit nearly all his money to the Anglo-Bengalee. While Montague stays in the country to close the deal with the architect, Jonas returns to London alone.

Part 17 (May 1844)
(45) John Westlock advises Tom to inform Jonas that he was innocent in his involvement in delivering the letter on the packet ship, (46) but when Tom and Ruth go to see Jonas, he is away in the country, so they have tea with Mercy and her sister. While they are there old Chuffey distractedly wonders who is dead upstairs. As they are about to leave, Jonas returns home, berates his wife for holding parties while he is gone, and refuses to hear Tom's apology. After Tom leaves, Mrs. Gamp frightens Jonas when she tells him of Chuffey's ranting. He hires her to watch the old man. Then he goes to a downstairs bedroom to sleep, ordering that he not be disturbed for the next day and a half. In the middle of the night he puts on the clothes of a country laborer and slips out into the street. (47) After riding all night on a coach to the west, Jonas gets off in the country and hides in a wood where he knows Montague will pass after his meeting with Pecksniff. Then, with a club fashioned from a fence post, he leaps out at Montague, clubs him to death, and leaves his body in the wood. Making his way back to London that night, he is frightened but has no regret. He returns to the small downstairs room at five in the morning. When Mercy awakens him, he learns that Nadgett has been inquiring about him.

Part 18 (June 1844)
(48) Martin is in London with John Westlock when Lewsome reveals his secret. It is simply that Lewsome, a physician, had supplied Jonas with some poisons in exchange for forgiving a gambling debt; shortly after he did so, Anthony Chuzzlewit died. (49) John and Martin go to Sarah Gamp to see if she can enable them to talk to Chuffey to corroborate Lewsome's suspicions, but she has been drinking, and before they can question her about Chuffey, she falls asleep.
(50) The next morning, Martin breaks off his friendship with Tom Pinch, regretfully accusing Tom of failing to keep his promise to protect Mary. Tom is disappointed and asserts that Martin will regret what he has done, but Ruth, who knows her brother's heart, gets Tom to admit that he loves Mary himself. The next day at work, Tom's employer finally reveals himself. It is old Martin Chuzzlewit.

Parts 19–20 (July 1844)
(51) When Mrs. Gamp comes to take charge of Chuffey, she is followed by old Martin, John Westlock, Lewsome, and Mark Tapley. They accuse Jonas of killing his father, but Chuffey, in a moment of lucidity, says that Anthony discovered his son's plot to poison him and destroyed the poison. He died of natural causes, grieving and blaming his own greed as the cause of Jonas's cruelty. His final words to Chuffey were "Spare him." On learning that he is not guilty of his father's death, Jonas gloats and orders his accusers to leave. But Nadgett and Chevy Slyme, now a policeman, are at the door. They charge Jonas with Montague's murder. Jonas offers Slyme £100 for five minutes alone in which to poison himself. Slyme takes the money, but gives it back when Jonas is still alive some time later. Placed under arrest, Jonas takes the poison in the cab on the way to the police station.
(52) At a meeting of the Chuzzlewits and those associated with them, old Martin announces that "the curse of our house . . . has been the love of self; has ever been the love of self." He reconciles with many of the family members and particularly with his grandson, young Martin, and he blesses Martin's love for Mary. He rejects Pecksniff as a consummate fraud and hypocrite, beating him over the head with his walking stick. Hypocritical to the end, Pecksniff forgives him. After the denunciation of Pecksniff, young Bailey appears before the assembly, miraculously recovered from his wounds. (53) John Westlock proposes to Ruth Pinch; they plan to move to the country, where John can practice architecture, and hire Tom to work with him. Tom will also live with them. At a celebratory dinner, the happy couples—John and Ruth, Martin and Mary, Mark and Mrs. Lupin—honor Tom Pinch, for whom the day has been one of unutterable joy.
(54) On the morning of Charity's wedding, old Martin tries unsuccessfully to elicit some sympathy from Charity for her widowed sister. As she waits for her wedding to begin, Charity learns that Augustus Moddle has avoided the marriage at the last minute by running away to the South Seas.

COMMENTARY

In his 1844 Preface to *Chuzzlewit*, Dickens noted a change in his manner of composition. "I have endeavored in the progress of this Tale," he wrote, "to resist the temptation of the current Monthly Number, and to keep a studious eye upon the general purpose and design." Although he did not write down his plans for each part—a practice he would initiate with *Dombey*—he did consciously relate everything in his narrative to a central theme, which, in the Preface to the CHEAP EDITION, he described as follows: "My main object in the story was, to exhibit in a variety of aspects the commonest of all the vices; to show how Selfishness propagates itself."

The extended title for the serial parts of the novel suggests that this thematic center was to be grounded in the story of old Martin Chuzzlewit and his extended family, which, in the opening chapter, has its lineage traced all the way back to Adam and Eve. But the narrative proper, which begins with the second chapter, seems to make Pecksniff the central character. John FORSTER's account confirms this as Dickens's intent: "The notion of taking Pecksniff for a type of character was really the origin of the book," Forster wrote, "the design being to show, more or less by every person introduced, the number and variety of humours and vices that have their root in selfishness."

With Pecksniff as its central figure, *Chuzzlewit* becomes a kind of comedy of humours, in the manner of Ben JONSON. John LUCAS (1970) identifies some of the humours, the obsessions that preoccupy various characters, as, for example, selfish greed (Anthony, Jonas), hypocrisy (Pecksniff), and expectations (young Martin, Slyme). Pecksniff, the exemplar of hypocrisy, may take in the innocent Tom Pinch for much of the novel, but he fools neither old Martin, the good-hearted "Volpone" of this Jonsonian comedy, nor the evil con men, Tigg and Jonas. The structure of the story also recalls humours comedy, beginning with the gathering of the selfish Chuzzlewits, going on to their dispersal into the world to exercise their various humours, and ending with another gathering, where rewards and punishments are meted out and Pecksniff's villainy is finally exposed.

As Jonsonian comedy, the novel is concerned with the external aspects of the characters, with their dramatic presence. Pecksniff is an apt center in this drama, for he is wholly defined by external appearances. All that is inside him, the narrator suggests, are the trite moral sentiments that frequently drop from his lips:

> It has been remarked that Mr. Pecksniff was a moral man. So he was. Perhaps there never was a more moral man than Pecksniff: especially in his conversation and correspondence. It was once said of him by a homely admirer, that he had a Fortunatus's purse of good sentiments in his inside. In this particular he was like the girl in the fairy tale, except that if they were not actual diamonds which fell from his lips, they were the very brightest paste, and shone prodigiously (2).

Pecksniff has no guilt about his hypocrisy, because he believes in his own fraud and does not admit his greed. His story does not involve introspection and moral growth. It is rather a series of dramatic actions, each overreaching those that precede it, until his hypocritical scheming is finally exposed. His progress is marked by scenes of physical comedy: his wind-blown entrance into the novel; his drunken collapse into Mrs. Todgers's fireplace; his exit from the novel as old Martin Chuzzlewit beats him with his walking stick. Appropriately, Pecksniff is an architect whose most fully executed designs are the schemes he devises to make money; his greatest construction is his own public character. Pecksniff stands with such great dramatic hypocrites as Tartuffe and Malvolio; the humours comedy that presents his story is the central focus of what R. C. CHURCHILL (1958) has described as "not only Dickens' best comic novel but the greatest work of comic genius in the whole of English literature."

Chuzzlewit is more than a comedy of humours. Several other comedic strands are woven into the novel. The social satire that begins the novel by tracing the genealogy of the Chuzzlewit family back to Adam and Eve runs through the novel, especially in the chapters exposing the self-serving greed and hypocrisy of the liberty-loving Americans. If young Martin is seen as its central figure, it becomes a comic BILDUNGSROMAN describing the hero's growth from immature self-centeredness to an awareness of and concern for others. Tom Pinch, the novel's central figure for some Victorian readers, adds a strand of sentimental comedy to the tough moralism of the Jonsonian story. His unworldly innocence is rewarded with a place in the hearts of the other characters, but he is not worldly enough to win the hand of Mary Graham. Mrs. Gamp, probably the greatest comic character in the novel, transcends generic containment and exists as one of Dickens's great comic figures, along with Pickwick, Micawber, and Scrooge, in a realm of pure imagination. Much of the comedy involving this attendant at the rites of birth and death is "black comedy," drawing humor from her garrulously outrageous defenses of her negligent disregard for the lives of her patients. So complex is the mix of comedic strands in the novel, that many critics have wondered whether *Chuzzlewit* is really less of an improvisation than the novels that preceded it and whether its stated thematic center can really bring together these disparate parts.

Just what Dickens meant by selfishness has prompted a good deal of discussion. Anthony and his son Jonas most fully represent the usual definition of the term. Business and the pursuit of wealth completely dominate their lives. They live in their place of business; the bedroom and dining furniture of their domestic life occupies corners in their warehouse. The "pursuit of wealth" has become for them "the one affair of life" and their philosophy is expressed in Jonas's perverse version of the golden rule, "Do other men, for they would do you" (11). Jonas never pretends to seek anything other than his own self-interest; he carries the principle to the rapacious extreme of patricide when his father does not die soon enough to suit him and leave him the family wealth.

Most of the other characters do more to disguise their selfishness. Tigg Montague's insurance scam pretends to be a legitimate business providing protection against the vicissitudes of fortune. His luxurious clothes and offices are part of a charade that promises the security of wealth to his clients, but he is more honest with the greedy Jonas, telling him, "Why should I disguise what you know so well, but what the crowd never dream of? We companies are all birds of prey: mere birds of prey" (27). The differences between Anthony Chuzzlewit and Son and the Anglo-Bengalee Disinterested Loan and Life Assurance Company seem only to be those of appearance and scale. Both ruthlessly pursue economic self-interest.

Selfishness, when applied to Martin Chuzzlewit or his grandfather, however, appears to have a very different meaning. Old Martin's refrain, "Oh self, self, self! at every turn nothing but self!" seems to extend beyond selfish greed to include self-obsession or self-centeredness. Young Martin's failing is not that he is rapaciously greedy. Although he hopes and expects to inherit his grandfather's money, he is not among the fawning and obsequious relatives, and his love for Mary Graham appears to lessen his chances of keeping the old man's favor. His fault, rather, is self-centeredness, an egotistical assumption that everything revolves around him. He takes Tom Pinch and Mark Tapley for granted. In his relationship with Mary Graham, he assumes that all sacrifice is his and he fails to understand why she gives him the ring. His egotism and class arrogance lead him to think that others exist to serve him. These are failings of a very different sort from the capitalistic rapaciousness of Jonas and Tigg or the hypocrisy of Pecksniff.

Old Martin is similarly self-obsessed, feeding his paranoia with the belief that everyone is out to get his money. He is not a hypocrite; his unconcern for appearance is evident in his open relationship with Mary Graham, which others, even Mrs. Lupin, view scandalously. But the contract he has made with Mary, giving her no hopes of inheriting his money, is a sign of an egotistical paranoia that takes no one on trust. While young Martin is off in America, learning through sickness and suffering of his common humanity, old Martin is learning that there really are disinterested and selfless Tom Pinches in the world.

The notion of self that is at the center of the novel, then, ranges from the rapacious self-interest of Anthony and Jonas on one extreme to the selflessness of Tom Pinch and Mark Tapley on the other. In between are the two Martins, self-centered egotists who are transformed by their experiences, and the various hypocrites whose pretenses of charity, mercy, and respectability mask their self-interest. Pecksniff is their prophet.

This moral continuum shapes the overall structure of the novel, but it is occasionally forgotten in the details of the story. Inconsistencies in character and plot undermine the thematic focus. For example, there are, as Lucas (1970) points out, two accounts of Anthony Chuzzlewit's death. The first, which Jonas himself believes, makes Anthony the victim of Jonas's poison, an end gruesomely consistent with the unmitigated self-interest in their do-or-be-done-to philosophy. But Chuffey's later account claims that Anthony, aware of Jonas's scheme, escaped the poison, and died of a broken heart. This revised version calls for the reader to accept a very different notion of Anthony's character than that presented earlier in the novel.

Several other characters make noteworthy changes in the course of the story, thematically reinforcing, perhaps, the central conversion of young Martin from egotism to altruism. Martin may be given enough interior development to make his transformation believable, but the changes in some of the others are harder to accept. Montague Tigg's transformation into Tigg Montague plays a wonderful counterpoint to Pecksniff's frauds. Appropriately, Pecksniff's final comeuppance is brought about by an even bigger fraud than himself, but it is hard to believe the vagabond of chapter three capable of such a compelling impersonation. Mercy Chuzzlewit's transformation from the conniving schemer who outwits her sister to win Jonas into the sympathetic victim after her marriage asks the reader to shift uncomfortably from the vigorous morality of the Jonsonian comedy to the sympathetic identification of sentimental fiction.

Perhaps the most difficult transformation to accept is that of old Martin Chuzzlewit, for by the end of the story it is not clear whether he was changed by experience or whether from the beginning he was a pious fraud who schemed to test his grandson and manipulate others so that the story would turn out as he wished. Since both versions of his story are left unresolved in the end, one is tempted to think that Dickens, as he improvised the story, may have changed his own sense of Martin's role midway through the novel.

Forster indicates that the American sections of the novel were also not planned from the beginning. Dickens introduced the American journey as a way to lift sales, for the novel was not selling as well as either he or his publishers had expected. Although some readers find these American chapters extraneous, an unnecessary interpolated tale taking up nearly one-sixth of the novel, most have seen them as extending and exaggerating the thematic issues in the British sections of the book. In America Martin finds a whole society devoted to self-interest and egotism but preaching a mythology of liberty, equality, and opportunity. Martin's journey of discovery is like a fifth voyage of Gulliver to discover a land where liberty excuses slavery, equality idolizes the British aristocracy, and opportunity offers only a chance to die in a fetid swamp named New Eden. In *Chuzzlewit*'s America, as Steven MARCUS (1965) points out, "the private self [was converted] into public property and into something wholly externalized." Martin notes that every American he meets has a title and is "one of the most remarkable men" in the country. These Americans don't converse; they orate. Their speeches invariably boast about the superiority of the United States over anywhere else. They are all surfaces; their personalities can be read in their faces. In Dickens's Dantesque description, Zephaniah Scadder, the land salesman who sells Martin a piece of Eden, has his hypocrisy and double-dealing written into the features of his face:

> He was a gaunt man in a huge straw hat, and a coat of green stuff. The weather being hot, he had no cravat, and wore his shirt collar open; so that every time he spoke something was seen to twitch and jerk up in his

throat, like the little hammers in a harpsichord when the notes are struck. Perhaps it was the Truth feebly endeavouring to leap to his lips. If so, it never reached them.

Two grey eyes lurked deep within this agent's head, but one of them had no sight in it, and stood stock still. With that side of his face he seemed to listen to what the other side was doing. Thus each profile had a distinct expression; and when the movable side was most in action, the rigid one was in its coldest state of watchfulness. It was like turning the man inside out, to pass that view of his features in his liveliest mood, and see how calculating and intent they were.

Each long black hair upon his head hung down as straight as any plummet line; but rumpled tufts were on the arches of his eyes, as if the crow whose foot was deeply printed in the corners had pecked and torn them in a savage recognition of his kindred nature as a bird of prey (21).

Scadder is literally two-faced, and the Eden on the architect's plan in his office maps a very different place from the swamp where Martin nearly dies.

Although rendered in satiric caricature, America is the site of Martin's conversion. He recovers from his illness to attend Mark through his and to realize how his preoccupation with himself has made him unaware and uncaring of others. Similar changes are taking place in other characters. Mark has met the extreme test of his good spirits and he will recover ready to return to the comforts of the Blue Dragon. Back in England, Mercy has met her match in marrying Jonas, and his brutality has intimidated and subdued her. And young Bailey, elevated from Mrs. Todger's houseboy to become Montague's footman and a turfy young man about town, is shocked by seeing Mercy's degradation. His near death and "resurrection" after the coach accident is a baroque parody of Martin's recovery story.

Over this black, life-and-death comedy, Mrs. Gamp presides like a ruling goddess. Her role in the plot is tangential. She is called in to lay out Anthony's body and to nurse Lewsome and old Chuffey. As a nurse, midwife, and preparer of bodies for burial, she presides over both birth and death, but her care is more for herself than for her patients and she is adept at obtaining a medicinal flask of gin or the clothes of the deceased persons she lays out. Her self-interest expresses her instinct for survival in the face of death, violence, and brutality. But most of all it is her language—wholly her own and at times incomprehensible—that identifies her. She repeatedly describes herself as "living in a wale," both the biblical "vale of tears" and also, perhaps, the belly of Jonah's whale. In what is probably her most famous speech, she explains to undertaker Mould her reasons for agreeing to work a double shift with two different patients: "I will not deny . . . that I am but a poor woman, and that the money is a object; but do not let that act upon you Mr. Mould. Rich folks may ride on camels, but it ain't so easy for 'em to see out of a needle's eye. That is my comfort, and I hope I knows it" (25). This idiosyncratic speech, characteristically larded with ob-

scure and confused biblical allusions, makes no sense, but it nonetheless contributes to the theme of selfishness in its oblique comment on the difficulties of the rich in transcending this "wale" to enter the Kingdom of Heaven.

Mrs. Gamp confirms her idiosyncratic view of things by appealing to the authority of Mrs. Harris, an imaginary friend she can call up to support her anecdotes or to provide corroborating evidence for her argument. Thus she lives in a self-created world, peopled by characters from her own imagination. The climax of Mrs. Gamp's story comes when Betsey Prig, her nursing partner, announces, "I don't believe there's no sich a person [as Mrs. Harris]." Mrs. Gamp responds with a spirited defense of her fantasy friend:

> "What!" said Mrs. Gamp, "you bage creetur, have I know'd Mrs. Harris five and thirty year, to be told at last that there ain't no sech a person livin'! Have I stood her friend in all her troubles, great and small, for it to come at the last to sech an end as this, which her own sweet picter hanging up afore you all the time, to shame your Bragian words! But well you mayn't believe there's no sech a creetur, for she wouldn't demean herself to look at you, and often has she said, when I have made mention of your name, which, to my sinful sorrow, I have done, 'What, Sairey Gamp! debage yourself to *her*!' Go along with you!" (49).

The originality of her vocabulary suggests that Mrs. Gamp's powers of creation extend beyond imagining her friend; she creates a whole new language. Mrs. Gamp is preeminently a creature of the city and the chaos of her language embodies the confusion of the city.

Dorothy VAN GHENT's (1950) classic essay describes the view from the roof of Todgers's as one characterizing "the Dickens world." From the roof, London appears as a "wilderness," a world in which inanimate objects take on life and appear to have nervous energy like the city itself. The city is a "maze" or "labyrinth" and to find Todgers's at the heart of this maze, "you groped your way for an hour through lanes and bye-ways, and courtyards, and passages" (9). The maze of Mrs. Gamp's language also mirrors this city; her creation of Mrs. Harris provides a way to counter the isolation and loneliness of urban life. Mrs. Harris offers Mrs Gamp the illusion of community, just as Todgers offers a fragile place of human refuge at the heart of the London labyrinth. Van Ghent asserts that "the Todgers's world requires an act of redemption," as does the world of *Chuzzlewit*—redemption from parricide, from Mercy's brutalization, from the frauds of Tigg and Pecksniff, from the dark obsession with money. The conversions and transformations that end the novel seek to redeem *Chuzzlewit*'s darkness, but they are not altogether satisfactory to counter the cruelty of urban life. Old Martin's domestic despotism may have just been part of a pious fraud and his softening a premeditated end to his story. Young Bailey's miraculous reappearance strains credulity. Though Mrs. Gamp desperately clings to her belief in Mrs. Harris, she too is troubled by Betsey Prig's realistic assessment of the truth.

CRITICISM

Alexander WELSH (1987) discusses the biographical origins of *Chuzzlewit* and considers several of the characters—Jonas, Tigg, Pinch, Pecksniff, and the two Martins—as projections of the author.

Nearly all the critics agree that *Chuzzlewit* is both a great comic novel and a seriously flawed one. R. C. CHURCHILL's (1958) claim that it is "the greatest work of comic genius in the whole of English literature" is the most extravagant assertion of its virtues. In the most sustained analysis of its comic structures and themes, James R. KINCAID (1971) describes *Chuzzlewit* as a novel that begins with the didactic intent of presenting varieties of selfishness and develops into a "comedy of accommodation" in which Mrs. Todgers and Mrs. Gamp model ways to survive positively in society. Lucas (1970) writes of *Chuzzlewit* as a flawed novel, in which Dickens was unable to bring together his realistic rendering of Victorian society with the moral fable he was telling at the same time. This lack of a coherent center to the novel is evident in loose ends in the plot and inconsistencies in the characters. Marcus (1965), while admitting the novel's contradictions, finds its characters and social analysis a marked advance on the earlier novels. His archetypal reading is particularly interesting for its discussion of the American scenes and Martin's transformation in the "anti-Paradise" of New Eden. Joseph GOLD (1972) also takes an archetypal approach, tracing Dickens's use of the story of Jonah in the whale as the archetype underlying the novel. F. S. SCHWARZBACH (1979) takes on the realistic elements in the book, discussing the city in the novel as a physical and symbolic representation of industrial society in the Victorian age.

ADAPTATIONS

Both Edward STIRLING and Charles Webb wrote competing adaptations that were staged in London as soon as *Chuzzlewit* completed its serial run. In both of these productions and in the 20 or so other adaptations produced by 1850, the lead actress played young Bailey and the leading male comedian Mrs. Gamp. The focus of much dramatic interest, Mrs. Gamp inspired farces and playlets of her own as well as playing an important role in adaptations of the novel. *Mrs. Sarah Gamp's Tea and Turn Out* (1846) by Benjamin Webster and *Dealings with the Firm of Gamp and Harris* (1846) by F. Fox COOPER were two of the plays that exploited the popularity of Dickens's boozy nurse.

Only one American adaptation of the novel appeared in the 1840s, an indication of the disaffection with Dickens brought on by his criticism of the United States in *Notes* and *Chuzzlewit*.

Most later adaptations continued to feature Mrs. Gamp, but Pecksniff sometimes displaced young Bailey from his earlier prominence. An adaptation from the 1880s, *Tom Pinch*, departed from the established version and told only the story of Tom and Ruth. A German production in 1864 by H. Chr. Klein, *Tartuffe Junior; oder Martin Geldermann und sein Erben*, linked Pecksniff with Moliere's famous hypocrite.

Two silent films appeared in 1912 and 1914, but no sound films have been produced from the novel. The BBC has made two adaptations: Constance COX's 13-part version (1964) and David Lodge's recent adaptation (1994) directed by Pedr James, with Paul Scofield (old Martin, Anthony), Tom Wilkinson (Pecksniff), Pete Postlethwaite (Montague), Elizabeth Spriggs (Mrs. Gamp), and John MILLS (Chuffey).

Martin Family Particular friends of Mincin, the Very Friendly Young Gentleman. *Young Gentlemen*.

Martin-Harvey, Sir John (1863–1944) Actor and theater manager who played in London, New York, and in many other cities in the late 19th and early 20th centuries. He played Sam Weller in "Jingle," an 1887 version of *Pickwick* in New York, and in 1935 played Magwitch in two productions of "The Scapegoat," an adaptation of *Expectations*. His greatest Dickensian role, however, was Sydney Carton in "The Only Way," a version of *Two Cities* which Malcolm MORLEY described as "the most successful of all plays taken from Dickens." Martin-Harvey performed Carton in numerous stage productions of this play between 1899 and 1923, and in a silent film production in 1926.

Martineau, Harriet (1802–1876) Novelist, journalist, social philosopher, and autobiographer. She was one of the first writers Dickens recruited for *HOUSEHOLD WORDS*, contributing many articles and stories to the magazine between 1850 and 1855. Although Dickens subscribed to many of Martineau's radical political and social views, he was not a consistent radical and differed with her on economic issues, especially on the role of government in regulating factories. After *Hard Times* and a series of articles in *Household Words* by Malcolm MORLEY on accidents in textile mills, she wrote *The Factory Controversy* (1855), a pamphlet in which she attacked Dickens and his magazine as sentimental proponents of "meddling and mischievous" factory legislation. She had become convinced that Dickens and W. H. WILLS were "grievously inadequate to their function [as editors], philosophically and morally." Her contributions to the periodical stopped in 1855; Dickens commented on her attack: "I do suppose that there never was such a wrong-headed woman born—such a vain one—or such a Humbug." In the 1850s she was widely thought to have been the model for Mrs. Jellyby.

Marton Village schoolmaster with whom Nell and her grandfather stay on their wanderings, "a pale, simple-looking man, of a spare and meagre habit, [who] sat among his flowers and beehives, smoking his pipe" (24). Later they meet him in the BLACK COUNTRY and go

Harriet Martineau, in an engraving by Daniel Maclise.

with him to the remote village where Nell dies (52–54, 73). *Curiosity Shop.*

"Martyr Medium, The"   Article for ALL THE YEAR ROUND (April 4, 1863), attacking the spiritualist Daniel Dunglas Home by reprinting passages from his book *Incidents in My Life* and then debunking them. *Miscellaneous.*

Marwood, Alice   Alias used by Alice BROWN. *Dombey.*

Mary (1)   Nupkins's housemaid, who later serves as Arabella Allen's maid and who eventually becomes Pickwick's housemaid and marries Sam Weller. *Pickwick.*

Mary (2)   Comfortable daughter of Old John the inventor. *Reprinted*, "Poor Man's Tale."

Mary (3)   Daughter of the dying drunkard. *Boz*, "Drunkard's Death."

Mary (4)   Incidental characters in *Boz*, "Seven Dials," "Greenwich Fair," "Vauxhall," "Gin-Shops."

Mary Anne (1)   Girl managing a gambling table at Ramsgate. *Boz*, "Tuggses."

Mary Anne (2)   Wemmick's "neat little" maidservant. *Expectations* (25).

Mary Anne (3)   Miss Peecher's favorite pupil, who always raises her hand before speaking. She "sufficiently divined the state of Miss Peecher's affections to feel it necessary that she herself should love young Charley Hexam" (II:1). *Mutual Friend.*

Marylebone   Affluent borough northwest of central London. Dickens lived here, on DEVONSHIRE TERRACE, from 1839 to 1851. Next door to his house was the **Marylebone Parish Church**, usually considered the original of the church where Paul Dombey was christened and Dombey and Edith married.

Maryon, Captain and Marion   Commander of the sloop *Christopher Columbus*. On the expedition to Silver-Store Island, Captain Maryon is taken ashore ill when they arrive at the island. His sister, **Marion**, one of the colonists and "the life and spirit of the Island," acts heroically during the pirate attack. Although Gill Davis loves and admires her, she is far above him in social station. She marries Lord Carton and Gill becomes one of the family retainers. "English Prisoners."

Master Humphrey's Clock   Weekly periodical edited and written by Dickens. Begun on April 4, 1840, it was planned to be a collection of stories and sketches produced by Master Humphrey and his circle of friends. The group gathered weekly to hold readings of manuscripts found in the case of Master Humphrey's clock. The original scheme was not successful, and Dickens altered the format to make the Master Humphrey material a frame narrative for two of his novels, *The Old Curiosity Shop* and *Barnaby Rudge.*

(1) In the opening chapter, Master Humphrey, a reclusive and crippled old man, and his three friends—a deaf gentleman, Jack Redburn, and Owen Miles—hear the first of the Giant Chronicles, "MAGOG'S STORY" of Hugh Graham and Mistress Alice. (2) The second story, "A CONFESSION FOUND IN A PRISON . . . ," chronicles a murder during the Restoration period in the 17th century. (3) When Pickwick applies for membership in the group, he offers a tale of witchcraft, "MR. PICKWICK'S TALE," (4) and proposes Jack Bamber for the other vacant place in the circle. (5) Meanwhile Sam and Tony Weller and Humphrey's servants form a similar storytelling group, "Mr. Weller's Watch," where Sam tells two anecdotes involving barbers. (6) Tony Weller introduces his mischievous grandson, little Tony, to the group; Master Humphrey tells of visiting ST. PAUL's; in the end the Deaf Gentleman finds Master Humphrey dead in his chair before the fire. The final installment of *Humphrey* appeared on December 4, 1841. The *Master Humphrey* material was first collected for the CHARLES DICKENS EDITION.

Matchett, Willoughby (d.1921)   Regular contributor to the DICKENSIAN during its first two decades of publication. He contributed articles on biographical topics, especially on Dickens at WELLINGTON HOUSE Academy; on critical issues in several of the novels, especially *Dombey, Dorrit,* and *Drood*; and on Dickens in relation to various modern authors.

Mathews, Charles J. (1776–1835) Comic actor, a great favorite of Dickens during his youth and early manhood. In the early 1830s Mathews staged a series of "at homes," one-man shows in which he played all the parts, without makeup, using different voices, mannerisms, and gestures to mark the different characters. These performances influenced Dickens's methods of CHARACTERIZATION and, especially, the PUBLIC READINGS later in his career.

Matiner, Misses Two single ladies attending the ball at the Assembly Rooms in BATH, "in hope of getting a stray partner now and then." *Pickwick* (35).

Matthews Servant boy to Mr. Gregsbury, "looking as if he had slept underground from his infancy, as very likely he had" (16). *Nickleby.*

Matz, Bertram W. (1865–1925) First Honorary Secretary of the DICKENS FELLOWSHIP; editor of the *DICKENSIAN* from its inception until 1925; editor for CHAPMAN & HALL; Dickens collector, bibliographer, and commentator. He wrote, collected, and edited many books and articles on Dickens—and some on other English writers—including the National Edition of Dickens's works (1907–08) and *Miscellaneous Papers* (1908), still a useful collection of Dickens's journalistic essays. He directed the project of making Dickens's DOUGHTY STREET house a Dickens museum. The Matz Collection of Dickens materials forms an important part of the DICKENS HOUSE library.

Maunders, Old Showman remembered by Vuffin, who "had in his cottage in Spa Fields in the winter time, when the season was over, eight male and female dwarfs setting down to dinner every day, who was waited on by eight old giants in green coats, red smalls, blue cotton stockings, and high-lows." *Curiosity Shop* (19).

Mawls An "impersonal boy," a pupil at "Our School." *Reprinted.*

Maxby Pupil at "Our School," favored because one of the ushers is attracted to his sister. *Reprinted.*

Maxwell, Mrs. Guest at the Kitterbell's christening party. *Boz,* "Christening."

Mayday Friend of the Traveller whose birthday celebrations awkwardly bring together guests who do not know each other. *Uncommercial* (20).

Maylie Family Middle-class family whose house in CHERTSEY is the target of Sikes's planned robbery (22). **Mrs. Maylie**, an upright and stately woman, "dressed with the utmost nicety and precision, in a quaint mixture of by-gone costume with some slight concessions to the prevailing taste" (29), is kind and sympathetic and takes in the wounded boy (30). Years before she had rescued from poverty her adopted daughter **Rose**, now 17 and beautiful. "So mild and gentle; so pure and beautiful; that earth seemed not her element, nor its rough creatures her fit companions" (29), Rose interests herself in Oliver's story and arranges the meeting on LONDON BRIDGE that leads to Nancy's murder (46). Rose is discovered to be the sister of Agnes Fleming, Oliver's mother (50). Although she considers herself unworthy of the love of **Harry**, Mrs. Maylie's son, he prevails upon her to marry him and for her sake he gives up a career in politics to become a country parson (50). *Twist.*

Maypole Inn Inn near CHIGWELL maintained by John Willet: "an old building, with more gable ends than a lazy man would care to count on a sunny day; huge zig-zag chimneys out of which it seemed as though even smoke could not choose but come in more than naturally fantastic shapes" (1). It is sacked during the GORDON RIOTS (54). Joe and Dolly Willet restore the inn after the riots (82). *Rudge.* The King's Head at Chigwell was the model for the Maypole.

Meadows, Kenny (1790–1874) Victorian illustrator, best known for *The Heads of the People* (1838–40), a series of portraits of literary characters to accompany writings by THACKERAY, JERROLD, and others. In 1838 he also did a series of 24 woodcuts of characters from *Nickleby,* under the title "Heads from *Nicholas Nickleby.*"

Meagles Family Middle-class family from suburban London whom Clennam meets at the quarantine station in MARSEILLES (I:1). **Mr. Meagles**, a retired banker, and his **wife**, are "practical people" who have traveled extensively, collecting souvenirs from their many journeys. Back in England Clennam often visits them at their cottage in TWICKENHAM, falls secretly in love with their daughter **Minnie ("Pet")**, but gives up his interest when she is courted by Henry Gowan (I:28). Pet is pretty and spoiled (perhaps to make up for **Lillie**, her twin sister who died in childhood): "round and fresh and dimpled and spoilt, and there was in Pet an air of timidity and dependence which was the best weakness in the world, and gave her the crowning charm a girl so pretty and pleasant could have been without" (I:2). She marries Gowan (I:34), who is snobbish and contemptuous of her parents and treats her with indifference. The kind old couple are also friends to Daniel Doyce; they introduce him to Clennam and aid in his dealings with the CIRCUMLOCUTION OFFICE. They have also taken in an orphan, Harriet BEADLE ("TATTYCORAM"), but they are insensitive to her discontent. She runs away to Miss Wade (I:27), but later returns to the Meagles (II:33). Meagles and Doyce are instrumental in securing Clennam's release from the MARSHALSEA (II:34). *Dorrit.*

Kenny Meadows's portrait of Mr. Mantilini from his set of extra illustrations, "Heads from Nicholas Nickleby" *(1839).*

"Mealy Potatoes"   Nickname of one of the boys David worked with at MURDSTONE AND GRINBY's wine-bottling warehouse. His complexion "was pale or mealy" (11). *Copperfield.*

Meckier, Jerome (1941–)   Professor, University of Kentucky; critic of Victorian and modern fiction. In *Hidden Rivalries in Victorian Fiction: Dickens, Realism, and Revaluation* (1987), he pairs novels by Dickens with novels by his contemporaries, showing how the novelists compete with each other by parodying and challenging each other's work. *Innocent Abroad: Charles Dickens's American Engagements* (1990) presents a biographical and historical account of Dickens's two American journeys.

"Medicine Men of Civilisation"   The procedures of savage medicine men may seem absurd to us, but many "civilized" customs are not far removed from the absurdities of the savages. English funeral customs, for example, are especially absurd and some savage rituals might improve the way Parliament proceeds. *Uncommercial* (28). Originally in *All the Year Round* (September 26, 1863).

Medievalism   Although Dickens was a great admirer of Thomas CARLYLE and adopted his criticism of industrial England as mechanistic and soulless, he did not share Carlyle's idealization of the Middle Ages. His disdain for the medieval past is implicit in the titles he chose for the false books in his library at GAD'S HILL. Under the general title *The WISDOM OF OUR ANCESTORS,* the series included individual volumes entitled *Ignorance, Superstition, The Rack,* and *Disease.* His satiric attack in *The Chimes* on the gentleman who extols the past in terms characteristic of the Young England movement also reveals Dickens's basically progressive, liberal perspective. Dickens's most sympathetic treatment of the Victorian Medieval revival probably appears in his humorous description of Wemmick in WALWORTH (*Expectations,* 25), whose small castle in the suburbs offers a refuge from the dehumanizing life of the Victorian city.

"Meditations in Monmouth Street"   Originally published in the *MORNING CHRONICLE* (September 24, 1836) as "Sketches by Boz, New Series No. 1." At the second-hand clothing shops in MONMOUTH STREET, "the burial-place of the fashions," Boz imagines the former owners of the clothes and shoes that are for sale. In particular he constructs the life story from boyhood to death of one man whose lifetime of suits are hanging together in one of the shops. *Boz.*

Medway   Chief river in KENT; ROCHESTER and CHATHAM are located near its mouth where it joins the THAMES. Pickwick meets Dismal Jemmy on a bridge over the river in Rochester (*Pickwick,* 5). Micawber speculates on entering the Medway coal trade (*Copperfield,* 17). The Traveller visits the Chatham Dockyard on the Medway (*Uncommercial,* 26).

Meek, George   Father of the infant **Augustus George** and narrator of the sketch "Births. Mrs. Meek, of a Son." He finds his household and his relationship with his wife, **Mary Jane**, totally disrupted by the event, especially by the interference of his mother-in-law Mrs. Bigby and the nurse Mrs. Prodgit. *Reprinted.* Originally in *HOUSEHOLD WORDS* (February 22, 1851).

Melchisedech   Solicitor to whom Tulkinghorn refers Trooper George. *Bleak House* (47).

'Melia   Dr. Blimber's servant who is kind to young Paul. *Dombey* (12, 14).

Mell, Charles   Assistant schoolmaster at SALEM HOUSE; "a gaunt, sallow young man, with hollow cheeks, . . . and his hair, instead of being glossy, was rusty and dry. He was dressed in a suit of black clothes which were rather rusty and dry too, and rather short in the sleeves and legs" (5). Mell meets David at the coach when he first arrives in London; on their way to the school they visit Mell's **mother** in an almshouse, where Mell plays the flute for her (5). Mell is dismissed when Steerforth reveals that his mother is in an almshouse, a fact he has learned from David (7). Mell later becomes Dr. Mell of the Colonial Salem-House Grammar School, Port Middlebay, AUSTRALIA; he presides at the dinner for Micawber there, which is also attended by his fourth daughter, **Helena** (63). *Copperfield*.

Mellows, J. Proprietor who presides over the demise of the DOLPHIN'S HEAD, an old coaching inn thrown into disuse by the coming of the railway. *Uncommercial* (24).

Melluka, Miss Polly Tresham's name for the the doll given to her by Jackson. *Mugby*.

Meltham Insurance actuary, described by Sampson as "the most profound, the most original, and the most energetic man I have ever known connected with Life Assurance." He pursues Julius Slinkton for the murder of the girl he loved, Slinkton's niece. Disguising himself as Alfred Beckwith and Major Banks, he exposes Slinkton's poisoning schemes and saves Margaret Niner, Slinkton's other niece, from dying like her sister. After he succeeds in exposing Slinkton, Meltham dies of a broken heart. "Hunted Down."

Meltonbury Son of Lady Meltonbury who used her influence to secure himself a government job. *Miscellaneous*, "Cheap Patriotism."

Melvilleson, Miss M. "Noted syren" who sings at the SOL'S ARMS; "she has been married a year and a half, . . . and . . . her baby is clandestinely conveyed to the Sol's Arms every night to receive its natural nourishment during the entertainments." *Bleak House* (32).

Memoirs of Grimaldi These memoirs of Joseph GRIMALDI (1778–1837), the great clown of Regency PANTOMIME, were written during the last years of his life. At the request of the publisher BENTLEY, Dickens selected the most engaging parts of Grimaldi's story, changed the first-person narration to third person, and added a preface in which he described his own fascination with clowns. The *Memoirs*, "Edited by Boz" and with illustrations by CRUIKSHANK, were published in two volumes in 1838. A modern edition, edited by Richard Findlater, appeared in 1968.

"Memory" Stryver's nickname for Sydney CARTON. *Two Cities*.

"Mender of Roads" The revolutionary also known as JACQUES FIVE. *Two Cities*.

"Mercury" The Dedlocks's footman. *Bleak House* (16).

Mercy Nurse who told horror stories to the Traveller when he was a child. *Uncommercial* (15).

Merdle, Mr. and Mrs. Financier, speculator, forger and swindler, Mr. Merdle develops enterprises that engage all of England and ruin Clennam, Doyce, Pancks, and the Dorrits. "He was a reserved man, with a broad, overhanging, watchful head, . . . and a somewhat uneasy expression about his coat-cuffs, as if they were in his confidence, and had reasons for being anxious to hide his hands" (I:21). Surrounded by powerful representatives of Society, Merdle suffers from a vague complaint that his physician is unable to diagnose (I:21). After his enterprises fail, he cuts his throat in a Turkish bath (II: 25). His **wife**, a society matron, provided "a capital bosom to hang jewels upon, . . . and he bought it for the purpose" (I:21). By her first marriage she is the mother of Edmund SPARKLER, and she thwarts her son's interest in Fanny Dorrit by paying her off (I:20), but when the Dorrits come into money, she seeks out their company in ITALY. *Dorrit*. The original of Merdle was John SADLEIR.

Meriton, Henry Second mate who survives the wreck of the *Halsewell*. *Reprinted*, "Long Voyage."

Merivale, Herman Charles (1839–1906) Playwright, novelist, and contributor to ALL THE YEAR ROUND. He acted in Dickens's last theatrical effort, a production of *The Prima Donna* in London on June 2, 1870, just a week before Dickens's death. He described Dickens's active involvement as director and stage manager of the production in a letter to the *Times* (P. COLLINS, 1981).

Merrylegs Signor Jupe's performing dog. The dog disappears with its master (I:6), but later returns to the circus to die, an event Sleary takes as a sign indicating that Jupe is also dead (III:8). *Hard Times*.

Merrywinkle Gentleman whose "name is inseparably connected with his complaints." He and his delicate wife are the Couple who Coddle Themselves. *Young Couples*.

Mesheck, Aaron Jewish confidence man who is finally tracked down at the Tombs in New York City by Sergeant Dornton, who describes this adventure in his "Adventures of a Carpet Bag." *Reprinted*, "Detective Police."

Mesmerism A therapy developed by Franz Anton Mesmer (1734–1815)—also called Animal Magnetism—that involved the use of hypnotic trances to effect healing. Mesmer theorized that the process brought cosmic forces to bear on animate bodies. Dickens's friend, the physician John ELLIOTSON, was the foremost British theorist of mesmerism and the founder of its journal, *The Zooist*. During the mesmeric mania of the 1840s and '50s, Dickens practiced mesmerism on his wife and others, the most celebrated case being his attempt to cure Mrs. DE LA RUE in GENOA. Dickens's involvement with mesmerism has been thoroughly explored by Fred KAPLAN (1975).

"Mesrour" Name given to Tabby by the children engaged in the seraglio fantasy. "Haunted House."

"Message from the Sea, A" Christmas number of ALL THE YEAR ROUND, 1860. Dickens and Wilkie COLLINS wrote the first, second, and fifth chapters. The story tells of Captain Jorgan, who brings a message in a bottle to Alfred Raybrock in the fishing village of STEEPWAYS in north Devon. The message, from Alfred's brother Hugh, seems at first to interfere with Alfred's planned marriage, but eventually it restores the lost brother, clears the bride's father of a robbery charge, and facilitates the marriage. *Christmas Stories.*

"Metropolitan Protectives, The" Article for HOUSEHOLD WORDS (April 26, 1851) by W. H. WILLS and Dickens on a night they spent at a police station. They describe the various cases that come before the police, many of them involving drunkenness, and how the police deal with them. The article was intended to assure readers of the magazine that they would be well protected during the upcoming Great Exhibition. *Stone.*

Micawber Family Loosely based on the family of John and Elizabeth DICKENS, the large Micawber family increases the financial demands on **Wilkins Micawber. Mrs. Emma Micawber**, "a thin and faded lady, not at all young" (11), has married beneath her social station, but she is intensely loyal to her improvident husband, repeatedly asserting, "I never will desert Mr. Micawber!" They have six children: **Wilkins, Jr.**, who sings at public houses; **Emma**, who ultimately marries Ridger Begs of Port Middlebay, AUSTRALIA; a younger **brother** and **sister**; and a pair of **twins**. *Copperfield.*

Micawber, Wilkins One of Dickens's great comic characters. David lodges with Mr. Micawber and his family in WINDSOR TERRACE when he is sent to London to work for MURDSTONE AND GRINBY (11). "A stoutish, middle-aged person, in a brown surtout and black tights and shoes, with no more hair upon his head . . . than there is upon an egg. . . . His clothes were shabby, but he had an imposing shirt-collar on. He carried a jaunty sort of stick, with a large pair of rusty tassels to it; and a quizzing-glass hung outside his coat" (11). After Micawber is released from the MARSHALSEA, where he was imprisoned for debt (12), he and his family set out for Plymouth with the hope that some employment for him will "turn up." From there he goes to CHATHAM to explore opportunities in the coal trade, to CANTERBURY where he embarrasses David by appearing at Uriah Heep's door (17), and then back to London where Traddles becomes his lodger (27). He ultimately finds work in the office of Wickfield and Heep in Canterbury (36), where he exposes Heep's villainy (52). In gratitude, Betsey Trotwood pays his debts and enables the family to settle in AUSTRALIA (54), where Micawber rises to become District Magistrate for Port Middlebay (63). His classic advice to David, "that if a man had twenty pounds a year for income, and had spent nineteen pounds nineteen shillings and sixpence, he would be happy, but that if he spent twenty pounds one he would be miserable" (11), may have been advice given to the young Charles Dickens by his own father, on whom Micawber is said to be based. *Copperfield.*

Michael (1) Narrator of "The Poor Relation's Story," who gives an idealized account of his life and suppresses the truth of his lonely poverty. *Reprinted.*

Michael (2) One of the inhabitants of ST. GILES, observed by Inspector Field on his tour of London's criminal slums. *Reprinted*, "Inspector Field."

"Middlesex Dumpling" Prizefighter who is prevented from fighting the Suffolk Bantam by the intervention of Magistrate Nupkins. *Pickwick* (24).

Midlands Although Dickens was a Londoner and made a literary world that has come to be known as "Dickens's London," he did occasionally write about the

Mr. Micawber, by Kyd (Joseph Clayton Clarke).

Midlands, the area of England beginning roughly at BIRMINGHAM and stretching north to Lancashire and Yorkshire. In this section of Britain the INDUSTRIAL REVOLUTION emerged in the first 30 years of the 19th century, as steam power was developed to operate the machines in the textile mills, iron founderies, and the other factories that opened in MANCHESTER, Leeds, Birmingham, Sheffield, and similar Midlands towns. The Birmingham that Pickwick visits (*Pickwick*, 50) is not described as an industrial city, but Little Nell's journey through the BLACK COUNTRY is an industrial *Walpurgisnacht* (*Curiosity Shop*, 43–45). In *Bleak House*, Rouncewell's iron foundry is only a short journey to the north from CHESNEY WOLD (63). *Hard Times*, Dickens's most sustained picture of the industrial Midlands, used PRESTON and Manchester as the prototypes for COKETOWN.

Miff, Mrs.   Attendant and pew-opener in the church where Dombey is married, "a mighty dry old lady, sparely dressed, with not an inch of fulness anywhere about her." *Dombey* (31).

Miggot, Mrs.   Laundress at GRAY'S INN. *Uncommercial* (14).

Miggs, Miss   The Vardens's maid, "a tall young lady, . . . slender and shrewish, of a rather uncomfortable figure, . . . of a sharp and acid visage" (7). She slavishly follows her mistress's whims, subscribing to her fanatic Protestantism, and she seeks the attentions of Simon Tappertit, jealously attempting to distract him from Dolly Varden. She aids the rioters during the imprisonment of Dolly and Emma Haredale (71). Discharged afterward by an enlightened Mrs. Varden (80), she spends the rest of her life as a turnkey in a women's prison (82). *Rudge*.

Mike   "Gentleman with one eye, in a velveteen suit and knee-breeches," who is one of Jaggers's clients. *Expectations* (20).

Mile End   Area one mile east of the CITY of London where the toll booth for the turnpike to the northeast was located. Tony Weller muses on the lives of turnpike keepers as he passes the gate (*Pickwick*, 22). Mrs. Jellyby meets here with "a Society called the East London Branch Aid Ramification" (*Bleak House*, 14).

Miles, Bob   One of the inhabitants of Rats' Castle, a thieves den in ST. GILES. *Reprinted*, "Inspector Field."

Miles, Owen   Fourth member of Master Humphrey's circle, a rich retired merchant who is Jack Redburn's constant companion. *Humphrey*.

Milkwash, John   The Poetical Young Gentleman: "His countenance is of a plaintive and melancholy cast, his manner is abstracted and bespeaks affliction of the soul: he seldom has his hair cut, and he often talks about

being an outcast and wanting a kindred spirit." *Young Gentlemen*.

Millais, Sir John Everett (1829–1896)   Painter, one of the founders of the PRE-RAPHAELITE movement in 1848. A protégé of RUSKIN in the 1850s, his affair with Ruskin's wife, Effie, led to a scandalous divorce. He married Effie in 1855, settled in Scotland, and later in his career gave up the Pre-Raphelitism of his earlier work. Dickens attacked his controversial painting "Christ in the Carpenter's Shop" in the 1850 Royal Academy Exhibition, as "mean, odious, repulsive, and revolting" ("Old Lamps for New Ones"). Dickens objected to the lack of idealization in the painting and described the realistically depicted boy Jesus as "a hideous wry-necked, blubbery, red-headed boy." Dickens later changed his mind about Pre-Raphaelite art, and he and Millais became friends. Millais recommended FILDES to Dickens as the illustrator for *Drood*.

Millbank   Area along the north side of the THAMES between Westminster and CHELSEA. In Dickens's time much of the area was an undeveloped urban wasteland; "as oppressive, sad, and solitary by night, as any about London. There were neither wharves nor houses on the melancholy waste of road near the great blank Prison. . . . Coarse grass and rank weeds straggled over all the marshy land in the vicinity. In one part, carcases of houses, inauspiciously begun and never finished, rotted away. In another, the ground was cumbered with rusty iron monsters of steam-boilers, wheels, cranks, pipes, furnaces, paddles, anchors, diving-bells, windmill-sails, . . . accumulated by some speculator" (*Copperfield*, 47). The Millbank Penitentiary was erected between 1813 and 1821 on the site of the present Tate Gallery. Bill Barker has spent some time there for his love of handkerchiefs (*Boz*, "Cab-driver"). David and Daniel Peggotty follow Martha Endell to this stretch of the river as she contemplates suicide (*Copperfield*, 47). SMITH SQUARE, where Lizzie Hexam lives with Jenny Wren, is in the vicinity (*Mutual Friend*, II:1).

Miller   Guest at DINGLEY DELL, "a little, hard, pipstone, pippen-faced man." *Pickwick* (6, 28).

Miller, Jane Ann   Widow who negotiates the adoption of Walter Wilding from the Foundling Hospital for the Vendales. "No Thoroughfare" (4).

Miller, J. Hillis (1928–)   American scholar, critic, and literary theorist; professor, Yale and University of California, Irvine. The novels of Dickens have figured significantly in his work, which ranges broadly over English and American literature, especially of the 19th and 20th centuries. Miller's *Charles Dickens: The World of His Novels* (1958), a phenomenological study concentrating on the language and symbolism in six Dickens novels, has been one of the most influential works of modern Dickens criticism. Miller also discusses Dickens's works in *The Form of Victorian Fiction* (1968), *Charles*

Dickens and George Cruikshank (1971), and in several of the essays collected in *Victorian Subjects* (1991).

Millers   One of Belinda Pocket's nursemaids. *Expectations* (22).

Mills, John (1908–)   English actor. His Dickensian roles include Pip in David LEAN's film of *Expectations* (1946), Joe Gargery in a 1975 stage version of the same novel, Jarvis Lorry in a television adaptation of *Two Cities* (1989), and Chuffey in the BBC adaptation of *Chuzzlewit* (1994).

Mills, Julia (1)   Dora Spenlow's bosom friend and confidante who acts as an intermediary during David's courtship of Dora; "Miss Mills having been unhappy in a misplaced affection, and being understood to have retired from the world on her awful stock of experience, but still to take a calm interest in the unblighted hopes and loves of youth" (33). She is taken to India (42) and returns as the wife of "a growling old Scotch Croesus, . . . is steeped in money to the throat, and talks of nothing else" (64). *Copperfield.*

Mills, Julia (2)   Reader who has made marginal notes in the romances in the library at "Our English Watering Place." *Reprinted.*

Milnes, Richard Monckton, Lord Houghton (1809–1885)   Poet, Conservative politician, bon vivant, bibliophile, friend of Dickens. Known for his wit and repartee, he and Dickens dined at each other's houses. Dickens appreciated his support for Liberal social causes and, especially, his support of COPYRIGHT legislation.

Milvey, The Reverend Frank   Young clergyman, "expensively educated and wretchedly paid" (I:10), who arranges the adoption of young Johnny by the Boffins (I: 16), conducts the funeral service for Betty Higden (III: 9), and marries Eugene Wrayburn and Lizzie Hexam (IV:11). His wife, **Margaretta**, is "a pretty, bright little woman, something worn with anxiety, who had repressed many pretty tastes and bright fancies, and substituted in their stead schools, soup, flannel, coals, and all the week-day cares and Sunday coughs of a large population, young and old" (I:10). *Mutual Friend.*

Mim   Traveling showman who exhibits Pickleson the Giant. He sells his deaf and dumb daughter to Marigold for six pairs of braces. "Marigold."

Mincin   The Very Friendly Young Gentleman. *Young Gentlemen.*

Mincing Lane   On this street in the CITY between FENCHURCH STREET and Eastcheap, the center of the tea trade, R. W. Wilfer worked in the offices of CHICKSEY, VENEERING AND STUBBLES. *Mutual Friend* (II:8).

Minerva House   Finishing school for girls in HAMMERSMITH, run by the Misses Crumpton, where the pupils acquire "a smattering of everything and a knowledge of nothing." It has many similarities with Miss Pinkerton's Academy in THACKERAY's *Vanity Fair. Boz,* "Sentiment."

Minns, Augustus   Well-to-do bachelor, age 48 who works at SOMERSET HOUSE. He has a "love of order" and an unmingled horror of dogs and children and he spends an uncomfortable evening at the home of his cousin Octavius Budden, whose dog and child both torment him. *Boz,* "Minns."

Mirror of Parliament   Newspaper established by Dickens's uncle, John Henry BARROW, in 1828, which provided verbatim transcripts of parliamentary proceedings. Dickens joined the paper early in 1832. In the two years that he was with the *Mirror,* he developed a reputation as an outstanding parliamentary reporter and he rose to become a kind of sub-editor. He left the *Mirror* in 1834 to become a parliamentary reporter for the *MORNING CHRONICLE.*

Miscellaneous Papers   Collection of previously uncollected articles, plays, and poems by Dickens, put together by B. W. MATZ in 1908 as volumes 35 and 36 of the National Edition of Dickens's Works. It contains 21 articles from the *EXAMINER,* 1838–49; 83 articles from *HOUSEHOLD WORDS,* 1850–59; 12 articles from *ALL THE YEAR ROUND,* 1859–69; six plays; and 19 poems. Matz's collection has been expanded by later work done by Walter DEXTER for the NONESUCH EDITION, by Harry STONE, and by various other scholars who have identified other works, but Matz's remains the basic collection of Dickens's journalistic and other uncollected writings.

Misnar, the Sultan of India   This play, written by Dickens when he was a boy of nine, is the earliest work known to be by him. It was based on one of the *Tales of the Genii,* a volume of oriental tales that Dickens read as a child, but no known copy of it has survived.

"Misplaced Attachment of Mr. John Douce, The"   Originally published as "Scenes and Characters No. 5. Love and Oysters" in *BELL'S LIFE IN LONDON* (October 4, 1835), this sketch describes a steady "old boy" widower and his infatuation for a 25-year-old woman in a blue dress who sells oysters. He becomes ridiculous to his longtime male companions, has his proposal turned down by the young lady, and eventually marries his cook. *Boz.*

"Miss Evans and the Eagle"   Originally appeared in *BELL'S LIFE IN LONDON* (October 4, 1835) as "Scenes and Characters No. 2." When Miss Jemima Evans and her beau, Samuel Wilkins, spend an evening at the EAGLE, they drink a bit too much and Samuel gets into a brawl with a whiskered young man who seems to him to be paying undue attention to Jemima. *Boz.*

"Missis, Our" Ferocious and disdainful manager of the refreshment room at Mugby Junction. She operates her "model establishment" as a "constitutional check upon the public." "Mugby" (3).

Mississippi River Dickens described "the hateful Mississippi" as "an enormous ditch, sometimes two or three miles wide, running liquid mud, six miles an hour" (*Notes*, 12). He located New Eden, the hellish frontier settlement where Martin Chuzzlewit nearly dies from fever, along its banks at what is now CAIRO, ILLINOIS (*Chuzzlewit*, 23).

"Mistaken Milliner, The. A Tale of Ambition" Story of Miss Amelia Martin, a milliner with ambitions to be a singer. Her debut at the WHITE CONDUIT TAVERN, however, is a disaster. Originally published as "Scenes and Characters No. 7" in *BELL'S LIFE IN LONDON* (November 22, 1835). *Boz*.

Misty, X. X. Speaker who addresses the second meeting of the Mudfog Association on the disappearance of dancing bears from the streets of London. *Mudfog* (2).

Mith, Sergeant Detective policeman from Scotland Yard, "a smooth-faced man with a fresh bright complexion," who tells "The Butcher's Story." *Reprinted*, "Detective Police."

Mithers, Lady She, along with her **husband**, is one of Miss Mowcher's clients. *Copperfield* (22).

Mitre Inn, The At this CHATHAM inn, the boy Charles Dickens was prompted by his father to stand on the dining room table and sing duets with his sister. Charley, narrator of "The Holly-Tree," fondly remembers the Mitre from his schooldays in the town.

Mitton, Thomas (1812–1878) Early friend of Dickens. They were law clerks together in LINCOLN'S INN in 1828–29. Mitton went on to become a solicitor and represented Dickens for many years.

Mitts, Mrs. Youngest woman at TITBULL'S ALMS HOUSE, she surprises her fellow inmates by marrying a Greenwich pensioner with one arm. *Uncommercial* (29).

Mivins ("The Zephyr") A prisoner in the FLEET PRISON. *Pickwick*.

Mizzler, Marquis of, and Lord Bobby Subjects of Chuckster's gossip. He claims to have inside knowledge that the differences between them arose over a bottle of champagne and not over a pigeon pie. *Curiosity Shop* (40).

Mobbs Pupil at DOTHEBOYS HALL who cannot eat fat. *Nickleby* (8).

Moddle, Augustus Melancholy "youngest gentleman" at Todgers's. He falls in love with Mercy Pecksniff and is devastated when she marries Jonas. Charity Pecksniff overcomes his scruples, but he agrees to marry her as a man with "a blighted heart" who will always love "Another" (32). Finally, unable to go through with the wedding, he runs away to Van Dieman's Land on the day of the ceremony (54). *Chuzzlewit*.

Model, The Artist's model that the narrator meets on a THAMES steamboat. *Reprinted*, "Ghost of Art."

Molly Jaggers's maid, "a woman of about forty . . . [whose] face looked to me as if it were all disturbed by fiery air, like the faces I had seen rise out of the Witches' caldron [in *Macbeth*]" (26). Jaggers had successfully defended her in a murder case and then taken her as his maid. She has very strong and deeply scarred wrists. She turns out to be Estella's mother. *Expectations*.

Moncreiff, William T. (1794–1857) Theater manager and playwright, best known for *Tom and Jerry*. His adaptation of *Pickwick*, "Sam Weller, or the Pickwickians," performed in London in the summer of 1837, did not stage the trial scene. Instead its great moments were the EATANSWILL election and a parade at the end celebrating the coronation of Queen Victoria. In 1839, he adapted *Nickleby* as "Nicholas Nickleby and Poor Smike: the Victim of the Yorkshire School." Moncreiff, believing himself to be the adaptor of novels for the stage whom Dickens attacked in *Nickleby* (48), issued a proclamation that defended his adaptations and asserted: "Having himself *unsuccessfully* tried the drama, there is some excuse for Mr. Dickens's petulance toward its professors." He later collaborated with Henry MORLEY on an article for *HOUSEHOLD WORDS*, "The Poor Brothers of the Charterhouse" (June 12, 1852).

Monflathers, Miss Snobbish principal of a girls school who uses Nell as an example of the vulgar people associated with the waxworks. *Curiosity Shop* (29, 31).

Monied Interest English businessman in the narrator's compartment on the train from London to Paris. *Reprinted*, "Flight."

Monks The name by which Edward LEEFORD is usually known. *Twist*.

Monmouth Street An extension of St. Martin's Lane through SEVEN DIALS in west London. Dickens describes "the only true and real emporium for second-hand wearing apparel" in this street in *Boz*, "Monmouth Street."

Monod, Sylvère (1921–   ) Professor, the Sorbonne; past president of the DICKENS SOCIETY and the DICKENS FELLOWSHIP. *Dickens the Novelist* (1967), an English translation and updating of his earlier *Dickens romancier* (1953), was one of the first works to use Dickens's notes,

NUMBER PLANS, diaries, and letters to explore his methods of composition. With George FORD, Monod has also edited *Bleak House* (1977) and *Hard Times* (1980). His critical introduction to *Chuzzlewit* appeared in 1985.

Monseigneur   A powerful lord who personifies the self-indulgent and disdainful French aristocracy at the time of the FRENCH REVOLUTION (II:7). *Two Cities.*

Montage   A technique used in motion pictures of moving rapidly through a series of brief pictures or cutting between images from parallel or contrasted story lines. D. W. GRIFFITH, who pioneered the technique in film, learned the principle of montage from Dickens. EISENSTEIN, in "Dickens, Griffith, and the Film Today," analyzes scenes from *Twist*, breaking them down into their montage images, to show how this fundamental technique of moving pictures was developed by Dickens. Zambrano (*Dickens and Film*, 1977) discusses Dickens's use of montage.

Montague, Julia   Singer who performs "I am a Friar" to an enthusiastic audience at the WHITE CONDUIT. *Boz*, "Mistaken Milliner."

Montague Place   Fashionable street in BLOOMSBURY, off Russell Square, where Mr. Perker lives. *Pickwick* (47).

Montague, Tigg   Name adopted by Montague TIGG when he becomes director of the ANGLO-BENGALEE DISINTERESTED LOAN AND LIFE ASSURANCE COMPANY. *Chuzzlewit* (27).

Montague Square   Area in MARYLEBONE where Mr. Jorkins "lived by himself in a house . . . which was fearfully in want of painting." *Copperfield* (35).

Monthly Magazine, The   Journal in which Dickens's first published story, "A Dinner at Poplar Walk," appeared in the December 1833 issue. The magazine, subtitled "The British Register of Literature, Science, and Belles Lettres" and edited by Captain J. B. HOLLAND, published eight more sketches by Dickens in 1834–35, all of which were collected in *Boz*. Although the *Monthly*, with a small circulation of about 600, did not pay its contributors, it did effectively start Dickens's literary career by placing a series of his sketches in print.

Montreal   Dickens spent two weeks here on his American journey in 1842. He found the Government House superior to the one in KINGSTON and remarked on the "solidity" of the granite quays along the St. Lawrence (*Notes*, 15). Although he appreciated Canadian hospitality, he considered Rosco's Hotel here "the worst in the whole wide world." In *Notes*, he describes at length the emigrants from England and Ireland that he observed on the boat from Quebec, praising their patience, self-denial, and untiring love for their children (15).

Dickens directed three plays at the THEATRE ROYAL in Montreal, the first of his AMATEUR THEATRICALS. He took parts in all three—Morton's "A Roland for an Oliver," MATHEWS's "Past Two O'Clock in the Morning," and POOLE's "Deaf as a Post." He was especially pleased by his wife's performance in Mathews's brief interlude.

Monument, The   Column designed by Christopher Wren in 1667 commemorating the Great Fire of London in 1666. Located at the spot where the fire broke out, it stands in Fish Street, east London. John Willet recommends sitting at the top of the Monument as the best cheap entertainment in London (*Rudge*, 13). Todgers's is located nearby (*Chuzzlewit*, 8–10). Tom Pinch considers asking directions of the man in the Monument when he first arrives in London (*Chuzzlewit*, 37). The Poor Relation remembers going with Little Frank to look at the outside of the Monument ("Poor Relation's Story").

"Monument of French Folly, A"   Article for *HOUSEHOLD WORDS* (March 8, 1851), comparing the well-managed and sanitary suburban cattle markets in France with the unsanitary urban markets in London, especially SMITHFIELD. Dickens attacked the stereotypical criticisms of the French practices which those against changes in English system used to defeat reform measures. *Reprinted.*

Moon   Physician who has Our Bore treated with "strong acids, cupped, and blistered." *Reprinted*, "Bore."

Mooney   Stargazer's scientific partner, an absent-minded astronomer who can only be brought down to earth by electric shocks. Stargazer wants him to marry his daughter, but Mooney declines the opportunity. *Lamplighter.*

Moore, Thomas (1779–1852)   Popular Irish poet and songwriter of the romantic period, best known for his *Irish Melodies* (1807–35). Dickens was particularly fond of his songs, which he sang to his children and quoted frequently in the novels, especially in the snatches of poetry quoted by Dick Swiveller in *Curiosity Shop.*

Mopes   Dirty, indolent, and surly hermit visited by the Traveller, Miss Kimmeens, and the Tinker at his decayed and ruined homestead, Tom Tiddler's ground. The Traveller tries to counter his misanthropy by proving to him that men must work and depend on each other. Dickens based the character on James Lucas, the notorious Hertfordshire Hermit, who attracted many visitors, including Dickens, to the family mansion at Stevenage, where he barricaded himself away from the world outside. "Tiddler."

Mordlin, Brother   Musical member of the Brick Lane Branch of the United Grand Junction Ebenezer Temperance Association who has put the words of Dibden's "Who Hasn't Heard of a Jolly Young Waterman?" to the tune of the Old Hundredth. He justifies his adaptation by "expressing his firm persuasion that the late Mr. Dibden, seeing the errors of his former life, had written that song to show the advantages of abstinence." *Pickwick* (33).

Morfin, Mr. Assistant manager at Dombey and Son, "a cheerful-looking hazel-eyed bachelor" (13), who anonymously offers aid to John Carker (33) and eventually marries Harriet Carker. *Dombey.*

Morgan, Becky Old woman who has been buried by David; Nell overhears him and the Sexton discussing just how old she was. *Curiosity Shop* (54).

Morgan ap Kerrig Mrs. Woodcourt's eminent Welsh ancestor. "He appeared to have passed his life always getting up into mountains, and fighting somebody; and a Bard whose name sounded like Crumlinwallinwer had sung his praises, in a piece which was called, as nearly as I could catch it, Mewlinnwillinwodd." *Bleak House* (17).

Morley, Henry (1822–1894) Journalist, man of letters; professor of English, University of London; editor and staff writer for HOUSEHOLD WORDS and ALL THE YEAR ROUND. Dickens originally recruited Morley in 1850 to write some articles on sanitation; he liked Morley's work so much that he offered him a position on the staff of the magazine. During the next two decades, Morley wrote over 300 pieces for the magazines on a great variety of subjects. Dickens said that "Morley always wants a little screwing up and tightening. It's his habit to write in a loose way," but he appreciated Morley's journalistic skills in researching and putting together a story. Morley, the only university graduate on the staff, said "Dickens has great genius, but not a trained and cultivated reason."

Morley, Malcolm (1891–1966) Actor, theater manager, playwright, and theater historian. His groundbreaking series of articles on theatrical versions of Dickens's novels, published in the DICKENSIAN between 1946 and 1957, remains some of the most important work on the topic. In another series of articles in the same journal on "The Theatrical TERNANs" (1958–61), Morley told the story of the family of actors and actresses who have such importance to Dickens studies.

Mormon Agent Organizer of the expedition of Mormons from England to the Great Salt Lake: "a compactly-made handsome man in black, rather short, with rich brown hair and beard, and clear bright eyes. From his speech, I should set him down as American." *Uncommercial* (22).

Morning Chronicle, The Leading Liberal daily newspaper in the first half of the 19th century, especially under the editorship of John EASTHOPE. Dickens worked as a reporter on the paper, then under the editorship of John Black, from 1834 to 1836. He did shorthand re-

porting of Parliament when it was in session, general reporting and theater reviews during parliamentary recesses. Dickens was fond of recalling the excitement of racing about the country to get a story and then to get it into print before the LONDON TIMES. Dickens also published nine early sketches in the *Chronicle* that would later be collected in *Boz*.

Mortair Member of the Medical Section of the Mudfog Association. *Mudfog.*

Mortimer Alias used by MICAWBER to escape his creditors. *Copperfield* (34).

Mortimer, Mrs. Friend of Louisa of the Cool Couple. *Young Couples.*

Mould Undertaker who buries Anthony Chuzzlewit and recommends Mrs. Gamp for the laying-out of the body (19); "a little elderly gentleman, bald, and in a suit of black, . . . [with] a face in which a queer attempt at melancholy was at odds with a smirk of satisfaction" (19). His **wife** and **two daughters** are "so round and chubby . . . that they might have been the bodies once belonging to the angels' faces in the shop below" (25). *Chuzzlewit.*

Mount Pleasant "Ill-favored and ill-savoured neighborhood" in east London where the Smallweeds live. *Bleak House* (21).

Mourning Coach-Horse Inn House-of-call for undertakers in the CITY where Nadgett pursues his investigation into the death of Anthony Chuzzlewit. *Chuzzlewit* (38).

Mowcher, Miss Dwarf hairdresser and manicurist who includes Steerforth among her fashionable clients; "a pursy dwarf, of about forty or forty-five, with a very large head and face, a pair of roguish grey eyes, and such extremely little arms, that, to enable herself to lay a finger archly against her snub nose as she ogled Steerforth, she was obliged to meet the finger half-way, and lay her nose against it" (22). She repeatedly exclaims, "Ain't I volatile?" Although, when she first enters the novel, she appears to be someone who will aid Steerforth in his seduction of Em'ly (22), she is outraged when she hears of it and offers to help Dan'l Peggotty in his search for his niece (32). She captures Littimer as he is trying to escape to AMERICA (61). *Copperfield.* The apparent change in Miss Mowcher's character was prompted by the objections of Mrs. Jane Seymour HILL, a dwarf chiropodist who complained to Dickens after the initial appearance of the character.

"M. R. F." Initials standing for My Respected Father, Eugene Wrayburn's sobriquet for his father. *Mutual Friend* (I:12).

"Mr. Barlow" The Traveller remembers his childhood tutor as someone who has blighted his life, a pedantic "instructive monomaniac" like the tutor Barlow in *Sanford and Merton*, a popular didactic work for children. Every time he is lectured at, instructed rather than entertained, or talked down to by a condescending letter writer, the narrator remembers the boring Mr. Barlow. *Uncommercial* (34). Originally in *All the Year Round* (January 16, 1869).

"Mr. Bendigo Buster on Our National Defences against Education" Satiric article for *HOUSEHOLD WORDS* (December 28, 1850) by Henry MORLEY and Dickens in which an old boxer, Bendigo Buster, describes the German educational system and warns his English readers, particularly those of the misguided journal for which he is writing the article, of the demoralizing effects of education. Do not follow the Germans, he counsels; stand with Turkey, Russia, Spain, Portugal, and southern Italy, which, like Britain, do not educate their children. *Stone*.

"Mr. Bob Sawyer's Party" One of Dickens's two PUBLIC READINGS from *Pickwick*. (The other was the Bardell v. Pickwick trial.) This reading was based on chapter 32 of the novel and was one of the most effective and popular of the comic pieces he performed.

"Mr. Booley's View of the Last Lord Mayor's Show" An allegorical interpretation of the LORD MAYOR's parade by Dickens's representative Englishman, the retired gentleman from ISLINGTON. From *HOUSEHOLD WORDS* (November 30, 1850). *Miscellaneous*.

"Mr. Bull's Somnambulist" Political satire on the Crimean conflict for *HOUSEHOLD WORDS* (November 25, 1854), in which Mr. Bull's household is afflicted with the somnambulism of its housekeeper Abby Dean (Lord Aberdeen, prime minister at the time). Her condition causes her to do nothing and to allow Bull's mortal enemy Nick (Russia) to steal a Turkey. *Miscellaneous*.

"Mr. Chops the Dwarf" PUBLIC READING based on "Going into Society," Dickens's Christmas story for *HOUSEHOLD WORDS*, 1858. Although he prepared the reading text in 1861, he did not perform it until 1868, and then only rarely.

Mr. F's Aunt The legacy left to Flora Finching by her deceased husband. See AUNT, MR. F.'S.

"Mr. Minns and his Cousin" Dickens's first published story. Under the title "A DINNER AT POPLAR WALK" this story appeared in the *MONTHLY MAGAZINE*, December 1833. It tells of Octavius Budden's unsuccessful attempt to curry favor with his well-to-do cousin Augustus Minns by inviting him to dinner. But Minns, who has an "unmingled horror" of children and dogs, is assaulted by both on the occasion and does not include the Buddens or their son in his will. *Boz*.

Mr. Nightingale's Diary One-act farce written by Dickens and Mark LEMON in 1851. The hypochondriacal Mr. Nightingale is saved from Slap's schemes to defraud him of his money by Gabblewig and Rosina Nightingale, who foil Slap by assuming various disguises. They are rewarded for their efforts when Nightingale blesses their marriage. *Miscellaneous*.

"Mr. Pickwick's Tale" Story told to Master Humphrey by Mr. Pickwick. John Podgers, a well-to-do burger of Windsor during the reign of James I, is asked to watch through the night for some witches who have been disturbing citizens in the neighboring town of KINGSTON. He turns down the opportunity, but his brash young nephew, Will Marks, accepts and becomes involved in a Cavalier intrigue to transport the body of a hanged cavalier from Kingston to the church of ST. DUNSTAN in London. After his secret mission, he tells the citizens of Kingston of his wild adventure with witches. *Humphrey*.

"Mr. Robert Bolton—the 'gentleman connected with the press' " At a gathering of the regulars at the GREEN DRAGON, Robert Bolton, a shorthand writer for the press, tells the story of Sawyer, a brutal baker who killed his son by boiling him in a laundry kettle. First published in *BENTLEY'S MISCELLANY* (August 1838). *Mudfog*.

"Mrs. Gamp" Dickens's PUBLIC READING from *Martin Chuzzlewit*, first performed in 1858. Although Mrs. Gamp was one of Dickens's most popular characters, he had difficulty developing a suitable text for the reading and this piece underwent more revision than any other in his repertory. Still, it was a mixed success. His portrayal of Mrs. Gamp was generally applauded, but Betsey Prig and Pecksniff were regarded as disappointing.

"Mrs. Joseph Porter" The second story published by Dickens, this sketch first appeared as "Mrs. Joseph Porter, 'Over the Way' " in the *MONTHLY MAGAZINE*, January 1834. It tells of the Gattleton's amateur production of *Othello*, which is disrupted by Mrs. Porter, their jealous and sarcastic neighbor. She encourages Tom Balderstone, who knows Shakespeare by heart, to disrupt the performance with unnecessary promptings, so that she can declare the evening "a complete failure." *Boz*.

"Mrs. Lirriper's Legacy" Christmas number of *ALL THE YEAR ROUND*, 1864, continuing the story of "Mrs. Lirriper's Lodgings." (1) In her opening monologue, Mrs. Lirriper tells of Major Jackman's friendship with Jemmy and of the model train they made together; of Joshua Lirriper, her husband's younger brother, a victim of drink and debt; of taking in Mr.

Buffle, the tax collector, and his family after their house burned down; of saving a grateful Mrs. Wozenham from bankruptcy; and of traveling to Sens, France, to learn the identity of a dying Englishman who has left her a small legacy. There they find Mr. Edson, Jemmy's father, on his deathbed. (2) In the final chapter, Jemmy, who does not know that the dying man is the father who abandoned him, makes up an idealized account of the man's life. *Christmas Stories*.

"Mrs. Lirriper's Lodgings"   Christmas number of ALL THE YEAR ROUND, 1863. Dickens wrote the first chapter, (1) in which Mrs. Lirriper tells of her 38 years as a lodging-house keeper, of the servants she has employed, and of her adopted son, Jemmy, whose mother died shortly after giving birth to him in the lodging house. She and her parlor boarder, Major Jackman, raised the boy. In the second and final chapter, also by Dickens, Jackman tells of Jemmy's achievements and retells Jemmy's story, the boy's fictional account of his life. *Christmas Stories*.

Mudberry, Mrs.   Neighbor "which kept a mangle" and informed Susannah Sanders that Pickwick would marry Mrs. Bardell. *Pickwick* (34).

Muddlebrains   Member of the Zoology Section of the Mudfog Association. *Mudfog*.

Mudfog   "A pleasant town" in a hollow by the river, "from which river Mudfog derives an agreeable scent of pitch, tar, coals, and rope-yarn, a roving population in oilskin hats, a pretty steady influx of drunken bargmen, and a great many other maritime advantages" ("Tulrumble"). The setting for several of Dickens's early sketches, it is based on CHATHAM. *Mudfog*.

Mudfog Association for the Advancement of Everything   Dickens's satirical version in BENTLEY'S MISCELLANY of the British Association for the Advancement of Science, an organization founded in 1831, with sections devoted to many scientific specialties. Dickens included two reports of the Mudfog Association in the magazine. Collected in *Mudfog*.

Mudfog Papers, The   Collection of Dickens's early sketches from BENTLEY'S MISCELLANY, 1837–38, published by Richard BENTLEY in 1880. The collection included "The PUBLIC LIFE OF MR. TULRUMBLE," "FULL REPORT OF THE FIRST MEETING OF THE MUDFOG ASSOCIATION . . . ," "FULL REPORT OF THE SECOND MEETING . . . ," "the PANTOMIME OF LIFE," "SOME PARTICULARS ABOUT A LION," and "MR. ROBERT BOLTON." Later editions also included "FAMILIAR EPISTLE FROM A PARENT TO A CHILD."

Mudge, Jonas   Secretary of the Brick Lane Branch of the United Grand Junction Ebenezer Temperance Association, "an enthusiastic and disinterested vessel, who sold tea to the members." *Pickwick* (33).

Mudie's Circulating Library   Chief circulating library in Victorian England, started in 1842 when Charles Mudie (1818–90) began lending books from his stationer's shop in London. For an annual fee of a guinea, his clients could obtain a year's subscription. Mudie encouraged the publication of novels in a three-volume format because this allowed three readers to read the same book simultaneously; he also screened the content of the novels and excluded those that might bring a blush to the cheek of the Young Person. By the 1860s, Mudie's influence on the publishing industry was so great that the three-volume format was nearly universal. Dickens, whose works appeared in serial numbers followed by a single-volume publication and whose subject matter was considered "vulgar" by some Victorian readers, did not conform to the library's standard format, so his novels were not among the "best renters" on Mudie's lists. Toward the end of his career, Dickens made more concessions to the libraries: *Great Expectations* fit exactly the three-volume format; *Mutual Friend* and *Drood* were also circulated by Mudie's. Although Mudie's Library continued in business until 1937, the three-volume format was discontinued in the 1890s.

Muff, Professor   Member of the Medical Section of the Mudfog Association, a hard drinker who claims that infinitesimal doses of drugs are just as effective as regular doses. *Mudfog*.

"Mugby Junction"   Christmas number of ALL THE YEAR ROUND, 1866. Dickens wrote the first four chapters. (1) "Barbox Brothers" tells of Young Jackson, who has just retired as the head of Barbox Brothers, a notary and bill-brokering firm. On an unplanned journey to Mugby Junction, he meets Lamps, a porter at the station who makes up songs for his invalid daughter Phoebe. Lamps becomes a guiding spirit for Jackson. (2) In "Barbox Brothers and Co." Jackson, also known as "Barbox Brothers," considers which of the seven train lines to take out of Mugby. Phoebe advises him to take the one to the city. There, on his birthday, he meets Polly, the daughter of Tresham, a friend from his young manhood who ran off with Beatrice, the one woman Jackson loved. He forgives them and returns to settle at Mugby Junction. (3) "Main Line: The Boy at Mugby" is narrated by Ezekiel, the boy from the refreshment room at Mugby Station, where inedible food is served and the customers are treated with contempt. Our Missus, who manages the operation, goes to France and returns to tell of the "despicable" practices in French refreshment rooms which serve edible food at moderate prices with polite service. (4) "No. 1 Branch Line: The Signal-man," the last of Dickens's contributions, is a ghost story. The narrator visits a signalman in an isolated cutting along the railway and learns that the man is troubled by an apparition that has appeared twice under his warning light. Tragedies followed both appearances. After the apparition appears for a third time, the narrator learns that the signalman has been killed by an engine. *Christmas Stories*. Four other chapters were contributed by other writers.

Mugby Junction Train station where the newly retired Young Jackson starts a new life by choosing to take one of the seven lines leading from the junction. "Mugby." Mugby is based on Rugby in Warwickshire.

Muggs, Sir Alfred Friend of Cornelius Brook Dingwall who recommends the Misses Crumpton's school to him. *Boz*, "Sentiment."

Mull, Professor Member of the Mudfog Association. *Mudfog*.

Mullins, Jack A regular at the SIX JOLLY FELLOW-SHIP PORTERS. *Mutual Friend*.

Mullion, John Brave member of the crew of the *Golden Mary*.

Mullit, Professor American professor of education that Martin meets at Pawkins's Boarding House. He writes pamphlets under the pseudonym "Suturb" (Brutus reversed). *Chuzzlewit* (16).

Muntle Mr. MANTALINI's real name. *Nickleby*.

"Murdered Person, The" Article for *HOUSEHOLD WORDS* (October 11, 1856), criticizing the public sympathy for the murderer and the lack of concern for the victim, even to the extent of blaming the victim. Dickens begins with the case of Mr. Dove, a penitent "pet prisoner," whose self-justifying statements reveal no remorse for the wife he killed. Similarly, those who support strict divorce and Sunday closing laws ignore the victims who suffer or are driven to crime by these constraining laws. Dickens develops this theme again in "FIVE NEW POINTS OF CRIMINAL LAW," in which he suggests that the underlying principle behind the points is "that the offender is the Murdered Person." *Miscellaneous*.

Murderer, Captain Protagonist of one of the tales told to the Traveller by his nurse. A serial killer who bakes his brides into meat pies, the Captain is eventually foiled by a dark twin who avenges her sister's death by taking poison just before she is killed and cooked into a pie. *Uncommercial* (15).

"Murderous Extremes" Article for *HOUSEHOLD WORDS* (January 3, 1857), lamenting the failure of bystanders to stop a murder in progress and suggesting that such passivity is the result of the public being told not to take the law into their own hands and that to do so is to risk being accused of interfering with the rights of the criminal. *Miscellaneous*.

Murdstone, Edward and Jane Brother and sister whose surname suggests the killing effect they have on the Copperfield family. **Edward**, second husband of Clara Copperfield, is described thus:

> He had that kind of shallow black eye . . . which, when it is abstracted, seems from some peculiarity of light, to be disfigured, for a moment at a time, by a cast. . . . His hair and whiskers were blacker and thicker, looked at so near, than even I had given them credit for being. A squareness about the lower part of his face, and the dotted indication of the strong black beard he shaved close every day, reminded me of the waxwork that had travelled into our neighbourhood some half-a-year before. This, his regular eyebrows, and the rich white, and black, and brown, of his complexion—confound his complexion, and his memory!—made me think him, in spite of my misgivings, a very handsome man (2).

After marrying David's mother, Murdstone installs his sister, **Jane**, as housekeeper to manage the household with "firmness":

> Like her brother, whom she greatly resembled in face and voice; and with very heavy eyebrows, . . . she brought with her two uncompromising hard black boxes, with her initials on the lids in hard brass nails. When she paid the coachman she took her money out of a hard steel purse, and she kept the purse in a very jail of a bag which hung upon her arm by a heavy chain, and shut up like a bite (4).

When David's instinctive dislike becomes active resistance to the Murdstone regime (4), Murdstone sends him to SALEM HOUSE school (5), and later, after his mother's death, to work at MURDSTONE AND GRINBY's wine bottling warehouse (10). Murdstone offers to take back David "unconditionally" from Betsey Trotwood and is refused (14). He later marries again and again breaks his wife's spirit (59). Jane Murdstone reenters David's life as Dora Spenlow's companion (26); she discovers David's letters to Dora and informs Mr. Spenlow of them (33). *Copperfield*.

Murdstone and Grinby Wine-bottling business partly owned by Murdstone, where David is sent to work after his mother's death (10–11). David describes the "secret agony of [his] soul" when he is reduced to the menial labor of pasting labels on wine bottles in the company of working-class boys from the streets of London (11). *Copperfield*. This traumatic episode in David's life is based on the most painful episode in Dickens's own childhood, when he was sent to work at WARREN'S BLACKING while his father was imprisoned for debt in the MARSHALSEA.

Murgatroyd A regular at the Green Dragon, an undertaker. "Bolton."

Murray, Eustace Clare Grenville (1824–1881) Journalist and novelist; member of the British diplomatic service; illegitimate son of Richard Grenville, second Duke of Buckingham and Chandos. He wrote many articles for *HOUSEHOLD WORDS* and *ALL THE YEAR ROUND,* most of them as "The Roving Englishman," describing foreign scenes and events while he was in the diplomatic service. He characterized Dickens as "one of the greatest and kindliest public teachers England has ever known."

Mutanhed, Lord   The "richest young man in Ba-ath . . . the one with the long hair, and the particularly small forehead." *Pickwick* (35).

Mutton Hill   The back door to Mr. Fang's police court led out of this street (also known as Mutton Lane), running between HATTON GARDEN and CLERKENWELL GREEN. *Twist* (11).

Mutuel, Monsieur   "A spectacled, snuffy, stooping old gentleman" with a "walnut-shell countenance" who is a friend of Madame Bouclet and is pleased by Langley's generous act in adopting Bebelle. "Somebody's Luggage."

Muzzle   Mr. Nupkin's "undersized footman, with a long body, and short legs." *Pickwick* (24, 25, 39).

"My Mahogany Friend"   Article for *HOUSEHOLD WORDS* (March 8, 1851), by Mary BOYLE, considerably reworked by Dickens. It tells of life at the Chase, the old house near the narrator's "Den," which the narrator gleans from a mahogany hat rack. *Stone.*

"My Uncle"   Article for *HOUSEHOLD WORDS* (December 6, 1851) by W. H. WILLS and Dickens, describing the pawnbroker and the people who patronize his business, a fuller and more sympathetic picture than that in *Boz,* "Pawnbroker's Shop." *Stone.*

Mystery of Edwin Drood, The   Dickens's 15th novel, left unfinished at the time of his death in June 1870, when he had nearly completed six of the projected 12 monthly parts. The six parts were published from April to September 1870 by CHAPMAN & HALL, with illustrations by FILDES. Charles COLLINS provided the cover illustration for the monthly numbers. Published in one volume, 1870. Although most of the commentary has attempted to explain how Dickens would have finished the novel, *Drood* can also be read as the culmination of themes and motifs in his earlier works.

SYNOPSIS

Part 1 (April 1870)
(1) At dawn three men lie in an opium den run by an old woman in the East End of London. John Jasper awakens from a drug-induced stupor and from incoherent Oriental visions. He checks his wretched companions and, satisfied that their mutterings are "unintelligible,"

In London, A Pilgrimage *(1872), Gustave Doré connected this woodcut of an opium den with the opening scene in* Edwin Drood.

places some money on a table and leaves. That afternoon he arrives late for the cathedral service, puts on his choir robe, and joins the procession as the words "Where the Wicked Man . . ." are intoned in the sanctuary.

(2) The Reverend Septimus Crisparkle worries that Jasper, music master and Lay Precentor of Cloisterham Cathedral, is ill. Jasper assures him that it is nothing, but he confides to his nephew, Edwin Drood, a young man nearly as old as his uncle, that "the cramped monotony of [his] existence grinds [him] away by the grain" and he has been taking opium. At dinner Jasper and Drood toast "Pussy," Jasper's music student and Drood's fiancée, whose picture hangs over the fireplace in Jasper's rooms. (3) The next day Edwin visits Pussy, whose real name is Rosa Bud, at Miss Twinkleton's School. Pretty, spoiled, and wilful, she is uncomfortable with her position as an "engaged orphan," bequeathed to marry Edwin in her father's will. Had they not been willed to each other, she says, they might have been friends. As it is, they try each other. She is not really interested in his career as an engineer or in going with him to Egypt to engage in developing an undeveloped country.

(4) Thomas Sapsea, a pompous, conceited auctioneer, invites Jasper to comment on the epitaph he has written

for his wife's tomb. It celebrates the way she "looked up to him" and admonishes those who read it to "with a blush retire" if they cannot do likewise. Jasper finds the epitaph "striking characteristic, and complete." Durdles, the maker of tombstones, measures the inscription for size and asserts, "It'll come in to an eighth of an inch." He takes the key to the Sapsea tomb and goes off to contemplate his carving. (5) On his way home, Jasper comes upon Durdles in the churchyard and asks him how he discovers forgotten tombs. Durdles taps with his hammer, demonstrating the different sounds by which he can distinguish the contents of the tombs. Back at his gatehouse rooms at midnight, Jasper fills a pipe with opium before going to bed.

Part 2 (May, 1870)
(6) The Reverend Luke Honeythunder, a large and over-bearing philanthropist, brings to Cloisterham his two wards, the twins Neville and Helena Landless. Septimus Crisparkle has his mother arrange a dinner in honor of their arrival, but Honeythunder dominates the conversation and all the guests are glad to see him return to London. (7) Neville tells Crisparkle, his tutor, of his unhappy childhood in Ceylon. Orphaned as children, he and Helena were abused by their stepfather and they tried several times to run away. Neville became "secret and revengeful," hating his stepfather to the point of wanting to kill him; Helena developed courage and resourcefulness, disguising herself as a boy and acting without fear. Neville asks Crisparkle to bear with them and help them. When Neville and his tutor return to the drawing room, Rosa is singing to Jasper's accompaniment. Suddenly she breaks off, saying she cannot continue. Later she tells Helena that she feels assaulted by Jasper and is afraid of him. (8) After escorting Rosa and Helena back to Miss Twinkleton's school, Edwin and Neville quarrel over Rosa. Jasper joins them just as they are about to come to blows. Although he separates them, he also encourages their dispute and the quarrel breaks out again over Rosa's picture when they get to Jasper's rooms. Neville throws the dregs of his wine at Edwin, tells him that he might appreciate Rosa properly had he known some hardships, and then leaves abruptly. The next day, after Edwin has left Cloisterham, Jasper reports to Crisparkle that the two are "murderous" toward each other. (9) Rosa's guardian, Mr. Grewgious, tells her that she is not bound by the will to marry Edwin. Rosa seems relieved, but indicates no unwillingness to go on with the wedding. She asks Grewgious to come back at Christmas when Edwin will again be in Cloisterham so that they can discuss their marriage plans with him.

Part 3 (June 1870)
(10) Crisparkle urges Neville to apologize for his behavior toward Drood. Neville is reluctant. Meanwhile Crisparkle gets Jasper to elicit an apology from Drood. Edwin writes asking Jasper to arrange a Christmas Eve dinner with Landless where the differences can be forgiven and forgotten.

(11) Meanwhile, Edwin goes to Grewgious's rooms in STAPLE INN on a foggy evening to ask if he can take any communication to Rosa when he goes to Cloisterham. Grewgious tells him that there can be "no coolness, no lassitude, no doubt, no indifference . . . in a real lover," and gives him a diamond and ruby ring that belonged to Rosa's mother. The ring was left for Rosa should she and Edwin marry. The ring makes Edwin consider just how serious his love for Rosa is.

(12) Jasper has arranged to visit the crypts under the cathedral with Durdles. He brings a bottle of liquor, gives it to Durdles, and the tombstone carver gradually beomes drunk. By the end of their tour, Durdles has fallen asleep in the crypt. He dreams that he hears Jasper's footsteps fading in the distance and the clink of a key falling from his hand. When Durdles awakens at two A.M., Jasper is gone and the key to the crypt is on the ground.

Part 4 (July 1870)
(13) Edwin comes to Cloisterham for Christmas. His conscience has been pricked by Grewgious and he intends to speak earnestly to Rosa. She too has been thinking about their relationship, and proposes that they be brother and sister to each other rather than lovers. He accepts her suggestion and thinks better of telling her about the ring.

(14) On Christmas Eve, Neville prepares for a solitary walking tour. He has purchased boots and a heavy iron-wood walking stick. He is uneasy about the dinner that evening at Jasper's house where he will meet Edwin again. Edwin spends a solitary day, thinking about what to tell Grewgious, whom he will ask to inform Jasper of the broken engagement. At dusk he meets an old woman in the street who begs money for opium. She tells him that someone named Ned is in danger. Jasper, meanwhile, spends the day preparing for his dinner guests.

On Christmas morning Jasper comes to the cathedral, where workmen are inspecting damage from the storm during the night. He is looking for Edwin, who went out with Landless during the storm and did not return. Neville has already set out on his trek. (15) As he is walking down a cart track several miles from Cloisterham, Neville sees eight men following him. He allows four to pass, but the other four follow behind. Without explaining the reason, they surround and apprehend him. When they are joined by Crisparkle and Jasper, Neville learns that Edwin is missing and that he was the last person known to see him alive. Neville claims that Edwin returned to Jasper's gatehouse; Crisparkle believes him, but Jasper suspects him of murdering Drood. As crews drag the river, searching for a body, Grewgious tells Jasper that Edwin and Rosa have decided not to marry. Jasper turns white and collapses. (16) When Edwin's body is not found, Jasper thinks Edwin may have gone away to avoid embarrassment over his change of plans, but when Crisparkle finds Edwin's watch and shirt pin by Cloisterham Wier, Jasper is convinced that Edwin has been murdered. There is insufficient evidence to hold Neville, but he remains the primary suspect in the crime. He leaves Cloisterham and goes to London.

Part 5 (August 1870)

(17) Mr. Honeythunder annoys Crisparkle by judging Neville guilty, giving up his guardianship of the boy, and condemning Neville's defenders. At Staple Inn, where Neville has taken a room, Crisparkle visits Grewgious, who keeps an eye on Neville. Grewgious tells him that Jasper has been lingering outside the inn.

(18) A stranger, Dick Datchery, appears in Cloisterham, rents rooms from Mrs. Tope next to Jasper's Gatehouse, and goes on a tour of the cathedral with Mayor Sapsea. He takes particular interest in the disappearance of Edwin Drood.

(19) Six months after Drood's disappearance, Jasper calls on Rosa for the first time. They are both dressed in mourning, for they have given up hope of Edwin's return. Rosa tells Jasper that she does not plan to begin music lessons with him again. He tells her, vehemently and repeatedly, that he loves her and implies that no one else can admire her and live. After he leaves, Rosa faints.

(20) When she regains consciousness, Rosa flees to London, where Grewgious takes care of her. Helena Landless has also come to London and Grewgious arranges a meeting between the two girls in the rooms of Lieutenant Tartar, Neville's neighbor at Staple Inn.

Part 6 (September 1870)

(21) Grewgious takes lodgings for Rosa with Mrs. Billican and asks Miss Twinkleton to come to London and act as her chaperone.

(22) Jasper spends the night in the opium den, where the old woman guides his fantasies and prompts him to speak during his opium trance. At dawn she shadows him as he leaves, following him to Cloisterham and his gatehouse. There she learns his identity from Datchery. The next morning, she attends the service in the cathedral and, from the shadows behind a pillar, she shakes her fist at him.

The manuscript, unfinished, ends here.

COMMENTARY

Dickens began *Drood*, his last novel, in the spring of 1870, four and a half years after he completed *Mutual Friend*. This is the longest gap between any two books in Dickens's career, a sign perhaps of his failing health and of his intense involvement with the PUBLIC READINGS during the final years of his life. He planned the new novel for only 12 monthly numbers, about two-thirds the length of his usual monthly serials, but he completed only half of them. When he died on June 9, 1870, he was working on the final pages of the sixth number.

He was excited by his idea for the book, telling John FORSTER that it was "not a communicable idea (or the interest in the book would be gone), but a very strong one, though difficult to work." The difficulties arose from the first number, which he underwrote by 12 pages. He remedied the shortfall by pulling a chapter from the second number and including it in the first. His notes for the novel also indicate that he had difficulty following his plan in later numbers and introduced several episodes earlier than he expected to. Though most of his original readers were not aware of these difficulties as they read the story, Wilkie COLLINS, in a harsh judgment of the book, described it as "Dickens's last laboured effort, the melancholy effort of a worn-out brain."

Collins may have been reacting to Dickens's subject matter, which, with its Oriental themes, opium trances, and mystery genre, seemed to be challenging Collins's own novel, *The Moonstone*, which had completed its serial run in ALL THE YEAR ROUND in 1868. Many of the commentators who have attempted to suggest the ways in which Dickens planned to complete the novel assume that the book was to be more on the order of a Collins mystery thriller than like Dickens's own earlier works. Dickens's initial inspiration, however, sounds a lot like the idea for some of his own earlier novels: "Two people, boy and girl, or very young, going apart from one another, pledged to be married after many years—at the end of the book. The interest to arise out of the tracing of their separate ways, and the impossibility of telling what will be done with that impending fate." Although Dickens dropped this plan or transformed it into the story of Rosa and Edwin, there is in their arranged relationship echoes of John Harmon and Bella Wilfer's arranged marriage (*Mutual Friend*) and of Pip's expectations for his marriage to Estella (*Expectations*).

In many ways *Drood* reminds its readers of Dickens's earlier novels. The intriguing opening chapter with its contrast between the opium den in London and the cathedral in Cloisterham recalls the contrast between city and country in *Bleak House* and the opposition of the private and public spheres in that novel's two narratives. In *Drood* the opium den may have connections to the Orient, but its primary function seems to be to represent the repressed inner world of Jasper, so different from his respectable outer appearance as the choir master of the cathedral, a contrast not unlike that between Bradley Headstone's controlled and mechanical respectability as schoolmaster and his passionate and murderous suppressed self. The cathedral is a projection of one side of Jasper's character; it also represents a way of life that has often been compared to the ecclesiastical world of Anthony TROLLOPE's Barsetshire novels. But Dickens is not concerned with the politics of Cloisterham or with the ways in which worldly concerns impact the religious community. He is more interested in the ways religious mysteries attempt to explain the human situation and the presence of evil in the world. *Drood* is closer to the world of Graham GREENE than that of Trollope.

The cathedral and the opium den act as the symbolic center in *Drood*, as the MARSHALSEA does in *Dorrit* or the dustheaps and the river in *Our Mutual Friend*. The DOUBLES in the novel also continue one of Dickens's repeated motifs. Like Sydney Carton, Harmon/Rokesmith, or Pip, who is both blacksmith and gentleman, Jasper is a divided figure whose separate lives are part of his mystery. This doubling in the central character is echoed in the Landless twins and, in comic parody, in Miss Twinkleton, who is described as having "two distinct and separate phases of being" (3).

What Dickens planned to make of these materials has been a matter of considerable dispute. The commentators can be broadly placed into two camps. The first group argues that *Drood* was to be a novel like Dickens's earlier ones, relating private and public realms; finding parallels in the domestic sphere to the larger public world. His interest was not so much in the mystery or the murder at the heart of his story as in the psychology of the characters involved in it, particularly John Jasper, who would be presented from the inside as a portrait of a murderer. The other school looks at *Drood* as something new in the Dickens canon, a mystery thriller in the manner of Collins, relying on a sensational plot with surprising turns at the end of the story. Adherents to this group often read the novel as if it were by Agatha Christie, looking for details in the text that provide clues to the surprises Dickens had planned. Several key questions have focused much of the discussion: What, exactly, is the central "mystery" in *Edwin Drood*? Is it Drood's disappearance, the identity of his presumed killer, or something about Jasper and his connection with Princess Puffer? What role was the ring that Grewgious gave to Edwin to play in the unraveling of the mystery? How would Durdles and his knowledge of the tombs underneath the Cathedral figure in the story? Who are the Landless twins and why are they in Cloisterham? Is Datchery a new character—perhaps a detective come to Cloisterham to solve the mystery of Edwin's disappearance—or is he one of the other characters in disguise, as his mismatched hair and eyebrows suggest?

Besides the text itself, literary detectives have the illustrations by Fildes and Collins to work from; reports of Dickens's intent from the illustrators, his family, and Forster; a fragment, known as "The Sapsea Fragment," that may have been planned for a future number, but was probably a discarded passage from the existing text; Dickens's other works; and numerous contemporary works by other authors that provide parallels to *Drood* or offer suggestions for interpreting Dickens's intentions. Forster (1872) offers the most clues:

> The story, was to be that of a murder of a nephew by his uncle; the originality of which was to consist in the review of the murderer's career by himself at the close, when its temptations were to be dwelt upon as if, not he the culprit, but some other man, were the tempted. The last chapters were to be written in the condemned cell, to which his wickedness, all elaborately elicited from him as if told to another, had brought him. Discovery by the murderer of the utter needlessness of the murder for its object, was to follow hard upon commission of the deed; but all discovery of the murderer was to be baffled till towards the close, when, by means of a gold ring which had resisted the corrosive effects of the lime into which he had thrown the body, not only the person murdered was to be identified but the locality of the crime and the man who committed it. . . . Rosa was to marry Tartar,

and Crisparkle the sister of Landless, who was himself, I think, to have perished in assisting Tartar finally to unmask and seize the murderer.

Forster's account is consistent with the existing text and with Dickens's usual interest in the psychology of the characters rather than in the elaborations of plot. His account identifies Edwin as the victim and Jasper as the murderer, the most probable directions suggested in the existing text. The very probability of Forster's solution disappoints those who want more mystery or who expect the story to turn upon unexpected events, but such surprises would not be characteristic of an author who "solved" the Harmon murder halfway through *Mutual Friend* and who was more interested in Headstone's criminality than his crime.

Forster's account makes Jasper the puzzling center of the story and commentators have wondered just what sort of man this murderer would reveal himself to be in his final meditations in the condemned cell. Is he a consciously malevolent man who conceals his villainy behind a mask of clerical respectability? A passionately out-of-control man insanely jealous of Edwin's relationship with Rosa? A person who must control others and who uses the powers of drugs and hypnotism to do so? A killer with ties to the Oriental cult of Kali who has a mission to murder Edwin? A man so deeply divided within himself that the respectable choir master is not even aware of the murderous activities of the opium addict? Commentators have advanced all of these interpretations to explain his character.

Clearly Jasper is a kind of Jekyll/Hyde figure. Both sides of his character appear in the opening chapter, where his murderous visions in London are countered by his singing later the same day in the cathedral service. The narrator's description of the doubleness in Miss Twinkleton's character may provide some important clues to understanding Jasper: "As, in some cases of drunkenness, and in others of animal magnetism, there are two states of consciousness which never clash, but each of which pursues its separate course as though it were continuous instead of broken (thus, if I hide my watch when I am drunk, I must be drunk again before I can remember where), so Miss Twinkleton has two distinct and separate phases of being" (3). Jasper the opium addict may be a totally separate person from the choir master; his murderous side may be unaware of his loving side that dotes on Edwin and later actively seeks to discover his nephew's murderer. Jasper is clearly subject to spells of drugged drunkenness and seems to be practicing animal magnetism when he frightens Rosa at the piano (7) and when he "suggests" to Crisparkle the location of Edwin's watch (16). There is a good deal of evidence, both in the novel and in external sources, leading to the suggestion that he is a Thug, a member of an Oriental cult of murderers, who kills Edwin in a ritual murder to avenge an earlier wrong. The surprising scene that was to end the novel might have been Jasper's realization and confession of his hidden side or Dickens's sympathetic interior portrait of the murderer coming to recognize his divided self and admitting the evil he has done.

Edmund WILSON (1941) suggested that the divided Jasper was also a portrait of his creator: "Mr. Jasper is, like Dickens, an artist: he is a musician, he has a beautiful voice. He smokes opium, and so, like Dickens, leads a life of imagination apart from the life of men. Like Dickens, he is a skilful magician, whose power over his fellows may be dangerous. Like Dickens, he is an alien from another world; yet, like Dickens, he has made himself respected in the conventional English community." Jasper's final revelation, then, was also to be the author's revelation of his own self-division, that he was, to use Wilson's phrase, "two Scrooges."

If *Drood* was to be Dickens's most complete self-revelation, there is reason to believe that Jasper may not be fully aware of his crime—even in his murderous persona, or that he may, like Pip, carry the guilt of Mrs. Joe's death without being guilty of actually carrying out the crime. Several commentators have suggested that Edwin, after becoming aware of Jasper's intent to murder him, ran off and disappeared or that Jasper failed in his attempt to kill Edwin. According to this view, the surprise at the end of the novel—a surprise both for the reader and for Jasper—was to be Edwin's reappearance, his resurrection from his presumed death. The power of the cathedral to renew life is suggested in the the pages Dickens wrote on the day before he died. After an episode in the murky visions of the opium den, Cloisterham is bathed in the redeeming light of the morning sun: "A brilliant morning shines on the old city. Its antiquities and ruins are surpassingly beautiful, with the lusty ivy gleaming in the sun, and the rich trees waving in the balmy air. Changes of glorious light from moving boughs, songs of birds, scents from gardens, woods, and fields—or, rather, from the one great garden of the whole cultivated island in its yielding time—penetrate into the Cathedral, subdue its earthy odour, and preach the Resurrection and the Life" (23). The resurrection theme recurs in all of the later novels, from Sydney Carton's sanctified execution to the baptismal drownings in *Expectations* and *Mutual Friend*. Edwin's return would have provided a surprising turn to end Dickens's last fable and a fulfillment consistent with the resurrection theme in all of his later novels.

CRITICISM

Nearly all of the commentary on *Drood* has been concerned with how the novel was to end, a topic that especially obsessed Dickensians around the turn of the century. The bibliographies of *Drood* commentaries compiled by B. W. MATZ and his daughter (*Dickensian*, 1911, 1928, 1929) list hundreds of books and articles offering solutions to the plot. Among the more influential later suggestions are Howard Duffield's "John Jasper—Strangler" (*Bookman*, 1930), which proposed that Jasper was connected to the Thugee cult of Kali and that the

murder was a ritual killing for revenge. Edmund Wilson (1941) accepted Duffield's conclusion, but extended his reading of the novel to describe Jasper as a projection of a divided and Dostoyevskian Dickens.

Felix AYLMER (1964) also found evidence for an Oriental connection to the murder, but in Egypt rather than India, and he offers an ingenious argument that Jasper is innocent of the crime and that Drood is not really dead.

Two recent completions of the story by Charles Forsyte (1980) and Leon Garfield (1980) develop conclusions more consistent with Forster's account of Dickens's plans for the story. Forsyte finds in Jasper a Jekyll/Hyde character; one of his selves loves Edwin and pursues the murderer, the other murders him. Garfield ends his Dickensian retelling with Jasper's dramatic confession of guilt to Crisparkle and then his execution. Addressing another of the *Drood* conundrums, the identity of Datchery, W. W. Robson (*Times Literary Supplement*, November 11, 1983), suggests that the surprise at the end of the novel would reveal that Datchery was Dickens himself. Two Italian mystery writers, Carlo Fruttero and Franco Lucentini, make a grand send-up of the Drood industry in *The D. Case or the Truth about the Mystery of Edwin Drood* (1989), when they gather a convention of literary detectives to decide how the novel was going to end. Of course, the detectives, all working in their own characteristic ways, arrive at different conclusions.

Noteworthy among commentaries not attempting to solve the mystery is Charles Mitchell's "*The Mystery of Edwin Drood*: The Interior and Exterior of Self" (*ELH*, 1966), which analyzes psycholgical themes in the existing text.

ADAPTATIONS

Before his death Dickens had raised the possibility of making a play from *Drood* with Dion BOUCICAULT. After Dickens's death, Boucicault considered going through with the project, but thought better of it. The first stage production was by T. C. De Leon, produced in October 1870 in Chicago and offering a solution received spiritualistically "direct from the shade of the deceased novelist." When his first adaptation was unsuccessful, De Leon rewrote the script and restaged the play in New York as *Jasper*. The first English production, Walter M. Stephens's adaptation at the Surrey Theatre, opened in November 1871. In this production Neville Landless, disguised as Datchery, pursued Jasper, who took poison to escape capture. Datchery also pursues Jasper in G. H. MacDermott's 1872 production, but in this play he is Bazzard in disguise. In another frequent solution to the mystery employed in the production at the Britannia Theatre in 1872, Jasper turns out to have botched the murder and Drood turns up alive, causing Jasper to suffer a fatal heart attack before the final curtain. Drood also reappeared in Robert Hall's *Alive or Dead* (1876), disguised as the lawyer who defended Jasper in court. An adaptation by Joseph L. Hatton and Dickens's son

Charles ended with the guilty Jasper taking poison. Although scheduled for production in 1880, it never actually reached the stage.

Notable among later stage versions are Beerbohm Tree's production of J. Comyns Carr's adaptation in which the addict Jasper, played by Tree, deleriously believes himself guilty of a murder he did not commit. An adaptation by Jane Bacon and Felix Aylmer (1951) presented an early version of Aylmer's ingenious defense of Jasper. A musical adaptation by Rupert Holmes (1985) in the style of Victorian music hall offered the audience an opportunity to vote on possible endings for the story.

The two best-known film versions—a silent film by Gaumont British (1914) with Tom Terriss as Edwin and a Universal sound film (1935) with Claude Rains (Jasper), Valerie Hobson (Helena), and Francis Sullivan (Crisparkle)—both end with Jasper's death. There were two other silent film versions (1909, 1912); another sound film was produced in Britain in 1993, which repeats the version of the story from the 1935 film.

Two television adaptations have appeared: a two-part American production for CBS (1952) and an eight-part serial for British Independent Television (1960).

Mystery Older woman companion of the Compact Enchantress on the train from London to PARIS. *Reprinted*, "Flight."

Mystery Story Although frequently confused with DETECTIVE STORIES, mystery stories do not always involve detectives; they are an older form, going back to such traditional and folk forms as the GHOST STORY. The mystery story can be defined as any work of prose fiction in which mystery or terror has an important role.

Some of Dickens's earliest writings deal with ghosts, supernatural events, or unexplainable experiences. Although *Boz* is a book devoted to urban realism, "The Black Veil" contains such mysterious elements and several of the INTERPOLATED TALES in *Pickwick*, such as "The Bagman's Tale" and "The Tale of the Bagman's Uncle," concern supernatural events. In several of the CHRISTMAS BOOKS, Dickens took the ghost story, traditionally told around the hearth on Christmas Eve, and brought it up to date, having the Ghosts of Christmas Past, Present, and Future, for example, visit Scrooge in his city house rather than in some lonely country mansion.

In a broader sense, nearly all of Dickens's novels can be considered mystery stories. As Northrop FRYE observed, "there is usually a mystery in Dickens's stories, and this mystery is nearly always the traditional mystery of birth, in sharp contrast to the mystery of death on which the modern whodunit is based." The mysteries at the heart of many Dickens novels engage questions of identity; the resolution to *Twist* involves uncovering the mystery of Oliver's parentage; Amy Dorrit must also learn of her heritage before she can fully understand who she is; Pip must learn the identity of his unknown ben-

efactor, and John Harmon must clear up the mystery of his murder and disappearance. Dickens's last, unfinished novel, *The Mystery of Edwin Drood*, the only one in which "mystery" appears in the title, might have combined the search for a mysterious identity with the solving of a murder, the form that characterizes many modern mystery stories.

In an older sense, mysteries were not things that human agents (detectives) solved, but things that religion attempted to explain. The ALLEGORY in some of Dickens's later novels, especially in works like *Expectations*, which connects the solution of Pip's identity with the miraculous return of Abel Magwitch, who redeems him from his self-indulgent idleness, seems to rely on this older sense of mystery.

Myth In suggesting that "Dickens was a mythologist rather than a novelist; he was the last of the great mythologists, and perhaps the greatest," G. K. CHESTERTON was stressing the primitive and religious dimensions of Dickens's storytelling. More than just pictures of 19th-century life, the novels use the materials of folklore, FAIRY TALE, and traditional story to explore the mysteries of life and death. Dickens spoke of the CHRISTMAS BOOKS as giving "a higher form" to old nursery tales, essentially turning them into myths of the industrial age in which such larger-than-life heroes as Scrooge learn the meaning of life by confronting a supernatural vision of death.

Myths reach beyond personal issues to address the concerns of a whole society or culture, what psychologist C. G. Jung called "the race." Much of Dickens's mythological symbolism derives from the BIBLE, especially from Genesis. His Victorian England is an Eden after the fall, a wilderness threatened by Noah's flood and in need of redemption. Dickens uses such ARCHETYPAL images as the river, the wilderness, the labyrinth, and the prison to express this mythological vision. His biblical imagery has been explored by Bert G. HORNBACK (1972) and Janet L. LARSON (1985).

Northrop FRYE considers more secular roots for Dickens's mythology in the tradition of New Comedy, a dramatic form from Hellenic Greece available to Dickens in the comedies of Moliere and Ben JONSON in which humours characters are driven by dominating obsessions like jealousy or greed. Dickens's characters, hardened by the industrial and urban world in which they find themselves, are also flat figures, dominated by singular obsessions. Dickens's heroes, Frye suggests, seek to overcome their situation and connect with a "hidden world of dreams and death, and . . . gain . . . a renewed life and energy."

The mythic impulse in Dickens, as Ian Duncan argues in *Modern Romance and Transformations of the Novel* (1992), defines his difference from Sir Walter SCOTT. Scott places the melodramatic plot of his novels into historical context, explaining the action as the result of historical forces; Dickens "remythologizes them." In *Two Cities*, for example, he traces the source of the FRENCH

REVOLUTION to the sexual violation of Madame De-Farge's sister by the Marquis of St. Evrèmonde.

Dickens's use of myth, as many critics have noted, ultimately serves a serious psychological project. Gwen WATKINS (1987), for example, sees his novels as devoted to a Jungian project, the search for a unified self. Industrialization, social change, and the loss of traditional beliefs and values made self-knowledge and identity problematic in Victorian England. Dickens searches for an underlying story, a myth, that will provide him with a sense of himself. Geoffrey THURLEY (1976) summarizes this search as follows: "Dickens is at the centre of all his own work. We can describe his entire *oeuvre* in terms of

a primal wish-fulfillment fantasy. . . . The elements of this myth can be summarized as follows. The child abandoned by feckless or unfortunate parents climbs out of the abyss of poverty and darkness towards security, peace, and light." In the early novels, Thurley observes, this progress is aided by benevolent uncles and impeded by evil ogres, but in the later novels the hero must take responsibility for his own difficulties and progress, and, by the end of his career, the resolution of the search has become "highly ambiguous." Repeated elements of this mythological search for selfhood include the orphan figure, the journey, and the revelatory or redemptive experience.

N

Nabokov, Vladimir (1899–1977) Russian-born American novelist, essayist, and professor of literature. In his course "Masters of European Fiction" at Cornell University, Nabokov, at the suggestion of Edmund WILSON, included *Bleak House* as one of the texts. His lectures on the novel, developing a detailed analysis of its structure, themes, and style, are included in his *Lectures on Literature* (1980), edited by Fredson Bowers and published after Nabokov's death.

Nadgett, Mr. Private investigator employed by Montague to check out policy holders in the Anglo-Bengalee Assurance Company. "He was the man at a pound a week who made the inquiries—he was born to be secret. He was a short, dried-up, withered old man, who seemed to have secreted his very blood. How he lived was a secret, where he lived was a secret" (27). He uncovers Jonas's attempt to poison his father (38) and proves Jonas's guilt in the murder of Tigg (51). He is Tom Pinch's landlord in ISLINGTON. *Chuzzlewit.*

Namby The sheriff's officer, "dressed in a particularly gorgeous manner, with plenty of articles of jewellery about him," who arrests Pickwick for refusing to pay the costs of *Bardell versus Pickwick. Pickwick* (40).

Nan Girl in the Liverpool slums waiting for a mercantile Jack. *Uncommercial* (5).

Nancy Prostitute and member of Fagin's gang, she recaptures Oliver after Brownlow takes him in by pretending to be the boy's sister (15), but later she provides Brownlow with information about Monks and Oliver (46). This leads to her murder by Sikes, who has been informed of her betrayal (47). In his preface to the novel, Dickens defended his portrayal of Nancy as "true": "It is emphatically God's truth, for it is the truth He leaves in such depraved and miserable breasts; the hope yet lingering there; the last fair drop of water at the bottom of a weed-choked well." *Twist.*

Nandy, John Edward Mrs. Plornish's father, "a little reedy piping old gentleman, like a worn-out bird; who had been in what he called the music-binding business, and met with great misfortunes, and who . . . had retired of his own accord to the Workhouse" (I:31). He occa-

sionally visits Mr. Dorrit and is greatly patronized by the Father of the Marshalsea. *Dorrit.*

Naples The Italian city where Steerforth takes and then abandons Little Em'ly (*Copperfield*, 46, 50). Dickens describes his visit to Naples in *Pictures* (12).

"Narrative of Extraordinary Suffering, A" Article for HOUSEHOLD WORDS (July 12, 1857), describing Mr. Lost, a retired businessman from Ware who gets lost in the maze of the railway system and Bradshaw's railway schedule. In his diary, Lost records an extraordinary series of railway journeys throughout Britain on which he is continually shunted from one line to another, never reaching his intended destinations. The whole experience reduces him to babbling idiocy. *Miscellaneous.*

Narrator The teller of the story. Dickens's usual narrator is an omniscient observer visible in the text in a style that is mannered and theatrical. Robert E. GARIS (1965) describes the Dickens narrator as governed by "the constant and overt intention to dazzle us with verbal devices, leading us through our impulse to applaud to a continual awareness of the artificer responsible, a self-exhibiting master of language." Kate Flint *Dickens*, (1986) discovers a more versatile narrator; describing the novels as "dialogic," she shows that the narrator adopts many different voices in the process of telling the story. Thus it might be more appropriate to refer to the Dickens narrators, rather than to a single narrator. Audrey JAFFE (1991) attempts to mediate these positions by analyzing the different voices adopted by the Dickens narrator which articulate varying degrees of omniscience and limitation.

Dickens occasionally employed a FIRST PERSON narration, notably in the autobiographical *Copperfield* and *Expectations*, in Esther Summerson's portion of *Bleak House*, and in several of the CHRISTMAS STORIES. Commentators on these works have often been interested in the ways in which Dickens modified or failed to modify his usual style to fit his story-telling characters.

Nathan Dresser in a private theater, "a red-headed and red-whiskered Jew." *Boz*, "Private Theatres."

Native, The Joey Bagstock's servant, "a dark servant . . . who Miss Tox was quite content to classify as a 'native,' without connecting him with any geographical idea whatever" (7), treated with contempt and abused by the Major. *Dombey.*

Neckett Sheriff's officer who arrests debtors and brings them to Coavins's sponging house (earning him the name **"Coavinses"** from Skimpole). Esther and Richard stop him from arresting Skimpole by paying the debt (6). After his death, **Charlotte** (**Charley**), his 13-year-old daughter, cares for the two younger children, **Emma** and **Tom**, and provides for them by doing laundry. Jarndyce rescues the children (15) and makes Charley Esther's maid (23). Charley nurses Esther through the smallpox (31, 35–37). Eventually she marries a miller (67). *Bleak House.*

Ned Chimney sweep who hires his small son out on burglaries with Sikes. *Twist* (19).

Ned, Lummy Subject of Bill Simmons's story, a guard on the Salisbury coach who escaped bankruptcy by running off to the "U-nited States," where he made and lost his fortune in a day as a result of bank failures. *Chuzzlewit* (13).

Neddy One of the turnkeys in the FLEET PRISON. *Pickwick* (42–44).

Neeshawts, Dr. Member of the Mudfog Association. *Mudfog.*

Little Nell The name by which Nell TRENT is better known. *Curiosity Shop.*

"Nemo" The alias used by Captain HAWDON when in London working as a law writer. *Bleak House.*

Nettingall, Misses Principals of a girls school in CANTERBURY attended by Miss Shepherd, who infatuates David. *Copperfield* (18).

Newgate Calendar, The A popular collection of biographies of infamous criminals imprisoned in NEWGATE PRISON. First published in 1773, it was frequently reprinted, expanded, and updated in the subsequent century. Fagin speaks of it as a kind of Who's Who of crime (*Twist*, 43). It is alluded to in several of the novels.

Newgate Novel Genre of fiction popular in the 1830s and '40s that fictionalized the lives of notorious criminals from the NEWGATE CALENDAR. Dickens's friends and fellow novelists Edward Bulwer LYTTON and W. H. AINSWORTH were the main practitioners of the form. Lytton's *Eugene Aram* (1832) and *Lucretia* (1846) and Ainsworth's *Rookwood* (1834) and *Jack Sheppard* (1840) prompted a controversy over such fiction. Those attacking the novels claimed that they promoted crime, and

they held up as proof a young man named Courvoisier who claimed that *Jack Sheppard* had motivated him to murder his master. Although *Oliver Twist* was not about a criminal from the *Newgate Calendar*, it was, like *Sheppard*, illustrated by George CRUIKSHANK and serialized in BENTLEY'S MISCELLANY, and it was often condemned with the other Newgate novels. Dickens answered these attacks in the Preface to the third edition (1841), in which he asserted that rather than crime it was "the principle of Good surviving through every adverse circumstance and triumphing at last" that was the central theme of the novel.

Newgate Prison London's main jail from the thirteenth century on, it was destroyed during the GORDON RIOTS in 1780 (*Rudge*, 64), and rebuilt in 1782. Dickens describes the prison in *Boz*, "Visit to Newgate." Oliver visits Fagin as he awaits execution in Newgate (*Twist*, 52). Wemmick takes Pip to tour the prison, leaving the "taint of Newgate" on him (*Expectations*, 32).

Newman Street Street running north from OXFORD STREET in central London, one of the "numerous streets which have been devoted time out of mind to profes-

Doré's famous rendering of the exercise yard at Newgate Prison for London, A Pilgrimage *(1872).*

sional people, dispensaries, and boarding-houses" (*Boz*, "Dancing Academy"). Mr. Turveydrop's Dancing Academy is located here (*Bleak House*, 14).

New Poor Law   The Poor Law Amendment Act of 1834. See POOR LAW.

New River Head   Uriah Heep takes lodgings in this section of ISLINGTON while he is staying in London. *Copperfield* (25).

"New Song"   Verses Dickens wrote in 1849 to his friend Mark LEMON, urging him to join him on holiday in BRIGHTON. *Miscellaneous.*

"New Year, The"   Originally published as "Scenes and Characters No. 11" in *BELL'S LIFE IN LONDON* (January 3, 1836), this sketch describes the New Year's Eve party hosted by Bobble, a senior civil servant, and the part in it played by Tupple, one of his junior clerks. *Boz.*

"New Year's Day"   Article for *HOUSEHOLD WORDS* (January 1, 1859) in which the narrator remembers several New Year's Days. On the first of these holidays, he was taken as a child to the World of Toys near SOHO Square, where he chose a magic wand; but he was disappointed when he couldn't transform anything with it. Later, the date itself becomes a kind of wand, calling up memories of New Year's Days past: a party where all the adults were lined up against a wall simultaneously drinking punch from glass cups; a day when he and his sister hid a man with a wooden leg behind the coal cellar; the day when he challenged Paynter, his rival for "the youngest Miss Clickett but one," to a duel; several New Year's Days spent at Miss Boles's country house; a day in an Italian villa; a cold day in Paris going to the theater. *Miscellaneous.*

New York   Reporting on his 1842 journey to AMERICA, Dickens describes the streets of this city—the fashionable people on Broadway, the lack of street entertainers, and the pigs who roam free—and his visits to the Tombs (the city jail), to a lunatic asylum, and to a Refuge for the Destitute (*Notes*, 6). Martin Chuzzlewit arrives in New York on the packet ship *SCREW* and stays at the Pawkins's boarding house (*Chuzzlewit*, 16).

New York Ledger   New York newspaper for which Dickens wrote "HUNTED DOWN" in 1851. He was paid £1,000 for the story.

Newcome, Clemency   Dr. Jeddler's cheerful, loving, and awkward servant who is dismissed after Marion Jeddler disappears. She marries Benjamin Britain and the two become proprietors of the Nutmeg Grater and Thimble Inn, an establishment named after objects bearing inscriptions that state her philosophy of life: "Forget

and Forgive!" and "Do as you would be done by!" They have three children—**Little Clem** and **two sons**. *Battle.*

Newsom, Robert (1944–)   Professor, University of California, Irvine. His influential *Dickens on the Romantic Side of Familiar Things*: Bleak House *and the Novel Tradition* (1977) analyzes *Bleak House* as representative of both Dickens's work and the novel as a literary form. Beginning with Dickens's assertion that he was concerned with "the romantic side of familiar things," Newsom discusses Dickens's ability to reveal the unexpected, unfamiliar, and miraculous dimensions of the mundane, and he discovers tensions in the novel between "the familiar and the strange, the real and the imaginary, the topical and the mythical, the empirical and the fictional, the modern and the ancient." *Bleak House* does not resolve these tensions, which are characteristic of many novels of the period, for the instability in Victorian society that the novel undertakes to present ultimately characterizes the novel itself. In "Embodying Dombey: Whole and in Part" (*Dickens Studies Annual*, 1989), Newsom discusses a similar tension in *Dombey*, but one expressed more primitively in the antithesis of physical wholeness and things falling to pieces. "The Hero's Shame" (*Dickens Studies Annual*, 1983) develops a psychoanalytic reading of the AUTOBIOGRAPHICAL FRAGMENT, its concern with shame—rather than guilt—and its ramifications in the novels.

Niagara Falls   The Dickenses spent 10 days at the falls on their American journey. The sight of the falls impressed Dickens with "Peace of Mind, tranquillity, calm recollections of the Dead, great thoughts of Eternal Rest and Happiness; nothing of gloom or terror." *Notes* (14).

Nicholas   Long-established butler at Bellamy's Coffee House near the Houses of Parliament: "An excellent servant Nicholas is—an unrivalled compounder of salad dressing; an admirable preparer of soda water and lemon; a special mixer of cold grog and punch; and above all an unequalled judge of cheese." *Boz*, "Parliamentary Sketch."

Nicholas Nickleby, The Life and Adventures of   (Serial Title: *The Life and Adventures of Nicholas Nickleby, containing a Faithful Account of the Fortunes, Misfortunes, Uprisings, Downfallings and the Complete Career of the Nickleby Family.* Edited by Boz.) Dickens's third novel, published in monthly parts from April 1838 to October 1839, with illustrations by BROWNE. Published in one volume by CHAPMAN & HALL, 1839. Dickens improvised this picaresque story, bringing together elements from SMOLLETT, theatrical melodrama, journalistic realism, and social satire. Although the novel lacks a central theme, it offers interesting scenes and

Squeers, the Yorkshire schoolmaster, at the Saracen's Head recruiting students for his school, in Browne's (Phiz's) illustration for the original edition of Nicholas Nickleby *(1838).*

characters and shows Dickens in the process of discovering his own novelistic voice.

SYNOPSIS

Part 1 (April 1838)

(1) When Godfrey Nickleby inherited £5,000 from his Uncle Ralph, he bought a small farm in Devonshire, where he settled with his wife and two sons, Ralph and Nicholas. When Godfrey died, £5,000 went to Ralph, who entered business in London, and £1,000 and the farm went to Nicholas. Nicholas married and there raised his two children, Nicholas and Kate, but he speculated with the money and lost it. He died penniless, leaving his wife and adolescent children to the protection of his brother.

(2) As the story begins, Ralph Nickleby pursues his business, a business of no clear definition or professional description, but one concerned with money, in a spacious house on GOLDEN SQUARE, in a section of London on its way down. At a public meeting of the United Metropolitan Improved Hot Muffin and Crumpet Baking and Punctual Delivery Company, Ralph and the other directors consider a petition to Parliament calling for the abolition of the existing muffin trade by forbidding street sellers—an action that will favor their enterprise. (3) When Newman Noggs, Ralph's clerk, brings him a letter announcing his brother's death and the arrival of his brother's widow and children in London, Ralph proceeds to his sister-in-law's lodgings at the establishment of Miss La Creevy, a painter of miniatures. He warns

Miss La Creevy that his relative is poor and that he will not be responsible for her rent, and he offers to aid Kate and Mrs. Nickleby only if Nicholas will go off to teach in a YORKSHIRE SCHOOL. Although Ralph clearly dislikes Nicholas, the boy is determined to prove his mettle and to help his mother and sister. Kate is skeptical about this plan, but Mrs. Nickleby is grateful to her brother-in-law for his help. (4) Later, at the SARACEN'S HEAD in SNOW HILL, Mr. Wackford Squeers interviews potential students and possible tutors. In his negotiation with Snawley, a potential client, Squeers makes it clear that most of his boys are illegitimate or stepchildren who are exiled to Yorkshire by their parents, and Snawley commits his two stepsons to the school. Ralph, who has dealt with Squeers in the past, comes to the inn with Nicholas and Noggs, and convinces the schoolmaster to hire his nephew for £5 a year. Nicholas is excited by his prospects, but Noggs seems strangely disturbed by Nicholas's optimistim.

Part 2 (May 1838)

(5) As Nicholas leaves on the Yorkshire coach, Noggs slips a note into his hand. Riding on the outside of the coach in cold winter weather, Nicholas is suddenly awakened when the coach overturns. (6) The other passengers praise him for his quick response in taking the reins of the horses while the coachman cut the traces. As they wait for another coach at a nearby inn, the passengers tell stories. A grey-haired man tells "The Five Sisters of York," a legend behind a stained-glass window in YORK Cathedral. A merry-faced gentleman then tells the story of "The Baron of Grogswig," the tale of a medieval German baron and his scolding wife. When the new coach arrives, they set out again, arriving the next evening at GRETA BRIDGE in Yorkshire. (7) There, at DOTHEBOYS HALL, Mrs. Squeers greets her husband with a steak dinner, while Nicholas is served short rations and has fears of what is to come. Smike, the boy of all work, reduced to near idiocy by mistreatment, hopes for a letter, but Squeers has brought none for him. Nicholas discovers the letter from Noggs in his pocket offering him aid should he need it. It brings tears to Nicholas's eyes.

Part 3 (June 1838)

(8) The next morning Nicholas watches as Mrs. Squeers administers treakle and brimstone to the boys and Squeers assigns their "lessons," various chores around the school. The boys are not the young gentlemen that Nicholas had imagined, but rather a group of maimed and abandoned waifs. Their meals are poor porridge and their schooling is limited and error-ridden. After dinner Squeers distributes the mail, berating the boys as he does so and driving them to tears. Smike tells Nicholas of a boy who died at the school, and Nicholas finishes his first day in despair, but he is determined to go on for the sake of his mother and Kate. He is convinced that his uncle is angry only at him. (9) When Miss Fanny Squeers, the schoolmaster's daughter, returns home and

hears of the new young master, she goes into the school-room, pretending to need her pen sharpened, and immediately falls in love with Nicholas. She arranges a tea for him, and invites her friend, Matilda Price, and Matilda's beau, John Browdie. At the tea Nicholas flirts with Tilda, angering both John and Fanny.

(10) Meanwhile, Ralph finds a position for Kate with Madame Mantalini, a milliner. At her interview Kate is disturbed by Mr. Mantilini's flirtatiousness and refuses to acknowledge him. She insists that she live at home with her mother and Ralph reluctantly agrees. He tells her that they can stay in a house he owns near the river.

Part 4 (July 1838)
(11) Kate has misgivings about her job, but Mrs. Nickleby talks of rich milliners. Noggs guides them to the dilapidated house near the river; he has furnished it with a few broken pieces of furniture.

(12) In Yorkshire, Nicholas angers Fanny Squeers by vowing that he has no romantic interest in her. (13) When Smike runs away from the school, Mrs. Squeers captures him. Squeers prepares to beat the boy before the whole school, but after the first blow, Nicholas intervenes and beats the schoolmaster. Then he packs up his belongings and sets out on foot for London. John Browdie, impressed by Nicholas's boldness, gives him some money for his journey. On the second morning Nicholas awakens to see Smike watching him. The boy has followed him from the school.

(14) In London Noggs attends an anniversary party for his neighbors the Kenwigs, where the honored guest is Mrs. Kenwigs's uncle, Mr. Lillyvick, a collector of water rates. The high point in the evening comes when Miss Petowker of the Theatre Royal, DRURY LANE, performs "The Blood-Drinker's Burial." As Noggs prepares punch for the party, he is called away to meet two strangers who have arrived at his lodgings.

Part 5 (August 1838)
(15) The strangers are Nicholas and Smike. Nicholas tells Newman his story and is outraged to hear of the lies that Fanny Squeers has written about him to Ralph Nickleby. He is diverted from his anger, however, by the cries of the Kenwigs' baby. He rushes downstairs to rescue the infant and impresses the Kenwigs with his aristocratic manner. (16) The next morning Nicholas seeks employment in London. He turns down a degrading position as secretary to Mr. Gregsbury, M.P., but later, under the pseudonym Mr. Johnson, he agrees to tutor the Kenwigs' daughters in French for five shillings a week.

(17) On her first day at Madame Mantilini's, Kate overhears a quarrel between Madame and her husband and is humiliated by some snobbish customers. At home, Mrs. Nickleby imagines Kate as Madame Mantilini's partner and Nicholas as Dr. Nickleby of Westminster School.

Part 6 (September 1838)
(18) At first Kate is befriended by Miss Knag, Madame Mantilini's forewoman, but when customers prefer Kate

to her, Miss Knag takes out her anger on Kate. (19) When Ralph asks Kate to preside at a dinner at his house, Mrs. Nickleby is delighted. The dinner is attended by Lord Frederick Verisopht, a naive young aristocrat whom Ralph intends to fleece, and by several of Ralph's disreputable aristocratic acquaintances, Mr. Pyke, Mr. Pluck, Mr. Snobb, and Colonel Chowser. When Kate is humiliated by the advances of Verisopht's rakish companion, Sir Mulberry Hawk, Ralph intervenes and seems to show some compassion for his niece.

(20) Nicholas finally locates Ralph at his mother's lodgings, where his uncle is recounting Fanny Squeers's lies about him and announcing that "this boy, head-strong, wilful, and disorderly as he is, should not have one penny of my money, or one crust of my bread, or one grasp of my hand, to save him from the loftiest gallows in all Europe." Warning his uncle that he will hold him responsible for any wrongs done to his mother or sister, Nicholas leaves London so that he will not be a burden on them.

Part 7 (October 1838)
(21) When Madame Mantilini's business fails and the establishment is closed, Kate must seek employment elsewhere. She takes a position as companion to Mrs. Witittery, a delicate and snobbish woman.

(22) Nicholas and Smike set out for PORTSMOUTH with the vague idea of going to sea. At an inn along the way, they meet Mr. Vincent Crummles, manager of a traveling theatrical troupe, who recruits them for his company. (23) The next day they join the company in Portsmouth. There they meet their fellow actors, including Crummles's daughter, an aging "Infant Phenomenon" who plays child roles. Nicholas is made playwright for the company and instructed to translate some French works and put them into English under his own name. He is also given roles in several of the troupe's repertory of plays.

Part 8 (November 1838)
(24) Nicholas (as Mr. Johnson) has a leading role in his first effort, playing opposite Miss Snevellicci, the leading lady of the company. He, Miss Snevellicci, and the Infant Phenomenon canvass Portsmouth for patrons, and their opening is a great success. (25) When Miss Petowker joins the company, Nicholas discovers that Lillyvick, smitten with the actress, has secretly followed her from London. They are married in a theatrical ceremony. Meanwhile, in the company's production of *Romeo and Juliet*, Nicholas plays Romeo, Smike the apothecary.

(26) Back in London, Verisopht and Hawk are both pursuing Kate. Ralph, to forward his scheme to fleece Verisopht, tells him where Kate lives. Sir Mulberry flatters Mrs. Nickleby to gain the same information.

Part 9 (December 1838)
(27) With the aid of his confederates Pyke and Pluck, Sir Mulberry contrives to get Mrs. Nickleby to the theater where Kate and Mrs. Wititterly have a box. There Mrs. Nickleby and Mrs. Wititterly are both awed by their ar-

istocratic company and Kate is abandoned to the un-wanted attentions of Sir Mulberry. She spurns him and tells him that her brother will resent his "unmanly per-secution" of her. (28) Hawk and Verisopht make regular calls at Mrs. Wititterly's, who is flattered to have aristo-cratic visitors, but she becomes jealous of Kate and ac-cuses her of being forward with them. When Kate appeals to her uncle for protection, Ralph says he can do nothing.

(29) In Portsmouth, Nicholas has risen to the head of the Crummles Company, arousing the jealousy of his fellow actors. When Noggs writes that Kate needs her brother's protection, Nicholas prepares to cut short his successful theatrical career and return to London.

Part 10 (January 1839)
(30) After a farewell dinner with the company and a final performance in the theater, Nicholas rushes back to Lon-don in response to another letter from Noggs telling him to return instantly. (31) When he arrives on the evening after Kate's futile appeal to her uncle, (32) Nicholas can-not find either Noggs or his mother and he wanders into a luxurious hotel near Hyde Park. There he overhears a stranger at an adjoining table speak insultingly about "Little Kate Nickleby." Nicholas challenges him and de-mands to know his name, but the stranger, Sir Mulberry, disdains him and as he leaves strikes him with his car-riage whip. Nicholas grabs the whip, breaks it, and strikes Hawk across the face with the handle, leaving an open wound from eye to lip. (33) The next morning Nicholas removes Kate from Mrs. Wititterly's and breaks off re-lations with his uncle.

Part 11 (February 1839)
(34) When the financially strapped Mantilinis come to borrow money from Ralph, they tell him of Nicholas's altercation with Hawk. Ralph is pleased to learn that Nicholas is in trouble. Squeers, recovered from the wounds that Nicholas gave him, tells Ralph about Smike, the boy he claims Nicholas abducted when he left Doth-eboys Hall. Ralph suggests that they may get revenge on Nicholas through Smike. (35) After placing his mother, Kate, and Smike at Miss La Creevy's, Nicholas goes off to the employment office to find work. There he meets Charles Cheeryble, a benevolent businessman who lis-tens to his story and introduces him to his twin brother Edwin. They hire him to assist Tim Linkinwater, their aging clerk. They also provide a cottage for the Nicklebys at BOW. (36) When Nicholas informs the Kenwigs of Lil-lyvick's marriage to Miss Petowker, they are deeply dis-appointed and despair about their children's prospects.

Part 12 (March 1839)
(37) Nicholas and Tim Linkinwater become comrades, and Tim proudly shows Nicholas's work to their em-ployers. At Bow, Mrs. Nickleby is "courted" by a strange gentleman in small clothes in the next cottage, who tosses cucumbers and other vegetables to her over the garden wall.

(38) One day as Smike is returning to Bow from Miss La Creevy's house in town, he meets Squeers and young Wackford in the street. Squeers grabs him and holds him captive at Snawley's house in SOMERS TOWN. (39) When John Browdie, in London on his honeymoon, learns of Smike's imprisonment, he slips into the house at night and frees the boy.

Part 13 (April 1839)
(40) Noggs and the Nicklebys are overjoyed to have Smike back. Nicholas is determined to find out if his uncle was behind Smike's capture, but he is diverted from this pursuit when he sees a young woman in the Cheerybles' office who had first caught his attention at the employment office. He becomes obsessed with find-ing out who she is. He engages Noggs to discover her identity and arrange a meeting with her. Noggs tracks down a Miss Cecelia Bobster, but she turns out to be the wrong person. (41) Meanwhile, Mrs. Nickleby's suitor comes over the garden wall and proposes to her before his keepers arrive to take him back. (42) While Nicholas is dining at the Saracen's Head with John and Tilda Browdie, Squeers, Fanny, and young Wackford appear. Fanny jealously attacks Tilda and Squeers accuses John and Nicholas of abducting Smike.

Part 14 (May 1839)
(43) When Nicholas steps in to quell a disturbance at the inn, one of the disputants turns out to be Frank Cheery-ble, nephew of the Cheeryble brothers, who has been defending the good name of a young woman of his ac-quaintance against the dispersions of another patron. Frank turns out to be a "good-humoured, pleasant fel-low" and shows an immediate interest in Kate.

(44) Ralph's hatred of Nicholas is intense, nearly as powerful as his avarice. As he makes his rounds to the Mantilinis and others, Ralph plans his revenge. (45) With Squeers and Snawley, he goes to the Nickleby's cottage and produces papers proving that Smike is Snawley's son. Smike refuses to go with them. Nicholas and John Browdie protect him from being forcibly taken away.

Part 15 (June 1839)
(46) The Cheerybles support Nicholas's effort to keep Smike from Snawley. They also ask Nicholas to act as their representative in dealing with a young woman, Ma-deline Bray, whom they have supported by buying draw-ings from her. She is the daughter of a debtor detained under the rules of the KING'S BENCH PRISON for a debt to Ralph Nickleby. Madeline turns out to be the young woman Nicholas has been seeking. (47) Meanwhile an old moneylender, Arthur Gride, conspires with Ralph Nickleby to marry the girl, for Gride has learned that her husband stands to inherit some property. Ralph broaches the proposition to Mr. Bray, offering to forgive his debt if he agrees to the marriage. (48) Unaware of Ralph's scheme, Nicholas admires Madeline's sacrificial concern for her father, but he despairs of winning the heart of so noble a woman. By chance he again meets the Crummles, who are in London on their way to a

theatrical tour in America, and he attends their farewell dinner.

Part 16 (July 1839)
(49) Nicholas worries about Smike's failing health, a condition worsened, it seems, by Frank Cheeryble's attentions to Kate. Meanwhile, Mrs. Nickleby's lunatic suitor emerges from her chimney during a family party and outrages Mrs. Nickleby by shifting his attentions from her to Miss La Creevy.

(50) After recovering from his injuries at the hand of Nicholas, Hawk returns from Belgium, where he has been recuperating. He vows to avenge his injury, but he gets into an altercation with Verisopht, kills the young lord in the ensuing duel, and is forced to escape again to the Continent.

(51) Noggs learns of Ralph Nickleby's scheme to marry Arthur Gride and Madeline Bray. When Nicholas tells him that Madeline is the young woman he has been seeking, Noggs tells Nicholas of the scheme and indicates that the wedding is scheduled to take place in two days.

Part 17 (August 1839)
(52) Although Nicholas despairs of preventing the marriage, Noggs encourages him to "hope, hope, to the last." Noggs meets Lillyvick, who has returned to London after Miss Petowker abandoned him to run off with a half-pay captain. Their hopes restored, the Kenwigs are reunited with their disconsolate relative. (53) Nicholas finds Mr. Bray eagerly anticipating the wedding that is to take place the next day and he fails to dissuade Madeline from her determination to sacrifice herself for her father. In a last attempt to prevent the marriage, Nicholas tells Gride what he knows of the scheme, threatens him, and attempts to buy him off, but Gride rejects his offers and throws him out of his house. (54) The next morning Nicholas and Kate confront Gride and Ralph Nickleby before the wedding. Although their opposition only incites Ralph's determination, the ceremony is prevented by Mr. Bray's sudden death. Nicholas carries off the insensible Madeline to the Nickleby cottage at Bow.

Part 18 (September 1839)
(55) Attended by Kate, Madeline slowly recovers. As Frank Cheeryble courts Kate, Smike's condition worsens and Nicholas takes him to Devonshire, hoping to effect his recovery there.

(56) Ralph blames Nicholas for thwarting his scheme and he vows revenge, but fortune has turned against him. Gride learns that his housekeeper, Peg Sliderskew, has absconded with the documents and papers relating to Madeline's property, and Ralph discovers that he has lost £10,000. He engages Squeers to recover Gride's papers and he plans his revenge on Nicholas. (57) As Squeers is about to secure the documents from Peg Sliderskew, Noggs and Frank Cheeryble intercede and take the papers themselves.

(58) Smike is not cured by going to Devonshire. He continues to decline. During his last days, he is alarmed by seeing the man who left him as a child many years

before at Squeers's school, and just before he dies he confesses to Nicholas his hopeless love for Kate.

Parts 19 and 20 (October 1839)
(59) Ralph's schemes unravel and are exposed. Squeers, his factotum, is imprisoned and his cohorts—the Snawleys and Gride—turn him away. In addition to this, the Cheerybles, aided by Noggs, are closing in on a truth unknown even to Ralph. (60) Summoned to the Cheerybles', Ralph is confronted by a former clerk, Brooker, who reveals that Smike was Ralph's son by a clandestine marriage. In revenge for maltreatment, Brooker had secretly left the child at Dotheboys Hall after telling Ralph that the boy had died.

(61) Meanwhile, Nicholas returns from Devonshire. He has admitted to Kate his love for Madeline and she to him her love for Frank, but they have agreed that they are not the social equals of those they love and have resolved not to marry. (62) Haunted by grief and remorse, Ralph wanders the streets, slowly making his way back to his house in Golden Square. There, in the attic, he hangs himself. (63) The Cheeryble brothers bless the unions of Frank and Kate, Nicholas and Madeline, Tim Linkinwater and Miss La Creevy. (64) When Nicholas carries the news to Yorkshire that Squeers has been sentenced to transportation, the boys at Dotheboys riot and rebel and the school is disbanded. (65) The good are rewarded, the bad punished, and the firm of Cheeryble and Nickleby continues into the next generation.

COMMENTARY

Although *Nickleby* is Dickens's third novel, it is, in many ways, still an apprentice work in which he is experimenting with the novel form and seeking his own place in the tradition he inherited. An exuberant story, filled with incident and invention and told with energy, *Nickleby* is Dickens's first attempt at a novel with a young man as its hero, a story that he repeated with variations in many of the later works, especially in *Chuzzlewit, Copperfield, Expectations,* and *Mutual Friend.*

The early years of Dickens's writing career were full of intense activity and experimentation. He often had several projects going at the same time and would begin a new novel while he was still at work on the old one. *Pickwick* and *Twist* overlapped for nine months in 1837, and *Twist* overlapped for nine months with *Nickleby* in 1838. When he began work on *Nickleby* in February 1838, Dickens was also finishing the *Sketches of Young Gentlemen,* and editing the *Memoirs of Grimaldi* and the monthly magazine BENTLEY'S MISCELLANY. With so many irons in the fire, he had trouble meeting his deadline on the 15th of the month for each installment of the novel, and he had no time to plan out the whole story beforehand. INTERPOLATED TALES like "The FIVE SISTERS OF YORK" in the second number suggest that Dickens may have filled out the monthly part with a previously written story and the desultory progress of the whole novel suggests that Dickens improvised the story as he wrote it.

Dickens's early novels can be seen, in part, as interpretations of his childhood reading: *Pickwick* of *Don Quixote, Twist* of HOGARTH's Progresses, and *Nickleby* of Smollett's picaresque tales. *Nickleby*'s alliterative title recalls *Roderick Random* and *Peregrine Pickle*, while its story of a young man seeking his place in the world recalls the similar journeys of Smollett's heroes. Roderick, Peregrine, and Nicholas are externally defined, physical heroes who gain their places in the world by conquest. Nicholas's fights with Squeers and Hawk recall the two-fisted assertiveness of Smollet's picaros. Yet even though he is physically assertive, Nicholas, also like Smollett's heroes, is more acted upon than acting. His uncle, Crummles, and the Cheeryble brothers do more to determine the course of his life than he does himself.

The improvisatory character of the novel is evident from the beginning. The first chapter sets up the picaresque situation when the young Nicholas is left on the edge of adulthood, fatherless and without financial resources, and must fend for himself. The second chapter satirizes parliamentary meetings and business speculation in its account of the United Metropolitan Improved Hot Muffin and Crumpet Baking and Punctual Delivery Company, but it adds nothing to the story of Nicholas and Kate. They return in the final chapters of the first number which introduce the attack on Yorkshire schools as Nicholas is employed by Squeers as an assistant master for Dotheboys Hall. From its first number the novel has the character of a miscellany, mixing the picaresque with SATIRE and social reform.

Dickens's initial idea for the novel was to attack Yorkshire schools in the way he had attacked the POOR LAW and workhouses in *Twist*. At the beginning of February 1838, he and Browne went to visit some of the infamous schools where unwanted children were banished by uncaring parents. Using "a plausible letter to an old Yorkshire attorney from another attorney in town, telling him how a friend had been left a widow, and wanted to place her boys at a Yorkshire school in hopes of thawing the frozen compassion of her relations," Dickens interviewed an attorney who advised him to tell the widow not to send her son to Yorkshire. His visits to the schools confirmed the advice, particularly in the case of Bowes Academy, which was run by William SHAW. Shaw, who had been prosecuted for mistreating his students, has often been identified as the original of Squeers, but Dickens claimed that his schoolmaster was "the representative of a class, and not of an individual. . . . Mr. Squeers and his school are faint and feeble pictures of an existing reality, purposely subdued and kept down lest they should be deemed impossible."

The chapters on Dotheboys Hall addressed a specific social grievance and Dickens, in his 1848 preface to the novel, took some credit for the decline in the number of Yorkshire schools in the 1840s. But Dotheboys Hall also represented broader social concerns. It extended his interest in children begun with his expose of the mistreated children in the workhouses and baby farms in *Twist*. While he was writing *Nickleby*, the mistreatment of children in the factories of northern England was a hotly debated issue. Pamphleteers and novelists like Mrs. Trollope in *Michael Armstrong* (1840) described the maimed and deformed children who worked on the cotton machines. Dickens's description of the physical infirmities suffered by the inmates at Dotheboys Hall links them with the controversial factory children:

> Pale and haggard faces, lank and bony figures, children with the countenances of old men, deformities with irons upon their limbs, boys of stunted growth, and others whose long meagre legs would hardly bear their stooping bodies, all crowded on the view together; there were the bleared eye, the hare-lip, the crooked foot, and every ugliness or distortion that told of unnatural aversion conceived by parents for their offspring (8).

The implicit connection between the factory children and the students at Dotheboys Hall extends the specific abuses in the schools to the mistreatment of children generally in Victorian England. The neglectful parents who abandoned their illegitimate or unwanted sons to Squeers's cruelties were representative of a society which provided no schools for the young and allowed children to work for 14 hours a day in the mines and factories.

When Dickens used up his material on the Yorkshire schools, he had Nicholas attack Squeers and desert Dotheboys Hall. Then he took up Kate's parallel story of working in Madame Mantilini's millinery establishment. The factory children and the young women who worked as dressmakers and milliners would become the subjects of important parliamentary investigations in the early 1840s, but in his treatment of Kate's story Dickens left social reform to take up stage melodrama. He does not dwell on the ill health or the working conditions of the milliners. There is no equivalent of Smike at Madame Mantilini's. Instead, Dickens describes Kate as a victim of sexual exploitation. In the millinery showroom and in Ralph Nickleby's drawing room, she is not a case study for a parliamentary report, but rather an embattled heroine from stage melodrama.

Appropriately, Nicholas follows her lead and soon finds himself the member of a traveling theater company. In the second quarter of the novel, Dickens comes closest to finding its thematic center, for *Nickleby* is, in many ways, a novel about life as theater. Handsome and active in defending the downtrodden Smike or his unprotected sister, Nicholas is a stage hero; he has little inner awareness and does not seem to grow as a result of his experiences. The villians, too, seem to be born to their theatrical roles as avaricious uncle (Ralph), aristocratic rake (Hawk), or miserly satyr (Gride). It may be this very theatricality that made the Royal Shakespeare Company's hugely successful 1980 dramatic adaptation so much more effective than the novel itself. In the stage melodrama we are not so aware of the lack of psychological depth as we are in reading the novel.

The Crummles episodes in Portsmouth act as a kind of play within the play, turning episodes from the rest of the novel into harmless theatrical illusion. In the theater, the exploitation and oppression of children is not really exploitation, for the Infant Phenomenon is not really a child. The disagreements between the actors may lead to duels, but no one really dies in these altercations, unlike Sir Frederick Verisopht, who is killed by Sir Mulberry Hawk in the larger story. Even the theatrical marriage of Miss Petowker and Mr. Lillyvick proves to be a sham, an unreal interlude between his life as a water-rate collector and her affair with the half-pay captain. As playwright and leading man, Nicholas (as Mr. Johnson) has a chance to author his own life and play its leading role, but that too proves illusory, for his plays are merely plagiarisms of French plays. Back in London, his challenge to Hawk is a brief theatrical gesture. It does not change the direction of his life; that will be left to the Cheerybles.

While Nicholas is on stage in Portsmouth, Kate is attending the theater in London, where she is "assaulted" by Sir Mulberry Hawk, the rakish stage villain. As an attendant to Mrs. Wititterly, Kate cannot withdraw from her public role and retreat to a more private sphere. The conventions of melodrama demand that she be trapped in her vulnerable position until Nicholas returns, challenges the villainous Hawk, and rescues her.

The second half of the novel is less interesting than the first. Dotheboys Hall, the Mantilini millinery establishment, and the Crummles theatrical troupe, despite the staginess in their presentation, were all based on realities of early Victorian England. Dickens' visits to the Yorkshire schools and provincvial theaters provided him with realistic observation to ground the melodrama in the story, but the heroes and villains of the second half have only a stage life. Nicholas' fight with Hawk and Frank Cheeryble's similar altercation at the Saracen's Head give both young heroes opportunities to defend the honor of the heroines. The machinations of the villains, from the seductions of the aristocratic rake and his accomplices Pyke and Pluck to the document shuffling of the old miser Gride, have a basis only in theater. Even though the Cheeryble twins were drawn from real people—the benevolent GRANT brothers of Manchester—their role in the novel is out of fairy tale or pantomime. They are, in ORWELL's (1939) words, "two gruesome old Peter Pans" who take over the direction of the story and arrest any chance Nicholas has of becoming the hero of his own life.

The most interesting characters in the novel are grounded in reality. For all his ogreish exaggeration, Squeers was drawn from schoolmaster William Shaw, who had a bad eye and had been sued by some of his clients for grossly mistreating their children. Crummles, typical of many theater people of the day, was inspired by T. D. Davenport, who advertised his daughter Jean as "the most celebrated Juvenile Actress of the day." Although the originals of the Kenwigs family have not been identified, Dickens's descriptions of them are grounded in the social realism that distinguished Boz's *Sketches*. And he based Mrs. Nickleby, probably the most mem-

orable character in the book, on his mother. Garrulous and self-absorbed, she is identified in her speech by her wishful thinking, associative logic, and digressive style. Her delusions make her diverting, sometimes dangerous to her children, but of no consequence in the plot. Her assessment of her lunatic neighbor is characteristic:

> "There can be no doubt," said Mrs. Nickleby, "that he *is* a gentleman, and has the manners of a gentleman, and the appearance of a gentleman, although he does wear smalls and grey worsted stockings. That may be eccentricity, or he may be proud of his legs. I don't see why he shouldn't be. The Prince Regent was proud of his legs, and so was Daniel Lambert, who was also a fat man; *he* was proud of his legs. So was Miss Biffin: she was—no," added Mrs. Nickleby, correcting herself, "I think she had only toes, but the principle was the same" (37).

Though her incoherence is comic, it also serves to veil the class snobbery, self-absorption, and egotism that makes Mrs. Nickleby incapable of recognizing or responding to the needs of her children.

Mrs. Nickleby is only one of several irresponsible parents in the novel, a motif that will become an important theme in many of the later novels. In *Nickleby*, as in *Twist*, Dickens seems still to be searching for this theme. The most interesting development in this exploration in *Nickleby* emerges in the role of Smike as a shadowing DOUBLE to Nicholas. Many readers have noted the seeming contradiction at the heart of *Twist*, where, on the one hand, Dickens describes the corrupting effect of a social system that leads children into deliquency and, on the other, presents Oliver as totally untouched by his environment. While Nicholas seems similarly unaffected by his weak father, dithering mother, and malevolent uncle, Smike shows the effects of childhood abuse and neglect in his maimed mind and body. As Nicholas's shadow and companion—as his double—Smike exaggerates and makes visible the inner wounds that Nicholas suppresses. Smike's uncertain parentage complements Nicholas's anonymity as Mr. Johnson; his unspoken love for Kate parallels Nicholas's reticence with Madeline Bray. Appropriately, Smike turns out to be Nicholas's cousin and his death, in the Nickleby home country in Devonshire, frees Nicholas to marry Madeline and Kate to marry Frank. Smike's doubling relationship with Nicholas is one of Dickens's initial explorations of a technique that in later works will become an increasingly important way to give dramatic expression to the inner life of his characters.

Even Ralph Nickleby is touched by the transforming power of Smike. Although he is the malevolent stage villain through most of the novel, Ralph becomes a novelistic character with an inner life as he faces the revelation that he is Smike's father and that the maimed boy is also a maimed part of himself. Like Scrooge recognizing his connection to the maimed Tiny Tim or Dombey coming to understand his responsibility for his son's illness and death, Ralph retreats to the attic room of his consciousness, where he stores the suppressed memories of his past, the room where Smike spent his childhood. There, alone with his thoughts and memories, he is transformed from a stage villain into a self-conscious novelistic character before he takes his own life (62). Smike plays an important part in enabling Dickens to reach beyond the theatrical conventions that dominate the novel and to experiment with their novelistic possibilities.

CRITICISM

Michael SLATER, in the Introduction to his facsimile edition of the novel (1982), provides a comprehensive discussion of the composition and sources for the work, especially for Dotheboys Hall and the Crummles theatrical troupe. Kathryn Chittick (*Dickens and the 1830s*, 1990) surveys the contemporary reception of the novel, generally more positive than later criticism of it. Describing *Nickleby* as "the most undisciplined of all his novels," John LUCAS (1970) discusses the parts which will be developed in the characters and themes of later works. Challenging those who find no thematic unity in *Nickleby*, Steven MARCUS (1965) considers it a novel about prudence and imprudence, in which Nicholas, victimized by the imprudence of his father and the false prudence of his uncle, must seek an identity for himself. Bernard Bergonzi's essay on the novel (in *Dickens and the Twentieth Century*, ed. J. Gross and G. Pearson, 1962) is especially good on the picarcaresque and theatrical elements in the novel. Leon Rubin's description of "the making of the historic Royal Shakespeare Company production" (*The Nicholas Nickleby Story*, 1981) offers insights into the themes of the novel and its theatrical character along with a fascinating account of the highly successful theatrical production.

ADAPTATIONS

Nickleby has been one of the most popular of Dickens's novels on the stage, partly because of Vincent Crummles and his theatrical troupe. The first adaptations, however, were produced so early in the novel's serial run that Crummles had not yet entered the story. Edward STIRLING's adaptation, which opened in November 1838, was modified over the following months to incorporate material from later parts of the novel as they appeared, and when the serial was completed, he produced another version, *The Fortunes of Smike, or, A Sequel to Nicholas Nickleby* (March 1840). Robert BOLTON (1987) counts 25 stage adaptations produced before the novel finished its serial run, including William T. MONCRIEFF's *Nicholas Nickleby and Poor Smike; or, the Victim of the Yorkshire School* (1839). Moncrieff, who had annoyed Dickens with an earlier dramatization of *Pickwick*, was probably the model for the plagiarist whom Nicholas meets in chapter 48 who has adapted 247 novels for the stage.

Nickleby has remained popular on the stage in the 20th century. Bolton (1987) documents a number of stage versions leading up to the Royal Shakespeare Company production in 1980. That eight-hour performance

by an ensemble cast was based on a script by David Edgar developed collaboratively with the company. Directed by Trevor NUNN and John Caird, the cast included David Trefall (Smike); Roger Rees (Nicholas); Edward Petherbridge (Noggs), and Susan Littler (Kate). Filmed for television in 1982, this celebrated production is available on videotape. Leon Rubin tells the story of the production in *The Nicholas Nickleby Story* (1981).

Three silent films were based on the novel: perhaps the earliest film adaptation of Dickens, a scene from Dotheboys Hall made by American Biograph in 1903; an Edison version of the Yorkshire school in 1910; and another adaptation by Thanhouser in 1912. Ealing Studios produced Alberto Cavalcanti's version in 1947, with a screenplay by John Dighton. The cast included Sir Cedric Hardwicke (Ralph Nickleby), Bernard Miles (Noggs), and Stanley Holloway (Crummles). Two BBC television serials have appeared: Vincent Tilsey's 10-part adaptation in 1957, and Hugh Leonard's 13-part serial in 1968. Saxon Lucas and D. Corr's "pop opera" *Smike* was broadcast on BBC television in 1973.

"Nicholas Nickleby at the Yorkshire School" Dickens's PUBLIC READING from *Nickleby*, it included the comic scene of Fanny Squeers's tea party and reached a triumphant climax in Nicholas's thrashing of Squeers.

Nickits   The former owner of Bounderby's country house whose improvidence caused the bank to foreclose on his mortgage. *Hard Times* (II:7).

Nickleby Family   Family at the center of the inheritance and identity plot of *Nickleby*. The two sons of **Godfrey Nickleby**, a Devonshire landholder and gentleman, inherit his property: **Ralph Nickleby**, the elder son, takes his money and goes into business; **Nicholas**, who inherits the farm, speculates with his inheritance and dies, leaving nothing for his **wife** and two children, **Nicholas Nickleby, Jr. and Kate**, "a beautiful girl of about seventeen." **Mrs. Nickleby** and the two children appeal for help to Ralph, who grudgingly provides a house for Mrs. Nickleby, places Nicholas in a YORKSHIRE SCHOOL as an assistant master, and secures a position for Kate in a millinery establishment. Nicholas eventually foils his uncle's plots. *Nickleby*.

Nickleby, Kate   Sister of Nicholas, Jr., "a beautiful girl of about seventeen." Her uncle Ralph places her in Madame Mantilini's millinery establishment and employs her himself to attend a dinner at his house where she is subjected to the unwanted advances of Sir Mulberry Hawk (19). Nicholas then leaves his position with a traveling theatrical company, returns to London, and confronts and wounds Hawk (32) and removes Kate from her humiliating position as companion to Mrs. Witterly. In the end, Kate marries Frank Cheeryble. *Nickleby*.

Nickleby, Mrs.   Mother of Nicholas and Kate Nickleby. Although she is well meaning and loves her children, she is a distracted and garrulous woman who fails to appreciate the dangers her children face and always expects things to turn out for the best. She even imagines that the lunatic who throws vegetables to her over her garden wall is an eccentric but acceptable gentleman suitor (37). *Nickleby.* She is loosely based on Dickens's mother.

Nickleby, Nicholas   Titular hero of *Nickleby*, whose youth and inexperience are contrasted with the worldly cynicism of his uncle Ralph Nickleby, the villain of the novel:

> The face of the old man was stern, hard-featured, and forbidding; that of the young one, open, handsome, and ingenuous. The old man's eye was keen with the twinklings of avarice and cunning; the young man's bright with the light of intelligence and spirit.... However striking such a contrast as this may be to lookers-on, none ever feel it with half the keenness or acuteness of perception with which it strikes to the very soul of him whose inferiority it marks. It galled Ralph to the heart's core, and he hated Nicholas from that hour (3).

Nicholas, anxious to prove himself to his uncle, accepts a position as an assistant master at DOTHEBOYS HALL, but his good-hearted sympathy for the mistreated boys, especially for Smike, prompts him to beat Squeers, the headmaster, and he is forced to leave the school (13). As Nicholas walks back to London, he is joined by Smike, who becomes his companion on his further adventures. After a spell with the Crummles Theatrical Company in PORTSMOUTH, where Nicholas serves as actor and playwright, he returns to London to defend his sister, Kate, from the attentions of Sir Mulberry Hawk. He impetuously assaults Hawk and wounds him (32). Nicholas finds work in London as a clerk for the Cheeryble brothers, who befriend him and his family (35). They support him as he saves Smike, who turns out to be Ralph's illegitimate son (60), from the persecutions of Ralph and Squeers. The Cheerybles also introduce him to Madeline Bray, whom he eventually marries. *Nickleby.*

Nickleby, Ralph   The villain of *Nickleby*, who takes an instant dislike to his nephew Nicholas and plots against him. A usurer who lives on GOLDEN SQUARE, Ralph banishes Nicholas by securing him an appointment as an assistant master at a YORKSHIRE SCHOOL (4). He places Kate in Madame Mantilini's Millinery business (17), and subjects her to the unwanted attentions of Sir Mulberry Hawk (19). After Nicholas foils his plots, rescues Kate, saves Smike from capture, and reveals that Smike is Ralph's illegitimate son (60), Ralph hangs himself in the attic of his house (62).

"Niger Expedition, The"   Article from the *EXAMINER* (August 19, 1848) in which Dickens reviews Cap-

tain William Allen's report of the failed expedition up the Niger in 1841. The expedition set out with three ships intending to negotiate with the tribal chiefs along the river to end the slave trade, open up commerce with Britain, establish an agricultural colony, and promulgate Christianity. After entering into some naive agreements with double-dealing tribal chiefs, the expedition was ravaged by fever, which killed nearly all of the Europeans. Dickens concludes that "no amount of philanthropy has a right to waste such valuable life as was squandered here.... Between the civilized European and the barbarous African there is a great gulf set." Looking forward to his satire of Mrs. Jellyby in *Bleak House*, he suggests that missionary efforts must begin in England: "the work at home must be completed thoroughly, or there is no hope abroad." *Miscellaneous.*

"Night Walks"   At a time in his life when he has difficulty sleeping, the Traveller takes walks through the streets of London, lasting from midnight until dawn. On these walks he sees the last stragglers in the streets as the pubs close and the city goes to bed. Going from HAYMARKET to WATERLOO BRIDGE, the narrator meditates on the suicides there; he proceeds on to the empty theaters on the Surrey side of the THAMES, then past NEWGATE, KING'S BENCH PRISON, and Bethlehem Hospital. There he meditates on dreams, wondering, "Are not the sane and the insane equal at night as the sane lie dreaming?" Passing the Houses of PARLIAMENT and WESTMINSTER ABBEY, he goes on to COVENT GARDEN market for some coffee before returning home to sleep as the people return to the streets at dawn. *Uncommercial* (13). The article first appeared in *ALL THE YEAR ROUND* (July 21, 1860).

Nightingale Family   Family at the center of the farce in *Mr. Nightingale's Diary*. **Christopher**, a hypochrondriac who is the victim of Slap's schemes, opposes the marriage of his niece **Rosina** to Gabblewig. When she saves her uncle from Slap's plots, she wins his consent to the marriage. *Nightingale.*

"Nightly Scene in London, A"   Article for *HOUSEHOLD WORDS* (January 26, 1856), describing the narrator's experience outside the workhouse in WHITECHAPEL, where he found five young women lying in rags in the street because there was no more room in the casual ward of the workhouse. He was told that there were starving people lying outside the workhouse every night, usually more than five. After giving each one some money for food and lodging, the narrator attacks "demented disciples who use arithmetic and political economy beyond all bounds of sense.... I utterly renounce and abominate them in their insanity; and I address people with respect for the spirit of the New Testament, who mind such things, and who think them infamous in our streets." *Miscellaneous.*

Luke Fildes's picture of the hungry and homeless in the streets of London, an engraving published in the Graphic *in 1869, depicts a scene similar to those described by Dickens on his night tours of London.*

Niner, Margaret Niece of Julius Slinkton, whom he plans to poison to get the insurance on her life. His plot is foiled by Sampson and Meltham. "Hunted Down."

Nipper, Susan Florence Dombey's sharp-tongued maid: "a short brown womanly girl, with a little snub nose, and black eyes like jet beads . . . who was so desperately sharp and biting, that she seemed to make one's eyes water" (3). When she speaks up for Florence to Mr. Dombey, she is discharged (44). She marries Mr. Toots (60). *Dombey.*

Nisbet, Ada (1907–1994) Professor, UCLA; literary scholar, bibliographer and critic; associate editor of *Nineteenth Century Fiction*, 1960–74; one of the key figures in the postwar generation of Dickens scholars. Nisbet wrote on a variety of Dickensian topics, especially about the reception of the novels, Dickens biography, and Dickens in America. *Dickens and Ellen Ternan* (1952) surveyed and evaluated the evidence pertaining to the novelist's relationship with Ellen TERNAN. Her Dickens bibliography in Lionel Stevenson's *Victorian Fiction: A Guide to Research* (1964) presented a comprehensive

description of scholarly and critical work on Dickens in English and in other languages; it has served as the foundation for later bibliographical work on the author. Nisbet's substantial collection of Dickens materials is housed in the Dickens Center at the University of California, Santa Cruz.

Nixon, Felix The Domestic Young Gentleman, he "lives at home with his mother," and the two chief subjects of his discourse "are himself and his mother." *Young Gentlemen.*

Nixon, Mr. and Mrs. Members of the audience at the Gattleton's private theatricals. *Boz*, "Porter."

"No. 1 Branch Line: The Signal-man" Short story about an apparition that appears to a railway signalman. See *Mugby* (4).

"No Thoroughfare" Christmas story for ALL THE YEAR ROUND (1867) by Dickens and Wilkie COLLINS. Dickens wrote all of the "Overture" and Act 3; Collins wrote all of Act 2; they collaborated on Acts 1 and 4.

SYNOPSIS

(1) 1835. Sally, a nurse from the FOUNDLING HOSPITAL is stopped in the street by a woman who asks her the name given to a child recently taken into the institution. Sally tells her "Walter Wilding."

1847. The same woman visits the Hospital and asks the matron to point out Walter Wilding to her.

1861. At the offices of Wilding and Co., the bachelor head of the firm, Walter Wilding, is hiring a housekeeper and making George Vendale a partner in the firm. Wilding's late mother established him in the business after reclaiming him from the Foundling Hospital. Now he has idealistic plans to make the firm like a family. When he hires Sarah Goldstraw as his housekeeper, he learns from her that he is not really his mother's son. Sarah was Sally, the nurse from the hospital; she knows that the real Walter Wilding was another child who was adopted shortly before the present Wilding was given his name. Wilding decides to seek out the real Walter and turn the wine business over to him, but every lead that he finds to the man's identity ends in a "no thoroughfare."

Meanwhile, Vendale carries on the firm's business dealings with Jules Obenreizer, a representative of the Swiss wine merchants Defresnier et Cie. As he does so, he falls more and more in love with Obenreizer's niece Marguerite.

Binfrey, Wilding's attorney, and Vendale advise Wilding to give up the search for the real Wilding and to keep Sally's information secret, but he rewrites his will to leave everything to the real Wilding should he be discovered within two years of his death. Then, weakened by the stress of his situation and increasingly depressed, he dies.

(2) When Vendale asks Obenreizer's permission to marry Marguerite, he is refused because of the social distance between an English gentleman and the daughter of a Swiss peasant. Obenreizer relents and says he will agree to the marriage should Vendale's income reach £3,000 a year. As Vendale goes over his accounts, he discovers that his firm has received a fraudulent receipt from Defresnier et Cie; to clear up the crime he must take the receipt to SWITZERLAND. Obenreizer arranges to travel with him. As they leave, Marguerite pleads with George, "Don't go!"

(3) On the journey, Vendale is concerned to protect the receipt. Obenreizer, who is guilty of the forgery, makes secret plans to steal it from him. He drugs Vendale and steals into his room in the night, but he cannot secure the document. Finally, as the two men cross the Simplon Pass in a dangerous February snowstorm, Obenreizer drugs Vendale and pushes him into a chasm, leaving him for dead, but the Englishman is rescued from an icy ledge by Marguerite, who has followed the two men to Switzerland.

(4) In April, two months after the episode on the mountain, Obenreizer, who has been dismissed by Defresnier et Cie, is working as a clerk for Maître Voigt, a Neuchatel attorney. He uses his position to gain access to the lawyer's files on a client named Vendale. When Obenreizer and Voigt are summoned to Brieg to meet with the English attorney Binfrey, they learn that Vendale did not die. Binfrey demands that Obenreizer give up his guardianship of Marguerite in exchange for not being prosecuted for attempted murder. Obenreizer reveals the secret from the files that Vendale is really Walter Wilding, a bastard adopted from the Foundling Hospital, and thus heir to Wilding and Co.

On the day of Marguerite and George's wedding in Brieg, the body of Obenreizer is brought down from the mountain where he died in a snowstorm.

Noakes Member of the statistical section of the Mudfog Association. *Mudfog.*

Noakes, Mrs. Landlady at the St. James Arms. *Strange Gentleman.*

Noakes, Percy Law student and "devilish good fellow" who organizes the steam excursion. *Boz,* "Steam Excursion."

"Noble Savage, The" Article from HOUSEHOLD WORDS (June 11, 1853), challenging the idea of the noble savage, claiming that it is an "enormous superstition" and a "monotonous humbug." Savages from Africa and America of the sort who have been exhibited in London submit to tyrants, mistreat women, and engage in mindless violence. "His virtues are a fable; his happiness is a delusion; his nobility, nonsense." *Reprinted.*

Nobody The hero of "Nobody's Story," representative of the ordinary working person. *Reprinted.*

"Nobody, Somebody, and Everybody" Article for HOUSEHOLD WORDS (August 30, 1856), attacking "Nobody . . . the great, irresponsible, guilty, wicked, blind giant of this time," who is accomplished at failure, takes no responsibility for his inaction or incompetence, and is responsible for bringing about the many fiascos of the recent Crimean War. "I want Somebody to be clever in doing business, not clever in evading it," the narrator asserts, "I want to see the working Somebody in every responsible position which the winking Somebody and Nobody now monopolize between them." *Miscellaneous.* This article helps to explain the NOBODY'S FAULT theme which Dickens developed in *Dorrit.*

Nobody's Fault Dickens's original working title for *Little Dorrit* when he conceived of the central emphasis in the book as the impersonality of the social and political system. He changed the title to *Little Dorrit* shortly before the first number was published.

"Nobody's Story" One of two stories that Dickens wrote for the Christmas number of HOUSEHOLD WORDS, 1853, this allegorical tale describes the suffering of Nobody and his oppression by the Bigwigs who blame him for the social ills. *Christmas Stories.*

Nockemorf The Bristol physician whose practice is purchased by Bob Sawyer. *Pickwick* (38).

"Noddy" One of Nicodemus BOFFIN's nicknames. *Mutual Friend.*

Noddy "A scorbutic youth" who attends Bob Sawyer's party. *Pickwick* (32).

Noggs, Newman Ralph Nickleby's clerk, "a tall man of middle-age, with two goggle eyes whereof one was a fixture, a rubicund nose, a cadaverous face, and a suit of clothes . . . much the worse for wear, very much too small. . . . [who] rubbed his hands slowly over each other: cracking the joints of his fingers, and squeezing them into all possible distortions" (2). From a well-to-do family in the north of England, Noggs has fallen into drink and debt and is forced to take on menial work. Noggs befriends Nicholas and acts as his "spy" into Ralph Nickleby's schemes. He warns Nicholas of the danger to Kate from Hawk (29) and provides information that enables the Cheerybles to expose Ralph. *Nickleby.*

Nogo, Professor Member of the medical section of the Mudfog Association. *Mudfog.*

Nonesuch Edition Limited edition of Dickens's works, edited by Arthur Waugh, H. Walpole, Walter DEXTER, and Thomas Hatton, published in 23 volumes, 1937–38. It reproduced all the original illustrations from the original plates and blocks; included several minor works not included in earlier editions, such as *The Life of our Lord* and the *Miscellaneous Papers* (as *Collected Papers*); and collected the fullest edition of the LETTERS prior to the Pilgrim Edition.

Norah Harry Walmer's seven-year-old cousin, with whom he elopes, intending to go to GRETNA GREEN. As an adult she marries an army captain and dies in India. "Holly-Tree."

Norfolk Street (1) In this street off Fitzroy Square in MARYLEBONE the Dickens Family had lodgings from 1829 to 1831.

Norfolk Street (2) This street leading from the STRAND to the river is the site of the lodging houses of Mrs. Lirriper and her rival Miss Wozenham. "Lirriper's Legacy."

Normandy Gaming booth operator and con man with "a very genteel appearance" who goes into society with Chops and ruins him. "Going into Society."

Norris Family Mr. Bevan's New York relatives who are Abolitionists but believe in segregation. They disdain Martin when they learn that he has been a steerage passenger on his journey to America. *Chuzzlewit* (17, 31).

"North American Slavery" Article for HOUSEHOLD WORDS (September 18, 1852) by Henry MORLEY and Dickens. The authors praise Harriet Beecher STOWE's *Uncle Tom's Cabin* as "a noble work; full of high power, lofty humanity; the gentlest, sweetest, and yet boldest, writing," and a work which prompts a desire to abolish slavery. They compare the cruel slavery in Cuba to the much more benign institution in the United States, pointing out that few slaves in the United States attempt to escape to freedom. The harsh treatment of free negroes in the North also discourages slaves from attempting to escape. Efforts to educate negroes and to create colonies such as the one in Liberia can enable the Americans to end slavery in a much more positive way than the British did. *Stone.*

Norton, Squire Villain who attempts to seduce Lucy Benson. *Village Coquettes.*

Norwood Wooded suburb southeast of London where Gabriel Parsons (*Boz*, "Tottle"), James Carker (*Dombey*), and Mr. Spenlow (*Copperfield*) reside.

Nubbles, Christopher (Kit) Shopboy at the Old Curiosity Shop, "a shock-headed shambling awkward lad with an uncommonly wide mouth, very red cheeks, a turned-up nose, and certainly the most comical expression of face I ever saw" (1). Devoted to Nell, he is dismissed by her grandfather, who suspects him of disclosing his addiction to gambling to Quilp (11). After Nell disappears, Kit secures employment with the Garlands, tending their pony Whisker (21), but Quilp conspires against him, and has the Brasses accuse him of robbery (59); Kit is sentenced to transportation (64), and is saved only at the last minute by the testimony of the Marchioness (66). After Nell's death, he marries **Barbara**, the Garland's maid; they have three children—**Barbara**, **Abel**, and **Dick** (73). Kit's **mother**, a kindhearted and hardworking laundress, is occasionally misguided and upset by the preaching at the Little Bethel chapel that she attends (41). His brother **Jacob** is "a sturdy boy of two or three years old" (10). *Curiosity Shop.*

Number Plans Although Dickens apparently improvised his way through his earliest novels, later on he kept notes for each of the individual SERIAL parts as he went along. In these notes he recorded directions for episodes, characters, and motifs that he planned to include in each number. He also noted developments in the plots, tried out names, and raised questions for himself. These plans are fairly complete for all the novels from *Dombey* on and there are some scattered notes for some of the earlier works. The originals of most of these notes are in the Victoria and Albert Museum; those for *Expectations* are in the Wisbeck and Fenland Museum, Wisbeck, England; those for *Mutual Friend* in the Pierpont Morgan Library, New York. Academic editions of the novels often include the notes in appendices. Harry STONE (1987) has compiled all the extant notes in a facsimile edition.

Number Twenty, Coffee-Room Flight   Debtor described by Sam Weller who, imprisoned for nine pounds, is let out into Fleet Market after seventeen years in the FLEET only to discover that he is much safer and happier in the prison. *Pickwick* (41).

Nunn, Trevor (1940–)   British Theater director; executive director, Royal Shakespeare Company. His production of *The Life and Adventures of Nicholas Nickleby* (1980) stands as the most ambitious and experimental theatrical adaptation of any Dickens work. The eight-hour production and the collaborative process developed to produce it are described in Leon Rubin's *The Nicholas Nickleby Story* (1981).

Nun's House   Miss Twinkleton's "Seminary for Young Ladies," housed in a former convent. *Drood* (3).

Nupkins   Prominent IPSWICH family. **George**, Mayor of Ipswich, principal magistrate and "grand personage," he hears the case against the Pickwickians for disturbing the peace, but he dismisses the charges when they reveal that Charles FitzMarshall who is courting his daughter, **Henrietta**, is the scoundrel Jingle. **Mrs. Nupkins**, "a majestic female in a pink gauze turban and a light brown wig," and her equally haughty daughter blame Mr. Nupkins for the scandal with Jingle. *Pickwick* (24, 25).

"Nurse's Stories"   The Traveller is drawn to the worlds of Crusoe, Gulliver, and the *Arabian Nights* by pleasant memories; he is also called against his will to remember the dark corners in the ghost stories told to him by his nurse. He especially remembers two such stories: those of Captain Murderer, the tale of a serial killer who baked his brides into meat pies, and Chips, the story of a shipwright who is driven to destruction by a talking rat that he received in a deal with the devil. *Uncommercial* (15).

Nutmeg Grater, The   Roadside inn kept by Benjamin Britain and Clemency Newcome after they marry. Later the name is changed to The Nutmeg-Grater and Thimble, referring to the two objects whose inscriptions state Clemency's philosophy of life. *Battle*.

O

Oakum-Head One of the "Refractories" in the Wapping Workhouse observed by the Traveller. Her hair is like the oakum that it is her task to pick. *Uncommercial* (3).

Obelisk, The A London landmark that in Dickens's time stood in the center of St. George's Circus in south London. David Copperfield meets the young man who steals his box and money near the Obelisk as he heads out of London toward DOVER. *Copperfield* (12).

Obenreizer, Jules Agent for a firm of Swiss wine merchants, Defresnier et Cie., "the great Obenreizer peculiarity was, that a certain nameless film would come over his eyes—apparently by the action of his own will—which would impenetrably veil . . . every expression save one of attention" (1). He fears that Vendale will expose his fraud and embezzlement and so tries to murder him in an Alpine pass. He is killed in an avalanche. "No Thoroughfare."

Obenreizer, Marguerite Jules's niece, daughter of Swiss peasants with "a wonderful purity and freshness of colour in her dimpled face and bright grey eyes, [who] seemed fraught with mountain air" (1). She foils her uncle's plot, saves Vendale's life, and later marries him (4). "No Thoroughfare."

O'Bleary, Frederick An Irish patriot boarding at Mrs. Tibbs's who hopes to better himself by marrying Mrs. Bloss. *Boz*, "Boarding House."

O'Boodleom Irish Member of Parliament who passes on information to the narrator from "The Best Authority." *Miscellaneous*.

O'Brien Passenger on the Gravesend packet. *Boz*, "River."

Odd Girl, The City girl whose first visit to the country is to a haunted house. "Haunted House."

"Ode to an Expiring Frog" Mrs. Leo HUNTER's poetic effusion, recited to Pickwick by her husband. *Pickwick* (15).

O'Donovan Resident, with his wife and child, of an Irish rookery in ST. GILES. *Reprinted*, "Inspector Field."

Offley's A well-known tavern in COVENT GARDEN that is one of the resorts of "old boys." *Boz*, "Dounce."

O'Killamollybore One of Tapenham's colleagues when he was a junior member of the government bureaucracy. *Miscellaneous*, "Cheap Patriotism."

Old Bailey Central criminal court for London and Middlesex, it was burnt down during the GORDON RIOTS (*Rudge*) and rebuilt in 1809. Dickens describes the court in *Boz*, "Criminal Courts." In the novels Fagin (*Twist*, 52), Kit Nubbles (*Curiosity Shop*, 63), Charles Darnay (*Two Cities*, II:2), and Magwitch (*Expectations*, 56) are tried at the Old Bailey.

Old Curiosity Shop, The Dickens's fourth novel, published weekly in *Master Humphrey's Clock* (April 25, 1840 to February 6, 1841), with illustrations by BROWNE, CATTERMOLE, MACLISE, and Samuel WILLIAMS. Published in one volume by CHAPMAN & HALL, 1841. One of the most controversial of Dickens's novels, *Old Curiosity Shop* has been praised as one of his most moving works and vilified as morbidly sentimental. With contrast as its organizing principle, the novel's formal structure pits the innocent and pure Nell against the carnal and corrupt Quilp. Dick Swiveller emerges as a kind of synthesis of these opposed forces, suggesting the possibilities for change and growth.

SYNOPSIS

Part 1 (April 25, 1840)
(1) One night while he is out walking, Master Humphrey meets a lost young girl. He guides her to her home, an old curiosity shop. There he reprimands the girl's grandfather for neglecting her, but the old man responds by affirming his love for the girl. As Master Humphrey leaves, Grandfather Trent leaves too, disturbing Humphrey by his apparent neglect. Afterward Humphrey is unable to forget the girl who "seemed to exist in a kind of allegory."

Part 2 (May 16, 1840)
(2) When he next visits the Old Curiosity Shop, Humphrey finds Grandfather Trent with his wastrel grandson Fred. Although Fred says he is there to see his sister Nell, he and his friend Dick Swiveller seem more interested in the old man's money. (3) When Nell arrives with the

Cattermole's illustration of the most memorable event in The Old Curiosity Shop—*the death of Little Nell.*

dwarf Quilp, she tells Fred that she loves him. Grandfather Trent confesses to Humphrey his dream of riches for Nell.

Part 3 (May 23, 1840)
(4) At the Quilp house on Tower Hill, Mrs. Quilp and her mother, Mrs. Jiniwin, gather with a group of women to discuss the tyranny of men. When Quilp returns, he drives the women away and threatens his wife, advising her to have nothing to do with the women.

Part 4 (May 30, 1840)
(5) The next morning the tyrannical dwarf torments his wife and mother-in-law before crossing the river to his warehouse and wharf, where he torments the boy who works for him. Nell interrupts these recreations when she brings him a letter.

Part 5 (June 6, 1844)
(6) Quilp reads the letter but does not answer it. Instead, he asks Nell if she would like to be the second Mrs. Quilp and marry him when his present wife dies. She shrinks from him. As they leave, Quilp's boy is fighting with Kit Nubbles, the shopboy from the curiosity shop who is devoted to Nell. At Quilp's house, the dwarf eavesdrops as Nell tells Mrs. Quilp of her worries about Grandfather Trent, who has taken to staying out all night.

(7) Fred Trent persuades Dick Swiveller to marry Nell as a way of getting to his grandfather's money. Swiveller plans to initiate the scheme by being cool to his current girlfriend, Sophy Wackles.

Part 6 (June 13, 1840)
(8) Meanwhile, Sophy has decided to pressure Dick to a commitment by holding a party where she can make him jealous of her attentions to Cheggs, a market gardener. Dick makes an early departure from Sophy's party, leaving Sophy to Cheggs.

Part 7 (June 20, 1840)
(9) Worried about her grandfather's unhappiness, Nell urges him to leave with her, even if they only become wandering beggars. Quilp refuses to lend the old man any more money and tells him that Kit Nubbles says he has been gambling away all he has. (10) Grandfather Trent sends Nell to inform Kit that his services are no longer needed and that he never again is to come to the curiosity shop.

Part 8 (June 27, 1840)
(11) Grandfather Trent falls ill. Meanwhile Quilp and his lawyer, Sampson Brass, take possession of the Old Curiosity Shop and Quilp takes over Nell's room. Kit keeps watch in the street and offers Nell and her grandfather his house as a refuge. (12) When the old man has barely recovered, Quilp tells him to prepare to leave. Nell and Grandfather slip out of the house at night and set out on their wanderings.

Part 9 (July 4, 1840)
(13) When Quilp discovers that they are gone, he is angry. Swiveller too is disconcerted, his plan to marry Nell thwarted before it has begun. As Quilp removes everything from the house, Kit takes Nell's bird. (14) Kit needs to work to help support his widowed mother and brother Jacob. He offers to hold the Garlands' horse while they are in the office of Notary Witherden signing apprenticeship papers for their son Abel.

Part 10 (July 11, 1840)
(15) Meanwhile, Nell and her Grandfather go into the countryside. Grandfather Trent urges them on so they can get as far as possible from the city. (16) They stop at a country churchyard, where they meet Tommy Codlin, proprietor of a traveling PUNCH AND JUDY show.

Part 11 (July 18, 1840)
(17) The next morning, Nell meditates on those buried in the churchyard. Then she and Grandfather join Codlin and his partner Short, who are on their way to a race meeting. (18) The next evening they stop at the Jolly Sandboys Inn, where many traveling performers have gathered.

Part 12 (July 25, 1840)
(19) As they approach the race meeting, Nell gathers wild roses into nosegays to sell, but she worries that Codlin will betray them, so, at an opportune moment when he is engaged with his puppets, she and her Grandfather slip away.

(20) Kit daily expects Nell to return, but after she has been gone a week, he accepts his mother's conclusion that they have escaped to a foreign country. He again minds the Garlands' horse while they are in Witherden's office.

Part 13 (August 8, 1840)
(21) The Garlands offer Kit £6 a year to be their servant. Quilp tries to discover Nell's whereabouts. After learning nothing from Kit, he plies Swiveller with liquor and

learns of Dick's scheme to marry Nell. (22) Kit goes off to Abel Cottage in Finchley to serve the Garlands.

Part 14 (August 8, 1840)
(23) When Swiveller tells Fred Trent that he has revealed their scheme to Quilp, Fred persuades Quilp to join them in their efforts to find Nell and her grandfather.

(24) Even though they are well away from the race meeting, Nell and Grandfather still fear being followed. They stop in an out-of-the-way village at the house of a poor schoolmaster who is troubled by the illness of his favorite pupil.

Part 15 (August 15, 1840)
(25) The next day the sick child dies. (26) Nell notes that the child left behind a loving grandparent who cared for him. Then she and her grandfather set out again and come upon a caravan whose hospitable owner, Mrs. Jarley, invites them to take tea and to travel with her.

Part 16 (August 22, 1840)
(27) The proprietor of a traveling waxworks, Mrs. Jarley hires Nell as a guide to the exhibition. In the town where they stop for the night, Nell is surprised to see Quilp in the street at midnight. He troubles her dreams. (28) The next morning, while the poet Slum writes verses to advertise the exhibition, Mrs. Jarley instructs Nell about each of the figures. She learns quickly.

Part 17 (August 29, 1840)
(29) Nell feels safe and happy working for the kind Mrs. Jarley. One day, while they are out walking, Nell and her grandfather are caught in a thunderstorm and take refuge at the Valiant Soldier Inn, where some gamblers are playing cards. Grandfather Trent takes Nell's purse and joins the game. (30) He spends all the money in the purse, so Nell must take some money from a secret cache in the hem of her dress to pay for their night at the inn. In the middle of the night, the rest of her hidden money is taken by a figure who slips into her room in the dark. It is her grandfather.

Part 18 (September 5, 1840)
(31) The next morning, Nell tells her grandfather that their money was taken during the night. He does not confess.

Mrs. Jarley sends Nell to Miss Monflathers's school to advertise the exhibition; the snobbish school mistress presents Nell to her pupils as a person debased by her association with the waxworks. (32) Meanwhile, Grandfather Trent gambles away all the money that Nell makes; she fears that if she does not give him money he will steal from Mrs. Jarley.

Part 19 (September 12, 1840)
(33) In their law office in BEVIS MARKS, Sampson and Sally Brass discuss Quilp's proposal that they hire Dick Swiveller as a clerk. Sally opposes the idea, but Sampson says they must cater to such an important client as Quilp, so Dick is hired and placed under the supervision of the intimidating Sally Brass. (34) When Miss Brass goes out,

leaving Swiveller in charge of the office, a diminutive servant girl emerges from the cellar and asks Dick to show the apartment for rent on the first floor. Dick rents it on good terms to a single gentleman who moves in immediately and goes to bed.

Part 20 (September 19, 1840)
(35) Brass is pleased with Dick's negotiation, but Sally thinks he should have bargained for even more. When the Single Gentleman sleeps for 26 hours straight, they bang on his door to rouse him. He takes Dick inside and tells him he does not want to be disturbed or spied upon. He won't give his name. (36) All relations with the lodger are henceforth undertaken by Swiveller. Dick gains Sampson's respect and shares an affectionate camaraderie with Sally. He wonders about the little servant. One day he secretly follows Sally to the cellar where he sees her mete out a meagre lunch to the girl and then beat her.

Part 21 (September 26, 1840)
(37) The Single Gentleman takes an unusual interest in Punch and Judy shows and invites them to perform in the street in front of the Brasses' house. When Codlin and Short perform for him, he learns of their connections with Nell and her grandfather and he offers to pay them for any information they can give of Nell's whereabouts.

Part 22 (October 3, 1840)
(38) Kit Nubbles is called into Mr. Witherden's office. There the Single Gentleman inquires about Nell and her Grandfather, telling Kit that he intends only good for them and asking him to keep their meeting secret. Swiveller tries unsuccessfully to learn from Kit about his connection with the Single Gentleman. (39) Kit and Barbara, the Garlands' maid, celebrate the half-holiday when they receive their quarter's pay by taking their mothers to ASTLEY'S and then to an oyster supper.

Part 23 (October 10, 1840)
(40) The next morning, Mr. Garland tells Kit that the Single Gentleman wants to hire him, pay him more than the Garlands do, and improve his prospects, but Kit refuses to go. So the Garlands lend him to the Single Gentleman, who needs Kit to go with him to fetch Nell and her grandfather. Kit, because of his falling-out with Grandfather Trent, proposes that his mother go in his place. (41) Kit finds his mother at the Little Bethel Chapel, and is surprised that Quilp is also there. Kit rushes her off to Witherden's office, where a coach is waiting to leave.

Part 24 (October 17, 1840)
(42) Meanwhile Nell has discovered that her grandfather plans to rob Mrs. Jarley's cash box. Telling him that she has had a troubling dream of his scheme, she gets him to slip away with her. (43) After walking through the night, they get a ride on a dirty canal boat that takes them to an industrial city in the middle of the BLACK COUNTRY.

Part 25 (October 24, 1840)
(44) There they spend the night in the factory town, befriended by a laborer who gives them a place to sleep by the warmth of a factory furnace. As they leave, the laborer presses two pennies into Nell's hand. (45) Passing through the industrial wasteland, Nell becomes sick and feverish. They run out of food and money. Everywhere they look, they see distress and death.

Part 26 (October 31, 1840)
(46) Tired and sick, Nell collapses in the road just as they meet Mr. Marton, the poor schoolmaster with whom they had stayed earlier. He carries her to an inn and orders a room, food, and care for her. The schoolmaster is on his way to a new post as clerk in a remote village to the north. After she recovers, Nell and her grandfather go there with him.

(47) Meanwhile the Single Gentleman and Mrs. Nubbles arrive at their destination, the town where the waxworks are on exhibition. Mrs. Jarley and William, her driver, are being married. She tells them that Nell and her grandfather have disappeared and she has been unable to discover where they have gone.

Part 27 (November 7, 1840)
(48) Quilp has followed Mrs. Nubbles to the country. After learning of her destination, he had taken the night stage. On the stage back to London, he rides on the roof and torments Mrs. Nubbles, who is inside, by peering in the window and making faces at her. When the coach arrives in London, Kit accuses him of being a "little monster." (49) At his home Quilp discovers his wife and Mrs. Jiniwin holding a wake for him, assuming that he has drowned in the river. He surprises those who have gathered for the occasion by walking into the room "like a dismounted nightmare."

Part 28 (November 14, 1840)
(50) Quilp accuses his wife of being a "widow in anticipation," and he chooses to become a "bachelor in earnest" by moving down to the wharf. At Brass's office, he hypocritically commiserates with Swiveller, who laments Sophy's marriage to Cheggs as he eats a piece of their wedding cake. Quilp ruminates on when might be the appropriate time to disclose to the Single Gentleman Dick's scheme to marry Nell. (51) At tea Quilp tells Sampson and Sally Brass that Kit is interfering with his plans, and asks them to get the boy out of the way.

Part 29 (November 21, 1840)
(52) Meanwhile, the schoolmaster arrives at the rural village with Nell and her grandfather. He arranges a house for them and a job for Nell as keeper of the keys to the church. The Old Bachelor, a patriarch of the community, introduces them to the village people and the schoolchildren. (53) Nell meets the old sexton of the church, who is both gravedigger and gardener. She finds peace among the tombs in the old, mouldering church.

Part 30 (November 28, 1840)
(54) The bachelor and the sexton tell Nell about the town, the church, and those buried in the churchyard.

She grieves for those who die and are forgotten, but the schoolmaster tells her that everyone lives in the memories of those who loved them. Nell decides to make tending graves one of her projects. (55) Everyone in the village is fond of her. The bachelor and the schoolmaster read to her in the evenings. Grandfather, realizing how much she has done for him, devotes himself to her. The schoolchildren know and love her.

Part 31 (December 5, 1840)
(56) When Kit comes to deliver a letter to the Single Gentleman living above Sampson Brass's office, Brass surprises him with praise and gives him two half-crowns.

(57) Left alone in the office, Dick Swiveller discovers the little servant peeking from behind the cellar door. He invites her in, orders a dinner, names her "the Marchioness," and recruits her for a cribbage partner.

Part 32 (December 12, 1840)
(58) As Dick and the Marchioness play cribbage, she describes the deprivation inflicted on her by the Brasses and tells him of their suspicion that he is not to be trusted. Later, when Sally and Sampson complain that some money is missing from the office, Dick suspects the Marchioness. (59) Sampson secretly hides a £5 note in Kit's hat and arranges it so that Dick discovers it there. Kit is charged with theft and Dick becomes the material witness.

Part 33 (December 19, 1840)
(60) Kit protests his innocence and asks to be taken to Witherden's office. On the way there, they meet a gloating and exultant Quilp. Though neither the Garlands nor Witherden believe the charge, the Brasses get Swiveller to corroborate the evidence against the boy and Kit is taken to jail. (61) In his cell, Kit remembers his happy days with Nell and weeps. His mother, brother Jacob, and Barbara's mother tearfully visit him in prison. Swiveller sends him a mug of beer.

Part 34 (December 26, 1840)
(62) Sampson visits Quilp at his wharf and is worried that the dwarf, who is singing exultantly about Kit's imprisonment, is being indiscreet. Undaunted, Quilp orders Sampson to fire Swiveller. (63) A clever prosecutor wins his case and Kit is found guilty of the crime. Swiveller takes Mrs. Nubbles home after the trial; when he returns to Bevis Marks, Brass pays him off and tells him not to return. That night, Dick falls ill with a raging fever.

Part 35 (January 2, 1841)
(64) For three weeks Swiveller is delirious. When he returns to consciousness, the Marchioness is caring for him. She has run away from the Brasses and has pawned all of Swiveller's clothes to buy medicine for him. She tells him that Kit has been sentenced to transportation and that she heard the Brasses, acting on instructions from Quilp, conspiring to frame the boy. (65) Swiveller has the Marchioness tell Abel Garland about the Brasses' plot.

Part 36 (January 9, 1841)
(66) The next morning, the Garlands, Witherden, and the Single Gentleman come to Swiveller's lodgings, bringing him food and people to care for him. They decide to try to get Sally Brass to testify against her fellow conspirators, but Sally is immovable. Sampson, however, agrees to testify against Quilp, and while he is writing his confession, Sally slips away. That evening Dick learns that he has inherited an annuity of £150 a year from his aunt.

Part 37 (January 16, 1841)
(67) At his wharf on a very foggy night, Quilp receives a letter of warning from Sally Brass. He curses Sampson, but he realizes that every "trouble and anxiety I have had of late times, springs from that old dotard and his darling child." Quilp plans his escape, but when he hears knocking at his gate, he panics, gets lost in the fog, falls into the river, and drowns.

(68) The Garlands hold a party to welcome Kit home from jail. His mother, his brother Jacob, Barbara's mother, and the Single Gentleman are all there. The pony Whisker nuzzles Kit and Barbara kisses him. Mr. Garland tells him to prepare for a journey to the village where Nell and her grandfather have been found.

Part 38 (January 23, 1841)
(69) The next morning in the carriage, the Single Gentleman tells Mr. Garland a story revealing that he is the estranged younger brother of Nell's grandfather. The two brothers had loved the same girl and he had gone abroad, giving up the girl to his brother. Now, after many years, he has returned to be reunited with him. (70) In the middle of a snowy night on the second day of their journey, they arrive at the village and rouse the sexton, who points the way to the ruin where Nell and her grandfather are living. Kit, carrying Nell's birdcage, goes to the house, drawn by a light in the window. As he knocks at the door, he hears a low moaning within.

Part 39 (January 30, 1841)
(71) Inside he finds Grandfather Trent, huddled before the ashes of a dying fire. Nell is asleep in an adjoining room. Neither Kit nor the grandfather's younger brother can rouse the old man from his preoccupation with Nell. When they go into the little room, they discover that Nell is dead. (72) She has been dead two days. On the Sunday of the funeral, the townspeople get a small boy to take Grandfather Trent into the country. Then they bury Nell in the church she loved. When Grandfather returns, he searches for her. Distracted and despairing, he takes his pack and staff and spends each day sitting by her grave waiting for her to return so they can resume their journey. One day the townspeople find him there dead.

Part 40 (February 6, 1841)
(73) Sampson Brass is sent to prison. Sally becomes a vagrant slum-dweller. Mrs. Quilp, enriched with her husband's money, marries an out-pensioner. Abel Garland marries a bashful young lady and the old bachelor from the village where Nell died comes to London to live with Mr. Garland, his brother. Dick Swiveller renames the Marchioness Sophronia Sphinx, pays for her education, marries her and moves to Hampstead. Fred Trent is drowned in Paris. The Single Gentleman seeks out all who were kind to Nell and his brother. Kit marries Barbara and he tells his children, Barbara, Abel, and Dick, "the story of good Miss Nell who died."

COMMENTARY

The Old Curiosity Shop has been rated as both the best and the worst of Dickens's novels, but no matter the verdict the novel almost always receives critical consideration. It has provoked strong reactions from its first appearance to the present. The idea for the story came to Dickens when he was visiting Walter Savage LANDOR in March 1840, and the old poet became one of young Nell's greatest admirers, suggesting that the "divine Nelly" was the best creation since Shakespeare's Cordelia. The story had its detractors as well; Edward Fitzgerald condemned "Boz's sham pathos," and the Irish politician Daniel O'Connell threw the book out of a train window in indignation when he realized that Nell was going to die. Most of Dickens's contemporaries, whether sophisicated readers or part of his broad popular audience, were deeply moved by the book. American readers are said to have gathered on the pier in New York as the ship arrived with the next serial installment to ask, "Is Little Nell dead?"

Many later critics have been less kind. Oscar Wilde is said to have quipped, "One must have a heart of stone to read the death of Little Nell without laughing," and Aldous Huxley chose Little Nell as a prime example of "vulgarity in literature"; her suffering, he claimed, lacked a context to give it significance. As a result it became merely bathetic SENTIMENTALITY. Although many contemporary critics continue to condemn the novel as overwritten and sentimental, others find significant ALLEGORY and a probing critique of Victorian culture in Nell's story. There is still no consensus about the quality or significance of the book.

Dickens began *Curiosity Shop* as a short story to be completed in a half-dozen chapters, but as he worked with the idea of the innocent child surrounded by old curiosities, it called for more expansive treatment. At the time he was seeking a way to give more continuity to *Master Humphrey's Clock*, for its miscellaneous and desultory character was turning away readers. As the story grew into a novel, Dickens knew that he had discovered the means to sustain reader engagement with his magazine. Still, at first he found the weekly deadlines and the shorter installments in the first of his weekly serials much more confining than the longer monthly parts of the earlier novels. After he got a feel for the weekly format and moved into the PICARESQUE journey narrative, however, the novel almost wrote itself. The only real difficulty Dickens encountered was telling the death of Little Nell.

John FORSTER takes credit for suggesting to Dickens, when he was about halfway through the novel, that Little Nell should die, but the idea seems present in the text from the start, as the paired illustrations by Samuel WILLIAMS of the sleeping Nell and by Cattermole of the dead Nell from beginning and end suggest. Dickens clearly improvised much of the novel and even if he had not consciously worked out the plot from the beginning, he had a least a subconscious awareness of the morbid logic at the heart of his story. Nell's death is foreshadowed throughout. Yet when he came to the final scenes, his grief for Mary HOGARTH, who had died three years earlier, made the writing difficult and painful. "It is very painful to me," he wrote to Forster, "that I really cannot express my sorrow. Old wounds bleed afresh when I think of this sad story." Yet Dickens, like many of his readers, sought out the painful indulgence. As he was writing about Nell's death, he refused all invitations to social engagements for fear of "disturbing the state I am trying to get into." Although he grieved for Mary's memory, his letters reveal that he was animated and lively at the same time.

The idea of an innocent young girl surrounded by old curiosities and old men immediately established the principle of contrast that pervades the novel. Youth and age, innocence and experience, good and evil, beauty and ugliness, passivity and violence, female and male are just a few of the polarities that are implicit from the opening scene. By the time he finished the story, Dickens realized that this principle of contrast was also the basis of allegory. In a passage added to the opening chapter when the novel was published as a single volume in 1841, Master Humphrey comments: "As it was, she seemed to exist in a kind of allegory; and having these shapes about her, claimed my interest so strongly, that . . . I could not dismiss her from my recollection, do what I would" (1). At several points later in the story, the narrator refers to Bunyan's *Pilgrim's Progress*, and some episodes on Nell's journey recall scenes from that well-known allegory.

Even though Nell is usually accepted as an allegorical rather than a realisitic character, she is nonetheless often dismissed as sentimental, a character for whom Dickens attempted to generate sympathy in excess of the facts of her situation. Certainly the narrator's clumsy attempts to heighten the effect of the narrative by preaching to the reader, as in his homily on sleep and death in chapter 12, often have an effect opposite to the one intended. But Dickens also shows considerable restraint in dealing with his highly charged subject matter. Nell's death, for example, occurs "offstage"; Dickens does not belabor the event itself. The modern reader must also remember the context which produced the novel. Victorian children, especially those who worked in mines and factories or scavenged with the street arabs of London, were threatened by industrialization and urbanization in ways that have been corrected by the social legislation of the last century and a half. The facts of Victorian life made many children an endangered species.

The novel does not attempt to treat these perils realistically. Even the scenes in the industrial Black Country are presented as surreal nightmare. The novel has more in common with FAIRY TALES, melodrama, pastoral, allegory, and such popular forms as PUNCH AND JUDY shows than with journalistic coverage or official reports. The young child leading the old man out of the corrupt city into the peacefulness of the country is an archetypal image, but it does not describe a sociological reality of the time. It articulates the ideal of a pastoral quest.

The simple journey plot is based in the opposition between city and country. The city—man-made and materialistic, corrupted by money, crowded and dangerous—threatens to draw innocence into its destructive vortex. By escaping to the peaceful countryside, Nell hopes to save her grandfather from destruction and to preserve her own innocence. But the problem is more complex than this simple dichotomy. As Quilp pursues Nell and her grandfather and they fall in with companions like Codlin and Short who threaten to expose them, the dangers of the city reach into the country. Also the countryside—a place of graveyards, dying schoolchildren, mouldering churches—achieves peacefulness at the expense of vitality. Rural villages are populated by old people on the edge of death; vitality and energy reside in the cities.

The dream allegory is dialectically structured around three defining characters: Nell, Quilp, and Dick Swiveller. Nell, the novel's thesis, is characterized by contrast to the old curiosities that surround her. From her first appearance lost on the streets of London, she is "little," an adjective used five times on the first page as she is introduced into the story. The curiosities around her include the old men—Master Humphrey and her grandfather—as well as the antique objects in the shop. She is solitary, "the only pure, fresh, youthful object in the throng" (1). Isolated amid the darkness and corruption of the city, Nell is abandoned by her grandfather and forced to plan her own retreat from Quilp's aggression.

The threat to Nell's innocence is not only external. As a girl of 13, Nell is on the edge of adulthood; her emerging sexuality also compromises her innocence. She responds to the threat of sexual maturity by retreat and denial. Withdrawing into her bower in the curiosity shop, she becomes, while sleeping, a prophetic image of the dead child at the end of the novel. She runs from Quilp, from her grandfather's weakness, from real and imagined threats of disclosure, and she denies herself comfort and food to provide for her grandfather. Her anorexic withdrawal is a gradual suicide to preserve her innocence and virtue. She is devoted to death. On her journey she seeks out graveyards, identifies with the schoolmaster's dying pupil, becomes a guide to a collection of corpselike waxwork figures, "a wax-work child" herself, as Miss Monflathers describes her (31). Nell is a childish, fairy-tale version of such earlier heroines doomed by virtue as Richardson's Clarissa.

Yet for all her weakness and passivity, Nell also has strength. On the journey, she is a parent to the old man, sustaining and providing for the two of them. The narrator ascribes her endurance to her virtue: "Nature often enshrines gallant and noble hearts in weak bosoms—oftenest, God bless her, in female breasts—and when the child, casting her tearful eyes upon the old man, remembered how weak he was, and how destitute and helpless he would be if she failed him, her heart swelled within her, and animated her with new strength and fortitude" (24). The journey stresses Nell's allegorical role; she becomes "the child" who shall lead her grandfather and others into the paths of righteousness. In the country, drawn to peace in country churchyards, Nell pursues the logic of her retreat from life as a choice of death.

Quilp represents the antithesis to Nell's death-wishing thesis. While she is passive, he is aggressively active, constantly seeking confrontations with his wife, his mother-in-law, his business contacts. Misogynous and sadistic, he describes his wife as "timid, loving Mrs. Quilp" (3) and delights in tormenting her. Even though she conspires with her female friends at tea "to resist that [male] tyranny" (4), she masochistically invites his mistreatment. He is a living version of Punch, the puppet who carries a stick to beat his wife and child. Quilp is as aggressively male as Nell is passively female. While Nell starves, he eats: "he ate hard eggs, shell and all, devoured prawns with the heads and tails on, chewed tobacco and watercresses at the same time and with extraordinary greediness, drank boiling tea without winking" (5). But as a deformed dwarf, he is an ugly parody of patriarchal power, capitalist greed, sexual oppression, and urban corruption, all aspects of his allegorical significance. As an impish ogre out of fairy tale, he embodies her childish fears more than he represents the social realities of the time. He is "a perpetual nightmare to the child, who was constantly haunted by a vision of his ugly face and stunted figure" (29), a projection of her fears of the city and her own sexuality.

Quilp's threat to Nell is explicitly sexual. He proposes to make her the second Mrs. Quilp, "to be my wife, my little cherry-cheeked, red-lipped wife" (6), and when he moves into the curiosity shop, he takes over Nell's "little room" for himself (11). The sexual threat posed by Quilp is a more assertive version of Fred Trent's scheme to marry the diffident Swiveller to her and a precursor to her grandfather's stealing into her room in the middle of the night to take money hidden in her clothes, a scene interpreted by some critics as a symbolic rape.

If Quilp is a monster of evil, a grotesque and deformed representation of aggression, violence, energy, capitalistic greed, and patriarchal oppression, Nell is a monster of virtue, innocent, selfless, otherworldly, suicidal. They represent such extremes—such absolutes—that they become separated from the others. Although Kit, the Garlands, and the old bachelor are members of Nell's camp of virtue, their goodness is more realistic and more compromising than hers. Kit is capable of transferring his affections to Barbara and surviving after Nell's

death. Likewise, Quilp's villainy is of a different order from that of Fred Trent or the Brasses. They inhabit the more realistic domain of con men and shady lawyers. Nell's isolation in the rural village inhabited by old men is mirrored by Quilp's solitary existence on the wharf by the THAMES. They are polarized DOUBLES, Little Nell and Little Quilp: energy versus passivity, city versus country, male versus female, adult experience versus childish innocence. Inevitably they die on the same night, Nell passing peacefully in her sleep, Quilp drowning as he tries to escape into the fog.

In the novel's dialectic, Dick Swiveller is the character who synthesizes the polarities of Nell and Quilp to the possibilities of compromise. He enters as a dissipated cohort of Fred Trent; in Trent's scheme to get his grandfather's money, Dick is to marry Nell. But Dick is too diffident to pursue that plot. He drops Sophy Wackles, but he makes no serious play for Nell. He is too intent on rosy wine and the songs that run through his head to pay serious attention to anyone else. Although he seems, like Quilp, to threaten Nell's virtue, he puts no energy into that scheme, or into his job with the Brasses. He lacks Quilp's aggressiveness and greed. If Quilp pursues self-interest, Dick could be said to pursue self-indulgence.

Dick swivels when he meets the Marchioness, the little kitchen drudge who emerges from the cellars of the Brass's house in BEVIS MARKS. Little like Nell, she is not a child of innocence; in a cancelled passage Dickens suggested that she was the child of Quilp and Sally Brass. But she draws Dick out of himself; focuses his antagonism to the Brasses, and makes his self-indulgent way of life useful as he teaches her to play cribbage and share a drink. By the end he has named, educated, and married her, and she has nursed him back to health. He did not drink himself to death while repeating old songs; she did not die in the tombs under the house in Bevis Marks. Together they transcend their separateness and isolation. Dick began as one of Dickens's self-creating comic figures who by imagination alone can transform gin into rosy wine and expand his single room into elaborate lodgings. In the end his imagination has expanded to name the mysterious Sophronia Sphinx and establish a new world for himself and his bride.

Curiosity Shop is a flawed novel, but it does not deserve Steven MARCUS's (1965) description as "Dickens's least successful novel, a work in which he seems to have lost much of his intellectual control, abandoning himself to all that was weakest and least mature in his character as a writer." Certainly Dickens searches for his theme and is vague about the allegorical significance of such characters as the Schoolmaster and Mrs. Jarley, but the central opposition between Nell and Quilp is clear and powerful. If Dick Swiveller seems less clearly defined and the nature of his achievement by the end not fully realized, he nevertheless remains one of Dickens's great comic characters, a novelistic figure whose ability to adapt to changing circumstances enables him to survive and grow. Meanwhile, both both Nell and Quilp, fixed as allegorical absolutes, are destroyed by their inability to learn from experience and change their lives.

CRITICISM

Curiosity Shop is the most discussed of the early novels. George FORD (1955) and Loralee MacPike (" 'The Old Curiosity Shape': Changing Views of Little Nell," 2 parts, *Dickens Studies Newsletter*, 1981) survey the widely differing responses to the novel and its heroine from the time of its publication. Since it evokes such divergent reactions, *Curiosity Shop* has been particularly interesting to reader-response critics: Michael STEIG has explored responses to the novel in several articles on Nell and, especially, Quilp, and on the role of grotesque comedy in the reader's reaction to the novel. His most recent article, "Abuse and the Comic Grotesque in *The Old Curiosity Shop*: Problems of Response" (*Dickens Quarterly*, 1994), reevaluates his earlier work in light of the differences between male and female responses to the novel. Analyzing the dynamics in reading the novel, Nicholas Morgan (*Secret Journeys: Theory and Practice in Reading Dickens*, 1992) finds the reader caught between the allegorical poles of angel and imp. The logic of the lives of both Nell and Quilp leads to death, he argues, and the reader must transfer sympathy from these allegorical figures to the survivors—Kit, Barbara, Swiveller, and the Marchioness.

The historical context of the novel is discussed by Paul SCHLICKE (1985) who considers the role of the traveling entertainers. In "The True Pathos of *The Old Curiosity Shop* (*Dickens Quarterly*, 1990), he discusses the historical background more broadly. Susan HORTON ("Swiveller and Snivellers: Competing Epistemologies in *The Old Curiosity Shop*" (*Dickens Quarterly*, 1990) considers the novel in relation to changing modes of shopping and popular entertainment. Ella Westland ("Little Nell and the Marchioness: some Functions of Fairy Tale in *The Old Curiosity Shop*," *Dickens Quarterly*, 1991), interprets the story as an allegory of economics in which Quilp represents "early-nineteenth-century capitalism; Nell comes to stand for capitalism's many victims," and the Marchioness offers a fairy tale of survival and modest triumph over the oppressive economic forces of the time.

Gabriel Pearson's classic essay on the novel (*Dickens and the Twentieth Century*, 1962), established the structural analysis that most later critics have followed. He is especially good on Dick Swiveller, whose ability to develop and adapt places him in sharp contrast to the unchanging Nell and Quilp. Garrett STEWART (1974) uses Swiveller as the "pivotal" figure in the novel and in Dickens's work generally, one of Dickens's "men of fancy" who recreate the world in imagination. S. J. Newman (*Dickens at Play*, 1981) sees incoherence as "the principle of narrative energy" in the novel and Swiveller as a figure who transforms the world in play. In a feminist reading, Gail Houston (*Consuming Fictions*, 1994) treats Nell and Quilp as representatives of the polarized gender roles in Victorian society. Characterized by his voracious appetite, Quilp is the "ultimate consumer who insists on possessing everything in the world around him," but "Nell's bodily desires must be contracted, and the Victorian narrative must transform her eros into thanatos."

Dickens Quarterly ran a 150th anniversary issue (March 1990) containing several articles on various aspects of the novel.

ADAPTATIONS

There were surprisingly few early theatrical adaptations of *Curiosity Shop*, in spite of Little Nell's popularity. Edward STIRLING adapted the story for the Adelphi Theatre while the novel was still running in serial, providing an ending in which Nell lives happily ever after. Malcolm MORLEY reports the probably apocraphal story that "such anticipation of her fate by the dramatist . . . annoyed Dickens so much that, having still several more chapters of the work to write, he reversed the Stirling pronouncement and killed the poor girl off."

The story came into its own theatrically in the late 1860s and 1870s when several versions of Nell's story appeared. John BROUGHAM's "Little Nell and the Marchioness" was first performed in AMERICA in 1867 with Carlotta CRABTREE playing both Nell and the Marchioness. Several other actresses combined the two roles during the following decade in plays that concentrated on the story of the child heroine, "An Angel on Earth," as one adaptation presented her. After the turn of the century, several theatrical adaptations appeared that gave Quilp or Dick Swiveller top billing.

There were several silent films from the novel, in 1903, 1911, 1912, 1914, and, most important, Thomas BENTLEY's version in 1921. Bentley also made the first sound picture from the novel in 1935, described by the *DICKENSIAN* as "the first British talking picture" based on Dickens. Although there have been few theatrical adaptations of the novel since World War II, a musical film, *Quilp*, directed by Michael Tucker with music by Anthony Newley, appeared in 1975. Newley also starred in the role of Quilp, with David Hemmings as Swiveller, Sara Jane Varley as Nell, and Michael Hordern as the grandfather.

The BBC has presented several radio and television adaptations of the novel, most notably a version in 13 episodes for television (1963) and William Trevor's nine-part television adaptation in 1980.

Old Curiosity Shop Several sites in London have been proposed as the original for the one in the novel; the popular tourist attraction in Portsmouth Street, however, is not among them.

Old Hell Shaft The abandoned mine shaft where Stephen Blackpool is found after his disappearance. *Hard Times* (III:6).

Old Kent Road The road David takes from London to DOVER in search of his aunt. *Copperfield* (13).

"Old Lady in Threadneedle Street, The" Article for HOUSEHOLD WORDS (July 6, 1850) by W. H. WILLS and Dickens describing a visit to the BANK OF ENGLAND in THREADNEEDLE STREET. Characterizing the visit as if to the household of "a dear, kind, liberal, benevolent Old Lady," they describe the activities in each of the rooms in the bank, comparing the institution to a publishing firm and a large circulating library. *Stone.*

"Old Lamps for New Ones" Article for HOUSEHOLD WORDS (June 15, 1850) attacking the medievalism of such groups as the Young England Movement and, especially, the PRE-RAPHAELITE BROTHERHOOD that disdained the progress of the preceding 300 years and, repeating the bargain made by the evil magician to obtain Aladdin's wonderful lamp in the ARABIAN NIGHTS, traded modern lamps for medieval ones. Dickens may also have had in mind John Ruskin, whose *Seven Lamps of Architecture* (1849) was current, when he chose the title for the article. Although Dickens apparently did not read Ruskin's book until later in the summer of 1850, Ruskin had already published one defense of the Pre-Raphaelites in a letter to the *Times* in May, shortly before Dickens published this article attacking them. Dickens begins with a famous attack on MILLAIS's painting "Christ in the House of his Parents," in which he claims that realism reduces a subject which should prompt "tender, awful, sorrowful, ennobling, sacred, grateful, or beautiful associations" into one which reveals "the lowest depths of what is mean, odious, repulsive, and revolting." Dickens then satirically suggests several other movements that might similarly promote retrogressive ideas. Pre-Perspective, Pre-Newtonian, Pre-Galileo, Pre-Harvey, Pre-Gower and Pre-Chaucer brotherhoods could apply similarly misguided principles to various scientific and humanistic studies and to literature, "cancelling all the advances of nearly four hundred years, and reverting to one of the most disagreeable periods . . . when the Nation was yet very slowly emerging from barbarism." *Miscellaneous.*

"Old Soldier, The" Doctor Strong's schoolboys' name for Mrs. MARKLEHAM. *Copperfield.*

Old Square The section of LINCOLN'S INN where the offices of Kenge and Carboy are located. *Bleak House* (20).

"Old Stage-coaching House, An" The Traveller stays at the DOLPHIN'S HEAD, a coaching inn "dying by inches" since the coming of the railway. The town, seven miles from the railway station, is deserted and melancholy, its buildings crumbling; a broken post chaise is even being used as a dwelling. *Uncommercial,* 24. Originally in ALL THE YEAR ROUND (August 1, 1863).

Old Street Road The street in east London, now simply Old Street, where Mrs. Guppy lives "in an in-dependent though unassuming manner" (9). *Bleak House.*

Old 'Un, The Daniel Peggoty's way of referring to Mrs. Gummidge's deceased husband. *Copperfield.*

Oliver Twist, or, The Parish Boy's Progress Dickens's second novel, serialized in 24 monthly installments in BENTLEY'S MISCELLANY between February 1837 and April 1839 (no installments June, October 1837; September 1838), with illustrations by CRUIKSHANK. In *Twist,* Dickens seemed to choose subject matter that turned *Pickwick* on its head. As his central figure he replaced the retired businessman with a child, and the innocent world of the earlier novel gave way to the dark criminal underworld of Sikes and Fagin. Although he was not fully successful in giving coherence to this story, it does evoke a compelling vision of childhood haunted by a mythic struggle between the forces of Good and Evil.

SYNOPSIS

Part 1 (February 1837)
(1) Oliver Twist is born in a workhouse. His mother dies before she makes her identity known to anyone there. (2) Oliver is brought up "by hand" in the workhouse for a year. Then he is farmed out to Mrs. Mann's baby farm, where he is systematically starved for the next eight years. On Oliver's ninth birthday Mr. Bumble, the parish beadle, takes the boy back to the workhouse to learn

Cruikshank's rendering the the most famous moment in Oliver Twist—Oliver *asking for more.*

a useful trade—picking oakum. The inmates there are also systematically starved. The hungry boys draw lots and Oliver is "chosen" to ask for a second bowl of gruel. His innocent request of the master, "Please, sir, I want some more," so astonishes and horrifies the workhouse authorities that they predict he "will be hung" and advertise his availability to apprentice to a trade.

Part 2 (March 1837)
(3) Mr. Gamfield, a chimney sweep, applies to take the boy. After some haggling the board agrees to turn Oliver over to him, but Oliver pleads with the magistrate, who refuses to approve the papers. (4) The next applicant is Mr. Sowerberry, an undertaker. Oliver, by this point "reduced . . . to a state of brutal stupidity and selfishness," makes no objection. Mrs. Sowerberry assigns Oliver a place to sleep among the coffins.

Part 3 (April 1837)
(5) The next day Oliver meets Noah Claypole, a charity boy also employed by Sowerberry. He taunts Oliver with the epithet "Work'us." After a month or so, Oliver is promoted to serve as a mute, a silent mourner supplied by the undertaker. His first funeral in this capacity is for a poor woman who starved to death while her husband was imprisoned for begging. After this sad event, Sowerberry tells Oliver that he'll "get used to it in time." (6) Resentful of Oliver's favored place, Claypole tells him, "yer must know, Work'us, yer mother was a regular right-down bad 'un." Furious, Oliver attacks Noah and knocks him to the floor, but Mrs. Sowerberry and the maid Charlotte subdue him and lock him in a cellar. Noah is sent to fetch Mr. Bumble.

Part 4 (May 1837)
(7) When Bumble arrives, Oliver is still defiant. Bumble cannot calm him, and asserting, "It's meat . . . You've over fed him, ma'am," he advises Mrs. Sowerberry to starve him into submission. When the undertaker returns, he beats Oliver. Early the next morning, Oliver runs away and sets out for London. On the way he says goodbye to Little Dick, one of his companions at Mrs. Mann's baby farm. (8) Oliver walks the 70 miles to London in six days, sleeping under hay ricks along the way. On the seventh day, he arrives in BARNET. There he meets "one of the queerest looking boys" he has ever seen, a short, ugly boy wearing a top hat and a man's overcoat with the sleeves folded back. Jack Dawkins, or "the Artful Dodger," buys some food for the hungry Oliver and then takes him into the city to the den of Fagin, a receiver of stolen goods, an old Jew who maintains a gang of juvenile pickpockets. There he is given supper and a place to sleep.

Part 5 (July 1837)
(9) The next morning, Oliver sees Fagin going through the treasures in a little strongbox. When Fagin realizes the boy is watching him, he is alarmed and tells him the things in the box are his savings. Later, the Dodger and Charley Bates return from working the crowd at an execution; they bring handkerchiefs and pocketbooks to Fagin. The boys play a game of picking Fagin's pockets.

(10) After many days in the hideout, Oliver is allowed to go out with the Dodger and Bates. When they see an old gentleman outside a bookshop absorbed in reading, the Dodger steals his handkerchief, gives it to Charley, and then the two of them run off. In an instant Oliver realizes what the gang is up to and he too begins running. The cry of "stop thief," goes up. Oliver is pursued through the streets. Even the Dodger and Bates join the chase. Finally, his strength spent, Oliver is knocked to the ground and arrested. The other two boys have disappeared. (11) Weak and faint, Oliver is unable to give his name, so he stands trial as "Tom White." Even though the old gentleman does not press charges, Oliver is convicted by Magistrate Fang. When the bookstore owner exonerates him, Fang reluctantly releases Oliver into the custody of the old gentleman, Mr. Brownlow.

Part 6 (August 1837)
(12) Brownlow takes Oliver to his home and puts the feverish child to bed. Mrs. Bedwin, a kind housekeeper, nurses him back to health. As he convalesces in the housekeeper's room, he is fascinated by a portrait of a young woman. Brownlow is startled to notice that Oliver is a "living copy" of the picture.

Meanwhile, the Dodger and Bates return to Fagin's den after the robbery. (13) The Jew is enraged when he hears what has happened. He throws a mug of beer at Bates, but it hits instead a dark, unkempt fellow, Bill Sikes, who has just entered the room. Fearful that Oliver will expose the gang, Fagin recruits Nancy, a prostitute who is Sikes's companion, to recover the boy. Posing as Oliver's sister, she learns the general location of Brownlow's house.

Part 7 (September 1837)
(14) When Oliver recovers, Brownlow buys him a new suit. One evening he asks the boy to give an account of his life, but before Oliver can tell his story, Mr. Grimwig, Brownlow's cynical chess companion, comes to visit. Later, when Brownlow wants to return some books to the bookseller, Oliver offers to go. Brownlow agrees, convinced that the boy will refute Grimwig's assumption that Oliver, with "a suit of clothes on his back, a set of valuable books under his arm, and a five-pound note in his pocket," will not return. (15) Oliver gets lost on the way to the bookstore. In a side street he meets Nancy who, with the help of Bill Sikes and the support of the crowd that gathers, overpowers him. Meanwhile Brownlow and Grimwig sit in the dark awaiting Oliver's return.

Part 8 (November 1837)
(16) Nancy and Sikes take Oliver to Fagin's new den, where the Dodger and Bates mock his fancy clothes. Fagin beats him, but Nancy takes away his club and vows that Fagin "will be the worse for it" if he harms the boy. The thieves take Oliver's new suit and restore the identical rags he had worn before, which they have found at a rag dealer's shop.

(17) The narrator compares the alternation of tragic and comic scenes on the stage to similarly abrupt changes in real life. Then the narrative shifts back to

Oliver's birthplace, where Bumble has stopped at Mrs. Mann's on his way to London. There he learns that little Dick is ill. The boy, whose limbs have "wasted away, like those of an old man," asks the Beadle to convey a message of love and good wishes to Oliver Twist. Bumble is outraged; "that out-dacious Oliver has demogalized them all," he exclaims. In London Bumble sees Brownlow's advertisement offering five guineas for information about Oliver. His account of the boy's "vicious parent, . . . treachery, ingratitude, and malice" saddens Brownlow, who forbids Oliver's name to be mentioned again in his household. Nevertheless, Mrs. Bedwin continues to believe in the boy.

Part 9 (December 1837)
(18) Fagin holds Oliver in solitary confinement. After several lonely weeks, Oliver is advised by the Dodger and Bates to join them in the "trade," but Oliver resists. Finally Fagin decides to educate Oliver to the trade by placing him in the constant company of the other two boys. (19) When Sikes and his accomplice Toby Crackit need a small boy for a robbery, Nancy proposes Oliver. Fagin likes the idea of implicating Oliver in a crime as a way to silence him. He is also convinced that his uneasiness about Nancy was unwarranted.

Part 10 (January 1838)
(20) Fagin warns Oliver that Sikes is a "rough man." When Nancy comes to fetch him, Oliver senses that he has "some power over the girl's better feelings," but she tells him that "this is not the time" to attempt to escape from Fagin. Sikes holds a pistol to Oliver's temple and warns him to do exactly as he is told. (21) Then Sikes and Oliver go westward out of the city, stopping on the way at an old ruined house. (22) Within they find Toby Crackit and Barney, a waiter from SAFFRON HILL. They rest until 1:30 in the morning, then set off again. After passing through CHERTSEY, they silently approach a large house. When Oliver realizes what is afoot, he pleads with Sikes to let him go. But Sikes cocks his pistol, removes the shutter from a small window at the back of the house, and tells Oliver to go through the house and unlock the street door. Then he lifts Oliver through the window and drops him inside. Oliver thinks of raising an alarm, but suddenly he sees two men, "a flash—a loud noise—a smoke—a crash somewhere." Sikes pulls him back through the window. As Sikes carries him off, Oliver loses consciousness.

Part 11 (February 1838)
(23) Bumble visits Mrs. Corney, the matron of the workhouse, and enunciates his welfare principle: "The great principle of out-of-door relief is, to give the paupers exactly what they don't want; and then they get tired of coming." Mrs. Corney agrees and invites him to tea. Bumble moves his chair until he can put his arm around Mrs. Corney and kiss her. This domestic scene is interrupted when she is summoned to the deathbed of an inmate. While she is gone Bumble inventories the items in her china closet. (24) The dying pauper confesses to Mrs. Corney that years earlier she stole a gold object

from the young woman who bore a child named Oliver. Mrs. Corney leaves the room reporting, "Nothing to tell, after all."

(25) When Crackit tells Fagin of the bungled robbery and that he and Sikes left the boy bleeding in a ditch, Fagin rushes out of the house "twining his hands in his hair."

Part 12 (March 1838)
(26) Fagin finds Nancy, apparently stupefied from drink, but she has no information about Sikes or Oliver. When Fagin arrives back at his den at midnight, a mysterious man named Monks is there waiting for him. The two men discuss the bungled robbery and Monks asserts that Fagin could have made a thief of the boy and had him transported for life. They are startled by the shadow of a woman on the wall, but when they search they find no one.

(27) Meanwhile, Bumble evaluates the contents of Mrs. Corney's room, exclaiming to himself, "I'll do it." When the matron returns, Bumble calls her "a angel" and proposes, envisioning them as the codirectors of the workhouse. Mrs. Corney accepts her "irresistible duck."

Part 13 (April 1838)
(28) After the robbery, Sikes leaves the wounded Oliver in a ditch. The boy recovers consciousness early the next morning and, weakened by loss of blood, he stumbles to the nearest house, the one they had attempted to rob. He knocks on the door and collapses on the front steps. The servants in the house, including Giles and Brittles, the two who had surprised him the night before, answer his knock and "capture" the thief. (29) The doctor, Mr. Losberne, examines Oliver and (30) discovers that the robber is a "mere child." Convinced that the boy is innocent, Losberne, Mrs. Maylie, and her niece Rose are determined to save him. That evening Losberne encourages Oliver to tell them his "simple history." The doctor confounds Giles and Brittles, making them uncertain of their identification of Oliver as the robber.

Part 14 (May 1838)
(31) The investigating officers from London, Blathers and Duff, get an evasive account from Losberne and hear contradictory stories from Giles and Brittles. By the time they question Oliver, the boy is feverish. They return to London without an arrest. (32) After Oliver recovers, Losberne offers to go with him in search of Mr. Brownlow. As they pass the ruined house where Oliver and Sikes stopped on the way to the robbery, Losberne impetuously goes into the building, but he finds only an old humpbacked man who claims that he has lived there for 25 years. In London they discover that Brownlow has gone to the West Indies. Disappointed, Oliver goes off with Mrs. Maylie and Rose to the country.

Part 15 (June 1838)
(33) Oliver thrives in the country, but Rose falls ill. When she takes a turn for the worse, Mrs. Maylie asks Oliver to mail letters to Doctor Losberne and to her son, Harry. As he is leaving the inn after dispatching the letters, Oliver stumbles against a tall stranger in a dark cloak,

Monks, who curses him, shakes his fist as if he is about to hit him, and then falls to the ground in a fit. Oliver's astonishment and fear are soon forgotten, however, in his concern about Rose, who hovers on the brink of death. Finally Losberne reports that Rose has passed the crisis and will live. (34) When Harry arrives, Oliver tells him the good news and Harry informs his mother that he loves Rose and plans to marry her, even if her birth is clouded by scandal.

One evening as Oliver is reading in a small room with a window opening on to the garden, he dozes off and dreams that he is back in Fagin's den. He hears the Jew say, "It is he, sure enough," and awakens to see two figures in the window, Fagin and the man who cursed him at the inn. They vanish as Oliver calls for help.

Part 16 (July 1838)
(35) Harry Maylie, Losberne, and Giles respond to Oliver's cry, but they can find no sign of the intruders. As Rose recovers she urges Harry to forget her, telling him that the stain on her name would blight his prospects. Harry gets her permission to press his suit once more within a year. (36) As he sets out for London, Harry secures Oliver's promise that he will write regularly and tell about himself and Rose.

(37) Meanwhile, Bumble has married Mrs. Corney and become master of the workhouse. Although he has been married for eight weeks, "it seems a age." Mrs. Bumble refuses to take his orders. She pommels him and humiliates him in front of the paupers. Bumble retreats to a public house and there meets a stranger who is seeking information about Oliver's mother. Bumble arranges to introduce the stranger, Monks, to someone who can throw some light on the subject of his inquiry.

Part 17 (August 1838)
(38) The next evening the Bumbles meet Monks at a ruined warehouse by the river. For £25, Mrs. Bumble reveals the things that Oliver's mother left, a locket containing "two locks of hair, and a plain gold wedding ring" inscribed with the name "Agnes." Monks drops the trinkets through a trap door into the river. Then he pledges the Bumbles to secrecy.

(39) Ravaged by illness, Sikes abuses Nancy and accuses his cronies of neglecting him. He sends Nancy to get some money from Fagin. While she is at Fagin's den, she overhears a private conversation between the Jew and Monks. She collects the money and then runs out into the street, crying and wringing her hands. By the time she delivers the money to Sikes, she has recovered her equanimity.

Part 18 (October 1838)
The next day Nancy has "the nervous manner of one . . . on the eve of some bold and hazardous step." She puts opium in Sikes's gin to make him sleep. Then she goes to a hotel near Hyde Park where she asks to see Rose Maylie. (40) Nancy tells Rose that she would be murdered if her whereabouts were known. She tells of overhearing Monks offer Fagin money to make Oliver a

thief; then, last night, of hearing Monks tell Fagin that all traces of Oliver's identity had been destroyed. She reports that Monks wants to destroy Oliver, his half brother. Monks also said that Mrs. Maylie and Rose would pay a fortune to know Oliver's identity. Rose offers to help Nancy escape from her dangerous life, but Nancy refuses all help. She arranges to walk on London Bridge on Sunday evenings between 11 and midnight should Rose want to communicate further with her.

(41) Oliver and Mr. Brownlow are reunited. Brownlow is overjoyed to see Oliver and learn his story. He and Rose plan to pursue Monks, but they agree not to tell Oliver.

Part 19 (November 1838)
(42) Noah Claypole and Charlotte come to London after taking money from Sowerberry's till. Fagin recruits Noah to steal coins from children. Fagin sends Noah, now using the pseudonym Morris Bolter, to observe the Artful Dodger's trial for picking pockets. The Dodger makes a mockery of the court, but he is formally indicted and taken off to jail. Noah takes the news back to Fagin.

Part 20 (December 1838)
(44) Fagin enlists Noah to spy on Nancy. The next Sunday evening, Bill Sikes remains at home, so Nancy, nervous and hysterical, cannot go out. (45) A week later, Noah follows her to LONDON BRIDGE. (46) There she meets Rose and Brownlow and takes them down some stairs at the end of the bridge. She offers to help Brownlow capture Monks on the conditions that Fagin not be involved and her identity as informer be kept secret. When she describes "a broad red mark, like a burn or scald" on Monks's neck, Brownlow indicates that he knows Monks's identity. Brownlow offers to help Nancy go to a safe haven, but she refuses. After Rose and Brownlow leave, she sinks down on the stairs and sobs. Then she returns to the street, soon followed by Noah who has overheard the conversation on the stairs.

Part 21 (January 1839)
(47) After Fagin gets Noah to tell Sikes what he saw and heard on the bridge, Sikes, wild with anger, rushes back to his rooms, awakens Nancy, and accuses her. She pleads with him to take up Brownlow's offer and go off with her to some distant place. But Sikes beats her twice across her upturned face with his pistol, knocking her to the ground. Then he seizes a heavy club and delivers the killing blow. (48) As the morning sunlight comes into the room, Sikes turns his back on the body, but he cannot get the horror out of his mind or forget the eyes staring at him. He burns the club, washes the bloodstains from his clothes, and leaves the house with his dog Bullseye. He goes to the countryside north of London, but wherever he goes he is haunted by the "widely staring eyes." Finally he decides to return to the city. Afraid that his dog will give him away, he attempts to drown the animal, but the dog escapes and runs off.

(49) Meanwhile Brownlow has captured Monks. Brownlow knows Monks is Edward Leeford, the son of

his oldest friend, Edwin Leeford. He tells Monks the story of his father's unhappy first marriage, the separation from his wife (Monks's mother), and the later relationship with Oliver's mother. He describes the will that Monks's mother destroyed after Edwin Leeford's death and the proofs of Oliver's identity that Monks destroyed. Threatening to prosecute Monks as an accessory to Nancy's murder, Brownlow gets Monks to write a confession and to restore Oliver as his father's heir.

Part 22 (February 1839)
(50) Fagin and Noah Claypole have been arrested. Three fugitives—Toby Crackit, Chitling, and Kags—have holed up in a derelict dwelling on JACOB'S ISLAND, a repulsive slum near the THAMES. Sikes's dog arrives there mud-covered and lame. A little while later Sikes appears, his blanched face buried in a handkerchief. When Charley Bates arrives, he backs away from Sikes and vows to turn him over to the mob that has gathered outside. Bates calls to the police from an open window. Sikes gets a rope and crawls out on to the roof of the house. The mob, directed by Bates's cries, breaks down the door. Sikes loops the rope around a chimney, but when he loses his balance and falls from the roof, the rope forms a noose around his neck. Bates sees his body swinging past the window. Bullseye jumps from the roof to his master, but misses the body and is dashed to death on a stone in the ditch below.

Part 23 (March 1839)
(51) Mr. Brownlow takes Oliver to his birthplace. There Monks corroborates the story of Edwin Leeford and Agnes Fleming, Oliver's parents, and gives an account of Edwin Leeford's will, which had left his estate to Oliver if "in his minority he should never have stained his name with any public act of dishonor, meanness, cowardice, or wrong." Monks paid Fagin to arrange Oliver's corruption. The Bumbles admit their complicity in suppressing Oliver's identity. Bumble tries to place the blame on his wife, but Brownlow informs him that under the law he is the more guilty party, because the law "supposes that your wife acts under your direction." Bumble responds by asserting, "If the law supposes that, the law is a ass—a idiot." Then Brownlow reveals the identity of Rose Maylie as the younger sister of Agnes Fleming, hence Oliver's aunt. Harry renews his suit for her hand, telling her that he has chosen to become a village parson so that he will be her social equal. The engaged couple join the others for a celebratory supper, but Oliver is sad, for he has learned that Little Dick is dead.

Part 24 (April 1839)
(52) Fagin is found guilty and condemned to death by hanging. In his cell he vacillates between stupefaction, defiance, and dementia. When Oliver comes with Brownlow to visit him in his cell, the old man shrinks from the boy and then imagines that the child can get him out of prison. As Oliver and Brownlow leave, Fagin sends up "cry upon cry that penetrated even those massive walls, and rang in their ears until they reached the open yard." By the time they leave it is dawn and the crowd is gathering for the execution.

(53) Three months later, Rose and Harry marry and settle in the country. Brownlow adopts Oliver and they settle nearby. Oliver agrees to give half of his father's estate to Monks so he can start a new life in the New World, where he squanders the money and dies in prison. Noah Claypole, pardoned for testifying against Fagin, takes up a career as a police informer. Charley Bates abandons crime to become a sheepherder in Northamptonshire. The Bumbles, relieved of their parochial positions, are inmates in the workhouse they once managed. The community of Brownlow and the Maylies, augmented by the frequent visits of Losberne and Grimwig, is "truly happy"; the two orphans, Oliver and Rose, "tried by adversity, remember its lessons in mercy to others, and mutual love, and fervent thanks to Him who had protected and preserved them." In the village church there is a white marble tablet inscribed with one name, "Agnes."

COMMENTARY

In *Twist* Dickens explores territory very different from that in *Sketches by Boz* or *Pickwick*. It represents a third kind of experiment by a novelist still in the process of learning his craft and discovering his voice. The novel does not follow Oliver's life long enough to make this a BILDUNGSROMAN, for we do not see how Oliver's childhood experiences shape his character as an adult, but the beginnings of that learning process are present in Oliver's story. *Twist* is one of the earliest novels to employ a child hero, a figure who will reappear in several of Dickens's later novels and in the works of other Victorian novelists. For its time *Oliver Twist* was an experimental novel.

Like Dickens's other early works, *Twist* was not carefully planned. A monthly serial for BENTLEY'S MISCELLANY, a magazine Dickens was editing at the time, *Twist* began appearing while *Pickwick* was in the midst of its serial run. The two novels overlapped for nine months and Dickens devoted half of the month to composing each of the monthly installments for the two books. After only a few months' respite at the end of *Pickwick*, Dickens began *Nickleby* in February 1838; that novel overlapped the last nine months of *Twist*'s serialization. At the same time, Dickens was editing the *Miscellany* and undertaking other writing and editorial projects. With so many demands, he had little time to plan his novels or to revise the monthly numbers. There are extensive revisions for some later editions of *Twist*, suggesting that Dickens was aware, at least later on, of the limitations to his demanding schedule. The revisions also reveal a more mature writer at work, for they toned down the sentimentality, cut out some of the strong language, and removed some of the apparent anti-Semitism in the presentation of Fagin.

Dickens also dealt with stresses in his personal life while working on the novel. The many projects he undertook and his unsettled contractual arrangements with various publishers indicate the financial pressures that Dickens faced as a young husband and father establishing himself as a professional writer. Some commentators have suggested that Oliver's vulnerability reflects the insecurity that Dickens felt at this early stage in his career. Only a few months after he began the novel, Mary HOGARTH, his young sister-in-law, died. Overcome with grief, Dickens suspended the publication of the monthly installments of his novels, one of the rare times that he failed to meet his publication schedule. Rose Maylie, first in a series of young women in the novels who were inspired by Dickens's memories of Mary Hogarth, is arrested in angelic innocence.

Oliver Twist, too, may be the first novel in which Dickens imaginatively recreated his experiences as a child working in the BLACKING FACTORY. Kidnapped from his respectable life with Brownlow and forced by Fagin to take part in Sikes's crimes, Oliver, like the young Dickens, feels helplessly entrapped in an alien world. Several commentators have suggested that *Twist* is the first of the "autobiographical" novels, the initial statement of Dickens' orphan myth that will be developed most fully in *Copperfield* and *Expectations*.

Dickens began the novel with topical satire, taking on the controversial New POOR LAW and the workhouse system that it instituted. In 1837–38 there were massive protests against the law, especially in the north of England. By abolishing outdoor relief, i.e., payments from the parish to supplement otherwise inadequate wages, and by requiring those who received benefits to enter a workhouse, the Poor Law was widely regarded as oppressive, a law which made poverty a crime and which imprisoned the pauper in "Poor Law Bastilles," workhouses made uninviting to discourage any but the most desperate from entering.

Bumble, Mrs. Corney, and Mrs. Mann are the heartless representatives of the workhouse system in the novel. To them Oliver is simply an "item of mortality" (1), his name merely the next one on an alphabetical list that Bumble uses to identify infant paupers. These nameless orphans have no history, no life story; if they survive the deprivation of the baby farm and the workhouse, they are sold as apprentices to the least demanding bidder. Oliver's innocence saves him from being released to a chimney sweep—an occupation notorious at the time for endangering and maiming the boys who worked at it—when the magistrate accidentally looks into his face and understands his fear. But the Board of Poor Law Guardians shows no similar humanity or understanding. They are convinced that Oliver is a "bad 'un" who will surely end up being hung.

Besides his attacks on the workhouse system, the law that established it, and the bureaucracacy that administered it, Dickens also satirized—in Magistrate Fang—the legal system that supported it. Fang was based on Magistrate LAING of HATTON GARDEN, notorious for his harshness and insolence. Dickens, who knew Laing only by reputation, visited his courtroom before writing of Oliver's hearing. His satire of the trial is said to have prompted the Home Secretary to remove Laing from the bench.

Dickens's subtitle, "The Parish Boy's Progress," suggests a larger satiric context for the topicalities in the opening numbers of *Twist*. Although Steven MARCUS (1965) and others have argued that Dickens had Bunyan's *Pilgrim's Progress* in mind as a model for his story, the Progresses of William HOGARTH were a more likely inspiration, for Dickens knew Hogarth's visual stories well and he shared the satiric and moralistic vision that prompted Hogarth's art. *Twist* begins as a story that promises to expose the ways in which oppressive social institutions corrupt children and turn them into thieves and criminals; Oliver's progress seems destined to follow a course much like that of Hogarth's idle apprentice, from idleness, to crime, and ultimately to the gallows. That Hogarthian theme governs the stories of the Artful Dodger, Noah Claypool, and most of the underworld characters in the novel, but Dickens was not so cynical as his mentor, nor, at this early stage of his career, so philosophically consistent in developing his satiric theme. When Oliver leaves the country and goes to London, the novel seems to shift from satiric exposé to mythic allegory. Instead of describing Oliver's progress to the gallows, the novel pits the innocent Oliver against the satanic Fagin and transforms his progress into a quest for identity.

Although *Twist* was attacked when it first appeared as one of the corrupting NEWGATE NOVELS, the Oliver of the quest story is very different from such Newgate figures as AINSWORTH'S Jack Sheppard, with whom he was often linked. The fictional biography of a notorious criminal from the *NEWGATE CALENDAR*, Jack's story is a realistic account, a downward progress from idleness to thievery, to transportation, and, finally, to the gallows. By the time Oliver reaches London, Dickens does not think of his child hero as a realistic figure, but rather as the allegorical "principle of Good surviving through every adverse circumstance, and triumphing at last" (1843 Preface). Although Oliver gradually comes to recognize and understand the presence of evil in the world, he is not corrupted by it. As an allegorical figure, he is not changed by experience; he remains angelic to the end, representative of innocence and goodness.

Although Dickens defended Fagin as a realistic representation of a whole class of criminal receivers of stolen goods, his allegorical intent is also apparent from Fagin's first appearance. Standing "before the fire. . . . with a toasting-fork in his hand . . . [his] villainous-looking and repulsive face . . . obscured by a quantity of matted red hair" (8), Fagin is satanic from the outset. Ironically, he is almost the first person to treat Oliver kindly and to take some "parental" interest in him. He provides food and lodging for the boy and devotes himself to Oliver's education. That Fagin should provide what the indifferent representatives of the Parish denied to Oliver heightens the satiric message and describes a world in which an indifferent society colludes with the powers of darkness to destroy the innocent. Evil has a metaphysical presence in the novel; goodness is less convincing. Graham GREENE (1950) describes the Manichaean allegory in *Twist* as "a world without God, . . . [where] we can believe in evil-doing, but goodness wilts into philanthropy."

Oliver has moments of epiphany when he loses his intellectual innocence, as, for example, when he realizes during the bookshop robbery that he is one of a gang of thieves and that the handkerchief game was part of his instruction in picking pockets (10). But Oliver is not changed by this knowledge. The more he knows of Fagin, Sikes, and Monks, the more evident the contradiction between the assumptions behind the satire and those behind the allegory. Satire is existential; it assumes that experience molds and changes people, that oppression and deprivation will turn an innocent child into a criminal. Allegory takes an essentialist view; its static characters represent fixed ideas and ideals. These contradictory modes at the heart of the novel create what has sometimes been formulated as a version of the nature/ nurture conflict, asking whether criminals are born or made. Dickens seems to take both sides of the issue, depending on whether he is writing about the Artful Dodger or about Oliver.

Dickens may recognize the contradiction at the heart of his story when he introduces chapter 17 with a discussion of the principle of alternation between tragic and comic scenes in the drama as one that is also true to life off stage. But moving back and forth between satiric and allegorical modes, and between the light world of Brownlow and the dark underworld of Fagin, his story sometimes seems headed in two different directions. He does use alternation effectively to provide suspense when he leaves Oliver lying wounded in a ditch for three numbers while he narrates the comedy of Bumble's courtship. But the novel loses coherence when Oliver takes up permanent residence with the Maylies and is no longer part of Fagin's urban hell. As long as Oliver was present in both allegorical dimensions, he provided a coherent center to the alternations between the light and dark worlds in the novel. But when he exited from Fagin's realm, Dickens was forced to turn the allegorical quest narrative into an inheritance story.

This difficulty may have resulted from Dickens's choice of a child hero. Even with his allegorical power to resist evil, there are limits to Oliver's experience. When Brownlow takes him to Fagin's cell on the night before the old man is to hang, the jailer warns him "It's not a sight for children, sir." Brownlow replies that "This child has seen him in full career of his success and villainy, I think it as well—even at the cost of some pain and fear—that he should see him now" (52). But Dickens was unwilling to expose his child hero to the murder of Nancy and the death of Sikes. There were some things beyond even the limits of Oliver's innocence.

While the dark side of the novel careens out of control with the account of Sikes and Nancy, Oliver is in protective custody at the Maylie's country house. Oliver's

existential quest to reconcile the bifurcation in his experience is replaced by Browlow's manipulation of Oliver's origins and identity. Oliver becomes the passive recipient of an 18th-century inheritance plot rather than the 19th-century hero who defines the terms of his own life. Earlier in the novel, he asserts himself to ask for more in the workhouse dining room, to resist being apprenticed to the chimney sweep, to defend his mother's honor against Noah Claypole's aspersions, to run away from Sowerberry and to resist becoming a thief. But by the end he has lost his assertiveness and he simply accepts Brownlow's version of his story.

Yet even in Eden, Oliver is not wholly without contradiction. In one of the most memorable and puzzling scenes in the novel, Oliver sees Fagin and Monks at the window of his country retreat, but when he raises the alarm no trace of their presence can be found (34, 35). We are left to wonder whether the experience was dream or reality and to speculate about whether the evil represented by the intruders is outside the window or within Oliver. The novel provides no answer to these questions, nor to some of the other mysteries in Oliver's story. Losberne, for example, cannot confirm Oliver's account of the house where he and Sikes spent the night on their way to Chertsey (32).

Even the formulaic inheritance plot cannot fully replace the experiential account of Oliver's search for identity. His father's will that made Oliver's inheritance contingent on his incorruptibility may explain Monk's motivation and Fagin's interest in the boy, but it cannot comprehend the depths of betrayal and fear that motivate the evil characters nor the goodness that protects Oliver and prompts Nancy to give her life for him. The mysteries of Good and Evil at the heart of the allegory are beyond novelistic explanation. Nor can the inheritance plot provide Oliver with a fully acceptable identity. He remains an illegitimate child, bearing his workhouse name, son of a mother identified on her tombstone only as "Agnes." In the end he is still a kind of social orphan.

In spite of its inconsistencies and contradictions *Oliver Twist* contains a number of memorable scenes and characters, many of them rendered in the compelling illustrations by Cruikshank. The success of these pictures suggests that Dickens may have thought of his story as a literary version of one of Hogarth's progresses. Especially memorable scenes include Oliver asking for more gruel at the workhouse, his arrival at Fagin's den, the robbery at Chertsey, Monks and Fagin at the window, Sikes's death, and Fagin in the condemned cell. These scenes do represent a downward progress from the workhouse to the gallows, even though Oliver is not the prisoner waiting to be hanged at the end of the story.

While Oliver is usually criticized as a simplistic allegorical character and a passive pawn in the inheritance plot, the contradictory modes in the novel make many of the characters around him, particularly those from the criminal underworld, intriguingly complex figures. Fagin has sometimes been viewed simply as an anti-Semitic stereotype. Certainly he is a product of anti-Semitic tradition, which Dickens seems to have accepted uncritically. Yet Dickens's revisions of later editions of *Twist*, and his inclusion of Riah in *Mutual Friend* indicate his willingness to redress a wrong when the injustice of his portrayal was pointed out to him. Even in his original depiction, Fagin does, in significant ways, transcend the stereotype. A mixture of satanic evil and sympathy complicates his character. His kindness to Oliver contrasts with the inhumane bureaucracy of the Poor Law administrators, and when Fagin instructs Noah Claypole in the principle of looking out for number one (43), he articulates the "philosophy" that the respectable proponents of laissez-faire who created the workhouse system share with the criminal underworld. But Fagin's application of the principle of self-interest—using hanging as a way of getting rid of those who know too much—takes the cruelty of the system to a brutal extreme. As the avatar of satanic evil, the vehicle for exposing the inhumanity of the system, and the scapegoat victim of society's attempt at self-preservation, Fagin elicits complicated responses and some limited sympathy.

The Artful Dodger is similarly complex. His criminality demands that he be punished for his crimes, but his oversized clothes remind us that he is a child forced into adult responsibilities by a society that neglects and abuses its children. His unrepentant assertiveness, especially at his trial (43), allies him with characters like Sam Weller and Young Bailey who survive by assertive self-creation. He commands admiration as much as condemnation.

Sympathy does not complicate our response to Sikes, even though we get an interior glimpse of him after the murder. But Nancy, the only interesting woman in the novel, elicits sympathy for her simultaneous compassion for Oliver and her loyalty to Sikes, a complexity characterized by Dickens as "a contradiction, an anomaly, an apparent impossibility, but it is a truth" (Preface). None of the good characters embody such intriguing contradictions.

Bumble, one of Dickens's great comic figures, comes from a different world from that of Fagin and Sikes. Their evil is metaphysical; his is earthly and opportunistic. He serves his own self-interest by trying to serve those in power, the perfect representative for an inhumane system that victimizes the poor while pretending to serve them. His stupidity makes him foolish and ineffective, causing him, for example, to misread Brownlow's interest in Oliver and to miscalculate Mrs. Corney's willingness to subordinate her own interests in marriage. His marital persecution may transform his role as satiric butt into clichéd domestic comedy as the henpecked husband, but his classic response to Brownlow's warning that the law will hold him accountable for his wife's actions is one of the most memorable—and most quoted—passages in Dickens: "If the law supposes that . . . the law is a ass—a idiot" (51). At moments like this, Dickens redefines the tradition.

CRITICISM

Two classic essays by English novelists provide quite different introductions to *Twist*. Graham Greene's "The Young Dickens" (1950) is a personal account of reading the novel as a child, "its simple and terrible explanation of our plight, how the world was made by Satan and not by God, lulling us with the music of despair"; Angus WILSON'S introduction to the Penguin edition (1966) discusses the literary sources for the story, its historical context, and the literary qualities of the text itself. J. H. MILLER (1962; 1991) treats *Twist* as a novel about surviving threats of extinction, suffocation, hanging, drowning, enclosure, and starvation, as Oliver journeys to the heart of the urban labyrinth, seeking to discover his identity. In the end his identity is recovered for him—a resolution, Miller points out, with which Dickens will soon become disatisfied in the novels that follow.

William T. Lankford (" 'The Parish Boy's Progress': The Evolving Form of *Oliver Twist*," PMLA, 1978) explains the inconsistencies and contradictions in the novel by analyzing Dickens's changing ideas as he worked on it. Steven Connor (" 'They're All in One Story': Public and Private Narratives in *Oliver Twist*," *Dickensian*, 1989) traces the thematic importance of the various stories within the novel and the role of storytelling itself. Steven MARCUS (1965) provides an especially useful discussion of Dickens's religion and the relation of the novel to *The Pilgrim's Progress*. In a special issue of the *Dickensian* on the novel (1974), Micheal SLATER analyzes its structure and satire. K. J. FIELDING, in a special issue of the *Dickens Quarterly* (1987), provides a thorough discussion of *Twist*'s anti-UTILITARIAN satire, showing how it responded to the contemporary understanding of Bentham's philosophy of self-interest.

ADAPTATIONS

One of the most dramatized of Dickens's novels, *Twist* spawned 10 adaptations before it completed its serial run, the first opening after only 12 of the 24 monthly numbers had appeared. The most noteworthy of these early productions was J. Stirling Coyne's at the ADELPHI THEATRE, starring as Oliver Mrs. KEELEY, who would become famous for her portrayal of Jack Sheppard, and as Sikes O. SMITH, who also performed Scrooge and the monster in "Frankenstein." Dickens was distressed by some of the stagings and considered adapting the novel himself, but he was discouraged from doing so by MACREADY, who thought the novel would not make good theater.

There were also non-theatrical pirates who produced prose mutations of the novel in cheap serial format, usually for working-class readers. The best known of such piracies was by "Bos" [T. P. Prest], *The Life and Adventures of Oliver Twiss, the Workhouse Boy* (1839).

Robert BOLTON (1987) counts more than two hundred stage versions by 1900 and estimates that there were probably double or triple that number. Oliver was most often played by actresses, among them Mrs. HON-NER and Mrs. Keeley. On rare occasions the role was taken by a child actor. Among the famous stage Fagins were Mr. HONNER, Frederick YATES, E. E. Saville, Beerbohm TREE, and Bransby WILLIAMS. J. L. TOOLE was famous for his portrayal of the Artful Dodger.

At least 23 film versions have been made, from the early silent "Modern Oliver Twist; or the Life of a Pickpocket" (1906) to Lionel Bart's musical *Oliver!*, adapted for the screen by Vernon Harris and directed by Carol Reed (1968). At least 18 silent films appeared, including French, Italian, and Hungarian versions. Best known of the silent films is Sol Lesser's *Oliver Twist* (1922), starring Jackie Coogan as Oliver and Lon Chaney as Fagin. The first sound version appeared in 1933 with Dickie Moore as Oliver. The best of the film adaptations, David LEAN's 1948 version for Cineguild, starred John Howard Davies as Oliver, Alec GUINNESS as Fagin, and Anthony Newley as the Artful Dodger. This film, censored when it first appeared in the United States for the stereotypical anti-Semitism in its portrayal of Fagin, continued the controversial history of stage productions of the story. Early adaptations were often linked with *Jack Sheppard* and several of them were scrutinized or censored for their portrayal of crime. Modern adaptations are occasionally criticized or cut for their anti-Semitism.

The single most popular dramatic version of the novel has probably been Bart's musical *Oliver!*, which opened on the London stage in 1960 and in film in 1968. Among television adaptations are Constance COX's 13-part serial for the BBC (1962) and James Goldman's version, directed by Clive Donner, for CBS (1982).

Olympic Theatre This establishment frequented by the Theatrical Young Gentleman, was in Wych Street off the STRAND in London's West End. Madame Vestris managed the theater in the 1830s. *Young Gentlemen.*

Omer "Tailor, Haberdasher, Funeral Furnisher" in YARMOUTH who arranges the funeral of Clara Copperfield Murdstone (9). "A fat, short-winded, merry-looking, little old man in black" (9), he employs Little Em'ly before she runs off with Steerforth. His daughter **Minnie** marries the shop foreman, Joram, who becomes a partner and then the proprietor of the business. *Copperfield.*

"Omnibuses" Originally appeared as "Street Sketches No. 1" in the *MORNING CHRONICLE* (September 26, 1834). Boz compares the tedium and annoyances of a long coach journey with the variety and amusement on a London omnibus. He describes the "native coolness" of the Cad who competes with the cads on other buses, an officious old man among the passengers, a "stout gentlemen in the white neckcloth," and a "shabby-genteel man with the green bag," all of whom are regular passengers. *Boz.*

"On an Amateur Beat" Walking from his lodgings in COVENT GARDEN to LIMEHOUSE, the Traveller imagines himself a police constable on his beat. Near TEMPLE BAR a swarm of ragged street children surround him; farther east he sees a crippled old woman whose bent form he has often observed before. Then he stops at the CHILDREN'S HOSPITAL and watches the dog Poodles going on his rounds from patient to patient. He ends his walk at a lead mill in Limehouse where nearly all the workers, in spite of precautions, sooner or later contract lead poisoning. *Uncommercial*, (35). Originally in *All the Year Round* (February 27, 1869).

"On Duty with Inspector Field" Article for *HOUSEHOLD WORDS* (June 14, 1851), describing the narrator's night with Inspector FIELD of the Metropolitan Police. Together they tour the thieves' dens and lodging houses in the center of London. They go to ST. GILES, the BOROUGH, the RATCLIFFE HIGHWAY, and WHITE-CHAPEL, observing the poverty, misery, and occasional defiance of the inhabitants of London's underworld. *Reprinted.*

"On Her Majesty's Service" Article for *HOUSEHOLD WORDS* (January 7, 1854) by E. C. Grenville MURRAY, edited by Dickens, which fictionalized Murray's experience as a consular official in Turkey and included an especially biting and bitter portrait of Sir Stratford Canning, Ambassador to Turkey, under the name Sir Hector Stubble. *Stone.*

"On Mr. Fechter's Acting" Article for the *ATLANTIC MONTHLY* (August 1869) enthusiastically describing the dramatic talents of Charles FECHTER, Dickens's friend and protegé, when the actor was beginning his theatrical tour of America.

"On Strike" Article for *HOUSEHOLD WORDS* (February 11, 1854) in which Dickens describes his visit to PRESTON duing the bitter and prolonged strike of the cotton weavers. In the train on his way there, he argues with a fellow traveller he calls Mr. Snapper. Dickens expresses his reservations about POLITICAL ECONOMY and his desire not to take sides in the strike; Snapper sides with the masters and asserts that one cannot be neutral. In Preston, Dickens reads the bills posted by the workers and attends one of their meetings; he is impressed with their restraint, the orderliness of the proceedings, and the "absence of anything like sullen discontent." He ends the article urging mediation between masters and men. *Miscellaneous.*

Once a Week Magazine started in 1859 by BRADBURY & EVANS after Dickens discontinued *HOUSEHOLD WORDS*, which they published, and started *ALL THE YEAR ROUND*. The magazine, which slavishly followed the model of its predecessor, continued in publication for several years.

"One Man in a Dockyard"   Article for *HOUSE-HOLD WORDS* (September 6, 1851) by R. H. HORNE and Dickens, describing the visit of John Strongitharm, "a man of good average size and strength," to ROCHESTER and CHATHAM. After visiting the castle and cathedral in Rochester and the military barracks, parade grounds, and fortifications in Chatham, he tours the dockyard with its sawmill, rolling mill, and shipbuilding activities. Awed by the scale of achievement, Strongitharm realizes that only "well-devised combinations of men [could] produce this majestic result." The power resides in all who contribute to the project and should not be ceded to "two or three genteel families." *Stone*.

Onowenever, Miss   The object of a youthful infatuation of the Traveller who "had pervaded every chink and crevice of my mind for three or four years." He remembers writing numerous imaginary letters to **Mrs. Onowenever**, the girl's mother, soliciting her daughter's hand in marriage, without "the remotest intention of sending any of those letters." *Uncommercial* (20).

Onwhyn, Thomas (1811–86)   Illustrator and artist, influenced by CRUIKSHANK and BROWNE. Using the pseudonym "Peter Palette," he illustrated some of the plagiarisms of Dickens's early works in the 1830s. He later became one of the *PUNCH* illustrators.

Orange, Mrs.   "A truly sweet young creature," friend of Mrs. Lemon, and wife of **James** in Nettie Ashford's tale. "Holiday Romance."

Orfling, The   Nickname of Mrs. Micawber's maid, CLICKETT. *Copperfield*.

Originals   Many of Dickens's characters were, at least in part, based on real people. Micawber, drawn from Dickens's father; Boythorn, from Walter Savage LANDOR; and Skimpole, from Leigh HUNT, are well-known examples. A good deal of effort, particularly around the turn of the century, was devoted to identifying originals. Alex J. Philip and Laurence Gadd (*The Dickens Dictionary*, 1928) include an extensive list of many of the proposed models. Many such attributions are highly speculative and questionable and have little value for furthering an understanding of Dickens and his works, but the study of originals can be more than source-hunting. Edwin PUGH (*The Dickens Originals*, 1912) studied several examples to show how Dickens transformed particular people into general types. Doris Alexander (*Creating Characters with Charles Dickens*, 1991) analyzes the psychological complexities in several of Dickens's transformations of real into imagined people.

Orlick, Dolge   Joe Gargery's journeyman blacksmith, "a broad-shouldered loose-limbed swarthy fellow of great strength, never in a hurry, and always slouching" (15). He holds a grudge against Pip and against Mrs. Joe, whom he secretly attacks and maims (16). When Miss Havisham hires him as a porter, Pip has him dismissed (29–30). Finally, he falls in with Compeyson and plots to murder Pip by luring him to the lime kiln on the marshes, a scheme foiled by Herbert Pocket, Startop, and Trabb's Boy (53). *Expectations*.

Orphans   Orphans appear in almost all of Dickens's novels; his heroes, from Oliver Twist to Edwin Drood, are almost always orphans or semi-orphans. The number of such children reflects, in part, a social reality of the time; children like Little Dick at Mrs. Mann's baby farm (*Twist*), the Neckett children sustained by the laundry work undertaken by Charley (*Bleak House*), or Jo the crossing sweeper (*Bleak House*) represent social realities of which Dickens, as a supporter of RAGGED SCHOOLS and other charities for children, was particularly aware.

The orphans are also, as many critics have pointed out, mythic figures, relatives of the orphaned children in fairytales and folklore. Dombey is haunted by fears that his son may become a changeling; Oliver is a kind of holy innocent who remains untouched by the evil world around him; David Copperfield, abandoned at birth by his fairy godmother, Aunt Betsey, must seek to recover his place in that fairy-tale fantasy. Geoffrey THURLEY (1976) sees the orphan as the central figure in "the Dickens myth," a wish-fulfillment fantasy in which the "orphan is miraculously rescued by magically empowered old gentlemen," a myth which is gradually transformed during Dickens's career to shift the responsibility for rescue to the hero himself. Orphanhood generates the quest for identity that is the central motif in nearly all the novels, and it provides a basis for much of the pathos and sentimentality. It is also essential to the Dickens story, for, as Amy Sadrin (*Parentage and Inheritance in the Novels of Charles Dickens*, 1994) points out, in the psychological myth that Dickens retells "fathers must die that their sons shall live."

Orwell, George (1903–1950)   Penname of Eric Blair, English novelist, essayist, political and social commentator; best known for *Animal Farm* (1946) and *1984* (1949). His essay "Charles Dickens" (1939) is one of the seminal works of Dickens criticism. Orwell describes Dickens as a subversive, but not a revolutionary, writer, for his criticisms of society showed "no consciousness that the *structure* of society can be changed." From his moral, apolitical point of view, Dickens called for a change of spirit, not a reformation of society. His perspective is narrow—that of a 19th-century bourgeois liberal. He has "no ideal of *work*," and sees the world from a consumer's point of view, but he identifies with the underdog and is generously angry on his behalf.

Osborne's Hotel, Adelphi   Hotel, formerly at the corner of John Adam Street, where Wardle holds the celebration for Pickwick's release from FLEET PRISON (*Pickwick*, 54). Mrs. Edson stays here before moving to Mrs. Lirriper's ("Lirriper's Lodgings").

"Our Almanac" Dickens's announcement in *HOUSEHOLD WORDS* (November 24, 1855) of the first issue of *The Household Words Almanac*. The project was not successful and only two issues of the Almanac appeared, in 1856 and 1857. *Stone*.

"Our Bore" Essay in *HOUSEHOLD WORDS* (October 9, 1852), describing a self-absorbed man who bores others with his tedious accounts of his travels, illnesses, and inside knowledge of nearly everything. *Reprinted*.

"Our Commission" Satirical article for *HOUSEHOLD WORDS* (August 11, 1855). Following a commission report on the adulteration of food, the article describes a report on the adulteration of government, public offices, and the representative chamber. The report finds all of these institutions adulterated by "unprincipled wholesale dealers. . . . When one of these dealers succeeded to a business or 'came in,' according the the slang of the trade—his first proceeding, after the adulteration of Public Office with Noodledom, was to consider how he could adulterate and lower his Representative Chamber." The solution, Dickens suggests, is for the public to reject all adulteration whatsoever. *Miscellaneous*.

"Our English Watering-Place" Sketch of an English seaside town (BROADSTAIRS) during the season. Old-fashioned and outdated, the town at first appears to have been left stranded by the moving tide of history, but by the time the narrator ends the piece, the tide is in and the town is "swelling up with life and beauty." Originally published in *HOUSEHOLD WORDS* (August 2, 1851) as "Our Watering Place." *Reprinted*.

"Our French Watering-Place" An account of the Channel crossing and the accommodations and amusements at a French seaside town (BOULOGNE). Originally published in *HOUSEHOLD WORDS* (November 4, 1854). *Reprinted*.

"Our Honorable Friend" Article for *HOUSEHOLD WORDS* (July 31, 1852), satirizing empty political rhetoric. Dickens describes "the honourable member for Verbosity" (said to be based on DISRAELI), whose "principles, to sum up all in a word, were Hearths and Altars, Labour and Capital, Crown and Sceptre, Elephant and Castle." The honorable member, "the first to bend sacred matters to electioneering tactics," challenges Tipkisson by making him out to be in favor of "Mosques and Mohammedanism." *Reprinted*.

Our Mutual Friend Dickens's 14th and last completed novel, published in 20 monthly numbers from May 1864 to November 1865 by CHAPMAN & HALL, with illustrations by Marcus STONE. Published in two volumes, February and November 1865; one volume, 1865. A panoramic novel set in the present, *Our Mutual Friend* satirizes the superficiality of society; the corrupt-

Gaffer and Lizzie Hexam scavenging on the Thames in James Mahoney's illustration for the first number of the Household Edition of Our Mutual Friend *(1874).*

ing power of money; the waste of urban, materialistic existence; and the predatory relations between human beings. Dickens represents this blighted world symbolically in the dust heaps of material wealth, the River THAMES polluted with dead bodies, and the human birds of prey who scavenge in the waste land. The parallel stories of John Harmon and Eugene Wrayburn offer a process of death and resurrection as a way of achieving a deeper, more spiritual sense of self.

SYNOPSIS

Part 1 (May 1864)
(I:1) In society's depths, at twilight, a boat with two figures in it floats on the Thames. Gaffer Hexam watches the water while his daughter Lizzie handles the oars. He discovers a floating corpse and takes it in tow. (I:2) Shortly afterward, on the surface of society, at the "bran new" home of the Veneerings, the fashionable members of society have gathered. Mortimer Lightwood, a lawyer, tells the story of the Man from Somewhere, young John Harmon, son of a wealthy and vindictive dust contractor. The rich old man had disowned his daughter for marrying against his wishes, and he bequeathed his whole estate to his son on the condition that he marry Bella Wilfer, a girl chosen because of her petulance. The dinner party is interrupted when Lightwood is informed that young Harmon, returning to England to claim his late father's fortune, has drowned. (I:3) Lightwood and his friend, the diffident Eugene Wrayburn, a lawyer with no practice, go with Charley Hexam, son of Gaffer, to LIMEHOUSE to view the corpse. There they meet Julius Handford, a stranger also inquiring about the dead man.

(I:4) A few days later, the Wilfer family, at their house in HOLLOWAY, discuss Bella, who has suddenly become a "widow." As they do so, a stranger, John Rokesmith, takes rooms in the Wilfers' house.

Part 2 (June 1864)

(I:5) Silas Wegg, a one-legged street seller of ballads and miscellaneous items, is at his regular post outside the corner house near CAVENDISH SQUARE. He imagines himself an employee of the house, hired to run errands. Mr. Boffin, Harmon's former employee who has inherited the Harmon estate in lieu of young Harmon, greets Wegg. After some casual conversation, he hires him to read to him at his house, BOFFIN'S BOWER, formerly HARMONY GAOL, the house of the elder John Harmon, the dust contractor. On his first evening at Boffin's, Wegg begins reading, with little understanding, *The Decline and Fall of the Roman Empire.*

(I:6) Abbey Potterson, proprietor of the SIX JOLLY FELLOWSHIP PORTERS, a riverside pub in Limehouse, rules the inn like an abbess. She has excluded both Gaffer Hexam and Rogue Riderhood, another river scavenger, from the pub because of rumors about their unsavory work. She tries to convince Lizzie Hexam to stop working for her father and to set out on her own, but Lizzie politely refuses to follow Abbey's advice. She does, however, give her brother some money and sends him away to pursue an education. When Gaffer returns home and discovers Charley gone, he is angry and disowns him.

(I:7) On his way to Boffin's Bower, Wegg stops off at the shop of Mr. Venus, a taxidermist and articulator of bones. He hopes to negotiate for the bone of his amputated leg which Venus has obtained. Venus confesses to Wegg that he is in love, but that the woman has refused him because of his profession.

Part 3 (July 1864)

(I:8) A simple and illiterate man, Nicodemus Boffin was the faithful employee of John Harmon for many years. He plans to use his newfound wealth to become cultured by having Wegg read to him. On the day that the Harmon property is to be turned over to him, Boffin asks Mortimer Lightwood, his lawyer, to make a tight will, leaving all of his property to Mrs. Boffin. Later, in the street, he meets Rokesmith, the stranger who took lodgings at the Wilfers', who offers to serve as his secretary. (I:9) The Boffins decide to use some of their money to adopt an orphan and call him John Harmon, in remembrance of the drowned man whose fortune they have inherited and whom they last saw as a seven-year-old child. They also decide to offer the disappointed bride, Bella Wilfer, a place in their home.

(I:10) The Veneerings prepare for a society wedding between "a mature young gentleman," Alfred Lammle, and "a mature young lady," reputed to have property, Sophronia Akershem. The ceremony is followed by a wedding breakfast at the Veneerings' house. On their honeymoon at SHANKLIN SANDS, Sophronia and Alfred bitterly confess that each has been misled about the financial situation of the other. Then they conspire to deceive the rest of the world as they have mutually deceived each other.

Part 4 (August 1864)

(I:11) The Podsnaps, the very models of the Philistine nouveau riche, hold a funereal party for their daughter Georgiana's 18th birthday. There the Lammles plot to exploit their relationship with Georgiana and insinuate themselves into the shy "young person's" confidence.

(I:12) At their cottage in HAMPTON, Wrayburn and Lightwood are interrupted by Rogue Riderhood, Gaffer Hexam's former partner, who is seeking Lightwood in order to claim Boffin's £10,000 reward for information about Harmon's murderer. Rogue asserts that Gaffer Hexam confessed the crime to him on the night that it occurred. (I:13) The three men wait with the police inspector in Limehouse for Gaffer to return from his work on the river. When he does not appear, Rogue sets out to find him and returns to say that he has found only Gaffer's empty boat with a broken oar. There was no sign of Gaffer.

Part 5 (September 1864)

(I:14) When Gaffer's boat is brought to shore, his body is discovered at the end of the tow rope.

(I:15) Mr. Boffin hires Rokesmith to be his secretary and, since he plans to move into a fashionable house on Cavendish Square, he offers Wegg a post as caretaker at Boffin's Bower. One evening, Mrs. Boffin interrupts Wegg's reading of *Decline and Fall* to tell Boffin that she has been frightened by seeing the ghostly faces of old Harmon and his two children. (I:16) As Boffin's secretary, Rokesmith is exemplary and puts all of Boffin's affairs in order. He is only difficult about one thing: He refuses to deal with Lightwood. He takes charge of the search for an adoptable child and accompanies the Boffins to the house of Betty Higden, where they meet her grandson, little Johnny, and arrange to take him in. When Rokesmith tells Bella that he is Boffin's secretary, she is unimpressed. (I:17) The Boffins move into their fashionable new house, where they are visited by members of society, invited to join charitable efforts, and solicited by all kinds of beggars who are attracted by their gold dust.

Part 6 (October 1864)

(II:1) Accompanied by his teacher Bradley Headstone, Charley visits Lizzie at her new lodging in SMITH SQUARE. They meet the "person of the house," Fanny Cleaver, known as Jenny Wren, a precocious and crippled 13-year-old who makes doll clothing and acts as parent to her alcoholic father. Charley urges Lizzie to find another lodging, but she is content with her place because it is near the river. On their way home, Charley and Bradley meet Eugene Wrayburn on the VAUXHALL BRIDGE. Charley, who introduced Eugene to his sister when he brought the lawyer to view Harmon's body, worries that Eugene is on his way to see Lizzie. (II:2) His concern is not unfounded. Eugene offers to educate Lizzie. She reluctantly accepts, after he argues that she should do it for her father's sake. After Eugene leaves, Jenny's drunken father comes home from work and is berated by his daughter.

(II:3) Veneering pays £5000 for the priviledge of running for the seat in Parliament for the borough of Pocket-Breaches. With the help of his friends, who "do a piece of work" for him, he is elected to the uncontested seat.

Part 7 (November 1864)
(II:4) Mrs. Lammle pursues her friendship with Georgiana Podsnap. She and her husband encourage a relationship between the girl and Fascination Fledgeby, an awkward young gentleman of apparently independent means. (II:5) After a difficult evening at the opera with the two reluctant lovers, Lammle first tries to insinuate his way into Fledgeby's confidence and then to bully him, but the secretive Fledgeby resists Lammle's manipulation. That afternoon Fledgeby goes to PUBSEY AND CO., his secret moneylending business in ST. MARY AXE, where Mr. Riah, a Jew, fronts for him. He finds Riah there with Jenny Wren and Lizzie Hexam in a small roof garden. Jenny taunts Fledgeby with the enigmatic invitation to "Come up and be dead!"

(II:6) Mortimer senses that something is troubling Eugene, and when Charlie Hexam and Bradley Headstone demand that Eugene end his relationship with Lizzie, Lightwood realizes what has been preoccupying his friend. He asks Eugene about his intentions, but Eugene claims that he has no designs and doesn't himself understand his interest in Lizzie.

Part 8 (December 1864)
(II:7) At Boffin's Bower where he is now the caretaker, Wegg is visited by Mr. Venus, who brings him his lost leg bone. Wegg proposes that they should collaborate in searching the dust mounds on the site for valuables. Venus is distraught because Pleasant Riderhood, Rogue's daughter who runs a pawnbroking business, has rejected his marriage proposal. He agrees to join Wegg in this "friendly move."

(II:8) Rokesmith chides Bella, who is now living with the Boffins, that she seems to have forgotten her family. To prove him wrong, Bella orders the coach and visits home, but her grand entrance spurs Mrs. Wilfer's haughtiness. With a bank note for £50 from Boffin, Bella buys her father a new wardrobe, goes with him for a secret dinner in GREENWICH, and turns the balance of the money over to him at the end of the evening. She tells him that she has become mercenary and is seeking a rich husband. (II:9) Soon after, on learning that little Johnny is very ill, the Boffins, Rokesmith, and Bella get the sick child from Betty Higden's house and take him to the Children's Hospital. But the illness is too far advanced; that evening, as Rokesmith watches over him, the child dies. (II:10) At a family conference the next day, Mrs. Boffin proposes that they not try to name another orphan child John Harmon, for the name has proved unfortunate. They choose instead to help Sloppy, another of Betty Higden's boys, in spite of his ungainliness.

Part 9 (January 1865)
(II:11) Bradley Headstone urges Lizzie to break off her relationship with Wrayburn and to be guided by her

brother and himself, but she rejects his advice. Headstone is reluctant to leave her house until he secures her promise that she will meet with him again.

(II:12) At her leaving shop and rooming house for sailors, Pleasant Riderhood is confronted by a sailor who wants to speak with her father. The stranger accuses Rogue of lying about Gaffer's involvement in the Harmon murder and promises to return with a paper for Rogue to sign relating the true facts of the case. (II:13) The stranger then goes out into the streets of Limehouse Hole, removes his disguise, and reveals himself as John Rokesmith. As he looks about him, he reconstructs the story of his death as John Harmon. Uneasy about the terms of his father's will, he had conspired to exchange identities with George Radfoot, a mate on the ship on which he was returning to England, so he could observe Bella anonymously. But Radfoot conspired with Riderhood to poison Harmon, a plot that failed when Harmon did not die and when Radfoot, dressed in Harmon's clothes, did. Harmon then decided to assume the identity of Rokesmith and honestly win the affections of Bella, to whom he is devoted. When he returns to the Boffins' house after his evening in Limehouse, Rokesmith proposes to Bella, but she rejects him. He promises to bother her no more.

Part 10 (February 1865)
(II:14) Rokesmith decides that bringing Harmon back to life would do no good, either for Bella, or the Boffins, or himself, so he buries him still deeper. Meanwhile, Betty Higden asks for help to outfit herself as an itinerant seller of sewing supplies so that she can leave London and free Sloppy to accept the opportunity offered by the Boffins. Mrs. Boffin reluctantly agrees to help her.

(II:15) Charley and Bradley intercept Lizzie by a churchyard in the CITY on her way home from work. There Headstone confesses to Lizzie that she is "the ruin" of him and he proposes to marry her. When she refuses him, he accuses her of an interest in Wrayburn. Afterward Charley berates her and tries unsuccessfully to change her mind. She is discovered in tears by Riah and Wrayburn, who both accompany her home. Wrayburn quizzes himself about his interest in her.

(II:16) On the first anniversary of the Lammle's marriage, society gathers to celebrate the occasion. Twemlow, a timid man with aristocratic connections who is a regular guest at the Veneerings' dinner parties, is introduced to Fledgeby, his distant kinsman. Mortimer reports the latest news in the story of the Man from Somewhere—that Lizzie Hexam has disappeared. Sophronia Lammle secretly asks Twemlow to intercede with Mr. Podsnap to save Georgiana from her scheme.

Part 11 (March 1865)
(III:1) While Riah waits for Fledgeby's instructions, Fledgeby warns Lammle to avoid the clutches of Pubsey and Co. Then Fledgeby instructs Riah to buy up bad debts, especially those of the Lammles. He also tries to learn from Riah where Lizzie is hidden. (III:2) That evening, Riah and Lizzie take Riderhood's affadavit that

Gaffer Hexam was not responsible for the Harmon murder to the Six Jolly Fellowship Porters. While they are at the pub, the body of Riderhood is brought in, drowned in a river accident. (III:3) Efforts to resuscitate Rogue succeed and he returns to life as belligerent as he was before, threatening to sue the steamer that ran him down and blaming his rescuers for not preserving his fur hat.

(III:4) At the Wilfers' wedding anniversary dinner, Mrs. Wilfer is uncomfortable and unhappy. After dinner Bella tells her father that Rokesmith proposed to her and was refused, that Lightwood would propose were she to encourage him, that Boffin has promised a good marriage settlement for her, and that Mr. Boffin daily "grows suspicious, capricious, hard, tyrannical, unjust" in his escalating love for money.

Part 12 (April 1865)
(III:5) Boffin has, in fact, become obsessive about money. He sets Rokesmith's wages at £200 per annum and demands that the secretary be available around the clock; he tells Bella that her good looks are worth money. Meanwhile, Mrs. Lammle takes an increasing interest in Bella.

(III:6) One evening, when Boffin doesn't appear for one of his reading sessions, Wegg invites Venus into the Bower. Boffin startles the two conspirators by showing up late with a collection of books about misers. He then goes out to the mounds alone and digs up a bottle. As he leaves, he informs Wegg that he has sold the mounds and that their removal will begin in the morning. (III:7) After Boffin is gone, Wegg confides to Venus that he has found a will of old John Harmon. Venus, distrusting his partner, insists on keeping the document; Wegg reluctantly gives in.

Part 13 (May 1865)
(III:8) Betty Higden continues her pilgrimage, plying her wares along the upper reaches of the Thames. Several times she faints and is near death, but the threat of being sent to the workhouse spurs her on. Once she is found by Rogue Riderhood, who is working as a deputy lockkeeper; he takes her money and then allows her to go on. Finally, near death, she is found by Lizzie Hexam. (III:9) When Bella, Rokesmith, Sloppy and the Milveys come up to the mill town where Lizzie is working for the funeral of Betty Higden, Lizzie asks them to keep her whereabouts secret. She tells Bella that her disappearance has nothing to do with the charges against her father and she confides that she is running from the attentions of Bradley Headstone and Eugene Wrayburn. Bella is moved by Lizzie's honesty and depth of feeling; she tells Rokesmith that meeting Lizzie has changed her.

(III:10) Eugene visits Jenny Wren, hoping to learn Lizzie's whereabouts from her, but Jenny won't tell him. Afterward, Jenny's drunken father, Mr. Dolls, comes to Eugene's rooms and offers to get Lizzie's address in exchange for drink. Meanwhile, Bradley Headstone follows Eugene through the streets, hoping that he will lead him to Lizzie. Eugene taunts Bradley by leading him on long, pointless perigrinations.

Part 14 (June 1865)
(III:11) Thinking that Lizzie may be hiding at Wrayburn's rooms, Bradley slips into the TEMPLE late at night and listens outside his antagonist's door, but he hears no woman's voice. As he leaves, he meets Riderhood. They share their dislike of Wrayburn and Bradley gives Rogue five shillings to inform him should he discover Lizzie's whereabouts.

(III:12) In desperate financial straits, the Lammles plan to make a move on Boffin by informing him of Rokesmith's proposal to Bella. They hope he will fire Rokesmith and replace him with Alfred. Riah, representing Pubsey and Co., pursues the Lammles insisting that they repay their debts. Although they plead with him, Riah is adamant, for he has been instructed by the secret owner of the firm, Fledgeby, to go after them. (III:13) Even Twemlow, who has cosigned a note for a friend, finds himself in the clutches of Pubsey and Co. Riah demands payment from him. Jenny is disgusted by Riah's hard-heartedness and calls him "the wicked wolf."

(III:15) Troubled by his involvement with Wegg, Venus discloses the friendly move to Boffin and allows Boffin to overhear Wegg's tirade against him as a "minion of fortune and worm of the hour." Boffin asks Venus to keep his change of heart secret from Wegg for the time being. As he goes home, Boffin meets Sophronia Lammle, who asks to speak to him in confidence.

Part 15 (July 1865)
(III:15) She tells him about Rokesmith's proposal to Bella, and the next morning Boffin fires the secretary for his "insolence" to Bella and for his mercenary designs on her and on Boffin's money. Bella is humiliated to be implicated in Boffin's meanness; she leaves his house and gives up the money the Boffins promised her. (III:16) Then she goes to her father's office and tells him what she has done. Rokesmith joins them there, proposes again, and this time he is accepted. The "three hobgoblins," Bella, John, and Mr. Wilfer, share a celebratory tea.

(III:17) The Lammles' belongings are auctioned off to pay their debts. Sophronia warns Twemlow that Fledgeby is the owner of Pubsey and Co. and that Riah is just Fledgeby's "mask." At the Veneerings' dinner party, the members of Society disparage the absent Lammles for living beyond their means. In the middle of supper, Wrayburn is called away from the table to get some information from Mr. Dolls.

Part 16 (August 1865)
(IV:1) At the Plashwater Weir Mill Lock on the upper Thames where Riderhood is the lockkeeper, Eugene Wrayburn comes through rowing a small boat. When he recognizes Rogue, he insults him. Eugene is being shadowed by Bradley, who is dressed like Rogue. He follows Eugene until he sees him meet Lizzie. Then, exhausted and suffering from unexplained nosebleeds, he returns to Rogue's lock house, where he spends the night.

(IV:2) The Lammles attempt to secure positions with the Boffins, replacing Rokesmith and Bella, but Mr. Boffin pays them £100 for their "service" of exposing Rokesmith and then dismisses them. Boffin also prevents Georgiana Podsnap from turning over £15 and her heirloom necklace to aid the Lammles.

(IV:3) Silas Wegg makes his move and comes down on Boffin, threatening to reveal the will he has found if Boffin will not share his wealth with him.

(IV:4) Bella and her father go off to GREENWICH, where Bella and John are married. The three spend the rest of the day celebrating.

Part 17 (September 1865)
(IV:5) John and Bella settle down to happy married life. Bella reconciles her mother and sister to her mendicant husband and dismisses John's questions about whether she would be happier if they were rich.

(IV:6) Eugene meets Lizzie by the river near the mill town where she has been in hiding. She pleads with him to leave her alone, but he also gets her to admit her love for him. After they separate, Eugene, in tears, goes down to a quiet spot by the river to settle his thoughts. There he is attacked by a man wearing a red neckerchief, beaten, and pushed into the river. Lizzie, who has also been settling her emotions by the river, hears the struggle and, finding a boat by the riverbank, she pulls the nearly lifeless body into the boat and prayerfully takes it to an inn. There the doctors see little chance that Eugene will live. (IV:7) After the attack, Bradley, dressed like Rogue Riderhood, returns to Plashwater Weir Mill Lock. There Rogue feeds him and watches him suspiciously as he sleeps. At their meal together, Bradley accidentally cuts his hand and spatters blood over Rogue's clothes. When Bradley leaves the lock, Rogue follows him, watches him change into his schoolmaster's clothes and throw the clothes he was wearing into the river. Rogue fishes the bundle of clothes from the river and returns to his lock. Back at school, Charley Hexam hears of the attack on Eugene Wrayburn and dissociates himself from Bradley.

Part 18 (October 1865)
(IV:8) Before he leaves England, bankrupt Alfred Lammle beats Fledgeby. When Jenny finds the moneylender wounded and sore, she adds pepper to the vinegar plaster that she places on his wounds. (IV:9) Jenny now believes in Riah's innocence, and when Fledgeby fires the old man, he returns with her to her house where they find Mr. Dolls dead from drink. After the funeral, Jenny is summoned to the bedside of Eugene Wrayburn. (IV:10) She and Mortimer attend Eugene on his deathbed. In his rare moments of consciousness, Eugene, to save Lizzie from public humiliation, asks that Bradley not be pursued. Many days later he asks Mortimer to propose to Lizzie for him. (IV:11) Mortimer goes to London to get John and Bella for the wedding, but John will not allow Lightwood to see him. At the train station, Bradley Headstone meets Bella and Mortimer on their way to the wedding. When he hears that Lizzie is to be married, he falls to the platform in a fit. Although Eugene is semiconscious and apparently close to death, during the ceremony Lizzie's love keeps recalling him to consciousness.

Parts 19–20 (November 1865)
(IV:12) When Lightwood acidentally meets the Rokesmiths and recognizes John as Julius Handford, the stranger he first met when he was inquiring about the drowned Harmon, Rokesmith must extricate himself from suspicion in the murder of John Harmon. He is identified for the police inspector as John Harmon. The next day John announces to Bella that they must move and he takes her to the Boffins' house, where they are reconciled with their old friends. (IV:13) The Boffins tell Bella how Mrs. Boffin discovered John Harmon's identity and how Boffin pretended to be a miser in order to make Bella aware of what she really wanted. Then they show Bella her new home.

(IV:14) Wegg comes down on Boffin, but Boffin, Venus, and Harmon expose Wegg's villainy and Sloppy throws the covetous balladmonger into a dustcart.

(IV:15) Several months later, Rogue appears at Bradley's school with the bundle of clothes. He insists that Bradley come to the lock. There Rogue tries to blackmail him; Bradley, desperately cornered, grabs Rogue around the waist and pulls him into the lock, where both men drown.

(IV:16) Mrs. Wilfer makes a grand visit to her daughter's grand house; Sloppy and Jenny share their humor together; the Wrayburns visit the Harmons; Eugene, much recovered, vows his love and loyalty to Lizzie and rejects society.

(IV:17) The members of society gather one last time at the Veneerings' house, before Mr. and Mrs. Veneering will escape from their creditors by running to the Continent. When Lady Tippins canvasses the assembled guests about the marriage of Eugene and Lizzie, they all agree that it was inappropriate, ill-advised, and a violation of society's rules. Only Mortimer and Twemlow dissent from the general chorus. Twemlow rises to the occasion, challenging Podsnap and describing Eugene as "the greater gentleman" for marrying Lizzie and making her "the greater lady."

COMMENTARY

When *Our Mutual Friend* began its run in monthly numbers in May 1864, it had been nearly a decade since Dickens completed his last monthly serial, *Little Dorrit*. In the meantime he had published two novels in weekly parts in ALL THE YEAR ROUND, but they were much shorter and required a different discipline from that required by the longer monthly numbers. Distracted by his PUBLIC READINGS and magazine editing and weakened from illness, Dickens found it difficult getting started again on a long novel. Although he began working on the germ ideas for *Mutual Friend* in the early 1860s, it took him over two years to write the first five numbers, the goal he set for himself before beginning publication.

John FORSTER reports that Dickens mentioned in his letters four years before publication "three leading notions" for the novel: "a man, young and perhaps eccentric, feigning to be dead, and *being* dead to all intents and purposes external to himself; . . . a poor impostor of a man marrying a woman for her money; she marrying *him* for *his* money; after marriage both finding out their mistake, and entering into a league and covenant against folks in general; [and] . . . some Perfectly New people." To these germs for Harmon, the Lammles, and the Veneerings, Dickens added "the uneducated father in fustian and the educated boy in spectacles" whom he had seen in CHATHAM, the models for Charley Hexam and his father. But the writing went very slowly and he worried that he had lost his creative power.

Influenced perhaps by his personal knowledge of the author's struggles to get the story on paper, Forster concluded that the novel "wants freshness and natural development." Henry James, one of the book's early reviewers, claimed that it was contrived and artificial, "a book so intensely *written*, so little seen, known, or felt." James also found the book lacking "philosophy," despite its overly-conscious creation. Other critics were kinder, but few of Dickens's contemporaries ranked the book with his best work.

Modern critics, particularly Marxist and social critics, have been much more positive, considering it one of the great social novels of Dickens's later period, along with *Bleak House, Little Dorrit*, and *Great Expectations*. Arnold Kettle (*Introduction to the English Novel*, 1951) praised the "profundity and consistency of the artistic structure" and Jack LINDSAY (1950) called it a "supreme work . . . one of the greatest works of prose ever written. A work which fully vindicates Dickens's right to stand, as no other English writer can stand, at the side of Shakespeare."

A satiric anatomy of Victorian society, *Mutual Friend* explores some of the same themes as THACKERAY's *Vanity Fair*, another panoramic satire of the period. Like the characters in Thackeray's novel, the Lammles demonstrate how to "live on nothing a year"; Podsnap reigns in patriarchal tyranny over his bourgeois household; the Veneerings' fashionable dinner parties are all surfaces and superficialities. Thackeray distanced his readers from his satire by setting *Vanity Fair* during the Napoleonic wars, 30 years before the time he was writing. In *Our Mutual Friend* Dickens writes about his own time. Beginning with the words, "In these times of ours," he goes on to anatomize life in the present, much as Anthony TROLLOPE would do a decade later in *The Way We Live Now* (1874–75). Dickens's subject is the emptiness and corruption of society in his time, which he surveys from top to bottom.

The first two chapters establish the range of Dickens's broad social canvas. He begins at the bottom with the lumpen-proletarians, Hexam and Rogue Riderhood, who scavenge bodies from the Thames for a living. Hexam, the narrator tells us, is "allied to the bottom of the river rather than the surface"(1), a realm in which human life is reduced to elemental, physical terms. A kind of urban cannibal, he responds to Lizzie's repulsion at their occupation by asserting: "As if it wasn't your living! As if it wasn't meat and drink to you!" (1) As one of the lower orders of humanity, he is reduced to the animal, a bird of prey who survives by feeding on his fellow man.

If Hexam is confined to the depths, the nouveau riche Veneerings in the next chapter, as their name implies, are all surface. The circle gathered at their supper table only *appear* to be friends, for they hardly know each other. Their relationship is summed up in the superficial image of their gathering in the mirror above the table. But there is a note of foreboding in this fashionable world as well; a "fatal freshness" (2) clings to the Veneerings, and their gloomy butler serves the wine as if it were a form of chemical poison.

As these two chapters establish the oppositions between high and low, surface and depth, they also connect them. The body that Hexam drags from the Thames turns out to be that of "the man from somewhere," the subject of the shallow and disembodied dinner conversation at the Veneerings. Up until that time John Harmon has been a kind of legal fiction, a creation of the story about his father's contrary will. With the news of his drowning, he becomes a physical presence, linking the river people with the society people as the "mutual friend" of the title. He is the subject that the two worlds have in common, even though they view him very differently. To the river people he is a corpse and a source of their physical survival. To the members of society he is merely the subject of a diverting story. The task of the novel will be to bridge this gulf in perception and attempt to reconnect the mental and physical, the animal and the human, surface and depth.

T. S. ELIOT derived his original title for *The Waste Land*, "He do the police in different voices," from *Our Mutual Friend*. Although Eliot seems to have been thinking of the novel as a source for the many urban monologues in his poem, its images of waste and decay may have been suggested by some of the images in Dickens's novel. The novel has sometimes been called Dickens's *Waste Land*, for its central symbols of the dust heaps and the river are the dominant features of a blighted urban landscape, symbols of an entropic society in its final days. There is no spiritual meaning to life in here. The rich, like Lady Tippins and the Veneerings, who take their physical comforts for granted, are bored and vacuous. Things have only monetary worth; the silver on the Veneerings' supper table is only valued "melted down." All value is reduced to its lowest physical terms. A human life is worth the money in its pockets or the price of its body parts to an articulator like Mr. Venus. Worth is determined in terms of salvage value as it is pulled from the river, scavenged from the dust heaps, or melted into its original form.

Written only five years after the first publication of Darwin's *Origin of Species* (1859), the novel's world is, in Tennyson's words, "red in tooth and claw." The river scavengers are "birds of prey" who compete with each other for the carrion they recover from the river; there is no "partnership," no mutual aid, between Gaffer Hexam and Rogue Riderhood. Mr. Venus's taxidermy business symbolically institutionalizes this predatory culture, his name ironically calling attention to the absence of love in this struggle for existence. The rich—indolent and idle—are similarly isolated. The Veneerings' debased notion of "friendship" calls attention to their lack of ties to others. Pushing out of existence anything they do not wish to know about as Podsnap does, they reject "mutual understanding." The natural selection of the competitive marketplace that has created them makes mutuality and sharing alien concepts:

> Traffic in shares is the one thing to have to do with in this world. Have no antecedents, no established character, no cultivation, no ideas, no manners; have Shares. . . . Where does he come from? Shares. Where is he going to? Shares. What are his tastes? Shares. Has he any principles? Shares. What squeezes him into Parliament? Shares. Perhaps he never of himself achieved success in anything, never originated anything, never produced anything! Sufficient answer to all; Shares. O mighty Shares! (I:10)

Like friendship, the idea of sharing has been ironically redefined as its opposite. Dickens's critique of this Darwinian world presages that of Peter Kropotkin, whose *Mutual Aid* (1902) challenged Darwin's conclusion that struggle rather than cooperation was the fundamental biological fact of the creation. By satirically reducing life to elemental terms and denying mutuality, Dickens was similarly challenging Darwin.

Even if all men do not share in the "Shares," they do share a common fate. Death is a constant attendant on the characters in *Mutual Friend*, low and high alike. Besides the death of Harmon/Radfoot that opens the story, several other important characters die along the way: Gaffer Hexam, Young Johnny, Betty Higden, Bradley Headstone, and Rogue Riderhood (twice). In the end, death, or virtual death, will give meaning and value to life.

The preoccupation with physical death in the "low" world is matched by a kind of spiritual death in the "high." Emptiness and vacuity characterize such figures as Lady Tippins. Eugene Wrayburn, the gentleman hero, is caught in a kind of living death, a paralysis induced by his relationship with his overbearing father and expressed in his cynicism, indolence, and sadism. The Darwinian world that has been reduced to an instinctive struggle for existence leaves Eugene with no sense of "design." There is no plan, no direction for his life. When Mortimer questions him about his intentions with Lizzie, Eugene responds: "I don't design anything. I have no designs. I am incapable of designs. If I conceived a design, I should speedily abandon it, exhausted by the operation" (II:6). While the "half-savage" river scavengers are reduced to an instinctive level of behavior to survive; the civilized members of society live aimless lives in a world without design.

These polarized ways of life articulate the two dominant responses to Darwinism in the 1860s. On the one hand, Darwin was accused of reducing human beings to animals; on the other, he was accused of describing a universe without design. Godless and without purpose, it was a universe without spiritual dimensions, ruled by struggle and death. In the surreal imagery of the novel, life is reduced to a semiliterate reading circle listening to nightly installments of *The Decline and Fall of the Roman Empire*.

A few of the characters challenge this domination of meaninglessness, materialism, and death. Betty Higden, who chooses to die rather than be reduced to dependency in the workhouse, provides a vision of a purposeful existence. The Boffins, although they later seem to succumb to the temptations of miserliness and fashion, begin the novel by attempting to use their inheritance to aid other people. Abby Potterson seeks to maintain a small community at the Six Jolly Fellowship Porters, even though she is not altogether successful in keeping the taint of Limehouse out of her public house. Lizzie Hexam, in spite of her impoverished childhood and her tyrannical father, maintains a sense of her own worth and continues to see visions in the fire. Her even more visionary companion, Jenny Wren, in spite of physical deformities, an alcoholic father, and impoverishment, makes "art" of her suffering by making dolls of the people she observes in the society around her. It is Jenny who articulates the paradoxical message at the heart of the story. In a scene where she and Lizzie have gone up to the roof of Pubsey and Co. to have a picnic and escape the turmoil of the city, she invites Fledgeby to join them and "come up and be dead!" (II:5) Her invitation suggests that "death" is a kind of liberation from the material life below, a transcendence of suffering into a realm of joy.

The parallel plots of the novel—the John Harmon and Eugene Wrayburn stories—both elaborate the message in the rooftop picnic scene. Both Harmon and Wrayburn go through death experiences to discover more meaningful lives. Harmon's death, which begins the novel, frees him from his identity as his father's son and heir. His disguise enables him to test Bella, but more important it enables him to discover and establish his identity for himself. By the time he proposes to Bella it is not because she has met his test, but rather because he has come to know his own heart. As the prince in a kind of fairy tale, Harmon is not very interesting. Bella, especially before her conversion into Harmon's little wife, is a more engaging character. Her name, with etymological roots suggesting both "beauty" and "war," describes her complexity. The child of a divided family in which the accepting father, R. W. Wilfer, is countered by the snobbish and irritable Mrs. Wilfer, Bella inherits these parental contradictions and speaks of herself as "always at war with myself" (III:5). She is petulant and money-grubbing as well as caring and self-denying. She is both the minx admired by old Harmon and the "boofer lady" loved by young Johnny.

Bella is one of several divided characters in the novel. Besides Harmon/Handford/Rokesmith, whose multiple names indicate the instability of his identity, there is Boffin the benefactor and Boffin the miser; Fanny Cleaver/ Jenny Wren, the sharp-tongued and visionary doll's dressmaker; Fledgeby and Riah, whose public personas reverse the hidden truths about them; the two Bradley Headstones, the mechanical teacher and the impassioned murderer; and the two Eugene Wrayburns, the aimless, cynical, sometimes sadistic man-about-town and, after his struggle in the river, the gentle and loving man.

Eugene's story, the engaging center of the novel, repeats in many ways that of John Harmon. Both young men are burdened by the dominance and expectations of their fathers. Harmon "dies" to escape his father's perverse will and Eugene adopts cynicism and idleness to thwart the expectations of his M.R.F. (Most Respected Father). Both refuse to accept their fathers' "designs" for their lives, but both are left without design when they choose to break away from paternal domination.

While Harmon becomes a shadowy figure caught up in the complications of the plot, Wrayburn emerges as a complex personality whose struggle to achieve personal independence and self-understanding is linked to the divisions in society that separate rich from poor, high from low, the governors from the governed. To Eugene's upperclass compatriots at the Veneerings', John Harmon is a character from another world—from "Somewhere"— whose story provides only a passing diversion. By entering that world, Eugene bridges the gulf between rich and poor and explores what the two worlds have in common—their mutuality. His quest is not purposeful; it lacks design, and he is intolerant of much that he finds in the underworld, particularly of Bradley Headstone, whose energy, passion, and single-mindedness are the qualities that Eugene has repressed in himself in his rebellion against his father. Eugene's taunting of Headstone matches Headstone's angry confrontations with the lawyer; their reciprocal games of cat and mouse mirror the mutuality between the two men who are "set against one another in all ways" (II:6). Their mutual struggle for dominance—to become, in a play on Riderhood's name for Eugene, the "other's governor"—is a life-and-death confrontation. It destroys Headstone and nearly destroys Eugene.

The difference between them is Lizzie, who is one of several characters who can be described as the "mutual friend" in the title. Like Boffin, Harmon, and Eugene, she bridges the gulf between high and low and facilitates mutual understanding. When she rescues Eugene from the river, she saves him from his destructive competition with Headstone and, with Jenny's aid, nurses him to health. The novel seems to suggest that Eugene's recovery depends on strength from the working class, spiritual vision from Jenny, and mutuality from the community of women. By marrying Lizzie, he transcends his upperclass diffidence and isolation, his male need for competition, and his purposeless engagement in games of mutual destruction.

As a counter to the Darwinian world of competition and struggle, mutuality seems largely to reside in the community of women. Male partnerships—like those between Riderhood and Hexam or Wegg and Venus—are

grounded in distrust and become mutually destructive. Women, who reject the predatory principle of competition, can create sites of nurture and cooperation. Abby Potterson, "abbess" of the community at the Six Jolly Fellowship Porters, has made such a place; Lizzie and Jenny support each other and provide a refuge for society's outcasts like Riah and Betty Higden; in their marriages Bella and Lizzie enable their husbands to leave behind dangerous struggles. Their community is apparent in the relationship between Jenny and Lizzie, the influence of Mrs. Boffin that makes Bella young Johnny's "boofer lady," and their mutual aid to Betty Higden. Lizzie's independence provides Bella with a model for her own transformation, and the meeting of the two women after Betty Higden's death (III:9) is an important turning point in the "long lane" of the novel.

The marriages represent modest achievements in establishing mutual understanding. They do not transform society. They do not save Rogue and Headstone from mutual destruction or the Lammles and Veneerings from bankruptcy and exile. The community presided over by the Golden Dustman and his wife at the end of the novel exists in the realm of fairy tale. The pious fraud by which he pretends to be a miser in order to change Bella, a later version of the Martin Chuzzlewit story, is manipulative and unconvincing. In the end the realistic "Voice of Society" has not been silenced. Lady Tippens, Podsnap, and their friends condemn Eugene for marryng beneath his class. Only Twemlow objects and praises Eugene's "feelings of gratitude, of respect, of admiration, and affection, [that] induced him . . . to marry the lady. . . . I think he is the greater gentleman for the action and makes her the greater lady" (IV:17). By recognizing the mutual love between Eugene and Lizzie, Twemlow transcends his isolation and reification. He is no longer just a leaf in the Veneerings' dining table, but a distinctly human voice, distinctly different from the other voices in the social chorus.

CRITICISM

The contemporary setting of *Mutual Friend* has made the background of the novel particularly interesting to historical critics. Richard Altick discusses the education controversies of the time as they affect the novel ("Education, Print, and Paper in *Our Mutual Friend*," in *Nineteenth-Century Literary Perspectives*, 1974), and Harvey SUCKSMITH ("The Dust-Heaps in *Our Mutual Friend*," *Essays in Criticism*, 1973), considers the actual contents of Victorian dustheaps and their symbolic significance in the novel. Arnold Kettle's Marxist analysis (*Introduction to the English Novel*, 1951) also locates the symbols in the novel in the realities of bourgeois Victorian culture. Jonathan Arac (*Commissioned Spirits*, 1979), on the other hand, finds the novel incoherent and lacking in organic connections between the characters and their social world.

Hillis MILLER, who has written about *Mutual Friend* on several occasions, argues (1958) that the novel, which seems to present merely "a collection of unrelated lives," in fact relates them in an "immense network of interrelations." He goes on to analyze the symbolism of money, dust, and regeneration. In his Afterword to the Signet edition (1961; 1991) Miller stresses the insubstantiality of money and the superficial values it imposes. Only those characters who "confront material and emotional depths, and then return to live their surface lives in terms of those depths can reconcile 'Society' and reality." Andrew SANDERS (1982) also finds the theme of regeneration important; he analyzes Eugene's baptismal resurrection from a life of idle boredom and spiritual death as the emblematic center of the novel. In *Form of Victorian Fiction* (1968), Miller analyzes the use of the mirror above the Veneerings' dining table as a symbolic way of showing how art reflects and transforms social reality. John Romano (*Dickens and Reality*, 1968) also uses the mirror to introduce his extended discussion of the realism in the novel. Connecting the mirror with Lightwood's story of the Man from Somewhere, Romano shows the inadequacy of art to fully comprehend the truth of what it reflects.

Beth Herst (*The Dickens Hero*, 1990) considers the various heroes and villains of the novel—Harmon, Wrayburn, Headstone—as culminating versions of the hero Dickens has developed from the earlier novels. Gail Houston (*Consuming Fictions*, 1994) analyzes the ways in which Victorian society's consuming greed valued waste and reified human beings. She finds a contradiction in the resolution, in which the novel's reified heroines are sacrificed to the growth and well-being of the heroes.

ADAPTATIONS

Like the other late novels, *Mutual Friend* inspired fewer stage adaptations than the earlier works. No stage versions appeared until six months after the novel completed its serial run, when two versions were staged, one in NEW YORK and the other in London. The latter, Henry Brougham Farnie's *Golden Dustman*, proved to be the most successful of the eight stage versions produced in the 1870s, especially after several long speeches were cut to reduce the four-and-one-half hour playing time. The American adaptation, George Fawcett Rowe's *Our Mutual Friend; or, Found Drowned* (1866) also played in London in 1871.

Two silent films, one by Edison (1911) and one by A. W. Sandberg (1919) were derived from the novel, but no sound films have appeared. Two BBC television serials have dramatized the novel, one by Freda Lindstrom in 12 parts (1959), with David McCallum as Wrayburn, and another by Julia Jones in seven parts (1976), with Leo McKern as Boffin.

"Our Next-Door Neighbour" First published in the MORNING CHRONICLE (March 18, 1836) as "Our Next-Door Neighbours," this sketch describes three parties who inhabit the lodgings in the house next door. The first is a gentleman who disturbs the street with his late-night drinking companions, the next a young man who disappears with the landlord's shirt and bedclothes, the last a widow and her consumptive son who gradually fails and dies. *Boz.*

"Our Parish" The first section of *Sketches by Boz*. In the first series the section included "The Beadle. The Parish Engine. The School-master"; "The Curate. The Old Lady. The Half-Pay Captain"; "The Four Sisters"; "The Election for Beadle"; "The Broker's Man"; "The Ladies' Societies." The last sketch, "Our Next-Door Neighbour" was added in the second series.

"Our School" Article for HOUSEHOLD WORDS (October 11, 1851). Dickens relates his memories of WELLINGTON HOUSE ACADEMY, now replaced by the railway. He remembers being first boy and winning a Latin prize; the "Chief, who was considered to know nothing," and the usher, "who was considered to know everything"; several students, Master Mawls, Dumbledon, and Maxby; and Phil, the school handyman, who "had a sovereign contempt for learning: which engenders in us a respect for his sagacity." *Reprinted.*

"Our Vestry" A humorous description of local government: its contentious elections for vestrymen, their insistence on self-government, their disputes over parliamentary procedure, and the debate over water between Tiddypot and Banger that nearly leads to blows. *Reprinted.* Originally in HOUSEHOLD WORDS (August 28, 1852).

"Our Wicked Mis-statements" Article for HOUSEHOLD WORDS (January 19, 1856) by Henry MORLEY and Dickens, responding to Harriet MARTINEAU's pamphlet, *The Factory Controversy: A Warning Against Meddling Legislation* (1855), in which she argued against a proposal to require cotton manufacturers to fence off their machinery to prevent accidents. Martineau accused *Household Words* of "unscrupulous statements, insolence, arrogance, and cant" in its statements of support for the proposal. After expressing esteem for Martineau, the authors challenge her misstatements and accuse her of special pleading for the Lancashire Association to Prevent the Fencing of Machinery, the organization that issued the pamphlet. Morley and Dickens challenge her figures for the number of accidents and go on to state the case for fencing machinery, pointing out that the manufacturers in Lancashire have been especially recalcitrant in taking preventative measures. *Stone.*

Our Young Folks Children's magazine published by TICKNOR & FIELDS, Dickens's American publishers. Dickens published "A Holiday Romance" in the magazine in 1868.

"Out of the Season" Stopping at a seaside resort (FOLKESTONE) out of the season, the author finds so many attractions and distractions that he gets no work done on the chapter he intends to write. *Reprinted.* Originally in HOUSEHOLD WORDS (June 28, 1856).

"Out of Town" Article for *HOUSEHOLD WORDS* (September 29, 1855) describing Pavilionstone (FOLKE-STONE), its great hotel, and the daily activity surrounding the arrivals and departures of the steamboats for France. *Reprinted.*

Ouvry, Frederic (1814–1881) Dickens's friend, solicitor, and advisor. He handled legal matters during the last two decades of Dickens's life, most significantly the separation from Catherine.

Overs, John A. (1808–1844) London cabinet-maker whom Dickens befriended and encouraged in his writing. Dickens contacted editors on Overs's behalf and wrote a preface for Overs's *Evenings of a Working Man* (1844).

Overton, Joseph Mayor of Winglebury, who manages to promote the confusion that prevents the duel and leads to the unexpected marriage of Alexander Trott and Miss Julia Manners. *Boz,* "Winglebury." He is named **Owen Overton** in *Strange Gentleman.*

Owen, John Pupil at Marton's school, "a lad of good parts, . . . but too thoughtless, too playful, too light-headed by far" (52). *Curiosity Shop.*

Oxford Illustrated Edition Edition of Dickens's collected works, issued in 21 volumes between 1947 and 1958, distinctive for its reengraved images of the original illustrations. Although the texts were not edited for schol-arly use, this edition has been the one most often cited in scholarly work prior to the appearance of individual volumes in the CLARENDON EDITION. The introductions in the Illustrated Edition are by various Dickensians of the postwar era. The edition did not include the miscellaneous papers, plays, or poems.

Oxford Market Dombey's footman Towlinson hopes to lead "an altered and blameless existence as a serious greengrocer" at this market north of OXFORD STREET between Great Tichfield Street and Great Portland Street. *Dombey* (18).

Oxford Street Known as Oxford Road in Dickens's day, this street dividing Mayfair to the south and MA-RYLEBONE to the north is where Gabriel Parsons walks hoping to meet his sweetheart (*Boz,* "Tottle"). Micawber imagines living at the west end of Oxford Street facing Hyde Park (*Copperfield,* 28). Jarndyce has London lodgings over an upholsterer's here (*Bleak House,* 13). Clennam and Meagles search for Miss Wade in the side streets in the neighborhood (*Dorrit,* I:27).

Oxford University Not a university man himself, Dickens seldom mentioned Oxford. He described some of its undergraduates in London when Steerforth and some of his Oxford acquaintances celebrate David's housewarming (*Copperfield,* 19–20). Dickens attacked Oxford and the Oxford Movement as representative of the narrow ignorance promoted at the University in "Report to the Commissioners . . ." (*Miscellaneous*).

Packer, Tom Private in the Royal Marines who fights against the pirates invading the Silver-store colony. "English Prisoners."

Packlemerton, Jasper One of the exhibits in Mrs. Jarley's Waxworks, a murderer "of atrocious memory, who courted and married 14 wives, and destroyed them by tickling the soles of their feet when they were sleeping in the consciousness of innocence and virtue" (28). *Curiosity Shop.*

Page, Norman (1930–) Professor, University of Nottingham; specialist in Victorian and modern literature. He has written and edited works on Hardy, Austen, Collins, Lawrence, TENNYSON, Housman, Kipling, and others. His *Dickens Companion* (1984), a work directed to graduate students and Dickens specialists, describes the resources available for Dickens studies and summarizes the composition, publication, and reception of each of Dickens's works. Page also includes a short critical bibliography for each work and a list of the characters with brief descriptions. His *Dickens Chronology* (1988) provides a year-by-year record of the events in Dickens's life.

Palace Yard Part of the WESTMINSTER HALL complex. John Harmon, disguised as Handford, gives his address as EXCHEQUER COFFEE-HOUSE, Old Palace Yard (*Mutual Friend*, I:3).

Palazzo Peschiere Dickens leased this "Palace of the Fishponds" during his stay in GENOA in 1844–45.

Pall Mall This fashionable street in central London houses a number of gentlemen's clubs. Here Montague Tigg has his lodgings and his fraudulent insurance company (*Chuzzlewit*, 27–28). Mr. Chops locates here when "Going into Society." Twemlow canvasses for Veneering by spending a whole day sitting in the window of his Pall Mall club (*Mutual Friend*, II:3). Also mentioned in *Boz*, "Winglebury"; "Golden Mary"; *Uncommercial* (16).

Palmer Player of many parts in the amateur theaters of London. *Boz*, "Private Theatres."

Palmer, Samuel (1805–1881) Artist engaged by Dickens to provide four sketches for *Pictures from Italy*

Samuel Palmer's panoramic drawing of Pompeii for Pictures from Italy.

after Clarkson STANFIELD withdrew, probably because of what he perceived as anti-Catholic bias in Dickens's text.

Palmerston, Henry John Temple, Viscount (1784–1865) Tory politician, pragmatic, imperialistic, and opportunistic, particularly hated by Dickens. When he became prime minister in the wake of the Crimean debacle of 1855, Dickens attacked him in *HOUSEHOLD WORDS* as "the Grand Vizier Parmastoon (or Twirling Weathercock)" in a series or articles entitled "The Thousand and One Humbugs." *Miscellaneous.*

Pancks Casby's agent and rent collector who "snorted and sniffed and puffed and blew, like a little labouring steam engine" (I:13). He squeezes the tenants in BLEEDING HEART YARD and takes the blame for Casby's avarice. He leads the effort to discover the Dorrit fortune (I: 35). He invests his money in Merdle's enterprises and Arthur follows his lead (II:13). He aids in exposing Rigaud (II:30) and Casby (II:32). *Dorrit.*

Pancras Road Street in CAMDEN TOWN, north London, where Miss J'mima Ivins and Mr. Samuel Wilkins meet their friends on the way to the EAGLE (*Boz*, "Miss Evans"); Heyling, in "The Old Man's Tale about the Queer Client," takes the Pancras Road in his final pursuit of his victim (*Pickwick*, 21); Jerry Cruncher resurrects a body in the St. Pancras Churchyard (*Two Cities*, II: 14).

Pangloss Government official in Liverpool, "lineally descended from the learned doctor of that name," who accompanies the Traveller to see some wounded soldiers from India. *Uncommercial* (8).

Pankey, Miss One of Paul Dombey's fellow boarders at Mrs. Pipchin's, "a mild little blue-eyed morsel of a child, who was shampoo'd every morning" (8). *Dombey*.

Pantomime In Britain, a form of popular theater beginning in the early 18th century and traditionally performed during the Christmas season. The basic pantomime plot revolves around a young lady with two suitors, a wealthy fop chosen by her father to marry her and a poor young man whom she prefers. When she is forced to choose between giving into her father or running off with her lover, a good Fairy transforms the whole group into the characters of traditional pantomime: the young lovers become Harlequin and Columbine, the interfering father Pantaloon, and his servant Clown. In the ensuing pursuit of the runaway couple, the "comic business" of the pantomime, the lovers escape their pursuers through tricks and contrivances until they are finally overtaken and subdued by Pantaloon and Clown. Then the Good Fairy reappears, secures the father's consent to the marriage, and the play closes with a grand celebration. In articles for his magazines ("The Pantomime of Life," "A Curious Dance around a Curious Tree," and "Paradise Revisited") and in his Introduction to the *Memoirs of Grimaldi*, Dickens recounted his childhood pleasure in the pantomime, particularly in the antics of Clown, and he reiterated his belief that the pantomime is "a mirror of life." Edwin EIGNER (1989) traces this influence in the novels, finding the structure and characters of pantomime as an informing principle in many of the novels.

"Pantomime of Life, The" Article from BENTLEY'S MISCELLANY comparing the types from PANTOMIME on the stage to people in real life. Collected in *Mudfog*.

Paper Buildings Section of the TEMPLE where Sir John Chester lives, "a row of goodly tenements, shaded in front by ancient trees, and looking, at the back, upon the Temple Gardens" (*Rudge*, 15).

"Paper Mill, A" Article for HOUSEHOLD WORDS (August 31, 1850) by LEMON and Dickens describing a visit to a paper mill at Dartford in KENT. As the narrator describes the process of making paper, he imagines himself as the rags that go through several stages of transformation to become writing paper. *Stone*.

Papers Boy working at Smith's bookstall. "Mugby."

Parables In the *Life of Our Lord*, Dickens's retelling of the gospel story for his children, he placed particular emphasis on Jesus's parables, stories that illustrated a moral or theological teaching and were often allegorical (see ALLEGORY). In Jesus' parables, for example, the father usually represents God. Dickens often used New Testament parables in his works. The satire in *Twist*, for example, ironically casts the workhouse and parochial officials as good Samaritans; *Hard Times* is structured on the parable of the sower. *Hard Times* itself is a kind of parable, illustrating the spiritual results of Gradgrind's individualistic materialism. Janet L. LARSON (1985) discusses both Dickens's use of biblical parables and the parabolic qualities in Dickens's own work.

"Paradise at Tooting, The" A bitter article for the EXAMINER (January 27, 1849) sarcastically attacking Mr. Drouet, proprietor of a baby farm in Tooting where a cholera epidemic had ravaged the infant population of 1,400, so that the "Tooting churchyard became too small for the piles of children's coffins." Dickens charges Drouet with neglect, overcrowding, and physical cruelty to the children. He charges the Poor Law guardians and inspectors with responsibility for the scourge. They allowed Drouet to maintain his vile establishment, which was "brutally conducted, vilely kept, preposterously inspected, dishonestly defended, a disgrace to a Christian community, and a stain upon a civilized land." *Miscellaneous*. Drouet's baby farm is a large-scale version of Mrs. Mann's establishment in *Twist*, where Oliver spends his early years and where his friend, young Dick, dies. Dickens addressed the Drouet case in two further articles, "The Tooting Farm" and "The Verdict for Drouet."

Paragon, Mary Anne The first in a series of impossible servants employed by David and Dora Copperfield. *Copperfield* (44).

Pardiggle, Mrs. Philanthropic associate of Mrs. Jellyby, "she was a formidible style of lady, with spectacles, a prominent nose, and a loud voice, who had the effect of wanting a great deal of room. And she really did, for she knocked down little chairs with her skirts" (8). She is the wife of **O. A. Pardiggle, F.R.S.**, "an obstinate-looking man . . . who was always talking in a loud bass voice about his mite" (30). Their five sons, **Egbert, Oswald, Francis, Felix**, and **Alfred**, "weazened and shrivelled" and "ferocious with discontent" (8), are pawns in their mother's philanthropy. Each has his allowance subscribed to various charitable enterprises. *Bleak House*.

Paris When Dickens first visited Paris in 1844 on his way to GENOA, he described the city in a letter to D'ORSAY as "the most extraordinary place in the world." He returned for frequent visits to the city, often with friends like MACREADY (1844), MACLISE (1850), and Wilkie COLLINS (1855). He describes a cold New Year's Day on one such visit in Paris in "New Year's Day." He was introduced in 1844 to many of the important French writers and artists, among them DUMAS, HUGO, Gautier, Sue, and Delacroix. He spent several months in Paris with his family during the winter and spring, 1845–46, while he was working on *Dombey*, writing back to John FORSTER that "Paul's death has amazed Paris." During this visit, Dickens went to the **Paris Morgue**, an institution described in *Uncommercial* (7, 19) and in "Railway Dreaming." He also made extended visits to Paris in 1855–56 and 1862–63.

The Dombeys spend a "dull" honeymoon in Paris (*Dombey*, 35) and Lady Dedlock is happy to leave behind the "desolation of Boredom" she finds there (*Bleak House*, 12), but Mrs. Lirriper is enthralled: "And of Paris I can tell you no more my dear than that it's town and country both in one. . . . It's pure enchantment" (*Legacy*, 1). Revolutionary Paris, the BASTILLE, ST. ANTOINE, and the Monseigneur's palaces are important settings in *Two Cities*.

"Parish Clerk, The"   Tale written by Pickwick while he is recuperating from his escapade at Miss Tompkins's School about Nathaniel Pipkin, a parish clerk and schoolmaster, who dreams of marrying Maria Lobbs. She flirts with him and he confesses his desire to her father, Old Lobbs, the local saddler, who rejects the idea out of hand. Maria marries her cousin and Nathaniel and Old Lobbs become friends. *Pickwick* (17).

Park Lane   Fashionable street in Mayfair where Nicholas attacks Sir Mulberry Hawk (*Nickleby*, 32); Miss Wade takes Tattycoram to her house in "a labyrinth near Park Lane" (*Dorrit*, II:27).

Parker   Police officer who accompanies Inspector Field and the narrator to the Old Mint. *Reprinted*, "Inspector Field."

Parker, Mrs. Johnson   "Mother of seven extremely fine girls—all unmarried." *Boz*, "Ladies' Societies."

Parker, Uncle   Wegg's name for one of the inhabitants of the corner house. *Mutual Friend*, I:5.

Parkes, Phil   One of the regulars at the MAYPOLE INN, a warden in Epping Forest. *Rudge* (1).

Parkins   Friend and confidante of Our Bore. *Reprinted*, "Bore."

Parkins, Mrs.   Laundress who disregards the requests of the narrator. *Reprinted*, "Ghost of Art."

Parkle   Barrister friend of the Traveller who lives in dusty chambers in GRAY'S INN. *Uncommercial* (14).

Parksop, Brother   George Silverman's grandfather. "Silverman."

Parley's Illuminated Library   Magazine that specialized in "re-originating" popular works of literature. Dickens sued the magazine for its plagiarism of the

Carol, won the case, but was unable to collect the damages when the magazine folded.

Parliament   In David Coperfield's description of working as a shorthand reporter taking down speeches in Parliament, Dickens drew on his own similar experiences with the MIRROR OF PARLIAMENT and the MORNING CHRONICLE: "Night after night, I record predictions that never come to pass, professions that are never fulfilled, explanations that are only meant to mystify. I wallow in words. . . . I am sufficiently behind the scenes to know the worth of political life. I am quite an Infidel about it, and shall never be converted" (*Copperfield*, 43). Dickens's years as a parliamentary reporter developed his ear for public speech, which he frequently parodied in the novels and his eye for the absurdities of the proceedings. In the "Parliamentary Sketch" in *Boz* and in gatherings like the Pickwick Club (*Pickwick*, 1) or the meeting of the United Metropolitan Improved Hot Muffin and Crumpet Baking and Punctual Delivery Company (*Nickleby*, 2), he satirized the inflated public rhetoric and the hair-splitting that he had observed in Parliament. Nearly all of his M.P.s are presented satirically, from Cornelius Brook Dingwall (*Boz*, "Sentiment") and Mr. Gregsbury (*Nickleby*, 16), to Veneering (*Mutual Friend*). As a member of the Whig Parliament devoted to carrying out investigations and producing bluebooks full of statistics, Gradgrind's "parliamentary duties" are said to be "sifting for odds and ends" at the "national cinder-heap" and "throwing the dust about into the eyes of other people who wanted other odds and ends" (*Hard Times*, II:11), a metaphor Dickens again uses to describe parliamentary activity in *Mutual Friend* (III:8).

Dickens satirizes parliamentary ELECTIONS in *Pickwick, Bleak House*, and *Mutual Friend*.

"Parliamentary Sketch, A"   A tour of Parliament and particularly of Bellamy's, the coffee house near the Houses of Parliament where members gather. This sketch combined two pieces originally in the EVENING CHRONICLE, "The House" (March 7, 1835) and "Bellamy's" (April 11, 1835). *Boz*.

Parliament Street   Street in Westminster where Dickens as a boy went into the Red Lion Pub and ordered a glass of ale. He describes a similar episode in *Copperfield* (11).

Paroissien, David H. (1939–)   Professor, University of Massachusetts; Dickens critic, editor, and historical scholar. He has edited and annotated *Pictures from Italy* (1973), *Selected Letters of Charles Dickens* (1984), and the Garland bibliography for *Oliver Twist* (1984). He has also written numerous articles on Dickensian topics, especially on the early novels. Particularly noteworthy is his survey of Dickens's ideas about literature and art, culled from comments in the letters and articles ("Literature's 'Eternal Duties': Dickens's Professional Creed," in *The Changing World of Charles Dickens*, ed.

R. Giddings, 1983). As General Editor of the *Dickens Quarterly*, Paroissien has coordinated special issues on several of the novels commemorating the 150th anniversary of their first publication.

Parsons, Gabriel Sugar baker and friend of Watkins Tottle who pays Tottle's debts on the condition that Tottle marry Miss Lillerton and pay him back from her estate. He gives up on Tottle when he fails to win Miss Lillerton. His own marriage to his wife, **Fanny**, is opposed by her parents and they marry secretly. *Boz*, "Tottle."

Parsons, Letitia Pupil at Minerva House who performs on the piano. *Boz*, "Sentiment."

Parvis, Arson Resident of Lanrean. "Message from the Sea."

"Passage in the Life of Mr. Watkins Tottle, A" Story originally published in the *MONTHLY MAGAZINE* (January, February, 1835), telling of a bachelor of 50 who is too timid and too poor to pursue his "uxorious inclinations." Prompted by his friend Gabriel Parsons, Tottle courts Miss Lillerton and finally proposes when Parsons releases him from his debts on the condition that he be paid back from Miss Lillerton's fortune. However, when Tottle learns that his intended has already accepted the proposal of the Reverend Charles Timson, Parsons abandons him; Tottle takes his own life a few weeks later. *Boz*.

Passnidge Murdstone's friend whom David meets at Lowestoft. *Copperfield* (2).

Patten, Robert (1939–) Professor, Rice University. In numerous articles and books, Patten has written on critical, bibliographical, and historical topics relating to Dickens. In *Dickens and his Publishers* (1978) he collects the facts of Dickens's publishing career and discusses how such factors as serial publication affected his work. *George Cruikshank: His Life, Work, and Times* (1992) treats Dickens's connections and collaborations with this important Victorian illustrator. Patten's many articles on Dickensian topics include several on *Pickwick*, especially on the INTERPOLATED TALES (one of them in *ELH*, 1967); an analysis of the religious dimensions to the *Carol* (*Dickens Studies Annual*, 1972); and an analysis of the links between *Dombey* and *Vanity Fair* ("The Fight at the Top of the Tree: *Vanity Fair* versus *Dombey and Son*," *Studies-in-English-Literature*, 1970). Patten has also edited *Pickwick* (1972).

Patty Spinster sister of the tenant of the Haunted House. "Haunted House."

Patrician's Daughter, The Dickens wrote a verse prologue for Macready's production of this first play by

J. Westland Marston in 1842. The prologue justifies setting a tragic story in the present. *Miscellaneous*.

Pavilionstone Dickens's name for FOLKESTONE, a former fishing village and smuggling town that has been transformed by the trains of the South-Eastern Railway Company bringing travelers on their way to the steamboats for France. *Reprinted*, "Out of Town."

Pawkins, Major and Mrs. New York family, typical of the Americans whom Martin Chuzzlewit meets in the New World. Mrs. Pawkins, proprietor of the boarding house where Martin stays in NEW YORK, is "very straight, bony, and silent" (16). Her husband, Major Pawkins, is a "great politician" and an "admirable man of business": "In plainer words he had a most distinguished genius for swindling, and could start a bank, or negotiate a loan, or form a land-jobbing company (entailing ruin, pestilence, and death, on hundreds of families), with any gifted creature in the Union" (16). *Chuzzlewit*.

"Pawnbroker's Shop, The" Originally published in the *EVENING STANDARD* (June 30, 1835) as "Sketches of London No. 15," this sketch describes the customers in a lower-class pawnbroker's shop in *DRURY LANE*: an old woman who regularly pawns and redeems bits of clothing; a drunken carpenter who abuses his wife and child; a mother and daughter who have fallen into poverty; a prostitute; and a drunken old woman. *Boz*.

Paxton, Joseph (1803–1865) Gardener, horticulturalist, designer of the Crystal Palace, member of Parliament. Paxton was the majority financial backer of the *DAILY NEWS*. Paxton's money came from speculation in railways, and Dickens feared that his financial interests would skew the editorial policy of the paper. He showed Dickens through the Crystal Palace while it was still under construction.

Payn, James (1830–1898) Novelist, poet, editor, and journalist, best known for *Lost Sir Massingberd* (1864) and *By Proxy* (1878). He published numerous articles in *HOUSEHOLD WORDS* and described his first meeting with Dickens in 1856 as "an epoch in my existence." Payn was friendly with Dickens, but he did not become one of Dickens's young men. He thought Dickens's separation from his wife a "sad blot" on his character and suggested that the novelist "was in a degree intoxicated with universal applause, as well as spoiled by the sycophants who hung about him, and sanctioned his vagaries." His recollections of Dickens appear in *Chambers's Magazine*, which he edited, (1874) and in *Some Literary Recollections* (1884).

Payne, Doctor Army doctor who is present at the interrupted duel between Dr. Slammer and Winkle. *Pickwick* (2, 3).

Paynter   The narrator's "enemy" in the competition for the attentions of "the youngest Miss Clickett but one." Although they arrange to duel, the two end up avoiding a fight and agreeing on the perfidy of Miss Clickett. *Miscellaneous*, "New Year's Day."

"Peacoat" ("Pea")   Officer who leads the narrator on a tour of the THAMES police. He may be the model for the Inspector in *Mutual Friend*. *Reprinted*, "Down with the Tide."

Peacock Inn   EATANSWILL Inn where Snodgrass and Tupman stay. *Pickwick* (13–14).

Peacock Inn   Starting point in ISLINGTON for coaches going north. Nicholas leaves from here on his way to DOTHEBOYS HALL (*Nickleby*, 5); the narrator of the "Holly-Tree" starts from here on his wintry journey to Liverpool.

Peak   Sir John Chester's valet, who, following his master's death and "true to his master's creed, eloped with all the cash and movables he could lay his hands on, and started as a finished gentleman upon his own account" (82). *Rudge*.

Peaks, The   Former name of Bleak House. *Bleak House* (8).

Peal of Bells, The   Village alehouse where Mr. Traveller stays. "Tiddler."

Peartree   Member of the EIGHT CLUB, this physician attends the poor gratis. *Drood*, Sapsea Fragment.

Pebbleson Nephew   Firm of London wine merchants purchased by Mrs. Wilding and renamed Wilding and Company. "No Thoroughfare."

Peckham   South London suburb, east of CAMBERWELL, where Walter Gay attends a weekly boarding school (4) and Mr. Feeder plans to board with his two maiden aunts while he explores "the dark mysteries of London" (14). *Dombey*.

Pecksniff, Charity (Cherry) and Mercy (Merry)
Daughters of Seth Pecksniff. Contrasted by their father as serious (Charity) and frivolous (Mercy), they are both scheming, vindictive, and hypocritical like their parent. Mercy, the younger daughter, "the most arch and at the same time the most artless creature" (2), marries Jonas Chuzzlewit to triumph over her sister and to best Jonas in marital quarrels (24), but he physically and psychologically abuses her, arousing the sympathetic attentions of Tom Pinch and Mrs. Todgers for her. After losing Jonas to her sister, Charity, shrewish and hypocritical, entraps Augustus Moddle into a proposal, but he runs off on their wedding day (54). *Chuzzlewit.*

Fred Barnard's iconographic representation of Pecksniff for the Household Edition of Martin Chuzzlewit *(1872).*

Pecksniff, Seth   Architect and surveyer, the very model of the hypocrite, who lives with his two daughters near SALISBURY in Wiltshire. "He was a most exemplary man: fuller of virtuous precept than a copybook. . . . His very throat was moral. You saw a good deal of it. You looked over a very low fence of white cravat . . . and there it lay, a valley between two jutting heights of collar, serene and whiskerless before you. It seemed to say, on the part of Mr. Pecksniff, 'There is no deception, ladies and gentlemen, all is peace, a holy calm pervades me' " (2). To forward his scheme of obtaining old Martin Chuzzlewit's money, he befriends young Martin and then, when the old man demands it, repudiates him (12). He marries his vain and frivolous daughter **Mercy** to Jonas Chuzzlewit, who brutally abuses her. He takes old Martin into his house and schemes to marry the old man's companion, Mary Graham. Then Tom Pinch, his loyal assistant and former student, discovers his hypocrisy (31). He loses his wealth in the collapse of Montague Tiggs's frauds and is denounced by old Martin (52). In the end he is reduced to writing begging letters. *Chuzzlewit.*

Peddle and Pool   Edward Dorrit's solicitors. *Dorrit* (I: 36).

Pedro   One of Jerry's troupe of performing dogs. *Curiosity Shop* (18).

Peecher, Emma   Schoolteacher at the school where Bradley Headstone is master. Small, neat, and methodical, "she could write a little essay on any subject, exactly a slate long. . . . If Mr. Bradley Headstone had addressed a written proposal of marriage to her, she would probably have replied in a complete little essay on the theme exactly a slate long" (II:1). *Mutual Friend*.

Peepy, The Hon. Miss Reputed to be the "Beauty of her day" in a time long past at "Our English-Watering Place." *Reprinted*.

Peerybingle Family Couple whose marriage is threatened by the appearance of a mysterious stranger: **John**, a carrier much older than his wife, "this John so heavy, but so light of spirit; so rough upon the surface, but so gentle at the core; so dull without, so quick within; so solid, but so good!" (1), and his young wife **Mary** (**Dot**), "called Dot for her tiny size. . . . though something of what is called the dumpling shape" (1). John's generosity to Dot and her good offices in preventing the unequal marriage of May Fielding and Tackleton by helping to reunite May and her true lover, Edward Plummer, renews their own marriage on the first anniversary of their wedding. They have an infant **son**. *Cricket*.

Peffer Snagsby's deceased partner in the law-stationer's business. *Bleak House* (10).

Pegasus's Arms, The The inn where the Sleary circus troupe stays in COKETOWN. *Hard Times* (I:6).

Pegg (aka Waterhouse) Liverpool crimp, an agent who traps or tricks men into serving as seamen or soldiers. *Uncommercial* (5).

Peggotty, Clara Daniel Peggotty's sister, David Copperfield's devoted nurse, "with no shape at all, and eyes so dark that they seemed to darken their whole neighbourhood in her face, and cheeks and arms so hard and red that I wondered the birds didn't peck her in preference to apples" (2). She pops the buttons on the back of her gown when she hugs the boy (2). While David's mother is marrying Murdstone, she takes David to YARMOUTH to the converted boat where her brother Daniel lives (3). When Murdstone dismisses Peggotty after Clara Copperfield's death, she marries the "willin' " Barkis and settles in Yarmouth (10). After Barkis dies (30), she returns to live with David and his aunt (34). *Copperfield*.

Peggotty, Daniel Clara Peggotty's "bacheledore" brother, a "rough-and-ready" fisherman, who lives in a house made from an overturned boat on the shore at YARMOUTH, where he has taken in his orphaned niece and nephew **Little Em'ly** and **Ham**, and the widow of his partner, Mrs. Gummidge. He refuses to be thanked for his generosity in taking them in and "if it were ever referred to, by any one of them, he struck the table a heavy blow with his right hand . . . and swore a dreadful oath that he would be 'Gormed' if he didn't cut and run for good, if it was ever mentined again" (3). When Em'ly abandons her fiancé Ham and elopes with Steerforth, Daniel makes it his mission to find her and restore her to the family (31). He and his niece are reunited after Steerforth abandons her (50), but Ham is drowned while attempting to rescue Steerforth from a storm at sea (55).

In the end Daniel, Em'ly, and Mrs. Gummidge resettle in AUSTRALIA (57). *Copperfield*.

Peggy (1) Housemaid. "Going into Society."

Peggy (2) Lord Chamberlain to King Watkins the First. "Holiday Romance."

Pegler, Mrs. The mysterious old country woman who occasionally appears in the streets of COKETOWN, looking at Bounderby's house or factory: "The flutter of her manner, in the unwonted noise of the streets; the spare shawl, carried unfolded on her arm; the heavy umbrella, and little basket; the loose long-fingered gloves, to which her hands were unused; all bespoke an old woman from the country" (I:12). She is revealed to be Bounderby's mother (III:5), ignored by him so that he could purvey his fiction of being a self-made man. *Hard Times*.

Pegwell Bay Beach resort south of RAMSGATE visited by the Tuggses. *Boz*, "Tuggses."

Pell, Solomon Shady lawyer of the Insolvent Court who arranges Sam Weller's imprisonment in the FLEET (43) and proves Susan Weller's will for Tony (55). "His forehead was narrow, his face wide, his head large, and his nose all on one side, as if Nature, indignant with the propensities she observed in him in his birth, had given it an angry tweak which it had never recovered" (43). *Pickwick*.

Peltirogus, Horatio Childhood playmate of Kate Nickleby, described by Mrs. Nickleby as a suitor for her daughter's hand. *Nickleby* (55).

Pendennis Autobiographical BILDUNGSROMAN by THACKERAY, serialized between 1848 and 1850, which is often compared to Dickens's autobiographical bildungsroman of the same period, *David Copperfield*. The novel tells of the youth and young manhood of Arthur Pendennis (Pen), who survives a disastrous infatuation for an actress, an affair with his housekeeper's daughter, an opportunistic relationship with an heiress, illness, and estrangement from his mother to eventually marry the patient and sensible Laura Bell, a young woman much like Agnes Wickfield.

Penny Dreadfuls A form of popular fiction developed in the 1830s and '40s, these sensational tales written for working-class readers were printed in an eight-page, double-column format, illustrated with crude woodcuts, and sold for a penny. Jo March in Louisa May Alcott's *Little Women* (1868) survives in New York by writing similar tales for the American market. Many of the penny dreadfuls recounted the lives of criminals, as in the NEWGATE NOVELS. Dickens was fascinated with motifs like the cannibalism in such popular stories as Sweeney Todd, one of the sensational penny dreadfuls. Scenes like the murder of Nancy and the pursuit and death of

Sikes contained many of the elements found in the cheap serials. It is not surprising that several of Dickens's novels were recast by writers like T. P. Prest, who produced *Oliver Twiss* under the pseudonym "Bos" for the penny market.

Penrewen Old resident of the village of Lanrean. "Message from the Sea."

Pentonville Fashionable suburb in north London where Nicodemus Dumps rents a "first-floor furnished" (*Boz*, "Christening"); Brownlow has his comfortable house (*Twist*, 12); Guppy has "lowly, but airy" lodgings at Penton Place (*Bleak House*, 9); Pancks lodges on the second floor of Rugg's agency (*Dorrit*, I:25). An experimental prison which separated the prisoners from each other, a strategy known as "the separate system," was established here in 1842. Dickens satirized the prison in *Copperfield* (61).

Peplow, Mrs. One of the muffin fanciers who spend their evenings at home. She sends her son **Master Peplow** out to buy muffins from a street seller. *Boz*, "Streets—Night."

Pepper ("The Avenger") Pip's servant boy. "I had even started a boy in boots—top boots—in bondage and slavery to whom I might be said to pass my days. For, after I had made this monster (out of the refuse of my washerwoman's family) and had clothed him with a blue coat, canary waistcoat, white cravat, creamy breeches, and the boots already mentioned, I had to find him a little to do and a great deal to eat" (27). *Expectations*.

Peps, Dr. Parker Doctor with an "immense reputation for assisting at the increase of great families" who attends Paul Dombey's birth and death. *Dombey* (I:16).

Perch Messenger for Dombey and Son, "whose place was on a little bracket, like a time-piece" (13) outside Dombey's office. He and his **wife** reside at BALL'S POND, where they raise their numerous children. *Dombey*.

Percy, Lord Algernon (1750–1830) Commander of the Northumberland Militia in London during the GORDON RIOTS. *Rudge* (67).

"Perfect Felicity" First in a series of articles for *HOUSEHOLD WORDS* (April 6, 1850) written in the voice of a raven who objects to being caged and misunderstood by humans who think he is happy and a "member of a Happy Family." He tallies his dislike of other family members—owl, pigeon, dogs, children, sparrows—and reveals his disgust with his situation in writing. *Miscellaneous*. See also "FROM THE RAVEN IN THE HAPPY FAMILY."

"Perils of Certain English Prisoners, The" Christmas number of *HOUSEHOLD WORDS*, 1857. Dick-ens wrote chapters 1 and 3, Wilkie COLLINS, chapter 2. The story is narrated by Gill Davis, a private in a Royal Marine detachment dispatched to the English colony on Silver-store Island to deliver supplies and bring out the annual production of silver from the mines in Honduras that is stored on the island. Aided by a native turncoat, Christian George King, a band of pirates attack the island, divide the residents and the soldiers, kill many of the colonists while taking the rest prisoner, and abscond with the silver. The prisoners are taken into the interior of Honduras and eventually, under the heroic leadership of Davis, manage to escape and reunite with their British protectors. *Christmas Stories*.

Periodicals Dickens began his writing career as a journalist and his first publications—stories and sketches later collected in *Boz*—appeared in various magazines and newspapers: MONTHLY MAGAZINE, BELL'S WEEKLY MAGAZINE, MORNING CHRONICLE, EVENING CHRONICLE, BELL'S LIFE IN LONDON. Throughout his career he also edited and wrote for magazines. Most of his journalistic essays appeared in THE EXAMINER, edited by FORSTER, and in his own magazines: BENTLEY'S MISCELLANY, HOUSEHOLD WORDS, and ALL THE YEAR ROUND. All of the novels were, in a strict sense, periodicals, appearing in either monthly or weekly SERIAL parts.

Perker Pickwick's and Wardle's solicitor, "a high-dried man, with . . . small restless black eyes, that kept winking and twinkling on each side of his little inquisitive nose." He arranges the payoff for Jingle in the Rachel Wardle affair (10), represents Pickwick in the Bardell suit, and negotiates Pickwick's release from the FLEET PRISON (45–47). *Pickwick*.

Perkins Resident of the village near the haunted house who "wouldn't go a-nigh the place." "Haunted House."

Perkins, Mrs. Resident of the neighborhood around SOL'S ARMS who, with her neighbor Mrs. Piper, takes a keen interest in the mysterious events at Krook's house. *Bleak House*.

Perkinsop, Mary Anne One of Mrs. Lirriper's maids, "worth her weight in gold, as overawing lodgers without driving them away." Miss Wozenham lures her away with higher wages. "Lirriper's Lodgings."

Perrault, Charles (1628–1703) French author who collected and retold eight traditional FAIRY TALES that became known in English as "Mother Goose's Tales." This collection, known to Dickens in the cheap chapbooks that circulated in England during his childhood, included "Bluebeard," "Cinderella," "Red Riding Hood," "Sleeping Beauty," "Hop o' My Thumb" and "Puss and Boots," stories to which he alludes frequently in the novels. Harry STONE (1979) discusses the importance of these stories in Dickens's work.

"Personal" Dickens' statement in *HOUSEHOLD WORDS* (June 12, 1858), responding to rumors regardng his marital difficulties and his relationships with Georgina HOGARTH and Ellen TERNAN. Addressed to those of his readers "who know me through my writings, and who do not know me otherwise," the statement concludes with the following declaration: "I most solemnly declare, then—and this I do, both in my own name and in my wife's name—that all the lately whispered rumours touching the trouble at which I have glanced, are abominably false." When his publishers, BRADBURY & EVANS, refused to publish the statement in *PUNCH*, Dickens broke off his relationship with them and began a new magazine to replace *Household Words*. *Stone*.

Perugini, Kate Married name of Kate DICKENS, Dickens's daughter, whose second husband was Carlo Perugini, a painter. Gladys STOREY's interviews with her were the basis for *Dickens and Daughter* (1939), one of the works that revealed Dickens's relationship with Ellen TERNAN.

Pessell Member of the medical section of the Mudfog Association. *Mudfog*.

"Pet" Nickname of Minnie MEAGLES. *Dorrit*.

"Pet Prisoners" Article for *HOUSEHOLD WORDS* (April 27, 1850) on PRISONS, criticizing the separate system of imprisonment currently in effect at the model prison in PENTONVILLE. Dickens objects to the expense of the experiment, pointing out that the prisoners are better fed and have better accommodations than workhouse inmates or the working poor. The money being spent on model prisons would be better spent, he suggests, on education for the honest poor and emigration for the criminals. He also argues that the separate system encourages false penitence, a criticism repeated in his portrayal of Littimer and Uriah Heep as prisoners in *Copperfield* (61). The separate system is also unnatural: By isolating naturally gregarious creatures from one another, the system induces both mental and physical illness. The silent system, which does not isolate prisoners, but rather enforces a discipline of silence, is a better system, Dickens asserts, and it is considerably cheaper. *Miscellaneous*.

Peter, Lord Imbecile lord who is courting Julia Manners for her money. He is unintentionally displaced by Alexander Trott and then killed in a drunken riding accident. *Boz*, "Winglebury."

Petowker, Henrietta Minor actress and friend of the Kenwigs "able to sing and recite in a manner that brought the tears to Mrs. Kenwig's eyes" (14). She joins the Crummles company, marries Mr. Lillyvick, the wa-

ter-rate collector (25), and then leaves him and runs off with a half-pay captain (52). *Nickleby*.

Pettifer, Tom Captain Jorgan's steward, whose hat contains the papers that explain the "Message from the Sea."

Peyrouton, Noel C. (1925–1968) Professor, Emerson College, Boston; Dickens scholar; founder and original editor of *DICKENS STUDIES*. Peyrouton wrote many articles for the *DICKENSIAN* and *Dickens Studies*, particularly on Dickens's trips to America and on other biographical topics. He was an associate editor for volume three of the Pilgrim Edition of the *LETTERS* (1974).

"Phib" Fanny Squeers's name for her servant PHOEBE. *Nickleby*.

Phibbs Cheapside haberdasher questioned by Inspector Wield about the murder of Eliza Grimwood. *Reprinted*, "'Dectective' Anecdotes."

Phil Morose janitor at Our School who "had a sovereign contempt for learning" which earns "respect for his sagacity" from the boys. *Reprinted*, "Our School."

Philadelphia On his visit to this "handsome, but distractingly regular" city, Dickens found himself succumbing to the Quaker influence: "the collar of my coat appeared to stiffen, and the brim of my hat to expand beneath its quakery influence. My hair shrunk into a sleek short crop, my hands folded themselves upon my breast of their own accord" (*Notes*, 7). He visited the Eastern Penitentiary to observe its system of solitary confinement and concluded the system's "slow and daily tampering with the mysteries of the brain, to be immeasurably worse than any torture of the body" (*Notes*, 7).

Philanthropy One of the most frequent themes in Dickens's work is the need for charity and caring for one's fellow human beings. When Scrooge reforms, he promptly gives money to the charity solicitors he has refused the night before and sends gifts to the Cratchits (*Carol*, 5). In the early novels especially, the hero is aided by benevolent older men like Brownlow (*Twist*) or the Cheeryble brothers (*Nickleby*), but such private philanthropy becomes increasingly problematic in the later novels, for it often has the effect of corrupting the recipients. Magwitch's money makes Pip an ungrateful snob (*Expectations*), and Jarndyce's gifts to Skimpole simply sustain his parasitism (*Bleak House*). Boffin must pretend to be a miser to enable Bella to see the corrupting effect of his kindness to her (*Mutual Friend*).

Dickens reserves his strongest scorn for the professional philanthropists who make a public display of their concern for others. Mrs. Jellyby practices "telescopic philanthropy": She can "see nothing nearer than Africa" (*Bleak House*, 4) and neglects her family while aiding the

Mrs. Pardiggle's intrusive and oppressive philanthropy, as depicted by Fred Barnard for the Household Edition of Bleak House *(1875).*

natives of Borrioboola-Gha. Mrs. Pardiggle, distinguished for her "rapacious benevolence," is a philanthropist who does "a little and ma[kes] a great deal of noise" (*Bleak House*, 8). Mr. Honeythunder's even noisier philanthropy "was of that gunpowderous sort that the difference between it and animosity was hard to determine" (*Drood*, 6).

Dickens, himself an active philanthropist, was aware of the dangers of over-zealousness. He lent his name to numerous charitable causes, spoke at their fundraising events and wrote about them in his magazines. Two charitable endeavors were particularly important to him: the URANIA COTTAGE project undertaken with Miss COUTTS, to rescue girls from the streets and start them in respectable life, and the GUILD OF LITERATURE AND ART, a project founded with LYTTON to provide for needy artists and writers.

Philistinism Matthew Arnold in *Culture and Anarchy* divided British society in his time into three groups: Barbarians, Philistines, and Populace. Philistines, the members of the Victorian middle class, believed that the greatness of Britain derived from its material wealth, and they devoted themselves to the pursuit of money. Dickens satirizes the pursuit of money throughout his novels, though he increasingly seems to think that money has displaced all other measures of value and that, for example, Magwitch can make a gentleman of Pip simply with money (*Expectations*). Dickens's fullest portrait of bourgeois philistinism appears in his attack on "Podsnappery" in *Mutual Friend*. Podsnap swells with monetary pride as he tallies the greatness of England and puts down everything foreign: "Mr. Podsnap was well to do, and stood very high in Mr. Podsnap's opinion. Beginning with a good inheritance, he had married a good inheritance, and had thriven exceedingly in the Marine Insurance way, and was quite satisfied. . . . Mr. Podsnap's world was not a very large world, morally; no, nor

even geographically: seeing that although his business was sustained upon commerce with other countries, he considered other countries, with that important reservation, a mistake, and of their manners and customs would conclusively observe, 'Not English!' " (11).

Phillips, Watts (1825–74) Irish playwright, novelist, and caricaturist. Phillips studied art with CRUIKSHANK, wrote some successful plays and some adaptations of Dickens's works for the stage, and wrote serial novels for popular magazines. His play about the French Revolution, *The Dead Heart* (produced in 1859 but written two or three years earlier), uses several plot ideas similar to *A Tale of Two Cities*, including the substitution of the hero for another on the guillotine. At the time critics accused Phillips of plagiarizing from Dickens, but Dickens may have read Phillips's play some time before he began his novel. Since the similarities between the two stories can be found in other works of the period treating the FRENCH REVOLUTION, it may be that neither Dickens nor Phillips was plagiarizing from the other but instead each was working with some of the same story conventions.

Philosewers Friend of the narrator who goes with him to inspect the social experiments of Friar Bacon. *Miscellaneous*, "Poor Man and his Beer."

"Phiz" Penname of Hablot K. BROWNE, Dickens's illustrator.

Phoebe (Phib) Fanny Squeers's maid, "a small servant girl with a hungry eye." *Nickleby* (12).

Phunky Assistant barrister and second to Serjeant Snubbin in Pickwick's defense. "Although an infant barrister, he was a full grown man" (31). *Pickwick*.

Physician One of the guests in Merdle's circle of important people, he serves as Merdle's personal physician, but he is unable to diagnose Merdle's complaint (I:21). He is called in to deal with Merdle's suicide (II:25). *Dorrit*.

Picaresque Novel Genre of realistic prose fiction recounting the adventures of a rogue hero, the picaro, an outsider to respectable society who lives by his wits. Although there are classical rogue stories like *The Satyricon*, the picaresque novel is usually said to begin in 16th-century Spain with *La Vida de Lazarillo de Tormes* (c.1554). Dickens was especially fond of the work of LE SAGE, a French picaresque novelist of the 18th century, and the English picaresque novels of the 18th century, especially SMOLLETT's *Roderick Random* and *Peregrine Pickle*. The episodic form of Dickens's early novels, which typically trace a series of loosely related adventures, use the journey as the basis of plot structure, and include resourceful lower-class characters such as Sam Weller, are derived from the picaresque tradition; however, Dickens's heroes are not down-and-out lumpen-proletarians, and there are few examples in Dickens's novels of the class war that prompts the European picaro's acts of trickery and revenge.

Piccadilly Known as Regent's Circus in the mid-19th century, Piccadilly Circus and the surrounding area was a fashionable residential district where Fascination Fledgby has lodgings at the ALBANY (*Mutual Friend*, III: 1,8) and the Lammles are married at ST. JAMES's church (*Mutual Friend*, I:10). Esther Summerson first arrives in London at the WHITE HORSE CELLAR in this district (*Bleak House*, 3). Piccadilly is also mentioned in *Nickleby* (64), *Rudge* (67), *Copperfield* (28), and "Somebody's Luggage."

Pickles Fishmonger who provides King Watkins the First with the salmon containing the magic fishbone. "Holiday Romance."

Pickleson ("Rinaldo di Velasco") Giant, performing under the name Rinaldo di Velasco, who tells Doctor Marigold of the deaf and dumb child Sophy and of the young man she eventually marries. "Marigold."

Pickwick Papers, The (Serial Title: *The Posthumous Papers of the Pickwick Club, containing a Faithful Record of the Perambulations, Perils, Travels, Adventures and Sporting Transactions of the Corresponding Members, edited by Boz.*) Dickens's first novel, published in 20 monthly numbers by CHAPMAN & HALL, April 1836 to November 1837 (omitting June 1836), illustrated by SEYMOUR (Parts 1 and 2); BUSS (Part 3), and BROWNE. Published in one volume, 1837. Dickens was commissioned by William HALL to write the letterpress for a series of sporting sketches by SEYMOUR, but after the artist's suicide, Dickens chose a new illustrator, took direction of the project, and gave the narrative more prominence. Gradually what began as essentially a series of comic sketches (see SKETCH) developed into a novel, and the novel, especially after the introduction of Sam Weller, became a runaway best-seller. By the end *Pickwick* had turned into a kind of comic BILDUNGSROMAN in which the innocent protagonist learns to compromise principle and affirm life. Although he experiences pain and suffering, Pickwick is not diminished or hardened by his trials.

SYNOPSIS

Part 1 (April 1836)
(1) At its meeting on May 12, 1827, the Pickwick Club forms a corresponding society to travel about the country and report its findings back to the group in London. The traveling group will be led by Samuel Pickwick, founder of the club and noteworthy for his theory of tittlebats. Three other gentlemen—Tracy Tupman, an admirer of the fair sex, Augustus Snodgrass, a poet, and Nathaniel Winkle, a sportsman—will accompany him. As Pickwick addresses the meeting, his speech is interrupted by Mr.

Alfred Crowquill's iconographic frontispiece for an 1852 edition of Pickwick Papers.

Blotton, who calls him a "Humbug." The dispute is resolved when Blotton agrees that he used the term only in its "Pickwickian sense." (2) As the Pickwickians set out on their travels the next day, Pickwick offends a cab driver by taking down notes of his conversation. He is rescued from the altercation by a stranger in a green coat who is also going to ROCHESTER. That evening, Tupman lends their traveling companion, Mr. Alfred Jingle, Mr. Winkle's Pickwick Club suit so the two of them can attend a dance. There Jingle offends Dr. Slammer of the local regiment; the next morning Slammer's second delivers a challenge to Mr. Winkle, believing that he was the offending young man. But at the duel Slammer does not recognize Winkle as his antagonist and the engagement is called off. (3) The next morning Jingle introduces to the Pickwickians a strolling actor who offers to tell them a story.

Part 2 (May 1836)
(3) The actor, Dismal Jemmy, tells "The STROLLER'S TALE," an account of a dying clown. When Dr. Slammer

and his friends arrive, they are taken aback to see Tupman and the stranger in the green coat, who was the offending party at the ball. When Jingle is identified as a strolling actor, however, Slammer declines to renew his challenge. (4) At a military exercise the next day, Pickwick gets caught between the opposing lines. He also meets the Wardles, who have come to view the proceedings. Mr. Wardle, a country squire, invites the Pickwickians to MANOR FARM. (5) On the way to the farm, they manage to frighten their horses and overturn their carriage, arriving late and tired after walking the last seven miles.

Part 3 (June 1836)
(6) The Pickwickians join the Wardles and their friends for cards and other games. Tupman pays his attentions to Rachael, the spinster sister of Mr. Wardle. The local clergyman recites his poem, "The IVY GREEN," and then he tells the story of "The CONVICT'S RETURN." (7) On a morning shooting expedition, Winkle wounds Tupman slightly, much to the consternation of Wardle's spinster sister. In the afternoon the Pickwickians attend the DINGLEY DELL versus Muggleton cricket match and the dinner that follows the game, where they again meet Mr. Jingle. (8) While his friends are at the cricket dinner, Tupman courts Rachael in the garden, where he is discovered by Joe, Wardle's sleepy servant boy. After the drunken group returns from the cricket celebration, Jingle charms the ladies with his stories. He learns that Tupman's courtship has been discovered and he advises Tupman to ignore Rachael and to be attentive instead to Emily, her neice. Meanwhile, Jingle pursues Rachael.

Part 4 (July 1836)
(9) When Rachael runs off with Jingle, Wardle and Pickwick give chase, but their carriage overturns just as it reaches the fleeing pair. Jingle sneers back at their misfortune. (10) In London, at the WHITE HART INN, Sam Weller is cleaning shoes when Wardle and Pickwick pay him to show them the room where Rachael and Jingle are staying. Wardle pays Jingle £120 to give up Rachael. As Jingle leaves he gives Pickwick the marriage license he has obtained, telling him it is "for Tuppy." Pickwick is outraged. (11) Back at Dingley Dell, Pickwick discovers that Tupman has left the farm and retreated in suicidal humiliation to the LEATHER BOTTLE in COBHAM. There they find him eating supper and looking well. They also find a stone with a strange inscription. Before going to bed, Pickwick reads "A MADMAN'S MANUSCRIPT," a document given to him by the clergyman at Dingley Dell. The next day the Pickwickians return to London to report to the Club on the inscribed rock that they have found.

Part 5 (August 1836)
(12) Pickwick surprises his landlady, the widow Bardell, with what she mistakes as a proposal of marriage. She throws herself into his arms just as the other Pickwickians arrive at his rooms. Pickwick has really been asking Mrs. Bardell about the advisibility of hiring a servant; that afternoon he engages Sam Weller, the bootblack from

the White Hart. (13) The Pickwickians go down to EATANSWILL to observe the election between the BLUES and the BUFFS. (14) Pickwick and Winkle stay at the home of Mr. Pott, the irascible editor of the *Eatanswill Gazette*. At the PEACOCK INN, where the rest of the Pickwickians stay, a traveling salesman tells them "The BAGMAN'S STORY."

Part 6 (September 1836)
(15) The Pickwickians are invited to Mrs. Leo Hunter's *fête champêtre*, a fancy dress affair where they will meet clever people and hear the hostess recite her "ODE TO AN EXPIRING FROG." When Jingle appears at the affair as Mr. Charles Fitz-Marshall, Pickwick is astonished and pursues him to the ANGEL in BURY ST. EDMUNDS. (16) There Sam learns from Jingle's servant, Job Trotter, that his master has a plan to elope that evening with one of the girls from Miss Tompkin's School. To foil the scheme, Pickwick hides in the school courtyard so that he can inform Miss Tompkins when the elopement is taking place. But he is discovered in the courtyard and no one at the school knows anything of Fitz-Marshall or his scheme. Sam and Wardle rescue Pickwick from this compromising situation. (17) Beset by rheumatism for three days after his escapade, Pickwick passes the time writing the story of "The PARISH CLERK," and reading it to Wardle.

Part 7 (October 1836)
(18) Winkle is surprised when Mr. Pott calls him a "serpent," and shows him an article in the rival newspaper implying that there is an affair between Pott's wife and Winkle. The misunderstanding is cleared up just as Pickwick is served notice that Mrs. Bardell has filed suit against him for breach of promise. (19) On a hunting expedition with Wardle, Winkle's reckless handling of the gun frightens Pickwick. After a picnic lunch, Pickwick, who has drunk too much cold punch, is left sleeping in a wheelbarrow. There he is discovered by Captain Boldwig, who takes him for a tresspasser and carts him off to the village pound. He is again rescued by Sam and Wardle. As they take him away he threatens to sue Boldwig. (20) Back in London Pickwick goes to Mrs. Bardell's attorneys, DODSON AND FOGG, and becomes so incensed that he accuses them of being scoundrels. His own attorney, Mr. Perker, is out of town, so Pickwick seeks out Perker's clerk, Mr. Lowten, at the MAGPIE AND STUMP tavern.

Part 8 (November 1836)
(21) An old man in the group of law clerks gathered at the Magpie and Stump tells "The TALE OF THE QUEER CLIENT." (22) In a coach driven by Sam's father, Tony Weller, Sam and Pickwick go to IPSWICH in search of Jingle. On the way Pickwick meets Peter Magnus, who is going to Ipswich to propose to a Miss Witherspoon, a lady he knows only through correspondence. At the inn, Pickwick and Peter Magnus eat dinner together. That night Pickwick loses his way in the inn and ends up in the wrong bedroom, where he surprises a middle-aged woman. (23) The next morning Sam runs into Job Trot-

ter, who tells him that Jingle has another nefarious plot. Sam plans to foil the scheme.

Part 9 (December 1836)
(24) When Peter Magnus meets Miss Witherspoon, he follows Pickwick's advice about the romantic strategy to follow; his suit is almost immediately successful. But when he introduces Pickwick to his prospective bride, she turns out to be the woman that Pickwick surprised the night before. Neither Pickwick nor Miss Witherspoon will reveal what happened and their reticence inflames the jealousy of Peter Magnus. Fearing that a duel will ensue, Miss Witherspoon files a complaint against Pickwick and Tupman with the local magistrate, Mr. Nupkins. They are arrested and taken through the streets. When Sam tries to rescue Pickwick, he is apprehended as well. (25) Sam has figured out that Jingle's plot involves the magistrate's daughter, and when Pickwick reveals the scheme to Nupkins, the magistrate dismisses the case against them. Together they expose Jingle's villainy. (26) Back in London, Pickwick sends Sam to Mrs. Bardell's to pay the rent, give notice of his intention to leave his rooms, and find out her feelings about the suit. Sam learns that she intends to go forward with the suit.

Part 10 (January 1837)
(27) Sam goes down to the MARQUIS OF GRANBY in DORKING to visit his father and stepmother. There he also finds Mr. Stiggins, Mrs. Weller's spiritual guide, who spends his time at the pub drinking and borrowing money from Tony. Sam advises his father to get rid of Stiggins, but Tony rejects his son's advice, telling Sam that he doesn't understand the intricacies of marriage. (28) The Pickwickians go down to Dingley Dell for Christmas, bringing with them a large cod fish and several barrels of oysters. There they celebrate the wedding of Wardle's daughter Isabella to Mr. Trundle and join in the Christmas festivities, playing games, drinking wassail, and kissing under the mistletoe. (29) At the end of Christmas Eve, Wardle tells the story of "The GOBLINS WHO STOLE A SEXTON."

Part 11 (February 1836)
(30) Christmas Day is cold and there are plans for skating. Two new guests, both medical students, arrive: Benjamin Allen, brother of Arabella who has caught the eye of Mr. Winkle, and Bob Sawyer. At breakfast they talk about the details of surgery. Later Bob Sawyer proves to be an accomplished figure skater, but Winkle is thoroughly incompetent and Pickwick calls him a "humbug." Pickwick does some sliding on the ice, falls through and is thoroughly soaked. When the Christmas party breaks up, Bob Sawyer invites Pickwick to a bachelor party at his rooms in London. (31) Back in town Winkle, Snodgrass, Tupman, and Sam are served supoenas by Dodson and Fogg to be witnesses for Mrs. Bardell. Pickwick is incensed at the unscrupulous lawyers, and he tells Perker that he will pay no money to go to Dodson and Fogg, no matter what the outcome of the trial, which is scheduled for February 14. Perker assures him that the best defense is planned and that Serjeant Snubbin will rep-

resent him in court. Pickwick tells Snubbin that he wants him as a lawyer only if he believes him innocent. (32) The Pickwickians attend Bob Sawyer's party in LANT STREET. By the end, their drunken songs are awakening the neighborhood in the wee hours of the morning and Sawyer's landlady, Mrs. Raddle, who is angry with her tenant for not paying his rent, throws all the revelers out into the street.

Part 12 (March 1837)
(33) Sam composes a valentine for Mary, the Nupkins' maid, and he signs it with Pickwick's name. Tony gets Sam to go with him to the Branch of the United Grand Junction Ebenezer Temperance Association, where they expose the drunken Stiggins as a hypocrite. (34) On St. Valentine's Day the trial of *Bardell v. Pickwick* takes place. The Pickwickians who came upon Mrs. Bardell in the arms of Pickwick prove to be damaging witnesses, for they are easily confused by the sharp lawyers. Sam tries to save the day for Pickwick with his smart and evasive answers, but the jury finds for Mrs. Bardell and awards her £750 damages. Pickwick vows never to pay the fine.

Part 13 (April 1837)
(35) Pickwick decides to go off to BATH. On the way he meets Mr. Dowler, who introduces him to Angelo Cyrus Bantam, M.C., the dandified Master of Ceremonies in the Assembly Rooms at Bath. (36) The Pickwickians and the Dowlers take a house together on the Royal Crescent. In a drawer in his room Mr. Pickwick finds a manuscript telling "The TRUE LEGEND OF PRINCE BLADUD." After everyone has gone to bed except Mrs. Dowler, Winkle is awakened by Mrs. Dowler's cabmen, who are bringing her home at three in the morning from a party. Winkle answers the door, but the wind blows it shut and he is left outside in his nightshirt with Mrs. Dowler. When the others in the house are finally awakened, Dowler accuses Winkle of running away with his wife and he chases him around the Crescent in the middle of the night. (37) Sam is invited to a "swarry" of Bath footmen. The splendor of their uniforms is matched only by their snobbery and condescension. Sam deflates the gathering with his racy language and apt epithets. The next morning Pickwick tells Sam that Winkle has disappeared and he asks Sam to find him.

Part 14 (May 1837)
(38) Winkle has gone to the BUSH INN at BRISTOL. While walking about the town he runs into Bob Sawyer, who has set up as an apothecary there. They spend the day drinking with Benjamin Allen and Winkle learns that Ben's sister Arabella is also in Bristol. When he returns to the Bush, Dowler is there, asking forgiveness and wishing to be reconciled. Sam also arrives and insists on taking Winkle back to Bath, but Winkle convinces Sam to stay with him in Bristol while they seek out Arabella Allen. (39) When Pickwick learns of Winkle's whereabouts, he joins the search for Arabella. Sam runs into Mary, the Nupkins' maid, who has taken a new place in Bristol, and learns from her that Arabella is kept

in seclusion in a neighboring house. Sam climbs a pear tree into Arabella's garden when she is on her evening walk and arranges an interview for Winkle the next evening. Winkle, Pickwick, and Sam all go on the expedition. Winkle is successful in speaking with Arabella, but the three must make a run for it when they are taken for robbers in the darkness. (40) After they return to London, Pickwick is arrested by a sheriff's officer. Perker advises him to pay the fine, but Pickwick is adamantly opposed to paying money that will enrich Dodson and Fogg and he chooses instead to enter the FLEET PRISON.

Part 15 (July 1837)
(41) At the Fleet, Pickwick is horrified by the dungeons where some of the prisoners are housed. He rents a bed from the warden for his first night and is awakened by three drunken prisoners—Mivens, Smangle, and an unnamed third man—who convince him to buy drink and cigars. (42) The next morning Pickwick is assigned a close, dirty room with a drunken clergyman and a butcher. When he discovers that he can pay to get a room of his own, he arranges to do so. He pays a pound a week to the prisoner whose room it is, and to hire furniture for the room he pays 27 shillings a week to the jailer, Mr. Roker. When he visits the poor side of the Fleet, the part of the prison for those who cannot afford to pay for their accommodations, Pickwick finds Jingle and Job Trotter among the prisoners. Shedding a tear, Pickwick gives Job some money. Then he returns to his quarters and dismisses Sam for the duration of his confinement. (43) Sam gets his father to issue an order to have him arrested for debt, and he arrives at the prison accompanied by an entourage of coachmen. As a matter of principle, Sam refuses Pickwick's help in satisfying his creditor. He says he does not want to enrich an evil man.

Part 16 (August 1837)
(44) The Pickwickians visit the prison. Winkle says that he must go away for a while and that he had hoped to take Sam with him, but now that Sam is a prisoner, he cannot do so. (45) Tony Weller, Susan, and Stiggins visit Sam. Stiggins gets sustenance from the prison bar and then sermonizes Sam. Pickwick takes Sam to see Jingle and Job Trotter and Sam learns that his master, an "angel in tights and gaiters," has provided them with a room and with food and clothing. The misery in the prison so depresses Pickwick that he decides to confine himself to his rooms. He stays there for three months. (46) On a day late in July, Mrs. Bardell and several of her friends make an excursion to the SPANIARDS in HAMPSTEAD for tea. While they are there, Mr. Jackson, of Dodson and Fogg's, appears and takes Mrs. Bardell off for an appointment, which turns out to be at the Fleet, where she is also imprisoned for the costs of the trial. Pickwick and Sam see her enter. Pickwick turns away without speaking; Sam sends for Perker.

Part 17 (September 1837)
(47) The next morning at 10 o'clock, Perker arrives at the Fleet. He tells Pickwick that he is the only person who can release Mrs. Bardell from prison. He counters Pickwick's angry resistance by suggesting that Pickwick will be recognized as the one who showed up the sharp practices of Dodson and Fogg. Then he produces a letter from Mrs. Bardell that absolves Pickwick and puts the blame for the action on the lawyers. When Winkle and his new bride, Arabella Allen, arrive, they ask Pickwick to reconcile Benjamin Allen and Mr. Winkle senior to their marriage. At last Pickwick is persuaded to pay the costs and leave the Fleet. As he goes he takes steps to release Jingle and Job Trotter. (48) Bob Sawyer and Ben Allen are discussing the possibility of Bob marrying Arabella as a way to get out of financial difficulties, when they learn of Arabella's marriage. Allen is incensed. It takes a lot of convincing from Pickwick, and a little liquor, to reconcile Ben and Bob Sawyer to the union. In the end, Allen agrees to go with Pickwick to inform Winkle's father of the marriage. (49) Back at his inn, Pickwick meets the one-eyed bagman again and hears "The STORY OF THE BAGMAN'S UNCLE."

Part 18 (October 1837)
(50) The next morning, Pickwick, Sam, Ben Allen and Bob Sawyer head for BIRMINGHAM on a journey marked by frequent stops to eat and drink. When they tell Mr. Winkle of the marriage, he receives the news stolidly, showing no emotion. They leave angry and disappointed. (51) On their return to London, rain forces them to stop for the night at the SARACEN'S HEAD in TOWCESTER. There they find Pott, editor of the *Eatanswill Gazette*, and Slurk, the rival editor of the *Eatanswill Independent*. The two editors engage in a brawl, which is broken up by Sam. (52) In London, Sam learns that Tony's wife has died, and he goes to console his father. Tony tells him that Susan had recognized before she died how her religion had interfered with her life and her relationship with Tony. He also tells Sam how he has been beset since Susan's death with widows seeking his attentions. Stiggins enquires about what Susan has left him, and he refuses to believe that he has been excluded from her will. Tony picks him up, carries him outside, and tosses him into a horse trough.

Parts 19–20 (November 1837)
(53) Early the next morning, Pickwick goes to Perker's office. There he accepts the gratitude of Jingle and Job Trotter as they set off for the West Indies. Then Dodson and Fogg come to be paid off. Although they are civil to him, Pickwick's anger mounts and he follows them as they leave, yelling "Robbers" after them several times. He returns to Perker's office with a great weight removed from his mind. (54) When Wardle learns that Snodgrass and his daughter Emily are in love, he is at first upset and irritable, but then he accepts the match. (55) Sam goes with Tony Weller to attorney Solomon Pell to execute Susan Weller's will. She has left £200 to Sam and the rest of her estate to Tony. After Pell proves the will, stockbroker Wilkins Flasher liquidates Tony's funds. When Tony puts together all of his money at the end of the day, he has £1,180. (56) He takes the money to Pickwick and asks him to take charge of it for him. At first Pickwick refuses, but then he calls Tony back, tells

him of Sam's affection for Mary, and agrees to do some good with Tony's money. He offers to set up Sam and Mary in business, but Sam is committed to serving Pickwick. Meanwhile, Mr. Winkle goes anonymously to see his new daughter-in-law. He is thouroughly pleased with her and is reconciled with his son. (57) Pickwick gives up traveling, disbands the Pickwick Club, and settles down in a house in DULWICH. There the wedding of Emily and Snodgrass is held and there he gathers together his many friends and colleagues. Sam and Mary marry, have children, and serve in Pickwick's house; the Winkles live nearby. Pickwick is known and respected by all in the neighborhood.

COMMENTARY

The Posthumous Papers of the Pickwick Club, or *The Pickwick Papers,* the shortened title by which it is usually known, is Dickens's first novel, published in serial form in 1836–37. In it one can trace the transition in Dickens's work from the journalistic sketches with which he began his writing career to the more sustained narrative that made him the great comic novelist of the century. *Pickwick* also contains some indications of Dickens's darker vision and of the concern with social issues that would stamp his work as characteristically Victorian.

The novel began as a project of artist Robert Seymour and young publisher William Hall to produce a series of sporting prints depicting the exploits of the Nimrod Club and to be accompanied by some prose narrative commentary. After Hall failed to interest several other authors in the project, he approached Dickens, a 24-year-old writer whose newspaper sketches, soon to be collected and published as *Sketches by Boz,* had brought him some favorable notice. Although Dickens was unfamiliar with the sporting themes in the original idea, he was quick to see opportunity in the proposal and he suggested that the subject matter not be limited to sporting scenes. The contract was agreed to in early March—Dickens was to receive about £14 for each 12,000-word monthly number—and Dickens submitted the first installment to Hall three weeks later.

Mr. Winkle is the character most clearly a product of the sporting design conceived by Seymour. He is a literary relative to the popular figures in the SPORTING NOVELS of R. W. SURTEES and Pierce Egan. But Pickwick and the wonderful, fast-talking villain of the early numbers, Mr. Jingle, carry a Dickensian stamp from the beginning. Seymour had to modify his originally lean idea of the hero when Dickens decided, in the first number, to make his hero a fat, older man. For the second number, Seymour had difficulty with the illustration of the dying clown, a subject far afield from the sporting scenes he was accustomed to drawing. The tension between illustrator and author may have contributed to Seymour's distress. In any case, on April 20, he shot himself, after completing the illustrations for the second number.

Dickens, who had married in April on the strength of the contract for *Pickwick,* was concerned that the project not be abandoned. He took an active role in redesigning the format and hiring a new illustrator. The number of illustrations for each monthly part was reduced from four to two and the number of pages of text was increased from 24 to 32. After working for a month with interim illustrator, R. W. Buss, in May Dickens interviewed applicants for an illustrator to replace Seymour. He chose a man younger even than himself, 20-year-old Hablot K. Browne. The artist who would become Dickens's most consistent collaborator, using "Phiz" as his artistic name to match Dickens' "Boz." Among the applicants for the position whom Dickens did not choose was William THACKERAY, who had recently returned to London from art school in Paris.

The new plan gave more prominence to the writer and less to the illustrator. By reducing the number of pictures and increasing the number of words, Dickens was able to include fewer episodes in each number and to develop them more fully. This change in format was important in enabling him to grow from a writer of brief sketches into a novelist following a continuing plot. By the fourth number a more unified story began to take shape with the introduction of Sam Weller and the beginning of the Bardell versus Pickwick story, the most sustained plotline in the book.

The episodic character of *Pickwick Papers* was influenced by other factors than its mode of publication. Dickens's models for the story were the novels of the PICARESQUE tradition, works like LE SAGE's Gil Blas and especially such 18th-century English novels as DEFOE's *Robinson Crusoe,* FIELDING's *Tom Jones* and *Joseph Andrews,* and SMOLLETT's *Roderick Random* and *Peregrine Pickle,* works he had pored over as a child. These episodic picaresque novels were filled with practical jokes, slapstick situations, and physical comedy, scenes which provided prototypes for many of the comic episodes in *Pickwick.* CERVANTES's *Don Quixote* and GOLDSMITH's *The Vicar of Wakefield* were also key influences, contributing to the idealism and the sentiment in Dickens's novel. Dickens was especially indebted to Goldsmith's novel for the prison scenes in *Pickwick.*

As Dickens gained assurance with his story, he also gained readers. Only 1,000 of the first number were printed, but sales began to pick up with the appearance of Sam Weller in the fourth number and after a year 20,000 copies of each part were being produced. By the end of its run in November 1837, nearly 40,000 copies of each part were being sold, a phenomenal number for a Victorian novel. Its success was more than literary. Pickwick was a cultural event and it became an industry. Robert PATTEN (1978) describes the frenzy: "There were Pickwick hats, canes, cigars, fabrics, coats, song books, china figurines, Weller corduroys and jest books, and Boz cabs. There were imitations, plagiarisms, parodies, sequels, extra illustrations, Pickwick quadrilles, stage piracies, and adaptations." Mrs. GASKELL gently satirized this literary mayhem in *Cranford* (1853) with a newspaper report that describes a man being run over by a train because he is so engrossed in the current installment of the novel.

From the beginning, as Philip COLLINS (1971) has commented, Pickwick was a "cult novel," having an appeal similar to the Sherlock Holmes stories. The ATHENAEUM described Dickens's recipe during the novel's initial run as "two pounds of Smollett, three ounces of Sterne, a handful of Hook, a dash of grammatical Pierce Egan—incidents at pleasure, served with an original sauce piquante." The sauce is what has sustained *Pickwick*'s special appeal, that quality that makes the world of the novel unique and that introduces in the very first number a new word into the language, the adjective "Pickwickian." Readers who get caught up in the Pickwickian worldview may become members of the cult or the Club, but not everyone is smitten. In her inauguration speech as president of the Dickens Fellowship, Margaret Lane admitted that *Pickwick* was the one Dickens novel she did not enjoy and could not finish. There may be some evidence to suggest that the Pickwick Club and the novel's celebration of male bonding has more appeal to men than to women, though the Pickwick Club formed by Louisa May Alcott's little women would seem to be evidence to the contrary.

If *Pickwick* initiated the Victorian novel by introducing serial publication as an appropriate mode for other novelists, it also articulated a Victorian consciousness. Appropriately, the novel was being published as Victoria took the throne. While it drew on 18th-century models, it transformed them, turning the crude bawdy humor of the picaresque into playful innocence. Mary Russell Mitford, recommending the novel to a friend, specifically pointed to the "Victorian" sensibility in the book:

> So you never heard of the 'Pickwick Papers'! . . . It is fun—London life—but without anything unpleasant: a lady might read it all *aloud*; and it is so graphic, so individual, and so true, that you could courtesy [sic] to all the people as you met them in the streets. I do not think there had been a place where English was spoken to which 'Boz' had not penetrated. . . . It seems like not having heard of Hogarth, whom he resembles greatly, except that he takes a far more cheerful view, a Shakespearean view, of humanity. It is rather fragmentary, except the trial (No. 11 or 12), which is as complete and perfect as any bit of comic writing in the English language. You must read the 'Pickwick Papers.'

Mitford's observation that the novel is fragmentary highlights a frequent criticism of the book. Many readers think that Dickens's object for the novel, stated in the Preface as "to place before the reader a constant succession of characters and incidents," is achieved at the expense of unity. The incoherence may be most evident in the INTERPOLATED TALES, stories that Dickens inserted into the novel, particularly in the first half. Their presence suggests that Dickens may have met his monthly deadlines by including material that he had written previously and not published.

This view has been effectively challenged. Several critics, most notably PATTEN (1967), have pointed out how the dark and gloomy subject matter of the interpolated tales contrasts with the light and sunny story of "the immortal Pickwick," who rises with "the first ray of light" and converts "obscurity" into "a dazzling brilliancy." The contrast between light and darkness that runs through the novel becomes central to the main line of the action in the last third of the book during the prison scenes. In the second half of the novel, the interpolated tales nearly disappear as a more coherent worldview, melding light and dark, emerges in the main action.

The Bardell versus Pickwick story has long been recognized as the main element of plot in what often seems a meandering story, but Sylvère MONOD (1968) has identified three subplots that also contribute to what Dickens described as "one tolerably harmonious whole": 1. the relationship between old Wardle and Pickwick; 2. the pursuit of Jingle; 3. the "Weller saga." Monod goes on to point out a number of episodes that have no relation to any of these plots, suggesting that the whole may not be quite as coherent as some ingenious commentators have suggested. Dickens, in the 1847 preface, seems to want it both ways: "I could perhaps wish now that these chapters were strung together on a stronger thread of general interest, still, what they are they were designed to be."

If *Pickwick* began as a novel designed by committee, this collaborative inspiration seems to be reflected in the collective hero of the opening numbers, the members of the peripatetic Pickwick Club. Each of the four corresponding members begins the novel as a humours character, a person defined by a single dominating obsession: Winkle is the sportsman, Snodgrass the poet, Tupman the lover, and Pickwick the scientific investigator. They are equally inept at their professions and the opening sketches suggest that the story will progress by mocking their pretensions. Winkle proves to know nothing about hunting. Snodgrass never writes a poem; Tupman loses Rachael Wardel to Jingle; and Pickwick—even with his spectacles on—is stumped by Bill Stump's stone.

Although he is satirized for his scientific pretensions, Pickwick, from the moment he first appears, differs from the other members of the club. If Winkle, Snodgrass, and Tupman are defined as latter-day representatives of the humours tradition, Pickwick redefines that tradition and begins a new one. His age makes him anomalous as a candidate for education in a collective Bildungsroman. He is, as the opening paragraph suggests, the sun itself, and his foolish quarrel with Blotton makes him a Humbug only in a Pickwickian sense. By the end of the opening chapter, Dickens has already defined a unique Pickwickian world where the rules of the Smollettian picaresque and the comedy of the sporting novels no longer apply.

Pickwick is paradoxical. As an older man, a scientific observer, a former man of business, and the mentor to a group of young men seeking to establish themselves in the world, he is expected to represent wisdom and experience, but he is as innocent as a child and his innate goodness makes him incapable of imagining the world in anything other than the most benevolent and optimistic terms. His inflated language, often grounded in a parody of the public utterances of politicians and academics, indicates how he transforms reality. Jingle can outwit him because he is incapable of seeing or imagining Jingle's villainy. The interpolated tales that he hears, which describe a world darkened by pain and suffering, are just tales, separate from the real experience of his life.

The protean Jingle, who cons his victims by impersonating their wishes, appears to Pickwick as a seasoned traveler, a man of the world whose knowledge of people and places enables him to speak with authority on any topic. Jingle's telegraphic manner of speaking, so opposite from Pickwick's prolix and airy generalizing, reduces experience to a series of discrete sensory data and his language to a series of nouns and verbs. He appears to model the empiricism that Pickwick has pretensions to, to be the voice of experience. But, as Pickwick painfully discovers, Jingle lacks benevolence and has no notion of serving others. When Pickwick is confronted with Jingle's selfishness, in the scene where Wardle rescues Rachael and buys off her "abductor," Pickwick is enlightened into anger; in a blind rage he stumbles into the arms of Sam Weller, the Cockney boots of the White Hart Inn who will replace Jingle as the representative of experience in the novel.

A product of the London streets and the son of a coach driver, Sam combines the knowledge of the traveler with that of the city boy. He is every bit as clever as Jingle, but his wit emerges in exemplary tales—like the story of the man who survived on crumpets—and in "Wellerisms," apt analogies from his experience that relate to the situations in which he finds himself. When he is urging the Ipswich magistrate to restrain his deputies and enjoy the company of the Pickwickians, for example, Sam comes up with the following analogy: "Business first, pleasure arterwards, as King Richard the Third said wen he stabbed t'other King in the Tower, afore he smothered the babbies" (25). His stories are more coherent than Jingle's and they point to a moral. He uses his wit to serve others, not just himself. Appropriately, he becomes Pickwick's servant. In the course of the story, as his name indicates, he becomes Pickwick's alter ego, playing experience to Pickwick's innocence. His entrance into the story changes the novel. The Pickwick Club is replaced as the central focus shifts to Samuel Pickwick and Samuel Weller, the idealistic Victorian Quixote and his cockney Sancho Panza.

With the introduction of Sam Weller, *Pickwick* found its center. Dickens may have begun the novel thinking of the project as a series of magazine sketches similar to those collected in *Sketches by Boz*. The sketches became a connected story when the chemistry between Samuel Pickwick and Sam Weller focused the action. Dickens's original audience responded to this change, for with the fourth number in which Sam first appears, sales of the novel markedly increased, the beginning of the mania that would make *Pickwick* a runaway best-seller.

The fifth number opens with the scene between Pickwick and Mrs. Bardell that begins the central action of the novel, the Bardell versus Pickwick trial. It clearly draws the differences between master and man. Pickwick is incapable of realizing how his evasive language misleads Mrs. Bardell. Although he is soliciting her opinion on the wisdom of keeping a servant, he puts the question abstractly: "Do you think it a much greater expense to keep two people, than to keep one?"(12) Mrs. Bardell misconstrues his meaning and faints into his arms. Sam Weller will not be similarly misled. When Pickwick asks him whether he has "any reason to be discontented with your present situation," Sam insists on knowing "whether you're goin' to purwide me with a better," and he goes on to negotiate the terms of his employment and his wages at £12 a year with two suits of clothes. There is no room for misunderstanding in Sam's dealings with Pickwick.

Pickwick comes to rely on Sam to extricate him from awkward situations, Sam to admire and love Pickwick. The story of their relationship becomes the story of the novel, but even Sam's confusing testimony at the trial cannot save Pickwick from himself. Appearances and the lawyers are against his master. While Pickwick chooses to go to jail as a matter of principle, Sam has himself imprisoned as a matter of love. In the Fleet, Pickwick must deal with darkness and suffering in fact—not just as part of an interpolated story. When Mrs. Bardell is also locked up because of his principles, Pickwick realizes that benevolence is more important to him than principle. He pays the fine, extricating all of the imprisoned Pickwickians, and he settles in Dulwich, a benign spirit presiding over a little community. Darkness and suffering are real in *Pickwick*, but they can be banished in the end to restore the Eden of Pickwick's imagination. The pattern of *Pickwick* will be repeated in several of the later novels, but never again will paradise be so completely regained.

CRITICISM

Pickwick established the serial as a standard mode of publication for later Victorian novels and its 20 parts (18 plus a final double number) was the format most often adopted. The story of how Dickens came to work in the serial form and how it developed as the novel went along is told by BUTT and TILLOTSON (1957) and Patten (1978). Patten's introduction to the Penguin edition of the novel (1972) adds critical commentary to his account of the novel's composition.

In a classic essay on *Pickwick*, W. H. Auden ("Dingley Dell and the Fleet" in *The Dyer's Hand*, 1962) describes the novel as an archetypal fable about the fall of man. When the innocent Pickwick discovers the presence of evil and suffering in the world during his time in the Fleet Prison, he loses his innocence. When Mrs. Bardell is imprisoned, he must give up his principles, sacrifice his honor, and collude with the evil system to end her suffering and his own imprisonment.

Barbara HARDY (*The Moral Art of Dickens*, 1970) challenges critics like Auden who find a mythic unity in the book. Describing it as a work of parts—some of them tedious and disconnected from the whole—she finds the power of the novel in its comedy and especially in the Pickwickian innocence that comes to terms with the harsh realities of Victorian England by denying and transforming them.

Steven MARCUS (1965) characterizes the novel's unique power as "transcendence . . . a representation of life which fulfills that vision, which men have never yet relinquished, of the ideal possibilities of human relations in community, and which, in the fulfillment extends our awareness of the limits of our humanity." This ideal is most fully realized, Marcus contends, in the bonds between Pickwick, Sam, and Tony Weller. James R. KINCAID (1971) describes Pickwick's transcendence as a result of his education at the hands of Sam Weller who introduces him to pain and poverty and teaches him the limitations of principle and the virtues of flexibility and realism.

Garrett STEWART (1974) devotes a third of his book to an analysis of parody and style in *Pickwick* as it sets a paradigm for the liberating power of imagination that Dickens explores in many of his novels.

ADAPTATIONS

Three stage adaptations appeared in London while the novel was still appearing in parts, one by STIRLING, one by William Leman Rede, and one by MONCRIEFF. All of them included much that was not in the novel, but only the last achieved some success in the theater, perhaps because it featured Sam Weller, played by W. J. HAMMOND. When Dickens protested against the play, Moncrieff defended his plagiarism by attacking the novel with praise: "to meddle with so extraordinary a writer, therefore, is as dangerous as it is enticing; the desultory nature of the adventures in which he has revelled, & the absence of that continuity of plot so essential in a dramatic piece, has also been the subject of much embarassment and has led the adaptor to draw on his own resources very frequently, when he would more gladly have availed himself of the superior material of his master."

The Pickwick mania prompted a great many sequels and other derivative works based on Dickens's novel. Philip COLLINS, in the *Cambridge Bibliography of English Literature* (1969), provides a substantial list of these stepchildren. Many of them are described in William Miller's "Imitations of Pickwick" (*DICKENSIAN*, 1936).

Pickwick has also been very popular as a source for dramatic material; its episodic nature has prompted many short pieces. Among later plays of note John Hollingshead's *Bardell v. Pickwick* (1871) claimed to be based on Dickens's popular PUBLIC READING. It starred

J. L. TOOLE as Buzfuz and Miss E. Farren as Sam Weller. Cosmo Hamilton's and Frank C. Reilley's *Pickwick* (1927–8) played in Washington D.C., New York, and London with Charles LAUGHTON in the title role. Wolf Mankowitz's musical *Pickwick*, with music by Cyril Ornadel and lyrics by Leslie BRICUSSE, opened in London in 1963.

Of the six silent films based on *Pickwick*, Thomas BENTLEY's 1921 adaptation was the most ambitious. It featured Frederick Volpe as Pickwick, a role he had played many times on stage, and Bransby WILLIAMS as Sergeant Buzfuz. The only sound film based on the novel is Noel LANGLEY's 1952 version, starring James Hayter (Pickwick), Nigel Patrick (Jingle), and Harry Fowler (Sam Weller).

On television *Pickwick* has appeared in numerous versions. Michael Pointer (*Charles Dickens on the Screen*, 1996) lists 15 different adaptations based on the novel. The earliest, a 25-minute excerpt from Anthony Coates's opera, *Mr. Pickwick*, was telecast in 1936. *Pickwick* was also the first of Dickens's novels serialized on the BBC, in seven parts in 1952. The BBC also produced a 12-part serial in 1985 starring Nigel Stock in the title role.

Pickwick, Moses   Operator of the coaches running between London and BATH and proprietor of several hotels in Bath, notably the WHITE HART where the Pickwickians stay *Pickwick* (35). Dickens took the name for his hero from Moses Pickwick.

Pickwick, Samuel   The retired businessman and confirmed bachelor who is the founder and chairman of the Pickwick Club. With his "bald head and circular spectacles" and dressed in old fashioned "tights and gaiters," the rotund Pickwick leads a group of young men, Winkle, Snodgrass, and Tupman, on a series of journeys around England to observe the world and report back to the club about their excursions. After a series of misadventures, in which Pickwick's innocence and naiveté make him the butt of the humor and the dupe of the schemes of Jingle, Pickwick takes a manservant, Sam Weller, who is as savvy about the world as Pickwick is innocent (12). Sam usually manages to rescue his master from the difficulties he finds himself in, but even Sam's clever testimony is unable to save Pickwick in the case of Bardell versus Pickwick (34). Outraged by the unscrupulousness of the lawyers, Pickwick refuses to pay the costs in the case as the court has ordered. So he is sent to FLEET PRISON, where this sunny and benevolent man confronts the darker side of humanity (40). When Mrs. Bardell is also imprisoned in the Fleet, Pickwick's good-heartedness overcomes his principles and he pays the money that releases Mrs. Bardell and himself from the prison (47). At the same time he arranges the release of Jingle and Job Trotter. Once out of prison, he settles down in DULWICH with Sam Weller and his bride as his servants (57). *Pickwick*.

Dickens said that the germinating idea for the novel was the character of Pickwick: "I thought of Mr. Pick-

Thomas Nast's Pickwick, for the American Household Edition (1873).

wick," he wrote in the 1847 preface to the novel, "and wrote the first number." The name was drawn from the proprietor of a Bath coach, Moses PICKWICK, mentioned in chapter 35 as the Pickwickians go to Bath. Pickwick has often been described as a character who changes in the course of the novel, losing his innocence due to his experiences, especially his time in prison. He is not embittered by what happens to him; rather he is changed from a comic butt to a benevolent angel in tights and gaiters. But Dickens suggested that the change was not so much in Pickwick as in the reader: "I do not think this change will appear forced or unnatural to my readers," he wrote, "if they will reflect that in real life the peculiarities and oddities of a man who has anything whimsical about him, generally impress us first, and that it is not until we are better acquainted with him that we usually begin to look below these superficial traits, and to know the better part of him."

Pickwickian This adjective for an uncomplimentary word that has lost its derogatory connotations comes from the episode in chapter 1 of Pickwick, where Mr.

Blotton calls *Pickwick* a "humbug" and then explains that the word was not to be taken as derogatory because he had not used it "in a common sense," but rather "in its Pickwickian sense."

Pic-Nic Papers, The Miscellany of poems, short stories, sketches, etc. by various writers, edited and introduced by Dickens for the benefit of the widow and children of John MACRONE, Dickens's first publisher. Dickens contributed the story "The Lamplighter." The three-volume work was published by COBURN in 1841.

Pictures from Italy Dickens's travel book based on the letters he wrote to John FORSTER during the year he spent with his family in GENOA from July 1844 to July 1845. The book describes their travels through FRANCE to get to ITALY and those through northern Italy. Dickens was particularly taken with VENICE, NAPLES, POMPEII—including an ascent of Vesuvius—and ROME. He comments on the places and people he sees, on the art, and on the Roman CATHOLIC CHURCH, vigorously expressing his belief that the poverty and oppression in Italy was largely due to the influence of the church. The letters were originally published in the *DAILY NEWS* between January 21 and March 11, 1846, and, in revised form, as a single volume by BRADBURY & EVANS in May 1846, with illustrations by PALMER. PAROISSIEN (1973) has edited and annotated a recent edition of *Pictures*.

Pidger Miss Clarissa Spenlow asserts that her sister's past relationship with this supposed suitor makes Miss Lavinia "an authority in affairs of the heart." *Copperfield*, (41).

Pierce, Captain Of the East Indiaman *Halsewell* who perishes with his **two daughters**, one of them named **Mary**, and many others when the ship is wrecked in a storm at sea near Seacombe on the Isle of Purbeck. *Reprinted*, "Long Voyage."

Piff, Miss One of the attendants in the Mugby Junction refreshment room. "Mugby."

Pig and Tinderbox Inn Inn where Professors Snore, Doze, and Wheezy are expected to stay during the meeting of the Mudfog Association. *Mudfog*.

Pigeon, Thomas Alias of TALLY HO THOMPSON, a horse thief in Sergeant Witchem's story *Reprinted*, "Detective Police."

Pilkins Dombey family physician who calls in Dr. Parker Peps for consultation. *Dombey* (1:8).

Pinch, Tom and Ruth Brother and sister whose simplicity, honesty, and altruism distinguish them from the greed and self-interest that dominates most of the characters in *Chuzzlewit*. **Tom**, Pecksniff's former pupil and general assistant, and the organist at the parish church, is "an ungainly, awkward-looking man, extremely short-sighted, and prematurely bald, . . . he might have been almost any age between sixteen and sixty" (2). Gentle and unselfish, he is a loyal friend to young Martin, who treats him condescendingly, and a devoted admirer of Pecksniff, blind to all his master's faults. When Tom discovers Pecksniff's scheme to seduce Mary Graham, with whom Tom is secretly in love, Pecksniff dismisses him (31). Tom goes to London and there rescues his sister **Ruth**, as gentle and trusting as her brother, from a demeaning position as a governess (36). The two set up housekeeping together, supported by Tom's employment as a librarian, a job provided anonymously by old Martin Chuzzlewit (39). Tom introduces Ruth to his friend and former fellow pupil John Westlock and they eventually marry (53). Tom lives with them and remains devoted to his friends—Ruth and John, young Martin and Mary Graham and their children—and to playing the organ (54). *Chuzzlewit*.

Pip (1)   Theatrical man invited to Tigg Montague's dinner for Jonas Chuzzlewit. *Chuzzlewit* (28).

Pip (2)   Name by which Philip PIRRIP, J., is generally known. His "infant tongue" could make of his given name "nothing longer or more explicit than Pip" (1). His benefactor later makes keeping the name a condition for receiving his great expectations (18). *Expectations*.

Pipchin, Mrs. (1)   Ogress and child-queller who operates a children's boarding house in BRIGHTON where Paul and Florence Dombey are sent to stay; "a marvellous ill-favoured, ill-conditioned old lady, of a stooping figure, with a mottled face, like bad marble, a hook nose, and a hard grey eye, that looked as if it might have been hammered at on an anvil without sustaining injury. . . . the secret of her management was, to give them everything they didn't like, and nothing that they did" (8). Forty years a widow of a man who had broken his heart pumping water out of Peruvian mines, she fails to intimidate young Paul, who surprises her with his direct and innocent questions (9). Mr. Dombey hires her as his housekeeper after his marriage to Edith (42). *Dombey*. Mrs. Pipchin is based on Mrs. ROYLANCE, Dickens's landlady in London when his father was in the MARSHALSEA PRISON.

Pipchin, Mrs. (2)   "An unsympathetic old personage of the female gender, flavoured with musty dry lavender, dressed in black crepe," who accompanies the narrator as a child to a toy market and buys a Harlequin's wand for him. Although Dickens does not explicitly connect this Mrs. Pipchin with the character in *Dombey*, the two women have similar roles and characteristics. *Miscellaneous*, "New Year's Day."

Piper, Mrs. Anastasia   Mrs. Perkins's friend and Krook's neighbor, who testifies at the inquest into Nemo's death: "a good deal to say, chiefly in parenthe-

ses, and without punctuation, but not much to tell" (11). *Bleak House*.

Piper, Professor   Member of the committee that interviews Elijah Pogram at the National Hotel. *Chuzzlewit* (34).

Pipkin, Nathaniel   Parish clerk in love with Maria Lobbs in Sam Weller's story of "The Parish Clerk." *Pickwick* (17).

Pipkin, Mr., M. R. C. S.   Speaker at the Anatomy and Medicine session of the Mudfog Association. *Mudfog* (2).

Pipson, Miss   "Fair Circassian" at Miss Griffith's school and a member of John's "seraglio." "Haunted House."

Pirated Editions   Strictly speaking, a pirated edition of a literary work is one that reprints the original work without recognizing or paying the author. In Dickens's day, there were several American publishers who specialized in pirating English works, since there was no INTERNATIONAL COPYRIGHT agreement to prevent them from doing so. Although reputable American publishers negotiated for advance copies of foreign works, their payments to the authors were reduced by the activities of the rogue publishers. On his American tour, Dickens spoke out for an international copyright agreement—and he was harshly criticized in the American press for doing so.

Even in England, with copyright laws in place, Dickens's works were pirated, or "re-originated," as one of the pirates described it. Such publishers as Edward Lloyd specialized in cheap imitations of popular works; his parts of "Bos's" *Oliver Twiss* followed on the heels of the parts of *Twist*. In exasperation, Dickens finally took one of the pirates to court over a "re-origination" of the *Carol*. He won his case, but the pirate declared bankruptcy, leaving Dickens with a moral victory and £500 in legal fees. Dickens learned to tolerate the pirates, as he did the playwrights who put his stories on the stage before they had finished their serial run, but he continued his support for copyright legislation that would protect writers from such thievery, both at home and abroad.

Pirrip, Philip, Jr. (Pip)   Narrator and protagonist of *Great Expectations*. Orphan son of **Philip, Sr.**, and **Georgiana**, who are buried in the local churchyard with five of their children, **Alexander**, **Bartholomew**, **Abraham**, **Tobias**, and **Roger**, Pip is raised by his sister, Mrs. Joe GARGERY. Pip's story begins on a Christmas when he is about seven and he befriends an escaped convict by stealing some food for him from his sister's larder (3). Sometime later he is taken to play with Estella, rich Miss Havisham's ward, who scorns him and makes him discontented with his common life and prospects (8).

While he serves his apprenticeship to his brother-in-law the blacksmith, Pip wishes for a better life, a wish that seems to come true when he is notified that he is the recipient of "great expectations" (18). His unknown benefactor—assumed by Pip to be Miss Havisham—supports his life as a gentleman in London, but when he reveals his identity several years later, he turns out to be Abel Magwitch, the convict Pip befriended as a child (38). As Pip plans Magwitch's escape from London and then witnesses his arrest, trial, and death, he realizes the shallowness of his expectations and the value of the life he rejected when he went to the city. In the end, he gives up Magwitch's money, works for his living, and is reconciled with Joe (59). *Expectations*.

Pisa   Dickens describes his visit to this Italian city and its famous leaning tower, "nothing like so high above the wall as I had hoped. It was another of the many deceptions practised by Mr. Harris, Bookseller, at the corner of ST. PAUL'S Churchyard, London. *His* Tower was a fiction, but this was a reality—and, by comparison, a short reality." *Pictures*.

Pitcher   A sickly pupil at DOTHEBOYS HALL. *Nickleby* (7).

Pitchlynn   Choctaw Indian chief, "a remarkably handsome man . . . with long black hair, an aquiline nose, broad cheek-bones, a sun-burnt complexion, and a very bright, keen, dark, and piercing eye," with whom Dickens discusses the decline of his people as they travel from LOUISVILLE, Kentucky, to ST. LOUIS, Missouri. *Notes* (12).

Pitt, Jane   Only friend of Old Cheeseman the Latin master. "Uncommonly neat and cheerful, and uncommonly comfortable and kind," she eventually marries him. "Schoolboy's Story."

Pittsburgh   Dickens visited this industrial city in Pennsylvania on his first trip to the United States in 1841. He compared it to BIRMINGHAM in *American Notes* (11).

Planter's House   ST. LOUIS hotel where Dickens stayed on his first American journey, "a large hotel . . . built like an English hospital." *Notes* (12).

Plashwater Weir Mill Lock   The lock where Rogue Riderhood is the keeper and where he and Bradley Headstone drown together (IV:15). *Mutual Friend*. It is probably based on the Hurley Lock, six miles downriver from HENLEY.

"Plate Glass"   Article for HOUSEHOLD WORDS (February 1, 1851) by Dickens and WILLS, one of several on various manufacturing processes. The article describes a tour of a plate-glass factory near Blackwall. *Stone*.

"Plated Article, A"   Stopping for the night at a dull town in Staffordshire, the narrator is entertained by a plate that describes in detail the processes by which Staffordshire pottery is made. *Reprinted*. From HOUSEHOLD WORDS (April 24, 1852).

"Plea for Total Abstinence, A"   After observing a temperance march in which the participants grossly overtax the horses pulling their wagons, the Traveller decides that teetotalers are "unable to use [horses] without abusing them" and he declares "total abstinence from horseflesh to be the only remedy of which the case admitted." *Uncommercial* (37). Originally in ALL THE YEAR ROUND (June 5, 1869).

"Please to Leave your Umbrella"   Article for HOUSEHOLD WORDS (May 1, 1858), describing a visit to HAMPTON COURT on a rainy afternoon. When he is asked to leave his umbrella at the door, the narrator imagines himself like Sterne's Sentimental Traveller and enters into a digressive meditation on what else is left behind when one is asked to leave his umbrella. At an OLD BAILEY trial he left behind his sense of absurdity; in Parliament, his knowledge of the difference between black and white. *Miscellaneous*.

Plorn   Nickname for Dickens's youngest child, Edward Bulwer Lytton DICKENS, born in 1852. Dickens sometimes gave the longer version of the name as Plornishmaroon or Plornishmaroontigoonter.

Plornish, Thomas   Frequently unemployed plasterer who lives with his wife, **Sally**, and their two **children** in BLEEDING HEART YARD, "a smooth-cheeked, fresh-coloured, sandy-whiskered man of thirty." He meets the Dorrits while imprisoned in the Marshalsea and offends Mr. Dorrit with his small tribute (I:6). Clennam employs him to sort out Tip Dorrit's debts (I:12) and to provide Cavaletto a place to stay (I:25). Mrs. Plornish establishes a small grocery shop in Bleeding Heart Yard and is devoted to her father, Old Nandy (II:13). *Dorrit*.

Pluck   One of Sir Mulberry Hawk's underlings; he and Pyke flatter Mrs. Nickleby into telling them Kate's whereabouts. *Nickleby* (27).

Plummer Family   Poor family in *Cricket* who suffer from Tackleton's exploitation. **Caleb**, a toymaker employed by Tackleton, is "a little, meagre, dingy-faced man, who seemed to have made himself a great-coat from the sack-cloth covering of some old box." He acts as the eyes of his blind daughter **Bertha**, describing their situation as far more comfortable than it is and Tackleton as far kinder than he is, so that Bertha falls in love with Tackleton and is jealous of May Fielding, who is to marry him. When Caleb reveals the truth, Bertha gains true sight, and knows the reality of their situation. Caleb's son, **Edward**, May Fielding's first love, is a sailor presumed dead in South America, but he returns in disguise and reclaims and marries May on the day she is supposed to marry Tackleton. *Cricket.*

Pocket, Herbert Pip's roommate at BARNARD'S INN after he comes into his expectations. Son of Pip's tutor, **Matthew Pocket**, Herbert is the "pale young gentleman" who fought with Pip over Estella (11). He has "a frank and easy way" and "a natural incapacity to do anything secret and mean" (22). He helps Pip to hide Magwitch and plan the escape. Pip secretly secures a position for Herbert with Clarriker's (37). Herbert marries Clara Barley, manages the Cairo office for the firm, and hires Pip as his clerk there (58). Matthew, Miss Havisham's cousin and a graduate of Harrow and Cambridge, is kind and unselfish but feckless and impractical; he has a habit of pulling his hair as a sign of frustration. He is the only one of Miss Havisham's relatives who speaks honestly to her and he has been banished from her presence. Pip tells Miss Havisham of Matthew's good character and she leaves him £4,000 in her will (59). His wife, **Belinda**, a knight's daughter, "had grown up highly ornamental, but perfectly helpless and useless" (23). She is so obsessed with social position that she pays no attention to housekeeping or to her young children **Alick**, **Jane**, **Charlotte**, **Fanny**, **Joe** and an unnamed **baby.**

Among the many Pocket relatives who hover around Miss Havisham, hoping for a share of her money is **Sarah**, "a little dry brown corrugated" cousin (11), who serves as her companion after Estella leaves. Miss Havisham leaves her a bequest of £25 for pills (57). *Expectations.*

Podder Member of the All-Muggleton Cricket Club. *Pickwick* (7).

"Poddles" One of the children in Betty Higden's minding school. *Mutual Friend.*

Podgers, John A comfortable and lazy citizen of WINDSOR in Mr. Pickwick's tale of the 17th century, who refuses an opportunity to watch through the night for witches. *Humphrey.*

Podsnap Family Family through whom Dickens satirizes the PHILISTINISM of the Victorian middle class. A pompous, self-satisfied insurance man, "**Mr. [John] Podsnap** was well to do, and stood very high in Mr. Podsnap's opinion. . . . He never could make out why everybody was not quite satisfied, . . . being particularly well-satisfied with most things, and, above all other things, with himself" (I:11). He ignores anything that would upset his complacency by denying it and pushing it away with a flourish of the right hand. He is the model for "Podsnappery," middle-class complacency and condescension. Particularly concerned about social propriety, he demands that nothing occur that would "bring a blush into the cheek of the Young Person," particularly to the cheek of his daughter **Georgiana**, "an under-

sized damsel, with high shoulders, low spirits, chilled elbows, and a rasped surface of nose, who seemed to take occasional frosty peeps out of childhood into womanhood, and to shrink back again"(I:11). When the Lammles scheme to marry her to Fascination Fledgeby, her snobbish and self-satisfied father is unaware of the danger to his daughter. She is saved from the union only when Mrs. Lammle warns Podsnap. **Mrs. Podsnap,** "a fine woman" with a "quantity of bone, neck and nostrils like a rocking horse," wears a majestic headdress on which she displays the "golden offerings" from her husband (I: 2). *Mutual Friend.* Dickens's friend, John FORSTER, is thought to be the model for Podsnap.

Poe, Edgar Allan (1809–1849) American poet, critic, short-story writer. Poe visited Dickens at his hotel in BALTIMORE in 1842, bringing as a gift his *Tales of the Grotesque and Arabesque* (1840). He admired Dickens's work and was influenced by such stories as "A Madman's Manuscript" in *Pickwick*, and the two spent the afternoon talking about literature. After he returned to England Dickens sought a publisher for Poe's work. Two years later Poe was angered when he was slighted in an article on American literature by John FORSTER, whom he thought must have been influenced by Dickens.

Poe's review of *Rudge* (*Graham's Magazine*, 1842) criticized the bifurcation of the murder plot from the GORDON RIOTS plot and suggested that the novel would have been better had Dickens confined the story to London and to a shorter span of time. But Poe praised the atmosphere of the novel. Dickens's raven, Grip, probably influenced Poe's poem "The Raven."

Poetry Dickens published some occasional verse in his periodicals and in some of the novels, such as "The Ivy Green" in *Pickwick* (6). These verses are collected in *Miscellaneous Papers.*

"Poetry of Science, The" Review for the EXAMINER (December 9, 1848) of Robert Hunt's *The Poetry of Science, or Studies of the Physical Phenomena of Nature*, a geological treatise to show, in Dickens's words, "that Science, truly expounding Nature, can, like Nature herself, restore in some new form whatever she destroys." The poetry that science discovers in nature amply compensates for the Dryades and other superstitions that it takes away. *Miscellaneous.*

Pogram, The Hon. Elijah Member of Congress whom Martin meets on the steamboat he takes when leaving Eden. Pogram is renowned as "one of the master minds of our country" for his "Defiance" which "defied the world in general to com-pete with our country upon any hook; and devellop'd our internal resources for making war upon the universal airth." *Chuzzlewit* (34).

Point of View Critical concept describing the vantage point from which an author presents his story. The NARRATOR can write in either a first- or third-person voice and can be limited in what he knows—as is the case, for example, when a character within the story narrates the action—or omniscient, standing outside the action and able to know what all of the characters are doing and thinking. These alternatives describe polar positions on a continuum; there are many possible points of view that are neither fully omniscient nor absolutely limited. Many critics have pointed out that Dickens's first-person narrators like David (*Copperfield*) and Pip (*Expectations*) sometimes know more than we expect them to and share some of the stylistic skills of Dickens's omniscient narrators. Audrey JAFFEE (1991) argues that his omniscient narrator is often less than omniscient.

Police   During Dickens's lifetime there were major changes in law enforcement and the police. During his childhood, policing was handled by constables, Bow Street Runners, and, in extreme situations like the GORDON RIOTS or the Peterloo Massacre, by the military. The river police force on the THAMES, described by Dickens in "Down with the Tide," was established early in the century. The Metropolitan Police Act of 1829 created a police force for the area around London and the Detective Department of the force was begun in 1842. There was substantial resistance to all of these changes and the police were under a great deal of scrutiny. In magazine articles like "Metropolitan Protectives" and "On Duty with Inspector Field," Dickens described the work of these new police agencies, making them more acceptable to his readers. The police and detectives in the novels, from the soldiers who pursue the escaped convicts at the beginning of *Expectations* to the Bow Street Runners Blathers and Duff in *Twist* (31) to Bucket (*Bleak House*) and the Police Inspector (*Mutual Friend*) reflect these changes and the growing professionalism in the police forces of the time.

Political Economy   The principles of classical economics, known in Britian as political economy, were a subject of intense debate during Dickens's lifetime, particularly in the 1830s and '40s. Following the REFORM BILL OF 1832, the Whigs took power after decades of Conservative rule; they introduced many measures to limit or end government interference in the economy, to establish free trade and a free market for labor. The economic philosophy behind this legislation, variously referred to as political economy, laissez-faire, and UTILITARIANISM, broadly reflected the ideas of such economists as Adam Smith, David Ricardo, and MALTHUS, and such utilitarian philosophers as Bentham. These ideas were popularized at the time by writers like Harriet MARTINEAU, whose *Illustrations of Political Economy* (1832–34) emphasized the principles in story form. Although Dickens supported some of the principles of the economists, especially free trade and the abolition of the CORN LAWS, he did not do so for reasons of economic principle. His concerns were humanitarian—getting bread for the poor—and political—opposing aristocratic privilege. He opposed the economists' cold-hearted rationalism, which dehumanized factory workers and turned them into "hands," allowed the expoitation of women and children under the guise of supporting a free market, and made the market rather than economic justice the determinant of a fair wage. He attacked the political economists as "philosophers" in *Twist*, satirized them in Filer and his associates in *Chimes*, and exposed the moral emptiness of the "hard facts school" in Gradgrind and Bounderby in *Hard Times*.

Political Squibs from The Examiner   Three political verses Dickens contributed anonymously to the EXAMINER in 1841 in support of the Liberal cause: "The Fine Old English Gentleman," "The Quack Doctor's Proclamation," and "Subjects for Painters." *Miscellaneous*.

Polly   Waitress at the Slap Bang restaurant who serves Guppy and Chick Smallweed. *Bleak House* (20).

Polreath, David   Elderly resident of Lanrean. "Message from the Sea."

Polygon   A block of run-down houses in SOMERS TOWN where the Dickens family lived 1827. Harold Skimpole lives here (*Bleak House* 43).

Pompeii   Dickens describes his visit to this Italian city, buried in the eruption of Mount Vesuvius in 79 AD, in *Pictures*. Mr. Meagles includes "morsels of tesselated pavement" from Pompeii among the souvenirs of his travels (*Dorrit*, I:16).

Ponto   Jingle's most intelligent hunting dog, who obeys a sign reading, "Gamekeeper has orders to shoot all dogs found in this enclosure." *Pickwick* (2).

Poodles   Mongrel dog in the East London Children's Hospital who cheers the patients as he makes his rounds from bed to bed. *Uncommercial* (30, 34).

Poole, John (1786?–1872)   Playwright, author of popular theatrical farces, one of which, *Deaf as a Post*, Dickens directed and performed in at MONTREAL in 1842. Toward the end of his life, Poole, wasted by alcohol, retired to Paris, where he lived in poverty. Dickens provided money for him from the performances of some of his benefit theatricals.

Poor Law   The Poor Law Amendment Act of 1834 (also called the New Poor Law), was one of the first major pieces of legislation passed by the Whig Parliament that took power after the REFORM BILL OF 1832. The act centralized welfare by grouping parishes throughout England and Wales into 21 unions and building workhouses for the poor in each. The law eliminated "outdoor relief"—receiving aid while remaining out of the workhouse—and it provided that conditions in the workhouse be such as to discourage paupers from seeking aid except as a last resort. The workhouses quickly became known as "Poor Law Bastilles," and many stories circulated of paupers like Betty Higden who chose death outside to the privations and indignities within the workhouse. Dickens satirizes the workhouses and attacks the poor law in the opening chapters of *Twist* (1–7), in the account of Mr. Nandy (*Dorrit*, I:31), and in the story of Betty Higden (*Mutual Friend*, I:17, II:14, III:8).

"Poor Man and His Beer"   Article for ALL THE YEAR ROUND (April 30, 1859), describing the social experiments of Friar Bacon, who has established a system of garden allotments that entitles the holders to be members of a cooperative club providing beer and social life and to borrow a pound each year to buy a pig. *Miscellaneous*.

"Poor Man's Tale of a Patent, A"   A smith describes the cumbersome and expensive process he went through to patent his invention. It had 35 stages and cost £96 7s. 6d. *Reprinted*. The article describes in detail the kind of frustrations imposed on Daniel Doyce by the CIRCUMLOCUTION OFFICE in *Dorrit*.

"Poor Merchantile Jack"   Traveller's account of visiting the slums of LIVERPOOL with a police superintendent and seeing the lodging-house keepers, publicans, and other inhabitants of the area, all of whom are waiting to prey upon visiting seamen. *Uncommercial* (5).

Poor Relation, The   MICHAEL (1), narrator of "The POOR RELATION'S STORY."

"Poor Relation's Story, The"   One of two contributions Dickens made to the Christmas number of HOUSEHOLD WORDS, 1852. Michael, the poor relation who narrates the story, tells his relatives a "castle-in-the-air" version of his life—his happy marriage to Christiana, his success in business with his partner John Spatter, and his affection for his cousin Little Frank. In fact, Michael is a penurious bachelor, living on the edge in Clapham Road after being defrauded by his business partner. *Christmas Stories*.

Poplar Walk   Street in STAMFORD HILL where Mr. Octavius Budden has his suburban retreat in Dickens's first published story, "A DINNER AT POPLAR WALK."

Poplars, The   Haunted house in the north of England rented by John, the narrator of the story. "Haunted House."

"Popular Delusion, A"   An article on BILLINGS-GATE Market and the fish trade in England written by

Dickens and W. H. WILLS for *HOUSEHOLD WORDS*, June 1, 1850. *Stone*.

Pordage, Mr. Commissioner   Representative of the British government on Silver-store Island, "a stiff-jointed, high-nosed old gentleman, without an ounce of fat on him, of a very high temper and a very yellow complexion. **Mrs. Commissioner Pordage**, making allowance for difference of sex, was much the same." He becomes governor of the island and a KCB. "English Prisoners."

Porkenham Family   The members of the Porkenham family—**Sidney**, **Mrs. Sidney,** and the **Misses Sidney**—are rivals to the Nupkins in IPSWICH society. *Pickwick* (25).

Porter, Mrs. Joseph   Gossipy and supercilious neighbor of the Gattletons whose talent for "scandal and sarcasm" makes her "courted, and flattered, and caressed, and invited" to her neighbors' amateur theatrical, even though she is, like her daughter **Emma**, disdainful of the proceedings. After encouraging Tom Balderstone to disrupt the proceedings with unnecessary promptings, she can declare the evening "a complete failure." *Boz*, "Porter."

Porters   A suitor of her youth at TUNBRIDGE WELLS recalled by Miss Twinkleton as "foolish Mr. Porters." *Drood* (3).

Portland Place   Fashionable residential street in MARYLEBONE. Mr. Dombey's house was nearby in a "dark, dreadfully genteel Street" (*Dombey*, 3). The extensive Tapkins family are "at Home, Wednesdays" at their residence in Portland Place (*Mutual Friend*, I:17).

Portman Square   The Podsnaps live "in a shady angle adjoining" this fashionable square in MARYLEBONE. *Mutual Friend* (I:11).

Port Middlebay   Town in AUSTRALIA where Mr. Peggotty, Mell, and the Micawbers settle after leaving England. Mr. Micawber becomes its magistrate. *Copperfield* (63).

Portsmouth   Dickens was born in this seaport on the English Channel in Hampshire, southwest England, on February 7, 1812. The Dickens's house at 1 Mile End Terrace, **Portsea** (now 393 Commercial Road), is now a Dickens Museum. The family left Portsmouth for London in 1838. Nicholas Nickleby and Smike appear with the Crummles' theater company during their run in Portsmouth (*Nickleby*, 22–25).

"Post-Office Money-Orders"   Article on the history, use and misuse of postal money orders written by

Dickens and W. H. WILLS for *HOUSEHOLD WORDS* (March 20, 1852). Dickens contributed a lengthy description of the Central Money-order Office in Aldersgate Street. *Stone.*

Potkins, William Waiter at the BLUE BOAR, ROCHESTER, where Pip dines with Pumblechook. *Expectations* (58).

Pott Editor of the *Eatanswill Gazette*, a contentious man, obsessed with his rivalry with Slurk, editor of the *Eatanswill Independent*. He is intimidated by **Mrs. Pott**, and he attacks Winkle when Slurk implies in print that his wife is infatuated with Winkle (18). Later his wife leaves him and the Pickwickians find him brawling with Slurk at the Saracen's Head in TOWCESTER (51). *Pickwick.*

Potter, Thomas City clerk who "makes a night of it" with his friend Thomas Smithers. After a good dinner and much drink, they are ejected from the theater for disrupting the performance, and end up in prison for disturbing the peace. *Boz,* "Making a Night."

Potterson, Abbey Proprietor of the SIX JOLLY FELLOWSHIP PORTERS, the pub along the THAMES in LIMEHOUSE near where John Harmon's body was found. She rules the pub like an abbess ruling a convent: she advises Lizzie to separate herself from her father and his work; she excludes both Gaffer Hexam and Rogue Riderhood from the fellowship in the inn; and she presides over the resuscitation of Rogue when he is pulled from the river. Her brother **Job**, steward on the ship on which John Harmon was a passenger, identifies the drowned man as Harmon (I:3). *Mutual Friend.*

Pottington Friend who challenges the narrator's news by appealing to "The Best Authority." *Miscellaneous.*

Pouch, Mrs. Joe A widow whom Trooper George might once have married. "Joe Pouch's widow might have done me good—there was something in her—and something of her—but I couldn't make up my mind to it." *Bleak House* (27).

Poulter Gabblewig and Rosina disguise themselves as Mr. and Mrs. Poulter, a couple who have benefitted so from the water cure at Malvern that they cannot stop walking. *Nightingale.*

Powler Family to which Mrs. Sparsit is boastfully connected through her late husband; they "could trace themselves so exceedingly far back that it was not surprising if they sometimes lost themselves" (I:7). *Hard Times.*

Pratchett, Mrs. Head chambermaid in the hotel where Christopher, the narrator of "Somebody's Luggage," works. **Mr. Pratchett** is in AUSTRALIA in "the Bush."

'Prentice Knights Secret society of apprentices headed by Simon Tappertit which is devoted to wresting power from their masters (8). During the GORDON RIOTS the society allies itself with the Protestant cause and changes its name to the United Bulldogs (36). *Rudge.*

Pre-Raphaelite Art School of painting established in 1848 by seven young artists and poets, the most noteworthy being Dante Gabriel Rossetti, William Holman Hunt, and John Everett MILLAIS. Through their work and their magazine, the *Germ*, they promoted an art that closely observed nature and expressed ideas, qualities they found in medieval and Renaissance art prior to Raphael. By 1850 their work had become controversial, its medieval and religious subject matter suggesting that they were philosophically allied to the Tractarians. In "Old Lamps for New Ones," Dickens attacked Millais's painting "Christ in the House of his Parents" for its degrading realism. He later altered his opinion of Millais's work and the two became friends, but he remained opposed to reactionary Victorian MEDIEVALISM.

Prescott, William H. (1796–1859) American historian, author of the *Conquest of Mexico* and other works. He was one of the group of American friends whom Dickens made on his American tour in 1842. Prescott visited Dickens in England in 1849.

Preston Dickens visited this textile manufacturing town in Lancashire in January 1854 during a long and bitter strike of the factory workers. His article about his trip, "On Strike," appeared in HOUSEHOLD WORDS, February 11, 1854 (*Miscellaneous*). Preston was one of the sources for COKETOWN in *Hard Times.* George Silverman's "infant home was a cellar in Preston" ("Silverman").

Price One of the debtors whom Pickwick meets at Namby's sponging house, "a coarse vulgar young man [with a] captivating freedom of manner, which is to be acquired in public-house parlours and at low billiard tables." *Pickwick* (40).

Price, Matilda ('Tilda) Lively Yorkshire miller's daughter who encourages Nicholas Nickleby to take a romantic interest in her friend Fanny Squeers (9). She marries John Browdie and brings her bridesmaid Fanny along on her wedding trip to London (39). *Nickleby.*

Prig, Betsey Professional nurse who is Mrs. Gamp's friend and associate: she "was of the Gamp build, but not so fat; and her voice was deeper and more like a man's. She had also a beard" (25). She divides the duties of caring for Lewsome with Mrs. Gamp and would have been part of a similar arrangement with Chuffey, had she not challenged the existence of Mrs. Harris, asserting,

"I don't believe there's no sich person" (51). Mrs. Gamp casts her off forever for this act of disbelief. *Chuzzlewit.*

Priestly, J. B. (1894–1984) English novelist, playwright; author and editor of numerous works of nonfiction; broadcaster and stage producer; president of the DICKENS FELLOWSHIP, 1970. Priestley's lower-middle-class characters and urban settings in his novels have been compared to those of Dickens, a novelist with whom Priestley is often connected. In advising young writers, Priestley urged them to "write for the common man and woman—like Hemingway, Dickens, Twain, and Poe did—for they are the ones who will keep your work alive long after you're gone." Priestley's pictorial biography of Dickens (1961) tells Dickens's life from a fellow Londoner's point of view. He stresses the comic side of Dickens and illustrates the general proposition, stated in *The English Novel* (1935), that Dickens's "later stories are better novels than the earlier ones, but they are not better Dickens." His analyses of Micawber and Swiveller as *English Comic Characters* (1925) offer sympathetic insight into Dickens's comedy, as does his centennial essay (in *Charles Dickens 1812–1870*, ed. Tomlin, 1969), which seeks to describe the "inimitable" qualities in Dickens's work. Priestley also prepared an edition of selected *Sketches by Boz* (1948) and wrote the general introduction to the Centennial Edition of Dickens's Works (1970).

"Prince Bull. A Fairy Tale" Dickens's allegorical fairy tale about the misconduct of the Crimean War when the red fairy Tape upsets all the plans of Prince Bull. *Reprinted.* Originally appeared in *HOUSEHOLD WORDS* (February 17, 1855).

Princess's Place The mews in London's fashionable West End where Miss Tox and Joey Bagstock live across the way from one another. *Dombey* (7).

Priscilla The Jellyby's maid who "drinks—she's always drinking." *Bleak House* (4).

"Prisoners' Van, The" Sketch describing two sisters, aged 14 and 16, who climb out of the prisoners' van on their way to jail for prostitution. The elder is brazen, the younger tearfully ashamed. *Boz.* It originally appeared in *BELL'S LIFE IN LONDON* (December 13, 1835).

Prisons Biographers suggest that Dickens's interest in prisons stemmed from the traumatic months in his childhood when his father was imprisoned in the MARSHALSEA for debt. DEBTORS PRISONS and criminal prisons appear in many of his works. Boz describes "A Visit to Newgate" and imagines himself a condemned prisoner awaiting execution, foreshadowing many of the prison scenes in the later novels: Pickwick's imprisonment in the FLEET (Pickwick 40); Fagin's condemned cell in NEWGATE (*Twist*, 51); the storming of Newgate by the Gordon rioters (*Rudge*, 64); Micawber's imprisonment for debt (*Copperfield*, 11); the symbolic Marshalsea of *Dorrit*, representing the physical and mental prisons that confine the human spirit; the BASTILLE, where Doctor Manette is buried for 17 years (*Two Cities*); the Newgate that Pip visits with Wemmick, leaving a "taint" upon him as he meets Estella in London (*Expectations*, 32). Moreover, according to John FORSTER, Dickens's last novel was planned to end with Jasper's meditations in his condemned cell.

Dickens visited prisons himself and entered into the controversies over prison reform in his journalistic writings and novels, as in his account of Heep and Littimer as "model prisoners" (*Copperfield*, 61), a satirical attack on the experimental PENTONVILLE Prison. Dickens joined the prison controversy of the 1840s with a chapter in *American Notes* (7) where he described the Eastern Penitentiary in PHILADELPHIA, an institution that used a system of solitary confinement, known as the separate system, to reform its inmates. Dickens criticized the system as cruel and unnatural and supported its alternative, the silent system, in which prisoners associated with their fellow prisoners but were not allowed to communicate with them. Attacked for his advocacy of the silent system, Dickens defended himself and reiterated his arguments against the separate system in "Pet Prisoners," a controversial article for *HOUSEHOLD WORDS* that criticized the application of silent principles at Pentonville. Philip COLLINS (1962) provides a comprehensive account of Dickens' ideas on prison reform and concludes that "it is impossible . . . to discover a consistent attitude, or a clear development in Dickens's various pronouncements on penal discipline. The most that one can say is that, throughout his career, he approved of severe penal measures, and inclined more towards a deterrent than a curative policy, and that the inclination became stronger, and was more vehemently expressed, the older he grew."

"Private Theatres" Dickens's satirical account of the private theaters in London that allow men of dubious talent to pay for the privilege of performing. The preparations for a particularly disjointed production of *Macbeth* are described in detail. *Boz.* The sketch originally appeared in the *EVENING CHRONICLE* (August 11, 1835).

Procter, Bryan Waller (1787–1874) Lawyer, poet, and dramatist who wrote under the penname Barry Cornwall. Friend of Byron, Leigh HUNT, and Charles Lamb, he wrote one tragedy, *Mirandola*, and *The Life of Edmund Kean.* He was, with Dickens, a member of Lady BLESSINGTON's literary salon at Gore House and the two were lifelong friends. Procter's work appeared in both *HOUSEHOLD WORDS* and *ALL THE YEAR ROUND.* His daughter, the immensely popular poet **Adelaide Anne Procter** (1825–64), also published in both of Dickens's magazines. She submitted her poems to Dickens under the pseudonym Mary Berwick and he accepted them not knowing who had written them. He wrote an introduction for a posthumous edition of her *Legends and Lyrics* (1866).

Prodgit, Mrs. Augustus George Meek's maternity nurse, "she wore a black bonnet of large dimensions, and was copious in figure." *Reprinted*, "Births."

Progress, The A literary form describing a journey that moves forward in distinct stages or steps. The English model for a progress narrative is Bunyan's *Pilgrim's Progress* (1673), next to the Bible the best-known literary work in Victorian England. Dickens and the other Victorian novelists allude to it frequently; Dickens makes his most extensive use of it in *Curiosity Shop*, in which Nell's allegorical journey recalls Christian's and where such scenes as escaping the city and passing through a wicket gate (16) allude explicitly to scenes in Bunyan's narrative.

In subtitling *Twist* "The Parish Boy's Progress," Dickens probably had in mind the progresses of William HOGARTH, who turned Bunyan's narrative on its head in a series of visual narratives that described the downward movement of their protagonists. "The Harlot's Progress" (1732), for example, described the corruption of a country girl who comes to London, and "The Rake's Progress" (1735) the dissolution into dissipation and madness of a young man-about-town. Although Oliver's story is predicted to follow a similar progress to the gallows, it takes a counter direction, prompting some critics to see Bunyan rather than Hogarth as Dickens's inspiration, but in the course of *Twist*, Oliver is displaced by Fagin as the central character of the progress as Fagin completes the predicted journey to the gallows.

Dickens also described Esther Summerson's autobiographical narrative as a progress (*Bleak House*), and even though her story has an upward movement, the story of Lady Dedlock also has many of the elements of one of Hogarth's progresses. Commentators have described several other novels as progresses, especially *Pickwick*, with its peregrinations throughout England, and *Expectations*, in which Pip's life story is broken into "stages."

Prologue to Westland Marston's Play *The Patrician's Daughter* Dickens wrote the verse prologue to this tragedy, a first play by an unknown playwright, in 1842. The lines, which justify a tragedy of contemporary common life, were spoken by MACREADY on stage.

"Proposals for a National Jest Book" Facetious article from *HOUSEHOLD WORDS* (May 3, 1856), proposing a national jest book that would record humorous anecdotes from parliamentary debates, court proceedings, and other public events. A Board of Jokery, composed of "younger sons, nephews, cousins, and cousin-germans, of the Aristocracy," would select the materials to be included, and each householder would be taxed £25 per annum to pay for his copy. Several samples of appropriate materials are included. *Miscellaneous*.

"Proposals for Amusing Posterity" A satirical article for *HOUSEHOLD WORDS* (February 12, 1853), describing some of the ways in which the present age is—by unequal justice, priviledge, and hypocrisy—recording jests for the grim amusement of posterity. *Miscellaneous*.

Prosee Eminent counsel who attends Perker's dinner party. *Pickwick* (47).

Pross, Miss Lucie Manette's maid, a thoroughly loyal servant to her "Ladybird" who "beneath the surface of her eccentricity [is] one of those unselfish creatures—found only among women" (II:6). She accompanies Lucie to Paris where she is surprised to meet her brother **Solomon** (also known as **John Barsad**) who is working as a spy in the French prisons. Earlier in the novel, as Barsad, he has testified against Charles Darnay at the trial in London (II:3). At the end of the story, Miss Pross is in the Manette's apartment in Paris when the Defarges come in search of Lucie. As she struggles with them, Madame Defarge's gun fires, killing its owner (III:14). *Two Cities*.

Prostitution Of the three common Victorian attitudes toward prostitution—condemnation, acceptance with regulation, and reformation—Dickens adopted the latter. He nearly always portrays the prostitute as a victim of economic necessity or duplicity, pities her as a remorseful creature outside the bounds of domestic happines, and seeks her reformation. His work at URANIA COTTAGE was founded on a commitment to changing the lives of the women there, but Dickens was also a realist who knew that such efforts were not always successful.

Prostitutes appear in his earliest work, Boz's realistic sketches of urban life, in the two girls being taken away in the "Prisoner's Van," in the gaudy but ravaged woman in "The Pawnbroker's Shop," and in the battered woman in "The Hospital Patient." These women represented the many prostitutes on the London streets at the time, constituting a social problem that engaged Victorian reformers like Dickens and shocked foreign visitors. Although we never see Nancy, Sikes's doxy in *Twist*, on the streets, Dickens identified her as a prostitute in a cancelled sentence in the 1846 Preface, and Brownlow's proposal to remove her from her degradation moves the remorseful girl, even though she rejects his offer. The economic necessity that drives these women into the streets also explains Lilian Fern's fall in the vision of the future in *The Chimes* (3), or the remorse of the prostitute who warns Little Dorrit off the streets (*Dorrit*, I:14). While Alice Marwood was driven to the streets to survive, her story also embodies the cherished Victorian tale of the poor girl seduced and then abandoned to prostitution by the rich man (*Dombey*, 34). Little Em'ly is Dickens's fullest development of this story, even though Emily is saved from the streets by Daniel Peggotty and by the example of her counterpart, Martha Endell (*Copperfield*, 47, 50). Dickens's most probing treatment of the theme of prostitution comes in the story of Edith Dombey, the rich and respectable lady who is doubled with her cousin, the prostitute Alice Marwood.

Fred Barnard's illustration for "The Prisoners' Van" in Sketches by Boz *depicts the contrasting reactions of two young prostitutes as they are taken away by the police.*

By paralleling the two women, Dickens suggests that mercenary marriage is a form of prostitution, something Edith herself recognizes when she tells her mother that Dombey has "bought" her (*Dombey*, 27). Michael SLATER (1983) surveys Dickens's treatment of prostitution and his attitude toward the prostitute.

Protagonist Chief character in a novel, play, or story. In the novel, the term is often preferred to *hero*, for the novel's central figure is usually an average person who is not faced with extraordinary tests or called upon to perform extraordinary deeds. Angus WILSON (1962) has said that "to examine the heroes and heroines of Dickens is to dwell on weaknesses and failures." Indeed, the central character in a Dickens novel has often been considered the least interesting figure in the book—conventional, with good intentions and without serious flaws, and less clearly defined than the characters around him. This accounting may describe fairly well such early Dickens protagonists as Nicholas Nickleby, but, as Beth Herst (*The Dickens Hero*, 1990) has shown, the later Dickens heroes are much more complex figures who be-

come the heroes of their own lives and achieve self-integration only by alienating themselves from society.

Provis Alias assumed by MAGWITCH when he returns illegally to England. *Expectations* (40).

Prowler Member of the Athenaeum and the Royal Society of Arts who passes along some particularly unbelievable gossip on "The Best Authority." *Miscellaneous.*

Pruffle Servant to the scientific gentleman at Clifton. *Pickwick*, 39.

Psychological Novel A novel emphasizing interior characterization, focusing on the personal history, circumstances, and motives that prompt its characters to act. Among Victorian novelists, George ELIOT is usually considered the major practitioner in this form. Commentators who stress the dramatic side of Dickens's work or his realistic depiction of Victorian society tend to describe him as a SOCIOLOGICAL NOVEList, and they often ignore the psychological dimensions of his work.

Although they do not employ an analytic narration similar to Eliot's, Dickens's works, as many recent critics have shown, are intensely psychological. His use of first-person narration and his understanding of personal history in *Copperfield, Bleak House*, and *Great Expectations*, and in such stories as "George Silverman's Explanation," is pre-Freudian. The central theme in all of his work—the search for an integrated sense of self—is fundamentally psychological. Although his plots are dramatic and focus on external events, his people individualized through physical traits, gestures, and mannerisms, these markers externalize an interior drama. The uncanny coincidences in the plots and such devices as REPETITION and doubling in characterization (see DOUBLE) convey the psychological import of the story. Among the critics who have analyzed the psychological dimensions of Dickens's work are Leonard MANHEIM, Taylor STOEHR (1965), Mark SPILKA (1963), Karen Chase (*Eros and Psyche: The Representation of Personality in Charlotte Bronte, Charles Dickens, and George Eliot*, 1984), and Gwen WATKINS (1987).

"Public Dinners" Comic sketch describing the charity dinner for the benefit of the Indigent Orphans' Friends Benevolent Institution, originally published in the *EVENING CHRONICLE* (April 7, 1835). *Boz.*

"Public Life of Mr. Tulrumble, The" Sketch describing the rise to eminence of Nicholas Tulrumble, a coal dealer who becomes mayor of Mudfog, and who for an unhappy six weeks surrounds himself with pomp and pretension until he realizes that he was much happier as just one of the regulars at the Jolly Boatman. First published in *BENTLEY'S MISCELLANY* (January 1837). *Mudfog.*

Public Readings Just after Christmas 1853, Dickens gave a reading of the *Carol* in Birmingham for charity, the first of many public readings of his works. He had previously given private readings of his CHRISTMAS BOOKS or of parts of his novels in progress for friends and family members, the best known being his reading of the *Chimes* in 1844. Several more charity readings in the mid-1850s were a prelude to a career as a professional reader that began in 1858 and continued, with almost annual seasons in London, regular provincial tours, and the famous American tour in 1867–68, until his death.

Dickens prepared performance texts for the readings, condensing the shorter pieces or extracting passages from the longer novels. His most frequent and popular readings were "The Trial from Pickwick," performed 164 times, and "A Christmas Carol," performed 127 times. The most notorious selection, "Sikes and Nancy," introduced into his repertory in 1868, recounted the murder of Nancy and the death of Sikes from *Twist*. It was sensational theater that horrified some of his listeners and so excited the performer that his doctor advised him

Dickens at his reading desk for his final performance on March 15, 1870.

against doing it. However, Dickens did not follow his doctor's advice, and he continued to perform "Sikes and Nancy" and other pieces up until a few months before his death. The strain of the performances is believed to have hastened his demise.

The readings were really performances rather than readings. Dickens knew his texts and played the different characters in different voices. Kate FIELD (1871) describes many of these performances that she attended during Dickens's American tour. Philip COLLINS (1975) provides an account of the readings and the performance texts. Emlyn WILLIAMS has recreated the public readings for modern audiences; recordings of several of his performances are available.

Publishers For most of his career Dickens worked with two publishers, CHAPMAN & HALL and BRADBURY & EVANS. As he was establishing himself and developing a reputation, he changed publishers frequently to take advantage of growing opportunities. His first publisher was John MACRONE, who issued both series of *Sketches by Boz*. Impressed with the success of the sketches, Chapman & Hall engaged Dickens to write the copy for the monthly numbers of *Pickwick*. Richard BENTLEY published *Twist* after it appeared in *BENTLEY'S MISCELLANY*, his magazine that Dickens was editing. He had the promise of a second novel, but Dickens turned that project over to Chapman & Hall, who became his regular publishers with *Nickleby* and *Master Humphrey's Clock*. When they talked of reducing his monthly payments because *Chuzzlewit* failed to meet expectations, Dickens moved to Bradbury & Evans. They published the novels from *Dombey* through *Dorrit* as well as *Household Words*. When they refused to include Dickens's "PERSONAL" statement regarding his marital separation in *PUNCH*, another of their publications, Dickens returned to Chapman & Hall, publishing with them the remaining novels and *ALL THE YEAR ROUND*, the magazine he created to break his magazine contract with Bradbury & Evans. Several of the collected editions of Dickens's works published during his lifetime were published cooperatively by both Chapman & Hall and Bradbury & Evans. Dickens published with several American firms; from 1867 on, his official American publisher was TICKNOR & FIELDS. The standard work on *Dickens and His Publishers* is by Robert PATTEN (1978).

Pubsey and Co.   The moneylending business in ST. MARY AXE that is run by Riah as a front for Fascination Fledgeby. *Mutual Friend*.

Puffer, Princess   Hag who presides at the opium den in the East End of London frequented by John Jasper. She shadows him to Cloisterham, perhaps to blackmail or spy on him (23). *Drood*.

Pugh, Edwin (1874–1930)   English novelist and critic; a member of the COCKNEY SCHOOL whose novels (e.g., *Man of Straw*, 1897; *Tony Drum, A Cockney Boy*, 1898) realistically described the life of the London poor. An avowed follower of Dickens, he wrote *Charles Dickens: The Apostle of the People* (1908), characterizing the novelist as a protosocialist, and *The Dickens Originals* (1911), an account of the real people who were transformed into Dickens characters.

Pugstyles   "Plump gentleman in a violent heat" who leads a deputation of constituents of Mr. Gregsbury, M.P., demanding that he resign. *Nickleby* (16).

Pumblechook, Uncle   Joe Gargery's uncle, a prosperous and hypocritical seed merchant: "a large hard-breathing middle-aged slow man, with a mouth like a fish, dull staring eyes, and sandy hair standing upright on his head, so that he looked as if he had just been all but choked" (4). He arranges Pip's initial meeting with Miss Havisham (7) and subsequently takes credit for Pip's great expectations (19), toadying to Pip's newfound wealth. But when Pip loses his prospects, Pumblechook treats him with patronizing pity (58). *Expectations*.

Punch often ran cartoons that parodied the famous original illustrations for Dickens's works. Here Tenniel, in an 1893 cartoon, recalls Leech's illustration for Christmas Present in A Christmas Carol *(Illustration 15), as he shows Sadstone [Gladstone] facing a Spirit of Christmas Present holding the torch of anarchy and surrounded by explosive political issues.*

Pumpkinskull, Professor   Member of the Mudfog Association. *Mudfog*.

Punch   Weekly magazine featuring satirical commentary, caricature, and parody, the most influential and long-standing of many Victorian comic magazines and miscellanies. Begun in 1841 by Mark LEMON, who edited the magazine until 1870, and published by BRADBURY & EVANS, *Punch* included many of Dickens's friends and associates among its staff and regular contributors. WILLS and JERROLD were among its founding group; LEECH, THACKERAY, TENNIEL, and HUNT counted among its regular contributors.

Punch and Judy   Popular puppet play performed by street performers in Britain since the late 17th century. The usual version of the story has Punch, an irascible, humpbacked creature, kill his child in a fit of anger. When his wife, Judy, attacks him with a stick, he takes it from her and beats her to death. He goes on to bludg-

Doré's vignette of a Punch and Judy performance in the streets of London.

eon his dog and the doctor, trick the hangman who is to execute him for his crimes into hanging himself, and, finally, he tricks even the devil. Dickens makes fullest use of Punch and Judy in *Curiosity Shop*: Nell travels with a pair of Punch and Judy performers, and Quilp has many

Punch-like qualities. Paul SCHLICKE (1985) discusses the Punch shows, Dickens's interest in them, and his use of the story in *Curiosity Shop*.

Pupford, Miss Euphemia   Principal of the Lilliputian College attended by Miss Kimmeens. "Tiddler."

Pupker, Sir Matthew, M.P.   Chairman of the United Metropolitan Improved Hot Muffin and Crumpet Baking and Punctual Delivery Company. *Nickleby* (2).

Purblind   Member of the Mudfog Association. *Mudfog*.

Purday, Captain   Retired naval officer in Our Parish who "always opposes the constituted authorities of the parish." *Boz*, "Our Parish."

Putnam, George Washington (1812–1896)   Dickens's faithful secretary on his first American trip in 1842. Putnam amused the Dickenses with his good humor and tall stories, and he was absolutely efficient in handling Dickens's correspondence and traveling arrangements. Putnam published his reminiscences of his time with Dickens in the *Atlantic Monthly*, 1870.

Putney   Suburban village on the Surrey side of the THAMES, west of London, where Dora Spenlow's aunts live. David and Dora are married in the parish church of St. Mary (*Copperfield*, 41–43). Arthur Clennam crosses Putney Heath on his way to visit the Meagles at TWICKENHAM (*Dorrit*, I:16).

Pyegrave, Charley   One of Miss Mowcher's aristocratic clients. *Copperfield*, (22).

Pyke   A "sharp-faced" cohort of Sir Mulberry Hawk. *Nickleby* (19).

Quarterly Review The major Tory quarterly journal of the 19th century, founded in 1809 to respond to the Whig *Edinburgh Review*. The *Quarterly* tended to regard Dickens as a mere popular entertainer beneath serious notice, a view made explicit in John Wilson Croker's unsigned review commenting on Dickens's vulgarity in the March 1843 issue. Abraham Hayward's review essay in the October 1837 issue, however, was a generally favorable assessment of Dickens's work, and Dickens noted that it contained "a great deal that I know to be true." He was bothered, however, by Hayward's famous prophesy: "The fact is, Mr Dickens writes too often and too fast. . . . If he persists much longer in this course, it requires no gift of prophecy to foretell his fate—he has risen like a rocket, and he will come down like a stick."

Quayle A philanthropic associate of Mrs. Jellyby, "a loquacious young man . . . with large shining knobs for temples," who hopes to marry Caddy Jellyby (4). *Bleak House*.

Quebec Dickens describes his visit to this "place not to be forgotten or mixed up in the mind with other places" in *American Notes* (15).

Queen Charlotte's Hospital Miss Tox inquires at this maternity hospital in Marylebone Road when seeking a wet nurse for Paul Dombey. *Dombey* (2).

Queen Square (1) BATH. Site of the house of Angelo Cyrus Bantam, the master of ceremonies in the Pump Room, whom Pickwick visits. *Pickwick* (35).

Queen Square (2) BLOOMSBURY. Jarndyce finds "a neat little furnished lodging in a quiet old house" for Richard Carstone here. *Bleak House* (18).

"Queer Client, Tale of the" Jack Bamber's story about George Heyling, a debtor in the MARSHALSEA PRISON, who vengefully pursued his cruel father-in-law because he blamed him for the deaths of his wife and child. *Pickwick* (21).

Queerspeck, Professor Member of the mechanical section of the Mudfog Association. *Mudfog*.

Quickear One of the policemen who goes with the Traveller to the haunts of sailors in LIVERPOOL. *Uncommercial* (5).

Quilp, Daniel Malevolent dwarf who lends money to Nell's grandfather, takes over the Old Curiosity Shop in payment, and then pursues Little Nell and her grandfather when they flee from him. "His head and face were large enough for the body of a giant. His black eyes were restless, sly, and cunning. . . . But what added most to the grotesque expression of his face, was a ghastly smile, which . . . revealed the few discoloured fangs that were yet scattered in his mouth, and gave him the aspect of a panting dog" (3). He torments his wife, **Betsy**, and mother-in-law, Mrs. Jiniwin, plays cruel practical jokes on Sampson Brass, and tries to destroy Kit Nubbles. He

Charles Green's rendering of Quilp and Dick Swiveller for the Household Edition of The Old Curiosity Shop *(1876).*

drowns in the THAMES, fleeing from the police who have uncovered his plot (65). After his death, his wife, "a pretty little, mild-spoken, blue-eyed woman" (4), inherits his riches and marries a young man (73). *Curiosity Shop*.

Quilp's Wharf   "A small, rat-infested dreary yard" on the Surrey side of the THAMES near Tower Hill where Quilp carries on his numerous occupations as ship-breaker, smuggler, moneylender, and so on (4). *Curiosity Shop*.

Quinch, Mrs.   Oldest pensioner at Titbull's Almshouses. *Uncommercial* (27).

Quinion   Manager of MURDSTONE AND GRINBY's wine-bottling warehouse who employs David Copperfield and introduces him to Mr. Micawber. *Copperfield* (11).

Rachael Coketown factory hand and faithful friend to Stephen Blackpool: "She turned . . . and showed a quiet oval face, dark and rather delicate, irradiated by a pair of very gentle eyes, and further set off by the perfect order of her shining black hair. It was not a face in its first bloom; she was a woman of five-and-thirty years" (I:10). Although she and Stephen love each other, his inability to secure a divorce from his drunken wife prevents their marrying. She tends Stephen's wife during her illness (I:13), but his promise to her not to join the trade union causes the other workmen to shun him (II:4). With Sissy, she discovers the injured Blackpool at the bottom of Old Hell Shaft (III:6). *Hard Times*.

Rachael, Mrs. The name of Esther Summerson's nurse before she marries CHADBAND. *Bleak House*.

Rackham, Arthur (1867–1939) English watercolorist and illustrator, known in particular for his mystical and fantastic illustrations to children's books. He illustrated the *Carol* (1915).

Raddle, Mrs. Mary Ann Bob Sawyer's landlady in LANT STREET and the sister of Mrs. Clubbins. "A little fierce woman," she orders about **Mr. Raddle**, a "faint-hearted, timorous wretch." *Pickwick* (32).

Radfoot, George Third mate aboard the ship that brings John Harmon back to England. He looks like Harmon, and the two plan to exchange clothes so that Harmon can secretly observe Bella Wilfer. When they arrive in England, he drugs and robs Harmon but is himself murdered, and his body is taken for Harmon's. *Mutual Friend*.

Rae, Dr. John (1813–1893) British surgeon and arctic explorer. Rae was a member of the expeditions in 1848–49 and 1851 that searched for Sir John Franklin and his crews. Rae's report to the Admiralty in 1854 concluded, from information obtained from some Eskimo, that the surviving members of Franklin's crew had resorted to cannibalism before dying of starvation. Dickens challenged Rae's conclusions in "The Lost Arctic Voyagers." Rae's reply to Dickens's article appeared in two installments in *HOUSEHOLD WORDS*: "The Lost Arctic Voyagers" (December 30, 1854) and "Dr. Rae's Report" (December 30, 1854). Rae's report to the Hudson

Scrooge meets "Old Scratch" in Arthur Rackham's fanciful illustration for Stave 4 of A Christmas Carol *(1915).*

Bay Company of his 1853–54 expedition to learn of Franklin's fate also appeared in *Household Words* (February 3, 1855).

Ragged Schools Free schools for inner-city children created by a movement begun early in the century but which became particularly active in the 1840s with the establishment of the Ragged School Union in 1844. Dickens and Miss COUTTS were active supporters of the schools; Dickens wrote a letter praising their work in the *DAILY NEWS* in February 1846 and he devoted many articles to their work in the early years of *HOUSEHOLD WORDS*. His article, "A Sleep to Startle Us" (March 13, 1852) describes a visit to the Ragged School at FIELD LANE. Although he disagreed with the Evangelical zeal of many in the movement (see EVANGELICISM), he thought these schools, by offering education rather than punishment, were taking a reasonable approach to the problems of juvenile crime and delinquency. His disagreements with the Evangelicals, however, dampened his interest, and in later years he was no longer convinced that the schools could change things. His satirical account of such a school in *Mutual Friend* (II:1) indicates his disillusionment with their work. Norris Pope (*Dickens and Charity*, 1978) surveys Dickens's involvement with these schools.

"Railway Dreaming"   Article for *HOUSEHOLD WORDS* (May 10, 1856), a meditation in a railway carriage about Parisians and their ways of doing things. Thinking of them as inhabitants of the moon, Dickens wonders at their eating habits and restaurants, and he praises the café as a place where a solitary person becomes part of a "community with the city life of all de-

grees." He ends with a lengthy description of the PARIS morgue. *Miscellaneous*.

"Railway Strikes"   Article for *HOUSEHOLD WORDS* (January 11, 1851) urging the engine drivers and firemen of the North Western Railway to reconsider their decision to strike. Their duties to the public and to other workmen outside the railway are more important, Dickens argues, than loyalty to their fellow railwaymen. The striking workers have been misled by "designing persons" to forget their individual responsibility to carry out their work. He also urges the public to contemplate no harsh measures against the strikers, for the workers will recognize that the strike is a "false step" and return to work with "the steadiness and patriotism of English workmen." *Miscellaneous*.

Railways   For the Victorians, the railway was the emblem of change and progress, the visible manifestation of the Age of Steam. It arrived suddenly and seemed to displace the old England of coaches and coaching inns almost overnight. This transformation occurred in the middle of Dickens's writing career and can be traced as

Carker's death, depicted here in Fred Barnard's illustration for the Household Edition of Dombey and Son *(1877), makes the railway a murderous agent of social and technological change.*

trains replace coaches in the novels. Pickwick's world is defined by the coach, but when Tony Weller reappears a few years later in *Master Humphrey's Clock*, he inveighs against "the rail [as] unconstitootonal and an inwaser o' priwileges. . . . a nasty, wheezin', creakin', gaspin', puffin', bustin' monster, always out o' breath, like a unpleasant beetle in that 'ere gas magnifier" (3). In *Dombey* the railway becomes an important symbol. The building of the railway creates a turmoil that divides the city and transforms CAMDEN TOWN (6). Dombey's journey to LEAMINGTON after his son's death describes a railway journey in sensuous detail; and Carker's death when run over by a train makes the railway itself an actor in the plot of the novel (55).

The railway's importance in *Dombey*, as Humphry HOUSE (1941) pointed out, coincided with the railway boom of the mid-1840s. In 1840, there were 1,857 miles of railway in Britain; by 1850, there were 6,621. After *Dombey*, railways routinely appear in the novels of contemporary life—*Bleak House, Mutual Friend*, and *Drood*. They have prominence in some of the shorter fiction: the two Idle Apprentices travel by train and spend some time in a railway station (*Lazy Tour*). *Mugby Junction* has a railway station as its major setting and its final chapter, "No. 1 Branch Line: The Signal-Man," tells a railway ghost story. Although Dickens is often connected with coaches, "his understanding of the sensual and social effects of the whole railway revolution," House (1941) points out, "was deeper and wider than that of his contemporaries."

Dickens frequently described railway journeys in his journalistic essays and travel books. "Railway Dreaming" describes the reveries of a passenger on a train as he observes the passing countryside; "Fire and Snow" a winter rail journey through the BLACK COUNTRY. In "An Unsettled Neighbourhood," Dickens describes the transformation of an urban district into a railway town; "An Old Stage-Coaching House" depicts a country village deserted when the railway replaces the coaches that used to stop in the town. "A Narrative of Extraordinary Suffering" is a facetious account of Mr. Lost, befuddled in his imaginary journeys via Bradshaw's railway schedule.

One of the more traumatic experiences in Dickens's life was the STAPLEHURST accident, which occurred when the train on which he was returning from France with Ellen TERNAN and her mother derailed on a trestle, killing 10 and injuring 50. He managed to get himself and his traveling companions safely out of the upset carriage, and he rescued several other passengers and aided the injured and dying. Although he is somewhat facetious in describing his experience in the afterword to *Mutual Friend*, he was very shaken by it. His son reported that afterward even a slight jolt on a railway journey would cause him to panic and grip the seat with both hands.

Rainbird, Alice One of the four child narrators of the stories in "Holiday Romance," she tells the story of Princess Alicia and her magic fishbone, which enables her to provide for the struggling family of King Watkins the First.

Rainbow Tavern, The This establishment in FLEET STREET, the second-oldest coffee house in London, is one of the resorts of the "Old Boys." *Boz*, "Dounce."

Rairyganoo, Sally One of Mrs. Lirriper's maids, suspected of being of "Irish extraction." "Lirriper's Legacy."

Ram Chowdar Doss Azuph Al Bowlar East Indian potentate who is the subject of Captain Helves's story on the steam excursion. *Boz*, "Excursion."

Rames, William Second mate of the *Golden Mary*.

Rampart, Sir Charles Commanding officer of Tibbs's volunteer regiment in 1806. *Boz*, "Boarding House."

Ramsey A defendant against whom DODSON AND FOGG have issued a writ. *Pickwick* (20).

Ramsgate A popular seaside resort on the north coast of KENT. Dickens visited here when vacationing nearby at BROADSTAIRS. The Tuggses are typical of the Londoners who took the steamboat down to Ramsgate for their holiday. *Boz*, "Tuggses."

Random, Honorable Charles Lord Stumpington's official private secretary. *Miscellaneous*, "Cheap Patriotism."

Rarx "A sordid and selfish" passenger on the *Golden Mary* who is obsessed with gold and loses his mind after the wreck. "Golden Mary."

Ratcliff THAMES-side slum notorious for crime in the East End of London. Nancy has moved from Ratcliff to FIELD LANE, an equally notorious district (*Twist*, 13). Bunsby's boat, the *Cautious Clara*, is lying in Ratcliff when Florence visits with Cuttle (*Dombey*, 23). The **Ratcliff Highway** is described in *Boz*, "Brokers," and by the Traveller (*Uncommercial*, 30).

Rathbone, Basil (1892–1967) British-born Hollywood screen actor, famous for his portrayals of Sherlock Holmes and of such villains as Sir Guy of Gisbourne in *Robin Hood* (1938). His Dickensian roles included Murdstone in George Cukor's MGM film of *David Copperfield* (1935), St. Evrémonde in the MGM *A Tale of Two Cities* (1935), and Scrooge in a 1957 television production.

"Rather a Strong Dose" Article for ALL THE YEAR ROUND (March 21, 1863) ridiculing William Howitt's *History of the Supernatural*. Although Howitt had been an admirer of Dickens's work and a frequent contributor to HOUSEHOLD WORDS, his amiable relationship with Dickens broke down in 1859 when Dickens rejected Howitt's spiritualism. Calling Howitt "the sans-culotte of the Spiritual Revolution," Dickens attacks his acceptance of all sorts of impostors and impossible occurrences and his dismissal of all rational explanations for the events he describes. *Miscellaneous.*

Ravender, William George   The courageous captain of the *Golden Mary,* who saves many of his passengers but dies himself in the effort. "Golden Mary."

Raybrock Family   Family in STEEPWAYS burdened with a long-standing suspicion of guilt and loss. **Mrs. Raybrock,** draper and postmistress of the village, believes her eldest son **Hugh** lost at sea, but when Captain Jorgan brings a message from him found in a bottle, the family are rescued from disgrace. The message enables Hugh's younger brother, **Alfred,** to marry **Kitty** Tregarthen. They have an infant son, **Jorgan.** Hugh also returns to his wife, **Margaret,** and his **daughter.** "Message from the Sea."

Raymond   Husband of Camilla, one of Miss Havisham's toadying relatives. *Expectations* (11).

Reade, Charles (1814–1880)   Popular novelist and dramatist and friend of Dickens, his SENSATION NOVELS followed a formula that combined a melodramatic plot with an issue of social reformation. *Hard Cash* (1863), serialized in ALL THE YEAR ROUND, exposed abuses under the insanity laws and in private mental institutions.

Reading   Greenleaf, the school run by the Misses Donny that Esther Summerson attends, is located near this town in Berkshire. *Bleak House* (3).

Realism   In the broadest sense, realism describes simply the attempt to represent faithfully in a work of literature or art the real world—in other words, to create verisimilitude. In regard to the 19th century, the term more specifically refers to the practice of writers (mainly novelists) who appeared around the middle of the century and called themselves realists— writers like Flaubert and Maupassant in France and George ELIOT and Anthony TROLLOPE in England. By describing the lives of common people as representative of the wider social life, the realists attempted to convince their readers of the truth of their pictures and to create sympathy for the people they wrote about. To these ends, many chose a style and technique that effaced the author or narrator and let the details of setting and story speak for themselves.

From the beginning of his career, well before the appearance of doctrinal realism, Dickens pursued some of the goals of the realists. His concern to accurately represent life in London in the 1830s informed the *Sketches by Boz* and is an important element in the novels. He also chose as subjects of his stories the common urban dwellers favored by the later realists. But in style and technique, Dickens did not subscribe to the canons of realism. His narrator is visibly present in the narrative, and the early works in particular are advertised as the unique work of "the Inimitable Boz." Dickens also

stresses the peculiarities of his characters and the bizarre and surprising turns in his stories, insisting in his prefaces that truth is stranger than fiction. The tendency to heighten reality and to exaggerate the peculiar, uncanny and bizarre are characteristics that Donald FANGER (1965) describes as those of "romantic realists," writers such as Balzac, Gogol, and DOSTOYEVSKY, whose historical position places them in a transitional period between ROMANTICISM and realism. As well as realistic verisimilitude, these writers sought to project a personal myth, creating their particular visions of London, Paris, or St. Petersburg, and, by heightening and intensifying the physical data from the world around them, to impose on it a Manichaean worldview, pitting good against evil, light against darkness, spirit against the material.

By the end of Dickens's career, realism was established as the dominant mode for serious fiction, and his later novels, particularly *Great Expectations,* are more realistic in style and technique; their tone of disillusionment is also characteristic of realistic fiction. John Romano (*Dickens and Reality,* 1978), by stressing these qualities in Dickens's later work, particularly in *Our Mutual Friend,* attempts to shift the balance in Dickens criticism away from its focus on the mythic and romantic to the realistic elements in his work.

"Received, a Blank Child"   Article for *HOUSE-HOLD WORDS* (March 19, 1853) by WILLS and Dickens describing the history and operations of the FOUNDLING HOSPITAL, a model among charitable institutions. *Stone.*

"Red Tape"   Article for *HOUSEHOLD WORDS* (February 15, 1851), attacking "Red Tape—the purpose of whose existence is to tie up public questions, great and small, in an abundance of this official article—to make the neatest possible parcels of them, ticket them, and carefully put them away on a top shelf out of human reach— . . . the peculiar curse and nuisance of England." Using the Window Tax as a prime example of such bureaucratic meddling, Dickens describes the ridiculous regulations defining a window and the disastrous effects of poorly lit and badly ventilated buildings, particularly on the health of the poor. *Miscellaneous.*

Red 'Us   This THAMES-side pub in Battersea was a popular Cockney resort. *Boz,* "River."

Red Whisker   David's rival for the attentions of Dora at her birthday picnic. *Copperfield* (33).

Redburn, Jack   Member of Master Humphrey's circle and a jack of many trades, he acts as "librarian, secretary, steward, and first minister; director-general of all my affairs, and inspector-general of my household" (2). He and the Deaf Gentleman are Master Humphrey's heirs. *Humphrey.*

Redforth, Lt.-Col. Robin   One of the four child authors in "The Holiday Romance." He tells the story of

Captain Boldheart, a pirate who defeats his enemy the Latin-grammar Master and a band of cannibals, and then rescues his sweetheart from a bathing machine at Margate.

Redlaw Protagonist of *Haunted Man*, a professor of chemistry who is visited by a phantom on Christmas Eve. He is a popular teacher and a benevolent man, but his life is darkened by past sorrows. The phantom offers to rid him of these painful memories on the condition that the chemist will also pass this gift on to those he touches. The gift turns out to be a curse, for without the capacity to remember past hurts and sorrows, Redlaw and those he influences lose their compassion, their ability to feel for the troubles of others. Redlaw's power is countered and reversed by Milly Swidger, his "better wisdom," who restores community to those affected by Redlaw by restoring the healing power of memory.

"Reflections of a Lord Mayor" Satirical article for HOUSEHOLD WORDS (November 18, 1854). After a state occasion, the LORD MAYOR of London, alone in his dressing room, addresses himself in his mirror on the question of whether the LORD MAYOR is an obsolete humbug, as a recent commission has claimed, or an important public figure, as members of the upper classes who attend his dinners proclaim. He decides in favor of the latter, goes to bed, and dreams of being made a baronet. *Miscellaneous.*

Reform Bill of 1832 One of the most important legislative actions of the century, the Reform Bill—sometimes referred to as the First Reform Bill to distinguish it from later bills in 1867 and 1884—reapportioned Parliament by reducing the property qualifications for electors, eliminating many pocket boroughs, and creating new electoral districts, particularly in the industrial north of England. At the time, the bill was often viewed as the dividing line between past and present, for it was passed only after much public pressure had forced reluctant members of Parliament to respond to the will of the populace. Furthermore, it unseated the long-standing Tory majority in favor of the reform-minded Whigs, thus opening up the political process for the reforms of the 1830s and '40s. Its passage can be described as the political beginning of the Victorian Age.

Dickens was a parliamentary reporter during the final stages of the effort to secure passage of the bill. Although his sympathies were clearly on the side of the Whig reformers, he did not find the reformed Parliament much more democratic than the old Tory House of Commons. His satires of the Boodles, Coodles, and Doodles who govern (*Bleak House*) or the Veneerings and their compatriots (*Mutual Friend*) suggested that a few powerful families still controlled the reins of power, even after Reform.

"Refreshments for Travellers" The Traveller laments the refreshments for travelers—watery soup, inedible pastries, and "glutinous lumps of gristle and grease, called pork-pie." The waiters at travelers' hotels show little interest in serving their customers and make no effort to accommodate their travel schedules. *Uncommercial* (6). Originally in ALL THE YEAR ROUND (March 24, 1860).

Regent Street Fashionable street connecting Oxford Circus and Picadilly Circus, completed in 1820, following a design by John Nash. Lord Frederick Verisopht has a suite of apartments here. *Nickleby* (10).

Regent's Canal Canal—opened in 1820—connecting Paddington with the THAMES at LIMEHOUSE. Site of the suicide of Watkins Tottle. *Boz*, "Tottle."

Regent's Park Dickens lived near the park at 1 DEVONSHIRE TERRACE during the 1840s. He had furnished lodgings at 3 Hanover Terrace in the spring and summer of 1861.

Religion Dickens's religion has been a topic of considerable controversy. Zealots in his own time accused him of blasphemy, and modern readers have sometimes found his religious sentiments just sentimental piety.

The novels are clear about the religious attitudes and practices that Dickens disliked. He frequently attacked Evangelical (see EVANGELICALISM) and Dissenting pietism: the pious hypocrisies of Stiggins (*Pickwick*), the ranting of Melchisedek Howler (*Dombey*), the oily self-righteousness of Chadband (*Bleak House*). In *Sunday under Three Heads* he attacked the negative Sabbatarianism that blighted the Clennam household (*Dorrit*) and denied innocent Sunday recreation to the poor. He also disliked formalistic religion, criticizing the Puseyites for their emphasis on ritual and Roman Catholicism for its superstitious mummery (*Pictures from Italy*). He blamed the CATHOLIC CHURCH for the deplorable poverty and oppression in the Catholic nations of southern Europe.

Rejecting both the extremes of Dissenting pietism and Catholic or High Anglican formalism, Dickens's religious ideas were closest to those of Broad Church Anglicanism. Although he was drawn to UNITARIANISM for a few years around the time he was working on *Dombey*, he remained orthodox in his belief in Christ's divinity, redemption, and resurrection, themes of central importance in the late novels from *Two Cities* on. He described himself as a New Testament Christian, rejecting the rigid and negative doctrines of Protestant sects that stressed the Old Testament, as the Calvinistic Mrs. Clennam did. In *The Life of Our Lord*, his retelling of the Gospels for his children, he stessed the moral teachings and parables in the New Testament. (See BIBLE.)

Peter ACKROYD (1990) offers a good summary of Dickens's religious views. Dennis WALDER (1981) treats them at greater length, tracing their implications for the novels. Janet L. LARSON (1985) considers Dickens's uses of the Bible. Critics who discuss religious themes in the novels include DYSON (1970), GOLD (1972), and SANDERS (1982).

Religious Hiccoughs The title Dickens gave privately to Chauncy Hare TOWNSHEND's *Religious Opinions* (1868), a volume Dickens edited for publication as Townshend's literary executor.

Repetition Dickens frequently uses stylistic repetition as a way of heightening the effect of his prose or emphasizing particular themes. The repetitions of "fog" in the opening paragraphs of *Bleak House* or the series of antitheses at the beginning of *Two Cities* are well-known examples of stylistic repetitions that introduce important themes. The repetition of the biblical quotation, "I am the resurrection and the life, saith the Lord," at the end of *Two Cities* prepares for Carton's sacrifice and underscores its significance.

Some of Dickens's repetitions were prompted by the serial form in which he worked. Repeating certain character traits or patterns of speech was a way to remind his readers of the identity of a character they might not have seen for several months.

Sylvere MONOD (1967) discusses Dickens's use of repetition. J. Hillis MILLER (*Fiction and Repetition*, 1982) analyzes several novels—though none by Dickens—to show how repetition develops meaning in fiction.

"Report of the Commissioners Appointed to Inquire into the Condition of the Persons variously Engaged in the University of Oxford" Satiric article for *HOUSEHOLD WORDS* (June 3, 1843). In a parody of the parliamentary report on child labor in the mines and factories, Dickens presents a report on the "Manufacture of Clergymen" at Oxford. He reveals the prevailing ignorance, particularly of "such comprehensive words as justice, mercy, charity, kindness, brotherly love, forbearance, gentleness, and Good Works," and attacks the preoccupation with forms of worship and the church hierarchy associated with the Oxford Movement and High Church Anglicanism. *Miscellaneous.*

Reprinted Pieces A collection of 31 of Dickens's essays, sketches, and stories from *HOUSEHOLD WORDS*, first collected into a single volume for the LIBRARY EDITION of Dickens's works in 1858.

Restoration House Elizabethan mansion in ROCHESTER, south of the cathedral, said to be the original of SATIS HOUSE in *Great Expectations*.

"Restoration of Shakespeare's 'Lear' to the Stage, The" Review for the *EXAMINER* (February 4, 1838) of MACREADY's production of *King Lear*, in which he replaced Nahum Tate's standard theatrical version of the play—a version that eliminated the Fool and restored Lear to his throne—with Shakespeare's original text. Dickens discusses the importance of the Fool and the pathos in the deaths of Cordelia and Lear. *Miscellaneous.*

Resurrection Men Grave robbers who, like Jerry Cruncher, dug up the bodies of the recently dead to sell to surgeons and medical students. These "honest tradesmen" were not always as honest as Cruncher makes them out to be. They sometimes obtained their specimens without the arduous task of digging. Dickens uses Cruncher's unusual avocation to parody the resurrection theme in the main story of *Two Cities*, (II:14).

Reynolds, Frank (1876–1953) Painter; illustrator for *PUNCH* and other magazines. Reynolds did colored illustrations for editions of *Pickwick* (1910), *Copperfield* (1911), and *Curiosity Shop* (1913). He produced a series of paintings on Dickensian subjects in 1912–13 that were reproduced as a portfolio of prints and distributed by the Old Black Swan Distillery.

Reynolds, G. W. M. (1814–1879) Popular novelist, editor, radical journalist and Chartist leader, best known for his *Mysteries of London*, an English imitation of Eugène Sue's *Mysteries of Paris*. His plagiaristic *Pickwick Abroad, Or The Tour in France* (1839) continued Dickens's novel by taking Pickwick on a continental grand tour.

Reynolds, Miss One of Miss Twinkleton's pupils at Nuns' House. *Drood* (9).

Riah ("Aaron") "An old Jewish man, in an ancient coat, long of skirt and wide of pocket" (II:5), who is employed by Fascination Fledgeby to carry on his money-lending business, PUBSEY AND CO. Riah befriends Lizzie and finds a job for her in the upriver mill town when she wants to hide from Headstone and Wrayburn. After he breaks with Fledgeby, he and Jenny Wren make a home together. *Mutual Friend*. In part, Riah was Dickens's response to Mrs. Eliza DAVIS's objection to the anti-Semitic stereotyping in the portrayal of Fagin.

Richard (1) Waiter at the SARACEN'S HEAD. *Nickleby* (4).

Richard (2) Meg Veck's fiancé, a blacksmith "with eyes that sparkled like the red-hot drippings from a furnace fire." In Trotty's dream of the future, he has become an unemployed drunk. *Chimes.*

"Richards" The name Dombey assigns to Polly TOODLE when she is working in his household. *Dombey* (2).

Richardson's Show The entertainment at the "heart" of GREENWICH Fair that mixed "a melo-drama (with three murders and a ghost), a PANTOMIME, a comic song, an overture, and some incidental music, all done in five-and-twenty minutes." *Boz*, "Greenwich Fair."

Richmond Town on the Surrey side of the THAMES, west of London, where Tupman settles down after the perigrinations of the Pickwick Club have ended (*Pickwick*, 57). Estella stays here at the home of Mrs. Brandley when she is coming out in London (*Expectations*, 33, 38).

Rickitts, Miss Pupil at Miss Twinkleton's school, "a junior of weakly consitution" (13). *Drood.*

Riderhood, Roger ("Rogue") A THAMES waterman, formerly Gaffer Hexam's partner; he has a "squinting leer" and fumbles at his "old sodden fur cap" as he speaks: "I am a man as gets my living and seeks to get my living by the sweat of my brow" (II:12). He attempts to implicate Hexam in Harmon's murder in order to claim the reward offered by Boffin (I:12), but Rokesmith makes him sign a confession confirming his own involvement in the murder (II:12). After he miraculously escapes from drowning (III:2), he takes a position as a lockkeeper at PLASHWATER WEIR MILL LOCK (IV:1) where he becomes aware of Headstone's attempt to murder Wrayburn. His scheme to blackmail Headstone leads to a struggle at the lock in which the two men drown together (IV:15). His daughter, **Pleasant**, an unlicensed pawnbroker and proprietor of a leaving shop in LIMEHOUSE Hole, is the object of Mr. Venus's frustrated affections. In the end she overcomes her aversion to Venus's business and marries him. *Mutual Friend.*

Rigaud (alias Blandois, alias Lagnier) Murderer and blackmailer, "a cosmopolitan gentleman. . . . He had a certain air of being a handsome man, which he was not; and a certain air of being a well-bred man, which he was not; it was mere swagger and challenge" (I:1). He is imprisoned in MARSEILLES for murdering his wife (I:1), but he is released and leaves France. In ITALY he attaches himself to the Gowans (II:1). After he obtains documents implicating Mrs. Clennam in the suppression of her uncle's will, he attempts to blackmail her, but his attempts are foiled when Mrs. Clennam's house collapses on him (II:33). *Dorrit.*

"River, The" Sketch which originally appeared in the *EVENING CHRONICLE* (June 6, 1835) as "Sketches of London No. 13." It describes boating parties on the THAMES, always marked by some misery or other, and a steam excursion to GRAVESEND. *Boz.*

"Rinaldo di Velasco" Stage name of the giant PICKLESON. "Marigold."

"Rob the Grinder" Nickname of Robin TOODLE, derived from his attendance at the school of the CHARITABLE GRINDERS. *Dombey.*

Robert Servant to John, twin brother to James in the German Courtier's tale. *Reprinted*, "At Dusk."

Robert, Uncle and Aunt Jane Guests at Christmas dinner. *Boz*, "Christmas Dinner."

"Robert Keeley" Tribute to the actor Robert KEELEY after his death, in *ALL THE YEAR ROUND* (April 10, 1869), by Dickens and Herman Merivale. Dickens describes Keeley as a comedian who was also a "master of pathos" and he discusses in particular his performances as Dogberry and Verges in *Much Ado about Nothing*, and Dolly Spanker in Dion BOUCICAULT's *London Assurance*. Uncollected.

Robinson (1) "A gentleman in a public office, with a good salary and a little property of his own" who courts the four Miss Willises in order to marry the youngest of them. *Boz*, "Four Sisters."

Robinson (2) Mrs. Tibbs's maidservant. *Boz*, "Boarding House."

Robinson (3) Clerk in Dombey's counting house. *Dombey* (51).

Roche, Louis (d. 1849) French native who was Dickens's "Brave courtier" on his trips to ITALY in 1844 and to SWITZERLAND in 1846, "a most faithful, affectionate, and devoted man."

Rochester Sister town to CHATHAM, in KENT, where Dickens spent the happiest and most memorable years of his childhood between 1817 and 1822. GAD'S HILL

Victorian engraving of the view across the Medway to Rochester.

PLACE, the house that Dickens purchased in 1856 and occupied from 1860 until the end of his life, is two miles outside of town on the GRAVESEND Road. Rochester is a major setting in several of the novels: The BULL INN is the first stop on the travels of the Pickwickians (*Pickwick*, 2–4); it is the market town in *Great Expectations* where SATIS HOUSE and Pumblechook's shop are located; it is CLOISTERHAM in *Drood*. It is also the setting of "Seven Poor Travellers" and the original of Winglebury (*Boz*, "Winglebury") and Dullborough (*Uncommercial*, 12).

Rockingham Castle   Castle in Northamptonshire, home of Dickens's friend Richard WATSON and his family, which he visited several times, in 1847, 1849, and 1852, and used as the original of CHESNEY WOLD in *Bleak House*.

Rodolph, Mr. and Mrs. Jennings   Singers who perform at the wedding dinner of Miss Martin's friend to the journeyman painter: "To hear them sing separately was divine, but when they went through the tragic duet of 'Red Ruffian, retire!' it was, as Miss Martin afterwards remarked, 'thrilling.' " *Boz*, "Milliner."

Rogers (1)   The parlor orator: "he was smoking a cigar, with his eyes fixed on the ceiling, and had that confident oracular air which marked him as the leading politician, general authority, and universal anecdote-relater, of the place." *Boz*, "Orator."

Rogers (2)   London constable. *Reprinted*, "Inspector Field."

Rogers (3)   Third mate of the *Halsewell*. *Reprinted*, "Long Voyage."

Rogers, Johnny   Workhouse inmate. *Reprinted*, "Workhouse."

Rogers, Miss   Subject of one of Mrs. Nickleby's uncertain recollections. *Nickleby* (37).

Rogers, Mrs.   Mrs. Bardell's genteel lodger. *Pickwick* (46).

Roker, Tom   The turnkey who arranges Mr. Pickwick's rooms at the FLEET PRISON. *Pickwick* (40–44).

Rokesmith, John   Pseudonym taken by John HARMON while he serves as Boffin's secretary and into the initial year of his marriage, before his true identity is revealed. *Mutual Friend*.

Rolland   Junior partner of Defresnier et Cie. who writes to Vendale concerning a forged receipt. "No Thoroughfare."

Rolls Yard   A spot in SYMOND'S INN off CHANCERY LANE where Mr. Snagsby "loved to lounge about of a Sunday afternoon" (10). *Bleak House*.

Roman Bath   The bath off the STRAND where David Copperfield has "had many a cold plunge" and to which he goes after learning of his Aunt Betsy's bankruptcy. *Copperfield* (35).

"Romance"   Song sung by Sam Weller to the coachmen gathered in the tavern opposite the Insolvent Court in Portugal Street. *Pickwick* (43). The song has been set to music by Sir Frederick Bridge.

Romanticism   A movement in literature, the arts, philosophy, and politics of the late 18th and early 19th centuries that revolted against neoclassical formalism, objectivity, and established rules and conventions, celebrating instead subjectivity, imagination, and spiritual freedom. Living when he did, Dickens was profoundly influenced by romanticism and was, in many ways, a romantic himself. The romantic writers who most influenced him were not the poets, but rather the prose essayists—Lamb, De Quincey, and, especially, CARLYLE.

Dickens's romanticism is probably most evident in his interest in personal growth and his belief in subjectivity and imagination. The importance of memory in David Copperfield's personal history or in Pip's inner awareness of his bad faith with himself and Joe (*Expectations*) makes these first-person narratives personal histories of the mental and emotional growth of their narrators. Like his romantic predecessors who sought the child in the man, Dickens, as Peter Coveny (*Poor Monkey, the Child in Literature*, 1957) points out, was "the central figure in the transference of the romantic child into Victorian literature." His heroes, like David Copperfield, Arthur Clennam, and Pip, are shaped in childhood, while child victims like Oliver Twist and Paul Dombey represent different versions of Wordsworth's "prison house" closing in on the growing boy.

For Dickens, as for the romantics, imagination provided the power to enable the child—or the man—to survive in the world. He attacked the schools of hard facts, the UTILITARIANISM and literalism that stunted fancy and nurtured only material self-interest. He celebrated the power of imagination to create the self and to change the world. Garrett STEWART (1974) discusses at length the role of imagination in Dickens's work.

Dickens did not accept all of the romantic assumptions. His celebrations of nature are, for the most part, perfunctory. He was a creature of the city; his values and perceptions were urban, not pastoral. The common people whose language he adopted were city dwellers. He did not accept romantic primitivism and usually found little nobility among savages. Although he wrote ghost stories, was interested in bizarre and mysterious events, and practiced MESMERISM, Dickens was fundamentally a rationalist about such issues. He rejected most supernatural explanations as superstition. Similarly, he rejected the romantic celebration of the past, especially the MEDIEVALISM of the Pre-Raphaelites (see PRE-RAPHAELITE ART) and others.

Donald Stone (*The Romantic Impulse in Victorian Fiction*, 1980) includes Dickens among the novelists it treats. Stewart (1974) offers the most sustained and provocative analysis of the romantic core in Dickens's works. Dirk den Hartog (*Dickens and Romantic Psychology*, 1987) discusses the influence of Wordsworth and other romantics on Dickens's ideas about the self.

Rome Dickens's account of his trip to Rome appears in *Pictures* (11). The Dorrit family's journey to Italy ends in Rome, where both Frederick and William die. (*Dorrit*, II:19).

Rookery, The The name of the house where David Copperfield was born, the choice of David's father even though the nests had long been deserted. *Copperfield* (1).

Rookery of St. Giles One of the most notorious slums in London in the 1830s and 1840s, much of the Rookery was cleared during the construction of new OX-FORD STREET in 1844–45. Dickens describes "the filth and miserable appearance of this part of London" in *Boz*, "Gin-Shops," and again in *Reprinted*, "Inspector Field." The Rookery has sometimes been suggested as the original of TOM-ALL-ALONE'S in *Bleak House*.

Rosa "Dark-eyed, dark-haired, shy village beauty" who shows visitors around CHESNEY WOLD and attracts the attentions of Watt Rouncewell. When Lady Dedlock chooses Rosa for her personal maid, she arouses the jealous anger of Hortense (12). When Tulkinghorn uncovers the truth about Lady Dedlock's past, she sends Rosa away to the Rouncewells (48), where she marries Watt (63). *Bleak House*.

Rose (1) Fiancée of a struggling young doctor. *Boz*, "Black Veil."

Rose (2) Lucy Benson's cousin, one of the *Village Coquettes*.

Ross, Frank Friend of Gabriel Parsons. *Boz*, "Tottle."

Rouncewell Family Family that illustrates the ways in which the social changes brought about by the IN-DUSTRIAL REVOLUTION affected the servants of the landed ARISTOCRACY. **Mrs. Rouncewell**, housekeeper at CHESNEY WOLD, is "a fine old lady, handsome, stately, wonderfully neat. . . . It is the next difficult thing to an impossibility to imagine Chesney Wold without Mrs. Rouncewell, but she has only been here fifty years" (7). Her older son has moved away and become an **iron-master**; he "would have been provided for at Chesney Wold, and would have been made steward in good season; but he took . . . to constructing steam-engines" (7). He runs for Parliament and defeats Dedlock's candidate (28). His son **Watt** falls in love with Rosa, Lady Dedlock's maid, and eventually marries her. Mrs. Rouncewell's younger son, **George** (**Mr. George**, **Trooper George**), ran away to the army and cut himself off from his mother. After leaving the army he opened a shooting gallery near LEICESTER SQUARE. Tulkinghorn and Grandfather Smallweed, who has loaned George money, pressure the Trooper to turn over to them a sample of Captain Hawdon's writing (34). George is arrested for Tulkinghorn's murder (49), but his friends the Bagnets help to clear his name and reunite him with his mother (56). He returns to Chesney Wold and becomes Sir Leicester's attendant (63). *Bleak House*.

"Round of Stories by the Christmas Fire, A"
The extra Christmas number of *HOUSEHOLD WORDS*, 1852. Dickens contributed two stories: "The Poor Relations' Story" and "A Child's Story." Among the other contributors were Elizabeth GASKELL and Harriet MARTINEAU.

Royal Charter Ship bound from Melbourne to LIVERPOOL that was wrecked off Llanallgo, Anglesey, Wales, on October 26, 1959. *Uncommercial* (2).

Royal East London Volunteers Gabriel Varden's militia. *Rudge* (41–42).

Royal Exchange ('Change) Dickens describes wandering in the CITY of London as a child: "I found myself on 'Change, and saw the shabby people sitting under placards about ships. I settled that they were misers, who had embarked all their wealth to go and buy gold dust or something of that sort, and were waiting for their respective captains to come and tell them they were ready to set sail" *Miscellaneous*, "Gone Astray." These shabby figures outside the Exchange reappear in several of the works: *Boz*, "Shabby-genteel People"; *Curiosity Shop* (4); and *Expectations* (22). Located at CORNHILL and THREADNEEDLE STREET, the old Exchange burned in 1838 and was rebuilt in 1842. In Dickens's time it served as a center for trading activity.

Royal George Hotel Inn at DOVER where Mr. Lorry meets Lucie Manette on their way to PARIS to retrieve her father. *Two Cities* (I:4).

Royal Literary Fund A charity devoted to providing aid to impoverished authors and their families. Dickens was active in the organization for many years. During the late 1850s, he, John FORSTER, and Charles Dilke spearheaded a movement to reform the institution, which they claimed spent too much money on administrative expenses and played favorites in choosing beneficiaries. Their demands for changes, however, were largely unsuccessful.

Roylance, Elizabeth The "reduced old lady" with whom Dickens had lodgings while the rest of his family was in the MARSHALSEA PRISON in 1824. She served as the model for Mrs. Pipchin in *Dombey*.

Rudge, Barnaby Simple-minded young man who wanders the countryside between CHIGWELL and London with his pet raven, Grip. "He was about three-and-twenty years old, and though rather spare, of a fair height and strong make. His hair, of which he had a great profusion, was red, and hanging in disorder about his face and shoulders, gave to his restless looks an expression quite unearthly. . . . His dress was of green, clumsily trimmed here and there . . . with gaudy lace" (3). Born the day after his father's disappearance and supposed murder, Barnaby is raised by his mother, **Mary**, who devotes herself to her son, protecting him from his father, **Barnaby Rudge, Sr.**, who went into hiding after murdering Reuben Haredale. The elder Rudge bedevils his wife by pursuing her and demanding money from her until he is finally caught by Geoffrey Haredale, imprisoned in NEWGATE, and executed. Young Barnaby, over his mother's objections and protests, joins the No Popery movement (48), is allied with Hugh and Dennis, and is arrested and sentenced to hang (58). He is saved from execution through the efforts of Gabriel Varden and Geoffrey Haredale (79). *Rudge*.

"Ruffian, The" The Traveller complains that ruffians are taking over the streets because the police tolerate them. As a result of this "constable contemplation," street crime is increasing. The Traveller describes his efforts to have a young woman arrested for using bad language in public and the difficulty he had convincing various authorities that he was seriously pressing charges. *Uncommercial* (30). Originally in *All the Year Round* (October 10, 1868).

Rugg Pancks's landlord, a debt collector and accountant who aids in the investigation that leads to the discovery of the Dorrit fortune. He takes care of Clennam's financial affairs when Arthur is imprisoned for debt (II: 26). His middle-aged daughter **Anastasia** lives on the proceeds of a successful breach-of-promise suit against a baker named Hawkins (I:25). *Dorrit*.

Rummun, Professor Member of the Mudfog Association. *Mudfog*.

"Rumty" Nickname of R. W. WILFER. *Mutual Friend*.

Russell, Lord John (1792–1878) Whig (later Liberal) politician; one of the architects of the REFORM BILL OF 1832; Prime Minister (1846–52; 1865–66). Dickens admired Russell and was, according to Russell's daughter, "a very great friend, and was always very welcome at any time."

Russia Cunard steamship on which the Traveller sails from NEW YORK to LIVERPOOL. *Uncommercial* (21).

Russian Prince, The One of Miss Mowcher's clients. *Copperfield* (22).

Sackville Street Fashionable street off PICCADILLY where Alfred Lammle lives. *Mutual Friend* (I:10).

Sadleir, John (1814–1856) Irish member of Parliament, banker, and swindler. When his financial schemes collapsed in 1856, while Dickens was working on *Dorrit*, he killed himself and became the unwitting model for Merdle.

Saffron Hill Street in HOLBORN, between Leather Lane and Farringdon Road, which was a notorious criminal district until 1867, when the area was altered by the construction of the Holborn Viaduct. Fagin's den of thieves is located here (*Twist*), and Phil Squod has worked here as a tinker (*Bleak House*, 26).

Saggers, Mrs. Second oldest inmate at Titbull's Alms-Houses. She irritates the other residents by leaving a pail outside her door. *Uncommercial* (29).

St. Albans Old Roman town in Hertfordshire where Dickens locates Jarndyce's Bleak House (6). Bill Sikes passes through the town when he is running from the murder of Nancy (*Twist*, 48).

St. Andrew's Church designed by Sir Christopher Wren in 1686, located near the HOLBORN Viaduct. On the way to the CHERTSEY robbery, Sikes notes the time on St. Andrew's clock as he and Oliver pass by (*Twist*, 21). Snagsby's partner Peffer is buried in the churchyard (*Bleak House*, 10).

St. Antoine Poor district near the BASTILLE, in PARIS, where DeFarge's wineshop is located. Many in the mob of revolutionaries are recruited from the hungry and unemployed people who live here. *Two Cities*.

St. Bartholomew's Hospital (Bartholomew's) Hospital in SMITHFIELD in the CITY where Jack Hopkins studies surgery with Doctor Slasher (*Pickwick*, 32) and Betsey Prig works as an occasional nurse (*Chuzzlewit*, 49). Arthur Clennam takes Cavalletto to Bartholomew's after he is injured in the street (*Dorrit*, I:13).

St. Clement Dane's Church in the STRAND where Mrs. Lirriper was married. "Lirriper's Lodgings."

St. Clement's, Ipswich Church next to the Nupkins' residence. Sam Weller meets Job Trotter in the churchyard (*Pickwick*, 23).

St. Dunstan's Church in FLEET STREET, also known as St. Dunstan's-in-the-West. The old church, torn down in 1831, was one of the sights of London. Its clock had a large gilt dial with two figures that struck the hours on a bell. As a child wandering in the CITY, Dickens stopped to watch "those obliging monsters strike upon the bells" (*Miscellaneous*, "Gone Astray"). Maypole Hugh also watches the figures (*Rudge*, 40), as do David and his aunt (*Copperfield*, 23). The new church, designed by John Shaw in 1831, is the church of *The Chimes* where Trotty Veck keeps his post.

St. Evrémonde Three men qualify for the title of **Marquis de St. Evrémonde** during the course of *Two Cities*. Charles Darnay's father, the elder of twins, first holds the title. He abuses the peasants on his estate and aids his younger brother's scheme to abduct and rape the daughter of one of their tenants. When the girl's brother attempts to defend his sister's honor, he is wounded by the younger twin and Dr. Manette is called in to tend the brother and sister, but both of the peasants die, the boy from his wound, the girl from brain fever (III:10). When the doctor later attempts to publicize the crimes of the St. Evrémondes, they have him imprisoned in the Bastille (III:10). After the death of the first Marquis, Charles's father, the younger twin, his uncle, becomes Marquis. A tyrant "with a face like a fine mask, . . . very slightly pinched at the top of each nostril," he is murdered in his sleep after his carriage runs over a child in the streets of Paris (II:7–8). Although Charles Darnay renounces the title, he is tried and convicted by the revolutionary court as an emigre and as the current Marquis de St. Evrémonde (III:9–10). *Two Cities*.

St. George's, Bloomsbury Site of the christening of the Kitterbell baby. *Boz*, "Christening."

St. George's, Southwark Church adjoining the MARSHALSEA, where Little Dorrit was christened and married. *Dorrit*, (I:6, II:34).

St. George's Fields Area on the south side of the THAMES around the OBELISK, which was open fields up until the beginning of the 19th century. The Gordon

343

rioters gathered here when they came to London to petition Parliament (*Rudge*, 48).

St. Giles Church at the center of a notorious slum area in London that included the ROOKERY and SEVEN DIALS, places that Dickens visited when touring the underworld with INSPECTOR FIELD (*Reprinted*, "Inspector Field"). Fascinated with the area and its criminal population, Dickens also describes it in *Boz* ("Seven Dials"). Sampson and Sally Brass are banished to St. Giles (*Curiosity Shop*, 73).

St. James's Christopher Wren church in PICCADILLY where the Lammles are married. *Mutual Friend*, (I:10).

St. James's Park Royal park south of the Mall, next to Buckingham Palace. Brooker confronts Ralph Nickleby in the park during a rainstorm (*Nickleby*, 44). Martin Chuzzlewit bids farewell to Mary Graham here as he prepares to set out for America (*Chuzzlewit*, 14). Meagles, Doyce, and Arthur Clennam discuss their troubles with the Circumlocution Office at a meeting in the park (*Dorrit*, I:10). Sally Brass is rumored to have "enlisted as a private in the second regiment of the Foot Guards and . . . been seen in uniform, and on duty, to wit, leaning on her musket and looking out of a sentry-box in St. James's Park" (*Curiosity Shop*, 73).

St. James's Square Fashionable square off PALL MALL, near St. James's Palace. The Gordon rioters threw valuables, including the keys to NEWGATE PRISON into the pond in the center of the square (*Rudge*, 70). Twemlow "devoted many anxious hours . . . in the cold gloom, favorable to meditation, of St. James's Square" trying to figure out his relationship with Veneering (*Mutual Friend*, I:2).

St. James's Street In this street in central London, off ST. JAMES'S SQUARE, the narrator of "To Be Taken with a Grain of Salt" has his lodgings (*Marigold*, 2); Josiah Bounderby stays in a hotel here (*Hard Times*, III: 3); "Our Bore" meets William the Fourth while walking here (*Reprinted*).

St. James's Theatre Theater on ST. JAMES'S SQUARE, where many of the plays Dickens wrote as a young man were produced. In 1836 *The Strange Gentleman* opened the season on September 29; *The Village Coquettes* opened on December 9. In 1837 *Is She His Wife?* opened on March 6.

St. Julien, Horatio Jem Larkins's stage name. *Boz*, "Private Theatres."

St. Louis, Missouri Dickens describes the French influence in the town and wonders about the climate: "I think it must rather dispose to fever, in the summer and autumnal seasons. . . . It is very hot, lies among great rivers, and has vast tracts of undrained swampy land around it" (*Notes*, 12).

St. Luke's, Chelsea Church where Dickens married Catherine HOGARTH on April 2, 1836.

St. Luke's Workhouse Located opposite the EAGLE INN in the CITY ROAD, the workhouse is the home of "the Orfling," the little servant girl who works for the Micawbers when they are in WINDSOR TERRACE. *Copperfield* (11).

St. Mark's In his "Italian Dream" of VENICE in *Pictures*, Dickens describes the cathedral as "A grand and dreamy structure, of immense proportions; golden with old mosaics; redolent of perfumes; dim with the smoke of incense; costly in treasure of precious stones and metals, glittering through iron bars; holy with the bodies of deceased saints; rainbow-hued with windows of stained glass; dark with carved woods and coloured marbles; obscure in its vast heights, and lengthened distances; shining with silver lamps and winking lights; unreal, fantastic, solemn, inconceivable throughout." "An Italian Dream."

St. Martin's-in-the-Fields On the steps of this church on TRAFALGAR SQUARE, the Traveller is surprised on one of his night walks by "a beetle-browed hair-lipped youth of twenty, and it had a loose bundle of rags on, which it held together with one of its hands." When the Traveller reaches out to touch him on the shoulder, "it twisted out of its garment . . . and left me standing alone with its rags in my hands" (*Uncommercial*, 13). David meets Daniel Peggotty on the steps of the church when the fisherman is searching for his runaway niece (*Copperfield*, 40). Earlier, David describes a pudding shop behind the church where he purchased currant puddings when he was working at MURDSTONE AND GRINBY (*Copperfield*, 11).

St. Mary Axe The area in the CITY of London where Fledgeby has the office of PUBSEY AND CO. Here Riah has the roof garden visited by Lizzie Hexam and Jenny Wren. *Mutual Friend*, (II:5).

St. Mary-le-Strand Eighteenth-century church by James Gibbs in the STRAND where John DICKENS and Elizabeth BARROW were married in 1807. He was a clerk in nearby SOMERSET HOUSE at the time.

St. Olave's, Hart Street Church in "the heart of the CITY," described by the Traveller as "Saint Ghastly Grim" because of the skulls that decorate the churchyard gate. *Uncommercial* (23).

St. Pancras The clock on the new St. Pancras church, erected in 1819–22, informs Mrs. Tibbs of the time (*Boz*, "Boarding House"). Roger Cly is buried in the churchyard of the old church, in which Jerry Cruncher goes on his "fishing" expedition (*Two Cities*, II:14).

St. Paul's Cathedral Main London cathedral, rebuilt after the Great Fire by Sir Christopher Wren in 1697. This London landmark is mentioned frequently in the novels. On one of its more notable appearances, it prompts John Browdie's remark, "Ecod, he be a soizable 'un be he" (*Nickleby*, 39). Lord George Gordon stops at the church on his way into London (*Rudge*, 37). Captain Cuttle, when he prepares the bower at the top of the Wooden Midshipman for Florence, tells her, "You're as safe here as if you was at the top of St. Paul's Cathedral, with the ladder cast off" (*Dombey*, 48). David Copperfield takes Peggotty to visit the cathedral, but she finds it does not compare in all particulars with the picture of the building on the lid of her workbox (*Copperfield*, 33). The cathedral is also mentioned in *Boz*, "Shops and Their Tenants"; *Twist* (18); *Nickleby* (3, 45); *Chuzzlewit* (38); *Copperfield* (23); *Bleak House* (19); *Dorrit* (I:3, II:34); *Mutual Friend* (I:8).

St. Peter's In the churchyard of this church in CORN-HILL, Bradley Headstone makes his impassioned proposal to Lizzie Hexam. *Mutual Friend* (II:15).

St. Peter's Basilica Although Dickens appreciated the beauty and majesty of St. Peter's Basilica in ROME, he was put off by some of the decoration: "the pillars of stately marble were swathed in some impertinent frippery of red and yellow," which had the effect of making the building look like "the opening scenes in a very lavish pantomime." He found "a much greater sense of mystery and wonder, in the Cathedral of San Mark at Venice." *Pictures*, "Rome."

Sala, George Augustus (1828–1896) Journalist and novelist; frequent contributor to HOUSEHOLD WORDS and ALL THE YEAR ROUND, whose work in these magazines was sometimes mistaken for that of Dickens; one of the most conspicuous of "Dickens's young men" who followed and imitated the novelist. Son of an actress who played in some of Dickens's AMATEUR THEATRICALS, he pleased the novelist with his conscientiousness and earnestness. He served for many years as a special correspondent for the London *Daily Telegraph*. Dickens sent him to Russia following the Crimean War as a special correspondent for *Household Words*, but the two quarrelled about the resulting articles and their friendship was broken off between 1856 and 1858. In his writings about Dickens in his autobiography, his memoir of Dickens (1870), and in *Things I Have Known* (1894), Sala credits the novelist's "friendship and encouragement" with making him a journalist and writer of books.

Salcy, the Family P. Theatrical family whose performance the Traveller attends in a French-Flemish town. "The members of the Family P. Salcy were so fat and so like one another—fathers, mothers, sisters, brothers, uncles, and aunts—that I think the local audience were much confused about the plot of the piece under representation." *Uncommercial*, 27.

Salem House Mr. Creakle's school in BLACKHEATH where Murdstone sends David Copperfield and where David meets Steerforth. *Copperfield* (5–7, 9, 13). It is based on WELLINGTON HOUSE ACADEMY.

Salisbury Wiltshire cathedral town near the village where Pecksniff lives. Tom Pinch, who considers Salisbury "a very desperate sort of place; an exceeding wild and dissipated city" (5), meets Martin Chuzzlewit there. He and Martin go to dinner at the best restaurant in town as the guests of John Westlock (12). *Chuzzlewit*.

Sally (1) Uncle Bill's niece. He teases her about keeping company with a young man. *Boz*, "London Recreations."

Sally (2) Workhouse inmate who assists at the delivery of Oliver Twist and steals the locket and ring from Oliver's dead mother. *Twist*, (1, 23, 24).

Sally (3) Compeyson's wife. *Expectations* (42).

Sam (1) Pecksniff's groom. *Chuzzlewit* (5).

Sam (2) Cab driver who resents Pickwick's questions, suspecting that he is a spy. *Pickwick* (2).

Samba, Quanko Attendant to Colonel Blazo, who finally bowls out Jingle in a West Indian cricket match: "Quanko Samba—last man left—sun so hot, but in blisters—ball scorched brown—five hundred and seventy runs—rather exhausted—Quanko mustered up last remaining strength—bowled me out." *Pickwick* (7).

Sampson Insurance man who narrates "Hunted Down," the story of Julius Slinkton, a poisoner who murders his victims for the insurance money.

Sampson, George Young man who is disappointed in his love for Bella Wilfer and transfers his affections to her sister Lavinia. "He put the round head of his cane in his mouth, like a stopper, when he sat down. As if he felt himself full to the throat with affecting sentiments" (I:9). *Mutual Friend*.

Sand, George (1804–1876) Penname of **Amandine Lucile Aurore Dupin**. French novelist, feminist, and radical; she advocated free love and was famous in her own time for her many love affairs, most memorably with the Polish composer and pianist Frederic Chopin. Dickens met her in 1860 in Paris and described her in a letter to WILLS as "a chubby, matronly, swarthy, black-eyed" woman, "whom you might suppose to be the Queen's monthly nurse," with "nothing of the bluestocking about her, except a little final way of settling all your opinions with hers."

Sanders, Andrew (1946–) Professor, Birkbeck College, University of London; scholar and editor of Victorian fiction; editor of *The DICKENSIAN, 1978–86. His* *wide-ranging survey, The Victorian Historical Novel 1840–1880* (1979), discusses *Rudge* and *Two Cities*, along with works by other novelists, major and minor. His *Companion to "A Tale of Two Cities"* (1989) provides a useful introduction to the text and backgrounds of that novel. In *Charles Dickens Resurrectionist* (1982), Sanders considers Dickens's personal religious beliefs about death and resurrection and analyzes the deaths in the novels as they embody these beliefs.

Sanders, Susannah Mrs. Bardell's friend, "a big, fat, heavy-faced personage," who testifies at the trial that her husband had often called her "duck" but never "tomata sauce." *Pickwick* (26, 34).

Sandling Village in near MAIDSTONE in KENT, generally thought to be the original of DINGLEY DELL in *Pickwick*.

Sanitary Reform Under this general rubric, a number of related reform issues were brought together: slum living conditions, water supplies and the handling of sewage, overcrowded living conditions, the ventilation of houses, and the diseases caused by these environmental conditions, especially cholera, typhus, and small pox. The leading reformer on these issues was Edwin Chadwick, whose *Report on the Sanitary Condition of the Labouring Population* (1842) prompted debate and legislative action, especially the Public Health Act of 1848. However, this bill was seriously flawed, for it excluded London from its provisions and hence sparked even more intense activity on the part of the reformers. In a speech to the Metropolitan Sanitary Association in 1850, an organization devoted to extending the provisions of the law to include London, Dickens said that the act was even worse than the tragedy of *Hamlet* with Hamlet left out: "the existence of a Public Health Act with the metropolis excluded from its operation suggested . . . the representation of *Hamlet* with nothing in it but the gravedigger."

HOUSEHOLD WORDS, begun during the years of intense debate to have London included in the act, crusaded on issues of sanitary reform, running numerous articles on various aspects of the topic. In an 1849 Preface to *Chuzzlewit*, Dickens wrote: "In all my writings I hope I have taken every possible opportunity of showing the want of sanitary improvements in the neglected dwellings of the poor." From Boz's descriptions of slum conditions to the hovels in the LIMEHOUSE of *Mutual Friend*, Dickens exposed the unhealthy sanitary conditions and disease in poor neighborhoods. His most focused attack appears in *Bleak House* in his description of TOM-ALL-ALONE'S and the disease carried by Jo from the inner city out to the suburbs.

Sapsea, Thomas Pompous and bombastic auctioneer and mayor of Cloisterham; "the purest Jackass in Cloisterham. . . . He possesses the great qualities of being portentous and dull, and of having a roll in his speech,

and another roll in his gait" (4). He hires Durdles to carve his epitaph to his late wife, **Ethelinda Brobity Sapsea**, which celebrates her appreciation of his importance (4). *Drood.*

Saracen's Head Coaching inn next to St. Sepulchre's Church, "just at that particular part of SNOW HILL where omnibus horses going eastward seriously think of falling down on purpose, and where horses in hackney cabriolets going westward not unfrequently fall by accident" (4). A terminal for coaches going north to YORKSHIRE, this inn served as Squeers's London headquarters. *Nickleby.*

Sarah Servant to the old lady in Our Parish. *Boz,* "Curate."

Satire Although there is a good deal of incidental satire in Dickens's novels and journalistic essays, he is not usually thought of as a satirist. His satire does not criticize its targets as irrational, a common satiric point of view, but rather as inhumane. He attacks rationalists, like the "philosophers" who know all about the poor but have no sympathy for their condition. Dickens's alternative to the rationalism of the utilitarians (see UTILITARIANISM) was a deep-felt concern for one's fellow man.

Sustained satires in the novels include the attack on proponents of POLITICAL ECONOMY, the "philosophers" of the POOR LAW in *Twist* and the hard-facts school in *Hard Times*; the satire of American greed and selfishness (*Chuzzlewit*), a journey that reads like the fifth voyage of Gulliver; and the attacks on CHANCERY (*Bleak House*), government red tape and aristocratic privilege in the CIRCUMLOCUTION OFFICE (*Dorrit*), and the pretentious Podsnappery and philistinism of the nouveaux riche (*Mutual Friend*). He satirized many of the same social ills in articles for *HOUSEHOLD WORDS* and *ALL THE YEAR ROUND,* especially the failure of government to address the needs of the poor. J. B. PRIESTLEY characterized the satiric Dickens in a speech to the DICKENS FELLOWSHIP in 1970: "Dickens is, in a way, the boy who saw the Emperor was not wearing any new clothes and that is why you find Dickens's enemies are the pillars of the Establishment, particularly the legal pillars, and senior academics, and all those who have been surrounding themselves for years by a cocoon of humbug and cant and pretense. Dickens went clean through that to the heart of the matter."

The standard work on *Dickens as Satirist* is by Sylvia MANNING (1971).

Satis House Miss Havisham's decaying mansion. The name, taken from a house in ROCHESTER, derives from the Latin for "enough." Estella explains the name to Pip as signifying "whoever had this house could want nothing else" (*Expectations*, 8). The house itself is based on another mansion in Rochester, Restoration House, where Charles II spent a night when returning to London from exile in France.

Saturday Review, The Conservative weekly review of "Politics, Literature, Science and Art," established by A. J. Beresford-Hope in 1855. Its anonymous reviews of fiction were often harsh, especially Fitzjames Stephen's reviews of Dickens. He attacked Dickens as a purveyor of "light literature" and was particularly offended by Dickens's satire of the CIRCUMLOCUTION OFFICE. Reviewing *Dorrit*, Stephen wrote: "The production among such readers [who will think little, and cultivate themselves still less] of false impressions of the system of which they form a part—especially if the falsehood tends to render them discontented with and disaffected to the institutions under which they live—cannot but be a serious evil, and must often involve great moral deliquency."

Saunders Bachelor friend of the Whifflers, the Couple who Dote Upon their Children; "whatever the attention of Mr. Saunders is called to, Mr. Sauders admires of course." *Young Couples.*

Sawyer Drunken baker who abuses his wife and then, when his son objects, murders the boy by boiling him in a laundry copper. *Mudfog*, "Bolton."

Sawyer, Bob Medical student at GUY'S HOSPITAL and bosom friend of Benjamin Allen. He has "that sort of slovenly smartness and swaggering gait, which is peculiar to young gentlemen who smoke in the streets by day, shout and scream in the same by night, call waiters by their Christian names, and do various other acts and deeds of an equally facetious description." He holds a bachelor party in his rooms in LANT STREET, the party is disrupted by his landlady, Mrs. Raddle, who is angry because he has not paid his rent (32). After finishing medical school, he buys the practice of Nockemorf at BRISTOL, where he desultorily and unsuccessfully follows his profession (38–39). Although Benjamin Allen plans to marry his sister Arabella to Bob, Winkle marries her first (50). In the end, Bob and Ben go to Bengal to start life afresh (57). *Pickwick.*

Saxby, Long A tall friend—"six foot ten"—of Cousin Feenix. *Dombey* (51).

Scadder, Zephaniah Duplicitous agent for the Eden Valley Land Company who sells Martin property in the development. The two sides of his face present totally different profiles: "Two grey eyes lurked deep within this agent's head, but one of them had no sight in it, and stood stock still. With that side of his face he seemed to listen to what the other side was doing. Thus each profile had a distant expression; and when the movable side was most in action, the rigid one was in its coldest state of watchfulness" (21). *Chuzzlewit.*

Scadgers, Lady Mrs. Sparsit's great aunt, "an immensely fat old woman, with an inordinate appetite for butcher's meat, and a mysterious leg which had now refused to get out of bed for fourteen years" (I:7). *Hard Times.*

Scaley One of the bailiffs who takes possession of Madame Mantilini's establishment. *Nickleby* (21).

Scarborough Seaside resort in YORKSHIRE where Meltham pursues Slinkton. "Hunted Down."

Scarton, Charley Actor in one of the private theaters who "is to take the part of an English sailor, and fight a broadsword combat with six unknown bandits, at one and the same time." *Boz*, "Private Theatres."

Schlicke, Paul Contemporary professor, University of Aberdeen, specializing in the role of popular entertainment in Dickens's works. In *Dickens and Popular Entertainment* (1985), he surveys the role of popular theater, street performers, circuses, and other entertainments in Dickens's novels and journalism. He analyzes the role of such performances in three novels: *Nickleby, Curiosity Shop*, and *Hard Times*. He has also prepared an annotated bibliography for *Curiosity Shop* (with Priscilla Schlicke, 1988) and an edition of *Hard Times* (1989).

"Schoolboy's Story, The" One of Dickens's contributions to the Christmas number of HOUSEHOLD WORDS, 1853, *Another Round of Stories by the Christmas Fire*. It tells of Old Cheeseman, a former student and master at the school who had been neglected as a child and exploited as a master, but he becomes a benefactor to the boys when he inherits a fortune. Then he marries Jane Pitt, his loyal friend in his school days. *Christmas Stories*. This story was one of Tennyson's favorites among Dickens's works.

Schwarzbach, F. S. (1949–) Professor, Washington University, St. Louis. Schwarzbach specializes in the Victorian city and in Dickens as a novelist responding to the urbanization of life in the 19th century. In *Dickens and the City* (1979), he finds an underlying mythic structure in the novels that describes a fall from a rural paradise into the urban hell of London that mirrors Dickens's own experience. Schwarzbach has also edited, with Ira Bruce Nadel, a collection of essays on *Victorian Artists and the City* (1980).

Scientific Gentleman The gentleman at CLIFTON who takes the flashing light of Mr. Pickwick's lantern for an unexplained natural phenomenon: ". . . the scientific gentleman seized his pen again, and committed to paper sundry notes of these unparalleled appearances, with the date, day, hour, minute, and precise second at which they were visible: all of which were to form the data of a voluminous treatise of great research and deep learning." *Pickwick* (39).

Scorpion Ship of the Latin-grammar Master, Captain Boldheart's enemy. "Holiday Romance."

"Scotland Yard" Originally published as "Sketches by Boz. New Series No. 2" in the MORNING CHRONICLE (October 4, 1836), this sketch describes the transformation of this area of London from the haunt of coal heavers to the site of fashionable shops and the offices of the police commissioners. *Boz.*

Scott, Tom Quilp's boy, an "eccentric spirit" with an addiction to standing on his head (5). After Quilp's death he becomes a professional tumbler (73). *Curiosity Shop.*

Scott, Sir Walter (1771–1832) Scottish historical novelist, poet; known as "the author of *Waverley*" (1814) and of the many Waverley novels that followed it; definitive novelist of the generation immediately preceding Dickens. Scott influenced Dickens and nearly every other Victorian novelist to write historical novels and to include a broad social panorama in their works. His efforts to embody historical forces in the lives of individuals and to connect public issues with the private lives of his characters inform the Victorian novel and shape even those novels without historical subjects.

Scott was also important to Dickens as a model of the professional writer who had been victimized during his career by unscrupulous publishers and by the lack of adequate copyright protection. In his speeches on COPYRIGHT in Ameria, Dickens used Scott, writing himself to death, as an example of the cruel results from the lack of a copyright law. Had there been such a law, Dickens told his listeners, "Scott might not have sunk beneath the mighty pressures on his brain, but might have lived to add new creatures of his fancy to the crowd which swarm about you in your summer walks and gather round your winter evening hearths."

"Scott and his Publishers" Two articles for the EXAMINER (March 31, 1839; September 29, 1839) in which Dickens supports the conclusion of John Gibson Lockhart, Scott's biographer, that the Ballantynes, Scott's publishers, mismanaged Sir Walter Scott's financial affairs. Dickens spells out the many loans that Scott made to the Ballantynes and the many debts that he forgave. He characterizes the Ballantyne family's retaliation upon Lockhart and Scott as "pitiful and disgusting." *Miscellaneous.*

Scradgers A "rather dirty little gentleman who looks like a converted Hyaena" and is a speaker at temperance rallies. *Miscellaneous,* "Whole Hogs."

Screw Steamship on which Martin Chuzzlewit and Mark Tapley travel—in steerage—to AMERICA. *Chuzzlewit* (15).

Screwzer, Tommy One of Cousin Feenix's many acquaintances—a "man of an extremely bilious habit." *Dombey* (61).

Scrivens Dandy who dresses like the Prince Regent and is a junior clerk in Tapenham's government department. *Miscellaneous,* "Cheap Patriotism."

Scroo Vice-President of the Display of Models and Mechanical Science section of the Mudfog Association. *Mudfog* (2).

Scrooge, Ebenezer Sharp-tongued and quick-witted businessman and miser, the surviving partner in the firm of Scrooge and Marley, "a squeezing, wrenching, grasping, scraping, clutching, covetous old sinner! Hard and sharp as flint, from which no steel had ever struck out a generous fire; secret, and self-contained, and solitary as an oyster" (1). Haunted by Marley's ghost on the seventh anniversary of his partner's death, Scrooge is visited by the three Spirits of Christmas, who show him visions of his life in Christmases past, present, and future. Scrooge is changed by the visions and learns "how to keep Christmas well" (5). *Carol.*

Scuttlewig, Duke of One of the friends claimed by the name-dropping Egotistical Couple. *Young Couples.*

Seamstress "A young woman, with a slight girlish form, a sweet spare face in which there was no vestige of colour, and large widely opened eyes" (III:13), who accompanies Sydney Carton to the guillotine. *Two Cities.*

Searle, Ronald (1920–) Illustrator for *PUNCH* and other magazines; book illustrator; famous for his St. Trinian's cartoons of fiendish schoolgirls. He illustrated *A Christmas Carol* (1961), *Great Expectations* (1962), and *Oliver Twist* (1962). He also did cartoons for the 1970 film *Scrooge.*

Senior, Nassau (1790–1864) Professor of POLITICAL ECONOMY at Oxford, frequent contributor to the *Edinburgh Review* and *QUARTERLY REVIEW.* In his review of HORNE'S *New Spirit of the Age* in the *Westminster Review* (1844), he commented on the economics of *A Christmas Carol:* "The process whereby poor men are to be enabled to earn good wages, wherewith to buy turkeys for themselves, does not enter into the account; indeed it would quite spoil the dénouement and all the generosity. Who went without turkey and punch in order that Bob Cratchit might get them—for, unless there were turkey and punch in surplus, some one must go without—is a disagreeable reflection kept wholly out of sight." The satire in *The Chimes* involving Trotty's bowl of tripe is a response to this criticism.

Sens, France "A pretty little town with a great two-towered cathedral and the rooks flying in and out of the loopholes" where Mrs. Lirriper and Major Jackman take Jemmy to meet his father, Edson, on his deathbed. "Lirriper's Legacy."

Sensation Novel Subgenre of the English novel in the 1860s; its main practitioners were Wilkie COLLINS, Charles READE, and Mrs. Henry Wood. Sensation novels, modeled in many ways on the novels of Dickens, dealt with topical issues or scandals, used the conventions of melodrama to provide a sequence of sensational incidents, and employed the serial form to enhance the mysteries and suspense in their plots. Dickens's attacks on the POOR LAW (*Twist*) and CHANCERY (*Bleak House*) suggested ways to address topical issues in fiction that Reade in particular would exploit in such novels as *Hard Cash* (1863), which dealt with abuses in the treatment of the insane. Collins's mystery "novels with a secret," in turn, influenced Dickens, suggesting the unknown benefactor in *Expectations* or the Harmon mystery in *Mutual Friend*. The concentration of sensational incidents in such fiction appears in Dickens in such sequences as the revelation of Magwitch's identity, the burning of Miss Havisham, and Orlick's capture of Pip in *Expectations*. Although Dickens cannot be strictly described as one of the sensation novelists, his close association with Collins and Reade and the publication of their work in ALL THE YEAR ROUND clearly influenced him.

"Sentiment" Originally published in BELL'S WEEKLY MAGAZINE (June 7, 1834), this story describes Lavinia Brook Dingwall's brief career at Minerva House, a finishing school where she is sent by her father, a self-important and fatuous M.P., to "recover" from an unfortunate love affair. Instead, she meets her lover at the school dance and elopes with him to live in poverty and misery near BALL'S POND. *Boz.*

Sentimentality From a modernist point of view, sentimentality has been defined as emotion in excess of the facts. The works of Dickens and other Victorians have often been judged by this modernist standard, and their portrayal of children and death—and especially of dying children—dismissed as grossly sentimental. Certainly Dickens and his contemporaries—and indeed 20th-century writers on occasion—were not without moments of false or overindulgent emotion, but the modern assessment of sentimentality often fails to take into account the 19th-century context in which Dickens was writing. The facts of infant mortality, child labor, limited educational opportunity and poverty were more extreme than we often imagine. The suffering of children was fact, not just the imaginings of exaggerated feeling.

Philosophical assumptions of the time also shaped Victorian sentimentality. Inheriting the romantic belief in the imagination, the Victorians idealized the power to imagine oneself in another's place. Shared feeling and a sympathetic understanding were considered defining human traits that led to emotional responses different from those conditioned by a cynical and rational modernism. Such "sentimentalism" was sought by the Victorians as a way of preserving traditional values in the face of a corrosive empiricism and rationalism. The imagination stifled by the hard fact school, Dickens believed, included the power to sympathize with others and to envision the way things might otherwise be. Fred KAPLAN (1987) traces the backgrounds and historical context of Victorian sentimentalism.

Septimus Mr. Booley's nephew, who accompanies Mr. Booley on his "journey" to the Ohio River. *Miscellaneous*, "Extraordinary Traveller."

Seraphina Schoolmaster's daughter, "the most beautiful creature that ever was seen," who is the heroine of Jemmy Lirriper's tale. "Lirriper's Lodgings."

Serial Publication Although occasional novels had been published in serial form prior to the Victorian Age, Dickens's *Pickwick Papers* was responsible for setting the fashion for later novels and for defining the standard form of the Victorian serial. Although *Pickwick* began as 24 pages of letterpress and four illustrations for each monthly part, Dickens revised the format after SEYMOUR's death to 32 pages of text accompanied by two illustrations. This revised plan allowed for more sustained development of the narrative, something essential in transforming the anecdotal sketch into a continuing novel. *Pickwick* was completed in 20 parts over 19 months, the last part constituting a double number. Dickens followed this format in all of his monthly serials except for *Twist* (which ran in BENTLEY'S MISCELLANY and had 24 somewhat irregular installments) and *Drood* (which was planned for 12 parts).

The weekly serials, all of which ran in Dickens's magazines, had much shorter installments, typically only one or two short chapters, and were sometimes unillustrated, as was the case with *Hard Times* and *Expectations*. This tighter format had the effect of concentrating the narrative on fewer plot lines and condensing the style.

Although suspense and cliff-hanging endings are assumed to be the major narrative characteristics of the serial, Dickens made rather sparing use of such devices. He saw the serial, instead, as an opportunity for sustained familiarity with a large number of characters, for developing parallel narratives with complex interconnections, and for shaping the narrative to the changing expectations of his audience. He did not write the novel and then cut it up into parts. Rather, he thought of the novel in terms of its monthly numbers; from *Dombey* on, he kept NUMBER PLANS in which he plotted out each part and made memoranda of what he wanted to include. William AXTON (1967) has also shown that he thought of the structure of the whole novel in terms of part divisions, making the fifth, 10th, and 15th numbers climactic turning points in the development of the story.

Michael Lund, in numerous articles and in *The Victorian Serial* (1991; with Linda K. Hughes), has done the most work on Victorian serial publication. Several Dickens scholars have studied the serial parts and analyzed the ways in which the serial form affected Dickens's methods of composition and novelistic form. See especially John BUTT and Kathleen TILLOTSON (1957), Archibald C. COOLIDGE (1967), Sylvère MONOD (1968), and Robert PATTEN (1978).

Serjeant's Inn An inn of CHANCERY in CHANCERY LANE to which Pickwick is taken as he is being committed to the FLEET PRISON. *Pickwick* (40).

Setting The physical and temporal context in which the action of a narrative takes place. Physically, the setting includes particular houses or rooms, like Bleak House or Miss Havisham's dining room with its decaying wedding feast. More broadly, it includes cities or countries: the France of *Two Cities* or the Coketown of *Hard Times*. Dickens's great setting is, of course, London, which he transformed in his imagination. He often adapted actual London streets and districts to fit the thematic requirements of his stories. Ralph Nickleby, a usurer, for example, lives on GOLDEN SQUARE and Jaggers's office (*Expectations*) is located on LITTLE BRITAIN, an actual street in the CITY that Dickens uses to suggest Jaggers's world as a microcosm of the nation. There are numerous books and atlases devoted to Dickensian TOPOGRAPHY, identifying the places that Dickens used in his novels, both those he used literally and those he adopted as models for fictional settings.

Temporally, the setting includes the time period in which the action occurs, its distance from or closeness to the time of narration, and the season of the year or time of day. The first chapter of *Mutual Friend*, for example, begins by establishing that the time is the present, autumn, and twilight, a setting symbolically relevant to an analysis of a civilization in "decline and fall." Humphry HOUSE (1941) showed that Dickens typically wrote about a vague period 10 or 15 years before the time of composition, though he was often inconsistent in particular historical details.

Seven Dials In Dickens's day, a notorious slum district surrounding ST. GILES Circus where seven streets come together. Boz describes the area in "Seven Dials" as "streets of dirty, straggling houses, with now and then an unexpected court composed of buildings as ill-proportioned and deformed as the half-naked children that wallow in the kennels." The area is also described

Gustave Doré's picture of a street in Seven Dials.

in *Boz*, "Monmouth Street." Mr. Mantilini descends to operating a mangle in this district (*Nickleby*, 64).

"Seven Dials" Originally "Scenes and Characters No. 1" in BELL'S LIFE IN LONDON (September 27, 1835), this sketch describes the crowded streets in this slum section of London, the women whose dispute ends in blows, the idle young men who lean against the lampposts, and the crowded tenement house where the residents quarrel with one another. *Boz*.

"Seven Poor Travellers, The" Christmas number of HOUSEHOLD WORDS, 1854. Dickens wrote the opening chapter, in which the narrator becomes a seventh traveler at Watts's Charity, who provides a dinner for the six travelers stopping there for the night. After supper the travelers tell stories; the narrator's is "The STORY OF RICHARD DOUBLEDICK." In the concluding chapter, also by Dickens, the narrator takes leave of the travelers and walks from ROCHESTER to GREENWICH, meditating on the significance of Christmas. *Christmas Stories*.

Sexton (1) Old man in the village where Nell ends her life who is both gravedigger and gardener in the churchyard. *Curiosity Shop* (53–55).

Sexton (2) A deaf old man, one of Gabblewig's impersonations in his scheme to expose Slap. *Nightingale*.

Seymour, Robert (1798–1836) Artist and illustrator, famous for his prints of amateur sportsmen ineptly engaged in hunting and fishing. His proposal to do a series of such prints involving a club of inept sportsmen was the generating idea that eventually became *Pickwick*. Seymour interested CHAPMAN & HALL in the proposal and they sought a writer to provide copy for the illustrations. After being turned down by William Clarke, they approached Dickens, who agreed to the proposal but broadened the subject matter from its sporting emphasis. In effect, Dickens insisted on having at least an equal role with the artist in determining the direction of the work. By the second number, he had, in "The Stroller's Tale" of the dying clown, introduced subject matter far afield from Seymour's original conception, a subject that was especially troubling to Seymour, who suffered from periodic bouts of depression. Dickens insisted that Seymour's first version of the plate illustrating the tale be redrawn. After he completed the illustrations for the second number, Seymour shot himself. His lack of self-confidence and history of mental illness clearly were the primary causes of his suicide, but the stresses in working with Dickens probably contributed to his action as well.

Many years later Mrs. Seymour and her son contended that Seymour had originated *Pickwick* and that Dickens did not give the artist proper credit or reward. Dickens challenged their claims, which were largely discredited, in the preface to the CHARLES DICKENS EDITION of his works, 1867.

Seymour's illustration for "The Stroller's Tale" in the second number of The Pickwick Papers. *His difficulties with the unfamiliar subject matter and Dickens's objections to his work troubled the artist shortly before his suicide.*

"Shabby-genteel People" Originally in the MORNING CHRONICLE (November 5, 1834) as "Street Sketches No. 4," this sketch describes Londoners who have fallen into poverty and try to keep up appearances, especially one shabby reader in the British Museum Reading Room. *Boz.*

Shadwell Just a month before he died Dickens took his American publisher, J. T. FIELDS, to visit an opium den in this dockside area of East London, which Fields described: "In a miserable court, at night, we found a haggard old woman blowing at a kind of pipe made of an old ink bottle; and the words that Dickens puts into the mouth of this wretched creature in *Edwin Drood* we heard her croon as we leaned over the tattered bed in which she was lying." In the novel, this old woman becomes the Princess Puffer, who croons a description of her business as she coaxes her clients to take another pipe of the opium that she has prepared: "I makes my pipes of old penny ink-bottles, ye see, deary . . . and I fits in a mouthpiece, this way, and I takes my mixter out of this thimble with this little horn spoon; and so I fills, deary." *Drood* (1).

Shaftesbury, Lord (1801–1885) (Anthony Ashley Cooper) Member of Parliament; prominent Evangelical (see EVANGELICISM); leader in issues of social reform, particularly in industrial and sanitary legislation; president of the RAGGED SCHOOL Union. Though he did not share Lord Shaftesbury's narrow religious convictions (see, for example, his disagreement about Sunday closing in "The Sunday Screw"), Dickens supported nearly all of Shaftesbury's reforms. The two men were friends and occasionally dined together. Shaftesbury was said to be without a sense of humor, and there is no indication that he read Dickens's novels, but he did read John FORSTER's *Life of Dickens*, remarking in his journal: "The man was a phenomenon, an exception, a special production. Nothing like him ever preceded. Nature isn't such a tautologist as to make another to follow him."

Shakespeare, William Dickens knew Shakespeare's plays well, both from reading them and from seeing them performed in the London theaters. Some of his earliest articles were reviews for the EXAMINER of productions of Shakespeare. Bentley, SLATER, and Burgis list nearly two full pages of allusions to Shakespeare in *The Dickens Index* (1988); the most frequently mentioned plays are *Hamlet, Julius Caesar, Macbeth*, and *Othello*.

Dickens is frequently compared to Shakespeare, particularly as a creator of character. The eminent Shakespearean Alfred B. Harbage explored the connections between the two writers in *A Kind of Power: The Shakespeare-Dickens Analogy* (1975).

"Shakespeare and Newgate" Article for HOUSEHOLD WORDS (October 4, 1851) by R. H. HORNE and Dickens, describing Samuel Phelps's reforms at Sadler's Wells Theatre, which had declined to the point where it had been taken over by a rowdy audience drawn to the theater by such debased and sensational plays as George Almar's *Jack Ketch*. Phelps cleared out the vendors who worked in the theater, prohibited foul language, and presented a repertory of Shakespeare and other classic dramatists. The new Sadler's Wells has become "a place in which to learn good things." *Stone.*

Shanklin The seaside resort on the Isle of Wight visited by Dickens in 1849. The Lammles spend their disillusioning honeymoon here (*Mutual Friend*, I:10).

Sharp Assistant master at SALEM HOUSE, "a limp, delicate-looking gentleman . . . with a good deal of nose, and a way of carrying his head on one side, as if it were a little too heavy for him" (6). *Copperfield.*

Sharpeye Policeman who accompanies the Traveller to the seamen's haunts in the Liverpool slums. *Uncommercial* (5).

Shaw, George Bernard (1856–1950) Irish dramatist, critic, novelist, and social commentator; a great admirer of Dickens and, like him, a prolific comic writer who devoted his works to correcting social ills. At a time when most Dickensians celebrated the comic Dickens of the early novels, Shaw praised the late Dickens of the dark social novels. He published introductions for *Hard Times* (1913) and *Great Expectations* (1937) and frequently derived characters and situations in his plays from Dickens. Dan H. Laurence and Martin Quinn have collected Shaw's writings on Dickens; they also discuss Shaw's indebtedness to the novelist in *Shaw on Dickens* (1985).

Shaw, William   One-eyed schoolmaster at Bowes Academy, YORKSHIRE, who served as the model for Squeers in *Nickleby*. Pretending to represent a prospective client, Dickens interviewed Shaw, who was already notorious and who had been accused of abusing and maiming some of his charges.

Shepherd, Miss   A boarder at the Misses Nettingalls' school with whom young David Copperfield is infatuated. "She is a little girl, in a spencer, with a round face and curly flaxen hair. . . . I am sometimes moved to cry out, 'Oh, Miss Shepherd!' in a transport of love." *Copperfield* (18).

Shepherd, The   One of Mrs. Weller's spiritual counselors, described by Tony Weller as "a fat chap in black, vith a great white face, a smilin' avay like clockwork." *Pickwick* (22).

Shepherd's Bush   URANIA COTTAGE, the refuge for fallen women sponsored by Miss COUTTS and directed by Dickens, was located on Acton Road in this section of west London.

Shepherdson   Thief arrested by Sergeant Mith in "The Butcher's Story." *Reprinted,* "Detective Police."

Sherman, Captain   Commander of the steamboat *Burlington* on Lake Champlain, the boat Dickens described as "superior . . . to any other in the world." Dickens attributed its "graceful comfort and beautiful contrivance" solely to its captain. *Notes* (15).

Sheridan, Richard Brinsley (1751–1816)   Sentimental comic dramatist, best known for *The School for Scandal* (1777). Dickens knew and admired Sheridan's plays, alluding to them on several occasions, most notably perhaps in the "Finches of the Grove" (*Expectations*, 34) taken from *The Critic*.

Shiny Villiam   Deputy hostler at the BULL INN in ROCHESTER, "so called, probably, from his sleek hair and oily countenance." *Pickwick* (5).

Ship, The   Riverside inn below GRAVESEND where Pip, Herbert, and Magwitch spend the night before attempting to board a steamship for the Continent (*Expectations*, 54). It was based on the Ship and Lobster Inn.

"Shipton, Mother"   One of Esther SUMMERSON's nicknames. Mrs. Shipton, or Mother Shipton, was a legendary prophetess, probably fictional, who was credited with having prophesied the deaths of Wolsey and Crom-

well and the invention of the steam engine and the telegraph.

"Shipwreck, The"   The Traveller describes a visit to the Welsh village of Llanallgo in late December 1859. Only two months before, the Australian trading and passenger ship, the *Royal Charter*, had broken up off the coast near this village, taking at least 500 lives. The Traveller describes the salvage operation, but he has come to the village to observe the selfless dedication of the local clergyman, Stephen Roose Hughes, who has buried the dead and ministered to the living tirelessly since the accident. The article is a tribute to his modesty, simplicity, and cheerful earnestness, his "true practical Christianity." *Uncommercial* (2). The article first appeared in ALL THE YEAR ROUND (January 28, 1860).

Shooter's Hill   Hill on the DOVER Road near BLACK-HEATH. Tony Weller retires to "an excellent public house near Shooter's Hill, where he is quite reverenced as an oracle" (*Pickwick*, 57). Jerry Cruncher catches up with the Dover mail coach as it is laboring up the hill (*Two Cities*, I:2). The Elmses, where Master Harry Walmers's father lived, is nearby ("Holly Tree").

"Shops and their Tenants"   Originally published in the MORNING CHRONICLE (October 10, 1834) as "Street Sketches No. 2," this sketch describes the series of commercial tenants who occupy the shops in a building that gradually declines from a draper's to a stationer's, to a bonnet maker's and tobacconist's, to a ladies' school, and, finally, to a dairy. *Boz.*

"Short" or "Short Trotters"   Nickname of HARRIS, Codlin's partner in the PUNCH AND JUDY show. *Curiosity Shop.*

Short Story   Although he was writing at the time when POE was defining the concentration and unity of effect that characterizes the modern short story, Dickens seems to take little interest in these technical issues. Some of his ghost stories in *Pickwick* may have influenced Poe, but Dickens held to a looser and more traditional notion of the short story than his American counterpart. Deborah THOMAS (1982) suggests that the feature distinguishing Dickens's idea of the short story was the "concept of oral narration." He connected such stories with those told aloud in the family circle or around the Christmas hearth.

His stories often fit into traditional forms like the GHOST STORY or the autobiographical narrative. In general terms, the stories are differentiated from SKETCHes by the presence of characters and plot, but there is a large border area in Dickens's shorter pieces where sketches and familiar essays use some of the techniques of story and where his stories take on the didactic or illustrative qualities of the essay.

If one accepts the oral and traditional nature of Dickens's storytelling, several of his shorter works are remarkable examples of the form. Sam Weller's anecdotes, like the story of "The Man as Killed His-self on Principle" (*Pickwick*, 44), are delightful examples of tall tales and legends. "Mrs. Lirriper's Lodgings," "Mrs. Lirriper's Legacy," and "Doctor Marigold" are humorous personal narratives revealing the characters of their first-person cockney narrators. "George Silverman's Explanation" and Miss Wade's "History of a Self-Tormentor" are confessional narratives, exposing through the personal histories that they relate the neuroses of their narrators. "The Schoolboy' Story," one of TENNYSON's favorites, is an evocative character sketch of a teacher by a former student that reveals the kindness of the teacher, Old Cheesman, and the growth in the narrator. Among Dickens's many ghost stories are two of his most successful shorter works, "No. 1 Branch Line: The Signalman" and the perfect *Christmas Carol*, one of the most memorable short stories in any language.

Most of Dickens's stories are collected in *Boz, Christmas Books, Christmas Stories*, and *Reprinted Pieces*. The standard critical work on the short stories is by D. THOMAS (1982). She has also edited a collection of the stories (1976).

"Short-Timers, The"   The Traveller's account of a visit to the LIMEHOUSE School of Industry, sponsored by the Stepney Union, where the children of the poor are educated for a variety of trades in a very successful educational scheme in which the children attend school for half the normal school hours. *Uncommercial* (21). Originally published in ALL THE YEAR ROUND (June 20, 1862).

"Shy Neighbourhoods"   One can know shy neighborhoods—poor neighborhoods in back streets and byways—by their pets, the birds, donkeys, dogs, cats, and fowl that one encounters while walking through them. *Uncommercial* (10). Originally in published in ALL THE YEAR ROUND (May 26, 1860).

"Signal-man, The"   See "MUGBY JUNCTION" (4).

Signal-man, The   A careful and professional employee of the railway, "whose post was in as solitary and dismal a place as ever I saw," who tells Young Jackson of the troubling apparitions that appear by his warning light. Twice they have appeared preceding tragic accidents. A third appearance occurs just before the signalman himself is run down by a train. *Mugby* (4).

"Sikes and Nancy"   Dickens's sensational and horrific PUBLIC READING of the murder of Nancy from *Twist*. Although he contemplated this performance piece as early as 1863, he did not perform it until November 14, 1868, when he gave a private reading for an invited audience to secure their advice about whether to include it in his regular program of readings. The reading was sensational and most of those attending advised him to perform it, but FORSTER, DOLBY, and his son Charley

urged him not to do so. His physician worried about possible hysteria in the audience and about Dickens's own health; Dickens's heartbeat increased during the exhausting performance, but he included it in the repertory of his farewell reading tour in 1869 and performed it regularly, almost compulsively. Legend at least blames the strain of performing "Sikes and Nancy" for hastening Dickens's death.

Sikes, Bill   Brutal thief and murderer; Fagin's accomplice; lover and murderer of Nancy; "a stoutly-built fellow of about five-and-thirty. . . . He had a brown hat upon his head, and a dirty belcher handkerchief round his neck: with the frayed ends of which he smeared the beer from his face as he spoke. He disclosed, when he had done so, a broad heavy countenance with a beard of three days' growth, and two scowling eyes; one of which displayed various parti-coloured symptoms of having been recently damaged by a blow" (13). He undertakes to carry out Fagin's scheme to corrupt Oliver by involving the boy in the CHERTSEY robbery (20–22). After Fagin tells him of Nancy's meeting with Brownlow, Sikes clubs her to death (47). Then, haunted by a vision of her eyes, he wanders in the countryside around London (48) before returning to JACOB'S ISLAND, where he accidentally hangs himself while attempting to escape from the mob (50). *Twist.*

Silver-Store   A British colony on an island off the Mosquito Coast of Honduras, established as a "safe and convenient place" to store the silver taken from mines on the mainland. "English Prisoners."

Silverman, Rev. George   Sixty-year-old clergyman who explains his life in "George Silverman's Explanation." Abused by his mother, who calls him "a worldly little devil," in the PRESTON cellar where he spent his early childhood, he becomes a self-denying and self-effacing adult. Even when he gives up the woman he loves and marries her to another man, he is accused of doing so for monetary gain. His story explains how his childhood prompted his otherworldliness, which in turn has isolated him from "the world."

Simmery, Frank   A gambling dandy, with whom Wilkins Flasher exchanges bets. *Pickwick* (55).

Simmons   Beadle in Our Parish, "the most important member of the local administration." *Boz*, "Beadle."

Simmons (2), Mrs. Henrietta   Mrs. Quilp's neighbor and sympathizer. *Curiosity Shop* (4).

Simmons, William   Van driver who gives Martin a lift from SALISBURY to Hounslow after he is dismissed by Pecksniff. *Chuzzlewit* (13).

Simpson (1)   One of Mrs. Tibbs's boarders, "as empty-headed as the great bell of St. Paul's." *Boz*, "Boarding House."

Simpson (2)   One of Pickwick's fellow inmates in the FLEET PRISON. *Pickwick* (42).

Simson   Guest of Percy Noakes on the "Steam Excursion." *Boz.*

Single Gentleman, The   Mysterious lodger who moves into the apartment on the upper floor of the Brasses' house in BEVIS MARKS in order to spy on the Brasses (34). He turns out to be Grandfather TRENT'S brother, who has returned from many years abroad and is reunited with his brother just shortly before his death (71–72). *Curiosity Shop.* In the frame story in MASTER HUMPHREY'S CLOCK, Humphrey surprisingly claims to be the single gentleman (6).

Six Jolly Fellowship Porters   (The Porters) The riverside pub in LIMEHOUSE where Abbey Potterson presides like an abbess over a community institution. *Mutual Friend.* It was probably based on the GRAPES INN.

Sketch   A traditional literary form, analogous to the visual art form from which it takes its name; the sketch is usually a short piece describing a character or a place, or evoking a mood. In traditional character sketches, the characters were types, representative rather than individualized figures. By combining the type with the individual, Dickens modified the convention and brought tension into his characters. Scrooge, for example, complicates the traditional miser with a zestful, self-seeking vitality, a paradoxical conception that enables Dickens to turn the character sketch into a conversion story.

In *Boz*, Dickens distinguished sketches from stories; the sketch lacks the plot and character development of the SHORT STORIES. The most immediate models for Dickens's sketches were those of Washington IRVING, whose *Sketch Book* influenced Dickens's early work in particular.

Sketches by Boz. Illustrative of Every-day Life and Every-day People.   Dickens's first book, collecting sketches and tales that he had published in various magazines between 1833 and 1836, and adding three previously unpublished pieces, "A Visit to Newgate," "The Black Veil," and "The Great Winglebury Duel." The First Series, published by MACRONE in two volumes in February 1836, with 10 illustrations by CRUIKSHANK (12 in a second edition), was reprinted in four editions within a year. Macrone published a Second Series, with 16 illustrations by Cruikshank, in 1837 (dated 1836), collecting pieces that had not been collected for the first series and adding one previously unpublished piece, "The Drunkard's Death." Dickens revised many of the sketches before they appeared in *Boz*. CHAPMAN & HALL published the first edition combining the two series in 20 monthly parts between November 1837 and June 1839 and in one volume, 1839. This edition added the previously uncollected "The Tuggses at Ramsgate" and arranged the items into the four sections—"Our Parish,"

Cruikshank's frontispiece for the first collection of Sketches by Boz *(1836).*

"Scenes," "Characters," and "Tales"—used in subsequent editions.

Sketches of Young Couples   A series of facetious sketches of various character types, directed to "the Young Gentlemen of England" to enable them to avert "the dangers" of the Leap Year and the upcoming marriage of Queen Victoria and to resist the designs of single ladies. The types presented were: "The Young Couple," "The Formal Couple," "The Loving Couple," "The Contradictory Couple," "The Couple Who Dote upon Their Children," "The Cool Couple," "The Plausible Couple," "The Nice Little Couple," "The Egotistical Couple," "The Couple Who Coddle Themselves," "The Old Couple." Published by CHAPMAN & HALL, 1840, with illustrations by BROWNE.

Sketches of Young Gentlemen   Series of facetious sketches of various types of young gentlemen, addressed to "the Young Ladies of the United Kingdom" to correct the libels of the *Sketches of Young Ladies* recently published by Quiz (Edward Caswell) and illustrated by Phiz (BROWNE). Dickens's sketches included: "The Bashful Young Gentleman," "The Out-and-out Young Gentleman," "The Very Friendly Young Gentleman," "The Military Young Gentleman," "The Political Young Gentleman," "The Domestic Young Gentleman," "The Censorious Young Gentleman," "The Poetical Young Gentleman," "The 'Throwing-off' Young Gentleman," "The Young Ladies' Young Gentlemen." Published by CHAPMAN & HALL, 1838, with illustrations by Browne.

Skettles, Sir Barnet, M. P.   Pompous and imposing father of **Barnet, Jr.**, Paul Dombey's schoolmate at Blimber's Academy. Sir Barnet (whose main interest in life is extending the circle of his acquaintance) and **Lady Skettles** invite Florence to stay with them in FULHAM while Mr. Dombey is in LEAMINGTON (24). *Dombey.*

Skewton, The Hon. Mrs. ("Cleopatra")   Edith DOMBEY's mother. Though a woman of 70, she dresses as though she were 27, and uses all of the cosmetic arts to present herself as "Cleopatra," the subject she modeled in a fashionable sketch in her youth. Though she pays lip service to "nature," she is all artifice, turning herself into a painted object, just as she turns Edith into an object and peddles her on the marriage market. *Dombey.*

Skiffins, Miss   Woman of "wooden appearance," uncertain age, and in possession of portable property, who marries Wemmick in an impromptu ceremony. *Expectations* (37, 55).

Skim, Mrs.   Proprietor of the Commercial Lodging House near ALDERSGATE STREET where Snoady stays when he comes up to London. *Miscellaneous,* "Lively Turtle."

Skimpin, Mr.   Junior barrister to Sergeant Buzfuz, representing Mrs. Bardell in the Pickwick trial. *Pickwick* (34).

Skimpole, Harold   Friend of John Jarndyce; dilettante, artist, and musician, who pretends to be an irresponsible "child." "He was a little bright creature, with a rather large head; but a delicate face, and a sweet voice, and there was a perfect charm in him. All he said was so free from effort and spontaneous, and was said with such captivating gaiety, that it was fascinating to hear him talk" (6). He takes no responsibility for his finances and sponges from Jarndyce and others. Esther and Richard loan him money to prevent his arrest by Neckett (6). He accepts a bribe from Bucket to disclose the whereabouts of young Jo (31). Later Jarndyce asks him not to accept money from Richard Carstone (61). Skimpole responds by describing Jarndyce in his memoirs as "the Incarnation of Selfishness" (61). His **wife** "had once been a beauty, but was now a delicate high-

nosed invalid, suffering under a complication of disorders" (43). Skimpole has several children and grandchildren, including three daughters, **Arethusa**, **Laura**, and **Kitty**, whom he characterizes, respectively, as his Beauty daughter, Sentiment daughter, and Comedy daughter (43). *Bleak House.* Skimpole was modeled on Leigh HUNT.

Slackbridge   Labor UNION organizer in COKETOWN who publicly castigates Blackpool for refusing to join the association. "An ill-made, high-shouldered man, with lowering brows, and his features crushed into an habitually sour expression, he contrasted most unfavourably, even in his mongrel dress, with the great body of his hearers in their plain working clothes." *Hard Times* (II:4).

Sladdery   Proprietor of a bookshop and lending library that caters to a fashionable clientele. *Bleak House* (2).

Slammer, Dr.   The fiery little surgeon of the 97th, "a little fat man, with a ring of upright black hair round his head and an extensive bald plain on the top of it," who challenges Jingle to a duel after the charity ball in ROCHESTER. The message, however, is delivered to Winkle by mistake. *Pickwick* (2–3).

Slang, Lord   Friend claimed by the name-dropping Egotistical Couple, Mr. and Mrs. Briggs. *Young Couples.*

Slap   Actor, known professionally as Formiville, who concocts several schemes to take Mr. Nightingale's property. *Nightingale.*

Slasher   Surgeon at ST. BARTHOLOMEW'S HOSPITAL who remarks that he "took a boy's leg out of the socket last week—boy ate five apples and a ginger bread cake—exactly two minutes after it was all over, boy said he wouldn't lie there to be made a game of, and he'd tell his mother if they didn't begin." *Pickwick* (32).

Slater, Michael   Contemporary scholar and critic; professor, Birkbeck College, University of London; Editor of the DICKENSIAN, 1968–77; Chairman of the Trustees of The Dickens House Museum; President of the DICKENS FELLOWSHIP. Slater is the author of *Dickens on America and the Americans* (1978), an illustrated account of Dickens's travels in America; *Dickens and Women* (1983), a biographical and critical account of the women in Dickens's life and the women characters in his novels; and *The Dickens Index* (with Nicholas Bentley and Nina Burgis; 1988), a reference guide to Dickens, especially useful for its explanations of references, allusions, quotations, and topicalities in the novels. Slater has also edited and provided substantial introductions to *The Christmas Books* (1971), *Nicholas Nickleby* (1978), and *Dickens 1970* (1970), a centenary collection of essays by major British scholars and critics on Dickens. He also compiled and edited *The Catalogue of the Suzannet Charles Dickens Collection* (1975).

Slaughter, Lieutenant Confederate of Captain and Mrs. Waters who "discovers" Cymon Tuggs hiding behind a curtain. *Boz*, "Tuggses."

Slaughter, Mrs. Greengrocer on Great Twig Street in the "Unsettled Neighbourhood." *Miscellaneous*.

Slavery Dickens altered the chronological organization of *American Notes* to devote a chapter to the issue of slavery, which he saw as the issue above all others defining American society. In doing so, as Jerome MECKIER (1990) points out, he challenged other British travel writers, particularly Harriet MARTINEAU, who explained slavery as an anomaly in an otherwise progressive nation. Dickens stressed the ways in which slavery brutalized all Americans and determined the character of the nation, and he then provided a catalog of particular instances of cruelty and brutality.

In *Chuzzlewit*, Dickens illustrates the brutality of the system with a former slave who was "shot in the leg; gashed in the arm, scored in his live limbs, like a crimped fish; beaten out of shape; had his neck gulled with an iron collar, and wore iron rings upon his wrists and ankles" (17). The contradiction of slavery in a free society is represented by the Norris family, abolitionists who assert the necessity of separating the races (17), and by the Watertoast Asociation, which dissolves when its members learn that an Irish politician they have supported is an advocate of emancipation (21).

An article written with Henry MORLEY for *HOUSEHOLD WORDS* in 1852, "North American Slavery," while just as opposed to slavery, takes a somewhat more positive view of the chances for abolition and the opportunities for America "to do what is right."

Sleary Proprietor of an equestrian CIRCUS, "a stout man . . . with one fixed eye, and one loose eye," and a lisping voice "like the efforts of a broken pair of bellows, . . . and a muddled head which was never sober and never drunk" (I:6). He cares for Sissy Jupe after her father deserts her (I:6), and he shelters Tom Gradgrind when he runs from Coketown (III:7). His daughter **Josephine**, "who had been tied on a horse at two years old, and had made a will at twelve, which she always carried about with her, expressive of her dying desire to be drawn to the grave by the two piebald ponies" (I:6), marries E. W. B. Childers. Sleary's philosophy, summed up in his assertion, "People mutht be amuthed" (III:8), expresses Dickens's views that imagination must temper hard facts and that amusement is essential even in the most earnest life. *Hard Times*.

Sleek, Dr. Teacher at the City Free School who proclaims the Orrery Exhibition, a kind of planetarium, is "improving" because it is "devoid of anything that could call a blush to the cheek of a youth." *Uncommercial* (20).

"Sleep to Startle Us, A" Article for *HOUSEHOLD WORDS* (March 13, 1852) describing the RAGGED SCHOOL in FIELD LANE and the dormitory for the homeless connected with the school. The narrator visits classes in tailoring, shoemaking, and mathematics, and he observes the 167 occupants of the dormitory as they prepare to sleep after attending the school. He ends by asserting: "An annual sum of money, comtemptible in amount as compared with any charges upon any list, freely granted in behalf of these Schools, and shackled with no preposterous Red Tape conditions, would relieve the prisons, diminish the county rates, clear loads of shame and guilt out of the streets, recruit the army and navy, waft to new countries, Fleets full of useful labour, for which their inhabitants would be thankful and beholden to us." *Miscellaneous*.

Sliderskew, Peg Arthur Gride's housekeeper, "a short thin weasen blear-eyed old woman, palsy-stricken and hideously ugly" (51). On the day Gride is to marry Madeline Bray, she steals the documents relating to Madeline's inheritance (56); Ralph Nickleby hires Squeers to retrieve the papers from her, but his attempt to do so is foiled by Frank Cheeryble (59). Peg is sentenced to transportation for her crimes (65). *Nickleby*.

"Slight Depreciation of the Currency, A" Article for *HOUSEHOLD WORDS* (November 3, 1855) which deplores the substitution of money for active public service. At a time when duty is especially called for, money alone cannot correct the inequities and injustices in society. *Miscellaneous*.

"Slight Question of Fact, A" Note for *ALL THE YEAR ROUND* (February 13, 1869), correcting an assertion in the *Pall Mall Gazette* that failed to recognize MACREADY's insistence on public decency in the theaters he managed. Dickens corrects the record. *Miscellaneous*.

Slingo Horse trader who employs Tip Dorrit. *Dorrit* (I:7).

Slinkton, Julius Poisoner who has murdered his niece and plots to murder Margaret Niner and Alfred Beckwith. He commits suicide when his schemes are discovered. "Hunted Down." Slinkton was based on the notorious poisoner Thomas Wainewright, whom Dickens had met.

Slithers Master Humphrey's barber, one of the members of "Mr. Weller's Watch." *Humphrey*.

Sliverstone, The Reverend and Mrs. Egotistical Couple in which "the lady's egotism is all about her husband and the gentleman's is about his wife." *Young Couples*.

Sloppy Orphan taken in by Betty Higden, "a very long boy, with a very little head, and an open mouth of disproportionate capacity" (I:16). He operates the mangle for Betty and reads the police reports to her in different voices. He is hired by Boffin to keep an eye on Wegg at the dust mounds (IV:3) and at the end of the novel he is attentive to Jenny Wren (IV:16). *Mutual Friend*.

Slout   Bumble's predecessor as master of the workhouse where Oliver Twist was born. *Twist* (27).

Slowboy, Tilly   The Peerybingle's clumsy servant girl and nursemaid, "always in a state of gaping admiration at everything, and absorbed, besides, in the perpetual contemplation of her mistress's perfections and the baby's." *Cricket*.

Sludberry, Thomas   Defendant in DOCTORS' COMMONS accused of brawling at a vestry meeting. *Boz*, "Doctors' Commons."

Sluffen   Cockney orator at the sweeps' annual dinner on the first of May. *Boz*, "First of May."

Slug   Member of the Mudfog Association. *Mudfog* (1).

Slum   Ragged poet who writes advertising verses for Mrs. Jarley's Waxworks (28). He is disappointed when she marries William (47). *Curiosity Shop*.

Slumkey, The Hon. Samuel   Successful Blue (Conservative) candidate in the election at EATANSWILL. *Pickwick* (13).

Slummery   Clever painter praised by the Plausible Couple as a way of pleasing Fithers, who has "forestalled [Slummery] in his department of art, and made it thoroughly and completely his own" and who is in their company. *Young Couples*.

Slurk   Editor of the *Eatanswill Independent*, organ of the Buff (Whig) party, and the archrival of Pott. "His manner was peremptory; his eyes were sharp and restless; and his whole bearing bespoke a feeling of great confidence in himself, and a consciousness of his immeasurable superiority over all other people." *Pickwick* (51).

Slyme, Chevy   Indolent and sullen nephew of old Martin Chuzzlewit who associates with Montague Tigg and believes his merits have not been properly appreciated. Later he becomes a policeman, and he is the officer who arrests Jonas (51). *Chuzzlewit*.

Smalder Girls, The   Acquaintances of Cousin Feenix. *Dombey* (47).

"Small Star in the East, A"   The Traveller visits a poor neighborhood in RATCLIFF near the river where underemployed laborers and dockworkers live in "a wilderness of dirt, rags and hunger." He sees a starving Irish family that includes a young woman suffering from lead poisoning, contracted while working in a nearby lead mill. An unemployed boilermaker's laborer and his wife, who sews pea-jackets, have only a loaf of bread and water to eat. The Traveller is so distressed by the starving children of a coal porter and laundress that he cannot continue his observations. However, when he discovers the East London Children's Hospital, he is heartened to find a dedicated young doctor and his wife caring for the children of their distressed neighborhood. *Uncommercial* (32). Originally in *All the Year Round* (June 19, 1868).

Smallweed, Joshua (Grandfather Smallweed)   Usurer to whom Trooper George owes money: "the name of this old pagan's God was Compound Interest" (21). Confined to a chair, he passes the time berating his wife, **Grandmother Smallweed**, and throwing cushions at her when she mentions money. Their twin grandchildren, **Bartholomew (Bart**, "**Small**," "**Chick Weed**") and **Judy**, bear the family "likeness to old monkeys with something repressing their minds" and are so small that "the two kneaded into one would hardly make a young person of average proportions" (21). Grandfather Smallweed uses George's debt to extract from the trooper a sample of Captain Hawdon's writing for Tulkinghorn (34). After the death of Krook, his brother-in-law, he discovers some papers among Krook's possessions and plans to blackmail Sir Leicester with them, but he is foiled by Bucket (62). *Bleak House*.

Smangle   A prisoner for debt in the FLEET PRISON, "a rakish vagabond." *Pickwick* (41, 42, 44).

Smart, Tom   A traveling salesman and the hero of "The BAGMAN'S STORY." He exposes Jinkins' scheme to marry the buxom widow innkeeper. *Pickwick* (14).

Smauker, John   Angelo Cyrus Bantam's footman, who invites Sam Weller to the footmen's "swarry" at BATH. *Pickwick* (35, 37).

Smif, Putnam ("America Junior")   Clerk in an American dry goods store who writes to Martin, asking his help in getting a passage to England so he can pursue his fame. *Chuzzlewit* (22).

Smiggers, Joseph   Perpetual Vice-President of the Pickwick Club. *Pickwick* (1).

Smike   Ralph Nickleby's son, who, unbeknownst to his father was left at DOTHEBOYS HALL by Brooker. There Squeers employs him as a drudge, and Smike is maimed in both body and mind by his mistreatment. "Although he could not have been less than eighteen or nineteen years old, and was tall for that age, he wore a skeleton suit, such as is usually put upon very little boys. . . . Heaven knows how long he had been there, but he still wore the same linen which he had first taken down; for, round his neck, was a tattered child's frill, only half concealed by a coarse, man's neckerchief. He was lame; . . . and . . . so dispirited and hopeless, that Nicholas could hardly bear to watch him" (7). After Nicholas defends him from Squeers's abuse, Smike follows him to London (13). Together they travel to PORTSMOUTH and join the Crummles troupe, in which Smike (as Digby) plays the apothecary in *Romeo and Juliet* (23, 25). After they return to London, Smike is captured by Squeers and rescued by John Browdie (38, 39). He develops a hopeless love for Kate Nickleby and pines away his life, dying in Devonshire (58). After his death, Brooker informs Ralph that Smike was his son (61). *Nickleby.*

Smith   London clerk who works at his desk " 'till five o'clock, working on, all day, as regularly as the dial over the mantel-piece whose loud ticking is as monotonous as his whole existence." *Boz,* "Thoughts about People."

Smith, M. P.   A new member of Parliament who "siezes both the hands of his gratified constituent, and, after greeting him with the most enthusiastic warmth, darts into the lobby with an extraordinary display of ardor for the public cause." *Boz,* "Parliamentary Sketch."

Smith, Albert (1816–1860)   British novelist, playwright, comic writer, editor; brother of Arthur SMITH. Smith's novels, especially such comic PICARESQUE serials as *The Adventures of the Scattergood Family* (1845) and *The Struggles and Adventures of Christopher Tadpole* (1847), were strongly influenced by Dickens's early works. Married to a daughter of the KEELEYs, Smith shared Dickens's love of the theater. He dramatized *Cricket* and *Battle of Life* with Dickens's approval. In the 1850s he gave public performances of his work, perhaps suggesting the idea to Dickens.

Smith, Arthur (d. 1861)   Business manager for Dickens's PUBLIC READINGS from 1858 to 1861; brother of Albert SMITH. Dickens described him as "the best man of business I know." When he died in 1861, Dickens felt his loss deeply.

Smith, O. (Richard John Smith) (1768–1855)
One of the leading actors at the ADELPHI THEATRE; famous for his portrayals of villains, he took the stage name "O" after playing a character named Obi in 1829. Smith performed in many of the Adelphi's adaptations of Dickens, playing Sikes, Newman Noggs, Hugh the Maypole hostler, Toby Veck, and John Peerybingle. He was best known for his portrayal of Scrooge in STIRLING's adaptation.

Smith, Samuel   Real name of Horatio SPARKINS. *Boz,* "Sparkins."

Smith, Sydney (1771–1845)   Liberal clergyman; Canon of ST. PAUL'S CATHEDRAL; famous wit; one of the founders of the *Edinburgh Review*; friend of Dickens. His *Lectures on Moral Philosophy* was one of Dickens's favorite books. The two men met in the 1830s, probably at Lady BLESSINGTON's salon. Although Smith was "deterred by the Vulgarity" of the penname "Boz," he thought the *Sketches* "written with great power. . . . The soul of Hogarth has migrated into the body of Mr. Dickens." He especially praised *Nickleby* and *Chuzzlewit.* Dickens named his seventh child after Smith.

Smith, Dr. Thomas Southwood (1788–1861)
Unitarian minister, medical doctor, Poor Law commissioner; energetic advocate of factory and SANITARY REFORM; one of the founders of the *Westminster Review,* the Society for the Diffusion of Useful Knowledge, and the Health of Towns Association. He sent Dickens the *Report of the Children's Employment Commission* in 1843 that sparked Dickens's indignation and led to *A Christmas Carol.* Smith was especially influential on Dickens's views regarding sanitary reform.

Smith Square, Westminster   Now Dean Stanley Street, the site of the house where Lizzie Hexam lived with Jenny Wren. *Mutual Friend.*

Smithers, Emily   The belle of Minerva House. *Boz,* "Sentiment."

Smithers, Miss   Boarder at WESTGATE HOUSE who is incited "into hysterics of four young lady power" by the discovery of Mr. Pickwick in the school's courtyard. *Pickwick* (16).

Smithers, Robert   City clerk and friend of Thomas Potter, with whom he "makes a night of it" and ends up arrested for disturbing the peace. *Boz,* "Making a Night."

Smithfield   London's wholesale meat market in the CITY. Oliver passes by the confusion of the market, "a stunning and bewildering scene," on his way to the CHERTSEY robbery (*Twist,* 21). Pip, on his first day in London, observes the "shameful place, being all asmear with filth and fat and blood and foam" (*Expectations,* 20). Dickens called for removing the market from the center of London in "A Monument of French Folly" (*Reprinted*). The market is also mentioned in *Nickleby* (4), *Rudge* (18), and *Dorrit* (I:13).

Smithick and Watersby   LIVERPOOL shipping firm and owners of the *Golden Mary*; they hire Ravender to sail the ship to California. "Golden Mary."

Smithie Family   Family attending the ball in ROCHESTER. *Pickwick* (2).

Smivey, Chicken   The name Tigg supplies to the pawnbroker for Martin Chuzzlewit when he is pawning his watch in London. *Chuzzlewit* (13).

Old Smithfield Market.

Smollett, Tobias George (1721–1771) English novelist, editor, and translator of CERVANTES and LE SAGE. Like David Copperfield, Dickens read Smollett's novels as a child. The influence of *Roderick Random* (1748) and *Peregrine Pickle* (1751) is especially evident in the loose PICARESQUE structure, physical comedy, alliterative titles, and young heroes of Dickens's early novels. Smollett's *Sir Launcelot Greaves* (1760–62), the first serialized novel in English, may have suggested that mode of publication to Dickens.

Smorltork, Count The foreign visitor whom Pickwick meets at Mrs. Leo Hunter's *fête champêtre*, who is collecting materials for a work on England. He was based on Count Pückler-Moskau and Friedrich von Raumer, who had both written books giving their observations of the English. *Pickwick* (15).

Smouch Assistant to Namby the sheriff; "a shabby-looking man in a brown great-coat shorn of divers buttons." *Pickwick* (40).

Smuggins Performer who obliges the harmonic meeting with a comic song. *Boz*, "Streets, Night."

"Smuggled Relations" Humorous article for *HOUSEHOLD WORDS* (June 23, 1855) describing a number of cases of relations who were kept secret: Cogsford "disguised" his mother as his housekeeper, Mrs. Bean; Benting never acknowledged his globe-trotting brother John; but the narrator and his wife Susannah are the most surprised to learn that their good friend Larver has been married for 10 years without their knowing it. *Miscellaneous.*

Snagsby Law stationer who hires Nemo to do occasional work for him as a law writer; "a mild, bald, timid man, with a shining head, . . . he tends to meekness and obesity" (10). His wife, **Sarah**, a zealous follower of the Reverend Chadband, suspects him of fathering Jo, the poor crossing sweeper whom he befriends and supplies with odd half-crowns (25). Bucket finally informs her that her suspicions are groundless (59). *Bleak House.*

Snap, Betsy   Uncle Chill's housekeeper, "a withered, hard-favoured, yellow old woman." "Poor Relation's Story."

Snapper   The name Dickens gives to a fellow traveler on the train to PRESTON who supports the masters in the Preston strike. *Miscellaneous*, "On Strike."

Snawley   Sanctimonious hypocrite who places his two sons in Squeers's school; "a sleek, flat-nosed man, clad in sombre garments, and long black gaiters, and bearing in his countenance an expression of much mortification and sanctity" (4). He poses as Smike's father in Ralph Nickleby's scheme to recover the boy (45). Prompted by his shrewish **wife**, Snawley confesses his involvement in Ralph Nickleby's plot (61). *Nickleby*.

Snevellici Family   Acting family who are members of the Crummles' theatrical company. **Mr. Snevellici**, dignified and addicted to drink, played "military visitors and the speechless noblemen," and occasionally beat his **wife**, who is "still a dancer, with a neat little figure and some remains of good looks" (30). Their daughter, **Miss Snevellici** is the leading lady in the Crummles troupe, "who could do anything, from a medley dance to Lady Macbeth, and also always played some part in blue silk knee-smalls" (23). She is enamored with Nicholas, but he does not reciprocate her flirtatious attentions. Eventually she marries a tallow chandler (48). *Nickleby*.

Snewkes   Friend to the Kenwigs. *Nickleby* (14).

Snicks   Life office secretary, a guest at Perker's dinner party. *Pickwick* (47).

Sniff, Mrs.   One of the disdainful attendants at the Mugby Refreshment Room. Her **husband**, "a regular insignificant cove," is so "disgustingly servile" to the public that her associates cannot understand how she ever "come so far to lower herself as to marry him." "Mugby" (3).

Sniggs   Mayor of Mudfog who dies at age 85, leaving vacant the position for Nicholas Tulrumble. *Mudfog*.

Snigsworth, Lord   Twemlow's aristocratic cousin who serves as Twemlow's calling card in society. *Mutual Friend*.

Snipe, The Hon. Wilmot   Ensign in the 97th Regiment who attends the ball at ROCHESTER. *Pickwick* (2).

Snitchey, Jonathan   Dominant partner in the law firm of Snitchey and Craggs, he refers to the firm as "self and Craggs." They handle the legal affairs of Doctor Jeddler and Michael Warden and advise Warden to flee to the Continent on the same night that Marion Jeddler disappears. **Mrs. Snitchey**, like Mrs. Craggs, distrusts her husband's law partner. *Battle*.

Snivey, Sir Hookham   Member of the Mudfog Association. *Mudfog*.

Snoady   Narrator of "The Lively Turtle," a smug and parsimonious man who splurges on a dinner of turtle soup and tender steak. Afterward he realizes that the turtle is representative of the best English virtues—a belief in comfort and a desire to be left alone—which oppose the radicals' desire for change. *Miscellaneous*.

Snobb   Guest at Ralph Nickleby's dinner party. *Nickleby* (19).

"Snobby"   Chuckster's demeaning nickname for Kit NUBBLES. *Curiosity Shop* (14).

Snobee   An unsuccessful candidate for Parliament. *Boz*, "Parlour Orator."

Snodgrass, Augustus   One of the members of the traveling Pickwick Club; "the poetic Snodgrass poetically enveloped in a mysterious blue cloak with a canine skin collar" (1). He secretly falls in love with Emily Wardle, marries her, and lives happily at DINGLEY DELL (57). *Pickwick*.

Snore, Professor   President of the Zoology Section of the Mudfog Association, an "ingenious gentleman [who] proposed to open a communication with fleas . . . so that they might be thoroughly imbued with a sense of the advantages they must necessarily derive from changing their mode of life, and applying themselves to honest labour." *Mudfog* (1).

Snorflerer, Dowager Lady   A friend claimed by the name-dropping Egotistical Couple, Mr. and Mrs. Briggs. *Young Couples*.

Snorridge Bottom   Town from which Gill Davis comes, between CHATHAM and MAIDSTONE. "English Prisoners."

Snow Hill   Steep and busy street leading from HOLBORN down to Farringdon Street. The SARACEN'S HEAD, where Squeers stays in London, was located on the hill (*Nickleby*, 4). Also mentioned in *Boz*, "Christening"; *Rudge* (67); *Twist* (26); and *Dorrit* (I:13).

Snow, Tom   Captain Ravender's black steward. "Golden Mary."

Snubbin, Serjeant   Mr. Pickwick's barrister in the breach of promise trial, "a lantern faced, sallow-complexioned man of about five-and-forty. . . . He had that dull-looking boiled eye, which is often to be seen in the heads of people who have applied themselves, during many years, to a weary and laborious course of study." *Pickwick* (31, 34). He was probably based on Serjeant Arabin, a well-known barrister of the time.

Snuffim, Sir Tumley   Mrs. Wititterly's physician. *Nickleby* (28, 33).

Snuffletoffle, Q. J.   Speaker at the Umbugology and Ditchwateristics Section of the Mudfog Association. *Mudfog* (2).

Snugglewood   Physician who applies leeches to cure Our Bore's brain disorder. *Reprinted*, "Bore."

Snuphanuph, Dowager Lady   "A fat old lady" who is Pickwick's whist partner at BATH. *Pickwick* (35–36).

Social Oysters   HIGHGATE social club to which Mr. Booley reports his Extraordinary Travels. *Miscellaneous*, "Extraordinary Traveller."

Social Problem Novel   A subgenre of British fiction that emerged in the 1830s, also known as the "Condition of England" novel, "fiction with a purpose," and the industrial novel. Influenced by the propaganda novels of William Godwin and the social philosophy of CARLYLE, novelists such as Frances Trollope (*Michael Armstrong, the Factory Boy*, 1839), DISRAELI (*Coningsby, Sybil, Tancred*, 1844–1847), and Elizabeth GASKELL (*Mary Barton*, 1848 and *North and South*, 1855) addressed the social issues of the day, particularly those brought about by the INDUSTRIAL REVOLUTION. Many of Dickens's novels were influenced by this thesis fiction. *Oliver Twist* and, especially, *Hard Times*, with the condition of England and particular issues of social reform central to their purpose, are examples of the genre.

Sociological Novel   A type of novel that defines its characters in terms of social class and broad social categories and assumes that society influences or determines the ways in which human beings act. Dickens's treatment of such social issues as the POOR LAW, EDUCATION, and industrialization; his close observation of the social world; and his many characters described in networks of social relationships to one another, have led commentators to characterize him as a sociological novelist. Philosophically, however, he was more an idealist than a REALIST, and he was inconsistent on the issues of how social forces shaped individuals and controlled behavior. His external rendering of his characters is often better described as a dramatic, rather than a sociological, technique.

Soemup, Dr.   President of the Anatomy and Medicine Section of the Mudfog Association. *Mudfog* (2).

Soho   Area surrounding **Soho Square** in the West End of London. Esther Summerson meets Caddy Jellyby in the Square (*Bleak House*, 23). Doctor Manette's London house is near the Square (*Two Cities*, II:6), as is the house of Jules Obenreizer ("No Thoroughfare").

Soloman Bell the Raree Showman   Title for a children's book that Dickens agreed to write for Christmas 1836, but which he was forced to abandon due to the pressures of other commitments.

Sol's Arms   Public house in CHANCERY LANE where Little Swills performs and where the inquests into the deaths of Nemo and Krook are held. *Bleak House* (11, 33). It is based on the Ship Tavern in Chancery Lane.

"Some Account of an Extraordinary Traveller"   Article from HOUSEHOLD WORDS (April 20, 1850), describing the travels of Mr. Booley to America, New Zealand, Australia, Egypt, India, and the Arctic—all by visiting the panoramas on display in London. *Miscellaneous*.

"Some Particulars Concerning a Lion"   Facetious article for BENTLEY'S MISCELLANY (May 1837) comparing the lion in the zoo with a literary lion and concluding that the latter is superior. Collected in *Mudfog*.

"Some Recollections of Mortality"   The Traveller is caught up in a crowd in PARIS who observe the body of an old man at the Morgue. The incident recalls two earlier experiences in the Traveller's life, first of seeing the body of a woman pulled from the REGENT'S CANAL in London, and then of serving at an inquest into the death of an infant. *Uncommercial* (19). Originally in ALL THE YEAR ROUND (May 16, 1863).

"Somebody's Luggage"   Christmas number of ALL THE YEAR ROUND, 1862. Dickens wrote the frame chapters, narrated by Christopher, a hotel waiter who acquires some luggage left by a former guest to the hotel. In the luggage he discovers some manuscripts, which he submits for publication. When the stories are about to be published, the owner of the luggage, an aspiring author who had no luck in placing his work, returns to the hotel and is so overjoyed to learn that the stories are in print that he gives Christopher £20. Dickens also wrote two of the stories. The first, "His Boots," tells of Langley, an Englishman who retreats to the French village of Vauban to forget a daughter that he has disowned. There he observes the love of Corporal Théophile for the orphan child Bebelle. When the corporal is killed in a fire, Langley adopts the child and forgives his daughter. The narrator of the second story, "His Brown-Paper Parcel," is a sidewalk artist who is so diffident and antisocial that he hires others to pretend that his work is theirs. *Christmas Stories*.

Somers Town   Area in northwest London, north of Euston Station. The Dickens family lived in the POLYGON in Somers Town in the 1820s when many foreigners (including Spanish refugees) and artists lived in the area. Boz describes it as the dwelling place of CITY clerks ("Streets—Morning"). Snawley's house, where Smike is held after Squeers captures him, is located here (*Nickleby*, 38). Skimpole occupies a dilapidated dwelling in the Polygon (*Bleak House*, 43).

Somerset House   In Dickens's time this building in the STRAND housed government offices, including those of the POOR LAW commissioners. Dickens's father and his uncle, Thomas BARROW, were clerks in the building, as is Minns (*Boz*, "Minns").

Son and Heir   Ship on which Walter Gay sails to Barbados; it sinks on the way. *Dombey* (13, 32).

Sophia   Ruth Pinch's disrespectful pupil, the daughter of a copper-founder. *Chuzzlewit* (9, 36).

Sophy   Doctor Marigold's daughter, a loving child who dies young. When he later adopts a deaf-and-dumb girl, he names her Sophy. He lovingly educates her and makes a wagon stocked with books for her to read, including a special book, *Doctor Marigold's Prescriptions*, that he has written for her himself. "Marigold."

Southampton Street   Mrs. Billikin's boardinghouse is located in this street that connects High HOLBORN with BLOOMSBURY SQUARE. *Drood* (22).

Southcote   Dickens's pseudonym for John Walker, a begging-letter writer who addressed a series of ingenious and lying appeals to Dickens. The novelist took him to court and testified against him, but the magistrate, impressed by "the excellence of his letters," discharged him. *Reprinted*, "Begging-letter Writer." (Originally in HOUSEHOLD WORDS [May 18, 1850].)

Southwark   Area south of the THAMES in London, usually referred to as the BOROUGH. **Southwark Bridge**, also called the IRON BRIDGE, is Little Dorrit's place of refuge.

Sowerberry   Undertaker who takes on Oliver Twist as an apprentice; "a tall, gaunt, large-jointed man, attired in a suit of threadbare black, with darned stockings of the same colour, and shoes to answer. His features were not naturally intended to wear a smiling aspect" (4). Although he treats Oliver as a valued assistant, his **wife**, "a short, thin, squeezed-up woman, with a vixenish countenance" (4), is less kind to the boy. After fighting with Noah Claypole and being held captive by Mrs. Sowerberry, Oliver runs away to London (8). *Twist*.

Sownds   Beadle at the church where Paul Dombey is christened (5) and his father married (31). *Dombey*.

Sowster   Oldcastle beadle who has "a very red nose, which he attributes to a habit of early rising—so red, indeed, that but for this explanation I should have supposed it to proceed from occasional inebriety." *Mudfog* (2).

Spa Fields   Open area in CLERKENWELL, east London, surrounding Spa Fields Chapel. In the 19th century, traveling showmen like Old Maunders made the area their winter quarters. *Curiosity Shop* (19).

Spaniards   Historic inn at the edge of HAMPSTEAD HEATH where Mrs. Bardell is having tea with her friends in the tea garden when Jackson apprehends her to take her off to prison. *Pickwick* (46).

Sparkins, Horatio   Name used by Samuel Smith, a draper's assistant, when he enters the high society of the Maldertons and impresses them with his philosophic banalities and genteel manners. *Boz*, "Sparkins."

Sparkler, Edmund   Mrs. Merdle's "chuckle-headed" son by her first marriage. "He had given so few signs of reason, that a by-word went up among his companions that his brain had been frozen up in a mighty frost which prevailed at St. John's, New Brunswick, at the period of his birth there, and had never thawed from that hour. . . . [He was] monomanical in offering marriage to all manner of undesireable young ladies" (I:21). He pursues Fanny DORRIT when she is just a poor dancer and Mrs. Merdle buys her off (I:20), but when the Dorrits come into money, he is allowed to marry Fanny (II:15), who treats him with disdain. He gets a position in the CIRCUMLOCUTION OFFICE. *Dorrit*.

"Sparks, Timothy"   Pseudonym under which Dickens published *Sunday under Three Heads*.

Sparks, Tom   Boots at the St. James's Arms who delivers the letters from the Strange Gentleman. *Strange Gentleman*.

Sparsit, Mrs.   Bounderby's housekeeper. A widow with aristocratic pretensions and "a Coriolanian style of nose" (I:7), she trades on her connections with the Powler and Scadgers families and hopes to marry Bounderby. When he marries Louisa, she is relegated to a position at Bounderby's bank where, resentfully, she sets out to undermine his marriage. She spies on Louisa, brings news of her rendezvous with Harthouse (III:3), and uncovers the identity of Mrs. Pegler as Bounderby's mother (III:5), an act for which she is dismissed from Bounderby's service (III:9). *Hard Times*.

Spatter, John   Business partner of Michael, the poor relation, whom he defrauds of the business. "Poor Relation."

Specks, Joe   The Traveller's boyhood friend in Dullborough. He has married the Traveller's childhood sweetheart, **Lucy Green**. The three of them reminisce about the past. *Uncommercial* (12).

Speddie, Dr.   Cumberland doctor who attends Thomas Idle's sprained ankle and tells Goodchild the story of Arthur Holliday. *Lazy Tour*.

Speeches   Dickens was an outstanding public speaker, described by Edmund YATES as "by far the best after-dinner speaker I have ever heard." His many speeches, particularly at the dinners of civic and philanthropic societies, have been collected and edited in an outstanding scholarly edition by K. J. FIELDING (1960; 1988).

Spenlow, Dora   Francis Spenlow's daughter, David Copperfield's "child-wife." David is infatuated by Dora from the moment he first meets her at her father's house in NORWOOD. "She had the most delightful little voice, the gayest little laugh, the pleasantest and most fascinating little ways, that ever led a lost youth into hopeless slavery. She was rather diminutive altogether. So much the more precious, I thought" (26). After her father forbids their courtship and dies (38), Dora goes to live with her two maiden aunts, **Clarissa** and **Lavinia Spenlow**. The courtship continues and leads to marriage, but Dora is hopelessly incompetent as a housekeeper and David abandons his attempts to teach her discipline before she fades and dies (53). *Copperfield*. Dora was based on Maria BEADNELL.

Spenlow, Francis   Partner in the firm of SPENLOW AND JORKINS; proctor in DOCTORS' COMMONS to whom David was articled. "He was got up with such care, and was so stiff, that he could hardly bend himself; being obliged, when he glanced at some papers on his desk, after sitting down in his chair, to move his whole body, from the bottom of his spine, like Punch" (23). He uses Jorkins as his "bad guy," blaming him for refusing to release David from his articles after Aunt Betsey's financial difficulties (35). When he invites David to his home in Norwood, David is immediately infatuated with his daughter Dora, but when Miss Murdstone, Dora's companion, discovers their courtship and reveals it to Mr. Spenlow, he demands that the affair be broken off and then dies that evening (38). *Copperfield*. Spenlow was based on Maria BEADNELL's father.

Spenlow and Jorkins   Firm of DOCTORS' COMMONS proctors to which David Copperfield is articled. Spenlow uses Jorkins, his invisible partner, as his excuse for refusing to allow David to resign his articles after Betsey Trotwood's financial difficulties. *Copperfield* (35).

Sphynx, Sophronia   Name that Dick Swiveller gives to the MARCHIONESS. *Curiosity Shop*.

"Spider, The"   Jaggers's nickname for Bentley DRUMMLE. *Expectations*.

Spigwiffin's Wharf   Fictional address along the THAMES in east London, between BILLINGSGATE and the CUSTOM HOUSE, where Ralph Nickleby provides a rundown house for Mrs. Nickleby and Kate. *Nickleby* (11).

Spiker, Mr. and Mrs. Henry   Dinner guests at the Waterbrooks': He is "so cold a man, that his head, instead of being grey, seemed to be sprinkled with hoarfrost," she, "a very awful lady in a black velvet dress, and a great black velvet hat, whom I remember as looking like a near relation of Hamlet's—say his aunt." *Copperfield* (25).

Spilka, Mark (1925–)   Professor, Brown University; Freudian critic who has written extensively on Lawrence, Hemingway, and literary theory, as well as on Dickens. In *Dickens and Kafka, A Mutual Interpretation* (1963), Spilka is not so much interested in Dickens's influence on Kafka as he is in the ways in which the similarities and differences between them illuminate the two writers. His comparison with Kafka did a great deal to open up the dark side of Dickens's work.

Spine, John   Celebrated novelist who reads some of his unpublished manuscript to Our Bore. *Reprinted*, "Our Bore."

"Spirit Business, The"   Article for HOUSEHOLD WORDS (May 7, 1853), a debunking report of several spiritualist publications from America that prove, Dickens concludes sarcastically, that "the spirit business cannot fail to be regarded by all dispassionate persons as the last great triumph of common sense." *Miscellaneous*.

"Spirit of the Fort"   The Traveller's name for the "wise boy" who tells him all about the nautical mysteries of CHATHAM. *Uncommercial* (26).

"Spitalfields"   Article for HOUSEHOLD WORDS (April 5, 1851) by WILLS and Dickens, describing Spitalfields, an area in east London, east of BISHOPSGATE, settled by French Huguenots in the 17th century and devoted to the manufacture of silk. The narrators visit a silk warehouse and then go on to the homes of two silk weavers. The first is a close and dark abode where the weaver, his wife, and another weaver to whom he rents space struggle to survive. The second, the home of a weaver of patterned silk, is light, airy, and clean, an example of the better opportunities offered in the silk business for students who have attended the School of Design. *Stone*.

Spontaneous Combustion   The controversial manner by which Krook dies (*Bleak House*, 32). Dickens was attacked for believing in superstition and bad science, most notably by George LEWES, after the appearance of the 10th number of the novel in which the horrific incident occurs. In response, Dickens listed authorities attesting to the authenticity of spontaneous combustion during the inquest in the 11th number, and he defended his use of the incident more fully in the preface to the 1853 edition. Trevor Blout ("Dickens and Mr. Krook's Spontaneous Combustion," *Dickens Studies Annual*, 1970), demonstrates that Dickens believed in the authenticity of the incident and carefully prepared and developed its symbolic role in the novel.

Sporting Novels   Popular genre of comic writing in the 1830s, whose chief practitioners were Pierce Egan

(1772–1849), whose *Life in London* (1821–28) recounted the adventures of Tom and Jerry, cockney devotees of the turf, and R. S. SURTEES (1805–64), who in 1831 created Jorrocks, a cockney grocer, squire, and follower of the hunt. These works were important predecessors to *Pickwick*. Originally planned as a series of sketches of sporting misadventures, *Pickwick* was to be another in this popular genre of comic writing. Protesting that he was not a sportsman, Dickens broadened the proposed subject matter for the novel, but the original idea is implicit in some of the early scenes and in the character of Winkle.

Spottletoe, Mr. and Mrs. Relatives of old Martin Chuzzlewit who follow him into the country with designs on his money (4). They are also present for Charity Pecksniff's abortive wedding (54). *Chuzzlewit*.

Sprodgkin, Mrs. Sally Parishioner of the Reverend Milvey who torments the clegyman "by conspicuously weeping at everything, however cheering, said by the Reverend Frank in his public ministrations." *Mutual Friend* (IV:11).

Spruggins, Thomas Candidate for beadle of "Our Parish" who is defeated by Bung, even though he has 10 children to Bung's five. *Boz*, "Election for Beadle."

Spyers, Jem Police officer who arrested Conkey Chickweed, the fraudulent publican in the story told by Blathers. *Twist* (31).

Squeers Family Family who operates DOTHEBOYS HALL, the YORKSHIRE school where Nicholas Nickleby is employed as an assistant master. **Wackford**, the ogre-ish headmaster of the school, "had but one eye, and the popular prejudice runs in favour of two. The eye he had was unquestionably useful, but decidedly not ornamental: being of a greenish grey, and in shape resembling the fan-light of a street door. The blank side of his face was much wrinkled and puckered up, which gave him a very sinister appearance, especially when he smiled, at which times his expression bordered closely on the villainous. His hair was very flat and shiny, save at the end, where it was brushed stiffly up from a low protruding forehead, which assorted well with his harsh voice and coarse manner" (4). He and his **wife**, "a large raw-boned figure . . . about half a head taller than Mr. Squeers" (7), view their pupils as "natural enemies" (8) and they mistreat and physically abuse them. Their two children are **Fanny**, a young woman of 23 who fails to interest Nicholas romantically and becomes vindictive toward him, and **Wackford, Jr.**, who is kept fat and well fed as an advertisement for the school. When Nicholas intervenes to stop Squeers from beating Smike (13), he is forced to leave the school. Squeers later comes to London and captures Smike (38). He is also employed by Ralph Nickleby to secure the papers that Peg Sliderskew has taken from Arthur Gride (57). In the end he is im-prisoned and transported (65). *Nickleby*. Squeers was based on William SHAW of Bowes Academy in GRETA BRIDGE, who had been sued by some of his clients for mistreating and blinding their children.

Squires, Olympia "Most beautiful" girl with whom the Traveller celebrated a birthday during his childhood by going to an Orrery exhibition. *Uncommercial* (20).

Squod, Phil Trooper George's assistant at the shooting gallery, "a little man with a face all crushed together, who appears, from a certain blue and speckled appearance that one of his cheeks presents, to have been blown up, in a way of business, at some odd time or times" (21). Originally an itinerant tinker, at the end of the novel he goes to live at CHESNEY WOLD with George. *Bleak House*.

Stables, The Hon. Bob Sir Leicester Dedlock's cousin, knowledgeable about horses. *Bleak House*.

Stagg Blind proprietor of the cellar where the 'Prentice Knights gather to drink and plot. "His eyes were closed, but had they been wide open, it would have been easy to tell, from the attentive expression of the face he turned towards them—pale and unwholesome as might be expected in one of his underground existence—and from a certain anxious raising and quivering of the lids, that he was blind" (8). He joins Barnaby Rudge, Sr., in his attempts to extort money from Mrs. Rudge (46). He is killed when he tries to run from the officers arresting Hugh and Dennis (69). *Rudge*.

Stagg's Gardens Fictitious area in CAMDEN TOWN where the Toodles family live admidst the chaos of railway construction. Although the inhabitants consider it "a sacred grove not to be withered by railroads" (6), the area is so utterly transformed that when Susan Nipper seeks out Polly's house a few years after her first visit there, it seems to have "vanished from the earth" (15) in the wake of the railroad. *Dombey*.

Stakes Real name of Mr. CHOPS the Dwarf. "Going into Society."

Stalker Police inspector who attends a meeting at the offices of HOUSEHOLD WORDS, "a shrewd, hard-headed Scotchman." *Reprinted*, "Detective Police."

Stalker, Mrs. Woman in the slum of ST. GILES who is cautioned by Inspector Field to make herself scarce. *Reprinted*, "Inspector Field."

Stamford Hill Suburb north of ISLINGTON where Octavius Budden lives at Amelia Cottage, Poplar Walk. *Boz*, "Minns."

Stanfield, Clarkson (1793–1867) Marine and landscape painter, described by Dickens as "the Natural

Historian of [England's] speciality, the Sea." He met Dickens in 1838, toured Cornwall with him in 1842, provided some illustrations for *Battle of Life* and *Haunted Man*, and painted scenery for several of Dickens's amateur theatrical productions. Although he agreed to illustrate *Pictures from Italy*, he withdrew from the project when he was offended by the anti-Catholic bias in the work. Dickens's obituary tribute to "Stanny" appeared in ALL THE YEAR ROUND (June 1, 1867) and in *Miscellaneous*.

Stanley, Edward, Lord (Earl of Derby) (1799–1869) Whig politician; chief Secretary for Ireland, 1830–33; Secretary for War and the Colonies, 1833–34, 1841–45. When Dickens was a parliamentary reporter, Stanley was especially impressed by the accuracy of Dickens's transcription of one of his speeches and he asked Dickens to retranscribe a speech that other journalists had misreported. Dickens first met CARLYLE at Stanley's house in 1840.

Staple Member of the DINGLEY DELL Cricket Club. *Pickwick* (7).

Staple Inn One of the INNS OF COURT, dating from the 16th century and located in GRAY'S INN Road. Snagsby walks here in summer "to observe how countrified the sparrows and the leaves are" (*Bleak House*, 10). Grewgious's chambers are in the inn, as are those he secures for Neville Landless (*Drood*, 11).

Staplehurst Railway Accident On June 9, 1865, while returning from FRANCE with Ellen TERNAN and her mother, Dickens was involved in a railway accident on the boat train from FOLKSTONE to London. The train was traveling near Staplehurst, in KENT, when it derailed at a gap in the tracks on a bridge where some repair work was being done. The workmen had misread the schedule and did not expect the train for another two hours. Several coaches went off the bridge; the coach in which Dickens was traveling was left hanging off the

A newspaper picture showing Dickens tending the injured during the Staplehurst railway accident.

bridge, still coupled to the coach behind it. Shaken but unhurt, Dickens escaped through a window and managed to get his companions out of the wreck. For the next few hours, he ministered to the injured and dying. Ten people were killed in the accident and about 50 were injured. Dickens was heroic in his efforts to aid them. Only after he was no longer needed did he remember the manuscript of *Mutual Friend*, on which he was working at the time and which he was carrying on the train. He climbed back into the compartment to get it. Although he was cool and collected during the accident, he was in shock afterward. Weakened and nervous during the rest of the summer, he never again felt easy about train travel.

Staples, Leslie C. (1896–1980) Secretary of the DICKENS FELLOWSHIP during World War II; editor of The DICKENSIAN from 1944 to 1968; president of the Fellowship, 1968. Staples began publishing articles on biographical, bibliographical, and topographic topics in the *Dickensian* in 1917. A collector of Dickens materials, particularly of the plagiarisms and piracies of Dickens's novels, Staples donated his collection to the DICKENS HOUSE library.

Stareleigh, Mr. Justice The judge who presides over the *Bardell versus Pickwick* case; he is "so fat that he seemed all face and waistcoat.... All you could see of him was two queer little eyes, one broad pink face, and somewhere about half of a big and very comical-looking wig." *Pickwick* (35). This character is said to have been based on Sir Stephen Gazelee and to have influenced his retirement from the bench.

Stargazer Astronomer, astrologer, and alchemist whose reading of the stars convinces him that the lamp-

Stanfield's vignette of The Nutmeg Grater for The Battle of Life *(1846).*

lighter Tom Grig is destined to marry his niece, Fanny Brown. He tries to marry his daughter **Emma** to his laboratory partner Mooney, but his maid Betsey Martin foils that scheme and enables the marriage of Fanny to Stargazer's son, **Galileo Isaac Newton Flamstead**. *Lamplighter*.

Starling, Alfred   Financially independent young man "who pretends to be 'fast.' " He is one of John's guests at the "Haunted House."

Starling, Mrs.   Friend of the Loving Couple, "a widow lady who lost her husband when she was young, and lost herself about the same time." *Young Couples*.

Startop   Pip's fellow pupil at Matthew Pocket's. Optimistic, spoiled, and delicate, he is the opposite of Bentley Drummle. He joins Herbert in rescuing Pip from the Limekiln (53), and rows the boat during the attempt to spirit Magwitch out of England (54). *Expectations*.

Steadiman, John   Chief mate of the *Golden Mary*, "aged thirty-two, . . . a perfect sailor," who takes command when Captain Ravender dies. "Golden Mary."

"Steam Excursion, The"   Originally in the MONTHLY MAGAZINE (October 1834), this story of an excursion down the river on a steamboat organized by the lighthearted law student Percy Noakes ends with a rough passage back to London that leaves those in the party exhausted and sick. *Boz*.

Steele, Tom   Subject of a story told by "Waterloo," the attendant on WATERLOO BRIDGE, an Irishman who jumped to his death from the Bridge. *Reprinted*, "Down with the Tide."

Steepways   Fictional name for Clovelly, a seaside village in Devon that steps down a steep hillside to the sea. "Message from the Sea."

Steerforth, James   Head boy at SALEM HOUSE school, David's boyhood hero, who was "reputed to be a great scholar, and was very good-looking, and at least half-a-dozen years my senior" (6). Steerforth acts as David's protector at the school, but he uses information that David has given him about Mell to publicly humiliate the schoolmaster and have him dismissed (7). David meets him again in London when Steerforth is a student at Oxford (24); he takes Steerforth to YARMOUTH and introduces him to Daniel Peggotty and Little Emily (21). Steerforth seduces Emily, runs off with her to ITALY, and then abandons her. David is disillusioned but forgiving:

> In the keen distress of the discovery of his unworthiness, I thought more of all that was brilliant in him, I softened more towards all that was good in him. . . . Deeply as I felt my own unconscious part in his pollution of an honest home, I believed that if I had been brought face to face with him, I could not have uttered one reproach. I should have loved him so well still—though he fasci-

nated me no longer—I should have held in so much tenderness the memory of my affection for him, that I think I should have been as weak as a spirit-wounded child, in all but the entertainment of a thought that we could ever be re-united (32).

David does not see Steerforth again until his body is washed ashore at Yarmouth during a terrible storm in which Ham also dies while trying to save him (55). **Mrs. Steerforth**, his mother, "an elderly lady, though not very advanced in years, with a proud carriage and a handsome face" (20), dotes on her son and arrogantly rejects Daniel Peggotty's appeal for aid and understanding (32). Estranged from her son, she suffers from "a fretful wandering of the mind" (64). *Copperfield*.

Steig, Michael (1936–)   Professor, Simon Fraser University; Freudian critic of Victorian literature; reader-response theorist and critic. Steig's *Dickens and Phiz* (1978) is the standard work on Dickens's relationship with BROWNE. He establishes their relation as a collaborative one and discusses Phiz's illustrations as the first interpretations of Dickens's novels, analyzing in illuminating detail many of Browne's pictures. In numerous articles, Steig has offered psychological and, more recently, reader-response discussions of Dickens's novels. Particularly interesting is the analysis of *Copperfield* in *Stories of Reading: Subjectivity and Literary Understanding* (1989) and a series of articles on *Curiosity Shop* (See CURIOSITY SHOP: Criticism).

Stetta, Violetta   Italian opera singer who is the subject of some of Chuckster's gossip. *Curiosity Shop* (40).

Stewart, Garrett (1945–)   Professor, University of California, Santa Barbara. His *Dickens and the Trials of Imagination* (1974) employs stylistic analysis to explore the important theme of imagination in Dickens's novels, especially *Pickwick, Curiosity Shop, Chuzzlewit,* and *Mutual Friend*. In *Death Sentences: Styles of Dying in British Fiction* (1984), Stewart discusses death scenes in 19th and 20th-century novels, beginning with a substantial chapter on Dickens.

Stiggins, The Rev. Mr.   The drunken hypocrite who is the "deputy shepherd" of the Brick Lane Temperance Meeting, "he was a prim-faced, red-nosed man, with a long thin countenance, and a semi-rattlesnake sort of eye—rather sharp, but decidedly bad" (27). Susan Weller, Sam's stepmother, is one of the women taken in by his piety. At a meeting of the temperance society, he is exposed by Tony Weller (33), who later kicks him into a horse trough (52). *Pickwick*.

Stiltstalking   Mrs. Tite Barnacle comes from this influential aristocratic family. Clennam meets **Lord Lancaster Stiltstocking**, "a noble refrigerator" (I:26), at HAMPTON COURT when he visits Mrs. Gowan. *Dorrit*.

Stirling, Edward (1809–1894)   British playwright, theater manager, and actor. He wrote over 200 plays, many of them adaptations and many of those from Dickens. His adaptations of *Pickwick, Twist, Nickleby, Curiosity Shop,* and *Chuzzlewit* were on the boards well before the novels completed their serial run; this haste to produce led to such absurdities as Smike inheriting a fortune in Stirling's version of *Nickleby.* After attending a performance of Stirling's *Nickleby* at the behest of ADELPHI THEATRE manager Frederick YATES, Dickens commented: "My general objection to the adaptation of any unfinished work of mine simply is that being badly done and worse acted, it tends to vulgarize the characters, to destroy or weaken the minds of those who see the impressions I have endeavoured to create.... No such objection can exist where the thing is as admirably done in every respect as you have done in this instance." Dickens saw several of Stirling's adaptations and, though occasionally unhappy with them, was usually quite positive. As well as the early novels, Stirling also adapted several of the CHRISTMAS BOOKS for the stage. He played Noggs in *Nickleby.*

Stoehr, Taylor (1931–)   Professor, University of Massachusetts, Boston; critic; editor of the works of the American social visionaries Paul and Percival Goodman. His *Dickens: The Dreamer's Stance* (1965) analyzes the style in Dickens's last six novels as characteristic of dream translations, illustrative of Dickens's "dream manner" or "supernaturalism." Using some of the techniques of dream analysis, Stoehr finds a characteristic plot with apparent and hidden strands that produce a series of discoveries leading to the hero's rebirth.

Stokes, Martin   Farmer friend of the Bensons who plays the country bumpkin in order to expose the schemes of Sparkins Flam and to save Lucy Benson from ruin. *Coquettes.*

Stone, Frank (1800–1859)   English painter, illustrator, and close friend of Dickens, who was his neighbor when Dickens lived at TAVISTOCK HOUSE. Stone was a prominent member of Dickens's theatrical troupe. He did three illustrations for *Haunted Man* and a frontispiece for the CHEAP EDITION of *Chuzzlewit.* He also painted some portraits of Dickens's children. He was the father of Marcus STONE, who also illustrated works by Dickens.

Stone, Harry (1926–)   Professor, California State University, Northridge; Dickens scholar and editor who has made important contributions to understanding Dickens's minor writings and his use of fairy tale and fantasy. In *Dickens and the Invisible World* (1979), Stone discussed Dickens's use of FAIRY TALES, legends, and other folk and fantasy materials, arguing that by the later novels, beginning with *Dombey,* Dickens had developed a "fairy-tale method" which he used as the underlying structure for his novels. In *The Night Side of Dickens: Cannibalism, Passion, Necessity* (1994), Stone exhaustively analyzes three areas of Dickens's psyche as it emerges in metaphors and suggestions of cannibalism,

Frank Stone's illustration of Milly Swidger with the Tetterby children for The Haunted Man *(1848).*

instances of "consuming passion that leads to misery and self-destruction," and characters who are the inevitable products of earlier acts and events. Stone's edition of *Charles Dickens' Uncollected Writings from "Household Words," 1850–1859* (1968) collects and annotates Dickens's contributions to articles which he coauthored or significantly edited. Stone has also edited a facsimile edition of *Dickens' Working Notes for his Novels* (1987), and several editions of minor works by Dickens. Important among his many articles are "Dickens and Harriet Beecher Stowe" (*Nineteenth Century Fiction,* 1958); "Dickens and the Jews" (*Victorian Studies,* 1959); "Dickens' Woman in White" (*Victorian Newsletter,* 1968) on Miss Havisham in *Expectations*; "The Love Pattern in Dickens' Novels" (in *Dickens the Craftsman,* ed. Partlow, 1970).

Stone, Marcus (1840–1921)   English artist and illustrator, one of the young men at GAD'S HILL in the 1860s. After Frank STONE died in 1859, Dickens became a second father to his son Marcus and the rest of the family. J. W. T. LEY (1918) describes Marcus as "Dickens' favorite among all the young men that worshipped him in the last decade of his life." Marcus was often invited to stay at Gad's Hill and he frequently accompanied Dickens on his walks. Dickens employed him to illustrate *Mutual Friend* and the LIBRARY EDITION of *Expectations,* which had not been previously illustrated. Stone also illustrated *Pictures from Italy, American Notes,* and *A*

Marcus Stone's picture of the Lammles on their disillusioning honeymoon for the original edition of Our Mutual Friend *(1864).*

Child's History of England for the Library Edition, and he drew frontispieces for the CHEAP EDITIONS of *Drood* and *Two Cities*. Stone described Dickens as "the best man I ever knew. He was such a good man that you put his greatness in second place when you knew him. He occupied himself daily in some sort of work for somebody."

"Stores for the First of April" Article for HOUSE-HOLD WORDS (March 7, 1857) in which Dickens calculates "what we have in store" for All Fool's-Day. He discusses a number of spiritualist accounts as appropriate stores, bitterly recounts the reports of bungling and mismanagement in the Crimea and the excuses given by those responsible, and goes on to describe a clergyman who wants to remove an exhibition of the Thugs in India from the British Museum because it encourages crime. *Miscellaneous.*

"Story of the Goblins who Stole a Sexton, The" INTERPOLATED TALE in *Pickwick*, a story told by Wardle on Christmas Eve at Manor Farm. When Gabriel Grub, a morose grave digger, spends Christmas Eve digging a grave and drinking himself into a stupor, he dreams that goblins torment him for his misanthropic behavior. He awakens the next morning in shame, leaves his village,

and wanders for ten years before returning a broken but repentant man. *Pickwick* (27). The story is usually considered a precursor to the *Carol*.

"Story of Little Dombey, The" Dickens's PUBLIC READING from *Dombey*. First performed in 1858, it was the first reading he drew from one of the longer novels. It presents the life and death of young Paul Dombey.

"Story of Richard Doubledick, The" Dickens's story for "The Seven Poor Travellers," the Christmas number of HOUSEHOLD WORDS, 1854. After being jilted, Richard Doubledick joins the army and is redeemed from a life of dissipation by Captain Taunton, an officer to whom he becomes a loyal friend and comrade-in-arms during the Napoleonic campaigns. When Taunton is killed, Doubledick vows to kill the French officer responsible for his death, but he is wounded, reunited with his love, and, through the influence of Taunton's mother, learns to love his enemies, including the French officer. "Seven Poor Travellers."

Storey, Gladys Close Friend of Dickens's daughter Kate (see Kate Macready DICKENS). Her controversial biographical work, *Dickens and Daughter* (1939), based on interviews with Kate Dickens during the last years of her life, was one of the first books to reveal Dickens's relationship with Ellen TERNAN. It convinced many formerly skeptical Dickensians that the rumors about the novelist's relationship with a young actress were true.

Stowe, Harriet Elizabeth Beecher (1811–1896) American novelist, best known for *Uncle Tom's Cabin* (1852). She sent Dickens a presentation copy of that novel in 1852, and in "North American Slavery" he described it as "a noble work" but criticized its "overstrained conclusions and violent extremes." The two met a year later when she was touring England, but they did not establish an ongoing friendship. By the end of his life, Dickens was less charitable toward Mrs. Stowe; when she published an article in 1869 on Lord Byron's affair with Augusta Leigh, Dickens wrote to FIELDS, his American publisher: "wish Mrs. Stowe was in the pillory." Harry STONE (1958) provides a detailed account of the relationship between the two novelists.

Strand, The One of the main commercial thoroughfares in London, connecting the CITY with the West End. HUNGERFORD Stairs, where Dickens worked as a boy at WARREN'S BLACKING, was located off the Strand, as were the offices of the *MORNING CHRONICLE*. The street is mentioned frequently in Dickens's works. Miss La Creevy's house, "halfway down the crowded thoroughfare," advertised her paintings with a "large gilt frame upon the street door" (*Nickleby*, 3). Martin Chuzzlewit has lodgings in the Strand (*Chuzzlewit*, 48). Dick Swiveller has "only one avenue to the Strand left open"; his creditors occupy all the other routes (*Curiosity Shop*, 8).

Strange Gentleman, The A dramatic version of "The Great Winglebury Duel," performed at the ST. JAMES'S THEATRE on September 29, 1836. A strange gentleman arrives at an inn on his way to GRETNA GREEN to marry Emily Brown. He has never met Emily; the marriage has been arranged by his father. His rival for Emily, Horatio Tinkles, challenges him to a duel. Attempting to avoid the duel and to meet Emily, the strange gentleman, Walter Trott, mistakes other guests at the inn and is mistaken by them. In the end he loses Emily to Tinkles, but he gains Miss Julia Dobbs.

Straudenheim The Traveller imagines the life of this inhabitant of Strasbourg as he watches him from his hotel window. *Uncommercial* (7).

Straw, Sergeant A detective police officer from Scotland Yard, "a little wiry Sergeant of meek demeanour and strong sense." *Reprinted*, "Detective Police."

Streaker Housemaid at the "Haunted House," capable of producing "the largest and most transparent tears."

"Streets—Morning, The" An hour-by-hour account of London in the morning, from the empty streets before dawn to the bustle at noon. Originally published as "Sketches of London No. 17" in the *EVENING CHRONICLE* (July 21, 1835). *Boz.*

"Streets—Night, The" Originally published in *BELL'S LIFE IN LONDON* (January 17, 1836) as "Scenes and Characters No. 17. The Streets at Night." The sketch describes a "dark, dull, murky winter's night" in suburban streets where the muffin and beer sellers peddle their wares door to door. Later, in a harmonic meeting, theatergoers gather in the small hours of the morning to sing and listen to "glees." *Boz.*

"Stroller's Tale, The" INTERPOLATED TALE told by Dismal Jemmy (James Hutley), a strolling actor. The tale describes the wretched poverty of a PANTOMIME clown, his abuse of his wife and family, and his alcohol-induced dementia during the final hours of his life. *Pickwick* (3).

Strong, Doctor Kind headmaster of the school in CANTERBURY that David Copperfield attends. An elderly man preoccupied with his Greek dictionary, Strong "was in his clothes not particularly well-brushed, and his hair not particularly well combed; his knee-smalls unbraced; his long black gaiters unbuttoned; and his shoes yawning like two caverns on the hearth-rug" (16). His young wife, **Annie**, "a very pretty young lady" (16) whom David at first mistakes for Strong's daughter, is suspected of having a secret affair with her cousin, Jack Maldon. Mr. Dick, who has become friendly with the doctor, puts these suspicions to rest (45). After Betsey Trotwood's financial losses, David goes to work as Doctor Strong's secretary (36). *Copperfield.*

Struggles Member of the Dingley Dell Cricket Club. *Pickwick* (7).

Stryver London barrister who defends Charles Darnay, "stout, red, bluff, and free from any drawback of delicacy" (II:4). He employs his old school friend Sydney Carton as his devil, his assistant in his legal practice. He briefly considers proposing marriage to Lucie Manette (II:12). *Two Cities.*

Stubbs Pony that Mr. Boythorn makes available to Esther Summerson, "a chubby pony, with a short neck, and a mane all over his eyes, who could canter—when he would—so easily and quietly, that he was a treasure." *Bleak House* (36).

Stubbs, Mrs. Percy Noakes's laundress, "a dirty old woman with an inflamed countenance." *Boz*, "Steam Excursion."

Stumpington, Lord Political appointee who takes over Tapenham's department with a change in government. *Miscellaneous*, "Cheap Patriotism."

Stumps, Bill Mr. Blotton claims that this working man, whom he has interviewed, is responsible for the inscription on the paving stone—which he translates to read "BILL STUMPS, HIS MARK"—that Pickwick has taken to be written in antiquity. *Pickwick* (11).

Styles   Member of the Statistics Section of the Mudfog Association. *Mudfog* (2).

Styles, John   Prisoner held up as a model of repentance by the proponents of the separate system of imprisonment. Dickens shows that his written statements are self-serving and hypocritical. *Miscellaneous*, "Pet Prisoners."

"Sucking Pigs"   Article for *HOUSEHOLD WORDS* (November 8, 1851), adding to the extreme ideologies attacked in an earlier article, "Whole Hogs," the sucking pig of Bloomerism, a movement led by Mrs. Amelia Bloomer, who advocated the wearing of bloomers, pant-like undergarments, as a way of liberating women. The excesses of the Bloomerites in dress, behavior, and rhetoric make them foolish. Bellows, the narrator of the piece, asserts that "if there were anything that we could dispense with in Mrs. Bellows above all other things, we believe it would be a Mission." *Miscellaneous*. This article is especially relevant to Dickens's criticism of Mrs. Jellyby and Mrs. Pardiggle in *Bleak House*.

Sucksmith, Harvey Peter   Contemporary British literary scholar, whose important study of Dickens's conscious artistry, *The Narrative Art of Charles Dickens* (1970), challenges, with detailed analyses of the rhetorical devices he used to achieve certain effects, the notion of Dickens as an unconscious artist.

Sudbury   Dickens reported a by-election in this Suffolk town for the *MORNING CHRONICLE* in July 1834 and then used it as the model for EATANSWILL in *Pickwick* (13). The Swan Inn in Sudbury is the original of the PEACOCK, where the Buffs have their headquarters.

"Suffolk Bantam"   Prizefighter who is stopped from fighting the Middlesex Dumpling by Magistrate Nupkins. *Pickwick* (23).

Sullivan, Francis L. (1903–1956)   British character actor, famous for his screen roles as Crisparkle in *Edwin Drood* (1935), Bumble in David LEAN's *Oliver Twist* (1948), and Jaggers in both the Universal Production (1934) and Lean's (1946) version of *Great Expectations*.

Sulliwin, Mrs.   Charlady in SEVEN DIALS: "Here's poor dear Mrs. Sulliwin, as has five blessed children of her own, can't go out a charing for one afternoon, but what hussies be a comin', and 'ticing away her own 'usband, as she's been married to twelve year come next Easter Monday." *Boz*, "Seven Dials."

Summerson, Esther   Narrator of the first-person sections of *Bleak House*. Raised by her aunt, Miss Barbary, as an orphan and told "It would have been far

better . . . that you had never been born" (3), Esther is shy and self-deprecating: "I know I am not clever. I always knew that. . . . I had always a rather noticing way—not a quick way. O no!—a silent way of noticing what passed before me, and thinking I should like to understand it better. I have not by any means a quick understanding" (3). After her aunt's death, John Jarndyce sends her to Greenleaf School and then appoints her as his housekeeper at BLEAK HOUSE in ST. ALBANS and as companion to Ada Clare (6). He praises Esther's industry, thoughtfulness, and maturity, addressing her with nicknames like **"Mother Shipton"** and **"Dame Durden"** that emphasize her role as a sexless housekeeper. He encourages her to learn about her parentage, in spite of Esther's reluctance to do so. In the course of the story Esther learns that she is the illegitimate daughter of Lady Dedlock and Captain Hawdon (36). Though Esther is pretty enough to be recognized by Guppy as Lady Dedlock's daughter, she depreciates her own beauty and is pleased when her face, scarred by smallpox, loses its beauty and resemblance to her mother. She refuses Guppy's proposal (9), and secretly loves Woodcourt, but she accepts Jarndyce's proposal out of gratitude to him (44). He recognizes her love for Woodcourt, however, and releases her to the doctor, providing a new Bleak House for them in YORKSHIRE (64). *Bleak House*. Esther's coy, self-deprecating character and voice have occasioned much controversy. Dickens has been attacked for holding up her uncomplaining deference as a feminine ideal and praised for his insightful analysis of women's role in Victorian society. Esther is perhaps the most controversial of all Dickens's characters.

Sumner, Charles (1811–1874)   American lawyer, writer, U.S. senator, law professor at Harvard, leader in the antislavery campaign. He served as Dickens's principal escort in BOSTON during the author's 1842 visit to AMERICA, Dickens dined with him in Washington during his 1867 reading tour. He described Dickens in 1842 as "a most delightful person, overflowing with genius, cordiality & kindliness. Under *thirty* (he will be 30 next month) & a more than conqueror of the world."

Sun Court   Street off CORNHILL, location of the GEORGE AND VULTURE, the inn where DODSON AND FOGG's clerk seeks out Pickwick. *Pickwick* (31).

"Sunday Screw, The"   Article for *HOUSEHOLD WORDS* (June 22, 1850), discussing a parliamentary bill to eliminate the collection and delivery of letters on Sunday. Dickens sees this bill as "the beginning of a Sabbatarian Crusade, outrageous to the spirit of Christianity, irreconcilable with the health, the rational enjoyments, and the true religious feeling of the community." He urges Lord SHAFTESBURY, whom he considers "most mischievously deluded on this question," to reconsider lending his influence to a movement which would turn Sunday into "a day of mortification and gloom." *Miscellaneous*.

Sunday under Three Heads   Pamphlet published in 1836, under the pseudonym "Timothy Sparks," with three illustrations by BROWNE; the full title was *Sunday under Three Heads. As it is; as Sabbath Bills would make it; as it might be made.* Prompted by the defeat in Parliament of Sir Andrew Agnew's Sunday Observance Bill, Dickens attacked such legislation for its class bias, pointing out that Agnew's bill would curtail only the recreations of the poor, not those of the rich. In describing Sunday as it is, he follows the activities of the day for both rich and poor, depicting it as the one day on which the poor have meat for their meal and the one day on which they can go out of doors to parks, into the countryside, or to the river for some healthful recreation. The Sabbath bills would turn Sunday into "a day of general gloom and austerity," leaving the poor, restless, discontented, and quarrelsome. Sunday might be made a time when the museums were open in the afternoon and when games and outdoor recreations, like those the author had once seen sponsored by a country clergyman, which engaged the whole community in healthful activity. "The Sabbath was made for man," Dickens reminds his readers in closing, "not man to serve the Sabbath."

Superintendent   Police inspector who takes the Traveller on a night visit to the slums of LIVERPOOL; "a tall well-looking well-set-up man of a soldierly bearing." *Uncommercial* (5).

"Supposing"   Under this title Dickens wrote several short articles for *HOUSEHOLD WORDS,* in each of which he addressed a social or governmental abuse by asking, What if the circumstances were changed? Or what if a different class of people were involved? The articles appeared on April 20, 1850 (on a potpourri of social and political issues); August 10, 1850 (on the misuse of government funds); June 7, 1851 (on class bias in the courts); February 10, 1855 (on mismanagement during the Crimean War). *Miscellaneous.*

Surrey Theatre   At this theater in Blackfriar's Road, Dickens attended a performance of *Twist* in 1838 that so distressed him that he "laid himself down upon the floor in a corner of the box and never rose from it until the drop-scene fell." This theater was also probably the one where Frederick Dorrit played the clarinet and Fanny Dorrit worked as a dancer (*Dorrit*, I:7, 20).

Surtees, Robert Smith (1805–1864)   Sporting novelist, best known for Jorrocks, a cockney grocer, huntsman, and squire whose "jaunts and jollities" Surtees described in the *New Sporting Magazine,* which he edited from 1831 to 1836. Jorrocks's popularity contributed to Robert SEYMOUR's scheme for a series of comic sporting plates that ultimately became *Pickwick Papers.* A huntsman himself, Surtees continued to publish sporting novels centered on Jorricks in the 1840s, among them *Handley Cross* (1843) and *Hillingdon Hall* (1845). LEECH illustrated several of his books.

Susan (1)   Mrs. Mann's maid. *Twist*, (17).

Susan (2)   Rosina Nightingale's maid. *Nightingale.*

Susannah   Wife of the narrator. *Miscellaneous,* "Smuggled Relations."

Suzannet Collection   Extensive collection of Dickens materials made by the Comte Alain de Suzannet (1882–1950), including editions of the novels, Dickens's reading texts; texts of Dickens's speeches; many letters and manuscripts, pictures and drawings, and miscellaneous Dickensiana. He and his wife donated many items from this collection to the DICKENS HOUSE Museum. Other items were sold at auction after his death. Michael SLATER (1975) edited a descriptive catalogue of the collection.

Swan, The   Coach stop in STAMFORD HILL, north London, where Minns disembarks on his visit to Poplar Walk. *Boz*, "Minns."

Sweedlepipe, Paul ("Poll")   Barber and bird fancier who is Mrs. Gamp's landlord and a friend of Young Bailey; "a little elderly man, with a clammy cold right hand, from which even rabbits and birds could not remove the smell of shaving soap. Poll had something of the bird in his nature" (26). *Chuzzlewit.*

Sweeney, Mrs.   Laundress at GRAY'S INN whose late husband had been a ticket porter for the same institution. *Uncommercial* (14).

Sweet William   One of the traveling performers—a conjurer who can put lead lozenges on his eyes and bring them out his mouth—whom Nell meets at the JOLLY SANDBOYS. *Curiosity Shop* (19).

Swidger Family   Family affected by Redlaw's power to eradicate the memory of suffering. **William**, keeper of the college where Redlaw lives and teaches, and his reprobate brother **George** are the sons of 87-year-old **Philip**, who "don't know what forgetting means." Redlaw's "gift" reduces the old man to dottering senility and makes George forget his sins against the family. They are returned to themselves by **Milly ("Mrs. William," "Mouse," "Swidge")**, George's wife. Her "better wisdom," rooted in her own sorrows, especially in the memory of her dead child, restores the memory and compassion of those affected by Redlaw's curse. *Haunted Man.*

Swillenhousen, Baron and Baroness von   Parents of the Baroness von Koëldwethout. *Nickleby* (6).

Swills, Little   Comic singer at the harmonic meetings at the SOL'S ARMS; "a chubby little man in a large shirt collar, with a moist eye, and an inflamed nose." *Bleak House* (11).

Swinburne, Algernon C. (1837–1909) English poet and critic. In GENOA in 1844–45, the Dickens children played with the "golden-haired son of the Swinburnes," who was home from his first term at Eton. Swinburne became an enthusiast for Dickens's work while he was at Eton and was an ardent Dickensian throughout his life. In a posthumously published essay on Dickens (1913), he shared his appreciation for the novels and provided several unusual insights into them, particularly into some of the incidental characters.

Switzerland Dickens traveled through Switzerland in 1845 and spent the summer of 1846 with his family there. David Copperfield recuperates from the loss of Dora in Switzerland (*Copperfield*, 58). The Dorrits pass through on their way to Italy (*Dorrit*, I:2). The narrator of "The Holly Tree" remembers a little Swiss inn, "a very homely place, in a village of one narrow zigzag street, among mountains," where a murder occurred while he was staying there (1). The Traveller describes a journey to Switzerland (*Uncommercial*, 7). In the Swiss Alps, Vendale discovers his true identity and Obenreizer meets his death ("No Thoroughfare").

Swiveller, Dick Dissolute and feckless associate of Fred Trent who has "the fire of his soul . . . kindled at the taper of conviviality" (2). He agrees to marry Nell so that Fred can get Grandfather Trent's money (7) and so that he can enjoy the pleasures of rosy wine and singing with his companions in the "Glorious Apollers." Dick gives up Sophy Wackles to forward this scheme, (8) but he fails to carry it out. Quilp has the Brasses hire him as a clerk (33), and he enlivens the office with his happy-go-lucky attitude and his quotations from popular songs (36). He befriends the Brasses' little servant girl, whom he calls "the Marchioness," teaching her the pleasures of beer and cribbage (57). When he is dismissed and falls ill, she runs away to him, nurses him through his fever, and provides the evidence to exonerate Kit Nubbles (64). With a small inheritance from his aunt, Dick educates her, names her Sophronia Sphynx, and marries her (73). *Curiosity Shop*.

Swoshle, Mrs. Henry George Alfred Mrs. Tapkins's married daughter, who calls on the newly rich Boffins. *Mutual Friend* (I:17).

Swosser, Captain, R. N. Mrs. Bayham Badger's first husband, a naval officer. *Bleak House* (13).

Sylvia Girl at the farm where Silverman stays after he is orphaned. He avoids her for fear of giving her the fever from which his parents died. "Silverman."

Symbolism In a sense, all literature is symbolic, suggesting meanings broader than the literal events and things that are described, and in its simplest sense a symbol is something (a character, an event, a place, or thing) that stands for something else.

In ALLEGORY the referent and the message are usually more important than the symbol and are usually expressed in figures that have well-established and understood meanings. The master in Jesus' parable of the talents, for example, clearly represents God, and the story is told to contrast the three servants as three different kinds of believers. Dickens uses such allegorical symbols in several of his novels, especially in *Curiosity Shop*, which is at times consciously modeled on John Bunyan's *Pilgrim's Progress* and is based in the traditional symbol of life as a journey. In his journalistic essays Dickens often employed such traditional symbols to develop political allegories as in the figure of John Bull, used to represent the average Englishman.

More often, especially in the later novels, Dickens employed symbolism of a more modern sort, using symbols that are ambiguous and that make the concrete symbol itself essential to its meaning. The fog in *Bleak House*, for example, may represent the confusion and obfuscation in the Court of CHANCERY, but it is also literally fog as it makes murky the city streets, turning them and the fields in Lincolnshire into mud. And its symbolic effects reach far beyond Chancery, devasting TOM-ALL-ALONE's and provoking Krook's confused mimicry, whose SPONTANEOUS COMBUSTION carries the apocalyptic suggestion that the world may succumb simultaneously to the agents of watery mud and fire. In its narrowest suggestion, the fog may look like the wigs worn by the lawyers and judges in the courtroom, but it is also a sign of social and primordial forces that are reducing everything to items of mortality caught, like the dinosaurs, in the mudslide of history. All of the later novels contain such richly suggestive symbols: the factories and circuses in *Hard Times*; the prisons in *Little Dorrit*; the worldly and visionary cities in *Two Cities*; the marshes, chains, Satis House, and river in *Expectations*; the dust heaps and the river in *Mutual Friend*; the opium den and cathedral in *Drood*. Almost all critics writing since Edmund WILSON have taken for granted that Dickens is a profoundly symbolic writer, using both traditional symbols from the BIBLE, folk literature, FAIRY TALES, and legend, as well as symbols derived from his own mythic apprehension of the world, richly suggestive, ambiguous, and paradoxical.

Symond's Inn "A little, pale, wall-eyed, woe-begone inn. . . . It looks as if Symond were a sparing man in his way, and constructed an inn of old building materials, which took kindly to the dry rot and dirt and all things decaying and dismal, and perpetuated Symond's memory with congenial shabbiness" (39). Vholes maintains his offices in this nondescript office building in CHANCERY LANE. *Bleak House*.

T

Tabblewick, Mrs. A beautiful woman, once believed by the Plausible Couple to be "the most beautiful woman ever seen." *Young Couples*.

Tabby Serving drudge at Miss Griffin's school. "Haunted House."

Tacker Assistant to Mould the undertaker, "an obese person, with his waistcoat in closer connection with his legs than is quite reconcilable with established ideas of grace. . . . He had been a tender plant once upon a time, but, from constant blowing in the fat air of funerals, had run to seed" (19). *Chuzzlewit*.

Tackleton Known as Gruff and Tackleton—derived from the name of his toymaking firm, begun with his deceased partner Gruff—Tackleton is the Scrooge of *Cricket*. A stern, cynical, and sarcastic old curmudgeon, "cramped and chafing in the peaceable pursuit of toymaking, he was a domestic Ogre, who had been living on children all his life, and was their implacable enemy." Though he has managed to secure the consent of the young and pretty May Fielding to an unequal marriage, Tackleton's plans are foiled when Edward Plummer, her first love, who was thought to have died in South America, returns and marries her on the morning of the day she was scheduled to marry Tackleton. When he observes John Peerybingle's generosity and understanding with Dot, Tackleton is changed and joins in the celebration of May and Edward's union. *Cricket*.

Tadger, Brother Member of the Brick Lane Ebenezer Temperance Association, "the little man in the drab shorts." *Pickwick* (33).

Tale of Two Cities, A Dickens's 12th novel, serialized unillustrated in weekly parts in ALL THE YEAR ROUND (April 30 to November 26, 1859). It was simultaneously issued in eight monthly numbers by CHAPMAN & HALL, illustrated by BROWNE. Published in one volume, 1859. Dickens's second HISTORICAL NOVEL, largely based on CARLYLE's *French Revolution, Two Cities* was intended, Dickens said, to make that "terrible time" more "popular and picturesque." Departing from his accustomed manner to concentrate on the incidents and MYTH in his story rather than on the characters, Dickens attempted to reconcile his historical theme with the personal story of Sydney Carton, whose sacrifice challenges historical inevitability.

SYNOPSIS

Book One. Recalled to Life

Part 1 (April 30, 1859)
(I:1) The book opens, in year 1775, with the now-famous words, "It was the best of times, it was the worst of times." In England, its American colonies on the verge of revolution, public order was maintained with muskets. In France, the Woodman (Fate) and the Farmer (Death) were already silently at work preparing for the revolution.

Fred Barnard's idealized portrait of Sydney Carton (1894).

(I:2) As the London-to-Dover coach labors up a muddy hill on a dark November night, a horseman brings a message for one of the passengers, Mr. Jarvis Lorry of Tellson's Bank. Lorry reads the brief note and sends the messenger back with the answer, "Recalled to Life." The coachmen speculate on the cryptic reply. The narrator says that Jerry Cruncher, the messenger, who works as a "resurrection man" on the side, stealing bodies from graves, would be "in a Blazing bad way" should recalling to life come into fashion. (I:3) Jerry is uneasy about the message. Jarvis Lorry, sleeping fitfully in the coach, dreams of digging out of a grave someone who has been buried for 18 years.

Part 2 (May 7, 1859)
(I:4) In Dover, Lorry meets Miss Manette, a young woman of 17 who has been informed that there is news respecting the property of her father, whom she has never seen. Lorry tells her how he handled the financial affairs of a physician of Beauvais and his English wife. When their child was orphaned 15 years ago, he brought the child, Miss Manette, to England. But, Lorry tells her, Doctor Manette did not die; he was a prisoner in the BASTILLE, and he has recently been released and is in the care of a former servant in Paris. Their secret mission is to bring him out of France. On hearing this news, Miss Manette faints.

Part 3 (May 14, 1859)
(I:5) A mob of the poor has gathered in the cobblestone street in front of a wineshop in Paris to sop up wine from a broken cask. During the desperate revelry, one of the celebrants writes the word *BLOOD* in wine on the wall. Meanwhile, in the wine shop, Madame Defarge, the owner's wife, knits; her husband sends three customers, all named Jacques, into a tower off the courtyard. When Lorry and Miss Manette arrive, Defarge directs them to the same tower. At the door of a garret room, they find the three Jacques peering through cracks around the door. In the darkened garret, they find Doctor Manette busily making shoes.

Part 4 (May 21, 1859)
(I:6) Yellowed from so many years in prison, like a creature revived from the grave, Manette does not recognize his visitors. When Defarge asks his name, he says, "One Hundred and Five, North Tower." When he sees his daughter's golden hair, he shows some signs of recognition. He takes some similar hairs from around his neck, compares the two and asks, "Was it you?" Gradually he allows her to embrace him. A few hours later, Lorry and Miss Manette set off in a coach, taking the old man and his shoemaking equipment with them.

Book Two. The Golden Thread

Part 5 (May 28, 1859)
(II:1) Five years later, Jerry Cruncher, Tellson's bank messenger, stands at his post outside the London office with young Jerry, his look-alike son. (II:2) He is sent to the OLD BAILEY where a treason case is in progress, and told to wait there for any message that Lorry may wish to send. In the dock Charles Darnay, a French emigré, stands accused of giving the French information about British troop movements. Everybody in the room is focused on the prisoner, except for Sydney Carton, a lawyer who lounges at the side of the room, looking at the ceiling and showing little interest in the proceedings.

Part 6 (June 4, 1859)
(II:3) The crowd has gathered in the courtroom, like flies around carrion, expecting Darnay to be sentenced to death. Two witnesses for the prosecution, John Barsad and Roger Cly, testify that they saw Darnay deliver information to the French. The Manettes, who met Darnay on the channel boat as the doctor was being brought out of France, are called to testify. The doctor remembers nothing, but Lucie is forced to testify that Darnay had jokingly suggested that George Washington would probably surpass George III in history. She had also seen him confer with some Frenchmen. Then Stryver, lawyer for the defense, points out his associate, Sydney Carton, and asks a prosecution witness to identify Carton as definitely not the gentleman in question. Carton's resemblance to Darnay is remarkable and the witness cannot do so. The jury deliberates and delivers its verdict. Jerry receives the note from Lorry, "Acquitted." He speculates that "Recalled to Life" would again have been appropriate. The flies disperse.

Part 7 (June 11, 1859)
(II:4) The doubles, Carton and Darnay, dine together. Carton's cynicism and despair clash with Darnay's optimistic integrity. During the meal, Carton drinks too much and becomes insolent. He describes himself as "a disappointed drudge" who cares "for no man on earth." After Darnay leaves, Carton studies himself in a mirror, seeing in his self-hatred the reasons for his dislike of Darnay, who looks so much like him.

(II:5) Carton goes to Stryver's office and the two work through the night on the cases for the next day. Carton does the hard work, priming Stryver on the issues in the cases. He drinks as he works. Stryver observes that Sydney has always been a background figure; even when they were schoolboys together at Shrewsbury, Carton did the assignments for the other boys. Sydney leaves the office at dawn, goes through the wasteland of the city, which seems to echo the "waste forces within him," and falls asleep in tears.

Part 8 (June 18, 1859)
(II:6) On a July afternoon, Lorry walks to SOHO to visit the Manettes. Only Miss Pross, Lucie's companion who is bothered by the "hundreds" of unworthy people interested in her "ladybird," is at home. When Lorry asks if Doctor Manette ever thinks of his time in prison, Pross says that Lucie sometimes walks in the night with her father till he recovers from such memories. Standing in the window of the Manettes' corner house, Lorry can hear the Manettes' footsteps approaching. Later, Charles

Darnay joins them. As they sit under the plane tree in the yard, Darnay tells a story about a prisoner who left the initials DIG carved on a wall in his cell; in the floor under the letters a manuscript he had buried there was found. The story upsets Dr. Manette. By tea time Carton has arrived and a storm is approaching. The storm sounds as if hundreds of footsteps are coming to the house.

Part 9 (June 25, 1859)
(II:7) In Paris, the rich gather at the house of Monseigneur, the powerful representative of the French aristocracy. In his private rooms, Monseigneur has four men to prepare his chocolate before he appears briefly to greet the fawning company. As the Marquis St. Evrémonde leaves the gathering and sets off for the country, his speeding carriage runs over a boy in the street and kills him. The Marquis worries about injury to his horses and berates the boy's father for not protecting the child. Defarge, the wine shop owner, consoles the boy's father with the thought that the child did not live to suffer poverty. The Marquis gives Defarge and the father gold coins, but as he sets out again, a coin comes flying through the carriage window. He demands to know who threw it, but Defarge and the grieving father have disappeared. Meanwhile, a woman sits knitting while the carriages of the aristocracy continue to pass by the poor in the streets. (II:8) The Marquis stops in the village near his chateau and asks a road mender why he was staring at the carriage. The man explains that he was staring at a figure covered in dust underneath the carriage who is no longer there. The Marquis goes on to his castle, where he asks whether his nephew Monsieur Charles has arrived from England.

Part 10 (July 2, 1859)
(II:9) His nephew has not arrived, so the Marquis dines alone. He thinks he sees something or someone outside the window, but the servant finds no one. When his nephew, Charles Darnay, arrives, they have an uncomfortable meeting. Charles knows his uncle was responsible for the trial in London and has tried to silence him "for the honor of the family." Charles urges the Marquis to right the wrongs done by the family, but his uncle says that to be feared and hated is a mark of respect. When Charles says that he plans to work rather than take any tainted family money and indicates that he knows the Manettes, the Marquis mutters, "So commences the new philosophy!" The next morning the body of the Marquis is found, stabbed to death, with a note: "Drive him fast to his tomb. This, from Jacques."

Part 11 (July 9, 1859)
(II:10) A year later, Charles Darnay is earning his living as a French language tutor in London. The chateau in France has faded into a dream. He tells Dr. Manette that he loves Lucie but that he has been reluctant to come between father and daughter. The doctor assures him that he will not stand in their way. Charles starts to reveal his identity, but the doctor stops him, saying that

if his suit prospers, the revelation can wait until the wedding morning. Lucie hears the sound of hammering from her father's room, but when she knocks at the door the sound ceases.

(II:11) Darnay is not Lucie's only suitor. Stryver confides to Carton as they are drinking together that he plans to propose to Lucie, even though he has criticized her in the past as only a golden haired doll.

Part 12 (July 16, 1859)
(II:12) Stryver heads for Soho to propose, stopping on the way to test his plan on Mr. Lorry. Speaking in his personal and not his business capacity, Lorry advises against it. Stryver is offended, but agrees to let Lorry sound out the situation and report back. By the time Lorry returns, the lawyer has convinced himself that he was never serious. Lorry repeats his earlier counsel.

(II:13) Sydney haunts the streets outside Lucie's house. One day, he confesses to her that she has given him a sense of how his life might have been better. She urges him to allow her to help him achieve a better life, but he says it is too late. He makes her promise to keep his confession secret, telling her that he "would embrace any sacrifice for you and for those dear to you."

Part 13 (July 23, 1859)
(II:14) Outside Tellson's, Cruncher and his son watch the funeral procession for Roger Cly, the spy who testified against Darnay. Cly has staged his own funeral in order to escape the wrath of the mob, and has secretly slipped off to France. Because it is a spy's funeral, the mob in the streets celebrates. They climb onto the hearse and, led by a dancing bear, turn the procession into a parade. Then the mob chases some other suspected spies through the streets. That evening, Jerry plans a "fishing trip" to resurrect Cly's corpse; he warns his wife not to spoil it by "flopping," that is, by kneeling down and praying. At one in the morning, he collects his tools and slips out of the house, unknowingly followed by his son. With two cohorts he goes to a dark cemetery, and his son watches as the three men fish Cly's coffin from a grave only to find it empty. The next morning young Jerry asks his father, who is in a foul mood, what a "resurrection man" is, and says he hopes to be one.

Part 14 (July 30, 1859)
(II:15) At the Parisian wineshop, in the tower room formerly occupied by Manette, Defarge, who calls himself Jacques Four, and the road mender, Jacques Five, who observed the Marquis' carriage, meet with Jacques One, Two, and Three. The road mender tells them of seeing a gaunt man, the father of the dead child, hanging underneath the coach of the Marquis and then, many months after the murder of the Marquis, seeing the same man apprehended, taken to prison, and then hanged in the village square. Defarge takes Jaques Five to see the king and queen at Versailles.

Part 15 (August 6, 1859)
(II:16) A confederate on the police force secretly tells Defarge that Barsad, the Englishman who testified with

Cly against Darnay, has been assigned to St. Antoine as a spy. When Barsad appears at the wineshop, Madame Defarge signals his presence to the patrons by placing a rose in her hair. He introduces several topics—oppression, the execution of the Marquis's assassin Gaspard, etc.—but he fails to get any expressions of revolutionary sympathy from them. He does suprise Defarge with the information that Lucie Manette is planning to marry the Marquis St. Evrémonde. Madame Defarge, who keeps a list of the enemies of the French people to be executed during the coming revolution by knitting them into a "shroud," records this information with her fateful needles.

Part 16 (August 13, 1859)
(II:17) On the evening before her wedding, Lucie asks her father for assurance that her marriage does not disturb him. He tells her for the first time how, while he was in prison, he imagined the child he had never seen. Sometimes he envisioned a son who would seek vengeance, but more often he imagined a daughter. In one of these visions she was married and kept her father's picture in her house. She would show the picture to her children, but she could not deliver him from prison. (II:18) Before the wedding, Charles Darnay meets with Dr. Manette in his room to reveal his identity as a member of the St. Evrémonde family. When they emerge, Manette is deathly pale. After Charles and Lucie leave for their honeymoon, the doctor relapses into his role as shoemaker-prisoner. For nine days, watched over by Pross and Lorry, he works at his bench and does not recognize them. Lorry's efforts to communicate with him are unsuccessful.

Part 17 (August 20, 1859)
(II:19) On the 10th morning, Lorry finds Manette restored to himself. Lorry consults with Manette, disguising the doctor's case to him as the story of someone else and asking if there is danger of a relapse. The doctor says that the attack was brought on by "a strong and extraordinary revival of the train of thought and remembrance that was the first cause of the malady," that the subject would not remember that cause, and that there was hope it would not recur. Lorry asks whether the tools of his traumatic trade—say, a blacksmith's tools—should be gotten rid of. This question makes Manette anxious. He finally agrees to the destruction of the shoemaker's tools for the sake of his daughter. When Manette leaves to visit Lucie and Charles, Lorry destroys the cobbler's bench.

(II:20) Sydney tells Darnay that he wishes to become his friend, but Darnay tells him that he already considers him a friend. When Charles tells Lucie of Sydney's request, he speaks of Sydney "as a problem of carelessness and recklessness." Lucie says that Sydney deserves more consideration and respect and "is capable of good things, gentle things, even magnanimous things."

Part 18 (August 27, 1859)
(II:21) For several years the Darnays live peacefully in their corner house in Soho, which is filled with the sound of echoing footsteps. They have a son, who dies, and a daughter, who lives. Sydney visits them half-a-dozen times a year and is a favorite of their child. By July 1789, when the child is six, Lorry tells them that French depositors are lining up to put their money into an English bank. As they sit in the window that evening, the echoing footsteps seem particularly loud.

Meanwhile, in France, the crowd led by the Jacquerie and the Defarges storms the Bastille. When they get into the prison, Defarge goes to One Hundred and Five North Tower and finds there a stone with *A. M.* on it. He searches the room, looking for a hiding place. The mob plans to take the governor of the prison to the Hotel de Ville for judgment, but they kill him on the way and Madame Defarge decapitates him. In the midst of the mob are the confused faces of seven prisoners who have been released and are being carried on the shoulders of the crowd. Above the mob, seven decapitated heads are carried aloft on poles.

Part 19 (September 3, 1859)
(II:22) Defarge announces that Foulon, an old man who suggested that starving people could eat grass, has been captured. St. Antoine converges on the Hotel de Ville; the mob takes Foulon into the street and hangs him from a lamppost. His head is displayed, stuffed with grass. Next they capture and execute Foulon's son-in-law and parade through the streets with his head.

(II:23) In the country village near the chateau of the St. Evrémonde family, everything is brown and wasted. The mender of roads directs a stranger to the chateau. That evening the castle burns and the townspeople refuse to fight the fire. They ring the town bell for joy, light candles in their windows, and threaten the local tax collector, Gabelle, who hides in his attic.

Part 20 (September 10, 1859)
(II:24) Three years later, in August 1792, Lorry has received a letter addressed to the Marquis St. Evrémonde. Lorry inquires among the French emigrés if any of them has knowledge of the Marquis. Although Darnay has promised Doctor Manette that he will never reveal his identity without the doctor's permission, he admits to Lorry that he knows the Marquis, and takes the letter. The letter is from Gabelle, whom Charles had employed to aid the tenants of the St. Evrémonde estates after his uncle's murder. Gabelle has been imprisoned and needs Charles's testimony to prove that he has the people's best interests at heart. Charles decides he must go to Paris. Leaving letters to Lucie and the doctor to be delivered after he is gone, he sets out for France.

Book 3. The Track of a Storm

Part 21 (September 17, 1859)
(III:1) Charles passes through barricades at each town as he moves closer to Paris. Finally he is forced to hire an escort to take him into the city. When they arrive at the walls of the city, he is addressed by the gatekeepers as "the prisoner" and is taken into custody. He asserts his status as a free man, but a recently passed law has made

all emigrés felons. He is taken to LA FORCE prison and placed in a dungeon where many aristocrats are being held.

Part 22 (September 24, 1859)
(III:2) Tellson's Paris office is located in Monseigneur's former house, the same building that now also serves as a kind of revolutionary headquarters. The Jacquerie have put a grindstone in the courtyard to sharpen their swords. Lorry, in Paris on bank business, looks into the courtyard with trepidation. After he thanks God that he has no friends in Paris, Lucie and Dr. Manette arrive and tell him that Charles is imprisoned in La Force. Lorry points out the revolutionaries in the courtyard to Manette, and the doctor goes to see what he can do for Charles. (III:3) Defarge appears at Tellson's with a letter from Charles to Lucie. He is accompanied by his wife and The Vengeance, her lieutenant. In Madame Defarge's presence, Lucie feels a shadow come over her. Lorry is troubled.

Part 23 (October 1, 1859)
(III:4) At first, Manette believes he can get Charles released quickly. He manages to secure a hearing; but just as it looks as if Charles will be freed, the court changes its mind.

Manette becomes the doctor to the prisons. He can visit Charles, but cannot get him released. Working among the carnage for more than a year, the doctor realizes that his suffering has given him strength. (III:5) Manette tells Lucie of a spot on the sidewalk outside a wood-sawyer's yard where Charles can see her from a prison window. She stands there each afternoon as the sawyer, the former road mender who calls his saw La Guillotine, torments her with his ritual of pretending the pieces of wood he cuts are heads. One wintry day she is on the corner as Madame Defarge and a revolutionary mob dance by doing the Carmagnole. She hides her eyes in horror. When she uncovers them, her father is there to tell her that Charles's trial is scheduled for the next day.

Part 24 (October 8, 1859)
(III:6) Darnay defends himself by telling how he gave up his French citizenship many years before in order to disown his family. He came back only to testify for Gabelle. The doctor testifies about Charles's life, ideas, and trial in England. Charles is released; he and his father-in-law are escorted home by a cheering mob. (III:7) That evening the family plans a quiet celebration. While Pross and Jerry go out to get wine and food, four rough men in red caps appear at the door to rearrest Evrémonde, who has been denounced by Citizen Defarge and his wife.

Part 25 (October 15, 1859)
(III:8) In the wineshop, Pross is startled to meet her brother Solomon, who is working as a spy in the prisons. Cruncher recognizes him as Barsad, the English spy. Then Carton, who has arrived secretly in Paris the night before, appears in the wineshop. He and Cruncher threaten to denounce Solomon to the tribunal. They

know that he gave false testimony at Darnay's trial in London and that he helped to fake the funeral of Roger Cly.

Part 26 (October 22, 1859)
(III:9) Cruncher confesses to Lorry his other life as a resurrection man and says that the horrors he has seen in France have made him penitent.

Meanwhile, Carton makes a deal with Solomon Pross to have access to Darnay, and he asks that Lucie not be told of the arrangement. Then he walks the streets all night, stopping briefly to purchase some drugs. The next morning, he goes to the court and hears the announcement that Darnay has been charged by the Defarges and by Doctor Alexander Manette. Defarge describes how he found Doctor Manette's manuscript hidden in 105 North Tower during the storming of the Bastille. An account of how he came to be imprisoned, the doctor's manuscript describes the crimes of the St. Evrémonde family.

Part 27 (October 29, 1859)
(III:10) Manette's narrative, written in prison in December 1767, is an account of the Christmas week of 1757. On December 22, he was accosted by the St. Evrémonde twins, the Marquis St. Evrémonde, Charles's father, and his brother, who was later assassinated by Gaspard. They took the doctor to a house outside Paris to attend two patients. One was a young woman of 20 or so, pregnant and crazed. She kept repeating: "My husband, my father, and my brother!" Then she would count to 12 and say "Hush!" The other patient was her brother, who died from a stab wound inflicted by one of the twins. As he died he told Manette that his sister had become crazed after her husband, worked to death by the twins, died in her arms. Then she was sexually violated by the younger brother. Following her brother's death, she lived for a week, attended by Manette. After the deaths of the two young peasants, the doctor was released by the St. Evrémonde twins and allowed to return home. There he wrote an account of the events he had witnessed and sent it to a minister of the crown. Soon afterward he was imprisoned in the Bastille.

Manette's manuscript unlooses the fury of the court. Charles Darnay, the current Marquis St. Evrémonde, is sentenced to die within 24 hours.

Part 28 (November 5, 1859)
(III:11) After the courtroom empties, only the Manettes, Barsad, and Carton remain. Lucie is allowed one last embrace from Charles. Dr. Manette begins to kneel before them, as if to ask their forgiveness, but they prevent him. Charles acknowledges his fate as the inevitable end of his family's crimes. As he is taken away, Lucie faints onto her father's breast. Carton carries her to the coach and escorts her home. There he embraces little Lucie, urges Manette to do everything he can to save Charles, and admits to Lorry that he has lost hope.

(III:12) Carton goes to the wine shop in St. Antoine. There the Defarges observe how much he looks like Darnay. He overhears Madame Defarge identify the violated peasant family in Manette's story as her own. She vows vengeance on Lucie, her daughter, and the doctor as well as on Charles. When the doctor returns from the prison, he has reverted to his shoemaker self. They know he has failed. Carton tells Lorry to prepare a coach to leave Paris at two o'clock the next afternoon.

Part 29 (November 12, 1859)
(III:13) Fifty-two people are scheduled to die in the group with Darnay. In his cell, Charles accepts his impending death and writes letters to those he loves—to all except Carton. He dreams of being with Lucie. Shortly after noon on the day of the execution, Sydney Carton appears in Darnay's cell. Carton exchanges clothes with him, and then, knowing that Darnay will resist, drugs him unconscious. Solomon Pross carries Charles away. Left behind, Sydney is led off to the room where the condemned are waiting. He meets a seamstress there, and they plan to go the guillotine together. Outside the prison, the waiting carriage admits the drugged Darnay. As it passes through the checkpoints going out of Paris, Lucie worries that they are being pursued.

Part 30 (November 19, 1859)
(III:14) Madame Defarge plans to arrest Doctor Manette, Lucie, and little Lucie. She does not tell Defarge, for she thinks him softhearted about the doctor. Only Pross is at the Manette apartment when she arrives. Pross knows that the longer she thinks that Lucie is there, the more time Lucie and the others will have to escape, so she prevents Madame Defarge from looking into the rooms of the apartment. In the ensuing struggle between the two women, Madame Defarge is killed with her own pistol. Pross locks the apartment, drops the key in the river, and leaves Paris with Cruncher.

Part 31 (November 26, 1859)
(III:15) The tumbrils proceed to the Guillotine. In the back of the third wagon are Sydney and the seamstress, speaking to each other and paying no attention to the crowd. Madame Defarge has not arrived for the execution; The Vengeance calls for her. Sydney and the seamstress give one another strength. If Sydney could have written his thoughts as he went to the knife, he would have described a vision of the happy family that his sacrifice has preserved and the years to come of their lives together. He approached his death knowing that "It is a far, far better thing that I do, than I have ever done; it is a far, far better rest that I go to than I have ever known."

COMMENTARY

Dickens wrote *A Tale of Two Cities* in weekly numbers to inaugurate *All the Year Round*. A tale of revolution, it emerged from a revolutionary period in Dickens's own life when he separated from his wife, initiated his affair with Ellen TERNAN, changed publishers, and began a new magazine. Just as he had turned his personal life into public event by publishing his "PERSONAL" statement about his marital break-up in *HOUSEHOLD WORDS,*

so the novel sought to connect public and private events and to explain the French Revolution in personal terms.

One of Dickens's favorite books was Carlyle's *French Revolution* (1837), a history he had read many times. Carlyle's idiosyncratic and impressionistic work broke from the tradition of rationalist historiography and stressed the irrational aspects of the revolution, what he called the "daemonic" element. Dickens did not wish to question Carlyle's history by turning it into fiction, but rather "to add . . . picturesque means of understanding that terrible time." To achieve this end, he planned a very different kind of novel from those he was accustomed to writing. Instead of allowing the characters to generate the story, he "fancied a story of incident . . . pounding the characters in its own mortar, and beating their interest out of them" (John FORSTER, 1872). This violent narrative strategy called for concentrated description, very limited dialogue, and a reliance on incident. The voice of the usual Dickensian narrator is subdued as the action itself takes precedence. Although Dickens relied on Carlyle's history for the incidents in his story and shared Carlyle's apocalyptic view of the revolution and its significance, he effaced his narrator, removing the voice of the prophetic interpretor who narrates Carlyle's account, to concentrate on the action itself.

The story Dickens planned to tell was one of extreme personal sacrifice. The idea of dying to save the life of a rival was suggested by Wilkie COLLINS's play *THE FROZEN DEEP*, in which the hero, Richard WARDOUR, discovers that one of his companions on an arctic expedition is his rival for the love of Clara Burnham. Overcoming his desire for revenge, he chooses instead to save the life of his rival, Frank Aldersley, and in the final scene he carries Frank to safety before dying himself. Dickens was deeply moved, especially by this final scene, when playing Wardour in 1857.

Dickens had developed similar themes in several of his stories, most notably in the sacrifices of Marion Jeddler, who gives up her fiancé to her sister (*Battle of Life*), and of Gill Davis, who risks his life, inspired by his admiration and love for Marion Maryon ("English Prisoners"). But these characters had not been called upon to die. The FRENCH REVOLUTION offered an extreme situation that made believable stories of such ultimate sacrifice. It was the same SETTING that inspired similar stories by Watts PHILLIPS in *The Dead Heart* (1859) and Edward Bulwer LYTTON in *Zanoni* (1842). As he contemplated his novel for the year and a half before he began writing, Dickens jotted down a series of possible titles, suggesting some of the themes that he planned to develop: *Buried Alive; Recalled to Life; The Thread of Gold; The Doctor of Beauvais; Memory Carton; The Tale of Two Cities.*

Dickens's version of the French Revolution is "a picturesque story." Scenes like the breaking of the wine cask in the streets of ST. ANTOINE (I:5), Darnay's English trial, resolved by his visual doubling with Sydney Carton (II:3), Cly's anarchic funeral procession (II:14), the murder and beheading of Foulon (II:22), and the frenzied dancing of the Carmagnole (III:5) concentrate history into vivid pictorial events. Murray Baumgarten ("Writing the Revolution," *Dickens Studies Annual*, 1983) has compared particular scenes in *Two Cities* with their counterparts in the *French Revolution* to show how Dickens made Carlyle's history visual.

The novel also includes some of Dickens's most quotable prose. The opening paragraph, with its antitheses and repetitions, and Sydney Carton's closing speech as he goes to the guillotine, are two of the best-known and most often quoted passages in all of Dickens's work.

In spite of its vivid pictorial scenes and quotable passages, *Two Cities* has not received much favorable criticism. Carlyle called it "wonderful," but many of Dickens's contemporaries were less impressed. Fitzjames Stephen was prompted by the novel to write one of the most telling attacks on any Dickens work; he faulted the structure and style, but he was most annoyed by the exaggerations in Dickens's history, especially in his descriptions of the excesses of the French aristocracy. Modern critics, for different reasons, have also been unkind to the novel. They have praised its structure and plotting, but decried its tedious characters and SENTIMENTALITY. The reservations of the critics, however, have not been shared by the broader popular audience. The novel has been a perennial best-seller, not only because it does double duty for English and history teachers, but also for its moving story. The sacrifice that so engaged Dickens has also moved many of his readers, and the scenes describing Sydney Carton's final hours have lodged themselves in the popular memory.

The famous passages that open and end the novel suggest its character and appeal. The antitheses at the beginning—"It was the best of times, it was the worst of times, it was the age of wisdom, it was the age of foolishness, it was the epoch of belief, it was the epoch of incredulity, it was the season of Light, it was the season of Darkness. . . ." (I:1)—present a pattern of opposition that will explode into revolution. These unqualified antitheses establish the tone of inevitability which supports Dickens's historical theme: "Crush humanity out of shape once more, under similar hammers, and it will twist itself into the same tortured forms. Sow the same seed of rapacious license and oppression over again, and it will surely yield the same fruit according to its kind" (III:15). At the same time, the antitheses draw attention to the similarities between the two cities of the title, which, in spite of the suggestion that they are opposed, are essentially similar: "In both countries it was clearer than crystal to the lords of the State . . . that things in general were settled forever" (I:1).

The generalizing effect of the opening chapter introduces the abstract character of the novel. *Two Cities* is, after all, history. Its particular story is intended to show the inevitable consequences of oppression and carries an implicit warning about the dangers of repeating the mistakes of the past. Thus, the plot embodies the rule of history, and the characters, even those based on actual persons, are representative figures. They are creatures of

MYTH and the novel is more allegorical than historical (see ALLEGORY). The Woodman Fate and the Farmer Death who emerge at the end of the first chapter to visualize the theme of historical inevitability are just the first of many allegorical figures. Monseigneur represents the French aristocracy, the many Jacques the oppressed peasantry. The very name *St. Evrémonde* carries the polyglot suggestion that its bearer is an "everyman," a representative of all the world.

The "personal" story of Doctor Manette, his daughter Lucie, and her husband Charles Darnay, although intended to individualize the historical drama, is less interesting than the allegory. Dickens's decision to concentrate on incident rather than character made his actors pawns rather than complex figures. Lucie is identified by her resemblance to her mother, her golden hair, and the allegorical suggestion in her name—*Lucie-light*. Charles is simply a secret aristocrat turned into an earnest bourgeois. The most intriguing thing about him would seem to be the connection of his initials to those of his creator. Doctor Manette, though he enacts a somewhat mechanical version of repressed memory, holds one of the keys to the novel, for buried in his memory—and in the manuscript hidden in the stones of the Bastille—is the myth that explains the revolution and reveals depths to character beyond the roles determined by history.

In what appears to be a kind of second beginning to the novel in the third chapter, Dickens defines the personal dimension of his story in the narrator's reflections on the theme of the buried life:

> . . . [E]very human creature is constituted to be that profound secret and mystery to every other. A solemn consideration, when I enter a great city by night, that every one of those darkly clustered houses encloses its own secret; that every room in every one of them encloses its own secret; that every beating heart in the hundreds of thousands of breasts there, is, in some of its imaginings, a secret to the heart nearest it! Something of the awfulness, even of Death itself, is referable to this. No more can I turn the leaves of this dear book that I loved, and vainly hope to read it all. No more can I look into the depths of this unfathomable water, wherein, as momentary lights glanced into it, I have had glimpses of buried treasure and other things submerged. . . . My friend is dead, my neighbour is dead, my love, the darling of my soul, is dead; it is the inexorable consolation and perpetuation of the secret that was always in that individuality, and which I shall carry in mine to my life's end.

This passage introduces some of the thematic implications of Doctor Manette's story, that each individual has a buried life, forever unknown to others and perhaps even to himself. The passage also calls attention to a technical problem that Dickens faced. Because the truth about Manette is buried, he is incapable of revealing it, except in the somewhat mechanical performance of switching between his two personas.

The only character whose submerged depths complicate the surface of his personality is Sydney Carton. A diffident, self-denigrating man, Carton is one of Dickens's wastrels, like Harthouse (*Hard Times*), Henry Gowan (*Dorrit*), or Eugene Wrayburn (*Mutual Friend*). Self-hating, dissipated, and cynical, he finds nothing to value in life, but he does work at his profession as Stryver's legal devil and he has occasional moments of vision when he imagines a better world. In one such moment, Carton, after a night in Stryver's office, goes out into the city, which appears to him "like a lifeless desert," a projection of the "waste forces within him." Then he has a vision,

> a mirage of honourable ambition, self-denial, and perservance. In the fair city of this vision, there were airy galleries from which the loves and graces looked upon him, gardens in which the fruits of life hung ripening, waters of Hope that sparkled in his sight. A moment and it was gone (II:5).

Called up from the depths of Carton's better self, this vision, along with his hopeless and self-denying love for Lucie, inspires his ultimate sacrifice.

The other "buried treasure" that *Two Cities* uncovers is Manette's manuscript, the "dear book" that reveals the depths of Manette's story and develops the myth that explains the revolution. That myth is a darkened version of the New Testament story, beginning at Christmas and ending with an "Easter" sacrifice, that explains the extreme violence of the revolution, the hysteria of Madame Defarge, and the need for Carton's sacrifice to "redeem the time."

The myth begins at Christmas 1757, when Doctor Manette is commandeered by the Marquis St. Evrémonde and his twin brother to attend two victims, a young man who has been stabbed in a sword fight with the Marquis and the wounded man's sister, whom the Marquis has raped. The Marquis is Charles Darnay's uncle; the victims are the brother and sister of Therese Defarge. Their deaths give birth to the cycle of violence that begins during that Christmas season and culminates in the revolution and Carton's sacrifice 35 years later. In this inversion of the gospel story, the rough beast that slouches to Paris to be born in 1757 is the violence and class hatred of the *ancien régime* that murdered Madame Defarge's brother and sister and buried the secret of the crime in the Bastille. Paris has become Babylon in the era of the beast, with the self-indulgent brutality of the aristocracy and the resentment of the peasants foretelling the revolution. Madame Defarge symbolizes the inevitable vengeance to come; as she knits her death list, she is an 18th-century sister to the Fates.

In a mad parody of the Christian sacrament that turns wine into blood, the poor in the streets of St. Antoine write *BLOOD* on the wall with wine from the broken casks (I:5). In London, Jerry Cruncher, a "resurrection man" with the same initials as Jesus Christ, performs a parody of the Easter story when he digs up Cly's grave only to find the tomb empty (II:14). Both Paris and London are in the grip of the beast. The blood lust that will

drive the Jacquerie into the streets attends Darnay's trial in London, where the spectators take a ghoulish interest in his punishment: "He'll be drawn on a hurdle to be half hanged, and then he'll be taken down and sliced before his own face, and then his inside will be taken out and burnt while he looks on, and then his head will be chopped off, and he'll be cut into quarters" (II:1). Dickens's version of the gospel story is told from the apocalyptic perspective of Revelation. In his latter-day novel, the two cities of the title are not very different from one another.

On an allegorical level, the contrasting cities, as Joseph GOLD (1972) points out, are the Earthly City—represented by both Paris and London—and the City of God, the latter present in the novel in Sydney Carton's visions. His earlier moment of epiphany is repeated just before he goes to the guillotine. In his memorable final scene, cast as a vision of the future rather than an account of past and present, Carton imagines a third city that will replace the two cities of the title: "I see a beautiful city and a brilliant people rising from this abyss, and, in their struggles to be truly free, in their triumphs and defeats, through long long years to come, I see the evil of this time and of the previous time of which this is the natural birth, gradually making expiation for itself and wearing out" (III:15). His self-sacrifice, which culminates this vision, breaks the hold of historic inevitability and starts the process that will engender this "beautiful city."

Two Cities is memorable not because it makes history picturesque, but because it challenges the very idea of history. Carton's final scene—the most memorable in the novel—replaces historical fact with vision and culminates the translation of history into myth. Although Dickens took many of the historical facts in his novel from Carlyle's *French Revolution*, his interpretation of "that terrible time" relies on a buried story, on the manuscript hidden in the wall of the Bastille by Doctor Manette and on the biblical story that breaks the hold of history with the sacrifice of a "truly free" individual. Carton's sacrifice provides the "Easter" ending to the novel's redemption myth.

Gold (1972) describes Carton's death as the culmination of Dickens's "translation of the Christian metaphysic into humanistic terms." Carton is drawn to the "loadstone rock" by his earthly love for Lucie, who has become the guiding light in his life, and by his vision of the beautiful city. Although before changing places with Darnay he meditates on the biblical promise "I am the resurrection and the life, saith the Lord; he that believeth in me, though he were dead, yet shall he live: and whosoever liveth and believeth in me, shall never die," he is not really a Christ figure. Rather he is more like the deeply flawed whisky priest in Graham GREENE's *The Power and the Glory* (1940), whose martyrdom arises from despair and an awareness of the darkness of his situation. A self-denigrating libertine, hopelessly in love with Lucie, Carton becomes an everyman in spite of himself. His vision of the future describes his blessedness as an immortality of influence on the Darnays and their descendants, who will remember his sacrifice. His final words state an optimistic challenge to historical fatalism, a challenge that may over time enable the two earthly cities to recover from the excesses of the best and the worst of times.

CRITICISM

The most thorough discussion of *Two Cities* as an example of a historical novel appears in Andrew SANDERS (1979); he compares the later novel with *Rudge* and discusses Dickens's fascination with the power of the mob.

Dickens's debt to Carlyle in the novel has been thoroughly explored by Michael GOLDBERG (1972) and by William Oddie (*Dickens and Carlyle*, 1972), who provides a detailed listing of Dickens's borrowings from the *French Revolution*. Oddie also points to important differences between the two works, especially to the fatalism in Dickens's novel which is not present in Carlyle. *Dickens Studies Annual* (1983) includes several articles discussing aspects of Carlyle's influence on the novel.

Sylvère MONOD (1968), the premier French scholar working on Dickens, praises Dickens's use of the two trial scenes to give structural symmetry to the story and his "conveying the emotions and evolutions of crowds and mobs," but he finds Dickens's history untrustworthy, the Anglo-French spoken by the French characters wearisome, and the story excessively pathetic and melodramatic. Gold (1972) offers a provocative reading of the mythic dimensions of the novel and of Dickens's use of Christian symbolism. Ruth Glancy's *A Tale of Two Cities: Dickens's Revolutionary Novel* (1991) is an informative and intelligent general introduction.

ADAPTATIONS

Although Dickens contemplated playing Sydney Carton on stage himself, he did not do so. The first production, which he authorized and supervised, opened at the Lyceum Theatre in London shortly after the novel completed its serial run. This production, with a script by Tom Taylor and starring Fred Villiers as Carton, had a successful run, even though it ended anticlimactically with the death of Madame Defarge rather than that of Carton. Another 1860 adaptation, *The Tale of Two Cities; or, The Incarcerated Victim of the Bastille*, changed the novel even more, ending with Sydney Carton's escape from the guillotine after a second change of clothes, this time with Barsad, who replaces him under the blade. Although there were several later 19th-century productions, the most famous adaptation, described by M. MORLEY as the "most successful of all plays taken from Dickens," did not appear until 1899. With a script by two clergymen, Freeman Wills and Frederick Langbridge, commissioned by the actor John Martin-Harvey, this play, *The Only Way*, dominated the dramatizations of the novel for the first half of the 20th century. Martin-Harvey played Carton for 36 years on the stage in both England and America, as well as in a silent film version (1925). *The Only Way* was also the basis of the first television adaptation of the novel (1948). F. Dubrez Fawcett (*Dickens the Dramatist*, 1956) reports that Martin-Harvey played Carton, the role which defined his theatrical career, "as an intellectual study, and a psychological one, gradually revealing him with ever-increasing power till he held the audience spellbound."

Silent films derived from the novel appeared in 1908, 1911, 1917, 1920, and 1925. Two sound films have been produced: David O. Selznick's 1935 version with Ronald Colman as Carton, and a 1957 British version (J. A. Rank), starring Dirk Bogarde and directed by Ralph Thomas.

The story was frequently adapted for radio in the 1940s and '50s. Notable television productions include a 1958 adaptation for CBS with a cast including Agnes Moorehead and Denholm Elliott, Constance Cox's 10-episode BBC adaptation (1965), and Pieter Harding's eight-part serial (1980), also for the BBC. A joint English-French television production made in 1989 for the anniversary of the Revolution starred James Wilby as Carton, Xavier Duluc as Darnay, and John MILLS as Lorry. The script by Arthur Hopcraft was directed by Philippe Monnier for Granada TV (Britain) and DUNE (France).

Talfourd, Sir Thomas Noon (1795–1854) Jurist and author; member of Parliament for Reading; judge. A friend of Wordsworth, Coleridge, and Lamb, he introduced Dickens to the literary circles of London at Gore House and Holland House and nominated him for membership in the ATHENAEUM CLUB. Dickens dedicated *Pickwick* to him, gratefully acknowledging Talfourd's efforts on behalf of the copyright bill. Talfourd represented Dickens in his suit against the pirates who plagiarized the *Carol*. He is usually regarded as the original of Traddles in *Copperfield*. Dickens's obituary for Talfourd appeared in HOUSEHOLD WORDS (March 25, 1854) and was reprinted in *Miscellaneous*.

Tamaroo Bailey Junior's successor as Mrs. Todgers's servant. Her name, from an old English ballad, was given to her by the boarders. *Chuzzlewit* (32).

Tangle Lawyer who "knows more of Jarndyce and Jarndyce than anybody, . . . supposed never to have read anything else since he left school." *Bleak House* (1).

Tape Red fairy godmother who tyrannizes over Prince Bull and disrupts his war against Prince Bear in Dickens's ALLEGORY of the Crimean War. *Reprinted*, "Prince Bull."

Tapenham Retired civil servant who narrates "Cheap Patriotism," describing the circumlocutions of the bureaucracy and reforms that do not change anything. *Miscellaneous*.

Tapkins, Felix Bachelor friend of the Lovetowns who flirts with Mrs. Lovetown. *Is She His Wife?*

Thomas Noon Talfourd, said to be the original of Traddles in David Copperfield.

Tapkins, Mrs.   Mother of **Antonina**, **Euphemia**, **Frederica**, and **Malvina**; a representative of an extensive and socially prominent family, she is among the first to call on the Boffins when they enter society. *Mutual Friend* (I:17).

Tapley, Mark   Ostler at the BLUE DRAGON; servant, companion, and friend to young Martin Chuzzlewit on his journey to AMERICA. His self-defined mission in life is to remain "jolly" in the most trying circumstances. He leaves the Dragon because he is too comfortable and there is no challenge to his optimism (5). Later he comes to Martin in London and volunteers to serve him in America (13), where he takes the nickname "Co," as a partner in the architectural firm of Chuzzlewit and Co. and where his optimism is severely tested by the duplicity and suffering encountered there. His selfless concern for others—for the family on the ship, for Martin in his illness—keeps him jolly. After returning to England, Mark

marries Mrs. Lupin the inn's landlady, and the Blue Dragon is renamed the Jolly Tapley (54). *Chuzzlewit.*

Taplin, Harry   Comic entertainer and singer who performs with Miss Amelia Martin at the WHITE CONDUIT. *Boz*, "Mistaken Milliner."

Tappertit, Simon (Sim)   Apprentice to locksmith Gabriel Varden, this narcissistic little man, "little more than five feet high, and thoroughly convinced in his own mind that he was above the middle size," is particularly vain about his legs, "which, in knee-breeches were perfect curiosities of littleness" (4). He is enraptured with his master's daughter Dolly and jealously dislikes Joe Willet as his main rival (24). Leader of the 'PRENTICE KNIGHTS, a drinking society of disaffected apprentices, he changes their name to the United Bull-dogs and allies them with the No Popery cause (39). He leaves his employment to join the rioters (51); during the riots his legs are crushed. He finishes life as a shoe-black and marries a rag-and-bone man's widow (82). *Rudge.*

Tappleton, Lieutenant   Dr. Slammer's second in the abortive duel with Winkle. *Pickwick* (2).

Tartar, Bob   President of the Society of Schoolboys, the group that decides to torment Old Cheeseman as a traitor. Tartar was thought to be the son of a wealthy West Indian planter. "Schoolboy's Story."

Tartar, Lieutenant, R. N.   Retired navy man who was once Crisparkle's school chum and is now Neville Landless's neighbor at STAPLE INN; "a handsome gentleman, with a young face, but with an older figure in its robustness and breadth of shoulder, . . . extremely sunburnt" (17). By the end of the unfinished novel, he is aiding Crisparkle and Grewgious in their defense of Landless and attracting Rosa Bud. *Drood.*

Tatham, Mrs.   "An old sallow-looking woman" who is a regular customer of a DRURY LANE pawnshop. *Boz*, "Pawnbroker's."

Tatt   Friend of Inspector Field; his diamond pin is stolen and recovered by Sergeant Witchem. *Reprinted*, "Detective Anecdotes."

"Tattycoram"   Nickname of Harriet BEADLE. *Dorrit.*

"Tattlesnivel Bleater, The"   Satirical article for ALL THE YEAR ROUND (December 31, 1859), mocking the pretensions of the popular press. The correspondents for the *Tattlesnivel Bleater*, after purveying misinformation on nearly every topic from the state of the Queen's health to the subjects of the paintings in the Royal Exhibition, offer the snivelling excuse that there is a conspiracy against them. *Miscellaneous.*

Tauchnitz, Baron Christian Bernard (1816–1895) German publisher who issued cheap reprints of English novels for continental readers. Tauchnitz often contracted to buy advance proofs of the novels; his standard payment was £50. Dickens's dealings with him were very friendly.

Taunton, Captain Richard Doubledick's officer and comrade-in-arms, who saves him from a life of dissipation. After Taunton is killed in battle, Doubledick visits **Mrs. Taunton**, the captain's mother, learning from her to love his enemies. "Doubledick."

Taunton, Vale of Rural area in Somerset where Mrs. Nickleby visited the Hawkinses while she was in school (*Nickleby*, 35). Vholes has a habit of telling people, "I have the privilege of supporting an aged father in the Vale of Taunton—his native place—and I admire that country very much" (*Bleak House*, 37).

Tavistock House House on Tavistock Square in BLOOMSBURY that the Dickens family occupied from 1851 to 1860. Dickens purchased the lease from Frank STONE, who moved into a neighboring house. The building was large, providing ample space for the large family; its spacious schoolroom could be converted into a theater for Dickens's theatrical productions.

Tavistock Street In Dickens's time, this street in COVENT GARDEN was residential. Mr. Minns had lodgings here. *Boz*, "Minns."

Tellson's Bank The long-established bank in FLEET STREET, near TEMPLE BAR, for which Jarvis Lorry is a senior clerk and Jerry Cruncher a messenger. "It was very small, very dark, very ugly, very incommodious. It was an old-fashioned place, moreover, in the moral attribute that the partners in the House were proud of its smallness, proud of its darkness, proud of its ugliness, proud of its incommodiousness" (II:1). There is also a PARIS branch, where Lorry conducts business during the FRENCH REVOLUTION. *Two Cities*.

Temeraire Terrible restaurant in Namelesston where the Traveller suffers through a "nasty little dinner." *Uncommercial* (33).

Temple, The Area in London between FLEET STREET and the THAMES. Owned by the Knights Templar in the Middle Ages, it later became the site of two INNS OF COURT—the Inner Temple and the Middle Temple. Sir John Chester's apartment is located in the PAPER BUILDINGS here (*Rudge*, 15). The library that Tom Pinch is employed to manage is located in some dusty rooms in the Temple (*Chuzzlewit*, 39); John Westlock courts Ruth Pinch in FOUNTAIN COURT (*Chuzzlewit*, 45); Stryver's chambers are in the Temple (*Two Cities*, II:5). Pip and Herbert Pocket have rooms on an upper story in GARDEN COURT (*Expectations*, 39). Eu-

Tavistock House, the Dickens family home from November 1851 to September 1860.

gene Wrayburn and Mortimer Lightwood (*Mutual Friend*, I:8), Charley ("Holly-Tree"), Slinkton ("Hunted Down"), and the bachelor in "The Ghost of Art" (*Reprinted*) all have chambers here.

Temple Bar In Dickens's day, prior to the installation of the Griffin in 1880, it was an arched gateway to the CITY, dividing FLEET STREET from the STRAND. He described it in *Bleak House* as "that leaden-headed old corporation: Temple Bar" (1). The 'Prentice Knights took an oath not "to damage or in any way disfigure Temple Bar, which was strictly constitutional, and always to be approached with reverence" *Rudge* (8). It is also mentioned in *Chuzzlewit* (45), *Copperfield* (46), *Two Cities* (I: 12; II:12, 24), and *Mutual Friend* (III:2; IV:10).

Tennent, Sir James Emerson (1804–1869) Liberal politician, supporter of the REFORM BILL and the abolition of the CORN LAWS; author; longtime friend of Dickens. A traveler and writer of travel books, Tennent climbed Vesuvius with Dickens and traveled around ITALY with him in 1853. Dickens dedicated *Our Mutual Friend* to him.

Tenniel, John (1820–1914)   Painter and illustrator, famous for his illustrations for *PUNCH* and for Lewis Carroll's *Alice* books. Tenniel and Dickens became friends when the artist was employed to provide five illustrations for *Haunted Man*. Later he acted in several of Dickens's AMATEUR THEATRICALS. As the political cartoonist for *Punch*, Tenniel frequently used Dickens characters in his cartoons, as in Illustration 75 (*Punch*).

Tennyson, Alfred, Lord (1809–1892)   The most famous English poet of his time, Tennyson succeeded William Wordsworth as poet laureate in 1850. Dickens met Tennyson in the early 1840s, probably through John FORSTER. Their relationship was most active in that decade, before Tennyson's marriage. Dickens invited Tennyson to vacation with his family in SWITZERLAND. Although the poet declined the invitation, he did visit Dickens in Lausanne. Tennyson particularly admired *Pickwick* and Old Cheeseman in "The Schoolboy's Story." Dickens thought *Idylls of the King* "the noblest" of Tennyson's works.

Ternan, Ellen ("Nelly") Lawless (1839–1914) Dickens's mistress, an actress from a theatrical family. With her mother, Frances Eleanor Jarman, and her sister

Tenniel's frontispiece for The Haunted Man *(1848) shows Redlaw encircled by contending angels and devils.*

Maria, Ellen was hired for the Manchester performances of Dickens's production of *THE FROZEN DEEP* in August 1857. Infatuated with the young actress, Dickens went to DONCASTER, where Ellen was playing in December, a trip obliquely described in *Idle Tour*. This was the beginning of a secret relationship that continued until Dickens's death. There is little documentary evidence of the relationship, causing a great deal of speculation about whether Ellen was, in fact, Dickens's mistress, whether they had a child, and just how responsive Ellen was to Dickens's attentions. The heroines of the late novels are sometimes taken as proof that Ellen scorned and tormented Dickens as Estella does Pip (*Expectations*).

Ellen often traveled with Dickens to France, and she was with him in the STAPLEHURST RAILWAY ACCIDENT. He left her £1,000 in his will. In 1876, after Dickens's death, Ellen married George W. Robinson, a clergyman and later headmaster of a school in MARGATE. By all accounts, she never mentioned her relationship with Dickens during her later life.

Dickens's relationship with Ellen was first revealed by Thomas Wright (*Life of Charles Dickens*, 1935) and by Dickens's daughter Kate (Kate DICKENS) in interviews with Gladys STOREY (1939). The most useful accounts of the relationship appear in works by Ada NISBET (1952) and Fred KAPLAN (1988), and in Claire Tomalin's *The Invisible Woman: The Story of Nelly Ternan and Charles Dickens* (1991).

Testator   Writer who furnishes his rooms in Lyons Inn with furniture he finds in the cellar and is visited by the drunken or spectral former owner of the items. *Uncommercial* (14).

Tetterby Family   Poor family cursed by Redlaw's power to eradicate memory. **Adolphus**, a struggling newsagent, is the father of the eight children, including **Adolphus Jr. ('Dolphus)**, a newspaper boy at the railway station, and **Johnny**, the second son, who minds **Sally ("Little Moloch")**, the baby of the family. Under the influence of Redlaw's power to erase memory, Adolphus's usual good spirits are lost, but they are restored again on Christmas morning by Milly Swidger. **Sophia** is the devoted mother of the family. *Haunted Man*.

Tewkesbury   Town in Gloucestershire where Pickwick, Ben Allen, and Bob Sawyer stop for dinner at the Hop Pole Inn on their way from BRISTOL to BIRMINGHAM. *Pickwick* (50).

Thackeray, William Makepeace (1811–1863) English novelist, comic illustrator, essayist, and lecturer; Dickens's friend and great rival. Their novels were often compared. On publishing *Vanity Fair* in 1848, Thackeray described himself as "all but at the top of the tree, . . . and having a great fight up there with Dickens." *Vanity Fair* was often compared with *Dombey*, especially in its treatment of businessmen; and the autobiographical

W. M. Thackeray, a portrait by Maclise.

PENDENNIS with *Copperfield*. The two first met in 1836 when Thackeray applied to take over for SEYMOUR as illustrator for *Pickwick*. The son of a colonial administrator in India and university educated, Thackeray thought Dickens "abominably coarse," but he admired and was occasionally awed by his work. Dickens especially admired *Vanity Fair* among Thackeray's works. In 1858 the two men quarreled over an attack on Thackeray by Edmund YATES. This GARRICK CLUB affair estranged Dickens and Thackeray until 1863, when the two were reconciled just a few weeks before Thackeray's death.

Thames, River The River Thames is so constant a presence in Dickens's work as to be taken for granted. From such early sketches as "The River" and "The Steam Excursion" (*Boz*) to *Mutual Friend*, in which the polluted Thames is one of the controlling symbols, the river holds an important place in Dickens's work. It is used symbolically in three novels in particular. In *Dombey*, the Thames links London to the sea, providing the avenue for Dombey's business and, for young Paul, the connection to the sea of immortality that he associates with the golden waves on the wall of his room. In *Expectations*, the river connects London with Pip's home country and links his childhood and later life. The climactic struggle between Magwitch and Compeyson on the river recalls their earlier struggle on the marshes and has the effect of bringing Pip's childhood and adulthood together. The polluted river in *Mutual Friend* acts both

as an extension of the wasteland, symbolized by the dust heaps, and as a source of life and renewal.

Thames Street Street running from BLACKFRIARS to the TOWER OF LONDON. Joe Willet goes to "some deep cellars hard by Thames Street" to pay the Maypole's bill (*Rudge*, 13). Mrs. Clennam's house is in this street or nearby (*Dorrit*).

"That Other Public" Satiric article for HOUSEHOLD WORDS (February 3, 1855), calling for "that other public" in both Britain and the United States to rise up against government corruption and mismanagement of the sort evident during the Crimean War in Britain and described as "smart dealing" by the Americans in *Chuzzlewit*. *Miscellaneous*.

Thavies Inn One of the Inns of CHANCERY near HOLBORN Circus. The Jellyby's house is located here. *Bleak House* (4).

Theatre Royal, Montreal On his 1842 journey to America, Dickens acted in and directed an evening of theater at this venue in MONTREAL. It was the first of his AMATEUR THEATRICAL productions.

Theatrical Fund Charity founded in 1839 to provide pensions for actors, actresses, and other theatrical performers. Dickens served as one of the trustees of the fund for many years and addressed its meetings on several occasions. Kenneth FIELDING (1960) includes 13 speeches given at various meetings of this charity—a charity that Dickens actively supported throughout his life.

Théophile, Corporal French soldier in VAUBAN who lovingly cares for the orphan Bebelle. After Théophile is killed in a fire, Langley finds the child lying on his grave. "Somebody's Luggage."

Thicknesse A regular at the Green Dragon; "a large stomach surmounted by a man's head, and placed on the top of two particularly short legs." *Mudfog*, "Bolton."

Thigsberry, Duke of By Chuckster's account, this patron to Violetta Stetta of the Italian Opera is even more generous than the newspapers make out. *Curiosity Shop* (40).

"Things that Cannot Be Done" Satirical article for HOUSEHOLD WORDS (October 8, 1853) celebrating the proposition that "Nothing flagrantly wrong can be done, without adequate punishment, under the English law." Dickens decries the light sentences given for acts of brutality and describes at length the example of a ne'er-do-well who has used the law to harass an heiress and extort money from her. *Miscellaneous*.

Thom   Practitioner of homeopathy and member of the Mudfog Association. *Mudfog*.

Thomas (1)   Pastry cook who catered the Gattleton's party. *Boz*, "Porter."

Thomas (2)   Waiter to the man who killed himself by eating crumpets. *Pickwick* (44).

Thomas (3)   Sir Leicester Dedlock's groom. *Bleak House* (40).

Thomas, Deborah A. (1943–)   Professor, Villanova University, who has written on both Dickens and Thackeray. *Dickens and the Short Story* (1982) identifies and analyzes the many short stories by Dickens, a part of his work neglected by most other critics. Thomas discusses both those stories published in his collections of short fiction and those inserted into the novels. She has also edited a collection of Dickens's short fiction (1976).

Thompson, Bill   Actor at the VICTORIA THEATRE. *Boz*, "Streets—Night."

Thompson, Harry   Acquaintance of Captain and Mrs. Waters who is bathing at RAMSGATE. *Boz*, "Tuggses."

Thompson, John   Dickens's manservant. When Dickens dismissed Thompson for dishonesty in 1867, after more than 20 years in his service, Dickens set him up in business.

Thompson, Julia   Friend of Felix Nixon, the Domestic Young Gentleman. *Young Gentlemen*.

Thompson, Mrs.   After she asks Mr. Fairfax, the Censorious Young Gentleman, what he thinks of Mrs. Barker, she agrees with him that the woman has something exceedingly odd in her manner. *Young Gentlemen*.

Thompson, Tally-ho (a.k.a. Thomas Pigeon)   Horse thief taken by Sergeant Witchem. *Reprinted*, "Detective Police."

Thomson, Sir John, M.P.   Eminent member of Parliament. *Boz*, "Parliamentary Sketch."

"Thoughts about People"   Originally published as "Sketches of London, No. 10" in the EVENING CHRONICLE (April 23, 1835). Boz describes three types of men that he observes in London: the anonymous clerks who live a life of routine, misanthropic old fellows who cut themselves off from others, and London apprentices who strut inoffensively in the streets on Sundays. *Boz*.

"Thousand and One Humbugs, The"   Series of satiric articles for HOUSEHOLD WORDS (April 21, April 28, May 5, 1855), attacking governmental incompetence during the Crimean War and the PALMERSTON administration that took power in February 1855, which Dickens described as "new versions of the best known stories" from the *Arabian Nights*. In the parody the Grand Vizier Parmarstoon (Palmerston) suceeded "Aabbadeen (or The Addled) [Lord Aberdeen], who had for his misdeeds been strangled with a garter." The Vizier's daughter Hansardadade—an allusion to Hansard's, the verbatim record of parliamentary proceedings— entertains the Sultan with the stories of "Scarli Tapa [Red Tape] and the Forty Thieves," in which the cave of riches is entered by the passwords "Debrett's Peerage. Open Sesame!" The other two parodies are "The Story of the Talkative Barber," and "The Story of the Barmacide Feast." *Miscellaneous*.

Threadneedle Street   Street in the CITY running from MANSION HOUSE to BISHOPSGATE, in which the BANK OF ENGLAND, "the Old Lady of Threadneedle Street," is located. The offices of the Cheerybles are loctated off this street (*Nickleby*, 35).

Three Cripples Inn   Tavern in SAFFRON HILL frequented by Fagin and his associates. *Twist* (26).

"Three 'Detective' Anecdotes"   In the first of the three anecdotes, Inspector Wield tells of "The Pair of Gloves" found under the pillow of a murdered woman that nearly incriminate their owner, young Mr. Trinkle. Next Wield tells of arresting on Derby Day at EPSOM a pickpocket, one of the Swell Mob, who had stolen a diamond pin. In the ensuing scuffle, Sergeant Witchem secures the pin by subterfuge and the thief is convicted and transported. In the third anecdote, Sergeant Dornton tells of arresting a medical student who was stealing from the cloakroom at the teaching hospital. *Reprinted*. Originally in HOUSEHOLD WORDS (September 14, 1850).

Three Jolly Bargemen Inn   Village pub that Joe Gargery frequents and where Pip gets two one-pound notes from the strange man who stirs his drink with a file. *Expectations* (10).

Thurley, Geoffrey (1936–)   Professor, University of Essex; poet, critic, translator, novelist. In *The Dickens Myth* (1976), Thurley discusses Dickens's works from *Twist* through *Expectations* as a mythic response to the social uncertainties of Victorian England, in which the individual is beset by the danger of falling into poverty and the obligations imposed by rising into affluence. The epitome of this myth is *Expectations*.

Thurtell, John   Notorious murderer who was executed in 1823 for the murder of William Weare. An account of his crime was included in the NEWGATE CALENDAR in 1828. Dickens cites him as an example of a murderer who maintained remarkable composure during his trial. *Miscellaneous*, "Demeanour of Murderers."

"Tibbs"   Penname used by Dickens for a series of sketches, under the general title *Scenes and Characters*, that appeared in BELL'S LIFE IN LONDON between September 27, 1835 and January 17, 1836. These sketches were later collected in *Boz*.

Tibbs, Mrs.   "Tidy, fidgety, thrifty" proprietor of a boarding house in GREAT CORAM STREET. Her small **husband**, inconsequential without her, disappears into the kitchen and never gets to tell about his life in the volunteer corps in 1806. After he engages in a series of romantic intrigues in the boarding house, the Tibbses separate by mutual consent and close the establishment. *Boz*, "Boarding House."

Tickit, Mrs.   The Meagleses' housekeeper and cook. *Dorrit* I:16.

Tickle   Inventor of "spectacles, which enabled the wearer to discern, in very bright colours, objects at a great distance, and rendered him wholly blind to those immediately before him." *Mudfog* (2).

Ticknor & Fields   Dickens's American publishing firm, in which James FIELDS was the senior partner. The firm published the DIAMOND EDITION of Dickens's works in 1867, illustrated by EYTINGE, and the American CHARLES DICKENS EDITION. They also published the texts of Dickens's PUBLIC READINGS during his American tour. Dickens wrote occasional pieces for their magazine, the ATLANTIC MONTHLY ("George Silverman's Explanation" and "On Mr. Fechter's Acting") and for their children's magazine, OUR YOUNG FOLKS ("Holiday Romance").

Tiddypot   Vestryman of Gumption House. *Reprinted*, "Our Vestry."

Tiffey   Senior clerk at Spenlow and Jorkins: "a little dry man . . . who wore a stiff brown wig that looked as if it were made of gingerbread." *Copperfield* (23).

Tigg, Montague   Vagabond and confidence man who fronts for Chevy Slyme in his attempts to extract money from his Chuzzlewit relatives. "He was very dirty and very jaunty; very bold and very mean; very swaggering and very slinking; very much like a man who might have been something better and unspeakably like a man who deserved to be something worse" (4). After leaving Slyme, he appears to be something better when he establishes the fraudulent Anglo-Bengalee Disinterested Loan and Life Assurance Company, takes luxurious offices and lodgings, and changes his name to Tigg Montague (27). He blackmails Jonas into putting his money into the scheme (38); Jonas murders him to escape his clutches (46). *Chuzzlewit*.

Tiggin and Welps   Firm for which the Bagman's Uncle works as a traveling salesman. *Pickwick* (49).

Tillotson, Kathleen (1906–   )   Professor, University of London, whose pioneering work on Dickens and other Victorian novelists set the direction for much later scholarship. *Novels of the Eighteen-Forties* (1956) surveyed the social and intellectual context for the novel boom in the decade and analyzed in detail four novels—one of which is *Dombey*—as representative of the period. In *Dickens at Work* (with John BUTT, 1957), she established methods of studying Dickens as a serial novelist, using manuscripts, proof sheets, and Dickens's working notes, and placing the novels into the immediate historical context of the time in which they were written. Tillotson edited the first volume in the CLARENDON EDITION, *Twist* (1966), and served as general editor for the project. She has also edited several volumes of the Pilgrim Edition of the LETTERS.

Tilted Wagon   Inn near Cloisterham where Neville Landless stopped for breakfast as he set out on his walking tour. *Drood* (15).

Timbered   Vice president of the Statistics Section of the Mudfog Association. *Mudfog* (1).

Timberry, Snittle   Member of the Crummles theatrical troupe who chairs the farewell dinner for the Crummles as they leave for AMERICA. He was especially adept at the "gymnastic performances" required by the writhings of a dying man. *Nickleby* (48).

Times   See LONDON *TIMES*.

Timkins   Candidate for beadle whose "nine small children" are insufficient to secure his success in the election. *Boz*, "Election for Beadle."

Timpson   Owner of the DULLBOROUGH coach, "Timpson's Blue-Eyed Maid." *Uncommercial* (12).

Timson, Rev. Charles   Unctuous clergyman and friend of Gabriel Parsons, he is the successful suitor for Miss Lillerton's hand. *Boz*, "Tottle."

Tinker   A ferocious ruffian who terrifies David on the road to Dover and steals his handkerchief. *Copperfield* (13).

Tinker   A wanderer resting on Tom Tiddler's ground who, like the Traveller, refuses to take Mopes's misanthropy seriously. "Tiddler."

Tinkler   Mr. Dorrit's valet, who travels with the family to Italy. *Dorrit*.

Tinkles, Horatio   Walter Trott's rival for Emily Brown. He challenges Trott to a duel and precipitates the disguises and mistaken identities of *The Strange Gentleman*. He is called Horace Hunter in "The Great Winglebury Duel."

Tinkling, William Eight-year-old narrator of the "Holiday Romance." He is "married" to Nettie Ashford and writes out the tales of the other three tellers.

Tiny Tim Bob CRATCHIT's crippled son, "as good as gold . . . he hoped the people saw him in church, because he was a cripple, and it might be pleasant to them to remember upon Christmas Day, who made lame beggars walk, and blind men see." *Carol* (3).

"Tip" Edward DORRIT's nickname. *Dorrit*.

Tip Gabblewig's servant. Slap recruits him to pretend to be Mr. Nightingale's son in one of his schemes. *Nightingale*.

Tipkisson Constituent who opposes the positions of "Our Honourable Friend." *Reprinted*.

Tipp Red-jacketed carman who works for MURDSTONE AND GRINBY. *Copperfield* (11).

Tippin, Mr. and Mrs. Musical performers at RAMSGATE. *Boz*, "Tuggses."

Tippins, Lady Widow of Sir Thomas Tippins, who was "knighted in mistake for somebody else" (I:10), she is a friend of the Veneerings and one of the voices of society. "A charming old woman," she dresses and presents herself as much younger than she is and maintains "a grisly little fiction concerning her lovers" (I:2). *Mutual Friend*.

Tisher, Mrs. Miss Twinkleton's assistant at Nun's House, "a deferential widow with a weak back, a chronic sigh, and a suppressed voice, who looks after the young ladies' wardrobes, and leads them to infer that she has seen better days" (3). *Drood*.

"Titbull's Alms-Houses" The Traveller visits the alms houses established by Sampson Titbull in 1723 in east London. He learns that the inmates resent the neglect of the trustees and are suspicious among themselves, but they are all surprised when Mrs. Mitts, youngest of the women inmates, resigns her place to marry a Greenwich pensioner. *Uncommercial* (29).

Tix, Tom Bailiff who, with Scaley, takes possession of Madame Mantalini's; "a little man in brown, very much the worse for wear, who brought with him a mingled fumigation of stale tobacco and fresh onions" (21). *Nickleby*.

"To be Read at Dusk" In this essay for the KEEPSAKE (1852), the narrator recounts anecdotes of strange occurrences that he overheard some couriers tell at the hospice on GREAT ST. BERNARD PASS. A Genoese courier tells of the disappearance of a young bride when she meets a man who possesses a face that has haunted her dreams. A German courier tells of a man who has a premonition of his brother's death. *Reprinted*.

"To Be Taken with a Grain of Salt" Dickens's contribution to the stories in "Doctor Marigold": a GHOST STORY told by the jury foreman in a murder trial, who sees the ghost of the murdered man throughout the trial until a guilty verdict is returned and the ghost disappears. "Marigold."

"To Working Men" Article for HOUSEHOLD WORDS (October 7, 1854), written in the wake of the cholera epidemic in London in August and September. Dickens calls on the working men whose families suffered most from the outbreak to rise up and demand legislation to improve sanitary conditions and the dwellings of the poor. Only such pressure from the people of the lower and middle classes, Dickens asserts, will make the politicians listen and act. *Miscellaneous*.

"Toady Tree, The" Article for HOUSEHOLD WORDS (May 26, 1855), denouncing "ruinous gentility and deference to mere rank." Using a series of hypothetical examples, Dickens shows various forms of such destructive deference: Dobbs, who refers to his titled friends by their nicknames; Hobbs, an inventor who has been denied recognition for his work but still kowtows to those in power; Pobbs, who puts his titled acquaintances down as "swells" but depends on their attentions to him. *Miscellaneous*. This article is particularly relevant to Doyce, the Meagles, and the Barnacles in *Dorrit*.

Tobin, Daniel Dickens's closest friend at WELLINGTON HOUSE. The two boys staged plays and performed boyish pranks together. After their schooldays, according to John FORSTER, Tobin worked as an occasional amanuensis for Dickens, but his requests for money finally exasperated the novelist, who broke off their relationship.

Todd's Young Man Baker's assistant who fascinates Betsy Clark. *Boz*, "Streets—Morning."

"Toddles" Pet name of a boy in Betty Higden's minding school. *Mutual Friend*.

Toddyhigh, Joe Childhood friend of the incoming LORD MAYOR of London. He falls asleep in the GUILDHALL during the lord mayor's banquet and awakens to overhear GOG AND MAGOG telling stories in the night. *Humphrey* (1).

Todgers, Mrs. M. Proprietor of a boardinghouse for commercial gentlemen, near the MONUMENT, where Pecksniff and his daughters stay in London. "A bony and hard-featured" lady, she is especially kind to Mercy, offering her a refuge from her marriage; "in some odd nook in Mrs. Todgers's breast, up a great many steps, and in some corner easy to be overlooked, there was a secret door, with 'Woman' written on the spring, which, at a touch from Mercy's hand, had flown wide open, and admitted her for shelter" (37). *Chuzzlewit*.

Tollimglower, Lady Childhood friend of old Mrs. Wardle. *Pickwick* (28).

Tom (1) Hackney coachman. *Boz*, "Hackney."

Tom (2) "Corpulent round-headed boy" who delivers messages and medicine for the young surgeon. *Boz*, "Black Veil."

Tom (3) The Gattleton's servant, who plays a fisherman in their theatricals. *Boz*, "Porter."

Tom (4) Gabriel Parsons's gardener. *Boz*, "Tottle."

Tom (5) Cad on the omnibus that Dumps takes from PENTONVILLE to BLOOMSBURY. *Boz*, "Christening."

Tom (6) One of the officers who arrest William Warden. *Boz*, "Drunkard's Death."

Tom (7) Waiter at the St. James's Arms. *Strange Gentleman*.

Tom (8) Wardle's coachman. *Pickwick* (4).

Tom (9) Clerk at the employment office where Nicholas seeks work; "a lean youth with cunning eyes and a protruding chin" (16). He quarrels with Frank Cheeryble at the SARACEN'S HEAD (43). *Nickleby*.

Tom (10) Coachman on the DOVER mail coach. *Two Cities* (I:2).

Tom (11) Sidewalk artist who narrates "His Brown-Paper Parcel." "Somebody's Luggage" (3).

Tom (12) Captain Boldheart's cousin. "Holiday Romance."

Tom, Captain NEWGATE prisoner visited by Wemmick and Pip. *Expectations* (32).

"Tom, Honest" A metropolitan representative in Parliament. *Boz*, "Parliamentary Sketch."

"Tom Tiddler's Ground" Christmas story for ALL THE YEAR ROUND, 1861. Dickens wrote the frame chapters and one of the stories, "Picking up Miss Kimmeens." A traveler comes to a remote rural village to visit Mopes the Hermit, who is said to be a miser who leaves coins about his property for passersby to pick up. When the traveler gets to Mopes's ruined homestead, however, he finds a misanthropic man, dirty and surly, who justifies himself as a model of misanthropy. The traveler, refusing to be intimidated by him, calls him "a Nuisance" and promises to show him that "every man must be up and doing, and that all mankind are made dependent on one another." Several passersby prove that humans are social beings, including the lonely child Miss Kimmeens, who ventures onto Tom Tiddler's ground in search of human contact.

Tom-All-Alone's "A black, dilapidated street, avoided by all decent people; where the crazy houses were seized upon, when their decay was far advanced, by some bold vagrants, who, after establishing their possession, took to letting them out in lodgings" (16). Jo the crossing sweeper inhabits this slum created because the property is tied up in a CHANCERY suit. *Bleak House*. Several locations in ST. GILES, DRURY LANE, and BLOOMSBURY have been suggested as the original. The name was taken from the house of a recluse outside CHATHAM, known to Dickens as a child.

Tomkinley Schoolmaster with whom Abel Garland went to MARGATE. *Curiosity Shop* (14).

Tomkins Pupil at DOTHEBOYS HALL. *Nickleby* (13).

Browne's (Phiz's) visualization of Tom-All-Alone's in one of his "dark plates," an engraving technique he developed to render the dark subject matter in Bleak House.

Tomkins, Alfred Clerk for a wine merchant who boards at Mrs. Tibbs's. *Boz,* "Boarding House."

Tomkins, Charles Fanny Wilson's fiancé. He is confused with the strange gentleman until things are sorted out and he and Fanny can set out for GRETNA GREEN. *Strange Gentleman.*

Tomkins, Miss Headmistress of the WESTGATE HOUSE school in BURY ST. EDMUNDS. *Pickwick* (16).

Tomlinson, Miss Post-mistress at ROCHESTER who attends the ball at the BULL INN. *Pickwick* (2).

Tommy (1) "A little greengrocer with a chubby face" who disagrees with "The Parlor Orator." *Boz.*

Tommy (2) A waterman—"a strange specimen of the human race, in a sackcloth coat, and apron of the same, who with a brass label and number around his neck, looked as if he were catalogued in some collection of rarities" (2); he summons the cab driver who later assaults Pickwick. *Pickwick* (2).

Tompkins, Charles Fiancé of Fanny Wilson caught up in the confusion at the St. James's Arms. *Strange Gentleman.*

Tong Village in Shropshire, three miles east of Shifnal, which was the original of the village where Little Nell dies. The Church of St. Bartholomew in Tong was the original for CATTERMOLE's engraving. There is, in the churchyard, a grave bearing the inscription "Reputed Grave of Little Nell."

Toodle Family Working class family whose vitality, fertility, and loving relationships contrast with the cold isolation and funereal atmosphere in the Dombey household. **Polly**, Paul Dombey's nurse; "a plump, rosy-cheeked wholesome apple-faced young woman" (2), is hired by Dombey on the condition that she take the name **Richards** and sever all connection with the Dombey family after she leaves (2). She is dismissed when she endangers Paul by taking him with her when she visits her family (6). Dombey secures a place for **Robin** (**"Rob the Grinder," "Biler"**), eldest of her five children, in the Charitable Grinders School (5). He later becomes a servant for James Carker, spying on Gills and Cuttle for him. Polly's **husband**, an engineer on the new railway, "a strong, loose, round-shouldered, shuffling, shaggy fellow" (2), offends Dombey when he offers his condolences after Paul's death and compares Dombey's loss to his own loss of a child (20). Polly's sister **Jemima** cares for Polly's children while she works for Dombey. *Dombey.*

Toole, J. L. (1830–1906) Late Victorian actor famous for his many Dickensian roles: Buzfuz, Artful Dodger, Bob Cratchit, Caleb Plummer, Trotty Veck, Ben Britain, and Tetterby. He was especially famous for his portrayal of the Dodger, which he played more than 3,000 times. Dickens praised his acting, and Toole responded with the comment: "To know from his own lips that he approved of my efforts to realize some of his creations on the stage has always given me great satisfaction."

Toorell, Dr. Member of the Anatomy and Medicine Section of the Mudfog Association. *Mudfog.*

"Tooting Farm, The" Article for the EXAMINER (January 27, 1849), following up "The Paradise at Tooting." Dickens reports that a verdict of manslaughter has justly been returned against Drouet. He asserts that the Board of Guardians, who complained that they were vilified by the press, were also "grossly in the wrong." He goes on to warn that such events as the cholera epidemic at the Tooting baby farm encourage the poor to embrace CHARTISM, and he calls for the abolition of baby farms and the amendment of the POOR LAW. *Miscellaneous.*

Tootle, Tom A regular at the SIX JOLLY FELLOWSHIP PORTERS. *Mutual Friend.*

"Tootleum-Boots" Mrs. Lemon's baby. "Holiday Romance" (4).

Toots Oldest student at Blimber's Academy, who, "when he began to have whiskers, left off having brains" (11). Obsessed with clothes and boxing, Toots aspires to become a young man of fashion; he repeatedly remarks, "It's of no consequence." Although slow-witted, Toots is a gentle and loving friend to Paul and Florence. He brings the dog Diogenes to Florence after Paul's death and falls hopelessly in love with her. In the end he settles for Susan NIPPER and regards her as a "most extraordinary woman" (62). They have three children: **Florence**, **Susan**, and another **daughter**. *Dombey.*

Toozellem, The Hon. Clementina Second wife of the 15th Earl of Stiltstocking. *Dorrit,* I:17).

Tope Chief verger at Cloisterham Cathedral. He and **Mrs. Tope** are landlords to both Jasper, in the gatehouse, and Datchery, who rents rooms at the Topes' house next door. *Drood.*

Topham, Francis William (1808–1877) Painter, illustrator, and engraver. Topham was a member of Dickens's amateur acting troupe before Dickens asked him to provide the frontispieces for the three volumes of *A Child's History of England.* Topham also did several watercolor paintings of scenes from *Curiosity Shop* and *Rudge.*

Topography Dickens often made use of actual places as the SETTINGS for his novels and stories, so that particular streets and buildings can be identified as the ones

Francis Topham's frontispiece for the first volume of A Child's History of England *(1852).*

that Dickens had in mind. On other occasions he mixes the fictional with the real, placing imaginary streets, houses, or inns in real towns or neighborhoods. These practices, of course, have prompted many ardent Dickensians to visit the actual places mentioned in the novels and to seek out the originals of the fictional places, identifying, for example, the Uncommercial Traveller's Dullborough as ROCHESTER and the country village where Nell dies as TONG in Shropshire. These topographic identifications are often disputed and the methods for arriving at them are various and, sometimes, questionable. COKETOWN, for example, has been identified as both MANCHESTER and PRESTON, obscuring, perhaps, Dickens's intent to create an imaginary factory town to meet the thematic demands of his story. It is important to remember that even "real" places became fictional when Dickens chose to make them part of his story.

Topographic activity was particularly intense in the early decades of this century, but many of the settings identified during those years have since disappeared. Alex Philip and Laurence Gadd include a useful index of the attributions made during this period in *The Dick-*

ens Dictionary (1928). Two useful recent guides to Dickensian places are London Transport's *The London of Charles Dickens* (1970) and Tony Lynch's *Dickens's England: A Travellers' Companion* (1986).

Topper Bachelor friend of Fred, Scrooge's nephew, who attends Fred's Christmas party and has his eye on one of Fred's wife's sisters. *Carol* (3).

Toppit, Miss American literary lady wearing "a brown wig of uncommon size" at the levee for Elijah Pogram. *Chuzzlewit* (34).

Topsawyer Mythical patron of the inn were David stops on his way to London, who, according to the waiter, drank "a glass of this ale . . . and fell dead." The waiter protects David from a similar fate by drinking David's glass of ale himself. *Copperfield* (5).

Tott, Mrs. Isabella ("Mrs. Belltott") One of the colonists on Silver-store Island, widow of a noncommissioned officer. "A little saucy woman, with a bright pair of eyes. . . . The sort of young woman, I considered at the time, who appeared to invite you to give her a kiss, and who would have slapped your face if you accepted the invitation." "English Prisoners."

Tottenham Court Road Street running north from ST. GILES Circus, in Dickens's time the site of many drapers shops. Horatio Sparkins is a clerk in such a shop (*Boz*, "Sparkins"). Boz also describes a wedding party in this road ("Hackney-Coach"). Miss Knag's brother Mortimer has a stationer's shop here (*Nickleby*, 18). Peggotty recovers Traddles's table and flower stand from a shop at the upper end of the street (*Copperfield*, 34).

Tottle, Watkins A timid bachelor of 50 with "uxorious inclinations," who is forced to propose to Miss Lillerton by his friend Gabriel Parsons. Tottle finally proposes, only to learn that Miss Lillerton has already agreed to marry the Reverend Charles Timson. *Boz*, "Tottle."

"Toughey" Nickname of JO, the crossing sweeper. *Bleak House.*

Towcester Stopping at this town in Northamptonshire on their way back to London from BIRMINGHAM, Pickwick and his friends observe the fight between Pott and Slurk, the rival editors from EATANSWILL, *Pickwick* (51).

Tower of London Quilp's domicile is located nearby on Tower Hill (*Curiosity Shop*, 4). Lord George Gordon (*Rudge*, 73) and Charles Darnay (*Two Cities*, II:6) are both imprisoned in the Tower.

Towlinson, Thomas Dombey's footman who marries Anne the maid and enters the grocery business. *Dombey.*

Town Arms   Headquarters of the Blue faction during the EATANSWILL election. *Pickwick* (13).

Townshend, The Reverend Chauncy Hare (1798–1868)   Clergyman; proponent of MESMERISM and author of *Facts in Mesmerism* (1840); devoted friend of Dickens. A gentle, affectionate man, Townshend has been said to be the original of both Cousin Feenix (*Dombey*) and Twemlow (*Mutual Friend*). He died while Dickens was on his reading tour in America. On hearing of his death, Dickens wrote to Georgina HOGARTH, "It is not a light thing to lose such a friend, and I truly loved him." Townshend named Dickens his literary executor and left him the task of editing and publishing his *Religious Opinions*, published with an introduction by Dickens in 1869.

Tox, Lucretia   Spinster friend of Mrs. Chick who secretly hopes to win the affection of Dombey; "a long, lean figure, wearing such a faded air, that she seemed not to have been made in what linen-drapers call 'fast colours' originally, and to have, by little and little, washed out" (1). She finds Polly Toodle as a nurse for young Paul (2), and remains loyal to Dombey, even after she is disowned by Mrs. Chick (29). Her neighbor, Joey Bagstock, flatters himself that she has designs on him. *Dombey*.

Tozer   Paul Dombey's roommate at Blimber's Academy. *Dombey* (12).

Tpschoffki, Major   Professional name of CHOPS the dwarf. "Going into Society."

Trabb   Obsequious tailor who provides Pip with a new suit of clothes when he sets out for London (19). His assistant, **Trabb's Boy**, "the most audacious boy in all that country-side" (19), mocks Pip's snobbery (30) and leads Herbert to the limekiln to rescue Pip from Orlick (53). *Expectations*.

Traddles, Thomas   David Copperfield's schoolmate at SALEM HOUSE, where he spends his time drawing skeletons on his slate: "the merriest and most miserable of all the boys. He was always being caned" (7). He is the "soul of honor" and defends Mr. Mell against Steerforth's aspersions (7). Traddles's life parallels David's in several ways. When David is learning to be a proctor in DOCTORS' COMMONS, Traddles is studying the law in London (25). David's hasty courtship of Dora is contrasted to Traddles's interminable engagement to Sophy Crewler, "the dearest girl" (27). Traddles also lodges with the Micawbers and he assists Micawber in unmasking Heep (52). He is the best man at David's wedding and acts as David's legal adviser. Eventually he marries Sophy and becomes a successful lawyer (59). *Copperfield*. Traddles is based on Sir Thomas Noon TALFOURD.

"Trading in Death"   Article for *HOUSEHOLD WORDS* (November 27, 1852) on the state funeral for the Duke of Wellington. Dickens objects to the expense and commercialization of Wellington's funeral and expresses the hope that it will serve to change the public mind, leading to less costly and more healthful funeral practices. *Miscellaneous*.

Trampfoot   Policeman who accompanies the Traveller on his tour of the LIVERPOOL slums. *Uncommercial* (5).

"Tramps"   The Traveller's catalog of the various kinds of tramps to be found on country roads in summer: savage tramps, slinking tramps, well-spoken tramps, spotless tramps, perplexed tramps, educated tramps, and handicraft men and sellers of sundry goods. *Uncommercial* (11). Originally in *All the Year Round* (June 16, 1860).

Traveller, Mr.   Narrator of "Tom Tiddler's Ground," he has come to visit the misanthropic Mopes with the intent of proving that human beings need one another. *Tiddler*.

Traveller, The   Narrator of *The Uncommercial Traveller*. (See UNCOMMERCIAL TRAVELLER.)

"Travelling Abroad"   The Traveller's account of a journey from London to PARIS, where he is unsettled by a visit to the morgue; to Strasbourg, where he imagines the life of Straudenheim, a merchant he watches from his hotel window; and, finally, to the mountains of SWITZERLAND. On the way to DOVER, near the mansion on GAD'S HILL the Traveller meets a "queer small boy" who has been told by his father—as Dickens himself was—"If you were to be persevering and were to work hard, you might someday come to live in it." *Uncommercial* (7).

Treasury   One of Merdle's powerful dinner guests. *Dorrit* I:21.

Tredgear, John   Resident of Landrean. "Message from the Sea."

Tregarthen, Kitty   Fiancée of Alfred Raybrock. Their marriage is made possible by the "Message from the Sea," which clears Kitty's **father** of complicity in the embezzlement committed by Lawrence Clissold.

Tremont House   "Very excellent" hotel in BOSTON where Dickens stayed during his 1842 visit. "It has more galleries, colonnades, piazzas and passages than I can remember, or the reader would believe." *Notes* (2).

Trent Family   Surname of the dispersed family at the center of *Curiosity Shop*. **Nell** (**Little Nell**), a gentle, angelic girl, "nearly fourteen," whose "very small and delicate frame imparted a peculiar youthfulness to her appearance" (1), lives in the Old Curiosity Shop with her **grandfather**, "a little old man with long grey hair, whose face and figure, . . . his spare and slender form [held] something of that delicate mould which I had noticed in the child" (1). The old man's addiction to gambling ruins him. After he loses the shop to Quilp (11), Nell leads him out of the city on a series of wandering adventures (12) as they run to escape Quilp's pursuit and Grandfather's addiction to gaming. They go to the races with some traveling performers (19), stay in the house of a poor schoolmaster (24–26), join Mrs. Jarley and her waxworks (27–28), pass through the BLACK COUNTRY (44–45), and, after meeting the schoolmaster again, end their journey in a remote rural village (52). There, in tranquility, both Nell and her grandfather die (71–72). Nell's brother **Frederick**, a wastrel and gambler, conspires to get the fortune he believes his grandfather has hoarded and to marry his sister to Swiveller (7). After Nell disappears, he goes abroad and his body ultimately turns up in the Paris morgue (73). Grandfather's brother, **the single gentleman**, returns from many years abroad to reconcile with his brother, but he finds them only after Nell has died and her grandfather is near death (71). In the frame narrative to the novel, he turns out to be **Master Humphrey**.

Tresham Young Jackson's former colleague. Tresham stole and married **Beatrice**, the woman Jackson loved. Years later the retired Jackson is reunited with Tresham, now a very sick man, through Tresham's daughter **Polly**. Jackson forgives Tresham and Beatrice. *Mugby* (2).

"Tresses of the Day Star, The" Article for *HOUSEHOLD WORDS* (June 21, 1851) by Charles KNIGHT, edited with some brief additions by Dickens, describing the new hummingbird exhibit created by John Gould for the Zoological Society. *Stone*.

"Tringham, Mr." Pseudonym used by Dickens to conceal his identity in his relationship with Ellen TERNAN.

Trimmers Friend of the Cheeryble brothers. *Nickleby* (35, 61).

Trinkle Son of a CHEAPSIDE upholsterer whose gloves make him the prime suspect in the murder of Eliza Grimwood; Inspector Wield discovers that he is not guilty of the crime. *Reprinted*, "Detective Anecdotes."

Trollope, Anthony (1815–1882) Prolific English novelist, best known for his series of Barsetshire novels; civil servant with the Postal Service; son of the novelist Frances Trollope and brother of Thomas Adolphus TROLLOPE. Although Trollope admired Dickens's success, he thought Dickens's novels pandered to the public and were deficient artistically. In *The Warden* (1855), the first of the Barsetshire novels, he satirized Dickens as Mr. Popular Sentiment, "a very powerful man" who used his novels to address social issues and who preferred "ridi-

cule" to "convincing argument," used simplification and exaggeration as his tools, and knew that "the artist who paints for the million must use glaring colours." Trollope praised Dickens on many occasions, but he harbored reservations about the artistic qualities of his work, and in his *Autobiography* (1883) he ranked Dickens below both THACKERAY and GEORGE ELIOT while acknowledging his immense popularity.

Trollope, Thomas Adolphus (1810–1892) English journalist, novelist; contributor to *ALL THE YEAR ROUND*; brother of Anthony TROLLOPE. Tom Trollope spent most of his adult life in Italy, working as an Italian correspondent for British newspapers. He first met Dickens in ITALY in 1845 and thought him "a dandified, pretty-boy-looking sort of figure," but after he knew Dickens better, he described him as "a strikingly manly man, not only in appearance but in bearing" and "perhaps the largest-hearted man I ever knew." Trollope's second wife was **Frances Eleanor Ternan**, sister of Ellen TERNAN. Although Dickens did not like her, he published two of her novels in *All the Year Round*.

Trott, Alexander Young man whose parents want him to marry Emily Brown for her money. However, when he is challenged to a duel by her true love, Horace Hunter, Trott is afraid to go through with the wedding. After he solicits the intervention of the mayor of Winglebury, his situation is confused with that of Lord Peter, who is masquerading as a madman to facilitate a rendezvous with Julia Manners. In the end, Alexander and Julia marry. *Boz*, "Winglebury." In *The Strange Gentleman*, Alexander becomes **Walker Trott**.

Trotter, Job Jingle's manservant, "a young fellow in mulberry-coloured livery . . . who had a large, sallow, ugly face, very sunken eyes, and a gigantic head" (16). He aids Jingle in his schemes, and his ability to call up hypocricial tears fools Sam twice. He is loyal to his master, accompanying him to the FLEET PRISON and, in the end, to the West Indies. *Pickwick*.

"Trotters, Short" Nickname of HARRIS, Codlin's partner in the PUNCH AND JUDY show. *Curiosity Shop*.

Trottle Member of the group listening to the story of Mr. Chops the dwarf. "Going into Society."

Trotwood, Betsey David Copperfield's strong-minded great-aunt who deserts him on the day of his birth because she was expecting the child to be a girl (1). "There was an inflexibility in her face, in her voice, in her gait and carriage, . . . but her features were rather handsome than otherwise, though unbending and austere" (13). Her formidable manner conceals a caring heart. When David runs from MURDSTONE AND GRINBY and seeks her out in DOVER, he discovers that his aunt has already taken the distracted Mr. Dick into her household (13). She agrees to become David's guardian (14), sends him to Doctor Strong's school in CANTERBURY (15), and starts him on the way to becoming a proctor in DOCTOR'S COMMONS (23). When she loses her money through Heep's machinations, she moves to London (24, 25). Although she realizes that David is "blind, blind, blind" (35) in his infatuation for Dora, she wisely refuses to interfere in their marriage and is a true friend to Dora (44). Her own life is shadowed by a bad marriage and a scapegrace **husband** who reappears periodically to demand money from her before he eventually dies (54). *Copperfield.*

Truck Member of the Mechanical Science Section of the Mudfog Association. *Mudfog* (1).

True Sun Newspaper begun in 1832, with Samuel Laman Blanchard as editor. For a few months in 1832 Dickens worked as a general reporter for the paper, while he was also writing for the *MIRROR OF PARLIAMENT* as a parliamentary reporter. The exact length of his tenure with the paper is uncertain.

Trundle Young man who marries Wardle's daughter Isabella during the Christmas festivities at Dingley Dell. *Pickwick* (28).

Trusty, Mrs. Rosina disguises herself as Mrs. Trusty, Captain Blower's nurse, in one of Gabblewig's impersonations. *Nightingale.*

Tuckle A footman who presides at the BATH "swarry": "a stoutish gentleman in a bright crimson coat with long tails, vividly red breeches, and a cocked hat." *Pickwick* (37).

Tugby Sir Joseph Bowry's porter who, in Trotty's dream, has married Mrs. Chickenstalker and evicts Meg from her lodgings when she cannot pay the rent. *Chimes.*

Tuggs Family When London grocer **Joseph Tuggs** inherits £20,000, he takes **Mrs. Tuggs** and his two children, **Simon** and **Charlotte** (who change their names to **Cymon** and **Carlotta** on coming into money) to RAMSGATE. There their naivete and snobbery make them easy prey to a trio of adventurers. *Boz,* "Tuggses."

"Tuggses at Ramsgate, The" First published in the *LIBRARY OF FICTION* (March 31, 1836), this story recounts how London grocer Joseph Tuggs, after inheriting £20,000, takes his family to RAMSGATE where the Waters—a con man and his wife—entrap young Cymon Tuggs in a compromising relationship with Mrs. Waters and extract £1,500 from Tuggs to hush the matter up. *Boz.*

Tulkinghorn Lawyer to the Dedlocks and other important families: "[T]he old gentleman is rusty to look at, but is reputed to have made good thrift out of aristocratic marriage settlements and aristocratic wills, and to be very rich. . . . He is of what is called the old school,

. . . and wears knee breeches tied with ribbons, and gaiters and stockings. One peculiarity of his black clothes . . . is that they never shine. Mute, close, irresponsive to any gleaming light, his dress is like himself" (2). Tulkinghorn pursues the mystery of Lady Dedlock's past, seeking Nemo's documents (11) and information from Jo and Hortense (22) and Trooper George (34) before confronting Lady Dedlock (40–41). Shortly after he returns to London from Chesney Wold, he is found murdered (48). Although George is detained for the crime, Hortense, disgruntled by Tulkinghorn's high-handed treatment of her, proves to be his killer (54). *Bleak House.* Tulkinghorn's house in LINCOLN'S INN FIELDS was based on John FORSTER's house.

Tulrumble, Nicholas Prosperous coal merchant of Mudfog Hall who is appointed mayor of Mudfog. Impressed by the LORD MAYOR's installation ceremony in London, he creates a grand ceremony for himself in Mudfog, but the occasion is disrupted by the drunken Ned Twigger, who reels into the procession in a suit of armor. Tulrumble gives up the position after six weeks when he realizes he was happier as just one of the group of men who gathered at the local pub. **Mrs. Tulrumble** and **Nicholas, Jr.** are not so ready to give up the magnificence of the mayoral life as Tulrumble is. *Mudfog.*

Tunbridge Wells Fashionable spa in KENT where Mr. Finching, "on a donkey," proposed to Flora Casby (*Dorrit,* I:24), and where "Foolish Mr. Porters" reputedly proposed to Miss Twinkleton (*Drood,* 3).

Tungay Creakle's assistant at SALEM HOUSE; "a stout man with a bull-neck, a wooden leg, over-hanging temples, and his hair cut close all round his head" (5). *Copperfield.*

Tupman, Tracy One of Pickwick's traveling companions, a middle-aged bachelor whose "ruling passion" is "admiration of the fair sex." "The too susceptible Tupman who, to the wisdom and experience of maturer years, superadded the enthusiasm and ardour of a boy, in the most interesting and pardonable of human weaknesses—love" (1). After his courtship of Rachel Wardle is foiled by Jingle (8), Tupman withdraws from such pursuits, eventually retiring to RICHMOND where he is much admired by "elderly ladies of single condition" (57). *Pickwick.*

Tupple Guest at the Dopple's New Year's Eve party who leads the round of toasts. *Boz,* "New Year."

Turk John's pet bloodhound. "Haunted House." Dickens owned a bloodhound with the same name.

"Turnham, Mr." One of the pseudonyms Dickens used to keep his identity secret in his relationship with Ellen TERNAN.

Turnstile Passage leading from HOLBORN to LINCOLN'S INN Fields; it once, as Snagsby tells his apprentices, led into open countryside. *Bleak House* (10).

Turveydrop Proprietor of a dancing academy and a model of deportment; "a fat old gentleman with a false complexion, false teeth, false whiskers, and a wig. . . . He was pinched in, and swelled out, and got up, and stopped down, as much as he could possibly bear. . . . He had a cane, he had an eye-glass, he had a snuff-box, he had rings, he had wristbands, he had everything but any touch of nature; he was not like youth, he was not like age, he was not like anything in the world but a model of Deportment" (14). Vain and indolent, he depends on his son **Prince**—named for the Prince Regent—to maintain the family income. Prince, "a little blue-eyed fair man of youthful appearance . . . [and] a little innocent feminine manner" (14), works himself to the point of exhaustion teaching dancing lessons. Turveydrop consents to Prince's marriage to Caddy JELLYBY when the couple agree to continue supporting him (23). *Bleak House*.

Twemlow, Melvin A member of society, this mild-mannered gentleman is one of Veneering's oldest friends because he is a cousin of Lord Snigsworth, who provides him with the small annuity on which he lives. Sophronia Lammle confides to him her scheme for Georgiana Podsnap (II:16). At the end of the novel Twemlow separates himself from the other voices of society, and by defending the marriage of Wrayburn and Lizzie Hexam he becomes the voice of human understanding (IV:17). *Mutual Friend*.

Twickenham Country village on the north side of the THAMES, west of HAMMERSMITH, where Lord Frederick Verisopht is killed by Sir Mulberry Hawk in a duel (*Nickleby*, 50). Arthur Clennam visits the Meagles in their cottage near the river here (*Dorrit*, I:16, 17, 26, 28).

Twigger, Edward ("Bottle-nosed Ned") Dissolute idler in Mudfog who is recruited by Mayor Tulrumble to appear in the mayoral procession in a suit of armor, but who is too drunk to perform sedately. He disrupts the procession and finally is chased home by his **wife**. *Mudfog*.

Twinkleton, Miss Principal of the Seminary for Young Ladies at Nun's House in Cloisterham attended by Rosa Bud and Helena Landless. She has "two distinct and separate phases of being": a scholastic model of decorum during the day and a sprightly persona each evening (3). She becomes Rosa's chaperone in London after Rosa flees from Jasper (21). *Drood*.

Twist, Oliver "Parish boy" hero of the novel that bears his name. Although he is born in a workhouse (1), apprenticed to an undertaker from whom he runs away (4), and falls into Fagin's den of thieves in London (8), Oliver maintains his innocence. His face convinces Brownlow that he is not a thief (11). Even after he is identified as one of the robbers at Mrs. Maylie's house, he convinces her and Doctor Losberne of his innocence (30). Fagin's attempts to corrupt Oliver are encouraged by **Monks** (see LEEFORD, EDWARD), who is revealed to be Oliver's half brother and stands to receive Oliver's inheritance should the boy be corrupted. After piecing together Oliver's parentage as the illegitimate child of Edwin Leeford and Agnes Fleming, Brownlow adopts the boy (50). *Twist*.

"Two Chapters on Bank Note Forgeries: Chapter II" Article for HOUSEHOLD WORDS (September 21, 1850) by WILLS and Dickens describing the history of counterfeit Bank of England notes and the ways in which counterfeiting has been reduced and nearly eliminated. *Stone*.

"Two Views of a Cheap Theatre" The Traveller's account of two visits to the BRITANNIA THEATRE, HOXTON, a new and spacious building, well ventilated and nicely arranged. On Saturday evening, he sees a PANTOMIME and a melodrama performed there and is especially impressed by the diversity in the audience, its attentiveness, and its enjoyment of the performance. On Sunday evening in the same building, he attends a religious service and notices that the audience is not so mixed as on the evening before; it is made up almost exclusively of "respectable" people. The Traveller suggests that the preacher might attract more working-class people if he was not so condescending in speaking of working men, if his stories were more believable, and if he made the New Testament the story that he chose to tell. *Uncommercial* (4). This article first appeared in ALL THE YEAR ROUND, February 25, 1860.

Tyburn Site near what is now Marble Arch, where public hangings took place from the 12th century until 1783. Maypole Hugh's mother had been executed here (*Rudge*, 75).

U

Uncommercial Traveller   Narrator of a series of sketches Dickens wrote for ALL THE YEAR ROUND in the 1860s. He describes himself in the following terms: "I am both a town traveller and a country traveller, and am always on the road. Figuratively speaking, I travel for the great house of Human Interest Brothers, and have rather a large connection in the fancy goods way" (1). *Uncommercial*.

Uncommercial Traveller   A series of sketches Dickens wrote for ALL THE YEAR ROUND in the 1860s. Seventeen of them were first published in volume form in 1861 under the general title *The Uncommercial Traveller*. In later editions more sketches were added: 11 more in the CHEAP EDITION (1865); eight more in the LIBRARY EDITION (1875); and one final addition in the Gad's Hill Edition (1890). The numbering used to identify particular sketches in this encyclopedia is that of the OXFORD ILLUSTRATED EDITION.

Undery   A solicitor who is one of those assembled at the "Haunted House." His name plays on that of Dickens's own solicitor, Frederic OUVRY.

Unions, Labor   The general perception of what Dickens thought of labor unions usually derives from *Hard Times*. In that novel Slackbridge, the unconvincing labor organizer, is, as G. B. SHAW (1913) described him, "a mere figment of the middle-class imagination. . . . Even at their worst trade union organizers are not a bit like Slackbridge." Dickens's failure with Slackbridge is usually taken as an indication that he did not understand unions and simply accepted the middle-class prejudice that unions were unnecessary and dangerous.

Dickens's position on unions, as developed in *Hard Times* and in his journal articles—especially "On Strike," "Railway Strikes," and "To Working Men"—is much more ambivalent. Stephen Blackpool's "muddle" in the novel suggests that Dickens shared CARLYLE's view that laissez-faire capitalism left the workers without leadership from those above them in society, vulnerable to demagogues like Slackbridge. In other instances, however—as in the essay "To Working Men"—he calls on members of the working class to take the initiative themselves to right the injustices that beset them. Though he attacks the outside agitators like Slackbridge and Gruffshaw ("On Strike"), he does not discount the workers'

grievances. Blackpool is at least as wronged by Bounderby as he is by Slackbridge. In spite of all the factory owners' statements about the interests of workers and owners being identical, Bounderby shows no recognition of any common bonds with Blackpool, an irony underscored as Dickens shows both of them to be the victims of failed marriages.

Dickens was also aware of the imbalance of power in the relations of owners and workers, a recognition that informs his ironic presentation of Mrs. Sparsit's views on the issue: "It is much to be regretted," she comments to Bitzer, ". . . that the united masters allow of such combinations. . . . Being united themselves, they ought one and all to set their faces against employing any man who is united with any other man" (*Hard Times*, II:1). Somewhat naively, perhaps, Dickens continued to believe that the issues between workers and masters could be settled through arbitration, for the interests of the two groups were linked, but he thought that the workers might have to take the initiative to make those above them recognize their common lot. Jack LINDSAY (1950) comes much closer to describing Dickens's views than most other commentators when he writes: "Dickens reveals an ambivalent attitude; he wants the workers to unite and insists that the people will take for themselves the rights that will never be given to them by Parliament, but at the same time he feels something frightening in the fact of mass organizations. He advocates trade unionism and shrinks from its results."

United States   See AMERICA.

Unitarianism   After returning from AMERICA in 1842, perhaps influenced by the religious liberalism of the New England Unitarians whom he met there, Dickens began attending a Unitarian chapel in London. He was drawn to Unitarianism by its emphasis on the moral teachings, rather than the theology, in the New Testament. It was the theological contentiousness in the Church of England at the time, particularly the quarrels between the Evangelicals (See EVANGELICALISM) and the Puseyites, that made Unitarianism attractive to Dickens. He attended the Unitarian chapel for most of the 1840s, while he was writing *Chuzzlewit*, *Dombey*, and, significantly, *The Life of Our Lord* for his children. The latter has sometimes been described as a "Unitarian gospel," but as Dennis WALDER (1981) points out, "This is to read into it a theological significance, hardly applicable, unless this simply means having a moral emphasis."

United Bull-Dogs   Name taken by the 'PRENTICE KNIGHTS when they ally themselves with the Protestant party during the GORDON RIOTS. *Rudge* (36).

United Grand Junction Ebenezer Temperance Association   The temperance society of which Stiggins is a leading member of the Brick Lane Branch and Mrs. Weller an ardent member. Sam and Tony visit a meeting of the association in *Pickwick* (33). Later in the novel, Dickens, apparently forgetting the name, changes *Ebenezer* to *Emmanuel* (52).

United Metropolitan Improved Hot Muffin and Crumpet Baking and Punctual Delivery Company   A company promoted by Mr. Bonney to corner the market in muffins and crumpets. Ralph Nickleby is one of its directors. *Nickleby* (2).

"Unsettled Neighbourhood, An"   Article for *HOUSEHOLD WORDS* (November 11, 1854), written from the point of view of an old resident of the neighborhood near the Norwich Railway Terminus Works, describing the turmoil in the neighborhood caused by the railway. *Miscellaneous*. This article is similar to the description of the transformation of STAGG'S GARDENS in *Dombey* (6, 15).

Upwich, Richard   Greengrocer who serves as a juryman at Pickwick's trial. *Pickwick* (34).

Urania Cottage   An asylum for former prostitutes in SHEPHERD'S BUSH, founded by Miss BURDETT-COUTTS in 1847. Dickens was involved in the project from the start, acting as planner and administrator, and took an active role in the day-to-day operation of the facility from 1846 to 1858. His "Appeal to Fallen Women" (1850) states his aims for the project; Alice Marwood in *Dombey*, Martha Endell and Little Em'ly in *Copperfield*, and the prostitute whom Little Dorrit meets on the streets (*Dorrit*, 1:14) are indications in Dickens's novels of his involvement with the issue of PROSTITUTION during this period.

Utilitarianism   An empirical and individualistic moral and social philosophy that was especially influencial in the mid-Victorian period. Also known as Philosophical Radicalism or Benthamism—after its founder, Jeremy Bentham (1748–1832)—Utilitarianism was grounded in the assumption that human beings sought to minimize pain and maximize pleasure, and set as its social goal "the greatest happiness of the greatest number." Although Dickens was sympathetic to the radicals' goals of reforming and rationalizing social and political institutions, he distrusted their use of statistics, their preference for the abstract generalization over the individual case, and their favoring of rationality over imagination. His most direct attacks on Utilitarianism in the novels appear in his critique of the "philosophers" behind the New POOR LAW in *Twist*, his attack on the statistical political economist Filer in *Chimes*, and his exposé of the moral emptiness of the school of fact in *Hard Times*.

V

Vale, Sam Comic actor whose popular portrayal of the Cockney Simon Spatterdash in *The Boarding House* at the DRURY LANE Theatre in 1822 is thought to be the original inspiration for the character of Sam Weller.

Valentine, Private Orderly to Captaine de la Cour, the "sole housemaid, valet, cook, steward, and nurse in the family of his Captain." "Somebody's Luggage."

"Valentine's Day at the Post Office" Article for *HOUSEHOLD WORDS* (March 30, 1850) by WILLS and Dickens, describing the operations of the Post Office. After posting three letters in red, yellow and green envelopes in FLEET STREET, they follow their progress as they are sorted and dispatched at the central office in St. Martin's-le-Grand. *Stone.*

Valentine Vox, The Ventriloquist Popular serial novel by Henry Cockton, published in 1839–40, that shows the influence of both *Pickwick* and *Nickleby*. Its loose series of adventures and its sketches of London life recall Dickens's early work in a general way; the story of Valentine's friend Goodman, who is kidnapped and imprisoned in a lunatic asylum, recalls in particular the story of Nicholas and Smike.

Valiant Soldier Inn Public house and gambling den run by Jem Groves, where Nell's grandfather is lured into gambling. *Curiosity Shop* (29).

Van Ghent, Dorothy (1907–) Professor, University of Vermont; poet; critic of the English and American novel. Her two influential essays on Dickens, "The Dickens World: The View from Todgers's" (*Sewanee Review*, 1950) and "On *Great Expectations* (in *The English Novel*, 1953), include telling discussions of Dickens's use of animism and reification. These related processes, in which the physical world comes alive and the human world is objectified, are at the heart of Dickens's vision of industrial England and crucial to his techniques of characterization.

Varden Family The conflicts within this bourgeois family reflect those in English society at the time of the GORDON RIOTS. **Gabriel Varden** is a London locksmith, "a round, red-faced, sturdy yeoman, with a double chin, and a voice husky with good living, good sleeping, good humour, and good health, . . . bluff, hale, hearty, and in a green old age" (2). He is a loyal friend to Mrs. Rudge and her son Barnaby, securing a pardon for the boy after the riots (79). A sturdy upholder of law and order during the riots, he heroically refuses to unlock the gates of NEWGATE PRISON (63). He is ruled by his wife, **Martha**, a fanatical Protestant who is "most devout when most ill-tempered" (7), but when she sees his steadfastness and courage during the riots, she is changed and abjures her fanaticism. Their pretty daughter **Dolly**, a coquette who draws the attentions of both Joe Willet and Simon Tappertit, is the friend and companion of Emma Haredale, acting as a go-between in the courtship between Edward Chester and Emma. Dolly is taken prisoner during the riots (59). She is rescued by Joe Willet and finally becomes his bride (71, 78). *Rudge.*

Vauban French village where Langley discovers the orphan Bebelle. "Somebody's Luggage."

Vauxhall Bridge The bridge across the THAMES connecting Westminster and Kennington. Charley Hexam and Bradley Headstone meet Eugene Wrayburn here (*Mutual Friend*, II:1). The bridge is also mentioned in *Boz*, "River," and "Somebody's Luggage."

Vauxhall Gardens This famous pleasure ground of the 18th and early 19th centuries—it was closed in 1859—was situated on the south side of the THAMES, near VAUXHALL BRIDGE. Dickens describes it in *Boz*, "Vauxhall."

"Vauxhall Gardens by Day" Originally published as "Sketches by Boz, New Series No. 4" in the *MORNING CHRONICLE* (October 26, 1836). When Boz goes to VAUXHALL GARDENS in the day, he is disappointed, for the attractions that appear so enchanting by night are tawdry and dingy by day. However, the ascent of two balloons by Mr. Green and his son provides some excitement before the day is over. *Boz.*

Veck, Toby ("Trotty") The cheerful ticket porter or messenger whose dream on New Year's Eve is the central story of *The Chimes*. "A weak, small, spare old man, he was a very Hercules, this Toby, in his good intentions." Driven to despair by the intimidating teachings of the political economists, he believes that he has no right to a place on earth. His vision of the Spirits of the Chimes teaches him that he is wrong to blame the poor for their poverty, and that society causes their misery. Restored to cheerfulness and hope, he and his daughter **Margaret** (**Meg**) plan her wedding and again look forward to the future. *Chimes*.

Vendale, George   Partner in Wilding and Co. and fiancé to Marguerite Obenreizer; "a brown-cheeked handsome fellow" (1). He goes to Switzerland to investigate a fraud by Marguerite's uncle Jules, who attacks him and leaves him in the mountains for dead. He is rescued by Marguerite and learns that he is the legitimate heir to the Wilding business. "No Thoroughfare."

Veneering, Hamilton and Anastasia   Nouveaux riche family, the principal representatives of high society in *Mutual Friend*; "bran-new people in a bran-new house in a bran-new quarter of London. Everything about the Veneerings was spick-and-span-new"(I:2). They have a "bran-new **baby**." Their dinner parties, which recur regularly through the novel, gather the members of society—Mortimer Lightwood, Eugene Wrayburn, the Podsnaps, Lady Tippins, Twemlow, Boots, and Brewer—to share the gossip of the day, hear the ongoing story of John Harmon, and provide a social chorus to the novel. Veneering buys his way into Parliament representing the borough of Pocket Breaches (II:3). In the end they are bankrupt and flee to France.

"Vengeance, The"   Madame Defarge's chief associate among the female revolutionaries, a "short, rather plump wife of a starved grocer" (II:22). *Two Cities*.

Venice   Dickens describes his impressions of this city in *Pictures* (8). After gaining their riches, the Dorrits travel to Venice, where Fanny meets Sparkler once again and Amy longs for London (*Dorrit*, II:3–7).

Venning, Mrs.   A British colonist on Silver-store Island; she is Fanny Fisher's mother. She is murdered by pirates during the raid. "English Prisoners."

Ventriloquist, Monsieur The   Performer at the Flemish fair, "thin and sallow and of a weakly aspect." *Uncommercial* (25).

Venus, Mr.   A taxidermist and articulator of bones who is hopelessly in love with Pleasant Riderhood. He makes Wegg's acquaintance by buying his amputated leg bone (I:7), and the two of them enter into a compact, "the Friendly Move," to blackmail Boffin (II:7). But Venus repents his involvement, reveals the plot to Boffin (III:14), and helps to incriminate Wegg. By the end Pleasant overcomes her objections to his occupation, and the two marry. *Mutual Friend*.

"Verdict for Drouet, The"   Article for the *EXAMINER* (April 21, 1849), continuing Dickens's earlier coverage of the cholera epidemic at the Tooting baby farm (see: "PARADISE AT TOOTING"). Dickens comments that even though the manslaughter conviction against Drouet has been overturned on a legal technicality, his guilt remains established and "the child-farming system is effectually broken up by this trial." *Miscellaneous*.

Verisopht, Lord Frederick   Foppish young aristocrat and companion to Sir Mulberry Hawk, who schemes to fleece him. He "exhibited a suit of clothes of the most superlative cut, a pair of whiskers of similar quality, a moustache, a head of hair, and a young face" (19). He and Hawk both pursue Kate Nickleby, but when he threatens to interfere with Hawk's plan to seek revenge on Nicholas and Kate, the two men duel and Verisopht is killed (50). *Nickleby*.

Vholes   Richard Carstone's solicitor, "a sallow man, with pinched lips that looked as if they were cold; a red eruption here and there upon his face; tall and thin; about fifty years of age; high-shouldered and stooping. Dressed in black, . . . there was nothing so remarkable in him as a lifeless manner" (37). He "puts his shoulder to the wheel" and sucks Richard ever deeper into the toils of Chancery, repeatedly remarking on how hard he works to support his three daughters (**Caroline**, **Emma**, and **Jane**) and his **father** in the Vale of TAUNTON. *Bleak House*.

Victoria, Queen (1819–1901)   When Victoria married Prince Albert in 1840, Dickens carried on a facetious fantasy with John FORSTER and Daniel MACLISE in which he pretended to be heartbroken that she had given her heart to another and not recognized his love for her.

The queen attended benefit performances given by his amateur theatrical troupe of *Every Man in His Humour* in 1848, *Not so Bad as We Seem* in 1851, and *The Frozen Deep* in 1857. Although the queen sent for him after the latter performance, Dickens begged to be excused from appearing before her, since he was still "in my Farce dress." He did have an audience with the queen at Buckingham Palace on March 9, 1870. She found him "very agreeable, with a pleasant voice and manner."

Victoria, The   The **Old Vic Theatre** in WATERLOO ROAD on the south bank of the THAMES, famous in the 19th century for its melodramas. The theater is described in *Sketches of Young Gentlemen* and "Amusements of the People."

Victualler, Mr. Licensed   "A sharp and watchful man" who is the host of an establishment for sailors in LIVERPOOL. *Uncommercial* (5).

Villa Bagnarello, Albaro   The Villa di Bella Vista, the house that Dickens rented for his family on their trip to ITALY in 1844. He described the overgrown and ill-cared for building as a "pink jail" and moved his family to the PALAZZO PESCHIERE in GENOA after only two and a half months in Albaro.

Village Coquettes, The Comic operetta by Dickens, with music by John HULLAH, produced at the ST. JAMES'S THEATRE on December 6, 1836. Set in 1729, the story involves two London men-about-town, Squire Norton and Sparkins Flam, who turn the heads of two village girls, Lucy Benson and her cousin Rose. The dandies plan to run off with the girls, but their plan is foiled by a neighboring farmer, Martin Stokes. The squire has a change of heart and blesses Lucy's marriage to her country lover, but Flam is unrepentant and in the end is disowned by his friend. *Miscellaneous*.

Villam Ostler at the Bull, WHITECHAPEL. *Pickwick* (22).

" 'Virginie' and 'Black-Eyed Susan' " Dickens's review for the EXAMINER (May 12, 1849) of Oxenford's English adaptation of Latour de St. Ytres *Virginie* and the revival of Douglas JERROLD's *Black-Eyed Susan*, both at the Marylebone Theatre. He has high praise for both plays, particularly the latter. *Miscellaneous*.

"Visit to Newgate, A" Sketch that first appeared in the first collection of *Sketches by Boz* (1836). On his journey through NEWGATE PRISON, the narrator notes the orderliness of the women's section; the swagger among the boys in the "school," the section for juveniles where he sees "not a wink expressive of anything but the gallows and the hulks"; and the idleness of the male prisoners. As he describes the condemned cells, the most detailed portion of the essay, the narrator imagines himself a condemned felon during his last night on earth, dreaming of freedom and awakening to realize he has only two hours to live. *Boz*.

Voigt, Maître Neuchâtel notary who holds the documents that reveal Vendale's identity and facilitates the unmasking of Obenreizer. "No Thoroughfare."

Vuffin Traveling showman whose exhibits include a giant and a limbless lady. *Curiosity Shop* (19).

Wackles, Sophy "A fresh, good-humoured, buxom girl of twenty," Dick Swiveller's first love. She and her sisters **Melissa** and **Jane** teach in **Mrs. Wackles**'s seminary for young ladies, Sophy instructing in "dancing, music, and general fascination" (8). When Sophy tries to encourage Dick's interest by her attentions to Cheggs, a market gardener, he leaves her, with some regrets, to pursue Fred Trent's scheme to marry him to Nell (8). *Curiosity Shop*.

Wade, Miss Discontented, distrustful, "self-tormenting" friend of the Meagles who convinces Tattycoram to leave them and live with her. She obtains from Rigaud the documents relating to Little Dorrit's identity, which Tattycoram returns when she leaves Miss Wade. Her autobiography, "The History of a Self-Tormentor" (II:21) tells of her painful illegitimacy and of her abusive relationship with Gowan. *Dorrit*.

Waghorn Member of the Mudfog Association. *Mudfog*.

Wakefield, Mr. and Mrs. Couple who go, with their daughter, on the steam excursion. *Boz* "Excursion."

Wakeley Coroner who inquires into the deaths of the pauper children at Tooting. *Miscellaneous*, "Paradise at Tooting."

Walcot Square Just off KENNINGTON Road in LAMBETH, south London, this square is the location of the house that Mr. Guppy has obtained, hoping to improve his prospects with Esther Summerson when he renews his marriage proposal. *Bleak House* (64).

Waldengarver The stage name used by Mr. WOPSLE in London. *Expectations* (31).

Walder, Dennis (1943–) Professor, Open University; South African scholar and writer who has written on the drama of Athol Fugard and other literary topics. *Dickens and Religion* (1981) discusses the religious elements in each of the novels, relating them to Dickens's own religious development.

"Walk in a Workhouse, A" After attending a religious service in a workhouse, Dickens walks through the rest of the institution observing and talking to the inmates. He sees many old people, some of them insane, more of them dispirited, even though their physical needs are reasonably taken care of. *Reprinted*. Originally in *HOUSEHOLD WORDS* (May 25, 1850).

Walker (1) A horse dealer from ISLINGTON who is in Solomon Jacobs's sponging house. *Boz*, "Tottle."

Walker (2) Auditor of the charitable society recognized by the senior officer at the public dinner. *Boz*, "Public Dinners."

Walker, H. Tailor who is converted to teetotalism and recruited into the Brick Lane Branch of the United Grand Junction Ebenezer Temperance Association. "When in better circumstances, owns to having been in the constant habit of drinking ale and beer, . . . is now out of work and penniless; thinks it must be the porter." *Pickwick* (33).

Walker, Mick "Oldest of the regular boys" who work with David at MURDSTONE AND GRINBY's, "he wore a ragged apron and paper cap. He informed me that his father was a bargeman, and walked, in a black velvet head-dress, in the LORD MAYOR's Show." *Copperfield* (11).

Walker, Mrs. Resident at No. 5 in the suburban street. *Boz*, "Streets—Night."

Wallace, William Fictional character based on William Downing Bruce (1824–75), an antiquarian scholar who exposed the deplorable state of the public records in England. *Stone*, "Doom of English Wills."

Walmers, Harry Eight-year-old gentleman whose elopement with Miss Norah is the subject of tale told by Cobbs, the boots of the Holly Tree Inn. Harry is the only son of **Mr. Walmers** of the Elmses, Cobbs's former employer. "Holly Tree."

Walter, Edward M'Neville Penname of Theodosius BUTLER. *Boz*, "Sentiment."

Walters, Charley A former inmate of the workhouse. *Reprinted*, "Workhouse."

Walters, J[ohn] Cuming (d. 1933) Journalist, editor of the *Manchester City News*; President of the DICKENS FELLOWSHIP. One of the active Dickensians in the early years of the 20 century, Walters wrote two books on *Drood* (1905 and 1912), arguing the thesis, controversial at the time, that Edwin was dead, murdered by Jasper, and that Datchery was Helena Landless in disguise. He also wrote a biographical study, *The Phases of Dickens* (1911).

Walton, Surrey One of the towns along the THAMES through which Betty Higden passes on her final journey. *Mutual Friend* (III:8).

Walworth The semirural suburb south of London where Wemmick has his castle and to which he retreats from the public life in the city (*Expectations*, 24). The "back part of Walworth" at the turn of the century is described as "a dreary waste" in *Boz*, "Black Veil." Mr. Tibbs retires to Walworth after separating from Mrs. Tibbs (*Boz*, "Boarding House"). The Traveller describes the high winds at Walworth in *Uncommercial* (6).

Wapping This dockside area in East London is mentioned in *Mutual Friend* (II:12). The Wapping workhouse is described in *Uncommercial* (3).

Warden, Michael Spendthrift neighbor of Dr. Jeddler with whom Marion is supposed to have eloped. He does learn to control his extravagance, and eventually he marries her. *Battle*.

Warden, William Drunkard whose drinking leads to the degradation of his wife and family and to his own suicide. His **wife** dies of a broken heart; his son **Henry** is killed by a gamekeeper; a second son, **William**, shoots the gamekeeper and is hanged; a third son, **John**, immigrates to America; and his daughter **Mary** deserts him. *Boz*, "Drunkard's Death."

Wardle Family The jolly old yeoman and owner of MANOR FARM at DINGLEY DELL, **Mr. Wardle** is "a stout gentleman, in a blue coat and bright buttons, corduroy breeches and top boots" (4); The Pickwickians meet Wardle at the military review in CHATHAM (4); he invites them to his house, where Tupman courts his spinster sister **Rachel** and is outwitted by the unscrupulous Jingle, who elopes with Rachel to gain her small fortune (5–9). Wardle's deaf mother, old **Mrs. Wardle**, "occupied the post of honour on the right-hand corner of the chimney-piece" in the manor house. The Pickwickians again visit Dingley Dell to celebrate CHRISTMAS and the marriage of Wardle's daughter **Isabella**, "a very amiable and lovely girl" (28–30). Wardle's other daughter, **Emily**, is secretly in love with Snodgrass through much of the novel, eventually marrying him after Pickwick's release from prison. The couple then settle at Dingley Dell. *Pickwick*.

Wardour, Richard Hero of Wilkie COLLINS's play *The FROZEN DEEP*, who gives up his life to save the life of his rival for the woman he loves. Dickens was very moved when he played the role in 1857, and was inspired to develop a similar situation in Sydney Carton's story in *Two Cities*.

Warren, The The mansion of the Haredale family near CHIGWELL that is burned down during the GORDON RIOTS. *Rudge* (1, 55).

Warren, Jonathan Early 19-century businessman, proprietor of the BLACKING WAREHOUSE where Dickens worked as a boy in 1824. He claimed to have invented the blacking recipe which his more famous brother **Robert** used to develop WARREN'S BLACKING. Jonathan established a blacking business at 30 HUNGERFORD STAIRS to challenge his brother's business, located at number 30, The STRAND. When James LAMERT became a manager in Jonathan's firm, he suggested that Dickens might be employed there.

Warren's Blacking A manufacturer of blacking. In 1824 when Dickens worked in the BLACKING WAREHOUSE, there were two firms claiming to possess Warren's original recipe for the product. The first, owned by Robert Warren and located at number 30, The STRAND, was later described by Dickens as "the famous one." The other, which had been sold by Jonathan WARREN to George Lamert and was located at 30 HUNGERFORD STAIRS, was the firm in which Dickens worked as a boy.

Warwick Castle Dombey makes an excursion to this castle south of Coventry with Edith Granger and Mrs. Skewton. *Dombey* (27). Dickens visited the castle with H. K. BROWNE in 1838.

"Warwick, The Earl of" The name Inspector Field gives to one of the thieves in ST. GILES. *Reprinted*, "Inspector Field."

Washington, D.C. Dickens describes the city, the Congress, and his meeting with President Tyler in 1842 in *Notes* (8): "Take the worst parts of the City Road in Pentonville, or the straggling outskirts of Paris, where the houses are smallest, preserving all their oddities, but especially the small shops and dwellings, occupied in Pentonville (but not in Washington) by furniture-brokers, keepers of poor eating-houses, and fanciers of birds. Burn the whole down; build it up again in wood and plaster; widen it a little; throw in part of St. John's Wood; put green blinds outside all the private houses, with a red curtain and a white one in every window; plough up all the roads; plant a great deal of coarse turf in every place where it ought *not* to be; erect three handsome buildings in stone and marble, anywhere, but the more entirely out of everyone's way the better; call one the Post Office, one the Patent Office, and one the Treasury; make it scorching hot in the morning, and freezing cold in the afternoon, with an occasional tornado of wind and dust; leave a brick-field without the bricks, in all central places where a street may naturally be expected; and that's Washington."

Waterbrook Agnes Wickfield stays in the house of this genteel solicitor—"a middle-aged gentleman, with a short throat, and a good deal of shirt collar"—and his **wife** while in London. *Copperfield* (25).

Waterhouse Alias of PEGG, the LIVERPOOL crimp, or receiver of stolen property. *Uncommercial* (5).

"Waterloo" Toll taker on WATERLOO BRIDGE who describes the suicides and other unusual people he has met on the bridge. *Reprinted*, "Down with the Tide."

Waterloo Bridge This bridge over the THAMES, between BLACKFRIARS BRIDGE and WESTMINSTER BRIDGE, was completed in 1817. The arches under the bridge provided "unfurnished lodgings" for the homeless, as they did for a fortnight for Sam Weller (*Pickwick*, 16). The drunkard Warden commits suicide by drowning under the bridge (*Boz*, "Drunkard's Death"). Dickens describes the bridge, its inhabitants and suicides, in *Reprinted*, "Down with the Tide."

Waterloo Station Railway station, opened in 1846, where Bradley Headstone learns of Lizzie Hexam's impending marriage from her friends who are going to the wedding. *Mutual Friend* (IV:11).

Waters, Captain Walter A confidence man who, with his wife, **Belinda**—"a young lady . . . with long black ringlets, large black eyes, brief petticoats, and unexceptionable ankles"—conspires to entrap Simon Tuggs in a compromising situation and extort £1,500 from the Tuggs family. *Boz*, "Tuggses."

Waters, Lieutenant Toots's name for Walter GAY. *Dombey* (50).

Watertoast Association of United Sympathisers An Anglophobic association of pro-Irish Americans encountered by Martin Chuzzlewit on his American journey, headed by General Cyrus Choke. "The Watertoast Association sympathised with a certain Public Man in Ireland [Daniel O'Connell], . . . because they didn't love England at all—not by any means because they loved Ireland much." However, when they learn that O'Connell opposes slavery, they disband the organization. *Chuzzlewit* (21).

Watkins Kate Nickleby's godfather. *Nickleby* (18).

Watkins, Gwen (1923–) Critic, biographer; wife of the Welsh poet Vernon Watkins, much of her writing is about the life and work of her late husband. *Dickens in Search of Himself* (1987) treats Dickens as a psycho-logical writer, discussing his works as documents in a self exploration, or as translations, in a psychoanalytic sense, of his subconscious life and experience.

Watkins the First, King Father of Princess Alicia in Alice Rainbird's story. "Holiday Romance."

Watson, Hon. Richard (1800–1852) Liberal politician, friend of Dickens. Dickens met Watson and his wife when he was in Lausanne in 1846, and he subsequently visited them at ROCKINGHAM CASTLE, their home in Northamptonshire, in 1849 and 1851. There he met Mary BOYLE, Mrs. Watson's niece, and organized amateur theatricals. On Watson's death in 1852, Dickens wrote: "I loved him as my heart, and cannot think of him without tears." CHESNEY WOLD in *Bleak House* is based on Rockingham Castle.

Watts, Richard Founder, in 1579, of the ROCHESTER charity that provides a bed and fourpence for six travelers each night. "Seven Poor Travellers."

Watty Bankrupt client who pesters Mr. Perker. *Pickwick* (31).

Waugh, Arthur (1866–1943) Chairman of CHAPMAN & HALL; journalist; author; father of Alec and Evelyn Waugh; one of the founders of the DICKENS FELLOWSHIP, and its president, 1909-10. He wrote on Tennyson, Browning, and other Victorian writers as well as Dickens. Described by the *DICKENSIAN* as "an authority [on Dickens] who does not labour or cavil over a minor bibliographical or topographical detail as some of us do," Waugh sometimes irritated other Dickensians with his critical judgments in his introductions to the Biographical Edition of Dickens (1902–1903).

Webster, Thomas (1800–1886) Artist who furnished the frontispiece for the CHEAP EDITION of *Nickleby*.

Wedgington, Mr. and Mrs. B. Acting and singing couple who give a charity performance at the seaside resort out of season. *Reprinted*, "Out of the Season."

Weedle, Anastasia One of the Mormon emigrants setting out for Utah; "a pretty girl, in a bright Garibaldi, this morning elected by universal suffrage the Beauty of the Ship." *Uncommercial* (22).

"Weevle" Alias taken by Tony JOBLING when he moves into Nemo's rooms in Krook's house. *Bleak House* (20).

Wegg, Silas Balladmonger and street vendor hired by Boffin to be his "literary man" and read to him (I:5) and to be caretaker of BOFFIN'S BOWER (I:15). "A knotty man, and a close-grained, with a face carved out of very hard material, . . . he was so wooden a man that he seemed to have taken his wooden leg naturally" (I:5). When he discovers a second will to the Harmon estate, he attempts to blackmail Boffin (IV:3), but his plot, a "friendly move" with Venus, is foiled and he is thrown out of Boffin's house and into a dust cart (IV:14). *Mutual Friend*.

Welbeck Street   Lord George Gordon lived at No. 64 on this street in MARYLEBONE. *Rudge* (37).

"Well-Authenticated Rappings"   Facetious article for *HOUSEHOLD WORDS* (February 20, 1858), describing three instances of unexplained events that have changed the narrator's attitude toward spiritualism. In two instances, a hangover and a case of heartburn are explained as spiritual visitations; in the third, a practical joke becomes a mysterious event. *Miscellaneous*.

Weller, Christiana (1825–1910)   Young woman pianist whom Dickens met in 1844 when he introduced her at a performance at the LIVERPOOL Mechanics Institute. He was immediately infatuated with her, seeing "an angel's message in her face . . . that smote me to the heart." He seemed to connect her innocence with that of Mary HOGARTH, for he wrote to T. J. Thompson, "I cannot joke about Miss Weller; for she is too good; and interest in her (spiritual young creature that she is, and destined to an early death, I fear) has become a sentiment with me." When Thompson confessed his love for the girl, a shocked Dickens encouraged him to propose to her, and he reconciled the couple twice during their engagement. But when Dickens visited the Thompsons in Lausanne in 1846, he was disappointed with Christiana, who seemed "to have a whimpering, pouting temper."

Weller, Mary   Dickens's nurse when the family lived in CHATHAM between 1817 and 1822. Dickens remembers the terrifying stories she told him as a child, particularly the tale of Captain Murderer, recounted in "Nurse's Stories" (*Uncommercial*, 15). In later life, Mary Weller recalled the recitations and songs performed by her young charge. She has usually been considered the original of Mary, the Nupkins's maid in *Pickwick*, and Clara Peggotty in *Copperfield*. Her younger sister **Anna** married Dickens's brother Frederick (see Frederick DICKENS) over the objections both of her parents and Dickens.

Weller, Samuel   Tony WELLER's son. He is Pickwick's manservant, and matches Pickwick's innocence with worldly savvy. He is working as the boots at the WHITE HART in the BOROUGH when Pickwick first meets him: "[H]e was habited in a coarse striped waistcoat, with black calico sleeves, and blue glass buttons, drab breeches, and leggings. A bright red handkerchief was wound in a very loose and unstudied style round his neck; and an old white hat was carelessly thrown on his head" (10). Sam is the embodiment of Cockney wit; he tells bizarre tales and has a "Wellerism," an outlandish

Browne's (Phiz's) rendering of the "First Appearance of Mr. Samuel Weller" depicts the Cockney servant who is often given credit for the runaway popularity of The Pickwick Papers *in 1836–37.*

comparison for nearly every occasion: " 'That's the pint, sir,' interposed Sam; 'out vith it, as the father said to the child, wen he swallowed a farden' " (12). Sam extricates his master from many embarrassing situations and uses his experience in the streets to compensate for Pickwick's naivete. But even his Cockney wit and clever testimony cannot prevent Pickwick from being sent to prison, so Sam contrives to have himself sent to the FLEET PRISON for debt (43) and he does not leave until Pickwick chooses to leave as well. In the end Sam marries **Mary**, the pretty housemaid that he has first met at the Nupkins's in IPSWICH, and he and his wife and their two sons, **Sam Junior** and **Tony Junior**, settle down in DULWICH as Pickwick's servants. *Pickwick*. Sam reappears in *Master Humphrey's Clock*, in which he and his father preside over "Mr. Weller's Watch," a circle of servants who gather below stairs while the circle of Master Humphrey gathers upstairs. Sam VALE, the Cockney actor, is thought to be the original from whom Dickens drew his character.

Weller, Tony   Sam WELLER's father, a coachman and the husband of **Susan**, proprietress of the MARQUIS OF GRANBY in Dorking: "[H]is face . . . had expanded under the influence of good living, and a disposition remarkable for resignation; and its bold fleshy curves had so far extended beyond the limits originally assigned them, that unless you took a full view of his countenance in front, it was difficult to distinguish more than the extreme tip of a very rubicund nose" (23). Like his son, Tony is a repository of Cockney wit and stories, many having to do with the evils of matrimony. He is plagued by the involvement of Susan—Tony's second wife and hence Sam's stepmother or, in the parlance of the day, his mother-in-law— with Stiggins and the Brick Lane Temperance Association. With Sam's help he exposes the hypocritical Stiggins (33). *Pickwick*. Both Sam and Tony reappear briefly in *Master Humphrey's Clock*.

Wellington House Academy The school in Hampstead Road, north London, that Dickens attended after leaving WARREN'S BLACKING. The sadistic headmaster of the school, William JONES, would become the model for Creakle of Salem House in *Copperfield*, but Dickens's two years there were largely happy ones. His fellow students remembered him as high spirited and involved in amateur theatrical performances, and he did well enough academically to win a Latin prize.

Wellington Street The offices of both *HOUSEHOLD WORDS* and *ALL THE YEAR ROUND* were located in this street off the STRAND.

Welsh, Alexander (1933–) Professor, University of California, Los Angeles; scholar and critic of Victorian fiction who has written on Scott, Eliot, and Thackeray as well as Dickens. *The City of Dickens* (1971) relates several central issues and historical concerns in Dickens's work: the city as both historical fact and spiritual ideal, the heroines as representatives of hearth and home and as angels of death, and the endings of the novels as they relate to the ending of life. *From Copyright to Copperfield: The Identity of Dickens* (1987) offers a biographical interpretation of the middle novels from *Chuzzlewit* through *Copperfield*, identifying a mid-career crisis, beginning with the American journey, as the source of the heroes and issues in these novels. In *The Hero as Quixote* (1981) Welsh traces the influence of CERVANTES on subsequent fiction, particularly on *Pickwick*.

Wemmick, John, Jr. Jaggers's clerk with a "post-office of a mouth" and a belief in "portable property." He keeps his business life in LITTLE BRITAIN completely separate from his personal life in WALWORTH. There, in a miniature castle surrounded by a moat, he lives with his deaf father, **John, Sr. ("Aged P.")**, whom he entertains by firing a cannon (25). He aids Pip in secretly setting up Herbert Pocket in business (37), warns him of Compeyson (45), and aids him in planning Magwitch's escape (48). He surprises Pip by inviting him to his "unplanned" wedding to Miss Skiffins (55). *Expectations*.

West, Dame Grandmother of Mr. Marton's favorite scholar, young HARRY (4) who dies while Nell is staying with the schoolmaster. *Curiosity Shop* (25).

Westgate House Jingle and Job Trotter trick Pickwick into hiding in the courtyard of this school for young women in BURY ST. EDMUNDS, leading to his embarrassing discovery there in the middle of the night. *Pickwick* (16).

Westlock, John One of Pecksniff's pupils and a staunch friend of Tom Pinch, even though they disagree about Pecksniff. He befriends both Tom and Martin when they come to London. He marries Ruth Pinch, and Tom lives with them (54). *Chuzzlewit*.

Westminster Abbey Britain's national church, located on Parliament Square across from the Houses of Parliament. Although Dickens requested to be buried in a private funeral in ROCHESTER, his family acceded to the wishes of Dean Stanley and the larger public who requested that he be buried in the Poets' Corner in the abbey. His body was interred there in an unannounced private ceremony on June 14, 1870.

Two political young gentlemen discuss the policy of charging an admission fee to the abbey (*Young Gentlemen*). The "poet" Slum compares himself to some lesser poets buried in the Poets' Corner in the abbey (*Curiosity Shop*, 28). Daniel Peggotty and David pass the abbey as they follow Martha Endell through the streets of London (*Copperfield*, 47). Pip and Herbert Pocket attend services at the abbey (*Expectations*, 22). Miss Abbey Potterson is thought by some regulars at her pub to be named after the abbey (*Mutual Friend*, I:6). The Traveller spends a quarter of an hour in the "fine gloomy society" of the abbey on one of his night walks (*Uncommercial*, 13).

Westminster Bridge This bridge across the THAMES, connecting LAMBETH with Westminster near the Houses of Parliament, is where Barnaby Rudge first meets the crowds of demonstrators when he enters London with his mother (*Rudge*, 47). The bridge is also mentioned in *Boz*, "River"; *Mutual Friend* (II:1); *Uncommercial* (13).

Westminster Hall Part of the original complex of the Houses of Parliament that was not destroyed in the fire of 1834. Here Geoffrey Haredale meets Lord George Gordon during the prelude to the riots (*Rudge*, 43). The Jarndyce case is heard in the old courts here (*Bleak House*, 19). John Harmon, disguised as Julius Handford, gives his address at the Exchequer Coffee House in this complex of buildings (*Mutual Friend*, I:3).

Westwood Hawk's second in the duel with Verisopht. *Nickleby* (50).

Wharton, Granville George Silverman's pupil, "a young gentleman near coming of age, very well connected, but what is called a poor relation." Silverman promotes his marriage to Adelina Fareway. "Silverman."

"What Christmas Is as We Grow Older" Essay for the Christmas number of *HOUSEHOLD WORDS* (1851), a meditation on the meaning of CHRISTMAS. Though he begins by remembering the Christmases of his childhood and young manhood, Dickens focuses the essay on remembering, with gentle comfort and peaceful reassurance, those who have died. *Christmas Stories.*

Wheezy, Professor   Vice-president of the Zoology and Botany Section of the Mudfog Association. *Mudfog.*

Whelks, Joe   Representative working-class theatergoer in Dickens's descriptions of "The Amusements of the People." *Miscellaneous.*

"Whelp, The"   Harthouse's epithet for Tom GRAD-GRIND. *Hard Times.*

"Where We Stopped Growing"   Important essay for *HOUSEHOLD WORDS* (January 1, 1853), meditating on the things from childhood that we never outgrow. Among his childhood reading, Dickens lists *Robinson Crusoe, The Arabian Nights, Bluebeard, Don Quixote,* and *Gil Blas* as unchanging memories. The whole region of COVENT GARDEN and its theaters is still "for me, a dissipated insoluble mystery." The woman in black and the woman in white who roamed the city streets still intrigue him, as do NEWGATE and the stories of voyage and travel. "If we can only preserve ourselves from growing up," he concludes, "we shall never grow old, and the young may love us to the last." *Miscellaneous.*

Whiff, Miss   An attendant at the Mugby Junction refreshment room. "Mugby."

Whiffers   A Bath footman at the "swarry" who has resigned his position because he has been asked to eat cold meat. *Pickwick* (37).

Whiffin   Town crier at EATANSWILL. *Pickwick* (13).

Whiffler, Mr. and Mrs.   Couple Who Dote upon Their Children—Georgiana, Ned, Dick, Tom, Bob, Mary Anne, Emily, Fanny, Carry, and an unnamed infant on the way. *Young Couples.*

Whilks   Neighbor and prospective client of Mrs. Gamp. *Chuzzlewit* (19).

Whimple, Mrs.   Landlady of the house where old Bill Barley and his daughter lodge and where Magwitch hides out. *Expectations* (46).

Whisker   Mr. Garland's independent pony who follows commands "after his own fashion, or not at all." *Curiosity Shop* (14).

White (1)   Police constable who works with Inspector Field. *Reprinted,* "Inspector Field."

White (2)   A "pale, bald child, with red whiskers" who is one of Mrs. Lemon's pupils. "Holiday Romance."

White, Betsy   Woman who preys on LIVERPOOL sailors. *Uncommercial* (5).

White, Tom   Name assigned to Oliver Twist by the court when he is unable to give his own name. *Twist* (11).

White, Young   Augustus Cooper's more worldly friend, who "had been flaring away like winkin'—going to the theatre—supping at harmonic meetings—eating oysters by the barrel—drinking stout by the gallon—even stopping out all night, and coming home as cool in the morning as if nothing had happened." *Boz,* "Dancing Academy."

White Conduit House   This popular resort in PENTONVILLE was the site of the annual dinner for the chimney sweeps. *Boz,* "First of May." Miss Amelia Martin makes her disastrous debut as a singer here. *Boz,* "Mistaken Milliner."

White Hart Inn (1)   BATH Inn where the Pickwickians stay, operated by Moses PICKWICK, probably the source for Dickens's hero's name. *Pickwick* (35).

White Hart Inn (2)   In the BOROUGH, one of the old coaching inns of London—"Great, rambling, queer, old places they are, with galleries, and passages, and staircases, wide enough and antiquated enough to furnish materials for a hundred ghost stories" (10)—where Jingle and Rachael Wardle put up and where Sam Weller is the boots. *Pickwick.*

The White Hart Inn in the Borough.

White Horse Cellar Coaching inn in PICCADILLY, from which the Pickwickians depart for BATH (*Pickwick*, 35) and where Esther Summerson arrives from READING (*Bleak House*, 3).

Whitechapel District in east London, site of many coaching inns in Dickens's time. Pickwick sets out for IPSWICH from the BULL INN (*Pickwick*, 20, 22); Joe Willet has dinner at the BLACK LION (*Rudge*, 13); David first arrives in London at the BLUE BOAR (*Copperfield*, 5). Oliver is taken to a house in Whitechapel after being recaptured by Nancy and Sikes (*Twist*, 19).

Whitefriars A slum in Dickens's time, this area between FLEET STREET and the TEMPLE was one of the places where the drunkard lived (*Boz*, "Drunkard's Death"). Jerry Cruncher's lodgings are in HANGING SWORD ALLEY (*Two Cities*, II:1). Pip gets Wemmick's warning not to go home at the Whitefriars gate to the Temple (*Expectations*, 44).

Whitehall Street running from Trafalgar Square to Parliament Square. Jingle alludes to the beheading of King Charles I as the coach passes Whitehall Palace (*Pickwick*, 2). John Harmon sees a notice announcing the discovery of his body at the Metropolitan Police headquarters in Whitehall Place (*Mutual Friend*, II:13).

Whitehead, Charles (1804–1862) Novelist, poet, literary editor, and friend of Dickens. His burlesque novel, *The Autobiography of Jack Ketch* (1834), brought him recognition and an invitation from CHAPMAN & HALL—which he declined—to be part of the project that eventually became *Pickwick Papers*. He recognized the quality of Dickens's early sketches and asked him to write for the LIBRARY OF FICTION, a monthly periodical he edited for Chapman & Hall. Dickens contributed "The Tuggses at Ramsgate." Later Whitehead published in BENTLEY'S MISCELLANY the novel *Richard Savage* (1842), a book much admired by Dickens.

Whitrose, Lady Belinda One of Jenny Wren's models for her dolls. *Mutual Friend*, (III:2).

Whittington, Richard (Dick) (d. 1423) LORD MAYOR of London who is associated with the legend of Dick Whittington and his cat. According to the story, Dick, while working as a servant to Mr. Fitzwarren, sent his cat, the only thing he owned, on one of his master's trading vessels. The cat saved the king of Barbary from a plague of rats and was purchased for an enormous sum, but meanwhile Dick had run away from mistreatment as a servant in Fitzwarren's kitchen. Stopping to rest at HIGHGATE, he heard the Bow Bells ringing, calling him to "turn again" and return to Fitzwarren's house. He did so, received payment for his cat, and became a wealthy businessman and eventually Lord Mayor.

Doré's rendering of Dick Whittington listening to the Bow Bells calling him back to the City of London.

Dickens refers to this legend frequently in the novels; it is central to the story of Walter Gay, who is compared to Whittington in his employment and whose story resembles Whittington's (*Dombey*, 4, 6, 9). See also *Curiosity Shop* (50); *Rudge* (31); *Chuzzlewit* (7); *Copperfield* (48); *Bleak House* (6, 31); *Dorrit* (II:12).

"Whole Hogs" Article for HOUSEHOLD WORDS (August 23, 1851), challenging all-or-nothing teetotalers, pacifists, and vegetarians, who insist that others accept the "whole hog" of their ideologies. Dickens criticizes the intemperance of the teetotalers' rhetoric, the naivete of the pacifists who would disarm Britain, and the absolutism of the vegetarians. He calls for more moderation in all three movements. *Miscellaneous*.

"Why" Article for HOUSEHOLD WORDS (March 1, 1856), posing a series of "why" questions that begin facetiously, asking why the young woman at the railway refreshment counter treats him with scorn and why writers speak of "what every schoolboy knows." By the end the questions are more serious, asking why he does not challenge such lazy characterizations as of the English as money loving and why he believes in the politics of Buffy and Boodle and the procedures of the British judicial system. *Miscellaneous.*

Wickam, Mrs. Paul Dombey's nurse after Polly Toodle is dismissed, "a meek woman . . . who was always ready to pity herself, or to be pitied, or to pity anybody else; and who had a surprising natural gift of viewing all subjects in an utterly forlorn and pitiable light." *Dombey* (8).

Wickfield Betsey Trotwood's lawyer, with whom David stays while in CANTERBURY attending Dr. Strong's school (15–19). His alcoholism makes him neglectful of his business and vulnerable to the schemes of his clerk, Uriah Heep, who manipulates his affairs and becomes a partner in the firm (35). His household is managed by his daughter **Agnes**, whose "quiet, good, calm spirit" brings a measure of tranquility to his life. But Heep also intends to become Agnes's partner, a design utterly offensive to David (25). After Heep's schemes ruin Aunt Betsey's fortune and Wickfield's reputation (34), Micawber, acting as a clerk for the firm, exposes Heep and restores order (52). Agnes, a friend and conscience to David throughout his life, eventually marries David (62). *Copperfield.*

Wicks Clerk to DODSON AND FOGG. *Pickwick* (20).

Widger, Mr. Bobtail and Mrs. Lavinia The Plausible Young Couple. *Young Couples.*

Wield, Inspector Charles A London police inspector, based on Inspector FIELD. *Reprinted*, "Detective Police."

Wiglomeration Jarndyce's term to describe the elaborate procedures and obfuscation of the court. "It's the only name I know for the thing. . . . Counsel will have something to say about it; the Chancellor will have something to say about it; the Satellites will have something to say about it; . . . the whole thing will be vastly ceremonious, wordy, unsatisfactory, and expensive, and I call it, in general, Wiglomeration." *Bleak House* (8).

Wiggs and Co. Owners of the ill-fated ship *Polyphemus* in one of the sea stories recounted by Walter Gay. *Dombey* (4).

Wigsby (1) Member of the Mudfog Association. *Mudfog.*

Wigsby (2) One of Our Vestrymen. *Reprinted*, "Our Vestry."

Wigzell, J. Pub owner who expands his business into a railway hotel with the coming of the railway. *Miscellaneous*, "Unsettled Neighbourhood."

Wilderness, The Riverside tavern near QUILP'S WHARF where the dwarf takes Dick Swiveller (21) and Sampson and Sally Brass (51). *Curiosity Shop.*

Wilding, Walter Head of Wilding and Co., a firm of London wine merchants that he has inherited from the woman he believes to be his **mother**. As a child he was an orphan. His mother recovers him from the Foundling Hospital thinking him her child, but after her death he learns that she was mistaken. He sets out to find her rightful heir, but dies in the attempt. "No Thoroughfare."

Wildspark, Tom Tony Weller's acquaintance who got off a manslaughter charge with "a alleybi." *Pickwick* (33).

Wilfer Family Suburban family of **Bella Wilfer**, the petulant and capricious young woman chosen by old John Harmon as the appropriate bride to will to his son. When she is disinherited by the presumed death of young Harmon, the Boffins take her into their house and she indulges her mercenary tendencies, encouraged by Boffin himself, who pretends to be a miser. She rejects Rokesmith's first proposal of marriage, indignant at his presumption (II:13), but when he is harshly treated by Boffin, she runs off and marries him (IV:4). She is not informed of the identity of her husband until many months later. She is especially close to her father, **Reginald ("R. W.," "The Cherub," "Rumty")**, a henpecked clerk for CHICKSEY, VENEERING, AND STOBBLES. His cherubic appearance, "chubby, smooth, innocent," bespeaks his gentle and self-effacing manner. "The modest object of his ambition [is] to wear a complete new suit of clothes, hat and boots included, at one time" (I:4). He and Bella go to a private supper in GREENWICH (II:8), and he is the only family member who attends her secret wedding (IV:4). His wife, **Mrs. Wilfer**, is as majestic as he is modest, "a tall woman, and angular. Her lord being cherubic, she was necessarily majestic" (I:4). She complains of being ill-used and feels herself above the station to which marriage has reduced her. Bella has two younger sisters, **Lavinia** and **Cecilia**. *Mutual Friend.*

Wilhelm German courier who tells the story of John, the twin who has a ghostly premonition of his brother's death. *Reprinted*, "At Dusk."

Wilkie, Sir David (1785–1841) Scottish genre and portrait painter; godfather of Wilkie COLLINS; friend of Dickens. Dickens was often compared to Wilkie, an artist known for his renderings of common people in their everyday lives. He had at least one of Wilkie's paintings at GAD'S HILL. In a tribute to Wilkie on the painter's death, Dickens spoke of him as one "who made the cottage hearth his grave theme, and who surrounded the lives, and cares, and daily toils, and occupations of the poor, with dignity and beauty."

Wilkins One of Captain Boldwig's gardeners. *Pickwick* (19).

Wilkins, Dick Scrooge's fellow apprentice at Fezziwig's. *Carol* (2).

Wilkins, Samuel "Journeyman carpenter of small dimensions" who "kept company" and eventually married Jemima Evans. *Boz,* "Evans."

Will Waiter at the St. James's Arms. *Strange Gentleman.*

Willet, John Slow but sure proprietor of the MAYPOLE INN near CHIGWELL, "one of the most dogged and positive fellows in existence—always sure that what he said or did was right" (1). He treats his son **Joe** like a child, causing him to run away to the army (31). Lord George Gordon and his lieutenants stop at the Maypole on their way into London (35–36) and the rioters ransack the tavern on their way to burn down the Warren, leaving John bound and dazed (54). In the army, young Joe loses an arm but proves his heroism. He returns in time to rescue Mr. Haredale, his daughter, and Dolly Varden during the riots (67, 71). Father and son are reconciled, and Dolly and Joe marry and restore the Maypole (72, 78, 80). *Rudge.*

William (1) Young man who dies from overwork, copying and translating for the publishers to support his widowed mother. *Boz,* "Neighbour."

William (2) Waiter at the SARACEN'S HEAD. *Nickleby* (5).

William (3) Sir Mulberry Hawk's groom. *Nickleby* (32).

William (4) The "twinkling-eyed, pimple-faced" waiter who eats most of David's dinner at the inn in YARMOUTH. *Copperfield* (5).

William (5) Coachman who drives David to London from CANTERBURY. *Copperfield* (19).

William, Sweet "A silent gentleman who earned his living by showing tricks upon the cards," one of the traveling performers whom Nell and her grandfather meet on the road. *Curiosity Shop* (19).

Williams A London constable. *Reprinted,* "Inspector Field."

Williams, Bransby (1870–1961) British actor, playwright, and music-hall performer. Williams began his career performing Dickens characters in music hall sketches in the 1890s and continued performing in these sketches and in numerous other Dickensian theatrical roles until the 1950s. Among the many Dickensian roles that he played on stage were Fagin (1909), Micawber and Daniel Peggotty (1921), and Magwitch (1947). In silent films he played Buzfuz in Thomas BENTLEY's *Adventures of Mr. Pickwick* (1921) and Gradgrind in Bentley's *Hard Times* (1915). He was the English BARRYMORE, playing Scrooge almost annually on BBC radio. He did readings of the *Carol* in which he performed all the roles, and he played Scrooge on BBC television (1946, 1950). As a playwright, he adapted plays from *Rudge, Dombey, Two Cities, Twist,* and *Copperfield.* In 1925 he founded the Tabard Players, a professional troupe devoted to the production of Dickens on stage.

Williams, Emlyn (1905–1987) Welsh actor, director, and writer, whose one-man show playing Dickens performing the PUBLIC READINGS began in 1951. He said of his inspiration for the performance: "I got the idea from Charles Dickens in 1951. . . . I was reading his autobiography [probably Edgar JOHNSON's biography], and I suddenly thought I'll dress up as Dickens and do what he did—tell a story from one of his books." In 1952 he wrote and performed a version of *Bleak House* in which he played all 35 characters. Williams later developed performances from Dickens's reading texts and from readings he himself extracted from the novels. By 1979 he had performed Dickens almost 2,000 times.

Williams, Raymond (1921–1988) Professor, Cambridge; Marxist critic and theorist, best known for *Culture and Society, 1780–1950* (1951) and *Keywords* (1976). In *The English Novel from Dickens to Lawrence* (1974), Williams saw Dickens, who developed characters and a literary form particularly adapted to express a new urban consciousness, as the defining figure in the novel as it responded to industrialization and urbanization. Williams also discussed Dickens in *The Country and the City* (1973) and in his introductions to *Dombey* (1970) and *Hard Times* (1966).

Williams, Samuel (1788–1853) Wood engraver and illustrator who contributed one illustration for *Curiosity Shop,* "The Child in her Gentle Slumber," and engraved illustrations by BROWNE and CATTERMOLE.

Williams, William A regular at the SIX JOLLY FELLOWSHIP PORTERS. *Mutual Friend.*

Williamson, Mrs. Landlady of the Winglebury Arms. *Boz,* "Winglebury."

Willing Mind Tavern Public house to which Daniel Peggotty goes. *Copperfield* (3).

Willis, The Misses Four inseparable sisters who become the talk of Our Parish when one of them, not publicly identified, marries Mr. Robinson. *Boz,* "Four Sisters."

Samuel Williams's illustration of "The Child in her Gentle Slumber" for the opening number of The Old Curiosity Shop *foreshadowed Cattermole's later picture of Nell on her deathbed (Illustration 66).*

Willis, Mr.   "A young fellow of vulgar manners" imprisoned in Solomon Jacobs's sponging house. *Boz,* "Tottle."

Wills, William Henry (1810–1880)   Journalist and editor, Wills contributed to BENTLEY'S MISCELLANY when Dickens was editor and became Dickens's secretary at the DAILY NEWS. He served as the "sub-editor" and part-owner of both HOUSEHOLD WORDS and ALL THE YEAR ROUND, taking responsibility for the day-to-day operation of both periodicals. Dickens described him as having "no genius, and [being], in literary matters, sufficiently commonplace to represent a very large proportion of our readers." The two complemented each other nicely and became intimate friends as well as business associates. Wills was privy to Dickens's affair with Ellen TERNAN, a loyal and discreet friend who fully deserved Dickens's tribute: "[We] doubt whether any two men can have gone on more happily, and smoothly, or with greater trust and confidence in each other."

Wilson (1)   The Iago of the Gattleton's private theatricals who is late for the performance because he is detained at the post office. *Boz,* "Porter."

Wilson (2)   The Parlour Orator's antagonist in the political debates of the Old Street Suburban Representative Discovery Society. *Boz,* "Orator."

Wilson (3)   Policeman on duty in the House of Commons. *Boz,* "Parliamentary Sketch."

Wilson, Angus (1913–1991)   British novelist and critic, best known for *Hemlock and After* (1952) and *Anglo-Saxon Attitudes* (1956). His fiction is often compared to Dickens's, especially for the characters. In "Charles

W. H. Wills.

Dickens: A Haunting" (*Critical Quarterly,* 1970), Wilson describes the hold his childhood reading of Dickens had on his imagination. His critical introduction to *The World of Charles Dickens* (1970) discusses Dickens's career chronologically, fitting its perceptive commentaries on the individual novels into a broad and sympathetic treatment of Dickens's life and career. His introductions to the Penguin *Twist* (1966) and *Drood* (1974) and the Signet *Expectations* (1963) similarly combine solid information about the author and texts with sympathetic and sharp criticism. Especially noteworthy among Wilson's many essays on Dickens and his works are "Dickens on Children and Childhood" (in Michael SLATER, 1970); "Heroes and Heroines of Dickens" (in J. Gross and G. Pearson, *Dickens and the Twentieth Century,* 1962); and "Dickens and Dostoyevsky" (*Dickensian,* 1970).

Wilson, Caroline   Pupil at Minerva House, "the ugliest girl in Hammersmith, or out of it." *Boz,* "Sentiment."

Wilson, Edmund (1895–1972)   American literary critic, novelist, playwright, poet, and social commentator. Wilson's essay "Dickens: The Two Scrooges" (a 1939 lecture, printed in *The Wound and the Bow*, 1941) established the modern critical approaches to Dickens and, as Ada NISBET (1964) points out, made it "customary to refer to individual critics as pre-or post-Wilsonian." Wilson challenged the modernists who viewed Dickens as a vulgar entertainer with a Dostoyevskian Dickens, divided between bourgeois optimism and deep personal pain and social despair. Wilson found this dualism, engendered by Dickens's childhood experiences in the BLACKING WAREHOUSE, running through his works, but most profoundly expressed in the dark later novels.

Wilson, Fanny and Mary   Two sisters on their way to GRETNA GREEN. Fanny is the fiancée of Charles Tomkins; Mary, of John Johnson. *Strange Gentleman.*

Wilson, Mr. and Mrs.   Godparents to the Kitterbell's baby. *Boz,* "Christening."

"Wind and the Rain, The"   Article for *HOUSEHOLD WORDS* (May 31, 1851) by H. MORLEY and Dickens, explaining the scientific principles behind wind and rain. *Stone.*

Windsor   This town in Berkshire is Esther Summerson's unhappy childhood home (*Bleak House*, 1) and the site of some of John Podger's 17th-century adventures in Pickwick's tale (*Humphrey*).

Windsor Terrace   Street in Finsbury, north London, where David lodges with the Micawbers. *Copperfield* (11).

Winking Charley   "A sturdy vagrant, in one of her Majesty's jails" who is a recurrent figure in the narrator's night thoughts. *Reprinted,* "Lying Awake."

Winkle, Nathaniel   One of the traveling Pickwickians, Winkle's pretense of being a sportsman gets him repeatedly into trouble and causes Pickwick to call him a "wretch" after one particularly inept performance with a gun (7). Winkle's confused testimony at the trial helps to convict Pickwick (34), but while Pickwick is in prison, Winkle marries Arabella Allen and, with Pickwick's help, he secures his father's blessing for the union (56). His father, **Winkle, Senior**, a BIRMINGHAM wharf owner, is "a little old gentleman in a snuff-coloured suit, with a head and face the precise counterpart of those belonging to Mr. Winkle, Junior, excepting that he was rather bald" (50). *Pickwick.*

"Winks"   Nickname for DEPUTY. *Drood* (23).

Winter, Mrs. Henry   Married name of Maria BEADNELL.

Winterbourne   House at BONCHURCH, Isle of Wight, where Dickens spent the summer of 1849.

Wisbottle   One of Mrs. Tibbs's boarders, "a high Tory . . . [who] knew the Peerage by heart." He feuds with the radical Mr. Evenson. *Boz,* "Boarding House."

Wisdom of Our Ancestors   General title for a series of fake books that Dickens had constructed for his library at GAD'S HILL. The individual volumes were: I. *Ignorance*; II. *Superstition*; III. *The Block*; IV. *The Stake*; V. *The Rack*; VI. *Dirt*; VII. *Disease.*

Wisk, Miss   Mr. Quale's fiancée, a woman with a mission "to show the world that woman's mission was man's mission; and that the only genuine mission, of both man and woman, was to be always moving declaratory resolutions about things in general at public meetings." *Bleak House* (30).

Witchem, Sergeant   Detective policeman, "shorter and thicker-set [than Sergeant Dornton], and marked with the small-pox . . . [with] a reserved and thoughtful air, as if he were engaged in deep mathematical calculations." *Reprinted,* "Detective Police."

Witherden   Notary to whom Abel Garland is apprenticed, "short, chubby, fresh-coloured, brisk and pompous" (14). He aids the Single Gentleman in tracing Nell and her grandfather (40) and brings about the comeuppance of the Brasses and Quilp (66). *Curiosity Shop.*

Witherfield, Miss   The middle-aged lady in curl papers who is surprised to find Pickwick in her hotel room in IPSWICH in the middle of the night. The altercation that arises the next morning between Pickwick and her suitor, Peter Magnus, leads to Pickwick's arrest for disturbing the peace. *Pickwick* (22, 24).

Withers   "Tall, and wan, and thin" page who pushes Mrs. Skewton's chair. *Dombey* (21).

Wititterly, Julia   The insipid lady from Belgravia to whom Kate Nickleby becomes secretary and companion after leaving Madame Mantalini's (21). She becomes jealous of the attentions paid to Kate by Sir Mulberry Hawk. Nicholas removes Kate from the house of Mrs. Wititterly and her devoted husband, **Henry**, after his fight with Hawk (33). *Nickleby.*

Wizzle   Guest invited to the steam excursion but unable to attend. *Boz,* "Steam Excursion."

Wobbler   Rude and desultory clerk at the CIRCUMLOCUTION OFFICE. *Dorrit* (I:10).

Wolf Associate of Tigg Montague who attends the dinner for Jonas Chuzzlewit: "literary character— . . . remarkably clever weekly paper—oh, remarkably clever!" *Chuzzlewit* 28.

Wolverhampton The description of the BLACK COUNTRY in the industrial midlands of England in *Curiosity Shop* (45) is based on Dickens's experience of the countryside between BIRMINGHAM and this industrial town in Staffordshire.

Wood Engraving Technique for printing illustrations that became increasingly widespread during Dickens's career. Dickens's primary illustrators—BROWNE and CRUIKSHANK—had their drawings etched on to steel plates from which they were printed, a technique widely used in the 1830s. Beginning in the 1840s, etching on steel was gradually replaced by wood engraving, in which the picture was cut into the end-grain of a hardwood such as boxwood or peartree. Firms of engravers like the Dalziel Brothers, who produced the engravings for the *HOUSEHOLD EDITION*, could quickly produce the blocks from an artist's drawings.

Wood Sawyer, The JACQUES Five, formerly a mender of roads, becomes a wood-sawyer during the Revolution and refers to his saw as La Guillotine. Lucie notices him at his wood yard near the LA FORCE prison when she goes to see her husband (III:5). *Two Cities*.

Wood Street Street in the CITY where the CROSS KEYS INN is located. This coaching inn was the terminal for coaches to and from ROCHESTER. Pip arrives in London and leaves again from this inn (*Expectations*, 20, 32). Cavaletto is run down by a fast mail coach in this street (*Dorrit* I:13).

Woodcourt, Allan "Young surgeon, . . . reserved, . . . sensible and agreeable" (13). He signs Nemo's death certificate (11). He falls in love with Esther Summerson before leaving for India, but he does not declare himself. His mother, **Mrs. Woodcourt**, warns Esther that the family's proud Welsh heritage makes her son an inappropriate match for someone like Esther (30). When he returns, Allan becomes a friend and advisor to Richard Carstone, and he tends Jo in his last illness (45, 47). Jarndyce secures him a practice in Yorkshire and secretly promotes his marriage to Esther (64). *Bleak House*.

Wooden Midshipman, The Wooden figure that acts as the sign for Sol Gill's nautical instrument shop. *Dombey*. Dickens based the effigy in his novel on one outside a shop in LEADENHALL STREET which can now be seen in the DICKENS HOUSE MUSEUM. The latter figure is mentioned by the Traveller in *Uncommercial* (3).

Woodensconce Member of the Mudfog Association. *Mudfog*.

Woolford, Miss Horse rider who gives a "graceful performance" at ASTLEY's. *Boz*, "Astley's."

Wopsle Parish clerk and friend of the Gargerys, he unites "a Roman nose, . . . a large shining bald forehead, . . . [and] a deep voice which he was uncommonly proud of" (4). He aspires to enter the church, but he ends up in the theater where he takes the stage name of WALDENGARVER. Pip watches him perform Hamlet in an obscure London theater (31); later, when Wopsle has been reduced to playing miscellaneous bit parts, Pip sees him at an even more obscure venue along the river (47). *Expectations*.

"Word in Season, A" Poem on religious conversion that Dickens wrote for Lady BLESSINGTON's annual, the KEEPSAKE, in 1844. *Miscellaneous*.

Workhouse Institutions for housing the poor, often referred to as Union Workhouses after the New POOR LAW of 1834, which divided the country into several districts, each uniting several parishes into a single unit with one workhouse.

"Work'us" Noah Claypole's derogatory epithet for Oliver. *Twist* (5–6).

"Worthy Magistrate, The" Article for *HOUSEHOLD WORDS* (August 25, 1855), attacking Mr. Hall, chief police Magistrate in the BOW STREET court, for his assertion that the English are a race of drunkards. *Miscellaneous*.

Wosky, Dr. Mrs. Bloss's doctor. "He had a very good practice, and plenty of money, which he had amassed by invariably humouring the worst fancies of all the females of all the families he had ever been introduced into." *Boz*, "Boarding House."

Wozenham, Miss Rival lodging-house keeper to Mrs. Lirriper. Although there has been "a little unpleasantness" between the two rivals over the years, they become good friends after Mrs. Lirriper saves Miss Wozenham from bankruptcy. "Lirriper's Legacy."

Wrayburn, Eugene Mortimer Lightwood's close friend, a barrister who has been in the profession for seven years without work, "in susceptibility to boredom . . . the most consistent of mankind" (I:12). An upper-class idler, melancholy and with no direction in his life, he is nonetheless uneasy about the expectations of his **M.R.F.** (**Most Respected Father**). He interests himself in the Harmon murder case, meets Lizzie Hexam (I: 2) and pursues her without any clear acknowledgment or understanding of his intentions (II:6). Over the objections of her brother, he educates her, and when Lizzie runs off to escape his attentions and those of Bradley

Headstone, he follows her, learning her whereabouts from Mr. Dolls (III:16). At the mill town on the upper THAMES where she is living, he is attacked by Headstone and rescued by Lizzie (IV:6), whom he marries during his gradual recovery. Her love brings more than his physical recovery; it gives purpose and meaning to his life. *Mutual Friend*.

"Wreck of the Golden Mary, The"   Christmas number of *HOUSEHOLD WORDS*, 1856. Dickens wrote the opening chapter describing the *Golden Mary*, a ship on its way from Liverpool to California that is rammed by an iceberg off Cape Horn. The passengers, led by Captain Lavender, survive 27 days in lifeboats before being rescued, but during that time a child, Lucy Atherfield, dies. Wilkie COLLINS collaborated with Dickens on the mate's narrative in this opening chapter and also wrote the final chapter, "The Deliverance," describing the rescue. Other writers contributed INTERPOLATED TALES to the number. *Christmas Stories*.

"Wren, Jenny"   The pseudonym used by Fanny CLEAVER. *Mutual Friend*.

Wright's Inn   Hotel next to the BULL in ROCHESTER, described by Jingle as "very dear—half-a-crown in the bill if you look at the waiter" (*Pickwick*, 2). It is the original of the Crozier in Cloisterham in *Drood* (18).

Wrymug, Mrs.   Client of the employment agency that Nicolas consults who requires her servants to be "serious" and join the Little Bethel Congregation. *Nickleby* (16).

Wugsby, Mrs. Colonel   One of the whist players at Bath. *Pickwick* (35, 36).

Y

Yarmouth, Norfolk Seaside town in Norfolk where Daniel Peggotty has his boathouse and where many crucial scenes in *David Copperfield* take place, most notably perhaps, the drowning of Ham and Steerforth (55).

Yates, Edmund (1831–1894) Journalist, novelist, and dramatist; contributor to ALL THE YEAR ROUND. Yates met Dickens in 1854 and became an intimate friend and protege of the novelist. His nomination to the GARRICK CLUB led to Dickens's dispute with THACKERAY. With B. R. Brough, Yates wrote a parody of *Hard Times*. In 1872, Yates toured America giving lectures that included his reminiscences of Dickens.

Yates, Frederick (1797–1842) Actor, theater owner, manager and director at the ADELPHI; father of Edmund YATES; friend of Dickens. He directed and acted in several early adaptations of Dickens's novels, playing Pickwick, Mantalini, Fagin, Quilp, and Sir John Chester. **Mrs. Yates**, Frederick's wife, an actress who played Nancy in *Twist*, Dolly Varden, and the widow Rudge, said after seeing Dickens perform in *The Lighthouse*, "O Mr Dickens what a pity it is you can do anything else!"

Yawler Schoolmate of David and Traddles at SALEM HOUSE who helps Traddles enter the legal profession. *Copperfield* (27).

York Setting for the tale of the "FIVE SISTERS OF YORK" (*Nickleby*, 6). John Chivery goes to York when he is seeking information on the Dorrit family fortune (*Dorrit*, I:25).

Yorkshire Dickens stayed at the GEORGE AND NEW INN at GRETA BRIDGE in 1838 when he was in this northern county—geographically the largest in England—with H. K. BROWNE gathering information on YORKSHIRE SCHOOLS for *Nickleby*. The inn serves as the coach stop for DOTHEBOYS HALL (*Nickleby*, 6) and was probably also the model for the HOLLY TREE INN. Allan and Esther Woodcourt's new BLEAK HOUSE is also located in Yorkshire (64).

Yorkshire Schools These notorious schools charged cheap fees and were used as dumping grounds for illegitimate and unwanted children. They garnered such children by advertising "no extra charges" and "no vacations." In 1823, at the trial of William SHAW for the gross neglect of students at his school at BOWES, where two children had become totally blind from infection, testimony revealed that the boys were served maggoty food, beaten, denied medical treatment, and housed five to a bed. Dickens began *Nickleby* with the idea of exposing such schools through the example of DOTHEBOYS HALL. He traveled to YORKSHIRE and, posing as a client, interviewed Shaw while preparing to write the novel.

"Young Blight" Mortimer Lightwood's office boy. *Mutual Friend*.

"Young Man from the Country, The" Article for ALL THE YEAR ROUND (March 8, 1862) in which Dickens reprints several passages from *American Notes* on the corruption in American politics, the suspicion of all who achieve high places, the love of smart dealing, and the slander in the American press. He ends by asking whether things have changed at all in 20 years. *Miscellaneous*.

Z

Zamiel Name given by the narrator to a fellow passenger on the express train for Paris, a "tall, grave, melancholy Frenchman, . . . got up, one thinks, like Lucifer or Mephistopheles, or Zamiel, transformed into a highly genteel Parisian." *Reprinted*, "A Flight."

"Zephyr, The" Nickname of MIVINS, one of Pickwick's fellow prisoners in the FLEET PRISON. *Pickwick*.

APPENDIX A

A BRIEF CHRONOLOGY OF DICKENS'S LIFE AND MAJOR WORKS

Publication dates are those for the first complete editions.

1812   Dickens born at Portsmouth.

1814   John Dickens, the novelist's father, transferred to London.

1817   John Dickens transferred to Chatham in Kent, where Charles spent the happiest years of his boyhood.

1821   Charles begins his education at William Giles's school in Chatham.

1822   John Dickens transferred to London.

1824   John Dickens arrested for debt and imprisoned in the King's Bench and then the Marshalsea prisons. Dickens is employed at the blacking warehouse. After his father's release from prison, Dickens enters Wellington House Academy.

1827   When his father again gets into financial difficulty, Dickens is withdrawn from Wellington House. He goes to work for the firm of Ellis and Blackmore as a solicitor's clerk.

1829   Dickens learns shorthand and works as a freelance court reporter at Doctor's Commons.

1830   After his 18th birthday, Dickens secures a reader's ticket to the British Museum. He meets Maria Beadnell.

1831   Dickens works as a parliamentary reporter for the *Mirror of Parliament*.

1832   Dickens works as a reporter for the *True Sun*. Illness prevents him from attending an audition at Covent Garden Theatre. He courts Maria Beadnell.

1833   Dickens breaks off his romance with Maria Beadnell. In December, his first story, "A Dinner at Popular Walk," is published in the *Monthly Magazine*.

1834   Dickens goes to work as a reporter on the *Morning Chronicle* and continues to publish stories and sketches in various London papers and magazines. He meets Catherine Hogarth.

1835   Dickens contributes series of sketches to the *Evening Chronicle* and *Bell's Life in London*. He is engaged to Catherine Hogarth.

1836   *Sketches by Boz*, first and second series. In March, *Pickwick* begins its serial run. Dickens and Catherine are married in April. Two short plays by Dickens, *The Strange Gentleman* and *The Village Coquettes*, are produced at the St. James's Theatre. Dickens meets John Forster.

1837   *The Pickwick Papers. Bentley's Miscellany* begins publication with Dickens as editor. Dickens's first child, Charles Culliford Boz, is born. The Dickens family move to 48 Doughty Street. In May Mary Hogarth dies and Dickens suspends publication of the monthly numbers of *Pickwick* and *Twist* for the month of June. Dickens is elected to the Garrick Club.

1838   *Oliver Twist; Sketches of Young Gentlemen; Memoirs of Grimaldi*. Dickens and Browne make an expedition to investigate Yorkshire schools. Dickens is elected to the Athenaeum Club.

1839   *Nicholas Nickleby*. Dickens resigns as editor of *Bentley's Miscellany*. The Dickens family takes its first holiday at Broadstairs and, in December, moves to Devonshire Terrace.

1840   *Master Humphrey's Clock*, vol. I; *Sketches of Young Couples*.

1841   *Master Humphrey's Clock*, vol. II; *The Old Curiosity Shop; Barnaby Rudge*. Dickens declines an invitation to run for Parliament as the Liberal candidate for Reading. Dickens and Catherine tour Scotland. In October, Dickens falls ill and undergoes an operation for a fistula.

1842   *American Notes*. Dickens and Catherine tour America, leaving in January and returning to England in July.

1843   *A Christmas Carol*. In October, Dickens presides at the inauguration of the Athenaeum Club in Manchester. While he is there, he conceives the idea for the *Carol*.

1844   *Martin Chuzzlewit; The Chimes*. Dickens changes publishers from Chapman & Hall to Bradbury & Evans. In July, the Dickens family travels to Genoa, Italy, for a stay of nearly a year. In December, Dickens returns to London to read *The Chimes* to a gathering of friends.

1845   *The Cricket on the Hearth*. The Dickens family returns to England in June. The first of Dickens's amateur theatricals, a production of Ben Jonson's *Every Man in His Humour* is staged at Frances Kelly's theater in September.

1846   *Pictures from Italy; The Battle of Life*. Dickens briefly serves as editor of a new Liberal newspaper, the *Daily News*. The Dickens family spends the summer and autumn in Switzerland and France. Dickens writes the *Life of Our Lord* for his children.

1847   The Cheap Edition, the first collected edition of Dickens's works, begins publication in monthly parts and separate volumes, published jointly by Chapman & Hall and Bradbury & Evans. The Dickens family returns to London from Paris in February. The amateur theatrical troupe tours to Manchester and Liverpool.

1848   *Dombey and Son; The Haunted Man*. In April the theatrical troupe gives several performances in London to benefit the effort to preserve Shakespeare's birthplace. From April to July, they tour several towns in the north of England and Scotland. Dickens's sister Frances (Fanny) dies.

1849   Dickens conceives the idea for a weekly magazine. He and his family spend the summer at Broadstairs, and then at Bonchurch on the Isle of Wight.

1850   *David Copperfield*. The first issue of *Household Words* appears in March. Dickens and Lytton create the Guild of Literature and Art, and the first theatrical performances to benefit the group are held at Knebworth.

1851   Catherine Dickens suffers a nervous breakdown in March; Dickens's father dies at the end of that month, and his infant daughter, Dora Annie, dies in April. The Dickens family moves to Tavistock House from Devonshire Terrace.

1852   *A Child's History of England*, vol. I; *Christmas Books*, collected for the first time for the Cheap Edition. The theatrical troupe tours the Midlands performing Lytton's *Not so Bad as We Seem*. The Dickenses take their first holiday at Boulogne.

1853   *Bleak House; A Child's History of England*, vol. II. Dickens spends the summer at Boulogne; in the autumn he tours Italy with Wilkie Collins and Augustus Egg. In December he gives his first public reading, a benefit performance of the *Carol* in Birmingham.

1854   *Hard Times; A Child's History of England*, vol. III. In January Dickens visits Preston in preparation for writing about industrial England.

1855   Dickens visits Paris with Collins in February and returns to that city in November with his family to spend six months there. He has a disillusioning reunion with Maria Beadnell, now the garrulous and middle-aged Mrs. Winter.

1856   Dickens purchases Gad's Hill Place.

1857   *Little Dorrit; The Lazy Tour of Two Idle Apprentices*. Dickens's personal life is troubled by growing marital discord. Dickens takes possession of Gad's Hill Place. After performing in Collins's *The Frozen Deep* at Tavistock House in January, Dickens takes the play to Manchester in August using professional actresses, among them Ellen Ternan. In September Dickens and Collins tour through the north of England, a trip described in *The Lazy Tour*.

1858   *Reprinted Pieces*, a collection of articles from *Household Words*, first appears as a volume in the Library Edition of Dickens's works. In May Dickens and Catherine separate. Dickens quarrels with Bradbury & Evans when they refuse to publish his "Personal" statement. Dickens begins public readings for his own benefit, first in London in April and, later in the year, on a tour of Britain, giving 87 readings at 44 different sites.

1859   *A Tale of Two Cities; Hunted Down*. Dickens leaves Bradbury & Evans and returns to Chapman & Hall, suspending publication of *Household Words* and beginning a new weekly magazine, *All the Year Round*. Dickens moves to Gad's Hill with his younger children and with Georgina Hogarth as his housekeeper.

1861   *Great Expectations; The Uncommercial Traveller*, first collection. Dickens makes an extensive reading tour throughout England during the fall. His son Charley marries Bessie Evans, daughter of his former publisher.

1862   Dickens gives a series of readings in London in June. He goes to Paris with Georgina Hogarth and his daughter Mamie for the winter.

1863   Dickens is saddened by the deaths of his mother, Thackeray, and his son Walter.

1865   *Our Mutual Friend; The Uncommercial Traveller*, second collection. Dickens suffers from lameness in his left foot. Returning from a holiday in Paris with Ellen Ternan, Dickens escapes injury in the Staplehurst Railway Accident.

1866   Although suffering from pain and exhaustion, Dickens makes an extensive reading tour during the spring and early summer.

1867   The first volumes in the Charles Dickens Edition of Dickens's works appear, an edition containing new prefaces and headlines for the pages, and the last edition published during Dickens's lifetime. After an exhausting provincial reading tour in the winter and spring, Dickens agrees, against the advice of Forster, to undertake an American reading tour late in the year. Early in November, he sets out from Liverpool for Boston.

1868   Troubled by a persistent cold and worn down by travel, Dickens nonetheless makes a triumphant tour of America, returning to England in May. On an English reading tour in the Fall, he gives his first performance of "Sikes and Nancy."

1869   Although his doctor urges him to discontinue the readings, particularly the performances of "Sikes and Nancy," Dickens persists until April, when illness forces him to return home.

1870   *The Mystery of Edwin Drood*. Despite failing health, Dickens undertakes a farewell series of readings at the beginning of the year. On March 9, he is received by Queen Victoria at Buckingham Palace; a week later, on March 15, he gives his final reading, a performance of the *Carol*. On June 8, after working on the sixth number of *Edwin Drood*, Dickens falls ill and dies the next day. He is buried in the Poets' Corner in Westminster Abbey on June 14.

1872–   Forster publishes *The Life of Charles Dickens*.
74

1874   *Christmas Stories*, the collection containing the Christmas writings of Dickens for *Household Words* and *All the Year Round*, appears as a volume in the Charles Dickens Edition.

1880   *The Mudfog Papers*, a collection of stories, sketches, and essays originally published in *Bentley's Miscellany*.

1908   *Miscellaneous Papers*, ed. B. W. Matz, two vols., a collection of Dickens's periodical essays, plays, and poems, assembled for the Gadshill Edition of Dickens's works.

APPENDIX B

A SELECT BIBLIOGRAPHY ABOUT DICKENS AND HIS WORKS

General Introductions and Reference Works

Ackroyd, Peter. *Introduction to Dickens.* London: Sinclair-Stevenson, 1991.

Bentley, Nicholas, Nina Burgis, and Michael Slater. *The Dickens Index.* London: Oxford University Press, 1988.

Fielding, Kenneth J. *Charles Dickens: A Critical Introduction.* London: Longman's, Green, 1958; 1965.

Hardwick, Michael and Mollie. *The Charles Dickens Encyclopedia.* Reading, Berkshire: Osprey, 1973.

Hayward, Arthur L. *The Dickens Encyclopedia.* London: Routledge, 1924.

Lucas, John. *Charles Dickens: The Major Novels.* London: Penguin, 1992.

Nelson, Harland S. *Charles Dickens.* Boston: Twayne, 1981.

Page, Norman. *A Dickens Companion.* London: Macmillan, 1984.

———— *A Dickens Chronology.* Boston: G. K. Hall, 1988.

Bibliographies

Bolton, H. Philip. *Dickens Dramatized.* Boston: G. K. Hall, 1987.

Collins, Philip. "Charles Dickens" section in the *New Cambridge Bibliography of English Literature.* Cambridge: Cambridge University Press, 1969; "Charles Dickens" section in *Victorian Fiction: A Second Guide to Research,* ed. George H. Ford. New York: Modern Language Association of America, 1978.

Eckel, J. C. *The First Editions of the Writings of Charles Dickens.* London: Chapman and Hall, 1932.

Gold, Joseph. *Charles Dickens: A Centenary Bibliography.* Toronto: University of Toronto Press, 1971.

Nisbet, Ada. "Charles Dickens" section in *Victorian Fiction: A Guide to Research,* ed. Lionel Stevenson. Cambridge, Mass.: Harvard University Press, 1964.

Pointer, Michael. *Charles Dickens on the Screen.* Lanham, Md.: Scarecrow Press, 1996.

Smith, Walter E. *Charles Dickens in the Original Cloth.* 2 vols. Los Angeles: Heritage Bookshop, 1981; 1983.

Biographies

Ackroyd, Peter. *Dickens.* London: Sinclair-Stevenson, 1990.

Allen, Michael. *Charles Dickens' Childhood.* London: Macmillan, 1988.

Forster, John. *Life of Charles Dickens.* 3 vols. London: Chapman and Hall, 1872–1874.

Johnson, Edgar. *Charles Dickens: His Tragedy and Triumph.* 2 vols. New York: Simon and Schuster, 1952. Reissued revised and abridged. New York: Viking, 1979.

Kaplan, Fred. *Dickens.* New York: William Morrow, 1988.

Ley, J. W. T. *The Dickens Circle.* London: Chapman and Hall, 1918.

Lindsay, Jack. *Charles Dickens.* New York: Philosophical Library, 1950.

MacKenzie, Norman and Jeanne. *Dickens: A Life.* New York: Oxford University Press, 1979.

Nisbet, Ada. *Dickens and Ellen Ternan.* Berkeley: University of California Press, 1952.

Patten, Robert. *Charles Dickens and His Publishers.* Oxford: Clarendon Press, 1978.

Smith, Grahame. *Charles Dickens: A Literary Life.* London: Macmillan, 1996.

Tomalin, Claire. *The Invisible Woman: The Story of Nelly Ternan and Charles Dickens.* New York: Alfred A. Knopf, 1991.

Works of Scholarship and Criticism

Adrian, Arthur. *Dickens and the Parent–Child Relationship.* Athens, Ohio: Ohio University Press, 1984.

Alexander, Doris. *Creating Characters with Charles Dickens.* University Park, Pa.: Pennsylvania State University Press, 1991.

Andrews, Malcolm. *Dickens and the Grown-up Child.* Iowa City, Iowa: University of Iowa Press, 1994.

Arac, Jonathan. *Commissioned Spirits: The Shaping of Social Motion in Dickens, Carlyle, Melville, and Hawthorne.* New Brunswick, N.J.: Rutgers University Press, 1979.

Axton, William. *Circle of Fire.* Lexington, Ky.: University of Kentucky Press, 1967.

Buckley, Jerome. *Season of Youth.* Cambridge, Mass.: Harvard University Press, 1974.

Butt, John and Kathleen Tillotson. *Dickens at Work*. London: Methuen, 1957.

Carey, John. *The Violent Effigy: A Study in Dickens' Imagination*. London: Faber and Faber, 1973.

Chesterton, G. K. *Charles Dickens*. London: Hodder and Stoughton, 1903.

————. *Charles Dickens: A Critical Study*. London: Methuen, 1906.

Chittick, Kathryn. *Dickens and the 1830s*. Cambridge: Cambridge University Press, 1990.

Cohen, Jane R. *Charles Dickens and His Original Illustrators*. Columbus: Ohio State University Press, 1980.

Collins, Philip. *Dickens and Crime*. London: Macmillan, 1962.

————. *Dickens and Education*. London: Macmillan, 1963.

————. *Dickens: The Critical Heritage*. London: Routledge & Kegan Paul, 1971.

Coolidge, Archibald C. *Dickens as a Serial Novelist*. Ames, Iowa: Iowa State University Press, 1967.

Dabney, Ross H. *Love and Property in the Novels of Dickens*. Berkeley: University of California Press, 1967.

Daldry, Graham. *Charles Dickens and the Form of the Novel*. Totowa, N.J.: Barnes and Noble, 1987.

Daleski, H. M. *Dickens and the Art of Analogy*. London: Faber and Faber, 1970.

Davies, James. *The Textual Life of Dickens's Characters*. Savage, Md.: Barnes and Noble, 1990.

Davis, Earle R. *The Flint and the Flame: The Artistry of Charles Dickens*. Columbia, Mo.: University of Missouri Press, 1963.

Davis, Paul. *The Lives and Times of Ebenezer Scrooge*. New Haven: Yale University Press, 1990.

Dyson, A. E. *The Inimitable Dickens*. London: Macmillan, 1970.

Eigner, Edwin. *The Dickens Pantomime*. Berkeley: University of California Press, 1989.

Engel, Monroe. *The Maturity of Dickens*. Cambridge, Mass.: Harvard University Press, 1959.

Fanger, Donald. *Dostoyevsky and Romantic Realism*. Cambridge, Mass.: Harvard University Press, 1965.

Flint, Kate. *Dickens*. Brighton, Sussex: Harvester, 1986.

Ford, George H. *Dickens and his Readers: Aspects of Novel Criticism since 1836*. Princeton: Princeton University Press, 1955.

————. *The Dickens Critics* (edited with Lauriat Lane, Jr.). Ithaca, NY: Cornell University Press, 1961.

Frank, Lawrence. *Charles Dickens and the Romantic Self*. Lincoln, Nebr.: University of Nebraska Press, 1984.

Garis, Robert E. *The Dickens Theatre*. Oxford: Clarendon Press, 1965.

Gissing, George. *Charles Dickens: A Critical Study*. London: Blackie, 1898.

Gold, Joseph. *Charles Dickens: Radical Moralist*. Minneapolis: University of Minnesota Press, 1972.

Goldberg, Michael. *Carlyle and Dickens*. Athens, Ga.: University of Georgia Press, 1972.

Hardy, Barbara. *The Moral Art of Dickens*. London: Athlone Press, 1970.

Hartog, Dirk den. *Dickens and Romantic Psychology*. London: Macmillan, 1987.

Harvey, John. *Victorian Novelists and Their Illustrators*. London: Sidgewick and Jackson, 1970.

Herst, Beth. *The Dickens Hero*. London: Weidenfeld and Nicolson, 1990.

Hollington, Michael. *Dickens and the Grotesque*. London: Croom Helm, 1984.

Hornbach, Bert G. *Noah's Arkitecture: A Study of Dickens' Mythology*. Athens, Ohio: Ohio University Press, 1972.

Horton, Susan. *Interpreting Interpreting: Interpreting Dickens's "Dombey."* Baltimore: Johns Hopkins University Press, 1979.

House, Humphry. *The Dickens World*. London: Oxford University Press, 1941.

Houston, Gail. *Consuming Fictions*. Carbondale, Ill.: Southern Illinois University Press, 1994.

Jackson, Thomas A. *Charles Dickens: The Progress of a Radical*. London: Lawrence and Wishart, 1937.

Jaffe, Audrey. *Vanishing Points: Dickens, Narrative, and the Subject of Omniscience*. Berkeley: University of California Press, 1991.

Kaplan, Fred. *Dickens and Mesmerism*. Princeton: Princeton University Press, 1975.

Kincaid, James R. *Dickens and the Rhetoric of Laughter*. Oxford: Clarendon Press, 1972.

Kucich, John. *Excess and Restraint in the Novels of Charles Dickens*. Athens, Ga.: University of Georgia Press, 1981.

————. *Repression in Victorian Fiction: Charlotte Brontë, George Eliot, and Charles Dickens*. Berkeley: University of California Press, 1987.

Larson, Janet L. *Dickens and the Broken Scripture*. Athens, Ga.: University of Georgia Press, 1985.

Leacock, Stephen. *Charles Dickens: His Life and Work*. Garden City, N.Y.: Doubleday, Doran, 1933.

Leavis, F. R. and Q. D. *Dickens the Novelist*. London: Chatto and Windus, 1970.

Lettis, Richard. *The Dickens Aesthetic*. New York: AMS, 1989.

————. *Dickens on Literature*. New York: AMS, 1990.

Lucas, John. *The Melancholy Man: A Study of Dickens's Novels*. London: Methuen, 1970.

McKnight, Natalie. *Idiots, Madmen, and Other Prisoners in Dickens*. New York: St. Martin's. 1993.

McMaster, Juliet. *Dickens the Designer*. London: Macmillan, 1987.

Magnet, Myron. *Dickens and the Social Order*. Philadelphia: University of Pennsylvania Press, 1985.

Manning, Sylvia. *Dickens as Satirist*. New Haven: Yale University Press, 1971.

Marcus, Steven. *Dickens: From Pickwick to Dombey*. London: Chatto and Windus, 1965.

Meckier, Jerome. *Hidden Rivalries in Victorian Fiction: Dickens, Realism, and Revaluation*. Lexington, Ky.: University Press of Kentucky, 1987.

Miller, J. Hillis. *Charles Dickens: The World of His Novels*. Cambridge, Mass.: Harvard University Press, 1958.

————. *Victorian Subjects*. Durham, N.C.: Duke University Press, 1991.

Monod, Sylvère. *Dickens the Novelist*. Norman, Okla.: University of Oklahoma Press, 1967.

Morgan, Nicholas H. *Secret Journeys: Theory and Practice in Reading Dickens*. Rutherford, N.J.: Fairleigh Dickinson University Press, 1992.

Newman, S. J. *Dickens at Play*. New York: St. Martin's, 1981.

Newsom, Robert. *Dickens on the Romantic Side of Familiar Things:* Bleak House *and the Novel Tradition*. New York: Columbia University Press, 1977.

Orwell, George. "Charles Dickens," *Inside the Whale*. London: Gollancz, 1940.

Pope, Norris. *Dickens and Charity*. New York: Columbia University Press, 1978.

Pugh, Edwin. *Charles Dickens: The Apostle of the People*. London: New Age Press, 1908.

Reed, John R. *Dickens and Thackeray: Punishment and Forgiveness*. Athens, Ohio: Ohio University Press, 1995.

Romano, John. *Dickens and Reality*. New York: Columbia University Press, 1978.

Rosenberg, Brian. *Little Dorrit's Shadows: Character and Contradiction in Dickens*. Columbia, Mo.: University of Missouri Press, 1996.

Sadoff, Dianne F. *Monsters of Affection: Dickens, Eliot, and Brontë on Fatherhood*. Baltimore: Johns Hopkins University Press, 1982.

Sanders, Andrew. *The Victorian Historical Novel, 1840–1880*. London: Macmillan, 1979.

———. *Charles Dickens Resurrectionist*. London: Macmillan, 1982.

Sandrin, Anny. *Parentage and Inheritance in the Novels of Charles Dickens*. Cambridge: Cambridge University Press, 1994.

Schlicke, Paul. *Dickens and Popular Entertainment*. London: Allen and Unwin, 1985.

Schwarzbach, F. S. *Dickens and the City*. London: Athlone Press, 1979.

Shaw, George Bernard. *Shaw on Dickens*, ed. Dan H. Laurence and M. Quinn. New York: Frederick Ungar, 1985.

Slater, Michael. *Dickens and Women*. London: J. M. Dent, 1983.

Smith, Grahame. *Dickens, Money, and Society*. Berkeley: University of California Press, 1968.

Spilka, Mark. *Dickens and Kafka, a Mutual Interpretation*. Bloomington: Indiana University Press, 1963.

Steig, Michael. *Dickens and Phiz*. Bloomington: Indiana University Press, 1978.

Stewart, Garrett. *Dickens and the Trials of Imagination*. Cambridge, Mass.: Harvard University Press, 1974.

Stoehr, Taylor. *Dickens: The Dreamer's Stance*. Ithaca, N.Y.: Cornell University Press, 1965.

Stone, Harry. *Dickens and the Invisible World*. Bloomington: Indiana University Press, 1979.

———. *The Night Side of Dickens: Cannibalism, Passion, Necessity*. Columbus: Ohio State University Press, 1994.

Sucksmith, Harvey Peter. *The Narrative Art of Charles Dickens*. Oxford: Clarendon Press, 1970.

Swinburne, Algernon C. *Dickens*. London: Chatto and Windus, 1913.

Tambling, Jeremy. *Dickens, Violence and the Modern State: Dreams of the Scaffold*. London: Macmillan, 1995.

Thomas, Deborah A. *Dickens and the Short Story*. Philadelphia: University of Pennsylvania Press, 1982.

Thurley, Geoffrey. *The Dickens Myth*. New York: St. Martin's, 1976.

Tillotson, Kathleen. *Novels of the Eighteen-forties*. Oxford: Clarendon Press, 1954.

Walder, Dennis. *Dickens and Religion*. London: Allen and Unwin, 1981.

Watkins, Gwen. *Dickens in Search of Himself*. London: Macmillan, 1987.

Welsh, Alexander. *The City of Dickens*. Oxford: Clarendon Press, 1971.

———. *From Copyright to Copperfield: The Identity of Dickens*. Cambridge, Mass.: Harvard University Press, 1987.

Wilson, Angus. *The World of Charles Dickens*. New York: Viking, 1970.

Wilson, Edmund. "Dickens: The Two Scrooges," *New Republic* (March, 1940). Collected in *The Wound and the Bow*. Boston: Houghton, Mifflin, 1941.

INDEX

Note: **Boldface** numbers indicate primary discussion of a topic. *Italic* numbers indicate illustrations.